HANDBOOKS

NEW ORLEANS

ANDREW COLLINS

FRENCH QUARTER AND
FAUBOURG MARIGNY

KERLEREC ST

N PRIEUR ST

ST ANN ST

ORLEANS ST

LAFITTE ST

ROBERTSON ST

N VILLERE ST

MARAIS ST

TREME ST

ST CLAUDE AVE

GOV NICHOLLS ST

N DERBIGNY ST

TREME

CLAIBORNE AVE

MAHALIA JACKSON
THEATRE OF THE
PERFORMING ARTS ★

Louis
Armstrong
Park

URSULINES AVE

N ROBERTSON ST

St. Louis
Cemetery
No 2

BASIN ST

N RAMPART ST

BURGUNDY ST

ST PHILIP ST

VOODOO
SPIRITUAL
TEMPLE ▼

LAFITTE'S
BLACKSMITH
SHOP ★

DONNA'S ▼

NEW ORLEANS
HISTORIC VOODOO
MUSEUM ▼

CAFE LAFITTE
IN EXILE ▼

ST PETER ST

St. Louis
Cemetery
No 1

TOULOUSE ST

**FRENCH
QUARTER**

ORLEANS
ST ANN
ST

BOURBON
PUB/
PARADE
DISCO ▼

DUMAINE ST

CORNSTALK
HOTEL ●

MADAME
JOHN'S
LEGACY ★

RAWHIDE
2010 ▼

GOOD
FRIENDS ▼

OZ ▼

FRITZEL'S EUROPEAN
JAZZ PUB ▼

735 NIGHTCLUB
AND BAR ▼

LOUISIANA OFFICE OF
TOURISM ▼

CAT'S MEOW ▼

PRESBYTERE ★

ST. LOUIS
CATHEDRAL ★

TUJAGUE ▼

MADISON AY

SEE "CENTRAL BUSINESS AND WAREHOUSE DISTRICTS" MAP

S VILLERE ST

PRESERVATION HALL ▼

THE
ARSENAL ★

1850
HOUSE ★

ST LOUIS ST

HISTORIC NEW ORLEANS
COLLECTION ▼

Jackson
Square

TREME ST

CROZAT ST

CONTI ST

BIENVILLE ST

CAJUN
CABIN ▼

DUNGEON
BAR ▼

LE PETIT
THEATRE DU
VIEUX CARRE ▼

THE CABILDO ★

WILKINSON ST

PONTALBA
APARTMENTS ★

LA SALLE

SAENGER
THEATRE ★

HERMANN-GRIMA
HOUSE ▼

BOMBAY
CLUB ▼

NAPOLEON
HOUSE CAFE ▼

CHARTRES

NEW ORLEANS
PHARMACY MUSEUM ▼

JACKSON
BREWERY ★

CHARITY
HOSPITAL

SARATOGA ST

ELK PL

CLEVELAND AVE

STATE PALACE
THEATRE ●

GERMAINE CAZENAVE WELLS
MARDI GRAS MUSEUM ▼

FLEUR DE LIS THÉÂTRE ▼

ANDREW JAEGER'S
HOUSE OF SEAFOOD ▼

CRESCENT CITY
BREWHOUSE ▼

STEAMBOAT
NATCHEZ ▼

S LIBERTY ST

RITZ-
CARLTON ●

DAUPHINE ST

CAN-CAN
CAFE ▼

UTOPIA ▼

WILLIAMS
RESEARCH
CENTER ▼

TOULOUSE
STREET
WHARF

TULANE AVE

LIBRARY LOUNGE/
FRENCH QUARTER BAR ▼

RED FISH
GRILL ▼

BOURBON ST

CAROUSEL BAR ▼

JEAN LAFITTE
NATIONAL HISTORICAL
PARK AND PRESERVE ▼

HARD ROCK
CAFE ▼

UNIVERSITY PL

LIVING ROOM ▼

KERRY IRISH PUB ▼

MOON WALK ★

GRAVIER ST

CANAL ST

ROYAL ST

EXCHANGE

IBERVILLE ST

HOUSE OF
BLUES ▼

COYOTE UGLY
SALOON ▼

N FRONT BLVD

Levee

COMMON ST

COMMON ST

LOUNGE
LIZARD ▼

LOYOLA AVE

PERDIDO AVE

O'KEEFE AVE

CBD

BARONNE ST

UNION ST

N PETERS ST

CUSTOM
HOUSE ▼

Woldenberg
Riverfront Park

CLAY ST

POYDRAS ST

ST CHARLES ST

CAMP ST

MAGAZINE ST

LANDMARK'S
CANAL PLACE ★

SOUTHERN
REPERTORY
THEATRE ▼

SHOPS AT
CANAL PLACE ▼

AUDUBON AQUARIUM
OF THE AMERICAS ▼

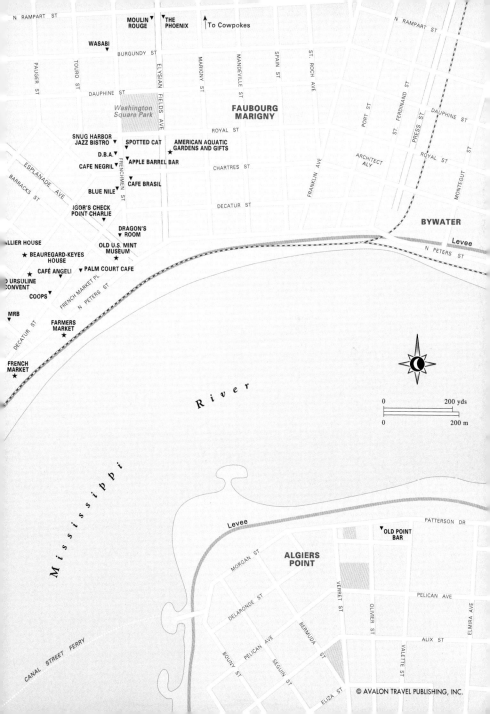

HANDSOME
WILLY'S
CLEVELAND AVE
CHARITY
HOSPITAL

MEDICAL
CENTER OF
TULANE

PERDIDO ST

LOUISIANA
SUPERDOME/
NEW ORLEANS
ARENA

NEW ORLEANS
CENTER

SEE "GARDEN DISTRICT AND UPTOWN" MAP

S PRIEUR ST
BERTRAND ST
CLAIBORNE AVE
LA SALLE
10

LOYOLA AVE

UNION
STATION

GREYHOUND
BUS STATION

MAGNOLIA ST

BUS
90

CBD

ERATO ST

MELPOMENE AVE

LA SALLE ST
FELICITY ST
TERPSICHORE ST
EUTERPE ST
POLYMNIA ST

Van
McMurray
Park

ST ANDREW ST
JOSEPHINE ST

PHILIP ST
BRAINARD ST
1ST ST
ST CHARLES AVE

LOWER GARDEN
DISTRICT

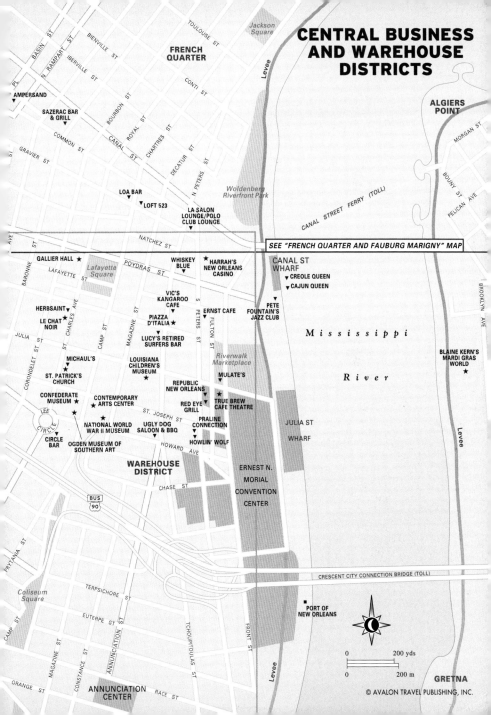

CENTRAL BUSINESS AND WAREHOUSE DISTRICTS

FRENCH QUARTER

Jackson Square

TOULOUSE ST

BIENVILLE ST

IBERVILLE ST

N RAMPART ST

BASIN ST

BOURBON ST

CONTI ST

ROYAL ST

CHARTRES ST

DECATUR ST

N PETERS ST

CANAL ST

COMMON ST

GRAVIER ST

Levee

ALGIERS POINT

MORGAN ST

BOUNTY ST

PELICAN AVE

BROOKLYN AVE

▼ AMPERSAND

▼ SAZERAC BAR & GRILL

▼ LOA BAR

▼ LOFT 523

▼ LA SALON LOUNGE/POLO CLUB LOUNGE

Woldenberg Riverfront Park

CANAL STREET FERRY (TOLL)

NATCHEZ ST

SEE "FRENCH QUARTER AND FAUBURG MARIGNY" MAP

BARONNE ST

LAFAYETTE

GALLIER HALL ★

Lafayette Square

POYDRAS ST

★ WHISKEY BLUE

★ HARRAH'S NEW ORLEANS CASINO

CANAL ST WHARF

▼ CREOLE QUEEN

▼ CAJUN QUEEN

HERBSAINT ▼

LE CHAT NOIR ★

ST CHARLES AVE

CAMP ST

MAGAZINE ST

S PETERS ST

FULTON ST

VIC'S KANGAROO CAFE ▼

★ ERNST CAFE

▼ PETE FOUNTAIN'S JAZZ CLUB

PIAZZA D'ITALIA ★

LUCY'S RETIRED SURFERS BAR ▼

M i s s i s s i p p i

JULIA ST

CORONDELET ST

MICHAUL'S ▼

ST. PATRICK'S CHURCH ★

LOUISIANA CHILDREN'S MUSEUM ★

Riverwalk Marketplace

R i v e r

BLAINE KERN'S MARDI GRAS WORLD ★

MULATE'S ★

REPUBLIC NEW ORLEANS ★

CONFEDERATE MUSEUM ★

CONTEMPORARY ARTS CENTER ▼

ST. JOSEPH ST

RED EYE GRILL ▼

★ TRUE BREW CAFE THEATRE

LEE CIRCLE

CIRCLE BAR ▼

NATIONAL WORLD WAR II MUSEUM ★

UGLY DOG SALOON & BBQ ▼

PRALINE CONNECTION ▼

HOWLIN' WOLF ▼

OGDEN MUSEUM OF SOUTHERN ART ▼

HOWARD AVE

JULIA ST WHARF

WAREHOUSE DISTRICT

CHASE ST

ERNEST N. MORIAL CONVENTION CENTER

BUS 90

PRYTANIA ST

Coliseum Square

TERPSICHORE ST

EUTERPE ST

ANNUNCIATION ST

TCHOUPITOULAS ST

FRONT ST

Levee

CRESCENT CITY CONNECTION BRIDGE (TOLL)

■ PORT OF NEW ORLEANS

CAMP ST

MAGAZINE ST

CONSTANCE ST

ORANGE ST

RACE ST

ANNUNCIATION CENTER

0   200 yds

0   200 m

GRETNA

© AVALON TRAVEL PUBLISHING, INC.

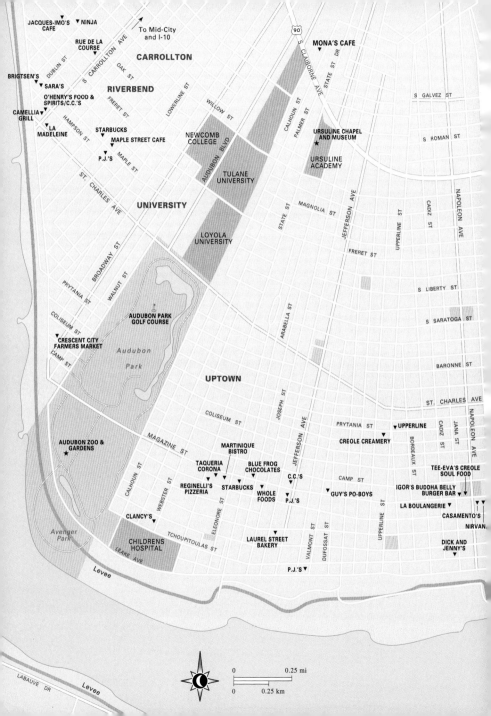

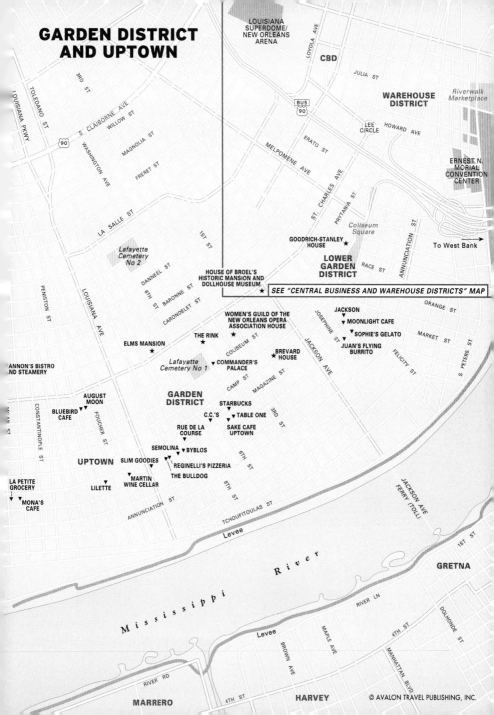

DISCOVER NEW ORLEANS

Although Hurricane Katrina dealt a devastating blow to much of greater New Orleans in 2005, many of those areas that define the Big Easy experience and capture the city's indomitable joie de vivre – the French Quarter, Central Business District (CBD), Garden District, and Uptown – had largely sprung back to life by early 2006. Despite receiving considerable storm and subsequent flooding damage, these sections that hold the majority of New Orleans's attractions, hotels, music clubs, and restaurants continue to thrive, as they have for generations.

Residents of New Orleans have long faced dire hardships – from yellow-fever epidemics throughout the 19th century to the ruthless, damaging Union occupation during the Civil War. But they've always recovered, in part by steadfastly embracing those traits that distinguish New Orleans from any other city in the world: a devotion to spirited music and fantastic food, a keen desire to preserve the

St. Louis Cathedral with Andrew Jackson statue

city's rich history, an inimitable sense of style and individualism, and a flamboyantly playful sense of humor.

New Orleanians kick into full celebratory mode at the drop of hat, but especially during Mardi Gras and the Carnival season leading up to it. This two- to three-week series of parties and parades is known for free-spirited licentiousness, with marchers clad in everything from pink afro wigs to papier mâché lion's masks gyrating and cartwheeling down St. Charles Avenue. But you'll also find a surprisingly sweet, low-key, familial warmth. On Mardi Gras Tuesday, for example, along the less-touristy Uptown stretches of the parade route, you'll always see throngs of parents hoisting their toddlers into makeshift wooden seats bolted to the tops of six-foot-tall stepladders, the better to catch the doubloons, beads, and other trinkets coming their way. If you didn't know any better, you might think you'd stumbled upon a small-town homecoming parade.

Mardi Gras float revelers

Live music is a major focus of Mardi Gras as well as the city's second-most popular event, Jazz Fest, but it's a theme that permeates the city's spirit and soul 365 days a year. The French Quarter, especially decadent Bourbon Street, may be touristy, but it's also a fantasy for music fans. Wander not just around the Quarter but also Frenchmen Street in Faubourg Marigny and Peters Street in the Warehouse District. Into the wee hours, you'll hear all kinds of tunes, from the sounds of a brass band emanating from a swanky jazz club to the sugary crooning of lounge singers covering Fats Domino or Harry Connick tunes at a corner pub. From block to block in the city's entertainment-driven neighborhoods, the specific sounds change, but the cacophony remains constant. It's all part of the music of New Orleans.

Food is just as integral to understanding New Orleans as music. Many visitors experience one, maybe even two or three, culinary epiphanies here. You may first *get* the whole New Orleans food scene while dining someplace fancy, perhaps one of the dozen or so restaurants around town that have been serving food since the

Fred's Lounge in Mamou, the heart of the Cajun Prairie

first Roosevelt administration. But gustatory greatness is just as often achieved by noshing on humble foods. You can saunter into a relatively uncelebrated tavern like Coops on Decatur Street, sit down at the bar, and order an Abita Turbo Dog brown ale and an oyster po'boy. You bite into it, and taste those tender, slightly briny, lightly battered oysters enveloped within a pod of feathery French bread. And you declare, to nobody in particular, that this is not only the best po'boy you've ever tasted, it's the best sandwich, period. It doesn't matter if anybody agrees with you. You have tracked down the holy grail of fried oysters, and nobody can take that away from you.

Of course, while New Orleans is the linchpin of the entire Gulf South, the rest of southern Louisiana offers similarly vivid experiences. From the Big Easy, you're within an afternoon's drive of the stately plantations of the Great River Road, the multitude of attractions and fine restaurants in politically and economically charged Baton Rouge, and the rich history, food, and music of Cajun Country, the western edge of which also bounced back valiantly from a major

one of Uptown's many genteel mansions

2005 hurricane (Rita). Just an hour north of New Orleans, the arty and sophisticated suburbs of the North Shore contain a bounty of charming downtown shops and galleries, both haute and down-home restaurants, and invigorating opportunities for biking, fishing, boating, and bird-watching. Side excursions to any of these vital nearby regions offer further opportunities to observe and experience everything that's special about southern Louisiana.

New Orleans, however, will always be the true heart of Louisiana. To appreciate the city fully, open your mind to all of the experiences the Big Easy sends your way. Ride on the vintage Canal streetcar through rapidly gentrifying Mid-City, or spend a night in a massive four-poster bed at an 1820s Creole cottage in Faubourg Marigny. Offer fervent hallelujahs in the many cathedrals of cool jazz. Stroll along Bourbon Street with a go-cup in hand. Slurp down a bowl of duck gumbo. Surrender to the genuine, if occasionally mischievous, charms of this sultry subtropical metropolis on the Mississippi. These are the sights, sounds, and tastes that will tell you that you're in a city that's absolutely without peer.

the French Quarter at night

Contents

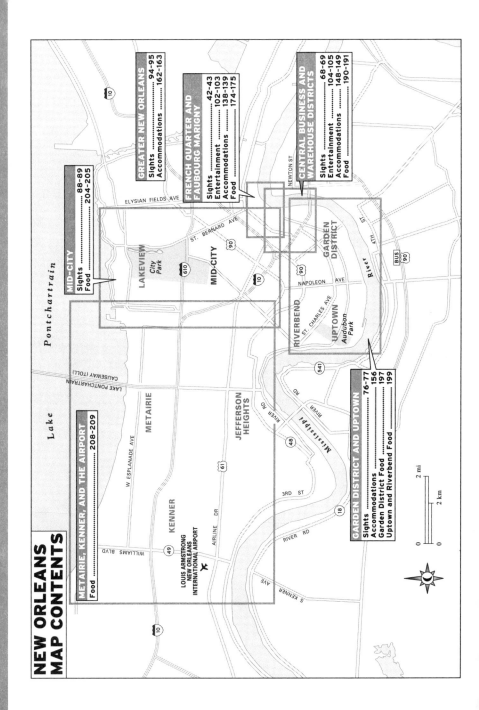

NEW ORLEANS
MAP CONTENTS

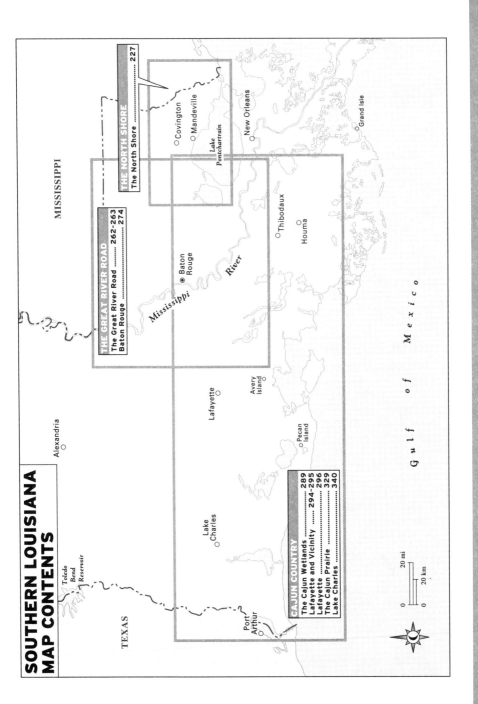

SOUTHERN LOUISIANA MAP CONTENTS

MISSISSIPPI

TEXAS

Toledo Bend Reservoir

Alexandria

Lafayette

Lake Charles

Port Arthur

Pecan Island

Avery Island

Baton Rouge

Mississippi River

Thibodaux

Houma

Covington

Mandeville

Lake Pontchartrain

New Orleans

Grand Isle

Gulf of Mexico

0   20 mi
0   20 km

The Lay of the Land

NEW ORLEANS

THE FRENCH QUARTER

It's the heart of New Orleans, and one of the most famous and historic neighborhoods in North America. And contrary to popular misconception, it's much more than the riot of boozy and floozy bars found along raucous Bourbon Street. This fabled district known also as Vieux Carré contains 98 blocks of distinctive brick and stucco buildings famed for their intricate wrought-iron balconies and romantic, cloistered courtyards. To be sure, this is where you'll find the city's more touristy businesses, but there's also a bounty of top-flight restaurants, acclaimed art galleries and antiques shops, and luxe hotels and inns. The blocks closest to the Mississippi River and Canal Street are the most commercial—don't overlook the quieter residential areas, where you'll be reminded that the French Quarter is very much a living, breathing, dynamic neighborhood popular with locals and visitors.

FAUBOURG MARIGNY AND BYWATER

The mostly residential and richly historic neighborhoods just downriver from the French Quarter, Faubourg Marigny and Bywater have become increasingly popular in recent decades among artists, young professionals, gays and lesbians, and other urban pioneers who have snapped up the hundreds of Creole and Caribbean-inspired cottages and homes. Faubourg Marigny is the more developed of the two neighborhoods, its commercial spine—Frenchmen Street—lined with sassy jazz clubs, funky bars, and trendy restaurants. The Marigny, as its often called, also contains some of the city's most atmospheric inns, making it an excellent accommodations option if you're seeking proximity to the Quarter without that neighborhood's crowds and higher prices. A few cafés and B&Bs have popped up in Bywater over the years, but this is more a place to live than eat or stay.

CENTRAL BUSINESS AND WAREHOUSE DISTRICTS

Following the Louisiana Purchase, the neighborhood just upriver from the French Quarter came to be named the American Quarter, as aspiring merchants and traders from throughout the United States settled and staked their fortunes here. Today the neighborhood is known as the Central Business District (or CBD) and the smaller, hipper, and adjoining Warehouse District. The former is largely the domain of office towers as well as a number of the city's larger hotels, many of them containing reputable restaurants. The latter has blossomed over the past 15 years into an intriguing quadrant of art galleries, museums, coffeehouses, and both laid-back and high-profile restaurants and bars operated by such locally prominent chefs as Emeril Lagasse and John Besh—there are several notable hotels in the Warehouse District, too.

THE GARDEN DISTRICT AND UPTOWN

Continue upriver from the CBD and you enter Uptown, which technically covers just about every block from Claiborne Avenue out to Audubon Park. This is a part of the city laid out largely during the 19th century, and it contains a mix or residential and commercial areas. Most of the shopping and dining are along Magazine Street—known for its funky antiques stores, chic boutiques, and eclectic restaurants—and St. Charles Avenue, which has a number of restaurants as well as quite a few inns and hotels. The neighborhood includes the exclusive Garden District, where graceful Victorian mansions overlook neatly manicured gardens and magnolia trees. Leafy Audubon Park is ideal for a stroll, or a visit to the zoo or fine golf course. And beyond the park, you reach the lovely campuses of Tulane and Loyola universities as well as the quirky Carrollton neighborhood, with its clutch of excellent cafés and shops.

MID-CITY

Most of the areas of New Orleans that received heavy flooding after Hurricane Katrina were residential neighborhoods generally not visited much by tourists, but Mid-City is the exception. This large swath of New Orleans that extends for many miles north of the Quarter and CBD had become increasingly gentrified and popular in the years leading up to Katrina, and although the storm damaged many homes and businesses here, much of the area came back resoundingly within a year after the hurricane. The main attractions in New Orleans's green lung, verdant City Park, have reopened, including the New Orleans Museum of Art and the New Orleans Botanical Garden. Strips with great restaurants, such as Esplanade and Carrollton avenues, also are enjoying resurgences. This is very much a neighborhood to watch, an area rife with fine 19th- and early-20th-century homes and with tremendous potential.

GREATER NEW ORLEANS

Although most visitors focus on the inner-city neighborhoods described above, metro New Orleans holds a number of worthwhile districts and communities as well as several worthwhile attractions. The portion of the area known as East New Orleans, along with the suburb of Chalmette, were badly flooded following Katrina, and it will take some time before they've recovered to any great degree. But in the suburbs of Metairie and Kenner (home to Louis Armstrong New Orleans International Airport), you'll find scads of mid-priced hotels, eateries, and shopping centers as well as Rivertown U.S.A., a kid-popular museum complex. Across the Mississippi River from New Orleans, the West Bank is home to several more suburbs as well as the immense Barataria Preserve, which is part of Jean Lafitte National Historical Park and contains many square miles of trails for hiking and waterways for boating.

ELSEWHERE IN SOUTHERN LOUISIANA

THE NORTH SHORE

The fastest-growing part of Louisiana, both in actual population and in apparent popularity, is the North Shore, a string of towns encircling Lake Pontchartrain, less than an hour's drive from New Orleans and loaded with great shopping, dining, and outdoor activities. The region is divided into two main parishes, St. Tammany and Tangipahoa, with the majority of attractions and charming accommodations and restaurants in St. Tammany. Things to do on this side of the lake include cycling along the St. Tammany Trace bikeway, visiting wineries, shopping for antiques and art in enchanting downtowns such as Covington and Ponchatoula, and visiting some of the more unusual museums in the state, such as the Abita Mystery House in Abita Springs and the Lake Pontchartrain Basin Maritime Museum in Madisonville.

THE GREAT RIVER ROAD

The twisting swath of villages fringing the Mississippi River between New Orleans and Baton Rouge is known as Plantation Country. Baton Rouge itself, although not a major tourist draw, does have a cluster of truly first-rate attractions (including the architecturally distinctive and historically significant State Capitol building), and just north of that, beautifully preserved St. Francisville is the quintessential antebellum Southern town, with dozens of fine old homes and a friendly, leisurely pace. This part of the state can easily be explored in just a day, if you choose just a couple of the major plantation museums along the Great River Road. The area is situated between New Orleans and Cajun Country, so it's a nice region to visit en route from one to the other. But you could also meander along the river for as long as a week and not run out of things to see and do.

CAJUN COUNTRY

After New Orleans, the Cajun Country is the most visited and intriguing part of the state. This area, also known as Acadiana, extends from just southeast of New Orleans, around the town of Houma, to the Texas border, out near the city of Lake Charles. The region's geographical and cultural center is the city of Lafayette, and this is a great place to begin your explorations of the region, as it has several excellent museums that interpret and introduce the heritage of the Cajun people. Wetlands towns such as New Iberia, St. Martinville, and Breaux Bridge are great for dining on Cajun food, exploring historic sites, and venturing into the swamps on guided boat excursions. Prairie towns such as Eunice and Opelousas are best known for their music heritage—these are great areas to learn about and listen to Cajun and zydeco music. The entire Cajun Country is characterized by exceeding warmth and hospitality, down-home informality, great food and music, swamps and bayous rife with wildlife, and an easy, comfortable pace. If you have time to visit just one section of the state outside of New Orleans, try to make it Acadiana.

Planning Your Trip

Situated in southeastern Louisiana along I-10, New Orleans hugs a crescent-shaped curve of the Mississippi River, extending north to enormous Lake Pontchartrain. The most historic and visitor-friendly parts of the city are the areas nearest the river. These include three adjoining areas: the French Quarter, the Central Business District, and Uptown, which contains the Garden District. Within the city of New Orleans, it's quite easy to get around most of the key neighborhoods using a combination of walking, streetcars and buses, and the occasional cab.

Southern Louisiana—the area covered in this book's side-trips to the North Shore, the Great River Road, and Cajun Country—extends about 200 miles east to west along the I-10 corridor, and only about 75 miles north to south. While the southern end of the state covers a decent-size area, the navigable and visited areas are quite easily reached from New Orleans. It's just a little over two hours from New Orleans to Lafayette, for example, and another hour or so out as far west as Lake Charles. Most of the plantations along the River Road lie less than an hour from New Orleans, as does Baton Rouge. St. Francisville, the base for exploring the River Road north of Baton Rouge, is about an hour and 45 minutes from New Orleans. The North Shore towns of Slidell, Mandeville, and Hammond are all less than 45 minutes from New Orleans.

WHEN TO GO

Louisiana and New Orleans are year-round destinations, although summer tends to be quietest, and this is especially true since Hurricane Katrina. Keep special events and festivals in mind when you plan your visit—Mardi Gras, always held sometime between early February and mid-March, is the best-known but by no means the only big party thrown in this city.

Even during the dreaded hot and humid summer, New Orleans throws several popular festivals. And with kids out of school at this time, family road trips throughout the southern half of the state are commonplace. This had long been a popular time for conventions, too, and although this business has cooled considerably in the aftermath of Katrina, expect it to pick up again in the coming years. Most attractions remain open year-round, although some reduce their hours or days in winter, and many businesses have more limited hours since Katrina.

Weatherwise, early spring and late fall are wonderful for visiting the state, and early spring is also the ideal time to take a swamp tour and see the state in its full splendor. Magnolia trees and flower beds come to life beginning in early March and stay colorful all through summer. Hurricane season runs from midsummer to the end of October, and it's always possible—especially with the increase in hurricanes in the Gulf of Mexico in recent years—for another biggie to hit soon. But purely from a statistical perspective, the odds of a hurricane's striking while you're in Louisiana, even during the hurricane season, are extremely slim. Winters in southern Louisiana are temperate and mild, and this is a great time to enjoy the charms of New Orleans.

WHAT TO TAKE

Packing for a trip to Louisiana is like planning for any other trip in the southeastern United States, or to any city or town with a warm and wet climate and some water access. If you're visiting only New Orleans, you can pack as you might for any warm-weather city—it gets hot and humid from April through October, so stick with light clothing constructed of breathable fabrics at these times. Only a handful of high-end restaurants in New Orleans require jackets, ties, or dresses, but even in summer, it's customary to wear nice jeans or slacks, sandals or loafers, and a collared shirt at any reasonably nice restaurant. This is a touristy place, and especially when the weather is hot, you can get away with casual attire, but printed T-shirts, cutoff shorts, and flip-flops are frowned upon at most of the nicer establishments in New Orleans, including some of the dressier hotel lobbies and lounges. That sort of attire is just fine at inexpensive, casual restaurants and bars. The temperature rarely falls below freezing in Louisiana, but in winter it can get nippy, so you should pack a light winter jacket and gloves if you're coming in January or February. But don't overdo it on the warm clothing, as you can also see highs in the 60s and 70s on many winter days.

If you're planning to spend time exploring southern Louisiana outside the cities, casual dress is even more the norm, and formal attire unheard of. There are a few things you should plan to bring with you if you're planning to go on a swamp tour, hiking or fishing trip, or any other outdoorsy exploration. It can rain frequently just about any time of year in Louisiana, so definitely pack a travel umbrella, a waterproof jacket, hat, and shoes, and a small waterproof travel bag (to carry a camera, for instance).

In few parts of the state are you very far from almost any kind of household, clothing, food, or travel supply—distances in southern Louisiana between gas stations, grocery stores, and department stores are usually fairly short, the exceptions being very small towns in rural parts of the state.

SIGHTSEEING TOURS

For a variety of reasons, southern Louisiana is rife with tour operators, and these can be a great resource, whether to explore a place that's difficult to find or enjoy on your own, or to get a more detailed history of what you're seeing. In some cases, it's actually less expensive to visit an attraction or a series of them on a group tour than on your own. Many of these excursions last the better part of a day and involve a large group and a bus ride, but many other options involve low-key strolls through the Garden District and some of New Orleans's most famous cemeteries.

Tour operators in New Orleans typically take credit cards, but some of the smaller operations do not, especially those companies giving walking tours. Always confirm the payment options before you show up. Many tour operators require or strongly recommend reservations, but again, there are plenty of exceptions to this rule.

Even if you're not a big fan of tour excursions, there are certain places in Louisiana, and particularly New Orleans, where it's helpful to visit as part of an organized group with a knowledgeable leader. Cemeteries are an obvious one—they can be in dicey or even downright unsafe areas, and as fascinating as they are aesthetically, with their mausoleums and aboveground graves, they're best appreciated when described by an expert guide. Certain historic neighborhoods with notable architecture but few formal attractions or homes open to the public—such as New Orleans's Garden District—are also best explored as part of a tour.

The vast and ravishingly beautiful swamps and marshes throughout the region are also best visited on a tour, for logistical reasons if nothing else. An outsider would have little luck navigating these complex waterways. But guides can also point out the flora and fauna around you and also find the best spots to see alligators, egrets, nutria, and other creatures of Louisiana swamps up close.

Many of the region's bus tours, which lead through the Plantation Country along the

Mississippi River between New Orleans and Baton Rouge, are just as well avoided if you're the kind of person who loves hopping into the car and motoring about on your own, exploring scenic highways and byways. Most of the sites visited on these tours are open to the public anyway, and you can just as easily show up on your own for a tour, traveling at your own speed. If you don't wish to rent a car, however, these tours provide a convenient way to see at least one and possibly several plantations without having to worry about directions, logistics, and car-rental drop-offs. They're especially handy if you're visiting New Orleans for only a short time, and there is the added advantage of hearing about the towns and historic sites that line the river on the drive from New Orleans out to the plantations.

See the *Sights* chapter for descriptions of individual tour operators.

Explore New Orleans

THE TWO-DAY BEST OF NEW ORLEANS

With two days to explore New Orleans, you can handily see the city's key neighborhoods and enjoy a sampling of its major attractions. This approach begins in the French Quarter and steers you through the adjacent CBD and Faubourg Marigny neighborhoods during the first day. Then it takes you through Uptown, from the Lower Garden District to Audubon Park and Riverbend. Seeing everything on this tour requires a bit of energy, but this is definitely a doable strategy and a highly worthwhile one, too.

DAY 1
French Quarter: Morning to Early Afternoon

You can orient yourself the first morning of your visit with a stroll through Jackson Square, the city's historic heart and soul, which is flanked by a number of historic buildings, most notably St. Louis Cathedral. From here, you can't really go wrong no matter which direction you walk in. Royal Street and Chartres Street are each lined with diverting shops and galleries. The down-home restaurant Coops, on Decatur Street, is a reliable bet for po'boys, gumbo, and other traditional local fare. Stop by the nearby Jean Lafitte National Historical Park and Preserve to gain a quick sense of the history of not only New Orleans but all of southern Louisiana. The Old U.S. Mint Museum is a must-see when it's open, but the building sustained considerable damage after Hurricane Katrina and was closed at press time, so check before visiting.

Central Business District (CBD): Late Afternoon

Stroll across Canal Street from the Quarter into the city's bustling Central Business District in the afternoon, heading to the neighborhood's Warehouse District. You'll find a handful of notable galleries and shops along Julia and Girod streets, but the biggest draw in this area is the outstanding Ogden Museum of Southern Art.

Faubourg Marigny and French Quarter: Evening

New Orleans is fabled for its great restaurants and lively bars, and no visit to the city is complete without an evening of noshing on great food and listening to local music. You can accomplish this along touristy Bourbon Street, which is at least worth a look, but for a more authentic and appealing experience, venture into the neighborhood just downriver from the French Quarter, Faubourg Marigny (just a 20-minute walk across the Quarter from the CBD). Here along Frenchmen Street you'll find a number of terrific bars as well as some outstanding restaurants, such as Marigny Brasserie and Praline Connection. After dining, continue venturing around Faubourg Marigny and the French Quarter, checking out some of the terrific bars and music clubs, from Donna's to Lafitte's Blacksmith Shop. Finish off your night, no matter what time it is, with the traditional New Orleans snack of chicory-laced café au lait and powdered beignets (doughnuts) at the open-air Cafe du Monde restaurant, right across from Jackson Square.

DAY 2
Garden District: Morning

Start off your day by paying a visit to the city's most aristocratic neighborhood, rife with gracious mansions fronted by magnificently landscaped yards. The best way to experience it all is to take one of the several morning guided walks offered by various tour operators, some of the best of them offered by Historic New Orleans Tours and Gray Line. Additionally or alternatively, consider a walk through the neighborhood's Lafayette Cemetery No. 1—the nonprofit preservation organization Save Our Cemeteries offers guided tours of the cemetery several mornings each week.

Lower Magazine Street: Early Afternoon

It's just a few blocks from the Garden District to the lower section of Magazine Street, the Big Easy's most intriguing stretch of shopping. Lower Magazine is packed with atmospheric antiques shops, plus a handful of affordable cafes and restaurants. Drop by Slim Goodies for a tasty lunch of terrific diner fare, and grab dessert at Sophie's Gelato. Of course, if it's a truly memorable meal you're seeking, plan for lunch in the Garden District at the famous—though rightfully pricey—Commander's Palace restaurant.

Audubon Park: Late Afternoon

Walk, catch a cab, or take the bus from Lower Magazine Street to leafy Audubon Park. You'll travel a few miles along Magazine, so walking is recommended only if you enjoy pounding the pavement, but the rewards in the form of cool shopping and great people-watching can be well worth the trouble. When you come to Audubon Park, you can saunter about this live-oak–shaded slice of greenery, take a nap on the grass, or—if you're still feeling energetic—stroll through the Audubon Zoo.

Riverbend: Evening

Finish up your day with some combination of cocktails and dinner at one of the hip hangouts in Uptown's Riverbend neighborhood, which is just a 15-minute walk from Audubon Park. Top picks include Jacques-Imo's Cafe or Brigtsen's, both of which offer superb contemporary Louisiana cooking. The former is more on the funky side, the latter more romantic and refined. From Riverbend, you can normally hop the St. Charles Streetcar back to the CBD or Quarter, but service has been suspended and will likely not resume until at least 2008.

EXPERIENCING MARDI GRAS

No festival so reveals the joyous spirit of New Orleans more than Mardi Gras, one of the world's most memorable events. Mardi Gras (French for "Fat Tuesday") is known in many parts of the world as Carnival. For some people, Mardi Gras is *the* time to visit New Orleans, but it's not for everyone; this rollicking celebration draws intense crowds. Though the parades are free, the city's hotels book up, and the costs of airfare and parking skyrocket—still, the people-watching, and the chance to catch beads and trinkets, can warrant the inconvenience.

Mardi Gras in 2006, just six months after Hurricane Katrina, was a modest affair compared with previous years, but a huge success, considering the state of New Orleans following the storm. The consensus is that if New Orleans could stage a festive, upbeat Mardi Gras so soon after facing such devastation, the future of this event looks highly promising.

Parades and Customs

Mardi Gras's most famous events are parades and gala balls sponsored and hosted by private clubs, called krewes. The parades and balls have a new theme each year, typically a historical or mythical event. About 65 krewes hold parades during the Carnival season.

A parade has a lead float, a king's float, then a couple of dozen more floats. The krewe's captain leads the procession on a float or on horseback, followed by that year's officers (kings, queens, and so on), followed by marching bands, motorcycle squads, teams of clowns, and other entertainers. A gala ball follows, during which the royal court and its officers, in flamboyant costume, are feted into the wee hours. The galas are private (and if you are invited, it's tuxedos or tails for men, floor-length gowns for women).

The Rex Parade uses the Fatted Ox, or Boeuf Gras, as its symbol, to represent the last meat feast before Lent. Rex is the king of Mardi Gras, and he arrives in New Orleans by riverboat on Lundi Gras (Fat Monday), when there's a huge party at Spanish Plaza, on the Mississippi River. Admission is free, but you must wear a Mardi Gras mask.

Those walking or riding in the parades toss throws like trinkets, bead necklaces, and doubloons (commemorative coins) to the spectators lining the route. It's said that during parade season, watchers are festooned with some 3 million plastic commemorative cups, 2 million gross beads, and well over 20 million doubloons.

Everybody ends up catching something during a Mardi Gras parade. Enhance your odds by screaming at the top of your lungs, wearing a costume, making eye contact, and having adorable kids by your side—that trick works so well, it's worth borrowing kids for the event. Along the main parade route you'll see hundreds of stepladders where people plop their young kids so they'll be able to see over the standing adults. The traditional call of parade watchers hoping to catch goodies and treats is "Throw me something, Mister," but you won't hear many people saying this anymore. Sometimes what you do hear is off-color and amusing.

King cakes, crumbly coffeecake-like confections iced in the colors of Mardi Gras, are sold at bakeries all over the city through Ash Wednesday. A small plastic baby is baked into each king cake, and the person whose piece of cake contains this trinket is responsible for providing next year's king cake.

Mardi Gras Tips

Here are some tips on making the most of attending Mardi Gras in New Orleans:

Hotels book up a full year in advance, but many people cancel—you can often find reasonably priced rooms on a few weeks' notice.

Mardi Gras season always kicks off on

the same day, but the date of Fat Tuesday varies from year to year. Everything begins on January 6, the Twelfth Night Feast of the Epiphany. Fat Tuesday is the day before Lent, when Christians traditionally feast on meat before giving it up for 40 days. Thus, Mardi Gras always falls 46 days before Easter, and before the first day of Lent, Ash Wednesday. In 2007, it falls on February 20; in 2008 it's February 5; in 2009 it's February 24; and in 2010, it's February 16.

For all practical purposes, Mardi Gras weekend extends from the Friday before Fat Tuesday through midnight on Fat Tuesday. As the clock tolls midnight on Tuesday, Mardi Gras comes to an abrupt end, and cleaning crews swarm the Quarter and the parade route, embarking on the Herculean task of removing debris, cups, and broken beads.

No official parades run through the **French Quarter**—the streets are simply too narrow. But there's plenty going on there, from smaller informal groups staging their own processions to spectators tossing beads off balconies to (often drunken) revelers on the streets below. The goings-on in the Quarter are not family-oriented, and partying, exhibitionism, and all-around debauchery are typical. However, Mardi Gras parades elsewhere in the city— particularly along St. Charles Avenue in Uptown and the CBD—are surprisingly **family-friendly.** You'll see wild dancing and costumes along the floats and plenty of parents with kids lining the route, and in these parts of town, nudity and off-color behavior are at a minimum.

Parade routes are listed in the *New Orleans Times-Picayune* and also at a number of websites, such as www.mardigrasneworleans.com. Many hotels distribute free guides to guests, and a handful of magazines dedicated to Mardi Gras are available at city bookstores and newsstands.

Celebrations Outside New Orleans

You can have a great time, while saving money and avoiding crowds, by checking out Mardi Gras in a smaller Louisiana city. **Lafayette,** in the heart of Cajun Country, has probably the second-biggest Mardi Gras in the state, and the city's Southwest Louisiana Mardi Gras Association Pageant and Ball welcomes the public. (Elsewhere, Mardi Gras balls are usually private, sometimes with ties to the debutante season.) **Baton Rouge** also has a good Mardi Gras, as do the communities along the **North Shore** of Lake Pontchartrain, in St. Tammany and Tangipahoa Parishes.

Many of Louisiana's smaller rural communities hold **Courir de Mardi Gras** (literally, "the Running of the Mardi Gras"). This event dates back to the Cajun migration, with roots in medieval France. During Courir de Mardi Gras, groups on horseback, in carriages, and in pickup trucks race about the countryside, knocking on doors and "begging" for ingredients for a massive communal pot of gumbo. They sing, dance, or engage in shenanigans in their attempts to solicit chicken, rice, sausage, and onions. At the end of the day, celebrants gather for a gumbo feast and fais-do-do (Cajun dance party).

THE JAZZ, BLUES, ZYDECO, AND CAJUN MUSIC TOUR

Southern Louisiana's rich music heritage is a big part of what makes this part of the country special and what separates it from other places. Beginning in New Orleans and working your way west across the state into Cajun Country, it's possible to experience virtually every type of music associated with Louisiana, from jazz and blues to zydeco and Cajun. You'll also find a handful of attractions along the way that interpret the history of music in the region.

If you're the type of traveler who can't get enough music, here's a five-day itinerary that highlights the very best places in the state to hear and learn about it.

Day 1: New Orleans

If you're absolutely mad about music, you should definitely time your visit to coincide with New Orleans Jazz Fest, which takes place over 10 days in late April and early May and pulls in some of the top performers in the world. But anytime of year, New Orleans is known to host legendary musicians and to hold less famous but still lively festivals and events with great music.

Festival or not, spend your first day learning a bit about music in the city. Stop by Old U.S. Mint Museum (which closed due to Katrina damage but is slated to reopen in mid- to late 2007), which has a terrific jazz exhibit on the second floor detailing the careers of such pioneers as Buddy Bolden, Jack Laine, and Jelly Roll Morton.

In the evening, New Orleans simply pops with music all night long, and to some extent, you should plan where to go according to who's in town (the publication *OffBeat,* on the Web at http://offbeat.com, has the best live-music listings). But some places where you're nearly always certain to hear outstanding music around town include Tipitina's, Howlin' Wolf, the Palm Court Cafe, Pete Fountain's Jazz Club, Donna's, and Snug Harbor Jazz Bistro.

Day 2: New Orleans

During the day, you might want to venture up to Armstrong Park, named for native jazz legend Louis "Satchmo" Armstrong—a statue

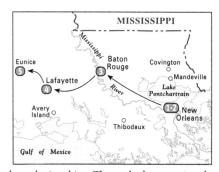

here depicts him. The park also contains the Mahalia Jackson Theatre of the Performing Arts, named for the famous gospel singer, which hosts concerts throughout the year. The National Park Service is developing the New Orleans Jazz National Historic Park, which eventually is to open inside Armstrong Park. The status of this development was unclear in the aftermath of Katrina, so stay tuned and keep checking the website for details at www.nps.gov/jazz.

Back in the Quarter, check out Preservation Hall, which since 1961 has been a favorite place to watch local jazz. Try to come back in the evening if there's a concert scheduled, but even during the day, you can admire the atmospheric old building and check out the walls covered with jazz posters and concert bills. It's a short walk to New Orleans Musical Legends Park on Bourbon Street, which contains statues of notable local jazz musicians. A great option for dinner and music, even though it's part of a national chain, is the always-hoppin'

House of Blues restaurant and club, on the edge of the Quarter near Canal Street. Nearly across the street, you'll also find one of the best sources of Cajun, jazz, zydeco, and blues CDs, vinyl, and tapes at the Louisiana Music Factory.

Day 3: Baton Rouge

En route to Cajun Country, stop in the capital city of Baton Rouge, which has an excellent variety of live-music clubs. Gino's Restaurant holds a wildly popular jazz jam 8–11 P.M. on Thursdays. Drop by Phil Brady's Bar for great blues music. College students and other music fans pack into the Cadillac Cafe and the legendary Varsity for hard-driving rock and blues.

Day 4: Lafayette

The largest city in Acadiana, Lafayette is an easy place to find great music. During the day, you can hear Cajun and zydeco performed at Vermilionville living history museum. And in downtown's Parc Sans Souci, the Lafayette Natural History Museum and Planetarium hosts popular lunchtime concerts featuring everything from jazz to percussion music. In the evening, head to one of the area's famous venues for Cajun food and dancing, such as Prejean's, Mulate's (in nearby Breaux Bridge), or Randol's.

Or check out one of the superb music clubs downtown, such as the Blue Moon Guest House and 307 Jazz and Blues Club. On the outskirts of town, El Sid O's Zydeco and Blues Club is one of the best places to hear live tunes in the region.

Day 5: Eunice

In northwestern Acadiana, about a 45-minute drive northwest of Lafayette, the small town of Eunice is ground-zero for learning about and listening to Cajun and zydeco music. Try to visit on a Saturday, when there's more going on in town. Start the day early by driving up to the nearby town of Mamou, where you can hear outstanding Fred's Lounge, which pumps up the volume 7:30 A.M.–2 P.M. Saturday (the bar is not open at night or any other days of the week). Begin by visiting the Prairie Acadian Cultural Center, a unit of Jean Lafitte National Historical Park and Preserve. It contains a wealth of exhibits on the origins and development of Cajun and Creole music. Then attend Rendezvous des Cajuns, the boot-stomping Cajun and zydeco variety show held early on Saturday evenings at the Liberty Center for the Performing Arts. If you're still up for live music in the evening, venture out to some of the first-rate clubs in the region, such as Slim's Y-Ki-Ki in Opelousas or D. I.'s Restaurant in Basile.

EATING YOUR WAY THROUGH SOUTHERN LOUISIANA

In a part of the country where travelers adore eating, it's almost impossible to tour southern Louisiana *without* experiencing fabulous meals. However, if you're truly serious about food, you can easily tailor your travels to take advantage of the region's leading shrines to noshing. Here's a sampling of restaurants—from low-budget dives to high-end hot spots—that should not be missed if dining well is your top reason for visiting. Keep in mind that New Orleans has so many incredible restaurants that it's nearly impossible to pick just a few, but the standouts suggested here rank among the best.

NEW ORLEANS

Commander's Palace

Few culinary traditions in America are more celebrated than enjoying a meal at this lavish restaurant, the flagship of the famed Brennan culinary empire. Highlights include turtle soup, bread pudding soufflé, and Creole-spiced filet mignon. Try your best to attend the weekend jazz brunch, which is great fun.

Galatoire's

If you had to pick one special-occasion restaurant in the French Quarter, this hallowed 1905 dining room is it. Feast on grilled pompano with sautéed crabmeat meunière or oysters Rockefeller and enjoy the rarefied ambience.

Quick Bites

Eating a muffuletta sandwich from Central Grocery is de rigueur in this town, as is partaking of the house-made gelato and ice cream at Angelo Brocato's. It requires a short trek into Bywater, but if you love home-style breakfast fare, stop by Elizabeth's for the specialty Loula May breakfast po'boy (fresh-baked French bread and spilling over with scrambled eggs, hot andouille sausage, and melted cheddar).

THE NORTH SHORE

The Dakota

Although it's attached to a humdrum Best Western hotel, this unassuming restaurant turns out some of the most creative food in the state, including such memorable dishes as New Orleans–style barbecued snails sautéed with fresh garlic, roasted tomatoes, rosemary, Abita beer, and butter. If you're looking to sample a wide range of chef's delights, opt for the tasting menu.

Longbranch

This handsome, historic restaurant in low-keyed Abita Springs opened in fall 2005, with talented young husband-and-wife chefs Allison and Slade Vines-Rushing at the helm. These creative kitchen geniuses turn out such tantalizing fare as salt-cured foie gras with local-strawberry jam and braised veal cheeks with sweet-potato gnocchi.

Quick Bites

In downtown Covington, Judice's turns out delicious short-order breakfasts and lunches, as does Old Mandeville's Broken Egg Cafe, where you might try bananas Foster waffles topped with pecans and fresh banana slices. And in Madisonville, funky Coffee's Boiling Pot is one of the best places in the state for authentic crawfish, crab, or shrimp boils.

THE GREAT RIVER ROAD

Juban's

You can watch local politicos and business leaders hobnob at this swanky Baton Rouge restaurant helmed by noted chef John Mariani. The restaurant is known for such signature dishes as crab and angel hair pasta fried crispy over a sauce of beurre blanc, and seafood-stuffed soft-shell crab topped with Creolaise sauce.

Grapevine Market and Cafe

This delightful little restaurant in the heart of Plantation Country doles out exceptional Cajun fare, from crawfish pie to barbecue shrimp to duck-and-andouille gumbo. The white-chocolate bread pudding draws raves among the desserts.

Quick Bites

Near the LSU campus in Baton Rouge, Louie's Cafe serves delicious home-style greasy-spoon fare 24 hours a day. Breakfast hits include the seafood Louie omelet (with crawfish, veggies, spiced butter, and herbed cream cheese), pecan pancakes, huge cheeseburgers, and po'boys. Charming St. Francisville is home to Magnolia Cafe, a lovely spot for pizzas, Mexican fare, and burgers, among other simple home cooking.

CAJUN COUNTRY

Cafe Vermilionville

A snazzy yet friendly restaurant set inside a stunning 1810s raised Creole cottage, Cafe Vermilionville is known for such creative Creole fare as crawfish beignets with a spicy Creole dipping sauce, and Louisiana speckled trout dusted with sweet-potato flour and finished with jumbo lump crabmeat and lemon-and-thyme beurre blanc. The restaurant also has one of the most respected wine lists in the area.

Catahoula's

It's worth the short drive north from Lafayette to tiny Grand Coteau to dine at this dapper restaurant that's set inside a vintage hardware-and-feed store. Exceptional regional fare is served, including raspberry roast duckling, seared ahi tuna on skewers, crabmeat cheesecake, and seafood Napoleon.

Quick Bites

In downtown Abbeville, Black's is one of the best restaurants around for enjoying oysters on the half shell plus other short-order Cajun treats. In Lafayette, Poor Boy's Riverside Inn serves outstanding po'boys, and Seafood Palace, a hole-in-the-wall in Lake Charles, serves some of the best fried seafood platters and gumbo in the state.

THE PLANTATION LOVER'S THREE-DAY WEEKEND

Louisiana's rich agrarian heritage has resulted in its incredible wealth of stunningly preserved plantation-museums, most of them set along the Great River Road, between New Orleans and the small town of St. Francisville. But you'll also find some notable plantation-museums in Cajun Country. With so many options, it's best to choose a few key properties to tour, perhaps spending the night in one or two of them. Here's a three-day itinerary that includes the state's most memorable plantations.

Day 1: Vacherie and Napoleonville

Start in the Mississippi River village of Vacherie with a visit to Laura: A Creole Plantation, which is known for its outstanding tours and fascinating legacy, as its slave cabins were where the folktales known as *Br'er Rabbit* were recorded in the late 1870s. The most interesting thing about a visit to Laura is that tour guides base their one-hour talk on the memoirs—which total about 5,000 pages—of the four generations of women who oversaw the compound's inner workings. Just upriver, stop for a tour of Oak Alley Plantation, whose stately exterior and 28 live oak trees provides one of the best photo ops in the South. As evening approaches, detour south off the Great River Road to Highway 1, which leads to little Napoleonville. Here you can spend the night at romantic Madewood Plantation, a 21-room Greek Revival mansion from 1846. The experience includes a tour of the buildings and grounds and a lavish candlelight dinner with your fellow guests.

Day 2: New Iberia and Sunset

From Napoleonville, plan a detour through Cajun Country by heading south on Highways 1, 398, and 662, and then west on U.S. Highway 90 to New Iberia. Here you can tour Shadows-on-the-Teche, a dignified white-columned brick house built by sugarcane farmer David Weeks in 1834. The best thing about Shadows is that the National Trust for Historic Preservation, which owns the house, also has a collection of about 17,000 paper documents relevant to the lives of the plantation's inhabitants and its day-to-day inner workings. Continue west on U.S. Highway 90 and then north on I-49 to the tiny village of Sunset, where you can spend the night at Chretien Point Plantation, a gracious 1831 plantation house set on 20 acres of lush grounds. Guests can choose from among five richly furnished rooms and also receive a full and hearty breakfast, a guided tour of the plantation house and grounds, hors d'oeuvres and cocktails each evening, and use of the large swimming pool. For dinner, plan to dine at Catahoula's, a wonderfully innovative contemporary restaurant in Grand Coteau that's just a 10-minute drive from Chretien Point.

Day 3: St. Francisville

From Sunset, take I-49 down to I-10, and follow this east to Baton Rouge, where U.S. Highway 61 leads north to the elegant, historic village of St. Francisville, the northernmost hub of plantation life on the Great River Road. Here you can tour **Rosedown Plantation State Historic Site,** a neoclassical columned manor house built in 1834. The Louisiana State Park service gives tours of the mansion and the beautiful formal gardens surrounding it. In the evening, plan to have dinner and spend the night in what is said to be the most haunted plantation in the state, **Myrtles Plantation,** which offers spooky evening mystery tours. The 1796 house is notable for its hand-painted stained glass, Aubusson tapestry, Baccarat crystal chandeliers, Carrara marble mantels, and gilt-leaf French furnishings.

SIGHTS

In truth, New Orleans is not a city rife with museums and attractions. But it's a wonderful place to explore, whether your interests lie in history, architecture, people-watching, shopping, or eating. In that sense, its neighborhoods, especially the oldest and most colorful, are living and working museums. And best of all, there's no admission fee for exploring them, and they're open 24/7, especially the French Quarter.

Still, you'll find a nice range of indoor attractions, from an excellent and underrated art museum to a slew of engaging house-museums set about the city. The city's top attractions tend to be its neighborhoods, from the French Quarter to the Garden District. You can get a peek inside some of the most intriguing houses by seeing them on guided tours.

Plenty of visitors, even those who come for just the weekend, make a trip out of the city to do one or two things (and sometimes both): take a swamp tour or visit some of the magnificent plantations flanking the Mississippi River between New Orleans and Baton Rouge. For these trips, you can go one of two routes: Either book a trip through one of the many tour operators in the city, or rent a car and drive on your own to the plantations or the departure point for the swamp tours. (If you're going on your own, see the side-trip chapters in this book: Swamp tours are well covered in the *North Shore, Cajun Country,* and *River Road* chapters, and plantation houses are covered in the *Cajun Country* and *River Road* chapters.) It's not especially practical to visit the Cajun Country as a day trip from New Orleans—the

SIGHTS

HIGHLIGHTS

◖ Most Iconic Landmark: The historic heart and soul of the French Quarter, and thus New Orleans, leafy and regal **Jackson Square** is fringed by such iconic buildings as St. Louis Cathedral, the Cabildo, the Arsenal, the Presbytère, and the Pontalba Apartments. It's the perfect place to get your bearings and begin exploring the Big Easy (page 45).

◖ Best Glimpse of History: The main branch of an impressive historical park, **Jean Lafitte National Historical Park and Preserve** is in the French Quarter along Decatur Street and contains a number of exhibits on the city's history. From here you can also attend one of the superb walking tours of the French Quarter (page 48).

◖ Best People-Watching: The historic **French Market,** parts of which date to 1813, runs for several blocks along Decatur Street and contains dozens of specialty-food and produce stalls and quite a few shops and eateries (including the famous Cafe du Monde). There are also flea markets and a farmers market on certain days (page 49).

◖ Best Tribute to Jazz Heritage: Although the **Old U.S. Mint Museum** was undergoing Katrina-related repairs as of fall 2006, this elegant neoclassical facility, which functioned both as a U.S. and Confederate mint during its early years, contains several outstanding museum exhibits, the best one tracing the city's jazz heritage (page 52).

◖ Most Bewitching Street: Bourbon Street receives more attention for its raucous nightlife, but **Royal Street** is the French Quarter's most alluring and engaging street, lined with fine antiques and art galleries, dapper cafes and restaurants, and several excellent hotels. Architecturally, it's one of the prettiest streets in America (page 53).

◖ Best Place to Take the Kids: An attraction that delights youngsters as much as adults, the spectacular, contemporary **Audubon Aquarium of the Americas** overlooks the Mississippi River and is filled with fascinating exhibits on important aquatic habitats around the world, from the Amazon rainforest to the Gulf of Mexico (page 60).

◖ Best Place to View Art: Nowhere can you find a more esteemed collection of Southern art than at the **Ogden Museum of Southern Art,** which moved into a dramatic new space in 2003 and displays 3,000 works by the region's leading talents (page 70).

◖ Best Activity for a Sunny Day: If there's one thing you should do on a balmy, sunny day, it's take **a walking tour of the Garden District,** a leafy, elegant neighborhood that's dotted with beautiful old homes and anchored by the historic Lafayette Cemetery No. 1 (page 80).

◖ Best Urban Oasis: After exploring Uptown's convivial restaurants or strolling along Magazine Street or St. Charles Avenue admiring historic homes, be sure to relax for a bit with a stroll through verdant, 340-acre **Audubon Park,** which is also home to the fine Audubon Zoo and Gardens, numerous sports fields and walking trails, and an excellent golf course (page 83).

◖ Most Enchanting Place for a Stroll: A 1,500-acre swath of greenery, **City Park** contains one of the city's top cultural attractions, the New Orleans Museum of Art. But it's also an excellent place for walking, especially through the park's New Orleans Botanical Garden. And there are several other draws here, from the outstanding restaurant Ralph's on the Park nearby to the Storyland children's playground (page 90).

LOOK FOR ◖ TO FIND THE SIGHTS YOU CAN'T MISS.

drive takes 2–3 hours each way. But you can easily visit the North Shore or River Road regions as day trips.

If you do opt to go it on your own, you may save money, especially if there are 3–4 of you sharing a rental car. Guided bus tours charge by the person, so 1–2 people may find it cheaper or similar in cost to book a tour, especially when you factor in the cost of gas and admission to the plantations and swamp tours, which are generally included in the tour fee.

There are always tradeoffs between making your own day trip and going with a guided tour. On any guided tour you're likely to be spending the trip with a fair number of other travelers, which can be good or bad depending on whether you're especially social. The tour buses draw heavily from among conventioneers and travelers who have booked package tours to New Orleans. If you're a particularly independent-spirited person, you might not enjoy this experience. On the other hand, some of the guides and drivers who lead these tours give excellent narration throughout the tour, and some of them are quite funny to boot. (Though you can also end up with a guide who tells awful, corny jokes and tries to an annoying degree to get everybody on the tour to chit-chat and participate.) Still, consider a tour if you prefer a carefree vacation: You don't have to study road maps, think about where you're going, or worry about picking up and returning rental cars and so on. Several of the city's best tour operators are described in this chapter.

Within the city itself, you can quite easily get around most of the key neighborhoods using a combination of walking, public streetcars and buses, and the occasional cab. If you're staying in the French Quarter or CBD/Warehouse District, you can easily hoof it to just about any attraction within either of these neighborhoods as well as in Faubourg Marigny. It's possible to walk to at least the Lower Garden District from the French Quarter and actually quite easy from the Warehouse District, but not all that many people do. You have to walk beneath the massive U.S. 90 bridge, and for several blocks there, it's a less-than-charming

St. Charles Avenue streetcar

© NEW ORLEANS CVB/JACK EDWARDS

stroll. It's easy and certainly more scenic just to take the St. Charles Avenue streetcar into the Garden District (the line is out of commission but expected to resume service sometime in mid- to late 2007).

The Garden District and Lower Garden District are at the lower end of Uptown, a long and winding neighborhood that extends for several miles west of the CBD. It's a fairly safe area, as safe as the Quarter or other well-visited neighborhoods, but distances are great, and you need to be in good walking shape to visit the entire Uptown district on foot. One practical idea is to take the streetcar to the Garden District and walk through it to reach Magazine Street. Walk uptown along Magazine as far as you feel like, taking in the many blocks of cool antiques and other shops, and use public buses when your legs need a break. Once you get to Audubon Park, walk over to St. Charles Street, which runs parallel to Magazine, and take the streetcar back to the CBD.

Mid-City, an area that has grown in popularity with visitors but was flooded significantly during Katrina, can be visited from the French Quarter quite easily by bus or streetcar. Just take Bus 48 up Esplanade Avenue, the road that divides the French Quarter from the next neighborhood downriver, Faubourg Marigny. Or take the streetcar up Canal Street from the other side of the French Quarter, where it meets with the CBD. Mid-City contains City Park, site of the New Orleans Museum of Art and the New Orleans Botanical Gardens. Hurricane damage in Mid-City wasn't as severe as in some of the worst parts of town, and a year after Katrina had struck, the majority of the homes and businesses in the neighborhood had either been reinhabited or had reopened, or they were close to coming back. Overall, Mid-City has come back nicely and is poised to continue growing, as those who are unable to return to the more badly damaged sections of the city continue to move into Mid-City.

Across the Mississippi from the French Quarter is the West Bank, which includes a small chunk of land, Algiers Point, that's actually considered part of New Orleans proper but is mostly a series of suburbs. Algiers Point has the famous Blaine Kern's Mardi Gras World museum and a few streets of interesting old houses—you can easily explore this neighborhood by taking the free (to pedestrians) ferry that runs all throughout the daytime and into the early evening between the foot of Canal Street and Algiers Point. A free shuttle bus on the West Bank takes any guests interested to Blaine Kern's Mardi Gras World.

At the risk of generalizing, the rest of New Orleans proper holds relatively little interest for visitors, and parts of the city are either unsafe, industrial, or simply not pleasant to explore. A handful of shopping centers and attractions are in the suburbs immediately outside New Orleans, such as Metairie, Gretna, and Harahan. It's not practical to explore these communities unless you have a car, although you can get to some of the key points in these cities using public buses. It takes some time getting to know the bus schedule, however, and few tourists use

them for such long trips—the fact is, few tourists, with or without private cars, spend much time exploring the close-in suburbs.

HOURS AND ADMISSION

Hours at many smaller attractions can be very complicated and can change frequently throughout the year, and this has become especially the case since Katrina. For this reason, an attraction's hours are listed only when they're fairly straightforward and reliable; in all other cases the hours are listed as either "limited" or "seasonal." It's always a good idea to phone ahead to ensure that the place will be open on the day that interests you.

Don't be put off by limited hours, though—in most cases, if you phone a week or two ahead and ask to see one of these smaller attractions by appointment, you'll be encouraged to set up a private visit. Most of these smaller establishments are operated by volunteers and supported by bequests and gifts; they typically charge a nominal entrance fee or perhaps request a donation.

Those attractions with a fairly steady flow of visitors offer the same hours you might expect of most local businesses and shops: 9 A.M.–5 P.M., 5–7 days a week (Sundays, Mondays, and Tuesdays are the most common days when attractions are closed; even some of the most prominent plantation museums close on Monday). In many cases, hours are reduced on Sundays. In summer you'll notice that some of these attractions stay open a bit later, and in winter some of them close at 4 P.M. or don't open until 10 or 11 A.M.

The admission given for each attraction in this book is for adults. At the vast majority of the attractions in the state, very young children are admitted free; grade-school kids, college students, and senior citizens very often receive discounts of 25–50 percent. Some places also give discounts to holders of AAA cards or military IDs—it's always a good idea to ask about discounts before paying.

Whatever these general rules of thumb, and whatever hours and admission are listed in this book, remember that hours (and other policies) may change with no notice. It's highly advisable that you phone ahead before visiting any attraction in Louisiana.

TOUR OPERATORS

One of the best general tour companies in the city is the ubiquitous but highly reliable **Gray Line** (504/569-1401 or 800/535-7786, www.graylineneworleans.com), which offers a wonderful variety of tours, including a Katrina-themed bus tour that takes you past some of the neighborhoods hit hardest by the storm and provides a fascinating look at the past, present, and future of safeguarding New Orleans against the wrath of nature. One of the more unusual Gray Line excursions is the Southern Comfort Cocktail Tour, a two-hour ramble through the Quarter in which strollers are regaled with stories of the Big Easy's colorful restaurants and taverns, along with the famous cocktails invented at them. Southern Comfort itself was created back in 1874 by M. W. Heron at a bar in the French Quarter. All Gray Line tours leave from the little lighthouse-style Gray Line booth at the foot of Toulouse Street by the river.

Blue Dog Seafood Tours (985/531-0000, www.bluedogtours.com) offers the ultimate tour for fish lovers. These boat rides take visitors through the swamps, where you'll see the crew hoist gill and hoop nets for fish, traps for crawfish, and even box traps for wild boar. The narrative also details how various residents of southern Louisiana—Cajuns, Isleños, Indians and escaped slaves, and Croatians and Vietnamese—historically eked out a living from fishing. The tour ends with a lavish feast of Louisiana seafood. Transportation to and from your hotel in New Orleans can be arranged for $15 per person; the tour and dinner cost $75 per person.

Cemetery tours are a favorite in New Orleans; they're usually entertaining but in some cases sensational, with mystical tales concerning voodoo and ghosts. If you'd prefer a straightforward graveyard tour that still has plenty of color and historical insights, try **Save Our Cemeteries** (504/525-3377 or 888/721-

7493, www.saveourcemeteries.com), a nonprofit organization that preserves and protects 31 of the city's burial grounds. It offers outstanding tours of both Lafayette Cemetery No. 1 and St. Louis Cemetery No. 1. These are well-done walks with excellent guides. The Lafayette tours are given at 10:30 A.M. on Monday, Wednesday, Friday, and Saturday and cost $6; the St. Louis tours are given at 10 A.M. on Sunday mornings only and cost $12.

Strongly recommended are the informative Garden District walks given by **Historic New Orleans Tours** (504/947-2120, www.tourneworleans.com). These tours are given at 11 A.M. and 1:45 P.M. daily, departing from the **Garden District Book Shop** (at The Rink, Washington Ave. and Prytania St.). The tours last about two hours, and the cost is $15. (The same company also does French Quarter, Haunted, and Cemetery Voodoo tours as well as Weekend Jazz Walks.)

One of the more interesting ways to appreciate New Orleans's two favorite attractions is via the *John James Audubon* (504/586-8777, www.aquariumzoocruise.com), a riverboat that plies the Mississippi between the Aquarium of the Americas, at the foot of Canal Street, and the Audubon Zoo, at Audubon Park. The boat has departures from the Aquarium to the zoo at 10 A.M., noon, 2 P.M., and 4 P.M. daily; departures from the zoo are 11 A.M., 1 P.M., 3 P.M., and 5 P.M. There are few more enjoyable ways to appreciate the city skyline than from this lazy boat ride. The fare is $17 roundtrip, and combination packages are available that include aquarium and zoo admission at a discounted rate.

Some of the other cruise boats offering excursions in New Orleans are also discussed in the *Entertainment* chapter, as these operators offer evening dinner and jazz cruises.

New Orleans Paddlewheels (Poydras St. Wharf, 504/529-4567 or 800/445-4109, www.neworleanspaddlewheels.com) has several types of river excursions aboard the **Riverboat *Cajun Queen,*** built in the late 1980s as an exact replica of a late–19th-century vessel that sailed along the Atlantic and Gulf coasts, and on the

Paddlewheeler *Creole Queen,* a 1983 boat based on an 1850s luxury paddle wheeler. Trips include Dixieland jazz cruises (with dinner included), hour-long river tours, and trips out to Chalmette battlefield, site of the Battle of New Orleans.

The **Steamboat *Natchez*** (Toulouse St. Wharf, behind Jackson Brewery, 504/586-8777, www.steamboatnatchez.com) offers daily cruises with live jazz along the river at lunchtime, during the afternoon, and in the evening.

ORIENTATION AND DIRECTIONS

New Orleanians rarely refer to compass directions when talking about how to get around the city or where something is. Part of the reason for this is that the city is bound on one side by the highly irregular Mississippi River, which, depending on which part of it you're facing, forms either the western, southern, or eastern border. Main roads tend to run parallel or perpendicular to the river, and since the river's direction changes, this means that New Orleans's street grid also changes its axis in different places. It can get very confusing trying to think in terms of east and west and north and south.

More often, the terms "lakeside" (meaning toward Lake Pontchartrain, and typically in a northerly direction) and "riverside" (meaning toward the Mississippi, and typically in a southerly direction) are used when referring to streets that run perpendicular to the river. For example, somebody might tell you to drive up Esplanade Avenue toward the lake. The terms "upriver" or "uptown" are used generally to refer to westerly directions, and the terms "downriver" or "downtown" are used for easterly directions. Canal Street, which people think of as running north–south, because it eventually connects the river to the lake, ac-

tually runs east–southeast toward the river. Looking across Jackson Square from midblock on Decatur Street directly toward St. Louis Cathedral, you're actually looking due northwest, not north, as one tends to think.

A little more confusion: "Uptown" is both an adjective describing the direction opposite "downtown" and also the name of a neighborhood itself. So, you can be headed "uptown" but not actually be going as far as Uptown the neighborhood, which is technically defined as the blocks between Louisiana Avenue and Lowerline Street. However, many New Orleanians simply call anything upriver from the CBD and Pontchartrain Expressway (that big elevated highway that runs along the side of the CBD and crosses over the Mississippi River to the West Bank) Uptown.

Got all that?

Don't worry too much if you don't. Just carry a map of the city with you at all times, as this is one place where such a document is absolutely indispensable whether you're walking, driving, taking public transportation, or even using cabs. New Orleans is very much a collection of neighborhoods, and people refer specifically to neighborhood names as much as or even more than they refer to street names or various coordinates.

A good starting point for orienting yourself before wandering the city's streets is the **Preservation Resource Center** (923 Tchoupitoulas St., 504/581-7032, www.prcno.org), in the Warehouse District. Here you can read helpful thumbnails that describe each of the city's neighborhoods and pick up a free map describing each. The center also has detailed information on the various types of architecture that define New Orleans, and the organization has been instrumental in helping get the city's most damaged historic areas repaired and rejuvenated since Katrina.

The French Quarter

Known also as the Vieux Carré (French for "Old Quarter" and pronounced VOH-cair-EE in these parts), the French Quarter comprised the entire city of New Orleans during its first century or so, and it has always been the great hub of activity and social life, especially for Creoles. When Americans began moving into New Orleans to stake their fortunes in the early 1800s, the descendants of French and to a lesser extent Spanish settlers shunned them bitterly. The adjacent Central Business District (CBD) grew up at that time as the so-called American Quarter, extending well into what is now the present-day Garden District.

The French Quarter's enduring architecture, much of it from the late 18th century and clearly influenced by the ruling Spaniards of that time, has long been appreciated by preservationists. This was one of the first neighborhoods in America where concerned locals began preserving old buildings and passing local laws that prohibited the alteration or razing of historic structures and the construction of buildings not in character with the rest of the neighborhood.

What also helped preserve the Quarter, at least throughout much of the 20th century, was its lack of prosperity. Especially after World War II, the neighborhood took a turn for the worst during the 1950s and '60s, and especially the Lower Quarter came to be thought of as something of a slum. A mix of hippies, gays, artists, antiques dealers, underprivileged families, a very few remaining descendants of early Creole families, and quite a few multigenerational Italian families (the most common of the neighborhood's immigrants during the early 20th century) lived here, and tourists visited some of the key nightspots, restaurants, and historic hotels nearest the riverfront and Canal Street but largely avoided the rest of it.

By about the mid- to late 1970s, preservation-minded locals began to promote the restoration of those sections of the Quarter that had fallen on hard times, and the city began talk-

French Quarter balcony

ing up the neighborhood more aggressively as a unique urban destination. Fancier hotels, inns, and restaurants opened, and Bourbon Street nightlife thrived, especially as New Orleans became increasingly notable as a business-convention destination.

The French Quarter's rise in popularity has been almost meteoric since the late 1980s, a phenomenon that has had the rather familiar effect of raising the entire district's standard of living but also of pushing out many of the less economically solvent residents into less expensive—and less desirable—areas. Real-estate prices for French Quarter buildings, both residential and commercial spaces, have skyrocketed, especially since Hurricane Katrina, as the Quarter emerged with relatively little damage compared with other areas. The cost of living along the most desirable blocks of the French Quarter is still quite a lot less than in prominent neighborhoods in other big U.S.

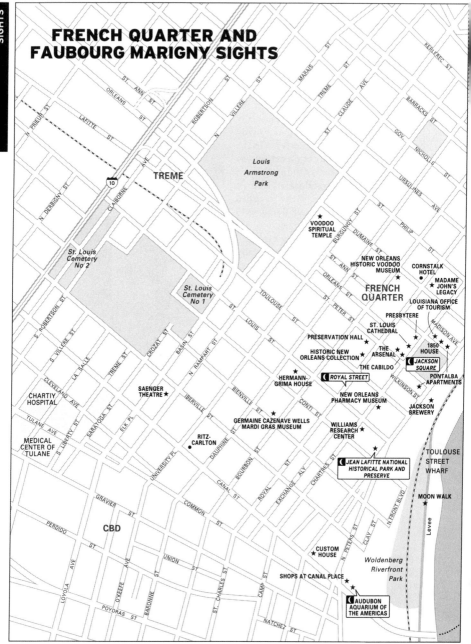

FRENCH QUARTER AND FAUBOURG MARIGNY SIGHTS

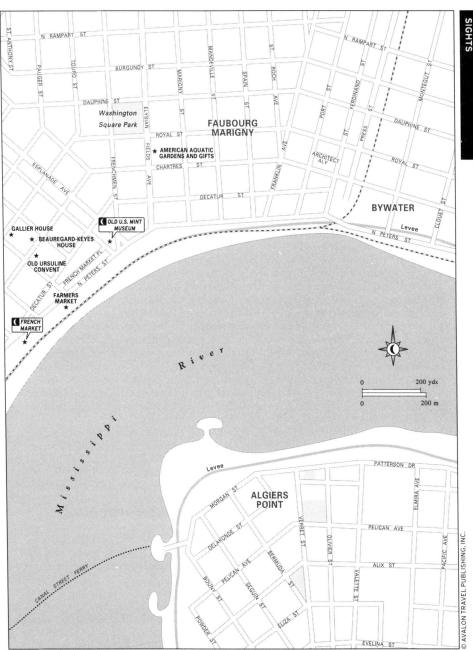

ST. ANTHONY ST
N RAMPART ST
PALIGER ST
TOURO ST
BURGUNDY ST
DAUPHINE ST
MARIGNY ST
MANDEVILLE ST
SPAIN ST
ROCH ST
AVE
N RAMPART ST
ST
ST
FERDINAND ST
PORT ST
PRESS ST
MONTEGUT ST

Washington Square Park
ROYAL ST
FAUBOURG MARIGNY
DAUPHINE ST

ELYSIAN FIELDS AVE
★ AMERICAN AQUATIC GARDENS AND GIFTS
ARCHITECT ALY
ROYAL ST

ESPLANADE AVE
FRENCHMEN ST
CHARTRES ST
FRANKLIN AVE

DECATUR ST
BYWATER

GALLIER HOUSE
★
◖ OLD U.S. MINT MUSEUM
Levee
N PETERS ST
CLOUET ST

★ **BEAUREGARD-KEYES HOUSE**

★
OLD URSULINE CONVENT
FRENCH MARKET PL
N PETERS ST

DECATUR ST
FARMERS MARKET
★

◖ FRENCH MARKET
★

Mississippi
R i v e r

0 _____ 200 yds
0 _____ 200 m

Levee
ALGIERS POINT
PATTERSON DR
ELMIRA AVE

MORGAN ST
VERRET ST
PELICAN AVE
PACIFIC AVE

DELARONDE ST
BERMUDA ST
OLIVER ST
ALIX ST
VALETTE ST

CANAL STREET FERRY
BOUNY ST
PELICAN AVE
SEGUIN ST
ELIZA ST

POWDER ST
EVELINA ST

© AVALON TRAVEL PUBLISHING, INC.

cities, but the city's reduced post-Katrina housing stock continues to drive up costs. And also keep in mind that costs are relative to income, and New Orleans salaries are lower than in many major U.S. cities—this was the case before the hurricane, and it's still the case today.

The gentrification trend in the French Quarter has spilled over downriver into neighboring Faubourg Marigny since the mid- to late 1990s, and even more recently up Esplanade Avenue toward Mid-City. Nevertheless, those blocks nearest the Marigny and also farthest from the river, up near North Rampart Street, tend to be the quietest, especially at night. You should regard your surroundings carefully wherever you wander in the French Quarter, but especially in these sections, where it's best to move about in groups or use cabs late at night.

Officially, the Quarter extends downriver from Canal Street to Esplanade Avenue, and lakeside (in the direction of Lake Pontchartrain) from the Mississippi River to Rampart Street. A dozen streets run parallel to Canal and Esplanade between them, and six streets run parallel to Rampart down to the river. On the riverside edges of the Quarter, North and South Peters streets run at a slight angle to the rest of the Quarter, roughly parallel to the bend in the river. All told, the French Quarter comprises 98 blocks, and there is not one single block that lacks architectural treasures and a rich history.

Most visitors focus on Decatur, Chartres, Royal, and Bourbon streets—the main thoroughfares running roughly parallel to and extending from the river, and on the Lower Quarter, meaning the blocks between Canal Street and about St. Ann Street, which marks the downriver border of Jackson Square. In this roughly 30-block quadrant you'll find the largest share of the French Quarter's hotels, restaurants, bars, shops, and tourist attractions, and you'll also find the most intense crowds.

If you walk along the streets parallel to Bourbon but farther toward the lake, you'll still find a smattering of hotels, restaurants, and bars, but few shops or attractions per se. But you'll see some wonderful old buildings, many of them private residences, especially on Dumaine and Burgundy streets. Rampart is a real hit-or-miss street. The side of Rampart away from the Quarter is not especially charming and, in fact, forms the border of the fabled Storyville (a red-light district during the early 20th century) and Tremé, a mostly poor and predominantly African American district characterized by several immense housing projects—this area was damaged heavily by the hurricane, and it may be years before it comes back fully. This side of Rampart also forms one border of Armstrong Park, which does have some interesting features. The Quarter side of Rampart has a hodgepodge of buildings, including some of the city's divier gay bars and also a couple of superb jazz clubs, Donna's and the Funky Butt.

The main cross streets of the Lower Quarter are, from Canal to Jackson Square, Iberville, Bienville, Conti, St. Louis, Toulouse, St. Peter, Orleans (a half street that runs only from Royal to Rampart), and St. Ann streets. Again, these streets are nearly choked with shops, restaurants, and other businesses catering primarily to tourists, which is not to say that they're lacking in appeal—you just have to wade through the crowds and overlook some of the cheesier and more commercial shops and restaurants that qualify more as tourist traps than bona fide points of interest.

Some of the finest antiques shops are along this stretch of Royal Street and the blocks just off it, where such establishments have thrived for more than a century, and you'll also find some excellent restaurants in these parts. Once you get beyond St. Ann and into the Upper Quarter, and wander the blocks between it and Esplanade (these being Dumaine, St. Philip, Ursulines, Governor Nicholls, and Barracks streets), you'll find not only some superb examples of 19th-century residential architecture but also some of the city's true hotel and restaurant gems, many of them less touristy than those in the Lower Quarter. The section of the Upper Quarter nearest the river has the most commercial activity, especially at Decatur and North Peters streets, where you'll find the famous French Market and quite a few shops and bars of interest. The Upper Quarter stretches of Royal and Chartres have some neat old hotels and a few eateries, but Bourbon, Dauphine, and Burgundy are mostly residential in the Upper Quarter.

It's difficult to capture the French Quarter's exact collective vibe—that changes from block to block. Architecturally, it feels like a cross between the Spanish and French cities of the Caribbean (such as Havana, the old part of San Juan, and Port-au-Prince, Haiti), Spain itself, and France. Little of the French Quarter bears any resemblance at all to even the historic residential neighborhoods found in other U.S. cities. Buildings tend to be painted in pastel colors and have frilly wooden or wrought-iron balconies with elaborate grillwork. Most of the oldest buildings in the neighborhood date to the late 1700s, when New Orleans was under Spanish control, as the previous French-style buildings that dominated before that time were mostly burned during one or both of the huge fires that engulfed the Quarter during this period, one in 1788 and a smaller one in 1794. This accounts for the distinctly Spanish look of many buildings.

But early Creoles (the term originally used to describe French colonists who had fled Haiti's black revolutions of the early 1800s) settled in and greatly determined the architectural and cultural flavor of the French Quarter as we know it. What you see today, at least in terms of architecture and layout, closely resembles the French Quarter of the 19th century.

⬛ JACKSON SQUARE

Jackson Square anchors the French Quarter and is a good place to begin your explorations. Originally known as the Place d'Armes (and then the Plaza de Armas, under Spanish rule), Jackson Square was renamed in honor of the seventh U.S. president, Andrew Jackson, who led the United States to victory during the Battle of New Orleans. A statue of Jackson, said to be the first equestrian statue ever erected to depict a horse balanced on its hind-quarters, anchors the square and ranks among

the city's favorite photo-ops (especially if you capture the image with St. Louis Cathedral in the background). The 14-foot-tall bronze was cast by artist Clark Mills in 1856 (at a then-astronomical cost of $30,000), the year that Baroness Micaela Almonester de Pontalba successfully lobbied city officials to transform Place d'Armes from a military parade ground into a civilized public garden. Note the inscription on the statue, which may seem unlikely on a statue in the South: "The Union Must and Shall Be Preserved." This was commissioned by Union Civil War General Benjamin Butler, the detested and brutal autocrat who ruled New Orleans with an iron fist during his short tenure there after the Union capture of the city midway through the war.

Jackson Square is a wonderful place to sit and read a newspaper, eat a muffuletta or a snack from one of the nearby cafes, and take in this earliest-laid-out section of New Orleans. Across Decatur Street from the square is a plaque marking the original riverfront—the Mississippi River nearly lapped at the edge of Jackson Square during the 18th century, before the course of the river shifted a bit south, and levees were constructed to protect the Quarter from flooding. Along the sidewalks that fringe Jackson Square on all sides (three of them are pedestrian ways with no motor vehicles), you'll find an eccentric bunch of mimes, artists, fortune readers, buskers, and other entertainers. And lined up along Decatur Street at the riverside of the square are horse-drawn carriages awaiting tourists booking excursions through the Quarter. (On that note, be careful of these carriages as they clip-clop through the neighborhood, especially if you're driving, and beware the messes they occasionally leave behind if you're on foot.)

Four buildings on the square—the Cabildo, the Arsenal, the Presbytère, and 1850 House—are part of the Louisiana State Museum system, as are the U.S. Mint and Madame John's Legacy in the Lower Quarter. Each charges a separate admission fee; buy tickets to two or more buildings, and you get a 20 percent discount. Some of the state museum facilities were still closed as of this writing, but other than the U.S. Mint, which received significant roof damage, most of the buildings were not badly damaged. The reason for closings and limited hours is staff shortages, and by 2007, it's expected that most of the museums will be back up and running, although likely with less extensive hours than before Katrina. See the individual descriptions for more details.

St. Louis Cathedral

The north (lakeside) end of the square is dominated by St. Louis Cathedral (615 Père Antoine Alley, 504/525-9585, www.stlouiscathedral.org, free tours 9 A.M.–5 P.M. Mon.–Sat., 1:30–5 P.M. Sun.), one of the most magnificent cathedrals in the United States. The current building was constructed in 1794 in the Spanish style, with two round spires rising from the facade, and then virtually rebuilt and remodeled in 1849, but simpler churches have stood on this site beginning with the arrival of the French explorer Sieur Jean Baptiste Le Moyne de Bienville, who established New Orleans as a permanent settlement in 1719—that first wooden structure was quickly dispatched by the forces of nature, when a hurricane swept through in 1723. During the 1849 remodel, huge steeples were added to the two symmetrical round towers, and the building has received additional restorations through the years. The cathedral was designated a minor basilica in 1964 by Pope Paul VI. Mass is said daily, and there's a gift shop, open 9 A.M.–6 P.M. daily.

The Cabildo

On the upriver side of the cathedral stands the Cabildo (701 Chartres St., 504/568-6968 or 800/568-6968, http://lsm.crt.state.la.us, open 10 A.M.–4 P.M. Tues.–Sun., admission $6), the building in which the formal transfer of Louisiana to the United States took place after the Louisiana Purchase. The Spanish first constructed the Cabildo as their seat of government in the 1770s, but it and its replacement were destroyed during both city fires. The current structure, made of brick and stucco and built in the Spanish style with Moorish in-

the Cabildo, site of the signing of the Louisiana Purchase

© NEW ORLEANS CVB

fluences, was erected in 1794, serving again as home to the Spanish administrative body, then as the Maison de Ville (Town Hall) during the very brief time the French reclaimed New Orleans. It would serve as the state supreme court headquarters for much of the 19th and early 20th centuries, and it was actually the site where the landmark *Plessy v. Ferguson* decision (which legalized segregation) was handed down. Many prominent visitors have been officially received in the Cabildo, from statesmen Henry Clay and the Marquis de Lafayette to such distinguished figures of the arts as Mark Twain and Sarah Bernhardt. The building looks more French than Spanish today, because the original flat-tile roof was replaced with a Second Empire mansard roof in the late 1840s.

The Cabildo became part of the Louisiana State Museum in 1911, but it suffered a devastating fire in 1988. After an exhaustive restoration, the building reopened in 1994, and it now contains a comprehensive and fascinating exhibit tracing the history of New Orleans through the past 200 years, with the focus falling especially on the early period. The exhibits are grouped into 10 chronological sections, beginning with the region's Native Americans and ending with Reconstruction. Various stages in between include Colonial Louisiana, the Louisiana Purchase, and several exhibits relating to different aspects of antebellum Louisiana life, such as Death and Mourning and Urban Life. Each section uses maps, photographs and drawings, historical documents, and informative narrative signs to describe the period and theme.

The Arsenal

Adjacent to the Cabildo on the riverside of the building, the Greek Revival Arsenal (600 St. Peter St., 504/568-6968 or 800/568-6968, http://lsm.crt.state.la.us, open 10 A.M.–4 P.M. Tues.–Sun., admission $6) was constructed in 1839 and became part of the state museum complex in 1915. It also was badly damaged during the Cabildo fire of 1988 and also carefully restored. Both permanent and rotating exhibits are installed in the first and second floors of the building; among the former, Louisiana and the Mighty Mississippi explores how flatboats, ferries, steamboats, and keel boats helped New Orleans grow into one of the world's great river ports during the 19th century. And the related exhibit Freshly Brewed: The Coffee Trade and the Port of New Orleans examines the economic importance of the city's coffee trade.

The Presbytère

Built in 1797 as a home for the priests of St. Louis Cathedral and standing just on the downriver side of it, the two-story Presbytère on Jackson Square (751 Chartres St., 504/568-6968 or 800/568-6968, http://lsm.crt.state.la.us/site/presbex.htm, open 10 A.M.–4 P.M. Fri.–Sun., admission $6) bears a structural resemblance to the Cabildo. It was never used for its intended purpose, as its financier, Don Andres Almonester (a Spaniard of considerable means who also funded the Cabildo and St. Louis Cathedral), died before it was com-

pleted. The new U.S. government eventually completed it and used it to house the Louisiana state courts during the 19th century.

Like the Cabildo, it became part of the Louisiana State Museum in 1911. It houses a colorful permanent exhibit on the history of Mardi Gras both in the city and Louisiana in general. Videos and audiotapes and a wide array of artifacts detail how Louisianans have celebrated Carnival through the years and how this event has grown to become one of the most popular festivals in the world.

Pontalba Apartments and the 1850 House

Baroness Micaela Almonster de Pontalba commissioned the two compounds of row houses flanking Jackson Square in 1849 (the lower building, on St. Ann) and 1851 (the upper building, on St. Peter), and they continue to bear her name as the **Pontalba Apartments.** She hired three different prominent architects, including James Gallier (who built many of the Quarter's most distinguished structures), but had a rocky relationship with them all. Samuel Stewart ultimately finished the construction, but the baroness closely supervised the process. Pontalba, in fact, completely renovated the entire property that surrounded the cathedral, convincing local authorities to change the name of what had been the Place d'Armes to Jackson Square (in honor of General Andrew Jackson, the victor of the Battle of New Orleans), and she came up with the idea of running two sets of row houses alongside it. She had inherited the land from her father, Don Almonester, the man who had financed the Cabildo, Presbytère, and St. Louis Cathedral after the devastating fire of 1788.

Each row of buildings, when it first opened, contained 16 separate houses on the upper levels and a series of shops on the lower levels. Her plan to build the Pontalba buildings and renovate the square and its existing buildings could be called one of the earliest examples of urban renewal, for the Quarter had fallen on hard times by the time she stepped in. For a period, her plan worked, but after the Civil War and well into the early

1900s, Jackson Square and the neighborhood immediately around it began to deteriorate, and the Pontalba Apartments functioned as rather unfashionable tenements.

In 1921, one of the early champions of preserving the Quarter, William Ratcliffe Irby, bought the Lower Pontalba Building from direct heirs of the baroness for $68,000, whereupon he willed the entire property to the Louisiana State Museum. Eventually, the city bought the upper building, on St. Peter Street. A full and badly needed reconstruction of the buildings was undertaken through the aid of the WPA (Works Progress Administration) throughout the 1930s, and the grand old town houses were subdivided into smaller apartments.

Number 523 was restored in 1955 by the museum to serve as an example of a fine New Orleans town house of the 1850s. Most of the furnishings therein were donated to the museum but are authentic to the exact period. Today the **1850 House** (523 St. Ann St., on Jackson Square, 504/524-9118 or 800/568-6968, http://lsm.crt.state.la.us, limited hours, call ahead, admission $3) is a small but popular museum that also has an excellent book and gift shop. The actual apartment occupies the two floors above the shop. Visitors can stand at edges of the doorways and peer into the rooms, gaining a sense of an 1850s row house owned by a family of somewhat considerable means. Some basic household goods are also displayed up close, such as a circa-1850 chamber pot—this is about as close as you'll ever want to get to one of those. Plaques on the third floor detail the lives of the home's inhabitants from 1850 to 1861. You leave the apartment via an exterior staircase that passes alongside the service quarters, through which windows allow viewing. These rooms include a ground-floor kitchen, which is actually more interesting than what you'll find on the upper floors, as examples of period-furnished Victorian living and sleeping quarters are quite easy to find in Louisiana (in museums, private homes, and inns), but Victorian kitchens are a good bit harder to come by.

Jackson Brewery

As you emerge from Jackson Square facing the river, make a right turn and stroll a block, looking across Decatur Street at the regal Jackson Brewery (600 Decatur St., 504/566-7245, www.jacksonbrewery.com) building, once the largest independent brewery in the South. German architect Dietrich Einsiedel designed the fanciful structure, with its imposing central tower, in 1891. The brewery closed in the 1970s, and the four-story building, with expansive views of the river, has been restored and refitted with shops, restaurants, and loft apartments.

◖ JEAN LAFITTE NATIONAL HISTORICAL PARK AND PRESERVE

A couple of blocks farther upriver (toward Canal Street) along Decatur, you'll reach the main office of Jean Lafitte National Historical Park and Preserve (419 Decatur St., 504/589-3882 for recorded information, 504/589-2133 for live assistance, www.nps.gov/jela, open 10 A.M.–4 P.M. daily, admission free), which was established in 1978 to preserve a variety of natural and historic resources and properties throughout the Mississippi River valley. The park actually has six distinct units, this one and two others in metro New Orleans (Chalmette Battlefield just east of the city, and Barataria Preserve on the West Bank) and three in the Cajun Country that deal with the history and culture of Cajun immigration; these latter sites are in Thibodaux, Lafayette, and Eunice. A seventh unit, the New Orleans Jazz National Historic Park, is being developed in Louis Armstrong Park, just opposite the north end of the Quarter, but its development has been delayed since Katrina and put on hold indefinitely. The center's best feature is its one-hour, one-mile walking tours, given at 10:30 each morning. These tours are limited to just 25 people and fill up quickly at busy times; availability is on a first-come, first-served basis. You pick up a free pass on the morning of the tour. Other special programs and lectures are held at different times

Jackson Brewery building

of year, and exhibits in the visitors center also rotate and focus on different aspects of New Orleans and Louisiana culture.

On a small grassy island along Decatur Street across from the park visitors center, note the dignified statue of the man who first plotted New Orleans at the site of the present-day French Quarter, Jean Baptiste Le Moyne de Bienville, brother of the explorer Pierre Le Moyne, Sieur d'Iberville. Jean Baptiste's decision in 1699 to establish a fortification on this miserable swampy spot raised the skepticism of many, but, of course, New Orleans has flourished to become one of the world's most charming (yet still swampiest and at times miserably hottest) cities.

◖ THE FRENCH MARKET

From the park, turn back toward Jackson Square and stroll past it along the riverside of Decatur, past a newsstand and an elevated walkway that leads to the riverfront, to reach one of the city's most famous attractions, the French Market (Decatur and North Peters streets), whose stalls run for several blocks from St. Ann to Barracks streets. Legend has it that this site stood as a Choctaw trading post long before the Spanish established an early market here in 1791. Parts of the current structure date to 1813. Originally, the stalls contained only a meat market, but subsequent structures were added all along North Peters Street throughout the 19th century, housing markets of fresh produce, flowers, spices, and other goods. Coffee stands were opened at opposite ends of the stalls, and one still remains to this day, the delightful **Cafe du Monde,** which serves café au lait and powdered beignets (French-style fried doughnuts) 24 hours a day. Many of the market's stalls still sell produce, meat, and other New Orleans foods, and these are also open 24 hours.

The part of the market nearest Jackson Square holds actual retail shops and a few eateries, some selling African and Latin American crafts and handiworks, others with souvenirs, candies, and other local goods. There's also a small shaded seating area, **Latrobe Waterworks Park,** with slate walkways, a fountain, and many benches and chirping birds—it's a peaceful spot to munch on some of the edibles you may have picked up at the **Farmers Market** section of the French Market.

The Farmers Market, an indoor market building, is oodles of fun for any food lover— it's a virtual eating shrine, and many of the foods here are bottled or packaged to be taken home or shipped just about anywhere in the world. Highlights include umpteen thousand types of bottled hot sauce, including several obnoxious novelty varieties, but also all the genuine Louisiana-made ones. Other goods include a wide array of imported teas, pecans dusted with all kinds of flavored sugars and seasonings (cinnamon, Amaretto, bourbon, maple sugar), Louisiana packaged foods and condiments (Tony Chachere's Creole Gumbo, for instance), many of the local spices and herbs used for Creole and Cajun cooking, sugarcane, cookbooks, ready-to-eat foods (you can get freshly ground alligator sausage in a bun), and sno-balls (those sweet frozen treats similar to Italian ice). All manner of produce is sold here, including mirlitons, Asian pears, persimmons, and eggplant. French Market Seafood (www.frenchmarketseafood.com) carries a tantalizing range of meats packed ready for your suitcase, including alligator jerky, oysters, and crabs. And rounding out this already enormous selection of delicious foods are big jars of Zatarain's crab boil, Creole mustard, freshly made pralines, raw honey, Zapp's potato chips, and just about anything else you can think of.

The lower half of the French Market, where it becomes more of an open-air bazaar (still covered much of the way) consists of a sprawling and slightly cheesy (not in the dairy sense of the word) **Flea Market,** not so much filled with secondhand treasures and garage-sale items as it is with T-shirts, beads, and other goodies typical of what you'll find in souvenir shops around the Quarter. It's not terribly exciting, but nothing much here costs much. On weekends, however, things become a little more interesting as a section of outdoor tables is set up next to the indoor section, and here you can find African masks, crafts, drums, and more one-of-a-kind pieces. Another weekend (Fri.–Sun.) feature of this end of the market shed is the **Artists Market,** which features works of dozens of mostly local sculptors, painters,

potters, and photographers. It's an affordable place, generally, to buy a genuine Louisiana-made work of art.

At the entrance to the French Market, along the median between North Peters and Decatur streets, note the striking 13-foot-tall gilt statue of Joan of Arc seated atop a stately horse. The original was designed in France in 1889 by Paris sculptor Emmanual Fremiet; this 1972 version, made from a cast of the original, was given to the city of New Orleans from the people of France and placed originally in the CBD outside the old convention center, which was razed and replaced with the controversial Harrah's casino. The developers agreed to refurbish and rededicate the statue outside the French Market as part of a deal to build their casino.

THE LOWER QUARTER

Decatur Street from Jackson Square through the Lower Quarter (to Esplanade) is a colorful stretch for strolling, less touristy than much of the neighborhood but still very much the domain of shops, eateries, and other commercial establishments. It's a funky stretch, sort of a holdover from the 1960s and '70s, when the Quarter became something of a hippie haven—you'll find some tattoo parlors, very divey bars, a few good restaurants (including Tujague's and Sbisa, both of which have been serving Creole food for more than a century), Central Grocery (a remarkable Italian-food store that's also home to the famed muffuletta sandwich), and some knickknack shops selling everything from toys to T-shirts to antiques (though not the fancy stuff found on Royal and Chartres streets).

Old Ursuline Convent

About three blocks down toward Esplanade Avenue along Decatur, make a left turn onto Ursulines Avenue, and then a right onto Chartres, stopping at the Old Ursuline Convent (1100 Chartres St., 504/529-3040, www.accesscom. net/ursuline, complex tours 10 A.M.–3 P.M. on the hour Tues.–Fri., 11:15 A.M., 1 P.M., and 2 P.M. Sat.–Sun., admission $5), which is be-

© NEW ORLEANS CVB/RICHARD NOWITZ

Old Ursuline Convent

lieved to be the oldest extant building in the Mississippi Valley. The convent was closed after Hurricane Katrina, but it's expected to reopen with its usual hours in early 2007. The convent is part of a large ecclesiastic complex called the **Archbishop Antoine Blanc Memorial,** comprising the convent, the adjacent Herb and Old Rose Gardens, St. Mary's Church, and several related outbuildings. It's all owned by the Catholic Archdiocese of New Orleans, and it's named for the first archbishop of New Orleans, Antoine Blanc, who held this post 1850–1860; before that, he was the city's fourth bishop, 1835–1850. During Blanc's administration, the St. Louis Cathedral was rebuilt to approximately its present incarnation, and nearly 50 Catholic parishes were opened all throughout Louisiana.

King Louis XV of France established the Old Ursuline Convent in 1745 to house the Ursuline nuns who first came to New Orleans in the late 1720s, making them the first nuns to establish a permanent foothold in what is now the United States. This convent was their second home, completed in 1752;

they moved to a new space at 4580 Dauphine Street in 1824, and then to their present Uptown home, at 2635 State Street, in 1912. In those early decades, the convent housed everybody from orphans of French settlers of the Natchez Massacre to wounded British soldiers to exiled Acadians (Cajuns, as they're known now) to the city's destitute masses. During the early 1800s, the nuns conducted a school for the education of daughters of wealthy Louisiana plantation owners—Baroness Pontalba was among the young ladies educated here. The Ursuline Academy still functions today at the convent's State Street locale and is the oldest continuously operated school for women in the United States.

The nuns and families of men engaged in the Battle of New Orleans in 1815 prayed for a miracle before the statue of *Our Lady Of Prompt Succor.* The Americans won that battle, and today a solemn Mass is conducted here each year to give thanks for these answered prayers, and a mosaic at the convent, created in 1997, depicts scenes from the battle. Perhaps more of a miracle is that the convent, along with the neighboring Royal Hospital and Royal Barracks, survived both of the French Quarter fires of the late 1700s.

The nuns could not afford to remain in the convent by the 1820s, as New Orleans had become by then a fantastically wealthy merchant port, and the real estate of the blocks around Jackson Square had become precious and expensive. They moved, and their convent was turned for a time into a Catholic boys school, then a temporary meeting place for the Louisiana State Legislature, and then the home of the archbishop of New Orleans. It was converted into a presbytère in 1899, after the purchase of a new archbishopric. The old convent is attached to **St. Mary's Church,** which Antoine Blanc had built in 1845 as a chapel for the archbishopric.

Beauregard-Keyes House

Opposite the convent, across Chartres Street, the Beauregard-Keyes House (1113 Chartres St., 504/523-7257, guided tours 10 A.M.–3 P.M. on the hour Mon.–Sat., admission $5) has a layered history. The handsome 1820s mansion was the home, after the Civil War, of the Confederate general P. G. T. Beauregard. It then became the home of novelist Frances Parkinson Keyes (pronounced KIZE). It's one of relatively few classic raised cottages in the French Quarter—the entrance and main floor are one level above the street. The house had a number of owners through the years, and by the mid-1920s was nearly slated for demolition before a group of women aware that Beauregard had lived here after the Civil War began a campaign to save it. In 1944, Frances Parkinson Keyes took possession of the house, and it was she who hired a firm to carefully restore it. She lived here until 1969, and one of her novels, *Madame Castel's Lodge,* actually portrayed Beauregard. In addition to that book, she wrote several of her 50-odd books here, including *Dinner at Antoine's, The Chess Players,* and *Blue Camellia.*

One of the lead attractions here is the formal garden, laid out by the wife of Switzerland's consul to New Orleans, who owned the house in the 1830s. You can see the formal parterre garden through brick "windows" with iron grills at the corner of Chartres and Ursulines streets. And, of course, a stroll through it is included in any of the guided house tours, which depart every hour on the hour. Roses, daylilies, crape myrtle, azaleas, sweet olive trees, irises, magnolia trees, and evergreen shrubs mix and bloom in one of the Quarter's loveliest gardens.

◖ OLD U.S. MINT MUSEUM

From the Beauregard-Keyes House, follow Chartres Street two blocks to Barracks Street, turning right and following this a block, crossing Decatur Street, where a walkway leads into the main entrance of the Old U.S. Mint Museum (400 Esplanade Ave., 504/568-6968, http://lsm.crt.state.la.us, closed temporarily, call for hours, admission $5, 20 percent discount when visiting multiple Louisiana State Museum buildings), another component of the Louisiana State Museum. This grand neoclassical building with a granite facade (the structure itself is composed of stucco and Mississippi River mud brick) was constructed in 1836 at a cost of about $185,000 at the behest of the U.S. president Andrew Jackson, who hoped it would financially jumpstart the exploration of the nation's western frontier. Especially in contrast to the rest of the French Quarter, it's a building of massive proportions (the walls on the ground floor are three feet thick) and stature.

A large chunk of the building's dramatic copper roof blew off during Katrina, and the building received considerable water damage, resulting in the museum's closure. Just one exhibition section, the New Orleans Jazz Collection, was damaged, and it's estimated only about 3 percent of the collection was affected. Renovations on the roof and interior are ongoing, but it's hoped the museum will reopen by mid-2007. The descriptions of exhibits below are based on the museum's layout before the storm; it's expected all of the exhibits will resume upon the museum's reopening.

This is the only building in the country to have functioned as both a U.S. and a Confederate mint. It also housed Confederate troops for a time during the Civil War, but with the Union occupation, the mint was shut down until Reconstruction, at which time it resumed service as a U.S. mint. During the Civil War it was also the site of a controversial punishment of Confederate loyalist William Mumford. Shortly after Union forces took possession of the city, troops erected the U.S. Stars and Stripes flag over the mint building. In an act that some people defended more as vandalism than treason, Mumford and a few friends stole the flag and dragged it through the city's mud- and manure-caked streets. For this act, Mumford was sentenced to death, and although a number of influential New Orleanians petitioned on his behalf after his trial, Mumford was hanged two months later from just below the mint's flagstaff.

In 1909 the mint was decommissioned, and in 1981 it was added to the state museum system. Today it contains a fascinating variety of exhibits that make it perhaps the most engaging of the several excellent facilities within the state museum collection. The building's history as a mint is chronicled on the first floor, and New Orleans's legacy as the birthplace of jazz is detailed on the second floor, as is a display of Newcomb pottery and crafts. A state historical center and archive occupies the third floor.

On the first floor, you can see the room in which coins and currency were actually minted. Many of the artifacts on display here come from other U.S. mints, such as the ones in Denver and Philadelphia—there are an 1868 coin press, historic photos, and other period materials and documents, plus several minted coins from the 1800s. There's also a small display dedicated to the building's architect, William Strickland, who trained under famous Greek Revival architect Benjamin Latrobe and who also designed the Tennessee State Capitol, as well as the mints in Charlotte and Philadelphia.

The jazz rooms on the second floor are filled with vintage photos and depictions of the city's early music legends, including such pioneers of the music form as Buddy Bolden, Jack Laine, John Robichaux, and Jelly Roll Morton (who lived not too far from here at 1443 Frenchmen Street, just above Faubourg Marigny). Exhibits trace the city's history and the emergence of quadroon balls, minstrels, funeral marches, brass bands, opera, and ragtime, all of which precipitated and to different degrees influenced the modern jazz movement.

Materials also discuss the contribution to jazz of Congo Square, which was designed in 1817 as an assembly space for slaves, running along Rampart Street between St. Ann and St. Peter streets. This place for funerals, worship, and other community gatherings inspired a brand of music that drew on the participants' African and West Indies heritage. It ceased to be by the 1850s, but today Congo Square is appropriately a neighborhood with several great jazz clubs. Another bearer of the jazz legend that's discussed is the New Orleans funeral as it pertains to musical celebrations of the African American community. There's also a large tribute to Louis Armstrong, who grew up here. Among the more interesting artifacts is a handwritten letter composed by a young and admiring jazz enthusiast to legendary New Orleans pianist Armand Hug—the letter was written by Harry Connick Jr.

A nice element of the jazz exhibit is that you hear some of the earliest jazz tunes piped in the whole time that you're touring the rooms. Also on the second floor are three huge and colorful murals depicting New Orleans's fabled Storyville red-light district, which was one of the city's cultivators of jazz, and an exhibition hall where rotating shows are mounted.

From here you can make a brief detour into Faubourg Marigny, or stroll up tree-shaded Esplanade Avenue a few blocks, making a left onto Royal Street.

◖ ROYAL STREET

Fittingly, Royal Street is one of the finest addresses in New Orleans, and it's also one of the most distinguished streets for antiques shops and art galleries in the United States. Many businesses are members of the Royal Street

Guild, a century-old collective of especially long-running and reputable shops, restaurants, and hotels. Rue Royale was christened by the French in the 18th century, and it served as New Orleans's "Main Street" for the city's first couple of centuries.

Gallier House

From Esplanade Avenue, which is how you'll be approaching the street if you're coming from the Old U.S. Mint Museum, Royal Street begins as mostly a lane of distinguished residences. On your left (the riverside of the street) a couple of blocks in, you'll come to the Gallier House (1118-1132 Royal St., 504/525-5661, www.hgghh.org, open 10 A.M.–4 P.M. Mon.–Fri., last tour leaves at 3:30 P.M., admission $6), part of a museum that also includes the Hermann-Grima House, on St. Louis Street—a combined $10 ticket gets you admission into both house-museums. The former home of famed New Orleans architect James Gallier, who designed the house in 1857, it's filled with exquisite furnishings from the 19th century, plus elaborate faux marble and faux bois (wood painted very carefully to resemble a more precious type of wood). The two-story stucco facade is noted for its ornate balustrade balcony and slender, finely crafted columns. The tour includes a look at the carefully restored slave quarters and a finely maintained garden, which sparkles with fountains and slate walks.

Cornstalk Hotel

From Gallier House, continue down Royal a couple of blocks. You'll pass the small and historic Cornstalk Hotel (915 Royal St., www.cornstalkhotel.com) on your right—it's fronted by an elaborate and much-photographed cast-iron fence, which dates to the 1840s and has an eye-catching motif of cornstalks choked with the vines of morning-glory blossoms.

Madame John's Legacy

At the end of the block, make a left off Royal onto Dumaine and walk down to No. 632, the site of another Louisiana State Museum house, Madame John's Legacy (632 Dumaine St., 504/568-6968 or 800/568-6968, http://lsm.crt.state.la.us, limited hours, call ahead, admission $3, 20 percent discount when visiting multiple Louisiana State Museum buildings). It's a fine example of a Louisiana French Colonial (or Creole) home from the late 18th century. Madame John's house was built to replace a home lost in the great fire of 1788. It survived the next, smaller fire of 1794 and is today one of just a few remaining pre-1800s buildings in the Quarter. The historic complex, which fronts Dumaine Street, comprises three buildings: a main house, a two-story *garçonniere* (living quarters, what we might call "crash pads" today, built by Creole families for younger men so that their assorted nighttime activities wouldn't disrupt the other family members), and a kitchen with cook's living quarters.

Typical of houses built in the late 1700s in New Orleans, Madame John's has a high double-pitched roof, and the main floor is one level above the street (to protect the living areas in case of flooding). On the street-level floor is the preserved brick basement that functioned as a work area and storehouse. Tours are self-guided, and the only interior on the property open to the public is the main house, which now serves as an art gallery displaying the work of some of the state's most prominent, largely self-taught folk artists. There's also an exhibit in the ground-floor basement area that traces the history of the house and its various occupants. Madame John was, in fact, not a real person but a character in a George Washington Cable story called *Tite Poulette,* an 1873 tale that dealt with a familiar theme of the author, people of mixed racial heritage who could pass for Caucasian. Cable, who was white, wrote sympathetically in favor of racial integration, much to the disgust of the majority of New Orleans's post–Civil War residents, living in the hostile and ugly times of Reconstruction. Cable ultimately moved to Northampton, Massachusetts. In a magazine article from the 1880s, this very house on Dumaine Street was identified by a local writer as the setting for *Tite Poulette,* and thenceforth locals referred to it as Madame

MARIE LAVEAU: VOODOO QUEEN OF NEW ORLEANS

Voodoo experienced its heyday in New Orleans in the 19th century. While most voodoo books and paraphernalia available in the French Quarter today are bought by curious tourists, there's no question that some still take the practice very seriously.

Misconceptions about voodoo abound and are often encouraged by its depiction in popular culture. Voodoo is based on the worship of spirits, called Loa, and a belief system that emphasizes spirituality, compassion, and treating others well. While there's nothing inherently negative about voodoo, its practice does allow its followers to perform rites intended to bring calamity upon their enemies. These traditions, such as piercing miniature effigies with sharp pins or burning black candles, are the most familiar among outsiders.

The origins of voodoo as a religious practice are indistinct. Voodoo rituals are based on a variety of African religious traditions, which were brought to the United States by West African slaves. In 18th-century New Orleans, where slaves were kept by French and Spanish residents, voodoo began to incorporate some of the beliefs and rituals of Catholicism as well.

Marie Laveau (circa 1804-1881) is the historical figure most connected with South Louisiana's rich voodoo tradition. A young and beautiful woman of French, African, and Native American extraction, she was New Orleans's high priestess of voodoo from roughly 1830 onward. She had numerous children, and at least one daughter continued to practice for many years after her mother's death, fueling rumors that the original Marie Laveau lived into the early 20th century. Her grave in St. Louis Cemetery No. 1, on Basin Street, is still a site of pilgrimage for voodoo practitioners.

Laveau combined the understanding ear of a psychologist with the showmanship of a preacher to become one of the city's most vaunted spiritual figures. As a young woman, Laveau practiced as a hairstylist in New Orleans, a position that afforded her the opportunity to work inside some of the city's most prominent homes and to earn the confidence of its most prominent women. As she soaked up the gossip of the day, she also dispensed both practical and spiritual advice to her clients, no doubt sprinkling her words with healthy doses of voodoo mysticism and lore. Word of Laveau's talents as a voodoo priestess spread rapidly, and soon she was staging ceremonies in the small yard of her St. Ann Street home. Her most notorious ceremony, held annually in a swamp cabin along Bayou St. John on June 23 (St. John's Eve), became the stuff of legend.

Laveau was the most famous priestess to captivate New Orleans's residents, but she wasn't the last. Throughout the centuries, a number of women and even some men have carried on the tradition of the voodoo priestess. According to legend, believers can invoke her powers by visiting her grave, marking the tomb with three Xs (a gris-gris, or charm), scratching the ground three times with their feet, knocking three times on the grave, and making a wish. Many people in New Orleans continue to celebrate St. John's Eve and believe that on this night, the spirit of the Voodoo Queen makes herself known.

John's Legacy. The house was donated by its last occupant, Mrs. Stella Hirsch Lemann, to the Louisiana State Museum in 1947.

New Orleans Historic Voodoo Museum

From Madame John's Legacy, walk back up Dumaine, crossing Royal Street, to reach the New Orleans Historic Voodoo Museum (724 Dumaine St., 504/523-7685, www.voodoo-museum.com, open 10 A.M.–8 P.M. daily, admission $7), where guided tours are given by historians versed in the city's rich voodoo lore. You're even greeted by a high priestess as you enter. The museum can arrange graveyard, vampire, and ghost tours. As you might guess, these excursions, highlighted by stories that are both amusing and scary, offer high entertainment value. But at the same time, the museum gives a very good overview of a practice still shrouded in secrecy and mystery and taken very seriously by its practitioners. Though the subject matter may be a tad on the ominous side, exhibits are neither gory nor frightening, and kids definitely enjoy this place.

The focus is on Marie Laveau, the anointed high priestess of voodoo who lived in New Orleans from the 1790s until her death in 1881. Laveau's father was a successful white planter, her mother a mulatto, so that Laveau herself was considered a quadroon. Laveau earned a living as a hairstylist for the Vieux Carré's wealthiest matrons, and in this capacity she developed her reputation as a leading voodoo priestess. During the museum tour you'll see her charmed wishing stump—touch it, and you're said to receive magical blessings. The museum contains ritual art and artifacts from Africa and Haiti, the two places from which New Orleans's distinctive brand of voodoo practice originated. You can arrange for private consultations and healing seminars with museum staff. Whatever your personal take on voodoo or other religions, keep in mind that many people practice voodoo with serious and solemn conviction, and this is not merely a sideshow, despite the emphasis on colorful stories and lore.

Historic New Orleans Collection

From the Voodoo Museum, return to Royal Street, and wander along this charming lane for several blocks before reaching one of the city's most underrated attractions, the Historic New Orleans Collection (533 Royal St., 504/523-4662, www.hnoc.org, open by tour only 9:30 A.M.–4:30 P.M. Tues.–Sat.), which is not only a vast repository of historical documents, but also a collection of restored buildings. It was also the city's first museum to reopen after Hurricane Katrina. General L. Kemper Williams and his wife, Leila, established this research facility in 1966, having long been avid collectors of important artifacts

and memorabilia pertaining to the city's history. The museum occupies a series of buildings in the heart of the Quarter, including the 1792 Merieult House (which was built after the first of the city's fires and which survived the second), a gracious house with Greek Revival architectural details. It contains the Williams Gallery and the museum shop on the first floor and the Louisiana History Galleries on the second level. Each gallery is dedicated to a specific period of the state's history (the French Colonial years, the Spanish Colonial years, Battle of New Orleans, etc.) and includes relevant maps, early editions of books, authentic furniture, and artwork illustrating that era. You can also admire art by nearly 50 New Orleans artists who have painted in the city during the past 200 years in the Laura Simon Nelson Collection. There are always one or two rotating exhibitions presented in the History Galleries. And the Monroe-Green Collection contains works by prominent Low Country artist William Aiken Walker, whose landscape, portrait, and still-life paintings of the 19th-century Atlantic and Gulf South offer great insights into its people and customs.

As you enter the complex's courtyard, you'll see the 1794 Counting House, another Spanish Colonial–style building that was given Greek Revival accents, and a second floor, in the 1830s. That and some other historic buildings all opening onto the central courtyard hold administrative offices, but the Williams Residence, an 1880s town house that the museum founders occupied until the death of L. Kemper in 1971, can also be toured—it's a room-by-room survey of how an upscale early–20th-century city home would have been furnished, a refreshing counterpoint to the majority of historic house-museums in New Orleans, which re-create the look of 19th or 18th centuries. That said, the Williams Residence does contain quite a few antiques, as a fine home of the early 20th century would. Watercolors by prominent local artist Boyd Cruise decorate many of the rooms. The Williamses were inveterate collectors of many things, among them vintage maps of New Orleans and the Louisiana Territory, and you can glimpse several of these in the study. The Williams Residence can be visited by tour only (tours given at 10 A.M., 11 A.M., 2 P.M., and 3 P.M. Tues.–Sat.) Tours cost $5. Guided tours are available of the History Galleries; these are given at the same times as the house tours and also cost $5.

A short walk over from the main campus of buildings, the **Williams Research Center** (410 Chartres St., 504/598-7171, www.hnoc.org, open 9:30 A.M.–4:30 P.M. Tues.–Sat., admission free) is an additional facility within the Historic New Orleans Collection, a library of documents, manuscripts, and photos on the history of the city. The research center often has a changing exhibit or two open to the public, along with a permanent exhibit titled Louisiana: Its Sites and Citizens, which explores the evolving daily life of the state's people through the years. Its research facilities are otherwise open only to scholars and others working on projects related to the Gulf South.

New Orleans Pharmacy Museum

A block downriver from the Williams Research Center is a small but fascinating attraction that looks almost like another posh boutique on a tony stretch of Chartres Street, the New Orleans Pharmacy Museum (514 Chartres St., 504/565-8027, www.pharmacymuseum.org, open 10 A.M.–5 P.M. Tues.–Sun., admission $5). It occupies a genuine apothecary shop from the 1820s; the original owner, Louis J. Dufilho Jr., was actually the first licensed pharmacist in the nation, having earned his certification in 1816. New Orleans, with its devastating outbreaks of yellow fever throughout the 19th century, became one of the nation's leading centers of medicine largely out of necessity; Louisiana was the first state to pass a law certifying pharmacists. Displays give a sense of what a pharmacy of that period looked like, including rows of 1850s hand-carved mahogany cabinets filled with everything from established drugs to "gris-gris" voodoo potions, and also tell the story of Louisiana's development in medicine and health care. The

various bloodletting equipment is particularly eye-opening—did you know that barbershops were one of the earliest practitioners of leeching blood, and that those cheerful red-and-white poles that stand outside barbershops to this day actually were used to indicate to the customers that bloodletting was available inside? Out back in a courtyard you can examine a garden of medicinal herbs, and find out which plants are still known to cure what ails you. Also on display is an 1855 Italian marble soda fountain. This is quite an extensive facility, with the two floors of this stately town house crammed with curious objects and informative displays.

CANAL STREET AND THE RIVERFRONT

From the Pharmacy Museum, follow Chartres Street a few blocks to Canal, the wide thoroughfare that separates the French Quarter from the Central Business District; it's also the terminus for the St. Charles Avenue streetcar (damaged by Katrina but expected to resume service in mid- to late 2007) as well as the place where you can pick up the streetcar that runs up Canal to Mid-City before turning onto Carrollton Avenue and continuing all the way to City Park. In the early part of the 20th century, streetcars ran all over New Orleans, and all of them (with one exception, the Napoleon Avenue line) either began or terminated here.

Canal Street's appearance offers a marked contrast to the Quarter. It's lined with massive buildings, including a few high-rise chain hotels, and it's anchored by a long median, called a "neutral ground" in New Orleans, because back when this street separated the French Quarter from the American Quarter (as the CBD was then known), the median was considered to be the home turf of neither district. The French despised the American upstarts, who had flocked here to make their fortunes after the Louisiana Purchase, and the Americans thought the French archaic and strangely insular, and they furthermore held Catholics in low regard and believed the French Quarter to be a den of pirates, sailors, free people of color, and others they considered beneath their stations in life.

Because of that broad neutral ground, Canal is one of the widest streets in America, spanning about 175 feet from one side to the other. The street was so-named for the shallow canal—really a ditch—that ran here along the western ramparts of the original city down to the river. As it developed into the neutral ground between the American and French quarters during the course of the 19th century, Canal gradually became the city's most prominent merchant thoroughfare, a department store–lined spine from which cross streets packed with smaller shops radiated. In the WPA *New Orleans City Guide* of 1938, the neighborhood's chronologists give the following description of the area's commerce:

The tendency of certain business activities to concentrate in one section of the city, although not quite so pronounced as it once was, is to be noted in the side streets in the vicinity of Canal. Most of the fur dealers are still to be found along North Peters and Decatur Sts. Royal St. has become one of antique shops which, resembling the bazaars of the Orient, line the street on both sides for blocks and pour out their strange and beautiful wares on the sidewalk. Coffee roasters and packers are to be found, for the most part, along Magazine and Tchoupitoulas Streets from Canal to Howard Ave. Farther uptown, Poydras St. from Camp to the river is the wholesale fruit, produce, and poultry center, while the principal meat packers are found near Magazine and Julia Sts. The section between Camp St. and the river, and Canal St. and Jackson Ave., contains most of the wholesale jobbing houses and many of the manufacturing plants. Carondelet St. has always been the street of the cotton brokers and bankers.

Little of what's noted here from the Depression years holds true today, except that Royal still has dozens of fine antiques shops, and Caron-

delet and the rest of the CBD blocks off it have developed into one of the South's leading centers of finance and banking. Otherwise, districts for fur, coffee, and food have disappeared or dissipated. The section bounded by Camp, the river, Canal, and Jackson, described as a manufacturing district in this passage, is in part, at least between Canal and the Crescent City Connection Bridge (to the West Bank), still abounding with old warehouse and factory buildings. But nowadays, this area known as the Warehouse District pulses with trendy clubs, new hotels, art galleries, a few museums, and the city's massive convention center. It is still, however, along the riverfront, the site of New Orleans's commercial port.

Note that street names change as you cross from the French Quarter into the CBD. North Peters becomes Tchoupitoulas (although South Peters Street runs through the CBD parallel to Tchoupitoulas, a block closer to the river), Decatur becomes Magazine, Chartres becomes Camp, Royal becomes St. Charles, Bourbon becomes Carondelet, Dauphine becomes Baronne, and Burgundy becomes University. Rampart continues from the Quarter into the CBD, but changes from North Rampart (in the Quarter) to South Rampart once it crosses Canal. This rule holds true for all New Orleans streets, with Canal acting as the dividing point between "north" and "south" streets.

If you turn right up Canal from Chartres Street, you'll mostly be passing storefronts occupied by tatty souvenir shops and fast-food restaurants, along with the lobby entrances to several hotels. The street used to feel a bit dodgy as you moved away from the river, but the opening in 2000 of the **Ritz-Carlton** (921 Canal St.) inside what had been the Kress and Maison Blanche department store gentrified things considerably. The Ritz was one of a number of businesses along Canal that was badly damaged in the aftermath of Katrina, but it reopened in December 2006 following a massive overhaul and renovation. On the opposite side of Canal, technically in the CBD, stands one of the South's true grandes dames, the **Fairmont New Orleans** (123 Baronne St.), which opened in 1893 and had undergone a massive restoration in the late 1990s but was also closed after being hit hard by Katrina, and more accurately vandalism after the storm. It's expected to be back in business sometime in 2007.

Still a bit farther up Canal are two of the city's most popular venues for concerts and plays, the **State Palace Theatre** (1108 Canal St., 504/482-7112 or 504/522-4435, www. state palace.com) and, just around the corner, the **Saenger Theatre** (143 N. Rampart St., 504/524-2490, www.saengertheatre.com), which was forced to close because of Katrina damage. It's hoped the theater will resume operation by 2007.

Were you to follow Canal Street toward the lake, it would take you more than three miles into Mid-City and eventually up to the cemeteries west of City Park; there a right turn onto City Park Avenue followed by a quick left onto Canal Boulevard leads you clear to Lakeshore Boulevard and the curving shoreline of Lake Pontchartrain.

Custom House

Back at the corner of Chartres and Canal, turn left and continue a block past Decatur until you reach the Custom House, which was constructed in the elaborate Egyptian Revival style as a courthouse in 1848, on the site of the old Fort St. Louis. During the 18th century, the fort had stood guard on what had then been the levee along the east bank of the Mississippi, whose banks are now found another 500 yards or so away down Canal Street. Between the city's founding in 1718 and the early 20th century, when the modern system of flood control and levees was built to rein in and control the Mississippi, the river shifted considerably; in other parts of the state, it made entire shortcuts and new arms and bends in the marshy terrain, forever altering its course and the landscape around it.

General P. G. T. Beauregard, who would figure prominently as a Confederate military leader during the Civil War, supervised the construction of this elegant and slightly intimidating structure, which takes up the entire block bounded by Decatur, Canal, North Peters, and Iberville streets. It was not actually completed by the time of the war. Beauregard, in fact, would never have the chance to see it through, and to add insult, the hated Union general Benjamin Butler used the Decatur side of the building as his administrative headquarters. The not-yet-completed upper floors served as a prison for Confederate soldiers, among them the martyred citizen William Mumford, who spent a couple of months here before his hanging at the U.S. Mint. When this granite structure was finally completed well after the end of the war, the price tag stood at about $5 million.

The stately 30,000-square-foot building was slated to become home of the **Audubon Insectarium** (Canal and Decatur Sts., www. auduboninstitute.org). The museum had aimed for a spring 2006 opening, but Hurricane Katrina has pushed this back indefinitely. When it does open, it's expected to contain the largest free-standing collection of insects in the United States, about 900,000 species. If just the thought of that makes your skin crawl, consider that visitors will have the opportunity to touch all kinds of live creatures, although many others will be presented through displays from a safe distance. As it does with the zoo and aquarium, the Audubon Institute intends to dispel the many preconceived notions humans have about animals—of course, the insect world has an especially serious image problem. As you might guess, the museum cafe will have an insect-themed appearance—although it will not actually serve anything with bugs. But at the museum's own bug-cooking demonstration "cafe," visitors will learn how many people around the world routinely snack on ants, grasshoppers, and other insects as an excellent, and some say delicious, source of protein. Less harrowing for squeamish visitors will be the massive butterfly room, where those fluttering, colorful insects will fly freely about a Japanese-style garden.

At the corner of South Peters Street, a block closer to the river, note the **Shops at Canal**

© NEW ORLEANS CVB/CARL PURCELL

Audubon Aquarium of the Americas

Place (333 Canal St., 504/522-9200, www .theshopsatcanalplace.com, shops open 11 A.M.– 7 P.M. Mon.–Sat., noon–6 P.M. Sun.), a fancy compound of retail shops, an art-house movie theater, and the Wyndham Canal Place hotel.

Audubon Aquarium of the Americas

From the Shops at Canal Place, walk another block to the foot of Canal Street, where you'll find one of the most popular attractions in the city, the Audubon Aquarium of the Americas (1 Canal St., 504/581-4629, www.auduboninstitute.org, open 10 A.M.–4 P.M. Wed.–Sun., admission $16), which overlooks the Mississippi River. The aquarium took a hard hit from Katrina but reopened in late May 2006 with brand-new—and much-improved—exhibits and a new roster of animals. Hours may be increased as visitation and staffing increase, so call ahead to confirm hours. This stunning, contemporary building provides a glimpse of several important aquatic habits, including the Amazon rainforest, Mississippi River, a Caribbean reef, and the Gulf of Mexico (which, ap-

propriately in this state, includes a replica of an offshore oil rig). Special tanks highlight certain species, such as sea otters, penguins, sea horses, jellyfish, a rare white alligator, and sharks—there's also a shark touch pool, where you can actually lay a hand on one of the gentler baby sharks.

The last ticket is sold an hour before closing. Parking (with a ticket validated either when you enter the aquarium or IMAX theater) is available for $4 for up to four hours.

The aquarium is also home to the **Entergy IMAX Theatre** (504/581-4629), which shows documentaries and other action-packed features (many of them in 3-D) on a screen that rises nearly six stories. Admission is $8 ($13.50 for a double feature), and combination tickets with the zoo and aquarium are available.

Woldenberg Riverfront Park

As you leave the aquarium or theater and face the river, you'll be standing at the edge of lovely Woldenberg Riverfront Park, a 14-acre redbrick promenade that extends along the riverfront from here to behind Jackson Brewery. It is actually along this stretch that Le Moyne, Sieur de Bienville, established the site of New Orleans in 1718. Crape myrtle and magnolia trees provide shade over the numerous park benches, affording romantic views out over the paddle wheelers docked along the riverfront. Like much of the river, this was an industrial eyesore of warehouses and wharves before being converted to this charming urban park. The one quay that remains in use, **Toulouse Street Wharf,** is the home for the palatial excursion riverboat, *The Steamboat Natchez,* from which calliope music plays on evenings before it departs for cruises along the river. Fringing the park is **Moon Walk,** a wooden boardwalk that extends along the riverfront, and indeed, it's a fine place on a warm evening to sit and admire the moon reflecting on the river. It was named, however, for the New Orleans mayor who had it constructed in the 1970s, Moon Landrieu (father of U.S. Senator Mary Landrieu).

Within the park, note the stunning *Monument to the Immigrant* statue, of Carrara white marble, created by noted New Orleans artist Franco Alessandrini; it commemorates New Orleans's role as one of the nation's most prolific immigrant ports throughout the 19th century and before that under the flags of France and Spain. Woldenberg Park has a few other sculptures of distinction, among them Robert Schoen's *Old Man River,* an 18-foot tribute to the Mississippi River carved out of 17 tons of Carrara marble; and *Ocean Song,* a series of eight 10-foot-tall pyramids.

Lafitte's Blacksmith Shop

Walk the length of Woldenberg Park, and then cut over to Jackson Square along the pathway that crosses beside Jackson Brewery. Head north up St. Peter Street, past Chartres and Royal streets, making a right onto Bourbon. Here you'll come to the ramshackle-looking Lafitte's Blacksmith Shop (corner of Bourbon and St. Philip streets), a lively neighborhood bar that occupies one of the few remaining buildings in New Orleans that survived both of the major late–18th-century French Quarter

fires. It's believed to have been built in the late 1760s or early 1770s.

ARMSTRONG PARK

From Lafitte's Blacksmith Shop, assuming you have not stopped for too long to enjoy a few cocktails, continue up St. Philip Street to Rampart Street, across from which stands Armstrong Park, the main entrance of which is at the corner of Rampart and St. Ann streets. Long considered the most dangerous tract of land close to the French Quarter, the park is slated to undergo an ambitious $8 million transformation, in which it will become **New Orleans Jazz National Historic Park** (www.nps.gov/jazz). The visitors center for the park is at the other end of the Quarter, by the French Market (at 916 N. Peters St.; call 504/589-4841 for further information). The status of the move to Armstrong Park has been unclear since Hurricane Katrina, so stay tuned on this one and check back to the national park site website.

When this new attraction finally opens, it will help not only the park but also the lakeside blocks of the French Quarter, including North Rampart Street, which can be spotty. The overhaul was to include the renovation of five historic buildings and landscaping of many acres of parkland. The park is opposite the site of historic Congo Square, where slaves of African descent regularly celebrated their music traditions with drumming and dancing gatherings during the early 19th century. When the park project is complete, there will be a jazz resource library and visitors center near the park's entrance. It's a fitting renovation for the nearest bit of greenery to the French Quarter, a part that tourists have been warned away from for decades because of the neighborhood's crime problems.

As you might expect, Armstrong Park does contain a splendid statue of Louis "Satchmo" Armstrong, the native New Orleanian who defined jazz as much as any musician. Another attraction within the park is the **Mahalia Jackson Theatre of the Performing Arts** (parking inside the park gates, Orleans Avenue entrance), which hosts performances sponsored by the New Orleans Ballet Association and the New Orleans Opera Association. The park is named for the world-famous gospel singer Mahalia Jackson, who was born in New Orleans in 1911, although she came into her own as a professional musician in Chicago in the 1930s and died in that city in 1972. After Katrina, the theater was handsomely restored.

St. Louis Cemetery No. 1

Near Armstrong Park is arguably the most famous and most intriguing of all of New Orleans's so-called cities of the dead, St. Louis Cemetery No. 1 (bound by Basin, Conti, Tremé, and St. Louis streets), which has been the final resting place for many New Orleanians since the late 18th century. The burial ground was established in 1789 and set outside what was then the city border, above Rampart Street, the theory being that proximity to the deceased was in part responsible for the rampant yellow fever and cholera outbreaks of this period. It would be many decades later that the medical establishment proved that mosquitoes carried yellow fever, and that it could not be spread from one person—living or dead—to another.

About 700 tombs are in this cemetery, interring many thousands of people, as most of these aboveground structures are owned by families or groups and designed to hold more than one set of remains. The tombs can be quite elaborate and are constructed typically of brick but covered in concrete or stucco. Some of the oldest ones are today little more than crumbled ruins. Bodies were buried aboveground because New Orleans sits below sea level and has a high water table—the earliest attempts to bury the dead in the city failed during floods, as the caskets simply floated to the surface. St. Louis Cemetery is in a dicey part of the city, and you shouldn't just wander over on your own, even during the day, although efforts have been made in recent years to rid this district of crime. It's much wiser to visit via a guided tour. Among the best are those offered through **Save Our Cemeteries** (504/525-

STORYVILLE

Just above the French Quarter along Basin Street, which parallels Rampart Street one block over, is a still-dicey neighborhood that has been infamous for well more than a century, Storyville. It was, from 1897 until 1917, the only officially sanctioned and legal red-light district in the country. For nearly 200 years, prostitution had thrived along streets all over New Orleans, a city that had more than its share of sailors, traders, laborers, and others seeking company during long spells away from home.

City politicos for years debated the best way to deal with this social fact of life, figuring that if they couldn't root out prostitutes and bordellos, they might as well sanction them – and tax them. It was city alderman Sidney Story who, in 1897, came up with the bright idea to create a legal red-light district, and after him the neighborhood was named.

By all accounts, the system worked wonderfully well. Potential customers could peruse a directory, the *Blue Book*, containing names of brothels and prostitutes, along with prices and the various services available, and photos of many of the women. The city's illegitimate music movement, jazz, flourished in the city's legitimate sex district, as many bordellos hired jazz musicians (including Jelly Roll Morton and King Oliver) to entertain. At its peak, the neighborhood licensed 750 ladies of the evening. And prostitution continued to be a big, albeit illegal business, in Storyville well into the 1960s, more than four decades after the red-light district was made illegal again.

You can get some sense of the neighborhood's history by watching the Louis Malle movie *Pretty Baby*, released in 1978 and starring a young Brooke Shields.

3377 or 888/721-7493, www.saveourcemeteries.org), which gives hour-long excursions through St. Louis Cemetery No. 1 at 10 A.M. on Sunday mornings. They depart from the

Royal Blend Coffee Shop (621 Royal St.), and reservations are not necessary. The cost (actually a suggested donation) is $12. Save Our Cemeteries also gives tours of Lafayette Cemetery, in Uptown. Note that although the city's historic cemeteries received some flooding during Katrina, they had all largely been repaired by spring 2006.

VooDoo Spiritual Temple

Just opposite Armstrong Park at the site of what was Congo Square is the VooDoo Spiritual Temple (828 N. Rampart St., 504/566-0274 or 504/522-9627, www.voodoospiritualtemple. org), which offers voodoo services, consultations, rituals, city tours ($18 per person), and lectures. Priestess Miriam runs this center of voodoo worship and healing, which also sells handcrafted voodoo dolls, gris-gris and mojo bags, blessed candles, aroma oils, talismans, and books and CDs related to voodoo.

BOURBON STREET

Leaving Armstrong Park or the VooDoo Spiritual Temple, walk along Rampart Street to St. Peter, making a left and continuing three blocks to the city's most extreme thoroughfare, Bourbon Street, which is either hated or loved by those who experience it—just about everybody seems to have a strong view regarding this unabashedly touristy row of nightclubs and drinking halls. Interestingly, although it's arguably the most recognizable street in New Orleans today, Bourbon was no more popular or important than the Quarter's other streets before its development into a nightlife sector. Bourbon Street is hardly mentioned in the WPA's exhaustively comprehensive *New Orleans City Guide,* written in 1938.

The street was named for France's royal dynasty, the Bourbons, in 1722, when the Quarter (which at that time was the entire city) was laid out. For the next 200 years, Bourbon was a pleasant street to live and shop on, but it was never anywhere near as prestigious as Royal Street, which runs parallel a block closer to the river, or Chartres Street. It wasn't until the early part of the 1930s that, especially along the section nearest Canal, Bourbon Street began to develop more commercial cachet, as a handful of prominent shops and department stores opened along the first few blocks of Bourbon. Its fame, or infamy, really, came about after World War II, during the 1950s, a straitlaced decade for much of the country. At this time, a handful of strip clubs began to prosper along Bourbon, becoming a top draw for visiting tourists.

It has evolved today into a more eclectic entertainment district, still with a handful of strip bars, but now with places known for music and other types of entertainment, and you'll also find a handful of prominent hotels and restaurants on or just off Bourbon. Since the late 1990s, the 100 and 200 blocks of Bourbon have seen a renaissance—this area, where there had been department stores for many decades, had become dark and ominous at night, when shops were closed. Visitors walking over from the CBD were often told to enter the Quarter down along Royal or Chartres streets and then walk up to Bourbon along Bienville or Conti streets, but these days it's safer and quite customary to approach Bourbon directly from Canal.

The blocks from Iberville to St. Ann streets are cordoned off during the evenings into a pedestrian mall—automobiles would find it impossible to drive along here anyway, as the streets fill with revelers, mostly visiting from out of town, who wander from bar to bar, go-cups (a.k.a. "geaux" cups) in hand. It's perfectly legal to saunter about the Quarter with an open container (as long as it's not made of glass), and many of the establishments here, especially along Bourbon, are open 24 hours. At St. Ann Street, the section of Bourbon closed to vehicle traffic at night ends. This cross street also marks the point at which Bourbon becomes a gay entertainment district for roughly a block or so, and it's where you'll find a handful of the city's most popular gay and lesbian discos.

Two blocks later, at St. Philip Street, Bourbon begins to take on the residential character the rest of the street possessed during its early decades. From St. Philip the next four blocks to the Quarter's boundary, Esplanade Avenue, Bourbon is surprisingly peaceful, even on weekend evenings, and it's a fine spot for admiring 19th-century homes.

Preservation Hall

A short detour off Bourbon Street, Preservation Hall (726 St. Peter St., 504/522-2841, www.preservationhall.com), between Bourbon and Royal streets, has been one of the most popular and respected places to hear true New Orleans jazz since 1961. The esteemed facility closed for a time after Katrina but reopened in early May 2006. The band and the venue were formed expressly to keep the legacy of the city's distinctive style of jazz music alive for generations to come, and many of Preservation Hall's early members were musicians who came of age during the early part of the 20th century, when this originally controversial style of music began to hit its stride. It's a charming, informal place, with seating on vintage wooden benches and folding chairs and a good bit of standing room—attending a concert here is like watching an informal jam session in a community center in some rural town in Louisiana.

Visitors who have watched the Preservation Hall band perform in more formal concert venues around the world (it tours more than 100 days annually) are sometimes surprised by just how laid-back and warm (and small) its home performance space is. The exterior of the 1750s house, which later housed a cobbler shop and then a grocery, with a second-floor galley running the length of the facade, is pleasantly decrepit stucco—it almost looks abandoned by day. From the hall you can stroll along a carriageway, its wall hung with vintage jazz posters and concert bills, out to the landscaped courtyard for a breath of fresh air.

Hermann-Grima House

If you've just entered Bourbon Street from Preservation Hall, you'll be standing at its junction with St. Peter Street. A right turn leads a block to the gay bars around the corner of St. Ann Street and then, a block or two farther, to Lafitte's Blacksmith Shop. Make a left turn onto Bourbon, and after two blocks you'll come to St. Louis Street. Make a right, and you'll soon be standing before another of the Quarter's best house-museums, the **Hermann-Grima House** (820 St. Louis St., 504/525-5661, www.hgghh.org, open 10 A.M.–4 P.M. Mon.–Fri., last tour leaves at 3:30 P.M., admission $6, $10 for combined ticket with Gallier House). The Hermann-Grima is a steep-roofed Federal-style mansion of the sort you'd more often see in Savannah or other old cities of British origin than New Orleans. Creole cooking demonstrations are held here on Thursdays, October through May—the Hermann-Grima House contains the only functional outdoor kitchen in the French Quarter, a holdover from its antebellum days (the house dates to 1831). Another unusual feature is the Quarter's only horse stable, adjacent to the charming courtyard garden. The house is run by the same people who operate the Gallier House, on Royal Street. The two house-museums have developed several self-guided tours, including **The African American Experience in 19th-Century New Orleans,** which interprets the lives of both enslaved and free people of color and how they lived, coped, and ultimately thrived in New Orleans in the 1830s through the 1860s.

Germaine Cazenave Wells Mardi Gras Museum

Return to Bourbon Street and continue along Bourbon to Bienville Street to reach the Germaine Cazenave Wells Mardi Gras Museum (813 Bienville St., 504/523-5433, www.arnauds.com/museum.html, open during restaurant hours, admission free), which is at the fabled restaurant Arnaud's, a favorite gathering place in New Orleans since World War I. The restaurant's owners opened the museum in the early 1980s as a tribute to Ms. Wells, who served as the queen of 22 Mardi Gras balls from the late 1930s through the late 1960s. On display are many of Wells's ball costumes, plus other Mardi Gras Royal Court attire. Wells was the daughter of Count Arnaud and Lady Irma Wells, who founded the restaurant in 1918. Displays of the gowns are augmented by photos of the many balls where they were worn.

New Orleans Musical Legends Park

Back on Bourbon, note the small New Orleans Musical Legends Park (311 Bourbon St.), which opened in 2003 and already includes a statue of jazz clarinetist Pete Fountain and trumpet great Al Hirt. Additional statues, busts, and plaques will be added through the years as notable jazz musicians are inducted.

From here, at the intersection of Bienville and Bourbon, you're just a couple of blocks from Canal, or you can walk back in the other direction along Bourbon or one of the parallel streets, such as Dauphine and Royal, to reach Faubourg Marigny.

Faubourg Marigny and Bywater

The neighborhood immediately downriver from the Quarter—across tree-shaded Esplanade Avenue—is Faubourg Marigny, a neighborhood sometimes credited as America's first suburb; it was settled during the first decade of the 19th century as a result of the Quarter's overcrowding, and in many respects, it continues to function as an extension of the Quarter.

Faubourg Marigny was originally a plantation, established in the early 18th century—it's named for the last owner of the plantation, Bernard Xavier Phillippe de Marigny de Mandeville, a profoundly wealthy French aristocrat who lived from 1785 to 1868. The enterprising de Marigny, realizing that the French Quarter had outgrown its boundaries, began subdividing his plantation as early as 1805, selling off quadrants to Creoles, immigrants, and free men of color. The neighborhood was soon completely cut up into short square blocks, and it thrived, at first as its own incorporated city and then as part of New Orleans, for many decades.

Like the French Quarter's, the neighborhood's fortunes waned after World War II, when it became popular to move away from inner-city boroughs and into the true suburbs—places such as Metairie and Kenner. The Marigny fell into a complete state of disrepair and poverty, despite being named a National Historic District in 1974.

As real-estate prices rose in the French Quarter in the late 1980s, savvy buyers—among them many artists, spirited professionals, and gays and lesbians—swooped in and snapped up the neighborhood's many charming cottages and houses. Before about 1995, bargains were still to be had in Faubourg Marigny; this is certainly not the case any longer, but the neighborhood still has lower real-estate costs than many other historic, centrally situated residential districts in other big U.S. cities.

There are really no formal attractions in Faubourg Marigny. A chief activity is simply strolling about admiring old houses, the bulk of which are Creole and French West Indies–style cottages and larger Greek Revival homes, many of them painted in a riot of bright colors and with intricate gingerbread, Gothic, and other Victorian details. Most of Faubourg Marigny is residential, but you'll find a handful of eateries and bars scattered throughout the district, especially along Royal Street, and you can also amble along one superhip commercial strip, Frenchmen Street, which is lined with cool music clubs, dark and shadowy Gen-X bars, funky ethnic restaurants, and affordable cafes. Although it's nowhere near as touristy as the French Quarter, Frenchmen Street's reputation has grown exponentially since the mid-1990s, and it can feel as crowded along here on a weekend evening as it does along some of the Quarter's busier streets.

A WALKING TOUR OF FAUBOURG MARIGNY

The neighborhood is bound by Esplanade Avenue, St. Claude Avenue, Press Street, and the Mississippi River, and from the Quarter it's most easily approached via Decatur Street. After crossing Esplanade, make a left onto Frenchmen, and this leads just a block or two to the little clutch of bars and cafes. From here, you're in a position to take a nice little residential tour of the neighborhood, keeping in mind that the Marigny is best known for its modest 19th-century cottages, not the grand high-style mansions more typical of the Garden District and even the Quarter. A pleasant loop is to walk downriver from Frenchmen Street along Chartres Street, crossing Elysian Fields Avenue, another wide street with a neutral ground, like Esplanade and Canal. A railroad extended clear along Elysian Fields Avenue from the 1830s through the 1950s, connecting downtown New Orleans and the Mississippi River with a resort area on Lake Pontchartrain (and also with ferry service across the lake to the cooler North Shore communities of Mandeville and Covington). Marigny was originally plotted as and named Elysian Fields after Paris's Champs Elysées (which, in French, means Elysian Fields).

Continue on Chartres for seven blocks to Press Street. Here turn left and walk up a block, returning to Frenchmen Street via Royal Street. Back at Elysian Fields, make a brief detour toward the river (taking a left from Royal) and stroll down a half block to visit **American Aquatic Gardens and Gifts** (621 Elysian Fields, 504/944-0410, www.americanaquaticgardens.com, open 9 A.M.–4 P.M. daily, admission free), a sprawling emporium with artfully arranged ponds, fountains, sculptures, terra-cotta, and plantings—it's worth strolling through even if you're not planning to buy anything.

Back on Royal, cross Elysian Fields Avenue, and as you approach Frenchmen, you'll see lovely **Washington Square Park** on your right, a delightful patch of tree-shaded lawns with park benches, surrounded by a wrought-iron fence. At Frenchmen, you can start a short tour of an especially charming part of the neighborhood: Continue upriver (west) along Royal, turn right up Touro Street, then left onto Dauphine, then left onto Pauger, and

© ANDREW COLLINS

Washington Square Park

then left onto Kerlerec Street. Two blocks later, bear left onto Chartres Street, which will lead you back in less than a block to Frenchmen, where you began this walking tour. This little jumble of turns takes you through a section where the neighborhood's houses have been restored with particular flourish.

The two most common architectural types you'll see along this tour are Creole cottages and shotgun houses. A Creole cottage typically has a four-room floor plan and a steeply angled roof, while a shotgun house is a long one-room-wide structure with a continuous gable roof that extends the length of the house. Some suggest that shotgun houses are the distant offspring of African "long houses." Creole cottages share some of the characteristics of the lacy little bungalows found throughout the French West Indies and other parts of the Caribbean, and, indeed, their popularity was heightened by the influx of Haitian refugees in New Orleans in the early 1800s. Creole cottages, in the United States anyway, are pretty much unique to New Orleans, while shotgun houses are found all through the South, especially in rural areas. However, New Orleans's shotgun houses are far more colorful, often characterized by frilly gingerbread detail, rich woodwork, and bands of colorful paint. Indeed, most U.S. architectural forms found in New Orleans represent the most florid styles within the genre.

If you like Faubourg Marigny, consider staying at one of its many lovely B&Bs and inns—this is an excellent base for exploring the city while avoiding the herds of tourists. Most of the inns here are highly charming and also less pricey than comparable properties a few blocks over in the Quarter. Do keep in mind that the Marigny has a number of unlicensed inns, which you should avoid. You can find out which of the city's licensed B&Bs are

in Faubourg Marigny by checking with the Professional Innkeepers Association of New Orleans (PIANO), whose website is www .bbnola.com.

BYWATER

The next neighborhood downriver from Faubourg Marigny is Bywater, which is also bound by Pratt, the river, and St. Claude, with its downriver boundary being the canal. Bywater has greatly cleaned itself up since the early 1990s, and as Faubourg Marigny has become prohibitively expensive for some, many homebuyers have moved farther downriver into this up-and-coming district, which also has a number of fine 19th-century homes, many in need of some TLC.

Central Business and Warehouse Districts

For at least a century after the U.S. purchase of Louisiana in 1805, American newcomers and the more established citizens of French descent maintained frosty and sometimes overtly hostile relations. Americans first settled in the neighborhood just upriver (technically southwest) of the French Quarter, now known as the Central Business District (referred to conversationally as the CBD). It was known then as the American Quarter, and the median running down Canal Street, which divides the two districts, gave rise to the term "neutral ground," which still today is what New Orleanians call any grassy median dividing opposing lanes of traffic on a wide street.

Although the CBD started out as a residential district, it was from the start a center of commerce, as the earliest residents were chiefly merchants and entrepreneurs keen on taking advantage of New Orleans's strategic location and America's recent acquisition of the territory.

Today the CBD is almost entirely without residential architecture, although some New Orleanians live in apartment buildings or, more recently, have moved into lofts and condos fashioned out of the old industrial

structures in the section of the CBD nearest the river, the Warehouse District. Just about every building in New Orleans taller than six or seven stories is in the CBD, and some of the tallest structures rise to more than 40 stories (One Shell Plaza is the tallest, at exactly 50 stories) and can be seen from as far away as the lakefront, the airport, and the Mandeville Causeway along Lake Pontchartrain. It's not a terribly interesting neighborhood to look at, any more than any other financial district dominated by office towers, but in recent years, several high-caliber hotels have opened in the CBD, and with them came some first-rate restaurants, helping to make the area more popular with visitors.

A WALKING TOUR OF THE CENTRAL BUSINESS AND WAREHOUSE DISTRICTS

This tour begins along St. Charles Avenue at Lafayette Square and continues mostly along the streets near the river, in the Warehouse District, before ending at the foot of Canal Street, where you can catch the ferry across the river to Algiers Point.

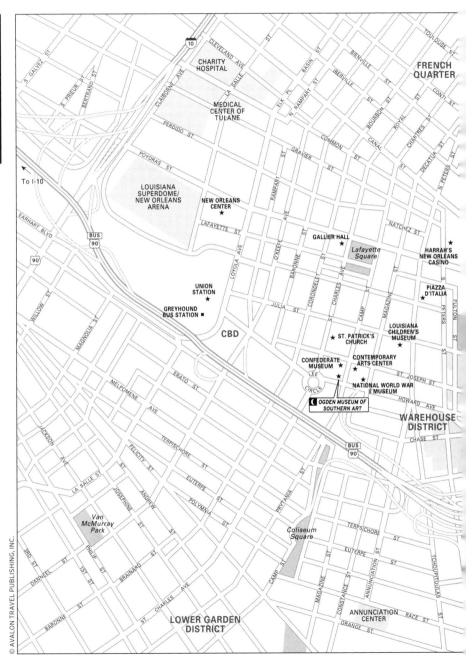

To I-10

CLEVELAND AVE
CHARITY HOSPITAL
TOULOUSE ST
FRENCH QUARTER
BIENVILLE
IBERVILLE
MEDICAL CENTER OF TULANE
CONTI ST
CANAL ST
BOURBON ST
ROYAL ST
CHARTRES ST
DECATUR ST
N. PETERS ST
COMMON ST
GRAVIER ST
PERDIDO ST
POYDRAS ST
LOUISIANA SUPERDOME/ NEW ORLEANS ARENA
NEW ORLEANS CENTER ★
EARHART BLVD
LAFAYETTE ST
NATCHEZ ST
GALLIER HALL ★
Lafayette Square
★ HARRAH'S NEW ORLEANS CASINO
BUS 90
90
UNION STATION ★
GREYHOUND BUS STATION ■
JULIA ST
PIAZZA D'ITALIA ★
WILLOW ST
MAGNOLIA ST
CBD
ST. PATRICK'S CHURCH ★
LOUISIANA CHILDREN'S MUSEUM ★
ERATO ST
CONFEDERATE MUSEUM ★
CONTEMPORARY ARTS CENTER ★
MELPOMENE AVE
LEE CIRCLE
★ NATIONAL WORLD WAR II MUSEUM
ST. JOSEPH ST
OGDEN MUSEUM OF SOUTHERN ART
HOWARD AVE
WAREHOUSE DISTRICT
CHASE ST
TERPSICHORE ST
FELICITY ST
EUTERPE ST
BUS 90
JACKSON AVE
POLYMNIA ST
LA SALLE ST
JOSEPHINE ST
ANDREW ST
PRYTANIA ST
Van McMurray Park
Coliseum Square
TERPSICHORE ST
EUTERPE ST
3RD ST
PHILIP ST
1ST ST
BRAINARD ST
DANNEEL ST
MAGAZINE ST
CONSTANCE ST
ANNUNCIATION ST
TCHOUPITOULAS ST
BARONNE ST
ST. CHARLES AVE
LOWER GARDEN DISTRICT
ANNUNCIATION CENTER
RACE ST
ORANGE ST

© AVALON TRAVEL PUBLISHING, INC.

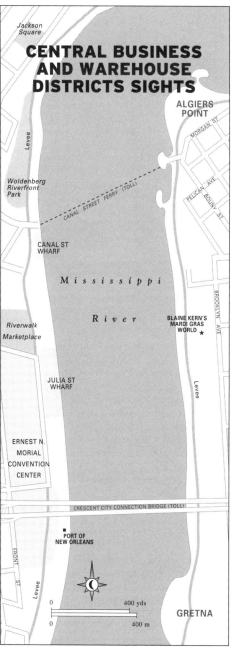

CENTRAL BUSINESS AND WAREHOUSE DISTRICTS SIGHTS

Jackson Square

ALGIERS POINT

MORGAN ST.

Woldenberg Riverfront Park

Levee

CANAL STREET FERRY (TOLL)

PELICAN AVE.

BOUNY ST.

CANAL ST WHARF

M i s s i s s i p p i

R i v e r

BROOKLYN AVE.

BLAINE KERN'S MARDI GRAS WORLD ★

Riverwalk Marketplace

JULIA ST WHARF

Levee

ERNEST N. MORIAL CONVENTION CENTER

CRESCENT CITY CONNECTION BRIDGE (TOLL)

PORT OF NEW ORLEANS

FRONT ST.

Levee

0   400 yds

0   400 m

GRETNA

If you're starting out from the French Quarter, follow Royal Street out of the Quarter to Canal and continue across Canal to St. Charles Avenue (which Royal becomes, once it enters the CBD). Follow St. Charles in the direction of uptown for several blocks, perhaps pausing briefly to admire the 1920s skyscraper at 333 St. Charles, which was built as the city's Masonic Temple and and is now home to the swanky Hilton New Orleans/St. Charles Avenue.

Lafayette Square

On your left soon after you cross wide Poydras Street you'll come to lovely and green Lafayette Square (bound by St. Charles Avenue, Camp Street, and North and South Maestri Places), which was laid out in the early 19th century as the American Quarter's version of the Place d'Armes (now Jackson Square). It was originally called Place Gravier but was rechristened in honor of the Marquis de Lafayette, who visited the city in 1825. Today the shaded and landscaped park with ample park-bench seating continues to be a pleasant place to relax or read a newspaper.

Gallier Hall

St. Charles Avenue itself is unremarkable as it runs through the CBD, lined with old and new office towers and hotels. It really doesn't begin to take form as a place to admire old homes and beautifully landscaped yards until you're well out of the CBD, in the Garden District. One building worth noting, however, is Gallier Hall (545 St. Charles Ave., 504/565-7457, www.gallierhall.com, free tours by appointment 9 A.M.–5 P.M. Mon.–Fri.), a hulking white Greek Revival building named for its architect, James Gallier, who designed the structure in 1850. Used as a special-events facility today, and as a spot where the city mayor greets members of the royal courts of Mardi Gras krewes (St. Charles Avenue is the main route for such parades), the building served as New Orleans City Hall from the late 19th through late 20th centuries. It's a stunning structure with massive Ionic columns.

St. Patrick's Church

From Gallier Hall, continue uptown along St. Charles Avenue, detouring briefly down Girod Street (a left turn), and then making a right onto Camp Street to see another of Gallier's creations, St. Patrick's Church (724 Camp St., 504/525-4413, www.oldstpatricks.org), the first place of worship built in the American Quarter and completed in 1838. The lavishly ornate interior is known for its high vaulted ceilings and fine stained glass.

Lee Circle

Back on St. Charles, continue as you were for a couple of blocks until you reach Lee Circle, formerly known as Tivoli Place, and now the hub for a small arts and museum district that has grown up on the streets just downriver from here since the mid-1990s. This is the one regal traffic circle in downtown New Orleans, and it imparts a slightly formal, urban air—a hint of Paris or London. Rising high over the traffic circle, which is a stop on the St. Charles streetcar line, stands a magnificent bronze statue of Robert E. Lee, the Confederate Civil War general; it sits atop a graceful marble column, the entire memorial rising 60 feet over the circle. It acts as a gateway to the Garden District and Uptown.

◖ Ogden Museum of Southern Art

Exit the circle via Howard Avenue, heading toward the river (a left if you're approaching it from St. Charles Avenue coming from Lafayette Square), and then make your first left onto Camp Street, which also marks the boundary of the Warehouse District, generally said to be enclosed by Camp Street and the river, from the Crescent City Connection Bridge to Poydras Street. Here on the corner, on your left, is the Ogden Museum of Southern Art (925 Camp St., 504/539-9600, www .ogdenmuseum.org, limited hours, call ahead, admission $10), which moved from a temporary space into a spectacular new building in 2003 and contains the largest collection of artwork from the American South in the United

© NEW ORLEANS CVB/CARL PURCELL

statue of Robert E. Lee, rising over Lee Circle

States. Much of the Ogden is an artful new construction, but it also incorporates parts of the old Howard Memorial Library, designed in the Richardsonian Romanesque style by native Louisianan architect H. H. Richardson, for whom that building style is named.

The complex includes the main building, which is a contemporary, five-story structure, along with the restored Patrick F. Taylor Library and the Clementine Hunter Education Wing, named for the famous Louisiana folk artist who grew up on a cotton plantation in Cloutierville (near Natchitoches) and produced about 4,000 works during her storied career. This is as complete a survey of Southern art as you'll find, with works from the 18th century to the present, spanning 15 Southern states as well as Washington, D.C. Works in every type of medium are represented among the nearly 3,000 items. Art of the Southern United States has been somewhat overlooked historically but has recently come strongly into its own. Some of the key artists represented here are noted Mississippi watercolorist Walter Anderson, 19th-century South Carolina portraitist

Thomas Sully, New Orleanian abstract expressionist George Dunbar, Depression-era photographer Walker Evans, and legendary folk artist (and country preacher) Howard Finster. The museum stays open in the evening 6–8 P.M. on Thursdays and presents live music.

Confederate Museum

Right next door to the Ogden Museum, inside the elegant Confederate Memorial Hall (ca. 1891), the Confederate Museum (929 Camp St., 504/523-4522, www.confederatemuseum.com, open 10 A.M.–4 P.M. Mon.–Sat., admission $5) holds the second-largest assemblage of Southern Civil War memorabilia in the country, including 125 battle flags, uniforms, weapons, and medical instruments, as well as the personal items of Robert E. Lee, P. G. T. Beauregard, Braxton Bragg, Confederate President Jefferson Davis, and other important Confederate figures during the war. As this war was the first ever recorded extensively through photographs, the museum has become especially known for its more than 500 tintypes, daguerreotypes, and other early photographic images. It is the oldest continuously operating museum in the state, having opened in 1891 in this Romanesque structure designed by another of the city's, and the South's, most distinguished architects, Thomas O. Sully (no relation to artist Thomas Sully, mentioned in the description of the Ogden).

Contemporary Arts Center

From the Confederate Musuem, continue down Camp to the corner of St. Joseph Street, and you can begin to sense the Warehouse District's artful gentrification, which is embodied by the Contemporary Arts Center (900 Camp St., 504/523-1216, www.cacno.org, gallery open 11 A.M.–4 P.M. Thurs.–Sun., admission free). A dramatic former warehouse with a redbrick facade and ranks of tall windows has been converted into this performing arts center with about 10,000 square feet of gallery space, in which rotating exhibits are given throughout the year. The CAC is behind the Lee Circle YMCA, just a block in from Lee Circle. CAC began in 1976 as a means to foster innovative, and often provocative, arts in New Orleans, and to that end, you can catch everything from bold photography and mixed-media installations to performances in modern dance, independent filmmaking, and edgy theater. Ticket prices for performances vary, but usually cost $10–20, and it's slightly cheaper if you buy tickets in advance rather than at the door. Performance times vary; some are given during the day, many at night. The excellent Cyber Bar and Cafe @ the CAC offers free Internet access to cafe customers; tea, beer, wine, and cocktails (this is New Orleans, after all) are available.

National World War II Museum

Turn right, toward the river, onto St. Joseph from Camp Street and continue a block, making a right onto Magazine, which leads to another of the city's more recent attractions. One of the nation's most exalted popular historians, the late Dr. Stephen Ambrose, founded the National World War II Museum (945 Magazine St., 504/527-6012, www.nationalww2museum .org, open 9 A.M.–5 P.M. Tues.–Sun. and open until 7 P.M. on Thurs., admission $14) here in 1991. The museum opened to the public on June 6, 2000—the 56th anniversary of the amphibious World War II invasion. This is the only museum in the United States dedicated to this event, which involved more than a million Americans. It may seem a random location for such a museum, but the Andrew Higgins factory, which now houses the museum, built ships during World War II, including some of the very vehicles that transported infantrymen to Normandy, an event that ultimately liberated Europe from Axis control. Ambrose, a professor at the University of New Orleans, lived in New Orleans until his death in 2002. He is best known for such riveting World War II histories as *The Good Fight, The Wild Blue* (about B-24 fighter pilots), and *D-Day: June 6, 1944.*

Louisiana Children's Museum

From the National World War II Museum, backtrack along Magazine Street, crossing St.

Joseph, and continue a block to Julia Street, which today is lined with art galleries, loft offices, and apartments. It's also home to the Louisiana Children's Museum (420 Julia St., 504/523-1357, www.lcm.org, open 9:30 a.m.–4:30 p.m. Wed.–Sat., noon–4:30 p.m. Sun., admission $7). New Orleans has become discernibly more kid-friendly through the years, and this enormous touch-friendly cache of interactive exhibits provides one of the better experiences for young ones. Many of the exhibits re-create grown-up activities or everyday errands on a kids' scale—there are a play grocery store, a miniature Port of New Orleans where youngsters can pretend to pilot a tugboat on the Mississippi and learn where all those bales of cotton and crates of sugar end up. Opportunities for children to deliver the news on a closed-circuit TV, play house inside a Cajun cottage, and experiment with different musical instruments reveal the extensive breadth of offerings. The target age for most of these exhibits is toddler up to about 12 or so, while a science lab that puts a fun spin on physics especially ignites the imaginations of the older kids. Visitors under 16 must be accompanied by an adult.

Ernest N. Morial Convention Center

Follow Julia down toward the riverfront, passing Emeril's, the famous restaurant of TV chef Emeril Lagasse, and make a right turn onto South Peters Street. As you walk from this point toward the massive Crescent City Connection Bridge, which arches high over the neighborhood, the Warehouse District's wine bars and art galleries give way to gritty machine shops, commercial bakeries, and other vestiges of the neighborhood's industrial past. Still, the architecture is interesting clear to the bridge, and along South Peters you can see that some of these old buildings have been converted to apartments and modern offices.

Turn left down Diamond Street, which leads to New Orleans's own city-within-a-city, the Ernest N. Morial Convention Center (900 Convention Center Blvd., off Lower Poydras

St., 504/582-3023, www.mccno.com), which has been a catalyst in reviving the neighborhood but which also received horrible media coverage during Hurricane Katrina, when it became a bleak temporary shelter for hundreds of displaced New Orleanians and visitors. The year it opened, it was the setting for the 1984 World's Fair. The sprawling skylighted convention center, the sixth-largest in the country, stretches out along the Mississippi River and below the Crescent City Connection Bridge, clear into the Lower Garden District. After Katrina, the center received a massive $60 million restoration, which has made it even more state-of-the-art than it was before the storm. Nevertheless, it's going to take some time for New Orleans to regain its pre-Katrina status as one of the nation's top convention destinations.

Port of New Orleans

Fronting the river outside the convention center is another behemoth, the Port of New Orleans (www.portno.com), which includes the huge cruise-ship terminal from which Carnival, Royal Caribbean Cruise Lines, Norwegian Cruise Line, the Delta Queen Steamboat Company, and RiverBarge Excursions launch ships all through the Mississippi River system and the Caribbean. This is principally an industrial port, however, and one of the world's leading hubs of international trade. It's the only deepwater port in the nation served by six major freight rail lines, and it leads the nation in market share for the import of plywood, steel, natural rubber, and—appropriate given the city's love of the stuff—coffee. About 2,000 ships come and go annually from and to the American Midwest via the river system, as well as to Latin America, Europe, Asia, and Africa. Additionally, about 6,000 ships pass by the port each year on their way up or down the Mississippi. One final claim to fame: The port encompasses the longest continuous wharf in the world, running about two miles from Henry Clay Avenue along the river to Milan Street; at any given time, up to 15 ships can tie up at the Port of New Orleans. Outside the port building is the dazzling contemporary sculpture *Mother River,* a 30-foot-tall work set inside a fountain that's meant as a tribute to the nearby Mississippi.

Piazza D'Italia

From the convention center, cut inland a block to Fulton Street, and make a right, following this interesting row of vintage warehouses for several blocks to Poydras Street, onto which a left turn leads a block (just beyond South Peters Street) to Piazza D'Italia (300 block on the west side of Poydras), a modern, outdoor park created in the style of a Romanesque square. It was laid out by renowned postmodern architect Charles Moore in 1978 to honor the contributions of New Orleans's thriving Italian community. A building facing Piazza D'Italia was converted into the 285-room Loews New Orleans Hotel in 2003, which helped to restore the original piazza into a public park.

Across Poydras from the piazza, **Harrah's New Orleans Casino** (8 Canal St., 800/533-6000, www.harrahs.com/our_casinos/nor) opened in a massive space along Canal Street in 1999. Its reception has been somewhat mixed, and many locals and visitors avoid the place entirely. The casino has free parking (with proof of playing), a 24-hour buffet, live entertainment, about 100 gaming tables, and 2,100 slot machines. There are a few good restaurants—including Besh Steakhouse, Gordon Biersch brewpub, and Bambu for Asian fare—which has helped make the casino more popular with nongamers. The casino also opened its own accommodation, the Riverfront Hotel, in September 2006.

Riverwalk

Another example of the city's once grungy and industrial downtown waterfront's being turned into a popular attraction for visitors is Riverwalk (foot of Poydras St., extending along the river to the Morial Convention Center, 504/522-1555, www.riverwalkmarketplace.com), which is connected to the New Orleans Hilton Riverside hotel. You reach it from the casino simply by walking a block down Poydras. The long, snaking building with great river views holds about 140 shops (a mix of chains and local stores), a large food court, and four sit-down restaurants. Parking is available at the Hilton garage, the World Trade Center garage, and along Convention Center Boulevard; it costs just $4 for up to four hours of parking at any of these facilities if you spend more than $10 at any Riverwalk store and have your parking ticket validated.

Leave Riverwalk the way you came in, and then make an immediate right off Poydras onto Convention Center Boulevard to reach Canal Street and the ferry for Algiers Point. Or, if you have a car parked near here, you might want to finish this tour by heading up Poydras about a dozen blocks to the Superdome.

Louisiana Superdome/ New Orleans Arena

The massive, 52-acre Superdome (1500 Poydras St., 504/529-8830, www.superdome.com) is home to NFL's New Orleans Saints, Tulane football, college football's Sugar Bowl, and other key gridiron events as well as major concerts and some of the city's most popular annual events (including the New Orleans Home and Garden Show and the Essence Music Festival). In the wake of Katrina, the Superdome is—like the Morial Convention Center—more infamous for its role as an evacuee center in the aftermath of the storm. The roof and interior were completely refurbished in 2006, in time for the Superdome to host the Saints' 2006–2007 season opener in September (which the Saints won handily over the Atlanta Falcons, with a crowd of more than 70,000 cheering them on).

The gargantuan arena is the largest stadium with a roof in the world, holding 72,000 fans for football (usually only about 20,000 for concerts, although seating was expanded to 87,500 for a Rolling Stones concert in 1981, setting a record for attendance at an indoor music concert). The roof alone covers about 10 acres and rises to a height of about 273 feet (nearly as tall as a 30-story building). The city commissioned construction of the dome in 1966, back when domed stadiums were all the rage, especially in places with excessively cold or hot climates and plenty of wet weather. Sultry, swampy New Orleans seemed a perfect fit, and of course the huge Astrodome in similarly hot and humid Houston had been a huge success when it opened a few years earlier. Construction wasn't actually begun on the Superdome until 1971, and it didn't open until four years later. Tours of the Superdome were given until the early 2000s but have been suspended indefinitely, so your only chance of seeing this pleasure dome is attending one of the many events here.

Just off Poydras, Loyola Avenue leads west a couple of blocks to the main branch of the U.S. Post Office and to the **Union Station** (Loyola Ave. and Earhart Blvd.) passenger terminal, a rather bland facility opened in the 1950s.

ALGIERS POINT

From the foot of Canal Street, you can catch the passenger and auto ferry, which makes frequent trips all day long across the Mississippi River to Algiers Point, on the West Bank but still part of the city proper. The mostly residential neighborhood with a vast cache of notable, if generally modest, 19th- and early-20th-century residences, has a handful of pleasant parks, a few B&Bs, pubs, and eateries, and a smattering of shops. Although it's easy to get to Algiers Point via the ferry, or by driving over the Crescent City Connection Bridge, this neighborhood has always felt and continues to feel distinct from the rest of the city, owing to that mile-wide boundary line, also known as the Mississippi River, that separates it from the French Quarter and CBD.

The little ferry service has been sending boats back and forth across the river since 1827, despite various bureaucratic efforts to eliminate it. Always the influential and very active Algiers Point Neighborhood Association has fought hard to keep the boat running, as such a cut in service could effectively wipe out the neighborhood's vibrancy. Service is offered 6 A.M.–midnight daily, and there's no charge for foot passengers (cars pay just $1 for round-trip passage).

The top reason visitors venture across the river to Algiers Point is to visit **Blaine Kern's Mardi Gras World** (233 Newton St., Algiers, 504/361-7821, www.mardigrasworld.com, open 9:30 A.M.–4:30 P.M. daily, admission $15), the largest builder of parade floats anywhere. Mardi Gras may take place over a relatively short period late each winter, but this place hums with activity every day of the year. Free shuttle buses to and from the museum greet passengers at the Algiers Point ferry terminal 9:30 A.M.–4:30 P.M. On the tour you'll see a video on the history of the city's Mardi Gras celebration.

The Garden District and Uptown

Technically, Uptown is really the area between Claiborne Avenue and Tchoupitoulas Street, running from Louisiana Avenue for nearly 40 blocks out to Lowerline Street, a few blocks beyond Audubon Park. But loosely speaking, any point upriver of the Crescent City Connection Bridge along or between St. Charles Avenue and Magazine Street could be considered Uptown, at least in relation to the Quarter and CBD. For the purposes of this book, the area has been broken down into the Lower Garden District, the Upper Garden District, Magazine Street, Audubon Park, and Tulane and Loyola universities, which have adjacent campuses on the other side of St. Charles Avenue from Audubon Park. Once you get beyond Lowerline, you're really in Carrollton, which was formed in the early 1800s as its own little distinct town but was eventually absorbed by New Orleans. The section where St. Charles Avenue meets with Carrollton Avenue, at the bend in the river, is known appropriately as Riverbend.

Uptown and the Garden District are remarkably diverse and best known for picturesque residential architecture and a slower and

© NEW ORLEANS CVB/RICHARD NOWITZ

Uptown home with wrought-iron gate

more relaxed pace than in the French Quarter and certainly the corporate CBD. The architecture is more traditionally American in this area, rich in the Greek Revival and Victorian styles typical of well-to-do Southern residential building, but it has also been strongly influenced by the city's French, Spanish, and West Indian roots.

A car is fine for exploring the Garden District and Uptown, as street parking is pretty easy to find all along St. Charles, many of the residential side streets, and along Magazine Street (although there it's mostly metered). However, the best way to truly experience the surroundings and get a sense of the vibe is to walk, so if you are using a car, try to park it in one or more central locales and hoof it from there.

Since St. Charles is one-way (toward Canal Street) in the CBD, if you're driving from the direction of Canal Street, take Carondelet Street, which runs parallel to St. Charles, several blocks toward Uptown, then left onto Howard Street, and right onto Lee Circle, bearing right onto St. Charles. Or take Magazine

Street, which is one-way toward Uptown from Canal and through the Warehouse District, beneath the Crescent City Connection Bridge, and into the Lower Garden District. Magazine continues one-way for about 10 blocks before becoming two-way once it crosses Felicity Street.

Magazine is a narrow two-lane street with dense pockets of commercial activity, so although it's a fascinating road to drive on, traffic does not move speedily. St. Charles is also only two lanes, but it's wider and divided by the neutral ground (median), on which the streetcar passes, and it has less commercial activity, so it tends to be a faster drive. Be aware, however, that streetcars have the right of way—be extremely careful not to block them when making a left turn from St. Charles onto a cross street. Wait on St. Charles with your left-hand turn signal on, and don't pull into the median until you're sure there are no streetcars coming and there's no oncoming traffic coming along the opposing lane of St. Charles. If you do sit in the median blocking the tracks while waiting for an opening in the opposing traffic, you're sure to hear the trolley driver clang the bells angrily at you. You can also take Tchoupitoulas, which parallels Magazine nearly alongside the Mississippi River, through Uptown. This is a mostly industrial stretch without much charm, but parts of Tchoupitoulas have begun to gentrify.

All of this advice aside, remember that you don't actually need a car to explore this area, despite the fact that it does cover a large expanse. It's quite feasible to rely chiefly on streetcars and buses to get in and around both the Garden District and Uptown.

Uptown is shaped like a broad U, with the CBD at the lower (eastern) end and the Carrollton/Riverbend neighborhood at the upper (western) end. The main thoroughfares are St. Charles Avenue and Magazine Street, which run more or less parallel, extending in a southwesterly and then westerly and then northwesterly direction from the CBD to Carrollton. Magazine Street and St. Charles each run about 4.5 miles through the

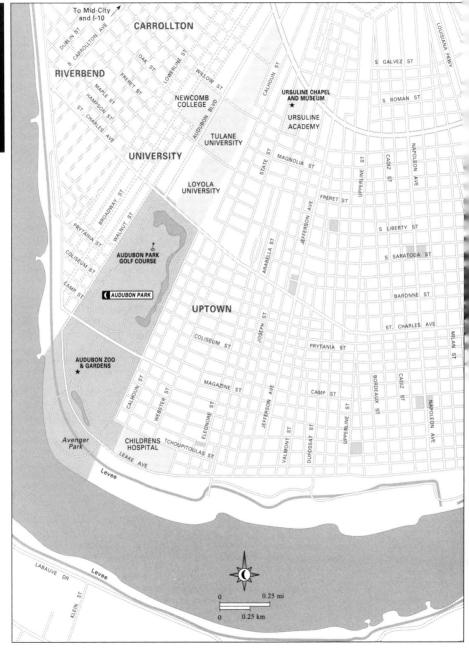

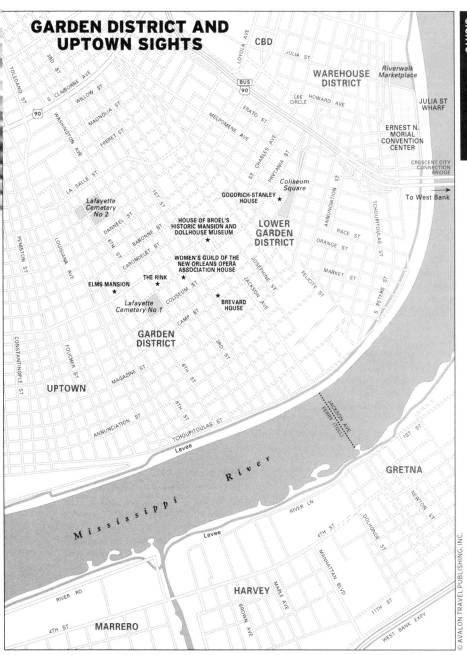

GARDEN DISTRICT AND UPTOWN SIGHTS

CBD

WAREHOUSE DISTRICT

Riverwalk Marketplace

LOYOLA AVE

JULIA ST

3RD ST

S CLAIBORNE AVE

WILLOW ST

TOLEDANO ST

MAGNOLIA ST

BUS 90

LEE CIRCLE

HOWARD AVE

JULIA ST WHARF

90

WASHINGTON AVE

FRERET ST

MELPOMENE AVE

ERATO ST

ST CHARLES AVE

PRYTANIA ST

ERNEST N. MORIAL CONVENTION CENTER

CRESCENT CITY CONNECTION BRIDGE

LA SALLE ST

Coliseum Square

ANNUNCIATION ST

To West Bank

Lafayette Cemetery No 2

1ST ST

GOODRICH-STANLEY HOUSE ★

RACE ST

TCHOUPITOULAS ST

DANNEEL ST

BARONNE ST

6TH ST

HOUSE OF BROEL'S HISTORIC MANSION AND DOLLHOUSE MUSEUM ★

LOWER GARDEN DISTRICT

ORANGE ST

PENISTON ST

LOUISIANA AVE

CARONDELET ST

WOMEN'S GUILD OF THE NEW ORLEANS OPERA ASSOCIATION HOUSE ★

JOSEPHINE ST

MARKET ST

FELICITY ST

S PETERS ST

ELMS MANSION ★

THE RINK ★

COLISEUM ST

JACKSON AVE

Lafayette Cemetery No 1

★ BREVARD HOUSE

CONSTANTINOPLE ST

FOUCHER ST

CAMP ST

3RD ST

GARDEN DISTRICT

UPTOWN

MAGAZINE ST

6TH ST

8TH ST

ANNUNCIATION ST

TCHOUPITOULAS ST

JACKSON AVE FERRY (TOLL)

1ST ST

Levee

GRETNA

NEWTON ST

RIVER LN

Mississippi River

DOLHONDE ST

4TH ST

Levee

MANHATTAN BLVD

11TH ST

RIVER RD

HARVEY

MAPLE AVE

BROWN AVE

WEST BANK EXPY

4TH ST

MARRERO

© AVALON TRAVEL PUBLISHING, INC.

Garden District and Uptown. At their nearest points, they're just three blocks apart, at the very eastern end of Uptown, but they diverge slightly as they move westward, and at some points, such as out near Audubon Park, it's about three-quarters of a mile from St. Charles to Magazine. Scores of cross streets connect Magazine and St. Charles, so you can always walk easily from one to the other. St. Charles is served by the famous St. Charles streetcar, and Magazine Street by several buses, making it easy to go the length of either street from the CBD.

More than just a convenient and affordable mode of public transportation, the **St. Charles Avenue streetcar** is itself very much an attraction—it's the oldest continuously operating streetcar line in the world, having first clanged and banged down the avenue in 1835. The streetcar is a charming way to travel throughout Uptown, but to see the whole neighborhood, it makes sense to take the bus along Magazine one way through Uptown, and the streetcar the other. Because St. Charles runs one-way toward Canal Street in the CBD, you pick up the streetcar at the corner of Canal and St. Charles to go Uptown, but the cars actually travel west through the CBD along parallel Carondelet Street.

St. Charles and Magazine differ greatly in character, and the blocks between them also vary quite a bit in appearance, history, and architecture as you wend through the Uptown District. Magazine is New Orleans's original shopping thoroughfare—the name means "shop" in French. St. Charles Avenue is lined with hotels, restaurants, grand residences, and a handful of modern midrise apartments in the Lower Garden District, but into the Upper Garden District it takes on a mostly residential appearance, and it remains this way until you get well into Uptown, around Audubon Park, where the lakeside of the avenue is fringed by the stately campus buildings of Loyola University. Hurricane Katrina severely damaged sections of the streetcar route and power system, and the line is still out of commission but expected to resume service sometime in mid- to

late 2007 (although a small stretch of the line through the CBD is planned to open by early 2007). The price tag for restoring the line was expected to exceed $11 million.

LOWER GARDEN DISTRICT

The area bounded by St. Charles Avenue and Tchoupitoulas Street, and the Crescent City Connection Bridge (Bus. U.S. 90) to Jackson Avenue, comprises the Lower Garden District, which was for a time just a nice way of describing the less-fancy area between the CBD and the true (Upper) Garden District. It is not so much the domain of ritzy mansions as is the Upper Garden District, but the area's handsome old cottages, town houses, and apartments have been touched increasingly by the wand of gentrification in recent years. In fact, the Lower Garden District has some of the finest examples of Greek Revival, Edwardian, and Queen Anne residential architecture in the city.

Along St. Charles Avenue, you'll find several hotels and restaurants, most of them moderately priced; parallel Prytania Street, a block south toward the river, has some of the same feel. The neighborhood also has several mostly generic-looking apartment buildings and hotels, which is another trait that distinguishes it from the more quaintly historic Garden District. One of the best spots for admiring architecture is Coliseum Square, which runs from Camp Street for four blocks between Melpomene Avenue and Race Street. Keep in mind that New Orleanians pronounce Melpomene, Terpsichore, Euterpe, and so on—the names of nine parallel streets from Coliseum Square nearly to Lee Circle—not the way they're pronounced when referring to the nine muses of classical Greek mythology, but rather MEL-puh-mean, TERP-sih-kore, and such.

The neighborhood stands on what had been part of the plantation of city founder Jean Baptiste Le Moyne de Bienville. It was divided into smaller plantations through the latter part of the 18th century and then subdivided into small city lots in the early 19th century. A developer and city planner named Bartheleme Lafon was hired to create the new neighborhood. Lafon, a fan of Greek classics, envisioned a grand district of fountains, tree-lined canals, parks, and open-air markets, and he named the nine streets extending from Place du Tivoli (known today as Lee Circle) and Coliseum Square after the nine muses. He laid out Coliseum Square with plans to house a great coliseum, and Annunciation Square to be anchored by a massive cathedral. Prytania Street was laid out lengthwise through the district as the main thoroughfare.

The neighborhood developed not quite according to Lafon's plans. Many large homes were constructed throughout the new blocks, especially around Coliseum Square, but the coliseum and cathedral never came to fruition, and the Lower Garden District has never developed the cachet of the adjacent Upper Garden District, where the city's wealthiest 19th-century Americans built their immense homes. By the late 1800s, quite a few smaller and simpler houses and cottages had been built throughout the district, many with fanciful Victorian trim, and Magazine Street had taken hold as one of the city's best destinations for shopping.

The Lower Garden District's fortunes waxed and waned through the early 20th century and then plummeted as much as just about any New Orleans neighborhood after World War II. Huge swaths of neighborhood nearest the river were cleared to make way for a commercial railroad depot and later for the infamous St. Thomas housing project (it has since been razed). The massive Crescent City Connection Bridge was built over the Mississippi near the border between the CBD and the Lower Garden District (today, for all practical purposes, it *is* the border). This project not only took out more houses, it effectively cut the neighborhood off from the CBD, creating a vast no-man's-land of asphalt beneath the wide bridge. A second bridge across the river was proposed for where the ferry now runs cars back and forth between the foot of Jackson Avenue and the West Bank town of Gretna, but locals helped to keep that bridge from ever being built.

In the early 1970s, concerned residents, worried that the already frail and disjointed Lower Garden District would crumble even further into a state of decay, banded together to form the **Coliseum Square Association** (www.coliseumsquare.org), which successfully fought off that second bridge proposal and also got the neighborhood listed on the National Register of Historic Places. The association gives an annual tour of homes each April—this is a terrific way to learn more about the neighborhood's wonderful architecture.

If you're exploring the area yourself, either drive to **Coliseum Square** and park near it, or take the St. Charles Avenue streetcar to around Melpomene or Euterpe Street and walk toward the river two blocks to reach the square. The blocks around the square, and also along St. Charles and Prytania, have the most attractive and interesting homes. There are no formal attractions or museums in this neighborhood, as most are private residences. Do note in particular the **Goodrich-Stanley House** (1729 Coliseum St.), a marvelously restored Creole cottage in which the famous African explorer Henry Morton Stanley (as in Stanley and Livingstone) lived as a young man.

To reach the Garden District from here, walk or drive in the direction of Uptown along Prytania Street or St. Charles Avenue, which are the two safest and most appealing ways to get there from the Coliseum Square area.

GARDEN DISTRICT

The Garden District is at once emblematic of New Orleans high society and of trendy urban living today—it's been home to novelist Anne Rice, edgy Nine Inch Nails singer Trent Reznor, football greats Archie and son Peyton Manning, and the cast of MTV's *Real World* in 2000. But pop culture aside, this is the New Orleans neighborhood where American aristocrats built their monuments of wealth during the prosperous boom times of the mid-19th century—by about 1900, most of the Garden District had been developed. The neighborhood's splendid homes line streets shrouded by towering live oaks, flowering magnolia trees, and graceful palms. The gardens surrounding these properties sometimes outshine the homes themselves.

ANNE RICE: NEW ORLEANS'S QUEEN OF THE DAMNED

Although she moved to California in 2005, author Anne Rice remains closely associated with the city she's long celebrated in her novels, New Orleans. Rice was born on October 4, 1941, in the city's Mercy Hospital (with the given name of Howard Allen O'Brien – unusual for a baby girl). She lived in New Orleans for the first 16 years of her childhood. A job transfer took her family to Richardson, Texas, where she completed high school and began dating fellow journalism student Stan Rice.

They married a couple of years later, and in 1961 the young couple moved to San Francisco's funky Haight-Ashbury District. Both studied creative writing at San Francisco State University, and Anne published her first short story, "October 4, 1948," in 1965. A year later she gave birth to a daughter, Michele. Stan began to receive considerable acclaim for his poetry, and when the Rices moved across San Francisco Bay to Berkeley in 1969, Anne wrote her first treatment of what would become her most famous work, *Interview with the Vampire*, in short-story form.

Tragedy struck in 1972 when Michele succumbed to leukemia. But within a year, Anne had focused her grief into converting *Interview* into a full-length novel. It was completed in 1973 and accepted by Knopf, the prestigious imprint of Random House, for publication in 1976. The film rights were sold to Paramount, but it would be 18 years later before the film, starring Tom Cruise, Brad Pitt, Kirsten Dunst, Stephen Rea, and Antonio Banderas, was completed and released. Most of the film was shot in southern Louisiana, including several scenes in the Garden District and specifically at Lafayette Cemetery No. 1.

The Rices continued to write prolifically throughout the 1970s and '80s, with Stan teaching and eventually chairing the Creative Writing department at San Francisco State University for many years. Anne Rice went on to produce such noted historical novels as *The Feast of All Saints* (1979) and *Cry to Heaven* (1982), but her greatest acclaim has come from building on *Interview* to develop seven more Gothic novels, *The Vampire Lestat* (1985), *The Queen of the Damned* (1988), *The Tale of the*

Like the Lower Garden District, this entire neighborhood is protected as a National Historic District. It began as part of Bienville's sprawling plantation and was converted to a series of smaller spreads during the mid- to late 18th centuries, before being further subdivided and sold to developers in the 1830s. It was laid out into quite large blocks, with the idea that it would appeal to "new" Americans of considerable means. The neighborhood thrived as an exclusive enclave of ostentatious mansions, most of which still stand today.

◖ A Walking Tour of the Garden District

The best way to experience the Garden District is on an organized walking tour, several of which are offered by different companies.

As with the Lower Garden District, there are few formal attractions open to the public here, but experienced guides can point out notable buildings and discuss their heritage and the often colorful stories behind them and their past and present owners. Strongly recommended are the informative walks given by **Historic New Orleans Tours** (504/947-2120, www.tourneworleans.com). These tours are given at 11 A.M. and 1:45 P.M. daily, departing from the **Garden District Book Shop** (at The Rink, Washington Ave. and Prytania St.). The tours last about two hours and cost $15. (The same company also does French Quarter, Haunted, Weekend Jazz Walks, and Cemetery Voodoo tours.) **The Rink** (Washington Ave. at Prytania St.) was the South's first roller-skating rink, built in the 1880s and converted many

Body Thief (1992), *Memnoch the Devil* (1995), *The Vampire Armand* (1998), *Blood and Gold* (2001), *Blackwood Farm* (2002), and *Blood Canticle* (2003). Together these nine works comprise *The Vampire Chronicles*. (*Queen of the Damned* followed *Interview* onto movie screens in 2002.)

Rice has also written a trilogy of novels that comprise *The Mayfair Witches* trilogy, and under pseudonyms A. N. Roquelaure and Anne Rampling has published several other works. Rice's own New Orleans home was the inspiration for Mayfair Manor, the home of the Mayfair Witches.

The Rices' second child, son Christopher, was born in 1979. (Christopher Rice wrote his first novel, *A Density of Souls*, in 2001. Like so many of his mother's works, it is set in New Orleans. The book received mixed reviews but has already earned the younger Rice a strong following. His second novel, *The Snow Garden*, was released in 2003.)

In 1989, Stan Rice retired from his SFSU job and the family moved back to Anne's hometown, New Orleans. They lived in a

stately 1857 Greek Revival and Italianate mansion at 1239 1st Street in the Garden District. Rice became a fixture in the neighborhood, having bought and restored St. Elizabeth's Orphanage (at 1314 Napoleon Ave.), a massive former boarding house and girls' orphanage built in 1865. She bought the 55,000-square-foot Second Empire building in 1993, and for several years it was open to the public for tours. Inside were books, furnishings, more than 800 dolls, and other collectibles amassed by the Rice family through the years. (The building is no longer owned by Anne Rice, and tours are not given any longer.)

On December 9, 2002, Stan Rice died after a battle with brain cancer. He left behind an impressive legacy of poetry and painting. Though Anne has since relocated to California, her deep connection to her hometown remains palpable, as evidenced on her website, www.annerice.com, which she updates regularly with notes, commentary, and other thoughts on New Orleans, writing, politics, and life in general.

years later into a row of boutiques and shops. The Garden District Book Shop is the most famous of these businesses, and it's an excellent place to pick up rare and out-of-print books on the city, as well as signed editions of Anne Rice novels.

Also very good are the guided walks given by **Gray Line** (504/569-1401 or 800/535-7786, www.graylineneworleans.com). These 2.5-hour tours leave at 10 A.M. daily from the French Quarter (you're first taken by bus from here to the Garden District) at the little Gray Line lighthouse kiosk behind Jackson Brewery. The cost is $20.

One of the more distinctive tours is of **Lafayette Cemetery No. 1** (Washington Ave. and Coliseum St., open 7:30 A.M.–2:30 P.M. Mon.–Fri., 7:30 A.M.–noon Sat., admission

free), which is one of relatively few "cities of the dead" in New Orleans that's relatively safe to explore, at least during the day. The guided tours offered by **Save Our Cemeteries** (504/525-3377 or 888/721-7493, www.saveourcemeteries.org), a nonprofit organization that preserves the city's burial grounds, are definitely the best way to go, and these cost $6. The one-hour walks are held at 10:30 A.M. Monday, Wednesday, Friday, and Saturday. Lafayette Cemetery No. 1 is especially popular with fans of Anne Rice's *The Vampire Chronicles* trilogy; it was featured in the movie *Interview with the Vampire*.

If you're exploring the area on your own, take the streetcar up St. Charles to Jackson Avenue, or drive and park anywhere in the neighborhood along Prytania or its side streets. The Garden District is bounded by St. Charles Avenue and Magazine Street, from Jackson Avenue for about a dozen blocks to Louisiana Avenue.

Right as you alight the streetcar at Jackson Avenue, you'll come to one small but noteworthy attraction, especially if you have an interest in miniatures. The **House of Broel's Historic Mansion and Dollhouse Museum** (2220 St. Charles Ave., 504/525-1000 or 800/827-4325, www.houseofbroel.com, open 10 A.M.–5 P.M. Mon.–Sat., admission $10) is set inside an imposing Victorian along the avenue. The first part of the house was built in the 1850s, and a major addition, which converted it to the immense three-story mansion that you see today, was built in the 1890s. This is a fine tour, not only to get a look at the living quarters and furnishings of an exceptional Garden District residence, but also to admire the hundreds of dolls, miniatures, and other collectibles that fill the rooms.

At the other end of the district on St. Charles, note the **Elms Mansion** (3029 St. Charles Ave., 504/895-9200, www.elmsmansion.com), built by a railroad tycoon after the Civil War and notable for its Flemish oak carvings and original tapestries. Tours are available only to groups and by appointment, but it's worth stopping to admire this Italianate Victorian from the street.

The most distinctive and impressive Garden District homes are set mostly along Prytania Street (a block from St. Charles) and the blocks just off it along 1st, 2nd, and 3rd streets. Some prominent structures also stand along Jackson Avenue. Architecturally, the grandest mansions tend to be in the Greek Revival style, but you'll also see a number of Italianate Victorians and even some traditional raised Louisiana cottages, which are, in fact, much larger than what most of us think of when we hear the word "cottage."

Followers of Anne Rice should make a point of stopping in front of **Brevard House** (1239 1st St.), a hybrid Greek Revival and Italianate mansion with spectacular cast-iron balconies. Here the novelist lived before moving to Cal-

ifornia in 2005; it's also where she and her husband raised their son, Christopher Rice, a novelist in his own right. Her husband, poet and artist Stan Rice, died in December 2002.

One of the only houses in the neighborhood that can be toured by the public, by appointment only, is the **Women's Guild of the New Orleans Opera Association House** (2504 Prytania, 504/899-1945, admission $5), which is furnished approximately as it looked when its last private owner, Nettie Seebold, died and willed the home to this organization. The circa-1865 home, also a mix of Italianate and Greek Revival styles, is filled with exquisite 18th- and 19th-century American furniture and artwork. It was built by noted New Orleans architect William A. Freret.

MAGAZINE STREET

New Orleans's original and enduring shopping street, Magazine Street (the name comes from the French *magasin,* which means "shop") follows the curve of the Mississippi River for about six miles from Canal Street through the CBD and then on through the Lower and Upper Garden Districts, Uptown, and on by Audubon Park. It's a shopping paradise, yet with very few chain or franchise businesses. Magazine is distinct because it embraces independent shops, restaurants, coffeehouses, and bars, and it's popular along different stretches with New Orleanians of every background, economic and social strata, age, and ethnicity. In some places it's collegiate and funky, others upscale and popular with the many professionals who live in the residential blocks between Magazine and St. Charles Avenue. The stretch of Magazine through the Lower Garden District is famous for its antiques shops, but you can find secondhand clothiers and furniture stores of varying quality all along Magazine.

The street begins in the CBD, at Canal Street, just a few blocks down from St. Charles, and forms one of the main spines through the Warehouse District. Here it's lined with old warehouse buildings, galleries, and a few nightclubs, shops, and restaurants. Beyond the Crescent City Connection Bridge, under which Magazine passes, the street is for about 10 blocks a rather downcast and mostly residential stretch. It doesn't really pick up and become busy with activity until you cross Felicity Street, at which point begins one of the South's most impressive and famous clusters of antiques shops. The lower stretch, between here and the bridge, does have loads of potential, and more than a few developers and preservation-minded homebuyers have begun buying up the tired-looking but promising town houses along here. There's little question that in time Magazine's gentrification will extend unbroken from the Warehouse District clear through Uptown, as whatever sections look slightly seedy today are tomorrow's hot spots for B&Bs, restaurants, antiques shops, and galleries.

AUDUBON PARK, TULANE, AND LOYOLA

As you continue upriver from Magazine Street and the Garden District, you reach the section of Uptown that takes in lush and leafy Audubon Park and the regal campuses of Tulane and Loyola universities. This is a great area to explore on a sunny day, as you'll find plenty of shade under the live oak trees in Audubon Park and dotting both college campuses.

◖ Audubon Park

The city's favorite place for strolling, right near the campuses of Loyola and Tulane, is leafy Audubon Park (St. Charles Ave. at Walnut St., 504/861-2537), a 340-acre spread with moss-draped oak trees, lush lawns with picnic areas, lagoons, and athletic facilities that include tennis courts, a golf course, and paved trails for jogging, in-line skating, and strolling. It's a wonderful spot for picnicking, strolling, and admiring the many impressive statues, many of them depicting animals and set within the park's zoo, and many created by WPA artists during the 1930s.

The park occupies what had been a plantation and also the estate of Jean Etienne De Boré, who developed a system of granulating sugar in 1794 that did for Louisiana's sugar business about what the cotton gin did for the

a fountain in Audubon Park

© NEW ORLEANS CVB/RICHARD NOWITZ

state's cotton trade. The city bought the tract of land in 1871, naming it New City Park, and eventually Audubon Park in honor of artist and ornithologist John James Audubon, who lived for many years both in New Orleans and outside Baton Rouge up near St. Francisville. The park quickly became famous after hosting the World's Industrial and Cotton Exposition in 1884, a 100th-anniversary celebration of the first shipment of Louisiana cotton to a foreign port. At this festival, the park's grounds and buildings were lighted with electricity, just six years after Thomas Edison first began experimenting with electric light bulbs.

The upper part of the park, between Magazine Street and St. Charles Avenue, consists of the park's golf course, as well as the winding lagoon and many gardens and benches. Below Magazine Street, toward the river, lies the **Audubon Zoo and Gardens** (6500 Magazine St., 504/581-4629 or 800/774-7394, www.auduboninstitute.org, open daily but with limited hours, call ahead, admission $12), which contains nearly 2,000 animals. It's a wonderful place to explore verdant, overgrown

© NEW ORLEANS CVB/RICHARD NOWITZ

Loyola University

gardens rife with just about every species of flora known to Louisiana. If you're taking the St. Charles Avenue streetcar, get off at stop 36 for the park and zoo. If you're coming by car, the zoo has plenty of parking.

A favorite attraction at the zoo is the Louisiana Swamp exhibit, the next best thing to taking a swamp tour and even better in one respect: You're guaranteed to see the creatures of the region's marshes and swamps up close and personal. The swamp exhibit is an actual re-creation of a Depression-era Cajun swamp settlement, complete with old bayou shacks and a trapper's cottage. In addition to learning about the animal life common to this environment, such as alligators and raccoons, you can see Spanish moss, cypress knees, and other flora common in the swamp.

Another exhibit that emphasizes both wildlife and its relationship to people and the environment is the Jaguar Jungle, which re-creates a Mayan rainforest and includes, in addition to the two dignified yet powerful jags themselves, storks, spider monkeys, and sloths. The display also features realistically rendered reproductions of stone carvings at famous Central American and Mexican archaeological sites, such as Chichén Itzá and Copán. In 2003, the jaguars mated successfully—a rare instance of such a thing in captivity. Other crowd-pleasers in other sections of the zoo include a pair of nearly 400-pound white tigers, an huge Indonesian komodo dragon, a few rather extroverted gorillas, and many monkeys. Kids love to ride the carousel (rides are $2), which features some 60 figures of endangered species.

Animal feedings are another big draw. These are scheduled all through the day in a variety of zoo venues; you can get a list at the admissions desk. Among the animals that are quite engaging to watch at feed times are giraffes and gators. You can also watch the staff feed live insects to tropical birds.

Loyola University and Tulane University

The campuses of New Orleans's two most famous institutions of higher learning sit adjacent to one another opposite the park. Loyola faces St. Charles Avenue just opposite Audu-bon Park, as does Tulane just a bit farther upriver, although much of its modern campus extends along the blocks farther toward the lake from St. Charles, off Freret and Broad-way streets. The presence of both schools has helped to infuse the businesses along Maga-zine Street and in the nearby Riverbend and Carrollton neighborhoods with a youthful, collegiate buzz.

Established by the Jesuit order in 1911, Catholic **Loyola University** (6363 St. Charles Ave., 504/865-3240 or 800/456-9652, www.loyno.edu) had been a Catholic prep school since 1904. Fronting St. Charles Avenue are the school's stately redbrick buildings with terra-cotta trim, built in the Tudor Gothic style. Loyola has an enrollment of 4,500 students.

Tulane University (6823 St. Charles Ave., 504/865-5000, www.tulane.edu), a private nonsectarian research university that comprises 11 schools and colleges, began as the Medical College of Louisiana in 1834, the need for it brought about in part by the city's constant struggles to contain deadly yellow fever epidemics. In 1847 it became the University of Louisiana, a public univer-sity. A huge 1883 bequest by a wealthy New Orleanian named Paul Tulane allowed the university to expand into a much more com-prehensive facility and to be reorganized as a private university; it was renamed Tulane in honor of this financial gift. The campus cov-ers about 110 acres of Uptown and includes more than 80 buildings.

Tulane ranks as one of the top schools in the South, with about 10,000 students. About a third of all students are from New Orleans, with most of the remainder hailing from all throughout North America; about 8 percent of the student body is from outside the United States. Notable divisions include the Tulane University School of Medicine, the second-old-est medical school in the Deep South, and the highly esteemed A. B. Freeman School of Busi-ness and the Tulane Law School.

The older Tulane buildings are set along or near St. Charles and include several Roman-esque structures of considerable architectural acclaim. It's a pretty campus to walk through, although neither it nor Loyola contains any public attractions or museums of note.

Ursuline Chapel and Museum

Along State Street, a few blocks northeast of Tulane's campus, the Ursuline Chapel and Museum (2701 State St., 504/899-7374, www.ursulineneworleans.org), part of the Ursuline Convent, is home to a gilded statue, *Our Lady of Prompt Succor,* which com-memorates a quite miraculous military vic-tory, the Battle of New Orleans, which took place during the War of 1812. In fact, the war had already ended a couple of weeks before the battle, but news of the peace treaty had not yet reached either the advancing British troops or the American defenders, led by fu-ture President Andrew Jackson. At the time, the city looked exceedingly vulnerable to at-tack, and New Orleanians solemnly prepared for the worst but hoped for the best. The more faithful among the citizens sat inside the Old Ursuline Convent on Chartres Street in the French Quarter and prayed to Our Lady of Prompt Succor all through the night of Janu-ary 7, 1815, for a successful outcome to the battle slated for the following day. The parish-ioners struck a moral deal: If their American army successfully fended off the Brits, they would dedicate the city to her.

The American army of 4,000, never taken seriously by the arrogant but impressively trained British troops, who were fresh from victory against Napoléon in Europe, faced about 8,000 enemy military men. Amazingly, Jackson led his troops—a motley mix of for-mer Haitian slaves, pirates, federal militia, and American frontier settlers—to a decisive vic-tory during which just a handful of Americans lost their lives, versus some 2,000 dead or miss-ing British troops.

The statue inside the chapel is a national shrine to this victory, and each year a spe-cial Mass is held on January 7 during which Our Lady and her infant are honored during a splendid high Mass.

The museum, which contains religious artifacts as well as correspondence between the convent and Thomas Jefferson, James Madison, and King Louis XV, may be toured by appointment.

CARROLLTON

Carrollton is today just another Uptown neighborhood of New Orleans, but this charming residential district with a couple of hip spans of eateries (it's especially strong on Asian restaurants) and shopping began as its own little town, incorporating in 1843. In those early years, Carrollton was a summer resort, separated from the city of New Orleans by several miles of plantations and swampland. Situated at a major bend in the Mississippi River, the town's popularity grew when a railroad line was built connecting it to New Orleans. Soon the place began to bustle with a racetrack, beer gardens, charming summer cottages, and a hotel. It served as the seat of Jefferson Parish for a time before being swallowed up by the mother ship, New Orleans, in an 1874 annexation.

The Carrollton Historic District today preserves an eclectic collection of mostly Craftsman, Colonial Revival, Greek Revival, and Italianate bungalows and houses, many of them painted in bright shades and most dating to the late 19th and early 20th centuries.

The southern end of South Carrollton Avenue, from St. Charles up to about Claiborne, is every bit as charming as St. Charles itself, with a grassy neutral ground that serves as the streetcar line, and huge oak trees draped with Spanish moss hanging over the street. The span of South Carrollton Avenue nearest St. Charles has a handful of good eating places. This subsection of Carrollton, known as **Riverbend,** also has a handful of funky clothing and gift boutiques, most of them along Dublin and Hampson streets.

If you walk down **Maple Street** in the opposite direction from Carrollton Avenue, downriver, you'll also encounter a small and enchanting entertainment-retail district, with many 19th-century cottages now housing coffeehouses, bars, and shops. This section is just a few blocks from Tulane's campus, and it tends to be frequented by students from there and Loyola.

A final street worth exploring in Carrollton is the town's old main thoroughfare, **Oak Street,** which runs toward the river off Carrollton Avenue, about six blocks from St. Charles. This funky strip of buildings has been the latest in the area to gentrify.

Mid-City

Mid-City can mean pretty much any part of New Orleans situated between I-10 and I-610, which form a triangle in the middle of the city, and also extending north toward the lake above I-610. This includes massive City Park, and the mostly residential blocks on either side of it, and it also takes in the interesting and up-and-coming neighborhood where Canal Street and Carrollton Avenue intersect, as well as Esplanade Ridge, the also up-and-coming neighborhood on either side of Esplanade Avenue from Rampart Street (at the edge of the French Quarter) to Bayou St. John and the southeast corner of City Park.

Mid-City, therefore, covers a chunk of New Orleans that's much, much larger than the French Quarter or CBD and is even bigger in total area than Uptown. However, other than City Park and the few patches of gentrification mentioned above, it's not generally a part of town that holds much interest for visitors, although simply driving or biking around Mid-City you're likely to pass by some fascinating blocks of distinguished residential architecture and to find some cool neighborhood restaurants and funky bars.

Mid-City is best explored by car, although most of the few key sites mentioned below can also be reached by city bus as well as the Canal Street streetcar line, which opened in 2004.

It is *possible* to begin this tour by walking Esplanade Avenue from the French Quarter, but it's about a 2.5-mile stroll to reach the New Orleans Museum of Art in City Park, and the middle span of this walk, from Rampart Street to Claiborne Avenue, known as Faubourg Tremé, is downcast and dodgy. If you're the sort of person who doesn't stand out obviously as a tourist and you feel comfortable walking through what is in places a lower-income urban neighborhood, consider walking at least one way, ideally during the late morning or midday. Even the somewhat transitional stretch of Esplanade passes by some beautiful old Greek Revival and Italianate mansions, and the stroll up Esplanade's tree-shaded neutral ground affords a much better sense of the area's rich history than driving or even taking a slow-moving bus. Do not make this walk after dark, however.

ESPLANADE RIDGE

As you head up Esplanade Avenue, in an area known historically as the Esplanade Ridge neighborhood, the first span of your walk, from Rampart Street to Claiborne, about six blocks, is the most severely dilapidated, although a number of buildings along this stretch have been restored in recent years, among them the impressive **Rathbone Inn** (1227 Esplanade Ave.) and the **Hotel Storyville** (1261 Esplanade Ave.). You'll soon reach Claiborne Avenue, over which the elevated I-10 highway zooms.

Cross under the interstate and continue up Esplanade. Along this stretch, which is still very much in a state of flux (although definitely improving), the avenue bears a considerable resemblance to St. Charles Avenue in Uptown. Indeed, just as the wealthiest Americans in the city built their mansions in the Garden District throughout the 19th century, quite a few wealthy Creole families erected stately homes along Esplanade.

Stop for a moment at the triangular sliver of a park where Miro Street crosses Esplanade and Bayou Road branches off from Espla-

nade diagonally. Here stands the marble-and-cement *Goddess of History—Genius of Peace* statue, along with a couple of park benches. This is a particularly pretty spot along Esplanade Ridge.

Degas House

Just up and across the street from the statue at Miro Street is the Degas House (2306 Esplanade Ave., 504/821-5009, www.degashouse. com), the only former residence of famed French impressionist Edgar Degas that's open to the public. You can stay in one of the seven lavish guest rooms, some with fireplaces and whirlpool tubs, or stroll (by appointment only) through the 1852 house in which the artist lived briefly from 1872 to 1873, while visiting relatives on his maternal side (his mother and grandmother were born in New Orleans). Tours include a walk through the house and the immediate neighborhood; they last about an hour, and a donation of $10 per person is suggested.

Continue up Esplanade about eight or nine more blocks, taking note of how the neighborhood continues to improve, the houses looking ever larger and more stately, and also more recently restored. Above Howard Avenue up until the edge of City Park, Esplanade Avenue is a lovely thoroughfare, and the cross blocks around Ponce de Leon and Maurepas streets have become a bustling little restaurant row since the late 1990s. There are several good spots here to grab a snack or a cup of coffee.

Fairgrounds Race Track

Just a few blocks east of Esplanade Avenue is the Fairgrounds Race Track (1751 Gentilly Blvd., 504/948-1285, www.fgno.com), the third-oldest thoroughbred-racing course in the nation. There's live racing from Thanksgiving through March, and an off-track–betting parlor is open year-round, where you can wager on events elsewhere in the country.

St. Louis Cemetery No. 3

Back on Esplanade, just up from the cluster of restaurants, you'll come to St. Louis Cemetery No. 3 (Esplanade Ave. between Lada Ct. and

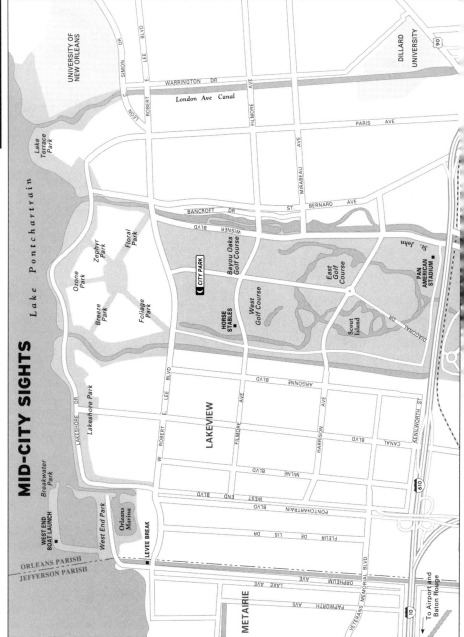

MID-CITY SIGHTS

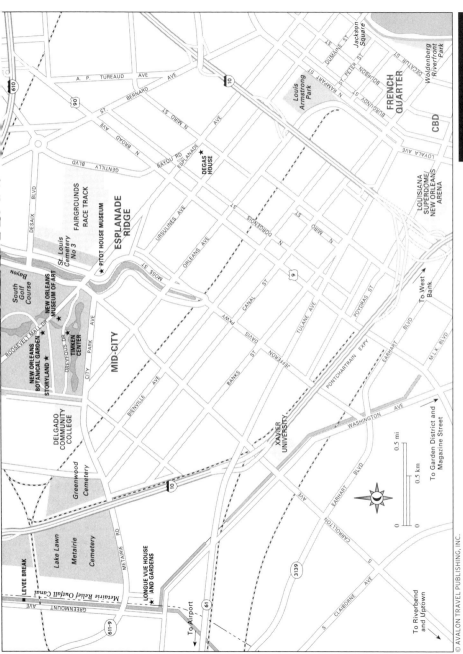

FRENCH QUARTER

Jackson Square

Woldenberg Riverfront Park

CBD

Louis Armstrong Park

LOUISIANA SUPERDOME/ NEW ORLEANS ARENA

ESPLANADE RIDGE

DEGAS HOUSE ★

FAIRGROUNDS RACE TRACK

St. Louis Cemetery No 3

PITOT HOUSE MUSEUM ★

South Golf Course

NEW ORLEANS MUSEUM OF ART ★

NEW ORLEANS BOTANICAL GARDEN ★

STORYLAND ★

TIMKEN CENTER ★

MID-CITY

DELGADO COMMUNITY COLLEGE

Greenwood Cemetery

Lake Lawn Metairie Cemetery

LEVEE BREAK ■

Metairie Relief Outfall Canal

LONGUE VUE HOUSE AND GARDENS ★

XAVIER UNIVERSITY

To West Bank

To Garden District and Magazine Street

To Riverbend and Uptown

To Airport

0.5 mi

0.5 km

© AVALON TRAVEL PUBLISHING, INC.

Moss St.), which is one of the safer ones in the city for exploring during the day. Just pop inside the small office by the entrance gate to pick up a map, and wander this narrow "city of the dead," which abuts the racetrack in places. As is true for all cemeteries and even most parks in New Orleans, you should not enter after dark, and it's wise to explore it with a friend or two.

Pitot House Museum

Turn right out of the cemetery and follow Esplanade just 150 yards farther, making a left onto Moss Street, which curves alongside the east bank of Bayou St. John to reach one of the only surviving Colonial plantations in the South, the Pitot House Museum (1440 Moss St., 504/482-0312, http://pitothouse.org, open 10 A.M.–3 P.M. Wed.–Sat., admission $5, includes guided tour), which overlooks the lazy, slow-moving bayou. The house is named for early occupant James Pitot, who was the first mayor of New Orleans after it was incorporated.

❰ CITY PARK

Retrace your steps back along Moss Street to Esplanade, make a left, and continue across the bayou, which puts you at the southeast edge of the 1,500-acre City Park (1 Dreyfous Ave., 504/482-4888, www.neworleanscity-park.com), which received moderate to heavy flooding and significant damage to some of its attractions during Katrina. Larger than New York City's Central Park, City Park contains a wealth of outdoors activities. Facilities include Bayou Oak Golf Course, one of the largest tennis facilities in the South, eight miles of lagoons ideal for fishing and canoeing or pedal-boating, an old-fashioned amusement park called Carousel Gardens, and a children's playground called Storyland, which features 26 larger-than-life sculptures, each based on a different fairy tale (open 10 A.M.–5 P.M. weekends, admission $3).

City Park sits on what had been, more than two centuries ago, a swampy oak forest, and it still contains the largest collection of mature live oaks in the world, some believed to date to the 1400s or earlier. You can stop by

the park's visitors center for a map and history of the entire compound, along with bits of information on some of the most famous oak trees, at the **Timken Center** (1 Dreyfous Ave., 504/483-9475), a Spanish Mission–style building that opened in 1913 as a gaming casino. It also contains public restrooms and a pleasant, casual restaurant.

New Orleans Museum of Art

The park's greatest cultural draw is the fabulous New Orleans Museum of Art (City Park, 1 Collins Diboll Circle, 504/488-2631, www.noma.org, open 10 A.M.–5 P.M. Tues.–Sun., admission $8), whose vast holdings (totaling about 40,000 objects) span many cultures and eras, from pre-Columbian and Native American to European postimpressionist. The museum is justly known for its excellent rotating exhibits—in 2003 it celebrated the 200th anniversary of the Louisiana Purchase with an exhibition called Jefferson's America and Napoleon's France. It's also an architectural marvel, consisting of an imposing Greek Revival building that dates to 1911 and a cleverly appended modern addition that was completed in 1993.

The permanent collection is as eclectic as it is extensive. The top (third) floor contains African, pre-Columbian, and Asiatic works in a rather compact network of smallish galleries. On the second floor you'll find the most extensive holdings—and you'll also gain a very clear sense of how the two wings of the museum fit together and coexist and contrast architecturally. The newer wing contains the impressive Lupin Foundation Center for Decorative Arts, a fascinating array of glassworks and ceramics, mostly of the 19th and 20th centuries. The second floor of the original museum has a few rooms decorated with period 18th- and 19th-century furnishings, as well as a survey of European and American artists from the present to several hundred years ago. Included are several paintings by Degas, three priceless Imperial Easter eggs created by Peter Carl Fabergé, and works by such notables as Monet, Gauguin, Picasso, Braque, Modigliani, Matisse, Kandinsky, Marsden Hartley, O'Keeffe,

© NEW ORLEANS CVB/CARL PURCELL

New Orleans Museum of Art

Man Ray, and Diane Arbus. There aren't necessarily a great many "must-sees" at NOMA, but the museum does a nice job giving an overview of art through the ages, and it also provides extremely detailed background information on the paintings and furnishings.

The museum's latest venture, completed in 2003, is the Sydney and Walda Besthoff Sculpture Garden, a five-acre run of gardens, magnolias, camellias, pines, and ancient live oak trees interspersed with 42 sculptures. Noted artists with works here include Henry Moore, George Rickey, Jacques Lipchitz, and George Segal. You traverse the grounds over bridges and footpaths that wind over lagoons and through gardens.

New Orleans Botanical Garden

The New Orleans Botanical Garden (1 Palm Dr., City Park, 504/483-9386, www.neworleanscitypark.com/nobg.php, open 10 A.M.–4:30 P.M. Tues.–Sat., admission $6) opened as a project of the WPA in 1936, bringing together the unique visions of landscape designer William Wierdon, building architect Richard Koch, and artist Enrique Alferez, each of whom

had a hand in the layout. The dozens of grand statues set throughout City Park were largely the work of Alferez, a local artist of immense talent who died in 1999 at the age of 98 after a career spanning seven decades, beginning in the 1930s. Many of his designs are reliefs of the female figure and garden benches, and most are surrounded by the park's lush landscaping. There are 2,000 types of plants here, including several themed gardens (aquatics, ornamental trees and shrubs, perennials).

In 2002, the park reopened its Conservatory of the Two Sisters, the first stage of a massive overhaul that will eventually see the entire Botanical Garden rejuvenated. The conservatory includes the Living Fossils Wing, in which you can observe today's plants displayed alongside their fossil ancestors. In the Tropical Forest Room, a roaring waterfall forms the backdrop for one of the largest collections of exotic flora in the South.

CANAL STREET AND CARROLLTON AVENUE

From the intersection of Canal and Carrollton, you can follow gracious palm-shaded Carrollton

Avenue west (upriver) for a little less than a mile through a neighborhood of mixed-income housing that contains a number of Victorian and early–20th-century houses and cottages in various states of refurbishment. This drive follows the path of the Canal Street streetcar, on which you can ride from City Park all the way to the foot of Canal, between the French Quarter and the CBD.

The neighborhood around the intersection of Carrollton Avenue and Canal Street is an interesting one, with a mix of fairly ordinary workaday shops and fast-food restaurants, along with quite a few notable cafes, ethnic restaurants, and interesting old houses. The incomparable Italian pastry and ice-cream shop **Angelo Brocato's** makes for an especially enjoyable snack break. Like St. Charles Avenue, Esplanade Avenue, and to a certain extent Carrollton Avenue, upper Canal Street was a place during the late 19th century where quite a few wealthy New Orleanians built impressive homes, many of them immense wood-frame Italianates and Greek Revivals. On the nearby side streets are a mix of mostly smaller shotgun houses, Creole cottages, and gingerbread Victorians. The neighborhood is neither touristy nor overly polished—just a genuine slice of residential New Orleans, and a neighborhood that's racially and ethnically diverse.

From here you could turn down Canal Street back to the Quarter, or continue along Carrollton Avenue under the I-10 freeway overpass and for another couple of miles to reach Carrollton. Or you could take Canal Street in the opposite direction of the Quarter, toward the lake, for nearly a mile, making a left onto City Park Avenue. This road takes you by New Orleans Country Club, Louisiana State Charity Cemetery, Metairie Cemetery, Greenwood Cemetery, and, right at the border between New Orleans and Metairie, the **Longue Vue House and Gardens** (7 Bamboo Rd., Old Metairie, 504/488-5488, www.longuevue.com, open 10 A.M.–5 P.M. Mon.–Sat., 1–5 P.M. Sun., admission $10), a lush and exotic 80-acre estate that once belonged to a cotton broker and now comprises a period-furnished Classical Revival manor house and spectacularly landscaped grounds. This is one of the most impressive attractions in the city, but many visitors never get here because it's slightly out of the way.

Greater New Orleans

Many visitors to New Orleans overlook the suburbs immediately east and west of the city, but there are several notable attractions in these areas. Alas, the areas east of New Orleans received heavy Katrina damage and may take quite some time to rebound. But Metairie and Kenner, the two largest suburbs just west of New Orleans, have largely recovered from storm damage and are worth a look. Across the river, there are also a handful of sights on the West Bank.

EASTERN NEW ORLEANS AND CHALMETTE

A handful of attractions are in eastern New Orleans and the neighboring communities, but this is the part of the city that was hit the hardest by Katrina, and some of the attractions are still not open (and some have no plans to reopen). It's best to explore these sites on their own, rather than as part of a linear tour, as distances between them are considerable, and the drives to and from these places are not especially intriguing. And given the severe damage to the area, it's wise to phone ahead before visiting.

Audubon Louisiana Nature Center

One attraction that's of particular interest to outdoor lovers is the 85-acre Audubon Louisiana Nature Center (Joe Brown Memorial Park, Dwyer Rd. and Read Blvd., 504/246-5672, www.auduboninstitute.org), which makes a nice change of pace from the urbanity of downtown New Orleans. The park and nature center have been closed since Hurricane Katrina, and there are no immediate plans to reopen them, but check the website for updates. You reach it by heading east for about 10 miles on I-10, then heading south onto Read Boulevard at Exit 244 (it's about a 15-minute drive from the Quarter). The park is a couple of blocks south on your left. Here you'll find an extensive network of nature trails, a butterfly garden, and a kids-oriented discovery loft with hands-on learning stations that shed light on the flora and fauna (including flying squirrels, snakes, and other local critters) of the region. When you're actually here wandering through the lush foliage and swamps, it's hard to imagine you're on the eastern edge of a major city.

Chalmette Battlefield and National Cemetery

The only one of the sites within the Jean Lafitte National Historical Park and Preserve that touches on Louisiana's military history, Chalmette Battlefield and National Cemetery (8606 St. Bernard Hwy., Chalmette, 504/281-0510, www.nps.gov/jela, limited hours, call ahead, admission free) commemorates the important victory by Andrew Jackson and his American troops during the Battle of New Orleans in 1815. The battlefield lies just six miles southeast of downtown New Orleans and comprises a 1.5-mile tour road (with six interpretive placards set along it at pull-offs) through the scene of the action, Chalmette National Cemetery, and the 1833 Malus-Beauregard House. The latter had no role in the battle, of course, having been built 18 years after it, but it's a dashingly handsome Creole mansion with long, graceful verandas and stout columns. It looks like the anchor of one of those classic southern Louisiana plantations, but, in fact, the house had no ties to a farm. It was built as a residence and occupied by a number of wealthy merchants and prominent figures, the last private owner being Judge René Beauregard.

Again not closely related to the Battle of New Orleans itself, Chalmette National Cemetery was actually commissioned as a graveyard for Union soldiers felled during the Civil War, although veterans of subsequent wars—the Spanish-American War, World Wars I and II, and Vietnam—are also interred here. You can visit the graves of four men who fought in the War of 1812, one of whom actually participated in the Battle of New Orleans. There's also an obelisk, Chalmette Monument, that stands high over the battlefield. The monument was commissioned in 1840 shortly after former President Jackson returned to the scene of the battle to mark its 25th anniversary, but construction wasn't begun until 1855, and the monument was not completed for another 53 years.

In terms of understanding the battle itself, how it evolved, and why the British failed so miserably, the placards and exhibits inside the visitors center are most useful. The park extends to the banks of the Mississippi, so you get a very clear sense of where the British came ashore and where the Americans awaited them. The Battle of New Orleans, fought on January 8, 1815, with most of the action in just two hours, was the last military conflict ever waged between U.S. and British troops.

Free talks on the battle are given daily. Check for interpretive programs, videos, and performances, scheduled regularly throughout the year, and when in New Orleans, be sure to drop in on the headquarters of the Jean Lafitte National Historical Park and Preserve, in the French Quarter at 419 Decatur Street. Here you'll find information on all of the park's six sites throughout southern Louisiana.

METAIRIE AND KENNER

Many visitors to the region see Kenner and Metairie as they arrive by air—Kenner is home to the Armstrong International Airport, and Metairie is the suburb you pass through en route to New Orleans. These are largely residential communities, but Old Metairie is worth a look for its shopping and dining, and Kenner is home to a leading family attraction, Rivertown U.S.A.

SIGHTS

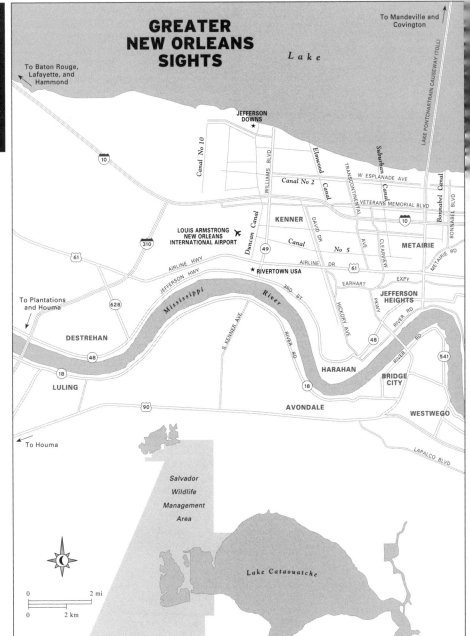

GREATER NEW ORLEANS SIGHTS

Lake

To Mandeville and Covington

LAKE PONTCHARTRAIN CAUSEWAY (TOLL)

To Baton Rouge, Lafayette, and Hammond

JEFFERSON DOWNS ★

Canal No 10

Canal No 2

Elmwood Canal

Suburban Canal

W ESPLANADE AVE

TRANSCONTINENTAL

VETERANS MEMORIAL BLVD

WILLIAMS BLVD

Bonnabel Canal

BONNABEL BLVD

KENNER

METAIRIE

LOUIS ARMSTRONG NEW ORLEANS INTERNATIONAL AIRPORT ✈

Duncan Canal

49

Canal

DAVID DR

No 5

CLEARVIEW AVE

METAIRIE RD

AIRLINE HWY

AIRLINE DR

★ RIVERTOWN USA

61

JEFFERSON HWY

61

EARHART EXPY

JEFFERSON HEIGHTS

3RD ST

HICKORY AVE

RIVER RD

To Plantations and Houma

628

Mississippi

River

S. KENNER AVE

RIVER RD

48

RIVER RD

541

DESTREHAN

48

HARAHAN

BRIDGE CITY

18

LULING

18

AVONDALE

WESTWEGO

90

LAPALCO BLVD

To Houma

Salvador Wildlife Management Area

Lake Cataouatche

0   2 mi

0   2 km

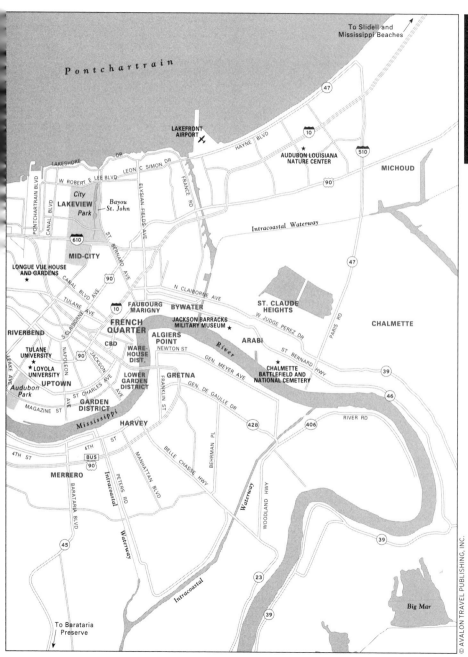

To Slidell and
Mississippi Beaches

Pontchartrain

LAKEFRONT
AIRPORT

47

10

510

MICHOUD

HAYNE BLVD

AUDUBON LOUISIANA
NATURE CENTER

90

LAKESHORE   DR

LEON C SIMON DR

W ROBERT E LEE BLVD

City
LAKEVIEW
Park

Bayou
St. John

ELYSIAN FIELDS AVE

FRANCE RD

Intracoastal Waterway

PONTCHARTRAIN BLVD

CANAL   BLVD

610

MID-CITY

ST. BERNARD AVE

47

LONGUE VUE HOUSE
AND GARDENS

CANAL BLVD AVE

90

TULANE AVE

N CLAIBORNE AVE

ST. CLAUDE
HEIGHTS

CHALMETTE

PARIS RD

10

FAUBOURG
MARIGNY

BYWATER

W JUDGE PEREZ DR

RIVERBEND

S. CLAIBORNE AVE

FRENCH
QUARTER

CBD

JACKSON BARRACKS
MILITARY MUSEUM

ARABI

ST BERNARD HWY

TULANE
UNIVERSITY

NAPOLEON

90

JACKSON

WARE-
HOUSE
DIST.

ALGIERS
POINT

NEWTON ST

River

GEN. MEYER AVE

CHALMETTE
BATTLEFIELD AND
NATIONAL CEMETERY

39

LOYOLA
UNIVERSITY

UPTOWN

Audubon
Park

ST CHARLES AVE

LOWER
GARDEN
DISTRICT

GRETNA

FRANKLIN ST

GEN. DE GAULLE DR

46

LEAKE AVE

4TH ST

MAGAZINE ST

GARDEN
DISTRICT

Mississippi

406

RIVER RD

HARVEY

BELLE CHASSE HWY

BEHRMAN PL

428

39

4TH ST

ST

4TH

BUS
90

MANHATTAN BLVD

Intracoastal

WOODLAND HWY

MERRERO

BARATARIA BLVD

PETERS RD

Waterway

Waterway

39

45

23

Intracoastal

Big Mar

To Barataria
Preserve

Old Metairie

Old Metairie nestles up against the New Orleans border and has some very upscale residential neighborhoods, despite being strangled on all sides by busy interstates and even busier Veterans Boulevard. It's a nice neighborhood for poking around, and a bike trail runs right through part of the area. It's also close to Longue Vue House and Gardens. To explore this area, take I-10 west from downtown to Exit 231A, and make a left onto Metairie Road, passing by New Orleans Country Club on your left and Metairie Cemetery on your right. You'll pass signs for Longue Vue House and Gardens after about a half mile. Continue straight across the canal, and Metairie Road winds through the Old Metairie section of town. If you venture off onto the cross streets, you'll pass through some elegant neighborhoods, many with fine old homes from the early 20th century. Metairie Road is also lined with good restaurants.

Rivertown U.S.A.

Just southeast of Armstrong International Airport, kids enjoy Rivertown U.S.A. (415 Williams Blvd., 504/468-7231, www.rivertownkenner.com, open 9 A.M.–5 P.M. Tues.–Sat., admission to each museum $3, $15 for all museums, $6 for a combined ticket to the Space Station and Planetarium and Observatory). This expansive educational and museum complex comprises the Daily Living Science Center, Space Station, Planetarium and Observatory, Wildlife and Fisheries, and Cannes Brûlée Native American Center. There's also a Mardi Gras Museum, a Saints Hall of Fame, a toy train museum, and a children's castle. In short, you won't have trouble finding two or three museums or exhibits with appeal, no matter what your interests.

In the Mardi Gras Museum, a particular favorite of out-of-towners, you can board a simulated Mardi Gras float, watch artisans at work on floats and costumes, and take a look at a wide array of beads, posters, costumes, and collectibles related to both the city Mardi Gras parades held throughout the state as well as the rural Courir du Mardi Gras celebrations, which are held mostly in rural Cajun communities. Cannes Brûlée Native American Center hosts a wide range of music, crafts, storytelling, and history demonstrations and lectures; in a re-created bayou setting, you can learn about the folk traditions, foods, medicinal plants, and crafts of the Native American cultures indigenous to Louisiana. More than 700 varieties of regional wildlife are on display, both mounted in dioramas and alive in a 15,000-gallon aquarium. Other museums detail Kenner's history, toy trains, and NFL football's New Orleans Saints.

A highlight for many visitors is the Science Center, which comprises the Louis J. Roussel Laser Planetarium and River Max Theater, the Freeport McMoRan Observatory, and an interactive museum dedicated to the exploration of space and the development of scientific technology. Visitors can explore touch-friendly exhibits on meteorology, electricity, the human body, gravity, and world geography. The planetarium has astronomy shows twice a day on Tuesdays and Fridays, and three times daily on Saturdays.

Rivertown is also home to the Rivertown Repertory Theatre, which presents a half dozen professional musicals and plays throughout the year. You reach Rivertown by taking I-10 west to Exit 223, Williams Boulevard; head south on Williams for about 2.5 miles.

THE WEST BANK

The West Bank comprises a stretch of suburbs and even a bit of New Orleans proper, including historic Algiers Point, although that section is covered as a side trip via the free (for passengers) ferry from Canal Street in the CBD across the river. New Orleans city limits continue along the West Bank of the river for several miles, extending about two miles inland, all the way out to English Turn, a big inverted C of the Mississippi River, roughly across from the town of St. Bernard. It's not a part of the city many people explore, as it holds few formal attractions and is not exactly a hotbed of dining or entertainment, but there are a few reasons to wander across the river.

In keeping with New Orleans's ever-confusing orientation, the West Bank section of New Orleans proper actually lies *east* as the crow flies across the river from downtown and the French Quarter. With a serpentine river such as the Mississippi, people refer to everything on one side as the West Bank and everything on the other as the East Bank (as the river *generally* flows in a north–south direction), but at many of its sharply curving points, the river can run east–west, west–east, and even south–north.

The West Bank is mostly a series of small but densely settled communities that include Gretna, Harvey, Marrero (which sits along the edges of Lake Cataouatche), and the even larger Lake Salvador. Farther west, as you follow U.S. 90, you'll pass through Westwego (one of the few Cajun settlements in metro New Orleans), and eventually out to the towns of Mimosa Park and Boutte, before U.S. 90 continues down into LaFourche Parish, the easternmost section covered in this book's Cajun Country side-trip chapter. You reach the West Bank from downtown New Orleans via the Pontchartrain Expressway, which rises over the Crescent City Connection Bridge; this is the final bridge over the Mississippi River before it empties into the Gulf more than 100 miles downstream, although there are a handful of car-ferry crossings farther downriver.

Barataria Preserve

Swamp tours can be great fun, but if you want to experience the wetlands of southeastern Louisiana at your own pace, and independent of a tour group, you should strongly consider spending a day at Barataria Preserve (6588 Barataria Blvd., or Hwy. 45, near Crown Point, Marrero, 504/589-2330, www.nps.com/jela, open 7 A.M.–7 P.M. daily during daylight savings time, 7 A.M.–5 P.M. the rest of the year, admission free), a division of the Jean Lafitte National Historical Park and Preserve.

Geologically speaking, the Mississippi Delta is still a newborn, having been formed with sediment and silt deposited at the mouth of the Mississippi 5,000 years ago. It's been a gradual process, with the area now encompassed by New Orleans having been built up just about 2,500 years ago. The river continues to deposit sediment, and the delta continues to expand, as it does in the Atchafalaya basin. Here at Barataria Preserve, you have the chance to explore and learn about one of the world's most substantial delta ecosystems, a series of bayous, marshes, swamps, and woodlands that appear at first to be almost virginal and untouched by man. Indigenous tribes, however, began settling on the delta from almost the moment it was dry and large enough to support human life. As Europeans arrived, they settled here to fish and trap as the Native Americans had, and later immigrants have cultivated the land in different ways, most recently for oil drilling. This was also the domain of the notorious pirate for whom the park is named, Jean Lafitte, who declared himself the King of Barataria during his heyday toward the end of the 18th century.

Barataria Preserve is a haven for an amazing variety of plant life, which thrives in this subtropical climate. Depending on water salinity, elevation, soil type, and moisture, different species thrive. Along the natural ridges and levees, there's dense hardwood forest, along with towering live oaks, but the habitat changes to palmetto groves on the lower back slopes of the levees. Water covers most of the lower regions of the levees throughout much of the year, and so in these swamp areas you'll encounter bald cypress trees, and then treeless marshes beyond the swamps.

The preserve makes an ideal habitat for anybody interested in getting outside for hiking and canoeing; fishing is allowed as long as you've obtained a valid permit. The preserve contains eight miles of hiking trails, 2.5 miles of which run across well-maintained boardwalk, allowing a close look at the swamp ecosystem and the many critters who live within. Just keep in mind that many of these animals are chiefly nocturnal, so you may not see much of them during the day. Animals that you may see during the day include gray squirrels, swamp rabbits, armadillos, and nutria, curious furry animals introduced from Argentina that have become something of a pest because of their vast quantities. Heron, ibis, and egrets fly freely through the swamp, and all sorts of scaly creatures, from turtles to frogs to snakes, slither and crawl about. Of course, as in any Louisiana swamp, you may very well encounter alligators, which like to sun along dry levees and riverbanks during warmer times of year; you may sometimes see them lying in shallow water, too, only their eyes and nostrils peeking out above the water. There's no reason to be alarmed as long as you give them their space and avoid making any aggressive gestures; alligators are not at all interested in human visitors, and most of them are quite used to seeing canoes and people.

Nine miles of waterway are dedicated exclusively to canoe use, on which no motorized craft is permitted. These are accessible at three separate canoe launches and afford a great chance to experience the terrain as the earliest humans to inhabit southeastern Louisiana would have, in total quiet. Just watch for snakes curled around the branches of overhanging trees—it's not a common problem, but snakes have been known to fall into boats passing beneath them. An-

other 20 miles of Barataria waterway is open to both motorized and nonmotorized boats, and there are several launches in the area for motorized craft. You can rent canoes just outside the preserve.

Barataria has picnic spots in several parts of the park, with restrooms both at the visitors center and at the parking area for the Pecan Grove and picnic tables.

The visitors center is open 9 A.M.–5 P.M. daily; trails and parking areas open at 7 A.M. and close at 7 P.M. from roughly early April to late October and 5 P.M. the rest of the year. Reservations are required for the Saturday morning canoe treks, the bird-watching excursions, the sunset strolls, and the moonlight canoe treks; call ahead for details on these engaging activities. Guided nature walks are given at 1:30 P.M. Sunday–Friday, and the 25-minute video *Jambalaya: A Delta Almanac* is presented throughout the day. Check for interpretive programs, videos, and performances scheduled throughout the year, and when in New Orleans, be sure to drop in on the headquarters of the Jean Lafitte National Historical Park and Preserve, in the French Quarter at 419 Decatur Street. Here you'll find information on all of the park's six sites throughout southern Louisiana.

ENTERTAINMENT

It's the reason plenty of visitors come to New Orleans: to be entertained. Usually, in this city, entertainment takes the form of watching a jazz, blues, or rock band captivate an audience in one of the city's seemingly endless array of lounges, bars, and live-music halls. Or it's attending Mardi Gras or Jazz Fest, two of the world's most exalted live-music events, or one of the many smaller festivals and parades held in the Crescent City throughout the year.

New Orleans's reputation as party central is well deserved, but enjoying a night on the town can involve a wide range of activities that appeal to many tastes. There is, of course, the city's salacious side, evidenced by the significant number of strip clubs, adult bookstores, and the like. You'll also find a big (though not particularly successful) casino in the Central Business District. You'll find a wide range of mod lounges, Old World watering holes, festive gay bars, and stately hotel cocktail lounges in New Orleans, with the greatest concentration in the Quarter. But New Orleans, and all of southern Louisiana for that matter, truly stands out for its rollicking live-music scene: It's one of the world's premier venues for jazz, blues, rockabilly, soul, zydeco, and Cajun music, and the city's venues vary from hole-in-the-wall dives to massive music halls. You'll find top-notch live music just about any night of the week.

ENTERTAINMENT

HIGHLIGHTS

《 Best All-Around Music Club: If you have the chance to watch live music at just one club, get out of the Quarter and drop by **Tipitina's,** a long-running locals' favorite that draws some of the top zydeco, jazz, blues, and Cajun talents around (page 104).

《 Best Gospel Brunch: Sure it's a little touristy, but the lively gospel brunch offered on Sundays at the riotously popular **House of Blues** is a hoot, and this outpost of the popular chain books great bands nightly, too (page 106).

《 Most Historic Jazz Venue: Opened in 1961, atmospheric **Preservation Hall** presents wonderful jazz concerts within its inviting vintage confines (page 110).

《 Most Elegant Setting for Live Music: Whirring ceiling fans and a beautiful mahogany bar are part of what makes the **Palm Court Cafe** such an inviting place to watch classic live jazz (page 110).

《 Coolest Hangout for Modern Jazz: On the quiet fringes of the Quarter, **Donna's** is a down-home jazz club that locals adore

for its smokin' tunes and smokin' barbecued ribs (page 110).

《 Best Neighborhood Joint: Thankfully reopened following considerable Katrina flooding, **Ernie K-Doe's Mother-in-Law Lounge** is a one-of-a-kind neighborhood favorite playing first-rate R&B music (page 111).

《 Best Gay Bar: The **Bourbon Pub/ Parade Disco** is the top game in town for the gay and lesbian crowd, with cocktails and mingling on the ground floor and dancing upstairs (page 112).

《 Most Refined Hotel Bar: You might want to dress a little for cocktails in the horsey, upscale **Polo Club Lounge,** a longtime fixture at the glamorous Windsor Court Hotel (page 113).

《 Best Hipster Hangout: In the supercool W New Orleans hotel, **Whiskey Blue** draws a well-dressed, trendy bunch for cocktails and conversation (page 113).

《 Most Historic Bar: **Lafitte's Blacksmith Shop** isn't merely old – it's inside the oldest building in the country that's still used as a bar (page 115).

LOOK FOR 《 TO FIND THE ENTERTAINMENT AND ACTIVITIES YOU CAN'T MISS.

Nightlife

The simplest way to partake of the city's nightlife is just to walk along Bourbon Street any evening. Inevitably, you'll hear the music simultaneously of two or more bars along this raucous stretch—it's a bit like being stuck between two radio stations. Bourbon is loud, occasionally obnoxious, and sometimes frightfully crowded. The street is closed to automobile traffic at night, except at the cross streets, where you do have to watch yourself. Most of the establishments along here stay open 24 hours, and you can carry your booze from bar

to bar, as long as you're nursing a plastic "go-cup" and not a bottle or other glass container. This scenario contributes to what is very often a drunken scene, where the soles of your shoes stick to the booze (and whatever else) stuck to the pavement. Bourbon Street is not for everybody, but you should at least check it out once during your visit, ideally on a busy evening. It's a caricature of New Orleans, but at the same time, it captures the almost ferocious enthusiasm with which people in this city indulge in music, drinking, dancing, and socializing.

Bourbon Street is virtually ignored by locals and die-hard music fans, however, as this rollicking, touristy stretch of clubs doesn't necessarily book the best acts in town, and it also brims with goofy strip joints, karaoke bars, and other giddy hangouts. You can find some genuinely excellent music spots in other parts of the French Quarter, and North Rampart Street, on the slightly dicey edge of the district, has some of the best improvisational jazz clubs in the country. You can always count on a good show at the city's longtime favorite music clubs, such as Tipitina's or the Palm Court. And the chain restaurant-club House of Blues, though every bit as touristy as Bourbon Street, can be counted on to present high-caliber bands.

You'll also find some great music acts at bars and taverns in the hipster-infested Warehouse District and at some of the hotel bars in the adjacent CBD. St. Charles Avenue and Magazine Street both have a handful of decent live-music venues Uptown, and in Faubourg Marigny, the trendy historic district just downriver from the Quarter, Frenchmen Street pulses with vibrant jazz, reggae, and rock venues. But just as you can find terrific food outside the tourist-oriented parts of the city, you can also find excellent music clubs in Mid-City, up near the lake, and in neighboring communities such as Metairie and Kenner.

You don't survive for long in New Orleans as a musician unless you've really got what it takes to keep people tapping their toes and leaning in on the edge of their seats, meaning that any veteran band in this town—whether or not you as a visitor have heard of it—could hold its own anywhere in America.

Even in bars that don't have live music, you'll almost always find a kickin' jukebox, a DJ spinning danceable beats, or piped-in tunes with that unmistakable New Orleans–inspired sound. People in this city need music the way they need water and air. So you're going to hear great music everywhere; you don't have to settle in on a bar with a live band to enjoy yourself.

New Orleans has some of the great hotel lounges in the country. These include swanky spaces in grande dame properties—the sorts of bars with walk-in cigar humidors and waiters in tails. But more recently, a crop of edgy boutique hotels has grown up in New Orleans, and many of these places have fashionable cocktail bars where it can be fun to convene with a group of friends.

The city's more youthful types tend to favor divey, hole-in-the-wall lounges Uptown and in Faubourg Marigny and also along bohemian Decatur Street in the Lower Quarter. You might detect a hint of self-consciousness or even attitude in some of these spots, especially if you're neither pierced nor tattooed (or if you're wearing tennis shoes and a rugby shirt). But at its core, New Orleans behaves like a genial small town, and even these sorts of places tend to welcome outsiders.

With the strip clubs in the Quarter, the gay bars mostly in the Upper Quarter, and the thousands of tourists and conventioneers who descend upon New Orleans each week, the city has an obviously sexual vibe—it's not difficult to pick people up in New Orleans, whether you're gay, straight, or bi, whatever your age or style. It's a city where many bars stay open 24 hours and serve very stiff drinks. And there's a pretty hard-core drug scene at even some of the most tourist-friendly clubs around town.

People like to cut loose in this city, and to lose themselves in the revelry, and that can be, of course, great fun. But with so little structure and so few rules, a weekend in New Orleans can be a bit too liberating for some people. On the plus side, many bars and clubs are within walking distance of hotels and inns, and cabs are easy to find outside most major venues, so you don't have to drive anywhere to have a good time. Try, though, to set some limits for yourself before a big night on the town. And should the opportunity arise to pick somebody up at a bar, exercise common sense—tell somebody with you where you're going, introduce your new friend to somebody else you know, even somebody else you've just met. Never give a stranger the impression that you're alone, unaccounted for, or in any way vulnerable.

By the same token, avoid walking back to

ENTERTAINMENT

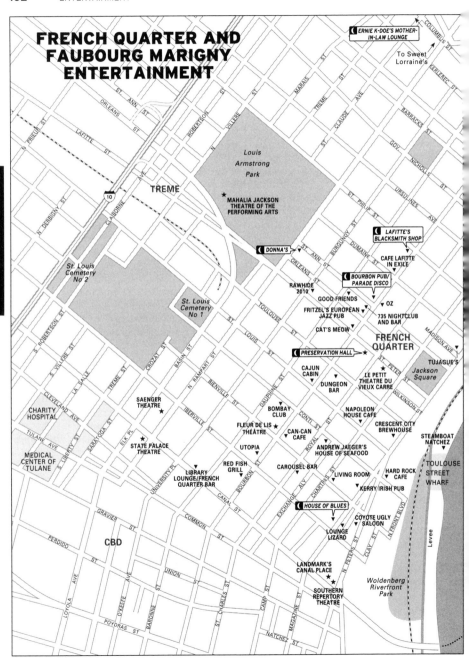

FRENCH QUARTER AND FAUBOURG MARIGNY ENTERTAINMENT

ERNIE K-DOE'S MOTHER-IN-LAW LOUNGE

To Sweet Lorraine's

COLUMBUS ST

KERLEREC ST

MARAIS ST

TREME AVE

CLAUDE AVE

BARRACKS ST

GOV NICHOLLS ST

ORLEANS ST

ST ANN ST

LAFITTE ST

N PRIEUR ST

ROBERTSON AVE

VILLERE ST

Louis Armstrong Park

URSULINES AVE

TREME

10

★ MAHALIA JACKSON THEATRE OF THE PERFORMING ARTS

ST PHILIP ST

BURGUNDY ST

DUMAINE ST

LAFITTE'S BLACKSMITH SHOP

CAFE LAFITTE IN EXILE

St. Louis Cemetery No 2

DONNA'S

ST ANN ST

ORLEANS ST

BOURBON PUB/ PARADE DISCO

N DERBIGNY ST

CLAIBORNE AVE

RAWHIDE 2010 ▼

GOOD FRIENDS ▼

OZ ▼

FRITZEL'S EUROPEAN JAZZ PUB ▼

735 NIGHTCLUB AND BAR

St. Louis Cemetery No 1

TOULOUSE ST

CAT'S MEOW ▼

LOUIS ST

MADISON AVE

PRESERVATION HALL ★

FRENCH QUARTER

TUJAGUE'S ▼

S ROBERTSON ST

S VILLERE ST

TREME ST

BASIN ST

N RAMPART ST

DAUPHINE ST

BOURBON ST

CAJUN CABIN ▼

ST PETER ST

Jackson Square

LA SALLE

CROZAT ST

BIENVILLE ST

DUNGEON BAR ▼

LE PETIT THEATRE DU VIEUX CARRE ★

WILKINSON ST

CLEVELAND AVE

SAENGER THEATRE ★

IBERVILLE ST

CONTI ST

BOMBAY CLUB ▼

NAPOLEON HOUSE CAFE ▼

CHARITY HOSPITAL

SARATOGA ST

ELK PL

FLEUR DE LIS THEATRE ★

CAN-CAN CAFE ▼

ROYAL ST

CRESCENT CITY BREWHOUSE ▼

STEAMBOAT NATCHEZ ▼

TULANE AVE

S LIBERTY ST

STATE PALACE THEATRE ★

UTOPIA ▼

ANDREW JAEGER'S HOUSE OF SEAFOOD ▼

TOULOUSE STREET WHARF

MEDICAL CENTER OF TULANE

UNIVERSITY PL

RED FISH GRILL ▼

CAROUSEL BAR ▼

CHARTRES ST

LIVING ROOM ▼

HARD ROCK CAFE ▼

LIBRARY LOUNGE/FRENCH QUARTER BAR ▼

CANAL ST

EXCHANGE ALY

KERRY IRISH PUB ▼

GRAVIER ST

COMMON ST

HOUSE OF BLUES ▼

COYOTE UGLY SALOON ▼

N PETERS ST

CLAY ST

N FRONT BLVD

Levee

LOUNGE LIZARD ▼

PERDIDO ST

CBD

UNION ST

Woldenberg Riverfront Park

LANDMARK'S CANAL PLACE ★

LOYOLA AVE

O'KEEFE AVE

ST CHARLES AVE

CAMP ST

MAGAZINE ST

SOUTHERN REPERTORY THEATRE ★

POYDRAS ST

BARONNE ST

NATCHEZ ST

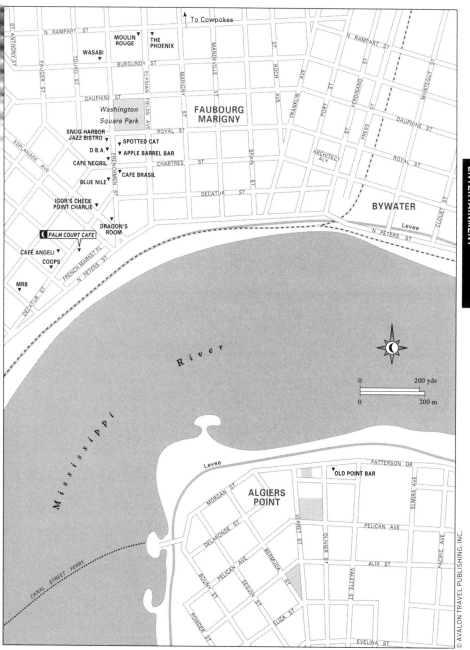

ENTERTAINMENT

To Cowpokes

N RAMPART ST

ST ANTHONY ST

TOURO ST

PAUGER ST

MOULIN ROUGE

WASABI

THE PHOENIX

BURGUNDY ST

DAUPHINE ST

ELYSIAN FIELDS AVE

MARIGNY ST

MANDEVILLE ST

ROCH ST

N RAMPART ST

MONTEGUT ST

DAUPHINE ST

Washington Square Park

FAUBOURG MARIGNY

FRANKLIN AVE

PORT ST

FERDINAND ST

PRESS ST

ESPLANADE AVE

SNUG HARBOR JAZZ BISTRO

D.B.A.

CAFE NEGRIL

BLUE NILE

FRENCHMEN ST

ROYAL ST

SPOTTED CAT

APPLE BARREL BAR

CAFE BRASIL

CHARTRES ST

SPAIN ST

ARCHITECT ALY

ROYAL ST

IGOR'S CHECK POINT CHARLIE

DECATUR ST

BYWATER

CLOUET ST

DRAGON'S ROOM

Levee

N PETERS ST

PALM COURT CAFE

CAFÉ ANGELI

COOPS

FRENCH MARKET PL

N PETERS ST

MRB

DECATUR ST

River

Mississippi

0   200 yds
0   200 m

Levee

OLD POINT BAR

PATTERSON DR

MORGAN ST

ALGIERS POINT

VERRET ST

ELMIRA AVE

DELARONDE ST

PELICAN AVE

OLIVIER ST

PELICAN AVE

BERMUDA ST

SEGUIN ST

ALIX ST

VALETTE ST

PACIFIC AVE

BOUNY ST

ELIZA ST

CANAL STREET FERRY

POWDER ST

EVELINA ST

© AVALON TRAVEL PUBLISHING, INC.

your hotel or inn alone from bars and clubs, even if you've only had a drink or two. It's prudent to take a cab even short distances if it's late and you're on your own. This isn't the menacing, crime-ridden city that some have made it out to be, but bad things do happen to visitors, sometimes in broad daylight, even in the heart of the French Quarter. And they're most likely to happen to visitors who have had a bit to drink and abandoned their common sense.

For the scoop on live music at local bars and clubs, check out the tourism publications found in just about every hotel, and also scan the listings of New Orleans's outstanding alternative newsweekly, *Gambit Weekly* (504/486-5900, www.bestofneworleans.com). The publication *OffBeat* (504/944-4300 or 877/944-4300, http://offbeat.com) is the best source in the state for learning about Louisiana's music scene, recordings by local artists, and where to catch live performances. The magazine's website is a font of great information. The *Times-Picayune* (800/925-0000, www.nola.com) comes out with a full calendar of nightly goings-on, plus festivals, art exhibits, and other timely events. It's in the *Lagniappe* section, which comes out Fridays. An excellent monthly glossy with great features and extensive listings on restaurants, sightseeing, and shopping is *New Orleans Magazine* (504/832-3555, www.neworleans.com).

Bars, clubs, and other nightlife venues are listed in their most appropriate categories (*Dance Club, Neighborhood Hangouts, Live Music,* etc.), but keep in mind that many of these places fit in multiple categories.

LIVE MUSIC
Rock and Blues
For catching rock (both hard-edged and down-home), jazz, zydeco, and blues, there may be no club in the city more acclaimed and also more festive than **Tipitina's** (501 Napoleon Ave., 504/895-8477), in Uptown. Purists may tell you that Tip's has lost its edge and no longer presents the best—or at least

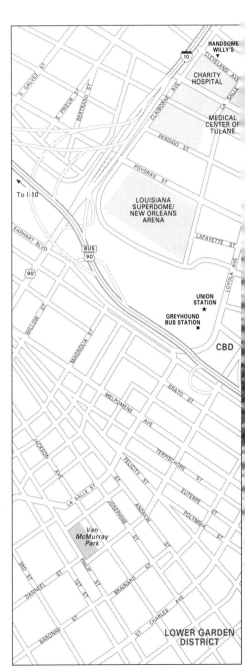

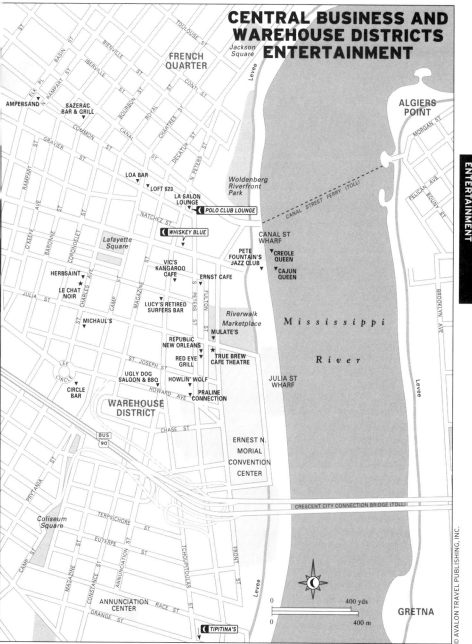

CENTRAL BUSINESS AND WAREHOUSE DISTRICTS ENTERTAINMENT

FRENCH QUARTER

Jackson Square

ALGIERS POINT

AMPERSAND

SAZERAC BAR & GRILL

LOA BAR

LOFT 523

LA SALON LOUNGE

POLO CLUB LOUNGE

Woldenberg Riverfront Park

CANAL STREET FERRY (TOLL)

WHISKEY BLUE

Lafayette Square

CANAL ST WHARF

VIC'S KANGAROO CAFE

PETE FOUNTAIN'S JAZZ CLUB

CREOLE QUEEN

CAJUN QUEEN

HERBSAINT

ERNST CAFE

LE CHAT NOIR

LUCY'S RETIRED SURFERS BAR

Riverwalk Marketplace

Mississippi

MICHAUL'S

REPUBLIC NEW ORLEANS

MULATE'S

River

RED EYE GRILL

TRUE BREW CAFE THEATRE

UGLY DOG SALOON & BBQ

HOWLIN' WOLF

JULIA ST WHARF

CIRCLE BAR

PRALINE CONNECTION

WAREHOUSE DISTRICT

BUS 90

ERNEST N. MORIAL CONVENTION CENTER

CRESCENT CITY CONNECTION BRIDGE (TOLL)

Coliseum Square

ANNUNCIATION CENTER

TIPITINA'S

0   400 yds

0   400 m

GRETNA

ENTERTAINMENT

© AVALON TRAVEL PUBLISHING, INC.

ENTERTAINMENT

© NEW ORLEANS CVB/JACK EDWARDS

Jazz was invented in New Orleans.

most distinctive—local acts, but anybody looking for an introduction to the city's eclectic music scene should head here. Entertainment varies greatly, but whoever's performing, you can probably dance to it.

Catch mostly top blues and funk acts at the **Howlin' Wolf** (907 S. Peters St., 504/529-5844), a cavernous nightclub in the Warehouse District, not far from the convention center. This is one of the city's biggest and most prominent music venues, and it also books rock, alternative, pop, R&B, and most every other style of band.

In the cavernous, historic Warehouse District space formerly occupied by Howlin' Wolf, **Republic New Orleans** (828 S. Peters St., 504/528-8282) is a music club and special-events facility that's often the site of concerts, parties, and other events.

Touristy though it is, the New Orleans outpost of the **Hard Rock Cafe** (418 N. Peters St., 504/529-5617) can be counted on for some pretty good rock acts. Again, it's a major tourist haunt, often packed with convention-

eers (it's just a block off Canal Street), but the **☾ House of Blues** (225 Decatur St., 504/529-2624) does many things well, and it's a great place to watch some of New Orleans's best blues, rock, zydeco, and other pop bands. The restaurant serves good food, the decor is colorful and fun, and the Sunday gospel brunch is especially enjoyable.

You can catch different types of music at the **Cat's Meow** (701 Bourbon St., 504/523-2788), from oldies to modern rock. Some nights there's karaoke. It can be a little cheesy, but the place has a loyal following.

A Faubourg mainstay, the **Blue Nile** (534 Frenchmen St., 504/948-2583) presents a broad mix of cool music, from jazz to world beat to Latin dance music to garage rock. With its plush lounge seating and tile floors, it's an elegant place to socialize and drink with friends early in the evening, and the music usually kicks off around 10 P.M.

In Uptown, the **Maple Leaf Bar** (8316 Oak St., 504/866-9359) serves up some of the best blues in town.

THE BIRTH OF JAZZ AND BLUES

Jazz wasn't invented in one definitive instant – it evolved over perhaps 20 or 30 years during the early part of the 20th century and in several parts of New Orleans's African American community. The state has produced several jazz luminaries, among them Jelly Roll Morton, Doc Souchon, Sidney Bechet, King Oliver, and crooner Harry Connick Jr.

Jazz music typically uses both individual and collective improvisation, syncopation, and distinctive vocal effects, and it has its origins in European, African, and Caribbean traditional music. Commonly you'll hear blues vocalizing sung to jazz instrumental accompaniment. Many people trace jazz to a popular cornet player named Buddy Bolden, who performed regularly in New Orleans from the mid-1890s until about 1910. Through the 1910s and '20s, ragtime-style jazz and other music forms with a spontaneous, upbeat tempo began to attract a following, albeit an underground one, in New Orleans.

This thoroughly modern and iconoclastic style of music was not, initially, well received by the mainstream, and in fact, hard as it is to believe now, it was shunned by organizers of Mardi Gras parades for years. During the early years, many people considered this music style to be scandalous and impudent – they criticized it at least as harshly as early critics of rock and roll denounced that music. Jazz was seen as a crude bastardization of more acceptable music styles. In 1901 the American Federation of Music spoke of efforts to "suppress and discourage the playing and publishing of such musical trash as ragtime"; the *Musical Courier* in 1899 referred to a "wave of vulgar filthy, and suggestive music which has inundated the land."

But through time, jazz would win the hearts of even the harshest naysayers, and today there's really no style of music for which the city is better regarded.

Blues music has its origins upriver a bit from New Orleans, about 300 miles north in the fruitful delta farming regions of northwestern Mississippi, especially the towns near Clarkdale. It's said that blues derives from the field hollers of cane and cotton workers in these parts. Eventually, the soulful vocals were joined with guitars, drums, and horns to become the modern form of blues celebrated today all through the South and especially in Louisiana. Huddie "Leadbelly" Ledbetter, who wrote such classics as "Goodnight Irene" and "Midnight Special," grew up in Shreveport, in the northwest corner of the state, and is often credited as the father of blues music.

Blues, along with New Orleans jazz, melded together in the 1950s to influence a new genre: rhythm and blues, or R&B. It is a distinctly commercial genre that was begun with the express intent of getting airplay on the radio and acclaim for its stars through record sales, and to that end it has always incorporated the catchiest and most accessible elements of the genres from which it borrows.

All around the state, and especially in Baton Rouge and New Orleans, clubs present live blues performers, and this often sorrowful, sometimes joyous, style of music also influences much of the jazz, rock, country-western, and gospel tunes heard elsewhere in the state.

Cajun and Zydeco

Right on Bourbon you can hear some great Cajun music at **Cajun Cabin** (503 Bourbon St., 504/529-4256), which has bands all week long. Another good stop for foot-stomping Cajun music is **Michaul's** (840 St. Charles Ave., 504/522-5517), which is also a restaurant serving decent Cajun fare.

Eclectic

Dos Jefes Uptown Cigar Bar (5535 Tchoupitoulas St., 504/891-8500) draws locals and students for live jazz and folk music. A few blocks down Tchoupitoulas, the smoky but loveable **Shiloh** (4529 Tchoupitoulas St., 504/895-1456) serves up a different style of music just about every night of the week, from hip-hop

THE MUSIC OF SOUTHERN LOUISIANA

Jazz was born in New Orleans, and the area between Lafayette and Lake Charles is famous for its Cajun and zydeco music, but just about every other style of music known to America has enjoyed a heyday in Louisiana, including blues, rock, gospel, and even opera, which took root here long before it did anywhere else in the country. In fact, the nation's first opera was performed in New Orleans in 1796.

Here's a rundown of some of the music genres you may not connect immediately to Louisiana but that have very deep roots here.

ROCK AND ROLL, POP, AND SOUL

Rock music was a natural outgrowth of blues, gospel, and country-western traditions, and some say it was born in New Orleans, where in the late 1940s a singer named Roy Brown sang a tune called "Good Rockin' Tonight," the first song that used "rock" as a term for this faster-paced, danceable variation on the blues. A book by music historian Robert Palmer called *Memphis Rock and New Orleans Roll* traces the development of rock music to these two cities along the Mississippi.

New Orleans's jazz traditions contributed the sassy roll to rock music, while Memphis contributed the harder-edged blues born in the Mississippi delta towns south of the city. The area between the two cities was rich with Pentecostal gospel sounds, which also influenced the development, ironically, of that devil music, rock 'n' roll. New Orleans's brand of rock music is especially influenced by piano playing, keyboards, and even accordion, which suggests a link between rock and zydeco.

Maybe the most famous Louisiana rock legend is Fats Domino ("Walking to New Orleans"), who emerged from the New Orleans club scene. Local session musicians have long attracted the attention of big-city record producers, who sent stars such as Little Richard to the Big Easy to make albums. Other rock, pop, and soul greats from the New Orleans area include Allen Toussaint, Percy Mayfield, the Dixie Cups, Ernie K-Doe, Irma Thomas, the Neville Brothers, Professor Longhair, Frankie Ford, Lee Dorsey, and Dr. John, many of whom recorded at the Cosimo Matassa music studio. More recently, New Orleans's music scene spawned the alternative pop-rock band Better Than Ezra, as well as the gangsta sounds of Master P and his empire of rappers, including his young son, Lil' Romeo (born in 1989).

Rock has been shaken up a bit with Louisiana influences, such as country and bluegrass, to form rockabilly music, made famous by the likes of Jimmy Clanton, Joe Clay, Floyd Kramer, Jerry Lee Lewis, Jim Reeves, Farron Young, Slim Whitman, and Hank Williams Sr. The term bandied about today for Cajun- and zydeco-tinged rock music is "swamp pop," and you'll hear it in the more current clubs all throughout Cajun Country.

COUNTRY AND BLUEGRASS

Country music, and its close cousin bluegrass (or perhaps child is a better term, since this style was born out of old-time country music traditions), share certain similarities with Cajun and even zydeco, but their routes are distinctly Anglo American (specifically Scots-Irish) rather than French, German, or African American. Many of the first Anglo settlers in Louisiana, who began arriving in the early 1800s, hailed from Kentucky and neighboring states and brought with them traditions of fiddling and ballad-singing.

Early barn dances and jamborees gave country music a widespread following, and the *Louisiana Hayride*, broadcast out of Shreveport's Municipal Auditorium on KWKH, popularized the genre in the 1940s and '50s, introducing Americans to Hank Williams, Johnny Horton, Johnny Cash, and Elvis Presley. The rocking honky-tonk style of country music, though not unique to Louisiana, thrives throughout the state. Western swing, which bands such as the Hackberry Ramblers perform today, mixes country music with Cajun, blues, jazz, and other genres in a distinctly Louisiana way.

The northern end of the state has especially strong country and bluegrass traditions, but you can find live performances at venues in New Orleans, as well as in the Florida Parishes, nine parishes that extend from Baton Rouge east along I-10 and then I-12 north of Lake Pontchartrain to the Mississippi border. Jerry Lee Lewis was born in Ferriday, and in Abita Springs, the *Piney Woods Opry* is a live radio-broadcast celebration of bluegrass. Former governor Jimmie Davis was one of the state's earliest country recording stars. Current country stars with Louisiana roots include Sammy Kershaw, Tim McGraw, Lonnie Wilson, Michael Rhodes, and the Whitstein Brothers.

GOSPEL

Gospel has deep roots in Louisiana, although it tends to be more often performed in the northern half of the state. Black gospel music, which has been celebrated in the state for many years, has its origins with the African slaves who first sung biblical songs and hymns known as "spirituals." Generally, these songs, which are performed in churches today, are performed a cappella, but other gospel music is accompanied by instruments and often has jazz, bluegrass, soul, and blues overtones. You can find performances not only at churches but at festivals and conventions. Some of the bigger music clubs in New Orleans, notably the House of Blues, feature gospel choirs from time to time.

CLASSICAL AND OPERA

Classical music and opera have been little influenced by Louisiana's other more homegrown music forms, but they've been appreciated in this region since the late 18th century, when the first opera ever performed in the United States made its debut in New Orleans. An early American classical composer, Louis Moreau Gottschalk, was born in New Orleans, and he incorporated African and Caribbean themes in his music. Classical concerts are held in just about every city in the state, and the Louisiana Sinfonietta, based in Baton Rouge and led by acclaimed composer Dino Constantinides, is especially well regarded. Notable Louisianans who have earned acclaim in this genre include opera singer Shirley Verret and virtuoso pianist Van Cliburn, from Shreveport.

RESOURCES

The publication *OffBeat* (http://offbeat.com) is the best source in the state for learning about Louisiana's music scene, recordings by local artists, and where to catch live performances.

Putumayo World Music (www.putumayo. com) has produced two excellent albums of Louisiana music, *Zydeco*, which focuses on that genre, and the broader *Louisiana Gumbo*, which includes great soul, R&B, and blues from throughout the state.

One great way to enjoy Louisiana music while visiting is on the radio. Favorites include KRVS-FM (88.7 in Lafayette, and 90.5 in Lake Charles), which specializes in zydeco and Cajun; WKJN-FM (103.3 in Baton Rouge), another Cajun favorite; and in New Orleans, WRNO-FM (99.5) for jazz, zydeco, and Cajun; WWNO-FM (89.9) for jazz; and WWOZ-FM (90.7, www.wwoz.org) for jazz, gospel, and zydeco.

You can learn more about the state's music scene from the state tourism office, or from the Louisiana Music Commission (www.louisianamusic.org), and the site www.cajunzydeco. net. Finally, the **William Ransom Hogan archive at Tulane University** (6801 Freret St., Jones Hall, Room 304, 504/865-5688) has a web archive of New Orleans jazz at www. tulane.edu/~lmiller/JazzHome.html. You can stop by and visit the archive in person; it's open 9 A.M.–4:45 P.M. Monday–Friday.

ENTERTAINMENT

to reggae to electronica. It's a great lounge for hanging out, dancing, or just zoning out and soaking up the tunes. **Mid-City Lanes Rock 'n' Bowl** (4133 S. Carrollton Ave., 504/482-3133) is practically a music (and bowling) institution, an offbeat place to catch live bands of all types; it's especially known for zydeco (on Thursdays), retro, and swing. It's in a neighborhood that was hit hard by Katrina, but it's come back better than ever.

You have to admire the perseverance of the folks who run **Handsome Willy's** (218 S. Robertson St., 504/525-0377), a rockin' music club and bar that opened in 2005, was virtually destroyed by Katrina the same year, and yet managed to reopen again by the end of 2005. It helps that the club developed a loyal following for booking great bands, from house music to funk to hip-hop—whatever gets people jumping out of their shoes. The club also serves pretty tasty pub fare, from tacos to meat loaf with mashed potatoes and gravy.

Located along the Marigny's nightclub strip, **Cafe Brasil** (2100 Chartres St., 504/949-0851) is nothing really to look at—just a big room with high ceilings, colorfully painted walls (with art for sale hung on them), bare floors, and a large dance area. What you come for is the hoppin' often-Latin dance music, plus hip-hop, reggae, and other styles, depending on the night.

In Uptown, drop by **Neutral Ground Coffeehouse** (5110 Danneel St., 504/891-3381) to catch live bluegrass performances. This atmospheric coffeehouse, said to be the oldest in the city, also has open-mic night on Sundays, and poetry readings on many nights.

Jazz

Since 1961, **❰ Preservation Hall** (726 St. Peter St., 504/522-2841) has been one of the city's top places to hear true New Orleans jazz. The Preservation Hall Band formed originally with members of the city's long-standing jazz elite, pioneers in the field who by the 1960s were already 70 or 80 years old. Top musicians continue to join Preservation Hall's

ranks, performing in the low-key and surprisingly intimate concert hall much of the year and touring cities all over the world for more than 100 days of the year. It's a must-attend for any jazz lover.

Fritzel's European Jazz Pub (733 Bourbon St., 504/561-0432) books some of the better jazz musicians along raucous Bourbon Street. This is a place to catch very traditional jazz. There's no cover, and just a one-drink minimum.

One of the most famous and delightful venues in the city for catching live jazz is the ❰ **Palm Court Cafe** (1204 Decatur St., 504/525-0200), in a handsome 19th-century building near the French Market with ceiling fans, an elegant mahogany bar, exposed-brick walls lined with photos of jazz greats, and a kitchen producing Creole fare that is quite tasty. Because seating is arranged at tables over dinner, reservations are a must. Each night a different one of the city's top jazz bands performs.

Another wonderful place for truly exceptional music is **Pete Fountain's Jazz Club** (New Orleans Hilton, 3rd floor, 237 N. Peters St., 504/525-6255), a show that can often book up early, so here, too, you should definitely call ahead to make a reservation (Fountain doesn't play every night, so call ahead to confirm when he's in town and performing). Pete Fountain is one of the legends of Dixieland jazz, having played with Al Hirt, the Dukes of Dixieland, and other top musicians of the genre. He first gained a national audience performing live on the *Lawrence Welk Show* in the late 1950s, and since then, he's been a guest on countless variety shows.

Up on dodgy Rampart Street, mixed in with a handful of mostly divey gay bars, you'll find one of the French Quarter's hottest jazz venues, ❰ **Donna's** (800 N. Rampart St., 504/596-6914). It pulls in outstanding brass-band music and also serves delicious barbecued ribs. It's arguably the best place in town for modern jazz.

The aptly named **Snug Harbor Jazz Bistro** (626 Frenchmen St., 504/949-0696)

© ANDREW COLLINS

Snug Harbor Jazz Bistro, Faubourg Marigny

a favorite place to catch late-night jam sessions; you'll find jazz and blues here most evenings.

Soul and R&B

Andrew Jaeger's House of Seafood (300 Decatur St., 504/581-2534) books some very good R&B acts. The famed **Praline Connection** (907 S. Peters St., 504/523-3973) presents a Sunday gospel brunch at its Warehouse District locale.

◖ **Ernie K-Doe's Mother-in-Law Lounge** (1500 N. Claiborne Ave., 504/947-1078) was the haunt of one of New Orleans's most flamboyant musicians, Ernie "K-Doe" Kador, who died in 2001. K-Doe was noted for such R&B smash hits as "Mother-in-Law" and "T'Ain't It the Truth," and his club in the Tremé neighborhood, a short cab ride from the Quarter (it's not generally safe to walk there), preserves his legacy by continuing to present first-rate R&B music by some of the city's legends. The lounge took a hard hit in the way of flooding after Katrina, but it reopened in summer 2006. The jukebox has an impressive selection of classic tunes, also.

is a cozy and classy spot in Faubourg Marigny where you can catch some of the city's top jazz acts and enjoy some pretty tasty food. Practically across the street is a far-less-famous jazz club that qualifies as one of the coolest little music finds in the city, the **Spotted Cat** (623 Frenchmen St., 504/943-3887), a happily cramped and sweaty dance hall with a long happy hour, a nice selection of those designer martinis, and great live bands. There's jazz much of the time, usually with a danceable beat, plus rock, blues, bluegrass, salsa—you name it.

Uptown, the **Columns Hotel** (3811 St. Charles Ave., 504/522-0581), a splendid plantation-style mansion with ornate decor, presents exceptional New Orleans jazz in its lovely Victorian Lounge.

Other excellent options for jazz include **Sweet Lorraine's** (1931 St. Claude Ave., 504/945-9654), a locals' favorite located on a quiet, historic street on the edge of the Marigny. Open 24 hours, **Mo's Chalet** (3201 Houma Blvd., Metairie, 504/780-2961) is

DANCE CLUBS

Among the high-energy haunts in the Quarter, the **Dungeon Bar** (738 Toulouse St., 504/523-5530) is a favorite place for popular dancing into the wee hours (it's open midnight–sunrise), as is tourist-filled **Utopia** (227 Bourbon St., 504/523-3800).

Ampersand (1100 Tulane Ave., 504/587-3737) is a favorite spot for students and other young stylish things in the Central Business District. It has dancing some nights, hip-hop and reggae theme nights, plus Latin, international, R&B, and other good tunes you can dance to.

HIP LOUNGES

A beautiful space known for its designer martinis, the **Bombay Club** (830 Conti St., 504/586-0972) feels a bit like the library of an exclusive club. A dining room serves quite good French-Asian bistro fare. A trendy spot across from House of Blues, the **Lounge Lizards** (200 Decatur St., 504/598-1500) is a bit less loud and frenetic but also presents a host of talented rock and blues bands most evenings.

One of the more scene-y options around town is the **Circle Bar** (1032 St. Charles Ave., 504/588-2616), with a retro decorative scheme and a cool crowd. It overlooks Lee Circle, near Hotel Le Cirque.

GAY AND LESBIAN

New Orleans, especially the French Quarter and Faubourg Marigny, has one of the greatest concentrations of gay bars in the country. Most have a decidedly male following, and there is no true lesbian bar in town, although Bourbon Pub and Oz get a number of women and men. Most, also, are small and neighborhoody in feel, with either a very quiet or very cruisy ambience.

The two most popular gay dance clubs sit opposite one another on Bourbon at the corner of St. Ann: the 🅒 **Bourbon Pub/Parade Disco** (801 Bourbon St., 504/529-2107) and **Oz** (800 Bourbon St., 504/593-9491). The former has a slick dance floor upstairs and a typically packed video bar on the ground level, while Oz has dancing on the ground floor and more loungelike spaces upstairs. Both have long wraparound balconies on the second floor, which are favorite perches from which to gaze at the throngs of revelers on Bourbon Street.

Just down Bourbon a block, **Cafe Lafitte in Exile** (901 Bourbon St., 504/522-8397) has been serving the gay community about as long as any bar in town. It draws more of a thirty- to fiftysomething crowd, a bit more mature than at Oz and Bourbon Pub. Here, too, you can people-watch from an upper balcony. Other fun hangouts for gay folks include laid-back **Good Friends** (740 Dauphine St., 504/566-7191), which has a pool table and a low-attitude demeanor, and **MRB (Mississippi River Bottom)** (515 St. Philip St., 504/524-2558), just a block off Decatur Street, which is known for its leafy patio. At **Rawhide 2010** (740 Bur-

CASINOS IN THE BIG EASY

It's not exactly Las Vegas, and the Louisiana cities of Shreveport and Lake Charles are considerably more popular as gambling hubs, but metro New Orleans does have a pair of 24-hour gaming facilities.

The mother ship for gamblers here, **Harrah's New Orleans Casino** (512 S. Peters St., 504/533-6000, www.harrahsneworleans.com) opened in the late 1990s under a cloud of controversy. It's one of the largest gaming facilities in the South, a massive property with 2,100 slot machines and 100 gaming tables, plus a full-service hotel. It has several excellent restaurants, including the vaunted Besh Steakhouse and the trendy Bambu, as well as the Gordon Biersch brewpub and a pretty good buffet.

The metro area's second big gaming hall is **Treasure Chest Casino** (5050 Williams Blvd., Kenner, 504/443-8000 or 800/298-0711, www.treasurechestcasino.com), which is actually a floating casino docked on Lake Pontchartrain and fairly near New Orleans International Airport. It offers live entertainment here nightly, a poker room, and a buffet restaurant.

gundy St., 504/525-8106) you'll encounter a mostly male crowd and a decidedly cruisy, lusty ambience.

The Marigny also has several gay bars, including the campy **Moulin Rouge** (940 Elysian Fields Ave., 504/944-1888), the city's premier venue for drag cabaret. Across the street, **The Phoenix** (941 Elysian Fields Ave., 504/945-9264) is a dark and cruisy place popular with leather-and-Levis types. For country-western two-stepping and line dancing, head to **Cowpokes** (2240 St. Claude Ave., 504/947-0505), the only such venue in New Orleans. Although the club welcomes everybody, it has a predominantly gay and lesbian following.

If you're out in Metairie, drop by

4-Seasons (3229 N. Causeway, 504/832-0659), the main gay and lesbian dance club and bar in those parts.

HOTEL BARS

Maybe the most famous hotel lounge in the city, the **Sazerac Bar and Grill** (123 Baronne St., 504/529-4733), at the grand Fairmont Hotel, is named for the noted drink, a concoction of rye whiskey and the local Peychaud's bitters. This is also a first-rate restaurant, serving creative New Orleans fare. The Fairmont and the Sazerac were closed after damage from Katrina, but both are expected to reopen in 2007. The elegant Windsor Court Hotel presents live jazz trios in its classy **Le Salon Lounge** (300 Gravier St., 504/596-4773), which specializes in hard-to-find wines, champagnes, and specialty liquors. It's also the only smoke-free lounge in town. The hotel is home to the very clubby ◖ **Polo Club Lounge** (504/523-6000), a horsey spot with oil paintings and polo photos and memorabilia.

The ultraswank **Loft 523** (523 Gravier St., 504/200-6532) books cool jazz or tango bands in its intimate lounge with exposed-brick walls and mod, low-slung furniture. There's dancing to a DJ late into the evenings when live musicians aren't performing. At the similarly fabulous International House, **Loa Bar** (221 Camp St., 504/553-9550) feels both hip and vaguely spiritual ("Loa" refers to deities or divine spirits in voodoo tradition), with its tall Gothic church mirrors and the glow of hundreds of candles. Where some modern bars feel overdesigned and uncomfortable, Loa offers plenty of sumptuous sofa seating, and the staff is surprisingly relaxed and friendly.

The W New Orleans attracts a cool clientele to its ◖ **Whiskey Blue** (333 Poydras St., 504/525-9444) cocktail lounge with leather club chairs, banquette seating, and slick contemporary decor. Noted nightlife celeb Randy Gerber, husband of Cindy Crawford, runs this and a similar operation in New York City.

At Ritz-Carlton, the **Library Lounge** (921 Canal St., 504/524-1331) is a quite fabulous fireside lounge with a walk-in humidor and a list of fine wines, scotches, and aperitifs—it's a nice place to unwind, or perhaps play backgammon, after catching a show or concert at a nearby theater. A cart loaded with expensive chocolates circles the room, doling out sweets to go with the cocktails. The hotel's **French Quarter Bar** (504/524-1331) presents live jazz many evenings and serves a full menu of New Orleans fare. And in the regal lobby lounge, you can listen to live piano and soulful crooning in the evenings and enjoy a sumptuous afternoon tea during the daytime.

At the Royal Sonesta Hotel, the **Can-Can Cafe** (300 Bourbon St., 504/586-0300) has long been acclaimed for its outstanding Dixieland jazz shows. Recline in a plush sofa at the **Living Room** (316 Chartres St., 504/581-1200), a supremely inviting lounge with book-lined shelves and game tables at the W New Orleans—French Quarter. Soak up the literary history and Old World ambience of the dignified Hotel Monteleone by having drinks in the colorful **Carousel Bar** (214 Royal St., 504/523-3341), in which an almost kitschy 1940s 24-seat bar—festooned with bright lights and garish decorations—slowly revolves around the center of the room.

RESTAURANT BARS

Many, even most, of the restaurants described in the *Food* chapter of this book also double as popular spots for cocktails, live music, and socializing, sometimes into the wee hours. The majority of them are better known for dining than for drinking. Here's a rundown of some of the best restaurants at which to hoist a mug (or, more likely, clink martini glasses):

Tujague's (823 Decatur St., 504/525-8676) is famous for its original cypress-wood bar and elegant French mirror, which was imported from Paris the year this classic Creole bar and tavern opened, 1856. The ancient cafe at the **Napoleon House Cafe** (500 Chartres St., 504/524-9752) is a great place to soak up the Quarter's rich history—it also serves cheap and delicious food in here. Another nice place to nosh while drinking is the oyster bar at Ralph Brennan's **Red Fish Grill** (115 Bourbon St.,

504/598-1200), a good place to begin a bar crawl along Bourbon Street.

Coops (1109 Decatur St., 504/525-9053) is a comfortably worn pub in the heart of the Quarter, near the French Market, with exemplary bar food—it draws a loyal bunch of locals and repeat tourists. **Crescent City Brewhouse** (527 Decatur St., 504/522-0571) has different types of live music most nights and is usually a lot of fun. The always-hopping **Cafe Angeli** (1111 Decatur St., 504/566-0077) serves up jazz on a nightly basis. Offbeat **Igor's Check Point Charlie** (501 Esplanade Ave., 504/949-7012) is a music club, restaurant, pool place, and self-serve laundry—what more could you ask for? The crowd tends to be youthful and countercultural, and the live bands tend to be blues and jazz, along with a healthy dose of alternative rock. The dark, seductive ambience of the **Dragon's Room** (435 Esplanade Ave., 504/949-1750) seems vaguely reminiscent of an opium den; it's above Siam Cafe Thai restaurant and serves as the perfect setting for colorful cocktails and catching groovy lounge music.

On the ground floor of Adolfo's, in the Marigny, the dark and cozy **Apple Barrel Bar** (611 Frenchmen St., 504/948-3800) is happily low-keyed yet hip, nice for cocktails before heading out to the noisier music clubs along Frenchmen. Just up the street, **Wasabi** (900 Frenchmen St., 504/943-9433) is half trendy sushi bar, and half refreshingly untrendy neighborhood bar serving great Japanese beer. At the festive Jamaican restaurant **Cafe Negril** (606 Frenchmen St., 504/944-4744), drop by many evenings for live reggae music and ska bands.

Suits and powerbrokers hobnob at the tiny but popular bar in **Herbsaint** (701 St. Charles Ave., 504/524-4114), one of the CBD's hippest restaurants. The Warehouse District's **Mulate's** (201 Julia St., 504/522-1492) is a giant, down-home Cajun dance hall with live bands and plenty of dancing. The laid-back **Ugly Dog Saloon and BBQ** (401 Andrew Higgins Dr., 504/569-8459), which occupies a slightly ugly Warehouse District building, has terrific happy-hour deals, tasty barbecue, and a chatty staff.

Uptown's **Clancy's** (6100 Annunciation St., 504/895-1111) is the quintessential feel-good neighborhood restaurant, with the quintessential feel-good neighborhood bar. **Igor's Buddha Belly Burger Bar** (4437 Magazine St., 504/891-6105) is similar in feel and concept to its sibling Check Point Charlie, although its relative proximity to Tulane and Loyola give it more of a collegiate ambience.

Out in Metairie, 9-to-5ers like to relax after work at trendy **P. F. Chang's China Bistro** (Lakeside Shopping Center, 3301 Veterans Memorial Blvd., Metairie, 504/828-5288).

SINGLES HAUNTS

All the rage of late, especially among under-30 tourists, is **Coyote Ugly Saloon** (225 N. Peters St., 504/561-0003), a hormonally charged pickup joint named for the giddy movie about, aptly, a bunch of beautiful women tending bar at a hormonally charged pickup joint (in New York City). **d.b.a.** (618 Frenchmen St., 504/942-3731), a hipster-infested hangout in Faubourg Marigny, is a good place to meet locals, hear live bands, and drink from a selection of about a zillion kinds of beer (plus many types of whisky and tequila). The crowd is young and laid-back but with a touch of style. It's much like its counterpart in New York City's artsy East Village.

Lucy's Retired Surfers Bar (701 Tchoupitoulas St., 504/523-8995, 5961 Magazine St., 504/895-0240) feels like a frat-sorority party most evenings, especially weekends. It's known as one of the city's more popular meat markets, and it's also a great place to suck down margaritas. A festive Aussie-inspired bar in the Warehouse District, **Vic's Kangaroo Cafe** (636 Tchoupitoulas St., 504/524-4329) has live music throughout the week and serves fairly traditional Down Under pub fare. It's on a quiet stretch of Tchoupitoulas, in a haggard old building, but it's quite festive inside. The crowd is young and raucous.

Handy to know about if you've got time to kill before a flight, **Hurricane's Sports Bar** (1414 Veteran's Memorial Blvd., Metairie, 504/833-0050) has a long weekdays happy hour (3–8 P.M.), which makes it a favorite of locals and travelers. There's also a long menu of burgers, pizzas, and other casual fare. There's live music many evenings, and it's also a popular placing for dancing late on weekends.

NEIGHBORHOOD HANGOUTS

In a touristy part of the Quarter but on a somewhat quiet block, **Kerry Irish Pub** (331 Decatur St., 504/527-5954) is cozy if not especially Irish-looking—it has live music many nights, brick floors, Tiffany hanging lamps, and dollar bills and other currency taped to the bar ceiling. Some music is Irish but other times you'll hear traditional folk performers. The highly atmospheric ◖ **Lafitte's Blacksmith Shop** (941 Bourbon St., 504/523-0066) occupies the oldest building in North America still used as a bar. It's a great place just to while away an evening, drawing a cool mix of locals and those tourists perseverant enough to wander beyond the busiest blocks of Bourbon. Across the river from the Quarter and CBD in Algiers Point, the **Old Point Bar** (545 Patterson St., 504/364-0950) is a great spot for cocktails and conversation; there's live jazz, Cajun, and rock many nights of the week.

A nice place to mix your appreciation of a good drink with your admiration of religious iconography, **St. Joe's** (5535 Magazine St., 504/899-3744) is a quintessential Uptown neighborhood bar with a twist: The place is filled with ancient wooden crosses, recovered church pews, votive candles, and other vestiges of Christianity. The vibe is funky and slightly irreverent, and there's a cool juke and a cheery patio out back. Another of the neighborhood's cool spots for mingling and hoisting a frosty mug of beer, **Le Bon Temps Rouler** (4801 Magazine St., 504/895-8117) draws in a full range of Uptowners, from college students to hipsters to music fans—there are live rock and blues bands some nights (usually no cover charge) and always a stellar jukebox. The place also turns out decent pub grub—quesadillas, chili cheeseburgers, wings, and so on. Out by the campuses of Tulane and Loyola, **T. J. Quills** (7600 Maple St., 504/866-5205)

is a favorite for inexpensive boozing, especially into the wee hours—it's a casual tavern where students stop off for a nightcap (or seven) on their way back from clubbing downtown.

A laid-back and decent enough Mexican restaurant, **Superior Grill** (3636 St. Charles Ave., 504/899-4200) becomes one of the hottest happy hours in town on Wednesdays. What's the big draw? Perhaps it's those three-for-one margaritas that keeps everybody smiling. You'll mostly find a locals bunch at the friendly **Half Moon Bar** (1125 St. Mary St., 504/522-0599), near Coliseum Square in the Lower Garden District. It's a nice place to shoot a game of pool or have a beer after antiques shopping or exploring this funky neighborhood.

A happy little dive with something of a hipster following and a truly age- and style-varied following, the **Red Eye Grill** (852 S. Peters St., 504/593-9393) is just a zero-decor hangout that feels colorful only because it's filled each night with friendly and enthusiastic revelers. It's not quite a singles scene, but meeting people is certainly the focus for some patrons. The place also serves hefty burgers and other good pub fare.

The **Ernst Cafe** (600 S. Peters St., 504/525-8544) has been a popular bar since the Warehouse District was, well, a warehouse district—the high-ceilinged corner bar opened in 1902. It occupies a handsome late-Victorian corner building with a long, curving wrought-iron balcony, and today it's mostly a place for after-work drinks and casual food. The location, near many hotels and the convention center, is a big draw.

RIVERBOAT TOURS

New Orleans Paddlewheels (27 Poydras St. Wharf, 504/529-4567 or 800/445-4109, www.neworleanspaddlewheels.com) offers excursions on the 1,000-passenger *Creole Queen* **Paddlewheeler** and the 600-passenger *Cajun Queen* **Riverboat.** The former offers Dixieland jazz dinner cruises several nights per week. Arrive at 7 P.M. for the two-hour excursion, which leaves port at 8 P.M. The latter offers two daytime cruises, at 10:30 A.M. and 2 P.M., respectively. This authentic, period-style *Creole Queen* paddle wheeler, powered by a massive 24-foot-diameter wheel, is decorated with Victorian-style furniture and a polished parquet dance floor. The fare is $16 for daytime excursions and $58 for dinner cruises (or $30 for just the cruise without dinner).

The **Steamboat *Natchez*** (Toulouse St. Wharf, behind Jackson Brewery, 504/586-8777 or 800/233-2628, www.steamboatnatchez.com) offers daily cruises with live jazz music along the river, with optional stops at the Audubon Aquarium of the Americas and the Audubon Zoo (admission to either attraction is included in these trips). The original *Natchez* was constructed in 1823 and served the important Mississippi River trade route between the cities of Natchez, Mississippi, and New Orleans. The present *Natchez,* which is 265 feet long and 44 feet wide,

was constructed in 1975 and bears a close resemblance to the grand steamboats of the 19th century. However, today's boat is quite luxurious, and it's fully air-conditioned, for which the 1,600 passengers it accommodates are surely grateful. Fares range from $17–28 for daytime excursions (typically at lunchtime and during the afternoon), and $32–55 for evening cruises; the higher fares include lunch or dinner.

As hokey as it may seem to hop aboard one of these tourist ships, these vessels all book first-rate Dixieland jazz bands, and these jaunts along the river afford spectacular views of the city's skyline. The food offered is generally good, if unspectacular (keep in mind that menus are designed for hundreds of passengers to dine at the same sitting.) Prime rib, Southern fried chicken, and catfish *louisiane* (with Cajun spices and a white-wine marinade) are typical.

Festivals and Events

Mardi Gras is just the tip of the iceberg—year-round, New Orleans and Louisiana offer a full dance card of festivals and special events worth building a trip around. As you might guess, the majority of these events revolve around food, music, and art, but you'll find celebrations of everything from the city's rich ethnic cultures to popular holidays with a Big Easy slant. Events held in summer, when tourism slows, often appeal more to other Louisianans, and they can be great fun.

Especially for Mardi Gras and Jazz Fest, but also for some of the other popular events in town (weekends leading up to Christmas, July Fourth, the French Quarter Festival, and Southern Decadence), the city can fill up fast, so it's wise to book well ahead. And if you're not interested in these most popular events, you should avoid visiting when they're scheduled. The biggest events tend to dominate the city and draw some serious crowds.

MARDI GRAS

If you're a fan of colorful, exciting festivals, there is—of course—no better time to visit New Orleans than during Mardi Gras and the Carnival season that leads up to it for several weeks. The wild goings-on during Mardi Gras in the New Orleans French Quarter have given the overall event a reputation for debauchery, and if you're seeking that kind of an experience, the Quarter on Fat Tuesday will not let you down. But Mardi Gras elsewhere in the city, notably in Uptown along the St. Charles Avenue parade route, is much more family-oriented and tends to be dominated by locals, or at least by Louisianans. Furthermore, just about every community in the state throws memorable Mardi Gras parades, parties, and other events leading up to the big day, and these, too, cater to locals and families and have a more wholesome feel.

For more information about the celebration

THE HISTORY OF MARDI GRAS

It's appropriate that New Orleans should have the most famous Mardi Gras – or Carnival – celebration in the United States. It was on Mardi Gras (French for "Fat Tuesday") that explorer Pierre Le Moyne, Sieur d'Iberville, first encamped here along the Mississippi River. Well, to be exact, Le Moyne chose a spot about 60 miles downriver from today's New Orleans, but his visit marked its beginning.

In New Orleans, records suggest that the city's early French inhabitants began holding parties and dances coinciding with Fat Tuesday as early as the 1720s. Further documentation exists of actual Mardi Gras parades first being held in 1827, but the krewes (private clubs that sponsor parades and gala balls) were not formed until 1857, when Krewe of Comus illuminated the city with its fiery torches. Comus started the tradition of pageant-style parades, with dancers and entertainers frolicking on the street alongside the floats and marchers.

You'll see three colors when watching Mardi Gras: purple, green, and gold. These hues represent justice, faith, and power, and were introduced to New Orleans Mardi Gras in 1872 by the first parade of Rex, which also gave Mardi Gras an official theme song, "If Ever I Cease to Love," from a burlesque play of that period.

Lafayette crowned its first king in 1897 and has been throwing the state's biggest Mardi Gras parades and balls outside New Orleans ever since. Mobile, Alabama, about a three-hour drive east of New Orleans, holds arguably the best Mardi Gras celebration in the country outside Louisiana – the genial Alabama city is recognized as the first in the nation to hold a Mardi Gras celebration, back in 1703. The Mobile event is, like those Mardi Gras celebrations held outside New Orleans, decidedly family-oriented.

One of the most notable 20th-century developments for New Orleans Mardi Gras was the formation of the Zulu Krewe in 1916. Its African-American members joined together to make fun of the exclusive Rex Krewe, and its king "ruled" with a scepter made of a banana stalk and a crown fashioned out of a can of lard. The Zulu Krewe continues to be one of the most-watched parades of Mardi Gras.

The celebration has seen both low and high points throughout the past century. It was cancelled for a couple of years during World War I and again for four years during World War II, and it enjoyed somewhat limited success during the Depression. By the 1950s, however, Mardi Gras was back in full swing, and it began to enjoy international acclaim, and the celebration was also expanded to the suburbs outside of New Orleans. It was in the late 1960s that the Bacchus Krewe altered tradition by inviting a celebrity to serve as its king (Danny Kaye was the first one, in 1969) and by replacing its private ball with a dinner dance to which both members and outsiders were invited (by ticket purchase).

Since that time, Mardi Gras has grown tremendously. Many new krewes and parades have come (and quite a few have gone) since the 1970s, and many more events and parties became open to the public. In 1992 New Orleans City Council passed an antidiscrimination ordinance that made it illegal for parading krewes to maintain a private membership. A few of the long-running krewes protested by cancelling their parades, but Rex complied and for the first time opened its membership to persons of all colors. The number of visitors from all over the world who descend upon New Orleans during Mardi Gras has skyrocketed. Attendance was down in 2006, the first Mardi Gras since Hurricane Katrina, but the event was still hugely popular and highly successful, and there's no reason to think that the event won't continue to delight thousands of locals and visitors for years to come.

ENTERTAINMENT

of Mardi Gras, see *Experiencing Mardi Gras* under *Explore New Orleans* at the beginning of the book.

JAZZ FEST

Officially called the **New Orleans Jazz and Heritage Festival** (www.nojazzfest.com), this music fan's dream come true has been going strong since 1969 and has grown to be nearly as popular as Mardi Gras. As with Mardi Gras, Jazz Fest was a resounding success in 2006, despite the aftermath of Katrina, and you can bet that this is one festival that will continue to draw huge crowds in the coming years. The event is held on two weekends in late April and early May. The 12 stages buzzing with jazz musicians of every persuasion and subgenre are the main reason to come, but it's also a time to attend music workshops and arts and crafts sales and demonstrations (about 300 craftspeople exhibit), and to sample an unbelievable array of great foods served at 150 stalls. Among the top acts who have performed in recent years, standouts include Fats Domino, Jimmy Buffett, Dave Matthews, Paul Simon, Bob Dylan, Etta James, Allen Toussaint, Pete Fountain, Buckwheat Zydeco, Deacon John, and various Marsalis brothers. On Monday and Tuesday in the middle of Jazz Fest, you can attend the low-key MO Fest, a showcase for local up-and-coming musicians held at Woldenberg Park. Six acts perform each afternoon.

Jazz Fest organizers always work out deals with dozens of local hotels, so if you book ahead, as only a limited number of rooms are blocked at each property, you can secure a pretty good rate, ranging from about $99 at some of the chain properties on the West Bank and in Metairie to $159 at lower-end downtown hotels (Hampton Inn, Courtyard Marriott), to well into the $200s for the upper-end business-oriented hotels in the Quarter and CBD. Just call the participating hotel that interests you (a full list is available at the festival website), and ask for the rate code NJF. The rates come with certain restrictions, such as deposits or, in some cases, full prepayment, plus minimum-night stays that vary from property to property.

Jazz Fest

© NEW ORLEANS CVB/CARL PURCELL

WINTER

Christmastime is simply huge in New Orleans, celebrated with great fanfare, as befits a city that loves to celebrate and clings dearly to long-held traditions. Many restaurants in town present special Reveillon dinner menus and there are jazz, gospel, choral, and just about every other kind of concert held throughout the month at a variety of clubs but also right on Jackson Square in front of St. Louis Cathedral. Food lovers should check the website of *Louisiana Cookin'* magazine (www.louisianacookin.com), as that publication sponsors a series of free cooking demonstrations at Le Petit Theater (616 St. Peter St.), held at 3 P.M. almost daily throughout the month. Chefs from top restaurants around town come by and show how to prepare everything from duck and andouille chowder to bread pudding with whiskey sauce.

The plantations on the river road gussy up with Christmas decorations and throw a variety of events and concerts, there's caroling along the New Orleans riverfront many eve-

ENTERTAINMENT

nings, Chanukah is celebrated at Congregation Temple Sinai (6227 St. Charles Ave., www.templesinaino.org), and huge bonfires are lit along the river in towns throughout southern Louisiana. One favorite tradition is the **Candlelight Tour of Historic Homes and Landmarks** (504/522-5730, www.christmasneworleans. com), held in mid-December and involving such attractions as the Old Ursuline Convent, the 1850 House museum, and the Gallier House. Also, from late November through the end of December, City Park comes alive for the **Celebration in the Oaks** (504/483-9415, www.neworleanscitypark.com/cito.php), a fabulous holiday light show that draws more than a half million visitors annually. You can drive through the park, walk the two-mile route, or see it on a horse-drawn carriage ride. Sights include a life-size re-created Acadian village with live zydeco and Cajun music, and the park's Storyland playground is given holiday decorations. This trip through the largest live-oak forest in the world is not to be missed during the holidays. For a full list of events and concerts held in the city, check the website www. christmasneworleans.com.

On New Year's Eve, you can take a special Mississippi River cruise aboard the **Steamboat Natchez** (504/586-8777 or 800/233-2628, www.steamboatnatchez.com); it features dancing and great food, and it's a terrific vantage point for catching the **New Year's Eve Midnight Fireworks** held along the riverfront.

Devotees of the city's most famous literary luminary rush to the Big Easy in late March and early April to attend the **Tennessee Williams/New Orleans Literary Festival** (504/581-1144, www.tennesseewilliams.net), which celebrates the playwright who gave us such iconographic works as *A Streetcar Named Desire* and *The Glass Menagerie*. The four-day gathering is replete with writing classes helmed by experts and notables, celebrity interviews, panel discussions, stagings of Williams plays, a walking tour, poetry slams, and the always enjoyable Stanley and Stella Shouting Contest. Attendees in recent years have included George

Plimpton, Dorothy Allison, Diane McWhorter, and Jim Grimsley.

Introduced to New Orleans during the 19th century by its many Sicilian immigrants, **St. Joseph's Day** is still celebrated with great élan in the city's Italian American community. The observance of this feast on March 19 traces back to the Middle Ages, when people built altars to St. Joseph, who they believed had answered their prayers and delivered them from famine. Modern participants continue to celebrate by constructing elaborate and riotously colorful altars in their homes and churches. An altar is also displayed in the CBD at the International House hotel (see its website, www.ihhotel.com/stjosephsday.html for details). Public St. Joseph's Day festivities occur in the CBD's Piazza D'Italia, at 300 Poydras Street. Smaller celebrations take place in private homes—signs welcome in friends and strangers alike to view family altars and enjoy cakes, breads, and other foods. Be sure to take them up on their hospitality.

SPRING
Far less touristy than some of the big New Orleans events and quite fun, mid-April's **French Quarter Festival** (800/673-5725, www.frenchquarterfestival.com) presents a few hundred local musicians on more than a dozen stages around the Quarter. Some excellent bands attend, performing everything from blues to zydeco to gospel. There's a fireworks display on the Mississippi, and dozens of booths serve food and drinks. Art exhibits and children's activities round out the fun.

The nation's fifth-largest 10K road race, **Crescent City Classic** (www.ccc10k.com) is held in New Orleans each April. Typically about 18,000 athletes from about 20 nations run through the French Quarter, up Esplanade Avenue, and to City Park.

In May, fans of one of nature's most perfect little fruits (no, it's not a vegetable) head over to Chalmette's **Tomato Festival,** a great time to sample Creole tomatoes (which were first grown in Haiti and popularized here when the early French settlers fled to New Orleans in

ENTERTAINMENT

the early 1800s). Despite the fact that Chalmette received severe damage from Katrina, the festival sponsor, Our Lady of Prompt Succor Catholic school, soldiered on in 2006 to keep the festival going.

Late May is the perfect time for foodies and wine buffs to visit the Big Easy for the five-day **New Orleans Wine and Food Experience** (www.nowfe.com), a mouthwatering event at which several hundred wines from more than 250 wineries are featured, along with food from about 100 of the city's top restaurants.

SUMMER

Fourth of July celebrations are staged in several area towns (Hammond, Bogalusa, Slidell, Mandeville, Thibodaux) as well as in New Orleans itself, with **Go 4th on the River** (www.go4thontheriver.com), an all-day extravaganza held at Woldenberg Park with live bands, cruises on vintage paddle-wheel riverboats, and special events all along the riverfront, from the French Market to the Riverwalk shops. You can also ferry over to **Blaine Kern's 4th of July Party** (504/361-7821, www.mardigrasworld. com), held at the world-famous Mardi Gras float-making factory and museum, on the West Bank just across the river from the Quarter. It offers barbecue and burgers, door prizes, and a spectacular fireworks show on the levee, which you can see from all around downtown.

The **Essence Music Festival** (www.essence.com/essence/emf) presents the music of dozens of African American musicians over three days and nights in early July. You can also attend about 15 different seminars and talks that touch on political, social, and religious issues, and you can browse Afrocentric crafts, art, books, souvenirs, and food at a festival market. The festival was held in Houston in 2006, but plans have called for a return to New Orleans in 2007. A short drive southwest of New Orleans at St. Gertrude Catholic Church in Des Allemands, mid-July marks the **Louisiana Catfish Festival** (985/758-7542), a time to appreciate that favorite freshwater fish of the South. It has catfish-cooking demonstrations and competitions, and more frightening,

catfish-eating contests, plus music, rides, and carnival games.

New Orleans celebrates the legacy of one of its most famous sons in early August with **Satchmo Summerfest** (800/673-5725, www.satchmosummerfest.com), which includes live music by brass, swing, and early jazz bands. The mostly free festival also includes a jazz Mass, local foods, and discussions and exhibits on Louis "Satchmo" Armstrong and his era.

FALL

Labor Day Weekend is the **Southern Decadence Celebration** (www.southerndecadence.com, 504/522-8047), a Mardi Gras–like gay and lesbian three-day festival held at venues throughout the Quarter and Faubourg Marigny, and including dance parties, drag shows, and a leather-gear block party. It's one of the wildest and most popular gay-and-lesbian celebrations in the country. Although Decadence fell during the weekend of Hurricane Katrina in 2005, a surprising number of revelers carried on. In 2006, it was back in full swing.

Across the river in early October, the **Gretna Heritage Festival** (504/361-7748, www.gretnafest.com) features live music, events at the German Heritage Center, a German beer garden, rides and games, an arts-and-crafts show, and other fun activities. There's also a big flea market, the **Collector's Fest** (504/486-7691), held in downtown Gretna a week or so before.

Late in October, the Audubon Institute (www.audoboninstitute.org) sponsors kids-oriented Halloween-themed activities at its facilities—these include **Boo at the Zoo** (including a zoo "ghost" train and trick-or-treating) and the similarly ghoulish **Scarium at the Aquarium.** In early November, the Audubon Zoo hosts the **Louisiana Swamp Festival** (800/774-7394, www.audoboninstitute.org). Arts and crafts are sold throughout the zoo, which also offers plenty of animal feedings and up-close animal activities, live Cajun and zydeco music, and the food of Louisiana's Cajun Country: boudin noir, cracklin's, seafood po'boys, fried alligator, and so on.

The Arts

Although New Orleans can claim one of the world's most dynamic live-music scenes, it's relatively less famous as a center of the performing arts. Still, you'll find a handful of very good theaters and performance halls in New Orleans and the towns surrounding it. There are only a few large-scale venues for formal concerts and theatrical performances, and, in fact, many big-name musicians favor comparatively small-time stages when their tour stops in this city. New Orleanians are loyal, knowledgeable, and excited about music, and performers appreciate the enthusiasm and enjoy playing a club that's small enough to encourage a close connection between the musicians and the fans.

There are a handful of mostly independent, fringe-style theaters in New Orleans, plus a few places where national touring companies perform Broadway hits and top-selling rock stars throw shows. Beyond that, it takes almost no planning and very little effort to find a place to catch a jamming live show in New Orleans, even on a Monday or Tuesday night. Just check the listings of some of the papers listed here to see who's on where, or simply stroll through the French Quarter. More than a dozen clubs along Bourbon Street have music bellowing from their doors every night of the week, and these places rarely charge a cover (although they will typically have a one- or two-drink minimum).

The colorful free entertainment paper *Gambit Weekly* (504/486-5900, www.bestofneworleans.com) is an indispensable resource for finding out what's playing around town. The publication *OffBeat* (504/944-4300 or 877/944-4300, http://offbeat.com) is the best source in the state for learning about Louisiana's music scene, recordings by local artists, and where to catch live performances. *Where Y'at Magazine* (504/891-0144, www.whereyat.net) is another good place for arts and nightlife listings (although beware that the online bar and restaurant listings can be wildly out of date), as is *Lagniappe* (504/826-3464, www.

nola.com), which is produced on Fridays by the *Times-Picuyane*.

For general information, listings, and calendars pertaining to the arts throughout New Orleans and Louisiana, contact the **Louisiana Division of the Arts** (225/342-8180, www.crt.state.la.us/arts). The organization's main function is to write grants for people involved in the arts in Louisiana, but the website also has useful links to local groups involved in arts-in-education, dance, design arts, folklife, literature, music, theater, and visual arts and crafts. The site has a detailed calendar that lists arts events of all types throughout the state.

THEATER AND CONCERT VENUES

At Tulane, check out what's showing at **Dixon Hall and the Lupin Theater** (Newcomb Pl. off Freret St., 504/865-5105, www.tulane.edu); it's usually a classical-music concert, or a student theater or dance production. Tulane also sponsors and hosts the annual **Shakespeare Festival** (www.neworleansshakespeare.com), a professional Actors Equity–affiliated organization that presents two Shakespeare works and usually one other work by a prominent playwright throughout July and August.

The **Jefferson Performing Arts Center** (1118 Clearview Pkwy., Metairie, 504/885-2000, www.jpas.org) hosts major Broadway-style shows and a variety of musical performances throughout the year.

In one of the CBD's few patches of greenery, **Lafayette Square** (off St. Charles Avenue), you can catch free concerts by some of the city's top bands every Wednesday at 5 P.M. Local bars and restaurants sell food and drinks, and area art galleries display some of their works for sale.

In Armstrong Park, the **Mahalia Jackson Theatre of the Performing Arts** (parking inside the park gates, Orleans Avenue entrance) hosts the main performances sponsored by the **New Orleans Ballet**

Association (504/522-0996, www.noba-dance.com), which books some of the world's most important ballet companies. The Theatre of the Performing Arts, named for New Orleans–born gospel singer Mahalia Jackson, is a popular venue for music concerts and festival events (it was closed, however, following Katrina and is not expected to re-open until at least 2008, following a complete restoration). The **New Orleans Opera Association** (504/529-3000 or 800/881-4459, www.neworleansopera.org) sponsors 2–4 classic works of opera each season, from October through April, with performances at Tulane University's McAlister Auditorium.

Le Chat Noir (715 St. Charles Ave., 504/581-5812, www.cabaretlechatnoir.com) is an innovative bar-cabaret-theater that stages intriguing, independent-minded plays, musicals, jazz shows, and performance pieces, many of them tending toward the festive and occasionally outrageous. Main productions are staged in the swanky Cabaret Room, which is modeled after a 1940s nightclub, with candles glowing atop each table; note the dress code—no jeans or shorts are permitted. Bar Noir is a less dressy space, where you can sip cocktails and mingle with the city's theater types and arts glitterati.

Le Petit Theatre du Vieux Carré (616 St. Peter St., 504/522-5081, www.lepetittheatre.com) dates to 1916 and is the oldest community theater in the nation. It stages some popular Broadway-style shows, musical revues, and the like. The theater company began simply as some friends who acted out plays in the living rooms of the earliest members, but soon the group began renting a space in the lower Pontalba Building. Growing popularity led the group to move into its current locale, a marvelous Spanish Colonial theater built in 1922. In addition to the main stage, a smaller venue mounts productions, and there's also a concert series.

At Loyola University, something interesting is often going on at the **Nunemaker Auditorium** (Monroe Hall, 3rd floor, 504/861-5441, http://music.loyno.edu/montage), a small performance space where students of the school's College of Music often give recitals.

In Kenner, **Rivertown Repertory Theatre** (325 Minor St., 504/468-7221, www.rivertownkenner.com), part of the Rivertown Museum complex, presents dramas, comedies, and Broadway musicals from September through May.

Major traveling Broadway-style productions have been staged frequently at the **Saenger Theatre** (143 N. Rampart St., 504/524-2490, www.saengertheatre.com), which also hosts big music concerts, comedy acts, and so on. Past performers have included Norah Jones, Margaret Cho, and Tori Amos. In summer, there's a Summer Classic Movie Series, which presents vintage (pre-1970) movies on the big screen. The Saenger was closed after damage from Hurricane Katrina; it's hoped the theater will resume operation by 2007. Around the corner, the **State Palace Theatre** (1108 Canal St., 504/482-7112 or 504/522-4435, www.statepalace.com) hosts the same types of events, including its own Classic Movie Series.

Southern Repertory Theatre (Shops at Canal Place, 365 Canal St., 504/522-6545, www.southernrep.com) occupies a handsome space on the third floor of the luxury Shops at Canal Place on the edge of the Quarter—this may seem an odd theatrical location, but this mall also has a first-rate movie theater that books artsy, independent films. Southern Rep stages a half dozen plays each year, most by noted Southern playwrights (Tennessee Williams, Lillian Hellman, Lorraine Hasberry, etc.) and local New Orleans writers.

The funky **True Brew Cafe Theatre** (200 Julia St., 504/344-1874) is a coffeehouse and bar that also stages a lot of one-man/woman shows, open-mic nights, comedy, and other innovative and thoughtful works.

CINEMAS

Megamovie complexes are all through the suburban towns of Metairie, Kenner, and across the river on the West Bank, but New Orleans also has some venues right downtown. One of the most popular is **Landmark Canal Place** (Shops at Canal Place, 333 Canal St., 504/581-5400), which specializes in art-house films but also shows a fair share of blockbusters. A throwback in this day of massive multiscreen cinemas is Uptown's **Prytania Theatre** (5339 Prytania St., 504/891-2787), an old-fashioned movie house that shows Hollywood blockbusters on its massive single screen, making it great fun for action flicks and movies with lots of special effects.

ARTS AND CRAFTS GALLERIES

Louisiana has a rich, multicultural tradition in the arts and crafts, and you'll find hundreds of outstanding galleries in New Orleans, with especially strong concentrations along Royal and Chartres streets in the French Quarter, in the Warehouse District, and along Magazine Street in Uptown. Other communities with important commercial art galleries include Covington on the North Shore, Lafayette, and Lake Charles.

You'll find a full listing of notable art galleries and art museums on the website of the **Louisiana Division of the Arts,** www. crt.state.la.us, under the link for Visual Arts and Crafts.

Recreation

Excellent opportunities for hiking, biking, camping, boating, fishing, bird-watching, and golfing lie within a short drive of downtown New Orleans, and numerous swamp tours start from the North Shore of Lake Pontchartrain and in the Cajun Country west and southwest of New Orleans. The state's mild winters are ideal for outdoor activities, while summer can be oppressively hot. But there's really no time of year that you won't see people outside enjoying themselves.

AMUSEMENT PARKS

The old Jazzland theme park underwent a massive $20 million transformation, completed in 2003, en route to becoming **Six Flags New Orleans** (12301 Lake Forest Blvd., 504/253-8100, www.sixflags.com/parks/neworleans). The park sat right in the middle of Hurricane Katrina's path, however, and was devastated by the storm. Six Flags was unable to open in 2006, and the company is still assessing damages and deciding how to proceed. This had been the premier Gulf Coast venue for thrill rides and amusements, and one hopes that eventually it will resume operations.

BIKING

With narrow streets and concerns about theft, New Orleans is not an ideal city for biking, and you'll see relatively few cyclists here. However, most of Louisiana is excellent biking terrain, generally flat and in many areas quite scenic. The only real drawback is the relatively high amount of auto traffic and the many narrow roads. Throughout this book's chapters covering side-trips, you'll find listings of bike-rental shops and also advice about picturesque and scenic routes.

A few bike clubs are in the region. The **New Orleans Bicycle Club** (www.neworleansbicycleclub.org) and **Crescent City Cyclists** (www.crescentcitycyclists.org) are geared toward racing but list a number of good cycling routes and bike shops on their websites, as well as articles on cycling. Also, the **Louisiana Department of Recreation, Culture, and Tourism**'s website www.bikelouisiana.com has detailed itineraries for biking throughout the state as well as other tips, information, and resources—it's a top-notch resource.

BIRD-WATCHING

From yuppies to senior citizens, families to singles, every kind of Louisianan seems to be taking up bird-watching these days, especially those folks who live around the coast. As hobbies go, this is one of the least expensive and most educational. Best of all, birds are abundant in the state year-round, though of course the species you're likely to see depends often on the season; there are hundreds of species throughout Louisiana.

Much of the best birding is along the coast and around Lake Pontchartrain, quite close to New Orleans, and throughout the Cajun Country wetlands and bayous. Species commonly spotted in many parts of southern Louisiana include pelicans, great blue herons, great and snowy egrets, green-winged teals, mottled ducks, American widgeons, turkey vultures, red-shouldered (and other) hawks, American kestrels, least sandpipers, several types of gull, several types of tern, mourning doves, nighthawks, belted kingfishers, purple martins, blue jays, wrens, mockingbirds, robins, cardinals, sparrows, and meadowlarks.

South Louisiana's two **Audubon Society** chapters are useful contacts for learning about birding in Louisiana. The New Orleans chapter's website, www.jjaudubon.net, contains a full South Louisiana Bird Guide, with detailed descriptions of 13 key birding areas (including New Orleans City Park) in and around greater New Orleans and the Cajun Country. An extensive chart lists the birds most prevalent in the Grand Isle and New Orleans areas—hundreds of birds are included, and you can click on bird names for a full page on that species with photos, descriptions, and tips on identification.

Popular spots for birding near New Orleans include the 20,000-acre **Barataria Preserve Unit of Jean Lafitte National Historical Park and Preserve,** (6588 Barataria Blvd./Hwy. 45, near Crown Point, Marrero, 504/589-2330, www.nps.gov/jela), which contains nearly 10 miles of trails and lies just south of the city. The park's Bayou Coquille Trail is a pavement-and-boardwalk trail that is known for myriad wildlife sightings. About four miles east of I-510, along U.S. 90, 23,000-acre **Bayou Sauvage National Wildlife Refuge** (www.fws.gov/bayousauvage) offers some excellent trails through marsh and hardwood forest, as well as a birding observation deck. At Tabasco Jungle Gardens, on Avery Island, you'll see one of the largest nesting areas for egrets anywhere in the country. In

the North Shore town of Covington, an hour's drive north of New Orleans, you'll find the **Wild Bird Center** (808 N. U.S. 190, Ste. F, 985/892-0585, www.wildbirdcenter.com/cov), a one-stop bird-watching shop with all sorts of books, binoculars, and related products.

GOLF

A number of excellent courses lie near New Orleans, especially above Lake Pontchartrain on the North Shore. Many of the best public golf facilities are described in this book's side-trip chapters. If you live or play regularly in Louisiana, it makes sense to join the **Louisiana Golf Association** (1003 Hugh Wallis Rd., Ste. G, Lafayette, LA 70508, 337/265-3938, www.lgagolf.org). The association's website contains information on Louisiana clubs, upcoming local tournaments, and many additional resources.

The **Louisiana's Audubon Golf Trail** (866/AGT-IN-LA—866/248-4652, www.audubontrail.com) leads duffers to 11 of the top public facilities in the state. You can reserve tee times online at any of the Audubon courses, which include Audubon Park Golf Club (a challenging executive course in New Orleans), Carter Plantation (a David Toms–designed course that opened on the North Shore in 2003), OakWing Golf Club (an Alexandria course that opened in 2002), Olde Oaks Golf Club (in Shreveport and codesigned by PGA star Hal Sutton), Cypress Bend (in Many, near Toledo Bend Resevoir), Calvert Crossing (in Calhoun, just west of Monroe), Gray Plantation (in Lake Charles, and named one of the best new courses of 2000 by *Golf Digest*), TPC of Louisiana (a spectacular layout that opened in New Orleans in 2004), Tamahka Trails (near Marksville), The Bluffs (near St. Francisville and codesigned by Arnold Palmer), the Atchafalaya at Idlewild (a 2005 course that opened in Patterson, near Houma), and The Island (south of Baton Rouge on the west bank of the Mississippi River, near Plaquemine).

The PGA tour's **Zurich Classic** (504/831-4653, www.pgatour.com) has taken place in late April or early May each year at **English Turn Golf and Country Club** (1 Clubhouse

Dr., 10 miles southeast of the French Quarter on the West Bank, off Hwy. 406, 504/392-2200, www.englishturn.com), a semiprivate club that is open to visitors by arrangement. Jack Nicklaus designed this world-class 18-hole course.

The Zurich is moving to the new **Tournament Players Club of Louisiana at Fairfield** (866/665-2872, www.tpc.com), a $20 million course created for professional tournament play that opened in 2004 but was closed for 2006 because of Katrina damage. It's expected to reopen in 2007. Famed golfing architect Pete Dye, with assistance from PGA touring professionals Steve Elkington and Kelly Gibson, designed the fabulous layout. The course sits along a 250-acre tract by Bayou Segnette State Park, a 20-minute drive from downtown New Orleans.

Audubon Park Golf Club (504/212-5290, www.auduboninstitute.org), mentioned above as part of Louisiana's Audubon Golf Trail, has been around since 1898, but this short par-62 course had languished in recent years. The course was completely overhauled in 2003 and is now looking better than ever. The 18-hole course is mostly par-3s, but there are four par-4 and two par-5 holes. At City Park, locals head to what many consider to be New Orleans's best links, **Bayou Oaks Golf Course** (1040 Filmore Ave., 504/483-9396, www.bayou-oaksgc.com), a complex comprising four 18-hole, par-72 courses; it also offers a lighted 100-tee driving range, a full pro shop and restaurant, and lessons. Few municipalities in this country have better public golf within city limits. The facility received considerable hurricane damage and remains closed, but is slated to reopen at some point; the driving range has already reopened.

A semiprivate course that's also quite popular is **Lakewood Country Club** (4801 General DeGaulle Dr., 504/393-2610, www.lakewoodgolf.com), which has hosted numerous PGA tournaments and is kept in spectacular shape. It's a much more costly day of golf, but serious duffers love it. This is another course that was badly damaged by Katrina and is being

renovated—it's slated to reopen in fall 2007. *Golf Digest* magazine has named semiprivate **Eastover Country Club** (5690 Eastover Dr., 504/245-7347, www.eastovercc.com), with two 18-hole courses to choose from, the best place to play in the city. The course was closed due to hurricane damage, and a projected reopening date has not yet been announced. Across the river in Gretna you can play **Timberlane Country Club** (Timberlane Dr., 504/367-5010, www.timberlanecc.com), a semiprivate course that's been innovatively cut through a stunning cypress swamp. Esteemed designer Robert Trent Jones Sr. designed the layout.

HEALTH CLUBS

A day pass for **Downtown Fitness Centers** (Canal Place, 333 Canal St., 504/525-2956; Sheraton Hotel, 500 Canal St., 504/525-2500) is $12, or $55 per week. These upscale fitness centers are outfitted with all the latest equipment. Another good option for visitors is expansive **Elmwood Fitness Center Downtown** (1 Shell Sq., 701 Poydras St., 504/588-1600), which has massage, spinning and aerobics classes, and a juice bar. Day passes cost $12. Elmwood also has locations in Metairie (Heritage Plaza, 111 Veterans Blvd., Ste. 475, Metairie, 504/832-1600) and Harahan (Elmwood Shopping Center, 1200 S. Clearview Pkwy., Ste. 1200, Harahan, 504/733-1600).

SPAS

Body Contours (220 Julia St., 504/598-9191, www.bodycontoursnola.com), in the Warehouse District, offers four-hands, Swedish, and deep-tissue massage, plus hot-stone therapy, either on-site or in the privacy of your hotel room.

Shine Spa and Specialties (622 Conti St., 504/581-4999) is a full-service day spa that also sells a wide range of earth-friendly skincare products. The environmentally sensitive **Earthsavers** (5501 Magazine St., 504/899-8555; Lakeside Shopping Center, 3301 Veterans Blvd., Metairie, 504/835-0225) has earned a loyal following for its all-natural exfoliants, skin moisturizers, and other skin-care products. The shop also offers spa services and aromatherapy.

If you have the sort of budget that means you can still relax after forking over more than $100 for a 50-minute massage, then by all means head to the luxe spa at the **Ritz-Carlton** (921 Canal St., 504/524-1331), the city's most opulent facility. Warm-stone reflexology, hydrotherapy, facials, and Magnolia Sugar Scrubs (a body polish using the essence of magnolia and botanical extracts) are among the sybaritic offerings.

Hip celebs often call at **Belladonna Day Spa** (2900 Magazine St., 504/891-4393, www.belladonnadayspa.com), an airy, modern bath-and-body shop that's also a top-notch unisex spa. Set inside a Victorian house, the interior treatment rooms are soothing and minimalist, with a Japanese ambience. Bindi herbal body treatments, shiatsu, and manicures and pedicures are among the most popular services.

SPECTATOR SPORTS

With the huge tourism base and wealth of hotel rooms, New Orleans has become a favorite host for major professional sporting events, from football's Super Bowl (most recently held in the city's Superdome in 2002) to the NCAA's Men's Final Four (in 1982, 1987, 1993, and 2003). The 73,000-seat **Louisiana Superdome** (1500 Poydras St., 504/529-8830, www.superdome.com) was built in 1975 and is the largest stadium in the world with a roof. It's the home stadium of the National Football League's **New Orleans Saints** (504/731-1700, www.neworleans-saints.com)—the team resumed play at the Superdome after its post-Katrina renovation in fall 2006. In case you're wondering about the team's name, it's a reference to the popular jazz anthem "When the Saints Go Marching In"—but also, New Orleans was awarded the NFL franchise on November 1, 1966, All Saints' Day. The stadium is also home to one of the most beloved college football matches, the **Allstate Sugar Bowl** (504/525-8573, www.allstatesugarbowl.com), which is played in late December or early January each year between two of the nation's top collegiate teams. The Bowl has also hosted college football's national championship numerous times, including in 2000, when Florida State defeated Virginia Tech. It's nearly impossible to find a hotel room in New Orleans when this event comes to town, so plan well ahead if you wish to attend.

Next door, the **New Orleans Arena** (1501 Girod St., www.neworleansarena.com) opened in 1999 and has seating for 20,000. It's a popular concert venue as well as the place to watch the NBA basketball team **New Orleans Hornets** (504/525-4667 or 866/444-4667, www.nba.com/hornets), which moved from Charlotte to New Orleans in 2002. Before that, New Orleans had gone many years without an NBA team. The arena also hosts the **New Orleans Voodoo** (504/731-1700, www.govoodoo.com), an Arena Football team.

Some of the city's colleges have very good sports programs. **Tulane** and the **University of New Orleans** field Division I college football teams, and both have excellent baseball teams. UNO also excels in women's volleyball, and Tulane is a major force in women's basketball. For information on the athletic program at Tulane, visit the school's athletic program website, http://tulanegreenwave.cstv.com. For UNO sporting-event information, check out www.unoprivateers.com.

Baseball fans come to watch the Minor League **New Orleans Zephyrs** (504/734-5155, www.zephyrsbaseball.com), the Triple-A affiliate of the Major League Washington Nationals. They play at 3,000-seat Zephyr Field (6000 Airline Dr., between Transcontinental and David drives), in downtown Metairie. With a pool and whirlpool tub, weekly fireworks displays, and games with players just one level away from big-league baseball, the Zephyrs enjoy some of the highest attendance of any Triple-A team. They're members of the Pacific Coast League.

Mid-City's **Fairgrounds Race Track** (1751 Gentilly Blvd., 504/944-5515, www.fgno.com), the third-oldest thoroughbred-racing course in

FISHING CHARTERS

Here in a part of the world where humans have reclaimed much of the land they live on from the Gulf, the Mississippi River, and its related bodies of water, fishing is not only hugely important to Louisiana's economy, it's one of the most popular sporting activities around. And it's a resilient industry, too, as evidenced by how quickly it bounced back after the devastation of Hurricane Katrina. But before you go casting your line into the Mississippi, consider booking a fishing trip with one of the many expert charters around the area. These guys know where to look and what to look for, and they can provide all the licenses necessary, plus tackle and a knowledgeable guide who can maneuver the state's maze of inland waterways. It's a great chance to hunt for redfish, trout, red snapper, and tuna. Many of these operators can clean and pack your catches at the end of the trip, and many area restaurants will cook and prepare your haul for you.

Captain Phil's Saltwater Guide Service (4037 Hugo Dr., 504/348-3264) is a reliable outfitter for trips out to the Gulf; he sails out of Lafitte, on the West Bank. **Griffin Fishing Charters** (800/741-1340, www.neworleansfishintours.com), also out of the atmospheric fishing village of Lafitte, is another excellent charter company that provides both fresh- and saltwater adventures.

If you'd prefer cruising through the bayous and lakes for redfish and speckled trout, consider **Papa Joe's Cajun Wetland Service** (382 W. Meae Dr., Gretna, 504/392-4409, www.fishneworleans.com). Joe's has a great website on which he keeps a diary of who sails with him each day, along with a lively record (and pictures) of their successes.

The area around Houma and coastal Terrebonne Parish has dozens of fishing marinas and charters, especially around the towns of Dulac and Cocodrie. The **Houma Area Convention and Visitors Bureau** (985/868-2732 or 800/688-2732, www.houmatourism.com) distributes a very useful free brochure on fishing in the area, listing charters and information on the most common species caught. In Chauvin, a 15-mile drive southeast of Houma, **Co Co Marina** (106 Pier 56, Chauvin, 985/594-6626 or 800/648-2626, www.rodnreel.com/cocomarina) provides fishing charters and also offers condo and boathouse-apartment rentals, modern and comfortable spots where you can stay before or after you set out for a day of casting a line.

the nation, offers live racing from Thanksgiving through March. An offtrack-betting parlor is open year-round, so you can wager on events elsewhere in the country. Key events at the track include Louisiana Champions Day, the New Orleans Handicap, and the Louisiana Derby.

TAKING TO THE WATER

Louisiana has nearly 400 miles of coastline, but if you count the many inlets and rivers, the state's total shoreline is many thousands of miles. About 15 percent of the state's 51,000 square miles are covered by water. River sports (such as canoeing and kayaking and rafting) are popular along the waterways of Jean Lafitte National Historical Park's Barataria Preserve, the Tchefuncte and Bogue Chitto rivers in St. Tammany Parish (on the North Shore), the Atchafalaya Swamp in Cajun Country, and the Calcasieu and Whiskey Chitto rivers near Lake Charles. The Mississippi River is not all that popular with recreational boaters, as it tends to be dominated by huge commercial freighters, and the extensive levee system separates it from the smaller and more interesting inlets and tributaries that are ideal for exploring by nonmotorized craft. You'll find aquatic outfitters and tour providers throughout the state; individual canoeing, kayaking, rafting, and tubing outfitters are listed in the regional side-trip chapters in this book. For information on boating safety and regulations throughout Louisiana, contact **Louisiana Department of**

Wildlife and Fisheries (LDWF) (2000 Quail Dr., Baton Rouge, LA 70808, www.wlf.state.la.us). The website provides information on registration, boating classes and safety, and the like.

The website **http://sportsmansresource.com** lists Louisiana boat-rental agencies, boating charters, and many other relevant resources.

A handful of marinas are in metro New Orleans, including the **Municipal Yacht Harbor** (401 N. Roadway St., New Orleans, 504/288-1431), which is on Lake Pontchartrain up near Breakwater Park and which was damaged quite famously during Katrina (photos of boats strewn all over the place appeared in many newspapers and televised accounts of the storm). The marina itself burned, and the marina situation along the lake is still unresolved. It will take a while to clean up this area.

Out in Venice, a two-hour drive down Hwy. 23 along the Mississippi River, there's **Cypress Cove Marina** (226 Cypress Cove Rd., 504/534-9289 or 800/643-4190, www.rodnreel.com/cypresscove), which also has a motel and restaurant, all of it rebuilt since Katrina. This may seem like a long way to go, but it's definitely a faster way to get by boat from New Orleans to the Gulf of Mexico than if you leave from New Orleans directly, either by way of the river or Lake Pontchartrain. From Cypress Cove it's just another 15 miles or so to the Gulf.

GENERAL RESOURCES

There are several excellent resources for learning more about the region's wealth of outdoor diversions. A good way to begin is by contacting the **Louisiana Department of Wildlife and Fisheries (LDWF)** (2000 Quail Dr., Baton Rouge, LA 70808, www.wlf.state.la.us). You can write to request brochures on the state parks and outdoor activities, or visit the useful website, which lists the phone numbers of the appropriate person or office for information on public boat ramps, songbirds, hunting licenses, and the like. Another state department with an informative website, the **Louisiana**

Department of Natural Resources (LaSalle Office Bldg., 617 N. 3rd St., Baton Rouge, LA 70802, 225/342-4500, www.dnr.state.la.us) can provide information on conservation, coastal restoration, and mineral resources throughout the state.

For the lowdown on each of Louisiana's 19 state parks, 16 state historic sites, and one state preservation area, contact the **Louisiana Office of State Parks** (P.O. Box 44426, Baton Rouge, LA 70804, 225/342-8111 or 888/677-1400, www.crt.state.la.us/crt/parks). The website has a helpful interactive map for state parks—click on the park in question, and you'll learn the property's acreage, history, facilities, parking and usage fees, hours, and distinctive features.

Day-use fees are $1 per person at state parks and $2 per adult at state historic sites. The $30 annual pass entitles the bearer to free day admission to all of the parks and historic sites. The parks website also gives fees for day-use facilities (such as group pavilions and meeting areas), and for camping, group camping, overnight cabins and lodges, swimming pools, and rental boats. Fees are the same for residents and nonresidents.

A wonderful way to learn about Louisiana's outdoors and become involved with keeping them clean is to join the state chapter of the **Nature Conservancy** (P.O. Box 4125, Baton Rouge, LA 70821, 225/338-1040, http://nature.org). This highly respected and influential organization was founded in 1951, and the Louisiana chapter has been instrumental in preserving 19 of the state's most precious natural settings. Some of the preserves are not open to the public, but six properties are, and you can generally visit them anytime during daylight hours. The properties open to visitors are Lafitte Woods Preserve (in Grand Isle), White Kitchen Preserve (in the Pearl River basin by Slidell, best visited via one of the area's swamp tours), Cypress Island (near Breaux Bridge on Lake Martin), Mary Ann Brown Preserve (30 miles north of Baton Rouge in the Tunica Hills), Abita Creek Flatwoods Preserve (in Abita Springs), and Lake Ramsay Preserve (near Covington). Preserves are open from an hour before dawn to an hour after sunset. Stay on marked trails, refrain from using bikes or vehicles (and from camping), and observe the conservancy's common-sense regulations concerning litter, bird-nesting sites, and so on.

Nature Conservancy properties are found all around Louisiana, but those open to the public are mostly near New Orleans and Baton Rouge, in the southeastern part of the state. White Kitchen is a dramatic section of Honey Island Swamp that's a favorite for bird- and wildlife-watching—while swamp tours offer the best look at it, you can also explore it via a boardwalk that cuts right through the marsh. Lafitte Woods preserves the best tract of oak and hackberry forest on the Grand Isle barrier island, about a two-hour drive south of New Orleans; this favorite spot for observing migratory songbirds has several walking trails and a 300-foot-long boardwalk overlooking acres of estuary and tidal ponds. The 2,800-acre Cypress Island is a favorite nature retreat in Cajun Country—it's famous for its rookery, which hosts as many as 20,000 herons, egrets, and ibis each year.

An equally important conservation advocate and resource is the **Audubon Society,** which has two chapters in the state. The **Orleans Audubon Society** (504/834-2473 or 877/834-2473, www.jjaudubon.net), based in Metairie, serves the Greater New Orleans area and has a website with loads of information on birding throughout southeastern Louisiana. Based in the state capital, the **Baton Rouge Audubon Society** (www.braudubon.org) oversees the Peveto Woods Sanctuary, down along the southwest Louisiana coast south of Lake Charles. The 40-acre tract is one of the state's many exceptional birding areas.

ENTERTAINMENT

ACCOMMODATIONS

After years of suffering through a hotel short-age, New Orleans saw unprecedented growth in its number of accommodations during the late 1990s. Most of the new hotels opened in the Central Business District and the adjoining, and increasingly trendy, Warehouse District, and many are geared toward business travelers and conventioneers. But even leisure travelers should take note: The best and most competitively priced selection of accommodations in the city has shifted from the French Quarter to the CBD. Furthermore, because it's taking longer for convention business to return to the city after Hurricane Katrina than leisure travel, many CBD hotels are struggling to fill rooms and offering especially attractive rates.

For proximity to everything New Orleans is famous for, the French Quarter remains the hub of accommodations, with dozens of hotels in all shapes and sizes. There are not many chain properties, and none that could be called cookie-cutter hotels. For this reason, even though the French Quarter has few places that could be called hip or modish, it remains a popular choice among all kinds of New Orleans visitors, because it's easy to find rooms in this neighborhood that embody the history and charm of this city's rich French-Spanish history.

Outside the CBD and French Quarter, greater New Orleans has significant numbers of charming inns and B&Bs, mostly in the Garden District, Faubourg Marigny, and Mid-City, as well as significant concentrations of budget- and midpriced chain hotels, mostly in neighboring Metairie and Kenner.

An excellent resource for finding out more

HIGHLIGHTS

◖ Best Value in the French Quarter:
With an enviable location along a relatively quiet stretch of Chartres Street and extremely reasonable rates, charming **Le Richelieu** hotel is one of the best deals around (page 137).

◖ Most Literary Hotel: Distinctive for its huge red neon sign on the roof, the handsome **Hotel Monteleone** has been a favored address among New Orleans literati for decades, hosting such luminaries as Eudora Welty, Truman Capote, William Faulkner, and Tennessee Williams (page 141).

◖ Best Service: The **W New Orleans – French Quarter** stands out not only for its stately historic architecture and contrastingly contemporary rooms but also for outstanding, friendly, and knowledgeable service – it's ideal if you're looking to be pampered (page 142).

◖ Fanciest Rooms: Ultra-swank and completely secluded from the crowds of the Quarter, **Hotel Maison de Ville** is a luxurious oasis of rooms and suites decked with fine antiques, Audubon prints, and marble bathrooms (page 142).

◖ Most Romantic Inn: Occupying what had been the 1820s home of a prominent New Orleans family, **Soniat House** is perfect for a getaway with someone special – the rooms abound with museum-quality furnishings, and you can enjoy breakfast in bed in the morning (page 143).

◖ Best Bed-and-Breakfast: A 10-minute walk from the French Quarter and steps from the funky restaurants and music clubs along Frenchmen Street, the charming and friendly **Elysian Fields Inn** occupies a striking 1860s house with warmly furnished rooms and top-flight amenities, and the owners are a joy (page 145).

◖ Best Business Hotel: If you're in town on business but would rather eschew the crowds of the larger convention properties, try the handsome **Renaissance Arts Hotel,** a sleek and airy hotel in the artsy Warehouse District (close to the convention center) with a high staff-to-guest ratio and first-rate amenities (page 151).

◖ Coolest Boutique Hotel: Whimsically and creatively decorated, the 119-room **International House** draws a hip crowd to its artful confines, which include a swish cocktail lounge and see-and-be-seen restaurant (page 152).

◖ Most Offbeat Retreat: A departure from the many antiques-filled, traditional B&Bs that you'll find Uptown, the **Green House Inn** delights visitors with funky, tropical decor and mod amenities (DVD players, Aveda bath products, private gym). Rates are very fair, too (page 157).

◖ Best Hidden Gem: Many tourists miss out on one of the best B&Bs in the city, the **1896 O'Malley House,** because it's a bit off the beaten path in the up-and-coming Mid-City neighborhood, but this handsome inn with delightful owners and beautiful furnishings is worth seeking out (page 159).

LOOK FOR ◖ TO FIND THE BEST LODGING.

ACCOMMODATIONS

about the city's many fine smaller properties is **PIANO–Professional Innkeepers Association of New Orleans** (www.bbnola. com), which has about 50 member inns and B&Bs. The organization's website has a very useful online reservations and availability function that enables you to search for properties with rooms open, even at the last minute.

FINDING A ROOM
Although room demand in New Orleans has tapered significantly since Katrina, and although more and more hotels have opened and fewer relief and other temporary workers are still in the city, it's still always a good idea to book your accommodations as far ahead as possible. And it's especially important that you do so when planning a stay at an inn or B&B, as such properties are fewer and farther between than motels and hotels, and they have fewer rooms. Southern Louisiana is famous for celebrations and festivals. Mardi Gras may be the most famous, but New Orleans also books up solid during Jazz Fest and has traditionally seen a hotel crunch when conventions have been in town. Although conventions are less of a factor now than pre-Katrina, they still happen. Lafayette and Baton Rouge book up less often, but they can also be popular during festivals, and in the aftermath of Katrina, both cities have received much more visitation and have thus had more demand for hotel rooms. Check the tourism websites—and this book—to learn when events are slated to occur throughout the state, so you can plan accordingly.

As for booking a hotel room for Mardi Gras, keep in mind that this festival culminates during the weekend, Monday, and Tuesday that precede Ash Wednesday, the date of which changes each year. But there are parades and related celebrations during the weeks from Christmas leading up to Mardi Gras, so it can sometimes be tough booking a room on weekends through early spring. Also, Mardi Gras is celebrated with great enthusiasm not just in New Orleans but in more or less every town in the state. During the apex of the celebration, expect rooms to be somewhat tough to score

in Lafayette, Baton Rouge, and other towns and cities. Still, you can usually find a vacancy somewhere in these communities, even if booking a few days before Mardi Gras.

Folks have different strategies for booking Mardi Gras rooms in New Orleans. First, keep in mind that the city will be nearly sold out Friday, Saturday, Sunday, Monday, and Tuesday nights of Mardi Gras week. The entire city clears out on Ash Wednesday, making it very easy to score rooms throughout the rest of the week and into the following week. However, the city is a mess the first few days after Fat Tuesday, so it might not be a wonderful time to visit. The week before Mardi Gras is fairly popular, but you can usually find hotel rooms without much difficulty during this time.

Many, many people book hotel rooms in New Orleans for Mardi Gras as much as a year ahead, but a good number of these folks cancel sometime during the year, with the great number of cancellations occurring within two months of the celebration. So don't get discouraged if you try reserving rooms several months out and find that all your favorite hotels are booked up—undoubtedly, some of these places will have rooms available closer to the date, and some will put you on a waiting list. The easiest and simplest way to book a Mardi Gras overnight is on one of the online travel sites, such as Orbitz or Expedia. Again, you may find almost nothing available if you check these sites 4–6 months before Mardi Gras, but be patient and check back often. Typically, you'll not only find more rooms available within a month or two of Mardi Gras, but you'll even find some reduced rates, as hotels with cancellations scramble to sell those last few rooms.

It's not a bad idea to check with some of the smaller inns and B&Bs in New Orleans, too. The very popular ones fill up quickly for Mardi Gras, but some perfectly nice ones often have availability right up to the big event. B&Bs and inns can be your best backup plan when a convention lands in New Orleans and steals away all the rooms of chain hotels. Do keep in mind that during Mardi Gras and Jazz Fest, you can expect to pay 150–250 percent more for a room than during slower periods.

WHAT IT WILL COST

Accommodations base their highest and lowest rates on two basic factors, both tied closely to supply and demand. Price ranges indicated in this book reflect the highest rates, double-occupancy, during high season. Don't be put off if you see a hotel listed in the $150–250 range when you're seeking something under $100 nightly. You'll find hotels in New Orleans whose highest rates hover around $200 nightly but drop to as low as $70 during slow times. It's always a good idea to phone ahead or visit a property's website and ask about special packages and seasonal, weekday, or weekend discounts.

Expect to pay more during holidays or during a few exceptionally popular weekends (Mardi Gras, Christmastime, etc.), for suites or rooms that sleep more than two, and for rooms with amenities such as fireplaces, hot tubs, and decks. Expect to pay less (often as much as 50 percent less) off-season (especially summer in sultry New Orleans), during the week at leisure-oriented country inns and B&Bs (especially in the Cajun Country and near plantations, which are popular weekend destinations), during weekends for urban hotels and motels in business-oriented areas (such as Baton Rouge and, to some extent, Lafayette), and for rooms with fewer amenities (shared baths, twin beds, brick-wall views, no TVs, etc.).

Rates at New Orleans hotels don't change a whole lot from weekday to weekend, but there are some exceptions. You can occasionally get a romantic inn or B&B, the sort of place that books up heavily on weekends, to cut you a break on weekdays, especially Mondays or Tuesdays, and especially if it's off-season. It never hurts to explain when booking that you'd like to come during a quieter time and are curious whether the inn could offer any deals or specials on slower days of the week. Conversely, in the corporate-oriented Central Business District, some of the upscale chain hotels that cater to convention trade and business travelers will offer reduced rates on weekends, at least during the slower tourist season (meaning summer and the period between Thanksgiving and Christmas).

Accommodations in this book are grouped according to the following price categories: Under $50, $50–100, $100–150, $150–250, and over $250. These ranges are based on the cost of an establishment's standard room, double-occupancy, during high season, which generally means fall and spring in southern Louisiana.

CHOOSING AN ACCOMMODATION

Unless you have your hopes set on a specific property, or a hotel with very specific amenities, it probably makes more sense to choose the area where you'd like to stay before choosing the exact accommodation. The loveliest room in a neighborhood that you find inconvenient or too touristy isn't going to feel lovely. Remember that you can get a lot more bang for your buck by staying slightly off the tourist track.

No matter what it says in a property's brochure, remember that nothing at your hotel—breakfast, a pool, an exercise room, turn-down service, local phone calls—is truly free. These extras may be included in the rate, but this means that rates at properties with oodles of perks, amenities, and facilities are going to be higher than rates at properties without them. These extras are all well and good provided you're really going to take advantage of them, but think seriously about booking a room at a country inn that's renowned for its lavish full breakfasts or an upscale hotel whose business and conference facilities are extensive. Do you eat breakfast? Are you in town on business?

As the old real-estate cliché goes, location is everything when it comes to finding the right place to stay—even if just for the night. Once you've established what you're willing to spend and what level of accommodation will suit you, think about where you plan to spend most of your visit. Are you looking to hide away with your mate in a romantic suite, rarely emerging until checkout? Or will you be spending as little time as possible in your room or even in the town where you're staying? Does a view matter? Being within walking distance of shops

ACCOMMODATIONS

or New Orleans's legendary nightlife? To satisfy one of these needs, you may have to sacrifice another.

One major caveat before relying heavily on state- or regionally produced travel planners and brochures: The organizations that produce these publications are often funded by a hotel tax that is added onto your room rate. Other tourist boards are member-based. As long as a lodging pays its taxes or pays membership dues to a particular board of tourism, it may be entitled to be included in any literature published by the state and local tourist boards. This means that these brochures and publications often will not or cannot refuse a listing to even the seediest, dreariest, and most horrible establishment.

What does this mean in practice? Having anonymously inspected a great number of the properties listed in New Orleans and elsewhere in southern Louisiana, I can say that 10–20 percent of them are highly suspect, and several of them make the hotel in *The Shining* look like a Ritz-Carlton. You would think that some sort of ratings system would be in place to keep properties that are truly unsanitary, substandard, or unsafe from being recommended unconditionally by organizations aiming to promote tourism, but such are the mysterious ways of governmental bureaucracies.

This is not to suggest that establishments omitted from this book are substandard—there are simply too many hotels to review in this guide, and thus what you'll find is a representation of the most appealing properties in the region, in every price category. Especially in New Orleans, which has scores upon scores of hotels, motels, inns, and B&Bs, I had to select only a fraction of the places that I actually feel quite confident recommending. To that end, I tried to write about those places representing the greatest value, which is figured roughly by considering the rates, the location, the facilities, and the level of cleanliness and staff professionalism I encountered. A change in management can raise or lower the quality of a property almost overnight, but it's safe to say that at press time I'd have

recommended every single property in this book to my mother (and that's saying a lot).

Hotels and Motels

The majority of the state's hotels and motels are perfectly nice, and a few are downright homey and charming. However, most of the unacceptable accommodations in Louisiana, as is true just about everywhere in the country, are lower-end chain motels, many of them off interstates or busy roads. There are exceptions, of course, as there are some truly awful B&Bs out there and some surprisingly unkempt and poorly run moderate to upscale hotels. You can increase your odds of picking a good property by keeping a few things in mind:

Look for *recent* stickers in lobby windows that indicate the hotel has been approved by AAA or the Mobil guides, and really check credentials of motels on busy roads within an earshot of a major highway (they're not only apt to be noisy, but they're more likely to be rendezvous points for any number of illicit activities). Motels that rent rooms by the hour are usually not very savory, and there are several of them in Louisiana.

At any property with which you're unfamiliar, ask to see the room before you check in, and if the front desk staff refuses or even hesitates, you can safely assume he or she is harboring secrets that shall be revealed to you only after you have left a credit-card imprint (the postage-stamp–size guest towels are frayed and threadbare and the air conditioner is broken). If you see plants or personal effects on the sills of guestroom windows, or rusty cars in the parking lot, you have no doubt stumbled upon a residential hotel with facilities that are probably not up to the expectations of most travelers (this may sound like a joke, but a few of these places are listed in the brochures produced by tourist boards).

A few chains are consistently reputable or have especially good products in Louisiana, including most of the high-end ones. Of economical and moderately priced chains, best bets include Clarion, Comfort Inn/Comfort Suites, Courtyard by Marriott, Four Points,

LEGAL AND ILLEGAL BED-AND-BREAKFASTS

Some of the most charming rooms in the city are found in unlicensed or illegal B&Bs or guesthouses. Many of these "underground" establishments advertise heavily. Probably no harm will come to you simply for staying at one, and certainly plenty of travelers do it, so why even think twice before booking a room at such a property? There are a couple of reasons.

Letting out rooms to tourists has long been a tradition in New Orleans, and its origins are harmless enough. Owners of the many grand and historic houses in the French Quarter and other visitor-friendly neighborhoods simply rented a room or two, or even several, as a way to earn a little extra income. Many travelers enjoyed staying at these informal accommodations, saving a little money, getting to know the hosts, and living as though they were residents of New Orleans.

The problem is that the city of New Orleans requires B&Bs to be licensed, and yet it seems to make little effort to enforce this rule. So the upstanding innkeepers around town who did go through the hassle of getting approval to open an inn, and then paid the various fees, are at a competitive disadvantage compared to those who run properties illegally.

As a consumer, the main risk you face staying at an illegal B&B is that you have little or no recourse for remedying any disputes that arise with the owners, and you have no legal protection should you be injured. Illegal short-term rentals often fail to comply with fire and safety regulations; if they do so, it's on a voluntary basis, since nobody inspects them. They also rarely carry the proper commercial insurance that a licensed inn is required to have, which poses a liability risk to visitors.

Outside of protecting your own best interests, you're actually helping the city of New Orleans and its historic neighborhoods by choosing to patronize only licensed and legal B&Bs. Illegal vacation rentals don't contribute their share of taxes to the city – and worse, in a city with a high crime rate and a number of urban problems, they do little to foster community cooperation and neighborhood pride. Think of it this way: Every illegal vacation rental is a building that should, per zoning laws, be resident-occupied. And when neighborhoods such as the Upper French Quarter and Faubourg Marigny are filled with transient vacation rentals, neighborhood stability is lost. It's in the best interest of these parts of town to have as many buildings occupied by residents, or by legitimate inns where the owners live on premises or have regular on-site staff.

The easiest way to ensure that the B&B you're interested in is licensed, legal, and up to proper standards is to choose one of the more than 40 properties that are members of **PIANO – the Professional Innkeepers Association of New Orleans** (www.bbnola .com), an organization that's been going strong since 2000. With so many excellent and reliable licensed inns in New Orleans, it's smartest to stick with PIANO members and avoid illegal B&Bs.

Hampton Inn, Hilton Garden Inn, Holiday Inn Express, Motel 6 (the best bare-bones chain in the state), and Quality Inn. There are some very nice Super 8 and EconoLodge motels in Louisiana, too, but these are less consistent in quality. Other economical and moderately priced chains that vary considerably in quality from property to property include Best Western, Budget Host, Days Inn, Ramada, and Travelodge. Independently operated budget motels are inherently no better or worse than chain properties—don't rule them out just because you've never heard of them. But do check them out ahead of time.

Inns and Bed-and-Breakfasts

To get a real feel for the area you're visiting, consider choosing a B&B or country inn over a larger chain property. It's sometimes believed that chains offer better rates, more consistent standards, better amenities for business travelers, and greater anonymity, but this is far from always—or even often—the case. Some smaller B&Bs, especially those that offer shared baths, have among the least-expensive rooms in Louisiana, and this rule holds especially true in New Orleans.

Furthermore, staying at a small historic property need not involve socializing with either your hosts or fellow guests, or placing phone calls and logging onto the Internet with your laptop from a common area. An increasing number of higher-end inns (this is less true of B&Bs in rural areas) have recognized the needs of business travelers and begun installing in-room direct-dial phones, data ports, cable TVs, VCRs, and even high-speed Internet access. If privacy is important to you, ask if any of the rooms have separate outdoor entrances. You might be surprised how many places do, often in carriage houses, former slave quarters, or other outbuildings set away from the main house.

All of this is not to suggest that more social and welcoming B&Bs and country inns are scarce—the kinds of places where guests compare notes on their finest antiquing conquests before a roaring evening fire, or conspire together to attack the area's most challenging hiking trails over a four-course full breakfast. The most successful innkeepers have learned to leave alone the independent travelers but gently direct the ones seeking local advice and connections, such as hard-to-score dinner reservations and directions to secret fishing holes that you'll never find in brochures or even in this book. If it's your wish, a B&B can offer both camaraderie and a personal concierge—and these perks come with no extra charges.

In the broadest sense, B&Bs are smaller than country inns. At B&Bs there tend to be fewer than 10 rooms (sometimes only one or two), the owners often live on the premises,

breakfasts tend to be intimate and social, common areas small and homey, and facilities and amenities minimal (rarely are there phones or TVs in guest rooms, nor is there a restaurant or exercise room). At inns you may find anywhere from several to 100 rooms, a full staff of employees (the owners often live off-property), breakfasts served in dining rooms and often at your own private table, spacious and more formal common areas, and an array of facilities and amenities.

More often than not, breakfast at a country inn is continental, while breakfast at a B&B is full (with a hot entrée and often 3–4 courses). It's less of a rule, but country inns typically charge more than B&Bs and, although they're often less personable and quirky, they maintain a higher standard of luxury and offer a greater degree of privacy. These are general differences, and in many cases the lines between country inns and B&Bs blur considerably. Regardless of these distinctions, inns and B&Bs share many traits: Usually they are historic or designed in a historic style, rooms typically vary in layout and are decorated individually in period style, and settings are often rural, scenic, or historic.

An excellent resource for finding out about great inns and B&Bs throughout New Orleans is **PIANO (Professional Innkeepers Association of New Orleans)** (www.bbnola. com), which lists more than 40 licensed properties throughout the city. A statewide organization that lists reliable places to stay in just about every parish is **Louisiana Bed and Breakfast** (225/346-1857, www.louisianabandb.com). It's always a good idea to choose inns that belong to professional organizations such as these, to which only properties that are run to a certain standard are admitted.

The French Quarter

Here in the city's activity heart you'll find the greatest density of hotels, many of them set inside adjoining rows of Victorian town houses, and a smattering of B&Bs. You'll be steps from the most famous nightlife, dining, and shopping in the city. And because this is a historic district, you won't end up in some bland cookie-cutter convention hotel—most of these are in the Central Business District (CBD), on the fringes of the Quarter. With a couple of exceptions, it's generally not a good idea to pick a place right on Bourbon Street, even if you love to party; the rates are often disproportionately higher at these places, and you're almost certain to hear plenty of street noise. If revelry is a high priority, opt for something on a nearby street; nowhere in the French Quarter are you far from places to eat and play. In general, hotel rates are quite high in the French Quarter, although many good deals can be found if you shop around, and you can often get a better deal here than at some of the luxury convention-oriented hotels in the CBD. If you've never been to New Orleans, and especially if you're just staying for two or three nights, it makes sense to book a room in this neighborhood, but consider some of the outlying areas, too, especially if you're more comfortable in a smaller inn or B&B, of which there are few in the Quarter. Parking is tight in the Quarter; most properties offer valet or self garage parking for $20–30 nightly.

HOTELS AND MOTELS
$100-150

Easy access to the property's superb restaurant, Stella, is reason enough to stay at the family-run **Hotel Provincial** (1024 Chartres St., 504/581-4995 or 800/535-7922, www.hotel-provincial.com), a well-priced upscale inn with 93 cheery rooms decorated individually with Louisiana antiques and reproduction French period furnishings. Many rooms open onto a sunny courtyard with two swimming pools. Service is efficient and friendly. This complex

of historic buildings includes a former 1830s military hospital.

A well-located and relatively affordable option right across from the Jackson Brewery building and next to Johnny's Po'boys, the **Historic French Market Inn** (501 Decatur St., 504/561-5621 or 888/538-5651, www.frenchmarketinn.com) contains 95 tastefully appointed rooms with floral bedspreads, brass beds, reproduction antiques, exposed-brick walls, and the usual slate of in-room amenities: TVs, phones with voice mail, irons and boards, hair dryers. In back, rooms lead out to one of the Quarter's trademark quaint courtyards, in this case anchored by a small pool. Continental breakfast isn't included but costs very little, and there's a snug coffeehouse next to the tiny lobby of this appealing 19th-century hotel.

◖ **Le Richelieu** (1234 Chartres St., 504/529-2492 or 800/535-9653, www.lerichelieuhotel.com) books up fast because it's been one of the Quarter's most popular midpriced hotels for many years. Indeed, standard one-bed rooms rent for under $100 nightly during the slower times. Rooms feel fairly typical of chain properties but with a bit more character, such as antique-style ceiling fans and reproduction antiques—the 17 suites offer lots of extra leg room with their large sitting areas. The 86-room European-style property sits along a quiet stretch of Chartres Street in the Lower Quarter, an easy walk from Bourbon Street activity, the French Market, and Faubourg Marigny. There's a cafe serving light food throughout the day (along with room service), a cocktail bar, and a garden swimming pool. It also offers free Wi-Fi and free and secure self-parking.

Quirky, offbeat, and offering one of the better rates in the French Quarter, the family-run **Olivier House** (828 Toulouse St., 504/525-8456 or 866/525-9748, www.olivierhouse.com) is just off the hubbub of Bourbon Street, set inside a towering 1839 Greek Revival town house. The 42 rooms and suites contain a mix of older and newer furnishings, and each has a

ACCOMMODATIONS

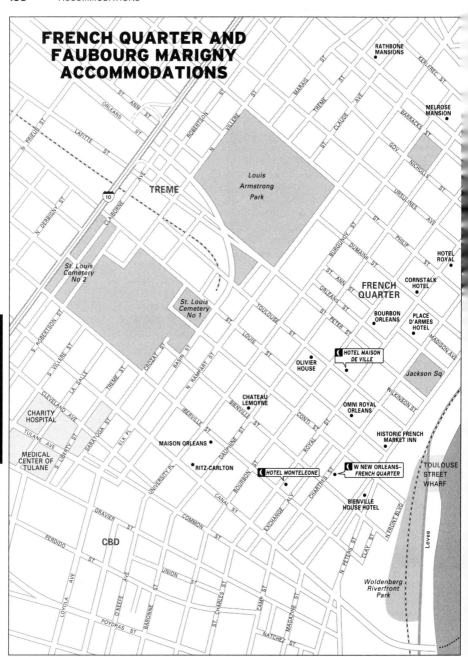

FRENCH QUARTER AND FAUBOURG MARIGNY ACCOMMODATIONS

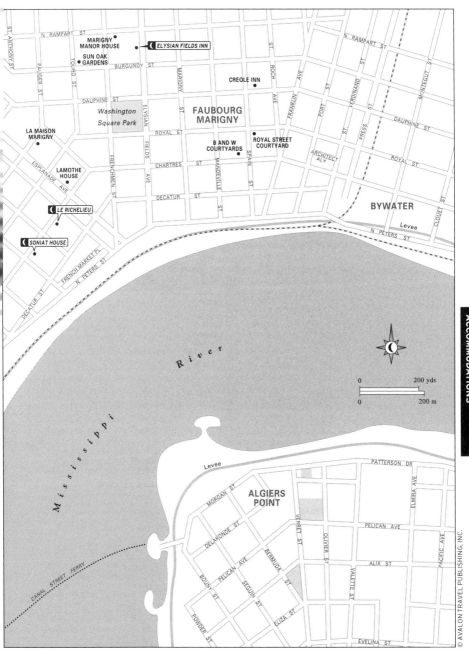

ACCOMMODATIONS

© AVALON TRAVEL PUBLISHING, INC.

different layout and decorative scheme; some are pet-friendly, and the whole property is well-suited to guests traveling with children. Suites have wet bars, kitchenettes, and some are split-level, with romantic upstairs sleeping lofts. A favorite room is the Garden Suite, whose downstairs flagstone living room has actual beds of flowers, a banana tree, and a spectacular gurgling fountain. It offers free off-street parking (almost unheard of in this part of the Quarter), a pool, and free local phone calls, making this friendly, low-key property an excellent value.

$150-250

The **Bourbon Orleans** (717 Orleans St., 504/523-2222 or 800/996-3426, www.wyndham.com) occupies most of a block at Bourbon and Orleans streets, making it party central—several gay and straight nightclubs are but a stone's throw from the Bourbon Street entrance. It makes sense, therefore, to book a room facing one of the side streets and not Bourbon if you want to get any sleep at night—all rooms have good soundproofing, but they can't always keep out all the noise of nearby revelry. This is one of the best properties close to Bourbon Street, as many of them are overpriced and a bit chaotic with the swarms of crowds outside the door. This Wyndham Historic Hotel, which dates to 1817, has a highly professional staff and 216 large rooms with tall windows, long flowing drapes, floral-print bedspreads, Queen Anne reproduction antiques, marble bathrooms, and high-speed Internet access. The property completed an ambitious $14 million renovation in 2004. The restaurant, Piallards, presents serviceable breakfasts and dinners, but this is by no means a destination dining option given all the great nearby culinary options.

The only accommodation right on Jackson Square, **Place D'Armes Hotel** (625 St. Ann St., 504/529-7142 or 800/366-2743, www.placedarmes.com) has a couple of other things going for it—for example, it's just a short walk from those heavenly beignets at Cafe du Monde. The property consists of nine adja-

view of St. Ann Street from the Bourbon Orleans hotel

cent 18th-century buildings, all carefully restored and containing a total of 83 rooms, all of them looking every bit as snazzy today as before Katrina. Many of them overlook delightful courtyards shaded by crape myrtle and magnolia trees, or the colorful street life of Jackson Square; many of these have balconies. All rooms have high-speed Internet, and there's Wi-Fi in common areas. Some bargain-priced smaller rooms have no view but perfectly charming furnishings. Continental breakfast (included in the rate and including fresh-squeezed orange juice) is served in a small tile-floor cafe, but you're also welcome to dine in the courtyard or back in your room.

Part of the acclaimed Melrose Hotel Group, a collection of four intimate, luxury New Orleans accommodations, the **Hotel Royal** (1006 Royal St., 504/524-3900 or 800/776-3901, www.melrosegroup.com) occupies a marvelous 1827 Creole town house that was a private home until the 1940s, then a launderette, and then a humdrum hotel until 2001, when it was completely refurbished. Although it's just a block off Bourbon Street, the hotel is in the Lower Quarter, down a few blocks from the more touristy and crowded areas. The 30 units have high ceilings and in many cases wrought-iron balconies and exposed brick; the least expensive rooms, which start at under $100 during slower times, look down over the romantic courtyard anchored by a fountain. The most exclusive rooms are the balcony suites, with wet bars and whirlpool tubs, but every room has individual climate control, coffeemakers, and irons and boards. A light continental breakfast is included.

The intimate **Bienville House Hotel** (320 Decatur St., 504/529-2345 or 800/535-9603, www.bienvillehouse.com) sits along Decatur Street, close to the River, Canal Street, and several good bars and eateries with a mellower ambience than those a few blocks up on Bourbon Street—that being said, you're not far from those either. By French Quarter standards, rooms here are large, airy, and looking especially dapper after a huge top-to-bottom overhaul recently. Bathrooms are attractive with white tile and upscale amenities. The best units offer sterling views of the river, but wherever you sleep, consider having coffee in the morning on one of the inviting rooftop sundecks; there's also a pool with a very civilized lanai surrounding it. The ground-floor restaurant, Louisiana Heritage Cafe, serves first-rate contemporary Creole cooking and also operates a cooking school, which offers a wide range of classes at 10:30 A.M. on Friday and Saturday.

The 【 **Hotel Monteleone** (214 Royal St., 504/523-3341 or 800/535-9595, www.hotel-monteleone.com), famous for its immense red neon rooftop sign, is a favorite because of its rich history—this 1886 property hosted Tennessee Williams many times, as well as Eudora Welty, William Faulkner, Truman Capote, and Richard Ford. For this reason, it's one of only three hotels in the country that has been named a Literary Landmark by the Friends of Libraries USA. You can sense the hotel's distinguished history simply by walking through the gracious marble lobby. Another plus is the great location on Royal Street, steps from rowdy Bourbon

Street action but safely away from the noise and commotion. Thanks to a massive renovation completed in 2003, the 573 rooms look better than ever, but keep in mind that many units are quite small and in some cases dark, and some look out at other hotel rooms (pricier rooms overlook the French Quarter or the Mississippi River, just a few blocks away). It's worth staying here if you can score a good deal—otherwise, some of the Monteleone's nearby competitors offer nicer, or at least brighter, rooms at similar or better prices. Amenities include three restaurants, the intimate Aria spa, and a wonderful rooftop pool (heated year-round) and fitness center.

With a prime spot in the Quarter, steps from dozens of great shops and restaurants, the **Omni Royal Orleans** (621 St. Louis St., 504/529-5333 or 800/843-6664, www.omni-hotels.com) has a devoted following but is less famous than some of its competitors and could even be called underrated. The lavish, rambling property contains 346 smartly furnished rooms with understatedly elegant decor, three phones, Wi-Fi, coffeemakers, and irons and boards; top rooms have balconies and whirlpool tubs, and just about all of them afford an impressive view of the Quarter. Public areas include a long, gracious marble lobby with tall arched windows and cushy chairs overlooking the colorful street life outside. It can get busy here, but the staff consistently keeps its cool and its humor. On the roof you'll find a fitness center and heated pool, along with a seasonal poolside cafe. A couple of natty bars are on the ground floor, along with the hallowed Rib Room restaurant, a retro-hip favorite of carnivores.

Not your typical Holiday Inn, the **Chateau LeMoyne** (301 Dauphine St., 504/581-1303 or 888/465-4329, www.holiday-inn.com) occupies a row of 1940s town houses, along with some vintage 19th-century structures built in the classic Creole style. It's been a hotel since 1971. Some rooms are in former slave quarters, and others contain such rich architectural details as cypress wood beams, exposed-brick walls, and lacy ironwork. Common areas include tree-shaded red-brick patios anchored by a pool. There's also a fitness center. There are 171 rooms with period reproductions and all the usual modern chain-hotel amenities you'd expect of a Holiday Inn, including high-speed Internet.

Over $250

A bit of a departure from many W Hotels, which tend to be sleek and modern, **◖ W New Orleans – French Quarter** (316 Chartres St., 504/581-1200 or 888/625-5144, www.whotels.com) occupies a stately old building with many rooms set around a magnificent courtyard. It captures the pizzazz and Old World charm of the French Quarter, but in other respects, it's definitely a W Hotel: The 98 rooms have plush feather beds with 350-thread-count linens, soft earth tones, framed black-and-white photos, TVs with high-speed Internet via infrared keyboards, DVD players, CD players, large work desks, cordless phones, Bliss Spa bath products, and fully stocked minibars with microbrew beers and iced teas. In addition to all these creature comforts, the W employs perhaps the most attentive and helpful staff of any property in the French Quarter—they'll do just about anything you ask to make your stay memorable. Sip cocktails and nosh on snacks in the mod Living Room, or book a table for dinner at Bacco, a stellar restaurant serving contemporary New Orleans-meets-Italy cuisine. You won't find a more alluring, skillful balance between French Quarter charm and high-tech sophistication.

Celebs and business leaders favor the super-posh **◖ Hotel Maison de Ville** (727 Toulouse St., 504/561-5858 or 800/634-1600, www.maisondeville.com), parts of which date to the 1700s (these are believed to be among the oldest extant buildings in the city). It's just off Bourbon Street, but once inside this cloistered property or one of the adjoining Audubon Cottages, you'd never know you're in the most raucous part of the city. There are 19 rooms and suites set among two main buildings, one of them a former slave quarters, with a central courtyard and fountain. Additionally, on nearby Dauphine Street, there are seven private cottages. In every unit you'll find museum-quality antiques, four-poster beds, framed Audubon prints, and marble bathrooms; some have exposed brick walls and fireplaces. The exceptional Bistro at Maison de Ville is one of the top special-occasion restaurants in the French Quarter, specializing in creative contemporary Creole fare.

The French Quarter isn't really all that authentically French these days, but don't tell that to the staff and creative team behind the deluxe **Maison Orleans** (904 Iberville St., 504/524-1331 or 800/241-3333, www.ritz-carlton.com), the 75-room "club level" annex of the adjacent Ritz-Carlton that replicates the dignity and flair of a 19th-century Parisian townhome. Rooms are decked in such stylish treasures as Louis XVI–inspired writing desks, brocade-upholstered wing chairs, and gilded mirrors. Guest have full use of the restaurants and other facilities of the much larger Ritz-Carlton hotel.

In 2000, the Ritz-Carlton opened a larger property, the 452-room **Ritz-Carlton** (921 Canal St., 504/524-1331 or 800/241-3333, www.ritz-carlton.com), right on busy Canal Street, inside the massive Kress and Maison Blanche department store buildings, on the very edge of the Quarter. The glazed terra-cotta, twin-towered building has long been one of the city's architectural landmarks. This is the perfect choice for the ultimate vacation of pampering: The Ritz has a 20,000-square-foot state-of-the-art spa, a chic health club and gym, a clubby Library Lounge with a walk-in humidor, two other handsome bars, and a grand full-service restaurant, Victor's Grill, which serves nonpareil contemporary continental cuisine. The well-trained staff tends to guests' every need, from overnight shoeshines to nightly turndown service. Richly furnished rooms feel right out of Old World Paris, with 300-thread-count Frette linens, goose-down pillows, Italian-marble baths, and floor-to-ceiling windows. Note that the Ritz-Carlton and its adjacent Maison Orleans suffered particularly severe damage after Hurricane Katrina, but both properties reopened in December 2006, having undergone massive renovations. They're both looking better than ever.

INNS AND BED-AND-BREAKFASTS
$100-150

The **Lamothe House** (621 Esplanade Ave., 504/947-1161 or 888/696-9575, www.lamothehouse.com) is perfectly situated if you want to be near the French Quarter but in a quieter locale—and quick access to the city's hottest neighborhood, Faubourg Marigny. It's set along oak-lined Esplanade Avenue, the border between the Quarter and Marigny, and it's an easy walk to clubs, restaurants, and shops in either neighborhood. Of course, at this cloistered Victorian inn you may simply want to curl up with your honey in your gracious hand-carved canopy bed, or lie on a chaise-longue in the lushly landscaped garden patio set around a small swimming pool with a hot tub. Rooms in this pretty-and-pink building contain such original architectural elements as intricately crafted ceiling medallions, marble-top nightstands, period artwork and wallpapers, and overstuffed Victorian couches. There's discounted off-street parking, and continental breakfast is included.

$150-250

An intimate, superluxurious small hotel that isn't cheap but isn't unreasonably priced either, the C **Soniat House** (1133 Chartres St., 504/522-0570 or 800/544-8808, www.soniathouse.com) sits on a quiet street close to the French Market and Faubourg Marigny. The hotel is set within an 1820s house built by one of New Orleans's most distinguished families. Rooms, overflowing with British, French, and Louisiana antiques, have such fancy extras as bath-side phones and extra reading pillows. You can relax in the elegant sitting room, with its well-stocked honor wine bar, or enjoy breakfast (which costs extra) either in your room or at a table by the lily pond in the courtyard. It's one of the only properties in town that's fully nonsmoking.

The **Cornstalk** (915 Royal St., 504/523-1515 or 800/759-6112, www.cornstalkhotel.com) is a quirky property, with rather small guest bathrooms that could stand some updating. This might be a turnoff for some, but the place has a loyal following of repeat guests (Bill and Hillary Clinton have stayed here, as did Elvis Presley) who appreciate this early-19th-century mansion's informative staff, antiques-filled rooms with sweeping drapes and high ceilings, Oriental rugs, and in some cases fireplaces. This Victorian inn is fringed by an oft-photographed ornate cast-iron fence, which dates to the 1840s and has a distinctive cornstalk design—-in fact, the hotel's yellow Italianate exterior has appeared in quite a few coffee-table books and movies. At the front of the house are a cheerful front garden, and upstairs a long balcony runs along the facade; both spots are perfect for people-watching or sipping a drink while admiring the passersby on Royal Street. The Cornstalk's an interesting place, and with rates that often dip well below $100 during slower times, it can be a pretty good deal, too, especially considering the plum location and free Wi-Fi.

It's not quite in the French Quarter, but if you can stand a 10-minute walk up Esplanade Avenue, the **Rathbone Mansions** (1227 and 1244 Esplanade Ave., 504/947-2100 or 800/947-2101, www.rathboneinn.com) can be a perfectly good base for exploring the area. The inns, which are nearly across the street from each other, are also a short drive south of City Park and the eateries along Esplanade Ridge; they're at the edge of historic Storyville, an area gradually undergoing an urban renaissance. The property consists of two lavish and expertly restored antebellum Greek Revival mansions. Many rooms have kitchenettes—some have balconies, and all have high ceilings and well-chosen antiques. A continental breakfast and afternoon wine-and-cheese reception are included, and the banana tree–shaded courtyard at the 1227 Esplanade property, with its whirlpool tub, makes a tranquil spot for whiling away an afternoon.

Over $250

An ultraposh inn on the border between the French Quarter and Faubourg Marigny, **Melrose Mansion** (937 Esplanade Ave., 504/944-2255 or 800/650-3323, www.melrosemansion.com) occupies one of the most dramatic buildings on regal Esplanade Avenue, a Gothic Victorian 1880s mansion with tall French windows, finger-lace ironwork, tall pillared balconies and verandas, and huge rooms, many of them full suites with sitting areas. The suites open onto grand balconies and have whirlpool tubs with separate showers, antique armoires, settees, and four-poster king-size beds. All rooms have marble bathrooms and gorgeous antiques and high-quality reproductions. Rates include nightly cocktails and hors d'oeuvres and a rather paltry continental breakfast. It offers a heated pool and 24-hour concierge. It's not hard to see why the hotel is such a favorite with honeymooners, but keep in mind that the rates are high, and the service and amenities don't always live up—it's a good choice, however, if you can snag a reduced rate during a slower time. It's part of the Melrose Group, which also includes the Hotel Royal and the Rivers Inn.

Faubourg Marigny and Bywater

This trendy, on-the-up neighborhood just downriver from the Quarter has much of the bustle of its more famous neighbor, including some excellent restaurants and nightlife. As with the French Quarter, the area received little or no flooding, except for some parts of Bywater farthest downriver. Many buildings in these neighborhoods received significant wind and storm damage, but most of this had been repaired by early 2006. Visitors unused to city living can be intimidated because it's a mostly residential neighborhood that can feel quiet at night, and it does have a few rough patches, especially as you get farther downriver. But this is also a real, historic New Orleans neighborhood, with a trove of stunning Creole cottages and Victorian treasures. There are no full-service hotels here, but you'll find oodles of cute inns and B&Bs. Prices here are about 65–90 percent of what you'd pay for comparable accommodations in the Quarter—the less central you are, the less pricey. In many cases, there's ample parking on the street, and some B&Bs have free off-street parking.

INNS AND BED-AND-BREAKFASTS
$50–100
One of the few pet-friendly inns in the city, the moderately priced **Royal Street Courtyard** (2438 Royal St., 504/943-6818 or 888/846-4004, www.royalstreetcourtyard.com) occupies a rambling historic Greek Revival compound with towering 14-foot ceilings. Among the eight rooms, several have fully equipped kitchens, and all have at least a refrigerator, cable TV, and a phone. This gay-popular inn is especially known for its verdant tropical courtyard, punctuated with fish ponds, blooming flower gardens, and a secluded hot tub. Innkeepers Phillip Lege and David Smith are wonderfully helpful and extremely popular with their guests. Continental breakfast is included.

An affordable, charming B&B a few blocks downriver from Washington Park and about eight blocks from the Quarter, the **Creole Inn** (2471 Dauphine St., 504/948-3230, www.creoleinn.com) is run by a museum curator and former professor with a great knowledge of the neighborhood's, and the city's, history and architecture. There are five rooms, two of which have two bedrooms and can accommodate up to four guests. Accommodations have high ceilings and hardwood floors, and a simple mix of antiques and rattan pieces, plus TVs with VCRs, cordless phones with voice mail, and private baths. It has a lounge where you can check email on a computer and a secluded patio with a fountain. Continental breakfast is included. This friendly, easygoing hostelry is one of the better values of any inn within walking distance of the Quarter, but keep in mind that one night's deposit is required and will be forfeited if you cancel within 60 days out.

© ANDREW COLLINS

Elysian Fields Inn

$100-150

Just inside Faubourg Marigny, a few steps from Esplanade (which forms the border with the Quarter), **La Maison Marigny** (1421 Bourbon St., 504/948-3638 or 800/570-2014, www.la-maisonmarigny.com) blends the homey ambience of a small B&B with the creature comforts of a luxury hotel. Each room has cable flat-screen TV with DVD player, high-quality bedding, plush bath towels, multispeed ceiling fans and central air and heating, phones, and Wi-Fi. Rooms have lavish dark-wood antique beds, handsome oak and mahogany furnishings, polished hardwood floors, attractive area rugs, and 12-foot ceilings—the place oozes with character without being overdecorated or frilly. There are just three guest rooms in this meticulously restored 1898 house, meaning that you're assured personalized service, but hosts Dewey Donihoo and John Ramsey also take care to respect guests' privacy. Breakfast is served in a sunny, foliage-choked courtyard.

If you really want to experience life in one of New Orleans's most charming and historic neighborhoods, an area that's well off the beaten tourist track but still just a short walk from the Quarter, consider a stay at the romantic **B and W Courtyards** (2425 Chartres St., 504/945-9418 or 800/585-5731, www.bandwcourtyards.com), an eight-room B&B set inside three 19th-century buildings with delightful connecting courtyards. This peaceful hideaway is a favorite with guests seeking privacy (it's not suitable for children), and innkeepers Rob Boyd and Kevin Wu are warm and enthusiastic hosts. Rooms are decked with fine antiques and fine linens, all with private bath, central air-conditioning and heat, Wi-Fi, and fresh flowers, and most of them open onto one of the courtyards. In the rear courtyard, you can soak in a whirlpool tub under the stars. There's also a nattily furnished long-term suite available.

The delightful ◖ **Elysian Fields Inn** (930 Elysian Fields Ave., 504/948-9420 or 866/948-9420, www.elysianfieldsinn.com) offers a lot of hotel for relatively reasonable rates. Accommodations in this striking 1860s mansion include eight guest rooms and a large suite with both a queen bed and a queen sleeper sofa. In-room amenities include Aveda bath products, Italian-marble bathrooms (most with whirlpool tubs), flat-screen TVs with VCR/DVD players, and central air/heat; the polished wood floors are fine Brazilian mahogany, and ceiling fans whir from the 10- to 14-foot ceilings. The rooms are filled with sleek and sophisticated Mission-style antiques and neutral-tone linens, and some units have sleigh beds or four-poster beds; the unfussy aesthetic is a nice departure from some of the city's more clutter-filled B&Bs. Were this property a few blocks over in the French Quarter, rates would be another $100 per night. But Elysian Fields isn't far from the Quarter, and it's just a couple of safe blocks from the hip dining and nightlife along Frenchmen Street.

A small house-museum with stunning gardens and two guest suites, **Sun Oak Gardens** (2020 Burgundy St., 504/945-0322, www.sunoaknola.com) is a colorful and striking Greek Revival Creole cottage painted in four colors and designated a city landmark. Wide-plank heart-pine floors, antiques culled from throughout southern Louisiana, and a small maze of patios and flowering gardens make this a marvel of historic preservation and one of the most distinctive architectural treasures in Faubourg Marigny, a neighborhood rife with great buildings. Up a winding staircase you'll reach the dormer suite, a cozy room with a pitched ceiling, bathroom with claw-foot tub, antique half-tester bed, and a sleeper sofa (the room can accommodate four guests). The Garden Suite overlooks the courtyard and has an iron half-tester bed and a loft sleeping area. Both units share a full kitchen with a dining area. It's an ideal B&B for friends traveling together and planning to stay for several days or more.

Near the northern edge of this funky neighborhood, **Marigny Manor House** (2125 N. Rampart St., 504/943-7826 or 877/247-7599, www.marignymanorhouse.com) sits along a quiet stretch that may feel a tad out of the way if you're not used to big cities but offers a wonderful sampling of vintage 19th-century residential architecture typical of New Orleans. The offbeat bars and restaurants of Frenchmen Street are a short walk away. The tan Greek Revival house, meticulously restored, has four neatly furnished, reasonably priced rooms with designer fabrics, marble-top chests, four-poster beds, and Oriental rugs over hardwood floors. One room has a balcony overlooking the brick fern-and-flower-bedecked courtyard.

Central Business and Warehouse Districts

This is New Orleans's rather modern downtown, which still means that you'll find a lot of buildings from the early 20th century, and some even older, especially down closer to the river in the Warehouse District. And except for the artsy Warehouse District, with its high-ceilinged brick buildings with tall windows, many of which reveal galleries and restaurants, much of the CBD feels rather corporate. Some parts of the neighborhood were flooded during Katrina, but most of it remained fairly dry. Nevertheless, a few hotels received major damage and remain closed. The section nearest the French Quarter, from Canal to Poydras streets, abounds with hotels, the most charming and distinctive of which are reviewed in this chapter. Many others—the Marriott, the Sheraton, the Inter-Continental, and a bunch of lower-end chain properties—are not included, partly because of space restrictions, but partly because they tend to court convention business, charge business rates, and offer a relatively cookie-cutter experience. They're often perfectly nice hotels with, in some cases, very fancy rooms, but you may end up paying $50–100 more per night for a room simply because it's inside a massive hotel with a huge staff and oodles of facilities that you might never use.

A pleasant trend of late, however, has

been an influx of smaller, more characterful boutique hotels opening inside early–20th-century office buildings—the Wyndham Whitney, the Drury Inn, and several others fit this description. You can find some elegant, imposing, grand, and occasionally economical hotels in the CBD, but you generally will not find a property that captures the jazzy personality or charming architecture of Old World New Orleans. Street parking is nonexistent to impossible in the CBD; most hotels offer garage or valet parking for $20–30 nightly. You can also find some lots, some staffed and some unstaffed, that charge anywhere between $5 and $20 per 24-hour period, but in these lots you typically will not have in/out privileges.

HOTELS AND MOTELS
$50-100
It's a cookie-cutter chain hotel that could just as easily be in central Dubuque as in the Central Business District, but the **Sleep Inn** (334 O'Keefe Ave., 504/524-5400 or 877/424-6423, www.sleepinn.com) has 129 clean rooms and a safe if uninspired location in the heart of downtown (the Superdome is four blocks away). Parking costs about $20 a day, but otherwise, this is an easy-on-the-budget option with an outdoor pool and continental breakfast.

About the only drawback to the well-run **AmeriHost Inn and Suites** (1300 Canal St., 504/299-9900 or 800/434-5800, www.amerihostinn.com) is a somewhat drab setting along upper Canal Street, a few blocks north of the French Quarter. On the other hand, this is one of the few hotels in New Orleans in this price range from which you can easily walk to Bourbon Street, the Superdome, and the many restaurants and shops downtown. The hotel is set inside an attractive 1920s brick building, and it offers a number of amenities, including a full-service restaurant, room service, an exercise room, a pool, continental breakfast, and in-room microwaves, refrigerators, irons and boards, and hair dryers. Valet parking is $10–15 nightly (it's more expensive on weekends).

$100-150
One of the better midrange chain hotels in the CBD, **Comfort Suites** (346 Baronne St., 504/524-1140 or 877/424-6423, www.comfortsuites.com) has only one drawback—its name is something of a misnomer. The rooms are not truly suites, though each features a half-partitioned sitting area with a desk and small sofa; some do have whirlpool tubs. Windows of many rooms are sealed shut and frosted, making it a bit dreary and stuffy in here. There's nothing special about this hotel, but rooms this size—with refrigerators, coffeemakers, and microwaves—at these rates are hard to find just a 10-minute walk from the Quarter.

Part of a popular Midwest-based chain, the only Louisiana locale of the **Drury Inn and Suites** (820 Poydras St., 504/529-7800 or 800/378-7946, www.druryinn.com) offers one of the best values in the CBD. This 156-unit hotel, with a mix of standard rooms and two-room suites, occupies a handsome 10-story 1917 building (formerly the Cumberland Telephone Building) five blocks from both the French Quarter and the Superdome. High ceilings and tall windows bathe the rooms in sunlight; each has a marble-accented bathroom, high-speed Internet access, and pleasant contemporary—if generic—furnishings. You can relax in the rooftop pool and hot tub, and you get discount admission to a health club across the street. Many of the building's original details, such as the ornamental lobby staircase and Waterford crystal chandeliers, have been carefully preserved. An expansive and hot continental breakfast and high-speed Internet are included in the rates, which often dip below $100 nightly, especially on weekends.

A cool, reasonably priced hotel in the slick Warehouse District, the **Ambassador New Orleans** (535 Tchoupitoulas St., 504/527-5271 or 800/455-3417, www.ambassadorneworleans.com) is situated within three neighboring red-brick warehouses that date to the 1850s. The look and feel blends the new and old. Ceiling timbers, steel beams, worn stucco, and brick are left exposed, and the 165 rooms have large writing desks, in-room safes, tall windows,

ACCOMMODATIONS

hardwood floors, and wrought-iron beds. On the ground floor, Banditos serves commendable Mexican food and has a lively tequila bar.

The **Hampton Inn and Suites New Orleans Convention Center** (1201 Convention Center Blvd., 504/566-9990 or 800/426-7866, www.hamptoninn.com) differs a bit from the usual modern chain properties—it's set inside a five-story redbrick building from the early 1900s that once contained a cotton mill. There's a shaded park beside the hotel, and the convention center, casino, Riverwalk shops, and Warehouse District are all close by. There are 288 guest rooms, many of them suites, some with minikitchens, whirlpool tubs, and separate bedrooms. High ceilings with tall windows keep things light and bright. A coin laundry, concierge, business center, pool, and fitness room round out the amenities.

Not many hotels in New Orleans offer better views of the Carnival parade route than **Hotel Le Cirque** (936 St. Charles Ave., 504/962-0900 or 800/684-9525, www.hotellecirqueneworleans.com), which towers over Lee Circle, right by the Ogden Museum of Southern Art and the National World War II Museum. Like the W hotels and the International House, this is a hotel for hipsters, with mod furnishings, monochromatic color schemes, and comfy Turkish robes in each room. But here, rates typically hover around $100 nightly and often dip well below that during slower times. This former YMCA has been handsomely retrofitted, but a simple design and smallish rooms help keep the prices down. As you might guess, this is a favorite address of artists, younger travelers, and others with a yen for style and a desire to save money.

$150-250

With a handy location near the French Quarter and along the streetcar line to the Garden District, the **Royal St. Charles Hotel** (135 St. Charles Ave., 504/587-1641 or 800/268-9749, www.royalsaintcharleshotel.com) makes sense if you're seeking a central location and stylish, understated accommodations. Original art fills the 143 contemporary rooms, which also hold bathrobes, minibars, custom-made lightwood

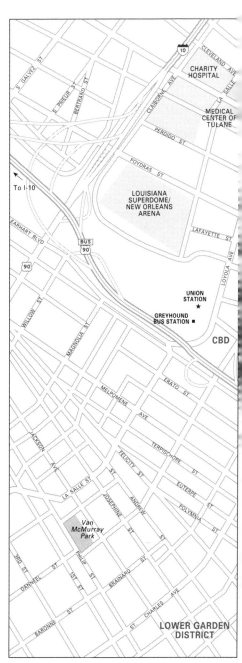

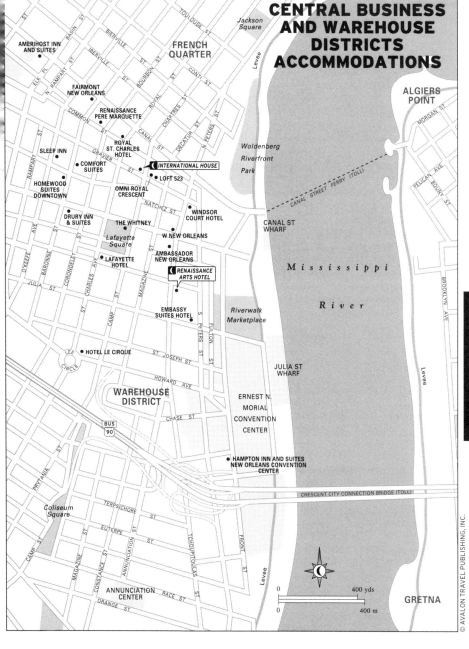

CENTRAL BUSINESS AND WAREHOUSE DISTRICTS ACCOMMODATIONS

FRENCH QUARTER

Jackson Square

ALGIERS POINT

AMERIHOST INN AND SUITES

FAIRMONT NEW ORLEANS

RENAISSANCE PERE MARQUETTE

ROYAL ST. CHARLES HOTEL

SLEEP INN

COMFORT SUITES

INTERNATIONAL HOUSE

LOFT 523

HOMEWOOD SUITES DOWNTOWN

OMNI ROYAL CRESCENT

Woldenberg Riverfront Park

WINDSOR COURT HOTEL

DRURY INN & SUITES

THE WHITNEY

Lafayette Square

W NEW ORLEANS

CANAL ST WHARF

AMBASSADOR NEW ORLEANS

LAFAYETTE HOTEL

RENAISSANCE ARTS HOTEL

Mississippi

EMBASSY SUITES HOTEL

Riverwalk Marketplace

River

HOTEL LE CIRQUE

JULIA ST WHARF

WAREHOUSE DISTRICT

ERNEST N. MORIAL CONVENTION CENTER

BUS 90

HAMPTON INN AND SUITES NEW ORLEANS CONVENTION CENTER

CRESCENT CITY CONNECTION BRIDGE (TOLL)

Coliseum Square

ANNUNCIATION CENTER

GRETNA

CANAL STREET FERRY (TOLL)

Levee

0   400 yds

0   400 m

ACCOMMODATIONS

© HILTON NEW ORLEANS/ST. CHARLES AVENUE

The Hilton New Orleans/St. Charles Avenue occupies a neo-Gothic building that once housed a Masonic temple.

furniture, in-room safes, and in-room faxes and modems. The hotel is part of a minichain called New Orleans Boutique Hotels, which also runs the Queen and Crescent Hotel (in the CBD) and the Garden District Hotel.

Intimate and hidden away on a narrow CBD street, the classy **Omni Royal Crescent** (535 Gravier St., 504/527-0006 or 800/843-6664, www.omnihotels.com) offers a low-key boutique-hotel ambience. The 98 rooms of this eight-story property have sturdy custom-made mattresses, imported bath amenities, terry robes, honor bars, and soft lighting; some have whirlpool tubs, and several suites have floor-to-ceiling windows, VCRs, and CD players. It has a rooftop pool and adjacent gym. The hotel was badly damaged after Katrina and had not opened at press time, but there are plans in place for it to reopen in 2007.

One of the few long-term-stay properties right in downtown New Orleans, the **Embassy Suites Hotel New Orleans** (315 Julia St., 504/525-1993 or 800/362-2779, www.embas-sysuites.com) sits just steps from the trendy art galleries and eateries of the white-hot Warehouse District. This 16-story building with 372 rooms makes a plush nest, especially for guests planning to stay more than a few days—each suite has high-speed Internet, kitchenettes with minirefrigerators and microwaves, work tables, and couches; the double suites sleep up to six guests, as they have sleeper sofas. Perks include full breakfast in the seven-story atrium lobby cafe, a 24-hour fitness center, and a lap pool and hot tub. There's also a full-service restaurant, Sugar House, serving traditional New Orleans fare. This is a great neighborhood—safe but lively and not nearly as touristy as the Quarter, which is just a short walk away.

The dashing **Renaissance Pere Marquette** (817 Common St., 504/525-1111 or 888/236-2427, www.renaissancehotels.com) rises 18 stories over the CBD, with 275 smartly furnished rooms. Dual-line cordless phones, CD players, hair dryers, irons and boards, 27-inch TVs, and morning papers are standard with every room.

Bathrooms, done in sleek marble, are huge. There's also an outdoor pool and gym.

The **Ⓒ Renaissance Arts Hotel** (700 Tchoupitoulas St., 504/613-2330 or 800/431-8634, www.renaissancehotels.com) opened in 2003 in the artsy Warehouse District, on the edge of the CBD. This upscale 217-room hotel occupies a five-story former warehouse. A distinctly urban, sleek addition to the city, it even has its own first-floor art gallery. Rooms are airy and spacious, with tall windows. Yes, it's part of the Marriott chain, but the hotel has a boutiquelike ambience, owing in part to the high staff-to-guest ratio and personal service. The in-house restaurant, La Cote Brasseries, is a neighborhood favorite for its creative French Creole cuisine.

New Orleans has seen an influx of longer-stay hotels in recent years, among them the **Homewood Suites Downtown** (901 Poydras St., 504/581-5599 or 800/468-3571, www.homewoodsuites.com), a 12-story building in the heart of the CBD. You'll find 30 two-bedroom suites and 136 one-bedroom units, all with full kitchens, breakfast tables, two cable TVs, two phones with data ports, irons and boards, continental breakfast, and evening cocktail and snack receptions Monday–Thursday. It also offers an indoor pool, exercise room, guest laundry, 24-hour convenience store, and business center. It's a popular spot for business travelers, but families or leisure visitors staying for several days can make good use of this hotel, which often offers reduced prices on slower weekends.

The former Hotel Monaco, an elegant boutique property that closed following Katrina, is set to reopen in 2007 as the **Hilton New Orleans/St. Charles Avenue** (333 St. Charles Ave., 504/524-8890 or 800/HILTONS, www.hhstcharles.com). The 250-room property occupies a 19-story 1920s building on St. Charles Avenue that once contained a Masonic temple. Decor is sophisticated and upscale, with fine linens, CD stereos, and colorful furnishings in each room. Suites have whirlpool tubs.

Slated to reopen in fall 2007, the **Hyatt Regency New Orleans** (Poydras St. at Loyola Ave., 504/561-1234 or 888/591-1234, www.hyatt.com) is expected to reclaim its role as one of the top business properties in town. The property will be part of a massive jazz-themed project that will include a National Jazz Center museum and performance space.

Set inside a vintage redbrick bank building near the bustling intersection of Poydras and St. Charles (an ideal locale for viewing Mardi Gras parades), **The Whitney** (610 Poydras St., 504/581-4222 or 800/996-3426, www.wyndham.com) offers one of the better values among upscale hotels in the CBD—rates often dip below $150 nightly. This is partly because the hotel is relatively small (just 93 units) as CBD hotels go, and the rooms themselves are a bit small. Still, with earthy color schemes, plush linens, ergonomic chairs and work desks, high-speed Internet, and handsome marble bathrooms, the accommodations are completely comfortable. The restaurant, Roth's Steak Knife, set inside the elegant former bank lobby, serves commendable food.

The stately **Lafayette Hotel** (600 St. Charles Ave., 504/539-9000 or 888/856-4706, www.thelafayettehotel.com) is the most appealing and best-situated of an empire of small, upscale boutique hotels set throughout New Orleans, all with elegant but in some cases staid decor and competent but unspectacular service. This hotel, inside a grand five-story 1916 building that served as a Navy barracks during World War II, sits beside attractive Lafayette Square and is right on the streetcar line. The 44 luxurious rooms are swathed in floor-to-ceiling drapes and designer fabrics. Also expect to find French doors opening onto small wrought-iron balconies, mahogany furniture, and British botanical prints—it's all very deluxe and proper. Suites have VCRs and whirlpool tubs. Some of the other properties that are part of the same company, New Orleans Fine Hotels—the Historic French Market Inn and Hotel Le Cirque—are also reviewed in this chapter, and check out the company web page (www.neworleansfinehotels.com) for details on the other lodging options, which include the Chateau Dupre (in the Quarter), the Holiday Inn Express (CBD), the Parc St. Charles (CBD), the Pelham Hotel (CBD), Astor Crowne Plaza (CBD), and the St. James (Warehouse District).

Over $250

In reader polls conducted by leading travel magazines, the 319-room **Windsor Court Hotel** (300 Gravier St., 504/523-6000 or 888/596-0955, www.windsorcourthotel.com) has been ranked among the top few hotels in the world. With that, the Windsor Court has a lot to live up to, and in some ways it's hard to understand what all the fuss is about. Sure, this hotel that opened in the early 1980s contains a $10 million collection of British art that includes originals by Gainsborough and Reynolds. There's a high staff-to-guest ratio, and these employees know how to please guests. And the large rooms, most of them full suites, contain high-quality Euro-elegant furnishings and Italian-marble baths, giving them the feel and look of a posh English country home. But you'll pay dearly to stay here, and the aesthetic doesn't really capture the jazzy exuberance of New Orleans—the hotel feels as though it were airlifted from London or New York City and dropped down in the heart of the CBD. Some people love it; others find it stuffy. Amenities include one of the most lavish and formal restaurants in the city, a full health club, a pool, and a 24-hour concierge.

More contemporary and urbane in ambience than W's French Quarter property, the 423-room **W New Orleans** (333 Poydras St., 504/525-9444 or 888/625-5144, www.whotels.com) occupies a 23-story downtown skyscraper near the shops of Riverwalk, the art galleries of the Warehouse District, and New Orleans's white elephant of a casino. The hotel is a favorite with young business execs, owing to its state-of-the-art wiring and high-tech gadgetry (in-room high-speed Internet, CD players, DVD players, cordless dual-line speakerphones), as well as its sexy and sleek Zoe restaurant and ultracool Whiskey Blue cocktail lounge. Rooms on the upper floors have exceptional river and city views. Bliss Spa bath products, marble baths, and monochromatic black, gray, and white color schemes complete the oh-so-cool look and feel.

There's no better time to visit the **Fairmont New Orleans** (123 Baronne St., 504/529-7111 or 800/527-4727, www.fairmont.com), or at least walk through it, than during the Christmastime holidays, when the lobby is transformed—a long canopy of white "angel hair" hangs the length of the marble entryway, with shiny ornaments, trimmed trees, and poinsettias as far as you can see. The entire hotel was dramatically renovated in the late 1990s at a cost of $51 million, and up until Hurricane Katrina, it had been living up to its Old World reputation as one of the most fashionable addresses in the South since 1893. The hotel closed after receiving extensive damage and is expected to reopen in 2007. The hotel has 700 rooms with marble baths, down pillows, and other cushy amenities, plus a rooftop health club with tennis, a pool, and spa. The Sazerac Bar and Grill is another highlight of this property that fringes the Quarter along Canal Street—it's named for the Sazerac cocktail, which was invented in New Orleans in 1859. The only drawback can be flaws in the service—it's a big hotel with a big-hotel feel, and sometimes staff can be slow with requests.

New Orleans had nothing even vaguely resembling a hip, contemporary hotel before **◖ International House** (221 Camp St., 504/553-9550 or 800/633-5770, www.ihhotel.com) opened in the late 1990s. Since then, a few other properties have taken a similarly enlightened approach to hospitality, but this beacon of beige, which occupies a 1906 Beaux-Arts building, remains one of the coolest addresses in town. The restrained decorating scheme of muted colors is not without whimsy: Seven times each year the lobby is reborn to celebrate a particular festival or holiday that's dear to New Orleans, from All Souls'/All Saints' Day in early November to the voodoo-based St. John's Eve in late June. Each of the 119 compact but light-filled rooms, which are all nonsmoking, has a CD player and a selection of disks featuring the music of New Orleans luminaries, and neatly matted black-

RECYCLE, REUSE

New Orleans has long had a tendency to reuse and adapt old buildings in innovative ways. This is especially true of the city's hotels and inns, several of which were constructed for entirely different purposes. Here are a few properties with especially colorful histories:

Drury Inn and Suites (820 Poydras St., 504/529-7800 or 800/378-7946, www.druryinn.com): This midprice chain inhabits the 1917 Cumberland Telephone Building and still contains the carefully preserved ornamental lobby staircase and Waterford crystal chandeliers that greeted past generations of phone company employees – a pre-dotcom example of office excess.

Hilton New Orleans/St. Charles Avenue (333 St. Charles Ave., 504/524-8890 or 800/HILTONS, www.hhstcharles.com): It's only right that visitors to this swanky Hilton feel like members of some exclusive club upon entering its luxe confines. Before it was converted into the Hotel Monaco (which closed following Hurricane Katrina and was in turn converted into the Hilton), this 19-story neo-Gothic wonder, built in 1926, housed the city's Masonic Temple. If only these walls could talk....

International House (221 Camp St., 504/553-9550, www.ihhotel.com): Before opening to house a stylish hotel in 1998, this timelessly beautiful 1906 Beaux-Arts building served as one of New Orleans's leading institutions of high finance, the Louisiana Bank and Trust Company. In the 1940s the building earned its present name, International House, when it became headquarters for a newly formed nonprofit trade group whose aim was fostering world peace. It was the forerunner not only to the World Trade Center that stands at the foot of Canal Street, overlooking the Mississippi River, but to more than 300 additional world trade centers that have been established in cities all over the world. It's only appropriate, of course, that International House is today a favorite destination of dignitaries, financiers, and world travelers.

Ritz-Carlton (921 Canal St., 504/524-1331 or 800/241-3333, www.ritz-carlton.com): Lay your head where Liz Claiborne and Cuisinart once reigned; this deluxe hotel, which sustained heavy Katrina damage but reopened in December 2006, is in a former department store building that once housed Kress and the Maison Blanche, built back in the days when people knew how to build department stores (1910, to be exact). It's only appropriate, by the way, that Liz Claiborne still has a strong following among fashionable shoppers in New Orleans; she's a direct descendant of Louisiana's first governor, William C. C. Claiborne.

The Whitney (610 Poydras St., 504/581-4222 or 800/996-3426, www.wyndham.com): Built in 1883, the Whitney was for many years one of New Orleans's most prestigious banking institutions. Now it's a 93-room boutique hotel, but you can still get a sense of the building's previous incarnation by exploring the ground-floor restaurant, 56 Degrees, which occupies the former bank lobby. Teller windows are still visible, flanking the kitchen. And the old safety-deposit vault is now a private dining room.

and-white photos of jazz greats line the walls. Other amenities include two-line speakerphones, high-speed Internet, vases filled with Louisiana wildflowers, and bathrooms with Aveda spa products. Suites have whirlpool tubs. There's no pool, but you can work out in the fitness center. Given the fashionable clientele it courts, it's no surprise that the hotel's Loa Bar is a favorite spot for well-coiffed, dressed-in-black sorts to rub elbows and mingle. And the restaurant, Lemon Grass, serves superb Pan-Asian fare.

The International House team, headed by owner Sean Cummings, also operates a more intimate and even more luxurious property nearby, **Loft 523** (523 Gravier St., 504/200-6523 or 504/553-9550, www.loft523.com), which may just be the most edgy and distinctive boutique hotel in the South. Starting from its airy, minimalist lobby with white walls and earthy tones, Loft 523 deviates from the typically ornate style of many New Orleans properties. This no-smoking place is sexy, and swank, with the emphasis squarely on contemporary urban design. The 16 SoHo loft–inspired rooms and two penthouse suites (with garden terraces) have low-slung, mod furnishings, luxuriant Frette linens, and plenty of high-tech gadgetry (Sony five-speaker CD stereos, DVD surround-sound TVs, Wi-Fi, cordless phones). Each of the glass-and-limestone showers has double showerheads and Aveda bath products. The hotel occupies an 1880s dry-goods warehouse in the CBD, its high ceilings and tall windows helping to create the artsy mood. The ground-floor bar is a swank spot for cocktails, but keep in mind that rooms on the second floor often pick up much of the noise from the ensuing revelry. Room service is available from the International House hotel, where you can also use the 24-hour fitness center.

The Garden District and Uptown

You'll find a great variety of accommodations in this huge neighborhood that extends for several miles upriver from the CBD. Closest in, for about 20 blocks past the CBD, you'll find a mix of inns, B&Bs, and full-service motels and hotels, most of them along St. Charles Avenue and Prytania Street. These places generally cost 10–30 percent less than comparable accommodations in either the Quarter or the CBD. The plus is that the neighborhood, even where it's somewhat built up, has its own charm and a less chaotic pace than downtown or the Quarter; it's also an easy streetcar ride or fairly short cab ride from the CBD and Quarter. The disadvantage, to some, is that you can't walk to the Quarter or CBD from here, at least not easily, and the neighborhood feels less urban—it's not as all-night and rockin'. If you're coming to New Orleans for the frenetic nightlife and nonstop revelry, you may feel out of touch over here. If you'd prefer a little more peace and quiet but still want to be near great dining and shopping, or if you're here with a family, this area, generally known as the Lower Garden District, makes a lot of sense.

Farther into the Garden District and Uptown, there aren't any full-service hotels, but you'll find several inns and B&Bs, set anywhere on the blocks between St. Charles Avenue and Magazine Street. Some of these places can feel quite removed from the city, and sometimes that's in a good way—you might find yourself staying on a gracious tree-lined street sandwiched between fancy homes, or a short walk from Audubon Park or the funky and laid-back shopping and dining along Magazine Street. Seasoned visitors to New Orleans, who've "been there and done that," often favor accommodations in this neighborhood over those in the more touristy or business-oriented neighborhoods downriver.

HOTELS AND MOTELS
Under $50

A popular budget hostel, the **Marquette House** (2253 Carondelet St., 504/523-3014, www.hiayh.org) is a quirky complex of 19th-century wood-frame buildings in the Garden District, a short walk from the St. Charles Avenue streetcar. The hostel has 155 beds and eight private rooms, and it has 24-hour access once you've checked in during more limited hours (call ahead for details, as the hours can vary). It offers fenced parking (for a small fee), a laundry, a patio and picnic area, storage lockers, and a communal kitchen. Dorm rooms are separated by gender and include about 10–15 beds a room. Rates start at $25 for dorm units, depending on the time of year and whether there's a big event in town. Reservations are absolutely essential if you're planning to come for Mardi Gras or Jazz Fest, and they're a good idea in summer, when many students are traveling to New Orleans. Tulane and Loyola are a short streetcar ride or long stroll away. The hostel does accept MasterCard and Visa. The Marquette is funky and well located, but it's developed a reputation in recent years for substandard cleanliness and uneven service. It's fine when you're seeking rock-bottom rates and don't plan to be in your room much, but the private rooms aren't much cheaper than some of the chain motels in the area and so probably not worth the bother.

$50-100

A great location close to the CBD and Garden District, and accommodations set inside historic 19th-century buildings, set the **Quality Inn and Suites St. Charles** (1319 St. Charles Ave., 504/522-0187 or 877/424-6423, www.qualityinn.com) apart from other midrange chain properties. It also has free off-street parking and Wi-Fi. The rooms themselves, as well as the level of service, are fairly standard (although all come with refrigerators and microwaves), but this is a dependable option with a nice swimming pool.

The unabashedly low-tech but supercharming (and affordable) **St. Charles Guest House** (1748 Prytania St., 504/523-6556, www.stcharlesguesthouse.com) makes the perfect roost if you're looking to save a few bucks and don't mind rooms without TVs or phones (although rooms do have Wi-Fi). The staff is friendly and helpful, always willing to offer advice and directions to the many Europeans, students, artists, and other independent-spirited travelers who stay here. The modest pension has 30 guest rooms set among four adjoining historic buildings; the rock-bottom–priced units share bathrooms (these start at just $50 nightly for a single). There's a pool and courtyard out back shaded by banana trees, and continental breakfast is included. The property received some roof and ceiling damage from Katrina and made a number of upgrades and renovations in 2006 as a result.

$100-150

The family-owned **Avenue Garden Hotel** (1509 St. Charles Ave., 504/521-8000 or 800/379-5322, www.avenuegardenhotel.com) has just 23 rooms set in a restored 1897 building with gracious balconies and ample charm. It's within walking distance of the CBD and a 10-minute streetcar ride from the French Quarter. The rooms mix reproduction New Orleans–inspired antiques with such up-to-date amenities as CD radio/alarm clocks, hair dryers, irons and boards, and voice mail; suites have VCRs, microwaves, refrigerators, and sofa sleepers—accommodations are simple but comfortable, more than satisfactory considering the price—rates often dip below $100 during slower times.

Popeyes and Copeland's restaurant magnate Al Copeland opened the art deco **Clarion Grand Boutique Hotel** (2001 St. Charles Ave., 504/558-9966 or 877/424-6423, www.clarionhotel.com), a 44-room low-rise property with a delightful and convenient location on St. Charles, smack in the middle of the Garden District. This is a great little hotel with fair rates and pretty good service compared with similar properties in New Orleans. It's also the only art deco hotel in the city. Try to get a unit with a balcony overlooking St. Charles (keeping in mind that traffic noise can be a bummer). Rooms have big windows that let in plenty of light, and all have refrigerators, microwaves, coffeemakers, safes, free Wi-Fi, dual-line phones with voice mail, and bold, attractive furnishings. Some rooms have hot tubs. Copeland's Cheesecake Bistro (which was closed at press time but slated to reopen in 2007) provides room service, and continental breakfast is included in the rates.

A top-notch property Uptown, the 100-room **Hampton Inn Garden District** (3626 St. Charles Ave., 504/899-9990 or 800/426-7866, www.hamptoninn.com) occupies an attractive midrise building that's a short streetcar ride from Audubon Park, Tulane, and Loyola. It's a bit farther from the CBD and French Quarter than most of the other hotels on St. Charles, but that's a plus if you're seeking a quieter

ACCOMMODATIONS

ACCOMMODATIONS

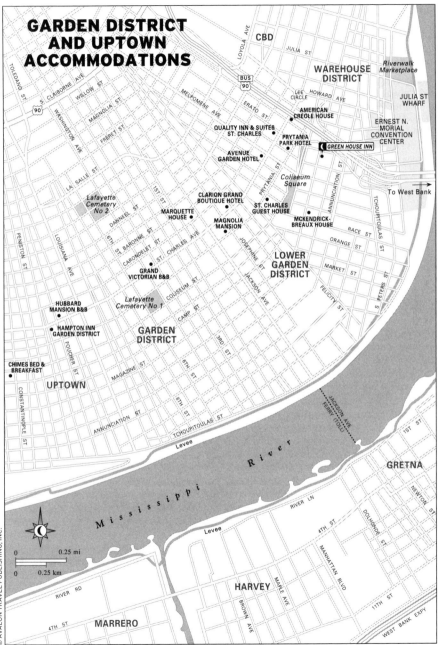

GARDEN DISTRICT AND UPTOWN ACCOMMODATIONS

CBD

LOYOLA AVE

JULIA ST

WAREHOUSE DISTRICT

Riverwalk Marketplace

BUS 90

LEE CIRCLE

HOWARD AVE

JULIA ST WHARF

MELPOMENE AVE

ERATO ST

AMERICAN CREOLE HOUSE

ERNEST N. MORIAL CONVENTION CENTER

S. CLAIBORNE AVE

WILLOW ST

MAGNOLIA ST

QUALITY INN & SUITES ST. CHARLES

PRYTANIA PARK HOTEL

GREEN HOUSE INN

WASHINGTON AVE

FRERET ST

AVENUE GARDEN HOTEL

TOLEDANO ST

90

Coliseum Square

ANNUNCIATION ST

To West Bank

LA SALLE ST

Lafayette Cemetery No 2

1ST ST

CLARION GRAND BOUTIQUE HOTEL

ST. CHARLES GUEST HOUSE

TCHOUPITOULAS ST

DANNEEL ST

MARQUETTE HOUSE

MAGNOLIA MANSION

MCKENDRICK-BREAUX HOUSE

RACE ST

LOUISIANA AVE

6TH ST

ST. BARONNE ST

CARONDELET ST

ST. CHARLES AVE

JOSEPHINE ST

ORANGE ST

S. PETERS ST

PENSTON ST

GRAND VICTORIAN B&B

COLISEUM ST

Lafayette Cemetery No 1

JACKSON AVE

LOWER GARDEN DISTRICT

MARKET ST

FELICITY ST

HUBBARD MANSION B&B

CAMP ST

HAMPTON INN GARDEN DISTRICT

FOUCHER ST

GARDEN DISTRICT

3RD ST

CHIMES BED & BREAKFAST

MAGAZINE ST

4TH ST

UPTOWN

CONSTANTINOPLE ST

ANNUNCIATION ST

8TH ST

TCHOUPITOULAS ST

Levee

JACKSON AVE FERRY (TOLL)

GRETNA

1ST ST

Mississippi River

NEWTON ST

RIVER LN

DOLHONDE ST

Levee

4TH ST

MANHATTAN BLVD

11TH ST

0   0.25 mi

0   0.25 km

HARVEY

WEST BANK EXPY

RIVER RD

MARLE AVE

4TH ST

MARRERO

BROWN AVE

© AVALON TRAVEL PUBLISHING, INC.

experience—this stretch of St. Charles is less developed and has fewer tall buildings. This Hampton Inn is above average as the chain goes, with particularly bright and well-kept rooms; some suites have whirlpool tubs.

One of the Garden District's nicer little properties, the **Prytania Park Hotel** (1525 Prytania St., 504/524-0427 or 888/498-7591, www.prytaniaparkhotel.com) has 62 attractively furnished rooms set in two buildings at the lower end of the neighborhood, an easy streetcar ride from the CBD (St. Charles Avenue is just a block away). The hotel has some great features, such as loft suites geared toward families, which have queen-size beds on the ground floor and sleeping areas in a loft up above. Another plus is the lobby store with snack foods. In every room you'll find refrigerators, microwaves, ceiling fans, and reproduction antiques, although the decor has become a bit dated through the years, and some improvements could greatly improve the place, especially in the bathrooms. The grounds are verdantly landscaped with cheery courtyards, and the staff is generally very helpful. If you don't mind giving up some of the amenities found at other hotels, such as a pool or restaurant, this is a decent find.

INNS AND BED-AND-BREAKFASTS
$50-100

The **⟨C⟩ Green House Inn** (1212 Magazine St., 504/525-1333 or 800/966-1303, www.thegreenhouseinn.com) offers a change of pace from so many of New Orleans's richly urbane inns and B&Bs. The decorative scheme of this Greek Revival 1840 town house is tropical and whimsical, from the pool out back shaped like a palm tree to the verdant and colorful landscaping. It's also one of the lower-priced properties in town, set in the Lower Garden District, an area that continues to gentrify as new homeowners move in and fix up the many great old houses in this neighborhood. Discounts are offered to college and grad-school students and to guests staying a week or longer. Rooms are well outfitted with king-size beds,

TVs with DVDs, minirefrigerators, phones with modems, Aveda bath products, Wi-Fi, ceiling fans and central air, and CD/clock radios—the kinds of amenities you'd expect of a much pricier hotel. The inn has a small workout room and a hot tub alongside the pool. The patio by the pool is clothing-optional. The Green House Inn has a loyal gay/lesbian following, but all are welcome.

$100-150

A longtime favorite set well Uptown, between the Garden District and Audubon Park (and within easy strolling distance of Magazine Street shopping and dining and the St. Charles Avenue streetcar), the **Chimes Bed and Breakfast** (1146 Constantinople St., 504/488-4640 or 800/729-4640, www.chimesneworleans.com) has just five lovingly furnished rooms facing a lush courtyard. Each has private bath, a queen-size mahogany or iron bed, stained- and leaded-glass windows, refrigerator, French doors, high ceilings, phones with answering machines, Wi-Fi, and cable TV; some have fireplaces, and two have twin beds that can accommodate kids or additional guests. This is a great base for exploring Uptown, a wonderful neighborhood that some visitors miss out on because they devote so much of their time to the French Quarter. The inn has a devoted repeat following and tends to book up early, so reserve as far ahead as possible. An expansive continental breakfast is included.

$150-250

The Garden District's fanciest accommodation is **Magnolia Mansion** (2127 Prytania St., 504/412-9500 or 888/222-9235, www.magnoliamansion.com), a stately 1850s wedding cake of a house designed by James H. Calrow, who also constructed Anne Rice's nearby former home at 1239 1st Street. The house served as the headquarters for the U.S. Red Cross from 1939 through 1954. It strikes a dashing figure from the street, with its 11 elaborate Corinthian columns and double-galleried veranda; moss-draped live-oak trees and magnolias tower over the grounds. There are nine rooms, which vary in price according to their size and amenities. All have TV with VCRs and high-speed Internet, and there's limited free parking (based on availability). Honeymooners and others celebrating special occasions favor this property for its over-the-top furnishings, such as floor-to-ceiling velvet drapes, mahogany four-poster beds, cast-iron claw-foot tubs, double whirlpool tubs, and Toulouse Lautrec–inspired murals; the Vampire Suite contains a massive hand-carved bed that's a replica of the one used in the movie *Interview with the Vampire*.

There are just three units at the **American Creole House** (1124 St. Charles Ave., 504/522-7777 or 800/999-7891, www.creolehouse. com), but each is a full suite with both a queen bed and queen sleeper sofa, a separate living/dining area, and either a full kitchen or kitchenette. The Balcony Suite, which overlooks St. Charles Avenue, is a favorite. These suites are ideal for business travelers in town for a while, families, or others seeking plenty of room to spread out. The inn is just a couple of blocks upriver from Lee Circle, an easy stroll to the CBD and Warehouse District.

McKendrick-Breaux House (1474 Magazine St., 504/586-1700 or 888/570-1700, www.mckendrick-breaux.com), on the edge of Magazine Street's antiques row in the up-and-coming Lower Garden District, nearly fell to the wrecking ball several years ago before preservation-minded owner Eddie Breaux turned it into a B&B. The three-story 1865 mansion, once part of a plantation, has been meticulously restored. Many rooms contain such architectural details as original ceiling medallions, claw-foot tubs, and plaster moldings. There are nine rooms and, unusual for New Orleans B&Bs, each can accommodate up to three guests, making this a great choice for friends traveling together or parents with one child. Three rooms open onto a foliage-filled courtyard; each has a private bath, high-

thread-count linens, original artwork by area artists, free local phone calls and data ports, cable TV, central heat and air, and robes, hair dryers, and irons and boards. Considering the amenities and first-rate staff, this is one of the best deals in the city, with rates beginning at about $150 nightly, which includes an extensive continental breakfast.

If you don't have the chance to visit the famed plantations along the River Road, you can at least get a sense of some of them with a stay at the **Grand Victorian B&B** (2727 St. Charles Ave., 504/895-1104 or 800/977-0008, www.gvbb.com). Each of the seven high-ceilinged rooms in this fanciful 1893 Victorian mansion are named for Louisiana plantation homes and contain the kinds of museumlike furniture you'd find at places such as Oak Alley and Nottoway. Destrehan Room contains a dramatic 1850s Renaissance Revival high-back bed, Evergreen a half-tester Eastlake Victorian bed—whatever room you choose, expect a big, oversize antique bed that you may not want to get out of each morning. The tall windows in the parlor overlook the clanging St. Charles Avenue streetcar, and continental breakfast is served in a sunny dining room or on the porte-cochere balcony.

The **Hubbard Mansion B&B** (3535 St. Charles Ave., 504/897-3535, www.hubbard-mansion.com) may look like one of those grand Greek Revival mansions along the Mississippi River—in fact, it's a brand-new construction, based on a fine antebellum mansion on a bluff in Natchez, Mississippi. An advantage for some guests is that the place has the modern amenities and solid feel of a new building, complete with thick walls and central air-conditioning. Rooms overflow with authentic period (and some reproduction) antiques, such as massive crown-canopy beds with rich linens, mahogany armoires, and marble-top dressers. This is a romantic nest, and it's right along St. Charles, a short trolley ride from downtown and the Quarter.

Mid-City

Within the city limits, it's also worth considering for a stay in up-and-coming Mid-City, a neighborhood that was hit rather hard with flooding during Katrina but that has rebounded better than ever. Mid-City comprises the blocks along or just off Esplanade Avenue north from the French Quarter to City Park, home to the art museum, as well as the area north along Canal Street and east-west–running Carrollton Avenue. In this area, you have about a dozen B&Bs and inns to choose from, most of them quite charming and stately. You can take the bus from here down Esplanade into the Quarter and Faubourg Marigny or take the streetcar up and down Canal Street and Carrollton Avenue, but it's generally easiest if you have a car when staying up here—walking to the French Quarter can be managed in about 15–30 minutes, but it can require walking through some dodgy sections and is not recommended after dark. A burgeoning little district of eateries and shops is just below City Park and near most of these inns, and the neighborhood itself is quite charming and getting more appealing every year.

INNS AND BED-AND-BREAKFASTS
$100-150

Don't let the Irish name fool you; the ◖ **1896 O'Malley House** (120 S. Pierce St., 504/488-5896 or 866/226-1896, www.1896omalleyhouse.com) isn't themed after the Emerald Isle. But it is named for one of the city's most prominent Irish citizens of the late 19th century, Dominick O'Malley, a newspaper publisher credited with exposing the corruption of local politicos. Innkeepers Brad Smith and Larry Watts own this gracious Colonial Revival mansion with original cypress-wood mantels, pocket doors, and other artful details. The congenial owners have done a fantastic job completely renovating the inn since they bought it in 2004, filling the gracious rooms with exceptional antiques, handsome

1896 O'Malley House

Oriental rugs, plush four-poster beds, and elegant armoires and bed stands, yet the rates here are far lower than what you'd pay for similarly handsome accommodations in the French Quarter or Garden District. Most rooms have whirlpool tubs, and all have cable TV and Wi-Fi. The house is in a steadily gentrifying section of Mid-City, just steps from the Canal Street streetcar and within walking distance of several restaurants. An especially bounteous continental breakfast is included.

Appropriately near the New Orleans Art Museum in City Park, **Degas House** (2306 Esplanade Ave., 504/821-5009, www.degas-house.com) is not only an inn but a museum—it's the world's only home or studio that housed French impressionist painter Edgar Degas that's open to the public. Degas lived in the house for about a year in 1872 while visiting his maternal relatives, who were successful New Orleans cotton merchants. The artist painted 22 works while living here. The B&B

contains nine rooms that vary considerably in size and luxury. All have full baths, soaring ceilings, and hardwood floors with well-chosen antiques; some larger suites have private balconies and whirlpool tubs, and one can accommodate extra guests on a sleeper sofa; three units have fireplaces. Guests get a free tour of the museum section of the house, which is hung with framed reproductions of many Degas works. All rooms have cable TV, Wi-Fi, and phones with voice mail, and continental breakfast is included.

$150-250

There are few spots in New Orleans, let alone places to spend the night, where you can experience the city while feeling totally removed from the hustle, bustle, and crowds. The fabled bed-and-breakfast **House on Bayou Road** (2275 Bayou Rd., 504/945-0992 or 800/882-2968, www.houseonbayouroad. com) sits about midway between the French Quarter and City Park, along Esplanade Ridge. Although intimate, the place is run with the polish and grandeur of a small luxury hotel, a big reason that actors, musicians, and other notables like to stay here when in town. There's a full concierge service, ample off-street parking, full and filling Southern breakfasts—they'll even arrange for you to be picked up and delivered here by limo from the airport. The two-acre property is set back from the road and lush with herb and flower gardens, courtyard patios, and ponds. The main house, a former indigo plantation, dates to 1798 and contains three guest rooms and suites; there are four more rooms in a sec-

© ANDREW COLLINS

House on Bayou Road

ond building as well as a luxury Creole cottage. Units have Wi-Fi and contain mostly 19th-century antiques, wet bars with complimentary sherry, some in-room Jacuzzis and fireplaces, and feather beds; the cottage has Audubon prints, a queen-size bed and sleeper sofa, a fireplace, DVD player, CD player, and Jacuzzi, plus a private porch with rocking chairs. Guests can also take a dip in the pool or relax in the hot tub. The property is a short drive from the Quarter, but there are also some great restaurants nearby in the Mid-City neighborhood.

Greater New Orleans

METAIRIE, KENNER, AND THE AIRPORT

Like New Orleans East, these suburbs west of New Orleans make sense as a place to stay only if you have a car and are looking to save some money. Rates out here generally run 20–40 percent lower than in the CBD for comparable chain hotels. It's also helpful to stay out here if you need to be near the airport. Quite a few new and well-maintained chain hotels have opened in Kenner (site of the airport) and, to a lesser extent, Metairie; there's a lot of business out this way, so the area makes sense for corporate travelers. It's also where you'll find several all-suites hotels that specialize in long-term stays. Although built-up and in some cases a bit industrial, Metairie and Kenner are not unpleasant places, and they are close to scads of good restaurants and shopping centers. All the hotels out this way offer free parking to guests for the duration of their stays. Guests can often leave their cars for a nominal charge (or even free of charge) after staying for at least one night. Last, this is a good base if you plan to spend only part of your time in New Orleans and the rest on the North Shore, visiting the plantations along the River Road, or even if you're heading to Baton Rouge during the day.

Hotels and Motels

$50-100: A meticulously kept midprice business hotel three miles from the airport, the **Hilton Garden Inn** (4535 Williams Blvd., Kenner, 504/712-0504 or 800/774-1500, www.hiltongardeninn.com) is right by the Treasure Chest Casino and the Pontchartrain Convention Center. It's not exactly a charming location, but it's convenient, and there are dozens of restaurants within a short drive. Interstate access is easy, and the price is right. Best of all, rooms have plenty of perks, such as microwaves, coffeemakers, refrigerators, voicemail and data ports, large work desks, and dual-line phones; suites have sleeper sofas in the sitting room, thus easily accommodating four guests. There are also a business center, pool, and gym.

The moderately priced **Comfort Suites Kenner** (2710 Idaho Ave., Kenner, 504/466-6066 or 877/424-6423, www.comfortsuites.com) is a relatively new building just off the interstate and very close to the airport. Rooms are spacious, all with wet bars, minirefrigerators, two phones, and high-speed Internet. There are indoor and outdoor pools, a hot tub, and a gym, and continental breakfast is included. A very reliable property all-around.

Just north of the airport and close to Esplanade Mall, the **Fairfield Inn Airport** (1801 32nd St., Kenner, 504/443-9800 or 800/228-2800, www.fairfieldinn.com) has four floors of modern, well-kept rooms with work desks and good lamps, high-speed Internet, iron and boards, and—in some rooms—refrigerators. A pool, exercise room, and whirlpool are on-site, and Colonial Golf and Country Club is a short drive away, along with several restaurants.

$100-150: Of the several long-term-stay accommodations out near the airport, the **TownPlace Suites by Marriott** (5424 Citrus Blvd., Harahan, 504/818-2400 or 800/364-1200, www.marriott.com) offers among the most luxurious and pleasant accommodations. The compound of spacious, contemporary townhomes sits right off Clearview Parkway (U.S. 90), near the Huey P. Long Bridge, which connects Harahan with the West Bank. The airport is five miles west, and downtown New Orleans is 10 miles east. Each of the 125 rooms has a fully equipped kitchen, and some have two bedrooms (all units can sleep up to four guests). There's a 24-hour gym, pets are welcome, continental breakfast is offered on weekdays, and there's a pool and barbecue area. The hotel is geared toward business travelers, but it also makes sense for families or friends traveling together and staying in town for an extended period. Rates are lowest if you rent by the week—they start as low as around $700 per

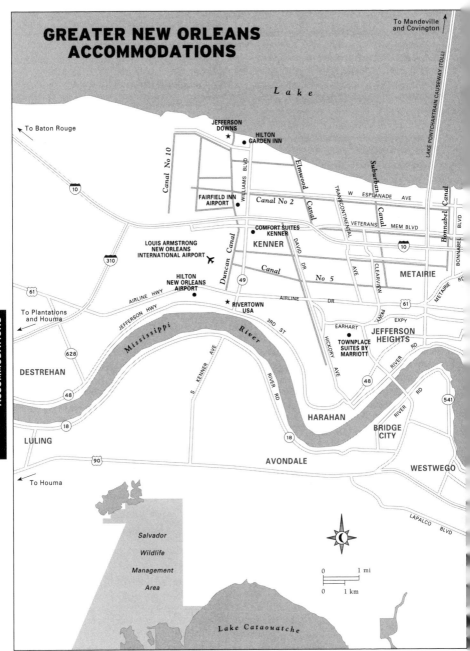

GREATER NEW ORLEANS ACCOMMODATIONS

ACCOMMODATIONS

To Mandeville and Covington

Lake

LAKE PONTCHARTRAIN CAUSEWAY (TOLL)

To Baton Rouge

JEFFERSON DOWNS
HILTON GARDEN INN

Canal No 10

WILLIAMS BLVD

Elmwood

Suburban

Canal

W   ESPLANADE   AVE

TRANSCONTINENTAL

Bonnabel Canal

BONNABEL BLVD

Canal No 2

FAIRFIELD INN AIRPORT

VETERANS   MEM BLVD

COMFORT SUITES KENNER

Duncan Canal

KENNER

DAVID DR

AVE

CLEARVIEW

10

METAIRIE

METAIRIE RD

LOUIS ARMSTRONG NEW ORLEANS INTERNATIONAL AIRPORT

310

Canal   No 5

61

HILTON NEW ORLEANS AIRPORT

AIRLINE HWY

49

AIRLINE   DR

61

EXPY

PKWY

RIVERTOWN USA

3RD ST

EARHART

JEFFERSON HEIGHTS

JEFFERSON HWY

Mississippi   River

RIVER RD

HICKORY

TOWNPLACE SUITES BY MARRIOTT

AVE

RIVER   RD

To Plantations and Houma

S. KENNER AVE

48

628

DESTREHAN

HARAHAN

RIVER   RD

541

48

BRIDGE CITY

18

LULING

18

AVONDALE

WESTWEGO

90

To Houma

LAPALCO   BLVD

Salvador

Wildlife

Management

Area

0   1 mi

0   1 km

Lake Cataouatche

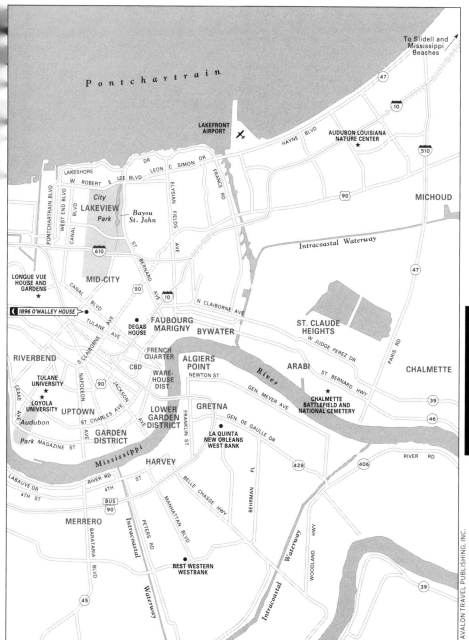

ACCOMMODATIONS

© AVALON TRAVEL PUBLISHING, INC.

week (or about $2,200 per month). The hotel was down for quite a while after Katrina, but it's a young property that's in great shape since it reopened.

Although the chain as a whole can be hit-or-miss in quality, the **Hilton New Orleans Airport** (901 Airline Dr., 504/469-5000 or 800/774-1500, www.hilton.com) is a lavish and well-run property practically a stone's throw from New Orleans International Airport. This is one of the priciest of the airport accommodations, but it does have its perks, including spacious rooms with marble-accented bathrooms, minibars, and such recreational amenities as a walking/jogging track, tennis court, pool, and fitness center. There is a charge for hotel parking.

THE WEST BANK

The large area on the West Bank of the Mississippi River, across from New Orleans, includes an area called Algiers Point that actually falls within New Orleans city limits; here, too, are the close-in suburbs of Harvey, Gretna, and Marrero. A fair number of chain properties are out this way, but it's not an especially convenient base for exploring the city, and only a handful of accommodations on the West Bank are included in this chapter. In general, you face the same pros and cons out here as you do by the airport or in New Orleans East; additionally, there's a toll charge for crossing the Mississippi River, and the West Bank suburbs feel quite removed from the city, even though some of them are actually a slightly shorter drive than from the airport into downtown New Orleans.

Hotels and Motels

$50-100: A great value if you don't mind being across the river, the 140-room **Best Western Westbank** (1700 Lapalco Blvd., Harvey, 504/366-5369 or 800/780-7234, www.bestwesternwestbank.com) is about a 20- to 25-minute drive from New Orleans proper. The advantages are saving a few bucks on a room that would cost you twice as much in the city and having free parking in a safe suburban area. It has a pool, hot tub, landscaped grounds, and a courtyard bar, guest laundry, continental breakfast, and weekly Cajun cookouts, and rooms have refrigerators.

About a 10- to 15-minute drive south of the city, **La Quinta New Orleans West Bank** (50 Terry Pkwy., Gretna, 504/368-5600 or 800/531-5900, www.lq.com) is a dependable midrange option with on-site laundry and continental breakfast.

FOOD

It's not especially unusual these days to say that a city's restaurants rank, collectively, among its top three or four attractions. With the culinary revolution that began in the 1980s and has continued unabated ever since, travelers increasingly spend as much time thinking about where they're going to eat during their vacation as they do planning their sightseeing. But food in New Orleans is more than a major attraction, it is—for more than a few visitors—the city's raison d'être. And this isn't a trend of the '90s or even '80s, unless you mean the 1880s. New Orleanians, and the travelers who adore this city, have been worshipping food as a virtual deity since at least the late 18th century, and in some circles before that. Food in this city is *that* good, and dining out is a pastime granted the utmost importance.

Serious as New Orleanians are about food—and they'll talk about it, debate it, praise it, and dissect it for hours on end—they actually observe the ritual of dining with great warmth, humor, and ease, typically consuming considerable quantities of wine and liquor along the way.

New Orleans claims plenty of handsome dining rooms: Old World spaces with dim lighting, dark-wood paneling, and gilt mirrors; slick new restaurants with curvaceous banquettes, recessed mood lighting, and larger-than-life abstract art. People here like to eat surrounded by pretty things just as much as everybody else. However, few New Orleanians would ever forgive a restaurant's so-so cooking simply because it has a beautiful interior or first-class white-glove service.

HIGHLIGHTS

◖ **Best Classic Creole Cuisine:** One of the few restaurants in Louisiana where men are expected to wear jackets, **Galatoire's** is the quintessential old-school New Orleans tradition, serving superb Creole fare from time-tested recipes (page 173).

◖ **Most Creative Cooking:** Forget about that Emeril fellow – Tom Wolfe serves some of the most dazzling contemporary fare in the South at **Peristyle,** which is tucked down a quiet street in a less-touristy part of the French Quarter (page 178).

◖ **Heftiest Sandwiches:** There's considerable debate about this category in New Orleans, but most folks agree that **Central Grocery** produces heavenly muffuletta sandwiches (page 182).

◖ **Funkiest Neighborhood Breakfast Joint:** Locals flock to **Elizabeth's,** in off-the-beaten-path Bywater section, for such memorable down-home country cooking as waffles with cooked apples, eggs with fried catfish strips, and addictive praline bacon (page 187).

◖ **Best See-and-Be-Seen Restaurant:** The domain of talented and much-adored chef John Besh, **Restaurant August** pulls in a stylish crowd of New Orleans movers-and-shakers, who delight in the restaurant's superbly crafted contemporary cuisine (page 189).

◖ **Best Special-Occasion Restaurant:** If you're celebrating a wedding anniversary

or about to propose, or you simply want to enjoy the best meal New Orleans has to offer in the most romantic setting, book a table at **Commander's Palace** (page 194).

◖ **Quirkiest Place for Great Cooking:** You have to walk through the bustling kitchen at funky **Jacques-Imo's Cafe,** a wonderful neighborhood restaurant in the Carrollton area of Uptown, known for innovative food, huge portions, and sassy service (page 196).

◖ **Best Brunch Venue:** Part of the fun of brunching at **Ralph's on the Park** is sampling the creative and beautifully presented nouvelle Creole cuisine, but the other benefit is that you can explore adjacent City Park, with its botanical garden and verdant paths, after you eat (page 203).

◖ **Best Desserts:** For more than a century **Angelo Brocato's** has doled out wonderful house-made ice cream and Italian pastries from its quaint Mid-City storefront space, which was virtually rebuilt in 2006 following heavy flooding from Hurricane Katrina (page 206).

◖ **Best Place to Eat in the Burbs:** In a nondescript section of the suburban New Orleans neighborhood of Metairie, **Drago's** has earned a cult following for its incredibly delicious barbecue oysters and other fresh Cajun and Creole seafood dishes (page 207).

LOOK FOR ◖ TO FIND THE BEST DINING.

FOOD

That's all well and good, but in this town, if you want your restaurant to survive, you worry about one and only one thing, and that's the food on the plate.

It then follows that New Orleans seems to have more divey and dilapidated restaurants serving heavenly food than any city in America. Just as people here won't support a fancy-looking eatery with mediocre cooking, they'll flock to some dumpy hole-in-the-wall on the worst crime-ridden block in the city if the place serves tasty food. The paint may be peeling, the floorboards may be slanted and cracked, the place may not even look sanitary. But the most catastrophic aesthetic miscues can be overlooked if the kitchen turns out a half-decent jambalaya or oyster-and-brie soup.

It's not unusual, of course, for a raffish and run-down restaurant serving good food to become popular *because* it's such a dump—diehard food lovers like the idea that they've worked a little and perhaps even taken their lives into their own hands to taste the best of a particular dish or style of cuisine. But in New Orleans, this sort of thinking is taken to great extremes. One suspects that more than a few restaurateurs have intentionally neglected the appearance of their dining rooms, just to boost their approval rating with hipsters seeking out peculiar places to eat.

These rules apply to the city's quirkier, home-style restaurants, mostly neighborhood joints with modest aspirations, run by cooks who simply want to make good food and share it with people. For a restaurant to become truly respected and well regarded, and ideally covered by the national food media, it generally does have to offer a charming ambience, fine service, and excellent food. The competition in New Orleans among destination restaurants—places that visitors make a special point of dining in—is fierce. Right off the bat, the city has about two dozen restaurants that have been famous for more than 50 years, and some of them for well more than a century.

Then you have the chef celebs, such as Emeril Lagasse, Susan Spicer, and virtually any member of the illustrious Brennan family. These highly regarded restaurateurs, along with many of their peers, each have at least two restaurants around town, and every time a name chef in New Orleans opens a new place, it garners immediate attention from the editors of glossy food and travel magazines. Finally, there are the so-called neighborhood restaurants, found mostly in Uptown and Mid-City, slightly off the tourist track. It's a bit of a myth that these places are little-publicized secrets that few tourists know about. Many of today's travelers rank dining out among their favorite activities when they visit a city, and they seek out those very neighborhood restaurants, especially in a place such as New Orleans. First-time visitors may not know as much about places such as Clancy's, Jacques-Imo's, Feelings Cafe, and Angelo Brocato's, but after their second and third trips to New Orleans, they're making regular forays to these and the many other superb neighborhood cafes around town.

DRESS

Casual attire is the norm outside New Orleans, except at a few high-end spots in Baton Rouge. New Orleans can be dressy, which can be uncomfortable during the warmer months and just plain annoying to many visitors who come here with casual duds expecting to have a gay old time. It seems to be more the old-time upper-crust local families, politicos, and business leaders who perpetuate the affection for formal dress at a handful of New Orleans's most upscale eateries. Or maybe it's all a plot hatched by the New Orleans clothing manufacturer Wemco, the largest producer of neckties in the world. In any case, if you don't like playing dress-up, don't—you'll find plenty of superb restaurants in town that don't require ties or jackets.

RESTAURANT PRICES

After the phone number of most restaurants included in this book, the average range of the cost of dinner entrées has been provided (e.g.,

$5–15). This is a general range that does not take into account the occasional high-priced special or unusual dish on a menu. For coffeehouses, gourmet markets, and some of the fast-food–oriented eateries in the book, no range has been given. And for restaurants where dinner is not served, the range of the cost of lunch entrées has been given.

Cuisines

TRADITIONAL CREOLE AND CAJUN

Creole cooking is the true ethnic cuisine of a city that has no single ethnicity, but by and large its influences are French and West African, owing to its having been prepared early on for French families by their African slaves. The bounty of fresh seafood in nearby waters led to Creole cuisine's reliance on fish and shellfish, and the city's Spanish, German, and later American influences also contribute to this distinctive cuisine that is found nowhere else in the world, although it bears some similarities to the Low Country cuisine of the Coastal Carolinas and Georgia. Traditionally, Creole cuisine has been wholly distinct from Cajun cooking, although they share French traditions and an emphasis on seafood. These days, the line between Creole and Cajun cooking has blended considerably, despite the fact that ardent supporters of both styles of cuisine insist the two are as different as night and day. The best Creole restaurants in New Orleans usually serve a few (or quite a few) dishes of Cajun origin, but most of southern Louisiana's Cajun restaurants, excepting some high-end nouvelle places, serve little in the way of the Creole cooking common to New Orleans.

Butter, cream, herbs, salt, and pepper are key components of Creole cuisine, the same being true to some extent for Cajun fare, although lard is used more often than butter and cream in the latter style. For both styles of cooking, the so-called holy culinary trinity of bell peppers, celery, and onions cooked in a roux of oil and flour is the foundation for countless dishes. Cajun cooking is often more spicy than Creole cuisine, although neither style uses truly hot seasoning as much as many visitors seem to imagine. Cooks in Louisiana use spices and chilies liberally, however, so if your tongue or digestive system is sensitive to this sort of thing, ask your server for advice on which dishes to avoid.

It's also often said that Creole cooking is "city" cuisine, while Cajun cooking is served mostly out in the country. In part for this reason, you won't find all that many true Cajun restaurants in New Orleans or even the towns around it—better to explore the Cajun parishes west and southwest of New Orleans to find these, especially around the cities of Houma, New Iberia, and Lafayette. Creole cuisine, on the other hand, is ubiquitous in New Orleans, and you can detect Creole influences at just about every kind of eatery in town, from Chinese restaurants to Italian trattorias to French bistros. Chefs are always finding inventive ways to sneak Creole recipes and ingredients into other styles of cuisine.

Most of the restaurants listed in this category throughout the chapter practice a fairly traditional form of Creole and, in some cases, Cajun cooking. The many establishments where you're likely to find contemporary cooking are listed under the heading "Creative and Contemporary." But the lines between old and new, traditional and innovative do blend easily.

CREATIVE AND CONTEMPORARY

Restaurants mentioned in this category serve a style of cuisine that has come to be called many things since nationally acclaimed chefs such as California's Alice Waters and New Orleans's own Emeril Lagasse became household names among gourmet-cooking junkies: Some call it New American or fusion, others eclectic, world-beat, or just plain contemporary. In this city, chefs will sometimes describe their cooking as "modern New Orleans" or "nouvelle Creole."

The city's truly famous institutions of dining, for the most part, still serve fairly traditional Creole cuisine, but the hottest and most-talked-about restaurants in the city fall under this "Creative and Contemporary" heading. Seemingly every month, one or two new places open, though a good many have not—despite sleek and arty dining rooms and fancy ingredients spun together in unusual and sometimes bizarre ways—lasted.

There's no set criteria for qualifying as a contemporary restaurant, and the styles of cuisine at these places vary considerably. But common denominators include relatively high prices ($20 and up for entrées) and menus that give lengthy and almost dramatic descriptions of each dish, its myriad accompaniments and contents, its style of preparation, and often the origins of key ingredients.

CASUAL COOKING

A mainstay of many restaurants around the French Quarter and other visitor-oriented neighborhoods around New Orleans, casual cooking could just as easily be called pub fare or bar food. These places serve food that's more substantial than short-order diner fare, and they serve it in an atmosphere where you do sit down at a table, order from a menu, and enjoy a full-service meal. But the food is simpler and typically less expensive than what you'll find in either traditional Creole restaurants or contemporary ones. In addition to bar-and-grill establishments, pizza parlors, low-frills seafood restaurants, brewpubs, and cafes serving more than just coffee and light snacks are included under this heading. In many cities, this style of food is little more than basic sustenance—but in New Orleans, even casual cooking is usually prepared with the freshest possible ingredients and the utmost culinary integrity. It doesn't matter who you are in this city, from a regular working Joe to a hotshot politician to the average tourist, you'll always be treated to high-quality cooking.

ETHNIC

For the most part, the restaurants included in this heading serve a specific national or ethnic cuisine, usually from an East Asian or Latin American country. But there are also listings within these headings for Middle Eastern, West African, and certain European styles of cuisine. If a place serves traditional Italian food, for instance, it's likely been listed here.

New Orleans doesn't have a widespread reputation for great ethnic fare, but that's really only because it's already so famous for its own distinctive local cuisine. This is, after all, one of the world's busiest ports, and the city has been a haven for immigrants from all over the globe for centuries. Some of the Vietnamese eateries in New Orleans rank among the best in the nation, and you can also find simply stellar sushi, dim sum, and Thai food. The proximity to Latin America has helped bring in a fine range of Mexican, Cuban, and pan-Latin restaurants. In fact, if you're visiting New Orleans for more than a couple of days and you love the cooking of a particular nation, it really makes sense to try it out here. You may reason that it's better to save ethnic dining for back home, at least if you come from an area with a similarly commendable selection of such restaurants, but many New Orleans Asian, Mexican, and Middle Eastern restaurants incorporate local ingredients (especially seafood) into their menus.

Alas, the French Quarter is extremely weak on ethnic food for exactly the reason just mentioned—most tourists in New Orleans have no interest in eating Szechuan or Cuban fare. It's more the locals who dine in the city's ethnic restaurants, and so these tend to be in the most residential of the city's neighborhoods: Uptown, Mid-City, and out in the neighboring communities of Metairie, Kenner, and Gretna. The scene is changing, however, as a handful of good ethnic restaurants have opened in the Central Business District and Faubourg Marigny since the late 1990s, and the trend seems to be headed into the Quarter.

FOOD

A CULINARY GLOSSARY

Louisiana is a state with its very own food vernacular, and many of the dishes, as well as the ingredients, that appear commonly on menus in New Orleans and elsewhere in the state are little known in the rest of the world. The popularity of Cajun and Creole cooking has spread dramatically in recent years, so that many foodies living on other continents now know roughly what jambalaya and étoufée are. Still, there are quite a few terms out there that you may not be familiar with. Here follows a quick reference guide to some of the most popular Louisiana foods, along with, where relevant, a guide to pronouncing them.

Andouille (an-DEW-ee): A lean pork sausage that carries a bit of a kick; it's a staple of gumbo, red beans and rice, and many other dishes.

Bananas Foster: Invented at Brennan's restaurant, this rich dessert consists of bananas simmering in hot rum over vanilla ice cream.

Beignets (BEN-yay): Similar to fried dough, but without holes, these square French doughnuts are deep-fried and then served with a dusting of powdered sugar. To many fans, it's an act of blasphemy to eat beignets without a cup of café au lait.

Blackened (fish, chicken, etc.): This is a Cajun preparation, traditionally used on redfish but more recently applied to just about any kind of fish or meat, that involves coating the fillet with a heady pepper-thyme-onion-garlic seasoning blend and then flash-frying it in a very, very hot cast-iron pan.

Boil (as in "crawfish boil" or "crab boil"): A quintessential Cajun seafood dish, in which shellfish is boiled in a spicy broth. It's a mess to eat, and therein lies the fun.

Boudin (boo-DHAN): A Cajun smoked sausage,

often served with mustard, that consists of ground pork roast, pork liver, chopped onions, cayenne pepper, and other spices.

Café au lait (CAFF-ay oh LAY): A cup of roughly equal parts coffee and steamed milk. In Louisiana, coffee is typically laced with chicory (CHICK-ree), a spice made of ground and roasted endive roots that adds just the tiniest edge.

Courtbouillon (COOH-boo-yahn): The Cajun version of cioppino, or a tomato-based bouillabaisse (seafood stew).

Cracklin's: Not much of the food listed here could be called healthy, but cracklin's are just plain awful for you. They taste good, though. Cracklin's are just bits of pork fat, sliced up and sautéed in a skillet.

Étouffée (AY-too-FAY): From the French word meaning "to smother," étouffée is one of the most popular Cajun dishes, typically made with shrimp or crawfish and a vegetable-based (often tomato) sauce. It's usually served over rice.

Filé (FEE-lay): Ground sassafras leaves; this spice introduced by the region's Choctaw Indians is a common ingredient in gumbo and other soups and stews.

Grillades (gree-LODS): Diced meat marinated in vinegar to produce a rich gravy; it's traditionally served with grits.

Gumbo: Of the many foods people associate with southern Louisiana, gumbo may be the most famous. This soup with African origins typically contains seafood mixed with spicy andouille sausage and often a bit of okra and filé seasoning. Okra, which in the Bantu language is called *nkombo* (hence the derivation of the soup's name), is less a staple of gumbo served at contemporary Creole restaurants today,

QUICK BITES

Dining establishments that fall within this heading offer some of the most delightful and unusual "only in New Orleans" experiences you can find. It could be a greasy-spoon diner, a shack serving fried oysters, a fast-food restaurant (no national chains have been included), a pastry shop, a deli, or a hot dog cart. The idea is that you get in and get out quickly, having, in many instances, devoured a memorable meal—maybe a soft-shell-crab po'boy, a burger slathered in blue cheese, or a cup of chestnut-flavored gelato. Some of these places are open 24 hours, others only for breakfast or lunch. Many of the best ones in New Or-where newer and sometimes unexpected ingredients are sometimes substituted. Duck and andouille sausage has become a favorite gumbo combination in recent years, and crawfish, crab, and crawfish are often used. Some gumbo is served with a side of white rice, which many diners mix in with their soup. Gumbo has a muddy, brownish consistency and colors, and it should be thick and spicy but not necessarily all that hot. The dish has become something of a clichéd metaphor representing the many cultures that have made New Orleans and southern Louisiana the complex blend that it is today.

Jambalaya (jahm-buh-LYE-uh): The Cajun equivalent of Spanish paella, this rice casserole typically contains andouille or tasso plus a variety of seafood.

Macque choux (mock shoe): A popular side dish of corn scraped off the cob and smothered in tomatoes, bell peppers, onions, and a variety of spices.

Mirliton (MER-lee-ton): Known as a chayote or christophine in other parts of the world, this pear-shaped squash is commonly stuffed with seafood or meat and served the way stuffed peppers are.

Muffuletta (muff-uh-LETT-uh): Central Grocery serves the best take on these Italian cold-cut sandwiches filled with provolone, spiced ham, salami, and green-olive relish. Some restaurants serve them hot, but loyalists consider this to be a no-no.

Oysters Rockefeller: An original recipe of Antoine's, oysters Rockefeller are served baked on the half shell and topped with a bit of spinach and an absinthe-flavored liqueur, such as Pernod.

Po'boy: The name for any sandwich made with French bread; common po'boys come filled with fried oysters, fried shrimp, andouille or other smoked sausages, roast beef, or meatballs. If you order a po'boy "dressed," it'll come with lettuce, tomatoes, pickles, and other dressings or condiments.

Praline (prah-LEEN): A sugary confection made with cream, butter, caramelized brown sugar, and pecans.

Red beans and rice: It is what it sounds like, but somehow this humble meal is elevated to a loftier status when served in Louisiana. Simmered in ham hocks and tasso or andouille sausage, the kidney beans and their gravy are served over white rice. Traditionally, Mondays are the favorite time for this dish, but there's really no time when a plate of red beans and rice doesn't hit the spot.

Remoulade (reh-moo-LAHD): A mayonnaise-based sauce flavored with mustard, capers, herbs, and/or horseradish and typically served with chilled shrimp or other meats.

Roux (rue): This is the base for many Cajun and Creole dishes: It's basically flour lightly browned in oil, which is then used to thicken just about anything.

Sazerac: A favorite cocktail, best sipped at the swell-egant Sazerac Bar in the Fairmont Hotel, consisting of rye whiskey, absinthe substitute, Peychaud's bitters, and sugar; the original recipe (from 1857) called for absinthe, but since that substance was banned in 1912, Pernod or the local Herbsaint typically pinch-hits.

Tasso: Another member of the Cajun/Creole sausage family, tasso is smoked beef or pork sausage used in many stews, pastas, and other dishes.

FOOD

leans are found in out-of-the-way neighborhoods, or they feel a bit run-down inside; hey, that's part of the fun.

At these sorts of restaurants, you probably aren't going to end up doing your heart any big favors—many of them specialize in deep-fried, sugar-laden, or heavily salted grub. They're mostly inexpensive, however, and they serve the sort of food that'll fill you up. Best of all, these above any other kind of restaurant in New Orleans are the sorts of places where you're likely to rub elbows with the locals—to really see up close how New Orleanians live, or at least how they eat. And in this city, if you watch the locals eat, you're learning a great deal about how they live.

JAVA JOINTS

New Orleanians were frequenting coffee-houses as part of their daily routine long before Starbucks caught on and Seattle became the nation's de facto caffeine capital. Starbucks outlets do appear all over the Crescent City, but the national chain has more sway with tourists than with locals, who tend to favor either indie options or local chains **CC's** (www.ccscoffee. com) and **P.J.'s** (www.pjscoffee.com).

You'll find about a dozen branches of CC's around town, including locations on Magazine Street and Louisiana Avenue Uptown, Royal Street in the Quarter, Poydras Street in the CBD, Esplanade Avenue in Mid-City, and in Metairie, Kenner, and other nearby 'burbs. There's a light selection of food served, including the usual muffins and pastries. Overall, CC's seems to have cozier seating than most of its competitors.

There are P.J.'s locales on Camp and Magazine streets in the CBD, Frenchmen Street in Faubourg Marigny, Magazine and Maple streets Uptown, and also in Metairie, Kenner, and many suburbs (as well as at the airport). The large Maple Street coffeehouse has a nice patio. Some locations serve substantial cafe fare. Many folks think P.J.'s is the big winner when it comes to hot and iced teas.

Rue de la Course is a smaller, funkier, and somewhat more interesting local chain, with several locations around town, three Uptown, one in the Quarter, and one in the CBD.

As for the seemingly ever-popular **Starbucks** (www.starbucks.com), you'll find branches on Canal Street in the CBD, on Magazine and Maple streets Uptown, and in just about all the 'burbs.

PICNIC SUPPLIES AND GOURMET GOODS

The line between restaurant, grocery, and specialty food shop blurs considerably in New Orleans. The best wine store in the area, Martin Wine Cellar, also has one of the best delis. Central Grocery, in the French Quarter, is most famous for its hefty muffuletta sandwiches, but don't overlook the fact that it carries wonderful and hard-to-find imported groceries. Some of the leading restaurants in the city also have gift shops where you can buy gourmet food, plus the usual souvenir T-shirts and ball caps.

The farmers market held inside the French Market is the most famous place to find gourmet edibles for sale in the city, but you can find a wide range of tasty local foods at just about any New Orleans grocery store, even a national chain.

If you love browsing market-fresh food, don't miss the **Crescent City Farmers Market** (www.crescentcityfarmersmarket.com), held four times a week at different locations around town and featuring a phenomenal roster of vendors and chefs. You'll find fresh oysters, soft-shell crabs, alligator, watermelons, blueberries, yams, Creole tomatoes, pecans, kumquats, orchids, fresh-cut flowers, pheasant, Creole cream cheese, Italian sugar cookies, sausages, maple syrup, red lentil balls, filé powder, and countless more delectables. It's held in the Warehouse District on Saturday (8 A.M.–noon) at 700 Magazine St., Uptown at 200 Broadway St. (near Audubon Park at Uptown Square) on Tuesday (10 A.M.–1 P.M.), at the French Market on Decatur in the French Quarter on Wednesdays, and in Mid-City at 3700 Orleans Avenue on Thursday (3–6 P.M., an hour later in summer). The Thursday and Wednesday markets have not yet resumed after Katrina, but it's expected they will reopen eventually. Farmers markets have been a part of life in New Orleans since the French and Spanish governments governed the city in the 18th century, and they remain just as vibrant to this day.

COOKING CLASSES

A great way to learn about the city's rich culinary heritage is to attend one of the many cooking demonstrations held throughout the city.

At the Riverwalk shopping center, **Creole Delicacies Gourmet Shop and Cookin' Cajun Cooking** (1 Poydras St., No. 116, Riverwalk, 504/586-8832 or 800/786-0941, www.cookincajun.com) is not only a cooking school but a first-rate shop for finding local ingredients and cookware. The two-hour classes include a full meal and a 10 percent discount in the gourmet shop. The **New Orleans School of Cooking** (524 St. Louis St., 504/525-2665 or 800/237-4841, www.nosoc.com) offers 2.5-hour classes, led by colorful chef Kevin Belton or one of his colleagues, that include a meal, recipes, and a great deal of lively storytelling. These cost $27. Both Creole and Cajun cooking are covered with these courses.

One of the more unusual settings for these demonstrations is Blaine Kern's Mardi Gras World museum on the West Bank. Here at the **Mardi Gras School of Cooking** (233 Newton St., 504/362-5225, www.gumbos.net), you learn and have a chance to prepare a wide variety of Creole and Cajun dishes. The demo kitchens are set amid the huge Mardi Gras floats, which are being constructed here year-round.

The French Quarter

TRADITIONAL CREOLE AND CAJUN

Among those few remaining New Orleans restaurants where men must wear a jacket in the evening and no patron may stroll in wearing shorts, **Galatoire's** (209 Bourbon St., 504/525-2021, $14–24), which opened in 1905 and has been run by the Galatoire family ever since, most deserves a visit, even if you have an aversion to dressing up. As much fun as the dining itself is watching the local politicos hobnob and broker deals, especially on Friday afternoons—the true regulars among Galatoire's many loyal patrons have been coming here for generations, often taking their seat at the same table. Despite its formal ambience and popularity among well-heeled locals, Galatoire's isn't all that expensive. From the enormous menu you can try everything from lavish high-end dishes such as grilled pompano with sautéed crabmeat meunière to broiled steaks and lamb chops béarnaise. But several chicken and seafood entrées weigh in around $15, including shrimp *au vin* and oysters Rockefeller. Crêpes suzette and banana bread pudding stand out among the rich desserts. The main dining room has always maintained a "no reservations" policy, although you can reserve a seat in the upstairs dining room, which was added after a major makeover in 1999.

It's probably not fair to describe **K-Paul's Louisiana Kitchen** (416 Chartres St., 504/524-7394, $27–39) as traditional, since much of the food at Paul Prudhomme's famous restaurant is prepared quite innovatively. The celeb chef, who was a kitchenhold name long before Emeril, was largely responsible for first popularizing Cajun cooking outside Louisiana, and this is still an excellent, although extremely pricey, place to sample such fare as turtle soup finished with hard-boiled eggs and dry sherry; bronzed swordfish with a sauce of roasted pecans, jalapeños, browned garlic butter, veal glaze, and lemon juice; or blackened stuffed pork chops with a mushroom zinfandel sauce. Sweet potato pecan pie and bread pudding with lemon sauce and chantilly cream are favorite sweet endings. The once-intimate dining room in this 1834 building took no reservations for many years, but a 1996 expansion added more seating, and nowadays you can reserve a table.

One of the true granddaddies of old-fashioned Creole cooking, **Antoine's** (713 St. Louis St., 504/581-4422, $21–39) opened its door in 1840 and hasn't missed a beat. Such dishes as oysters Thermidor (baked on the half shell and served with bacon and tomato sauce) and avocado stuffed with shrimp *ravigote* (marinated peeled and boiled shrimp with a chilled sauce of Creole mustard, horseradish, mayonnaise, capers, and hard-boiled eggs) were invented here. Be forewarned: The menu is in French, but the solicitous waitstaff will happily explain what's what. The list of options seems endless, with cheeses, sauces, salads, and side

FOOD

FOOD

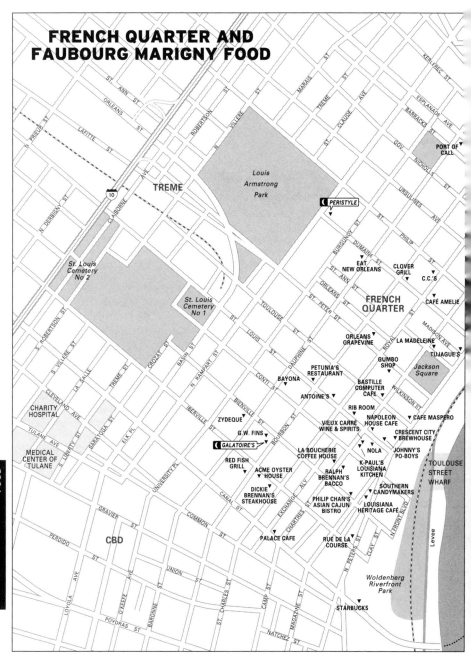

FRENCH QUARTER AND FAUBOURG MARIGNY FOOD

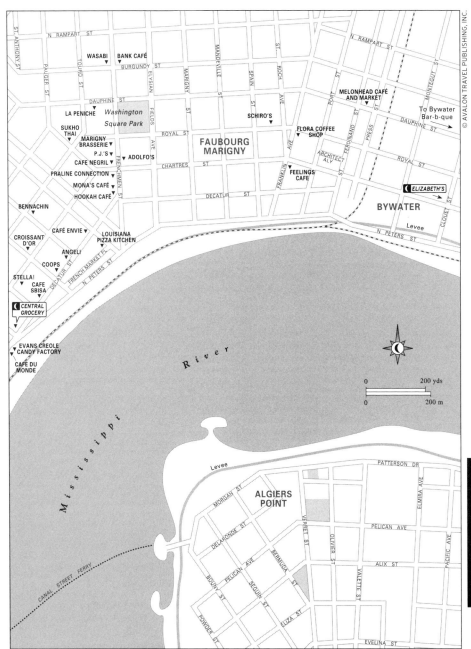

FOOD

REVEILLON

December is a wonderful time to visit New Orleans for several reasons, not the least of which is the moderate weather. But for food-lovers, the big draw is Reveillon, an ancient Creole (and Catholic) celebratory feast dating to the 1830s, which originally was held on Christmas and New Year's Eves but now happens throughout the month of December and is celebrated by all walks of life, regardless of any particular religious affiliation. Still, for many people, the most special Reveillon dinners are held Christmas or New Year's Eve.

The Christmas meal was traditionally held after midnight Mass at St. Louis Cathedral. Families would return home and spend time together sharing a fairly austere meal of egg dishes, sweetbreads, and a rum cake. This has historically been the more restrained of the two Reveillon meals, as the New Year's Eve feast has always consisted of elaborate desserts, plenty of whiskey and wine, and lots of laughing, singing, and dancing.

Dozens of restaurants in New Orleans offer Reveillon menus throughout the month of December. These are prix-fixe menus, usually four or five courses, and many establishments do offer Reveillon on Christmas or New Year's Eve, although you should reserve well ahead if you plan on attending on the eves or on Christmas or New Year's Day. Favorite venues for this celebration include Begue's, Dickie Brennan's Steakhouse, Galatoire's, Palace Cafe, Rene Bistrot, The Rib Room, Tujague's, Upperline, and 7 on Fulton.

At traditional Tujague's, the choices are limited and the menu straightforward: shrimp remoulade, a soup of the day, boiled brisket of beef with horseradish sauce, braised lamb shanks in a Creole stew, banana-bread pudding, and chicory-laced coffee; the meal costs about $30 per person. More cutting-edge places around town have fancier and more unusual offerings, such as 7 on Fulton ($40 per person), where you might start with grilled quail with pear, greens, and crispy bacon, followed by diver scallops with foie gras, chestnuts, mushrooms, and a sunchoke purée; the meal ends with spiced apple cake or a caramelized-banana crepe. For more information on Reveillon, log on to www.frenchquarterfestival.com.

---

of vegetables all available á la carte along with crab omelets, chateaubriand for two, backfin lump crabmeat au gratin, broiled trout with crawfish and white wine, and so on. Deciding what to eat is only half the challenge—figuring out *where* to eat can also test your decision-making skills: There are 15 dining rooms, some for private parties but most open to the public. The Rex Room is decked in Mardi Gras photos, while the Japanese Room, which was opened a century ago but closed during World War II for four decades before a 1984 revival, is a study in Japanese decorative arts.

Tujague's (823 Decatur St., 504/525-8676, $15–22) is a neat old corner bar and tavern that's been around since 1856, making it the second-oldest continuously operated restaurant in New Orleans. It sits opposite the French Market, and it serves many of the local Louisiana produce and seafood sold there. In fact, little on this menu varies from what diners might have ordered for lunch or dinner more than a century ago: beef brisket in Creole sauce, shrimp rémoulade, herb-and-greens gumbo, pecan sauce. In addition to the usual cocktails and wines, Tujague's serves its own microbrewed beer. Drinking here has quite a legacy, as the cypress-wood bar is original, and the handsome French mirror was shipped here from Paris the year the restaurant opened. Even if you don't come for a meal, at least stop in to chat with the other locals and tourists who frequent this hallowed institution.

Cafe Sbisa (1011 Decatur St., 504/522-5565, $14–25) is a dark and clubby space with the feel of a big-city brasserie—tile floors, mirrors, amber lighting, and well-dressed staff impart an air of informal elegance. In 1899, the

Sbisa family opened this cheerful bistro inside an 1820s building near the French Market. It's an excellent place to try the New Orleans seafood classic court bouillon (a bouillabaisse-like stew of Gulf fish, shrimp, mussels, crabmeat, crab claws, and Creole seasonings), but neither will you go wrong with trout Eugene (topped with shrimp, crawfish tails, and crab fingers with herbed rice and asparagus) or honey-roasted chicken with three-cheese pasta and mustard greens. One of the favorite places to dine is on the second-floor balcony overlooking Decatur Street and the French Market. This longtime New Orleans standby has never lost its popularity, in part because prices are quite reasonable, especially considering the big quantities of food. But the restaurant has not yet reopened following Hurricane Katrina, so check ahead.

A dainty little restaurant that serves prodigiously huge crepes, **Petunia's Restaurant** (817 St. Louis St., 504/522-6440, $11–23) occupies a pink three-story 1830s town house whose sunny (and also pink) dining rooms reveal the builder's masterful woodworking. You can get pastas, traditional Creole fare (a nice jambalaya, for instance), and blackened fish, but the crepes are what sets this place apart from others around town. The St. Francis, filled with shrimp, crabmeat, ratatouille, and a creamy cheese sauce, earns plenty of accolades. Save room for the St. Louis dessert flambé, with vanilla ice cream, bananas, cherries, and pecans afire. Breakfast is another of Petunia's specialties—consider eggs St. Louis (English muffins topped with grilled tomatoes, crabmeat, poached eggs, and homemade hollandaise sauce).

Even in the Quarter, it's rare to find a restaurant with as illustrious a history as the **Napoleon House Cafe** (500 Chartres St., 504/524-9752, bistro $12–24, cafe $4–7). Everything here—the tile floor, the scruffy plaster walls with peeling paint, the wobbly old wooden tables, and the eclectic prints, vintage photos, paintings, and chandeliers with orange light bulbs—contribute to the old-timey air. The front room is a bar where a light cafe menu is offered. Through the bar is a cozy dining room, and then a lush and characterful courtyard with partially covered seating. If alone, dine at the bar, read a book, chat with the friendly bartenders, eavesdrop, and try to grasp this room's 200-year-old history of entertaining New Orleanians. The building was first owned by New Orleans mayor Nicholas Girod, who offered the home as a residence to exiled Napoléon Bonaparte in 1821; supposedly, the Little Corporal was quite interested, but he died before he could ever move to New Orleans. You can try a wide range of foods in both of Napoleon House's dining areas: The cafe serves tapenade, feta, and goat cheese spread; boudin with Creole mustard, Corsican salad (red leaf lettuce, Kalamata olives, cherry tomatoes, toasted walnuts, red onion, gorgonzola, and raspberry vinaigrette), and the trademark house muffuletta, served hot with ham, Genoa salami, pastrami, Swiss cheese, provolone, and Italian olive salad. In the bistro, consider grilled salmon topped with citrus cream and served with Louisiana cane syrup glaze and sweet potato straw, or a delicious smoked rabbit with tasso jambalaya. There's an excellent wine list, too.

CREATIVE AND CONTEMPORARY

An eclectic, highly regarded restaurant on a quiet stretch of Dauphine, **Bayona** (430 Dauphine St., 504/525-4455, $14–21) fuses traditions, recipes, and ingredients from a handful of cultures all known for great food. Chef Susan Spicer, who was named best chef in the Southeast in 1993 by the prestigious James Beard Foundation, dreams up such imaginative combos as lamb loin with a goat cheese–zinfandel sauce, and seared ceviche with peppered fruit salsa and ancho-mango coulis. Desserts are no mere afterthought here—notable is crème brûlée with Chartreuse, star anise, and ginger, or try the toasted pecan roulade with caramel mousse and pecan syrup. There's a huge, commendable wine list. The setting, an 18th-century Creole cottage filled with trompe l'oeil

FOOD

murals of the Mediterranean countryside and a plant-filled courtyard, is the quintessence of romance.

ℂ Peristyle (1041 Dumaine St., 504/593-9535, $22–26) is the domain of one of the city's top chefs, Tom Wolfe, who comes up with some wonderful French-influenced American recipes, such as a starter of grilled Louisiana quail salad with pancetta, watercress, spinach, montasio cheese, and sherry vinaigrette, or a main dish of grilled marinated tuna steak with crispy potato cakes, pickled fennel relish, and a preserved lemon–chive fumet. It's in a vintage building on a quiet street at the edge of the Quarter, near slightly ominous Rampart Street, but the interior is elegant and soft, with terrazzo marble floors. This is chiefly a dinner restaurant, but lunch is served on Fridays.

The **Rib Room** (Omni Royal Orleans Hotel, 621 St. Louis St., 504/529-7046, $18–36), despite a dull name that conjures visions of old-hat restaurants from yesteryear, may just be the best steak house in the city. The dining room is unabashedly retro, with its soaring ceilings with timber beams, an exposition kitchen under a curving brick archway, big comfortable leather chairs, huge arched windows overlooking Royal Street, and pepper mills the size of fire hydrants. The staff is both deft and fun-loving—many employees have been here for three or four decades. The food is heavenly and in some instances, such as the pan-seared foie gras with ginger-pear relish, visionary. There's a tender filet mignon whose preparation changes each week. Nouvelle foodies may scoff at this place, but it's a cool and hip dining venue almost in spite of its legacy.

Red-meat lovers swear by the hefty cuts served at **Dickie Brennan's Steakhouse** (716 Iberville St., 504/522-2467, $16–33), which is known for bacon-wrapped tournedos of beef served over smoked gouda–and–garlic mashed potatoes. Steamed Maine lobsters, blackened prime rib, and the double-cut pork chop over smoked bacon–and–apple hash topped with grilled onion are also big draws. This is a clubby, upscale space, but (neat) casual attire is customary and the mood relaxed.

There aren't many restaurants on exuberant Bourbon Street worth going out of your way for, but Ralph Brennan's **Red Fish Grill** (115 Bourbon St., 504/598-1200, $16–32), set inside a former department store just a block into the Quarter from Canal, is an exception. This first block of Bourbon has revived in recent years; it was once dominated by department stores, and after closing time the stretch felt dark and ominous. This restaurant opened in 2000 and has helped to recharge the block. The cavernous main dining room reverberates with piped-in rock music, and huge redfish mobiles dangle overhead—this is no wallflower of a restaurant, but the noisy and festive ambience makes it fun for friends dining together, singles, and anybody heading out afterward for a tour of Bourbon Street's nightlife. To one side is a spacious oyster bar with huge oyster half-shell sculptures; you can order from the main menu in here, too. The barbecued oysters are a great starter, served with a tangy blue-cheese dipping sauce, and the kitchen also turns out an amazingly delicious chocolate bread pudding. But few dishes here beat the hickory-grilled redfish served over crawfish and potatoes and topped with a lemon-butter sauce.

Inside the swank W Hotel French Quarter, **Ralph Brennan's Bacco** (310 Chartres St., 504/522-2426, $10–25) offers stylish dining at unusually low prices. The dining room, with its recessed lighting, white napery, and natty patrons and staff, complements the informal but hip W Hotel and feels like the perfect place to see and be seen without feeling that you have to dress to the nines. The food is modern Italian, but quite a few dishes have notable Creole accents. Beef carpaccio with arugula, white truffle oil, and parmigiano-reggiano, or soft-shell crab with creamy crawfish risotto and sweet-and-spicy pepper jelly are fine choices. Bacco also offers a handful of $10 entrées, including crawfish–and–blood orange penne pasta, and herb-roasted chicken.

One of the top restaurants to open in the Quarter in the past few years (in 2001, to be exact), **G. W. Fins** (808 Bienville St., 504/581-3467, $19–29) is a bit of a departure from most seafood-based New Orleans restaurants: Although many local dishes are offered here, the kitchen serves fresh fish flown in from all over the world, from Alaskan halibut to Scottish salmon. The setting, a converted warehouse with lofty ceilings, warm woods, and cushy booths, is contemporary and upbeat—it feels more CBD than French Quarter. Specialties worth seeking out include wood-grilled escolar with eggplant ragout and tomato fondue, New Bedford sea scallops with mushroom risotto and mushroom butter, and sautéed mangrove snapper with daikon cakes and a lemongrass reduction. There's nothing overly convoluted or cutesy about the cooking, just fresh fish with modern ingredients presented with flair.

Everybody knows about **NOLA** (534 St. Louis St., 504/522-6652, $18–35), Emeril Lagasse's restaurant in the French Quarter, although not everybody loves it. When you're a big fish in an even bigger sea, it's hard not to be noticed and also criticized. After all, Emeril isn't the only dazzling chef in New Orleans—he isn't even the only great one on his block. When all is said and done, however, NOLA delivers great cooking and a lively dining experience that pretty much lives up to its billing, and service is generally reliable. Just keep in mind that it can be hard to get a table, so book ahead, and expect a wait even when you show up on time for your reservation. It's not a big restaurant, although there are a few seats at the bar, which can be useful if you're dining alone or coming in without a reservation. The restaurant typically sets aside a very limited number of tables for walk-ins. If you're hoping to nab one, you should plan to arrive a good half hour before the restaurant opens at 6 P.M. The menu changes often, but some favorites include a stuffed chicken wings appetizer with a house-made dipping sauce, citrus-horseradish–crusted red drum roasted on a cedar plank and served with lemon butter sauce and a Creole tomato salad, and—as a finale—the NOLA buzz bomb, a dense flourless chocolate cake with bittersweet chocolate mousse and brandied apricots wrapped in chocolate ganache.

With a gorgeous bilevel interior inside the former Werlein's Music Store, the **Palace Cafe** (605 Canal St., 504/523-1661, $18–25) ranks among the most cosmopolitan-looking of the several outstanding Brennan family restaurants in New Orleans. It can get touristy, as it's close to several convention hotels, but don't be put off by the location—the kitchen consistently prepares some of the best and most exciting New Orleans fare in the city, and the staff is highly personable and efficient. Signature dishes are many: There's an oyster pan roast poached in rosemary cream and topped with bread crumbs, crabmeat cheesecake baked in a pecan crust with wild mushrooms, *panéed* rabbit with tasso ham and gruyère cheese over fettuccine with leeks and carrots, and catfish pecan meunière. It's all good, and every dish is presented with a great flourish. The restaurant serves a particularly enjoyable Sunday jazz brunch. Of the city's high-end (but not super-expensive) special-occasion restaurants, Palace Cafe leads the pack.

It's right on busy Decatur Street, inside the Bienville House Hotel, but **Louisiana Heritage Cafe** (320 Decatur St., 504/529-2345, $15–30) feels discreet, its entrance rather difficult to find and its reputation solid but rather hushed. This is also the site of the Louisiana Heritage School of Cooking, and cooking classes on regional cuisine are offered here on Friday and Saturday at 10:30 A.M. If you're here for a meal, expect such classic southern Louisiana fare as seafood beignets served with remoulade sauce, and blackened catfish smothered with crawfish étoufée.

A cute, warmly furnished spot with plenty of outdoor seating and live music some evenings, **Cafe Amelie** (912 Royal St., 504/412-8965, $19–29) serves simple but creative American fare, such as panfried crab cakes drizzled with a light citrus sauce and crispy Muscovy duck with warm bitter-orange vinaigrette. The menu is short, but there are usually some specials. At lunch, don't miss the leg of lamb sandwich with rosemary mayo and fresh greens. The interior is a converted carriage house with beamed ceilings and French doors.

Stella! (1032 Chartres St., 504/587-0091,

$16–29) is a Quarter favorite, in spite of (or perhaps because of) its discreet, slightly out-of-the-way location. Although it's set inside the Hotel Provincial, Stella! is a way down Chartres Street from the busier half of the neighborhood—you sort of have to know about it to find it. Not everybody loves the silly name either, but the tribute to Stanley Kowalski can be forgiven, as the food is anything but silly. Once inside this dapper, clubby dining room, you'll be treated to truly creative fare, such as sublime seared Hudson Valley foie gras with quenelles of Granny Smith apples, toasted brioche, huckleberry jam, and a burgundy reduction, or an entrée of Creole spice–dusted grouper and cornmeal-crusted frogs' legs with seafood jambalaya risotto and lemon Tabasco honey butter. Some of these dishes may sound overwrought, but ingredients complement each other nicely.

An occasional complaint about the French Quarter is that there aren't enough reasonably priced yet sophisticated restaurants. The intimate **Orleans Grapevine** (718-720 Orleans Ave., 504/523-1930, $12–21) fits the bill perfectly. It's a classy yet casual bistro a block from the craziness of Bourbon Street, set inside a restored 1809 building. There's a great list of wines by the glass, and then the kitchen turns out such pleasing fare as a green salad with port-poached pears, roquefort, and port vinaigrette; baked brie topped with praline sauce; and apple-glazed, cedar-roasted salmon with roasted root vegetables and potatoes.

CASUAL COOKING

Acme Oyster House (724 Iberville St., 504/522-5973; also 3000 Veterans Memorial Blvd., Metairie, 504/522-5973; $5–12) has since 1910 been a reliable option for fresh bivalves. Always packed with tourists, it can be crazy in here in this casual place with red-checked tablecloths, but it's worth braving the frenzy for very good po'boys, gumbo, and other straightforward fare. Is it oyster nirvana, as some people claim? No, in truth, it's not any better than a lot of oyster bars around town, but its rich history and convenient lo-

cation make it a fun place. You can also get shrimp and soft-shell-crab po'boys, burgers, jambalaya, gumbo, and a first-rate oyster-artichoke bisque.

Johnny's Po-boys (511 St. Louis St., 504/524-8129, $4–8), opened in 1950, is an unprepossessing little place with tables sheathed in red-checkered cloth and surrounded by bentwood chairs. It's open only till 4 each afternoon but fills up daily for breakfast and lunch. It's best known for its namesake sandwiches, but you can also get platters of fried seafood. Classic po'boys include tuna, country-fried steak, and the Judge Bosetta (with ground beef, Italian and hot sausage, and swiss cheese).

The owner of **Coops** (1109 Decatur St., 504/525-9053, $5–17) sought to create a space that's equal parts bar and restaurant, and indeed this untouristy and underrated hangout on raffish Decatur Street succeeds on both counts, offering the convivial spirit of a neighborhood pub and food that's pub-style but consistently high caliber. The oyster po'boys here are as good—and as big—as any around town, and you don't have to battle with the lines typical of more popular places. So prodigious are these French-bread cargo ships that it's nearly impossible to put the thing down once you've managed to grasp it; there's too great a threat that its contents will drop unceremoniously to the table. Other home-style favorites include rabbit-and-smoked-sausage jambalaya, crab claws marinated in Italian vinaigrette, and fried alligator bits. There's a pool table in back, and dark-wood tables and exposed brick give the place a warm feel, as does the superfriendly and welcoming staff. Just one caveat—the cramped and unpleasant bathrooms, reached through the rear courtyard, leave much to be desired.

Cafe Maspero (601 Decatur St., 504/523-6250, $5–10) is more atmospheric and spacious than Johnny's—seating is under brick arched ceilings, at big wooden tables, or you can dine at the bar. The place is famous for its sandwiches, such as the roast beef and swiss, the veggie muffuletta, and the smoked sausage. But New Orleans fare, from jambalaya to catfish platters, is also popular. Purely from a food perspective, Maspero is a bit overrated, but it's still a reliable find for reasonably good food. The strawberry daiquiris are so refreshing it's easy to forget the high alcohol content; these drinks are strong.

Another place that's so touristy it's hard to believe it can really live up to the hype, the **Gumbo Shop** (630 St. Peter St., 504/525-1486, $7–20) does deliver the goods, from kicky shrimp Creole over rice to first-rate crawfish étouffée to a nicely prepared filet mignon with sautéed mushrooms. Of course, the gumbos really are terrific. The complete Creole dinners are a steal—you get an appetizer, vegetable, entrée, and dessert, with several choices in each category.

Crescent City Brewhouse (527 Decatur St., 504/522-0571, $8–20) occupies the first two floors of a white-brick building on Decatur. As brewpubs go, it serves surprisingly decent and varied food, but you come mostly to sample the various microbrews, which are prepared Bavarian-style, with simple, natural ingredients (just water, malt, hops, and yeast)—the light Weiss beer is a house favorite. Offerings from the menu include lemon chicken wings, fried calamari and caponata, shrimp po'boys with fiery habanero ketchup, seared scallops with roasted pepper–and–vermouth cream, and raspberry roast duck.

An affordable and romantic eatery in the Lower Quarter, **Eat New Orleans** (900 Dumaine St., 504/522-7222, $8–15) sits at a relatively peaceful corner just a block from Bourbon, inside a handsome wood-frame house with big bay windows facing both Dumaine and Dauphine streets. The cheery restaurant opened in summer 2006, replacing the long-running Quarter Scene, which closed following Katrina. Tennessee Williams had been a regular, and the restaurant continues to have a strong following with the gay community. The food is straightforward and fairly traditional, mostly of the Cajun and Creole variety, including first-rate red beans and rice, shrimp-and-grits, seafood gumbo, and a delicious torte filled with blue cheese and figs. Like its predecessor, Eat has no liquor license, but you're welcome to bring your own, and there's never a corkage fee.

A dark and divey corner tavern that's so popular for its hefty burgers that there's sometimes a line outside the door, **Port of Call** (838 Esplanade Ave., 504/523-0120, $6–14) serves the full range of traditional American comfort foods, including pizza, steaks, and huge baked potatoes topped with all kinds of goodies (they come with the burgers). The burgers, made with freshly ground beef and piled high with melted cheddar, really are that good.

You'd think there'd be more places to scarf down a big meal late after a night of drinking and dancing, but **Angeli** (1141 Decatur St., 504/566-0077, $6–14) is one of the only decent places in the Quarter that's open into the wee hours (till 2 A.M.). A wide range of munchies and light bites are offered, including pizzas, wraps, wings, waffles, designer coffees, all kinds of beers, and addictive flatbread with sun-dried tomato pesto and parmesan cheese—pretty much any food you might crave late at night. Often, old black-and-white movies are shown against a rear wall of the dining room, which draws an eclectic crowd that's especially interesting (ravers, gays, club kids, yuppies, artists) the later you eat here. There's usually light jazz playing in the background, and the busy street-corner location allows for optimum people-watching.

Louisiana Pizza Kitchen (95 French Market Pl., 504/522-9500; also 615 S. Carrollton Ave., 504/866-5900; 2112 Belle Chasse Hwy., Gretna, 504/433-5800, pies $7–9, entrées $7–14) serves food throughout the day, which surprisingly few substantial eateries in the Quarter do (most are open for lunch and dinner but close in between, and several serve dinner only). It's right on the edge of the French Market, facing the U.S. Mint Museum. The gray-brick room has walls decked with local art (for sale) and black-and-white–checked floors—it's a vaguely art deco look. Pizzas are of the

FOOD

FOOD

© ANDREW COLLINS

A tradition for more than a century, Central Grocery is famed for its muffuletta sandwiches.

thin-crust variety baked with little grease, and toppings tend toward creative. The pizza topped with applewood-smoked bacon and chives with mozzarella cheese, sour cream, and Roma tomatoes is a classic. The crawfish pie is also great. Pita wraps, pastas, calzones, and hefty salads (try the one with blue cheese and roasted pecans) round out the menu.

ETHNIC

The French Quarter has precious few ethnic restaurants, but a new standout that's worth investigating is **Bennachin** (1212 Royal St., 504/522-1230, $8–14), one of the only West African eateries in the South (odd when you consider the region's, and especially Louisiana's, clear ties to West Africa through its many decades of importing slaves from Senegal). It's actually been in New Orleans for some time, but the restaurant, whose owner hails from Cameroon, moved from its original Mid-City locale to the Quarter in 2003, inside what had been a Turkish restaurant. Recommended dishes include stews of beef, ginger, peanuts, and spinach; a red bean soup that

seems like an appropriate progenitor to New Orleans cuisine; and couscous with a tart yogurt sauce. There's always a daily lunch special for under $6.

Philip Chan's Asian Cajun Bistro (301 Decatur St., 504/522-4964, $16–49) is exactly what the name says, even if that sounds a bit unusual, especially in the French Quarter, which is largely bereft of good Asian restaurants. Phillip Chan made a name for himself with the elegant Chopstix restaurant in Atlanta, and he presents some truly imaginative food at this stylish restaurant, such as a po'boy packed with sweet-and-sour crawfish at lunch, and such dinner items as Peking duck with hoisin sauce; "drunken" Louisiana shrimp with a tomato, basil, cilantro, and mint wine broth; and Asian wok-fried lobster tail with mushrooms, scallions, and ginger.

QUICK BITES

People sometimes overlook the fact that **Central Grocery** (923 Decatur St., 504/523-1620) really is a grocery store, in this case carrying a mouthwatering array of fine imported Italian foods, many of them hard to find in the United States. But, of course, the place is most famous for being home of the incredibly delicious muffuletta sandwich, made with Italian bread coated in sesame seeds that's then stuffed with ham, salami, mortadella, provolone cheese, and a generous helping of olive salad (made of chopped green and Kalamata olives, carrots, capers, garlic, and olive oil). The restaurant claims to have invented this dish—skeptics are less sure, but there's little denying that Central Grocery makes one of the best, and it serves it cold, in contrast to many delis and restaurants around town. There are more than a few fans who simply cannot visit New Orleans without having at least one of these sandwiches, and ardent devotees have been known to have them shipped to far-flung corners of the globe. There's no dining room per se, just a counter in back with a few benches. A bag of Zapp's potato chips goes especially well with a muffuletta. As for the grocery section, you'll find imported oils and vinegars, fine cheeses, gourmet pastas, anchovies, nuts, and just about every other gourmet product you might find at a neighborhood grocery store in an Italian city.

Lucky Dogs, those little brown-and-red weiner-shaped hot dog carts in the French Quarter, are ideal for a quick snack—there's usually one along Decatur near Jackson Brewery. On a literary note, the bizarre antihero of John Kennedy Toole's unusual New Orleans epic novel, *A Confederacy of Dunces,* worked as a vendor for Lucky Dogs.

For delectable barbecue (something New Orleans isn't known for), plan a meal at **Zydeque** (808 Iberville St., 504/565-5520, $6–19), a huge, crowded, down-home joint with unbelievably tender pulled pork, slow-cooked chicken, and more. Everything comes with the usual tasty sides, such as baked beans, mustard greens, and coleslaw. The pecan pie á la mode makes for a sweet ending.

It's late, you're hungry (maybe even a little tipsy), and you have a craving for greasy food. It's times such as these when you'll count your lucky stars that a place such as the **Clover Grill** (900 Bourbon St., 504/598-1010, $3–7) never closes and never stops frying wonderfully fattening and gooey cheeseburgers, pecan waffles topped with bananas, vanilla malts, and bowls of grits swimming in melted butter. Part of the fun at this loud, dishy diner—where the menu is filled with jokes and the wisecracking staff is quick to make fun of customers—is enjoying the constant merriment. Three of the city's most popular gay bars lie within a block of the Clover Grill, and so drag queens and disco bunnies typically make up a chunk of the clientele.

A source of delectable sweets, the **Croissant D'Or** (617 Ursulines Ave., 504/524-4663) is a classic French bakery that also serves light lunch fare, homemade soups, fresh salads, and good breakfasts. It's in the Lower Quarter, near the Old Ursuline Convent, and it makes a nice break from exploring the neighborhood's rich architecture.

Although part of a Texas-based chain, the Jackson Square outpost of **La Madeleine** (547 St. Ann St., 504/568-0073; also 601 S. Carrollton Ave., 504/861-8662; 1327 St. Charles Ave., 504/410-8500; 3300 Severn Ave., Metairie, 504/456-1624; 4–7) feels so authentically New Orleans that many visitors think the chain originated here. This and the other locations around town serve very good and reasonably priced French cafe food, such as French onion soup, crème brûlée, baguette sandwiches of several varieties, and pesto-pasta salads. You'll also find excellent coffee and such toothsome breakfast treats as ham Florentine crepes and custom omelets.

JAVA JOINTS

What began as a humble coffee stand to serve the customers and employees of the produce stalls in the French Market in 1862, **Cafe du Monde** (1039 Decatur St., 800/772-2927; also Riverwalk Marketplace, 1 Poydras St., 504/587-0841; Esplanade Mall, 1401 W. Esplanade Ave., Kenner, 504/468-3588; New Orleans Centre, 1401 Poydras St., 504/587-0842; 3301 Veterans Memorial Blvd.,

Metairie, 504/834-8694; Oakwood Mall, 197 Westbank Expy., Gretna, 504/587-0849) has grown into one of the most legendary food operations in the country, included in coffee-table books, written about in newspapers and magazines, and discussed on television programs. Part of its mystique and popularity is that the place is open 24/7, except for Christmas, and that it serves so few foods (although it serves them all well). The mainstays are beignets (French-style fried doughnuts dusted with powdered sugar) and dark-roasted coffee laced with chicory and traditionally served "au lait" (a cup filled half with hot milk, half with coffee) but also available black. You can also order fresh-squeezed orange juice, white or chocolate milk, iced coffee (a recent innovation, having made its debut in 1988), and sodas (an even more recent innovation, and some say an abomination). The cafe is mostly an open-air operation consisting of dozens of small marble tables surrounded by green vinyl chairs and covered with a tentlike roof. Waiters clad in white shirts with black bow ties and white-paper hats whisk about gracefully, delivering plates of beignets at breakneck speed. In cold weather, the area is warmed with heating lamps, but you can also grab one of the few tables in a small and fully enclosed dining area. There are now a handful of satellite locations of Cafe du Monde, mostly in area shopping malls, which keep shorter hours and definitely lack the ambience of the original.

The Quarter has a branch of the city's most famous coffeehouse chain, **CC's,** at 941 Royal Street, at the corner of Dumaine Street. It's a cozy spot, meaning that seating is a bit limited, but it's also warmly lighted and charmingly furnished, with several cushy armchairs.

Bastille Computer Cafe (605 Toulouse St., 504/453-3125) is perfect when you need to log onto the Net; it's in an old brick cottage in the heart of the Quarter. Here you can grab a coffee and rent a computer or use your own laptop to access the web. Bastille

has a full slate of CD burners, business services, and design, scanners, digital photo editing, and every other service you could possibly need—even computer lessons are available here.

A wonderful place to while away an afternoon and people-watch, **Cafe EnVie** (1241 Decatur St., 504/524-3689) brews a strong coffee, serves plenty of interesting teas, and prepares decent salads and sandwiches, too. It offers free Wi-Fi and lots of seating.

Near the many antiques shops along Chartres and Royal streets, **La Boucherie Coffee House** (339 Chartres St., 504/581-6868) www.laboucheriecoffeehouse.com, is a nice place to take a break from your retail ramble. You can pick up great pastries and sweets here, too, along with salads, sandwiches, and soups.

PICNIC SUPPLIES AND GOURMET GOODS

For more than a century, **Evans Creole Candy Factory** (848 Decatur St., 504/522-7111 or 800/637-6675) has been crafting delicious pralines. Still today, you can watch the candymakers working on a fresh batch of pralines through the big windows of this shop in the French Market, which is also an excellent source for hand-dipped chocolates, dark-chocolate turtles (Creole pecans topped with caramel and dipped in chocolate), chocolate-covered maraschino cherries, and other tempting sweets.

Southern Candymakers (334 Decatur St., 504/523-5544), also in the French Market, is a full retail shop with pralines, marzipan, peanut brittle, fudge, and lots of other sweets that will do horrible things to your teeth but will make the rest of you quite happy. You can stop by for a free sample, too.

It's not a real chore finding alcohol in the French Quarter, but when it's your own bottle of wine, liquor, or beer that you're seeking, look no farther than **Vieux Carré Wine and Spirits** (422 Chartres St., 504/568-9463), which has an especially impressive selection of wines. The store will deliver purchases within the Quarter and CBD.

Faubourg Marigny and Bywater

TRADITIONAL CREOLE AND CAJUN

One of the city's definitive gay restaurants, **Feelings Cafe** (2600 Chartres St., 504/945-2222, $15–26) is set on a quiet street in a charmingly decrepit-looking old building several blocks past Frenchmen Street (it's a 10- to 20-minute walk from the Quarter). It's known best for its Sunday brunch (try the crab cakes with poached eggs and Hollandaise sauce) but serves first-rate Creole and continental fare at every meal. Specialties include seafood-baked eggplant (a slice of fried eggplant topped with a combination of dirty rice, shrimp, crabmeat, and crawfish and covered with a rich seafood butter sauce), blue cheese steak, and Gulf fish *moutarde* (sautéed local fish with lemon butter, topped with Dijon mustard, hollandaise, roasted almonds, and new potatoes). Peanut-butter pie is the trademark dessert. The setting is a shabby-chic dining room with art (for sale on the walls), along with a shady patio and a piano bar. It's a real locals' favorite, worth venturing a bit off the beaten path.

For a sublime blend of soul and Creole cooking, drop by the **Praline Connection** (542 Frenchmen St., 504/943-3934; also 907 S. Peters St., 504/523-3973), famous for both its crawfish étouffée and its bread pudding. This is one of several great eateries, along with a number of hopping bars and music clubs, that you can find along ultrahip Frenchmen Street. There are a few Praline Connections around town these days, but the original on Faubourg Marigny's Frenchmen Street tends to draw the greatest praise. In two simple dining rooms, the staff, clad in natty white shirts, black bow ties, and black fedoras, moves about efficiently with hot platters of red beans and rice, collard greens, bread pudding with caramel sauce, étouffée, smothered pork, and other hearty—and often quite spicy—renderings of both soul and Creole cooking. Local beers and wines are sold, and you can pick up the ingredients and seasonings here to pre-

Praline Connection

pare your own renditions of these foods back home. The Warehouse District branch is a full-on gospel and blues hall with live music and a fabulous brunch.

CREATIVE AND CONTEMPORARY

Marigny Brasserie (640 Frenchmen St., 504/945-4472, $16–26) is a slick, modern space whose kitchen puts a contemporary spin on both Louisiana and French ingredients and recipes. The grilled filet mignon over roasted-garlic mashed potatoes with a bordelaise sauce reflects the kitchen's simple approach to fine, contemporary food. Several light salads are available, including a delicious strawberry and spinach salad with walnuts and stilton cheese. The stylish bar is a relaxing place to sip cocktails before heading to one of the nearby music clubs.

The **Bank Cafe** (2001 Burgundy St., 504/371-5260, $16–24) occupies a handsome former bank building with 22-foot-high ceilings and a snazzy art decor bar. Large works of art add color to the otherwise sleek, minimalist

FOOD

THE CELEBRATED CRAWFISH

Nicknamed "mudbugs" or "crawdaddies," crawfish are easily the most celebrated of Louisiana's many varieties of seafood. These humble three- to four-inch freshwater crustaceans, found in swamps, bayous, and rivers, are worshipped with palpable fanaticism and served year-round at restaurants throughout the state, but especially in the Cajun Wetlands. They bear a strong resemblance to their much larger saltwater cousins, lobsters.

Louisiana is home to about 30 varieties of crawfish, better known as crayfish in other parts of the world. Two species, the white river crawfish and the red swamp crawfish, are harvested commercially. Live crawfish are first harvested around December; a good season lasts into midsummer. Peak months are March–May. This is the best time to visit a restaurant in Acadiana for authentic crawfish boils.

For many outsiders, crawfish are an acquired taste, typically first encountered as ingredients in native Cajun fare such as étouffée. Eating them boiled, by breaking their shells and extracting their tender and faintly sweet meat, takes a bit of effort and can be quite messy – it's all part of the fun. The crawfish are boiled live in a concoction of water, seasoning (Zatarain's makes the most famous brand), cayenne pepper, Tabasco or other hot sauce, lemon juice, olive oil, salt, and bay leaves. Among true devotees, this is by far the best way to eat crawfish.

You can also find crawfish served fried in po'boys or platters, in a thick bisque, in salads, and as "dressing" atop redfish, drum, snapper, and other local seafood. In fact, there really aren't too many savory dishes served in Cajun Country that *aren't* made with crawfish.

The earliest settlers in the Cajun Wetlands began eating and farming crawfish as early as the 18th century, but commercial crawfish farming didn't take hold in the state until the 1930s and '40s, when the state's flood-control projects created concentrated populations of crawfish. The town of Henderson had the first major crawfish farm. At first, fishing operations relied on the natural bounty of crawfish that flourished in the Atchafalaya Basin, but harvests often fell short of demand, which increased – and continues to increase – steadily every year. In the 1960s, Louisiana State University developed a system for successfully raising crawfish in man-made ponds. Water level is critical to crawfish farming, and these controlled ponds allow the manipulation of water levels, virtually guaranteeing successful harvests even during years when low rainfall in the Atchafalaya Basin leads to weak crawfish crops.

Many of those employed in crawfish fishing come from families that have been in this business for multiple generations. They fish with traps similar to lobster traps – these pillow-shaped wire containers have a pair of funnels that allow crawfish to wander in.

Most farmers raise crawfish using man-made ponds during periods when they're not engaged in other types of farming; it's an especially popular practice among rice farmers. It's usually possible to harvest more than 1,000 pounds of crawfish per acre, and most commercial ponds range 20–40 acres.

Today, more than 90 percent of the crawfish farmed commercially in the United States come from Louisiana, where about 1,600 farmers and nearly 1,000 commercial fisherman produce the crop (California and Texas are the two other states with significant crawfish-farming operations). In a good year, the combined annual yield of crawfish – both raised in farms and fished from natural wetlands – exceeds 100 million pounds and has an impact on the state economy approaching $125 million.

© NEW ORLEANS CVB/CARL PURCELL

crawfish dinner

space. The kitchen serves excellent Mediterranean-inspired food, including Moroccan-style braised lamb shank with couscous, *gremolata,* pine nuts, parsnip, and carrots; and fennel-and-lemon–crusted roasted chicken with kale, whipped potatoes, and roasted-garlic pan sauce. Try the saffron–black pepper flan with fresh local strawberries for dessert. There's also an excellent Sunday brunch.

CASUAL COOKING

Despite the name, **Bywater Bar-b-que** (3162 Dauphine St., 504/944-4445, $5–12) is more than just a place to get tasty smoked ribs, pulled pork, and tangy barbecued chicken. This campy restaurant with a shrine to Barbie dolls and a "no-smoking" section that consists of a chair nailed upside down to the ceiling also serves pastas, grilled veggies, pizzas, and—at breakfast—eggs Benedict, huevos rancheros, and plenty of other yummy edibles. The diminutive restaurant is in the Bywater neighborhood, about a dozen blocks downriver from Frenchmen Street. It's definitely worth checking out if you're in these parts and deserving of a special trip if you are a fan of barbecue.

Way out on the east end of Bywater in a modest white-frame house by the levee, easygoing (**Elizabeth's** (601 Gallier St., 504/944-4810, under $6) requires an even longer journey from the Quarter, but it does serve exceptional breakfasts and lunch (it's not open for dinner). Owner-chef Heidi Trull comes up with all sorts of imaginative specials and also manages to chat with many of her customers, some of whom travel here from the farthest reaches of the city. The Loula May breakfast po'boy is a local specialty—it comes served on fresh-baked French bread and spilling over with scrambled eggs, hot andouille sausage, and melted cheddar. Order cheese grits or a side of praline-flavored bacon to go with it. Lunch favorites include turkey club sandwiches, fried catfish po'boys, and sides of fresh-cut sweet-potato fries.

During normal dining hours, **La Peniche** (1940 Dauphine St., 504/943-1460, $6–14) is nothing special—just a friendly, reasonably priced neighborhood cafe serving satisfying breakfast, lunch, and dinner fare—country-fried steak, pecan waffles smothered with peanut butter, good burgers, and coffee. At 3 in the morning, however, especially after you've just stumbled out of a bar or caught a case of the late-night munchies, La Peniche feels like paradise—the place is open 24 hours except for one 43-hour span from Tuesday at 2 P.M. till Thursday at 9 A.M. Note, however, that the restaurant has had much more limited hours owing to short staffing and slower demand since Katrina, so check ahead to confirm how late La Peniche is open. Even if you're not able to dine here all night, the dishy staff and colorful local following make it a fun place to eavesdrop or make new friends.

ETHNIC

On the edge of Faubourg Marigny, just a few blocks up Frenchmen Street from the main cluster of bars and restaurants, **Wasabi** (900 Frenchmen St., 504/943-9433, $9–19) serves excellent sushi and a delicious grilled squid dish. The deep-fried jumbo soft-shell crab stir-fried with jalapeños, onions, and Asian spices is a real treat. Also try baby octopus salad, soft-shell crab rolls, or one of the many daily-changing specials. The dark and cozy space is actually half mellow-cool neighborhood bar and half Japanese restaurant.

For some of the best Thai food in the city, drop by cozy **Sukho Thai** (1913 Royal St., 504/948-9309, $8–14), where friendly service and walls hung with local art create a hip yet informal vibe.

Big portions of traditional Italian and Creole fare are heaped onto the plates at **Adolfo's** (611 Frenchmen St., 504/948-3800, $12–21), a longtime neighborhood standby that's especially strong on seafood dishes such as crab-and-crawfish cannelloni and sautéed soft-shell crabs. There's usually a very nice rack of lamb on the menu, too, often paired with a rosemary-garlic sauce. It's a small place, and reservations are a must if you have four or more in your party. Downstairs, the Apple Barrel Bar is a dark and cozy spot to nurse a cocktail before or after dinner.

FOOD

Mona's Cafe (504 Frenchmen St., 504/949-4115; also 4126 Magazine St., 504/894-9800; $5–12) serves great, cheap Middle Eastern food and is also a richly stocked Lebanese grocery. Start with some snacks, such as zaater bread (baked with ground thyme, oregano, sesame seeds, sumac, and olive oil), mixed hummus and foul (mashed fava beans with garlic, hot peppers, lemon, and olive oil), and spinach pie. Chicken kabobs, gyros, lamb chops, and grape-leaf platters rank among the several excellent entrées.

Next door to Mona's, **Hookah Cafe** (500 Frenchmen St., 504/943-1101, $5–10) is not only a great place to hear live jazz and other cool music, it's also an excellent venue for Indian and Middle Eastern cuisine. Other draws include highly entertaining belly-dancing shows and the opportunity to go boho and smoke (tobacco) out of a hookah pipe. Hookah is slightly hokey, but that's part of the fun. The menu is tapas-style and eclectic, with the likes of whipped butternut squash with cashews, lentil pâté with pita chips, sesame-crusted lamb with papaya-mint sauce, and goat-cheese dumplings with orange-ginger sauce. And food is served here till 2 A.M. on Fridays and Saturdays, and till midnight other days (except Monday, when it's closed).

New Orleans architecture, music, and even food have been influenced by the Caribbean, but **Cafe Negril** (606 Frenchmen St., 504/944-4744, $10–15) is one of the only places in the metro area that serves an entirely West Indies menu. The space along the Frenchmen Street entertainment strip is bright and colorful (there's a larger-than-life Bob Marley mural on one wall), and the food is quite good and well seasoned, with an emphasis on seafood (such as Jamaican jerk fish of the day). The ceviche starter is excellent, and regulars swear by the West Indies curried goat stew.

QUICK BITES

Set inside a strikingly restored historic building in the heart of the neighborhood, **Schiro's Community Cafe** (2483 Royal St., 504/944-6666, $4–10) serves many needs of locals—it's not only a restaurant serving three meals every

Melonhead Cafe and Market

© ANDREW COLLINS

day but Sunday, but it's also a small grocery store and launderette. Baked stuffed catfish, which is served on Fridays, is a specialty that even nonlocals will travel here for, but anytime it's a nice spot for sandwiches, burgers, and other munchies.

In Bywater, **Melonhead Cafe and Market** (2801 Dauphine St., 504/942-4226) is a cute spot at Dauphine and St. Ferdinand with juice, smoothies, soups, free wireless, and healthful sandwiches and edibles. There are plenty of vegan items here, plus excellent breakfast fare. It's in a characterful yellow building with a cheery, fun ambience, right on the border with Faubourg Marigny.

JAVA JOINTS

Sharing a corner with a couple of gay bars on the border between the Marigny and Bywater, **Flora Coffee Shop and Gallery** (2600 Royal St., 504/947-8358) is a cool little place with sidewalk seating, worn-in furnishings, big portions of coffee elixirs, and light snacks. It's a nice place to read a book or chat with locals. The local chain **P.J.'s** has a sunny storefront cafe at 524 Frenchmen Street.

Central Business and Warehouse Districts

CREATIVE AND CONTEMPORARY

A boisterous power-lunch room that's also a hit with the dinner crowd, trendy **Herbsaint** (701 St. Charles Ave., 504/524-4114, $17–26) sits along a nondescript stretch of St. Charles, its setting brightened by tall windows, soft-yellow walls, a tile floor, and a young and good-looking staff. Start with fried frogs' legs or a plate of herb gnocchi with wild mushrooms, sage, and roasted garlic. The grilled organic chicken with lemon risotto and artichokes is a top main course. The wine selection is terrific; also offered are many cool cocktails (lime gin fizz, for instance) and wine-tasting flights of three vintages.

Restaurant Cuvée (322 Magazine St., 504/587-9001, $18–28) has one of the finest wine lists in the South, plus A-one Creole cooking infused with contemporary French, Spanish, and other Mediterranean ingredients. Start with char-grilled local oysters served with parmigiano-reggiano and white-truffle oil, pause to enjoy a salad of pepper-crusted tuna carpaccio with fresh heart of palm and teardrop tomatoes, and then move on to a spectacular main dish of mustard-and-herb-crusted fillet of salmon with lump crabmeat, brie orzo, and lemon confit. The lighting fixtures in this elegant dining room, with exposed brick walls, dark-wood trim, and white linens, are fashioned from wine bottles of prestigious vintages. It's an ideal locale for a special occasion but without the pretension that mars some of the CBD's top dining establishments.

◖ **Restaurant August** (301 Tchoupitoulas St., 504/299-9777, $21–37) is presided over by talented and charismatic chef John Besh, the Louisiana born-and-bred kitchen wizard who earned fame on the North Shore with his restaurant Artesia. He opened this Warehouse District restaurant in 2001, inside a handsome late-1800s Creole French building, and it's been tough to get a table here ever since. Besh presents uncomplicated yet richly nuanced con-

temporary American fare, with healthy doses of both local and Mediterranean ingredients. The light salad of lavender-grilled figs, Serrano ham, goat cheese, and arugula makes for one of the restaurant's most celebrated starters. You might follow with slow-cooked Louisiana grouper cheeks with artichokes, sweet peas, apple bacon, and wild onions, or an imaginative lasagna layered with rabbit, veal sweetbreads, and chunks of fresh lobster. Do save room for goat-milk cheesecake with rosemary-honey ice cream and a hint of bee pollen.

René Bistro (817 Common St., 504/412-2580, $15–22) is another of the stellar and relatively young hotel restaurants that's generating lots of buzz around the CBD. Chef René Bajeux is widely regarded as one of the top French cooks in the United States, having previously served as executive chef at the Windsor Court. His menu, which has few dishes more costly than $20, focuses on classic French bistro fare but with many creative twists—you won't go wrong with the sautéed skate served with an artichoke and green bean salad and topped with a caper emulsion. Sautéed foie gras with a white-truffle flan and reisling reduction has fans of goose liver swooning. There's live jazz many evenings, and the Sunday brunch ranks among the tastiest such affairs in the city.

Wolfe's in the Warehouse (Marriott Convention Center, 859 Convention Center Blvd., 504/613-2882, $19–32), run by the same chef at the French Quarter's acclaimed Peristyle, Tom Wolfe, turns out some amazing fare, including tender Kobe-beef short ribs, and a crepe filled with Hudson Valley foie gras and duck glazed with Steen's Cane Syrup. The restaurant had been open only a month before Katrina hit, but it reopened quickly and has done well ever since. It's set inside a charming mid-19th-century cotton warehouse.

A reliable pick for creative Creole-inspired Italian fare, **Tommy's Cuisine** (746 Tchoupitoulas St., 504/581-1103, $14–26) is a charming

FOOD

space in the Warehouse District close to the many art galleries of Julia Street. The warmly lighted dining room with paneled walls, mirrors, and old-fashioned sconces creates an appealing scene for sampling oysters Tommy (baked in the shell with romano cheese, pancetta, and roasted red pepper), soft-shell crabs with linguini, Roma tomatoes, and a reggiano-crawfish sauce, or chicken roasted with white wine, olive oil, rosemary-garlic jus, and a hint of lemon. The pecan praline bread pudding with a bananas Foster sauce and vanilla ice cream is like a glorious combination of the city's greatest desserts.

The bigger and louder of Emeril Lagasse's acclaimed restaurants, **Emeril's** (800 Tchoupitoulas St., 504/528-9393, www.emerils.com) takes its hits from critics who complain about haughty service and high prices, but this is the domain of one of the world's most famous chefs, and it's always packed. All in all, if you can get a table here (book well ahead), go for it—Emeril didn't become famous for no reason. He's a great cook with a great kitchen staff, and the food here is more complex and imaginative than at NOLA, his French Quarter restaurant. Try citrus-and-tea–glazed duck with savory caramelized onion–bread pudding and *haricots verts,* or grilled filet mignon with truffle-creamed potatoes, sautéed asparagus, crispy root vegetable chips, and a red-wine reduction. Desserts include a laudable Key lime pie with berry coulis as well as crepes filled with homemade mascarpone cheese and topped with orange sauce. The space is airy, high-ceilinged, and dramatic, the quintessence of Warehouse District chic.

7 on Fulton (Riverfront Hotel, 700 Fulton St., 504/525-7555, $18–32) has been opened by renowned local restaurateur Vicky Bayley and is helmed by noted chef David English. It's in the trendy Riverfront Hotel and serves an imaginative mix of contemporary Southern- and continental-inspired dishes, such as crispy-skinned duck breast with a honey glaze alongside dirty rice with bits of duck-leg confit, and grilled Angus strip steak with braised short ribs and oxtail-mushroom ravioli, and barbecue

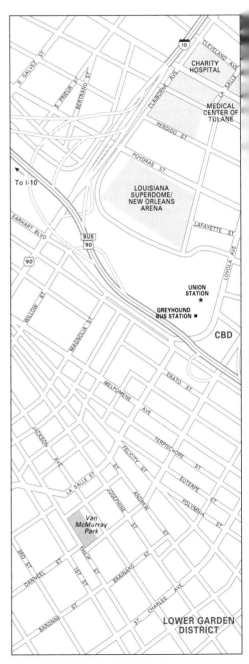

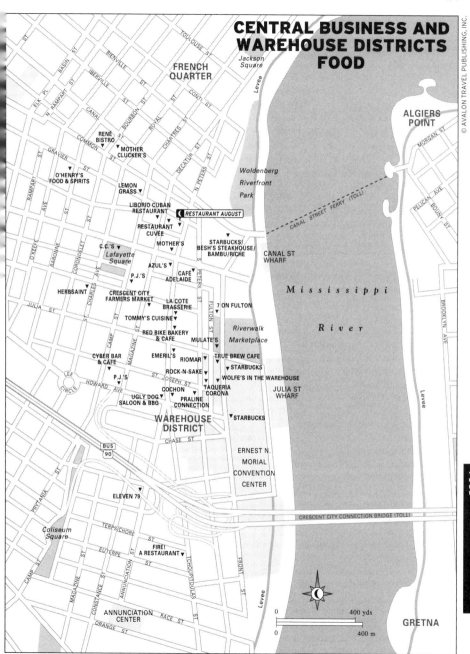

CENTRAL BUSINESS AND
WAREHOUSE DISTRICTS
FOOD

© AVALON TRAVEL PUBLISHING, INC.

FRENCH
QUARTER

Jackson
Square

ALGIERS
POINT

RENÉ
BISTRO
▼ MOTHER
CLUCKER'S

O'HENRY'S
FOOD & SPIRITS

LEMON
GRASS ▼

Woldenberg
Riverfront
Park

LIBORIO CUBAN
RESTAURANT ▼
◖ ▼ RESTAURANT AUGUST
▼ RESTAURANT
CUVÉE

C.C.'S ▼
Lafayette
Square

AZUL'S ▼
▼ MOTHER'S

CAFÉ
ADELAIDE

STARBUCKS/
BESH'S STEAKHOUSE/
BAMBU/RICHE

CANAL ST
WHARF

CANAL STREET FERRY (TOLL)

P.J.'S ▼

HERBSAINT ▼
CRESCENT CITY
FARMERS MARKET

LA COTE
BRASSERIE ▼

7 ON FULTON

Mississippi

TOMMY'S CUISINE ▼

RED BIKE BAKERY
& CAFE ▼

*Riverwalk
Marketplace*

River

CYBER BAR
& CAFE ▼

EMERIL'S ▼

MULATE'S ▼

RIOMAR ▼

TRUE BREW CAFE ▼

P.J.'S ▼

ROCK-N-SAKE ▼

▼ STARBUCKS

ST. JOSEPH ST.

COCHON ▼

UGLY DOG ▼
SALOON & BBQ

TAQUERIA
CORONA ▼

▼ WOLFE'S IN THE WAREHOUSE

JULIA ST
WHARF

PRALINE
CONNECTION

WAREHOUSE
DISTRICT

▼ STARBUCKS

CHASE ST.

ERNEST N.
MORIAL
CONVENTION
CENTER

BUS
90

ELEVEN 79 ▼

CRESCENT CITY CONNECTION BRIDGE (TOLL)

*Coliseum
Square*

FIRE!
A RESTAURANT ▼

ANNUNCIATION
CENTER

0   400 yds

0   400 m

GRETNA

Levee

FOOD

shrimp with fried polenta sticks. High ceilings and tall windows create an airy feel.

The popular chef John Besh struck gold again with **Besh's Steakhouse at Harrah's** (512 S. Peters St., 504/533-6111, $24–45), a lavish, clubby space that keeps gamers happy and gives the big spenders something to blow their cash on. This is a loud, fancy, big-portions kind of place, where you can expect tasty 40-day–dry-aged New York strip steak with blue-cheese butter and onion rings, or a surf-and-turf of fillet of beef and grilled lobster-tail sandwich. Harrah's latest culinary addition, **Riche** (512 S. Peters St., 504/533-6000, $22–44), opened in September 2006 at the new Fulton Street Promenade, which adjoins Harrah's brand-new 26-story luxury hotel. Celebrity chef and cookbook author Todd English opened this fancy spot that feels and looks like a proper French brasserie, complete with such authentic yet updated French fare as seven-onion soup with Gruyere cheese, and hanger steak with shallot-watercress butter and cornmeal-battered shrimp. You can also hear lively music in the adjacent 528 By Todd English jazz club.

Set inside the glamorous Loews New Orleans Hotel, **Cafe Adelaide** (300 Poydras St., 504/595-3305, $24–36) is a highly touted newcomer from the Brennan family, offering great food at breakfast, lunch, and dinner. Start the day with honeycomb waffles topped with toasted-pecan syrup. At dinner, you might start with the oyster-and-artichoke cakes. Main dishes of note include lemongrass-glazed yellow-fin tuna with charred-orange and caramel sauce, and Creole-spiced fillet of beef with Creole-tomato jam and mushroom fricassee. Lighter fare, as well as a long list of colorful cocktails, is available in the trendy Swizzle Stick Bar.

Noted chef Donald Link, of Herbsaint, runs **Cochon** (930 Tchoupitoulas St., 504/588-2123, $12–17), which opened in April 2006 in the Warehouse District and serves a stellar blend of Cajun and contemporary American victuals, specializing in small, tapas-style portions. There's an in-house butcher, as the restaurant receives whole pigs and butchers them there, using all parts. Highlights on the menu include fried chicken livers with pepper-jelly toast, smoked ham hocks with braised greens, and a wood-fired oyster roast. There are some larger plates, too, such as smoked beef brisket with horseradish potato salad. Save room for the orange ice-box pie or banana pudding. You can watch chef Link cook through the open kitchen.

In the classy Renaissance Arts Hotel, **La Cote Brasserie** (700 Tchoupitoulas St., 504/613-2350, $15–28) is a snazzy restaurant decked out with abstract artwork and done in bright colors, creating an appropriate setting for Chuck Subra's refined modern French and Creole fare. Try the sea scallops marinated with lemongrass, star fruit, and watercress, or herb-roasted Cornish hen with Louisiana crawfish–andouille hash. The Sunday brunch is exceptional, especially Croque Madame, a sautéed ham, gruyère, and fried-egg sandwich.

If the name of **Fire! A Restaurant** (1377 Annunciation St., 504/566-1950, $14–27) sounds a bit curious, consider that this hip restaurant occupies a dramatic old firehouse with high ceilings and atmospheric redbrick walls. The food tends toward the modern and unusual, with specialties such as tempura squash blossoms over greens with sweet chili and horseradish-Dijon dipping sauce; flatbread topped with grilled pineapple, prosciutto, and spicy Hoisen sauce; and Asian-spiced shrimp skewers over jicama-cucumber slaw with mango vinaigrette.

Quirky **Eleven 79** (1179 Annunciation St., 504/299-1179, $11–20) has a strong local following for its Creole-inspired Italian fare. The grilled calamari with pecorino-cheese polenta is heavenly, and you won't go wrong either with oysters panne served with a white rémoulade. The diminutive, charming restaurant occupies a restored bungalow in the shadows of the Pontchartrain Expressway bridge, just on the edge of the Warehouse and Lower Garden Districts. It took a big hit following Katrina but finally reopened to joyous diners in September 2006.

Although it can fill up with business travelers (it's two blocks from the convention center), bustling **RioMar** (800 S. Peters St., 504/525-3474, $14–20) maintains a warm and personal ambience, owing largely to the well-trained staff and welcoming dining room, set inside a vintage industrial building with a slate floor and barrel-vaulted archways. The specialty is seafood prepared Latin American–style. You could make a small meal of the ceviche sampler, with four types of raw seafood each cured in a different Latin tradition: Spanish (with octopus and olive oil), Panamanian (with habanero peppers and lime), Ecuadorian (with shrimp, tomato, and citrus juice), and Peruvian (with tomatoes, onions, and cilantro). Entrée highlights include littleneck clams steamed with parsley and chorizo, and yellowfin tuna served rare and wrapped in Serrano ham with a chickpea purée and Romesco sauce. Pork chops and steaks are also served.

Azul's (Ambassador Hotel, 535 Tchoupitoulas St., 504/599-2111, $14–22) opened in 2006 and has earned a loyal following for its extremely tasty Cuban fare, including shrimp with a sweet-chili glaze and truffle oil.

At the ultraswank International House hotel, **Lemon Grass** (217 Camp St., 504/523-1200, $14–24) is a dark and sexy dining room with dark and sexy patrons. The food, which is generally excellent, is almost an afterthought for many of the hip diners who come here to see and be seen. Still, don't overlook such tempting starters as the spring roll of minced chicken, jicama, and wood-ear mushrooms served with a light citrus sauce, or crab cakes served with a wonton and sweet Creole mustard–chili coulis. Main courses include wok-smoked salmon steak with grilled vegetables, and Asian curry gulf shrimp over angel-hair pasta.

CASUAL COOKING

Like the famous original outside Lafayette, **Mulate's** (201 Julia St., 504/522-1492, $13–19) serves tasty Cajun fare alongside rollicking Cajun music. You'll often see big groups of people and families seated in this enormous dance hall and restaurant on the edge of the Warehouse District, a short walk from the casino and the Quarter. It can feel a little bustouristy in here, but if you're not able to make it out to the real Cajun Country, this is a nice opportunity to experience authentic music and food from the region. Specialties from the long, long menu include catfish Mulate (topped with crawfish étouffée), crabmeat au gratin, and—when you just can't make up your mind—Mulate's Cajun Seafood Platter, which includes stuffed crab, fried crawfish tails, butterflied shrimp, fried catfish, fried oysters, jambalaya, corn macque choux, and home-style fries.

ETHNIC

By many accounts, **Rock-n-Sake** (823 Fulton St., 504/581-7253, $15–22) serves some of the freshest and most interesting sushi in the South, including spicy crawfish rolls, giant clams, wasabi-infused *tobiko,* and baby softshell crab. Tofu teriyaki "steak," udon noodles with thinly sliced beef and onions, snow crab salad, barbecued eel over rice, and chicken *katsu* round out the menu. The dining room is noisy and vibrant, a bit like a nightclub (plenty of regulars come to sip sake martinis, melon balls, and other pretty cocktails), with Mardi Gras masks and large contemporary paintings covering the walls, and loud rock and pop music blasting in the background. The staff and the crowd tend to be young and in-the-know.

Check out **Liborio Cuban Restaurant** (321 Magazine St., 504/581-9680, $11–19) when the mood for hearty, authentic Cuban fare strikes. New Orleans has a long and close relationship with Cuba, or at least it did during the 18th and 19th centuries, and this casual Warehouse District restaurant does the island nation's robust cuisine justice. The kitchen serves a terrific paella with shrimp, squid, and pork, as well as stuffed Cuban steaks, lobster-stuffed steak, hefty Cuban sandwiches, and caramel flan for dessert.

In the massive Harrah's Casino, **Bambu** (365 Canal St., 504/533-6000, $12–22) serves well-prepared Asian fusion fare, with dishes from Japan, China, Vietnam, Thailand, and elsewhere. It's a good late-night option. Local chef Ricky Toy, who has worked at Brennan restaurants and at Whole Foods, prepares honey-wasabi shrimp, Cantonese-style barbecue duck, and bananas Foster crepe smothered with a rich chocolate sauce.

QUICK BITES

The celeb photos lining the walls of **Mother's** (401 Poydras St., 504/523-9656, $4–12), a glorified cafeteria with brash lighting, Formica tables, and chatty servers, attests to its longstanding popularity—it opened in 1938, and still it draws a mix of downtown office workers, hungry tourists, and local politicos. The most famous dishes here are the roast beef or baked ham po'boys, but you can also get very good gumbo, jambalaya, étouffée, and other humble Creole and Cajun fare. It opens at 5 A.M., which is good to know if you happen to be returning to your CBD hotel late with hunger pangs after barhopping.

An easygoing down-home hangout in the Warehouse District, the **Ugly Dog Saloon and BBQ** (401 Andrew Higgins Dr., 504/569-8459, $4–10) can be counted on for cheap drinks (especially during the weekday happy hours), great crawfish boils on Sundays in late winter, and a nice range of barbecued favorites, such as pulled-pork sandwiches. Fancy it ain't.

JAVA JOINTS

The **Cyber Bar and Cafe** (900 Camp St., 504/528-3828), at the Contemporary Arts Center, is more than a convenient spot to check your email and surf the Web. The artsy, attractive place has all kinds of coffee drinks plus beer and wine, and it's an excellent spot for sandwiches, snacks, and desserts (baked fresh at several New Orleans bakeries).

Attached to a funky theater and performance space, **True Brew Cafe** (200 Julia St., 504/524-8441) is most crowded before and after performances but makes a nice respite any time of day. Soups, salads, and sandwiches are offered, plus the usual array of baked goods and coffee drinks.

The Garden District and Uptown

TRADITIONAL CREOLE AND CAJUN

There are only so many of New Orleans's most vaunted institutions of fine dining that you can possibly try during any one visit—even if you have the time, you may not have the appetite. If you must put one place at the top of your list, make it **C Commander's Palace** (1403 Washington Ave., 504/899-8221, $25–40), the flagship eatery in the famed Brennan family empire, and *the* place to try turtle soup, Gulf fish seared in a cast-iron pan, and bread pudding soufflé—especially if you're uninitiated to such famous New Orleans foods. Lunch really isn't superexpensive (there's a wonderful three-course prix fixe for about $30 at lunch, and $35 at dinner), making it a good time to test the waters. At dinner, consider the Creole-spiced filet mignon served over truffled buttermilk–mashed potatoes, caramelized onions, smoked mushrooms, and tasso *marchands de vin*. The weekend jazz brunches are the stuff of legend. Reservations, as far ahead as possible, are a must. Commander's was looted badly after Hurricane Katrina and didn't reopen for nearly a full year.

In an off-the-beaten-path location beyond the Crescent City Connection bridge and a few blocks south of the convention center in the Lower Garden District, **Le Citron Bistro** (1539 Religious St., 504/566-9051, $12–18) occupies an ancient Creole cottage that's nearly 200 years old (a rarity in this part of town—in fact, it's the oldest building in town above Canal Street). The kitchen turns out such tempting treats as pannéed (breaded and lightly fried) rainbow trout, catfish St. Jean Baptiste (topped with lump crabmeat salad, fried sweet-potato

© NEW ORLEANS CVB/RICHARD NOWITZ

jazz brunch at Commander's Palace

chips, and papaya sauce), and shrimp-and-oyster pasta. The food is simple, hearty, and reasonably priced.

CREATIVE AND CONTEMPORARY

In the space that used to hold Sugar Magnolia, **Jackson** (1910 Magazine St., 504/529-9599, $18–26) is a similarly appealing neighborhood restaurant that opened in February 2006. The ambitious menu of creative Creole fare has been making this a destination dining experience even for foodies all over the city. Sample such delicious items as center-cut filet mignon with a cabernet-orange reduction, and sesame-crusted tuna with lime-wasabi mayo. There's a popular brunch on weekends, and on Thursday nights the restaurant hosts wine tastings on its lovely balcony with views of Magazine Street.

Uptown has become such a great dining destination in recent years that what had been a discreet locals' hangout for many years, **Clancy's** (6100 Annunciation St., 504/895-1111, $16–27), has almost come to

feel a tad touristy. No matter the increasing crowds—the staff works hard to fit everybody in and make both regulars and newcomers feel right at home. The loosely Creole-meets-Italian menu changes often but usually has a few reliable standbys, such as fried oysters with brie, smoked soft-shell crab with lump crabmeat, and filet mignon with stilton and a red-wine demi-glace. There are several dining areas in this rambling building, the quietest and most romantic being upstairs, the more convivial and social in the front room adjacent to the bar.

One of the first eateries to get tourists out of the French Quarter and up to Riverbend, **Brigtsen's** (723 Dante St., 504/861-7610, $19–26) occupies a lovely Victorian cottage with a warm, homey dining room with Victorian-style wallpaper and soft lighting. The restaurant is perhaps most famous for its amazingly good and ever-changing seafood platter, which on a typical night might include grilled drum fish with shrimp and corn macque choux sauce, crabmeat Thermidor, baked

FOOD

oysters Rockefeller, baked oyster with bacon and leeks, deviled crab, and eggplant caponata (all for a quite reasonable $25). Other commendable dishes include a starter of braised rabbit in phyllo pastry with creamed spinach, bacon, leeks, and white truffle oil, and braised venison on a potato pancake with roasted vegetables and apple cider pan gravy.

On bustling Oak Street, funky **€ Jacques-Imo's Cafe** (8324 Oak St., 504/861-0886, $14–22) presents a mix of eclectic contemporary dishes and New Orleans standbys. You walk through the bar and the kitchen to reach the rambling, loud dining room. Loyal fans can't rave enough about the charismatic staff and the ever-changing list of specials, which has featured smothered rabbit with onion-strewn grits, and country-fried venison chop with wild-mushroom pan gravy. The fried mirlitons with oysters and rich oyster-tasso hollandaise sauce are also commendable. Every meal comes with delicious butter-topped cornbread muffins and two sides, such as mashed sweet potatoes and smothered cabbage. Finish off your meal with energy-pumping coffee-bean crème brûlée. Reservations are available only for large groups, and the place fills up quickly. So expect quite a wait on most nights—pass the time at the charming bar.

One of the most convivial restaurants in the city, **Upperline** (1413 Upperline St., 504/891-9822, $18–25) is run by colorful owner JoAnn Clevenger, who loves to mingle with patrons and talk about her wonderful art and photography collection, which fills the restaurant's eclectically furnished dining rooms. Chef Ken Smith prepares Creole food with plenty of inventive twists and global spins: beef tournedos with stilton, balsamic mushrooms, and thyme is one exceptional entrée, and grilled Gulf shrimp with warm salad niçoise and tapenade also scores high marks. One of the best ways to enjoy a meal here is to order the seven-course Taste of New Orleans dinner ($35), which includes duck étouffée, oyster stew, fried green tomatoes with shrimp rémoulade (a true Big Easy classic prepared to perfection here), andouille gumbo, spicy shrimp with jalapeño cornbread,

roast duck with ginger-peach sauce, and warm bread pudding with toffee sauce. It's hard to say who will be angrier at you for indulging in such a meal: your doctor or your dentist.

In a cozy, lacy Uptown cottage on a narrow stretch of Magazine Street, **Martinique Bistro** (5908 Magazine St., 504/891-8495, $13–19) is a little gem of an eatery that woos diners with its sweetly romantic dining room and cloistered courtyard. Even if the food weren't wonderful, you could feel happy just spending a couple of hours here with a date. But the Caribbean-inspired French fare is outstanding—it's prepared by chef Hubert Sandot, who is, in fact, of both West Indies and French descent. Specialties include shrimp with sun-dried–mango curry, sesame-crusted salmon with sweet banana sauce, and jerk lamb shank braised in a sauce of riesling and papaya. Many wines are sold by the half bottle.

A high-ceilinged storefront restaurant along a lively stretch of Magazine, **Lilette** (3627 Magazine St., 504/895-1636, $17–23) is one of the neighborhood's more idiosyncratic and enjoyable restaurants, a setting equally suitable for a special occasion or a meal after or before shopping (both lunch and dinner are served). Unlike many or even most of the city's upscale contemporary dining establishments, Lilette's kitchen rarely attempts to improve upon Creole or Cajun cooking and instead borrows heavily from France and Northern Italy for inspiration. The grilled hanger steak with thin-cut fries and marrowed bordelaise sauce tastes fresh from a Paris bistro. More complex is the entrée of roasted Muscovy duck breast with cabbage, chorizo sausage, and black-olive sauce.

A dapper little eatery that's quickly developed a lofty reputation among foodies, **La Petite Grocery** (4238 Magazine St., 504/891-3377, $20–26) serves modern takes on French favorites. As the name suggests, the restaurant occupies what had been a small neighborhood grocery store. Behind flowing velvet drapes lies a romantic, subtly lighted dining room where you might sample grilled fillet of beef over roquefort and garlic-potato gratin, New Orleans–style bouillabaisse, and tomato-and-mint–braised

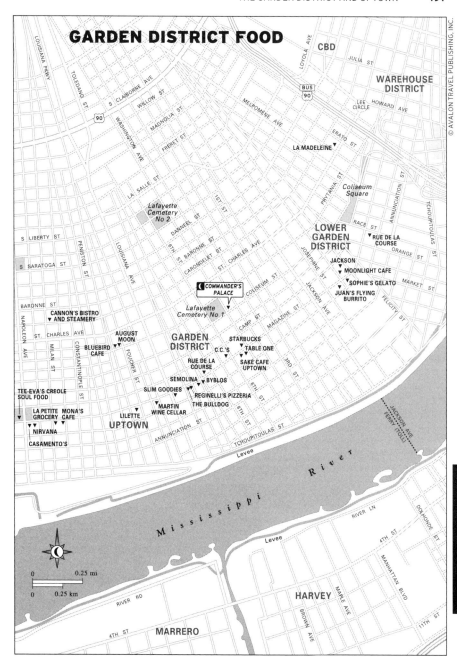

GARDEN DISTRICT FOOD

CBD

WAREHOUSE DISTRICT

LA MADELEINE

Coliseum Square

LOWER GARDEN DISTRICT

RUE DE LA COURSE

JACKSON
MOONLIGHT CAFE
SOPHIE'S GELATO
JUAN'S FLYING BURRITO

COMMANDER'S PALACE

Lafayette Cemetery No 1

Lafayette Cemetery No 2

CANNON'S BISTRO AND STEAMERY

AUGUST MOON
BLUEBIRD CAFE

GARDEN DISTRICT

STARBUCKS
C.C.'S
TABLE ONE

RUE DE LA COURSE
SAKE CAFE UPTOWN

SEMOLINA
BYBLOS

TEE-EVA'S CREOLE SOUL FOOD

SLIM GOODIES
REGINELLI'S PIZZERIA
THE BULLDOG
MARTIN WINE CELLAR

LA PETITE MONA'S
GROCERY CAFE
LILETTE
NIRVANA
UPTOWN
CASAMENTO'S

Mississippi River

Levee

JACKSON AVE FERRY (TOLL)

FOOD

RIVER LN

Levee

HARVEY

0   0.25 mi

0   0.25 km

RIVER RD

4TH ST   MARRERO

lamb shank with roasted red onions and ricotta gnocchi. The steamed mussels in butter and white wine make a memorable starter.

Dick and Jenny's (4501 Tchoupitoulas St., 504/894-9880, $14–23) keeps regulars happy with its neighborhood feel, outgoing staff, and reasonably priced contemporary city fare. Grilled filet mignon with lobster and brie is a dazzling main dish, and don't miss the crab cake served atop a fried green tomato. The only kicker is one you might expect of such a popular place: There's almost always a pretty long wait for a table (and reservations are not accepted).

The domain of one of the city's most talented chefs, **Table One** (2800 Magazine St., 504/872-9035, $16–27) is helmed by Gerard Maras, who has worked at some of the best restaurants in town. This bilevel restaurant has seating on the sidewalk, too, and serves stellar but reasonably priced French and New Orleans cuisine, such as braised duck with currants and shrimp remoulade.

Make the trek way Uptown to **Maple Street Cafe** (7623 Maple St., 504/314-9003, $13–19), a dapper neighborhood restaurant serving first-rate contemporary versions of continental and Mediterranean cooking. A bountiful Greek salad makes a refreshing starter, while pepper-crusted sliced breast of duck drizzled with blueberry cognac sauce is typical of the main dishes, which change often. Oyster amandine is a favorite starter. The narrow two-tier dining room has a tile floor and cream-colored walls. There's also dining in a small courtyard.

A lovely pale-blue Riverbend cafe with marvelous cooking and convivial service, **Sara's** (724 Dublin St., 504/861-0565, $12–19) occupies one of the neighborhood's many delightful little cottages, on a row with several cheery shops. It's a source of delicious, offbeat cuisine that fuses Indian, Mediterranean, Thai, French, and Creole flavors. Jamaican-spiced lamb chops, pecan-crusted chicken with a citrus-ginger reduction, and *saag paneer* (house-made Indian farmer's cheese) with baby spinach and spices reflect the kitchen's deft handling of these varied cuisines. Cool off with a mango daiquiri.

In Riverbend, **One Restaurant** (8132 Hampson St., 504/301-9061, www.one-sl.com, $14–23) is the quintessential neighborhood bistro with contemporary cooking that could hold its own anywhere in the city. A specialty is the charbroiled oysters topped with roquefort cheese, but also consider the tuna carpaccio salad with Vietnamese vegetables. Among the entrées, don't miss the braised country pork ribs with a mushroom demi-glace and truffle-scented potato croquettes. The restaurant is inside a historic Victorian cottage, and inside diners can watch chefs at work in the open kitchen.

Set directly along the St. Charles Streetcar line in the Garden District, **Cannon's Bistro and Steamery** (4141 St. Charles Ave., 504/891-3200, $14–28) is an airy, casual place with large windows and hanging plants inside. Try crab cakes Katrina (topped with fettuccine and a rich crawfish sauce), grilled salmon with bordelaise sauce, and chicken pecan salad with a blue cheese vinaigrette. Other specialties come from "the steamer" menu, where there are lobster and Gulf shrimp.

Semolina (3226 Magazine St., 504/895-4260; also 5080 Pontchartrain Blvd., 504/486-5581; 3501 W. Chateau Blvd., Kenner, 504/468-1047; Clearview Shopping Center, 4436 Veterans Memorial Blvd., Metairie, 504/486-5581; $8–18) is a burgeoning local chain of slick-looking upscale pasta restaurants. You'll find some fairly traditional Italian-style dishes here, but the menu spans the globe, offering such unusual fare as Thai curry shrimp over angel hair, a baked cake of macaroni and cheese (one of its most popular innovations), Greek-inspired gyro pasta served in a sour cream-tzatziki-feta sauce, and the more ubiquitous (in New Orleans, anyway) jambalaya pasta.

CASUAL COOKING

So concerned about the freshness of its bivalves is **Casamento's** (4330 Magazine St., 504/895-9761, $6–14) that this famous yet surprisingly humble restaurant on mid-Magazine Street closes down June–August, when oysters are

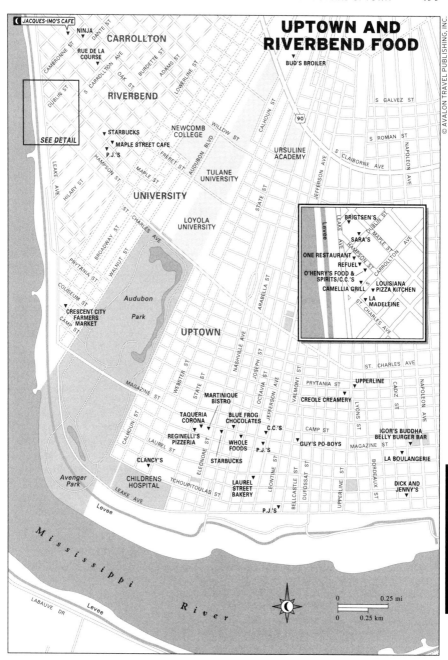

UPTOWN AND RIVERBEND FOOD

© AVALON TRAVEL PUBLISHING, INC.

JACQUES-IMO'S CAFE

NINJA

CARROLLTON

RUE DE LA COURSE

BUD'S BROILER

RIVERBEND

S GALVEZ ST

S ROMAN ST

STARBUCKS

NEWCOMB COLLEGE

MAPLE STREET CAFE

P.J.'S

URSULINE ACADEMY

S CLAIBORNE AVE

NAPOLEON AVE

TULANE UNIVERSITY

UNIVERSITY

LOYOLA UNIVERSITY

SEE DETAIL

BRIGTSEN'S

SARA'S

ONE RESTAURANT

REFUEL

O'HENRY'S FOOD & SPIRITS/C.C.'S

LOUISIANA PIZZA KITCHEN

CAMELLIA GRILL

LA MADELEINE

ST. CHARLES AVE

Audubon Park

CRESCENT CITY FARMERS MARKET

UPTOWN

ST. CHARLES AVE

UPPERLINE

CREOLE CREAMERY

MARTINIQUE BISTRO

TAQUERIA CORONA

BLUE FROG CHOCOLATES

C.C.'S

IGOR'S BUDDHA BELLY BURGER BAR

REGINELLI'S PIZZERIA

WHOLE FOODS

P.J.'S

GUY'S PO-BOYS

LA BOULANGERIE

CLANCY'S

STARBUCKS

Avenger Park

CHILDRENS HOSPITAL

LAUREL STREET BAKERY

DICK AND JENNY'S

P.J.'S

Levee

FOOD

Mississippi River

LABAUVE DR

Levee

0   0.25 mi

0   0.25 km

Casamento's

S. Carrollton Ave., 504/866-9741; also 301 Baronne St., 504/522-5242; 710 Terry Pkwy., Gretna, 504/433-4111; 8859 Veterans Memorial Blvd., Metairie, 504/461-9840; $6–14) has a big menu with many types of deli-style sandwiches, plus a handful of Creole specialties. You can grab a table and enjoy the view over tree-lined Carrollton. The house specialty is a burger topped with pastrami and melted swiss. The other locales, throughout greater New Orleans, are less atmospheric.

A favorite late-night destination for hungry, pizza-craving college students, **Reginelli's Pizzeria** (741 State St., 504/899-1414; also 3244 Magazine St., 504/895-7272; 817 W. Esplanade Ave., Kenner, 504/712-6868; 5608 Citrus Blvd., Harahan, 504/818-0111; $6–12) serves some of the best pies in New Orleans, along with massive calzones, focaccia sandwiches, and big salads. The Parthenon pizza, topped with garlic herb sauce, mozzarella, artichokes, roma tomatoes, onions, fresh mushrooms, and feta cheese, is a winner.

Moonlight Cafe (1921 Sophie Wright Pl., 504/522-7313, $6–13) is a funky little retro tavern with simple wooden tables, alternative music, and a colorful crowd. The menu lists a seemingly endless variety of finger foods, such as burgers, baba ghanouj, charbroiled salmon kabobs, shrimp po'boys, gyros, and wraps. There's a great beer selection, too.

The **Bulldog** (3236 Magazine St., 504/891-1516; also 5135 Canal Blvd., 504/488-4180; $5–8) is a reliable bet if you're thirsting for an interesting beer on tap—the restaurant stocks brews from all around the world. There's good food at this British-inspired pub, too, from Mexican fare to New Orleans treats to good old-fashioned barbecue. The hickory-smoked barbecue burger with cheddar is quite good, as are the chicken fajitas.

ETHNIC

Youthful and raffish **Juan's Flying Burrito** (2018 Magazine St., 504/569-0000; also 4724 S. Carrollton Ave., 504/486-9950, $4–8) has wooden booths, brick walls, and an artsy, alternative staff and crowd. Art covers the walls,

out of season. Italian immigrant Joe Casamento opened the place in 1919, installing the trademark tile floors that give the restaurant its clean, distinctive look today. Casamento's stands out from other oyster bars in several ways: It makes its own sandwich bread, and it serves excellent home-style Italian food, such as spaghetti and meatballs. As for those oysters, you can order them fresh on the half shell, in a stew, or on a loaf (basically a monstrous po'boy). The soft-shell crab platter is yet another commendable specialty.

A daft favorite of slackers, artists, and students, **Igor's Buddha Belly Burger Bar** (4437 Magazine St., 504/891-6105, $5–11) occupies a colorful space that includes both a dining room and a self-service laundry (just like Igor's Marigny hangout, Check Point Charlie). The half-pound burgers are seriously good, and on Mondays Igor's serves free red beans and rice until it runs out of the stuff. It's one of the better late-night options on Magazine.

Just an old-time burger and cocktail tavern with decent—not great—food but a warm ambience, **O'Henry's Food and Spirits** (634 and loud music fills this spot, one of the best quick bites along the lower stretch of Magazine, close to antiques shops. The fare is a mod take on Tex-Mex, with such filling fare as the Veggie Punk burrito (with potatoes, jalapeños, jack cheese, lettuce, and salsa) and shrimp tacos. You'll also find a nice range of beers and margaritas.

Taqueria Corona (5932 Magazine St., 504/897-3974; also 3535 Severn Ave., Metairie, 504/885-5088; and 1827 Hickory Ave., Harahan-River Ridge, 504/738-6722; $3–12) is a snug, homey Mexican joint low on ambience but big on flavor. These taquerias, with several locales around the city, serve serious regional Mexican fare, not just the usual Americanized Tex-Mex. You might start with the piquant black-bean soup with sour cream and cilantro, followed by *pollo asado* (a half-pound chicken breast marinated and charbroiled, served with *pico de gallo*). You could also just get a plate of tacos, which come in many varieties: chorizo, shrimp, tongue, fish, chicken, pork, ground beef, and cheese. Pitchers of sangria and margaritas are a bargain.

Some folks swear that the original **Byblos** (3218 Magazine St., 504/894-1233; also 2020 Veterans Memorial Blvd., Metairie, 504/837-9777; $9–17), an excellent Middle Eastern restaurant in an Old Metairie shopping center, is better than the newer location on Magazine Street. Both are very nice, however, and the Magazine Street version is more atmospheric.

Ninja (8433 Oak St., 504/866-1119, $10–22), which occupies what looks a bit like a modern suburban house, serves outstanding Japanese fare and sushi—it's in Carrollton, along up-and-coming Oak Street. There's a high-ceilinged, open dining room on the second floor and a bar downstairs.

Closer to town on the edge of the Garden District is another stellar Japanese restaurant, **Sake Cafe Uptown** (2830 Magazine St., 504/894-0033, $12–20). Yellowtail tartare with Russian caviar is a specialty.

For some of the better Chinese food in town, enjoy a meal at **August Moon** (3635 Prytania St., 504/899-5122, $6–13), which also serves a number of dishes from Vietnam. The restaurant is also a good bet if you're a seafood fan, with choices such as panfried rice noodles with shrimp, and catfish cooked in a clay pot with jasmine rice, but also consider the Mandarin duck and lemongrass tofu dish.

New Orleans doesn't have a wealth of Indian restaurants, but **Nirvana** (4308 Magazine St., 504/894-9797, $9–17) definitely serves the needs of curry and *naan* fans. At lunch, there's a phenomenal $6.95 lunch buffet that has a justifiably fanatical following.

QUICK BITES

If you love a good, no-nonsense diner, **Slim Goodies** (3322 Magazine St., 504/891-3447, $4–11) is worth seeking out. This colorful hole-in-the-wall on Magazine serves some of the best breakfasts in the neighborhood (order the hearty sweet-potato pancakes), along with giant sandwiches and salads. Try the soulful Robert Johnson burger (with bacon and blue cheese), the veggie-favored "stalt" (smoked tempeh, avocado spread, lettuce, and tomato), or a "horned devil" salad of mixed greens, swiss and provolone cheeses, tomatoes, ham, and deviled eggs. For dessert, there's the "cloud," a chocolate brownie topped with ice cream and whipped cream.

A garishly painted yellow takeout stand on Magazine, **Tee-Eva's Creole Soul Food** (4430 Magazine St., 504/899-8350) hits the spot when you're hungering for short-order soul chow, pralines, pies, or sno-balls. Famous treats here include the homemade pecan pralines as well as sweet potato–pecan pie. There's also a savory crawfish pie that's awfully tasty.

A longtime, famous stalwart for delicious comfort food, **Camellia Grill** (626 S. Carrollton Ave., 504/866-9573, $4–8) was one of many businesses badly looted after Katrina, and it's one of the most famous in the city that has not yet reopened. However, a new owner bought the restaurant in summer 2006 with plans to reopen it by early 2007. The down-home restaurant has always specialized in burgers—the house classic is called a Doc Brinker, and it comprises two burgers with melted swiss

FOOD

on rye bread with sides of chili and slaw. A long list of pies, cakes, and ice-cream treats are offered for dessert, and breakfast is also an enjoyable meal in this funky old house in the Riverbend section of Uptown. The seating is limited to stools set around a zigzag-shaped counter. The new owner also has ambitions to open additional Camellia Grill branches elsewhere in the region in the near future.

A loveable dive on a quiet Uptown street corner, **Guy's Po-Boys** (5257 Magazine St., 504/891-5025, under $6) offers daily-changing sandwich specials, great shrimp po'boys, and other comfort chow. The bare-bones decor somehow adds to the experience.

Do as many locals do and drop by **Bluebird Cafe** (3625 Prytania St., 504/895-7166, $3–9) for tasty no-frills breakfast fare, including spicy huevos rancheros and light-as-a-feather waffles.

Bud's Broiler (3151 Calhoun St., 504/861-0906; also 605 Lapalco Blvd., Gretna, 504/393-8160; 2008 Clearview Pkwy., Metairie, 504/899-2837; 2800 Veterans Memorial Blvd., Kenner, 504/466-0026; 6235 Elysian Fields Ave., 504/282-6696, www.budsbroiler.com) is a great place for delicious, if not necessarily healthy, charbroiled burgers and the like.

Although it deserves ample praise for being the city's best wine shop and one of its top gourmet grocery stores, **Martin Wine Cellar** (3500 Magazine St., 504/896-7420; also 714 Elmeer Ave., Metairie, 504/896-7350; $4–9) does one thing as well as any restaurant in the city: deli sandwiches. The food here is more typical of Sonoma's wine country than New Orleans—there are no crawfish or oysters on the menu, but you can get such toothsome sandwiches as the Steamboat (corned beef, ham, hickory-smoked bacon, swiss cheese, onions, and Creole mustard on an onion roll), plus zesty tomato-pesto salad. The list of sandwich options goes on and on, and they're served in fairly massive portions. You order your meal at the counter and then take a seat in the plant-filled glass-brick dining room amid the legions of yuppies and epicureans. Apart from the deli, there's a large wine and liquor store, plus shelves stocked with all sorts of imported and local savories

and sweets. The second locale, just off Veterans Boulevard in Metairie, is a short drive from the west side of City Park.

If you need a quick break from antiques shopping on Lower Magazine Street, head to **Sophie's Gelato** (1912 Magazine St., 504/561-0291), a cute gelateria where all the gelato is made fresh, in-house. Flavors change seasonally, depending on what sorts of ingredients are available, but you might try pineapple-cranberry.

For traditional ice cream, check out the **Creole Creamery** (4924 Prytania St., 504/894-8680), a handsome retro-hip Uptown ice-cream parlor serving such tantalizing flavors as lavender-honey, red-velvet cake (yes, this is actually a flavor of ice cream), bananas Foster, triple-shot mochaccino, pink-grapefruit sorbet, and chamomile. And these guys are constantly dreaming up new and often deliciously bizarre flavors.

JAVA JOINTS

Uptown has the greatest concentration of coffeehouses in the city, especially along Magazine Street, where you'll find several atmospheric branches of the local chains, P.J.'s, CC's, and Rue de la Course. There's also a Starbucks along Magazine, if you must go with Seattle java. Strictly in terms of ambience, as all of these places have pretty good coffee and a variety of light snacks, the mid-Magazine branch of **Rue de la Course** (3121 Magazine St., 504/899-0242; also 1140 S. Carrollton Ave., 504/861-4343) is the most atmospheric and inviting of these places, especially if you're in the mood to read or peck away on your laptop. Tables have study lamps and many have access to electrical outlets. You can also dine at one of several tables along the busy sidewalk. Rue de la Course doesn't offer a tremendous amount in the way of food, just pastries and cakes, but the coffees and chai tea are top-notch.

A hip spot in the Riverbend area of Uptown, **Refuel** (8124 Hampson St., 504/872-0187) serves a rich array of coffee and tea drinks plus top-notch breakfast and lunch fare. Try the Belgian waffles with strawberries to start off the day, or a chunky Cuban sandwich on a baguette at lunch. The crab-cake salad is also quite good, served with lime-spiked avocado and citrus aioli.

PICNIC SUPPLIES AND GOURMET GOODS

This part of town being where most of the city's well-heeled professionals live, it's hardly surprising that it has some of New Orleans's largest and best-stocked gourmet grocery shops, including Martin Wine Cellar (described under *Quick Bites*). **La Boulangerie** (4526 Magazine St., 504/269-3777) is a delightful storefront French bakery with great food. Here you can taste some of the lightest, flakiest croissants around, along with light sandwiches and delectable pastries. It opened a second location in the CBD in 2003 at 625 St. Charles Avenue.

Blue Frog Chocolates (5707 Magazine St., 504/269-5707) specializes in sensuous, wonderful imported European candies and truffles, including whimsical Italian flowers fashioned out of candy. It's in a dainty blue wood-frame house Uptown.

The gourmet grocery chain **Whole Foods** (5600 Magazine St., 504/899-9119; also 3420 Veteran's Blvd., Metairie, 504/888-8225) opened a massive branch along Magazine Street in 2002; it's fairly close to Audubon Park. There's also an in-store cafe serving creative sandwiches, salads, and the like.

A couple of blocks off Magazine Street, **Laurel Street Bakery** (5433 Laurel St., 504/897-0576, $5–10) is worth a visit for its fresh-baked scones, cinnamon rolls, pastries, bagels, quiche, and the like. You'll find a nice selection of fresh artisanal breads here.

Mid-City

CREATIVE AND CONTEMPORARY

Cozy **Cafe Degas** (3127 Esplanade Ave., 504/945-5635, $12–19) serves such superb French cuisine as salade niçoise, seafood brochette, and Cajun-style bouillabaisse. There's nothing overly trendy or complicated about Degas—the cooking is authentic and reminiscent of true French bistro fare. In warm weather you can enjoy a meal on the lush garden patio, which is the perfect place to end an afternoon of exploring Mid-City.

Another of the bumper crop of fine restaurants along historic Esplanade Ridge is **Lola's** (3312 Esplanade Ave., 504/488-6946, $11–18). The small BYOB eatery takes no reservations and no credit cards—it's a small-scale operation whose owners focus on food above all else. And this Mediterranean-inspired cooking stands up to any in the city: Consider fragrantly seasoned paella heaped with chorizo and shellfish, the refreshing chilled gazpacho, and the fresh ceviche. Nearly across the street, Whole Foods grocery has an exceptional selection of well-priced wines.

In a handsome old building across from leafy City Park, **Ralph's on the Park** (900 City Park Ave., 504/488-1000, $22–32) is the Brennan family's only dining operation in Mid-City, and it's absolutely worth the trip. First off, it's far from the madding crowds of the Quarter and CBD, making for a more relaxed and convivial dining experience. It's also set inside a lovely, historic building that dates to 1860. Then there's the elegant food, such as pork tournedos and oysters with tasso-popcorn rice and spiced pecans, and lamb T-bone grilled medium-rare with black lentils and golden beets. It's one of the best brunch options in town, too.

CASUAL COOKING

Around the corner from Angelo Brocato's (see *Quick Bites*), **Kjean** (236 N. Carrollton Ave., 504/488-7503, $4–10) seafood had occupied a rather ragged little shanty serving no-nonsense food at low prices before Katrina's flooding destroyed the building. The owners are building a new restaurant on the

FOOD

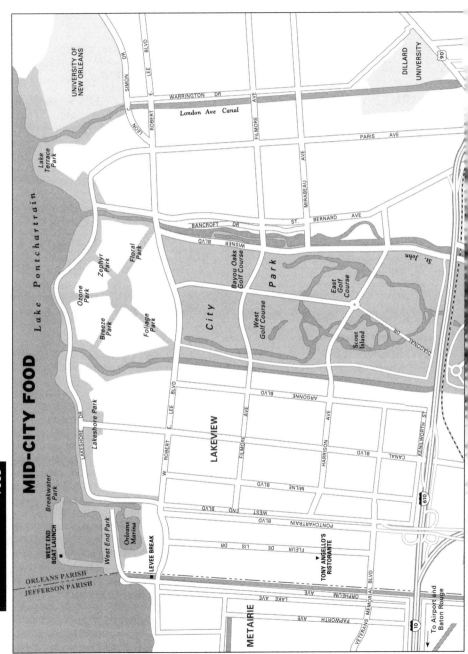

MID-CITY FOOD

Lake Pontchartrain

UNIVERSITY OF NEW ORLEANS

DILLARD UNIVERSITY

90

G. SIMON DR

E. LEE BLVD

LEON

ROBERT

WARRINGTON DR

London Ave Canal

FILMORE AVE

PARIS AVE

MIRABEAU AVE

ST. BERNARD AVE

Lake Terrace Park

BANCROFT DR

WISNER BLVD

Bayou Oaks Golf Course

City Park

St. John

Floral Park

Zephyr Park

Ozone Park

Breeze Park

Foliage Park

West Golf Course

East Golf Course

Scout Island

DIAGONAL DR

Lakeshore Park

LAKESHORE DR

E. LEE BLVD

W. ROBERT

FILMORE AVE

ARGONNE BLVD

BLVD

LAKEVIEW

HARRISON AVE

CANAL BLVD

KENILWORTH ST

610

MILNE BLVD

WEST END BLVD

PONTCHARTRAIN BLVD

Breakwater Park

West End Park

Orleans Marina

WEST END BOAT LAUNCH

LEVEE BREAK

ORLEANS PARISH
JEFFERSON PARISH

FLEUR DE LIS DR

TONY ANGELLO'S RISTORANTE

METAIRIE

LAKE AVE

PAPWORTH AVE

ORPHEUM AVE

VETERANS MEMORIAL BLVD

10

To Airport and Baton Rouge

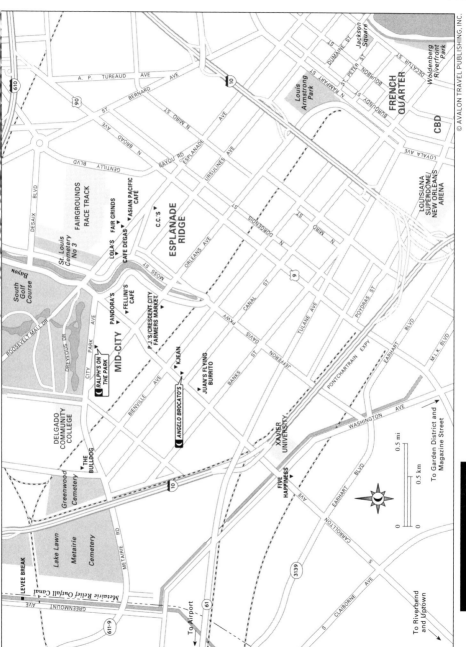

© AVALON TRAVEL PUBLISHING, INC.

site, which should open by 2007. This is the perfect place when you just need a quick bite. Grab a number at the counter and order an oyster or shrimp po'boy. It's also a market, selling freshly caught fish, pig's feet, and a variety of raw and prepared foods.

Fellini's Cafe (900 N. Carrollton Ave., 504/488-2155, $8–17), occupies an old service station in the heart of Mid-City, not far from Canal Street or the park. The pizzas here are the main draw—they're creative and relatively light, with all kinds of tasty toppings. But also consider one of the salads or pasta dishes. There's a lovely shaded patio off to the side of the rather intimate dining room.

ETHNIC

You have to travel a bit to find **Tony Angello's Ristorante** (6262 Fleur de Lis Dr., 504/488-0888, $8–15), which is set inside a pedestrian-looking house near the canal separating New Orleans from Metairie, up near the lakefront. The restaurant received massive amounts of water during Katrina's flooding and is in the process of being rebuilt. For home-style, red-sauce Italian fare, it's hard to think of a better place to enjoy a meal. The staff treats everybody like family. Despite its humble appearance, the restaurant attracts many prominent New Orleanians (Harry Connick Jr. is said to be a regular) for its filling and hearty cooking. The novelty dish that has really made Tony Angello's famous is the Feed Me platter—just utter these words, and you'll be served a vast sampling of house specialties, brought out one plate after the other. It's best to tackle this multicourse adventure with a friend or two.

Asian Pacific Cafe (3125 Esplanade Ave., 504/945-1919, $8–14) is set inside a cute painted-lady house next to Cafe Degas and serves tasty French-Asian fare. You might start with smoked duck and roast marinated shrimp with a light balsamic sauce, followed by lamb chop sautéed with shallot-olive paste and garlic *panko* (Japanese bread crumbs), served au jus. The staff is charming and eager to please.

Close to the Metairie border and the campus of Xavier University (just off I-10 and Airline Highway), **Five Happiness** (3605 S. Carrollton Ave., 504/482-3935, $9–16) serves commendable Mandarin and Szechuan fare in a bright dining room festooned with Chinese artwork and decorations. Crispy whole fish available with a variety of sauces is a house favorite, with the type of creature varying according to what's fresh on any given day. The bird's nest of minced shrimp, dried black mushrooms, and water chestnuts enmeshed within a "sandwich" of iceberg lettuce leaves is as tasty as it is artful. Don't be put off by the neighboring fast-food restaurants and auto-repair shops—this is the real deal.

QUICK BITES

After a day of exploring City Park, take a snack-break detour at **Angelo Brocato's** (214 N. Carrollton Ave., 504/486-0078), an Old World bakery that's famous not only for its superb Italian pastries but for tantalizing house-made ice cream, Italian ice, and gelato in all kinds of tempting flavors, such as *panna cotta,* chestnut, and rum custard. The Mid-City hole in the wall celebrated its 100th anniversary in 2005, only to be smacked hard by the wrath of Katrina. The storm caused the place to close for nearly a year, but the virtually rebuilt Angelo Brocato's reopened in July 2006, much to the relief of sweet-toothed devotees. It's just off Canal Street and a few blocks south of City Park, and it also serves fabulous cannoli and cookies. It feels like something out of Brooklyn, and it's in the heart of a small cluster of eateries and shops that suffered grave Katrina damage, some of which have yet to reopen.

How do you eat a sno-ball? On a hot day, wait for some of the ice to melt and then slurp it up with a straw, then use a spoon to eat the shaved ice on top. You can practice this technique at **Pandora's** (901 N. Carrollton Ave., 504/486-8644), a humble take-out window serving up sno-balls in dozens of flavors (strawberry cheesecake, watermelon, praline cream), plus soft-serve ice cream, hot dogs, chili, tamales, and the like.

JAVA JOINTS

A cheerful neighborhood coffeehouse near the Fair Grounds racetrack and just off Esplanade Avenue, the amusingly named **Fair Grinds** (3133 Ponce de Leon St., 504/948-3222) serves all the usual hot and iced coffee drinks, plus a variety of snacks. The homey space with racetrack collectibles, framed photography, and green walls is well suited for working on your laptop or reading, as there are reading lamps on many tables and comfortable seating.

PICNIC SUPPLIES AND GOURMET GOODS

Opened on the site of the former Mid-City branch of Whole Foods (which now has a much bigger locale Uptown on Magazine Street), the **Market at Esplanade** (3135 Esplanade Ave., 504/872-0275) is a one-stop shop for gourmet treats, natural foods, and other tempting groceries, perfect if you're on your way to nearby City Park for a picnic. The market also serves tasty gelato in several enticing flavors.

Greater New Orleans

METAIRIE, KENNER, AND THE AIRPORT
Traditional Creole and Cajun

Try to make a reservation a few days in advance for 【 **Drago's** (3232 N. Arnoult Rd., Metairie, 504/888-9254, $11–35), a riotously popular restaurant with limited seating and parking. The emphasis here is on seafood, much of it prepared with a Louisiana slant. The lobster dishes are particularly noteworthy. Try lobster Marco (whole lobster stuffed with fresh sautéed shrimp and mushrooms in a light cream sauce over angel hair pasta). Apart from the usual seafood, blackened duck over linguini with oysters and cream is delicious. You can sit at the bar, which affords clear views of the grill guys charbroiling oysters (which many regulars eat a couple dozen of as a full meal), or dine in one of the noisy but festive dining rooms. The high volume of business has just one drawback: The waitstaff often seems harried and (understandably) frazzled.

Creative and Contemporary

One of a handful of South Shore suburban restaurants that actually merits making a special trip from downtown, **Vega Tapas** (2051 Metairie Rd., 504/836-2007, $5–13) is the classiest of several restaurants in a small strip in Old Metairie. Tomato-red walls and high ceilings create an elegant but informal ambience for sampling tapas, most with a vaguely Mediter-ranean but always innovative spin: smoked salmon and avocado salad with a horseradish-tarragon dressing, eggplant napoleon layered with oven-dried tomatoes, house-made mozzarella, arugula, and sun-dried–tomato pesto; and sautéed sweetbreads and cremini mushrooms with prosciutto and a sherry beurre blanc. One of the few big-ticket restaurants near the airport, **Le Parvenu** (509 Williams Blvd., Kenner, 504/471-0534, $14–24) draws even foodies who rarely leave downtown for creative and beautifully presented contemporary Creole fare. Try the sautéed snapper with herbed crabmeat and a lemon beurre blanc.

Zea Rotisserie (1525 St. Charles Ave., 504/520-8100; also Zea Rotisserie and Brewery at 1655 Hickory Ave., Harahan, 504/738-0799; Esplanade Mall, 4450 Veterans Memorial Blvd., Metairie, 504/780-9090) specializes in meaty fare served on a spit and handcrafted microbrewed beers. But the menu is really quite eclectic, offering a wide range of foods from all over the world, among them wood-grilled rainbow trout, sweet-pepper chicken wings, and spare ribs (available with hickory barbecue sauce or sweet-and-spicy Thai style). It's a cavernous place, usually echoing with chatter and lively conversation.

Casual Cooking

The Galley (2535 Metairie Rd., Metairie, 504/832-0955, $7–16) is a casual and fun seafood

FOOD

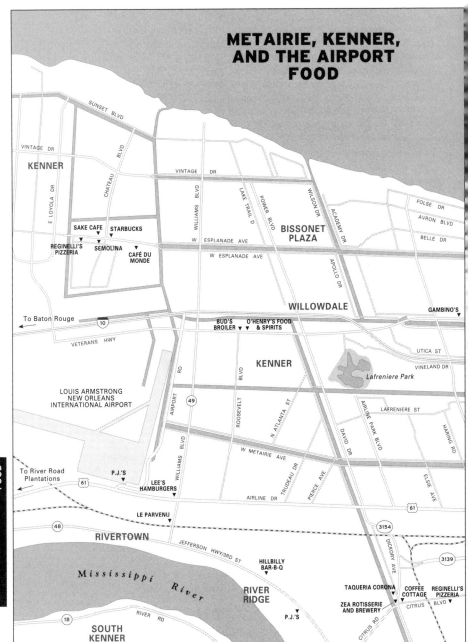

METAIRIE, KENNER, AND THE AIRPORT FOOD

SUNSET BLVD

VINTAGE DR

KENNER

CHATEAU BLVD

E LOYOLA DR

VINTAGE DR

WILLIAMS BLVD

LAKE TRAIL D

POWER BLVD

WILSON DR

ACADEMY DR

FOLSE DR

AVRON BLVD

BELLE DR

SAKE CAFE ▼   STARBUCKS ▼

REGINELLI'S PIZZERIA ▼   SEMOLINA ▼   CAFÉ DU MONDE ▼

BISSONET PLAZA

W ESPLANADE AVE

W ESPLANADE AVE

APOLLO DR

To Baton Rouge ←   10

VETERANS HWY

WILLOWDALE

BUD'S BROILER ▼ ▼   O'HENRY'S FOOD & SPIRITS

GAMBINO'S ▼

UTICA ST

VINELAND DR

LOUIS ARMSTRONG NEW ORLEANS INTERNATIONAL AIRPORT

AIRPORT RD

49

ROOSEVELT BLVD

N. ATLANTA ST

KENNER

Lafreniere Park

LAFRENIERE ST

AIRLINE PARK BLVD

HARING RD

DAVID DR

W METAIRIE AVE

TRUDEAU DR

PIERCE AVE

ELSIE AVE

To River Road Plantations ←   61

P.J.'S ▼

WILLIAMS BLVD

LEE'S HAMBURGERS ▼

AIRLINE DR

61

LE PARVENU ▼

48

RIVERTOWN

3154

3139

JEFFERSON HWY/3RD ST

DICKORY AVE

Mississippi River

HILLBILLY BAR-B-Q ▼

RIVER RIDGE

TAQUERIA CORONA ▼   COFFEE COTTAGE ▼   REGINELLI'S PIZZERIA ▼

ZEA ROTISSERIE AND BREWERY ▼   CITRUS BLVD

P.J.'S ▼

CITRUS RD

RIVER RD

18

SOUTH KENNER

FOOD

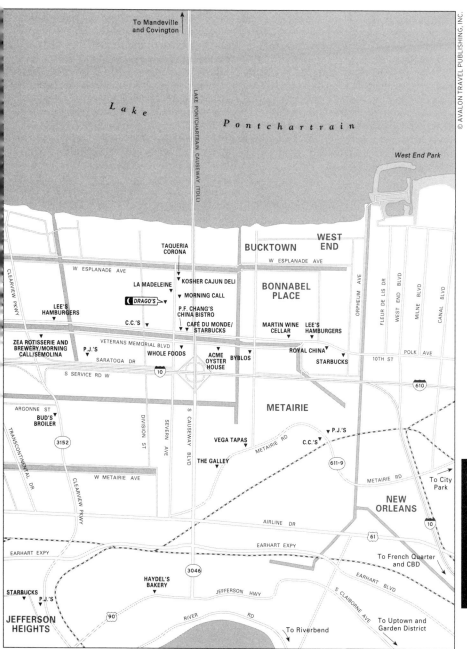

© AVALON TRAVEL PUBLISHING, INC.

To Mandeville and Covington

LAKE PONTCHARTRAIN CAUSEWAY (TOLL)

L a k e   P o n t c h a r t r a i n

West End Park

WEST END

BUCKTOWN

W ESPLANADE AVE

W ESPLANADE AVE

TAQUERIA CORONA

KOSHER CAJUN DELI

LA MADELEINE

MORNING CALL

DRAGO'S

BONNABEL PLACE

LEE'S HAMBURGERS

P.F. CHANG'S CHINA BISTRO

C.C.'S

CAFÉ DU MONDE/ STARBUCKS

MARTIN WINE CELLAR

LEE'S HAMBURGERS

CLEARVIEW PKWY

ZEA ROTISSERIE AND BREWERY/MORNING CALL/SEMOLINA

P.J.'S

VETERANS MEMORIAL BLVD

WHOLE FOODS

SARATOGA DR

ACME OYSTER HOUSE

BYBLOS

ROYAL CHINA

STARBUCKS

10TH ST

POLK AVE

ORPHEUM AVE

FLEUR DE LIS DR

WEST END BLVD

MILNE BLVD

CANAL BLVD

S SERVICE RD W

10

610

METAIRIE

ARGONNE ST

BUD'S BROILER

3152

TRANSCONTINENTAL DR

DIVISION ST

SEVERN AVE

S CAUSEWAY BLVD

VEGA TAPAS

THE GALLEY

METAIRIE RD

C.C.'S

P.J.'S

611-9

METAIRIE RD

NEW ORLEANS

To City Park

CLEARVIEW PKWY

W METAIRIE AVE

AIRLINE DR

61

10

EARHART EXPY

EARHART EXPY

To French Quarter and CBD

3046

HAYDEL'S BAKERY

EARHART BLVD

JEFFERSON HWY

S CLAIBORNE AVE

To Uptown and Garden District

STARBUCKS

P.J.'S

JEFFERSON HEIGHTS

90

RIVER

RD

To Riverbend

FOOD

shack with great food. Shrimp and crabmeat au gratin is a top pick, and several tasty sides are available (mac and cheese, sweet potato fries).

More than a few fans of the genre swear that **Hillbilly Bar-B-Q** (208 Tullulah Ave., River Ridge, 504/738-1508, $4–11), on a side street near the Mississippi—a short drive southeast of the airport—has the best barbecue in metro New Orleans. The meats are smoked over Kentucky hickory after receiving a kicky dry-spice rub, and all the usual sides (slaw, beans, potato salad) are available.

Ethnic

The upscale and trendy Pan-Asian chain **P. F. Chang's China Bistro** (Lakeside Shopping Center, 3301 Veterans Memorial Blvd., Metairie, 504/828-5288, $9–20) has a branch out by the mall in Metairie. The always-packed restaurant is well regarded for its big arty drinks and such creative fusion fare as pan-fried shrimp dumplings with chili-pepper soy sauce, orange-peel chicken with chili peppers, and scallops wok-fried with a light lemon sauce.

The restaurant in greater New Orleans for authentic dim sum, **Royal China** (600 Veterans Memorial Blvd., Metairie, 504/831-9633, $8–15) is a rather ordinary-looking Chinese restaurant that presents a lavish and tasty assortment of about 50 of these creative small plates, including crab–and–cream-cheese wontons, stir-fried squid in black-bean sauce, and sweet rice-flour crepes with red-bean paste and powdered sugar. There's a full menu of other, more expected Chinese dishes, too, but dim sum is the restaurant's raison d'être.

A superb option for sushi is **Sake Cafe** (817 W. Esplanade Ave., Kenner, 504/468-8829, $11–20). Try the Kenner roll, a tempura-battered treat with crab stick, avocado, and whitefish. Deals on beer, sake, and sushi abound during the daily happy hour, held 3–6 P.M.

Quick Bites

Kosher Cajun Deli (3519 Severn Ave., Metairie, 504/888-2010, $4–11) fits the bill when you're craving chopped liver, smoked fish, and other deli favorites. It's a basic deli lunchroom in an attractive storefront near Causeway Boulevard. You'll also find a nice selection of gourmet prepared foods and groceries.

A miniempire of burger joints that delights carnivores, **Lee's Hamburgers** (904 Veterans Memorial Blvd., Metairie, 504/836-6804; 4301 Veterans Memorial Blvd., Metairie, 504/885-0110; 2100 Airline Dr., Kenner, 504/472-0966; $3–9) cooks juicy patties smothered in several toppings. You can also get chili-cheese fries and, at some locales, more substantial fare such as fried shrimp and grilled chicken platters. For fans of local fast food, this is a must.

Java Joints

Similar in concept to the French Quarter's Cafe du Monde, **Morning Call** (3325 Severn Ave., Metairie, 504/885-4068; also Clearview Shopping Center, 4436 Veteran's Memorial Blvd., Metairie, 504/779-5348) is open 24/7 and serves a short menu whose specialties include piping-hot café au lait and beignets. Unlike Cafe du Monde, it's never overrun with tourists, but by the same token, Morning Call doesn't have nearly as interesting a location—it's in a small shopping center across from Lakeside Shopping Center. The interior is quite elegant, though. Long mirrored marble counters line one side of the room; the other contains small wooden tables. Servers in white paper caps skirt about the room, delivering plates of food. Next door is the Lakeside Newsstand, which is also open 24 hours.

Coffee Cottage (5860 Citrus Blvd., Jefferson, 504/818-0051) is a cute spot in Jefferson, known for its homey decor and terrific desserts, such as tiramisu, white-chocolate mousse cake, and Key lime pie. It's also a source of excellent creative sandwiches and salads, varying from Creole chicken salad tossed with pecans and Creole mustard to honey ham–and–cheese focaccia sandwiches.

Picnic Supplies and Gourmet Goods

Haydel's Bakery (4037 Jefferson Hwy., Jefferson, 504/837-0190) has long been a favorite stop for desserts: Mardi Gras king cakes, pecan pies, white-chocolate bread pudding, almond croissants, and praline cheesecake. The trademark Cajun Kringle is a hallmark of this bakery: It's a ring-shaped pastry jammed with pecan filling.

Gambino's (4821 Veterans Memorial Blvd., Metairie, 504/885-7500) is known for its huge six-layer Doberge cakes, which come in chocolate, lemon, or caramel. Cookies, king cakes, biscotti, and sublime pralines are also available.

THE WEST BANK
Creative and Contemporary

Reason alone to trek out to Gretna, **Red Maple** (1036 Lafayette St., 504/367-0935, $12–21) is helmed by one of the city's rising culinary stars, Randy Barlow, who's worked in several top restaurants. The place began as a gruff working-class bar in the 1960s and gradually evolved into a simple restaurant, but these days it's become a serious dining operation with first-rate modern New Orleans fare. Steaks and seafood dominate the menu. In warm weather, grab a table on the garden patio.

Casual Cooking

If you've taken the ferry across the river from the CBD into Algiers Point and find yourself with a case of the munchies, duck into the **Dry Dock Cafe** (133 Deleronde St., Algiers Point, 504/361-8240, $6–16), an easygoing neighborhood bar and grill that serves a mighty nice burger and some similarly enticing salads and comfort fare, such as fried seafood plates and crawfish bisque.

Ethnic

If you love real (not watered-down) Chinese food, consider making the trek across the river to **China Blossom** (1801 Stumpf Blvd., Suite 8, Gretna, 504/361-4598, $7–16), which despite being in a suburban shopping center has a pleasant, somewhat upscale interior—the service is accommodating and friendly, too. The cuisine here mixes traditional Asian ingredients and techniques with quite a few foods from Louisiana. You might begin with crawfish Na (a crepe filled with crawfish tails, minced pork, diced onions, and mushrooms), and then move on to marinated prawns grilled and served over glazed pecans, fried oysters, catfish in a ginger-and-garlic sauce, or sweet-and-sour pork. There's really not a bad dish on the menu.

Another great Gretna Asian restaurant is **9 Roses** (1100 Stephens St., 504/366-7665, $7–14), which features such delectable Vietnamese dishes as whole steamed fish with scallions, ginger, and a tangy soy sauce.

The West Bank, especially Gretna, is a good bet for Italian cooking, and **Tony Mandina's** (1915 Pratt St., Gretna, 504/362-2010, $8–14) does this genre justice. The menu strays from the traditional with a handful of exceptional locally influenced seafood dishes. Come for angel hair marinara, grilled lemon-pepper chicken, *strata del mare* (seafood layered with pasta, mozzarella, and red sauce), and eggplant Dominic Jude (battered eggplant medallions layered with shrimp and crabmeat and topped with shrimp Alfredo sauce).

Java Joints

If you're over exploring Gretna and need a coffee break or a light lunch, consider **Common Grounds** (335 Huey P. Long Ave., 504/227-2200), which has rotating art exhibits and tasty food.

FOOD

SHOPPING

It's not necessarily the main thing tourists do in New Orleans, but then again there are few visitors who leave without sampling the aisles of exotic produce and hard-to-find spices that fill the French Market, or without browsing the antiques stores along Magazine Street, where you can buy the very quality and style of furnishings found in some of those grand plantation homes out on the River Road.

Shopping in New Orleans tends to be a by-product of other popular aspects of the city's heritage—dining, music, art, historic preservation. The city doesn't have as important a fashion retail scene as most other major U.S. metropolises, nor is it teeming with chain stores. You'll find one or two branches of all the big ones, but often in malls well away from the city's most interesting neighborhoods. Thank-

fully, key shopping areas such as the French Quarter and Uptown's Magazine Street have largely resisted chain development and emphasize independently owned shops, many of them selling products you're likely to find only in New Orleans.

This chapter is organized by neighborhood, and within these sections by types of retail. Greater New Orleans has several large shopping centers and malls, which are listed individually within the neighborhood sections below. In each of these write-ups, a few key, representative stores are mentioned in passing; some notable shops at malls and shopping centers are described later in the section in greater detail within their own appropriate subcategory (*Clothing, Souvenirs and Gifts,* etc.).

New Orleans has a vast array of food items

HIGHLIGHTS

◖ **Best Local Crafts:** The definite source for locally produced furniture, crafts, and decorative items, **RHINO Contemporary Craft Co.** represents dozens of talented locals – RHINO stands for "Right here in New Orleans," which is where its goods are produced (page 215).

◖ **Most Prestigious Art Gallery:** In a handsome space along Royal Street, **Martin-Lawrence Galleries** carries museum-quality works by such luminaries as Chagall, Warhol, and Picasso (page 216).

◖ **Most Distinctive Source of Art:** The fanciful, colorful pieces at **Royal Cameo Glass** have been created by some of the nation's top glass artists, and they're among the most beautiful works of art you'll find at any gallery in New Orleans (page 217).

◖ **Finest Royal Street Antiques Shop:** If you've ever wanted to decorate your home in the fashion of those regal mansions that line the streets of the Garden District, you need to check out the elegant pieces at **Keil's Antiques,** which is known especially for its shimmering chandeliers (page 217).

◖ **Best Music Source:** You'll find the best in local and regional blues, jazz, zydeco, and Cajun tunes at **Louisiana Music Factory,** which also stocks all kinds of cool memorabilia (page 218).

◖ **Best Mardi Gras Memorabilia:** The quirky and flamboyant **Little Shop of Fantasy** is your one-stop for all things Mardi Gras, from elaborate masks to gaudy costumes (page 220).

◖ **Best Place to Watch Artists at Work:** The **New Orleans School of Glassworks and Printmaking Studio** is a working studio, where you can watch talented artisans at work before purchasing their wares (page 221).

◖ **Finest Magazine Street Antiques Shop:** With so many wonderful shops along Magazine Street, it's tough to pick a single highlight, but **Bush Antiques and Beds au Beau Rev** leads the pack with its astounding selection of beds from Europe and the United States, some dating back two centuries (page 222).

◖ **Best Jewelry Shop:** An esteemed local chain, **Mignon Faget** carries stunning jewelry, much of it designed with traditional Louisiana icons, such as fleur de lis cufflinks and oyster pendants (page 223).

◖ **Best Source of Architectural Treasures:** When old New Orleans homes are torn down, **Ricca Demolishing** salvages many of the beautiful architectural remnants and sells them to the public – it's a great place to find cypress doors, wrought-iron gates, and vintage hardware (page 223).

LOOK FOR ◖ TO FIND THE BEST SHOPPING.

for sale, from packaged candies and goodies to gourmet groceries to prepared foods and picnic supplies. (Most of the places selling food are listed in the *Food* chapter of this book, rather than here, because they tend to sell ready-to-eat food as well.) Many of the city's souvenir shops, too, carry New Orleans spices and sauces, pralines and other confections, and other gourmet gifts.

Most goods and retail products, as well as groceries, specialty foods, wine, souvenirs,

and gifts, cost the same or less in New Orleans than in other big cities. You don't run a huge risk of being gouged, even when buying T-shirts and shot glasses or other silly gifts in even the most touristy shops. Competition is pretty fierce in the French Quarter, and sales tactics are rarely aggressive or sleazy. If you're shopping for antiques and art, however, do keep in mind that the stores along or near Royal and Chartres streets have a reputation for carrying some of the most expensive furnishings in the South, and, some argue, at excessively marked-up prices. Magazine Street is considered a less pricey source of art and antiques, and even there you're not going to find any amazing bargains. It's almost always a seller's market when it comes to fine furnishings and antiques in New Orleans. True bargain hunters will have better luck heading to the North Shore town of Ponchatoula, an hour away, where it's said that more than a few New Orleans antiques dealers buy many of their wares in the first place.

Shops in the French Quarter tend to open late in the morning and close early in the evening, though souvenir-oriented shops usually stay open into the late-evening hours. Many shops in the Quarter are open daily, with some—especially antiques stores and art galleries—closing one day a week, typically Monday or Sunday. The same rules apply to Magazine Street and the Warehouse District. Otherwise, shops throughout New Orleans keep hours fairly typical of what you'll find in other big cities, opening at 9 or 10 A.M. and closing around 5 or 6 P.M., with some of the major retail chains open until 9 or 10 P.M. It's the rare shop in New Orleans that doesn't accept plastic, and many shops in the city's more visitor-friendly areas will ship your purchases back home. You may be surprised how easy it is to get even some perishable food items over-

nighted safely to just about anywhere, from muffuletta sandwiches at Central Grocery to the seafood and meats at the French Market.

ANTIQUES ORGANIZATIONS AND PUBLICATIONS

Whether you're a novice or an expert, your antiquing success will be enhanced if you consult a few publications before setting out. The country's leading resource is *Antiques and the Arts Weekly* (The Bee Publishing Co., Box 5503, Newtown, CT 06470, 203/426-3141), a mammoth 200-page feast of detailed auctions (with photos), museum and gallery exhibits, book reviews, antiques show calendars, shopping tips, and engaging features. Subscriptions are $74 annually. The paper has a fine website, www.antiquesandthearts.com, whose most helpful and unusual resource is an exhaustive list of antiquarian books and their authors. The paper's emphasis is somewhat on New England, where it is based, but there's plenty of information on shops and auctions in Louisiana, too.

Regionally, the *Antiques Gazette* (985/429-0575, www.theantiquesgazette.com), based in Hammond, is a terrific resource with hundreds of listings for shops through southern Louisiana and bordering states. A one-year subscription costs $18, but the paper is distributed free at many shops and tourism office centers.

The French Quarter

Royal Street is the most exclusive address for shopping in the French Quarter, known for upscale antiques and first-rate art galleries. Parallel Chartres Street has some of the same kinds of stores, as do the blocks connecting them. The ritzier shopping is in the Lower Quarter; once you venture past around St. Peter Street, you'll find funkier boutiques, such as mod clothiers, eccentric costume shops, edgy galleries, and places with a distinctly youthful vibe. Decatur Street is similarly offbeat when it comes to retail, and it's

also a good area for finding cheesy T-shirts, Tabasco and other Louisiana food products, crawfish-embroidered everything, souvenir "go-cups" (the plastic mugs tourists carry around the Quarter filled with daiquiris and hurricanes), and every other imaginable trinket and souvenir. In such an irreverent and party-oriented city, it's not surprising that many of the souvenir shops emphasize sex, drinking, and off-color humor in their gifts, toys, cards, and novelties. Decatur Street also leads to the mother ship of New Orleans

© NEW ORLEANS CVB/RICHARD NOWITZ

shops on Royal Street

shopping, the French Market, which contains retail shops, a lively farmers market, and a flea market.

MALLS AND SHOPPING CENTERS

Jackson Brewery (600 Decatur St., 504/566-7245, www.jacksonbrewery.com), also known as Jax Brewery, contains about 50 shops and eateries inside a dramatic 1891 former brewery nearly across from Jackson Square. From the upper floors, you can take in very nice views of the Mississippi River. You'll find a mix of interesting shops (JAX Art Gallery, selling prints and posters of local artists, and Street Scene, which sells hand-painted reproduction wood carvings of vintage New Orleans) and touristy ones (such as Cajun Clothing Co., where you can pick up your very own crawfish-embroidered polo shirt), plus the city's only Virgin Megastore, and a couple of chains such as Chico's clothing and Sunglass Hut. There's a small food court, and Pat O's on the River is a favorite spot for cocktails at sunset.

The posh **Gallery of Shops** (901 Canal St., 504/524-1331), at the Ritz-Carlton hotel, contains several high-end shops and fashion boutiques. It's an appropriate setting, as the shops occupy the first floor of the former Maison Blanche department store. Farther down Canal, the **Shops at Canal Place** (333 Canal St., 504/522-9200, www.theshopsatcanalplace.com) is the fanciest full-scale mall in the immediate downtown area, with branches of such acclaimed emporia as Saks Fifth Avenue, Coach, Kenneth Cole, L'Occitane, Brooks Brothers, Gucci, Ann Taylor, Williams-Sonoma, and Pottery Barn. There's also an excellent movie theater that specializes in indie and foreign films but also plays some blockbusters.

If you're a big fan of massive shopping malls, by the way, consider a trek to Metairie, which has one of the region's top such venues. The **Lakeside Shopping Center** (3301 Veterans Blvd., Metairie, 504/835-8000, www.lakeside-shopping.com) contains more than 120 shops, among them Aldo, Banana Republic, Coach, Guess, Hollister, Nicole Miller, J. Crew, Restoration Hardware, and Williams-Sonoma. The anchors are Dillard's and JC Penney. There's also a lively P. F. Chang's restaurant.

ART AND ANTIQUES

The mission of ⟨C RHINO **Contemporary Craft Co.** (Shops at Canal Place, 310 Canal St., 504/523-7945) is to promote and sell the handcrafted decorative arts, furniture, objets d'art, and clever creations of local talents. RHINO stands for "Right Here in New Orleans," and, indeed, that's where all the goods here come from. The famous "Blue Dog" artist George Rodrigue operates his **Rodrigue Studio** (721 Royal St., 504/581-4244) in a warmly lighted space nearly behind St. Louis Cathedral. You can buy everything from original oil paintings to inexpensive Blue Dog gifts. The inspiration for these works is the owner's terrier, Tiffany, who died some years ago. **Gallery Nine-Forty** (940 Royal St., 504/558-0000) specializes in New Orleans–themed works, including many compositions related to Mardi Gras.

LOUISIANA TAX-FREE SHOPPING

If you're visiting from another country, you're entitled to a refund of the state sales tax, and in certain cases, the local sales tax, on goods bought in Louisiana. This policy, unique among the 50 states, was introduced as a way to help promote visitation by foreign travelers, and depending on how much shopping you do, you really can save a bit of money.

The refund is available to visitors who have a valid foreign passport *and* an airline or other international round-trip ticket of up to 90 days' duration. Canadians are the one exception to the passport rule; they may provide proof of residency by showing a driver's license or birth certificate. If you come from any other country, you must supply a passport. Resident aliens, foreign students, U.S. citizens living in other countries, and citizens with dual citizenship in the United States and another country are not eligible. The refund does not apply to services, hotel charges, car rentals, food and beverages, or personal goods bought for use while in Louisiana, and only purchases made at participating shops qualify.

To take advantage of this program, ask for a refund voucher at the shop where you make your purchase – any participating merchant will be able to provide you with this, once you show your passport (or other ID, if Canadian). It's important to remember that you will not be given the refund at the time of purchase – this happens at the Louisiana Tax Free Shopping Refund Center at New Orleans International Airport. At the actual shop you'll pay the full price, including tax, for your purchase, and you'll be issued a voucher in the amount of the refund due you. You must present the voucher and all original receipts for every purchase to qualify for the refund.

Refunds under $500 are issued in cash; refunds over $500 are issued by check and mailed to your home. You can also mail in your vouchers and receipts to receive a refund. In this case, you must mail the original vouchers, copies of the receipts, your travel ticket, a copy of your passport, a statement explaining why you didn't collect the refund at the airport, and a statement explaining where the merchandise is now to **Louisiana Tax Free Shopping Refund Center** (Box 20125, New Orleans, LA 70141). For additional information, log on to www.louisianataxfree.com.

Look for original works by M. L. Snowden, Peter Max, LeRoy Neiman, Frederick Hart, and other notables of the contemporary art world at **Hanson-King Gallery** (523 Royal St., 504/556-8240). There's a branch of the world-famous 🄲 **Martin-Lawrence Galleries** (433 Royal St., 504/299-9055) along Royal Street. The roster of star artists with works here is astounding: Picasso, Chagall, Warhol, Erté, and so on. Owned by one of the most respected artists in Louisiana, the eponymous **Michalopoulos Gallery** (617 Bienville St., 504/558-0505) carries dozens of James Michalopoulos's vibrant, architectural renderings, with their trademark skewed angles and impressionistic brushwork. Many of his works feature Creole houses or classic French Quarter town houses. Sharon Stone, Bruce Willis, and Bonnie Raitt are among his most notable col-

lectors. Michalopoulos is also one of the owners of the excellent North Shore restaurant Etoile, where many of his works are displayed.

Callan Fine Art (240 Chartres St., 504/524-0025) has lovely 18th- and 19th-century impressionist and other fine paintings, with the works of the French Barbizon movement a particular specialty. One unusual venue is **Stone and Press Gallery** (238 Chartres St., 504/561-8555), which specializes in artists of the first half of the 20th century who work in etching, lithography, and wood engraving, as well as mezzotints painted by many contemporary luminaries. It's one of only four galleries in the South that's a member of the International Fine Print Dealers Association. Photo giants such as Ansel Adams, Edward Curtis, Elliott Erwit, Henri-Cartier Bresson, and Helmut Newton have works available at the prestigious

Gallery for Fine Photography (241 Chartres St., 504/568-1313).

A French Quarter fixture since 1938, **New Orleans Silversmiths** (600 Chartres St., 504/522-8333) handcrafts gold, platinum, and sterling silver and also carries many vintage pieces, as well as corkscrews, candlesticks, and other fine works. The Quarter's only gallery dedicated to studio glass, **(Royal Cameo Glass** (322 Royal St., 504/522-7840) shows pieces created by some of the nation's leading artists in this medium. Acclaimed artist Louis Sahuc sells his fine black-and-white images at **Photo Works New Orleans** (839 Chartres St., 504/593-9090)—there are beautiful shots of the city as well as other places Sahuc has traveled.

Since 1899, **(Keil's Antiques** (325 Royal St., 504/522-4552) has been specializing in 18th- and 19th-century antiques from France and England, from marble mantels and magnificent crystal chandeliers to garnet chokers. You might expect to find some first-rate French antiques in the Quarter, and indeed, the **French Antique Shop** (225 Royal St., 504/524-9861), which moved to New Orleans from Paris in 1939, has an extensive and impressive array of fine Gallic furnishings from the 18th and 19th centuries as well as some striking Asian vases and accessories. Specialties include gilt-leaf mirrors, salvaged mantels, dining-room tables, and bronze statuary. The tiny and terrific **Brass Monkey** (235 Royal St., 504/561-0688) carries a wonderfully odd assortment of antique collectibles, from Limoges boxes to ancient walking sticks to vintage medical paraphernalia—expect the unexpected.

The sleek showrooms of **Hurwitz Mintz** (227 Chartres St. and 211 Royal St., 504/568-9555; 1751 Airline Dr., Metairie, 504/378-1000), which has been a fixture in New Orleans since the 1920s, are something to behold; they occupy several large shop windows along prominent blocks of Chartres and Royal streets. Inside the windows you'll find curvaceous and striking modern furniture arranged cleverly and colorfully. Hurwitz Mintz isn't an antiques shop, as it carries all the major

lines of today's furniture makers, from Drexel-Heritage to Henredon, but it is a great place to find reproduction antiques, as well as striking postmodern and abstract sofas, beds, chairs, and tables that complement the antiques you may already own. Prices are surprisingly reasonable, especially given the prime locations in the Quarter.

SOUVENIRS AND GIFTS

Your best bet for souvenirs is simply to stroll the length of Decatur Street and pop inside a few shops, as there are many of them, and they're pretty similar. For more of the same, check out the stalls at the Flea Market at the French Market building.

The **Museum Shop at the Historic New Orleans Collection** (533 Royal St., 504/598-7147) sells all manner of Louisiana memorabilia and artifacts, many with a historical bent. You'll find a huge supply of regional books, plus tote bags, letter openers, commemorative minted coins, pens, and so on. The **Little Toy Shop Too** (513 St. Ann St., 504/523-1770) is a great store in the Pontalba Building filled with very cool things, including precious miniatures, collectibles, toy soldiers, and imported European toys, as well as games and gifts that aren't so fine and breakable, which you could actually entrust to the hands of playful kids.

Perhaps the best, or at least the silliest, of the quirky gift and novelty shops along Decatur, **Funrock'n** (Decatur and Governor Nicholls Sts., 504/524-1122 or 866/255-0491) carries bizarre and tacky knickknacks you probably never knew you needed: Elvis lamps, *Day of the Dead* lunch boxes, "Satan Was a Lesbian" refrigerator magnets, *The Scream* posters, iron-ons, cards, and other peculiarities.

CLOTHING

With locations in the Quarter and Uptown, **Hemline** (609 Chartres St., 504/592-0242; 3308 Magazine St., 504/269-4005) is a favorite women's clothing boutique carrying Diesel, BCBG, Diane von Furstenberg, and other trendy labels. Search for top-of-the-line designer wear (DKNY, Prada, etc.) at **Prima**

LOUISIANA FOOD FINDS

Some of your most memorable – and distinctive – purchases may be products you can nosh on. From New Orleans out through the Cajun Country, dozens of businesses specialize in manufacturing specialty foods and drinks. Here's a roundup of favorite Louisiana-made food products:

Abita Beer: Abita Springs, on the North Shore about an hour from New Orleans, first became famous for its crystalline artesian wells. It's this perfectly pure water that's used by **Abita Brewery** (800/737-2311, ext. 2, www.abita. com) to craft such classic Louisiana elixirs as Abita Amber, Turbodog, and the seasonally popular Mardi Gras Bock. Tours of the brewery are available at 1 P.M. and 2:30 P.M. Saturdays and at 1 P.M. only Sundays; no reservations are required.

Blue Plate Mayonnaise: Made by Luzianne, which is based right in the heart of the CBD on Magazine Street, Blue Plate mayo is made with local cottonseed oil and has been a favorite condiment in these parts since the late 1920s. Luzianne is also the second-largest independent coffee manufacturer in the United States.

Camellia Beans: The magic ingredient in rich and delicious red beans and rice, Camellia-brand dried kidney beans are manufactured in the New Orleans suburb of Harahan and sold throughout the state. Although red kidney beans are the big seller, Camellia also sells black, navy, split pea, lentil, lima, field pea, and crowder pea varieties.

Community Coffee and Tea: Better known these days in Louisiana for its string of festive coffeehouses, Community Coffee and Tea is, first and foremost, a coffee and tea producer. Its packaged ground coffee and bagged and iced teas have a deeply loyal following. You can pick these products up at any Community Coffee (a.k.a. "CC's") espresso cafe or at most specialty food and gift shops.

Crystal Hot Sauce: Tabasco isn't the only game in town when it comes to pepper sauces. The slightly milder Crystal brand hot sauce has its diehard fans. It's made right in New Orleans by the Baumer Foods plant, which also produces fruit preserves, Creole mustards, marinades, and many other foods.

Dixie Beer: Made inside a rambling brewery building on New Orleans's Tulane Avenue, this rich and tasty beer sold in longneck bottles is arguably the most popular beer of the Deep South. The Jazz Amber Lite and Blackened Voodoo lager are distributed nationally. Sipping a Dixie Beer while slurping down raw oysters is a classic Louisiana tradition.

French Market Coffee: Chicory, a faintly bitter herb root grown mostly in northern Europe, is dried, ground-roasted, and then blended with French Market coffee beans to create the inimitable flavor that so many java drinkers cherish. Once you've had French Market Coffee, which is sold all around town and especially in the French Market's Cafe Du Monde, you may never be able to go back to your usual beans.

Donna's Closet (1218 St. Charles Ave., 504/525-3327; also 4409 Chastant St., Metairie, 504/885-3327); there's a plus-size shop adjacent at 1206 St. Charles.

You can shop for fun if slightly hokey Cajun clothing, complete with a crawfish logo, at **Perlis** (6070 Magazine St., 504/895-8661; Riverwalk, foot of Poydras Street, 504/581-6746; Jackson Brewery, Decatur Street, 504/523-6681). The popular chain **Urban Outfitters** (400 N. Peters St., 504/558-9459) has an outpost along busy North Peters Street.

BOOKS AND MUSIC

Across from the House of Blues music club, the ◖ **Louisiana Music Factory** (210 Decatur St., 504/586-1094) is a noted music shop with a great selection of jazz, Cajun, and zydeco music. You'll find both used and new CDs, plus books, videos, posters, and other music memorabilia. It does a brisk mail-order business.

You can relax in an armchair while perusing the secondhand tomes at **Beckham's Bookshop** (228 Decatur St., 504/522-9875),

Melinda's Original Habanero Pepper Sauce: Louisianans love their hot sauces, and Melinda's – based in Metairie – manufactures a blend that differs a bit from the usual suspects. Here the fiery flavors of habanero peppers are blended with lime, onions, carrots, and garlic to create a kicky but complex condiment. Melinda's Mango-Habanero version is terrific for barbecuing.

Pralines: These exquisite melt-in-your-mouth, disk-shaped candies are made with cream, butter, caramelized brown sugar, and pecans. They're sold at virtually every food-related gift shop in southern Louisiana, but one of the best sources of authentic pralines is **Evans Creole Candy Factory** (848 Decatur St., 504/522-7111 or 800/637-6675, www.evanscreolecandy. com), in the French Quarter.

Steen's Syrup: This sugarcane syrup-processing plant in the small town of Abbeville, near Lafayette, has been going strong since 1910. Buy a bottle of this thick sweetener to pour over pancakes or bake into cakes and cookies. It's also a key ingredient in K. C. Masterpiece-brand barbecue sauces.

Tabasco Sauce: The mother of all U.S. hot sauces, Tabasco hardly needs a description here. Louisiana families are known to go through a decent-size bottle of the stuff every week or two, and the Tabasco company – based on Avery Island in the heart of the Cajun wetlands – also makes a number of related sauces, mustards, jerkies, and snacks.

Free tours of the **Tabasco factory** are also available (337/365-8173 or 800/634-9599, www.tabasco.com, 9 A.M.–4 P.M. daily).

Tony Chachere's: One of the leading two Cajun and Creole prepared-foods companies in Louisiana, Tony Chachere's (pronounced SASH-er-eez) is based in the Cajun town of Opelousas and known for a vast array of sauces, boxed products, and the like. The carefully blended food mixes, such as Creole butter beans and rice, are especially good, but also check out the tasty seasoning blends.

Zapp's Potato Chips: There's nothing that complements a muffuletta sandwich from Central Grocery better than a bag of Zapp's Potato Chips (well, that and a can of Barq's root beer or cream soda). These supercrunchy and shockingly fattening chips truly zip with flavor. Popular types include Cajun Crawtator (made with the same seasonings commonly found in crawfish boil), Hotter 'n Hot Jalapeno, Cajun Dill, Sour Cream and Creole Onion, Bee-Licious (made with honey-mustard), and Sweet Cinnamon Sweet Potato.

Zatarain's: A notable spice producer based in the West Bank suburb of Gretna, Zatarain's has been turning out tasty food mixes and spices since 1889. The jambalaya mix is particularly good, as are the crab and crawfish boils, but don't overlook such noble and notable delicacies as root beer-extract, frozen sausage-and-chicken gumbo, and cornbread-stuffing mix.

a good source of rare and hard-to-find antiquarian titles. There's a strong collection of first editions. William Faulkner actually lived for several months at what is now **Faulkner House Books** (624 Pirate's Alley, behind St. Louis Cathedral, 504/524-2940). Here, in 1925, he wrote *Soldiers' Pay*. The store stocks rare first editions of his works, plus collections of his letters. It's also a fine source of contemporary fiction by both local and faraway authors. **Crescent City Books** (204 Chartres St., 504/524-4997) contains two floors of out-of-

print and antiquarian titles. It's an exceptional source of local history and literature, scholarly books, and hard-to-find titles on philosophy, ancient history, and literary criticism—a real book lover's bookstore.

COSMETICS
Arguably the best among several wonderful perfumeries around town, **Hové** (824 Royal St., 504/525-7827) has been proffering high-quality imported and locally made fragrances, lotions, soaps, and bath oils since the 1930s.

Outrageous **Fifi Mahony's** (934 Royal St., 504/525-4343) is your one-stop salon and makeup counter for that occasion when you're trying to make a statement. Pop in and browse the wigs that come in every color of the rainbow (and then some), plus body glitter, Tony and Tina cosmetics, wild hair-care products, and offbeat handbags. **Shine Spa and Specialties** (622 Conti St., 504/581-4999) is a full-service day spa that also sells a wide range of earth-friendly skin-care products.

ONLY IN NEW ORLEANS

Mardi Gras masks are a big business in New Orleans year-round, and ◖ **Little Shop of Fantasy** (517 St. Louis St., 504/945-2435) offers one of the better selections. Many of the masks and Mardi Gras costumes and accessories are made locally, others by artists from all over the world. Some of these items are strictly for collecting, not wearing, unless you're willing to risk getting beer splashed across a $1,200 mask during a crazy Carnival party.

Well, you're in New Orleans, and there are few cities with a sexier vibe, so why not drop by the Quarter's premier sex boutique,

Chartres Street Conxxxion (107 Chartres St., 504/586-8006), a 24-hour emporium of movies, books, lingerie, oils, equipment, and assorted playthings. It's popular with straights, gays, and everybody who identifies somewhere in between.

Laura's Candies (331 Chartres St., 504/525-3880) is New Orleans's oldest candy store. Great food and a lovely place, with a bigger variety of sweets than some of the other local shops. You can watch cigars being made at the **New Orleans Cigar Factory** (415 Decatur St., 504/568-1003; 206 Bourbon St., 504/568-0168), which sells many styles and has a walk-in humidor.

Rhonda and Walt Rose, owners of **Louisiana Loom Works** (616 Chartres St., 504/566-7788), hand-weave all of the colorful rag rugs at this shop, where you can examine the wares and watch the production process. They also take custom orders and will ship your rug within about a month. **Quilt Cottage** (801 Nashville Ave., 504/895-3791) not only sells finished quilts but also carries an astounding array of fabrics and supplies for making your own quilts; classes are also offered.

Central Business and Warehouse Districts

Most of the CBD is dominated by high-rise hotels and office towers and has few shops of note, although the riverside of the neighborhood, known as the Warehouse District, does contain a handful of art galleries and other fine shops. There are also two large shopping malls at opposite ends of the neighborhood, the Riverwalk, down by the river, and the New Orleans Centre, up by the Superdome.

MALLS AND SHOPPING CENTERS

The **Riverwalk Marketplace** (1 Poydras St., 504/522-1555, www.riverwalkmarketplace.com) is, shopwise, like many other midscale shopping malls; it's notable for its sweeping river views and especially good food court. It has a number

of stalls proffering local or at least local-feeling goods, souvenirs, and crafts, although it's a less atmospheric locale for souvenir shopping than the French Market in the Quarter. Among the many chain shops you'll find are Banana Republic, Gap, Ann Taylor Loft, Nine West, Body Shop, Brookstone, Rocky Mountain Chocolate Factory, and so on. There are 140 shops, plus many restaurants.

ART AND ANTIQUES

The Warehouse District has some of the South's most important fine arts galleries, among them **Arthur Roger** (432 Julia St., 504/522-1999), which specializes in modern works and presents highly popular openings and shows. A bit north, in the CBD, **Stella**

Jones Gallery (201 St. Charles Ave., 504/568-9050) is the city's top arts exhibit space for the works of African American artists. At the ❰ **New Orleans School of Glassworks and Printmaking Studio** (727 Magazine St., 504/529-7277, www.neworleansglassworks. com), you can watch highly skilled glassblowing and printmaking artisans at work and then browse their wares.

DESIGNER

Picked up so many goodies that you can't fit everything in your suitcase? Just drop by **Pursestrings** (Riverwalk Marketplace, 1 Poydras St., 504/588-9097) to browse the many colorful and stylish travel bags and totes, plus a wide selection of briefcases, luggage, and handbags. Among New Orleans's many very good jewelry shops, **Adler's** (722 Canal St., 504/523-5292; Lakeside Shopping Center, 3301 Veterans Memorial Blvd., Metairie, 504/523-1952) has the most loyal following—it's been serving the Crescent City since 1898. Fine watches, crystal, china, and silver are among the fine offerings.

If you need a jacket for your dinner at Galatoire's, consider **Rubenstein Brothers** (102 St. Charles Ave., 504/581-6666), a classic outfitter carrying such exclusive lines as Dolce and Gabbana, Armani, and Kenneth Cole.

Magazine Street and Uptown

Few American streets offer the astonishing variety of shops and boutiques that you'll discover along Magazine Street, which follows the curve of the mighty Mississippi River for about six miles from the city's Central Business District out to Audubon Park. Sassy secondhand clothiers, colorful oyster bars, jamming music clubs, and convivial java joints line the way, but it's the lower stretch of Magazine—from about Canal to Jackson streets—that possesses the city's most fascinating and offbeat antiques district. Magazine Street's prime antiquing row begins around Felicity Street and wends its way upriver to about Jackson Avenue, but there are plenty more pockets of antiques shops farther up.

Commercial activity along Magazine Street slows, intensifies, softens, regains strength, and then seems to disappear suddenly, like so many stages of a passing storm. Magazine Street is broken into little chunks of commerce interrupted by equally interesting rows of historic cottages and houses, in some cases grand and in others quite modest. The greatest thing about this street, apart from its sheer abundance of retail (and dining), is its quirky variety. The customer base along Magazine spans all economic brackets, all ages, and all styles.

© ANDREW COLLINS

Magazine Street offers a fascinating variety of shopping and dining.

The presence of a Starbucks at the corner of Washington and Magazine signals that even this fiercely independent shopping street is not immune to change, for better or for worse.

A massive branch of the gourmet health-food grocery chain Whole Foods opened in 2001 near Audubon Park, but otherwise major chain development has been pretty minimal. That may change, as Wal-Mart opened a branch just a couple of blocks off Magazine, in the Lower Garden District. It stands where housing projects once stood, and, interestingly, the developer who pushed for the Wal-Mart is a longtime proponent of historic preservation who argued that the benefits of bringing such a store into the neighborhood outweighed the negatives. As charming as Magazine Street is, for example, it has relatively few shops carrying everyday goods at low prices, and in general, Uptown lacks the discount shopping that many of its lower-income residents would benefit from.

As it turns out, you can't see the Wal-Mart store, or even sense its presence, as you stroll up curious Magazine Street, where you can find an auto repair shop sitting across the street from an Oriental rug shop, or the prestigious Neal Heaton Auction House across from a Popeyes. This is a real urban street, not just a place for tourists to spend money, and so the scenery and the people-watching are happily varied and unpredictable.

ART AND ANTIQUES

Those in the know come to **Collections II and Rousset Antiques and Textiles** (2104 Magazine St., 504/523-2000) in search of museum-quality 18th-century French tables and chairs, especially Louis XVI style, plus delicate embroideries, silks, paisleys, and toiles. Additionally, and at significantly lower prices, the store features an array of beautiful dinnerware and dining accessories, from reproduction pieces to antiques, all hand-chosen during the owners' regular forays into Paris, Provence, and Normandy. Come to quirky **Antiques-Magazine** (2028 Magazine St., 504/522-2043) to admire the astounding variety of hanging chandeliers and light fixtures and sconces, tending toward the frilly and decadent sorts that can make or break a room—most of them date from the mid-19th

century into the middle of the 20th, with an especially strong art deco and Victorian presence. Antiques-Magazine sells mostly smaller items and collectibles, including costume jewelry, cut-glass decorative arts, and art glass.

((**Bush Antiques and Beds au Beau Rev** (2109 Magazine St., 504/581-3518) is one store where you may want to sleep on your purchase—the dozens of beds sold here are quite spectacular and come from all over Europe and North America, from a mid-19th-century iron-and-brass four-poster to a whimsical cast-iron, green-painted sleigh bed. Other specialties include religious art (even some altars and ecclesiastical chandeliers) and decorative French ironwork that will remind you of the intricate grills and balustrades found on the exteriors of so many New Orleans homes. Head out back to the rear patio and browse the extensive collection of folk art. **Simon of New Orleans** (2126 Magazine St., 504/561-0088) carries a wide selection of folk and primitive art as well as French and Italian antiques.

The **Shop of the Two Sisters** (1800 Magazine St., 504/525-2747) is a large corner shop, set inside a handsome Greek Revival town house, packed to the rafters with eclectic regional furnishings, mirrors, lighting fixtures, and objets d'art—many of them from faraway lands. A designers' favorite, **Ray Langley Interiors** (2302 Magazine St., 504/522-2284) has a handsome showroom of modern, functional furniture—the sort of stuff you might see in some of the city's stylish boutique hotels.

The **Thomas Mann Gallery** (1812 Magazine St., 504/581-2113) is filled with whimsical contemporary art, glassware, jewelry, colorful stemware, and other works in different media. Mann's works are sold in galleries throughout the country, but this is the local flagship. **Eclectique Antiques** (1123 Josephine St., 504/524-6500) is a very large and impressively stocked emporium carrying a great variety of lamps, shades, and lights. The selection crosses many styles and periods. **Dunn and Sonnier** (2130 Magazine St., 504/524-3235) specializes in flower bulbs, iron garden furniture, and eclectic, mostly American-looking antiques. It's a bright and happy shop that's somewhat unusual for the neighborhood.

With more than 7,000 square feet of showroom space, **Top Drawer Antiques** (4310 Magazine St., 504/832-9080) is one of largest antiques shops Uptown, with original and reproduction pieces, plus paintings and accessories.

SOUVENIRS AND GIFTS

Orient Expressed Imports (3905 Magazine St., 504/899-3060) is a funny little gift shop with amusing tchotchkes, hand-smocked children's clothing, carved *santos,* and fine linens. A favorite stop for novelty items, curious gifts, fun clothing, and generally irreverent and teen- to adult-oriented oddities, **Winky's** (2038 Magazine St., 504/568-1020) is a good place to find that boxing-nun action figure you've been searching for. The **Bead Shop** (4612 Magazine St., 504/895-6161) occupies a quirky little Creole cottage—it's the perfect crafts boutique for a city that celebrates Mardi Gras with such enthusiasm.

Cameron Jones (2127 Magazine St., 504/524-3119) sells kinetic, colorful, and contemporary housewares, plant stands, wine racks, and other cool fixtures and elements for the home.

◖ Mignon Faget (3801 Magazine St., 504/891-2005; the Shops at Canal Place, 333 Canal St., 504/524-2973; Lakeside Shopping Center, 3301 Veterans Memorial Blvd., Metairie, 504/835-2244) has an almost cult following among New Orleans's devotees of fine jewelry. Faget has won countless awards for her creations, many of which incorporate icons and images familiar to Louisiana, such as oyster pendants, red-bean charm necklaces, and fleur de lis cuff links.

Jim Russell Records (1837 Magazine St., 504/522-2602) is a local institution, known for its more than half million LPs, 45s, and 78s in all music genres. It's where ardent record collectors go to find the rarest and most obscure vinyl.

If you're looking for an *indelible* souvenir of New Orleans, there's always **Crescent City**

ELSEWHERE IN THE AREA

If you're a serious fan of antiques and bric-a-brac shopping, it's worth making the trip to Kenner, out near the airport, to check out the **Original Jefferson Flea Market** (2134 Airline Hwy., 504/461-0128), a massive showroom with 45 individual dealer shops selling every imaginable kind of furniture, collectible, and accessory.

Near Mid-City park, **◖ Ricca Demolishing** (511 N. Solomon St., 504/488-5524) is one of several wrecking companies in New Orleans that have seen a huge, if unfortunate, boom in business as a result of Hurricane Katrina. This 50,000-square-foot emporium has long been an amazing source of cypress doors and mantels, all sorts of hardware, gates, brackets, and other materials salvaged from historic New Orleans homes.

Tattoo (4800 Magazine St., 504/269-8282). This safe and reputable piercing parlor is a fixture along funky upper Magazine Street. It offers a full range of designs, from traditional to edgy.

Beautiful and, in some cases, very fine and expensive handmade pens as well as fine stationery, note cards, diaries, and related writers' tools are found at elegant **Scriptura** (5423 Magazine St., 504/897-1555).

CLOTHING AND COSMETICS

House of Lounge (2044 Magazine St., 504/671-8300) sells vintage gowns and dresses—it's a fabulous collection of pieces that would make for quite an entrance. Bedroom smoking jackets, feather boas, and colorful corsets may be just what you're looking for to spice up your love life. A whimsical and offbeat clothier, **Frock Candy** (3336 Magazine St., 504/818-2940) sells funky and reasonably priced women's club gear, makeup, T-shirts, and jewelry. It's a hit with local clubgoers. A stylish plus-size boutique, **Mrs.**

Spratt's (4537 Magazine St., 504/891-0063) carries sizes 1X–5X, including pieces from some top labels.

At **Ballin's** (721 Dante St., 504/866-4367) fashion-forward shoppers pick up the latest sportswear and evening attire from Vera Wang, Marisa Bartelli, and other top designers. **Pippen Lane** (2929 Magazine St., Uptown, 504/269-0106) sells all sorts of cute and fun kids' apparel, including linens and shoes. There's also fanciful hand-painted furniture and thought-provoking, educational toys. Head to **Gaetana's** (7732 Maple St., 504/865-9625) for sensible but stylish modern women's wear and accessories. There's a branch of the famed wedding dress–maker Vera Wang at **Mimi** (5500 Magazine St., 504/269-6464), a high-end clothing boutique.

Quirky **Aidan Gill for Men** (2026 Magazine St., 504/587-9090) is an unusual spot with old-fashioned barbershop memorabilia, upscale bath products, and ties and other accessories for men. The environmentally sensitive **Earthsavers** (5501 Magazine St., 504/899-8555; Lakeside Shopping Center, 3301 Veterans Blvd., Metairie, 504/835-0225) has earned a loyal following for its all-natural exfoliants, skin moisturizers, and other skin-care products. The shop also offers spa services and aromatherapy.

THE NORTH SHORE

Separated from the South Shore by enormous Lake Pontchartrain, the North Shore comprises a string of fast-growing middle- to upper-middle-income suburbs, north of which lies a patchwork of rural, wooded towns extending about 40 miles to the Mississippi border. The region is a hidden gem, less famous than the Cajun Country, the plantation towns along the Mississippi River, and, of course, New Orleans. But Louisianans themselves, as well as many who live in other nearby Southern states, have long known of the North Shore's charms—chief among them being that it's simply less touristy than other parts of the state.

It's misleading and perhaps unfair to call the North Shore's most prominent communities—Slidell, Mandeville, Covington, Ponchatoula, and Hammond—suburbs. Although these towns contain their share of gated communities and strip shopping malls, they're also a trove of nature preserves, forests dense with towering pine and hardwood trees, and funky historic districts abundant with independent shops and eateries. The architecture, topography, and even climate are distinct from the rest of southern Louisiana, bearing a closer resemblance to the charming vintage towns of Mississippi, Alabama, and Georgia.

Like coastal Mississippi and New Orleans, the North Shore took a hard hit from Hurricane Katrina in August 2005. The storm walloped the eastern end of the North Shore, particularly Slidell, whose downtown was totally flooded and whose many residential blocks fronting Lake Pontchartrain were leveled by massive winds as well as flooding. Farther west along

© ANDREW COLLINS

HIGHLIGHTS

◖ **Best Place to Learn About the Sea:** Although it began as a rather modest museum in the charming village of Madisonville, the **Lake Pontchartrain Basin Maritime Museum** has grown into one of the North Shore's best attractions, with excellent exhibits on the region's maritime history. The museum is also actively restoring the nearby Madisonville lighthouse, and it hosts the wildly popular Madisonville Wooden Boat Festival (page 234).

◖ **Most Eccentric Museum:** The quintessence of quirkiness, the funky **Abita Mystery House** contains a memorable stash of folk art and recycled goods, and it never ceases to surprise first-time visitors. A favorite exhibit is the House of Shards, constructed of broken bottles, license plates, machine parts, and pottery scraps (page 235).

◖ **Best Place to Imbibe: Pontchartrain Vineyards and Winery,** in rural Folsom, not only produces the finest vintages in the state, but it also presents informative tours, popular concerts, and other enjoyable events on its courtly, bucolic grounds (page 236).

◖ **Best Place for Boot-Stompin':** A rollicking variety show, the **Abita Springs Opry** is broadcast on radio and TV stations throughout the South. It takes place at Abita Springs Town Hall once a month in the spring and fall, and at these concerts you'll hear wonderful folk music, country, gospel, and bluegrass (page 237).

◖ **Most Enjoyable Way to Burn Calories: Bicycling on Tammany Trace,** a 31-mile rails-to-trails bikeway that extends through several towns across the North Shore, offers cyclists, walkers, and others a scenic, traffic-free ride past towering oak, magnolia, and pine trees and through verdant wetlands. This is the best biking in the state (page 239).

◖ **Best Place to Talk to the Animals:** Don't mistake the **Global Wildlife Center,** which is on the Tangipahoa and St. Tammany parish line, for a mere zoo. About 3,000 (mostly African) wild animals here roam freely amid the 900 rural acres, and visitors view them on covered-wagon safaris (page 253).

◖ **Best Opportunity for Window-Browsing:** Magazine Street in New Orleans might be more famous, but going **antiques shopping in Ponchatoula** offers better bargains and a tremendous variety (page 254).

LOOK FOR ◖ TO FIND RECOMMENDED SIGHTS, ACTIVITIES, DINING, AND LODGING.

the shore, the areas of Lacombe and Mandeville (including historic Old Mandeville) nearest the shore also sustained heavy damage from flooding and wind. And farther inland, Covington, Abita Springs, Folsom, and points north—where the terrain is dominated by massive pine trees—damage was sporadic but significant as many limbs and entire trees fell on homes. A year after Katrina, most of the region had been cleaned up and businesses in most communities had reopened. The one town where a number of businesses remain closed is Slidell, and some parts of this community will take years to rebuild. However, many of Slidell's shops, restaurants, and hotels have reopened, and just as in

New Orleans across the lake, things continue to improve on a daily basis.

You'll find relatively few formal attractions in this region, although the Global Wildlife Center in Folsom ranks among the must-sees in the entire state, and Honey Island Swamp near Slidell is de rigueur among enthusiasts of swamp touring—tours on the swamp, which was also slammed hard by Katrina, resumed surprisingly quickly after the storm, proof, perhaps, of just how quickly nature can adapt and heal itself. This is also one of Louisiana's top areas for golfing, bird-watching, biking, canoeing and kayaking, and fishing. Fans of indoor recreation shouldn't feel left out, either—there

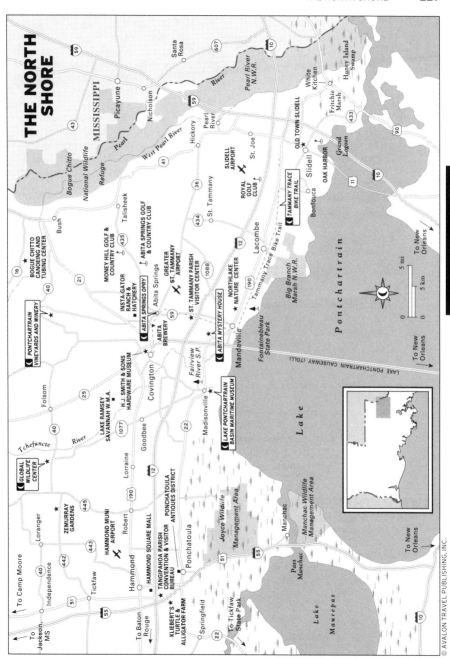

THE NORTH SHORE

THE NORTH SHORE

MISSISSIPPI

Bogue Chitto National Wildlife Refuge

Santa Rosa

Picayune

Nicholson

Pearl River

Pearl River N.W.R.

White Kitchen

Honey Island Swamp

Fritchie Marsh

West Pearl River

Hickory

Pearl River

Old Town Slidell

Grand Lagoon

Bush

Talisheek

St. Joe

SLIDELL AIRPORT

OAK HARBOR

Slidell

Bonfouca

BOGUE CHITTO CANOEING AND TUBING CENTER

St. Tammany

ROYAL GOLF CLUB

TAMMANY TRACE BIKE TRAIL

MONEY HILL GOLF & COUNTRY CLUB

ABITA SPRINGS GOLF & COUNTRY CLUB

GREATER ST. TAMMANY AIRPORT

NORTHLAKE NATURE CENTER

Lacombe

Tammany Trace Bike Trail

To New Orleans

PONTCHARTRAIN VINEYARDS AND WINERY

Abita Springs

ST. TAMMANY PARISH VISITOR CENTER

INSTA-GATOR RANCH & HATCHERY

ABITA SPRINGS OPRY

ABITA BREWERY

ABITA MYSTERY HOUSE

Mandeville

Big Branch Marsh N.W.R.

Pontchartrain

Folsom

H.J. SMITH & SONS HARDWARE MUSEUM

Covington

Fairview River S.P.

Fontainebleau State Park

LAKE PONTCHARTRAIN (TOLL)

To New Orleans

LAKE RAMSEY SAVANNAH W.M.A.

Goodbee

Madisonville

LAKE PONTCHARTRAIN BASIN MARITIME MUSEUM

Tchefuncte River

Lorraine

GLOBAL WILDLIFE CENTER

Loranger

ZEMURRAY GARDENS

HAMMOND MUNI AIRPORT

Robert

PONCHATOULA ANTIQUES DISTRICT

Lake

Joyce Wildlife Management Area

Manchac

Manchac Wildlife Management Area

To Camp Moore

Independence

Tickfaw

Hammond

HAMMOND SQUARE MALL

TANGIPAHOA PARISH CONVENTION & VISITOR BUREAU

Ponchatoula

To New Orleans

To Baton Rouge

To Jackson, MS

KLIEBERT'S TURTLE & ALLIGATOR FARM

Springfield

To Tickfaw State Park

Pass Manchac

Lake Maurepas

5 mi
5 km

© AVALON TRAVEL PUBLISHING, INC.

are few parts of the state with a better variety of antiques shops, and the North Shore outranks every other part of the state except New Orleans when it comes to upscale dining.

Spring and fall are probably the biggest months for visiting the North Shore, although many New Orleanians come up here in summer, because it's slightly cooler and the towering pine trees provide plenty of shade. If you're visiting Louisiana for the first time and using New Orleans as your base, consider making at least a day trip to the North Shore and perhaps spending a night or two—this strategy is especially recommended if you tire quickly of city life. Because the area is relatively affordable and within a 90-minute drive of many of southern Louisiana's and coastal Mississippi's key towns and attractions, it's also convenient to use the North Shore as a base for further exploring.

MEDIA

Most people in these parts rely on New Orleans's *Times-Picayune* (www.nola.com), although Hammond also has a daily newspaper, *The Daily Star* (www.hammondstar.com). Nondaily papers on the North Shore include *The St. Tammany News Banner* (www.thesttammanynews.com), in Covington; the *Ponchatoula Times* (www.ponchatoula.com/ptimes), in Ponchatoula; and the *Sentry-News* (www.thesttammanynews.com), in Slidell. New Orleans's jam-packed alternative newsweekly *Gambit Weekly* (www.bestofneworleans.com) also has plenty of coverage on dining, nightlife, events, and attractions on the North Shore.

GETTING THERE

The North Shore is at the junction of four interstates: I-10, I-12, I-59, and I-55. This makes driving here from a number of key points—New Orleans, the Gulf Coast, Baton Rouge, Birmingham, and Jackson, Mississippi—extremely easy and direct. From New Orleans you can come either by way of I-10, which deposits you at the east end of the region in Slidell, or by way of the Lake Pontchartrain Causeway, which places you more centrally in the area. Note that there's no toll for crossing this bridge from south to north, toward the North Shore, but you will be charged a toll of $2 for crossing north to south. Driving here is your best bet; you need a car to really explore this region.

New Orleans International Airport is very close to the Lake Pontchartrain Causeway on the South Shore—the drive from the airport to Mandeville takes about 45 minutes. **St. Tammany Tours** (800/543-6262) runs shuttle buses from the airport to the North Shore, available 24 hours by reservation. The cost is $27 per person, one-way.

Greyhound (800/231-2222, www.greyhound.com) connects several towns along the North Shore to New Orleans and New Orleans International Airport, although transfers are sometimes necessary. Towns on the North Shore served by Greyhound are Amite, Hammond, Mandeville, Ponchatoula, and Slidell. **Amtrak** (800/872-7245, www.amtrak.com) has two trains that pass through the region. The Crescent stops in Slidell on its daily run between New Orleans and New York City—it connects the region to Hattiesburg, Mississippi; Birmingham; Atlanta; and Washington, D.C. The City of New Orleans stops in Hammond during its daily run between New Orleans and Chicago, with other major stops including Jackson, Mississippi, and Memphis.

St. Tammany Parish

The state's fastest-growing parish mirrors other upscale suburbs in the South, such as the boomtown north of Atlanta and Houston, but on a smaller scale. You'll hear the same discussions here about traffic problems, growth management, and community planning, but the growing pains have—to this point—been less dramatic here. One reason is that Lake Pontchartrain provides a massive natural barrier between metro New Orleans and the North Shore. This side of the lake is also the site of some enormous tracts of protected wetlands, so the areas along the east and west branches of the Pearl River, along the lakefront in Lacombe and eastern Mandeville, and in several other parts of the parish will never be developed commercially. That all being said, many experts believe that St. Tammany Parish will grow even more in the wake of Hurricane Katrina, as those who desire proximity to New Orleans without actually living in the Big Easy continue to relocate here.

Early visitors to St. Tammany Parish, which took its name in 1812 from the esteemed Delaware Indian chief Tamanend, were drawn here by the lush pine forests and primeval swamps harboring abundant wildlife. Curative artesian water in Abita Springs and cooler temperatures tempted many well-to-do urban dwellers in search of a healthful escape—throughout the 19th century, first steamships and then trains brought hundreds of New Orleanians to the *autre cote du lac* (other side of the lake), primarily during the sultry summers. Inns and restaurants catering to city folk popped up, especially in Mandeville and Abita Springs.

The land had been occupied by Choctaw Indians, who are said to have named the area's rivers, and it was the French among the Europeans who investigated the region during the early explorations of New Orleans. Permanent European settlements began to take root throughout the 1800s, and in addition to the parish's early development as a summer resort, timber, agricultural, and boatbuilding industries thrived here.

The 23-plus-mile Causeway bridge, the longest in the world, first connected Mandeville to the town of Metairie (and the adjacent city of New Orleans) in 1959, which greatly spurred the parish's growth. But St. Tammany really boomed during the 1990s, as a number of businesses moved out here, and many more residents with jobs in New Orleans, Metairie, and other South Shore towns chose to live here, tempted by the natural beauty, excellent schools, low crime, and generally high quality of life.

A number of artists and writers have lived in St. Tammany Parish, including novelist Walker Percy, who lived in Covington (the library there holds a symposium on Percy every April). Actor John Goodman has a home in Mandeville.

SLIDELL

The largest town in the parish, Slidell (population 32,000) is also the closest to New Orleans. In fact, it's just a short hop from East New Orleans, meaning that it stood directly in the path of Hurricane Katrina and did, in fact, sustain a severe hit from the storm. Storm or not, Slidell continues to grow. This commuter suburb, well known for its excellent public-school system, is home to many workers who drive each day across the bridge to the South Shore or across the state line into Mississippi. The town is most often visited because of Honey Island Swamp, on the eastern edge of the community, which is fed by the West Branch of the Pearl River (the East Branch forms the border between Louisiana and Mississippi).

The city was established in 1882 as a base camp for construction of the New Orleans and Northeastern Railroad, which ran to Meridian, Mississippi, and connected rail travelers ultimately to New York City and other Northeastern cities. The site was chosen by virtue of its being the nearest high ground to New Orleans

THE NORTH SHORE

SWAMP TOURS

Swamp tours are big business all through southern Louisiana, and of all the tours you can take while visiting New Orleans, these boat rides through some of North America's most pristine and spectacular swamps might be the most memorable. The top destinations for swamp tours are Slidell, Houma, and towns along the Atchafalaya Swamp basin east and south of Lafayette, but you can also find swamp tour operators along the River Road south of Baton Rouge and throughout metro New Orleans.

Tours are of several types, some of them using airboats, some using quieter excursion vessels. The airboats travel at amazing speeds, but they do tend to scare away wildlife.

The narrative accompanying the tour can vary from highly educational to corny, with tall tales about swamp creatures and Cajun folklore. But on a good swamp tour, you'll come away not only having observed a wide variety of wildlife firsthand, but also with a new understanding of the topography and ecology that has shaped New Orleans and southern Louisiana. After all, at one time, all of New Orleans looked more or less like Honey Swamp and the Atchafalaya Basin.

LOGISTICS

Rates for swamp tours vary depending on duration, the boat, and the number of passengers. You can expect to pay about $15–25 per adult for a two-hour tour, and kids under 12 are often discounted. Most swamp-tour outfitters give tours year-round, but the best time to go is spring (April and May, especially) and fall (September and October). In winter, animals are less active (alligators are dormant) and the swamps not nearly as lush and vibrant. In summer, it can be awfully hot riding around a swamp in a metal boat for a couple of hours, and the river flow is sometimes low, but you should have ample opportunity to sight wild animals and enjoy verdant foliage.

Although many tour companies offer several tours throughout the day, it's important always to make a reservation, even if only a few hours ahead; tours do book up at busy times. There's a chance, with some outfitters, that you'll be able to show up and get on a tour, but most prefer that you call ahead, and sometimes you won't even be able to find where a tour starts without calling for directions.

Many swamp-tour operators can, for a fee, drive you between New Orleans and the debarkation point. Honey Island Swamp Tours, out of Slidell, charges $45 per adult for a swamp tour that includes van transportation back and forth to New Orleans; the price for a tour where you show up yourself is $23 per adult. Many other companies giving tours on the North Shore, down near Houma, and in the eastern end of the Atchafalaya Swamp basin, offer similar deals.

HONEY ISLAND SWAMP TOURS

One of the most respected operators in the state, Honey Island Swamp Tours (985/641-1769, www.honeyislandswamp.com) was established by Dr. Paul Wagner, an environmental consultant with a Ph.D. in wetland ecology. He sold the business in 2005, but the guides here continue to run it in the same spirit as Dr. Wagner. The company can handle nearly 150 guests per trip, using up to seven boats.

These tours are geared toward the thinking traveler, and they pass through some of the most primeval terrain in the region. One nice thing about the swamps on the North Shore, as opposed to those down in the Atchafalaya Basin or south of New Orleans, is that you see dense groves of very tall trees all through Honey Island — it gives the swamp a lush and dramatic appearance. Honey Island is the second-largest swamp in Louisiana; while Atchafalaya is larger, it's been significantly altered by pipelines, canals, and levees. The Pearl is one of the only rivers in the state that does not have a levee system and it is encouraged to flood, which nourishes the wetland and keeps the swamp healthy. About the only evidence of human alteration as you float down the Pearl and into Honey Island Swamp is the I-10 highway bridge that crosses the river, and the rows of fishing camps built on stilts along several stretches of the river.

Honey Island Swamp is an estuary and a very different ecosystem from the other swamps in the state. It's called an overflow river swamp, and it looks more like a miniature Amazon than like another Gulf Coast swamp. It's very quiet and peaceful, and you'll see lots of turtles out sunning (usually red-eared sliders, though some of the snapping turtles here live to be 150–200), along with herons, ibis, egrets, hawks, kingfishers, and the occasional owl. Cypress and tupelo are among the most common trees in this and other Louisiana swamps, but you'll also see plenty of green ash, river birch, and red gum trees.

Wood duck is the most common waterfowl. A furry beaverlike creature called nutria, which was introduced to Louisiana from Argentina by the McIlhenny family of Avery Island, is common in Honey Island as well as most of the other swamps in Louisiana. They're cute to look at, but nutria have unfortunately become a nuisance.

Honey Island Swamp Tours covers about seven or eight miles during its excursions, and although the company never promises passengers that they'll observe alligators, the odds of seeing them are strong, as long as it's not winter.

SWAMP TOUR OPERATORS ELSEWHERE IN LOUISIANA

Also on the North Shore, **Mockingbird Swamp Tours** (985/748-7637 or 985/519-1340, www.mockingbirdswamptours.com) runs excursions along Bayou Manchac and the swamplands between Lake Pontchartrain and Lake Maurepas.

Many of the best swamp tours are given outside Slidell on the North Shore, or near Houma in the southern heart of Cajun Country, but there are some reliable operators in the metro New Orleans region. At the famous Evergreen Plantation on the Great River Road, **Airboat Adventures** (Hwy. 18, Edgard, 504/454-3882 or 888/467-9267, www.airboatadventures.com) gives swamp/plantation combo tours.

For a more intimate experience, try **The Last Wildnerness** (225/659-2499, www.lastwildernesstours.com), which uses a small Cajun fishing boat to give tours of the Atchafalaya Basin, departing from Bayou Sorrel, not far from Nottoway on the River Road. Guide Dean Wilson takes passengers well off the beaten path, even by swamp standards, and into tight and shallow bodies of water that larger craft can't reach. Last Wildnerness also rents canoes and offers canoe tours.

A favorite in Houma is **A Cajun Man's Swamp Cruise** (985/868-4625, www.cajunman.com), conducted by Ron "Black" Guidry, who leads passengers on an entertaining tour through Black Bayou. Guidry is fluent in French and English, and he plays guitar and accordion and sings Cajun ditties while maneuvering his boat through the swamps.

Between Vacherie and Thibodaux, **Torres' Cajun Swamp Tours** (985/633-7739, www.torresswamptours.com) is a popular operator.

In the heart of Cajun Country, **Champagne's Swamp Tours** (1008 Roxy Dr., St. Martinville, 337/845-5567 or 337/230-4068, www.champagnesswamptours.com) takes passengers out in a 20-foot aluminum crawfish skiff with a very quiet engine. The tour leaves from Lake Martin Landing and passes through a dramatic flooded cypress and tupelo forest, as well as the largest nesting area of wading birds in the state. Another highly recommended company, in nearby Breaux Bridge, is **McGee's Landing** (337/228-2384, www.mcgeeslanding.com).

on the other side of Lake Pontchartrain. Early industries included brick and creosote manufacturing, lumber milling, and shipbuilding—in fact, Slidell shipyards built a number of military vessels used in World Wars I and II.

It's easy to reach Slidell from New Orleans via I-10, which cuts across the eastern edge of Lake Pontchartrain, but it's more interesting and not all that much longer to take U.S. Highway 90 East, which is Exit 240 from I-10 just a bit northeast of the French Quarter. The highway winds through the swampland that predominates in eastern New Orleans and, after crossing a short channel that connects Lake Pontchartrain to Lake Borge (which feeds into the Gulf of Mexico), intersects with U.S. Highway 190, which will run you right into downtown Slidell.

Olde Town

Slidell has a modest but engaging Olde Town district, mostly a jumble of 19th-century Victorian clapboard and brick buildings with some newer 1950s and '60s cottages. It's not overly trendy, but it's real, and feels like a genuine slice of Louisiana. This area experienced significant Katrina flooding, and a number of businesses in the Olde Town district haven't yet opened, but many others have. The anchor in Olde Town is the **Slidell Cultural Center** (444 Erlanger St., Slidell, 985/646-4375, www.slidell.la.us/slidellcenter.php, open 9 A.M.–4 P.M. Mon.–Fri., 10 A.M.–2 P.M. Sat., admission free), which exhibits traveling national and regional art exhibitions in a handsome gallery space. Because the center sustained severe damage from Hurricane Katrina, it moved temporarily to the historic Slidell Train Depot (1827 Front St., Slidell). Check first before visiting whether the center is back in its original location.

Slidell Museum

The town's other attraction is the Slidell Museum (2020 1st St., Slidell, 985/646-4380), a modest history museum with artifacts and documents, some dating as far back as the 1600s, that trace the region's history. It's set in Slidell's

old town jail. Also damaged by the hurricane, the museum was closed for renovations during 2006 but is expected to reopen in 2007.

En Route to Lacombe

From the Olde Town area, turn south onto U.S. Highway 11 and follow it to the next major intersection, which is Highway 433, onto which you should make a right turn. If you feel like checking out one of the several interesting residential neighborhoods that fringe Slidell's extensive canal system, make an immediate left onto Palm Drive and follow this road as it wends by waterside homes and skirts the bank of Bayou Bonfouca. You'll eventually hit Canulette Road, which brings you back onto Highway 433, where a left turn sets you back in the same direction you were going before the detour onto Palm Drive. Highway 433 winds beneath towering pine trees and over a wonderful old pontoon bridge that was featured in the early-1970s James Bond thriller *Live and Let Die* before eventually joining with U.S. Highway 190; a left turn here leads you toward Mandeville by way of the small town of Lacombe.

LACOMBE

The ancestral home of both Choctaw and Colapissa Native Americans, Lacombe is set along a picturesque bayou. Much of the southern section of town is occupied by **Big Branch Marsh National Wildlife Refuge** (Bayou Paquet Rd., off Transmitter Rd., which is off U.S. 190, Lacombe, 985/882-2000, www.fws.gov/bigbranchmarsh). Lacombe is less built up than either Slidell to the east or Mandeville to the west, and it's also home to a few of the parish's better restaurants. The main drag through Lacombe is U.S. Highway 190, and if you continue on it in a westerly direction, you'll soon enter Mandeville.

MANDEVILLE

Considered by many to be greater New Orleans's most exclusive suburb, Mandeville is popular with visitors for its high-end shopping and many great restaurants, but the most distinctive draw is quirky Old Mandeville, a district of restored cottages, eateries, and shops down along Lake Pontchartrain, just east of where the Lake Pontchartrain Causeway connects the town with the South Shore.

From Lacombe via U.S. Highway 190, you'll first pass through the heavily wooded Fontainebleau State Park; the turnoff into the park is on your left a short while after you cross the town line. Beyond the park, continue on U.S. Highway 190 as it passes through a more residential area, and make a left turn onto Jackson Street, which leads south a few blocks until it ends at Lakeshore Drive, onto which you make a right turn. Lakeshore Drive, which runs directly along the Lake Pontchartrain shoreline, offers a wonderful architectural tour of some of Mandeville's most beautiful and—in many cases—historic homes. This area took a hard hit from Hurricane Katrina, so keep in mind that many of the fine homes and buildings nearest the lake will be in various stages of renovation for the near future. Still, Old Mandeville has largely recovered from the storm and looks as bewitching as ever.

Lakeshore runs for several blocks, but at Gerard Street, turn right and perhaps park your car along the street, as this puts you in the heart of historic Old Mandeville, a perfect spot for a stroll. This charming community of generally modest but frilly wood-frame bungalows thrived in the early part of the 20th century as a summer resort for well-to-do New Orleans families who arrived here by train via either Slidell or Hammond, or by ferry across Lake Pontchartrain (this was long before the construction of the causeway). At the little rail station in Old Mandeville, now a trailhead for the Tammany Trace bike path, hundreds of visitors would debark each weekend. Mandeville Trailhead has a farmers market on weekends, and there's an amphitheater that hosts concerts and activities. Most of the houses in Old Mandeville date to the first two or three decades of the 20th century. Ferries docked at long piers jutting from the intersection of Gerard and Coffee streets. A massive wooden waterslide and a number of bathhouses were along the shore, where summer visitors splashed about

in Lake Pontchartrain. Today, housing prices in Old Mandeville have risen steadily—these little cottages fetch a goodly sum, even the ones that need quite a lot of work.

The best walking route is up Gerard Street for several blocks before you make a left turn onto Monroe Street for one block; at Lafitte Street, head back down south toward the lake. Any of these short blocks in Old Mandeville are great for walking, and all are lined with handsome old cottages and homes.

Hop back in your car and backtrack to Lakeshore Drive, turning right and continuing to West Beach Parkway, onto which you turn right. Follow the road a few blocks north and then turn left onto Monroe Street, which runs across Causeway Boulevard, which leads onto the Lake Pontchartrain Causeway to the town of Metairie on the South Shore. The first span of the causeway opened in 1956, and it was doubled into two spans in 1969. *The Guinness Book of Records* names the 1969 span as the longest bridge in the world, at 23 miles, 1,538 yards. The two spans run parallel to each other, about 80 feet apart and in most places not too high over the water; the entire bridge sits atop 9,000 pilings. For first-timers, a drive across this very, very long bridge can be intriguing, but any local who commutes this way can tell you that the novelty wears off quickly. About 30,000 cars cross over the bridge each day. It's testament to the solid engineering of the bridge that it received no major damage from Katrina.

Monroe Street continues west of Causeway Boulevard a short distance, and you then make a left turn onto Live Oak Street, a right onto Copal Street, and a left onto Fountain Street, which leads to prodigious **Seven Sisters Oak** (200 Fountain St., Mandeville, admission free). This enormous tree is said to be more than 1,000 years old (and some say 1,500 years); it's more than 37 feet in circumference—big enough that it withstood the fury of Hurricane Katrina with little trouble at all. The oak sits in the front yard of a private home whose owners have very graciously made it accessible to the public—do keep in mind that you're on private property. You can park right in the home's driveway, beside the tree, and there are no formal hours, but visiting from late morning to late afternoon would seem to be the most considerate time to take a look. If you think those handsome live oak trees at Oak Alley Plantation or in New Orleans's Audubon Park are impressive, you'll be awed by this massive tree. You can follow Copal or any of the cross streets for a bit, if you're in the mood to admire some more of Mandeville's fine homes. Retrace your steps to Live Oak Street and head north, making a left turn on West Causeway Boulevard, which cuts in a northwesterly direction to Highway 22, onto which a left turn will take you into the mostly residential community of Madisonville.

MADISONVILLE

Named for President James Madison, this growing town of both full-time residences and summer and weekend cottages and houseboats, many of them on or near the Tchefuncte River (meaning "Three Forks" and pronounced chuh-FUNK-tuh), has a cute downtown along the water. On Friday evenings there's an antique car show held downtown. Shortly after Highway 22 crosses the river (coming from Mandeville), make a left turn onto Main Street, and follow this winding riverside road to where it dead-ends, at a parking area and boat launch. You can see the circa-1900 Madisonville lighthouse, a 38-foot structure that sits on an island just off from the shoreline, from the parking area, and you may occasionally see river wildlife along this largely untraveled road. The Lake Pontchartrain Basin Maritime Museum is working to restore the lighthouse and, ultimately, to install a road that would greatly increase public access to this landmark building. You can also park downtown and stroll along the river, admiring the handsome homes and the sailboats docked in front of them.

◖ Lake Pontchartrain Basin Maritime Museum

On your way down Main Street you'll pass the still-nascent Lake Pontchartrain Basin Maritime

© ANDREW COLLINS

tree lit for the holidays along the banks of Bayou Tchefuncte in downtown Madisonville

Museum (Main St., Madisonville, 985/845-9200, www.lpbmaritimemuseum.org, open 10 A.M.–4 P.M. Tues.–Sat., noon–4 P.M. Sun.; admission $3), which occupies a beautiful building and contains several excellent exhibits documenting the region's seafaring heritage. These include a diorama on rural life on a Cajun bayou, a video on the origins of local watercraft, a re-created blacksmith shop that would have produced Civil War ships, an exhibit on the Louisiana Purchase, a display of vintage outboard motors, and some other interesting displays. Especially worth a look is the Port Century exhibit, which chronicles how steamboats played a vital role in the growth of the region. The museum is also restoring the Lightkeepers Cottage at the Tchefuncte River Lighthouse, and inside the museum there's an exhibit on the lighthouse. One of the best features of the maritime museum is that it offers boatbuilding classes, where you actually learn to construct an authentic Cajun-style pirogue, a lake skiff, or other craft common to Louisiana's waters. The museum also hosts a wide range of events, lectures, and classes.

Fairview-Riverside State Park

The town's main attraction is the historic **Otis House,** which is set inside lush 99-acre Fairview–Riverside State Park (Madisonville, 985/845-3318 or 888/677-3247, www.lastate-parks.com, admission $1), just off Highway 22, on the east bank of the Tchefuncte. The lovely green park sits at a sharp S-bend of the river and is shaded by dozens of massive live oak trees. Facilities include campsites for tent and RV camping, a playground, and a picnic area. Fishing, boating, and waterskiing are popular along the river. The Otis House dates to 1880 and was the family home for a wealthy sawmill owner. It contains period furnishings, artwork, and fine original architectural detailing, and it's open for tours 9 A.M.–5 P.M. Wednesday–Sunday; admission is $2.

COVINGTON

From downtown Madisonville, follow Highway 21 north across I-12 and into the dapper downtown of Covington, which though smaller than Slidell and Mandeville has grown to become one of the North Shore's most popular suburbs. Founded in 1813 as the town of Wharton but soon renamed for War of 1812 hero General Leonard Covington, this bustling community is the seat of St. Tammany Parish and contains one of the liveliest little downtowns in the state. Downtown is situated where the Bogue Falaya and Tchefuncte rivers meet—it's an utterly charming little town with an artsy personality.

H. J. Smith and Sons Hardware Museum

Downtown Covington is the site of the H. J. Smith and Sons Hardware Museum (308 N. Columbia St., Covington, 985/892-0460, open store hours Tues.–Sat., admission free), a small exhibit space inside the H. J. Smith store, which has been up and running since 1876. It includes local artifacts, vintage hardware, and exhibits relevant to both the store's and the town's history. You'll see a 1920s gas pump, a hand-operated washing machine, and a 20-foot-long cypress dugout canoe.

Insta-Gator Ranch and Hatchery

Despite the rather morbid slogan "From Hatchling to Handbag," the Insta-Gator Ranch and Hatchery (23440 Lowe Davis Rd., Covington, 985/892-3669, www.insta-gator-ranch.com, open by reservation Tues.–Sun., admission $12) makes for an interesting little side trip. It's home at any given time to more than 2,000 alligators, most of them intended to be harvested (i.e., killed) and used for handbags, boots, purses, and food. Sound awful? In fact, this ranch and other licensed farms greatly help the wild-alligator population in Louisiana, and the ranching program was developed by the U.S. Fish and Wildlife Service in conjunction with the Louisiana Wildlife and Fisheries. Ranches and farms such as this one are required to return a number of their young to the wild. As long as there's a market for alligator goods, there will be alligator harvesting; by licensing qualified establishments to raise and farm alligators, the state is able to forbid alligator hunting in the wild, thereby ensuring the propagation of the species in Louisiana.

ABITA SPRINGS

It's just a short drive east from Covington, via Highway 36, to the small and funky community of Abita Springs. Acclaimed during the late 19th century for its curative waters, Abita Springs began as a health resort favored by wealthy New Orleanians looking to escape from the sultry and overcrowded city. As a laid-back country town that's more countrified in character than neighboring towns along the shore but still within commuting distance of the Big Easy, Abita Springs might be the perfect healthful escape. Spring water is still bottled here, but the town's most famous elixir nowadays is Abita Beer, which is brewed right in town and distributed all around the state and which has developed a following nationwide.

◖ Abita Mystery House

The touch-friendly Abita Mystery House (22275 Hwy. 36, Abita Springs, 985/892-2624

THE NORTH SHORE

or 888/211-5731, http://ucmmuseum.com, open 10 A.M.–5 P.M. daily, admission $3) is a leading oddity of the area—a museum of very curious curiosities, with the facade of an old gas station but comprising several quirky (and rather musty) buildings. This truly bizarre attraction is the brainchild of local artist John Preble, who has painstakingly assembled the quirky and often comical exhibits within. His creations mix folk art, recycled goods, and an array of collectibles to remarkable effect. Among the displays are a stuffed 24-foot-long "bassigator" who would answer to the name Buford were he an actual living thing. The House of Shards has been built largely with scraps of bottle, license plate, machine parts, and pottery. You'll also find strangely fascinating dioramas constructed largely from discarded parts and pieces that depict everything from voodoo worship to alligator wrestling. The letters "UCM" don't appear to stand for anything, by the way—it's named this way so that you'll pronounce it the "you-see-em museum." Less out there is an early-20th-century Creole cottage, fully restored, and now the site of arts workshops and classes. The museum sits along pine- and oak-shaded grounds and is adjacent to a leafy park with a footbridge across a rushing stream and an elegant 1884 picnic pavilion. This is one of the North Shore's best attractions for kids.

Abita Brewery

Nearby on Highway 36, Abita Brewery (21084 Hwy. 36, Abita Springs, 985/893-3143 or 800/737-2311, www.abita.com), offers free tours and tastings at 1 and 2:30 P.M. on Saturdays and at 1 P.M. Sundays. Abita Brewing Company opened in 1986, taking full advantage of Abita Springs's famed water. These tours are low-key and fun, a good opportunity to learn about the brewing process—it's the sort of place where the staff generally takes time to chat with visitors. Abita produces five kinds of beer, varying from the dark and rich Turbo Dog to the pleasantly fruity Purple Haze to the light and bubbly Abita Amber; there are also several seasonal beers.

FOLSOM

Folsom is a small, rural town north of Covington, reached via Highway 25. The town feels a world away from the towns along Lake Pontchartrain, and a few worlds away from the South Shore. Here the gentle, rolling countryside is known for its stables—many horse enthusiasts come to Folsom, and there are riding shows throughout the year. The town is partly in Tangipahoa Parish, where you'll find its most famous attraction, the Global Wildlife Center, which you can reach by heading west on Highway 40 from Folsom's village center. (See the *Tangipahoa Parish* section for a full description of Global Wildlife.)

◖ Pontchartrain Vineyards and Winery

From Folsom, follow Highway 40 east as it rolls through the rural, northern end of the parish to reach Pontchartrain Vineyards and Winery (81250 Old Military Rd./Hwy. 1082, Bush, 985/892-9742, www.pontchartrainvineyards. com, open for tours and tastings Wed.–Sun.). It's quite a beautiful place, set amid the horse farms of Bush and eastern Folsom. Begun in 1997, the winery has already won some major awards. It's the only serious winery in the state, and its food-friendly wines are served at some of the major restaurants in the area. Depending on when you go, you might end up participating in the harvest or catching one of the many concerts held there during the summer and fall, including the Jazz'n the Vines series, which has jazz performances about once every two weeks (the concerts cost $10). Tasting is held in a French Provincial–style brick building and visitors center, which overlooks the gentle hillside planted with grapes. The short but informative tours are more personable than most of those you'll find in major wine-producing areas such as Napa and Sonoma.

Landry Vineyards

There's also a smaller winery in town, Landry Vineyards (11650 Tantela Ranch Rd., Folsom, 985/294-7790, www.landryvineyards.com), that sells wine at a number of markets and restaurants in the area. Visitors are welcome to come by on Saturdays for a tour, and the owners of this family-run, 20-acre winery were planning eventually to open a tasting room. This is a nice opportunity to visit a low-keyed winemaking operation and talk with owners Jeff and Libby Landry about the process.

SHOPPING

St. Tammany Parish is notable for shopping, both for its one-of-a-kind independent boutiques and stores and its abundance of chains and superstores along the main roads in Slidell, Mandeville, and Covington. Fans of art galleries and boutiques will want to focus on downtown Covington, an artsy retail mecca, as well as on the old sections of Mandeville and Slidell.

Covington

Great little galleries and design shops line Covington's Main Street, which is one of the most charming little downtowns in the state of Louisiana. It's small-town friendly but rather hip. Connecting Covington to Mandeville is U.S. Highway 190, a band of strip malls that's handy if you're looking for fast-food restaurants, big-box stores, and movie theaters.

The **St. Tammany Art Association** (320 N. Columbia St., Covington, 985/892-8650) occupies a beautiful old building downtown, where it shows and sells the works of its more than 30 talented artists. **Mi Casa** (405 N. Columbia St., 985/875-9483) makes custom slipcovered furniture and carries art and decorative pieces from Mexico, including colorful Day of the Dead figures.

A few blocks from Columbia Street is a smaller pocket of cool boutiques, set along Lee Lane. These include the **Linen Closet** (315 Lee La., Covington, 985/893-2347), which carries fine bedding, pillows, duvets, and the like.

Slidell

Not quite as well known as the North Shore's antiquing mecca, Ponchatoula, Olde Town Slidell does have a few impressive antiques shops, most of them tucked into a quadrant

bounded by Front, 1st, 2nd, and Erlanger streets. It's best just to park the car and stroll about this neighborhood. This area received severe wind damage and flooding from Katrina, and some shops were lost; the downtown is gradually being rebuilt.

ENTERTAINMENT AND NIGHTLIFE

Covington, Slidell, and Mandeville all have a handful of popular bars and music clubs, and Old Mandeville is home to one of the state's only professional theaters. It's pretty easy to find live music just about any night of the week, and St. Tammany Parish's relatively young and professional population accounts for a high "hip" factor at many bars and clubs.

The must-attend for live-music lovers is downtown Covington's **Columbia Tap Room** (434 N. Columbia St., Covington, 985/898-0899, www.columbiastreettaproom.com), which presents first-rate rock, folk, and blues bands throughout the week. This is a cool corner bar with big plate-glass windows, through which you'll almost always see a rollicking, happy crowd. More down-home and happily ungentrified—depending on which band is playing that night—is **Ruby's Roadhouse** (840 Lamarque St., Mandeville, 985/626-9748), which presents everything from rock to Cajun. The two local branches of **Daiquiris and Creams** (1729 Gause Blvd., Slidell, 985/641-4656; 1737 U.S. 190, Mandeville, 985/624-3030) present live music many nights and are popular spots for cocktails and schmoozing.

In Covington, the **Skyfire Theatre** (332 N. New Hampshire St., Covington, 985/875-7577, www.skyfire.tv) shows everything from live theater to midnight movies to top Hollywood films; there's a wine bar on premises.

FESTIVALS AND EVENTS

Some of the state's best-attended festivals are held in St. Tammany Parish.

◀ Abita Springs Opry

No matter where you are in Louisiana (or in several neighboring states), you can listen to or watch the North Shore's most acclaimed musical event, the Abita Springs Opry (formerly the Piney Wood Opry) (985/892-0711, www.abitaopry.com), which is broadcast on radio and TV stations throughout the Deep South. It's held once a month during the spring and again during the fall, and you can catch the performance live at the Opry's broadcasting headquarters, the Abita Springs Town Hall. Tickets cost $12–15, depending on seating, and shows begin at 7 P.M. You'll hear country, bluegrass, and gospel bands and musicians strum and hum the night away. This event is quite distinct from the many Cajun and zydeco concerts held elsewhere in the state—the Opry's mission is to preserve and celebrate the folk music of the piney woods regions of Louisiana, Mississippi, and Alabama.

Mardi Gras

Covington has two parades through downtown and a picnic and festival on Fat Tuesday in Bogue Falaya Park. But in these towns noted for boating, it's only appropriate that the most popular Mardi Gras events are boat parades. In Slidell, the **Krewe of Bilge** is a colorful procession of boats along the town's canals near Lake Pontchartrain, and in Madisonville, the **Krewe of Tchefuncte** passes along the Tchefuncte River. As at land-based Mardi Gras parades, spectators line the road (or river or canal) and beg costumed revelers riding on what you could literally call "floats" to toss them beads and trinkets.

Other Events

The North Shore's reputation as a bird-lover's paradise is capitalized on each April with the **Great Louisiana Bird Fest** (985/626-1238, www.northlakenature.org), which is built around a series of naturalist-led "field trips" to St. Tammany Parish's top birding venues—you'll see countless local and migrating species and *might* just spy the extremely rare red-cockaded woodpecker, or even an American bald eagle.

From March through October, the last Friday of each month, downtown Covington has

the **Columbia Street Block Party,** complete with music, food, and family-oriented activities. Anybody with a green thumb should check out the **Spring Garden Tour,** a self-guided trail through several of downtown Covington's most beautiful gardens during April. In May, head to Madisonville for the annual **Cruisin' on the River Antique Car Show** (www.madisonvillechamber.org), a lively event that draws auto enthusiasts of all ages.

Bogue Falaya Park on the edge of downtown Covington is the site of **Old Fashioned Family Fourth** (985/892-1873) with live music, food, and fireworks. Yet another of Louisiana's excellent food festivals, the **Mandeville Seafood Festival** (www.seafoodfest.com) kicks off in late June and early July beneath the moss-festooned live oaks fringing Mandeville Harbor. Here you can try local seafood prepared umpteen different ways, enjoy the verdant setting, and listen to live music. In late October, boating enthusiasts should not miss the **Madisonville Wooden Boat Festival** (985/845-9200, www.lpbmaritimemuseum.org), during which hundreds of beautiful, mostly handcrafted wooden boats sail, motor, or row along Madisonville's Tchefuncte River. These craft include both antiques and newer models, varying in size 10–70 feet. You'll find live music; a marine flea market with nautical art, boating supplies, and foods; a boatbuilding workshop for kids; and a boatbuilding contest and race.

The second weekend in November is the **Covington Three Rivers Art Festival** (985/871-4141, www.threeriversartfestival.com), a juried arts and crafts show drawing about 150 vendors. This is one of the most prestigious such events in the South. Slidell's **Christmas Under the Stars** (985/646-4375) has become a North Shore tradition. It kicks off in Olde Town's Griffith Park in early December with the lighting of the neighborhood's many old trees and some music concerts, and it continues with storytelling, theater, choral performances, and other events for about 10 days leading up to shortly before Christmas. All events are free, and virtually all are geared heavily toward families.

© ANDREW COLLINS

Tammany Trace bike path in downtown Covington

RECREATION

In addition to shopping and dining, enjoying the outdoors is the key draw for visitors to St. Tammany Parish, which is noted for its swamps and wildlife preserves, an exceptional bike trail, a few fine golf courses, and excellent fishing and boating both along several bayous and immense Lake Pontchartrain.

◖ Bicycling on Tammany Trace

St. Tammany Parish has one of the best biking resources in the South, the Tammany Trace (985/867-9490, www.tammanytrace.org), a 31-mile rails-to-trails bikeway that runs from Slidell west to Mandeville and then north to Abita Springs before curving west again into downtown Covington. The path—which is paved and also serves the interests of joggers, strollers, inline skaters, wheelchair users, and horseback riders—is the first rails-to-trails conversion in Louisiana; it follows the path of the old Illinois Central Railroad, winding beneath boughs of pine, oak, and magnolia trees and across 31 bridges and through some of the

state's verdant wetlands. The trail cuts right through or near all of the downtown retail and dining districts in the area. Hurricane Katrina took down a number of trees along the trail and also damaged some bridges—most notably, the Bayou Lacombe Bridge was destroyed, and plans are under way to build a new one.

The key trailheads have public restrooms, parking, and interpretive signs and displays about the region. These are found in Slidell on the west side of town, where Thompson Road extends south from U.S. Highway 190; in the heart of Old Mandeville, where you'll also find an amphitheater and a small interpretive center (and several eateries within walking distance), and farther north in Mandeville just off Highway 59 by Exit 65 off I-12 (just beyond the St. Tammany Parish visitor information center, off Koop Dr.). You can also pick up the trail and find parking in downtown Abita Springs, right around where Highways 59 and 36 intersect, and in downtown Covington.

Motorized vehicles are not permitted on the trail, and inline skaters should yield to cyclists, who should yield to joggers, who should yield to walkers, who should yield to horses; pedestrians should stay to the right, as should any slower traffic. The trail may be used 7 A.M.–sunset.

You can rent bikes at the **Abita Mystery House** (22275 Hwy. 36, Abita Springs, 985/892-2624), **Spokesman Professional Bicycle Works** (1848 N. Causeway Blvd., Mandeville, 985/727-7211), and **Kickstand Bike Rental** (690 Lafitte St., across from Old Mandeville trailhead, Old Mandeville, 985/626-9300). Rates are usually around $6 or $7 per hour for a standard mountain bike, or about $15–20 per day.

Fishing

There's plenty of great catfish and other freshwater fishing in the muddy bayous of St. Tammany Parish, especially in the preserves and state parks mentioned here. There are also charter-fishing operations that take travelers out through Lake Pontchartrain into the Gulf of Mexico. An excellent one, based in Slidell, is **Angling Adventures of Louisiana** (53105 Hwy. 433, Slidell, 985/781-7811 or 877/422-6352, www.aaofla.com). Charters angle chiefly for redfish, speckled trout, and flounder; all fishing tackle is provided, and the tours cost about $350 for one or two people and around $600 for four.

Fairview-Riverside State Park (Hwy. 22, Madisonville, 985/845-3318 or 888/677-3247) offers great river fishing and crabbing from its banks along the Tchefuncte River; you can also put in a boat here or at one of the other launches in Madisonville. Upriver you're likely to encounter bass, white perch, bluegill, and bream, while down closer to where the river joins Lake Pontchartrain, you can catch channel catfish, redfish, and speckled trout.

Golf

St. Tammany Parish has some of the best golf courses in the whole state, beginning with the private **Money Hill Golf and Country Club** (100 Country Club Dr., Abita Springs, 985/892-8250, www.moneyhill.com), which hosted the 1999 U.S. Open qualifier and has received numerous awards from major golf publications. Nonmembers can play this course by arrangement. **Oak Harbor** (201 Harbor Blvd., Slidell, 985/646-0110, www.oakharborgolf.com) is one of the best public golf courses in the South. The course and surrounding area were badly hit by Katrina, but the course reopened in 2006 after a massive renovation.

Other reputable public or semiprivate courses in the parish include **Abita Springs Golf and Country Club** (73433 Oliver St., Abita Springs, 985/893-2463, www.abitagolf.com) and **Royal Golf Club** (201 Royal Dr., Slidell, 985/643-3000), which was also damaged by the hurricane but had been refurbished and reopened by early 2006.

Hiking and the Outdoors

One of the most impressive outdoor sanctuaries in southeastern Louisiana is 15,000-acre **Big Branch Marsh National Wildlife Refuge** (headquarters at 61389 Hwy. 434, Lacombe, 985/646-7555, www.fws.gov/bigbranchmarsh). There are several access points for the refuge along the northeastern shore of Lake Pontchartrain. Off U.S. Highway 11, just as you cross the lake and enter Slidell, there's a boat launch; a second launch is off Highway 434, which runs due south from the village of Lacombe down through the refuge and right to the shore of Lake Pontchartrain.

There are several boat ramps and parking areas through Slidell and Lacombe, most of them along bayous that snake inland from the lake and through the refuge. Bayou Liberty Road, which runs west from U.S. Highway 11 in Slidell, and Bayou Paquet Road, which continues west into Lacombe, are good roads for access to the refuge; on the western border of Big Branch, you'll find parking areas right off U.S. Highway 190, near Cane Bayou on Lamieux Boulevard. The refuge ends at Cane Bayou, which is the Lacombe/Mandeville town border, but you then enter Fontainebleau State Park, through which U.S. Highway 190 runs.

Keep in mind that much of Big Branch is open to hunting (for deer and wildfowl), so be alert and dress accordingly during hunting season. Permits are required for all hunting and fishing, and there are a number of regulations, including the prohibition of several kinds of boats (including motorized craft). Fishing here is restricted to recreational casting and crabbing—no nets, traps, or trotlines are allowed.

Fontainebleau State Park (67825 U.S. 190, Mandeville, 985/624-4443 or 888/677-3668, www.lastateparks.com) is—at 2,800 acres—the region's largest recreation area, with facilities such as both primitive and improved campsites, swimming, a playground, and a fishing pier. It's a great park for birdwatchers and hikers, as trails meander through the pine-shaded forest, passing through an ancient grove of live oaks and the crumbling brick ruins of an 1830 sugar mill that was opened by Mandeville's founder, Bernard de Marigny de Mandeville, who operated a sugar plantation here for several decades during the 19th century. He named the plantation Fontainebleau, after the regal French forest hunting ground used by royalty.

The park has direct access onto Lake Pontchartrain, and it's a popular spot for sailboarders and other water-sports enthusiasts. There's a beach along the lake, but swimming is best conducted in the nearby swimming pool, which has full changing facilities. The Tammany Trace bike trail runs through the park, drawing bikers, walkers, and inline skaters. A signed park nature trail identifies some of the many types of trees you'll find here, and visitors can also sometimes observe turkeys, opossums, and rare red-cockaded woodpeckers. A guide to bird-watching inside the park is available at the park's visitors center, and park naturalists conduct guided hikes and nature programs year-round. Entrance fees at all state parks is $1 per person.

Near the park, the **Northlake Nature Center** (U.S. 190, just east of Bayou Castine, Mandeville, 985/626-1238, www.northlake-nature.org) is a 400-acre nature preserve with trails that cut through stands of massive pine and hardwood trees. It's yet another great spot for bird-watching.

Sailing and Boating

You can take canoe and tubing trips along the Bogue Chitto, which runs primarily through Washington Parish (between the North Shore and the Mississippi border) and just a bit into the northeastern corner of St. Tammany Parish. **Bogue Chitto Canoeing and Tubing Center** (10237 Choctaw River Rd., Bogalusa, 985/735-1173, www.tubingboguechitto.com) rents tubes and canoes and gives river tours from spring through fall. These are lazy and relaxed river trips that are great fun for kids or adults, and there's no worry of dangerous rapids.

Another great way to get onto the water is by booking a trip through **South Coast Kayaks** (985/867-9530, Covington, www.southcoastkayaks.com), which offers classes as well as four-hour and full-day guided trips on Lake Pontchartrain, Lake Maurepas, Manchac Swamp, Honey Island Swamp, and the Tchefuncte River—to name just a few great places to take to the water. You get a 20 percent discount if you supply your own boat and gear, but otherwise, South Coast can provide everything.

ACCOMMODATIONS

The parish has quite a few enchanting B&Bs, most with 1–3 guest rooms—they occupy just about every setting in the parish, from the rural piney woods communities in the north to the historic downtowns of Covington and Mandeville. You'll also find a nice selection of modern chain hotels just off the interstate in Slidell and Covington.

Hotels and Motels

$50-100: Hampton Inn (56460 Frank Pichon Rd., Slidell, 985/726-9777 or 800/426-7866, www.hamptoninn.com) is a three-story, 80-room property in tip-top condition and with reasonable rates. About a quarter of the units have refrigerators and microwaves.

Another very nice Slidell property is the **Holiday Inn Hotel and Suites** (372 Voter's Rd., Slidell, 985/639-0890, www.holiday-inn.com), which has 57 rooms and 34 suites, and a restaurant, indoor pool, fitness center, and business center.

© ANDREW COLLINS

Blue Willow Bed and Breakfast, Covington

The **Best Western** (625 N. U.S. 190, Covington, 985/892-2681 or 877/766-6700) is a pleasant 75-room property beside the wonderful Dakota restaurant and just a short way north of I-12. Many rooms have microwaves and refrigerators.

$100-150: ◖ **Courtyard by Marriott** (101 Northpark Blvd., just off N. U.S. 190, Covington, 985/871-0244, www.courtyard.com) is perhaps the best chain property in St. Tammany Parish, constantly renovating and offering a DSL Internet connection. It's on the edge of an office park, overlooking a pond and shaded by towering pine trees.

Inns and Bed-and-Breakfasts

$50-100: About a block from Old Mandeville's handsome lakefront, **Pollyanna** (212 Lafitte St., Mandeville, 985/626-4053) occupies a sweet pale-blue cottage with a pair of cheerfully decorated rooms with pitched ceilings, floral-print fabrics, and a smattering of antiques. Each unit opens onto a main lounge with a minibar (included in the rate). Conti-

nental breakfast is served on weekdays, a full English-style breakfast on weekends.

$100-150: Just steps from the great shopping in downtown Covington, **Camellia House B&B** (426 E. Rutland St., Covington, 985/893-2442, www.camelliahouse.net) offers one gorgeously furnished guest suite with an adjoining sunporch containing a refrigerator, microwave, and dining nook stocked with delicious breakfast food and home-baked cookies. The room, inside a lovely early-20th-century house, is filled with stylish antiques, a plush bed with well-chosen linens, cable TV and a phone with a data port, and a bright and modern bathroom with a shower and pedestal sink; the room has its own exterior entrance, which leads onto the home's wide veranda and also has access to a pool and hot tub. The sunporch has its own twin bed and trundle bed, so you can fit a total of four guests in here. Hosts Linda and Don Chambless are friendly and know a great deal about the area.

Almost catty-corner from Camellia House, Maureen and Tom Chambless (Don's brother) own **☙ Blue Willow Bed and Breakfast** (505 E. Rutland St., Covington, 985/892-0011, www.bluewillowbandb.com). Here you'll find a pair of suites, each with private exterior entrances through a gated brick courtyard, which has its own hot tub. And then there's also a third suite, with its own private entrance, reached through a screened-in porch. All rooms have high ceilings, polished hardwood floors, and decadent four-poster beds and smart furnishings, cable TV and VCR, Wi-Fi, as well as breakfast setups that include pastries, yogurt, cereal, orange juice, coffee, and more. These properties are steps from Tammany Trace bike trail and the Bogue Falaya River and Park.

A secluded getaway in the deep woods **☙ Little River Bluffs** (11030 Garden La., Folsom, 985/796-5257, www.littleriverbluffs.com) anchors a 60-acre wooded property on the artesian-fed Little Tchefuncte River. This is a naturist's dream, with swimming in and kayaking on the river, hiking through the woods, and sunbathing on a sugary-white sandbar. Great blue herons, egrets, otters, and other wildlife inhabit this lush woodland that feels light-years away from New Orleans (which, in fact, is just 55 miles south). There are three accommodations, the A-frame River Chalet, which sits on a bend in the river; the Meadow Cabin, tucked under a canopy of tall pine trees; and the Treehouse, which also overlooks the river. Each has a full kitchen and fireplace; two have whirlpool tubs. These rustic cabins are totally romantic and relaxing. There's a two-night minimum.

Just around the corner from Pollyanna in Old Mandeville, **Mar Villa Guest House** (2013 Claiborne St., Mandeville, 985/626-5975 or 877/650-3920, www.marvilla.com) is a wonderfully charming renovated cottage next to the similarly wonderful Broken Egg restaurant. This pink 1870s Victorian with gingerbread trim contains original heart-pine floors, beaded-wood ceilings, and hand-crafted cabinetry. There are three simple but charming units with phones, cable TV, and tile bathrooms with large clawfoot tub/showers. A veranda overlooks the shaded backyard. Several restaurants are within walking distance, as well as the trailhead for the Tammany Trace bike and walking path.

Just north of Slidell, the **Woodridge B&B** (40149 Crowes Landing Rd., Pearl River, 985/863-9981 or 877/643-7109, www.woodridgebb.com) occupies a grand brick house with elegant columns and grounds dotted with century-old live oak trees. Each of the five large rooms in this building, which once housed a private school, have private baths, air-conditioning, cable TV, and ceiling fans. Antiques—varying from a pineapple four-poster bed to a sturdy oak chest—fill the rooms, which also have Wi-Fi. And guests can relax in the sun on the landscaped patio or swim in a large in-ground pool. A full country breakfast is included. The inn is just a few minutes' drive off I-59, Exit 3.

A relative newcomer to the area, **Maison Réve Farm** (76251 Hwy. 1077, Folsom, 985/796-8103, www.maisonrevefarm.com) is a stunning contemporary mansion built in the style of a French chateau and offering three comfy, upscale rooms as well as beautiful common areas. The Cotes du Rhone and Des Amis rooms each have their own whirlpool tub, and the Bon Ton room has an oversize shower. One of the big draws here is the rich and artful full Southern breakfast presented each morning. The B&B sits on 30 secluded acres laced with gardens and footpaths. Congenial owners Dan and JoAnn are extremely enthusiastic not only about the area but about their handsome home, and they're always happy to tell guests about the best dining and sightseeing secrets in the area. Keep in mind that there's a two-night minimum on weekends, and the inn is not suited to children and can not accommodate pets.

$150-250: Perhaps better known for its wonderful restaurant, **Annadele's Plantation** (71495 Chestnut St., Covington, 985/809-7669, www.annadeles.com) is also a lovely B&B, with four luxurious suites, one with French doors that open onto a balcony overlooking the garden. Hardwood floors, magnificent chandeliers, Oriental rugs, and fine antiques fill the rooms. The property is poised on a swath of gardens and greenery overlooking the Bogue Falaya River, shaded by tall cypress and magnolia trees. It's a short drive from Covington's dapper downtown.

Over $250: At the very high end, **Villa Vici Getaways** (Covington, 985/674-0909, www.villavicigetaways.com) is a pair of luxury cottages a few blocks from each other in downtown Covington. Charropin Beach sleeps two, and St. John Place sleeps four, and both require a two-night minimum. The owners have a rather off-putting payment policy: Half is due upon making your reservation (which is nonrefundable), and the balance is due 30 days before your arrival—this, too, is nonrefundable. Considering the rates of $200–250 nightly for St. John's and $300–350 for Charropin Beach, you better be sure you want to stay at these places before you book. Charropin is set on a 13-acre gated estate with a private beach on the Bogue Falaya River; it also overlooks a swimming pool. It has a private kitchen with top-notch amenities and a full bath with whirlpool tub. St. John Place is an upscale apartment with sleek contemporary furnishings, a full kitchen, laundry, and a living room with a sleeper sofa. The rooms both convey a thoroughly chic aesthetic.

Camping

The entire North Shore is popular for camping, with facilities at both of St. Tammany Parish's state parks as well as a few commercial campgrounds. **Fairview-Riverside State Park** (Hwy. 22, Madisonville, 985/845-3318 or 888/677-3247) has 81 tent and RV sites with water and electric hookups, as well as a separate primitive tent-camping area. It's set along a picturesque bend of the Tchefuncte River. Offering even more sites, and types of sites, is 2,800-acre **Fontainebleau State Park** (U.S. 190, Mandeville, 985/624-4443), where you'll find 126 tent and RV sites with electrical and water hookups, barbecue grills, and picnic tables, plus a bathhouse and waste station. There are also some primitive tent-camping areas and numerous undesignated campsites scattered throughout the park, some near the beach along Lake Pontchartrain. There are also group campsites, as well as a camping lodge that sleeps 10 and has a kitchen and two baths. You can make reservations for the lodge or any of the tent sites at Fairview and Fontainebleau State Parks by calling 877/226-7652 or logging onto www.lastateparks.com.

Among commercial campgrounds, Covington's **Land-O-Pines** (17145 Million Dollar Rd., Covington, 985/892-6023 or 800/443-3697, www.land-o-pines.com) is the most popular. There are sites for RVs and tents, or you can rent cottages that sleep up to eight guests and have kitchens and cable TV. The park is open to day-use visitors for $6 per person. Land-O-Pines has a large pool and long, twisting waterslide, plus a kiddie pool, camp shop, playground, game room, launderette, volleyball court, horseshoe pits, fishing ponds, river with white sandy beach, softball field, snack bar, minigolf, and basketball court—you won't run out of things to do at this place.

Another good option is **New Orleans East KOA** (56009 Hwy. 433, Slidell, 985/643-3850 or 800/562-2128, www.koa.com), which has a large plot of RV sites and a pool, minigolf, and fishing. This facility closed in 2006 as a result of hurricane damage but is undergoing renovations and is expected to reopen in 2007.

FOOD

The North Shore's definitive draw may very well be its wealth of exceptional restaurants in every price range. The very best dining experiences on this side of the lake compare favorably with the best in New Orleans, only with lower prices. You'll find some first-rate Creole and Cajun eateries, along with excellent contemporary American, French, Italian, and Asian restaurants. Apart from New Orleans, no other part of the state offers such a variety of accomplished dining venues. Most of the better-known spots are in Mandeville and Covington, but you'll find great places to eat in every town in the parish. Although St. Tammany Parish is less touristy than some parts of the state, it is a hub of upwardly mobile professionals, and this accounts not only for the high number of restaurants but also for the dapper crowds that fill these places many nights, especially on weekends. Reservations are a good idea in this part of the state.

Upscale

One of the top dining venues on the culinarily impressive North Shore, **The Dakota** (629 N. U.S. 190, Covington, 985/892-3712, $17–29) may not look dazzling with its location beside a Best Western motel, but the contemporary American cooking here is anything but ordinary. Start with New Orleans–style barbecued snails sautéed with fresh garlic, roasted tomatoes, rosemary, Abita beer, and butter, perhaps moving on to the Mixed Nest, roasted quail with andouille-cornbread stuffing and a herb glaze paired with grilled duck breast with raspberry-pepper sauce. Food such as this would set you back a good bit more in New Orleans. If you're looking to sample a wide range of chef's delights, opt for the tasting menu, which generally runs about $40–45 per person.

At **Annadele's Plantation** (71495 Chestnut St., Covington, 985/809-7669, www.annadeles.com, $22–34), a favorite dish is the sautéed pompano topped with crabmeat, fried leeks, and a beurre blanc sauce. Also consider panko-crusted blue crab cakes with scallion-chipotle aioli, or Cajun-marinated duck breast and confit of duckling leg with Grand Marnier–honey glaze. You can relax with a cocktail in the elegant Bogue Falaya lounge, and on Sundays, drop by for the fabulous brunch.

Over in Lacombe, chef Constantin Kerageorgiou has made **La Provence** (25020 U.S. 190, Lacombe, 985/626-7662, $19–32) a veritable temple of gastronomy for years. With its stucco facade, red-tile roof, and authentic furnishings, the place really does look as though it were airlifted to the North Shore from the south of France. And wait until you taste Kerageorgiou's sublime food, such as fricassee of rabbit (a recipe of the chef's mother), domestic lamb marinated and roasted with fresh Provençal herbs, stewed rabbit, and creamy

eggplant flan with a tomato-and-basil fondue and Moroccan olives.

In the heart of Abita Springs, **Longbranch** (21516 Hwy. 36, Abita Springs, 985/871-8171, $27–35) opened late in 2005, replacing what had been one of the North Shore's most famous restaurants, Artesia. Young husband-and-wife chefs Allison and Slade Vines-Rushing operate this handsome restaurant that's already garnered a huge buzz for its sophisticated, creative cooking. The couple, originally from the region, worked at some of the top restaurants in New Orleans and then in New York City before moving back to Louisiana to open Longbranch. You might start with salt-cured foie gras with local-strawberry jam and a warm country biscuit before moving on to braised veal cheeks with sweet-potato gnocchi, or wild striped bass with caramelized artichokes, tomato confit, and a spicy lobster sauce. The restaurant is inside a former hotel, built in the late 1800s to accommodate visitors to the area's curative springs.

Creative but Casual

Affordable, arty, and hip, **Etoile** (407 N. Columbia St., Covington, 985/893-8873, $10–25) is a wine bar and restaurant that's adjacent to an esteemed Louisiana Star wine shop. The airy room has bare concrete walls, skylights, high ceilings, and striking oil paintings by co-owner James Michalopoulos, who is noted regionally. The menu tends toward the eclectic—seared wasabi-crusted tuna over daikon root and peanuts tossed in a rice-wine parsley vinaigrette makes a great starter. The risotto du jour is always appetizing, but so is crisp oyster salad with baby spinach and a blue cheese vinaigrette. There's an impressive wine list, and there's a handsome mosaic bar.

A romantic, low-key eatery with a pair of small art-filled dining rooms, **Ristorante del Porto** (205 N. New Hampshire St., Covington, 985/875-1006, $10–17) is perhaps the North Shore's best-kept dining secret—and it's an outstanding value, considering the high quality of ingredients and their deft preparation. Contemporary international fare with

THE NORTH SHORE

an Italian slant is on offer here, from slow-roasted fennel-spiced pork with cannellini beans and kale to house-made pappardelle pasta with rabbit ragu and butternut squash. There's a wonderful wine list with many under-$25 vintages.

◖ **Judice's** (421 E. Gibson St., Covington, 985/892-0708, $5–9) is a bustling, art-filled breakfast-and-lunch cafe with a long copper-topped counter and pewter-colored pressed-tin ceilings, and tables covered with vintage photos and memorabilia. This is a local institution, great on Saturday after the farmers market. Dine on shrimp rémoulade with fried green tomatoes, English muffins topped with poached eggs and a cabernet mushroom sauce, and a wide range of pancake, French toast, and egg dishes, plus salad and sandwiches. It's a fun spot for people-watching. Dinner, with an emphasis on light Italian fare, is served on weekend evenings.

A favorite of celebrities and New Orleans foodies, **Sal and Judy's** (U.S. 190, Lacombe, 985/882-9443) is an old-fashioned trattoria serving inexpensive, hearty red-sauce Italian food. Some naysayers claim the service can be indifferent, but others swear this is the best Old World Italian experience in metro New Orleans.

In Old Mandeville, **Nuvolari's Ristorante** (246 Gerard St., Mandeville, 985/626-5619, $14–25), serves exceptionally good traditional Italian food with an emphasis on fish and shellfish. You might start with baked gnocchi in pesto cream or house-made crab ravioli. Among the main dishes, consider linguine *frutta di mare* (tossed with local shellfish and mushrooms in a sherry cream sauce) or salmon piccata topped with a lemon-caper-butter sauce. Deft, friendly service helps make this one of the town's best bets for an enchanting meal. The wine list is commendable, too.

Seafood, Pizzas, and Pub Grub

Related to the famous Abita Brewery, the **Abita Brew Pub** (72011 Holly St., Abita Springs, 985/892-5837, $7–18) serves tasty comfort food that complements or even incorporates the locally crafted beers. Crab claws are served with a dipping sauce that includes rosemary, barbecue sauce, and Turbo Dog, a richly dark beer. Other good bets include pecan-crusted catfish, barbecue ribs, and very good crawfish cakes. A large mural on one wall depicts the area's Tammany Trace bike path, which plenty of patrons use to reach this down-home hangout in the village of Abita Springs. There are several outdoor tables, plus a tavern inside with pop and alternative tunes piped in and sports on TV—the crowd tends toward the young and hip.

In the same town as the brewpub, **Abita Bar-B-Q** (69399 Hwy. 59, Abita Springs, 985/892-0205, $5–11) serves credible pulled-pork sandwiches and platters and some of the choicest hot boudin sausage you'll ever feast on. This low-keyed place serves all sorts of great barbecue fare, from beef brisket to ribs—you're guaranteed to make a mess of yourself here, but you'll probably have fun doing it.

Isabella's Pizzeria (70452 Hwy. 21, Covington, 985/875-7620; also 4250 Hwy. 22, Mandeville, 985/674-5700; large pies $10–15) is a spacious, family-friendly restaurant with live music some nights. It's got a cosmopolitan feel for a local pizza parlor. Specialty pies include the shrimp pesto pie, and you can also sample some hearty pasta dishes or sandwiches (the muffulettas here are commendable).

Times Bar and Grill (1827 Front St., Slidell, 985/639-3335; also 1896 N. Causeway Blvd., Mandeville, 985/626-1161; $6–13) occupies the railroad station on the edge of Olde Town Slidell; it's well-known for its hefty burgers but also serves pastas, soups, salads, and other casual fare.

A loveable dive in downtown Madisonville, ◖ **Coffee's Boiling Pot** (305 Hwy. 21, Madisonville, 985/845-2348, $6–13) is a rambling little dining room where you can sample the most delicious boiled crabs au gratin you'll ever find; boiled crawfish and shrimp are other specialties. Celebrity chef Emeril Lagasse supposedly favors this place.

Mike Schaeffer's Seafood (158 S. Military Rd., Slidell, 985/646-1728, $5–15) is a very good, casual eatery in a renovated country-elegant wood-frame building not too far from Honey Island Swamp. A wide range of po'boys is available, from the familiar meatball or softshell crab to the rather strange french-fry variety, plus sides of macaroni, stuffed crab, and sweet-potato fries. Entrées include catfish-and-shrimp platters, steaks, barbecued baby-back ribs, and chicken parmesan with spaghetti. Thursday and Sunday are all-you-can-eat catfish nights. It has a full bar, including a large selection of frozen daiquiris.

Ethnic

(**Trey Yuen** (600 N. Causeway, Mandeville, 985/626-4476; also 2100 N. Morrison Blvd., Hammond, 985/345-6789, $8–15) gained enormous fame a few years back when a major national travel magazine declared it one of the top few Asian restaurants in the country. It's no easy feat living up to this acclaim, and not everybody thinks that this restaurant with enormous and attractive branches in both Hammond and Mandeville is quite so amazing, but there's no denying that it's a great option for well-prepared Chinese food. What sets this place apart from other Asian eateries in the area is its use of regional ingredients—you might, for example, try marinated spiced alligator stir-fried with green onions and fresh mushrooms in a light oyster sauce. Other dishes use crawfish, softshell crab, and other local delicacies. More conventional but also excellent is the spicy flaming chicken with baby corn, snow peas, water chestnuts, and a piquant garlic sauce. Both Asian-style dining compounds—though enormous in that banquet-hall sort of way—are characterized by stunning Japanese landscaping and fine Asian artwork inside.

Osaka (792 I-10 Service Rd., Slidell, 985/643-9276, $7–14) is the best choice around here for sushi and Japanese food.

Quick Bites

The (**Broken Egg Cafe** (200 Gerard St., Mandeville, 985/624-3388; also 500 Theard St., Covington, 985/893-4412; $4–8) is an adorable breakfast and lunch spot right in Old Mandeville, near the lake. The restored 1920s cottage contains a warren of dainty dining rooms with hardwood floors and teapots filled with fresh flowers. Among the delicious breakfast options are bananas Foster waffles sprinkled with pecans and fresh banana slices, and the Grand Isle omelet with fresh shrimp, onions, and tomatoes, topped with salsa and guacamole. A number of hefty sandwiches and salads are served at lunch, including a tasty barbecue burger with cheddar and sautéed onions. Order a side of blackberry grits or spicy chorizo sausage.

Roadside short-order restaurants dot the region, including **Char-Lou's** (27470 U.S. 190, Lacombe, 985/882-7575, under $6), an unassuming, squat dining room with a few outdoor picnic tables where you can order barbecue ribs, po'boys, hot boudin, fresh seafood, and other cholesterol-laden, fattening delights.

In downtown Madisonville, **Badeaux's** (109 Hwy. 22, Madisonville, 985/845-7221, under $6) offers similarly enticing if not exactly healthful food. You order from either of two takeout windows, and there's also a modest dining area. The lack of charm is part of the charm here.

A nice option for simple, hearty comfort food, the **Back Porch Grill** (414 N. New Hampshire St., Covington, 985/892-5252, $6–12) sits right near the Covington trailhead of the Tammany Trace bike path, in the heart of downtown. It's a good bet for chicken and other leafy salads as well as filling sandwiches, soups, and casual cooking. Desserts are made on the premises.

Java Joints

You'll find the usual national (Starbucks) and Louisiana (CC's and P.J.'s) coffeehouse chains in abundance throughout Slidell, Mandeville, and Covington, but for something a little more atmospheric, in downtown Covington drop by **St. John's Coffeehouse** (535 E. Boston St., Covington, 985/893-5553), a spacious yet homey java place on the busiest street corner, with old-fashioned tile floors, ceiling fans, reading lamps on many tables with ladderback

THE NORTH SHORE

chairs, a shelf of books to browse through, and some sidewalk seating. It can't be beat for people-watching. A wide range of iced and hot drinks are served—from root-beer floats to iced mochas, as well as sandwiches and light food. This is a great place to chat with locals. There's live music many evenings.

Picnic Supplies and Gourmet Goods

Often compared with Martin Wine Cellar in New Orleans and Metairie, **Hugh's Wine Cellar** (4250 Hwy. 22, Pine Tree Plaza, Mandeville, 985/626-0066) is an outstanding wine shop that also carries fine liqueurs, cognacs, and the like, along with artisanal cheeses and other gourmet foods and gifts.

Occupying a bright yellow storefront in downtown Covington, **Columbia Street Natural Foods Market** (415 N. Columbia St., Covington, 985/893-0355) sells prepared foods, organic produce, cheeses, free-range chicken, and lots of other goodies, along with sandwiches, wraps, and sushi to go.

Covington has a small but lovely **Farmers Market** on the grounds of its town hall, held 9 A.M.–1 P.M. Saturdays and 2–6 P.M. Wednesdays—everything fresh, from Creole cream cheese to produce to pies to homemade dog biscuits to jams and jellies, is proffered. It's a friendly market, a good place to chat with and meet locals.

INFORMATION AND SERVICES
Visitor Information

Information on these towns can be obtained from the **St. Tammany Parish Tourist Commission Visitor Center** (68099 Hwy. 59, just north of I-12, Mandeville, 70471, 985/892-0520 or 800/634-9443, www.neworleansnorthshore.com). This is one visitors

center that's worth dropping by in person, as it occupies a cleverly designed wood-frame building in an authentic Louisiana swamp.

Getting Around

There's virtually no public transportation in St. Tammany Parish, and a private car is a must for exploring. Only in downtown Covington and Olde Town Mandeville will you find accommodations within walking distance of a fair number of shops and eateries, and even in these communities your options are limited. Unfortunately, traffic can be torturously slow in some parts of the parish, especially U.S. Highway 190 between Mandeville and Covington and in Slidell, and Highway 59 between Mandeville and Abita Springs. However, U.S. Highway 190 from the western edge of Slidell into Mandeville is relatively less traveled and quite scenic, as are several of the parishes' state highways, such as Highway 22 (from Mandeville west through Madisonville and clear to Ponchatoula in Tangipahoa Parish), Highway 21 (from Madisonville northeast up through Covington and on through Bush and Bogalusa), and Highway 433 (in Slidell from U.S. Highway 90 winding northwest to U.S. Highway 190). For speed, I-12 can be a lifesaver, and it's usually free from major traffic jams—it runs west to east across the parish, connecting the junction of I-59 and I-10 in Slidell with Mandeville and Covington before continuing to Tangipahoa Parish and I-55. By way of I-10, it's just a 40-minute drive from downtown New Orleans to Slidell, and by way of the causeway across Lake Pontchartrain, it's a 45-minute drive from New Orleans to Mandeville. Rush-hour traffic jams along both these routes are common, so figure an extra 20–30 minutes depending on when you make these drives.

Tangipahoa Parish

As opposed to St. Tammany Parish, which runs chiefly east–west around the northeastern perimeter of Lake Pontchartrain, Tangipahoa (pronounced TAN-jah-puh-ho) Parish forms a south–north rectangle, extending from the north shore of Lake Pontchartrain up to the Mississippi state border. The towns down nearest to the lake, Ponchatoula and Hammond, are the most popular with visitors and also the most populated. As you travel north, you'll encounter smaller and sleepier communities with a mostly rural feel, except for the presence of I-55, which cuts along the west side of each of these towns.

The smaller towns in Tangipahoa Parish all have wonderful old vintage rail stations, and all of them have found new uses these days, from a police station in Amite to a senior center in Independence to an antiques and gift shop in Ponchatoula.

PONCHATOULA

Ponchatoula is a quiet little town famous for its plethora of antiques shops. It's the oldest incorporated community in Tangipahoa Parish (dating to 1861), and although it's the closest town in the parish to New Orleans, it feels miles from the big city. You can reach the town coming from New Orleans via I-55, or from St. Tammany Parish to the east, via either Highway 22 or I-12 from Madisonville.

The big excitement downtown occurs when the City of New Orleans Amtrak train from Chicago speeds through, keeping pedestrians and autos momentarily from crossing the track that pierces the heart of the commercial district. Freight trains also cut through downtown rather often. There's been a rail depot here since 1854, when the Jackson and Great Northern Railroad was first begun; the original depot was burned by Union forces in 1863, and the present depot dates to the 1890s.

These days the depot houses the **Country Market** (E. Pine St. and Railroad Ave., Pon-chatoula, 985/386-9580), which sells homemade jams, jellies, breads, candies, and other gourmet goods, including praline syrup, green-tomato jam, and fig preserves. Antiques and crafts are also available, and on display is a 1912 steam locomotive that was used during the town's heyday. An old mail car has been converted to an art gallery, and flying high above the depot atop a 177-foot pole is a massive U.S. flag, measuring 30 by 60 feet. One final curious sight here is a large caged-in pool of water in which you can observe Ponchatoula's resident alligator.

MANCHAC

For a quirky detour, drive south from Ponchatoula along I-55, and glance out to your left as you approach Manchac, a tiny fishing village largely accessible only by boat. You'll see numerous cottages dotting the swampland here, each with a small dock, all of them either supported on stilts or situated on the rare piece of high ground. Take the Manchac exit off I-55; follow the road to the right toward the lakeshore to reach Middendorf's Restaurant, one of the North Shore's best seafood restaurants. Follow Old U.S. Highway 51 south over the Manchac Pass, and you'll find a little nest of activity on your left that includes a daiquiri bar and a rollicking little lounge called Gator's, which is also a debarkation point for swamp tours. Manchac is mostly the domain of local fishermen, and it has the feel of utter seclusion. It's hard to believe that New Orleans International Airport lies just 35 miles south.

TICKFAW STATE PARK

Tickfaw State Park (27225 Patterson Rd., Springfield, 225/294-5020 or 888/981-2020, www.lastateparks.com, open 9 A.M.–dusk daily, admission $2 per vehicle) is at the end of a remote and twisting narrow road west of Springfield, in the middle of what seems like nowhere, about 15 miles west of Ponchatoula.

LOUISIANA ON FILM

Louisiana's lush landscape, antebellum plantation houses, and well-preserved urban areas make for breathtaking, often curious, and always memorable backdrops in motion pictures. It's no surprise that the Louisiana Office of Film and Video (www.lafilm.org) is one of the most aggressive in the country when it comes to attracting producers and directors.

One of the first and most colorful Louisiana films was a dramatization of the life of pirate Jean Lafitte, 1938's *The Buccaneer,* which starred Fredric Marsh and was directed by Cecil B. DeMille. Starlet Dolores del Rio starred in the famous Cajun tale *Evangeline* in 1929. Based on the Henry Wadsworth Longfellow poem about two young Acadian lovers separated during their peoples' expulsion from Canada, it was filmed in St. Martinville on the banks of Bayou Teche. Perhaps the most famous early classic filmed in the state is 1938's *Jezebel,* for which star Bette Davis won the Oscar for Best Actress. It was filmed in part around Lake Charles. Marlene Dietrich played a stunning French countess in the 1941 adventure comedy, *The Flame of New Orleans,* which was filmed in the Big Easy.

And in the category of "it's so bad it's good," Lon Chaney Jr. plays a live mummy accidentally dug up in a rural Louisiana bayou in *The Mummy's Curse* (1944). One of the oldest Tarzan movies, 1918's *Tarzan of the Apes* made use of the jungle terrain around Morgan City.

Few James Bond fans will ever forget the hair-raising boat chase through the bayous of Slidell in the 1973 007 thriller *Live and Let Die,* which opens with a traditional jazz funeral in New Orleans. The gripping family drama *Eve's Bayou* (1997), with Samuel L. Jackson and Lynn Whitfield, was shot in Covington, Madisonville, and Napoleonville.

Sometimes a Louisiana locale stands in for another part of the South. Such was the case with the 1999 Melanie Griffith and Lucas Black comedy, *Crazy in Alabama* – which was actually crazy in Houma. One scene was set in New Orleans at Lafitte's Blacksmith Shop, the wonderful old Bourbon Street bar.

Dozens of other notable movies have been filmed in these parts. Here's a partial list:

- *A Streetcar Named Desire* (1951) with Vivien Leigh, Marlon Brando, Kim Hunter, and Karl Malden; filmed in New Orleans

- *King Creole* (1958) with Elvis Presley and Walter Matthau; filmed in New Orleans

- *The Long Hot Summer* (1958) with Paul Newman, Joanne Woodward, and Orson Welles; filmed in Clinton and Jackson

- *Hush… Hush, Sweet Charlotte* (1964) with Bette Davis and Olivia de Havilland; filmed in Baton Rouge, and at Houmas House Plantation in Burnside

- *The Cincinnati Kid* (1965) with Steve McQueen, Edward G. Robinson, and Ann-Margret; filmed in New Orleans and Covington

- *Nevada Smith* (1966) with Steve McQueen and Karl Malden; filmed in New Orleans, Baton Rouge, and Lafayette

- *Hotel* (1967) with Rod Taylor and Karl Malden; filmed in New Orleans

- *Easy Rider* (1969) with Peter Fonda and Dennis Hopper; filmed in New Orleans, Lafayette, and Morgan City

- *Sounder* (1972) with Teddy Airhart and James Best; filmed in Clinton, St. Helena Parish, and East Feliciana Parish

- *The Drowning Pool* (1975) with Paul Newman and Joanne Woodward; filmed on Oaklawn Plantation in Franklin, in Lafayette, and Lake Charles

- *Casey's Shadow* (1978) with Walter Matthau and Alexis Smith; filmed in Lafayette

- *Pretty Baby* (1978) with Brooke Shields, Keith Carradine, and Susan Sarandon; filmed in New Orleans

- *The Toy* (1982) with Richard Pryor and Jackie Gleason; filmed in Baton Rouge and Hammond

- *No Mercy* (1986) with Richard Gere and Kim

Basinger; filmed in Baton Rouge and New Orleans

- *The Big Easy* (1987) with Dennis Quaid and Ellen Barkin; filmed in New Orleans

- *Blaze* (1989) with Paul Newman and Lolita Davidovich; filmed in Baton Rouge, New Orleans, and Winnfield

- *Fletch Lives* (1989) with Chevy Chase and Hal Holbrook; filmed in New Orleans, Burnside, Gonzalez, and Thibodaux

- *Sex, Lies, and Videotape* (1989) with James Spader and Andie MacDowell; filmed in Baton Rouge

- *Steel Magnolias* (1989) with Julia Roberts, Sally Field, Dolly Parton, Shirley MacLaine, and Olympia Dukakis; filmed in Natchitoches

- *Miller's Crossing* (1990) with Gabriel Byrne and Marcia Gay Harden; filmed in Hammond and New Orleans

- *Wild at Heart* (1990) with Nicolas Cage and Laura Dern; filmed in New Orleans

- *JFK* (1991) with Kevin Costner, Kevin Bacon, and Tommy Lee Jones; filmed in New Orleans

- *Passion Fish* (1992) with Mary McDonnell and Alfre Woodard; filmed in Elton, Jennings, and Lake Arthur

- *The Pelican Brief* (1993) with Julia Roberts and Denzel Washington; filmed in New Orleans

- *The Client* (1994) with Susan Sarandon and Tommy Lee Jones; filmed in New Orleans

- *Interview with the Vampire* (1994) with Tom Cruise and Brad Pitt; filmed at Lafayette Cemetery No. 1 and elsewhere in New Orleans, at Oak Alley Plantation in Vacherie, and in Shreveport

- *Dead Man Walking* (1995) with Susan Sarandon and Sean Penn; filmed in Angola Prison, Baton Rouge, New Orleans, and Slidell

- *Something to Talk About* (1995) with Julia Roberts and Dennis Quaid; filmed at Oak Alley Plantation in Vacherie

- *The Apostle* (1997) with Robert Duvall and Farrah Fawcett; filmed in Lafayette

- *Lolita* (1997) with Jeremy Irons and Melanie Griffith; filmed in New Orleans

- *Out of Sight* (1998) with George Clooney and Jennifer Lopez; filmed in Angola Prison and at Krotz Springs

- *Primary Colors* (1998) with John Travolta, Emma Thompson, and Larry Hagman; filmed in New Orleans and at Oak Alley Plantation in Vacherie

- *The Waterboy* (1998) with Adam Sandler and Kathy Bates; filmed throughout Louisiana

- *Double Jeopardy* (1999) with Tommy Lee Jones and Ashley Judd; filmed in New Orleans

- *Inspector Gadget* (1999) with Matthew Broderick and Rupert Everett; filmed in Baton Rouge

- *Monster's Ball* (2001) with Billy Bob Thornton and Halle Berry; filmed in Angola Prison and LaPlace

- *Runaway Jury* (2003) with John Cusack, Gene Hackman, Dustin Hoffman, and Rachel Weisz; filmed in New Orleans, Kenner, and Metairie

- *Ray* (2004) with Jamie Foxx; filmed in New Orleans, Hammond, and Baton Rouge

- *A Love Song for Bobby Long* (2004) with John Travolta and Scarlett Johansson; filmed in New Orleans

- *The Skeleton Key* (2005) with Kate Hudson, Gena Rowlands, and John Hurt; filmed in New Orleans

- *All the King's Men* (2006) with Sean Penn and Jude Law; filmed in Morgan City, Baton Rouge (at the State Capitol building), and New Orleans

THE NORTH SHORE

This 1,200-acre park sits astride three miles of the Tickfaw River, and you can saunter along about a mile of boardwalk through the lush wetlands, which encompass four different ecosystems: cypress/tupelo swamp, bottomland hardwood forest, mixed pine/hardwood forest, and the Tickfaw River itself. You'll sometimes see heron and egrets swooping into the swamp to grab a crawfish snack. Other wildlife commonly seen in the park include turtles, snakes, wild turkeys, opossum, and wildfowl—and, rarely, you might spot a coyote, deer, fox, or beaver. Rent a canoe for the best chance to really dig deep into the swamp and see wildlife. A nature center (open 9 A.M.–5 P.M. daily) contains excellent exhibits on the park's flora and fauna, and park rangers lead interpretive walks through the swamp and present discussions in the park's amphitheater—call ahead for a schedule. Nighttime educational and entertainment programs are geared toward overnight guests; there are 14 air-conditioned cabins (each with two bedrooms and sleeping accommodations for up to eight people), with fireplace, full kitchen, and bathroom. You'll also find 30 RV campsites and 20 tent sites. Just outside the park gate you'll find a sno-ball and ice cream stand, an eatery selling po'boys and other light fare, and a minigolf place.

HAMMOND

The parish's largest community (with 18,000 year-round residents, another 16,000 college students throughout the school year, and thousands more retirees during the wintertime), Hammond lies just north of Ponchatoula and takes its name from an enterprising Swedish immigrant named Peter Hammond, who arrived in the 1820s and came up with a sappy idea upon observing the region's abundance of pine trees: He started a business that processed the resin from pine trees to make tar, pitch, turpentine, and coal. He also chopped down the trees and used the wood for barrels and kegs.

The city's growth didn't begin in earnest until 1854, when the Jackson and Great Northern Railroad was run through Hammond—the tracks still extend through the parish, roughly parallel to U.S. Highway 51 and I-55, from the western shoreline of Lake Pontchartrain to the Mississippi border at Kentwood. A slew of small manufacturing concerns grew up around Hammond after the arrival of the railroad. Perhaps the most successful was a shoe factory begun by Charles Emery Cate, which during the early part of the Civil War provided thousands of Confederate troops with footwear. It was likely for this reason that Union troops torched the community during their swing through the area in 1862. Hammond gradually rebounded and prospered after the war and incorporated as a city in 1889.

Today it's the commercial and residential hub of Tangipahoa Parish, home to one of the nation's fastest-growing colleges, Southeastern Louisiana University (SLU), and a burgeoning population of retirees. A virtual caravan of "snowbirds" arrives from the cold Midwestern states late each fall, working its way south down the I-55 corridor. Here the retirees rent houses or mobile homes, or park their own RVs at one of the many campgrounds set throughout the area. The mild climate and relatively low cost of living is a boon, as is being close enough to New Orleans to make frequent day trips but far enough away to avoid the occasional inconveniences of urban life. Another reason for the popularity of Hammond with not only retirees but all people is that the city has a fast-growing health-care industry.

SLU formed in 1925 as Hammond Junior College and is nationally renowned for its top-notch Collegiate School of Business, as well as strong programs in industrial technology, nursing, and education. The campus dominates the area north and west of downtown, off Oak Street and University Avenue.

Like many North Shore towns, Hammond has worked hard at improving its downtown in recent years, and today you'll find a good number of thriving independent eateries and shops, as well as an abundance of historic buildings, on either side of the rail tracks that split the district north–south. Art deco, Queen Anne, and Renaissance Revival styles dominate the architectural streetscape. Perhaps most striking is the 1912 Illinois Central Railroad Depot and, across the street, the Grace Memorial Episcopal Church. Also note the Central Rexall Drug Store at 125 Thomas Street; there's been a pharmacy here in this turn-of-the-20th-century building since 1917. Downtown's most famous building is the Columbia Theatre, which dates to the 1920s and was completely renovated and reopened in January 2002. It's a massive redbrick-and-limestone building with Jacobean and Renaissance Revival architectural elements. The very first talkie, *The Jazz Singer,* was screened here during the theater's earliest days.

Probably the favorite Hammond attraction is **Kliebert's Turtle and Alligator Farm** (41067 W. Yellow Water Rd., Hammond, 985/345-3617 or 800/854-9164, www.klieberttours. com, open noon–dark daily Mar.–Oct., admission $6). Kliebert (pronounced KLEE-bair) is just southwest of town, easily reached by either the Highway 22 exit from I-55 or, if coming from the north, from Exit 28 off I-55; just follow signs from either exit, as it's a short drive from the interstate. It's best to call ahead to confirm hours and let someone know you're coming. This is one of the only alligator farms in southern Louisiana open to the public. Louisiana bans hunting and poaching of alligators in the wild, so these farms raise and harvest the animals, helping to protect the wild species. All farms are required to return to the wild a significant percentage of the alligators born here. At Kliebert's you can get a firsthand look at the gators and turtles; there's also a sanctuary where egrets and herons nest in trees over the alligator habitats.

U.S. 51 NORTH

The string of small towns that extend along U.S. 51 north of Hammond offer little in the way of formal attractions, but there are a few worthy B&Bs and eateries. Also, from the town of Tickfaw, just north of Hammond, you can make the drive east on Highway 442 to reach two of the region's top attractions, the Global Wildlife Center and Zemurray Gardens. Tickfaw is a little bump of a village, although there's a very nice and affordable B&B in the center of town.

Zemurray Gardens

From Tickfaw, you can follow Highway 442 and then Highway 40 for a total of about 10 miles to reach the immense Zemurray Gardens (23115 Zemurray Garden Dr., Loranger, 985/878-2284, open six weeks each year, 10 A.M.–6 P.M. daily mid-Mar.–mid-Apr., admission $5), which is famous for brilliant stands of azaleas and a nature path that passes through a dense forest of magnolias, cypress, and poplar trees, and flowers of all kinds. It also passes by Mirror Lake and by lovely cast-bronze statues. Anchoring the garden complex is an early-20th-century Arts and Crafts lodge.

Global Wildlife Center

From Zemurray Gardens, continue east on Highway 40 for roughly another four miles to reach the Global Wildlife Center (26389 Hwy. 40, Folsom, 985/624-9453, www.globalwildlife. com, open daily, admission $10). There are few more engaging and unusual sites in Louisiana, and yet relatively few visitors to greater New Orleans ever learn about, let alone visit, this remarkable facility, which is well worth the trip off the beaten path. The center covers about 900 rural acres, and once you're within the grounds, it's hard to imagine you're in Louisiana or even in North America—giraffes, zebras, antelope, llamas, camels, and three dozen other species of mostly African wildlife (nearly 3,000 animals all together) roam freely across the property. You see the animals by boarding covered wagons, which are pulled across the grounds by tractors, in tours that last about 90 minutes.

There's really no set routine or path—the safari guides simply go where the animals are, and in many cases you're allowed to come extremely close to the wildlife. It's an excellent opportunity for photographers. Reservations are not required (except for groups), but visitors are asked to call an automated information line (985/796-3585) for the weekly-changing schedule of guided tours.

The center has a huge gift shop selling all manner of wildlife toys, prints, books, stuffed animals, and so on (proceeds benefit the care of the animals here) and a small concession stand; you can also buy little cups of feed, with which you'll have the opportunity to tempt some of the tamer animals close enough for a memorable photo op.

From the Global Wildlife Center, you can continue east on Highway 40 to reach the village of Folsom (described in more detail in the *St. Tammany Parish* section of this chapter), or you can return to Tickfaw.

Amite

Amite (pronounced AY-meet) occupies the site of an important Choctaw Indian settlement along the Tangipahoa River—in fact, the last of the great Choctaw leaders of this area, Chief Baptiste, is said to have welcomed the earliest French settlers here. The derivation of the town's name has two explanations: Either it's the Choctaw name for "red ant" or it comes from the French for "friendship."

Amite grew to greater significance as settlers from the United States began visiting the region in the 1810s, and it became one of the railroad towns in the 1850s with the construction of the Jackson and Great Northern Railroad. It grew popular during the summer with prosperous New Orleanians seeking cooler climes and fresh air, especially during the frequent plagues of yellow fever that swept through New Orleans. Most of the impressive summer retreats built here before the Civil War have burned or been torn down, but a few still stand. During the war, Union troops entered Amite and burned the rail depot and destroyed the tracks that led from the depot 10 miles north to Camp Moore. Amite served as a base for Union occupation during Reconstruction after the war.

Amite became the seat of Tangipahoa Parish in 1869. The original courthouse still stands (it houses Cabby's Restaurant). The city boomed as a supply and trade center for southeastern Louisiana's cotton farmers, but it also became notorious through Reconstruction as the site of frequent political and economic unrest, fights, and assaults. By the middle of the 20th century, cotton farming gave way chiefly to dairy farms—Tangipahoa Parish leads Louisiana in milk production, as well as in strawberry farming. One of the biggest industries in Amite today is oyster processing; the town hosts the popular Oyster Festival each March. It's also the home of an immense 24-acre foundry and machine shop that produces sugar mills, dock fittings, and marine decks.

You'll find a smattering of handsome early-20th-century buildings in the small downtown, which runs mostly along the rail tracks.

Tangipahoa

Right in the small village of Tangipahoa is **Camp Moore Confederate Museum and Cemetery** (U.S. 51, 0.5 mile north of town, Tangipahoa, 985/229-2438, www.campmoore.com, open 10 A.M.–3 P.M. Tues.–Sat., admission $2), which was established in 1861 as the largest Confederate training camp in Louisiana during the Civil War (called the War Between the States in these parts). The camp trained 6,000–8,000 soldiers at any given time, for a total of at least 25,000. The cemetery here contains the graves of the nearly 1,000 soldiers who died of disease at the camp—two measles epidemics spread through the camp during its tenure. The camp was taken over by Union forces and shut down in fall 1864.

SHOPPING
◖ Antiques Shopping in Ponchatoula

Ponchatoula is Tangipahoa Parish's mecca for shopping, noted for its antiques shops set around the center of town. It's a great source of bargain-hunting—plenty of the high-end dealers on Magazine and Royal streets in New Orleans are said to make trips up to Ponchatoula, buy goods here, and then resell them at higher prices in the French Quarter. Nearly 20 antiques shops make up Ponchatoula's impressive little downtown shopping district, all of them within a compact several-square-block area. The best strategy is to park your car in one of the spaces along Pine Street or Railroad Avenue and walk around. Most shops are along Pine Street, between about 8th and 3rd streets, and most are open about 10 A.M.–5 P.M. Monday–Saturday and noon–5 P.M. on Sundays.

ENTERTAINMENT AND NIGHTLIFE

The college town of Hammond contains the largest share of area bars and nightspots—this part of the North Shore isn't a major nightlife hub, but there are a few engaging hangouts.

Hammond is also home to the beautifully restored 900-seat **Columbia Theatre** (220 E. Thomas St., Hammond, 985/543-4366, www. columbiatheatre.org), an elegant 1928 building that now serves as the city's and Southeastern Louisiana University's premier performing arts center. Events here include pop concerts, performances by the Louisiana Philharmonic, and both touring and local plays and musicals.

FESTIVALS AND EVENTS

Tangipahoa Parish hosts several of the state's better-attended events, and if you don't mind the occasionally intense crowds, these can be an excellent time for a visit.

The **Strawberry Festival** (www.lastrawberryfestival.com) constitutes a number of events that take place in and around Hammond February–mid-April, but the main celebration occurs that final weekend and includes a car show, parade, road race, history exhibits, crafts, food, and so on. Strawberry Festival events leading up to the big weekend include talent shows, dances, a jambalaya cook-off, and other family-oriented fun. This is considered to be one of the nation's largest three-day festivals.

The **Amite Oyster Festival** (985/748-5161) takes place in mid-March at the Tangipahoa Parish Fairgrounds; the bivalve is celebrated and sampled during this weekend-long event. In late April, the town of Independence celebrates its immigrant heritage with the **Italian Festival** (985/878-1902, www.theitalianfest.

com), a great opportunity to sample tasty foods and enjoy music and crafts demonstrations.

Major **Fourth of July** fireworks celebrations are held in Hammond and Ponchatoula.

Oktoberfest (Le Fleur de Lis Complex, Ponchatoula, www.ponchatoulaoktoberfest.com) is a big event in Tangipahoa Parish; it's one of the largest such celebrations in the state. The **Tangipahoa Parish Free Fair** (Tangipahoa Fairgrounds, Amite, 985/878-3890, www.tangifair.org) draws crowds in early October for games, food, and music. And Hammond hosts the popular **Louisiana Renaissance Festival** (985/429-9992, www.larf.org) each November.

ACCOMMODATIONS

Situated at one of the South's pivotal interstate junctions, the meeting of I-55 and I-12, Hammond has dozens of chain motels, including a number of properties opened since the late 1990s. With New Orleans just 60 miles south and Baton Rouge 50 miles west, and strong motel competition responsible for very competitive rates, this can be an ideal base for visitors to southeastern Louisiana. You'll also find a number of mostly reasonably priced B&Bs spread throughout the parish.

Hotels and Motels

$50-100: Well managed and with spacious rooms, the **Comfort Inn in Amite** (1117 W. Oak St., Amite, 985/748-5550 or 800/228-5150, www.comfortinnofamite.com) opened in 2001 and is the best chain lodging option in the northern half of the parish. It has a pool, fitness room, guest laundry, and hot breakfast is included.

Opened in 2002, the top-notch **Hampton Inn** (401 Westin Oaks Dr., Hammond, 985/419-2188 or 800/426-7866, www.hampton-inn.com) is just west of downtown off I-55 at U.S. 190. The three-story, interior-corridor property has 78 rooms, all with microwaves, refrigerators, irons and boards, and coffeemakers. There are also a coin laundry, business center, fitness room, and pool.

The **Super 8 Hammond** (200 Westin Oaks

Dr., Hammond, 985/429-8088 or 800/800-8000, www.super8.com) is an economically priced option right off I-55 and U.S. Highway 190. The hotel has large, by budget-motel standards, rooms, some with refrigerators and microwaves; there are several fast-food restaurants within walking distance.

Inns and Bed-and-Breakfasts

$50-100: In Tickfaw, the **G. W. Nesom House** (U.S. 51 at Hwy. 442, Tickfaw, 985/542-7159, www.gwnesom.com) is a dramatic Eastlake-style Queen Anne Victorian with a hipped roof and a turret wing. Antiques fill the common areas, three guest rooms, and lavish Bridal Suite of this 1903 house, with sweeping first- and second-floor verandas. A full breakfast is included.

Built in the late 1930s, **Country Lane** (62058 Simpson La., Roseland, 985/748-9062, www.bbonline.com/la/countrylane) feels completely rural and secluded, yet it's just a couple of miles from I-55 and downtown Amite. The key draw is the stable with eight stalls and two grassy paddocks and access to 500 acres of rolling country ideal for horseback riding. It's an easygoing B&B with four guest rooms and two suites, each done with country furnishings, quilts, and rather frilly curtains and fabrics. Some pets are permitted by arrangement.

In downtown Ponchatoula, steps from the antiques district, the **Guest House B&B** (248 W. Hickory St., Ponchatoula, 985/386-6275) offers a simple and comfortable accommodation. There's just one lovingly maintained cottage, complete with its own kitchen; it's filled with local antiques and is very private, making it ideal for a longer stay, or even to use as a base to explore New Orleans.

$100-150: ◖ **Michabelle** (1106 S. Holly St., Hammond, 504/419-0550, www.michabelle.com) is a wonderfully decadent B&B on the south side of Hammond's historic downtown on a tree-shaded street. This imposing white Greek Revival mansion adroitly blends classic French style with Old South charm. The four rooms are rife with late-Victorian antiques, Oriental rugs, and gilt-framed paintings. There's an excellent restaurant, whose dining room has a trompe l'oeil ceiling of floating cherubs against a cerulean sky. The grounds are marked by lush gardens, and a three-tier fountain gurgles out front.

Camping

There are six campgrounds in Tangipahoa Parish. Reliable options include **Hidden Oaks Family Campground** (21544 U.S. 190 E, Hammond, 985/345-9244 or 800/359-0940), which rents canoes and inner tubes for use on its lake. Secluded **Tchefuncte Family Campground** (54492 Campground Rd., Folsom, 985/796-3654 or 888/280-1953, www.tchefunctecampground.com) sits along the serene Tchefuncte River; it's an ideal spot if you love swimming.

Indian Creek Campground and RV Park (53013 W. Fontana Rd., Independence, 985/878-6567) also rents cabins. The **New Orleans/Hammond KOA** (14154 Club Deluxe Rd., near I-55 at I-12, Hammond, 985/542-8094 or 800/562-9394) overlooks a small lake and offers a wide range of recreational activities, including a pool, minigolf, fishing, and volleyball.

FOOD

Tangipahoa Parish has fewer high-profile and high-end restaurants than St. Tammany Parish, but great dining is still very much a hallmark of the region, from down-home lunchrooms to family-style seafood and steak restaurants to a handful of trendier spots, found mostly in Ponchatoula and Hammond.

Upscale

◖ **Michabelle** (1106 S. Holly St., Hammond, 985/419-0550, $16–22), a classy inn, also has a first-rate restaurant with both prix-fixe and à la carte menus. The dining options change often but might include rainbow trout with crabmeat served with a smoked-mussel cream sauce, followed by roast breast of turkey marinated with wild herbs and served with dried cherries and raisins. Chocolate pecan pie is a favorite way to finish things.

Tucked inside a cozy 1880 cottage a few blocks east of the rail tracks in Hammond, the **Jacmel Inn** (903 E. Morris St., Hammond, 985/542-0043, $13–20) is a romantic place for a special yet not necessarily superexpensive dinner. The kitchen turns out a mix of contemporary Creole, Cajun, and loosely Italian fare, including an exquisite starter of escargot served with mushrooms, brandy, ginger, and garlic butter. The bouillabaisse is a classically prepared main dish bursting with local seafood. Several pasta dishes and steaks are also offered.

Creative but Casual

C'est Bon (131 S.W. Railroad Ave., Ponchatoula, 985/386-4077, $6–12) is a great restaurant located in Ponchatoula's downtown antiques district. Try the raspberry-baked brie or the stuffed quail; you can also get burgers and sandwiches, several pasta dishes (such as crawfish lasagna), and a tasty bourbon-pecan chicken. The dining room is intimate and clubby, with dark-red wood paneling and exposed brick; it overlooks the rail tracks.

Tope Iä (104 N. Cate St., Hammond, 985/542-7600, $12–28) is a glamorous little restaurant with an attractive young staff and an inviting bar, too, that's nice if you're dining alone. Deft preparation and fresh ingredients account for the success of the kitchen. You might start with blackened alligator or potato hush puppies with hot-pepper jelly, followed by Cajun-marinated duck breast tossed with artichoke hearts, sun-dried tomatoes, mushrooms, and penne in a light marinara sauce, or soft-shell crawfish Atchafalaya stuffed with crawfish and topped with hollandaise sauce. It's a popular lunch spot, too.

Seafood, Pizzas, and Pub Grub

In Independence, a small town between Tickfaw and Amite that's known for its tight-knit population of Italian immigrants, **Gina's** (319 4th St., Independence, 985/878-9479, $4–8) is a tiny lunch spot that serves hearty, home-style fare, such as spaghetti, lasagna, and meatballs.

It's open only for lunch, and it's a great place to observe the local color.

Out in the country near Folsom and the Global Wildlife Center, you'll find yet another unusual Louisiana culinary experience, **White's Steak and Fish House** (56034 Virgil White La., Husser, 985/748-3710, $6–12), a long, low, and rather drab bunkerlike building in a blip of a village called Husser. It's about a 30-minute drive northeast of Hammond, and it's open only Thursday–Saturday evenings. But people come from miles around to sample the steak and seafood, served from a buffet. There's no alcohol.

In downtown Ponchatoula, **Paul's** (100 E. Pine St., Ponchatoula, 985/386-9581, $3–9) is a bare-bones lunchroom with paneled walls, Formica tables, and a few stools at the counter. The place is known for strawberry daiquiris (a favorite potable in this parish known for strawberry farms), great breakfasts, and rather ordinary diner cooking, such as barbecued chicken, red beans and rice, or stuffed crab. It's nothing fancy, but you can count on honest home cooking and friendly service.

In the tiny fishing village of Manchac, south of Ponchatoula off I-55, **Middendorf's Seafood** (30160 U.S. 51, Manchac, 985/386-6666, $6–14) serves perhaps the freshest seafood in the state, from platters topped with fried oysters, shrimp, and crab to po'boys. The modest dining room has varnished wooden walls and a sprinkling of nautical photos and prints.

Ethnic

La Carreta (108 N.W. Railroad Ave., Hammond, 985/419-9990, $7–14) is a very attractive and hip Mexican eatery by the rail tracks in Hammond, a favorite of college students and yuppies. There's a big redbrick patio with a fountain, and inside, the high-ceilinged space is decked with colorful serapes. This is a great alternative to the cookie-cutter eateries out near the interstate. Steak burritos with green salsa, shrimp fajitas, *chiles rellenos,* and *carnitas* are among the kicky offerings. There's live music on Wednesdays.

The most distinguished Asian restaurant in the parish is ❪❫ **Trey Yuen** (2100 N. Morrison Blvd., Hammond, 985/345-6789, $8–15), offering well-prepared Chinese food that has garnered some national attention. It also has a branch in the St. Tammany Parish town of Mandeville.

Quick Bites
Lee's Grill (401 W. Thomas St., Hammond, 985/345-3091, $4–10) is a slice of retro Louisiana. This great old building with a stainless-steel facade was a real drive-in way back when; now you can eat inside (although there's still a take-out window and lots of parking). Specialties include banana splits, seafood platters, po'boys, half-pound burgers, and very good salads.

Java Joints
The popular New Orleans chain **P.J.'s Coffee and Tea** (224 W. Thomas St., Hammond, 985/345-1533) has a bright and upbeat location downtown, a short drive from the university (and, as you'd expect, it draws plenty of student types). You can get the usual coffees and teas, plus already-prepared Greek and chef's salads, cookies, bagels, and sandwiches.

Picnic Supplies and Gourmet Goods
Independence's rich Italian heritage is evident when you stop by **Blaise's A Taste of Italy** (315 4th St., Independence, 985/878-1951), which specializes in homemade ricotta, anise, and almond Italian cookies, and delicious liqueur cakes made with rum, amaretto, or hazelnut or peach brandy.

INFORMATION AND SERVICES
Visitor Information
The towns in this region are served by the **Tangipahoa Parish Convention and Visitor Bureau** (42271 S. Morrison Blvd., Hammond, 985/542-7520 or 800/542-7520, www.tangi-cvb.org).

Getting Around
Tangipahoa Parish sits at the crossroads of I-12, connecting Baton Rouge to Slidell, and I-55, which connects New Orleans to Mississippi. As with St. Tammany Parish, a private car is indispensable for exploring the area. Very few accommodations are within walking distance of sights and restaurants, and there are no practical public-transportation options.

THE GREAT RIVER ROAD

A drive along the Great River Road reveals some of the most striking and curious contrasts between the past and the present, and rural life and industry, that you'll find anywhere in the country. The name Great River Road, in southern Louisiana, does not refer to just one highway but rather a series of roads running along both sides of the Mississippi River, from New Orleans up through the rural plantation country northwest of the city on through the state capital, Baton Rouge, and then up to the charming Old World towns of St. Francisville and New Roads. Just a bit north of here, the east bank runs into the Mississippi state border, and the river continues to function as a state border for about 2,000 miles until it cuts into interior Minnesota.

When most people in these parts refer to the Great River Road, they're speaking most specifically of the stretch that begins west of New Orleans, about where I-310 crosses the Mississippi River, and that ends south of Baton Rouge, around the towns of Plaquemine and Sunshine. The city of Baton Rouge falls squarely between the two sections of river known for Louisiana's most dramatic antebellum plantation houses. North of Baton Rouge, St. Francisville is a delightful and well-preserved southern river town that feels grander and more inviting than any of the towns along the stretch of River Road between New Orleans and Baton Rouge. It's really its own ball of wax, and nearby New Roads, which is situated along a false river (a former bend in the Mississippi that naturally cut itself off over time), is often visited with St. Francisville.

HIGHLIGHTS

◖ Best Photo Op: Few images in Louisiana are more recognizable than the stunning alley of live oak trees that brackets the Greek Revival home at **Oak Alley Plantation.** Visitors can tour the house and explore the beautifully landscaped grounds (page 265).

◖ Most Fascinating Plantation Tour: The engaging tours of **Laura: A Creole Plantation** are what set this property apart from others along the Great River Road. Here you'll learn not only about the four generations of women who presided over the property but also the lives of the slaves who lived here (page 265).

◖ Best Plantation Gardens: Whether you're a fan of elegant old homes filled with fine art and antiques, or an aficionado of formal gardens, you'll find plenty to see and do at the dramatic (and lush) **Houmas House Plantation and Gardens** (page 267).

◖ Coolest-Looking Government Building: Unlike any other state capitol in the country, the art deco **Louisiana State Capitol** soars 34 stories over the Baton Rouge skyline. You can view the scenery from an ob-servation deck and also see exactly where notorious politico Huey Long was assassinated (page 275).

◖ Most Informative History Museum: The **Louisiana State University Rural Life Museum** shines a light on the often overlooked history of culture, folkways, and everyday life among rural Southerners through the centuries. The 25 acres of semiformal gardens are part of the draw (page 275).

◖ Most Beautiful Historic Neighborhood: A residential area filled with stunning Victorian homes and a small commercial downtown known for its antiques shopping are what lure travelers to the **St. Francisville Historic District,** which is in Louisiana's third-oldest town (page 280).

◖ Fanciest Plantation: St. Francisville's preeminent plantation museum, **Rosedown Plantation State Historic Site** is operated by the Louisiana State Park system and encompasses about 30 acres of formal gardens as well as a neoclassical 1834 manor house of which thoughtful and engaging tours are offered (page 282).

LOOK FOR ◖ TO FIND RECOMMENDED SIGHTS, ACTIVITIES, DINING, AND LODGING.

This is a part of the state that was not, generally, damaged heavily by Hurricane Katrina, and it was missed entirely by Hurricane Rita. That being said, some of the areas of the River Road did receive wind damage and flooding, and moreover, Baton Rouge was significantly affected by Katrina, even if the hurricane hit well east. The state's capital city, Baton Rouge is where many evacuees of New Orleans relocated after the storm—it's been estimated that the area saw a 15–20 percent spike in the months following—and for this reason, the city has seen a surge in population. Evidence of this is apparent throughout the city, where there's been a big increase in construction and where numerous restaurants, shops, and hotels have either opened or are in the construction and planning phases.

Along the River Road between New Orleans and Baton Rouge, the mostly rural communities in this region have experienced relatively little change. You may have already heard a bit about the striking plantation homes that dot the Great River Road, from relatively modest raised cottages to enormous Greek Revival wedding cakes with dozens of outbuildings and rows of 200-year-old live-oak trees draped with hanging moss. This is no myth. The region is rife with these fabulous homes. And therein lies one of the first notable contrasts. You can leave the big and crowded cities of New Orleans and Baton Rouge and, in less than 30 minutes, find

© ANDREW COLLINS

entrance to Louisiana State University campus, Baton Rouge

yourself standing on a plantation with more acreage than the French Quarter and fields of sugarcane for as far as the eye can see.

But the Great River Road, even in the sparsely populated areas, is not exactly quaint, or frozen in time. Along considerable stretches of the road, you'll see huge and in places alarming reminders that you're in a state whose economy is more dependent on heavy industry than sugarcane. Oil refineries, chemical plants, and other fortresses of mining and manufacturing line the river, sometimes within a stone's throw of old plantations. The peculiar juxtaposition is fascinating even when it's not very scenic.

Another reminder that the days of paddle-wheel riverboats and quiet agrarian living have long since passed is the high grassy levee that runs virtually uninterrupted along the Mississippi River, all through Louisiana and right up into the states to the north. As you drive along the still narrow, still mostly peaceful River Road, you can't actually see the river. Back in the 1870s, folks could sit out on the veranda at Oak Alley or Nottoway plantations,

sipping mint juleps and watching the steamboats chug up and down the river. No more. On the other hand, in the 1870s you had to worry about floods wiping out crops, destroying or damaging homes, and otherwise tearing up the landscape.

The levee system effectively bound the Mississippi River, whose course had changed gradually but constantly for thousands of years, into a permanent straitjacket, and it largely eliminated the threat of floods—in fact, the levee was not breached in this part of the state during or after Katrina. The levee is an attraction in itself, and in many spots dirt roads lead up over the levee to the batture (pronounced BATCH-er, no doubt to the horror of French-speaking people everywhere), a term that describes the strip of land between the riverbank and the levee. Here on this fertile and regularly flooded area you'll often find populations of deer or, in many areas, cattle grazing. A path runs along the top of the levee in most places, on which you can jog, walk, or ride a bike.

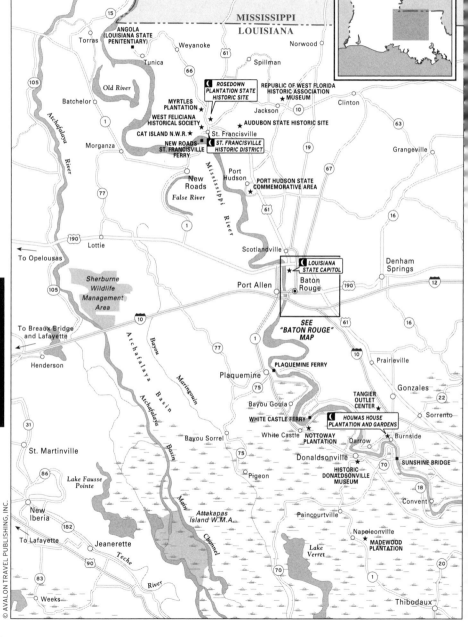

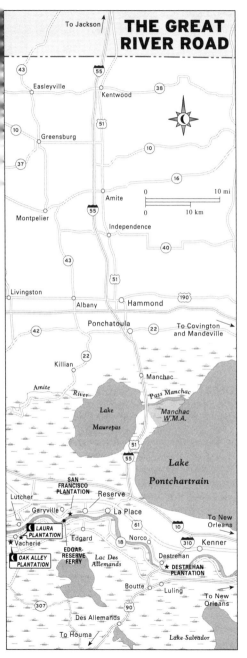

Well into the 19th century, the Mississippi River was the main highway, of sorts, between New Orleans and Baton Rouge, and even with improved roads and then automobile transportation, travelers still had to ride along the twisting, narrow lanes hugging the tight curves of the river well into the 20th century. Governor Huey Long finally pushed through construction of a straight and wide road, the Airline Highway, between New Orleans and Baton Rouge in the 1930s. This diverted traffic, commerce, and people from many of the towns along the River Road.

In the 1950s, the industrial plants began building their hulking structures along the river, and population actually grew rapidly in places, although never nearly to the density found in Baton Rouge or New Orleans. Eventually, an even faster, wider, and more direct highway was built between the two cities, I-10. The River Road was left looking like a rural byway from the Depression era, pockmarked with dozens of huge refineries and factories and fringed by massive levees. That's the road you see today. It's not quaint, you can't see the river from your car, but it's still a fascinating place for a road trip.

One thing to keep in mind as you visit sites on both sides of the river: The ferry is a charming way to switch back and forth across the Mississippi—it's a short ride, although it doesn't always run as often as people would like. Several ferry crossings are along the Mississippi, as well as several bridges. Fares on ferry boats and tolls on bridges are collected only when crossing westbound.

In addition to the plantations described in this chapter that are open for tours, the River Road passes within view of a number of additional properties not open to the public, but they're worth taking a look at from the street. You can obtain a detailed driving-tour map and brochure, "Up a Lazy River," which pinpoints many sites and towns along the Great River Road, from any of the offices of tourism in parishes along the river between New Orleans and St. Francisville. You can also see this map online at www.lariverroad.com.

Plantation Country

The most popular part of the Great River Road for most visitors to New Orleans is the stretch from Destrehan, near I-310, to just below Baton Rouge. It's about a 100-mile drive if you travel the roads hugging the curve of the river (whereas, as the crow flies, it's a distance of only about 60 miles).

There aren't a great many attractions along this span, and relatively few places to stay and eat, but you could definitely spend three full days exploring all the plantations open for tours and frequenting some of the better places to stay and eat. As a single-day excursion from New Orleans, you'd be wise to focus your explorations on the west bank communities of Vacherie (home to Laura and Oak Alley Plantations) and Donaldsonville (which has some great places to eat and is close to Nottoway Plantation). If you have just a couple of hours to spare, you can still get a feel for the area by visiting a plantation close to New Orleans, Destrehan.

For a more substantial River Road exploration, consider spending one or two nights at one of the plantations or B&Bs in the area (these are mostly around Vacherie and Donaldsonville). There's also a modern Best Western in Donaldsonville, and a few chain hotels in Gonzales and Sorrento, two suburbs along I-10 between Baton Rouge and New Orleans, an easy drive from most of the plantations.

DESTREHAN

One of the oldest house-museums on the Great River Road, and also one of the nearest to New Orleans, **Destrehan Plantation** (13034 River Rd., Destrehan, 985/764-9315, www.destrehanplantation.org, open 9 A.M.–4 P.M. daily, admission $10) was built in 1787, although the sweeping Greek Revival mansion you see today, with its eight front columns and double galleries, is the result of a major renovation and expansion in the 1830s. Robin de Logny commissioned the construction of the house, hiring a freed mulatto named Charles

(no last name is known) to build it; this process took three years, and de Logny died just two years after moving in. The estate passed into the hands of de Logny's son-in-law. Jean Noel Destrehan, a French aristocrat, bought the house and added the twin wings on either side of the facade in 1810. He and his brother-in-law, Etienne de Boré (the first mayor of New Orleans), earned fame for perfecting a means of granulating sugar, thus helping to turn southern Louisiana into one of the top sugarcane-farming regions in North America. De Boré owned a plantation several miles downriver, in what is now the Audubon Park section of New Orleans. Details still visible in this rambling structure include hand-hewn cypress timbers and the distinctive hipped roof typical of West Indies architecture. The house is just 25 miles west of New Orleans and a mere 10-minute drive from New Orleans International Airport, making it popular with visitors who don't have time to explore the entire River Road but would still like to see a grand Louisiana plantation.

GRAMERCY

San Francisco Plantation (2646 River Rd., Garyville, 985/535-2341 or 888/322-1756, www.sanfranciscoplantation.org, open 10 A.M.–4 P.M. daily, admission $10) sits on the east bank of the river, about 25 miles upriver from Destrehan. The house was constructed by Edmond Bozonier Marmillion in 1856, and it's considered the only plantation on River Road that has been authentically restored to its original appearance. The exquisite hand-painted ceilings in five rooms are an important detail, but also note the extensive faux marbling, and the fine antiques made by Mallard and John Henry Belter.

VACHERIE

Vacherie has two of the most prominent plantations open to the public in the South, Oak Alley and Laura.

⟨ Oak Alley Plantation

Oak Alley Plantation (3645 Hwy. 18, Vacherie, 225/265-2151 or 800/442-5539, www. oakalleyplantation.com, open 9 A.M.–5 P.M. daily, admission $10) is about 15 miles upriver, and across the river (take the bridge from Gramercy), from San Francisco Plantation. One of the best photo ops in the South, this incredible alley includes 28 live oak trees, planted in two rows bordering the front walk. Dating from about 300 years ago, these trees have been here much longer than the present mansion, which is beautiful but certainly wouldn't stand out as it does today without the graceful, arching trees framing it. An early French settler, clearly with some aristocratic aspirations, planted the oaks in the early 1700s to lead from the river down a path to his rather modest house. More than 100 years later, the property's owner, Jacques Telesphore Roman, used his considerable sugarcane fortune to construct the present Oak Alley mansion. The entire property now comprises about 25 acres; much of the original plantation, which had been well larger than 1,000 acres, is now undeveloped forest, but about 600 acres is still leased to sugarcane farmers.

As you approach the property, you'll pass the rather modest front gate that marks the beginning of the alley of oaks; you can't enter the property here, as the actual driveway for automobiles lies a short distance farther down the road (just follow the signs). But you can park your car along the dirt driveway leading up and over the Mississippi River levee and walk up to the gate to snap a picture and admire the trees and the house in the distance. If you walk up the short dirt drive to the top of the levee, you get a very nice view of the river—there's often a tanker or freighter chugging along, contributing to that peculiar contrast between modern industry and 19th-century plantation living that characterizes the whole region. Once you drive onto the grounds, you buy your tickets at a booth and proceed to the Big House, as the mansion is called, for a guided tour. The tours themselves are fairly straightforward and not overly exciting, unless you happen to get

an especially colorful guide. But after the tour you can spend as much time as you care to exploring the grounds and relaxing amid the oaks, crape myrtles, and azaleas, or admiring the peacocks and friendly bobtail cats wandering about the property.

The plantation has been in several movies, including *Primary Colors,* where it served as the home of Larry Hagman's would-be presidential candidate; at the front gate, before the alley of oaks, the characters of Governor Jack Stanton (John Travolta) and Henry Burton (Adrian Lester) meet with Hagman's Governor Fred Picker. The plantation was also featured prominently in the film of Anne Rice's *Interview with the Vampire* in 1994, starring Tom Cruise and Brad Pitt; in the 1995 Julia Roberts vehicle *Something to Talk About;* and in the 1985 made-for-TV adaptation of William Faulkner's *The Long Hot Summer.* Oak Alley has a popular breakfast/lunch cafe and bed-and-breakfast, and RVs may park on the ground overnight for $10; there are no hookups or campground services and facilities, however, so RVs must be entirely self-contained.

⟨ Laura: A Creole Plantantion

Just downriver from Oak Alley you can embark on one of the most unusual plantation-tour experiences in the country, Laura: A Creole Plantation (2247 Hwy. 18, Vacherie, 225/265-7690, www.lauraplantation.com, open 9 A.M.–5 P.M. daily, admission $10), which differs from most of the others along River Road in a couple of ways. First, it has a fascinating legacy, as its slave cabins were where the folktales known as *Br'er Rabbit* were recorded in the late 1870s. A young man named Alcée Fortier, who lived near Laura, took a great interest in the stories recounted by former slaves living on the plantation, and he set about writing down the tales exactly as he heard them here on the plantation. Fortier went on to become a professor at Louisiana State University, where he published the collection of stories under the title *Louisiana Folktales.* His friend Joel Chandler Harris then published the considerably more famous *Tales of Uncle Remus,* based on his interviews with slaves in the Carolinas and Georgia. The stories came to be known as the *Br'er Rabbit* tales because one of the two main characters in Fortier's and Harris's collections was Lapin (French for "rabbit").

But maybe the most interesting thing about a visit to Laura is that tour guides base their one-hour talk on the memoirs—which total about 5,000 pages—of the four generations of women who oversaw the compound's inner workings; it's a condensation of the fascinating life of the Creole women who ran the plantation, along with intimate and telling details about their children and extended family and their slaves. The memoirs were compiled in the 1930s by Laura Locoul Gore, who grew up on the plantation and represents the final generation of women at Laura. The tour of Laura offers a provocative and colorful look into the high and low points of Creole life in the early 19th century. At most of the other plantations in this area, tours discuss the original owners, the architecture of the house, and its basic history, but these tours often are based on general second- and third-hand information, and they rarely discuss the lives of the slaves and the day-to-day, firsthand observations of the plantation's occupants.

Another difference at Laura is the plantation house itself, which is not one of the typical glowing white Greek Revival mansions found in this region, but rather a relatively modest though still large raised Creole house that has been, intentionally, only partly restored in order to give guests a more realistic sense of what the house looked and felt like when it was occupied by Laura and her ancestors. The house suffered a major fire in 2004, but staff still managed to give tours the very next day, and restoration work has continued unabated. As good as this museum is, the quality of your tour varies from guide to guide, as is true at all plantations, but most of the interpreters here do a very nice job.

DONALDSONVILLE

Donaldsonville is a neat little river town with a bustling historic district and many significant commercial and residential structures, both large and small. The town has a handful of good restaurants and places to stay and makes a good base for exploring this whole region, as it's just about 60 miles upriver from New Orleans, 35 miles downriver from Baton Rouge, and within 25 miles of Oak Alley on one side and Nottoway on the other.

River Road African-American Museum

The town's latest attraction is the River Road African-American Museum (Williams and Lessard Sts., Donaldsonville, 225/474-5553, www.africanamericanmuseum.org, open 10 A.M.–5 P.M. Wed.–Sat., 1–5 P.M. Sun., admission $4), which moved here in September 2003 from a smaller building at Tezcuco Plantation, which was lost in a fire in summer 2002. (Luckily, the African-American Museum itself wasn't lost in this fire, but the grounds at Tezcuco are no longer open to the public.) At this new museum you'll find a wide variety of exhibits and collections related to the River Road's rich African American heritage. These include a monument to the many black soldiers who fought for the Union during the Civil War at Fort Butler, right in Donaldsonville, on the banks of the Mississippi (another organization, the Fort Butler Foundation, is planning to restore the site of Fort Butler and eventually turn it into a museum and national historic park). Also on display is a tribute to Leonard Julien, who in 1964 invented the sugarcane planting machine, an innovation that vastly reduced the number of men, wagons, and tractors necessary to plant a field of sugarcane. And you'll learn about Madam C. J. Walker, who became America's first female self-made millionaire by inventing a hair-care product in 1900. The museum pays tribute to the thousands of slaves who were brought to towns along the Great River Road and displays artwork, African masks, exhibits on musicians, and many other documents and photos.

Historic Donaldsonville Museum

You can learn more about the general history of the area at the Historic Donaldsonville

Museum (318 Mississippi St., Donaldsonville, 225/746-0004, www.hdm1806.org, open 9 A.M.–5 P.M. Mon.–Fri., 10 A.M.–5 P.M. Sat., and noon–5 P.M. Sun., donation suggested), which is housed within the stately Italianate Lemann Store Building. A variety of artifacts, including some from the original Lemann department store, are displayed, as well as a replica of the town's old movie theater, a re-created corner grocery store, a Civil War display, and a gallery of collectibles and keepsakes donated by local townspeople through the years.

Houmas House Plantation and Gardens

The nearest plantation to Donaldsonville is just across the river and then a few miles downriver. The setting of the Bette Davis film *Hush... Hush, Sweet Charlotte,* stunning Houmas House Plantation and Gardens (40136 Hwy. 942, River Rd., Darrow, 225/473-7841 or 888/323-8314, www.houmashouse.com, open 10 A.M.–5 P.M. Mon.–Wed., 10 A.M.–8 P.M. Thurs.–Sun.—closes an hour earlier Nov.–Jan., admission $20 for mansion and gardens, $10 for gardens and grounds only) includes a dramatic 1840 Greek Revival mansion, set on an extensive property of oak-shaded grounds. At the plantation's peak, it encompassed 20,000 acres of sugarcane crops. An Irishman named John Burnside bought it for the princely sum of $1 million in 1858 and promptly declared his immunity during the Civil War, on the grounds that he was a British subject. Union forces honored the declaration and left Burnside and his house alone during their march up the Mississippi River from New Orleans to Baton Rouge. By the end of the century, a new owner, Colonel William Porcher, increased sugarcane production to 20 million pounds per year, more than any other operation in the state. Houmas House fell gradually upon hard times during the early 20th century but the house and remaining grounds (much of the property was subdivided and sold off through time) were bought by George B. Crozat in 1940, and he set about restoring the place. Hollywood came calling in the early 1960s,

and a new owner took over in 2003, furthering the restoration efforts and helping to turn this into one of the most appealing plantation museums in the region. Houmas House employs excellent guides who offer detailed tours of the plantation house, which is filled with antiques and artwork and decorated much as it might have looked during its prime in the mid-19th century. On Thursdays through Sundays, it's possible to take one of these tours in the early evening, which is unusual as Louisiana plantations go. But even if you don't tour the house, it's worth checking out the dramatic grounds and beautifully kept gardens.

NAPOLEONVILLE

If you're not in a rush, consider making a detour to this small town on Bayou LaFourche, which you reach via either Highway 70 (if you're coming from Vacherie on Highway 18 or from the East Bank by way of the Sunshine Bridge) or down Highway 308 (if coming from downtown Donaldsonville). The draw here is **Madewood Plantation** (4250 Hwy. 308, Napoleonville, 504/369-7151 or 800/375-7151, www.madewood.com, open 10 A.M.–4:30 P.M. daily, admission $10), a 21-room Greek Revival mansion from 1846 that's most famous as a bed-and-breakfast but is also open for tours. The mansion is finely appointed, but tours are a bit less extensive than at some other plantations, so it may not be worth coming all the way here simply to see the house, unless you're considering staying overnight (highly recommended) or you happen to be passing through the area, perhaps en route between Thibodaux and Donaldsonville.

WHITE CASTLE

Famous because it's the largest plantation home in the South, the 65-room **Nottoway Plantation** (30970 Hwy. 405, White Castle, 225/545-2730 or 866/668-6929, www.nottoway.com, open 9 A.M.–5 P.M. daily, admission $10) is one truly immense Greek Revival mansion, with an interior of about 53,000 square feet. John H. Randolph built this wedding cake of a house in 1859, where it acted as the centerpiece of a 7,000-acre sugarcane plantation. A favorite of tour groups, Nottoway is also heavily in the business of events and weddings; it functions as a small hotel, with 15 rooms, and has a popular restaurant. It's a marvel, but you probably won't come away with the same intimate sense of the place as you might at Laura or one of the smaller and lower-key properties in the region. Nottoway lies about 12 miles upriver from Donaldsonville, on the same side of the river.

SHOPPING

In La Place, **Jacob's World-Famous Andouille** (505 W. Airline Hwy., La Place, 985/652-9080 or 877/215-7589, www.cajunsausage.com) is the original source for this Louisiana treat. You can stop inside the shop, which has been going strong since the 1920s, or buy smoked meats and other gourmet ingredients via the Internet or mail-order.

Just off I-10 in Gonzales, a suburb between New Orleans and Baton Rouge that's just 10 miles north of Donaldsonville and close to a cluster of chain hotels and restaurants, **Tanger Outlet Center** (Hwy. 30 at I-10, Gonzalez, 225/647-9383 or 800/406-2112, www.tangeroutlet.com) is a favorite diversion for shopaholics. Among the scores of chain outposts here are Bass, Gap, Guess?, Jockey, Jones New York, Levi's, Liz Claiborne, Samsonite, Nine West, Farberware, and Mikasa.

FESTIVALS AND EVENTS

Aside from its tourist following, this area is strung with villages and towns with low populations, and big gatherings and festivals are few and far between. Some of the plantations have annual events, such as Oak Alley's **Spring Arts and Crafts Festival** in late March, and Laura Plantation's **Br'er Rabbit Folk Festival** in October. A few towns have rather modest Mardi Gras parades, including Lutcher and Gramercy. Donaldsonville hosts the **Sunshine Festival** (225/473-4814) each November, a country fair with live bands, local foods, a "kiddie land" with rides, and arts and crafts. Christmas is one of the best times to explore the River Road,

as on many evenings towns along the river hold **Christmas Bonfire** parties throughout December, during which participants enjoy food and music as they build huge piles of wood. By Christmas Eve, the more than 100 bonfires constructed along the river are set ablaze. Check the website www.festivalofthebonfires.org for details. Oak Alley also joins in the fun with its own Christmas bonfires twice in early December. The bonfires are a longtime Louisiana tradition along the river. Some say the tradition was begun as a way to welcome the Cajun version of Santa Claus, PaPa Noel, while others suggest that the fires were lit to help travelers along the river on Christmas Eve make their way to midnight Mass.

ACCOMMODATIONS

There aren't a tremendous number of lodging options along the Plantation Country section of the Great River Road. If you prefer the anonymity and value of a modern hotel, your only centrally situated choices are in the towns of Gonzales, just off I-10, and Donaldsonville, a bit farther south. But you can stay on the premises of some of the historic plantations, and at Nottoway and Madewood, you can actually book a room inside the main house.

Hotels and Motels

$50-100: Just on the west bank of the river near the Sunshine Bridge, Donaldsonville's **Best Western Plantation Inn** (2179 Hwy. 70, Donaldsonville, 225/746-9050 or 800/528-1234, www.bestwestern.com) is a modern and appealing base with clean and attractive rooms with colonial-inspired furnishings. The setting off Highway 70 is unremarkable but inoffensive. The 62 rooms have microwaves, refrigerators, and hair dryers, and continental breakfast is included. There are also a pool and guest laundry.

Convenient to I-10, about midway between Baton Rouge and New Orleans, the **Holiday Inn Gonzales** (1500 Hwy. 30, Gonzales, 225/647-8000 or 800/946-5432, www.holiday-inn.com) is also very accessible to the plantations on River Road—about 20 miles from Oak Alley, and just 10 from Donaldson-ville. There are 171 rooms, plus a fitness center and pool; continental breakfast is included. A branch of the excellent local seafood chain Mike Anderson's is on premises.

Inns and Bed-and-Breakfasts

$100-150: There are five comfortable guest units in turn-of-the-20th-century cottages on the grounds of **Oak Alley Plantation** (3645 Hwy. 18, Vacherie, 225/265-2151 or 800/442-5539, www.oakalleyplantation.com). Don't be put off by the simple white exteriors of these attractive but plain cottages; the richly furnished, antiques-filled interiors capture the warmth and history of plantation living on the River Road, and some units have full kitchens. A full country breakfast is included. Oak Alley also operates a neighboring property, the former Bay Tree Plantation B&B, which has rooms in two buildings and a separate and quite luxurious cottage; all have private baths, some with whirlpool tubs. The rooms do not have phones or TVs.

One of the most charming places to stay in the area, ◖ **Bittersweet Plantation** (404 Claiborne Ave., Donaldsonville, 225/473-1232, www.jfolse.com) offers five luxury suites with such creature comforts as CD players and VCRs; a refrigerator and mini-bar stocked (no extra charge) with red and white wine, soft drinks, and other goodies, and in some cases the rooms have working fireplaces and whirlpool tubs. The inn is run by famed Louisiana chef John Folse, and you can bet that breakfasts here are a highlight of an overnight stay. Also, dinners for guests can be arranged by reservation.

$150-250: ◖ **Nottoway Plantation** (Hwy. 1, Whitecastle, 225/545-2730 or 866/527-6884, www.nottoway.com), the largest plantation house in the South, has 15 guest rooms set among the main house, the boys' wing, and the overseer's cottage. If it's a special occasion, you might consider booking the Master Bedroom Suite, which contains the original bedroom furnishings of the house's builder and first owner, John Hampton Ran-

dolph. There are two other large and beautiful suites, including the Bridal, which has three rooms, a whirlpool tub, and a private pool; and the Randolph, an airy third-floor room with clear views over the Mississippi. The catch with the Randolph and the Master Bedroom Suite are that they're open during the day for tours, meaning that you must check out by 9 A.M. and can't check in until 5 P.M. Other rooms vary from a modest and cozy room with a sleigh bed to one of the huge original bedrooms, with a fireplace and a grand mahogany four-poster double bed. A guided tour of the house along with full breakfast are included, and overnight guests may also explore the house on their own in the early evening and enjoy the oak-shaded grounds and large swimming pool.

A vintage, handsome 1890s inn in downtown Donaldsonville, **Cabahanoose** (602 Railroad Ave., Donaldsonville, 225/474-5050, www.cabahanoose.com) offers four sumptuously outfitted suites with high ceilings, separate sitting rooms, and wide-plank pine floors that date to the house's original construction. One room's decor is themed after mallard ducks and has a relaxing balcony, while another is themed after the region's sugarcane-farming industry. All of these rooms are quite large and ideal for a truly romantic retreat away from busy cities or more touristy and crowded parts of southern Louisiana. At night, you'll find brandy and chocolates in your room.

Over $250: One of the grand plantation homes that also offers overnight accommodations, ◖ **Madewood** (Hwy. 308, Napoleonville, 800/375-7151, www.madewood.com) sits along Bayou LaFource, about 20 miles from Donaldsonville and the Mississippi River. It's just 15 miles northwest of Thibodaux, making it a good base if you're planning to explore both the Great River Road and Houma's Cajun wetlands. Madewood stands out among other plantations offering overnight stays for a couple of reasons. Five of the guest rooms are set right in the mansion, and even the three in the Charlet House, an 1830s Greek Revival raised cottage, feel highly romantic if less ornate. Second, overnight accommodations here include an evening wine-and-cheese reception followed by dinner with your fellow guests at a long oak dining-room table. After this you can retreat to the parlor for coffee or a liqueur before sleeping off the huge and elaborate meal to make room for breakfast. Staying here is a social experience, insofar as meals are concerned, but also a romantic one, as the rooms are truly spectacular, with high ceilings, tall four-poster beds, long flowing drapes, Oriental rugs, and fine ceiling medallions and plaster moldings. There are no phones or TVs in the rooms of this 1846 mansion, but there is Internet access.

FOOD

You won't find a vast number of restaurants along the River Road between New Orleans and Baton Rouge, but there are a few nice options, especially around Donaldsonville. It's also a fairly short drive up to the I-10 towns of Gonzales and Sorrento to find a wide variety of chain and fast-food restaurants.

Traditional Creole and Cajun

In White Castle, the grand **Nottoway Plantation** (Hwy. 1, seven miles south of Plaquemine, White Castle, 866/527-6884, $16–25) presents fine if not especially exciting old-Louisiana cooking in its resplendent and stately dining room, called Randolph Hall. Prime rib of beef au jus, crawfish étouffée, smoked and grilled quail, and blackened crab cakes over eggplant are favorite dishes. The adjacent Randolph Parlor is a civilized place to wind down an evening, perhaps over cordials or cigars.

Cafe LaFourche (817 Bayou Rd., Donaldsonville, 225/473-7451, $11–22) is an attractive steak and seafood house in downtown Donaldsonville. It's a simple but elegant place with a black-and-white floor, a good bet for authentic and reasonably priced Cajun fare. The 16-ounce "swamp steak" (a rib eye topped with fresh seafood) is a house specialty, but don't overlook the platter of shrimp, scallops, and oysters with spicy marinara sauce over angel hair pasta, or the soft-shell crab smothered with crawfish étouffée. Fried seafood platters,

po'boys, and a very good turtle soup are also offered, and sticky pecan cheesecake ranks among the tastiest desserts.

Creative and Contemporary

The ◖ **Grapevine Market and Cafe** (211 Railroad Ave., Donaldsonville, 225/473-8463, $10–22) is a delightful little restaurant opened by the same folks who operate the legendary Cafe Des Amis in Breaux Bridge. Breakfast, lunch, and dinner are served in a cozy dining room that's filled with local artwork and has cushy lounge seating or out on a patio. It's a great spot for coffee and desserts or a full-on Cajun-style meal. Crawfish pie is a specialty here, but consider the barbecue shrimp, duck-and-andouille gumbo, drum fish stuffed with spinach and andouille, or the signature eggplant wheels, which are topped with a variety of delicious sauces, from crawfish au gratin to smothered onions and tasso ham. The white-chocolate bread pudding has drawn raves among the desserts, as has the lemon ice-box pie.

Casual Cooking

◖ **The Cabin** (Hwys. 22 and 44, Burnside, 225/473-3007, $6–17) is as much a museum of the area's Cajun culture as it is a restaurant. Walls of this former slave cabin (circa 1850), with its original cypress roof, are papered with old newspapers, as was the tradition in the 19th century. The rustic dining room is packed with interesting memorabilia, including vintage farming tools, old paintings, and furniture. There's also dining in an inviting courtyard out back. This is a great place to try blackened redfish, a Louisiana specialty that's prepared to perfection here. Also try the soft-shell crab, scampi, pork sausage, barbecue beef po'boys, and crawfish omelets.

Nobile's (2082 W. Main St., Lutcher, 225/869-8900, $7–19) offers a nice range of home-style Louisiana favorites, from country steaks to fresh shrimp—it's not fancy, but the chef uses only the freshest vegetables and ingredients. The restaurant occupies a handsome 1870s building and for more than a century provided sustenance to the many workers employed in the area's cypress industry.

Loyal fans insist that nobody prepares fresher seafood in this part of the world than **Hymel's** (8740 Hwy. 44, Convent, 225/562-9910, $8–20), a zero-ambience roadhouse where you can dive into boiled crawfish and crabs, fried shrimp and oysters, and fresh oysters on the half shell.

Quick Bites

Right by Laura Plantation, **B&C Cajun Restaurant** (2155 Hwy. 18, Vacherie, 225/265-8356, $5–12) serves some of the tastiest seafood around, including wonderful oyster po'boys, fried alligator, and seafood gumbo.

D. J.'s Pizza (Hwy. 20, Vacherie, 225/265-7600, $6–14) serves a nice range of pizzas, plus meatball po'boys, pastas, and leafy salads.

It's open only for breakfast and lunch, but the cheery restaurant at **Oak Alley Plantation** (3845 Hwy. 18, Vacherie, 225/265-2487, $5–13) serves top-notch victuals, from chicken fricassee and shrimp Creole to seafood po'boys and a tempting dessert of bread pudding with whiskey sauce. Blue Bell brand ice cream is served in Oak Alley's Plantation Cafe.

Java Joints

In La Place, a branch of the acclaimed New Orleans–based coffeehouse chain **P.J.'s** (1808B W. Airline Hwy., La Place, 985/359-7575) serves designer drinks, great sandwiches, and excellent pastries and desserts.

INFORMATION AND SERVICES
Visitor Information

For information on Gramercy, Lutcher, Vacherie, and Convent, contact **St. James Parish Tourism** (5800 Hwy. 44, Convent, 225/562-2266, www.stjamesla.com). The **Ascension Parish Tourist Commission** (6967 Hwy. 22, Sorrento, 888/775-7990, www.ascensiontourism.com) handles tourism in the towns of Gonzales, Sorrento, Darrow, and Donaldsonville. Tourism for Destrehan and Luling are handled by the **St. Charles Parish**

Department of Economic Development and Tourism (P.O. Box 302, Hahnville, 985/783-5140, www.stcharlesgov.net/departments/tourism.htm). Check in with the **Iberville Parish Tourist Commission** (23405 Church St., Plaquemine, 225/687-5190, www.ibervilleparish.com) for information on Plaquemine, Sunshine, and White Castle. There's also information on the entire River Road region available at www.takemetotheriver.com, or by calling 866/204-7782.

Tours

New Orleans Tours (4220 Howard Ave., New Orleans, 504/212-5951 or 866/596-2698, www.notours.com) is one of the largest and most reliable operators for tours from New Orleans out to the plantations. It offers a variety of half- and full-day bus excursions out to Laura, Oak Alley, and other antebellum homes along the River Road. Also excellent is **Tours by Isabelle** (P.O. Box 740972, New Orleans, LA 70174, 877/665-8687, www.toursbyisabelle.com), which is favored by many of the plantations in the region. Isabelle's plantation tours are available in several versions, tailored to how much you want to see and how much time you have to explore. This company does post-Katrina tours of New Orleans, too, along with swamp and airboat excursions.

GETTING AROUND

This is a part of the state with little or no public transportation but a very good network of roads, so plan to visit the area using a car. If you're staying in New Orleans, check with your hotel concierge or bed-and-breakfast for information on companies that offer half- or full-day tours out to some of the plantations.

To reach the lower towns along the Great River Road from New Orleans, follow I-10 west to I-310, and exit onto Highway 48 (Exit 6), which puts you right by Destrehan. From here, you can follow Highway 48 northwest along the east bank of the river, or you can cross the I-310 bridge and follow Highway 18 along the west bank. Keep in mind that River Road is not just one road—it's a combination

BONNET CARRÉ SPILLWAY

The only real break along the Great River Road levee south of Baton Rouge occurs about 25 miles upriver from New Orleans, near the small town of Norco. Here the Bonnet Carré Spillway acts as a floodgate protecting New Orleans from devastating upriver flooding. (Hurricane Katrina damaged the levees inside New Orleans and did not cause flooding upriver, so Bonnet Carré Spillway did not play much of a role in that particular storm.) The Mississippi River actually sits at a higher elevation than the land around it, including New Orleans and Lake Pontchartrain. The Bonnet Carré Spillway is situated at a point where the river passes close to Lake Pontchartrain, just under six miles from its southwestern shore. The spillway connects to a floodplain of about 8,000 acres, which is crossed by I-10, U.S. Highway 61, and rail tracks, all of which are elevated on stilts. If the river gets too high, the floodgates at the spillway can be opened to divert water from the river across the floodplain and into Lake Pontchartrain, sparing New Orleans and other cities downriver. Except during times of flooding, when the gates are partially or entirely opened, you can drive across the paved road that runs across the floodplain, parallel to the spillway.

The floodplain over which water is diverted to Lake Pontchartrain was chosen not only because it was a short distance between the lake and the river, but because it had already been compromised four times by major floods along the river. The Bonnet Carré Spillway was built after one of the worst floods in the state's history, a 1927 wash that rendered the levee useless. Work on the $14 million project commenced in 1929 and was completed 2.5 years later.

Operated by the Corps of Engineers, the spillway is opened when either the river flow or the height of the river is severe enough that it stresses the levee system. This can happen even when the floodwaters have not risen very far. If waters rise even to a moderate flood stage for a prolonged period, they can saturate the earthen levees, which may begin to erode. Thus far, the spillway has been opened nine times, in 1937, 1945, 1950, 1973, 1975, 1979, 1983, and 1997.

Bonnet Carré isn't the only major structure of its kind in Louisiana; well upriver from Baton Rouge, near the town of Morganza, the Morganza Floodway can be opened to divert water across a floodplain and into the Atchafalaya Swamp basin.

---

of numbered highways that run alongside both banks of the Mississippi River. So as you drive along, it's best to have a map with you and to stick with the roads that hug the river, not just to a particular route number.

Along the west bank, Highway 18 is the River Road for many miles, as far as Donaldsonville, but north of that, the river's west bank is traced by Highway 405 and Highway 988 up to Port Allen, opposite Baton Rouge. Along the east bank from Destrehan, the river is traced by Highway 48, then Spillway Road across the Bonnet Carré Spillway (which can be closed because of high water and flooding, in which case traffic is detoured along the interior to U.S. Highway 61 (Airline Highway), and then along Highways 628, 636, 44, 942, 75, 141,

75 again, and then 991 clear to Baton Rouge. Several bridges and ferries connect roads on either bank of the river between Baton Rouge and New Orleans, making it very easy to get back and forth.

The highlights of the River Road are mostly in St. James and Ascension parishes, which are about midway between New Orleans and Baton Rouge. If you're planning to spend most of your time in this area, around Donaldsonville and Vacherie, it's quickest to drive up I-10 for 50 miles to Exit 182 (Sorrento), and then follow Highway 22 for 10 miles down to Donaldsonville, or follow Highway 70 (off Highway 22) seven miles over the Sunshine Bridge to Hwy. 18, which leads another 15 miles to Vacherie. From the Highway 22 exit off I-10, it's about 30 miles to Baton Rouge, and 85 to Lafayette.

One thing to keep in mind about Highway 22, on the chance that you're also planning to spend time in the New Orleans North Shore area, near Hammond and Mandeville, is that you can take this winding country highway all the way from Donaldsonville through Sorrento (rather than hopping onto I-10) and through the Amite River area up to the antiques mecca of Ponchatoula, and eventually to Mandeville. It's a scenic, twisting drive past bayous and river homes, and it's a nice alternative to the interstates. Total mileage from Donaldsonville to Ponchatoula via Highway 22 is 50 miles, and the drive takes about 90 minutes. You'd save about 15 minutes if you went by way of I-10 to I-55, but that drive is 65 miles and much less interesting. (See the *Essentials* chapter for details on reaching New Orleans and Baton Rouge from other parts of the country by train, plane, and bus.)

Baton Rouge

The city's state capital, Baton Rouge makes a great base for exploring the entire length of the Great River Road within Louisiana, but it also has a number of worthwhile attractions in its own right. The city also has dozens of chain hotels and motels, plus a wide range of restaurants; it's an affordable place to stay, but its accommodations generally lack character.

Unfortunately, there aren't too many back ways to drive from New Orleans to Baton Rouge—you can take the old Airline Highway (U.S. Highway 61), but most of the stretch is commercially robust, with numerous traffic lights and no real sense of the towns you pass through. You can also bypass the I-10/U.S. Highway 61 corridor and slip up along the Great River Road (described under *Getting Around* in the *Plantation Country* section), but this really only makes sense if you give yourself a full day or even an overnight stop and explore some of the plantations and related diversions. Without stops, the drive from Baton Rouge to New Orleans along the River Road takes several hours—and just imagine that before Huey Long rammed through the Airline Highway, this was the only road between the two cities.

Baton Rouge is more of the typical new Southern city than New Orleans is. It sprawls in virtually every direction, not necessarily unpleasantly. Many of the older, outlying residential neighborhoods are quite charming to drive through, and in general, Baton Rouge feels clean, prosperous, but perhaps lacking a distinct identity all its own. It's a political city and a collegiate city, and government and education provide its personality more than the streets, buildings, and topography. But you'll find a few of Louisiana's most enriching and engaging attractions in Baton Rouge: The Capitol, the Rural Life Museum, the Old State Capitol, and U.S.S. *Kidd* are first-rate, well worth planning an overnight here. If you have time only to pass through the city en route elsewhere, it is possible to see these four attractions in a half day.

SIGHTS
Old State Capitol

Once the seat of the state government, the Old State Capitol (100 North Blvd., Baton Rouge, 225/342-0500 or 800/488-2968, www.sos. louisiana.gov/museums, open 10 A.M.–4 P.M. Tues.–Sat., noon–4 P.M. Sun., admission $4) was constructed in 1850 and is one of the state's few prominent examples of large-scale Gothic architecture. Inside you'll find a vast and wonderfully presented warren of interactive and multimedia exhibits on a wide variety of topics, including Huey Long's assassination, the history of elections and campaigns in Louisiana, the Louisiana Purchase, citizenship and voting, and state history. It's the sort of museum that's as enjoyable for kids as

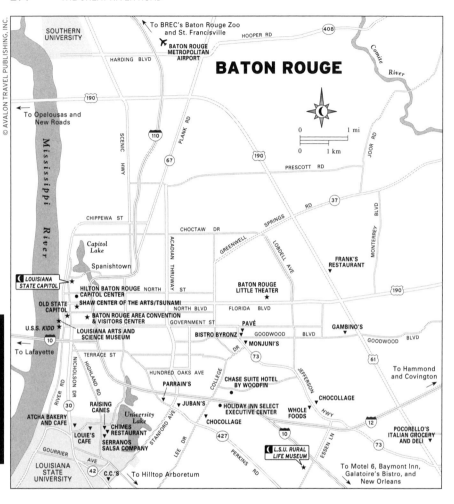

for adults, and the variety of documents, artifacts, collectibles, and curios displayed here is impressive.

U.S.S. *Kidd*

The U.S.S. *Kidd* (Government St. and S. River Rd., Baton Rouge, 225/342-1942, www.usskidd.com, open 9 A.M.–5 P.M. daily, admission $7) is the only ship anywhere on exhibit that's still in its wartime camouflage paint. This World War II–era Fletcher-class destroyer was awarded 12 battle stars for serving during World War II and the Korean War; it was struck by a Japanese kamikaze plane during the World War II Battle of Okinawa— an attack that killed 38 members of the *Kidd*'s crew. It has been carefully restored and can now be toured, along with two military aircraft from past wars, an exhibit on *Old Ironsides* that includes a full-size section of the U.S.S. *Constitution*'s gun deck, and the largest model-ship collection in the South.

Louisiana Arts and Science Museum

Downtown's Louisiana Arts and Science Museum (100 S. River Rd., Baton Rouge, 225/344-5272, www.lasm.org, open 10 A.M.–4 P.M. Tues.–Fri., 10 A.M.–5 P.M. Sat., 1–5 P.M. Sun., admission $6 for galleries, or $8 for galleries plus one show in the Space Theater) occupies the city's vintage rail terminal and is geared largely toward kids. This touch-friendly museum has a Challenger Learning Center where visitors can learn about space explorations through simulated missions as well as a gallery on the culture of ancient Egypt. There are also a variety of science and art exhibits, a planetarium, and the ExxonMobil Space Theater, which shows movies on a 60-foot-high dome screen.

Shaw Center of the Arts

In the Shaw Center of the Arts (www.shaw-center.org), the **LSU Museum of Art** (100 Lafayette St., Baton Rouge, 225/346-5001, www.lsumoa.com, 10 A.M.–5 P.M. Tues.–Sat., 1–5 P.M. Sun., admission $8) contains an eclectic mix of works, from American and British paintings from the 19th and 20th centuries to Newcomb pottery to Chinese jade and antiquities. The Shaw Center also contains the LSU School of Art Gallery, the Manship Theatre, and several other arts organizations as well as two restaurants and a P.J.'s Coffeehouse.

(Louisiana State Capitol

The Louisiana State Capitol (State Capitol Dr., off N. 3rd St., Baton Rouge, 225/342-7317, www.crt.state.la.us, open 8 A.M.–4:30 P.M. daily—observation deck closes at 4 P.M., admission free), a nifty 34-story art deco wonder, was completed in January 1932 and took 14 months to build with a price tag of about $5 million (not exactly chump change in those days). It is, at 450 feet, the tallest U.S. capitol building. One of the highlights of a visit here, and a surprising number of visitors seem to overlook it, is touring the 27 acres of spectacularly landscaped gardens. You can also ride the elevator to the 27th-floor observation deck, which affords spectacular views of the countryside, and look around the

Louisiana State Capitol

entrance and the chambers (when the state legislature is not in session), and see exactly where the flamboyant governor and U.S. senator Huey P. Long was assassinated.

A historic residential neighborhood just east and south of the Capitol Building, **Spanishtown** is worth a drive or walk through to admire the 19th- and early-20th-century wood-frame houses.

North of the Capitol grounds and downtown, the river is lined with massive oil refineries, their towers lighted like newfangled Christmas trees at night—it's a striking display of lights, and although it's enormously industrial and maybe even unpleasant to look at by day, the nighttime view is almost artful.

(Louisiana State University Rural Life Museum

A fourth important attraction in Baton Rouge, the Louisiana State University Rural Life Museum (4650 Essen La., just south of I-10, Baton Rouge, 225/765-2437, http://rurallife.lsu.edu, open 8:30 A.M.–5 P.M. daily, admission $7) is a short drive southeast of downtown. This living-history museum is set on the 450-acre **Burden**

THE GREAT RIVER ROAD

Research Plantation, and it is dedicated to preserving and interpreting the lifestyles and cultures of preindustrial Louisiana. Numerous buildings and exhibits show different aspects of early Louisiana living, including a gristmill, sugarcane house and grinder, church, school-house, blacksmith shop, and outdoor oven. Inside a large barn you can examine tools and vehicles spanning more than 300 years. There are a few historic houses that reveal Louisiana's rich tradition of folk architecture, which was common in rural areas during the state's earliest years. You can also tour the extensive Windrush Gardens, a 25-acre plot of semiformal gardens abundant with winding paths, ponds, and flora found typically in 19th-century plantation gardens. Special events are held all year-round, during which docents offer demonstrations using some of the vintage farming and household equipment.

Hilltop Arboretum

Another opportunity for roaming the outdoors and enjoying Baton Rouge's generally moderate climate, the Hilltop Arboretum (11855 Highland Rd., Baton Rouge, 225/767-6916, www.lsu.edu/hilltop, open dawn–dusk daily, admission free) occupies 14 gorgeous acres on LSU's campus and is noted for one of the most extensive collections of Louisiana shrubs and trees in the state.

BREC's Baton Rouge Zoo

A favorite attraction among kids is BREC's Baton Rouge Zoo (3601 Thomas Rd., Baton Rouge, 225/775-3877, www.brzoo.org, open 9:30 A.M.–5 P.M. daily, admission $5.50), which is home to more than 1,800 animals. Highlights include the white tigers, giraffes, and elephants as well as the aquarium of Louisiana species. The Cypress Bayou Railroad carries passengers through the zoo.

ENTERTAINMENT AND EVENTS
Entertainment and Nightlife

The **Baton Rouge Little Theater** (7155 Florida Blvd., Baton Rouge, 225/924-6496, www

.brlt.org) presents musicals throughout the year. Fans of gaming can test their luck at **Casino Rouge** (1717 River Rd. N, Baton Rouge, 225/709-7777 or 800/447-6843, www.casino-rouge.com), a huge 24-hour facility with more than 1,600 slots and plenty of table games plus a handful of popular restaurants and a lounge offering live music on Friday and Saturday nights. The city's other big casino is the **Belle of Baton Rouge** (103 France St., Baton Rouge, 800/676-4847, www.belleofbatonrouge.com), which is housed inside a three-deck riverboat docked permanently on the Mississippi River.

Gino's Restaurant (4542 Bennington Ave., Baton Rouge, 225/927-7170) holds a highly regarded jazz jam on Thursday 8–11 P.M. Head to **Phil Brady's Bar** (4848 Government St., Baton Rouge, 225/927-3786) for its well-attended Thursday night blues jams.

College students and other music fans pack into the **Cadillac Cafe** (5454 Bluebonnet Rd., Baton Rouge, 225/296-0288) and the legendary **Varsity** (3353 Highland Rd., Baton Rouge, 225/383-7018) for hard-driving rock and blues.

The city's favorite gay and lesbian dance club is **Splash** (2183 Highland Rd., Baton Rouge, 225/242-9491), in a slightly dodgy neighborhood near LSU's campus. Another popular option is **George's Place** (860 St. Louis St., Baton Rouge, 225/387-9798), a lively video bar and neighborhood hangout.

Festivals and Events

On the Fourth of July, come to Baton Rouge for the **Star-Spangled Celebration at the U.S.S. Kidd,** which includes tours of the museum, an air show, live music, and fireworks over the Mississippi River.

ACCOMMODATIONS

Baton Rouge has about two dozen major chain hotels and motels, most of them set just off I-12 and I-10, on the southeast side of town.

Hotels and Motels

Under $50: Bargain hunters should go with the nicest of three **Motel 6** (I-10 at Siegen La., Baton

Rouge, 225/291-4912 or 800/466-8356, www. motel6.com) properties in the Baton Rouge area. This one is within a walk or short drive of several restaurants and shopping centers.

$50-100: In southeastern Baton Rouge, the **Baymont Inn and Suites** (10555 Rieger Rd., at I-10 and Seigen La., Baton Rouge, 225/291-6600 or 877/229-6668, www.baymontinns. com) is a reasonably priced hotel with an outdoor pool and nice-size rooms with recliner armchairs and good work spaces.

$100-150: An upscale 330-room business-oriented hotel near a cluster of shops, restaurants, and office buildings, the **Holiday Inn Select Executive Center** (4728 Constitution Ave., Baton Rouge, 225/925-2244 or 888/465-4329, www.holiday-inn.com) is well situated and has extensive amenities and facilities, including a full-service restaurant and bar, 24-hour room service, a pool and patio, and in-room coffeemakers, irons and boards, and two phones.

The **Chase Suite Hotel by Woodfin** (5522 Corporate Blvd., Baton Rouge, 225/927-5630 or 888/433-9669, www.woodfinsuitehotels. com) is an all-suite property in the same compound as a Barnes and Noble superstore and a massive cineplex. Although geared toward long-term stays, the hotel also offers special weekend packages geared toward the leisure trade. Suites have full kitchens, CD players, and TVs with VCRs, and other hotel features include a pool, continental breakfast, a sports court, and health club privileges.

Baton Rouge's most impressive property is the **◖ Hilton Baton Rouge Capitol Center** (201 Lafayette St., Baton Rouge, 225/344-5866 or 877/862-9800, www.hiltoncapitol-center.com), which opened in 2006 in the historic buildings that once housed the Heidelberg Hotel. Developers spent about $50 million creating this elegant property with 293 smartly furnished rooms, a full spa and fitness center, and a lavish restaurant, Kingfish.

FOOD

Where there are politicians, there are almost always good restaurants, and Baton Rouge con-firms this rule with its wide variety of very nice places to eat. It's also a student town, and you can find several good and relatively affordable spots for a meal around the campus of LSU.

Traditional Creole and Cajun

A branch of one of the most famous restaurants ever to delight gourmands in New Orleans, **Galatoire's Bistro** (17451 Perkins Rd., Baton Rouge, 225/753-4864, $14–32) opened in a shopping center in Baton Rouge in fall 2005, drawing mixed responses from locals and long-time fans. Some say that the opening of such a vaunted institution in as prosaic a setting as a shopping center is a form of sacrilege, but once you're inside amid the sumptuous decor, it's hard not to feel swept up by the restaurant's charms. More important, there's the incredible food, from crabmeat *sardou* (artichoke bottoms piled high with lump crabmeat and served on a bed of spinach with hollandaise sauce) to filet mignon topped with a rich béarnaise sauce. Starters such as oysters en brochette and shrimp rémoulade further delight those who have discovered the Baton Rouge Galatoire's. A final plus is that the service at the Baton Rouge branch lives up to that of the original.

Creative and Contemporary

Perhaps the most stylish restaurant in Baton Rouge, and thus a favorite of politicos and business execs, **◖ Juban's** (3739 Perkins Rd., Baton Rouge, 225/346-8422, $16–30) has been serving innovative Louisiana-influenced fare since the early 1980s, when owner-chef John Mariani's temple of fine cuisine was named one of America's "Best New Restaurants" in the pages of *Esquire.* The restaurant is known for such signature dishes as crab and angel hair pasta fried crispy over a sauce of beurre blanc, and seafood-stuffed soft-shell crab topped with Creolaise sauce and duck breast pan-seared with Louisiana fig glaze and fried plantains. Pecan-smoked salmon with capers and boursin cheese makes a nice starter.

Bistro Byronz (5412 Government St., Baton Rouge, 225/218-1433, $8–19) blends the warm ambience of a neighborhood tavern with the elegant decor of a sophisticated eatery. It's a New Orleans–style place with great food that's nonetheless eclectic and available in several price ranges. You might go for one of the sandwiches (a burger, or the classic corned beef Reuben), try the sesame-crusted tuna salad with Asian vinaigrette, or opt for something more substantial, such as chicken artichoke bake with mozzarella sauce or traditional cassoulet with white beans, tasso ham, and duck sausage confit.

Casual Cooking

Casual **Parrain's** (3225 Perkins Rd., at the foot of the I-10 exit, Baton Rouge, 225/381-9922, $12–21) serves first-rate seafood such as crab au gratin, catfish *perdu* (semiboneless fried catfish topped with crawfish étouffée), whole fried Cornish game hen with slaw and dirty rice, and crawfish po'boys. The restaurant is also home to the convivial Hammerhead Bar, which has one of the better happy hours in town.

Excellent, traditional Italian fare is the specialty of **Monjuni's** (711 Jefferson Hwy., Baton Rouge, 225/231-1595, $8–13), which is particularly renowned for its hearty pasta. Other good bets include the hefty muffuletta sandwiches, the marinated-artichoke sandwich, and the meatball "nachos" served on crisp garlic-toast rounds. The ceiling of this colorful spot is decorated like an arbor, with faux hanging grapes.

The **Chimes Restaurant** (3357 Highland Rd., Baton Rouge, 225/383-1754; also 10870 Coursey Blvd., Baton Rouge, 225/296-4981; $7–14) has a big import-beer selection, with about 120 beers from more than 60 countries. The original is near the edge of LSU campus, and a new branch opened on Baton Rouge's east side in 2006.

Ethnic

Serranos Salsa Company (north gates of LSU, 3347 Highland Rd., Baton Rouge, 225/344-2354, $8–15) presents tasty Latin American and Mexican fare. You might try Cuban-style pork *carnitas* (smoked orange-and-lime–marinated pork roast with garlic and spices), tequila-marinated lime shrimp, or fish tacos with serrano-chile cream sauce and *pico de gallo*.

Tsunami (100 Lafayette St., Baton Rouge, 225/346-5100, $8–19) at Shaw Center has great sushi; it's the same people as the branch in Lafayette. Excellent options are the Sunflower (sashimi tuna with a ponzu sauce, black *tobiko* caviar, and a quail egg), and rib-eye steak with caramelized-onion butter and a side of wasabi-mashed potatoes. The Grand Isle roll (tuna, yellowtail, and scallion) is one of the better *maki* rolls offered.

Quick Bites

A favorite place of students craving sustenance late into the evening, ◖ **Louie's Cafe** (209 W. State St., Baton Rouge, 225/346-8221, $5–11) serves delicious home-style greasy-spoon fare 24 hours a day. Breakfast hits include the seafood Louie omelet (with crawfish, veggies, spiced butter, and herbed cream cheese), pecan pancakes, huge cheeseburgers, and po'boys. Louie's has long been famous for its hash browns—try the version with sautéed mushrooms, colby cheese, and sour cream. Watching the chefs cook here is part of the fun—grab a seat at the U-shape counter and watch the line chefs prepare mounds of hash browns and other foods.

Simple and casual **Frank's Restaurant** (8353 Airline Hwy., Baton Rouge, 225/928-4575, $4–8) serves tasty breakfast fare, including house-smoked sausages, and also sells stuffed brisket, fried turkey, and other fine meats to go.

Raising Canes (3313 Highland Rd., Baton Rouge, 225/387-2662, $3–7) is a local fast-food chain that's famous for its boneless chicken breast, chicken finger sandwiches, and special sauce. A few branches are around town, but the one by LSU is the most atmospheric, and it's open late, too.

Java Joints

About a dozen branches of the Louisiana chain **CC's Coffee** (800/525-5583, www.ccscoffee.

com) are set around Baton Rouge. The one just beyond the south gates at LSU (4410 Highland Rd., Baton Rouge, 225/761-9220) is a favorite of students, has free high-speed Internet, and sometimes has live entertainment.

Picnic Supplies and Gourmet Goods

Gambino's (8646 Goodwood Blvd., Baton Rouge, 225/928-7000) is known for its huge six-layer Doberge cakes, available in chocolate, lemon, and caramel. Cookies, king cakes, biscotti, and sublime pralines are also available.

Many people in Baton Rouge say that **Pocorello's Italian Grocery and Deli** (12240 Coursey Blvd., Baton Rouge, 225/293-3737) serves the best muffulettas outside New Orleans; you can also pick up meatball-and-eggplant po'boys, stuffed artichokes, and other prepared foods and imported Italian groceries.

Middle Eastern snacks, groceries, baked goods, and other fare are served and sold at **Atcha Bakery and Cafe** (3221 Nicholson Dr., Baton Rouge, 225/383-7482).

Maybe the definitive source of gourmet chocolates in the Baton Rouge area, **Chocollage** (3056 College Dr., Village Square, Baton Rouge, 225/924-1748; also 7939 Jefferson Hwy., Baton Rouge, 225/216-2462) sells fine Belgian truffles and candies.

Head to the upscale gourmet chain **Whole Foods** (7529 Corporate Blvd., Baton Rouge, 225/218-0452) to stock up on tasty snacks for a picnic or to nosh on in your hotel room.

INFORMATION AND SERVICES

For information on Baton Rouge, contact the **Baton Rouge Area Convention and Visitors Center** (730 North Blvd., Baton Rouge, LA 70802, 225/383-1825 or 800/527-6843, www.bracvb.com); there's also a tourism information center stocked with brochures on the ground level of the Louisiana State Capitol building.

GETTING AROUND

From New Orleans, it's a straight 80-mile shot up I-10 to reach Baton Rouge; the drive takes an hour and 15 minutes. It's easiest to explore the area by car. Even in Baton Rouge, which has a somewhat compact downtown in which you can walk among a few attractions, the hotels are mostly outside of downtown to the east, off the interstate, making a car handy and public transportation impractical. (See the *Essentials* chapter for details on reaching New Orleans and Baton Rouge from other parts of the country by train, plane, and bus.)

THE GREAT RIVER ROAD

St. Francisville and Environs

Technically, it would be fair to describe St. Francisville as being the northernmost community of the Great River Road's Plantation Country, but this leafy, dignified town near the Mississippi border actually looks and feels a bit different from the other communities with plantations along the road. The terrain is hilly and studded with pine and hardwood forest, and the plantation homes here are not set along the levee but rather back a few miles on or near the region's main highway, U.S. Highway 61.

This picturesque town is also separated from the Plantation Country described in that section by Baton Rouge. The latter has dozens of chain hotels and motels, plus a wide range of restaurants, making it a good base for exploring St. Francisville and the towns in these parts if you're unable to find a room up here.

Two small communities within a short drive of St. Francisville, New Roads and Jackson, also bear exploration. If you have only one or two nights to visit this part of the River Road, focus on St. Francisville if it's Louisiana's antebellum plantations that most interest you.

ANGOLA: THE LOUISIANA STATE PENITENTIARY

About 25 miles northwest of the beauty and gentility of St. Francisville is perhaps the most notorious (at least historically) prison in the United States, Angola, which has been dubbed the "Alcatraz of the South," among many less flattering things. These days, Angola has been reformed, and its notoriety has died down, but it's still the largest state prison in the country – definitely not a place you want to spend time involuntarily.

In its effort to clean up, Angola has created the quite interesting and surprisingly forthcoming **Louisiana State Penitentiary Museum** (follow Hwy. 66 from U.S. 61, 225/655-2592, www.angolamuseum.org, open 8 A.M.-4:30 P.M. Tues.-Fri., 9 A.M.-5 P.M. Sat., donation suggested), which examines the facility's history as well as its onetime reputation as the "bloodiest prison in America."

The 18,000-acre prison sits in a bend of the Mississippi River, surrounded on three sides by water and by the gently rising Tunica Hills on the other; it's just a few miles south of the Mississippi border. Much of Angola is farmland, and inmates are required to work the fields five days a week, eight hours a day. Corn and soybeans are the main products grown here, but there are many other crops, plus a herd of cattle numbering about 1,500.

One of the best times to plan a visit is October; every Sunday of that month, the prison hosts the **Angola Rodeo** (225/655-2030, www.angolarodeo.com), which was begun in 1965 and is the longest-running prison rodeo in the country. The event takes place in a 7,500-seat stadium, and professional judges and rodeo stock are brought in – this is no amateur show. In the late 1990s, an arts-and-crafts show was added, which takes place beginning at 9 A.M. (the rodeo doesn't start until 2 P.M.) and includes a variety of wares and decorative items produced by inmates. This, like the rodeo itself, has become a phenomenally popular event. In 2001, the rodeo expanded to run on two Sundays each April as well as on the four Sundays in October.

ST. FRANCISVILLE

St. Francisville is the second-oldest incorporated town in Louisiana, although it was born out of rather inauspicious beginnings. Back in the 1730s, Spanish Capuchin monks developed a small settlement across the Mississippi River in what is now Pointe Coupee Parish (home to the town of New Roads). The monks found, however, that they could not develop a reliable burial ground on this side of the river, because its low elevation left it vulnerable to frequent floods, which washed away the cemetery. The monks began rowing the bodies of the deceased across the Mississippi and burying them on the relatively high bluffs that now form the foundation for downtown St. Francisville.

A permanent settlement was established in 1785 when the king of Spain issued land grants in an effort to settle a large area north and west of New Orleans, which came to be called the Distrito de Nueva Feliciana, part of the colony of Spanish West Florida. The small town of St. Francisville was formally laid out along the very same bluff the Capuchin monks found so useful. Below the proper town of St. Francisville, down the hill from the bluffs, a second settlement known as Bayou Sara thrived during the early 19th century, as the small bayou for which it was named provided a safe anchorage for flatboaters transporting goods down the Mississippi. Cotton and other trade made Bayou Sara the most important port on the Mississippi between Natchez and New Orleans by 1860, but the Civil War, a fire, major floods, and the onset of the railroad industry rendered Bayou Sara a virtual ghost town by the end of the 19th century.

◖ St. Francisville Historic District

St. Francisville was not affected by the misfortunes of its neighbor down the hill; rather,

Tickets to the rodeo cost $10, and proceeds go to cover expenses and also into a fund that provides for education and recreational supplies for inmates at Angola.

The museum and the rodeo notwithstanding, Angola's legacy is a grim one. The prison was run privately when it was founded in 1844, then occupied by Union troops during the Civil War, and then run privately again by a Confederate general named Samuel James from 1869 until 1900. Brutality was rampant in these years – it's reported that the average lifespan of inmates at Angola was just five years.

The state took over Angola in 1901, but medical treatment and living conditions remained poor for many years. Music played a vital role for many Angola inmates, the most famous being the blues pioneer Leadbelly, who served time here for brandishing a knife during a fight. Leadbelly's blues music was so well received that it caught the attention of record makers, who recorded his hit "Good Night Irene" here while the promising talent served his time. Leadbelly was soon freed from prison, and in the late 1930s he developed a tremendous musical reputation in New York City and later Paris.

Amazingly, for about 50 years, Angola operated with no paid guards. Instead it was staffed with so-called "trusty guards," favored inmates who were furnished with weapons and were notorious for ignoring or perpetuating prison violence. In the 1960s and early '70s, stabbings, beatings, and deadly fights were commonplace, occurring once a day on average.

Angola began its most dramatic period of reform in 1973, when it eliminated the "trusty guard" system and began changing many of its policies. It finally obtained accreditation from the American Correctional Association (ACA) in 1993. Angola's most recent claim to fame is that it incarcerated Matthew Poncelet, whose plight inspired the Susan Sarandon and Sean Penn movie *Dead Man Walking*.

THE GREAT RIVER ROAD

many of the men who earned vast riches in the Mississippi River shipping industry built fancy homes along the bluff and even farther inland. Today St. Francisville's lovely historic district contains nearly 150 structures built during the town's shipping heyday in the 19th century. Some of these houses are quite large, and the district contains a wide range of Victorian residential styles. It's an easy neighborhood for a walk, flat and with little street traffic. Among the buildings preserved here are three of the state's most beautiful churches, the **Our Lady of Mt. Carmel Roman Catholic Church** (on the west end of the district, just off Ferdinand St.), which was completed in 1893 according to a design by Civil War Confederate general P. G. T. Beauregard; the **Grace Episcopal Church** (farther east along Ferdinand), which was built in the Gothic style in 1858; and the **United Methodist Church** (Royal and Fidelity streets), a stately 1899 structure.

Many of the houses in this district have magnolia and other flowering trees lining the sidewalks and perimeters of their yards, or ornate iron fences. These aren't all mansions, as a number of charming smaller cottages are mixed in with the larger homes. It's truly one of the prettiest neighborhoods to stroll through in Louisiana. Down the hill from the district you can see what remains of Bayou Sara, including a handful of modest cottages and shotgun houses and a 19th-century rail station and warehouse that now house a deli and gift shop.

Along the main drag, Ferdinand Street, you'll find a number of antiques shops, as well as the **West Feliciana Historical Society** (11757 Ferdinand St., St. Francisville, 225/635-6330), which doubles as the tourist information center for West Feliciana Parish. Inside you can pick up brochures and examine historic photos, documents, and memorabilia that tell the story of St. Francisville and Bayou Sara. Among the antiques shops in the area, try not to miss the **Audubon Antique Gallery** (7143 U.S. 61, at Hwy. 10, St. Francisville, 225/635-3977), a large multidealer emporium with an outstanding selection of regional furnishings and accessories from the 19th and early 20th centuries.

◖ Rosedown Plantation State Historic Site

St. Francisville has a handful of plantation homes open to the public for tours, the most famous and prominent being Rosedown Plantation State Historic Site (12501 Hwy. 10, St. Francisville, 225/635-3332 or 888/376-1867, www.lastateparks.com, open 9 A.M.–5 P.M. daily with the final tour at 4 P.M., admission with house tour $10), on the east side of downtown, right off U.S. Highway 61. Built by one of the nation's wealthiest men of his day, Daniel Turnball, this neoclassical columned manor house was constructed in 1834 as the centerpiece of a massive cotton plantation that at one time totaled nearly 3,500 acres and required the labor of 450 slaves. Turnball furnished his palace with the finest furnishings from Europe, the East Coast, and New Orleans. He also laid out, through time, about 30 acres of formal gardens.

Rosedown remained in the Turnball family for a remarkably long period by Louisiana plantation standards, until 1956, despite the fact that the family lived in near-poverty after the Civil War, leasing much of the land to sharecroppers. Descendants of Turnball lived in the second-floor quarters of the house even after opening the plantation to visitors for touring beginning in the 1930s. The remaining heirs sold the house upon the death of Turnball's last direct descendant, Nina Turnball, in 1956, and the new owner, Catherine Fondren Underwood, set about restoring the home as near to its original appearance as possible. The plantation now encompasses 371 acres and includes the mansion as well as several outbuildings. State park staff and volunteers give guided tours.

Myrtles Plantation

One of the more colorful attractions in town is Myrtles Plantation (7747 U.S. 61, St. Francisville, 225/635-6277 or 800/809-0565, www.myrtlesplantation.com, open 9 A.M.–5 P.M. daily, call for information on evening mystery tours, admission $10), which bills itself as being among the most haunted houses in the United States. It's also operated as a bed-and-breakfast, so if you're curious about ghosts, here's your chance to spend the night among, as legend has it, several of them. Apart from this considerable lure, the 1796 house is notable for its hand-painted stained glass, Aubusson tapestry, Baccarat crystal chandeliers, Carrara marble mantels, and gilt-leaf French furnishings. Little expense seems to have been spared in its construction. Engaging historical tours that touch on the house and its grounds are given during the day, but the considerably more colorful Mystery tours given many evenings are the real draw.

Cat Island National Wildlife Refuge

St. Francisville's leading attractions aren't all man-made. Cat Island National Wildlife Refuge (401 Island Rd., off Ferdinand St. in the Bayou Sara section of St. Francisville, 225/635-4753, www.fws.gov/catisland, open dawn–dusk daily, admission free), which was established in fall 2000, is a favorite haunt of hikers, wildlife photographers, fishing enthusiasts, and others who appreciate being out in the wilderness. The 10,000-acre expanse of forested wetlands sits along the southernmost unleveed span of the Mississippi River, and most years it floods completely, usually between December and June. Vehicles are prohibited on refuge roads during periods of flood. The refuge's greatest resource is its wildlife, from black bears and white-tailed deer to bobcats and river otters. Fish commonly caught in the preserve's waters include largemouth bass, bream, and catfish.

Port Hudson State Commemorative Area

Technically in Jackson but actually close to

downtown St. Francisville, which is about 10 miles north, Port Hudson State Commemorative Area (236 U.S. 61, Jackson, 225/654-3775 or 888/677-3400, www.lastateparks.com, open 9 A.M.–5 P.M. daily, admission $2 per person) was built in memory of what's been dubbed the "longest true siege in American military history." During the Civil War, in response to a Union effort to control the Mississippi River and thereby split the Confederacy into two distinct geographic halves, Confederate forces built a military fortification on the river bluffs at the tiny town of Port Hudson. On May 27, 1863, the Union army, with 30,000 troops and fresh from victory in Baton Rouge, began a fierce attack on the 4.5-mile string of earthwork fortifications manned by 6,800 Confederates. The South managed to hold its ground for an amazing 48 bloody and tragic days of fighting that saw casualties in the thousands on both sides. Upriver, however, the city of Vicksburg fell to Union hands, so Confederate commander Franklin Gardner, realizing the defense of Port Hudson was now a moot point, negotiated a surrender, thus ending the siege.

Today at Port Hudson there's an extensive state park preserving the original fortifications and interpreting the battle in a museum. Living-history events and war reenactments are held throughout the year. Other features include six miles of trails.

NEW ROADS

To reach New Roads from St. Francisville, you head west on Ferdinand Street about a mile past Our Lady of Mt. Carmel church to the ferry landing at the end of the road (clearly marked signs point the way). Take the ferry, which runs frequently from early morning until midnight and costs $1 westbound (the direction you travel to get to New Roads); the ride is free eastbound.

New Roads is a small, dapper village that looks like a classic Mississippi River town, except for one thing: It's not on the Mississippi. The long, curving body of water on which the town is situated is the False River, which was formed when a sharp S-shape bend in the Mis-

sissippi River, which essentially doubled back on itself, was breached when the river took a more direct course. The remaining 22-mile curve, now cut off from the river, became what's called an oxbow lake. New Roads sits along the False River's west bank, and many stately Creole-style houses and commercial buildings in town overlook the water, which is popular for boating and swimming. Because it's not a flowing industrial river constantly muddied from silt and soil on the river bottom, the False River is an appealing shade of blue.

In New Roads's scenic little downtown you'll find a smattering of shops and eateries, notably some excellent antiques shops, all along a quite walkable little strip on Main Street. There are no formal museums in town, but you can obtain a free self-guided walking/driving tour from the Pointe Coupee Parish Chamber of Commerce.

JACKSON

After exploring St. Francisville and New Roads, if you have time, consider making the enjoyable side trip east to Jackson from St. Francisville via Highway 10 (a distance of about 12 miles). There are a few historic sites and antiques shops you can look at in Jackson, a bump of a village that has a frozen-in-time feel and some interesting old buildings (including a town hall crowned by an onion dome).

Up a block from Main Street is the **Republic of West Florida Historic Association Museum** (College and High Sts., Jackson, 225/634-7155, http://atos.stirlingprop.com/jackson, open 10 A.M.–5 P.M. Tues.–Sun., donation suggested), which includes an old cotton gin, a working railroad, military aircraft, scientific and musical artifacts, and several outbuildings containing a variety of history-related exhibits; it flies the several different flags that have flown over this community through the years.

Just up from the museum on the right is the sprawling and quite grand **Centenary State Historic Site and Historic College** (3522 College St., Jackson, 225/634-7925 or 888/677-2364, www.lastateparks.com, open

9 A.M.–5 P.M. daily, admission $2 per person), a pine-shaded campus of what opened in 1826 as the College of Louisiana. It closed 20 years later because of declining enrollment, at which time the Methodist/Episcopal-operated Centenary College of Brandon Springs took over the gracious campus and buildings. During the Civil War, the college closed, and the buildings were used first by Confederate and then by Union troops. Centenary reopened after the war but suffered low enrollment and finally moved to Shreveport, where it remains today, in 1908. Sadly, the Main Academic Building and the East Wing were demolished in the 1930s, so today all you can visit is the school's redbrick Greek Revival West Wing.

As you leave town, head back on Highway 10, but just a mile out of town, after the road crosses over a bayou, make a left onto Highway 965, at the sign pointing toward Audubon State Historic Site. Follow this road for several miles beneath a dense canopy of oak and pine trees, by a few private plantation homes. You can pause along the way for a visit at **Audubon State Historic Site** (Hwy. 965, Jackson, 225/635-3739 or 888/677-1400, www.lastateparks.com, open 7 A.M.–9 P.M. daily, admission $2 per person), which you reach about five miles after you turn onto Highway 965. In this dense, junglelike 100-acre park you'll find good hiking trails through the magnolia and poplar trees, as well as the 1806 Oakley House, a distinctive West Indies–style colonial house where famed wildlife painter James J. Audubon lived briefly in 1821; records indicate that he worked on at least 32 of his wildlife paintings while living in the house. Other facilities include a picnic shelter and several outbuildings from the original plantation. Guided tours of the house are given throughout the day.

About two miles west of Audubon State Historic Site, you come to U.S. Highway 61, onto which a right turn takes you back up 1.5 miles to St. Francisville. The entire loop, depending on how long you stop at the museums, can be done in an hour or a few hours.

FESTIVALS AND EVENTS
In Jackson, the **Pecan Ridge Bluegrass Festival** (225/629-5852) is held in May, July, and September and draws top musicians in this genre. Come to St. Francisville in mid-March for the **Audubon Pilgrimage** (225/635-6330, www.audubonpilgrimage.info), a chance to celebrate and explore the life of painter John James Audubon. There are historic tours and a wine-and-cheese festival. The famed **Angola Prison Rodeo** (225/655-2607, www.angolarodeo.com) takes place in late April.

ACCOMMODATIONS
In St. Francisville and New Roads, you'll find a nice range of inns and B&Bs, some quite simple but a number of them luxurious and somewhat pricey.

Hotels and Motels
Under $50: The **Best Western St. Francisville** (U.S. 61 at Hwy. 10, St. Francisville, 225/635-3821 or 800/826-9931, www.bestwestern.com) may be a modern chain hotel, but it's warm and inviting nonetheless. It lies just outside the historic district on U.S. Highway 61, on a large well-manicured property set well off the road and overlooking a five-acre lake. Amenities include a pool and in-room coffeemakers, irons and boards, and voice mail.

Inns and Bed-and-Breakfasts
$50-100: St. **Francisville Inn and Restaurant** (5720 Commerce St., St. Francisville, 225/635-6502 or 800/488-6502, www.stfrancisvilleinn.com) looks like a cover of *Southern Living,* complete with a front yard shaded by towering moss-draped live oaks. But for its location next to a convenience store and across from a Dollar General discount shop and a Ford dealer, you'd swear it's the late 19th century as you stand on the grounds. The rambling Victorian house dates to the late 1870s. Next door is Parker Memorial Park, and the gracious homes of the historic district are within walking distance. Rooms are simply furnished but pleasant and well priced;

all have private baths, cable TV, Wi-Fi, and phones, and one has a whirlpool tub. A full buffet breakfast is included. A popular restaurant is also on-site.

$100-150: The **Barrow House Inn** (9779 Royal St., St. Francisville, 225/635-4791, www. topteninn.com) comprises a pair of houses, one from the late 1700s and the other from around 1810. Among the two buildings, which are in the heart of St. Francisville's historic district, are several rooms and suites, each decorated with 1840s–1870s antiques. Fluffy four-poster canopy beds, darkwood armoires, and Oriental rugs are among the furnishings. In one house, a sun room contains a collection of 21 first-edition Audubon prints. Breakfast is served on fine china with silver flatware—you're given a choice of continental or one of three full New Orleans–style breakfasts.

In Jackson, a short drive east of St. Francisville, the dignified **Old Centenary Inn** (Hwy. 10, Jackson, 225/634-5050, www.oldcentenary inn.com) is a luxurious 1935 Colonial Revival inn with eight antiques-filled rooms, each with phone, TV, and VCR, and a private bath with two-person whirlpool tub. A full breakfast is included. It's a great value, in part because Jackson is less touristy than St. Francisville. The same owners operate a smaller four-bedroom Greek Revival inn called **Millbank** (3045 Millbank St., Jackson, 225/634-5901, www. oldcentenaryinn.com), which also has a restaurant on-site.

$150-250: For the chance to stay in what many believe to be the most haunted house in Louisiana, book a room at 【 **Myrtles Plantation** (7747 U.S. 61, St. Francisville, 225/635-6277 or 800/809-0565, www.myrtles-plantation.com), one of the most popular touring plantations in the St. Francisville area. The ornately furnished 1796 main house contains six handsome and expansive rooms and suites. The General David Bradford Suite has two adjoining verandas and a huge four-poster bed; it's among the most luxurious of the accommodations. Less pricey is the old caretaker's cottage, which has its own porch, and the four garden rooms, each with an antique Chippen-

dale claw-foot tub, in outbuildings behind the main house. Myrtles Plantations also has a fine full-service restaurant, the Carriage House.

FOOD

This entire area is full of good dining options. The emphasis is less on Creole and Cajun fare and more on both creative and traditional Southern and continental cooking, but you'll find a healthy variety of classic Louisiana ingredients on most of these menus.

Traditional Creole and Cajun

Morel's Restaurant (210 Morrison Pkwy., New Roads, 225/638-4057, $12–22) serves a mix of traditional Creole and continental dishes, such as grilled catfish *piperade,* served on steamed rice and finished with a Creole sauce and sautéed bell peppers. The shrimp rémoulade on fried eggplant is a typically tantalizing appetizer.

Built on the False River as the parish's first automobile dealership in 1917, 【 **Satterfield's Riverwalk** (108 E. Main St., New Roads, 225/638-5027, $8–20) is today one of the region's most reliable and popular places for well-prepared Creole and Italian fare. There's seating on a deck overlooking the river at black wrought-iron chairs and tables, and in an elegant but casual dining room with tall windows affording great views. House specialties include fillet of beef topped with a crawfish-tarragon-cream sauce, grilled catfish with fresh homegrown vegetables, and trout amandine. Lighter salads and sandwiches are also available.

Creative and Contemporary

Northeast of Baton Rouge, and east of St. Francisville and Jackson, it's worth making the drive to the **Front Porch Restaurant and Bar** (9173 Hwy. 67 S, Clinton, 225/683-3030, $13–22) to sample some of the area's best and creative cooking. Try wood-grilled tuna topped with Key lime butter, roasted chicken with a roast-garlic and mushroom sauce, and broiled mushrooms stuffed with crab and shrimp and topped with buttered rum.

Casual Cooking

Ma Mama's (124 W. Main St., New Roads, 225/618-2424, $8–17) is a great spot for home-style Italy-meets-Louisiana cooking, such as soft-shell crab bites or crawfish balls to start, perhaps followed by parmesan shrimp pasta, baked spinach lasagna, pork chops, or a rib-eye steak. The restaurant occupies a dapper historic building in the center of town.

As you pull into Jackson on Highway 10 from St. Francisville, note **Bobby's Drive-In Restaurant** (1427 Charter St., Jackson, 225/634-7190, $4–9), a great place to get your fix of fried chicken, curly fries, oyster po'boys, dirty rice, and barbecued ribs. You can eat in your car or in the very modest dining room with green-and-white–checked plastic tablecloths, linoleum floors, and a few stuffed and mounted animals. It ain't fancy.

Quick Bites

Pick up a barbecue-brisket po'boy, sausage sandwich, plate of boudin bites, or a combo plate at **Road Side BBQ and Grill** (4641 Main St., Zachary, 225/635-9696, $4–10); Zachary is a bit north of Baton Rouge.

 Magnolia Cafe (5689 Commerce St., St. Francisville, 225/635-6528, $6–10) serves a nice mix of sandwiches, Mexican fare, and pizzas—a slightly unlikely trinity of great kinds of food. Seafood enchiladas, French dip po'boys, and burgers are popular items. There's live music on Friday nights.

Java Joints

In New Roads, break for coffee, a light lunch, or snacks at **Espresso Etc.** (110 E. Main St., New Roads, 225/618-8701), a warm and cozy storefront cafe right in the center of town. Quiche, sandwiches, salads, and sweets are among the offerings, and you can also browse for jewelry, art, and crafts by local artists.

INFORMATION AND SERVICES

Information on St. Francisville and Jackson can be obtained from the **West Feliciana Parish Tourist Commission** (P.O. Box 1548,

© ANDREW COLLINS

Ma Mama's restaurant, New Roads

St. Francisville, LA 70775, 800/789-4221, www.stfrancisville.us), which has a small visitors center inside the West Feliciana Historical Society. Information on New Roads can be obtained from the **Greater Pointe Coupee Chamber of Commerce** (P.O. Box 555, New Roads, LA 70760, 225/638-3500, www.pc-tourism.org), which has a rack of brochures in the lobby of its office at 160 East Main Street. And Jackson's tourism is handled by the **East Feliciana Parish Tourist Commission** (P.O. Box 667, Jackson, LA 70748, 225/634-7155, www.felicianatourism.org).

GETTING AROUND

From Baton Rouge, it's a 30-mile drive up U.S. Highway 61 to reach St. Francisville. As with the rest of the Great River Road, a car is your best way to get around. (See the *Essentials* chapter for details on reaching New Orleans and Baton Rouge from other parts of the country by train, plane, and bus.)

CAJUN COUNTRY

After New Orleans, southern Louisiana's Cajun Country, anchored by the city of Lafayette, attracts the most attention from visitors of any part of the state. It's here that you can discover the rich and distinctive heritage of the Cajun people, who were expelled from Canada in the mid-1700s before eventually relocating to this terrain of swampland, rivers, and fertile prairies. Beyond Lafayette and the region's other urban anchor Lake Charles, the Cajun Country is largely a collection of small to mid-size towns, many of them rural and quite historic in character. Restaurants serving Cajun specialties (crawfish pie, fried oysters, blackened redfish) and presenting live Cajun and zydeco music proliferate in this region, which is also known for its lively swamp tours, rustic bed-and-breakfasts, quaint house-museums, and relatively affordable antiques and crafts shops and art galleries.

There are a few basic commonalities between this area and New Orleans, but all too often outsiders lump the two areas together, as though Cajun culture is simply an extension of New Orleans, and that Creoles and Cajuns are one and the same. In fact, this part of Louisiana was settled for different reasons and by different people than was New Orleans, and everything from the food to the music to the accents in this part of the state are different, not only from the rest of the state but from anywhere in the world. Other than Lake Charles and the very western edge of the region, which received considerable damage from Hurricane Rita, the Cajun Country emerged largely unscathed after the two devastating storms of

© ANDREW COLLINS

HIGHLIGHTS

◖ **Best Place to Understand Cajun History:** Operated by the National Park Service, the modern **Acadian Cultural Center** tells the Cajun story with state-of-the-art exhibits and an excellent movie on the Acadian banishment from Canada. It's a must for getting a sense of Southwestern Louisiana's rich and moving history (page 293).

◖ **Best Living History Museum:** Cajun Louisiana's answer to colonial Williamsburg or Plimoth Plantation, the fascinating **Vermilionville** outdoor museum recounts the Cajun experience through historic and repro-duction buildings, music-and-dance presenta-tions, crafts demonstrations, and great food served at La Cuisine de Maman restaurant (page 295).

◖ **Best Small-Town:** Make a point of ex-ploring downtown St. Martinville, a charming community centered around gracious Church Square. It's where the very first Cajuns arrived from Canada around 1764. You can view the Acadian Memorial, the Evangeline Oak (which commemorates the story of *Evangeline*), and tour the small but excellent African American Museum and St. Martinville Cultural Heritage Center (page 300).

◖ **Best Cajun Plantation:** Arguably Louisiana's most interesting plantation mu-seum that's not on the Great River Road, the dignified, neoclassical **Shadows-on-the-Teche** overlooks Bayou Teche in New Iberia's charm-ing downtown. Tours tell the courageous tale of Mary C. Weeks, the widow who ran this suc-cessful sugarcane plantation (page 303).

◖ **Best Island That's Not Really an Island:** Technically a salt dome rather than an island in the common sense of the word, **Avery Island** is owned by the McIlhenny fam-ily and is the site of two seminal attractions: the McIlhenny Tabasco Company (of which tours are available) and the Jungle Gardens and Bird City, a lush wildlife preserve where gators, egrets, deer, and other creatures roam freely (page 304).

◖ **Best Place to Learn About Life in the Swamps:** Another fine component of Jean Lafitte National Historical Park and Preserve, Thibodaux's **Wetlands Acadian Cultural Center** reveals the manner in which Cajun settlers adapted to the region's swamps and marshes, earning their livelihood by trap-ping and fishing (page 326).

◖ **Best Music-Heritage Site:** In down-town Eunice, the **Prairie Acadian Cultural Center** is the westernmost member of Jean Lafitte National Historical Park and Preserve, and it's key to understanding Acadiana's rich zydeco and Cajun music heritage. Exhibits also dispel the common notion that Cajuns settled only in wetlands and reveal the heritage of those many Cajuns who moved onto south-western Louisiana's prairie (page 331).

◖ **Most Memorable Music Venue:** A toe-tapping Cajun variety show held at Eunice's Liberty Center for the Performing Arts, the two-hour *Rendezvous des Cajuns* radio pro-gram features great Cajun and zydeco tunes, storytelling, and jokes. It's a wonderful way to see and hear the region's famous music up close (page 331).

LOOK FOR ◖ TO FIND RECOMMENDED SIGHTS, ACTIVITIES, DINING, AND LODGING.

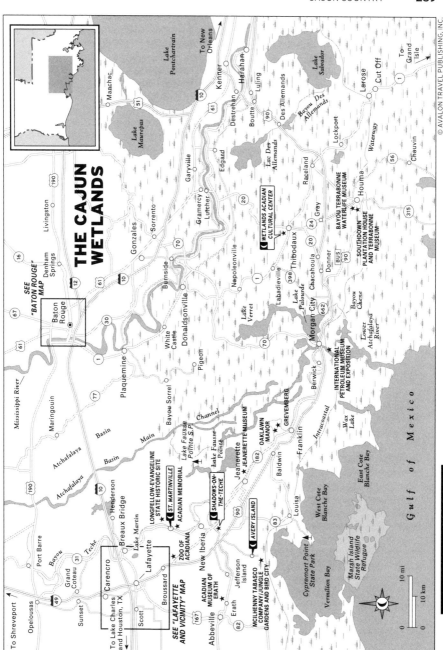

© AVALON TRAVEL PUBLISHING, INC.

THE CAJUN WETLANDS

2005. In fact, quite a few New Orleanians affected by Katrina relocated to Lafayette and some of the surrounding communities. Lake Charles had already largely recovered from Rita by spring 2006, but the coastal area south of Lake Charles, encompassing Cameron Parish, was virtually wiped off the map and will take years to rebuild.

HISTORY

The area now known as Acadiana, or Cajun Country, was inhabited by several Indian tribes before European trappers and settlers began establishing outposts here. The Attakapas and Chitimacha, who were bitter enemies, were the principal tribes around what is now Lafayette, St. Martinville, New Iberia, and Morgan City. The earliest Europeans in the area were mostly French trappers and then a handful of cattle ranchers, who began setting up small trading posts and farms in the early 1700s. It was not until around 1760 that the earliest Cajuns moved to the region, arriving by boat and establishing the town of St. Martinville.

The word "Cajun" is a corruption of "Acadian," the name for French settlers who had lived in Canada's Maritimes provinces, especially Nova Scotia, during the 17th and 18th centuries. The settlers came mostly from the Vendée region of far western France, and they began arriving in Canada during the very early 1600s, well before English colonists had established a foothold in Massachusetts. When Great Britain secured control of the Canadian region in 1713, the thousands of Acadians living in Nova Scotia resisted and in some cases flouted the authority of the British crown. Acadians developed a reputation for being fiercely independent, and they refused to submit to England's authority or learn English. To sign the oath of loyalty to the British Crown would have rendered an Acadian obligated to fight on behalf of the British against the French during the French and Indian Wars.

After years of tension between British authorities and Acadian residents, the British colonial government established a ruthless program, which came to be known by the French

as the *Grand Dérangement* (literally the "Great Disturbance"), in which the government rounded up the region's French settlers and expelled them from Canada. In many instances the British told men, women, and children to gather at a local church, where they were to hear an important announcement. Upon their entering the church, the doors were locked and the French families imprisoned, and then they were led to waiting ships bound for Europe, the Caribbean, and the East Coast colonies that would eventually become the United States.

Some colonies turned away the ships carrying refugees, and in other places they were accepted as indentured workers with no rights. Everywhere they were subject to great suspicion and prejudice. In Colonial America at this time, Catholics were severely distrusted and, often, persecuted by the Protestant church-state, although attitudes did begin to shift after the American Revolution, when French Catholics played a vital role in the colonists' overthrow of British rule.

In two major waves, one small one in 1764 and the other in 1785, about 3,000–4,000 expelled Acadians and their descendants moved to southern Louisiana to start anew. Contrary to popular opinion, very few of the state's Cajuns came here directly from Nova Scotia (it's estimated between 150–200 settlers); most had returned to France to live but failed, for the most part, to assimilate back into French society, having become a distinct people after living in Nova Scotia for several generations. They were truly without a home, and Louisiana welcomed them as much as anything because the young territory was eager to attract settlers, especially in the southwestern part of the region, which was considered to be dangerous frontierland occupied by aggressive Attakapas Indians.

Interestingly, during the two major Cajun arrivals, Louisiana was under Spanish rather than French control. The Cajuns cared little who governed the territory and more that they would be moving someplace where people spoke French and practiced Catholicism. The Spanish government, like the French one before it, was pleased to attract any significant mass of settlers, and they were particularly happy that the Cajun refugees were interested in developing and working farms. The Cajuns were just one group of refugees or hard-luck immigrants, along with whites and freed blacks from Haiti and residents of the Spanish Canary Islands, who helped to change the territory from a financially dubious backwater into an agricultural and trade powerhouse by the time America admitted Louisiana into the Union as the country's 18th state, in 1812.

The city of Lafayette, with a population of about 112,000 (as of 2005—it's likely quite a lot higher now since many people displaced by Hurricanes Katrina and Rita have moved here), acts as the capital of the Acadiana, which comprises 22 southern Louisiana parishes, from Calcasieu and Cameron parishes on the western border with Texas to the parishes around New Orleans in the east—the total population of these 22 parishes is nearly 1.3 million. Cajuns remain a relatively close-knit group—about 400,000 residents of Louisiana identify themselves as primarily Cajun, and of the roughly 700,000 nationally who claim Cajun ancestry, about 75 percent live in Louisiana or neighboring Texas. In Vermilion and Acadia parishes, which are southwest and west of Lafayette, more than 45 percent of the residents claim to be of Cajun descent, although even though they make up a minority of residents, they have a disproportionate influence on the region's culture and politics. More than a third of the residents in Assumption, Cameron, Evangeline, Iberia, Jefferson Davis, Lafourche, St. Landry, and St. Martin parishes also claim to be Cajun. Lafayette Parish, despite being the hub of the area, is only about 25 percent Cajun, a figure that's declining each decade as greater numbers of outsiders settle there. By contrast, fewer than 1 percent of all New Orleanians claim to be of Cajun descent.

ORIENTATION AND PLANNING

Acadiana is shaped roughly like a scythe and follows U.S. Highway 90 west to southeast, from Lake Charles to Houma. The long, rect-angular handle of the scythe extends from Lake Charles to Lafayette along both U.S. Highway 90 and the parallel U.S. Highway 190 corridor, from Kinder to Opelousas. This part of Acadiana is considered to be the Cajun prairie, where early settlers earned their livelihood farming. The curving blade of the scythe extends southeast along the U.S. Highway 90 corridor from Lafayette down through New Iberia and Morgan City and then about as far east as Houma. This region is considered the Cajun wetlands, where the settlers derived their livelihood chiefly from fishing and trapping. From Houma, it's just a 60-mile drive to New Orleans.

This chapter is broken down into four general regions, Lafayette and Central Acadiana, Eastern Acadiana, the Cajun Prairie, and Lake Charles. Lafayette and Central Acadiana encompass parts of both prairie and wetlands but are, geographically and culturally, more the latter. This area contains a great many attractions, restaurants, accommodations, and charming, historic small towns. If you have only a little time out this way, be sure to spend time in Lafayette and the surrounding area.

The Cajun prairie includes the towns northwest and west of Lafayette, including Opelousas and Eunice along the U.S. Highway 190 corridor, Rayne and Crowley along the U.S. Highway 90 corridor, and Lake Charles out near the Texas border. Opelousas and Eunice are notable for their musical heritage, as both traditional Cajun and zydeco music have flourished here. Lake Charles is a growing city, and the towns between it and Lafayette have a smattering of things to see and do. It's the farthest section from New Orleans, although it's worth checking out if you're visiting the state by way of Texas, which it borders.

Eastern Acadiana takes in the string of towns between the Atchafalaya River and Houma and contain far fewer attractions than Lafayette and environs. However, this is ground zero for fishing and swamp-touring enthusiasts, and it's also close to the Plantation Country (see the *Great River Road* chapter). If you're seeking just a taste of Cajun culture and would prefer not to stray far from New Orleans, a night or two out near Houma or Thibodaux might suit you perfectly. You can also travel through this part of the region en route from New Orleans to Lafayette along U.S. Highway 90, a wide, limited-access highway on which you can usually make very good time.

It's fairly easy to spend four or five days in this part of the state, especially if you hit all the major attractions between Lafayette and Houma and you venture up to Eunice to explore the region's zydeco and Cajun music heritage. If you have more time, consider a longer exploration of Cajun Country, perhaps venturing as far as Lake Charles. If you enjoy the outdoors and the music and food heritage of the area, you're unlikely to run out of things to see and do. But if you came to Louisiana craving the lively pace and big-city buzz of New Orleans, you might be best limiting your time in Cajun Country to a few days or less. Greater New Orleans and Acadiana enjoy more differences than similarities, but therein lies much of the charm of Louisiana's Cajun Country.

Lafayette and Central Acadiana

The heart of Cajun Country, Lafayette and Central Acadiana includes the city of Lafayette and towns in its immediate vicinity, stretching about as far down as the Atchafalaya River—the communities most popular with visitors include, in order of their proximity to Lafayette, Breaux Bridge, St. Martinville, New Iberia, Abbeville, and Franklin.

LAFAYETTE

Lafayette is the most important city in Acadiana and what many people consider to be its hub. As with the surrounding towns in the region, the cultural makeup is really less purely Cajun than outsiders sometimes imagine. Certainly there are many people here of Cajun descent, and many who speak the local Cajun dialect of French as their preferred first language, but residents of the region are also strongly of African, Spanish, Northern European, and Native American origin.

The city is easily reached from New Orleans, Houston, and the rest of the region—it's just off I-10 and I-49, a little more than two hours west of the Crescent City, and it contains the bulk of the region's chain motels and hotels, fast-food and other restaurants, and shops and services. There's also a decent-size regional airport with direct service to a handful of Southern cities.

This is a thoroughly modern city, not an especially quaint or old-fashioned one. The city sprawls, and much of it feels suburban and overrun with strip malls. However, it's also home to some excellent museums on Cajun culture, and it has some first-rate Cajun music clubs and restaurants. And the formerly depressed downtown area has received a major makeover in recent years, with new museums, clubs, and restaurants.

It's subtropical in climate, owing to its location just 40 miles north of the Gulf of Mexico and 15 miles west of Atchafalaya Swamp. Attakapas Indians inhabited the area for many decades dating as far back as the late 1600s, but their dominance was overturned by a legion of three opposing southern Louisiana tribes who formed an alliance to defeat the notoriously warlike Attakapas; these included the Opelousas, Choctaw, and Alabamons.

Although it's the Cajun capital of the state, it was not actually settled by Acadian exiles until the Spanish government assumed control of the region in the 1760s, by which time a few French trappers and farmers had already put down roots here. The earliest group of Acadians, who had moved from Canada to a hodgepodge of East Coast ports and Caribbean islands, first arrived in nearby St. Martinville in 1764. But when the larger wave of Cajun arrivals hit Louisiana in 1785, with the blessing of the territory's Spanish government, Lafayette truly grew into a center of Cajun life. These many hundreds of

ANDREW COLLINS

Acadian Cultural Center

Cajuns arrived from France, to which they had returned after their brutal expulsion from the Canadian Maritimes.

The earliest known permanent European settlement in what is now Lafayette was established by the English and known as Petit Manchac; it was a small trading post on the banks of the Vermilion River, approximately where it is crossed today by the Pinhook Avenue bridge (right beside the Hilton hotel). It wasn't until 1821, when an Acadian descendant named Jean Mouton donated land for the construction of a Catholic church, that the settlement really took hold as a major center of Cajun life.

Lafayette Parish was created (from the western edge of what had been St. Martin Parish) by the state legislature in 1823, and the young town, then known as Vermilionville, for the major bayou that passed through it, was named the parish seat. In 1884, the fast-growing settlement was rechristened Lafayette in honor of the French marquis de Lafayette, who acted so heroically in the American Revolutionary War.

Today Lafayette is the hub of an eight-parish area with a metro population of about 600,000,

about 110,000 of them within city limits. It's one of the state's faster-growing cities, with a blossoming economy to go with it. Per-capita income in Lafayette Parish grew by 54 percent between 1990 and 2000, and today Lafayette has the third-highest per-capita income in Louisiana. The low cost of living and central location have made it a desirable tech city.

◖ Acadian Cultural Center

A great place to begin a tour is the National Park Service's superb Acadian Cultural Center (501 Fisher Rd., Lafayette, 337/232-0789, www.nps.gov/jela, open 9 A.M.–5 P.M. daily, admission free), which offers an excellent general overview of Cajun history and culture. It's a short drive southeast of downtown Lafayette, just off U.S. Highway 90 by Lafayette Regional Airport. Well-labeled and often large-scale exhibits, artifacts, and photos are set throughout the museum space in this contemporary building designed to resemble a Cajun cottage. You can easily spend an hour in here absorbing the lore of Cajun music, family life, cooking, language, and fishing, and exploring

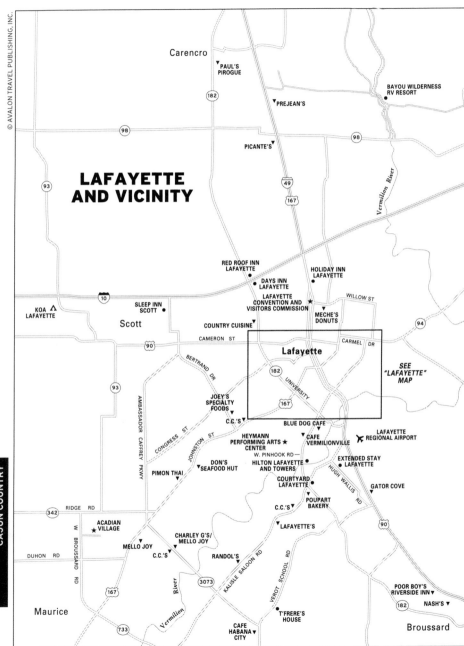

© AVALON TRAVEL PUBLISHING, INC.

CAJUN COUNTRY

Carencro

PAUL'S PIROGUE

BAYOU WILDERNESS RV RESORT

182

PREJEAN'S

98

98

PICANTE'S

49

167

Vermilion River

LAFAYETTE AND VICINITY

93

RED ROOF INN LAFAYETTE

HOLIDAY INN LAFAYETTE

10

DAYS INN LAFAYETTE

WILLOW ST

KOA LAFAYETTE

SLEEP INN SCOTT

LAFAYETTE CONVENTION AND VISITORS COMMISSION

MECHE'S DONUTS

94

Scott

COUNTRY CUISINE

CAMERON ST

CARMEL DR

90

Lafayette

SEE "LAFAYETTE" MAP

BERTRAND DR

182

93

UNIVERSITY

AMBASSADOR CAFFREY PKWY

JOEY'S SPECIALTY FOODS

167

C.C.'S

BLUE DOG CAFE

CONGRESS ST

JOHNSTON ST

HEYMANN PERFORMING ARTS CENTER

CAFE VERMILIONVILLE

LAFAYETTE REGIONAL AIRPORT

W. PINHOOK RD

DON'S SEAFOOD HUT

HILTON LAFAYETTE AND TOWERS

EXTENDED STAY LAFAYETTE

PIMON THAI

COURTYARD LAFAYETTE

HUGH WALLIS RD

GATOR COVE

RIDGE RD

342

C.C.'S

POUPART BAKERY

90

W BROUSSARD RD

ACADIAN VILLAGE

LAFAYETTE'S

DUHON RD

MELLO JOY

CHARLEY G'S/ MELLO JOY

167

C.C.'S

RANDOL'S

KALISLE SALOON RD

VEROT SCHOOL RD

POOR BOY'S RIVERSIDE INN

3073

182

NASH'S

733

Vermilion River

T'FRERE'S HOUSE

Broussard

Maurice

CAFE HABANA CITY

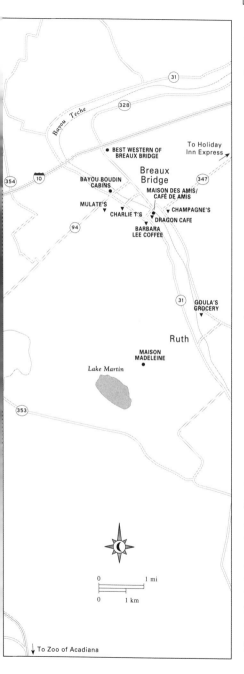

the serpentine route Acadians journeyed from Nova Scotia to southern Louisiana. In a large theater, the 40-minute movie *The Cajun Way: Echoes of Acadia* is shown hourly until 4 P.M. and is definitely worth making time for; it offers a gut-wrenching but inspirational look at the plight of Cajuns and their astounding resolve balanced with their love of celebration and tradition that has kept them a distinct cultural group to this day. Check for interpretive programs, videos, and performances scheduled regularly throughout the year, and when in New Orleans, be sure to drop in on the headquarters of the Jean Lafitte National Historical Preserve, in the French Quarter at 419 Decatur Street. Here you'll find information on all of the park's six sites throughout southern Louisiana, including two other centers, on wetland Cajuns and prairie Cajuns, in the towns of Thibodaux and Eunice, respectively.

◖ Vermilionville

Within view of the Acadian Cultural Center, Vermilionville (300 Fisher Rd., Lafayette, 337/233-4077 or 866/992-2968, www.vermilionville.org, open 10 A.M.–4 P.M. Tues.–Sun., admission $8) is another must-see for understanding Cajun culture. This 23-acre living-history compound comprises five restored historic houses, 12 reproduction period buildings, and exhibits on indigenous people, the area's wetlands, and Cajun and zydeco music (which is performed live here regularly). You can attend cooking demonstrations, eat in the casual restaurant and bakery, and walk through a nature trail identifying Louisiana plant life. This setup differs a bit from the smaller Acadian Village, another Lafayette living-history center in a different part of town, which has fewer staff members and holds fewer demonstrations. Vermilionville is, rather oddly, set near the airport and several modern warehouses, but once you enter the re-created village, it feels quite authentic; there's even a lazy bayou running through the property. Different buildings, some authentic from the period and others exact replicas, include a chapel and presbytére (where a clergyman would have lived),

CAJUN COUNTRY

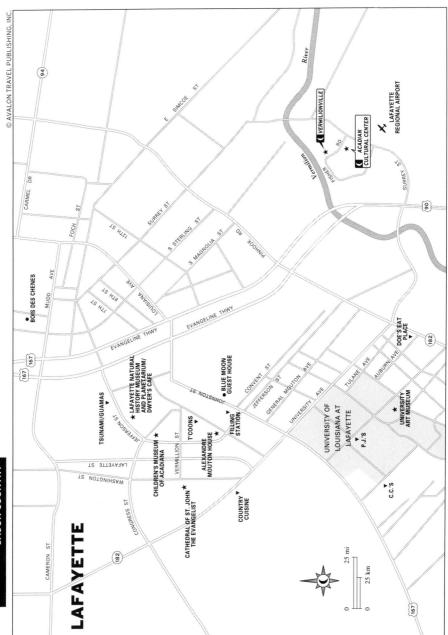

LAFAYETTE

an Acadian barn where volunteers engage in boatbuilding and net- and trap-making, and several residences, the oldest dating from 1790. Every element of Vermilionville sheds light onto the culture of the area's original Cajuns, from the homestyle cooking of La Cuisine de Maman restaurant to live music-and-dance programs. The guides here are knowledgeable and enthusiastic, too.

Acadian Village

Similar in approach to Vermilionville but a bit smaller in scope is Acadian Village (200 Greenleaf Dr., Lafayette, 337/981-2364, www .acadianvillage.org, open 10 a.m.–5 p.m. daily, admission $6), which is on the southwest side of town, easily accessible as you head down U.S. Highway 167 toward Abbeville. This complex is a replicated Cajun village from the late 1800s, with several buildings moved here from their original sites throughout the region. These include a general store, a circa-1800 cottage brought over from St. Martinville, a blacksmith shop, a replica of an 1850 chapel, and several period houses. The layout and setting is somewhat more picturesque than Vermilionville, and the experience here offers an excellent and highly entertaining sense of what an actual bayou village might have looked like 150 years ago. At Acadian Village, you mostly explore on your own, at your own pace, rather than being led by docents, which can make for a refreshing change of pace if you're a bit tired of being led in groups through plantations and museums. The buildings here are packed with old artifacts, metalworking tools, everyday tools, household goods, and textiles—you could spend a while here just poking around. The disturbingly realistic re-created doctor's office may leave you thankful for the advances that have been made since the 19th century in medical diagnostics and procedures.

There's a large picnic pavilion, which sometimes hosts special events and demonstrations. Alongside the narrow bayou that cuts through the village, you're likely to see turtles sunning themselves on logs, and guinea hens and rather aggressive geese wandering about. An interest-

Jefferson Street, downtown Lafayette

© ANDREW COLLINS

ing side attraction is the Mississippi River Museum, set in a modern building on the edge of the village; it contains murals depicting Indian life and European settlement throughout the Mississippi River Valley, plus 200- and 400-year-old canoes fashioned of cypress wood, which virtually never rots, is resistant to termites, and can last for eons. The museum, which is free with admission to Acadian Village, also contains taxidermic wildlife and old maps and charts of the area.

Downtown Sights

Downtown Lafayette, which is contained roughly within a triangle bound by West University Avenue (Hwy. 182), Johnson Street (U.S. 167), and Congress Street, has gradually been revitalized since the mid-1990s and has a handful of attractions, plus a growing number of places to eat and shop. This business district is where banks and oil companies built offices throughout the 20th century, making it Acadiana's commercial center.

The **Alexandre Mouton House/Lafayette Museum** (1122 Lafayette St., Lafayette,

CAJUN COUNTRY

337/234-2208, open 9 A.M.–4:30 P.M. Tues.–Sat., 1–4 P.M. Sun., admission $3), the 19th-century home of Louisiana's first Democrat governor, occupies one of the most striking buildings downtown. Furnishings from different generations of the Mouton family fill the house.

A couple of blocks north and west of the Mouton house museum, near the third-oldest oak tree recognized by Louisiana's Live Oak Society, the **Cathedral of St. John the Evangelist** (914 St. John St., Lafayette, 337/232-1322, 9 A.M.–noon and 1–4 P.M. Mon.–Fri., admission $3) is a striking Dutch Romanesque church of considerable proportion. It dates to 1916 and has an aboveground cemetery dating to a century before that. Tours are available by appointment, but you're also welcome to drop by and look around on your own. A gift shop sells inspirational jewelry, crafts, and cards.

On the northeast side of downtown, an easy walk from the cathedral, you'll find one of the city's newest attractions, opened in 2003, the **Lafayette Natural History Museum and Planetarium** (433 Jefferson St., Lafayette, 337/291-5544, www.lnhm.org, open 1–9:30 P.M. Tues., 1–5 P.M. Wed.–Fri., 10 A.M.–6 P.M. Sat., and 1–6 P.M. Sun., admission $5), which is housed within a stunning many-windowed three-story building in the city's up-and-coming downtown; the 72,000-square-foot space had housed an old department store. It's a classic hands-on place where kids and adults can poke, prod, handle, and experiment with scientific objects, and examine collections of Native American crafts, paintings, and pottery of Louisiana artists, rare books, photographs, meteorites and tektites, and other curious artifacts. The planetarium, with its 40-foot dome, presents a wide range of astronomy programs. The museum also sponsors a series of lunchtime concerts in downtown's Parc Sans Souci (at 201 E. Vermillion St.), which include live blues, folk, and percussion music.

Also popular with younger visitors is the nearby **Children's Museum of Acadiana** (201 E. Congress St., Lafayette, 337/232-8500, open 10 A.M.–5 P.M. Tues.–Sat., admission $5), whose many fanciful exhibits touch on Acadian history as well as natural science, space, nutrition, and the arts. Kids can explore a mock grocery store or bank or a real ambulance, stage their own shows in a kid-size TV station, and admire art in a gallery with rotating exhibits.

The **Acadiana Center for the Arts** (101 W. Vermilion St., Lafayette, 337/233-7060, www.acadianaartscouncil.org) opened in 2005 inside a sleek building in the heart of downtown. It includes a museum exhibition space, a performing arts center, and educational facilities. It's yet another piece in the downtown renaissance. Art exhibitions are staged here throughout the year.

After New Orleans and Baton Rouge, Lafayette has the third-largest presence of college students of any community in southwestern Louisiana, with the **University of Louisiana at Lafayette** (104 University Circle, Hwy. 182 and U.S. 167, Lafayette, 337/482-1000, www.ull.edu), which enrolls about 16,000 students. The campus is just south of downtown. Cypress and oak trees dot the attractive campus, which has a mix of older and newer buildings. Visitors should be sure to check out the **University Art Museum** (710 E. St. Mary Blvd., Lafayette, 337/482-5326, www.thehilliard.org), which moved into a large and new 40,000-square-foot space in fall 2003. This move is helping to turn what had been a fairly modest facility into the premier art museum in the Gulf Coast region between Houston and New Orleans. UAM mounts important traveling exhibitions throughout the year and has a diverse and growing permanent collection with notable works by regional, national, and international artists dating from the past four centuries.

BROUSSARD

Broussard is a small community just south of Lafayette via U.S. 90. The main attraction here is the **Zoo of Acadiana** (116 Lakeview Dr., Broussard, 337/837-4325, www.zooofacadiana.org, open 9 A.M.–5 P.M. daily, admission $8), which opened in 1992 and is home to about 800 animals representing more than 50 species. You walk through the junglelike park along tree-shaded boardwalks and paths, observing the animals in realistic enclosures that replicate nature as much as possible. There are also a petting zoo and a train. Favorite activities include the feedings of Australian parrots, playful otters, black bears, and alligators. Monkeys, llamas, and giraffes are among the most popular animals to watch. Between November 24 and December 30 (excluding Thanksgiving and Christmas, when the zoo is closed), the zoo stays open until 9 P.M. for the Safari of Lights, when the entire zoo is decorated for the holidays.

BREAUX BRIDGE

It's a 15-minute drive east of Lafayette, via either I-10 or the more scenic but slower Highway 94, to reach Breaux Bridge, which is also the first major Cajun community you'll come to if you approach the region from New Orleans and Baton Rouge via I-10. Breaux Bridge is a low-key country Cajun town with a small but vibrant downtown district that makes for a pleasant stroll and offers some interesting window-browsing. A couple of small parks are downtown, one of them with plaques discussing the many bridges that have crossed Bayou Teche at this point, hence the name of the town. In 1799 an Acadian immigrant named Firmin Breaux constructed the first crossing in town, a modest footbridge. The town was not officially laid out until a descendant of Breaux, a woman named Scholastique Picou Breaux, drew up plans and began subdividing her farmland into smaller lots and selling them to other settlers.

Apart from a couple of excellent places to eat and some charming B&Bs, the town's main claim to fame is **Lake Martin** (off Hwy. 170, three miles south of downtown Breaux Bridge and reached via Hwy. 31), the largest nesting area for wading birds in the state. You can walk along a nature trail by the water, watch for the many varieties of birds (as well as nutria, snakes, turtles, and alligators), or take one of the excursions here offered by **Champagnes' Swamp Tours** (337/845-5567, www.champagnesswamptours.com) or **Cajun Country Swamp Tours** (337/319-0010, www.cajuncountryswamptours.com), both of which are highly reputable outfitters.

ST. MARTINVILLE

About 15 miles south of Breaux Bridge via Highway 31 or south of Lafayette via U.S. Highway 90 to Highway 96, small but bustling St. Martinville (population 7,200) is the quintessential Cajun town, set on Bayou Teche and abundant with historic houses and sites that relate to the region's establishment as an Acadian stronghold. The earliest Acadians arrived at this spot in 1765, making their way here up Bayou Teche from the Gulf of Mexico. The region was already home to Attakapas Indians, long rumored to practice cannibalism, and it was with some trepidation that a handful of trappers set up a frontier trading post here in the mid-1750s. They were followed by cattle farmers, encouraged to settle by the authorities in New Orleans, who sought a source of beef with which to feed the city's growing population.

The earliest Acadian refugees, having been first exiled to colonies along the East Coast, came to Louisiana hoping, correctly, to find a relatively welcome environment—at the very least, a population that was mostly French and Catholic. They first piled into New Orleans, poor and without a concrete plan. The local government furnished the Acadians with basic food, provisions, and farming tools and granted them a parcel of land in the Attakapas District, the name at that time for what is now St. Martin, St. Mary, Iberia, Vermilion, and Lafayette parishes.

During this first year of Cajun settlement, France ceded Louisiana to the Spaniards, but the new government welcomed the Cajuns with great enthusiasm. For military reasons, they wanted to see the Attakapas District grow into a self-sustaining part of Louisiana, and during the Spanish reign, St. Martinville and the many neighboring towns grew with new arrivals of Cajuns as well as refugees from the revolution in France, Spaniards from the Canary Islands, enterprising Creole families from New Orleans and Mobile, and slaves from West Africa.

Through time, Attakapas became a formal parish, whose name was changed to St. Martin Parish in 1807, the town of St. Martinville having been christened by a Catholic priest. The community grew from a loose collection of farms and a few larger plantations into a proper town, the urban core of which formed along the streets emanating from Church Square, still today downtown's charming focal point. In 1817, St. Martinville, now a prominent trading center in the new U.S. state of Louisiana, became the sixth city in the state to incorporate. Growing contingents of Italians, Germans, and Creoles who had fled from Haiti joined the chiefly French and Cajun inhabitants. Around this time, steamboat travel made it relatively easy for visitors to travel to and from St. Martinville on the Bayou Teche, which until well into the 19th century served as the principal "highway" in and out of the region. By the mid-1850s, St. Martinville had earned the nickname Petit Paris for its bounty of fine hotels and cultural venues, including an impressive theater.

Although this small, bustling city remains a center of cultural and social life in the Cajun Country, it has never really grown to become much more substantial or populous than it was during the 19th century—this is a big reason the town feels so warm and inviting today. It's bypassed by major highways, and it never grew into a center for southern Louisiana's oil refining and banking the way nearby Lafayette did. Walking through town today, you might not think to call it a city, even though, governmentally, St. Martinville is just that. These days St. Martinville is, in addition to being a significant tourism center, a hub of sugarcane and crawfish harvesting, as well as a factory base for the undergarment manufacturer Fruit of the Loom—it's St. Martinville's largest employer, with nearly 3,000 workers. The town is also known for Louisiana Hot Sauce, a Tabasco rival found on many kitchen and restaurant tables throughout the South.

BAYOU TECHE

Bayou Teche runs through the Cajun towns of Breaux Bridge, St. Martinville, and New Iberia, forming the natural western levee of the basin. "Teche" is an old Attakapas Indian name for "snake." Native American legends offer different origins for the name, including one that suggests that a snake actually created the river: Chitimacha warriors destroyed a massive venomous serpent many miles in length, and as the beast died from its wounds, it writhed and deepened a twisting track in the mud that became the riverbed of Bayou Teche.

The Teche begins just east of Opelousas in the town of Port Barrie, where it flows from Bayou Courtableau. Roughly paralleling I-49, it meanders through the towns of Arnaudville and Cecilia before cutting beneath I-10 and entering Breaux Bridge. It's along this stretch, from Arnaudville to Breaux Bridge, that the banks of the river are shaded by tall oak trees, dramatically draped with moss. A couple of miles downstream from St. Martinville, the Teche passes through Keystone Locks and Control Structure, constructed by the U.S. Army Corps of Engineers to increase the bayou's water level, making it navigable for boats heading upstream to Port Barrie.

You can drive alongside much of the Teche along several state highways, especially from New Iberia south through Jeanerette and Franklin. It eventually passes through yet another flood-control structure before finally emptying into the Lower Atchafalaya River.

◖ Exploring Downtown St. Martinville

To explore St. Martinville, start by parking anywhere near Church Square, which anchors downtown at Bridge and Main streets. Presiding over Church Square is the house of worship for which the town and parish are named, **St. Martin de Tours Catholic Church** (Bridge and Main Sts., St. Martinville), which dates to

1765 and is one of the oldest churches in the Gulf South. It contains a replica of the Grotto of Lourdes, which was added in 1870.

A centerpiece of the town is the restored **Duchamp Opera House** (200 S. Main St., St. Martinville, 337/394-6604), the very building that, when built in the 1830s, helped to establish the town's reputation as a cultural hub; throughout the 19th century, it was the site of traveling shows, operas from New Orleans, and local theatrical performances. Throughout most of the 20th century it functioned as a department store but has been refurbished to its original purpose and now is home of the Evangeline Players theater group as well as a venue for other shows. Also here is a multidealer antiques shop.

A couple of blocks behind Church Square, at the corner of Evangeline Boulevard and South New Market Street, you can see one of the most visited and photographed icons of Cajun history, the **Evangeline Oak,** a massive tree named for the protagonist of Henry Wadsworth Longfellow's tragic epic poem of Cajun heartbreak, *Evangeline.* The tree sits overlooking Bayou Teche, marking the apocryphal site where lovers Evangeline and Gabriel, separated during the ruthless Cajun exile from Canada, eventually reunited.

Right beside the park with the Evangeline Oak is the **Acadian Memorial** (New Market St., St. Martinville, 337/394-2258, www.acadianmemorial.org, open 10 A.M.–4 P.M. daily), a tribute to the Acadians who settled here. Features include a 12- by 30-foot mural by Robert Dafford that depicts the arrival of Acadians between 1764 and 1788; the mural has a twin in Nantes, France, that shows the Louisiana-bound refugees boarding a ship from France in 1785. There's also a granite-and-bronze Wall of Names, which lists about 3,000 people who were identified in early state records as having been Acadian refugees. In the Acadian Memorial garden, an eternal flame burns from the center of a polished granite oval. Next door to the memorial, in the **St. Martinville Cultural Heritage Center** (121 New Market St., St. Martinville, open 8 A.M.–4 P.M. Mon.–Fri.),

you can use the memorial's multimedia center to research genealogy and history on Acadians, and you can tour a small but nicely done museum on the history of Cajuns in southwestern Louisiana. Donation suggested.

Inside the St. Martinville Cultural Center, the **African American Museum** (121 New Market St., St. Martinville, 337/394-2273, open 10 A.M.–4 P.M. daily, donation suggested), which opened in 2001, uses clever multimedia exhibits and illustrated displays to interpret the history and heritage of the West African slaves who were brought to Louisiana, sold, and moved to this part of the state. The focus is especially on the Wolof, Bambara, and Mandiga tribes of Senegal. Many slaves bound for Louisiana were shipped out of Africa by way of Goree Island, about two miles off the shore from Dakar, Senegal. Documents discuss the plight of the hundreds of thousands of Africans and their descendants who lived as slaves in Louisiana from 1699 until 1862, when Union forces occupied the state. It's explained that slaves brought to the New World on French ships generally endured less harsh and brutal conditions than on British ships, because the French traders were paid bonuses if they kept their captives alive—even so, the mortality rates on slave ships was extremely high, and it was not uncommon for half of the women and men forced onto ships in Africa to perish on the journey. Exhibits also explain the origin of the term Creole and *gens de couleur libres* (free people of color).

Longfellow-Evangeline State Historic Site

About a mile north of Church Square is the historic Maison Olivier plantation house, which can be visited by guided tour and anchors the first state park established in Louisiana, Longfellow–Evangeline State Historic Site (1200 N. Main St., St. Martinville, 337/394-3754 or 888/677-2900, www .lastateparks.com, open 9 A.M.–5 P.M. daily, admission $2). In addition to the plantation house, the park contains a farmstead (also open for tours) and a small historical museum. All are set along a lovely meadow with paths leading beside Bayou Teche. Originally a *vacherie* (cattle ranch), the plantation was turned into an indigo farm and eventually a highly profitable sugar plantation on which Maison Olivier was built around 1815. The house is a classic raised Creole cottage, a style of architecture unique to Louisiana that incorporates French, Caribbean, and Creole influences. Mostly mid-1800s antiques fill the house. A small footbridge crosses a narrow bayou to the Acadian Farmstead, which illustrates how a typical Cajun farmhouse might have been furnished in the early 1800s. The small Cajun history museum is not especially thrilling, with static, rather dated exhibits, but it does provide some insights into the region's heritage, and it's also where you check in to sign up for a tour of the plantation house or farmstead. Near the museum is a small and very rustic Cajun cabin that gives a nice sense of the difference between the lifestyles of wealthy Creoles and the lower-income Cajuns—the cabin is furnished with original Louisiana cypress pieces, and a small garden in back is planted with medical and culinary herbs popular in this part of the state for many decades.

Lake Fausse Pointe State Park

The second state-operated attraction in town is geared more toward the many outdoors enthusiasts drawn to the Atchafalaya Swamp basin. Lake Fausse Pointe State Park (5400 Levee Rd., St. Martinville, 337/229-4764 or 888/677-7200, www.crt.state.la.us, day use $1 per person) sits about 18 miles southeast of downtown St. Martinville, just off West Atchafalaya Levee Road. From town you head east on Highway 96, then right onto Highway 679, left onto Highway 3083, and then right onto the levee road; continue along here for seven miles to reach the park, which sits on the east side of Lake Fausse and fringes Atchafalaya Swamp—it may take a little effort to get here, but the drive is through beautiful wetlands. Before massive levees were built on the eastern and western sides of Atchafalaya Swamp, the

entire area occupied by this park was part of the swamp, whose boundary extended from Bayou Teche clear to the Mississippi River. Chitimacha Indians lived in this area first, followed by French trappers, Acadian farmers, and then settlers from mainland Spain and the Spanish Canary Islands.

Although Lake Fausse is popular for boating and fishing, it's generally a tranquil place that has for decades been a favorite haunt of wildlife photographers and bird-watchers—there are many areas within the park that seem almost primeval in their serenity and lush foliage. Facilities include a boat launch, a boat dock with rentals, picnic pavilions, a camp store, 18 overnight camping cabins (with screened-in porches, air-conditioning, and piers out over water) and numerous primitive tent sites, an RV camping area (with water and electricity hookups), a conference center, and an extensive network of hiking trails.

NEW IBERIA

Although much smaller than Lafayette and 30 minutes farther south, New Iberia is another excellent base for exploring the Acadiana. It's very close to Avery Island, Abbeville, and St. Martinville (which is nine miles north, via Hwy. 31), and New Iberia is less dominated by retail chain sprawl than Lafayette. It has a few key attractions in its own right, and a gentrifying downtown commercial district with a handful of noteworthy shops and cafes.

The seat of Iberia Parish, New Iberia—along with the several surrounding villages—was land occupied by the Attakapa Indians before Acadians began trickling in during the 1760s after their landing at St. Martinville. The same decade, Spain took possession of Louisiana, and in 1779 a group of immigrants from the Spanish city of Málaga settled the town, attempting to farm flax and hemp. Their agrarian endeavors failed, but settlers remained, and the town—today the only permanent settlement in the state established by Spaniards—took the name New Iberia, after Spain's Iberian Peninsula.

Farming did eventually flourish here, with sugarcane becoming the dominant crop as it did elsewhere in Acadiana—still today, Iberia Parish produces more sugarcane (much of it in nearby Jeanerette) than any other parish in Louisiana. New Iberia's most prominent attraction, Shadows-on-the-Teche plantation, was built as the administrative center in 1834 of a prolific network of sugarcane-farming operations. Cattle farming grew into an important industry through about the 1860s, and the area's several salt domes, the most famous being Avery Island, also become important to the economy. The town is home to the oldest extant rice mill in the United States, Conrad Rice Mill. This is a bit odd, as the state's major rice-producing area is well northwest of New Iberia, along the U.S. Highway 90/I-10 corridor between Lafayette and Lake Charles.

The best way to get a feel for downtown New Iberia is to park along the main drag, West Main Street, and wander its blocks. This is a one-way street, the northbound part of Highway 182, so if you're approaching New Iberia by way of Highway 14 from U.S. Highway 90, which you likely would if coming from Lafayette or Houma, turn right onto St. Peter Street (the southbound part of Highway 182) as you enter downtown, and continue for several blocks to Lewis Street (there's a Pizza Hut on the corner); make a left turn, and then a quick left again onto Main Street (Hwy. 182 northbound). The first several blocks of this drive pass by a dazzling array of finely preserved mostly 19th-century homes in several styles, from the classic Greek Revival to painted-lady gingerbread cottages.

◖ Shadows-on-the-Teche

Right about at Center Street (Hwy. 14), you'll come to the city's leading attraction and one of the true must-see museums of Acadiana, Shadows-on-the-Teche (317 E. Main St., New Iberia, 337/369-6446, www.shadowsontheteche.org, open 9 A.M.–4:30 P.M. daily, admission $7, free to members of the National Trust for Historic Preservation), a dignified white-columned brick house built by sugarcane farmer David Weeks in 1834. Weeks died of an unknown malady during a trip to New Haven before ever

Victor's Cafeteria, New Iberia

living in the house. His wife, Mary C. Weeks, ran the house and oversaw the plantation for years afterward. The house is much smaller than some of the leviathan plantation houses along the Great River Road, and that's one reason it makes for a better tour—you aren't treated to an endless march through rooms and outbuildings. But the best things about Shadows is that the National Trust for Historic Preservation, which owns the house, also has a collection of about 17,000 paper documents relevant to the lives of the plantation's inhabitants and its day-to-day inner workings. Guides at Shadows draw on these records to help paint a vivid picture of life here, and often the most fascinating bits of information to modern visitors revolve around seeming minutiae, such as inventories of the kitchen pantry, rather than the grandest or fanciest antiques. Some of the volunteer guides who give house tours are actual descendants of David and Mary C. Weeks. In addition to having a well-documented history, Shadows-on-the-Teche is one of the better-furnished plantation homes around. Other details inside the Classical Revival house include a lavish Italian marble floor in the formal dining room and the wide galleries at the exterior facade.

The home's last private owner, David Weeks Hall, worked hard to find a way to have the house saved as a museum; as fate would have it, he died in 1958 exactly one day after the National Trust for Historic Preservation agreed to take the house. Hall was something of a renaissance man and a well-known figure among the assorted literati who passed through New Iberia during the first half of the 20th century. You can still see the autographs of many of his distinguished guests on a door in his ground-floor studio—among the signatures are those of Elia Kazan, Walt Disney, Cecil B. DeMille, and Henry Miller. Across the street from the plantation in a former bank building, a visitors center presents a brief film on the Weeks family and history of the plantation, and rotating exhibits offer further insights into the property.

Center Street in New Iberia is so named because it was the center of the vast Weeks plantation, which once extended many miles south from this building, clear out to Weeks Island (a.k.a. Grand Cote), the actual sugarcane-farming operation that so enriched the Weeks family. One of the many interesting details that comes out during the tour is that the Weeks family actually had to pay dearly for processed sugar. Sugarcane was harvested here in southwestern Louisiana but refined in factories on the East Coast, so Louisiana families had to buy it back at a considerable cost in its refined form (ironic when you consider that unrefined "sugar in the raw" today now commands high prices in supermarkets and gourmet-food shops). Like many others in Louisiana, the plantation was occupied by Union troops during the Civil War. Soldiers camped around the grounds, and officers lived on the ground floor. It was an uneasy time for the Weeks family, and the matron of the family, Mary C. Weeks, died in the house during the Union occupation. The house's verdant grounds sweep right back to the muddy Bayou Teche, and you can stroll through the beautiful, somewhat formal gardens, which feature about 25 varieties of trees.

Other Downtown Sights

From Shadows-on-the-Teche, continue your stroll up Main Street, where you'll transition from the more residential section of town into the commercial district. Note the ornate art deco **Evangeline Theatre** on your right; it opened in 1930 as a motion-picture house and closed in 1960, sitting dormant until 1994, when it underwent a full restoration. To get a good look at **Bayou Teche,** cross the waterway at Bridge Street—on a warm day you'll often see boaters speeding along the murky brown water, which is not polluted but rather brown from the sediments constantly being stirred up on the river bottom. As a tour guide at Shadows-on-the-Teche noted, "You know your gumbo roux is just right when it's the color and consistency of Bayou Teche."

On the south side of downtown, you can tour the Konriko company's **Conrad Rice Mill** (307 Ann St., New Iberia, 337/364-7242 or 800/551-3245, www.conradricemill.com, open 9 A.M.–5 P.M. Mon.–Sat., admission free), America's oldest rice operation, having been founded in 1912. This factory museum has exhibits on the region's Cajun culture and specifically on how rice proved to be a key crop in the southwestern Louisiana economy. Parts of the mill building date to 1914, although it has received several additions through the years. During the factory tour through this rambling old mill, you get to see how rice is packaged, formed into rice cakes, and processed today. There's also the inevitable company store, where you can buy a broad assortment of rice products, along with T-shirts and related souvenirs.

◖ Avery Island

Perhaps the most visited section of New Iberia, the community of Avery Island is home to a pair of seminal Cajun Country attractions, Jungle Gardens and the Tabasco Factory. Avery Island is not an island in the sense that most people think of one—namely, it is not surrounded by water. It is, in fact, a salt dome, which rises rather gently above the surrounding wetlands and has been a source of commercial salt since the 1860s. The earliest salt works on the island were short-lived but important for Confederate troops during the Civil War. It was in 1862 that a significant cache of rock salt was discovered here—the first such deposit in all of North America. Union troops, upon securing the area, immediately destroyed the salt mines, which were not reopened until 1880. Avery Island continues to be a source of commercial salt. But salt is not Avery Island's claim to fame; rather, it's another savory condiment, Tabasco Sauce, which Edward McIlhenny first bottled on Avery Island in 1868.

To reach Avery Island, follow Highway 329 about six miles southwest from U.S. Highway 90 in New Iberia. You'll come to a small guardhouse where a nominal toll of $1 is collected, the money going toward the maintenance of the community roads, and then you proceed to the driveways for the Tabasco factory (on your left) and, beyond that, for Jungle Gardens.

The tour of the **McIlhenny Tabasco Company** (Avery Island, 337/365-8173 or 800/634-9599, www.tabasco.com, open 9 A.M.–4 P.M. daily, admission free) is actually pretty underwhelming, but then again, it's free. The tour begins with a shamelessly promotional video expounding on the virtues of Tabasco Sauce, suggesting that you simply cannot eat enough of the stuff. You'll see images of happy and hungry folks gleefully squirting gobs of Tabasco onto just about every food but ice cream. You're then given a small souvenir bottle of the vaunted condiment before proceeding along a wall of windows through which you can observe the inner workings of the factory, where a jumble of machines and conveyor belts bottles, caps, and labels the sauces. You walk through a small museum of Tabasco memorabilia at the end of your tour, and you can then wander across the parking lot to the faux–old-fashioned Country Store. Here you can buy Tabasco neckties, golf balls, sweat pants, boxer shorts, plus various food products made with the sauce. It's all good, clean, hot fun, and the experience is especially nice for kids who may be getting a little tired of tour-

ing historic house-museums. And now for the obligatory Tabasco trivia tidbit: The company holds the second-oldest food trademark in the country (issued in 1870), according to the U.S. Patent Office (Tabasco is mum on who holds the oldest).

Slightly less famous but of arguably much greater interest on Avery Island is the McIlhenny family's 250-acre **Jungle Gardens and Bird City** (Avery Island, 337/365-8173 or 800/634-9599, www.tabasco.com, open 8 A.M.–5 P.M. daily, admission $8). A narrow four-mile country lane winds through this garden complex, which you can do in less than an hour by car or in the course of a few hours if you decide to hoof it. You can also park in several spots along the drive and get out to walk around. Thousands of subtropical plants and trees, including massive moss-draped live oaks (in case you haven't tired of these yet), grow throughout these wild gardens, which are home to deer, turtles, nutria, raccoons, black bear, and alligators (during the warmer months, it's fairly easy to spot the gators, and you can often get close enough for a picture, although—as common sense dictates—you should absolutely not approach these animals directly).

But the big draw at Jungle Gardens is Bird City, a massive nesting ground for graceful (and big) great white egrets. You reach this area by parking at the designated spot (you will receive a trail map when you pay your admission at the Jungle Gardens gift shop on entering the park). Long platforms are set on stilts rising out of a large marshy pond, and the egrets build nests here—they're most prolific from December through July, when you may see many hundreds of these creatures squawking, gathering branches, mating and courting, flying overhead, and putting on a spectacular show. A three-story observation deck sits opposite the nesting platforms, close enough—especially if you have a decent zoom lens—to snap some wonderful pictures. The gardens also include the most complete collection of camellias in the world and a Buddhist temple containing a statue dating to the 12th century. Although the gardens are open year-round, they're less thrilling

CAJUN COUNTRY

in winter, from November through February, when much of the plant life is dormant, not to mention the hibernating alligators.

Jefferson Island

Another of New Iberia's coastal salt domes, Jefferson Island is home to the beautifully restored **Rip Van Winkle Gardens** (5505 Rip Van Winkle Rd., New Iberia, 337/359-8525, www.ripvanwinklegardens.com, tours given 9 A.M.–4 P.M. daily, admission $10), and it also has a strange but interesting past. A popular American actor of the 19th century, Joseph Jefferson, built his winter home here in 1870. In the late 1950s, the estate's then-occupant, J. Lyle Bayless, an expert on camellias and enthusiastic horticulturalist, laid out the 20-acre Rip Van Winkle Gardens around the house and eventually built a conservatory and another fine house here, right on the shore of adjacent Lake Peigneur. In a bizarre incident in 1980, however, an oil rig on the lake broke through to an underground cavern that was part of the salt mines beneath it, and the entire lake drained furiously like a bathtub with its stopper pulled. Nobody was killed, but the rig and drilling equipment disappeared and the mines filled with water. The house, gardens, conservatory, and visitors center Bayless had built were destroyed in the disaster. The gardens were eventually reestablished, however, by new owners, and now the property is back open and beautiful, with the grounds and many buildings having been fully restored, including the original Joseph Jefferson home. Tours reveal a breathtaking 25-acre spread of semitropical plant life, including brilliant magnolias, azaleas, hibiscus, and camellias plus hundreds of annuals. There are also overnight accommodations available in cottages on the property.

JEANERETTE

About 12 miles southeast of New Iberia via Highway 182, Jeanerette is the capital of the state's sugarcane industry, and you can learn a bit about this legacy at the small but informative **Jeanerette Museum** (500 E. Main St., Jeanerette, 337/276-4408, open 10 A.M.–noon and 1–4 P.M. Mon.–Fri., donation suggested), which contains photos and illustrated exhibits as well as artifacts and memorabilia related to this livelihood. There are also exhibits on African American history, Mardi Gras, and the cypress-logging industry.

A huge sugarcane-processing plant is right on Bayou Teche along Highway 182. You can't go inside, but on winter days during the processing season, you can watch some of the harvesting process from the road.

For as watery a place as the Cajun wetlands are, it's actually not all that easy to find direct access to the open Gulf waters. One of the best opportunities for this sort of exploration is to head down to **Cypremort Point State Park** (Beach La., off Hwy. 319, Cypremort Point, 337/867-4510 or 888/867-4510, www.crt.state.la.us, 6 A.M.–9 P.M. Sun.–Thurs., until 10 P.M. Fri.–Sat., $2 per vehicle), which fronts a cove on Vermilion Bay, an arm of the Gulf of Mexico. To reach the park from U.S. Highway 90 in Jeanerette, make a right turn onto Highway 318, following this until it joins with Highway 83; continue south on Highway 83 into the village of Cypremort, making a left turn onto Highway 319, which leads another five miles or so to the park entrance; the whole drive takes about 30–40 minutes from downtown Jeanerette.

Within the 185-acre park you'll find a half-mile stretch of man-made beach, one of the only ones in the region, along with a motorized-boat launch (actually just outside the park entrance), a sailboat launch, and picnic pavilions. There's also a fishing pier, from which you can cast a line for flounder and redfish. Swimming and beach-bumming are favorite activities here, but it's also a hot spot for sailboarding, sailing, and most any other type of recreational seafaring. This is a remote park, and wildlife sightings are not uncommon of muskrats, deer, and gators and even the occasional rare Louisiana black bear.

FRANKLIN

Franklin, about 16 miles southeast of Jeanerette via U.S. Highway 90, has long been one of

LOUISIANA'S SUGARCANE INDUSTRY

Based chiefly in Acadiana, the state's sugarcane industry extends across 25 Louisiana parishes and encompasses about 450,000 acres of farmland (an area roughly two-thirds the size of Rhode Island). Revenue for Louisiana in a typical year exceeds $1.5 billion, the result of harvesting 15 million tons of sugarcane, which represents about 20 percent of the sugar planted in the United States. There are about 700 sugarcane farms throughout southern Louisiana today, employing about 11,000 workers, and another 16,000 people work in other capacities in the state's sugarcane industry.

The earliest Louisianans engaged in this industry were Jesuit priests who planted crops along what is now Baronne Street in New Orleans's Central Business District. This was in 1751, nearly a half century before the city's earliest mayor, a sugar planter named Etienne de Boré, developed the first method of granulating sugar commercially at his plantation, which stood where Audubon Park is today. The industry has suffered setbacks in the form of floods, occasional disease epidemics, and some prolonged deep-winter freezes, but it has for the most part been a steady crop for Louisiana for the past 200 years.

Growing sugarcane is a time-consuming and labor-intensive process. The rows of stalks are planted each fall, and the buds produce shoots of cane the following spring. By late summer, the fresh cane shoots have grown to a size conducive to sugar production, and from the fall through early winter they are harvested. The good news is that the stalks will regenerate 2-4 more times before the field must be allowed to lie fallow for a year and then replanted. This means that one field planted with sugarcane can be harvested annually for 3-5 years.

The cane is then cut and loaded onto wagons, where it's brought to one of the many sugar refineries throughout southern Louisiana; there the raw cane is washed and crushed, the juice collected and reduced over boiling heat until it becomes a thick liquid, which is then separated into crystals (raw sugar) and molasses (used to produce livestock feed). Raw sugar is then sold to refineries, where the crystals are melted and the impurities removed. A byproduct of the cane refining is bagasse, a fuel that is used to power cane-processing factories.

the most prosperous sugarcaning communities anywhere, and the success of this industry during the 19th century is reflected by the about 400 homes and other notable structures in the city's beautiful historic district. The neighborhood, set along the main thoroughfare, Highway 182, makes for a pleasant afternoon or early-evening stroll, the sidewalks lighted with old-fashioned street lamps. With all the wealthy plantations and prominent families in Franklin through the years, it's little wonder that the town has produced five Louisiana governors (most recently Mike Foster, as well as his grandfather Murphy Foster, who served in the 1890s), three U.S. senators, a chief justice of the Louisiana Supreme Court, and several other prominent figures.

Franklin is still a big sugar producer, and it also has three plants producing carbon black, a petroleum-based compound essential to the production of tires and many mechanical rubber goods as well as plastics, paints, and printing inks.

The leading attraction in town is **Grevemberg** (407 Sterling Rd., Franklin, 337/828-2092, www.grevemberghouse.com, open 10 A.M.–4 P.M. daily, admission $6), a Greek Revival mansion built in 1851, its four fluted Corinthian columns and gracious second- and ground-floor galleries striking a regal pose over the flowering grounds. Inside you can view an estimable collection of mostly 19th-century antiques, plus antique toys, Civil War memorabilia, reproduction period wallpapers, and numerous decorative pieces.

Franklin's other leading house-museum is

CAJUN COUNTRY

owned by politician Mike Foster, who served as Louisiana's governor 1995–January 2004, when he was prevented from running again by term-limit laws. **Oaklawn Manor** (Irish Bend Road, off Hwy. 182, Franklin, 337/828-0434, open 10 A.M.–4 P.M. daily, admission $10) is a brick fortress with 20-inch-thick walls built in 1837 in the Greek Revival style. It stood as the heart of a massive sugarcane plantation during its heyday and is today known for its formal gardens, which bear a resemblance to those of Versailles. You'll also see a number of aviary houses set along the ground, which contain both domestic and tropical birds. The house was featured in the 1975 crime flick *The Drowning Pool,* which starred Paul Newman, Joanne Woodward, and Melanie Griffith. It was the producers at Warner Brothers Studios who had the aviary built for the film, but it fits in perfectly with Oaklawn today. Inside you'll find antique bird prints by John James Audubon, John Gould, and Prideaux John Selby, along with a collection of priceless antiques.

ABBEVILLE

Although it's not a large city, Abbeville feels more urbane and bustling than some of the other towns around Acadiana. It was founded in 1843, and the downtown area now comprises a large historic district with a mix of attractive commercial and residential architecture. It's also home to **Steen's Syrup Mill** (Abbeville, 800/725-1654, www.steensyrup.com), the world's largest sugarcane-syrup plant. Several engaging shops and eateries are downtown, which sits along Bayou Vermilion on its course from Lafayette down to Vermilion Bay. Anchoring the town center is one of Acadiana's most picturesque places of worship, **St. Mary Magdalen Catholic Church,** a redbrick Romanesque structure built in 1911 and possessing a high steeple and an ornate interior. It sits at the corner of Pere Magret Street and Quia des Beaux Arts.

Abbeville can be reached either from Lafayette south via U.S. Highway 167 (20 miles) or from New Iberia west via Highway 675 to Highway 14 (20 miles). A great way to take in

St. Mary Magdalen Catholic Church, Abbeville

© ANDREW COLLINS

Abbeville is to head down in the late afternoon, stop in one of the two excellent oyster bars in the center of town for an inexpensive and delicious meal, and then catch a theatrical performance at the **Abbey Players Theatre** (State and Lafayette streets), which was built in 1908 and originally housed a bar.

ERATH

East of Abbeville, roughly midway between it and U.S. Highway 90 in New Iberia, is the small town of Erath, worth a look to check out the small but informative **Acadian Museum of Erath** (203 Broadway, Erath, 337/937-5468, www.acadianmuseum.com, open 1–4 P.M. Mon.–Fri., donation suggested), set inside a small complex of early-20th-century storefronts right off Highway 14. The museum contains three rooms with exhibits on the area's history. The first traces the founding of Canadian Acadia in 1604; the second tackles the Grand Dérangement, or deportation of Acadians from Canada; and the last one explores the rebirth of Acadiana in southwestern Louisiana. The museum was closed after being badly damaged by the flooding of Hurricane Rita, but it is expected to resume operations. Call ahead first.

SHOPPING

Shops selling Cajun-related gifts, arts and crafts, music tapes and CDs, and books are easy to find throughout Acadiana, especially attached to the museums. One of the best sources of these types of goods is the **farmers market** held in downtown New Iberia's Bouligny Plaza (off Main Street); it's held 4–7 P.M. Tuesdays and 8–11 A.M. Saturdays. You'll find baked goods, produce, candies, blacksmith wares, herbs, hand-dipped candles, crafts, and local art. (Bayou Teche Farmers Market takes place across from Victor's.)

New Iberia is one of the best towns for shopping in the area, as it's home to a handful of very nice independent shops and boutiques, including several antiques shops. Stroll along Main Street and the blocks just off it. Be sure to check out **Books Along the Teche** (110 E. Main St., New Iberia, 337/367-7621), a small but first-rate independent bookstore that specializes in the books of James Lee Burke, author of the Dave Robicheaux detective novels.

In downtown Lafayette, **Jefferson Street Market** (538 Jefferson St., Lafayette, 337/233-2589) is a collection of shops and designers selling imported textiles, custom-crafted cypress furnishings, folk art, decorative items, local art, antiques, and similar items—it's a must if you're looking to pick up authentic southwest Louisiana items for the home. A small cafe is on-site, Keller's Bakery, where you can pick up gourmet sandwiches and snacks. Another important shopping stop downtown is **Sans Souci** (219 E. Vermilion St., Lafayette, 337/266-7999), a gallery featuring the works of members of the Louisiana Crafts Guild—you'll find clothing and textiles, small furniture, pottery, ceramics, glass, wood, and many other types of decorative items. Downtown's **Whoojoo Glass Studio** (532 Jefferson St., Lafayette, 337/269-9310) sells the colorful wares of Craig McCullen, who specializes in stained-glass art. Kaleidoscopes and elegant lamps also are for sale. The store is right by **Jefferson Street Market** (538 Jefferson St., Lafayette, 337/233-2589), a collection of stalls selling the works of several different local craftsmakers and artisans. You'll find folk art at **Schexnayder Galerie,** handmade wooden furniture at **Ted Jacques,** and handwoven and hand-dyed Acadian textiles at **Artisans of Louisiana.**

A great source of stylish women's clothing and accessories as well as shoes and gifts, **Artesia** (2513 Johnston St., Lafayette, 337/232-8441) is close to the University of Louisiana at Lafayette campus.

In the small town of Maurice, **Vivian Alexander Gallery and Museum** (6165 Picard La., Maurice, 337/898-0803, www.vivianalexander.com) showcases the unusual "egg" purses and other "egg" artworks created by artist Alex Caldwell and his staff of local artisans. The gallery functions both as a shop and a museum, and it's open daily by appointment.

In the heart of downtown Breaux Bridge you'll find a handful of boutiques, among them **Breaux Bridge Trading Co.** (202 Guilbeau St., Breaux Bridge, 337/332-5381), a multidealer complex of antiques shops.

ENTERTAINMENT AND NIGHTLIFE

In this part of the world, it's the restaurant that doesn't have live music, at least on weekends, that's the exception. You can catch Cajun song and dance and zydeco at a number of places all through the area, but Lafayette and the neighboring towns seem to support any kind of music that you can tap your toes to.

Much of the action is centered in Lafayette, which is also home to the stately **Heymann Performing Arts Center** (1373 S. College Rd., Lafayette), which hosts a variety of entertainment mounted by the **Performing Arts Society of Acadiana** (337/237-2787, www.pasa-online), including pop concerts, dance troupes, theater, and opera. Also calling the arts center home is the esteemed **Acadiana Symphony Orchestra** (337/232-4277, www.acadianasymphony.org), whose season includes about a dozen concerts and runs September–July.

As for nightlife, many of the region's top restaurants also do double-duty as live-music clubs. Check out the **Blue Dog, Cafe Des Amis, Clementine's, Mulate's, Prejean's,** and **Randol's** for some of the best listening (see the listings in the *Food* section).

El Sid O's Zydeco and Blues Club (1523 N. St. Antoine St., Lafayette, 337/235-0647) has some of the best live music anywhere in Acadiana. **307 Jazz and Blues Club** (307 Jefferson St., Lafayette, 337/262-0307) is a favorite for top-notch live entertainment—it's one of the top venues along bustling Jefferson Street. The **Blue Moon Guest House** (215 E. Convent St., Lafayette, 337/234-2422) has a large, outdoor deck where musicians of all types perform Thursday–Sunday to an eclectic crowd of all ages. The place is usually packed with locals and visitors. **Marley's** (407 Jefferson St., Lafayette, 337/235-2004) is a crowded old-fashioned pub with big-screen TVs, often airing football and basketball games. Downtown Lafayette is the region's hub of gay nightlife, with **Sound Factory** (209 Jefferson St., Lafayette, 337/269-6011) and **Jules** (533 Jefferson St., Lafayette, 337/264-8000).

In downtown New Iberia, **Napoleon's** (129 W. Main St., New Iberia, 337/364-6925) is a swanky little cocktail bar with armchairs, paintings of the "Little Corporal" himself, and jazz and folk bands regularly. **Landry's Restaurant** (2138 U.S. 90 W, New Iberia, 337/369-3772) presents live Cajun bands on weekend evenings.

FESTIVALS AND EVENTS

Outside New Orleans, no part of the state enjoys a good festival more than Lafayette and Central Acadiana. Scores of engaging events are held in towns all through the region, virtually year-round. Sultry summer is the one time when it seems fewer things are going on, but it's always worth checking with the local tourist boards to find out whether there's a party or gathering scheduled during the time of your visit. Lafayette also stages the second-largest Mardi Gras celebration in the state.

Mardi Gras

Mardi Gras events are all through the region in the weeks leading up to Fat Tuesday, with an especially high concentration of them occurring in Lafayette. You can attend everything from the **Krewe des Chiens Mardi Gras Ball** (337/984-7611, www.paradefordogs.com), a procession of pooches that includes music, food, and a silent auction (to raise money for homeless dogs), to the **Krewe of Vermilion Children's Parade** (337/893-8121) in the town of Erath, to **Mardi Gras Parade and Fais-Do-Do** (337/232-7667, www.cityofscottla.com) in the small town of Scott. In Lafayette, you can attend the carnivalesque **Le Festival de Mardi Gras à Lafayette,** which takes place adjacent to Cajundome and the Cajunfield. It has live bands, rides, a games midway, and other festivities. Sometimes the smaller and less formal Mardi Gras events are the most enjoyable and can afford outsiders the best chance to meet and talk with locals and learn about the different Mardi Gras customs.

Spring and Summer

In April, bicycle riders flock to the area for **Cycle Zydeco: Louisiana's Cajun/Creole Food and Music Cycling Festival** (www.cyclezydeco.com). This phenomenally popular four-day bike tour moves at a leisurely pace through Lafayette and surrounding countryside, so participants can enjoy live music, food, and booze at a number of venues. The event keeps getting more and more popular, and participation is limited to the first few hundred who sign up (the exact limit is set each year). The sign-up process usually begins in the late fall (keep checking the website for details), and the event is often full within 48 hours, so if you're interested in this, it's imperative that you sign up early.

Musical performers from all over the French-speaking world descend on Lafayette each April for **Festival International de Louisiane** (337/232-8086, www.festivalinternational.

com), a massive five-day party that showcases all kinds of local and French music, plays in French, and other Francophone fun.

Things really heat up in early April at New Iberia's **Hot Sauce Festival** (337/365-7539), at SugArena on Highway 3212. A big part of the fun is attending the Sauce Piquante Cook Off, in which participants compete in three categories: seafood, nonseafood, and most festively decorated booth. Other activities include a petting zoo, an arts-and-crafts show, live music, and a hot-air balloon rally.

Also in April, head to Abbeville for the **Carousel of Arts** (337/898-4114, www.vermilion.org), a music, fine-arts, and theater festival with an arts-and-crafts show and a spirited gumbo cookoff.

Fans of mudbugs gather at the **Breaux Bridge Crawfish Festival** (337/332-6655, www.bbcrawfest.com) in early May to sample the tasty treats and listen to live Cajun and zydeco music. It's one of the most popular events in the region.

Over 11 days in late May and early June, the family-oriented **Cajun Heartland State Fair** (337/265-2100, www.cajundome.com) is a lively indoor celebration with carnival rides, a petting zoo, and live entertainment and food.

Of all places, the little town of Erath throws one of the biggest and most festive **Fourth of July celebrations** (337/937-5861, www.erath4.com) in the area, with pageants, carnival rides, and fireworks. It takes place over several days leading up to the Fourth.

Lafayette's **Le Cajun French Music Festival and Awards Show** (337/233-9690, www.cajunfrenchmusic.org) is a three-day early-August event dedicated to the promotion and preservation of Cajun song and dance as well as French heritage. It has music, an awards show, food, and demonstrations.

Fall and Winter

In mid-October, just as the hot weather begins to break (usually), Lafayette holds its rollicking **Festivals Acadiens,** a chance for visitors to learn about Cajun culture through its rich musical traditions. You can learn the Cajun waltz or two-step, and how accordions, *tit fers,* and fiddles figure into the sounds of Cajun song and dance. Outside Mardi Gras, this is one of the most well-attended and popular festivals in the region. The event comprises several smaller ones throughout the area, including the Festival de Musique Acadienne, the Bayou Food Festival, the Louisiana Crafts Fair, Downtown Alive!, and Kids Alive! Events are held at lovely Girard Park near the University of Louisiana at Lafayette.

Come October, Abbeville celebrates its **Louisiana Cattle Festival** (337/893-9712, www.louisianacattlefestival.org), which is dedicated to the area's legacy as a cattle-ranching hub in the late 1700s. You'll find food, music, a street fair, and a queen's pageant. November's **Broussard Community Fair** (337/837-6363, www.beausoleil-broussard.com) is a great time to visit this small and charming town southwest of Lafayette.

Breaux Bridge kicks off the holiday season with a **Cajun Christmas Bayou Parade** (337/332-8500, www.bayouparade.com) in late November—a long parade of lights stretches down along Bayou Teche, and there's a fireworks display.

All through December, many of New Iberia's grandest homes are trimmed with lights and decorations for **Christmas on the Bayou** (888/942-3742, www.iberiaparish.com), which includes holiday concerts downtown, parades, and celebration. Lafayette offers similar activities at its **Cajun and Creole Christmas** (800/346-1958, www.lafayettetravel.com), which runs through the month at a variety of venues.

ACCOMMODATIONS

This part of the Cajun Country has dozens of B&Bs, varying from small and rustic cabins overlooking swamps and bayous to regal Greek Revival manor houses filled with museum-quality antiques. The greatest number and variety of such properties are in Lafayette, Breaux Bridge, New Iberia, and St. Martinville. Lafayette also has dozens of chain motels and hotels, many of them along U.S. Highway

90 just south of I-10 or along the city's main commercial drags, such as Pinhook and Kaliste Saloom roads. A small cluster of chain hotels is also off U.S. Highway 90 at Highway 14 in New Iberia.

Lodging costs are much lower in Acadiana than in New Orleans, with most mid- to upscale chain hotels charging nearly but still less than $100, except during very busy times, and many perfectly decent lower-end properties charging under $50. B&B prices vary more, but even the most luxurious properties in the area generally keep their rates under $150, while inns that cost $50–100 nightly make up the majority.

A new upscale boutique hotel, the Juliette, is planned for downtown Lafayette, with an anticipated opening of 2007. Also under construction downtown is a 110-room Homewood Suites (www.hilton.com), which is also to open in 2007 right across from the courthouse and within walking distance of museums, restaurants, and nightlife.

Hotels and Motels

Under $50: Although it's a chain with an uneven track record, the **Days Inn Lafayette** (1620 N. University Ave., Lafayette, 337/237-8880 or 800/329-7466, www.daysinn.com), just off I-10 north of downtown, offers among the best values in the region. The place was completely revamped in 2000 and has clean, attractive rooms whose fox-print–covered walls may not have you believing you're at a Ritz-Carlton but do at least brighten things up. Amenities include a pool; in-room writing desks, microwaves, and refrigerators; and a courteous staff.

Another very inexpensive option along the same strip as the Days Inn is the **Red Roof Inn Lafayette** (1718 N. University Ave., Lafayette, 337/233-3339 or 800/733-7663, www.redroof. com), a generic but reliable budget property.

The **Sleep Inn Scott** (2140 W. Willow St., Scott, 337/264-0408 or 877/424-6423, www. sleepinn.com) is a midpriced chain just off I-10 a few miles northwest of Lafayette, a good choice to be closer to Lake Charles and away

from the heavily trafficked I-10 exits north of downtown. Rooms are compact, but some suites have whirlpools, and perks include a morning paper and continental breakfast; all units have built-in work areas.

A terrific all-around option with a quiet location on the southwest side of town, an area less overrun with strip malls than out by the interstate, the **Courtyard Lafayette** (214 Kaliste Saloom Rd., Lafayette, 337/232-5005 or 800/321-2211, www.marriott.com/lftcy) has pleasantly landscaped grounds, a friendly staff, warm and inviting public areas, and 90 spacious and well-lighted rooms with work desks, voice mail, in-room movies, and irons and boards.

Extended Stay Lafayette-Oil Center (807 S. Hugh Wallis Rd., Lafayette, 337/232-8313 or 800/398-7829), part of a chain of economical properties designed for guests staying several days or more, is just across U.S. Highway 90 from Lafayette Regional Airport, on the south side of town, which puts you a bit closer to New Iberia and St. Martinville than most of the city's hotels. The other big advantage to this hotel is that its amenities work well if you're traveling with friends or family or staying a while: Rooms are 300 square feet, with recliner chairs, kitchens equipped with dishes and silverware, and ample space for up to four guests.

Built in the late 1990s, the **Comfort Suites New Iberia** (2817 Hwy. 14, New Iberia, 337/367-0855 or 877/424-6423, www.comfortsuites.com) is one of the best values in town. Rooms are bright and large with both beds and sleeper sofas, and it has an indoor pool and exercise room. The big, pink, vaguely Carribean-style building, with 50 guest rooms, is just off U.S. Highway 90, a short drive from downtown New Iberia and Avery Island.

Practically next door to the Comfort Suites is the **Best Western Inn and Suites of New Iberia** (2714 Hwy. 14, New Iberia, 337/364-3030 or 800/780-7234, www.bestwestern. com), a 150-room low-rise built in the early 1980s but completely overhauled in 1999. Amenities include a restaurant and lounge and outdoor pool.

Outside of Lafayette and New Iberia, chain hotels are limited to a handful of spots, including the **Best Western of Breaux Bridge** (2088-B Rees St., Breaux Bridge, 337/332-1114 or 888/783-0007, www.bestwestern.com), a run-of-the-mill 50-room property just off I-10, a short drive north of town.

Also in this category is the **Best Western Forest Motor Inn** (1909 Main St., Franklin, 337/828-1810 or 800/828-1812, www.bestwestern.com), a qualitatively similar motor court with 88 rooms, an Olympic-size outdoor pool, a restaurant, business services, and a convenient location just outside Franklin's historic district.

There's also a very nicely maintained **Holiday Inn Express** (2942 Grand Point Hwy., Breaux Bridge, 337/667-8913 or 800/465-4329, www.hiexpress.com), just off I-10 near the town of Henderson. It's the closest hotel in Acadiana to Baton Rouge via I-10.

$100-150: The fanciest chain property in the area, the ❰ **Hilton Lafayette and Towers** (1521 W. Pinhook Rd., Lafayette, 337/235-6111 or 800/774-1500, www.lafayette.hilton.com) sits on the banks of Bayou Vermilion and has 330 warmly furnished rooms with French Provincial–inspired furnishings. The 15-floor hotel offers nice views of the countryside and is centrally situated, close to the airport and downtown. It has a pretty good full-service restaurant and a hotel bar that's popular with locals and has live bands fairly often. Other pluses include a 24-hour business center, a fitness center, in-room high-speed Internet, room service, and a full laundry service.

The Hilton's main competitor, the **Holiday Inn Lafayette** (2032 N.E. Evangeline Thruway, Lafayette, 337/233-6815 or 800/465-4329, www.holiday-inn.com), differs markedly in location and ambience. It's a low-rise property just off I-10 and the junction with I-49, and it sits on 17 landscaped acres with picnic areas, playgrounds, and a large game room—the setting and activities make it a favorite with families. Other features include a large health center, an indoor pool, and a full restaurant.

Inns and Bed-and-Breakfasts

Under $50: A quasihostel, the affordable ❰ **Blue Moon Guest House** (215 E. Convent St., Lafayette, 337/234-2422, www.bluemoonhostel.com) is a great choice for budget travelers and music fans—it's a clean, centrally situated Acadian-style wood-frame house with four private rooms and two bunk rooms that can accommodate a total of up to 30 people, and the outdoor deck and bar in back is one of Lafayette's favorite venues for Cajun music, jazz, blues, and the like. The dorm-style units are first-come, first-served and can be converted into private rooms if there's availability; if you're seeking one of the private rooms, it's best to email ahead and make a reservation. The late 1890s house, with hardwood floors and sunny rooms with both double and single-size bunk beds and in some cases private beds, is open to guests of all ages, including families. The owners, who speak English and French, run a laid-back and friendly place where guests tend to mingle and get to know each other. It has Internet access and an attractive, nicely outfitted self-service kitchen. The live music is typically offered Wednesday–Sunday. If you're looking for a charming, authentic slice of local color at the cost of a local budget motel (the dorm rooms are supercheap at $18 per person), the Blue Moon is perfect.

$50-100: Steps from St. Martinville's Evangeline Oak, the **Old Castillo B&B** (220 Evangeline Blvd., St. Martinville, 337/394-4010 or 800/621-3017) is a stately redbrick Greek Revival inn that was built in the 1800s as a private home but was soon converted into a hotel. During most of the 20th century, the building served as the city's only high school for girls, run by the Mercy nuns. It has five rooms with high ceilings, hardwood floors, and fine antiques.

You can't get much closer to the swamp country than by staying at the **Riverside Cottage B&B** (2091 Atchafalaya River Hwy., Breaux Bridge, 337/228-2066), a tranquil country house with three spacious suites, each with a private balcony overlooking the gentle Atchafalaya River. Rooms have sleeper sofas and can accommodate up to four guests, and each also has a private entrance, cable TV, phone, refrigerator, microwave, and coffeemaker. Two of the rooms are floral-themed, and the Country Suite has a rich hardwood floor and wood paneling. Furnishings are simple, warm, and unfussy, and guests enjoy plenty of privacy here, making it a favorite spot with couples seeking a secluded retreat from civilization.

With rates lower than most of the cookie-cutter motels around the area, **Bayou Boudin Cabins** (100 W. Mills Ave., Breaux Bridge, 337/332-6158, www.bayoucabins.com) makes a fun and funky alternative. There are eight cozy cabins right by Bayou Teche, close to downtown and within walking distance of famous Mulate's Restaurant, and there's a home-style cafe right on the premises, serving seafood boudin, cracklin's, andouille gumbo, and the like. The cabins are rustic but endearingly furnished—one has old newspaper for wallpaper, another contains a handmade pencil-post queen-size bed. Some have screened porches, another is decked in 1950s-style furnishings, and they all have cable TVs. A full breakfast is included.

$100-150: Stay at the stately **Hanson House** (114 E. Main St., Franklin, 337/828-3217 or 877/928-3271, www.bigdogz.com/hh) for the chance to experience the high-style romance of an antebellum mansion—there aren't many buildings like this in Cajun Country. The Greek Revival home, built by an evidently quite successful British ship's captain in 1849, sits along Franklin's main drag, in the heart of the town's historic district—it's between Lafayette and Houma, making it a good choice for exploring the length of the Cajun wetlands. Furnishings are eclectic, varying from ornate Victorian carved-wood beds and dressers to more modern pieces from the 1940s and '50s; both private and shared baths are available. An extensive and filling Southern breakfast is included.

One of St. Martinville's architectural gems, **Bienvenue House** (421 N. Main St., St. Martinville, 337/394-9100 or 888/394-9100, www.bienvenuehouse.com) was built in 1830 and today contains four lovely rooms with a mix of country-inspired and more formal antiques. Breakfasts here are a lavish affair, and many of the town's restaurants and shops are within a short walk.

Upscale 🄲 **Maison Des Amis and Chez Des Amis** (140 Bridge St., Breaux Bridge, 337/507-3399, www.cafedesamis.com) comprises a pair of the most elegantly furnished homes in Cajun Country. Maison Des Amis has a two-bedroom suite and a standard room, while Chez Des Amis is a smaller cottage with a pair of standard guest rooms. Furnishings are well chosen and stylish, from plush linens and pillows to fine dark-wood Victorian antiques. Each cottage is filled with the artwork (for sale) of prominent Louisiana artists and has a sitting area, and guests enjoy a full breakfast in the acclaimed Cafe Des Amis. The inns are along Bayou Teche, a short drive from the nature preserve at Lake Martin.

With a convenient downtown location in New Iberia, just across the street from Shadows-on-the-Teche, **Le Rosier** (314 E. Main St., New Iberia, 337/367-5306 or 888/804-7673, www.lerosier.com) contains six romantically furnished rooms. The hosts are friendly, and there's an equally convivial Dalmatian doggie on hand to greet guests. Rooms have DSL lines and desks. It's a very charming house with a spacious breakfast area. The six very secluded units are inside an outbuilding in back of the main house. It's a first-class operation all around. The inn also has a small restaurant serving tapas and light fare in the evening.

In Lafayette, **Bois des Chenes Bed & Breakfast** (338 N. Sterling St., Lafayette, 337/233-7816) occupies an 1820s plantation house a short drive from downtown. Three of the suites, each with private bath, cable TV, and minirefrigerators, are inside an 1890s carriage house behind the main home. The upstairs unit can accommodate five guests, and the other two suites—on the ground floor—are each double occupancy. Each is decorated elegantly in a different regional style: country Acadian, Louisiana Empire, and classic

© ANDREW COLLINS

Bois des Chenes Bed & Breakfast, Lafayette

Victorian. In the main home, there are two full suites with the same amenities; one has a working wood fireplace (and it does come in handy on those chilly winter evenings).

Set near the bird-watching paradise of Lake Martin, **Maison Madeleine** (1015 John D. Hebert Dr., Breaux Bridge, 337/332-4555, www.maisonmadeleine.com) occupies a handsomely renovated 1840s Creole cottage as well as a *garçonierre* (cottage). There are three guest accommodations, each with shared bath, and rooms are decorated with fine antiques. Rates include a full breakfast. If you're a photo buff or an avid birder, this is the spot for you.

Over $250: The Gougenheim (101 W. Main St., New Iberia, 337/364-3949, www.gougenheim.com) is an impressive, elegant 1894 building on Main Street, very near Victor's Cafeteria. It was constructed as the Washington Ballroom, where it hosted many wedding receptions and important social functions, and it was beautifully restored by its current owners and converted into a B&B in 2001. There's a large veranda that wraps around the second floor, and four large guest apartments: a one-bedroom, a two-bedroom, and two with three bedrooms. Hardwood floors, detailed woodwork, exposed brick, and posh furnishings give this the feel of a small luxury hotel; some units have spiral staircases leading up to sleeping lofts. Amenities include large TVs with VCRs, designer kitchens with granite counters and stainless-steel appliances, and private balconies overlooking downtown New Iberia's historic district.

Camping

In quiet Carencro, **Bayou Wilderness R.V. Resort** (201 St. Clair Rd., Carencro, 337/896-0598, www.bayouwildernessrvresort.com) is north and east of Lafayette and has 120 full pull-through RV sites set on 50 acres of wooded grounds. The resort has oodles of activities and recreational diversions, including a pool with slides, a whirlpool tub, a tennis court, shuffleboard, a playground and video arcade, and trails through cypress groves and by natural fishing ponds. There's also a

CAJUN COUNTRY

well-stocked camp store. The property is right by Bayou Vermilion.

Right in the center of things (well, just west of town), **KOA Lafayette** (537 Apollo Rd., Scott, 337/235-2739 or 800/562-0809, www.koa.com) is right off I-10 and has a wealth of facilities, including two pools, minigolf, Cajun driving tour cassettes that you're free to borrow, and fishing in a 10-acre stocked lake. In addition to the 175 level concrete sites, you can stay in one of the 20 camp cabins.

Another popular camping area in the region is **Maxie's Campground** (U.S. 90, Broussard, 337/837-6200, www.maxiescampground.com), which is southwest of Lafayette, within easy striking distance of Avery Island, New Iberia, and St. Martinville—it's very near the Zoo of Acadiana. There are 70 RV sites with full hookups, plus laundry facilities and restrooms with showers. This is less a resort and more a picturesque, tree-shaded meadow where you can safely and comfortably park your RV.

FOOD

To somebody visiting from another part of the country or even a different country entirely, the food served at most restaurants in Acadiana might not seem a significant departure from that served in New Orleans. The Cajuns use a lot of local fish—oysters, soft-shell crabs, crawfish, shrimp, redfish, catfish. And you'll find gumbo, bread pudding with rum sauce, red beans and rice, étouffée, jambalaya, and plenty of other foods common to New Orleans on menus in Lafayette, New Iberia, and elsewhere. The difference, really, is that while it's not hard to find the main dishes of Cajun cooking on menus all throughout New Orleans, you don't often find the full range of New Orleans cuisine on Cajun menus—although alligator fritters, cracklin's, and boudin are far easier to find in Breaux Bridge or Abbeville than in the French Quarter. The true Creole classics of the Big Easy, such as oysters Rockefeller, bananas Foster, shrimp rémoulade, turtle soup, and fish slathered in rich cream sauces are less common out this way, found only at a handful of upscale places that specialize in a more urbanized form of Louisiana fare.

This is not to say that the food served in Cajun restaurants is any less fresh, authentic, or tasty—only that preparations tend to be simpler and more straightforward, even if portions at Acadiana restaurants are consistently every bit as overwhelming as in New Orleans. Happily, prices at Cajun Country restaurants are much lower than at comparable places in New Orleans—even at the most sophisticated eateries in Lafayette, it's rare to see entrées on menus costing much more than $20. Similarly, dress is more casual, and the ambience of restaurants less formal—in fact, some of the most respected eateries in Acadiana for food have almost depressingly drab dining rooms. It's as though Cajuns are a bit suspicious of a restaurateur who would go to great lengths to gussy up a place, as though maybe it's an attempt to mask substandard food.

That all being said, the dining scene in Acadiana, especially in fast-growing Lafayette and sophisticated New Iberia, is changing, just as it is everywhere. A number of places serving innovative, impressionistic versions of traditional Cajun cooking have opened in these parts in recent decades, and their legions will no doubt multiply in the coming years.

Traditional Creole and Cajun

Lafayette's (1025 Kaliste Saloom Rd., Lafayette, 337/216-9024, $11–26) is a fairly standard-issue steak-and-seafood place doling out huge portions of extremely fresh seafood. The fare served here is generally rich and heavy, in many cases deep-fried—just the way plenty of people in these parts like it. Sample coconut shrimp, crawfish-and-artichoke bisque, mahimahi Creole-style with a sauce of crawfish, shrimp, wild mushrooms, parsnips, and hollandaise sauce, tandoori-style tilapia, and whole semiboneless applewood-smoked-bacon–wrapped quail with a stuffing of crawfish, crab, and shrimp. Lafayette's is set in a sprawling, modern building made to look like a plantation house, with dining rooms set around a central bar. Prices are reasonable, and servers are young and friendly.

A longtime favorite for Cajun music and authentic food, **Mulate's** (325 Mills Ave., Breaux Bridge, 337/332-4648 or 800/422-2586, $13–19) is a cavernous, noisy, and happy place built with cypress logs brought over from nearby Henderson Swamp—it's on busy Highway 94, on the northwest side of town, an easy drive from Lafayette or Exit 109 off I-10. Specialties from the long, long menu include catfish Mulate (topped with crawfish étouffée), crabmeat au gratin, and—when you just can't make up your mind—Mulate's Cajun Seafood Platter, which includes stuffed crab, fried crawfish tails, butterflied shrimp, fried catfish, fried oysters, jambalaya, corn macque choux, and home-style fries. It's tourist central at this place, but it's hard not to enjoy yourself here, even if you don't love crowds—the music is infectious.

Set in a grand 1890s building, **Clementine's** (113 E. Main St., New Iberia, 337/560-1007, $13–23) is New Iberia's classiest restaurant, a white-linen and fine-flatware sort of place, but the dress and mood are still casual. The walls are lined with the paintings of locally prominent artists—the restaurant is named for painter Clementine Hunter. The cooking tends toward traditional Cajun and Creole, with a few nods to today's contemporary styles, such as crawfish cakes with a kicky Creole-style sauce, corn-and-crab bisque, and tender black Angus steaks. Still, it's the straightforward chicken-and-andouille gumbo that really stands out. There's a well-thought-out wine list. You'll find this high-ceilinged, elegant restaurant right on Main in the heart of the historic district. There's live music on weekend evenings.

In downtown Broussard, **Nash's** (101 E. 2nd St., Broussard, 337/839-9333, $10–20) occupies a stately 1908 house surrounded by mature oak and cedar trees. The kitchen specializes in both traditional upscale Creole and Italian fare, a breed of cooking that's relatively common in New Orleans but unusual in Acadiana. You might start with crab cakes topped with a Creole horseradish cream or Italian sausage served over caramelized onions with roasted peppers and Italian red gravy. Worthy entrées include shrimp-and-eggplant parmigiana over angel hair pasta, cornmeal-dusted oysters, filet mignon, or grilled amberjack with a lemon-butter sauce served over shrimp fettuccine.

◖ Prejean's (3480 I-49 Access Rd., Lafayette, 337/896-3247, $15–25), directly south of Evangeline Downs racetrack, is as popular for its live Cajun music as for the very good food. The rambling dining room is presided over by a friendly and efficient staff. Of the big Cajun dance hall–slash–dining rooms in the region, Prejean's serves the best, and most inventive, Cajun and Creole food, including such specialties as mesquite-grilled yellowfin tuna Rockefeller with lobster sauce, skillet-cooked shrimp, crab, and crawfish in crab-butter cream topped with jack cheese, catfish Catahoula (stuffed with shrimp, crawfish, and crab), alligator Grand Chenier (white tailmeat with a crab-shrimp stuffing), and a mixed grill of mesquite-grilled elk chop, blackened venison chop, and buffalo tenderloin, each with its own sauce. Chocolate crème brûlée ranks among the favorite desserts. The whole time you're enjoying the dinner, you can enjoy live music and dancing at the front of the dining room. Lunch is also served, and the breakfasts at Prejean's are legendary—try the sweet-potato pancakes or the crawfish-and-andouille eggs scramble.

Another of Lafayette's great Cajun dance halls and restaurants, **Randol's** (2320 Kaliste Saloom Rd., Lafayette, 337/981-7080, www.randols.com, $7–18) has been a fixture in these parts since the 1970s. The food is pretty standard Cajun: crawfish boils, fried soft-shell crabs, and so on, plus some specialties such as an ahi tuna napoleon with crisp wontons, wild mushrooms, and sweet onions, and trout Lucile (smothered with a crab, shrimp, and crawfish cream sauce). But Randol's offers some of the freshest seafood around, which ensures an enjoyable dining experience. Another big, big draw is the lively Cajun and zydeco music.

Don's Seafood Hut (4039 Johnston St., Lafayette, 337/981-1141, $13–28) has pressed-tin ceilings and an attractive interior despite its prosaic setting on busy Johnston Street, surrounded by shopping centers. There's a very nice wine list, too. A specialty here are the gumbos, plus the bacon-wrapped oysters, oysters Bienville (topped with a wine-and-cream sauce of mushrooms and shrimp). There's also a branch outside New Orleans in the town of Metairie.

Creative and Contemporary

If you have a chance for only one dinner in the Cajun Country, give strong consideration to 【 **Cafe Vermilionville** (1304 W. Pinhook Rd., Lafayette, 337/237-0100, $18–28), a snazzy yet friendly restaurant set inside a stunning 1810s raised Creole cottage that brightens up an otherwise dull road clogged with strip malls. During its early years, it served as Lafayette's only inn; now chef Ken Veron serves his innovative style of fine Cajun cooking within its historic walls. The menu changes often, but here are a few recent favorites to whet your appetite: There are the starters of smoked duck and figs au poivre, or the crawfish beignets with a spicy Creole dipping sauce. The salad with bronzed shrimp, artichokes, and montrachet goat cheese is a knockout. Among the entrées, consider Louisiana speckled trout dusted with sweet-potato flour and finished with jumbo lump crabmeat and lemon-and-thyme beurre blanc, or marinated chicken breast broiled over an open flame and topped with crawfish tails and French mushrooms and then served with a roasted garlic-and-chive butter. Cafe Vermilionville has one of the most respected wine lists in the area.

Charley G's (3809 Ambassador Caffery Pkwy., Lafayette, 337/981-0108, $18–35) serves superb nouvelle Cajun fare, with smoked-duck-and-andouille gumbo a particular favorite. Other treats include coconut shrimp with pepper jelly, wood-grilled redfish with fried green tomatoes, lump crabmeat, and succotash, and crispy roast duck with ginger-peach glaze and roasted-corn pudding. With the ambience of a clubby, big-city restaurant in New Orleans's Central Business District, this is arguably the fanciest restaurant in Lafayette, a fine setting to celebrate a special occasion. There's live piano

many evenings, and the bar is a popular gathering spot among cigar aficionados.

In Lafayette, whence famous "blue dog" artist George Rodrigue hails, the **Blue Dog Cafe** (1211 W. Pinhook Rd., Lafayette, 337/237-0005, $13–22) is filled with the canine art so beloved by so many people. But the real reason to dine inside this cheery, rambling house along a busy road on the south side of town is to sample the creatively rendered Louisiana cuisine, from velvety corn-and-crab bisque to tender seafood wontons—and those are just the starters. Dig in to honey-glazed duck and some of the best crawfish étouffée in town when you're truly hungry.

Some of the most creative cooking in the area is served at **Cafe Des Amis** (140 E. Bridge St., Breaux Bridge, 337/332-5273, $12–20), a snazzy yet laid-back storefront eatery set in a 19th-century building. Oven-glazed duckling glazed with cane syrup and pepper jelly and sesame-encrusted drum topped with shrimp and sautéed in fresh chopped tomatoes and lime juice are house specialties, but don't overlook sushi-grade tuna served rare with a black peppercorn crust. The restaurant serves breakfast and lunch, too, including Saturday morning zydeco concerts; there's also live acoustic music on Wednesday evenings.

It's worth the short drive north to 【 **Catahoula's** (234 Martin Luther King Dr./Hwy. 93, Exit 11 from I-49, Grand Coteau, 337/662-2275 or 888/547-2275, $14–24), which is named for the state dog of Louisiana, a special blue-eyed dog descended from the dogs used by explorer Hernando de Soto during his journey through southern Louisiana in the 1530s—the walls of the restaurant, which occupies an old hardware-and-feed store, are lined with photos of these majestic dogs. Exceptional regional fare is served, including raspberry roast duckling, seared ahi tuna on skewers, crabmeat cheesecake, and seafood Napoleon.

Casual Cooking

Not surprisingly, you'll see an actual varnished pirogue hanging from the ceiling at **Paul's Pirogue** (209 E. St. Peter St., Carencro,

337/896-3788, $5–18), a wood-paneled, rustic dining room in downtown Carencro. You'll find both communal and individual tables at this storefront spot with friendly, low-key service. The special combo dinners are the big draw here—with the crawfish version you get crawfish salad, bisque, étouffée, *boulettes* (fried dumplings), and a generous pile of boiled crawfish, along with fried or stuffed potatoes and dessert. It's a delicious, messy affair. Less overwhelming but equally tasty are the simpler dishes, such as shrimp-and-crab étouffée, Paul's pepper (a bell pepper stuffed with crabmeat), snapper Kori (served under a mound of sautéed crabmeat), and fried frogs' legs.

A famous import from Natchez, Mississippi (it's been there since 1941), **Doe's Eat Place Lafayette** (530 W. Pinhook Rd., Lafayette, 337/266-5332, $8–22) occupies a vintage building in the city's Oil Center. The airy dining room is filled with local artwork, and there's some serious eating to do here. Doe's is noted for two things: juicy steaks and hearty tamales.

Soul food doesn't get much better than what you'll taste at **Country Cuisine** (709 N. University Ave., Lafayette, 337/269-1653, $5–13), a simple low-frills restaurant that has a set menu but also comes up with a nice mix of daily specials. Favorites include barbecued ribs and chicken, shrimp and okra, meatball stew, stuffed pork chops, and a wide range of sides—black-eyed peas, smothered potatoes, cabbage, mac and cheese, and baked beans.

◖ Poor Boy's Riverside Inn (240 Tubing Rd., Lafayette, 337/235-8559, $7–21) began as a mere sno-ball stand in the early 1930s but has grown into one of the most treasured spots in the region for delicious home-style cooking. The po'boys are the stuff of legend, but you can also pick up tasty steaks and traditional lump crabmeat in garlic butter. There are also themed meals, such as the Oyster Lover dinner, which comes with an oyster shooter, salad, oyster gumbo, oyster pie, oyster jambalaya, oyster en brochette, fried oysters, oysters Bienville, and oysters Rockefeller—got all that? It's a favorite with everyone in these parts from oil

workers to gourmands. The same owners operate New Iberia's similarly good **Little River Inn** (833 E. Main St., New Iberia, 337/367-7466, $7–21).

There's also superb seafood at **Gator Cove** (2601 S.E. Evangeline Thruway, Lafayette, 337/264-1374, $8–19), which you can't miss, as the name of the restaurant is painted in huge letters along the roof of the low-slung building. You'll find all the usual Cajun faves here: fried alligator bits, boiled crabs and crawfish, seafood-stuffed shrimp, fried seafood platters, and Cajun-style steaks.

Lagniappe, Too (204 E. Main St., New Iberia, 337/365-9419, $7–14) is a cute art-filled sunny cafe just a block or two from Shadows-on-the-Teche. It's very casual, with red-and-white–checked plastic tablecloths and large windows overlooking busy Main Street. You'll find a classic menu of Cajun gumbos, bisques, po'boys, salads, seafoods, and grills. Have a slice of banana-mango cake to finish off your meal. Everything on the menu is prepared fresh from scratch. It's mostly a lunch place, but dinner is served on Friday and Saturday nights.

◖ Black's (319 Pere Megret, Abbeville, 337/893-4266, $4–11) is arguably the most atmospheric of Abbeville's handful of outstanding oyster bars—it's a large tavern with high ceilings and tall brick walls and plain wood tables. Fresh oysters on the half shell cost just $4.50 a dozen, but you can also get alligator bits, soft-shell crab loaves, and delicious grilled chicken salad with homemade ranch dressing. The dining area and bar are filled with mounted fish and posters of local scenes.

The **Seafood Connection** (999 Parkview Dr., New Iberia, 337/365-2454, $5–11) may occupy a humble cinder-block building with no windows and long rows of plain tables bathed in fluorescent light, but this phenomenally popular restaurant is staffed by supernice servers and excellent fry cooks who turn out some of the tastiest fish and shellfish around. Here you can order fresh platters of boiled crab and crawfish, stuffed shrimp or crab, and fried soft-shell crab, oysters, and frog's legs. It's open daily and quite late by New Iberia standards, and it's a great value. Just keep in mind that virtually everything on the menu once swam in the sea, so landlubbers should look elsewhere.

The **Filling Station** (900 Jefferson St., Lafayette, 337/291-9635, $5–12) occupies a funky old neon-lit gas station on Jefferson, with a glass-brick deco-inspired bar and a big front patio where patrons dine on great American and Mexican food. The enchiladas are filling and delicious.

Nearby **T'Coons** (740 Jefferson St., Lafayette, 337/232-3803, $6–14) is close to the courthouse and draws plenty of lawyers and politicos for the great breakfasts of grillades and grits, as well as hearty lunches of smothered rabbit and other Cajun favorites.

Ethnic

Rather close to the famous Cajun restaurant Prejean's (but on the opposite side of I-49), **Picante's** (3235 N.W. Evangeline Thruway, Lafayette, 337/896-1200, $4–13) is a stellar Mexican restaurant with a youthful, friendly staff and spicy fare varying from fairly typical Tex-Mex dishes to a few items with distinctly local flair: Huge Cajun chimichangas are packed with crawfish étouffée and Mexican rice, and topped with avocados, sour cream, and a corn cake. Another fine offering is the chile-and-cheese–stuffed steak. The decor is fairly standard for the genre, with colorful Mexican art—a high point for many regulars is karaoke and live music, offered several nights a week.

Cafe Habana City (2848 Verot School Rd., Lafayette, 337/857-7527, $8–17) brings the delights of Cuban fare to Cajun Country. The cheerful dining room with pastel-hued walls conjures images of the Caribbean, and the food goes ever further. Try marinated pork with mojo sauce, Cuban-style pork tamales, or grilled shrimp marinated in citrus sauce. Be sure to order a side of sweet or savory plantains.

Pimon Thai (3904 Johnson St., Lafayette, 337/993-8424, $7–16) is one of a handful of good Asian restaurants in Acadiana. Traditional coconut-lemongrass-chicken soups, chicken satays, and green and red curries with shrimp, chicken, or beef are among the offerings.

On weekends, you can listen to live zydeco and Cajun music while brunching on tasty and relatively authentic Chinese and Japanese fare at **Dragon Cafe** (107 S. Main St., Breaux Bridge, 337/507-3320, $6–18), a colorful place in the heart of Breaux Bridge's historic downtown, which is also open for lunch and dinner most days. There's a sushi bar, too. The place is especially renowned for its elaborate flaming desserts.

Showcasing excellent Central and South American cooking in downtown Lafayette is **Guamas** (3028 Jefferson Blvd., Lafayette, 337/267-4242, $9–18). The menu focuses on Cuban, Puerto Rican, Colombian, and Venezuelan cooking, such as the addictive *bolsitas* (deep-fried fritters filled with ground beef and served with a guava dipping sauce). Save room for the *tres leches* cake for dessert. The colorful dining room has paintings of butterflies, frogs, and other tropical creatures.

Tsunami (412 Jefferson St., Lafayette, 337/234-3474, $8–19) is the kind of hip and sleek sushi restaurant you might expect to find in a much bigger city, with its swanky vibe, dark and urbane lighting, and bamboo wall separators. Great dishes here include grilled salmon with a gingered mango-avocado salsa and rib-eye steak with caramelized-onion butter and a side of wasabi-mashed potatoes. The Grand Isle roll (tuna, yellowtail, and scallion) is one of the better *maki* rolls offered. Tsunami may very well offer a vision of where downtown Lafayette is headed in terms of sophistication and worldliness.

Quick Bites

Hungry Lafayette diners have been enjoying the home-style breakfast and lunch fare of **Dwyer's Cafe** (323 Jefferson St., Lafayette, 337/235-9364, $4–9) since 1927. The low-key downtown restaurant opens at 5 each morning and features a terrific fresh-daily plate lunch that includes a mix of entrées and vegetables, plus great burgers, biscuits and gravy, eggs, and other hearty, honest fare.

Charlie T's (530 Berard St., Breaux Bridge, 337/332-2426, under $6) is a wonderful deli serving smoked and specialty meats, boudin, cracklin's, and other Cajun delicacies.

In downtown New Iberia, a sign outside **Victor's Cafeteria** (109 W. Main St., New Iberia, 337/369-9924, $5–8), a plain, almost dowdy lunch and breakfast room, proudly announces "Dave Robicheaux eats here." But even if you're not an ardent fan of the fictional Cajun detective made famous by novelist James Lee Burke, you should drop by to sample the hearty, home-style cooking, including a fabulous crawfish pie and an ever-changing roster of fresh-baked pies and cakes. Breakfast is served daily 6–10 A.M. and lunch every day but Saturday. There's often a line to get in, but it moves quickly.

With a 1950s theme and staff dressed accordingly, **Duffy's Diner** (1106 Center St., New Iberia, 337/365-2326, $4–12) is a fun place to take kids—the ice-cream treats and malts are luscious and largely portioned. In addition to the usual diner favorites, Duffy's serves commendable fried seafood, oyster po'boys, and other Cajun fare.

Myran's Maison de Manger (Hwy. 31S, Arnaudville, 337/754-5064, $4–10) is a funky, much-loved short-order place with great shrimp po'boys, cherry milkshakes, and fried chicken. Don't mind the linoleum floor and fluorescent lights. Very down-home, simple place.

Java Joints

The local coffeehouse of choice is **Mello Joy** with four branches (625 Jefferson St., 337/232-0006; 3809 Ambassador Caffery Pkwy., 337/988-3058; two at Mall of Acadiana, 5725 Johnston St., 337/988-2373; all in Lafayette); it has a particularly homey and inviting location in the heart of downtown. Mello Joy brews its own excellent coffee and also serves plenty of other drinks, but it's also a reliable bet for house-made soups and gumbos, creative salads and sandwiches, ice cream, and heavenly pies.

A branch of the popular New Orleans cof-

© ANDREW COLLINS

Dwyer's Cafe, Lafayette

feehouse, **P.J.'s Lafayette** (200 E. St. Mary St., Lafayette, 337/572-9555) sits adjacent to the bustling campus of University of Louisiana Lafayette. The spacious cafe with a sunny upstairs terrace and ample seating beneath the shade trees along St. Mary Street is often packed with students and professors. In addition to coffees and teas, you can get very good sandwiches and desserts here, too.

P.J.'s formidable rival, also based in New Orleans, **CC's** (3810 Ambassador Caffrey Pkwy., Suite 100, 337/981-4343; 2668 Johnston St., Suite C-4, 337/269-9281; 340 Kaliste Saloom Rd., Suite D, 337/233-0429; 1042 Camellia Blvd., 337/981-6167; 100 Rex St., 337/235-7686; all in Lafayette), has several locations in Lafayette, all of them providing free high-speed Internet service, not to mention excellent coffee and light food.

In Breaux Bridge, **Barbara Lee Coffee and Tea** (110A Bridge St., Breaux Bridge, 337/332-3594) is a cute and friendly downtown cafe where you can grab a quick bite, perhaps a cup of gumbo or a fresh salad. Pastries and cakes are also served.

CAJUN COUNTRY

Picnic Supplies and Gourmet Goods

Champagne's Breaux Bridge Bakery (105 S. Poydras St., Breaux Bridge, 337/332-1117) has been a snacking institution in Breaux Bridge since 1888—the wonderful cakes, breads, cookies, and other baked goods are worth stocking up on before an outing or on your way to your inn or hotel.

Also useful for salads, boudin, and Cajun groceries and food products is **Rees Street Market** (241 Rees St., Breaux Bridge, 337/332-2243).

Goula's Grocery (1014 Ruth Bridge Hwy., Breaux Bridge, 337/332-6006) is famous for its hot boudin and hot cracklin's, along with other fine meats and Cajun delicacies—it ships all over the country.

In Lafayette, **Joey's Specialty Foods** (503 Bertrand Dr., Lafayette, 337/237-3661 or 877/466-8873, www.cajun-joeys.com) is another great source of local packaged and prepared foods—it does a brisk mail-order business from its website. Game and meats, box and picnic lunches, hot sauces, candies, deli fare, and all kinds of seafood are available.

Another great source for local Cajun foods is **Herbert's Specialty Meats** (8212 Maurice Ave., Maurice, 337/893-5062).

Poupart Bakery (1902 W. Pinhook Rd., Lafayette, 337/232-7921) is a favorite spot for breakfast Danishes and pastries. This bakery serves delectable cream cheese croissants, French bread, cheesecakes, chocolate cakes, and coffees.

Another local tradition is **Meche's Donuts** (306 E. Willow St., Lafayette, 337/232-2782), a great place for coffee and doughnuts.

INFORMATION AND SERVICES

The **Lafayette Convention and Visitors Commission** (Box 52066, Lafayette, 70505, 337/232-3737 or 800/346-1958, www.lafayettetravel.com) serves as an umbrella tourism organization for most of the Acadiana towns between Opelousas and Morgan City, and between Jennings and Henderson. The LCVC has a large visitors center on the median of U.S.

Highway 90, just a bit south of I-10, where you can ask for advice on where to stay and pick up hundreds of brochures, walking-tour maps, and visitor guides.

Most of the other nearby parishes also have tourism organizations, the most prominent being the **Iberia Parish Convention and Visitors Bureau** (2704 Hwy. 14, New Iberia, 70560, 337/365-1540 or 888/942-3742, www.iberiaparish.com) and the **St. Martin Parish Tourist Commission** (Box 9, St. Martinville, 70582, 337/298-3556, www.cajuncountry.org). Also, for more detailed information on Franklin, contact the **Cajun Coast Visitors and Convention Bureau** (Box 2332, Morgan City, LA 70381, 985/395-4905 or 800/256-2931, www.cajuncoast.com). You can also stop by either of the Cajun Coast tourism office visitors centers, one a few miles west of Morgan City in Patterson (at 112 Main St., 985/395-4905 or 800/256-2931), and the other in Franklin (15307 U.S. 90, 337/828-2555).

The free *Times of Acadiana* (337/237-3560, www.timesofacadiana.com) serves Lafayette and environs with scads of listings and entertainment coverage. Another great freebie is the *Independent Weekly* (www.theind.com), which is strong on arts, dining, and entertainment.

GETTING AROUND

Within the area, you really need a car to maximize your flexibility and maneuverability. **Lafayette Transit System (LTS)** (337/291-8570, www.lafayettelinc.net/lts) does provide bus service around that city, but since many of the area's main attractions are in outlying towns not served by LTS, this is an impractical option.

From New Orleans, there are two main routes to Lafayette and environs. You can either take the straight, easy 135-mile shot across I-10 through Baton Rouge, which takes a little more than two hours. Or you can opt for the more circuitous 160-mile route via U.S. Highway 90, which takes around three hours. Eventually U.S. Highway 90 will become an extension of I-49, which runs from Shreveport southeast to Lafayette, and already many improvements have been made to this road—in many places it's now a limited-access highway with a 70 mph speed limit. (See the *Essentials* chapter for details on reaching New Orleans and Lafayette from other parts of the country by train, plane, and bus.)

Houma and Eastern Acadiana

Houma is the base for exploring the eastern end of the Cajun wetlands—it's also the only incorporated town in all of Terrebonne Parish, an enormous but sparsely populated parish that includes many of the fishing and oil-rigging outposts down along the Gulf. There's a wide variety of dining options here, plus a handful of chain hotels and B&Bs, and from here you're within striking distance of numerous swamp-tour and fishing excursions.

HOUMA

Houma doesn't have a great many attractions, although downtown, bounded roughly by Park Avenue and Verrett Street, and by Canal Street and Barrow Street, does have a good many historic buildings of architectural significance, including churches, Victorian storefronts, and houses—many of these buildings date to the late 19th century, which is when the city was established. You can get a free copy of the illustrated Houma Downtown Walking Tour from the Houma Convention and Visitors Bureau.

Bayou Terrebonne runs through the heart of Houma, fringing the northern end of downtown and intersecting with the Intracoastal Waterway, which snakes through a good bit of Terrebonne Parish. It's the main bayou in a vast network of waterways that converge in Houma.

Bayou Terrebonne
Waterlife Museum

Probably the best way to get a sense of the various industries and livelihoods that have formed the foundation for life in the Cajun wetlands is to tour the Bayou Terrebonne Waterlife Museum (7910 W. Park Ave., Houma, 985/580-7200, www.houmaterrebonne.org/

waterlife.asp, open 10 A.M.–5 P.M. Mon.–Fri. and noon–4 P.M. Sat., admission $3), where interactive and well-laid-out exhibits discuss fishing (both occupational and recreational), shellfish harvesting, oil and natural gas mining, and hunting and trapping. You'll see a mounted 13.5-foot alligator, an exhibit and documents on hurricanes, a shrimp boat, and a display on Louisiana cypress trees. It's housed inside a former barge and freight warehouse, built in the 1880s, on Bayou Terrebonne.

Southdown Plantation House
and Terrebonne Museum

Make time to visit Southdown Plantation House and Terrebonne Museum (1208 Museum Dr., off Hwy. 311, Houma, 985/851-0154, www.southdownmuseum.org, open 10 A.M.–4 P.M., last tour an hour before closing, Tues.–Sat., admission $5), a 19th-century manor house that once anchored a large sugar plantation. The eclectic exhibits inside trace local history, including a large collection of Boehm and Doughty porcelain birds and flowers and the re-created Washington, D.C., office of Allen J. Ellender, a U.S. senator from 1937 through 1972. The house also contains original 19th-century furnishings of the Minor family, who lived here during the plantation years.

MORGAN CITY

Originally part of the territory inhabited by both the Attakapas and Chitimacha Indians, who first named the Atchafalaya River (meaning simply "long river"), Morgan City has been famous for the past two centuries for shrimp fishing, and in the past century as a base for workers on the many offshore oil rigs

THE ATCHAFALAYA BASIN SWAMP

The Atchafalaya (pronounced UH-cha-fuh-lye-uh) is the main distributary of the Mississippi River and an active, living delta through which flows the 135-mile-long Atchafalaya River. At about 15 miles in width, the basin is the largest overflow swamp in the United States and covers about 850,000 acres, about a third of the total land mass of Louisiana.

A swamp is any low ground overrun with water but punctuated by trees; marshes are similar but have few or no trees. This swamp began forming around A.D. 900, when the Mississippi River began to change its course, which had favored an easterly shift once it reached southern Louisiana. For many centuries the river then flowed through the present-day Bayou Lafourche, which passes through the city of Houma and eventually empties into the Gulf.

Annual flooding forced heavy waters into the low-lying and dense forest on either side of the Mississippi River. Eventually natural levees formed and contained the water permanently. In recent centuries, the Mississippi River has shifted still farther back toward the southeastern section of the state.

Historically, this swamp cultivated some of the richest and most fertile soil in the South, not to mention prolific fishing grounds, making it the perfect place for the exiled Acadian refugees who arrived in the mid- to late-18th century and established roots all through the basin. The geography of the swamp effectively cut the early Cajun settlements off from the rest of the state, helping them to preserve their distinct heritage and language. They remain a remarkably close-knit society to this day.

Atchafalaya swamp's appearance and character both changed dramatically throughout the 20th century. Discoveries in the 1920s of vast oil and natural-gas reserves brought prosperity to the region, as well as large numbers of newcomers. Major floods, most notably in 1927, have at different times forced small communities within the basin to abandon their homes and settle on higher land. And in 1973 the federal government constructed an 18-mile-long bridge through the swamp, extending I-10 from New Orleans and Baton Rouge to Lafayette. The work of the U.S. Army Corps of Engineers, which involved erecting massive floodgates at the intersection of the Mississippi and Atchafalaya rivers, is what prevented the Mississippi from seeking a permanent shortcut through the swamp to the Gulf.

The construction of these flood-control systems and levees, as well as oil pipelines and other man-made structures, has not only forever altered the swamp but has at times threatened its well-being. The largest bottom-land hardwood forest in the country, Atchafalaya is still home to fertile and productive fish and wildlife habitats. More than 50,000 egrets, ibises, and herons nest in the region, with about 300 additional bird species represented. The basin claims about 65 species of reptile and 90 types of fish. Other inhabitants include deer, alligators, bobcats, turtles, alligator gar fish, bald eagles, bears, nutria, wood ducks, cranes, raccoons, possums, osprey, and coyotes.

in the Gulf. This town on the east side of the Atchafalaya River, about 20 miles from where it empties into the Gulf, was first settled as a sugarcane plantation operated by a noted Kentucky surgeon and planter named Walter Brashear. The town took his name and became important during the Civil War, when Union troops occupied it, treasuring its strategic location as a gateway to the Atchafalaya Swamp and a means to cut off Confederate supply lines from Texas.

The town really took off in the 1870s, however, when entrepreneur Charles Morgan dredged the Atchafalaya Bay Channel deep enough for large ships, instantly turning the town into a major trade center for animal fur, shrimp and other seafood, and timber from cypress trees. Brashear was renamed in his honor in 1876. Morgan City was truly immortalized, however, by Hollywood, when it chose this subtropical land with lush swamps as the locale for the first *Tarzan* movie in 1917, starring Elmo Lincoln. The city's boom period began in the 1930s, when its shrimp-fishing industry developed into one of the most prolific in the world. Shortly after World War II, Kerr-McGee Industries drilled Louisiana's first offshore oil well, far out into the Gulf, and Morgan City became the point from which workers and equipment were moved out to this and the many rigs that followed. Today the city possesses the largest commercial marine fleet in the world (Tidewater) and also the world's largest helipad (operated by Petroleum helicopters), which is used for transporting workers and supplies back and forth between Morgan City and the offshore oil rigs in the Gulf. The importance of these two industries continues to be celebrated every Labor Day weekend during the Louisiana Shrimp and Petroleum Festival.

Morgan City is oil country, a hard-working place. The most interesting area is the old downtown, which is set just back from the river below the massive Highway 182 and U.S. Highway 90 bridges over the Atchafalaya River. A striking thing about this downtown area is that all along Front Street, a 22-foot-tall concrete retaining wall runs between town and the river; it was built in 1985, replacing a 13-foot wall that was easily overcome during major floods in 1973. On the riverside of the wall are some warehouses and docks, with a number of shrimp boats tied up along the pier. Doors in the wall allow traffic to flow between the river and the town. During bad storms, the doors are shut, and Morgan City is cut off from the rising tide, as is the Berwick area on the other side of the river. The flood wall is much uglier than a levee, although it's certainly a more efficient use of space, since the wall is just a couple of feet thick, whereas levees take up a considerable swath of land along the riverbank.

Morgan City couldn't exactly be called bustling, and many of its downtown storefronts sit vacant today, but it's an interesting old town. To connect with the other side, take the older and smaller of the two bridges across the river, over which Highway 182 runs—this puts you squarely in Berwick, a town with several seafood-processing plants and marine businesses. The downtown historic district runs about four blocks deep from the Atchafalaya River, between the U.S. Highway 90 bridge and Railroad Avenue. You can obtain a free self-guided walking-tour map from the Cajun Coast tourism office.

International Petroleum Museum and Exposition

One attraction that's definitely worth a look is the fascinating International Petroleum Museum and Exposition (111 1st St., Morgan City, 985/384-3744, www.rigmuseum.com, tours 10 A.M. and 2 P.M. Mon.–Sat., admission $5), a.k.a. "Mr. Charlie Rig," built as the first submersible oil-drilling rig in 1952. The museum's claim to fame is that it's the only place in the world where visitors can walk along an authentic oil rig. Mr. Charlie himself was used from the early 1950s until 1986. Here's how it worked: The 220-foot-long mobile oil barge, which could accommodate 58 workers, would be towed to a shallow-water location (no deeper than 40 feet), where massive tanks inside the barge would be filled with water. The barge would sink to the Gulf floor, and drilling would commence. At the end of the drilling cycle, the water tanks would be pumped out and filled again with air, whereupon the rig would float to the surface and be towed to its next location. It's often said that this very rig revolutionized the oil-drilling industry, allowing greater flexibility and maneuverability for drilling off-shore—unquestionably, it changed the nature and the fortunes of life in southwestern Louisiana. These days, you can tour the entire rig, which rests above water. On the 90-minute tour you get a real sense of what it's like to live and work on one of these self-contained industrial islands in the Gulf.

Other exhibits at the museum discuss how crude oil is mined and refined and a history of how mankind began tapping into the earth's vast oil reserves in the 19th century. The museum sits in the Atchafalaya River, right at the junction with the Intracoastal Waterway.

Berwick and Patterson

Across the river from Morgan City is the smaller fishing and industrial town of Berwick, and beyond that on U.S. Highway 90 is Patterson. Neither place has much in the way of attractions or interest to travelers, but together these communities were a major source of commercial cypress for many years. At one time, Patterson had the largest cypress sawmill in America.

THIBODAUX

The area's second-largest community after Houma (which is 15 miles south), Thibodaux was settled by early trappers and fishermen and has a handful of mostly ordinary chain-oriented motels and restaurants. The main reason for a visit is to explore the excellent Wetlands Acadian Cultural Center.

◖ Wetlands Acadian Cultural Center

The Wetlands Acadian Cultural Center (314 St. Mary St., Thibodaux, 985/448-1375, www. nps.gov/jela, open 9 A.M.–6 P.M. Tues.–Thurs., 9 A.M.–5 P.M. Fri.–Sun., and 9 A.M.–7 P.M. Mon., admission free), yet another facility of the outstanding Jean Lafitte National Historical Park and Preserve, touches on the plight of those Cajuns who settled in swamps and marshes and along bayous throughout the southeastern side of the Atchafalaya Basin. Most of the Cajun refugees who put down roots in this region, which includes the swamps and marshes around Thibodaux and Houma, earned their living as trappers, hunters, and fishermen, as opposed to the Cajuns who moved to the prairies to farm.

Inside the center you'll find a wide variety of well-displayed artifacts that tell the story of the Acadian settlement, along with diagrams, charts, photography displays, and similarly useful and easy-to-follow documents. As with all of the Jean Lafitte sites, a great effort has been made to illustrate what everyday life was like for early Cajuns and subsequent generations right through the present day. Other facilities include a 200-seat theater that mounts a variety

of programs and lectures on Acadian culture, as well as plays performed by the Thibodaux Playhouse, a local theatrical group. In a crafts demonstration room you can watch local artisans build boats, carve out duck decoys, make fishing nets, and create local household and decorative items. The center has an excellent bookshop stocked with books on Cajun history (including many titles appropriate for children) and local music CDs. Check for interpretive programs, videos, and performances, scheduled regularly throughout the year, and when in New Orleans, be sure to drop in on the headquarters of the Jean Lafitte National Historical Preserve, in the French Quarter at 419 Decatur Street. Here you'll find information on all of the park's six sites throughout southern Louisiana.

ENTERTAINMENT AND EVENTS
Entertainment and Nightlife

Houma's **A-Bear's Cafe** (809 Bayou Black Dr., Houma, 985/872-6306) is a great place to catch live Cajun and old-time rockabilly music. **Bayou Delight** (4038 Bayou Black Dr., Houma, 985/876-4879) also features Cajun and rockin' oldies.

Festivals and Events

It may sound an odd mix, but the **Louisiana Shrimp and Petroleum Festival** (800/256-2931, www.shrimp-petrofest.org) in Morgan City is quite a hoot, with fireworks, music, seafood, a children's village, and a blessing of the fleet. It's held in late August or early September.

In mid-October, head down to Houma for the **Downtown on the Bayou Festival,** which features four stages of Cajun, zydeco, jazz, country, rock, and gospel music. Drawing more than 90,000 visitors each year, it's one of the region's top draws.

ACCOMMODATIONS

There aren't a huge number of accommodations options in this part of the state, but there are several modern chain properties in Houma and Thibodaux as well as a handful of inns. Keep in mind that this area isn't especially far from either New Orleans or the plantation towns along the Great River Road, so you can always consider these areas for additional lodging options as well as Lafayette and environs.

Hotels and Motels

$50-100: A nice, inexpensive, and well-kept motel with a large pool in back, the **Ramada Houma** (1400 W. Tunnel Blvd., Houma, 985/879-4871 or 888/989-8367, www.bayoucountryinns.com) is within walking distance of several restaurants and has its own decent place to eat on-site. The 153-room property has a lounge, an outdoor pool, a hot tub, and pleasantly landscaped grounds. The same owners also operate the **Plantation Inn** (1381 W. Tunnel Blvd., Houma, 985/868-0500 or 800/373-0072, www.bayoucountry inns.com), a somewhat more upscale modern hotel with a lounge and restaurant.

An affordable option in downtown Houma, the **Fairfield Inn** (1530 Martin Luther King Blvd., Houma, 985/580-1050 or 800/228-2800, www.fairfieldinn.com) has three stories of airy, clean rooms with free local calls, work desks, and very good lighting. It also has continental breakfast, same-day dry-cleaning, an indoor pool and hot tub, and an exercise room.

Inns and Bed-and-Breakfasts

Under $50: A charming cottage on the banks of the Intracoastal Waterway, **Honduras House B&B** (1023 Saadi St., Houma, 985/868-1520) offers three simply furnished rooms with Victorian antiques and private baths (one is wheelchair-accessible). The largest accommodation has a full sitting room and a porch overlooking the water. Also on-site is Melvin's Restaurant, which serves casual regional fare.

$100-150: Grand Bayou Noir (1143 Bayou Black Dr., Houma, 985/873-5849, www.grandbayou noir.com) sits on four acres studded with gracious oak and fruit trees, fronting the peaceful Bayou Black. Guest rooms in this imposing 1930s Colonial Revival house

have private baths and elegant antiques, plus cable TV; one suite has a private balcony and sitting area.

FOOD

The food options in this area are similar in style, flavor, and variety to those around Lafayette and environs, although expect things to be even more informal in this region.

Traditional Creole and Cajun

Don't be put off by the location amid fast-food restaurants. **Savoie's** (1377 Tunnel Blvd., Houma, 985/872-9819, $5–24) is the real thing—a first-rate, down-home Cajun seafood restaurant that's also acclaimed for its steaks and continental-style dishes, such as veal Monica (topped with crayfish). Po'boys and the fried speckled trout platter are additional favorites at this rustically decorated spot with a young, friendly waitstaff. Its name is pronounced SAV-wahs.

Another great standby for Cajun fare, **A-Bear's Cafe** (809 Bayou Black Dr., Houma, 985/872-6306, $7–17) has been serving good, no-nonsense food (red beans and rice, catfish, boiled shrimp) since the early 1960s in an atmospheric 1920s building. On Friday nights there's live Cajun music.

Arguably the best fish house in an area known for them, **Eastway Seafood West Cajun Restaurant** (1029 W. Tunnel Blvd., Houma, 985/876-2121, $8–20) serves a vast range of creatures from the sea, in both traditional Cajun and somewhat more contemporary preparations. You'll find rare grilled tuna, red snapper, frogs' legs, oysters on the half shell, and some toothsome desserts, including traditional bread pudding with rum sauce and homemade peanut-butter or chocolate fudge. The Cajun mudbug-and-corn soup is a house specialty.

Casual Cooking

Red Fish Pizza (224 S. Hollywood Ave., Houma, 985/872-1400, $6–14) serves some of the tastiest gourmet pies around, along with bounteous salads and fresh pasta dishes.

Quick Bites

A Houma institution, **Boudreau and Thibodeau's Cajun Cookin** (5602 W. Main St., Houma, 985/872-4711, $5–17) serves some of the tastiest home-style local fare in the area, from po'boys to crawfish boils to massive (and fattening and delicious) breakfasts. You won't go home hungry after a platter of country-fried steaks or the soft-shell crab and stuffed-crab combo. The place is festive and borderline silly, with goofy Cajun jokes printed on both the walls and the menu ("… you know you're Cajun if there's more furniture on your porch than in your living room"). Perhaps the best thing about this place is that it's open 24 hours, a rarity in these parts.

A multitude of homemade ice creams are served at **Scarlet Scoop** (300 Barrow St., Houma, 985/872-5114), a local parlor that's a favorite place for a break before or after exploring the area.

Stop by down-home **Rita Mae's Kitchen** (711 Federal Ave., Morgan City, 985/384-3550, $4–10) for short-order fried seafood, gumbos, plate lunches, and other soul-food specialties. It's nothing fancy, but the food is consistently tasty and the small dining room in this tin-roofed cottage is bright and cheerfully decorated, with black-and-white tile floors and both counter and table seating. It's in the heart of Morgan City's historic downtown, a few blocks from the river, and the kitchen turns out three meals a day.

INFORMATION AND SERVICES

The **Houma Area Convention and Visitors Bureau** (114 Tourist Dr., off U.S. 90, Gray, 985/868-2732 or 800/688-2732, www.houmatourism.com) has a visitors center with brochures and information on Houma and surrounding towns.

For information on Morgan City and Berwick, contact the **Cajun Coast Visitors and Convention Bureau** (P.O. Box 2332, Morgan City, 70381, 985/395-4905 or 800/256-2931, www.cajuncoast.com). You can also stop by either of the Cajun Coast tourism office visitors centers, one a few miles west of Morgan City in Patterson (112 Main St., 985/395-4905 or 800/256-2931), and the other in Franklin (15307 U.S. 90, 337/828-2555).

Free and found at many hotels and restaurants, Houma's *Gumbo Entertainment Guide* (985/876-3008) is a monthly paper filled with event and nightlife listings and other lively goings-on.

GETTING AROUND

Within the area, a car is the best way to get around. From New Orleans, it's a 60-mile drive along U.S. Highway 90 to reach Houma or Thibodaux. (See the *Essentials* chapter for details on reaching New Orleans from other parts of the country by train, plane, and bus.)

The Cajun Prairie

Although Cajuns are more commonly associated with swamplands and rivers, and with the communities between Lafayette and Houma, a considerable number of these early refugees moved north and west of this area in search of arable land suitable for farming. These Cajuns settled chiefly between Lafayette and Lake Charles, and between Opelousas and Kinder, or as far west as De Quincy. Here they raised cattle and grew a variety of crops, including sugarcane, cotton, and vegetables. Without the mysterious lure of the swamps in or near the Atchafalaya Basin, the Cajun prairie lacks the tourist cachet of the wetlands, and because these towns were settled later than St. Martinville, Breaux Bridge, and some of the other historic communities near Lafayette, the region is decidedly less quaint and cutesy.

However, the area between Eunice and Opelousas has long been famous for cultivating the Cajun and zydeco music that's such an integral part of Cajun life today, and in all the towns and cities in the prairie region, you'll find a wealth of great restaurants serving

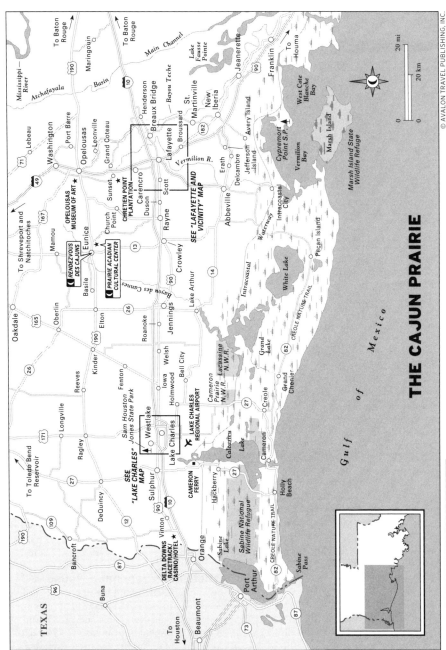

THE CAJUN PRAIRIE

© AVALON TRAVEL PUBLISHING, INC.

authentic Cajun chow. There are fewer key museums and attractions in this part of Cajun Country, but it's definitely a region that bears exploring, and its largest city, Lake Charles, has quite a lot to see and do, including some of the state's most popular casinos.

The modest, agrarian towns along U.S. Highway 190 form something of a Cajun and zydeco music trail. You'll find only a handful of places to stay and eat in each town, but the live-music clubs in these parts play some of the best music in the region, and on Saturday mornings you can show up at the Savoy Music Center and Accordion Factory and have a wonderful time listening to local musicians jamming together.

OPELOUSAS

Named for the Opelousas Indians, this city of 22,000 at the junction of U.S. Highway 190 and I-49 was established by the French as the administrative capital of Le Poste des Opelousas in 1720, just a couple of years after the founding of New Orleans. Little came of the area during the first century, as it shifted from French to Spanish governance, but by the time of the Louisiana Purchase, a mix of Cajuns, English, Scotch-Irish, and German settlers had established farmsteads here, taking advantage of the richly fertile lands. The area surrounding Opelousas was named St. Landry Parish in 1804 after a particularly beloved bishop.

As a farming region, Opelousas and the rest of the towns along U.S. Highway 190 became heavily populated with African slaves, who were needed more here than in the wetland areas of Cajun Country, where trapping and fishing were central to the economy. Today's Opelousas is a rich mix of Cajun, African American, and Northern European traditions, with a healthy celebration of the area's Native American heritage thrown in. The big stops here are local music clubs specializing in zydeco and Cajun song and dance.

Opelousas Museum of Art

Be sure to check out what's on display at the Opelousas Museum of Art (100 N. Union

Michelle Prudhomme House, Opelousas

St., Opelousas, 337/942-4991, open 1–5 P.M. Tues.–Fri., 9 A.M.–5 P.M. Sat., $3 donation requested), which presents rotating exhibits lent from major museums around the region as well as private collections. It's worth dropping by just to get a look at the striking Federal-style building, constructed of brick in the early 1800s as a tavern.

Le Vieux Village

Le Vieux Village (828 E. Landry St., Opelousas, 337/948-6263, open 9 A.M.–4 P.M. daily, donation requested) is a compound of historic buildings, most of them moved from their original locations in the area to this site in the center of town. Among the draws at this self-guided living-history museum is one of the oldest Methodist churches west of the Mississippi River.

Michelle Prudhomme House

The city is also home to one of the oldest houses in the state, the Michelle Prudhomme House (Prudhomme Circle, next to Opelousas General Hospital, Opelousas, 337/948-6263, open by appointment, donation requested), a raised Colonial that was built around 1810. The same family lived in this house until the 1970s, when it was sold and then nearly faced with demolition to make way for a parking garage. Preservationists saved the structure. It contains some original furnishings. And on the front lawn, there's an original pigeonier, one of only about 20 still standing in the state.

GRAND COTEAU

This historic village can be visited as a quick stop en route from Lafayette up I-49 to Opelousas. Grand Coteau's main attraction, just west of town, on the other side of I-49, is **Chretien Point Plantation** (665 Chretien Point Rd., Sunset, 337/662-7050 or 800/880-7050, www.chretienpoint.com, open 1–5 P.M. weekdays, 10 A.M.–5 P.M. weekends, admission $10), a gracious 1831 plantation house set on 20 acres of lush grounds; it's one of the most stately such homes away from the Great River Road. The name of the plantation is pronounced CRAY-chee-en. Visitation is by one-hour tours, and these are led by knowledgeable docents dressed in period attire. The plantation's dramatic staircase served as the model for Tara's in the film adaptation of *Gone with the Wind,* and designers of the mansion drew their own inspiration from another famous structure, the Palace of Versailles in France—this is evident in the arched Palladian lunette windows above the exterior doors and windows. Dignified Tuscan columns are set around the home's brick exterior—one of the columns was torn off by a Union cannonball in the heat of Civil War battle, and the front door still has a number of bullet holes. In addition to touring the house, you can also book an overnight stay here (see *Accommodations*).

EUNICE

A farming community about 20 miles west of Opelousas, Eunice is the musical heart and soul of Acadiana, an important stop for any traveler interested in the heritage of zydeco and Cajun music. It's the youngest town in St. Landry Parish and also the second-largest (only Opelousas is larger), with a population of about 12,000.

(Prairie Acadian Cultural Center

Eunice's small but historic downtown is also home to the westernmost unit of Jean Lafitte National Historical Park and Preserve, the Prairie Acadian Cultural Center (250 W. Park Ave., Eunice, 337/262-2862, www.nps.gov/jela, open 8 A.M.–5 P.M. Tues.–Fri. and 8 A.M.–6 P.M. Sat., admission free). The center tells the story of the Cajuns who settled north and west of the Atchafalaya Swamp, in the southern Louisiana prairie communities along the present-day U.S. Highway 190 and I-10 corridors, from Opelousas and Lafayette west to Kinder and Lake Charles. Here they raised cattle and other livestock, cultivated rice, cotton, and sugarcane, and led lives quite different from those of their wetland relatives. The exhibits at this interpretive center bear some resemblance to those at the Acadian Cultural Center in Lafayette, and to those at the Wetlands Acadian Cultural Center in Thibodaux, but here there's more focus on the region's dependence on agriculture and on its musical roots. The center's theater hosts frequent Cajun and zydeco concerts as well as lectures, videos, and other programs on the area's heritage. Weaving, spinning, musical-instrument–making, and other crafts demonstrations are given regularly, and you can watch local cooks prepare authentic Cajun, soul, and Creole meals in an exhibition kitchen at 4 P.M. on Saturdays. The bookshop here has an outstanding selection of Cajun and zydeco CDs and tapes. Check for interpretive programs, videos, and performances, scheduled regularly throughout the year, and when in New Orleans, be sure to drop in on the headquarters of the Jean Lafitte National Historical Preserve, in the French Quarter at 419 Decatur Street. Here you'll find information on all of the park's six sites throughout southern Louisiana.

(*Rendezvous des Cajuns*

Next to the center is the famous **Liberty Center for the Performing Arts** (S. 2nd St. and Park Ave., Eunice, 337/457-7389), an old movie house and vaudeville theater built

CAJUN COUNTRY

CAJUN AND ZYDECO MUSIC

Cajun and zydeco are terms often confused with one another or used to describe the same music, but they have distinct origins and subtle but important differences. Both have their origins in southwest Louisiana's Cajun Country, and they have each enjoyed a huge surge in worldwide popularity since the 1980s. They're also sometimes credited with being the progenitors of modern country-and-western music, which is a relatively new phenomenon when compared with Cajun and zydeco.

Cajun music derives, as one would guess, from the French culture of Cajun settlers who came to southwestern Louisiana primarily during the 18th and early 19th centuries – it's nearly always sung in French – but this upbeat, danceable music form also has German, Anglo American, and African influences. Originally Cajun tunes revolved around fiddles, but the influence of German settlers led to the use of push-button accordions during the

late 1800s, and now both these instruments are the keystones of any good Cajun band. Nowadays Cajun bands typically include a bass and drums. A *tit fer* is another instrument common to the genre – this iron triangle struck with a spike is used to add rhythm.

When live Cajun is performed, you'll generally see folks dancing either waltzes or two-steps. Like many of the country tunes that have been inspired by it, Cajun music often tells the tale of something tragic or unhappy, such as failed romances, early deaths, or other hardships common to life among the Acadian immigrants of early southern Louisiana.

But many songs are funny and self-effacing, playing on an often unfortunate circumstance for laughs. Many of today's Cajun tunes have their origins in the Acadian folk music of Canada and also in the traditional fiddling tunes of France. It is truly folk music, and the early traditions were never written down but passed along from generation to

Dancers and onlookers enjoy the live Cajun music at Fred's Lounge in Mamou.

generation, just as many old Cajun tales were. The earliest recordings of Cajun music date to the late 1920s. Top venues for Cajun today include Randol's and Prejean's restaurants in Lafayette and Mulate's in Breaux Bridge.

One of the most famous and distinguished Cajun-Western bands is the Hackberry Ramblers, whose albums have been nominated for Grammies in recent years. Back in 1933, fiddler Luderin Darbone and accordionist Edwin Duhon formed the band, mixing the toe-tapping sounds of traditional Cajun music with western swing and folky hillbilly influences. They used to power the electric sound system at local dance halls by hooking up to Darbone's Model-T Ford. They released their first album with RCA Bluebird in 1935, and they continued to perform and record for decades. In the early 1980s, a renewed interest in Cajun music was born, and the Ramblers, based in Lake Charles, enjoyed a popular resurgence. The music now tends toward a faster-paced, rollicking honky-tonk vibe. In 2003, the Ramblers were filmed performing at Eunice's weekly *Rendezvous des Cajuns* on NBC's *Today* show to celebrate the band's 70th anniversary. Leading the performance were fiddler Darbone and accordionist Duhon, still going strong at ages 90 and 92 respectively.

While Cajun is a predominantly Anglo music form, its cousin zydeco has its roots with the African American sharecroppers and farmers of the same region. The two music styles clearly influenced each other, with zydeco evolving from a tradition called "La La," a term for an early style of music played among African Americans in homes and at some clubs that used only an accordion and a washboard for instruments. Zydeco is much more closely linked to blues and R&B music. It's a younger music genre than Cajun; it uses either an accordion or push-button piano and also incorporates a *frottoir* (literally "rub board," or washboard), as opposed to the *tit fer* (triangle) used in Cajun music.

Many of the Creole African Americans in southern Louisiana came from the Caribbean, which also helped to shape this music style. In Afro-Caribbean culture, there's a syncopated style of a cappella music called *juré* that is sometimes cited as zydeco's true predecessor.

In the middle of the 20th century, zydeco came to be influenced by the burgeoning R&B and blues music of the South, and it continues to evolve and change as zydeco musicians borrow from rock, jazz, soul, and even rap and hip hop. Clifton Chenier, of Opelousas, is often considered the father of modern zydeco – he toured throughout the United States and Europe in the 1960s, helping to spread the popularity of this inimitable style.

The name zydeco is said to derive from the French phrase, *les haricots sont pas salés,* meaning "the snapbeans are not salty." The first two words, *les haricots,* are pronounced lay-ZAH-ree-coh, which has been shortened through the years to zydeco, pronounced ZAH-dee-coh. The phrase in question referred to a period of such financial hardship that one could not afford to so much as season basic foods – and so, as with Cajun music, zydeco often touches on themes of struggling to persevere and make do during difficult times.

Both zydeco and Cajun music are best appreciated live, ideally someplace where you can get out on the dance floor and cut loose, or at the very least – if you're shy – tap your toes a bit. Both forms go hand-and-hand with eating, and you'll find that many of the best Cajun and soul restaurants of southern Louisiana, especially near Lafayette, have live zydeco and Cajun music many nights of the week. The little town of Eunice, about 45 miles northwest of Lafayette, is one of the best places to catch live performances – here the Liberty Center for the Performing Arts hosts live Cajun and zydeco music on Saturday evenings. You can also hear great zydeco tunes locally by tuning your radio to 103.7 FM, KOCZ.

Rendezvous des Cajuns, at the Liberty Center for the Performing Arts, Eunice

© ANDREW COLLINS

in 1924 that was restored, after having fallen into a state of neglect, in 1986, when local citizens banded together to revive it. Back in the day, such illustrious performers as Tex Ritter, Fattie Arbuckle, Roy Rogers, and Jimmy Clanton performed here. Today it's the site at 6 P.M. on Saturday nights of *Rendezvous des Cajuns,* a two-hour live radio variety show with Cajun and zydeco music, along with storytelling, jokes, recipes, and other tidbits of Cajun lore. It's a memorable way to become acquainted with the region and its rich musical history. Admission to the radio variety show is $5, and you can buy tickets at the theater that day beginning at 4 P.M.

Eunice Museum

Along the same block as the Liberty Center is the Eunice Museum (220 S. C. C. Duson Dr., Eunice, 337/457-6540, open Tues.–Sat., admission free), which marks the site where town founder C. C. Duson sold the community's first lots in 1893. The museum occupies Eunice's original rail depot, and it's filled with artifacts, toys, displays, a loom and spin-

ning wheel, and rotating exhibits relevant to the town's and region's growth.

Cajun Music Hall of Fame and Museum

Next to the Eunice Museum, the Cajun Music Hall of Fame and Museum (240 S. C. C. Duson Dr., Eunice, 337/457-6534, open 9 A.M.–5 P.M. Tues.–Sat. summer and 8:30 A.M.–4:30 P.M. Tues.–Sun. winter, admission free) honors more than 30 prominent Cajun musicians and their contributions to the genre. The exhibit space is filled with photos, old musical instruments, and other displays tracing the heritage and development of Cajun music.

SHOPPING

In the historic town of Washington, you'll find a number of antiques shops in the center of the village, the most famous being **Old Schoolhouse Antique Mall** (123 S. Church St., Washington, 337/826-3580), a 40,000-square-foot building housing about 100 individual dealers and shops. You'll find some of the state's best selections of glassware, jewelry, and furniture at this place, which also contains a small cafe fashioned after a neighborhood drugstore soda fountain.

ENTERTAINMENT AND NIGHTLIFE

All through the U.S. Highway 190 corridor and the towns north and south of this stretch, you can find bars and clubs playing rollicking, bone-shaking music, from swamp pop to traditional Cajun to zydeco—it's one of the premier live-music regions in the country, which is remarkable when you consider that most places with notable music scenes are in highly populated urban centers, where clubs can pack in large audiences. In the Cajun prairie, people play music because they love to, not with the expectation that they'll get rich.

Here's a quick roundup of some of the top places to hear live music in the region. Eunice is the hub of all this activity. The **Purple Peacock** (U.S. 190, Eunice, 337/546-0975) is a favorite place to catch live rock and roll. The **Liberty Center for the Performing Arts** (2nd St. and Park Ave., Eunice, 337/457-7389) hosts *Rendezvous des Cajuns* 6–8 P.M. on Saturdays (see *Eunice* for details). Another big draw is the **Savoy Music Center and Accordion Factory** (U.S. 190 E, three miles east of Eunice, 337/457-9563), which holds informal jam sessions 9 A.M.–noon on Saturday. **Acadiana Sounds Recording Studio** (203 S. 2nd St., Eunice, 337/457-1786) also contains Dee's Cajun Gifts—it's a great place to pick up CDs and tapes of zydeco and Cajun music.

Slim's Y-Ki-Ki (8471 Hwy. 182, Opelousas, 337/942-6242) has been one of the area's favorite zydeco dance halls since shortly after World War II; it's open mostly on weekend evenings and brings in some of the top bands in Louisiana. The big, low-slung building is sparse on decor (except for a few palm trees painted on the walls), but there's a huge wide-open dance floor where you'll always see enthusiasts cutting loose to the music (and you're welcome to come out and try dancing yourself). If the lot is too crowded, park in the Piggly Wiggly grocery-store lot across the street. This is one of the best places in the region to hear zydeco, and you should try to get here while you can, as a number of the area's music clubs have closed down in recent years, victims of aging owners and clients and of the fact that many younger people from the area are more interested in other types of popular music.

In Basile, about 10 miles west of Eunice via U.S. 190, **D. I.'s Restaurant** (6533 Evangeline Hwy., Basile, 337/432-5141) is famous for its live Cajun performances, which include prominent local bands most evenings and renowned jam sessions on Wednesday nights.

Another legendary spot for Cajun music is **Fred's Lounge** (420 6th St., Mamou, 337/468-5411), a smoky little joint in downtown Mamou that offers live tunes on Saturday mornings as it hosts a local radio broadcast. These events have become de rigueur among area Cajun music fans. This squat redbrick building is something of a dive, but it's been featured in major magazines and on television programs around the country and internationally. The late Fred Tate, who died in 1992, opened the bar in 1948, and it operated with regular bar hours for many decades. Now it's just open on mornings of the radio show broadcast, 7:30 A.M.–2 P.M. Saturdays. And don't think the early-morning hours discourage revelers from drinking.

Northwest of Lafayette and 15 miles southwest of Opelousas, the little hamlet of Church Point is home to **Le Vieux Moulin** (402 Canal St., Church Point, 337/684-1200), which has live music on Saturday mornings and sells handmade Cajun instruments. Its name means the Old Mill.

FESTIVALS AND EVENTS
Mardi Gras

Courir de Mardi Gras is a style of Mardi Gras celebration that's particular to some of the more rural towns in the parish, such as Eunice, and it's also celebrated at the Vermilionville living history museum in Lafayette. During this Mardi Gras Run, participants set out through a town on horseback, in wagons, and even in pickup trucks on a mad dash to obtain ingredients for a massive pot of gumbo. Probably the most famous and fun version of Courir de Mardi Gras is the one held in Church Point, a small town about 25 miles northwest of Lafayette. For details on this event, call 337/684-2739 or visit www.churchpointcourirdemardigras.com.

Spring and Summer
In Opelousas, **Main Street Revived** is an evening R&B concert held at the corner of Bellevue and Main on Friday nights from late March through late May. Up in Ville Platte, get your taste buds geared up in late June for the **Festival de la Viande Boucanée,** or Smoked Meat Festival (337/363-6700), which includes military demonstrations, a jet fly-by, an arts-and-crafts show, and the World Championship Smoked Meat Cook-Off. In late April, Arnaudville celebrates those delectable Louisiana crustaceans with the **Annual Étouffée Festival** (337/754-5912); the weekend-long event includes an étouffée cook-off, Cajun music, and carnival rides.

Fall and Winter
Rayne holds the not-to-be-missed **Frog Festival** (337/334-2332, www.rayne.org/chamber.html) each September, which features live Cajun bands, rides, an accordion contest, and frog racing and jumping. Labor Day weekend in Opelousas is the time for the **Southwest Louisiana Zydeco Music Festival** (337/942-2392, www.zydeco.org), three days of great concerts, plus foods and arts and crafts.

Music lovers should not miss the **Eunice Folklife Festival** (337/457-7389, www.eunice-la.com) in late October, which includes two long days of great Cajun, zydeco, country-and-western, bluegrass, and gospel acts. Also in mid- to late October, you can wander over to Crowley for the **International Rice Festival** (337/788-4100, www.crowley-la.com) or to Opelousas for the **Annual Louisiana Yambilee Festival** (337/948-8848, www.cajuntravel.com), a country fair with rides, music, a parade, and pageants.

Mid-November in Port Barre, about 10 miles

east of Opelousas on U.S. Highway 190, you can attend the **Cracklin' Festival** (877/948-8004, www.cajuntravel.com), which features a cracklin' cook-off, music, rides, and more food.

ACCOMMODATIONS
It's not terribly far to reach this area from Lafayette or Lake Charles, which have plenty of accommodations. But you'll also find a handful of accommodations right in the heart of the region, in Opelousas, Eunice, and even Washington.

Hotels and Motels
Under $50: About midway between Lafayette and Lake Charles, just off I-10, the **Comfort Inn Jennings** (607 Holiday Dr., Jennings, 337/824-8589 or 877/424-6423, www.comfortinn.com) makes for a safe and comfortable base.

Eunice doesn't have many accommodations, but the **Best Western Eunice** (1531 W. Laurel Ave., Eunice, 337/457-2800 or 800/962-8423, www.bestwestern.com), an attractive two-story hotel built in 1995, is a reliable option. There are 35 rooms along with an outdoor pool and hot tub.

In Opelousas, your best bet is the **Holiday Inn** (5696 I-49 N. Service Rd., Opelousas, 337/948-3300 or 800/465-4329, www.holiday-inn.com), a 75-room midrise hotel with an indoor pool, hot tub, business center, and on-site restaurant. All rooms in this 2001 property have coffeemakers and two-line phones, and some have whirlpool tubs. It's right off the interstate.

Inns and Bed-and-Breakfasts
$50-100: In Eunice, the **Potier's Prairie Cajun** (110 W. Park Ave., Eunice, 337/457-0440 or 337/457-8592, www.potiers.net) occupies a small brick 1920s building that had been Eunice Hospital eons ago. It's a funky place in the middle of downtown, not especially fancy but with a fantastic location and reasonable rates, and considerably more character than a standard chain motel. The 10 rooms have private bath and simple but comfortable local

furnishings from the early 20th century; each is stocked with fixings for continental breakfast. A small gift shop off the lobby sells Cajun crafts and local souvenirs. A whirlpool tub is in the common courtyard.

Washington has a couple of simple but charming little B&Bs that all make for enjoyable, quiet overnight stays—each is within walking distance of downtown antiques shops. **Camellia Cove B&B** (211 W. Hill St., Washington, 337/826-7362) is a graciously restored 1825 house set on two acres of lush gardens and lawns. There are two large guest rooms on the second floor, each filled with antiques and having a private bath, and a decadent full breakfast is included in the morning.

On a quiet street near Washington's largest antiques mall, **Country House B&B** (608 Carriere St., Washington, 337/826-3052 or 877/862-8038) is operated by June Lowrey, a delightful host and first-rate artist (her works hang in some of the accommodations). This property, towered over by tall shade trees, consists of the main house, which has a suite with private bath, and then a private cottage with its own kitchen.

$150-250: In Sunset, near Grand Coteau and just a short way west of I-49 en route from Lafayette to Opelousas, you'll find one of the South's most elegant inns, (**Chretien Point Plantation** (665 Chretien Point Rd., Sunset, 337/662-7050 or 800/880-7050, www.chretienpoint.com), which is also one of the top touring house-museums in Acadiana. Guests can choose from among five richly furnished rooms and also receive a full and hearty breakfast, a guided tour of the plantation house and grounds, hors d'oeuvres and cocktails each evening, and use of the large swimming pool. Hand-carved antique beds—some of them four-posters, all with plush bedding and pillows—Oriental rugs and hardwood or brick floors, and garden or pool views enchant guests, many of whom come here to celebrate a special occasion. One room has a whirlpool tub. Although Chretien Point is open for tours, it receives fewer visitors than most of the major River Road plantations, making

it ideal for a quiet and truly relaxing retreat, especially during the warmer months, when guests can take a dip in the swimming pool out back.

FOOD
With few exceptions, restaurants in this part of Acadiana are even less formal than those in Lafayette. What there's no lack of are great eateries serving home-style Cajun and soul food, including quite a few places that have live jazz, Cajun, and zydeco tunes.

Traditional Creole and Cajun
In Jennings, **Boudin King** (906 W. Division St., Jennings, 337/824-6593, $6–16) specializes in its namesake, prepared daily using pork, long-grain rice, and spicy seasonings, but it's also a handy stop for crispy fried chicken, filé-crawfish gumbo, red beans and rice with smoked sausage, and other regional delights. The same owners offers similarly good food at **Cajun Way Family Restaurant** (1805 Parkers Ave., Crowley, 337/788-2929, $6–16), another great stop on the way between Lafayette and Lake Charles.

Just off I-10, between Lafayette and Lake Charles, quirky Rayne is home to the even quirkier **Chef Roy's Frog City Cafe** (1131 Church Point Hwy., Rayne, 337/334-7913, $9–15), a rambling barn-red restaurant by the Days Inn, serving superb seafood and Cajun fare—not to mention fried frogs' legs, a popular dish here in the frog capital of Louisiana. Some top picks here include fried coconut-beer shrimp served with a tangy orange sauce, shrimp fettuccine, crawfish au gratin, and crab White Lake (eggplant fried and topped with crab stuffing). There's also a drive-through window, where you can order margaritas and daiquiris, shakes and ice cream, and fresh-boiled seafood (when in season).

In Eunice, you can catch live Cajun and zydeco tunes on Tuesday evenings at (**Nick's** (123 S. 2nd St., Eunice, 337/457-4921, $8–20), an elegantly restored downtown bar and grill from the 1930s, close to the museums and Liberty Theater. This is an airy space with an original tile bar, high ceilings, a lovely outdoor patio, and an adjoining dance hall with a corrugated-metal wall, pressed-tin ceilings, and plenty of beer signage. There's live music on Saturdays and jam sessions some other nights of the week. In season, treat yourself to a massive platter of boiled crawfish. Any time of year, this is a great choice for traditional Cajun cooking, with specialties that include corn-and-crab bisque, smoked-duck salad, eggplant pirogue stuffed with shrimp au gratin sauce, and ribeye steaks topped with crawfish étoufée. The service is friendly and helpful.

Creative and Contemporary

◖ **Steamboat Warehouse** (525 N. Main St., Washington, 337/826-7227, $10–22) occupies a beautiful old redbrick warehouse with original cypress beams across its soaring ceilings. It overlooks Bayou Courtableau and has a small dock jutting over the river that's perfect for sipping a predinner cocktail (try the mango margarita) and taking in the lush foliage fringing the river. Talented young chef Jason Huguet helms the kitchen and is responsible for such memorable fare as softshell crabs amandine, chicken topped with a crawfish cream sauce, and steak Annie (charbroiled filet mignon covered with a stuffing of lobster, crab, shrimp, and crawfish). But typically there are even more tantalizing specials listed each evening, including an ever-changing roster of desserts. The restaurant also has a few overnight cottages for rent.

Casual Cooking

Ray's Diner (2979 S. Union St., Opelousas, 337/942-9044, $5–13) has won numerous awards for serving the best crawfish étouffée in the area, plus steaks, boiled crawfish and crabs, and hearty breakfast fare.

Since the late 1920s, the **Palace Cafe** (135 W. Landry St., Opelousas, 337/942-2142, $4–11) has been doling out honest home-style fare, including daily blue-plate specials and wonderfully crispy and juicy fried chicken.

In Eunice, **Mama's Fried Chicken** (1640 W. Laurel Ave., Eunice, 337/457-9978, $5–13) really does serve the best fried chicken in town, but you can also get tasty crawfish étouffée, plate lunches with plenty of vegetable sides, and red beans and rice.

Try **Frenchie's** (427 6th St., Mamou, 337/468-4000, $6–10) for a tasty meal—it's right across the street from the famous Saturday-morning music club, Fred's, and serves delicious po'boys and Cajun fare.

Quick Bites

East of Opelousas, **Bourque's Supermarket** (581 Saizon St., Port Barre, 337/585-6261, under $6) is noted for its delicious stuffed bread filled with jalapeño peppers and gooey cheese and sausage. Boudin and cracklin's are also served in this low-key roadside shop.

A quaint lunchroom that also sells antiques and collectibles, cozy **Back in Time** (123 W. Landry St., Opelousas, 337/942-2413, $4–8) serves a wide range of soups, salads, and sandwiches, plus desserts made on the premises and flavored coffees.

Smoky southwest Louisiana barbecue is the draw at **Allison's Hickory Pit** (501 W. Laurel Ave., Eunice, 337/457-9218, $3–7), a tiny place that's only only for lunch Friday–Sunday.

In Eunice, **Ruby's** (221 W. Walnut Ave., Eunice, 337/550-7665) is a cozy storefront cafe that turns out great plate lunches, hearty Southern breakfasts, homemade biscuits and jam, and tasty sandwiches and salads. It's downtown, close to Eunice's museums.

Picnic Supplies and Gourmet Goods

The famous purveyor of Louisiana prepared foods and spices, **Tony Chachere's Creole Foods** (519 N. Lombard St., Opelousas, 337/948-4691 or 800/551-9066, www.tonychacheres.com) is right in downtown Opelousas and is open for free tours a few times a day; call ahead for times. You can also shop here for Chachere's mixes (such as Creole butter beans and rice), hush-puppy batter, and seasoning blends. Note that Chachere's is pronounced SASH-er-ees.

INFORMATION AND SERVICES
Visitor Information

For information on the towns of Opelousas, Eunice, Grand Coteau, and Washington, contact the **St. Landry Parish Tourist Commission** (Box 1415, Opelousas, 70571, 337/948-8004 or 877/948-8004, www.cajun-travel.com).

Getting Around

The entire region is best explored by car. I-10, which leads from Lafayette to Lake Charles, is a wide interstate highway with a 70 mph speed limit, as is I-49, which leads north from Lafayette to Opelousas. A slower road is U.S. Highway 190, especially where it passes through the downtowns of Eunice, Basile, and several other towns in the area, but it offers a more scenic view of the region.

Lake Charles and Environs

From Eunice, it's a 60-mile one-hour drive to reach Lake Charles, a city of 75,000 that's the hub for western Acadiana and the seat of Calcasieu (pronounced CAL-kuh-shoo) Parish. The city's strongest draw is with gamblers, who flock to Delta Downs horse-racing park just west of town, in Vinton, and three casinos in the city itself. The story of Lake Charles's encounter with a fall 2005 hurricane is less famous than New Orleans's, as the damage here from Hurricane Rita, which struck about a month after Hurricane Katrina hit the other side of the state, wasn't as severe. Still, by any measure, Rita was a monster. The Category 3 storm tore down trees (some of which smashed roofs of houses), blew down signs and a number of buildings, and badly damaged plenty of property around the city, including one of the casinos (Harrah's), whose riverboat casino remains shuttered while repairs take place. By the end of 2005, Lake Charles appeared—superficially—to be largely back to normal, and by fall 2006, little obvious evidence of the storm remained in the city itself. South of the city, however, along the Gulf Coast in Cameron Parish, normalcy still hasn't returned, and it's not expected to anytime soon. The lazy beach communities along here as well as the small town of Cameron were destroyed by the storm, just as badly as coastal Mississippi communities were ripped apart by Katrina. To this end, the scenic Creole Nature Trail—a popular driving tour past Cajun wildlife preserves—remains partially closed off. Still, communities

in Louisiana have a way of eventually bouncing back after any storm, and it's believed that in time, even Cameron Parish will rebuild.

But Lake Charles is also a base for outdoors enthusiasts, who enjoy the lake and its nearby wildlife preserves. The actual body of water known as Lake Charles is a rippling blue lake where on warm days you're apt to see sailboats and sailboarders riding the waves, and sunbathers enjoying the only inland white-sand beach on the Gulf Coast. South of the city, bird-watchers, anglers, and hikers have long flocked to Sabine National Wildlife Refuge (the Gulf of Mexico's largest refuge for wildfowl) and Cameron Prairie National Wildlife Refuge. But again, these areas are open only to varying degrees because of damage from Hurricane Rita.

As in Lafayette, Attakapas Indians originally lived on the land where Lake Charles and its neighboring towns are situated; the region's original name (still the name of the parish) Calcasieu was a war cry of the Attakapas, and it meant roughly "screaming eagle." The earliest settlers were Frenchmen attracted not only to the area's fishing and trapping but to the vast stands of virgin forest. French settler Martin LeBleu built a permanent homestead about six miles west of Lake Charles in 1780, and soon after, an Italian named Carlos Salia (who changed his name to the Gallic version, Charles Sallier) also set up a home here. It's said that Sallier befriended the infamous pirate Jean Lafitte, who came to rely on the large lake near

CAJUN COUNTRY

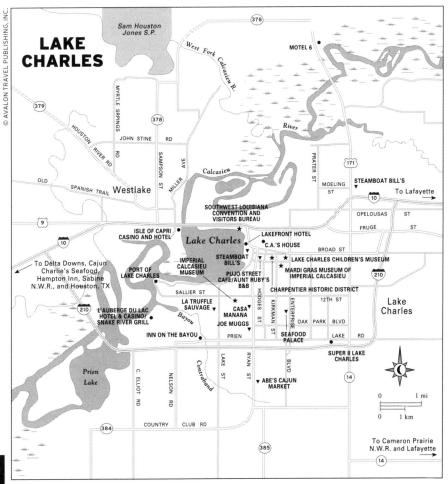

© AVALON TRAVEL PUBLISHING, INC.

LAKE CHARLES

Sam Houston Jones S.P.

West Fork Calcasieu R.

MOTEL 6

379

MYRTLE SRPINGS

378

JOHN STINE RD

SAMPSON ST

MILLER AVE

Calcasieu River

PRATER ST

171

STEAMBOAT BILL'S

MOELING ST

To Lafayette

10

HOUSTON RIVER RD

OLD SPANISH TRAIL Westlake

OPELOUSAS ST

FRUGE ST

9

10

SOUTHWEST LOUISIANA CONVENTION AND VISITORS BUREAU

ISLE OF CAPRI CASINO AND HOTEL

Lake Charles

LAKEFRONT HOTEL

C.A.'S HOUSE

BROAD ST

IMPERIAL CALCASIEU MUSEUM

STEAMBOAT BILL'S

PUJO STREET CAFE/AUNT RUBY'S B&B

LAKE CHARLES CHILDREN'S MUSEUM

MARDI GRAS MUSEUM OF IMPERIAL CALCASIEU

210

PORT OF LAKE CHARLES

To Delta Downs, Cajun Charlie's Seafood, Hampton Inn, Sabine N.W.R., and Houston, TX

SALLIER ST

CHARPENTIER HISTORIC DISTRICT

12TH ST

Lake Charles

210

L'AUBERGE DU LAC HOTEL & CASINO/ SNAKE RIVER GRILL

LA TRUFFLE SAUVAGE

CASA MANANA

JOE MUGGS

Bayou

HODGES ST

KIRKMAN ST

ENTERPRISE

OAK PARK BLVD

LAKE RD

INN ON THE BAYOU

PRIEN

SEAFOOD PALACE

SUPER 8 LAKE CHARLES

Prien Lake

C. ELLIOT RD

NELSON RD

Contraband

LAKE ST

RYAN ST

BLVD

14

ABE'S CAJUN MARKET

0   1 mi

0   1 km

384

COUNTRY CLUB RD

385

To Cameron Prairie N.W.R. and Lafayette

14

CAJUN COUNTRY

Sallier's homestead as a great place to store stolen treasures, as it was just 30 miles from the Gulf of Mexico via the Calcasieu River yet well out of sight of authorities. Lafitte began referring to this body of water as "Charlie's Lake," and through time the town grew to be officially named Lake Charles.

Officially, however, Lake Charles's status as a town sat in limbo for some time. After the Louisiana Purchase of 1803, this greater area, known as Río Hondo Territory, existed with-

out a clear government, as neither the Spanish nor the new U.S. government claimed the area. The Admas-Onis Treaty of 1819 finally resolved the issue, naming the Sabine River, about 30 miles west of Lake Charles, as the official border between the state of Louisiana and the Spanish territory of Texas.

Lake Charles progressed as a center of cattle farming and lumber, settled early on by hundreds of Cajuns who came by way of Lafayette and the wetlands of the Atchafa-

L'Auberge du Lac, Lake Charles

laya Basin. The introduction of rail service in 1880 further popularized Lake Charles and helped to make it an important way station between New Orleans and Houston. Around the turn of the 20th century, considerable reserves of sulfur were discovered in the area west of Lake Charles, and thus the mining town of Sulphur was born. The market for sulfur dried up by the mid-1920s, but by now Lake Charles had grown into one of the state's most important cities.

In 1926 Calcasieu channel was dredged, making it possible for large ships to make their way from the Gulf of Mexico to Lake Charles, and this helped spur the development of the petrochemical industry that's still so important in Lake Charles today.

SIGHTS
Casinos
The **Isle of Capri Casino and Hotel** (100 Westlake Ave., Lake Charles, 800/843-4753, www.isleofcapricasino.com) sits along the northwestern shore of the lake and has an all-suite hotel, three restaurants (including the popular Calypso's Seafood Buffet), and plenty of gaming, plus lounges and a theater that books live, mostly Louisiana-based musicians and bands.

On the northeast side of the lake, **Harrah's Lake Charles Casino** (505 N. Lakeshore Dr., Lake Charles, 800/427-7247, www.harrahs.com) was heavily damaged by Hurricane Rita; it was being rebuilt, but no timetable for a reopening had been announced at press time. However, Harrah's did reopen its accommodations in February 2006, renaming it the Lakefront Hotel.

On the south side of the lake you'll find the newest and most luxurious casino resort, **L'Auberge du Lac** (777 Ave. L'Auberge, Lake Charles, 337/395-7777 or 866/580-7444, www.ldlcasino.com), which opened in 2005. The grand, 26-story gaming property contains 1,600 slots, more than 60 gaming tables, and both elegant and casual bars and restaurants. There are also some 750 luxury hotel rooms, a large pool and sandy beach area, an event center hosting major music and comedy acts, and an acclaimed golf course, Contraband Bayou.

Museums

Downtown Lake Charles has a handful of attractions, including the **Lake Charles Children's Museum** (327 Broad St., Lake Charles, 337/433-9420, www.child-museum.org, open 10 A.M.–5 P.M. Tues.–Sat., admission $5); and the **Mardi Gras Museum of Imperial Calcasieu** (809 Kirby St., 2nd floor, Lake Charles, 337/430-0043, open 1–5 P.M. Tues.–Fri., admission $3.50), which has the largest collection of Mardi Gras costumes anywhere. You can learn about the city's history at the **Imperial Calcasieu Museum** (204 W. Sallier St., Lake Charles, 337/439-3797, open 10 A.M.–5 P.M. Tues.–Sat., admission $2), which contains an art gallery and extensive collection of early Louisiana Colonial furniture, a re-created late-19th-century barbershop, and a collection of original Audubon prints. On the grounds, the enormous **Sallier Oak,** which dates to the late 1600s, stands guard over the museum and is a member of the Live Oak Society.

Charpentier Historic District

In a city that developed into a major lumber center during the 19th century, it's hardly surprising that Lake Charles is rife with fine Victorian wood-frame homes, many of them in the Charpentier Historic District, which is bound roughly by Belden Street to the north, Louisiana Avenue to the east, Kirby and 7th Streets to the south, and Ryan Street to the west. Many of the people who came to Lake Charles in the 1880s to work in the timber industry hailed from the Midwest, and the architectural style that grew up in this district is more typical of the gingerbread, Gothic, Eastlake, and Queen Anne houses found in Michigan and Indiana than elsewhere in Louisiana. Excellent self-guided walking/driving tours of this neighborhood are available from the Southwest Louisiana Convention and Visitors Bureau.

Sam Houston Jones State Park

Northwest of downtown, 1,100-acre Sam Houston Jones State Park (107 Sutherland Rd., Lake Charles, 337/855-2665 or 888/677-7264, www.crt.state.la.us/parks, open 9 A.M.–dusk daily, admission $1 per person) is set around a rich pine forest with a fenced-in 10-acre deer habitat, many hiking trails, two boat launches, fishing areas, a picnic grove, and a small but nicely done nature center (open 9:30 A.M.–3:30 P.M. Wed.–Sun.). There's also a campground with 12 vacation cabins, 62 RV sites, and 19 tent sites. The nature center has three rooms, each focusing on a different habitat. Inside you'll find many kinds of animals, including snakes both venomous and nonvenomous (which you can sometimes hold). Wildlife sometimes seen around the park includes alligators (which are less common here than around central Acadiana), red foxes, flying squirrels, mink, coyotes, skunks, raccoons, red-eared slider turtles, and plenty of snakes. Fishing enthusiasts will find catfish, bluegills, largemouth bass, and spotted gar. The park sustained a lot of damage from Hurricane Rita, but it had reopened by spring 2006.

VINTON

On I-10 at the Texas/Louisiana border, Vinton is best known as the home of **Delta Downs Racetrack, Casino, and Hotel** (2717 Hwy. 3063, Vinton, 800/589-7441, www.deltadowns.com), which began as a venue for year-round racing, an off-track–betting parlor, and slot machines. Next came a huge casino gaming development, followed in 2006 by a dramatic new luxury hotel.

SHOPPING

Downtown Lake Charles has quite a number of antiques shops, many of them on or near Ryan Street, both at Broad and 12th streets. A full brochure listing local shops is available from the Southwest Louisiana Convention and Visitors Bureau.

ENTERTAINMENT AND EVENTS
Entertainment and Nightlife

Crystal's (112 W. Broad St., Lake Charles, 337/433-5457) is the gay and lesbian club in town.

Festivals and Events

Lake Charles has huge Mardi Gras celebrations, so that's always a good time of year to come and enjoy the revelry. The biggest event in the area is the **Contraband Days Festival** (www.contrabanddays.com), a 12-day event in early May that includes a variety of live-music performances, helicopter rides, a "doggie log race," rides and games, and plenty of food. In mid-July, music lovers attend the **Cajun French Music Association Annual Food/Music Festival** (800/456-7952), a two-day event held at the Burton Coliseum that showcases plenty of great Cajun music plus great food, from boudin balls to cracklin's.

ACCOMMODATIONS

You'll find dozens of chain properties and a handful of inns in Lake Charles. A few motels are also off I-10 between Lafayette and Lake Charles.

Hotels and Motels

Under $50: You'll find the lowest rates in town at the clean and simple **Motel 6** (335 U.S. 171, Lake Charles, 337/433-1773 or 800/466-8356, www.motel6.com), which is about eight miles north of downtown Lake Charles.

Superior to the typical properties that are represented by this chain, the **Super 8 Lake Charles** (1350 E. Prien Lake Rd., Lake Charles, 337/477-1606 or 800/800-8000, www.super8.com) was built in 2000 and has large rooms, interior corridors, and in-room coffeemakers, microwaves, refrigerators, irons and boards, and hair dryers. The hotel is on the south side of town, just off I-210, which bypasses Lake Charles from I-10.

$50-100: Although Harrah's Lake Charles casino was damaged and closed indefinitely after Hurricane Rita, Harrah's reopened and renamed its accommodations in February 2006, and the **Lakefront Hotel** (505 N. Lakeshore Dr., Lake Charles, 337/437-1500 or 888/782-9525, www.harrahs.com) makes an excellent choice. It contains 263 upscale rooms as well as 10 suites, and it's a good base for visiting the area's other gaming facilities, which

are within an easy drive, or taking advantage of downtown attractions. There's also a full-service restaurant.

One of the most interesting lodging options in Lake Charles, because of its location, is **Inn on the Bayou** (1101 W. Prien Lake Rd., Lake Charles, 337/474-5151 or 800/642-2968, www.innonthebayou.com), which sits right on Bayou Contraband, so named because Jean Lafitte allegedly hid his spoils along here. This modern motel has a 550-foot boat dock with deep-water access, fishing, and a large pool and sundeck. Rooms are typical of what you'd find at a midprice chain hotel, but they do all have large work desks, Wi-Fi, and plenty of room, and all are equipped with free high-speed Internet.

The luxurious **L'Auberge du Lac** (777 Ave. L'Auberge, Lake Charles, 337/395-7777 or 866/580-7444, www.ldlcasino.com) opened in 2005 inside a stunning 26-story building on the southern edge of the lake, with expansive views of the entire area. Amenities, apart from the enormous gaming facility downstairs, include a large pool with its own sandy beach and "lazy river" water course, a full-service spa and salon with fitness center, a championship golf course, and a slew of very good restaurants. There are 750 spacious rooms here, each with high-speed Internet, big TVs, luxurious bathrooms, and terrycloth robes.

Similarly posh, in nearby Vinton, the **Delta Downs Racetrack, Casino, and Hotel** (2717 Delta Downs La., Vinton, 888/332-7829, www.deltadowns.com) opened its fancy accommodations in spring 2006. The midrise property has handsome rooms outfitted with high-end armoires and wood furnishings, and bathrooms with stand-alone glass-door showers and large tubs (whirlpool tubs in some). There's gaming and horse racing on-site plus several restaurants and a large pool. The only drawback is that the property lies 25 miles west of Lake Charles, so you have to schlep back and forth to visit attractions and restaurants (there's not a whole lot to do in Vinton apart from visit this resort).

In Sulphur, just west of Lake Charles but

right at the beginning of the Creole Nature Trail (far enough north where it wasn't damaged), the **Hampton Inn** (210 Henning Dr., 337/527-0000 or 800/426-7866, www.hampton-inn.com) is a reliable bet, with a pool, fitness center, and business services. The outstanding seafood restaurant Cajun Charlie's is next door.

Inns and Bed-and-Breakfasts

$50-100: In Lake Charles's lovely Garden District, **C. A.'s House** (618 and 624 Ford St., Lake Charles, 337/439-6672 or 866/439-6672, www.cas-house.com) is one of the most distinctive—and distinguished—accommodations in this area dominated by chain hotels. There are four opulently furnished rooms in C. A.'s House, a 1900 white Colonial Revival mansion with four columns running along the grand facade and lushly landscaped grounds. There's also an attractive two-story suite with a full kitchen and private entrance. Guests in either the inn or the carriage house have access to the property's hot tub and to a heated pool. Guests enjoy free use of kayaks and bikes, and there's Wi-Fi throughout.

The same folks who own Pujo Street Cafe and Market run one of western Acadiana's most inviting inns, **Aunt Ruby's B&B** (504 Pujo St., Lake Charles, 337/430-0603, www.auntrubys.com), a reasonably priced spot with six upscale rooms, all with private baths, cable TV, and phones. Opened originally as the city's first boarding house, this 1911 home in the Charpentier Historic District has a garden-filled front yard and a relaxing veranda. The lake, and the casinos, are just a few blocks west. Full breakfast is included.

FOOD

Lake Charles has a few upscale and urbane places to eat, but it's mostly a casual town. You'll also find several restaurants (including inexpensive all-you-can-eat buffets) at the casinos.

Traditional Creole and Cajun

It's worth the short trip from Lake Charles to Sulphur to sample the spicy and filling Louisiana cooking at **Cajun Charlie's Seafood** (202 Henning Dr., Sulphur, 337/527-9044, $7–18), which is especially famous for its extensive lunch buffet, during which you can scarf down as much as you want of fried seafood, sweet potatoes, bread pudding with rum, whitefish, catfish, hush puppies, jambalaya, and the list goes on and on. Dinner is no less of an event, with many of the same foods available in larger portions à la carte. The dining room is packed to the rafters with fun bric-a-brac—old farm tools, vintage advertising signs, mounted wildlife, fishing nets, and even an old pirogue hanging from one rafter. In the adjoining gift shop you can browse for books, dolls, gift boxes of boudin, and cards.

Creative and Contemporary

◖ **Pujo Street Cafe and Market** (901 E. Ryan St., Lake Charles, 337/439-2054, $10–24) is a beautiful space with high pressed-tin ceilings and exposed brick walls, black-and-white photos, French doors, and crisp white napery. It feels like something out of New Orleans's Warehouse District. The large central bar makes for a nice gathering point. The food is fresh and innovative: Try the crawfish salad with spinach, roma tomatoes, red onion, and honey Dijon dressing, or the Caribbean-style sea bass with mango salsa and scallion rice.

Sublime Northern Italian and Southern French cuisine is served at **La Truffe Sauvage** (815 Bayou Pines W, Lake Charles, 337/439-8364, $26–34), www.latruffesauvage.com), which occupies a romantic cottage on the west side of downtown, just a few blocks below the lake. The white-glove restaurant with live piano on Tuesday evenings is the setting for some of the state's finest cooking outside New Orleans. Start with the yellowfin tuna carpaccio with extra-virgin olive oil, fresh lemon, avocado relish, and parmigiana-reggiano cheese, or the duck consommé with crab-and-mushrooms ravioli. Main courses include braised lamb shank with risotto Milanese, natural jus, and horseradish *gremolata,* and the signature dish: pan-roasted scallops and duck foie gras with green lentils, white truffle oil, and 50-year-aged balsamic vinegar.

At the posh L'Auberge du Lac casino, the **Snake River Grill** (777 Avenue L'Auberge, Lake Charles, 337/395-7565, $16–32) is a Jackson, Wyoming, import, serving creative Rocky Mountain–inspired food. The menu changes often, but typical dishes might be the steak tartare pizza with garlic aioli, the parmesan-truffle shoestring potatoes (a great side dish for sharing), and dry-aged, bone-in buffalo strip steak with sweet-potato fries and juniper butter.

Casual Cooking

For well-prepared, traditional seafood, head to **Steamboat Bill's** (1004 Lakeshore Dr., Lake Charles, 337/474-1070; also 732 N. Martin Luther King, Lake Charles, 337/494-1700, $7–14), a waterfront restaurant that's usually packed with hungry diners. Choose from soft-shell crab dinners, boiled crawfish plates, shrimp étoufée, red beans and rice, and other great southern Louisiana fare.

❨ Seafood Palace (2218 Enterprise Blvd., Lake Charles, 337/433-9293, $5–13) is a hole-in-the-wall with great gumbo and some of the best short-order seafood in the area.

Ethnic

In the south side of downtown Lake Charles, **Casa Manana** (2510 Ryan St., Lake Charles, 337/433-4112, $7–15) serves commendable Tex-Mex food, which is saying a lot in a city just 30 miles from the Lone Star State—if you don't serve decent Mexican fare in these parts, you don't survive. The chow here is Americanized but spicy and well portioned. Consider the tamale combo, portabella mushroom fajitas, baby-back ribs, and eggplant San Miguel (breaded and topped with shrimp and a *pico de gallo*–cheese sauce).

Java Joints

Inside the Books-a-Million bookstore south of downtown, **Joe Muggs** (2934 Ryan St., Lake Charles, 337/436-3577) is a pleasant stop for cappuccinos, espressos, flavored coffees, chai teas, sweets, and sandwiches.

Picnic Supplies and Gourmet Goods

If you find yourself craving the flavors of Acadiana at home, give **Abe's Cajun Market** (3935 Ryan St., Lake Charles, 337/474-3816) a call, or just drop by the market before you leave town. Abe's is famous for the *turducken,* a true exercise in excess. This fowl conglomerate consists of a deboned turkey, which is stuffed with a deboned duck, which is stuffed with a deboned chicken, which is stuffed with your choice of cornbread or crawfish. The massive platter serves 15–20 people and can be shipped to you anywhere in the United States for about $90, including shipping. Other delicacies available at Abe's include étoufée, gumbo, Cajun sausage, Cajun-stuffed pork chops, beef jerky, and jambalaya.

INFORMATION AND SERVICES
Visitor Information

Pick up information on Lake Charles and surrounding towns at the **Southwest Louisiana Convention and Visitors Bureau** (1205 N. Lakeshore Dr., Lake Charles, 337/436-9588 or 800/456-7952, www.visitlakecharles.org).

Getting Around

It's best to explore Lake Charles by car. The interstate I-10 connects Lake Charles with Lafayette and with Houston, Texas. See the *Essentials* chapter for details on reaching New Orleans, Lafayette, and Lake Charles from other parts of the country by train, plane, and bus.

BACKGROUND

The Land

Louisiana, especially the southern end of the state, is—in geological terms—brand-spanking new. It's largely made up of sediment deposited by the Mississippi River or left in the wake of the continuously shifting Gulf of Mexico shoreline. It's tied with Florida for having the second-lowest mean elevation of any state (about 100 feet, which trails only Delaware), and its highest point—535-foot "Mount" Driskill, up north near Grambling and Minden, is not very high at all.

In southern Louisiana, elevations are as low as eight feet below sea level in New Orleans, a point made abundantly clear during the flooding aftermath of Hurricane Katrina, to perhaps 300 feet in a few slightly elevated areas north of Lake Pontchartrain. The soil around most of the southern parishes is sandy, except along the delta land that has been formed by Mississippi River sediment. The topography is mostly coastal marsh, alluvial plains, and grassy prairie. To get an idea of what the hillier northern part of the state looks like, visit the North Shore area above Lake Pontchartrain, especially the upper towns nearest the Mississippi border, where you'll encounter dense longleaf and shortleaf pine forest and some gentle hills. The entire state sits along an extremely gradual slope, which drops, on average, a couple of feet per mile from north to south.

© ANDREW COLLINS

The Mississippi River has always played a vital role in the appearance, development, and economy of New Orleans and of the state as a whole. Through the northern two-thirds of the state, it runs crookedly and tortuously north–south and forms the border between Mississippi and Louisiana. At 31 degrees latitude, the Mississippi–Louisiana border jogs along a straight west–east line to the Pearl River, which then forms the state border going north–south to the Gulf of Mexico. From the point where the Mississippi River is no longer the state border, it winds southeast through the lower third of the state, cutting directly through Baton Rouge and New Orleans. All along this route, the land for several miles on either side of the river lies in Louisiana and has been formed entirely by river sediment.

The section of the Mississippi that flows through Louisiana is famous in large part because it's the mouth of the river and it figures so large in the history of New Orleans. But this stretch represents just a fraction of the entire river, whose source is Lake Itasca, in northern Minnesota. All told, it wends 2,350 miles, bordering Minnesota, Wisconsin, Iowa, Illinois, Missouri, Kentucky, Arkansas, Tennessee, Mississippi, and—finally—Louisiana, before it empties into the Gulf of Mexico. At this final phase, in southern Louisiana, the mighty river and its many tributaries form a fan-shaped delta. All told, the Mississippi River is the definitive drain for about 40 percent of the United States, acting as the watershed basin for parts of 31 states and three Canadian provinces. Waterways as far east as New York and as far west as Montana eventually empty into this vast pool of water. There are only four drainage basins larger than this one in the world: the Amazon, in South America, and the Congo and the Nile, in Africa. It's the world's third-longest river.

Louisiana's shoreline is incredibly jagged and comprises 6.5 million wetland acres, more than 40 percent of the entire nation's marsh ecosystem. Unlike the considerably more stable Gulf shorelines of Texas, Mississippi, Alabama, and Florida, Louisiana's coast is continuously shifting, the result of the evolving play between

MUDDY WATERS

Contrary to popular belief, the muddiness of the Mississippi River, and of many of the other rivers and bayous in the state, is not a sign of pollution or any other unhealthy condition. The rivers become muddy because the fast-moving current is constantly transporting natural and easily eroded bottom sediments. In fact, according to the most recent studies on the river, there are no serious problems at all with contamination and pollution.

An odd thing about the state's rivers is that many of them flow at a higher elevation than the floodplains that surround them. The sediment brought downriver and deposited in Louisiana has built up the riverbanks, forming natural levees. When the river runs high, as much as one-third of the state, and at least half of southern Louisiana – including all of metropoilitan New Orleans – would be one massive pool of water were it not for the intricate system of man-made levees and spillways constructed all along the river and its tributaries.

the Gulf currents and the flow of the Mississippi and other tributaries. The current Mississippi Delta, which extends across the southern Louisiana shoreline, took about 6,000 years to form. Its largest tributary, the Atchafalaya River, flows into the western end of the delta, southeast of Lafayette and southwest of Houma. The Atchafalaya's delta will eventually fill in much of northern Atchafalaya Bay and come to resemble the fully formed Mississippi River delta.

In addition to the Mississippi and Atchafalaya, the state's other major rivers are the Red (which flows from northwest Louisiana through Shreveport before joining the Mississippi), the Ouachita (in northeastern Louisiana), the Sabine (which forms the border between Texas and Louisiana), and the Pearl (which flows through southeastern Louisiana, where it forms the border with Mississippi, and into the Gulf). A bayou is simply the Louisiana term for what the rest of the country might call a brook, but, in fact, many bayous in Louisiana are large enough that they'd be called rivers elsewhere in the country. The word derives from the Choctaw term for a river, *bayuk,* and some larger bayous include Teche (which flows through the Cajun Country through St. Martinville and Breaux Bridge), Vermilion (which flows through Lafayette), LaFourche (which runs through Houma), and Boeuf (which passes near Opelousas in St. Landry Parish).

If you're not already feeling a little soggy from reading all this, keep in mind that Louisiana also contains about 150 lakes, some of which are man-made, including the nation's fourth-largest man-made lake, 186,000-acre Toledo Bend Reservoir, which forms much of the east-west border between Texas and Louisiana. Toledo Bend is a popular recreational area, especially with fishing enthusiasts and boaters. In the southern part of the state, many of these "lakes" are really salt- or brackish-water lagoons that were once bays or inlets of the Gulf but were eventually somewhat or entirely sealed off by the formation of barrier beaches or delta ridges from the Gulf and rivers. The largest and most famous of these is Lake Pontchartrain, which is traversed by the longest bridge in the world, the 23-plus-mile Lake Pontchartrain Causeway. Barataria Bay, south of New Orleans, is another example of this kind of lake, as are Lake Maurepas, just west of Lake Pontchartrain and connected to it by Bayou Manchac, and Lake Salvador, just southwest of New Orleans and fringed by Jean Lafitte National Historical Park and Preserve.

Like the famous river that flows into it, the Gulf of Mexico is no slouch when it comes to superlatives. It's the fifth-largest sea in the world, covering nearly 600,000 square miles.

CLIMATE

The weather has been a hot topic in Southern Louisiana for as long as people have lived here—long before Hurricanes Katrina and Rita barreled through the state in 2005. Hurricanes have always been a threat to the Louisiana shoreline, and given the increasing numbers and magnitude of these storms in recent years, one suspects Louisiana will have plenty of brushes with violent storms in the future. Hurricane season begins in June each year and lasts through November.

Southern Louisiana is jokingly called the northernmost coast of Central America, and not just because of its banana-republic politics—it also has a climate that's more similar to Costa Rica's than to that of most of the United States. Almost all of the southern part of the state is considered a semihumid, subtropical zone—it almost never receives snow (and then only a dusting), and in New Orleans, when the temperature occasionally dips to freezing on the coldest winter evenings, locals bundle up as though they're about to run the Iditarod. The state's average rainfall is about 55 inches per year, but some of the southern parishes average closer to 70 inches of rain annually—compare that with about 35 inches of rain each year in Seattle, and just 15 inches or so in dry areas of the country such as Los Angeles. Yes, you can expect to get rained on during a typical visit in New Orleans—it's rainy all year, with the highest totals in the summer and the lowest in October and November, but there are no bone-dry months here.

With a low atmospheric ceiling and high humidity, nighttime to daytime low and high temperatures don't usually span a great range. The mean temperature for the year is about 60 degrees in the southern part of the state, but New Orleans usually feels warmer, even if the temperature isn't necessarily higher, because it's less breezy and the considerable concrete in its roads and buildings tends to absorb and retain heat. Average high temperatures in New Orleans in summer are about 92 degrees, with nighttime lows averaging a still very hot 75 degrees. In winter, throughout December, January, and February, highs average a quite pleasant 65 degrees, with lows a manageable 48 degrees. Winter is a wonderful time to visit. Summer can be simply unbearable on the most humid days, even considering that virtually every public accommodation, restaurant, shop,

NEW ORLEANS CLIMATE

MONTH	AVERAGE HIGH	AVERAGE LOW	AVERAGE RAINFALL
January	61	42	5.0
February	64	44	6.0
March	72	53	4.9
April	79	59	4.5
May	84	65	4.6
June	89	71	5.8
July	91	73	6.1
August	90	73	6.1
September	87	70	5.5
October	79	59	3.0
November	71	51	4.4
December	64	45	5.8

Note: Temperatures are in degrees Fahrenheit; rainfall in inches.

and attraction in New Orleans and the rest of the state is air-conditioned. Especially in the touristy French Quarter, which can be littered with garbage along Bourbon and outside bars on weekend mornings, it can feel and smell positively foul to walk around on a summer day. Spring and fall are fairly genial times to visit southern Louisiana, keeping in mind that temperatures can easily reach into the 90s during warm spells but that they more typically average in the upper 70s in September and October, and again in April and May.

New Orleans itself averages about 110 days a year with completely sunny skies, and about the same number of days with rain. Otherwise, it's partly cloudy or partly sunny, depending on whether you're an optimist or a pessimist about weather.

History

PRE-EUROPEAN LOUISIANA

In northeastern Louisiana, not too far from the city of Monroe, archaeologists have identified a series of ancient ceremonial mounds that some in the scientific community believe are the earliest physical evidence of human settlement on the entire continent. More recent but still prehistoric mounds dot the landscape of the state, especially in the northern and eastern regions. These mounds were a fixture in the early Native American farming communities that proliferated in these parts for the 2–3 millennia before European settlement.

Louisiana's Hopewell indigenous tribes thrived in the Gulf South from about 200 B.C. until nearly A.D. 900, with Mississippian tribes succeeding them in the 1500s. Native Americans of the 1600s and 1700s, when Europeans first began exploring the region, comprised three distinct branches, each with its own culture and language: Caddoan, Muskogean, and Tunican. It was this last branch, which included the Chitimacha, Attakapa, and other tribes, that mostly inhabited what is now southern Louisiana, with Muskogean and Caddoan Indians living in the central and northwestern parts of the state, respectively.

The effect of French and then Spanish settlement on indigenous people living in Louisiana was, as it was wherever Europeans explored the New World, devastating. Many tribes were annihilated by disease, others squarely routed out, enslaved, or massacred by settlers. Still, some Native Americans managed to hang on and thrive in Louisiana, many of their members intermarrying with African Americans. Today there are Chitimacha, Houma, Tunica-Biloxi, Coushatta, and Choctaw settlements in the state. Many geographical names in Louisiana have indigenous origins, among them Bogalusa (which means "black water"), Opelousas ("black leg"), and Ponchatoula ("hanging hair").

Most people think of the French explorer René-Robert Cavelier, Sieur de La Salle, as the earliest European settler in the region, and he was the first to establish a permanent stronghold in the name of his own country, in 1682. But 140 years earlier, Spaniards led by explorer Hernando de Soto first visited what is now Louisiana. They didn't stay, but they did leave behind diseases that proved fatal to many of the indigenous people they encountered.

La Salle entered Louisiana down the Mississippi River from the north and claimed for France all the land drained by not only this massive river but also its vast network of tributaries. This parcel covered about 830,000 square miles and ran from the Gulf of Mexico to Canada, and from the Rocky Mountains to Mississippi. He first termed the region Louisiana (well, technically, Louisiane, which is its name in French) after France's reigning monarch of that period, Louis XIV.

1700-1766

Louisiana's period of French rule was barely more than three generations—France would cede the territory to the Spanish in 1762 before occupying it again for a short period preceding the Louisiana Purchase. Neither the first nor second periods of French rule proved to be profitable for France, and on the whole, one could say that the entire episode was a failure from a colonial perspective. On the flip side, the French occupation planted the seeds for the emergence of New Orleans as one of young America's most fascinating cities.

New Orleans was not the first settlement in Louisiana by the French, although explorer Pierre Le Moyne, Sieur d'Iberville, did establish a toehold near the city on March 3, 1699 (Mardi Gras day, coincidentally). That same year, the French built a permanent fort about 90 miles east in Biloxi (now Mississippi), and, three years later, another 60 miles east in Mobile (now Alabama). The first permanent French settlement to go up in what is now Louisiana, in 1714, was Natchitoches, a still-charming small city in northwestern Louisiana, about 300 miles northwest of New Orleans. By the late 1710s, however, France had already failed to invest substantially in its new settlement and, unable to fund a full-fledged colony, the monarchy transferred control of Louisiana to Antoine Crozat, a French financier of considerable acclaim.

Crozat was able to make little headway with Louisiana, and just five years later, control of Louisiana was shifted to Compagnie d'Occident, led by a wealthy Scotsman named John Law. It became quickly apparent to Law and other authorities, however, that the southern Mississippi was vulnerable to plays for control by the two key competing European powers in colonial America, Great Britain and Spain. To protect their interests, the French built a new fort in 1718 along the lower Mississippi, christening the settlement La Nouvelle-Orléans, after Philippe, Duc d'Orléans. A handful of settlements were added along the Mississippi River to the north, and in 1722 France named young New Orleans the territorial capital of Louisiana.

Nouvelle Orléans's beginnings were almost pathetically modest. The site, at a sharp bend of the Mississippi River more than five feet *below* sea level, was little more than bug- and alligator-infested swampland, which the city's earliest residents shored up with landfill and dams. Part of the settlement covered one of the few bumps of higher ground along the river's banks. The site was chosen in part because a bayou (now known as Bayou St. John) connected the Mississippi River at this point to Lake Pontchartrain, which itself emptied into the Gulf. For eons, the area's Native Americans had used the bayou as a shortcut for getting from the river to the Gulf without having to paddle all the way south, nearly another 100 miles, to where the Mississippi entered the Gulf.

Today's French Quarter, also known as the Vieux Carré (literally, Old Square), for the first several decades encompassed all of New Orleans. It was anchored by the Place d'Armes, which would later be renamed Jackson Square. The river's course in relation to the city has changed slightly since the city's founding—in the early days, Jackson Square faced the riverfront directly, whereas today a significant strip of land and levee acts as a barrier between it and the river.

Law can be credited with making the earliest effort to interest European settlers in Louisiana. His first successful campaign brought not Frenchmen but Germans to the new territory. Law would convince Germans to move to Louisiana as indentured workers, meaning they were bound to work for an established period, and once their service commitment was complete, they were granted freedom. Law's Occidental Company used all the usual trickery and false advertising common throughout Europe in those days to attract immigrants and investors: It promised vast riches, huge mining reserves, and easy agricultural opportunities, virtually none of which was accurate.

During Law's first few years of controlling Louisiana, his company managed to convince about 7,000 mostly German and French residents to migrate to Louisiana. A significant percentage of these migrants died from disease or starvation, as the colonial authorities were in no position at all to feed, clothe, and house

the arrivals. If you stayed in Louisiana during these early days, in all likelihood you did so only because you hadn't the means to return to Europe. Word of the false promise of Louisiana spread quickly back to France, but authorities allowed Law and his company to administer the territory until 1731, when the French monarchy finally stepped in to resume control.

Law was responsible for first importing West African slaves to Louisiana. His Compagnie d'Occident also owned the French Compagnie du Senegal, which controlled all French slave trade. During roughly a 10-year period, about 3,000 mostly Senegalese slaves were taken from their homeland to Louisiana. Slaves worked on the handful of early plantations and also on the countless smaller subsistence farms that developed around southern Louisiana, most engaged in the production and export of indigo and tobacco.

Back in control of the colony from 1731 through 1762, France failed utterly to turn Louisiana into a profitable venture. Furthermore, its strategic importance diminished sharply as England developed an upper hand during the French and Indian War, which had begun in 1754, toward controlling Canada. In 1762, France hatched a diplomatic scheme to help impel Spain to join it and rout the British: It secretly handed over the Louisiana Territory to Spain in the Treaty of Fontainebleau. In fact, the territory stayed in the family, as France's King Louis XV simply transferred the land to his own cousin, Spain's King Charles III.

The move ended badly for both France and Spain. France lost the war with Britain in 1763 and lost control of Canada. And Spain ended up with a lemon. One might argue, of course, that France really didn't lose a colony so much as it rid itself of what had become an enormous and depressing financial burden. Furthermore, as part of the peace treaty between the joint powers of Spain and France with their victor, Great Britain was awarded all of Louisiana east of the Mississippi River, which became known as West Florida. Spain kept a much larger tract, which included all of Louisiana west of the river, along with a critical little area along the lower Mississippi River called Ile d'Orleans, which included the city of New Orleans. France was free of any part of Louisiana.

1766-1803

The actual physical transfer of Louisiana, and especially New Orleans, to Spain was an unmitigated disaster fraught with rebellion, virtual martial law, and ugly acts of violence. It didn't help that the residents of New Orleans had no idea that they had become subjects of Spain until 1766, when the first Spanish governor, Antonio de Ulloa, arrived that March and, like a wicked stepmother, immediately instituted a strict rule upon the city's inhabitants.

Almost as immediately, there were insurgencies, and in 1768 the situation became particularly dire when locals actually drove Ulloa and his cronies clear out of town. Spain hired a tyrannical military man, General Alejandro O'Reilly, to beat down the rebellion, which he did, quite successfully, in August 1769. He managed to get Spain in firm control of New Orleans, a rule that would last until the United States orchestrated the Louisiana Purchase in 1803, for although France technically owned Louisiana at that time, Spaniards continued to govern the city's day-to-day affairs right through to the end.

The Spanish, like the French, made every possible effort to boost the colony's population, sending plenty of Spaniards to Louisiana throughout their period of rule. From a cultural standpoint Louisiana remained squarely French, as the colonists from France far outnumbered any newcomers. The only reason the appearance of the French Quarter today more closely resembles Spanish colonial than French colonial architecture is that two huge fires burned much of the city during the Spanish occupation, and many of the new buildings that went up were constructed by Spanish authorities. The first fire hit the Quarter in 1788, apparently started by candles at a religious observation; about 850 buildings burned, and about 200 of those were again lost in a smaller fire in 1794. It's Spain's influence that resulted

in the wrought-iron balconies, shaded courtyards, and other features that typify French Quarter architecture.

Ironically, the majority of the newcomers to Louisiana during the Spanish period were actually French, or French-speaking, refugees. The most famous group were the Acadians, who had been cruelly expelled from the Maritime Provinces of Canada after the British victory. The French immigrants living in Acadian Canada were typically rounded up and forced onto ships—some were sent back to France, and others were reluctantly taken in by certain British colonies in what is now the United States. Many died in passage or of poverty encountered where they landed. Spain, looking to boost the population of the Louisiana colony, enthusiastically welcomed the Acadians, who arrived in two major waves, the first in 1764 and an even larger one in 1785. Most of them settled in the marshes and swamplands of south-central and southwestern Louisiana. In Louisiana, the name Acadian gradually morphed into Cajun, as we all know it today, and Lafayette, Louisiana, became the hub of Cajun settlements.

A lesser-known group of refugees that also came to New Orleans and Louisiana in great numbers from 1791 through 1803 were white French settlers and some free people of color from the French colony of Saint-Domingue (now Haiti), who fled the island during the violent black revolution of the 1790s.

Louisiana's makeup changed a bit during the American Revolution, as Spain worked in concert with the American colonists to undermine their rivals, the British. They sent supplies and munitions to the colonists, and in 1779, after formally declaring war on Britain, their Louisiana militia captured all of the British settlements of West Florida. This included all of the Gulf Coast region between the Mississippi River and the Perdido River, which today forms the east-west state border between Alabama and Florida. Per the terms of the Treaty of Paris in 1783, Spain's assistance was, at the war's conclusion, rewarded with a chunk of land that included all of both East Florida (today's Florida) and West Florida (which today includes Alabama, Mississippi, and the nine Louisiana parishes east and north of the Mississippi River, now sometimes referred to as the Florida parishes).

With the young United States now in control of all the land east of the Mississippi River (except for East and West Florida), New Orleans and the entire Louisiana Territory grew dramatically in strategic importance. New Orleans became the seaport serving America's interior, as important rivers throughout Ohio, Kentucky, and Tennessee all fed to the Mississippi.

In yet another secret treaty, however, Spain in 1800 decided to transfer all of the Louisiana Territory, including New Orleans, back to France. The actual residents of New Orleans never even knew they were residents of a French colony for the three years they were back under the country's rule, as in 1803, the United States bought Louisiana from France for a mere $15 million. Even by the standards of that day, $15 million was a paltry sum for such an enormous parcel of land—approximately one-third of the land that now makes up the present-day continental United States. Because Spain still possessed East and West Florida, the nine Louisiana parishes east and north of the Mississippi River remained in Spanish hands until 1810, when the American residents of West Florida declared their independence and asked to be annexed by the United States.

1804-1865

Upon buying Louisiana from France, the United States immediately split the territory in two at the 33rd parallel, which today forms the northern border of Louisiana. All land south of that point became known as the Territory of Orleans, and, confusingly, all land to the north became known as the Territory of Louisiana.

America named William C. C. Claiborne governor of the Orleans territory, which he ruled from the territorial capital, New Orleans. He endured a difficult period, attempting to introduce the American democratic political system to a people entirely unused to self-determined government. In 1790, about 10,000

new refugees from Saint-Domingue moved into New Orleans, doubling the population but adding further chaos to the city. In many respects, it's this final wave of French-speaking people from Haiti—white colonists of French descent and free people of color *(gens de couleur libres)*—that ultimately established the French-Caribbean character that exists to this day in New Orleans.

For a time, New Orleans deviated from rural Louisiana in its relative tolerance of racial diversity—the *gens de couleur libres* were, in many cases, well educated and quite able to forge good livings as builders, designers, artisans, and chefs. These early Creole immigrants were in a large way responsible for the intricate and fanciful Creole cottages and other buildings still found throughout the city and southern Louisiana, and these same immigrants helped to develop New Orleans's inimitable Creole cuisine, which blended the traditions of France, Spain, the Caribbean, Africa, and even the American frontier and Native Americans.

Intermingling was considerable in this early New Orleans society, as wealthy Europeans and Creoles commonly had mistresses, some who were *gens de couleur libres,* quadroons (one-fourth black), octoroons (one-eighth black), or some other mix of Anglo, Latin, African, and Native American descent. It's largely for this reason that the term Creole, when applied to people, is rather confusing. The name was first applied to upper-crust French settlers born in Louisiana but descended from mostly wealthy European families, as the very word derives from the Spanish "criollo," a term that described people born in the colonies rather than born in Europe or, for that matter, Africa. These days, just about any New Orleanian or Louisianan who can claim some direct combination of French, Spanish, Caribbean, and African blood can justly consider him- or herself a Creole, the exception being the descendants of the original French-Canadian refugees from Acadia, known as Cajuns.

The United States accepted the Territory of Orleans as the state of Louisiana on April

JEAN LAFITTE AND LOUISIANA'S PIRATES

Piracy and its slightly more acceptable cousin, privateering, have been a part of southern Louisiana lore since the time of the region's settlement. This infamous and often ruthless practice developed in the Gulf of Mexico in the 16th century, when high-seas thieves began targeting Spanish galleons loaded with silver and gold and headed for that country's colonies in the New World. During times of war, European nations legitimized piracy, authorizing the crews of these renegade vessels to stop and seize the ships of opposing nations.

Louisiana developed into a hotbed of piracy because of its geography and topography: The state's irregular, marshy shoreline was punctuated with hundreds of hidden, protected coves, which made perfect havens for pirates. They could elude authorities, smuggle and hide their spoils, and build and repair ships in secret. During the 19th century, the most infamous of these bodies of water was Barataria Bay, a massive body of water just east of present-day Grand Isle; its northern edge lies about 40 miles due south of New Orleans as the crow flies. The bay sits at the north-central tip of the Gulf of Mexico, about 500 miles north of Mexico's Yucatán Peninsula, 650 miles northwest of Cuba, 450 miles west of Florida's Gulf Coast, and 450 miles east of Texas's Gulf Coast. Strategically, no location offered better access to so many lucrative colonial shipping routes.

In this bay, the infamous Baratarians established a colony of illicit doings that included warehouses and docks. Pirate ships returned here with their bounties, and then auctioned them to visitors from New Orleans. Sometimes, they hauled their goods directly to New Orleans, where they found a vast and eager market. Everything, including precious metals, foods, spices, rum, and African slaves were sold by the Baratarians, who were led during the height of their success by the Lafitte brothers, Jean and Pierre.

Unofficially, and even officially for a time, authorities in New Orleans turned a blind eye to Jean Lafitte and his operations, unwilling to shut off the constant stream of valuable and heavily discounted goods into the city. It was not until Lafitte's disregard for the law became too flagrant that Governor William Claiborne finally ordered his arrest, offering a $500 reward for his capture.

30, 1812—it thereby became the 18th state of the union, preceded only by Vermont, Kentucky, Tennessee, and Ohio after the original 13 states. The political system, with Claiborne as governor and New Orleans the capital, continued largely as it had from the time of the Louisiana Purchase.

America wasted no time in exploiting its new purchase, as thousands of entrepreneurial-minded settlers flocked to the busy port city during the first decade after the Louisiana Purchase. They were not welcomed in the French Quarter at all, and in fact the original Creoles would have nothing to do with American settlers for many decades. Some of these upstarts immediately started amassing great riches in shipping and trade enterprises, building lavish homes in the American Quarter, which is now the Central Business District. Canal Street divided the two enclaves, and the median down this street came to be considered New Orleans's "neutral ground." Today, the city's residents refer to any street median as neutral ground.

By the early 1800s, a century's worth of immigrants from all walks of life had contributed to one of the most racially, culturally, and economically diverse populations in the nation. Freed prisoners from France, Haitian refugees, slaves, European indentured servants, American frontiersmen, Spanish Canary Islanders, nuns, military men, and others now formed New Orleans's population and that of many of the communities upriver.

Britain and the United States had remained hostile to one another since the Revolution, and shortly after Louisiana became a state, the two

In 1814, a fleet of American military ships descended upon the Baratarians' headquarters, seizing eight schooners, about 40 houses, nearly 100 men, and countless spoils. Jean Lafitte and the other leaders of the group heard of the impending attack before its onset and successfully hid from authorities before making their escape.

The War of 1812 was in full swing at this point, and late in 1814, the British launched plans to ascend the Mississippi River and attack New Orleans. Lafitte's exploits were legendary across the high seas at this point, and the British decided to approach him with an offer, figuring that he'd happily jump at the opportunity to exact his revenge against U.S. authorities. Lafitte was offered $30,000 and a captainship in the British Navy if he would join in their attack on the Americans.

Lafitte declined. Whether out of some deep loyalty to the United States or, more likely, because he believed he stood to gain more by aligning himself with the U.S. government, he tipped off Governor Claiborne about the impending British attack. He then volunteered his own considerable militia and fleet to defend New Orleans against the British – if Claiborne would agree to drop all charges against Jean and Pierre Lafitte and their fellow Baratarians.

Claiborne relayed the offer to General Andrew Jackson, who had arrived to lead the defense of New Orleans against the British, and Jackson accepted without hesitation. In January 1815, during the Battle of New Orleans, Jean Lafitte and his cohorts performed admirably, greatly assisting American forces in turning back the British attack. Claiborne and Jackson kept their word, and U.S. authorities left the Baratarians alone from that point on.

The final fate of the Lafitte brothers is unrecorded. All that is known is that several years later, they moved their operations to Galveston Bay in Texas, but few additional details can be confirmed. In 1819, the U.S. Congress passed a law declaring piracy a crime punishable by death, and the government finally began pursuing and prosecuting pirates more vigorously. These circumstances may have helped to curtail the Lafittes' operations. Whatever became of the dashing buccaneer, his legacy – and tales concerning his exploits – live on.

nations entered into the War of 1812, which would last three years. By 1814, New Orleans figured heavily in the campaign, as the faltering British decided to go after several key ports along the Gulf Coast and the Mississippi River in an effort to cut off the supply-and-trade system serving the interior United States. New Orleans, defended by Major General Andrew Jackson, was attacked by the British on January 8, 1815—several days after British and American leaders had signed a peace treaty ending the War of 1812. Still, many believe that the British would not have formally ratified the treaty had they been able to pull off that final battle. Andrew Jackson's victory in the Battle of New Orleans helped to propel his political career, and in 1828 he was elected the seventh president of the United States.

The year 1812 was significant in New Orleans for another reason—it received the first steamboat, aptly called the *New Orleans,* ever to navigate the Mississippi River system; the boat steamed all the way from Pittsburgh via the Ohio River. Steamboats would greatly alter the nature of commerce in New Orleans, as up until 1812 trade had been conducted by small vessels propelled chiefly by the river current, meaning that they could not return upstream once they arrived in New Orleans. In many cases, the boats were simply scrapped once they arrived.

Robert Livingston and inventor Robert Fulton were given a monopoly on the steamboat business for the first few years, but the two abandoned their stronghold in the face of outraged legal challenges, and the number of steamboats arriving and departing New Orleans grew rapidly; by the mid-1840s, more than 1,000 different steamboats were calling on New Orleans each year. Steamboats left New Orleans for the Midwest and the East Coast carrying tobacco, cotton, sugarcane, and many other goods. New Orleans also became a major trade port with the Caribbean Islands, from which it imported fruit, tobacco, rum, and—illegally, after their importation was banned in 1808—slaves.

Louisiana's population stood at about 150,000 by 1820, having increased greatly since statehood with the arrival of settlers from other parts of the United States, who moved here to pursue new land and to farm. The population grew to 350,000 by 1840, and to 700,000 by 1860, the start of the Civil War. During this period, the state became a U.S. superpower owing to its phenomenal agricultural growth, chiefly in cotton and sugarcane. Both small farms and massive plantations grew these crops, using largely slave labor. Cotton was grown just about everywhere in the state, but somewhat less in the swampy southern regions, where sugarcane thrived in the warmer and wetter climate. In fact, sugarcane was always a more lucrative crop than cotton. The state also became a major rice grower—the crop was first planted in the southern and Mississippi River areas to feed slaves, but it proved profitable and was developed into a valuable commercial crop by the end of the 19th century.

With the outlying areas seeing huge growth in agriculture, the region's key port and gateway, New Orleans, grew dramatically. By 1820, it had already become the largest city in the South with a population of about 27,500, surpassing Charleston. After New York City, it was America's leading immigrant port of entry from 1830 until the Civil War, as immigrants headed to the interior Ohio and Mississippi river valleys by way of the city. It also ranked only second in the United States, again behind New York City, in its volume of commercial traffic, which increased tenfold from 1815 to 1840, from $20 million to $200 million. During several of these years, New Orleans actually exceeded New York City in wealth. Cotton, tobacco, grain, and meats were shipped down the Mississippi through New Orleans from the agricultural interior, and huge quantities of manufactured goods, sugar, and coffee were sent back upriver to settlers and other ports via the Gulf of Mexico.

By the 1850s, New Orleans had grown to become the fourth-largest city in the United States and a leading cultural hub. Visitors from other parts of the country were struck by the city's distinctly Spanish architecture and Parisian ambience—it was a city of high fashion, opera and theater, lavish dining, and sophisticated parties. Already by this time, the city was beginning to celebrate Mardi Gras with parties and simple parades.

The hot and humid summers proved to be breeding grounds for yellow fever and other subtropical maladies, and although many residents died from the disease during these years, the city's population still grew to a staggering 170,000 by 1860.

The dynamic changed in the middle of the 19th century with the construction of railroads and canals, which made it possible for Midwestern states to move their products to the eastern United States more quickly and cheaply than by way of New Orleans and the Gulf. The city continued to prosper as a shipper of cotton and sugarcane. Louisiana relied heavily on slave labor to ensure the profitability of its agricultural markets, and New Orleans prospered hugely in this ignominious trade. Had the Midwestern states remained as dependent on New Orleans for trade as they were in the early part of the century, it's quite possible the state would not have sided with the South in favor of secession during the Civil War, but by 1860, Louisiana's interests were completely in step with the rest of the South's.

As the state capital, New Orleans enjoyed significant economic and political advantages that alienated it from the rest of Louisiana. After years of debate about this issue, the legislature finally resolved to move the capital to Baton Rouge, about 60 miles upriver, in 1849, where it has remained to this day the state political seat, excepting a 20-year period during and after the Civil War.

When South Carolina seceded from the Union in December 1860 after the election of Republican Abraham Lincoln, who sought to curb the spread of slavery, it set off a flurry of similar withdrawals among other southern states, with Louisiana seceding on January 26, 1861, the sixth to do so. It then joined in the effort toward war in becoming a member of the Confederate States of America.

Although much of the fighting took place in the coastal and mid-Atlantic states, New Orleans and Louisiana were vulnerable to Union attack for exactly the same reason they were attacked by the British during the War of 1812. If the Union army could capture and control the Mississippi River, it could cut off supply lines between the Confederacy and any states west of the river, and it could enjoy a continuous supply line to the interior Midwest. Anticipating just such an attack, the Confederates built fortifications along the river south of New Orleans.

In April 1862, Captain David G. Farragut led a flotilla of Union Navy ships to the mouth of the Mississippi, where it proceeded north toward New Orleans. He made it with little trouble, shelling and ultimately disabling the Confederate fortification and sailing rather easily to capture the South's largest city. Immediately, New Orleans was named the Union capital of all the territory held by the Federal army in Louisiana, which soon included Baton Rouge, taken by Farragut's troops shortly after. The Confederate state government moved west about 60 miles to Opelousas and then scrambled nearly another 200 miles northwest to Shreveport, where it remained until war's end.

A corrupt northern fat cat, Union Major General Benjamin F. Butler, assumed control of New Orleans and Union-occupied Louisiana, running things a bit like the Spanish had—he was hated by all, including more than a few Union troops, and eventually was removed from office. By war's end the state itself stood politically divided, the Mississippi River valley (including New Orleans and Baton Rouge) in Union control, and the western and northern regions still under Confederate control.

1865-1900

The period immediately after the Civil War, known as Reconstruction, was a grim one, and its policies that attempted to create an integrated society of whites and free blacks actually backfired, although it's much easier to criticize these measures with more than 140 years of hindsight.

President Lincoln signed the Proclamation of Amnesty and Reconstruction into law in December 1863, and so even before the war had ended, a civil government was established in those parts of Louisiana held by Union troops. When the war ended, this civil government assumed control of the state. Early on, it seemed as though little had changed for blacks, even though slavery had been formally abolished by this civil government. A number of the former Confederate leaders of prewar Louisiana held office in this new civil government, which immediately passed the infamous Black Codes. These edicts placed enormous restrictions on the rights and freedoms of the state's African Americans, who were also denied the right to vote.

These conditions led to an extreme seesaw of power between the Republican and (largely ex-Confederate) Democratic sides of the government, which would bitterly divide Louisianans and precipitate tragic violence for the rest of the 19th century and well into the 20th. Blacks struck back against the government in New Orleans, first by rioting violently in 1866 until finally the federal government stepped in to impose order. These same issues, revolts, and riots flared up in other Southern states, and Congress responded by drafting the Reconstruction Acts in 1867 and 1868, which President Andrew Johnson vetoed, but which passed with a two-thirds majority nonetheless. And so, formally, began the period of Reconstruction in the American South.

Reconstruction dictated that the 10 ex-Confederate states that had been returned to the Union would lose their rights to self-govern,

DEAL OF THE CENTURY

By 1876, the divide between Republican and Democratic voters had narrowed, not only in Louisiana but all over the country. The U.S. presidential election at the time, with Republican Rutherford B. Hayes pitted against Democrat Samuel Tilden, makes the Bush-Gore debacle of 2000 look relatively mild.

In three states – Louisiana, South Carolina, and Florida – both parties claimed victory in the state gubernatorial elections, and thus the electoral votes due either Hayes or Tilden. To win the presidency, Hayes needed the electoral votes of all three states.

The lawmakers struck a rather sleazy but sly compromise. If the Democrats from all three states agreed to hand over the electoral votes to make Hayes the president, the Republicans would cede the three gubernatorial elections to the Dems. Louisiana elected Governor Francis R. T. Nicholls (a Republican would not occupy the governor's office again until 1980). This deal effectively ended Reconstruction in Louisiana – although Hayes was a Republican, he withdrew federal troops from New Orleans in appreciation of those much-needed final electoral votes.

The majority of those who registered to vote that year were, in fact, black; whites, discouraged and disgusted by the process, largely stayed away from the polls.

Pro-Union white Southerners (called scalawags by their detractors), opportunity-seeking whites from the North (called carpetbaggers and hated even more by their detractors), and former slaves held the clear majority of political seats in Louisiana (and many other Southern states) during the eight years of Reconstruction. Among these Republican officeholders were Louisiana's first elected black governor, P. B. S. Pinchback; the first black U.S. senator, Blanche K. Bruce; as well as black members of the U.S. Congress and black holders of just about every state political post.

In the meantime, the most ardent opponents of Reconstruction, including quite a few prominent ex-Confederate leaders, went to extreme lengths to sabotage, tear down, and otherwise render ineffective the state's Republican leadership. From this effort came the development of such antiblack groups as the Ku Klux Klan (in northern Louisiana), the Knights of the White Camellia (in southern Louisiana), and the especially terror-driven White League. These and other groups, sometimes systematically and sometimes randomly, intimidated, beat, and many times lynched blacks and more than a few white sympathizers. The White League took credit for the assassination of several Republican elected officials. About 3,500 members of the White League actually attempted to overthrow the state government during what came to be known as the Battle of Liberty Place in New Orleans in 1874. During a fierce riot, they took over the city hall, statehouse, and state arsenal until federal troops arrived to restore order. For the next four years, the troops remained in New Orleans, overseeing the city's—and the state's—order.

During the course of Reconstruction the voting situation in Louisiana grew increasingly volatile, as whites intimidated or threatened blacks to keep them from voting and rallied voter support among anti-Republican whites. More and more officials and congressmen sym-

and the federal military would instead step in to govern until these states rewrote their constitutions with laws and language that Congress deemed acceptable. In effect, Louisiana was no longer a state until it submitted to the wishes of the federal government. The federally controlled state government then drafted a new constitution in March 1868, which wholly deferred to the sentiments of Congress: Adult males of all races were granted the right to vote—excepting fully declared ex-Confederates, who actually had their voting rights revoked—and blacks were assured full civil rights. Interestingly, when the new constitution was presented to Louisiana citizens, voters approved it overwhelmingly.

pathetic to the South gained office, and they in turn pardoned and restored voting rights to many of the ex-Confederates.

White Democrats were swift in removing from blacks any rights they had gained during Reconstruction, and then some. In 1898, the state constitution was rewritten. Without expressly denying suffrage to blacks, it required poll taxes, literacy, and property ownership in order to vote, which disqualified most of the state's black voters.

While Reconstruction had a profoundly negative effect on the plight of blacks, a few strides were made during the 19th century. Many blacks ended up returning to work at a subsistence level on the farms where they once had been slaves, but some headway was made in education and social relief. The federal government established the Freedmen's Bureau, which helped to fund public schools for blacks throughout the South and issued other forms of assistance and economic relief.

The economy of the rural South faltered greatly after the Civil War, and various depressions, labor problems, and episodes of social unrest conspired to put many large and small farm owners out of business. For much of the 19th century, a large proportion of southern farms were run by sharecroppers, whereby the owners of the land—many of them northerners who had bought failed farms—gave tenants equipment and materials to farm the land and live on a fairly basic level. The workers were also entitled to a small cut of the crop yield. Farm production in Louisiana began to increase under this system, but it was still far lower than before the Civil War, and even with bounteous crops, many farmers could not make ends meet.

New Orleans, whose economy had been devastated by the war, gradually staged an economic comeback during the course of the next half century. The renewed growth in cotton and sugarcane trafficking helped to jump-start the city's shipping and trade economy, and the mouth of the Mississippi River was deepened and made accessible to much larger ships, many of which sailed from ports much farther away than in earlier times. Railroads were built across much of Louisiana, and in 1914, the opening of the Panama Canal brought new trade to New Orleans by way of Latin America. The city's population stood at 290,000 by 1900, with the state population up to about 1.4 million.

1900-WORLD WAR II

Louisiana's economy began to diversify throughout the early 20th century, much more so than in most other agrarian southern states. Significant sources of oil were discovered in the northwestern part of the state, and natural gas sources were developed all over Louisiana. In 1938, huge oil deposits were discovered off the coast, and a massive oil-drilling industry grew up in southern Louisiana, especially in the towns southeast of Lafayette and southwest of Houma. Salt and sulfur mining also grew into a big contributor to the economy, chiefly in the southern belt extending from Lake Charles to southeast of Lafayette.

The farming economy continued to suffer through the early 1900s, however, and a severe recession took hold throughout the 1920s. The growing anguish and desperation among rural farmers helped to promote the ascendancy of one of the most notorious and controversial political figures in American history, Huey P. Long, a colorful, no-nonsense straight talker whose fervently populist manner played well with poor farmers and laborers. Long declared war on big corporations, especially Standard Oil, and took up the cause of small businesses and the common man. His actions early in his political career squarely favored those he claimed to want to help. Long was elected governor in 1928 and then U.S. senator in 1930, although he kept the governor's seat until 1932, when a handpicked successor took office. Still, he pretty much called the shots in state politics right up until his death. Long was assassinated in 1935 by Dr. Carl Weiss, the son-in-law of one of his political archenemies.

Long was instrumental in developing state public assistance and public works programs across Louisiana during the Great Depression, but he was also infamous for his nepotism and corruption, routinely buying off colleagues and tampering with the political process. The "Kingfish" ran the state like a fiefdom, and he actually ended up preventing federal funds from reaching the state during his last few years in office as a U.S. senator. Long may have died in 1935, but his brother, Earl K. Long, succeeded him as governor, as did his son, Russell Long. Until the early 1960s, anti- and pro-Long factions continued to dominate Democratic party politics and therefore, because Democrats controlled just about everything in Louisiana, state politics.

World War II boosted the Louisiana economy with its need for mineral and oil resources. It was during this period that Louisiana developed the massive refineries and chemical plants still found along much of the Mississippi River and all through the lower third of the state (especially Lake Charles and Baton Rouge), and it was also during the 1940s that the state's population demographic changed so that more Louisianans lived in cities than in rural areas.

At the same time, many rural citizens, especially blacks fed up with the state's segregation and racial mistreatment, left the South to seek factory jobs in Chicago, Oakland, and other northern and western cities. Other Louisianans moved to southeastern Texas, where jobs at refineries, factories, and shipyards in Beaumont, Orange, and Port Arthur abounded.

NEW ORLEANS TODAY

During the second half of the 20th century, New Orleans steadily blossomed into one of the nation's—and the world's—most popular vacation destinations. Mardi Gras evolved, especially during the 1960s, from a largely regional celebration into an international festival, and Jazz Fest became similarly popular. The economy came increasingly to depend on tourists, and then, throughout the 1970s and 1980s, convention business. Hurricane Katrina has, of course, dampened both tourism and convention business, and the city now finds itself working hard to regain its stature as a leading leisure and business destination.

Beyond tourism, New Orleans has several other important industries going for it. Even before Katrina, the city, as with the rest of Louisiana, had experienced quite a few booms and busts since World War II. The city is today the largest port in the United States, and it's second in the world only to Rotterdam in its value of foreign commerce and waterborne commerce. The state continues to rely heavily on such natural resources as salt, agricultural products, sulfur, petroleum, and natural gas, and many of the ships transporting these goods leave by way of New Orleans.

The intense trade presence has spawned an important commercial byproduct: banking, although it's believed that at least some of this and other corporate businesses may move permanently to Baton Rouge or other cities in the wake of Katrina. Still, the CBD remains one of the nation's leading centers of finance, with more dozens of commercial banks. During the strongest oil years of recent times, from the early 1970s through the early 1980s, the city's banks and other industries raked in plenty of money financing offshore oil production. From the mid-1980s to the early 2000s, however, a nationwide slump in oil prices cost New Orleans and, even more acutely, Lafayette countless jobs. The oil industry has been doing well again in recent years, although Katrina's devastation has put a damper on the industry's growth in these parts. Still, the oil and natural gas industries play vital roles in both the city's and the state's economy—the state contains just under 10 percent of the nation's known oil reserves, and it's the country's third-largest producer of petroleum (it's also the nation's third-largest refiner). And that's not even considering the possibility of additional oil reserves farther out at sea in the Gulf.

Farming, though diminished considerably during the past century, still represents a significant chunk of the state economy, although it has relatively little direct effect on New Orleans. Louisiana has about 27,000 farms, more than 2,000 of them with more than 1,000 acres. Crops vary greatly, depending on terrain and climate. The leaders are sugarcane, rice, soybeans, cotton, and corn. Sugarcane is a particularly important crop, and Steen's Syrup Mill in Abbeville, southwest of Lafayette, is the world's largest syrup plant. The massive Domino sugar refinery outside New Orleans is the largest such refinery in the nation. Other popular crops include wheat, sorghum, sweet potatoes, strawberries, blueberries, peaches, and hot peppers.

What has saved New Orleans's and Louisiana's economy in recent decades is tourism, which even after the lean months right after the terrorist attacks of September 11, 2001, continued to score high numbers right up until Hurricane Katrina struck New Orleans. Even though most of the historic, tourism-driven sections of New Orleans were back up and running within weeks of Katrina, the storm still has had a gravely chilling effect on the city's economy, and Hurricane Rita has also caused huge losses in tourism in St. Charles and the surrounding area. One way or another, New Orleans always seems to find a way to attract visitors, and the city's future as a tourism destination is solid. What's less certain is how strongly the city can recover as a popular convention destination—numbers were already declining before the storm, as other cities around the country had constructed new convention centers. Since the storm, the convention trade has gradually begun to pick up, but the numbers are far below what they were before Katrina, and it's difficult to say when and if those numbers will return to pre-Katrina levels.

Tourism has been an important source of revenue for New Orleans and the rest of southern Louisiana for centuries, but its prominence has grown dramatically during the past 50 years. Pre-Katrina, nearly 100,000 Louisianans worked in the state's tourism industry, and travelers spent more than $5 billion during their visits to the state each year; post-Katrina tourism estimates have not yet been determined. A glamorous byproduct of tourism is the local film industry, which is still going strong since Katrina.

New Orleans is a predominantly Democratic, politically left-of-center city, generally quite progressive on social issues. The state on the whole, however, tends to be more conservative on social issues, and the proportion of Democrats to Republicans is closer.

Hurricane Katrina and Recovery

Arguably, nothing in the past 50 years has had more impact on the city than Hurricane Katrina. Within two months of New Orleans's horrifying brush with the storm in August 2005, most of the areas of the city popular with visitors—the French Quarter, Central Business District (CBD), Garden District, and Uptown—were already in decent shape. Many restaurants, hotels, shops, and attractions had reopened, and many of the residents of these neighborhoods had returned. These areas were largely spared the worst Katrina flooding, and they rebounded quickly (albeit with a significant number of exceptions) to look more or less normal. New Orleans went on to enjoy well-attended and lively Mardi Gras and Jazz Fest celebrations in 2006.

A year after Katrina, the population of New Orleans stood at about half of what it was prior to the hurricane, and the crowds—both in terms of residents and visitors—hadn't returned in anywhere near pre-Katrina numbers. Some parts of the city that experienced extensive damage, such as Mid-City and City Park, had come back significantly by this point.

In the hardest-hit neighborhoods, generally residential parts of the city that fall north and east of the French Quarter and CBD, there remain hundreds of contiguous blocks lined with empty, decimated homes and businesses. Contrary to the perception conveyed by at least some of the news coverage of Katrina, the hardest-hit neighborhoods are not coming back any time soon—and the destruction affected residents of all income brackets, ages, races, and creeds. It's true that these are mostly neighborhoods that visitors saw little of in the past, and so most visitors aren't keenly affected by their demise in the present. But New Orleans as a whole will take years to rebuild.

People and Culture

The strongest influence on the growth of this city may, arguably, be French, but no one nationality represents a decisive majority here, and, in fact, New Orleans's most historic neighborhood, the French Quarter, is more Spanish Colonial in appearance than French.

The city's distinctive style of cuisine and music, the pervasive infatuation with things carnal and pleasurable, the Gothic literary traditions, and the long-standing practice of voodoo-tinged Catholicism are legacies contributed not only by the French and Spanish settlers who occupied New Orleans throughout the 18th century, and by the Choctaw Indians who preceded them, but by the vast numbers of Acadian refugees ("Cajuns"), slaves brought from West Africa, American frontiersmen and traders, German farmers, Irish and Italian laborers, Slavs, Creole refugees from Haiti, and, more recently, Vietnamese. All told, the flags of France, Spain, England, the Confederacy, the Union, and even, briefly, independent Louisiana have flown over New Orleans.

These various groups haven't just left their mark on a particular neighborhood during a specific period, they've migrated to New Orleans in significant enough numbers to have a pervasive and lasting influence. The cultural gumbo has resulted in some rather odd traditions that last to this day. Many street and neighborhood names are pronounced differently in New Orleans than anywhere else in the world, from Conti (CON-tie) and Cadiz (KAY-diz) streets to the Michoud (MEE-shoh) neighborhood. Sometimes French and Spanish names are pronounced roughly as the French and Spanish would pronounce them, and sometimes they're pronounced as virtually nobody else on the planet would pronounce them.

The cuisine unique to New Orleans, which by itself is the biggest reason many visitors travel to this city, borrows widely from myriad cultures. Ingredients and dishes like filé (a

© NEW ORLEANS CVB/CARL PURCELL

Neighborhood festivities celebrate New Orleans's unique culture and community spirit.

powder of dried sassafras leaves popularized by the Choctaw), jambalaya (a rice casserole very similar to Spanish paella), okra (a podlike vegetable introduced by African slaves), and crawfish (a small freshwater crustacean that's prevalent in local waters) are as common in New Orleans restaurants as hamburgers and apple pie in most U.S. cities.

The city's irrepressibly buoyant music is also distinctly local. Jazz was invented here, a conglomeration of mostly African-American traditions that has rural counterparts elsewhere in southern Louisiana in the form of zydeco and Cajun music. Blues, rock, and even opera were also embraced in New Orleans long before they were in most of the rest of the country.

ESSENTIALS

Getting There and Around

GETTING THERE

New Orleans's airport is well served by most major airlines and has direct flights to most of the nation's largest cities. It's centrally located, usually not terribly expensive, and pleasant to fly in and out of, so if you're coming for a short period or from a long distance, flying here makes plenty of sense. New Orleans also has direct Amtrak train service and Greyhound bus service from many big cities, but these modes of transport are often quite time-consuming and, especially in the case of trains, not always less expensive than flying.

Airports

Louis Armstrong New Orleans International Airport (900 Airline Hwy., off I-10, Kenner, 504/464-2650, www.flymsy.com), 15 miles west of downtown New Orleans, is a massive facility serving the entire Gulf South with service on about two dozen airlines. It's easy to find direct flights from most major U.S. cities (more than 35 in all) and also to such international cities as San Pedro Sula, Honduras, and Toronto, Canada. That being said, as of fall 2006, capacity was down significantly since Hurricane Katrina, and the airport's operations were at just under 65 percent of pre-Katrina status.

© ANDREW COLLINS

Sample direct-flying times to New Orleans from major cities: Atlanta, 90 minutes; Chicago, 2 hours and 15 minutes; Los Angeles, 4 hours; Miami, 2 hours; and New York City, 3 hours.

New Orleans International Airport received a $850 million makeover between 1998 and 2001, which helped it accommodate a number of additional flights by Southwest Airlines, Midwest, jetBlue, and Air Canada. All sorts of food concessions have been added, including a huge Vieux Carré–inspired food court.

In southern Louisiana, commercial service is also available to Baton Rouge, Lafayette, and Lake Charles. **Lafayette Regional Airport** (200 Terminal Dr., off U.S. 90, two miles southeast of downtown, 337/266-4400, www.lftairport.com) is served by American, Continental, Delta, and Northwest, with frequent direct flights to Atlanta, Dallas, Houston, and Memphis. **Baton Rouge Metropolitan Airport** (9430 Jackie Cochran Dr., eight miles north of downtown off I-110, 225/355-0333, www.flybtr.com) is served by the same carriers and to the same four key cities as Lafayette Airport. **Lake Charles Regional Airport** (500 Airport Blvd., off Hwy. 385, about 10 miles south of downtown, 337/477-6051, www.flylakecharles.com) is served by Continental, with direct service to Houston.

Generally, it's more expensive to fly to one of the smaller regional airports than to New Orleans.

An alternative airport that's worth considering if you ever have trouble scoring a flight to New Orleans, or if fares are especially high there because of a special event (such as Mardi Gras or Jazz Fest), is **Jackson International Airport** (601/939-5631, www.jmaa.com) in Jackson, Mississippi, a three-hour drive north of the city. It's a fairly large airport serviced by eight airlines, with direct service to Atlanta, Baltimore/Washington, Charlotte, Chicago, Cincinnati, Dallas, Detroit, Houston, Memphis, and Orlando. A bit smaller but slightly closer to New Orleans (a little under three hours away) is **Mobile Regional Airport**

(800/357-5373, www.mobairport.com), which is served by American, Continental, Delta, Northwest, and US Airways.

Transportation to and from the Airport

Getting from New Orleans International Airport to the French Quarter, a 15-mile trip that takes 25–35 minutes depending on traffic (which can be horrendous at peak travel times), is a relatively costly proposition. There are cabs, which you can pick up at the taxi stand outside baggage claim, that charge a fixed rate of $28 for 1–2 passengers and $12 per person thereafter. It makes very good sense if you're alone to offer to split the ride with another single person standing near you. Similarly, there's an airport limo service. This costs $35 for 1–2 passengers and $10 per person (up to eight passengers capacity). You'll generally wait 10–20 minutes at the terminal's limo desk for this service, while cabs are usually there waiting for passengers outside the baggage claim.

For just $13 per person, you can take the **Airport Shuttle** (504/522-3500 or 866/596-2699), which departs from New Orleans International Airport every 10 minutes and drops passengers at any downtown, CBD, or Garden District hotel.

For just $1.10, you can catch the **Jefferson Transit Airport-Downtown Express Bus** (504/364-3450, www.jeffersontransit.org) from the airport to New Orleans.

If you're taking a cab someplace other than downtown New Orleans (meaning the CBD or French Quarter), you'll pay $1.70–2.50 per mile (you can attempt to negotiate a better fare). For trips to Orleans, Jefferson, and Kenner parishes, cabs charge $2.50 for the first one-sixth mile and $0.20 for each additional one-sixth mile and 40 seconds on the clock. There's also a flat charge of $1 per additional passenger. For St. Charles Parish, which comprises the towns west of Kenner and the airport, cabs charge $1.70 for the first one-fifth mile and $0.20 for each additional one-fifth mile or 40 seconds on the clock. Drivers must provide air-conditioning (and cannot charge for it), cannot refuse passengers for very short trips, and cannot charge for a "normal" amount of luggage.

Cruise Ships

New Orleans's popularity as a cruise-ship destination and as a point of embarkation has risen steadily during the past two decades. Many people like leaving from New Orleans because it's such an enjoyable place to spend two or three days before or after the cruise. It's also a convenient debarkation point for cruises in the Western Caribbean—these typically call at Cozumel/Cancún, Jamaica, the Cayman Islands, and sometimes Key West. And when Cuba inevitably is opened up to U.S. tourism, ships from New Orleans will no doubt sail to Havana.

Cruise lines that regularly sail from New Orleans, typically leaving from the cruise terminal near the Hilton at Canal Street, include the youthful and budget-oriented **Carnival Cruise Line** (888/227-6482, www.carnival. com). Carnival operates the *Sensatiori* and the *Conquest,* which offer year-round Western Caribbean cruises.

Slightly more upscale than Carnival and appealing to a slightly more mature demographic, **Royal Caribbean Cruise Line** (800/398-9819, www.royalcaribbean.com) offers five- to 10-night Western Caribbean cruises November–May on the 2,500-passenger *Grandeur of the Seas.* **Norwegian Cruise Line** (800/543-2805, www.ncl.com) offers Western Caribbean cruises November–May on the *Norwegian Sun.*

A small cruise ship is the R/B *River Explorer* (888/456-2206, www.riverbarge.com), a 198-passenger vessel that plies the Mississippi, Cumberland, Missouri, and Ohio rivers, the Atchafalaya Basin, and the Gulf Intracoastal Waterway, offering trips lasting 4–10 days.

The only cruise line based in New Orleans is a distinctly American and rather unusual one: the **Delta Queen Steamboat Company** (800/543-1949, www.deltaqueen.com). This line includes three modern paddle-wheel steamboats, which call New Orleans their home port but sail the entire river system of the central United States. Cruises from New Orleans can run as far as Pittsburgh and Minneapolis and include such ports as St. Louis, Cincinnati, Louisville, Nashville, Chattanooga, Memphis, and Galveston. These luxurious, beautifully crafted boats have the feel of a lavish Victorian grand hotel, and even if you don't sail on one, it's great fun to watch them plying the Mississippi River. The *Delta Queen* itself is the oldest in the fleet, having been built in 1927 at a cost of about $1 million; the 285-foot vessel holds up to 174 passengers. The *Mississippi Queen* holds 414 passengers and was launched in 1976; it holds the world's largest calliope, which you can hear from a great distance. Finally, the **American Queen,** the largest steamboat ever built, commenced service in January 2003 and can carry 436 passengers.

Interstate Train Service

Amtrak (800/872-7245, www.amtrak.com) trains run across southern Louisiana, with stops (going east to west) in Slidell, New Orleans, Hammond, Baton Rouge (via a Greyhound bus connection), Schriever (near Houma and Thibodaux), Lafayette, New Iberia, and Lake Charles. This is a fairly hassle-free way to get to the region from Atlanta, Memphis, Houston, Pensacola, and a number of other big cities.

Three trains serve southern Louisiana, all of them including New Orleans as a stop. The City of New Orleans originates in Chicago and terminates in New Orleans; it also stops on the North Shore in Hammond. Other big cities along this route include Jackson, Mississippi; Memphis; and Centralia, Illinois. The Crescent runs between New York City and New Orleans, with major stops that include Philadelphia, Washington, Charlottesville, Charlotte, Atlanta, and Birmingham. It also stops in Slidell. The Sunset Limited is an east–west train that runs between Orlando, Florida, and Los Angeles, California, stopping in New Orleans as well as Schriever, New Iberia, Lafayette, and Lake Charles. Other big cities along this route include Jacksonville, Pensacola,

Mobile, Gulfport, Houston, San Antonio, El Paso, Tucson, and Palm Springs.

Taking the train isn't necessarily cheaper than flying, but it can be a relaxing and fascinating way to see the countryside. Amtrak offers a number of promotions and special passes; the latter can allow you to stop and overnight in cities served by Amtrak, making this a surprisingly practical way to visit several parts of the country on one affordable ticket. For example, the **North America Rail Pass,** which costs about $999 for peak travel periods (May 26–October 15) and $709 for off-peak (the rest of the year), entitles the bearer to 30 days' worth of unlimited rides and stopovers throughout the United States and Canada. There are rental-car agencies at Amtrak stations in most big cities.

Interstate Bus Service

If it's been a while since you traveled by bus, be prepared for a surprise: Many improvements have been made, movies are shown, and the rides are quite comfortable (and far less expensive than Amtrak).

Greyhound (800/229-9424, www.greyhound.com) is the definitive interstate bus provider for Louisiana, with frequent and flexible service connecting to all neighboring states and throughout the country.

In southern Louisiana, Greyhound stops at dozens of cities and towns, the major ones being Baton Rouge, Crowley, De Ridder, Franklin, Gonzales, Hammond, Houma, La Place, Lafayette, Lake Charles, Mandeville, Morgan City, New Iberia, New Orleans, Opelousas, Ponchatoula, Raceland, Slidell, St. Francisville, and Thibodaux. There's almost no decent-size community covered in this book that can't be reached from New Orleans via Greyhound. As opposed to Amtrak, Greyhound buses have multiple daily runs between New Orleans and many neighboring states. Travel times can be significantly longer (although not always), but fares are generally much cheaper.

Typical travel times on Greyhound from major cities around the United States to New Orleans: Atlanta, 10–12 hours; Austin, 10–12 hours; Chicago, 19–23 hours; Dallas, 12–14 hours; Denver, 30–34 hours; Houston, 7–9 hours; Little Rock, 12–15 hours; Los Angeles, 40–44 hours; Memphis, 7–10 hours; Nashville, 12–16 hours; Orlando, 14–17 hours; Pensacola, 4–6 hours; St. Louis, 16–17 hours; and Washington, D.C., 23–27 hours.

Greyhound offers the **Discovery Pass,** which you can buy in increments of 4–60 days, allowing unlimited stopovers throughout the duration of the pass. Different types and prices of passes are available to U.S., Canadian, and international travelers.

DRIVING

Southern Louisiana is at most points about 300 miles across; from the southernmost town covered in this book (Houma) to Louisiana's northern border with Mississippi, it's only about 120 miles by car. Because either interstate or limited-access highways run in relatively straight lines among the key destinations in southern Louisiana, and these roads typically have speed limits of 65–70 mph, the region is relatively easy to get around. It's not difficult to cross southern Louisiana in one afternoon.

Metro New Orleans (meaning the South Shore towns, below Lake Pontchartrain) is about 20 miles across and 10 north to south. Traffic can be as difficult here as in typically large U.S. cities (it's not markedly worse or better than average), but under average circumstances, it's fairly easy to get from one end of New Orleans to the other in 30–40 minutes. Downtown New Orleans is at the geographic center of metropolitan New Orleans, meaning that from here to any other point, it's usually not more than a 20- to 30-minute drive, barring traffic problems.

A car is your best tool for exploring southern Louisiana. If you're visiting only New Orleans, the pluses and minuses related to using a car about balance each other out. Against using a car, consider the following: Traffic can be frightful, many streets are one-way, street parking is scarce, garage and hotel parking is expensive, the central neighborhoods are walkable, cabs are easy to come by if not always

DRIVING DISTANCES FROM NEW ORLEANS

The Acadian Peninsula, New Brunswick, Canada	2,114 miles		Mobile, Alabama	143 miles
Anchorage, Alaska	4,451 miles		Nashville, Tennessee	530 miles
Atlanta, Georgia	470 miles		Natchitoches, Louisiana	274 miles
Baton Rouge, Louisiana	81 miles		Natchez, Mississippi	176 miles
Chicago, Illinois	929 miles		New York, New York	1,309 miles
Dallas, Texas	521 miles		Orleans, California	2,610 miles
Denver, Colorado	1,398 miles		Pensacola, Florida	200 miles
Gulfport, Mississippi	76 miles		Phoenix, Arizona	1,528 miles
Houma, Louisiana	58 miles		St. Louis, Missouri	678 miles
Houston, Texas	347 miles		San Antonio, Texas	544 miles
Jackson, Mississippi	186 miles		Shreveport, Louisiana	338 miles
Lake Charles, Louisiana	205 miles			
Little Rock, Arkansas	444 miles			
Los Angeles, California	1,900 miles			
Louisiana, Missouri	757 miles			
Memphis, Tennessee	394 miles			
Minneapolis, Minnesota	1,290 miles			
Mexico City, Mexico	1,292 miles			
Miami, Florida	863 miles			

Six places that share New Orleans's approximate latitude: Tallahassee, Florida; Austin, Texas; Chongqing, China; Lhasa, Tibet; Kuwait City, Kuwait; Cairo, Egypt.

Six places that share New Orleans's approximate longitude: the Galápagos Islands, Ecuador; Guatemala City, Guatemala; Mérida, Mexico; Memphis, Tennessee; St. Louis, Missouri; Thunder Bay, Ontario.

completely reliable, and public transportation is decent, especially from the French Quarter to the most popular of the city's outlying neighborhoods, Uptown and Mid-City.

The pros for using a car: Rental cars are generally a bit less expensive than elsewhere in the country, there's ample and sometimes free parking in some outlying neighborhoods, a car is handier than public transportation for exploring Uptown and Mid-City, a car is unquestionably useful if planning any side trips from the city, New Orleanians are relatively easygoing drivers (at least compared with drivers in many other big cities),and one day's rental car is often cheaper when shared among two or more people than shuttle or taxi transportation from the airport to downtown.

Again, if you're having trouble deciding whether to use a car or not, the most significant factor is probably this: Are you planning to stay within the city limits the entire time, or do you expect to take some trips to other parts of the state? If you're planning only one or two days outside the city, you can always rent a car in downtown New Orleans for a day or two and then enjoy life without it the rest of your stay.

If you're visiting New Orleans from another part of the South, and you're staying long enough that it's worth driving for eight hours or so, consider that the following cities all fall roughly within a 550-mile drive of the Big Easy: Atlanta, Houston, Dallas, Jackson, Little Rock, Memphis, Mobile, Nashville, Pensacola, and San Antonio. Within this perimeter, if you're traveling as a group of two or more, and you're staying in Louisiana for more than five days, it's probably most economical to drive, even if you rent a car from home as an alternative to logging extra miles and wear-and-tear on your own car.

For general information on commuting, road closings and construction, getting to and from Louisiana, and getting around the state, contact the **Louisiana Department of Transportation and Development** (Room 301, Box 94245, Baton Rouge, LA 70804, 225/379-1100). Its website, www.dotd.state. la.us, offers extensive information on numerous publications, traveler resources and road conditions, licenses and permits, and upcoming roadwork and projects.

An excellent resource for online transportation information in the state is www.apta. com/links/state_local/la.cfm, which has links to countless sites.

Road Names and Labels

Conversationally, Louisianans tend to call most numbered roads "Highway," as in "take Highway 61 to Baton Rouge" or "follow Highway 25 to Folsom." This is true both for U.S. and state highways. In this book, interstate highways are indicated with an "I" before the number (e.g., I-10, I-510, etc.), all U.S. highways are referred to with a "U.S. Highway" or simply "U.S." before the number (U.S. Highway 90, U.S. 61, etc.), and all other numbered state and local roads are referred to with a "Highway" or "Hwy." before the number (Highway 1, Hwy. 14, etc.).

Scenic Drives

Southern Louisiana has a good many scenic drives. Alas, there are also plenty of major routes that make for lousy sightseeing and suffer from heavy congestion.

Of interstate highways, I-10 is a convenient if rather dull highway that runs from the southwestern end of the state, near Lake Charles, due east to the southeastern part of the state, near Slidell, where it joins I-59 and I-12. At Baton Rouge, I-10 curves down and loops through

New Orleans before curving back up again to Slidell; I-12 runs due east from Baton Rouge to Slidell, bypassing New Orleans. Lafayette is situated along I-10, midway between Lake Charles and Baton Rouge. Coming from the northwest, I-49 leads down from Shreveport, meeting I-10 in Lafayette; plans are for I-49 eventually to continue south from Lafayette, loop through Cajun Country (roughly following the course of present-day U.S. Highway 90), and rejoin I-10 just west of New Orleans. Much of the work on this interstate has been completed, and so the route's present incarnation (U.S. Highway 90) is mostly a fast limited-access four-lane highway with a 70 mph speed limit. Last, I-55 enters the state just north of Hammond from Mississippi, joining I-12 and then, just west of New Orleans, I-10.

All of the interstate drives in Louisiana are flat, straight, and at times monotonous, but each has some interesting aspects. A significant stretch of I-10 west of Baton Rouge and east of Lafayette passes through the Atchafalaya swamp basin, and along here the highway is completely elevated above the swamp, built along tall piers. It's rather unlike any other stretches of interstate in this country, and it's quite interesting the first time you drive it. There's not a great deal of variation along this drive, however, and the novelty does wear off after you've driven it a few times. People who have grown up in southern Louisiana would think you're just plain crazy for finding this drive interesting even the first time you try it. Similarly, a long section of I-10 between Sorrento (east of Baton Rouge) and Kenner (west of New Orleans) also rides high along stilts through swampland, and the same is true for parts of U.S. Highway 90 down near Houma.

Because Louisiana is basically flat, roads rarely curve or rise or offer expansive views, but many of them are novel because they pass alongside hulking levees or over swamps or other bodies of water. You have to search a bit to see the beauty in some of these drives. One that immediately comes to mind is the Great River Road, actually a series of numbered highways that hug both banks of the Mississippi River from just outside New Orleans through Baton Rouge and up into Mississippi. Visitors are sometimes surprised to realize that you cannot generally see the actual river along this drive, as the road sits well below the levee; however, there are many spots where you can pull over or even drive atop the levee and catch a nice view, and many bridges and free ferry crossings are set along this road. What you will see is a surreal clash of the old and the new: Rural villages, massive power plants and refineries, and sprawling 19th-century plantation estates sit side by side throughout this region.

Culturally fascinating is U.S. Highway 190, offering varied glimpses of southern Louisiana life from Slidell west through the North Shore towns above New Orleans and then paralleling I-12 to Baton Rouge and cutting across the Cajun prairies through Opelousas, Eunice, and Kinder. You pass everything from pristine wildlife preserves to upscale bedroom communities to rural Cajun towns on this route. From the Cajun town of New Iberia, Highway 14 is an interesting drive west through Abbeville and eventually on to Lake Charles. At the Texas border south of Port Arthur, Highway 82 hugs much of the barely developed Gulf shoreline in the southwest corner of the state before cutting northeast to join Highway 14 at Abbeville. From Lafayette, Highway 182 offers a more interesting alternative to U.S. Highway 90 as it cuts through the heart of Cajun Country, entering New Iberia and Franklin and then crossing the Atchafalaya River in Morgan City and continuing down to Houma.

Highway 1, near Houma at the small city of Raceland, can be traced either north through Thibodaux and eventually up to where it becomes part of the Great River Road and cuts up into Baton Rouge and then New Roads, or south through the sparsely populated towns leading to Grand Isle on the Gulf of Mexico. From New Roads, north of Baton Rouge, Highway 10 makes for a picturesque drive through rolling pine groves east through the Florida parishes to Bogalusa at the Mississippi border. The pine-studded North Shore is, in fact, an entire network of lovely country drives beneath massive canopies of shade trees; Highways 25, 21, 41, 22, and 16 all make for engaging road trips. Crossing the 23-plus-mile Lake Pontchartrain Causeway, the world's longest bridge, can also be fascinating if you've never done it before; after the third or fourth time, however, this drive starts to feel a bit dull, and you can imagine how boring it must be for the thousands of commuters who cross the causeway twice a day. Finally, if you follow U.S. Highway 90 east out of New Orleans, the very road on which actress Jayne Mansfield was killed in a car accident in the late 1960s, you'll pass through some still pristine bayou and swampland along the north shore of Lake Borgne (an arm of the Gulf of Mexico), and eventually continue into coastal Mississippi.

The worst roads for driving in southern Louisiana are generally the U.S. highways, which had been the main thoroughfares before the interstate system was built, mostly after World War II. On these roads, you're apt to encounter long and bleak traffic-choked stretches of strip malls, fast-food restaurants, and auto-repair shops. Ugly and slow-moving roads around metro New Orleans include U.S. Highway 61 (a.k.a. Airline Highway, and it's awful pretty much the whole way from New Orleans to Baton Rouge), Veteran's Memorial Boulevard (in Metairie and Kenner), Esplanade Avenue (in Metairie and Kenner), U.S. Business Highway 90 (from Westwego along the West Bank to Algiers Point), U.S. Highway 90 through Lafayette, and U.S. Highway 190 through Baton Rouge.

U.S. Highway 190 above the Lake Pontchartrain Causeway, north of Mandeville to downtown Covington, is a short and not entirely unpleasant bit of road dominated by shopping centers—it is mainly notable, though, for its unbelievably dense and slow traffic, particularly heading southbound on weekday mornings and northbound in the late afternoons. This is a situation in which two towns have grown rapidly, and because they're surrounded and also intersected by large tracts of swamp and marshland, there's no simple way to build new and bigger roads. This phenomenon hasn't taken root in too many other parts of the region yet, but as southern Louisiana grows, the problem will start popping up elsewhere.

Speed Limits and Driving Laws

Speed limits along the interstates are generally 70 mph, but they drop a bit to 65 or 60 mph along those spans of elevated roadway passing over the swamps and bayous, and they drop further to 50 or 55 mph through congested areas, such as New Orleans and Baton Rouge. Other limited-access highways tend to range 55–70 mph, depending on congestion. As in most states, however, officers typically don't pull over offenders who keep within 5–8 mph of the posted limit. The two-lane state and U.S. highways all through the region generally have speed limits of 55 mph along narrow rural stretches and 65 mph in wider spots. These roads, especially in rural areas, are sometimes very heavily patrolled by police, and it's highly unsafe to speed on these—they're narrow with virtually no shoulder and can be bumpy. You're most likely to encounter speed traps when entering villages or approaching major intersections along these highways; reductions in the speed limit are typically well marked and preceded by Speed Zone Ahead or Reduced Speed Ahead signs. The wise driver will heed these warnings.

In New Orleans as elsewhere throughout Louisiana, a right turn after coming to a complete stop at a red light is permitted except where posted. Pedestrians crossing the street onto which you're turning have right of way, and at several congested intersections in New Orleans, right turns on red are prohibited (and signed accordingly). Following the same rules, left turns at red lights are permitted *only* if you're turning from a one-way street left onto another one-way street.

Parking

Parking in New Orleans is a gamble—keep as few of your belongings in your car as possible if parking on the street or in an unattended lot. If you can't remove everything and/or don't have a car alarm and/or are deeply concerned, just pay the $15–30 per night most hotels and commercial lots charge. At some properties you'll pay less, at some smaller inns you may have free parking, but many, especially in the Quarter or near it, have no parking at all. There's really no consistent rule, and you should investigate this when booking a hotel room, as the added daily price can add up.

Downtown in New Orleans you'll find a fair amount of meter parking, but this is primarily short-term, costing $0.25 per 12-minute interval, usually with a maximum of one or two hours in one space. Note that at rush hour (7–9 A.M. and 4–6 P.M.), many of the main streets downtown are no-parking zones. Finding street parking in the Quarter is extremely difficult, especially in the Lower Quarter. And in the Upper Quarter, most of the street parking is restricted for residents with permits. In Faubourg Marigny, it's fairly easy to find a spot on the street, and it's not too bad in most of the Garden District and Uptown, although you'll find meters along Magazine and some of the more commercial stretches of St. Charles.

The parking lot next to Jackson Brewery charges about $15 per day; it puts you very close to several hotels and virtually anything in the Quarter, and it's a well-lighted and fairly conspicuous place, making it a less likely target of crime. There are a few other lots right near it. However, during busy times of year, these lots fill up fast, especially if it's a weekend. Also, there are no in-and-out privileges.

Outside the Quarter and CBD, you can often find street parking (metered and otherwise, but beware streets that restrict overnight parking to cars with resident permits), and some shops and eateries Uptown and in other parts of the city have lots or dedicated spaces. As in most major cities, parking safety is an issue here; New Orleans is a tourist town, and visitors are traditionally seen as good targets. The unattended parking lots around the CBD can seem like a bargain, but remember that the owners of the lots bear no legal liability for stolen, damaged, or lost cars and other belongings.

One smart parking option, especially if you're staying for a few days or more, is to park at one of the long-term lots out by the airport (they run as low as $5 per day) and take a cab, bus, or shuttle into the city. You really can get by easily without a car in New Orleans, so it makes sense just to park it somewhere safe and out-of-the-way. The airport lots are fenced in and secure, too.

Obviously, you should not park in a designated handicap-parking spot unless you have the proper placard to hang from your rearview mirror; to obtain an official handicap placard for your rental car, call 504/483-4610. Call 504/826-1900 for general questions about parking in New Orleans, 504/826-1880 for questions about parking tickets and violations. If you've parked in a rush-hour no-parking zone, blocking a driveway, by yellow fire-lane rectangles, within 20 feet of a corner or crosswalk, within 15 feet of a fire hydrant, or in a street-cleaning, loading, or service zone, you will be ticketed and possibly towed. They're quite vigilant about this in New Orleans. Parking in the neutral ground (median) is prohibited, although you'll sometimes see locals do it.

Taxis

In New Orleans, taxis charge a flat rate from the airport to downtown. Rates within the city are $2.50 to start, plus $1 per mile thereafter. Keep in mind that cabs charge a flat rate of $3 per person *or* the meter rate, whichever is higher, during certain peak-visitor events, such as Mardi Gras and Jazz Fest. You don't hail cabs on the street in New Orleans or anywhere else in Louisiana, but you will often find them waiting at major intersections near Bourbon Street and other nightlife-heavy areas in the Quarter, near hotels (most hotel doormen can easily call or hail you a cab), and near casinos or other attractions. This is the sort of city where it's easy to lose track of time, especially if you're bar-hopping, so it's always a smart idea to have the name and number of at least a couple of cab companies.

Cab drivers have a good but not stellar reputation in New Orleans. They're generally trustworthy and friendly, but a high percentage of passengers are from out of town, and so it's not uncommon—as is true in many touristy cities—for cab drivers to pad the bill slightly by taking you on a circuitous route. This doesn't happen often, but to minimize the likelihood of being victimized by this sort of ploy, do your best to act as though you know where you're going (ideally, know the quickest route ahead of time and specify that way) and speak up if you're concerned about why a driver is taking you an unusual way. There's no need to be paranoid—if the driver explains that traffic or construction blocked the more conventional route, you can probably believe her or him. Jot down the driver's badge ID number, which is posted in all cabs, when you get into any cab, and report any driver who fails to perform satisfactorily. A number of gypsy cabs operate in New Orleans. These are private, generally unlicensed cabs that roam the city looking to pick up passengers. You have no guarantees as to service, safety, and reliability when using gypsy cabs, so it's best to avoid them entirely and use taxis operated by licensed and established cab companies instead.

Reliable cab companies in New Orleans include **White Fleet Cab** (504/822-3800), **Checker-Yellow** (504/943-2411), and **United Cabs** (504/522-9771). Other cities and larger towns throughout the region all have at least one local cab company.

Car Rentals

Just about all the major car-rental agencies are represented at New Orleans International Airport, including Alamo, Avis, Budget, Dollar, Enterprise, Hertz, and National.

Rates for car rentals in New Orleans typically start around $30 per day for economy cars but can easily rise to $40 or more per day during busy times, when conventions are in town, and so on. Weekly rates begin at about $150 per week for an economy car and $190 for a midsize car.

MASS TRANSIT

For visitors, using mass transit in rural areas, or even in smaller cities throughout the region, probably doesn't make sense compared with using your own or a rented car. Baton Rouge is the one place outside New Orleans where you could conceivably get by on the transit system, the **Capital Area Transit System (CATS)** (225/389-8282, www.brcats.com). But if you're just visiting Baton Rouge for a day or two, this option isn't especially practical, as you'd spend a good bit of time learning the routes and waiting for connections.

Most attractions in southern Louisiana's other decent-size city, Lafayette, are in outlying areas, so using the **Lafayette Transit System** (337/291-8570, www.lafayettelinc.net/lts) makes even less sense.

No communities in southern Louisiana have commuter rail, subways, or light rail.

In New Orleans, however, mass transit, in the form of buses and streetcars, can be extremely useful.

Buses and Streetcars

New Orleans is served by an extensive network of buses and streetcars operated by the **New Orleans Regional Transit Authority** (504/248-3900, www.norta.com). The fare is $1.25 plus $0.25 per transfer; express buses cost $1.50. You must pay with exact change (depositing coins or inserting $1 bills into the fare box at the front of the bus or streetcar) or a VisiTour pass (see below) upon boarding the bus. Bus and streetcar fares were suspended in New Orleans after Hurricane Katrina, but the free ride was discontinued in fall 2006. Neither food nor drink are permitted on buses or streetcars, nor are smoking or playing a stereo without headphones. Because they're historic, the St. Charles Streetcars are exempt from ADA (Americans with Disabilities Act) compliance, and passengers with disabilities may have trouble boarding. But all other RTA buses and streetcars are equipped to accommodate people with disabilities. Additionally, the RTA provides vans with lifts and curb-to-curb taxi service for those unable to use buses or streetcars because of a disability; call 504/827-7433 for further information.

Hurricane Katrina greatly affected the city's streetcar service. The famous **St. Charles Streetcar** line is still not up and running yet, and it's not yet known when it will be operational, but best estimates are not until at least summer 2007. So check before planning to ride this line. Normally, and it can be assumed that things will be back to normal eventually, the historic St. Charles line runs 24 hours a day along St. Charles Avenue, from Claiborne Avenue to Canal Street—it's a wonderful, scenic, atmospheric way to get between the CBD and Uptown. The fare is $1.25, plus $0.25 per transfer. The St. Charles line has been in operation, amazingly, since 1835, and the olive-green cars date to the 1920s, when they were built by the Perley Thomas Company (these cars were not damaged by the storm and are being used on the city's Canal line). The St. Charles line began as the main railroad line connecting the city of New Orleans with the resort community of Carrollton, which is today part of the city. At its peak in service, New Orleans's streetcar service spanned about 200 miles.

The **Riverfront Streetcar** runs the rather short but scenic 1.9-mile route along the riverfront; it operates 7 A.M.–10:30 P.M. weekdays and 8 A.M.–10:30 P.M. weekends. These modern red streetcars were built by New Orleans metal- and woodworkers.

The city's newest line is the **Canal Streetcar,** a line that ran for many years right into the 1960s and then resumed service in 2004. It extends from the foot of Canal, by the ferry terminal for Algiers Point, all the way up to City Park Avenue; a spur line connects along North Carrollton Avenue out to Esplanade Avenue, by City Park and the New Orleans Museum of Art. Many of the streetcars used on this route were damaged badly by Katrina, but the Canal Streetcar began running again early in 2006 using many of the historic St. Charles Streetcars that were not damaged by the storm.

Many bus routes were still not operational after Katrina, but these are to neighborhoods in the city where nobody is living or working. As neighborhoods reopen, public transportation to these areas will be reintroduced. Service to the parts of the city where visitors are most likely to visit—the French Quarter, Faubourg Marigny, CBD, Uptown, and Mid-City—is back. Useful bus routes include the **Magazine Line** (bus number 11), which runs along the six-mile stretch of galleries, shops, and restaurants from the Warehouse District through Uptown; the **Jackson-Esplanade Line** (bus number 91), which runs from the Garden District to the CBD and then passes from the edge of the French Quarter (at Rampart and Esplanade) north along historic Esplanade Ridge and into City Park; the **Canal Bus** (bus number 42), which runs up Canal to City Park Avenue, and the **St. Charles Bus** (bus number 12), which follows the route of the temporarily nonoperational St. Charles Streetcar, from Canal Street through the CBD along St. Charles Avenue all the way into Uptown and Riverbend at Carrollton Avenue.

If you're going to be using public transportation a lot, it's worthwhile to buy a **VisiTour pass,** which is sold by the Regional Transit Authority (RTA, 504/248-3900). The pass entitles the bearer to unlimited use of all streetcars and buses and costs $5 for a one-day pass and $12 for a three-day pass. You can buy these passes from the concierge or front desk of many hotels, or call the RTA Rideline

(504/248-3900) for the name of a ticket outlet near you. There are RTA VisiTour kiosks in the Riverwalk shops and the Jackson Brewery shops, too.

Ferries

You can get from the CBD (at the foot of Canal Street) to the West Bank (at Algiers Point) via the frequently running **Algiers Ferry,** which operates 6 A.M.–midnight. The ride is free for pedestrians and $1 per automobile.

Elsewhere along the Mississippi River, there are either inexpensive (usually up to $1 for cars and $0.50 for pedestrians, with fares collected only for westbound service) ferry crossings at many points up and down the river and in a few other parts of southern Louisiana. You can view a full list of crossings, with times and fares, at the **Louisiana Department of Transportation and Development** website, www.dotd.state.la.us/operations/ferry.shtml. There are 13 ferry crossings on the Mississippi River, with others across the Ouachita, Atchafalaya, and Calcasieu rivers, as well as across Bayou Boeuf. These rides are typically quite short, and reservations are not taken. The ferries cross frequently, usually from early morning till well into the evening.

Tips for Travelers

STUDENTS

New Orleans is one of the all-time destinations among college-age travelers, with the rest of the southern part of the state, especially Cajun Country, also quite popular. It helps that the area has so many colleges and universities. New Orleans is home to Dillard University, Louisiana State University Medical Center, Loyola University, Tulane, the University of New Orleans, and Xavier University. Other colleges and universities found throughout the southern part of the state include Louisiana State University (Baton Rouge), McNeese State University (Lake Charles), Nicholls State University (Thibodaux), Southeastern Louisiana

University (Hammond), Southern University (in Baton Rouge, it's the largest predominantly African American university in the United States), and University of Louisiana (Lafayette), which also has a branch up in Monroe, in the northeast part of the state.

Within New Orleans, the restaurants, clubs, and shops along Frenchmen Street in Faubourg Marigny, Decatur Street in the French Quarter, all through the Warehouse District, Magazine Street all through Uptown and the Upper and Lower Garden Districts, and Maple Street Uptown all have a decidedly collegiate and youthful vibe. Bourbon Street is truly age-varied, but you're more likely to see conventioneers and

A GUIDE TO LOUISIANA PRONUNCIATIONS

How do you pronounce "New Orleans"? It's sometimes heard as N'AW-luhns in movies and TV commercials, but New Orleanians most definitely do not pronounce it this way, and you shouldn't either – it sounds disrespectful, as though you're making fun of locals. The more conventional incorrect pronunciation is NOO or-LEENS. Say it this way and you'll be marked as an outsider (probably a Northerner), but at least you won't be accused of being a jerk. Locals pronounce the city's name in a handful of relatively similar ways, the simplest and most common being noo OHR-lins or thereabouts. You don't have to say it with a big, silly drawl or with delicious emphasis, as if you're a damsel in a Tennessee Williams play. Just say it quickly and casually. You might hear some locals, especially those with aristocratic tendencies, pronounce it noo OHR-lee-ahns.

When it comes to the name of state, things get a bit more straightforward. You have two options: LOO-zee-ann-ah or le-WEE-zee-ann-ah. Both pronunciations are common and considered acceptable.

Having settled that, we move on to the rest of the rivers, lakes, towns, and streets of New Orleans and Louisiana. Pronouncing these place-names can be extremely tricky for outsiders. "Correct" pronunciation isn't really the point here – according to your French teacher, Chartres Street, in New Orleans's French Quarter, would be pronounced shart. But the correct local pronunciation is CHAR-ters or CHART-uz.

If you're the sort of traveler who would rather not sound like an outsider, or at least you'd prefer to sound like a veteran traveler, keep the charts of Louisiana place-name pronunciations on the pages that follow handy, and do your best to learn the major ones. Locals won't generally torment you for pronouncing words as an outsider, and in many cases there are two or more commonly accepted (though often hotly debated) ways to pronounce the same word, especially taking into consideration one's accent – Louisiana has several regional accents. However, if you can say things in a manner that's relatively local-sounding, even if you have a Yankee or international accent, you may be taken a little more seriously by the Louisianan you're addressing.

The pronunciation keys on the following pages are approximate and most definitely imperfect, again owing to the many regional nuances among locals, who sometimes have grown up on the same block but still favor one pronunciation to another. Syllables set in capital letters are stressed (as in CHAR-ters).

If a common street or place-name is not listed, assume it's pronounced more or less the way it is elsewhere in the United States (for example, St. Louis Street in the French Quarter is pronounced here the way the Missouri city is, saynt LOO-iss, not the way the French would).

---

yuppies parading along here more than you are college students.

STA Travel (www.statravel.com) is the definitive resource for student-age travelers—its website is a font of information on student deals all around the world. There is one STA travel agency in the state: **STA Louisiana State University** (LSU Union, Suite 143, Raphael Semmes Rd., Baton Rouge, 225/578-0840). There had been a second STA agency near Tulane University in New Orleans, but that is closed for now, since Katrina.

There's one youth hostel in New Orleans and the only official one in the state, **Marquette House** (2253 Carondelet St., 504/523-3014, www.hiayh.org), which is in the Lower Garden District. It's part of **Hostelling International–American Youth Hostels** (202/783-6161, www.hiayh.org), which is a useful general resource for learning about hostels throughout the United States.

Many Louisiana museums and attractions offer student discounts; always bring your university or school ID card with you and ask even if such reduced prices or admissions aren't posted.

GAY AND LESBIAN TRAVELERS

New Orleans is something of a bastion of gay-friendliness in perhaps the most socially conservative and gay-hostile part of the nation, the Gulf South. Louisiana as a whole, along with its nearest states, Texas, Arkansas, Mississippi, and Alabama, offers no legal protection against discrimination on the basis of sexual orientation, and attitudes of many people living in smaller towns throughout the state are less than welcoming toward gays and lesbians.

New Orleans, on the other hand, has gay newspapers, a busy nightlife district that rubs right up against the more mainstream nightlife district in the French Quarter, a gay bookstore, and numerous lesbian and gay organizations and gay-owned businesses. Locals tend to be rather blasé about the sight of two women or two men walking hand in hand in the Big Easy, especially in the Quarter, Faubourg Marigny, and Uptown, which tend to have the highest lesbian and gay populations. Tourists, however, sometimes from less tolerant places, have been known to react less comfortably. And rarely, but occasionally, New Orleans has been the site of gay-related attacks and crimes, or more often fights or arguments along Bourbon Street, where drunken revelers sometimes lose their cool, and where the city's straight and gay nightclub rows collide (at St. Ann Street, to be precise).

According to Census 2000, Orleans Parish (home to New Orleans) ranked 11th in the United States in counties by percentage of same-sex couples (defined as households headed by unmarried same-sex partners). New Orleans also ranked 25th among incorporated places with the highest actual number of same-sex couples, with a total of 1,768 of them. These stats don't pertain to single people, and they're also dependent on couples voluntarily identifying themselves as gay. But both figures give a sense of how popular New Orleans is among gays and lesbians.

Statewide, New Orleans has by far the highest percentage of same-sex couples among the state's incorporated places, with several neigh-

NEW ORLEANS STREET NAMES

Burgundy (street): bur-GUN-dee
Cadiz (street): KAY-diz
Calliope (street): CALL-ee-ope
Carondelet (street): care-OHN-deh-LET
Chalmette (suburb): SHALL-mett
Chartres (street): CHART-ers
Clio (street): CLYE-o
Conti (street): CON-tie
Decatur (street): de-KAY-dur
Iberville (street): IBB-bur-ville
Loyola (school): lye-O-luh
Marigny (street/neighborhood):
    MAH-rah-nee
Melpomene (street): MEL-po-MEEN
Metairie (suburb): MED-uh-ree
Michoud (street/neighborhood): MEE-shoh
Milan (street): MYE-lan
Pontchartrain (lake): PONCH-uh-train
Prytania (street): prih-TAN-ya
Socrates (street): SO-crates
Tchoupitoulas (street): chop-ah-TOO-lehs
Terpsichore (street): TERP-sih-core
Toulouse (street): tuh-LOOS
Tulane (street/school): TOO-lane
Vieux Carré (neighborhood):
    VYOO ka-RAY

boring towns trailing just behind. Outside the immediate region, Baton Rouge ranked second in the southern part of the state, followed by the towns of Bogalusa, Hammond, New Iberia, and Houma. Quite a few gay people also live in Lafayette and Lake Charles, which with Baton Rouge contain the other gay nightlife options in the state.

Two annual events, Mardi Gras in the late winter and the Southern Decadence Celebration over Labor Day weekend, draw the greatest numbers of gay and lesbian visitors to New Orleans, but the city is always popular, and many of the B&Bs and hotels—especially in Faubourg Marigny—are gay-owned.

For information on nightlife and the scene throughout Louisiana and the Gulf South, consult the free biweekly *Ambush Magazine*

PRONOUNCING LOUISIANA PLACE-NAMES

TOWNS AND CITIES

Amite: AYE-meet
Basile: bah-ZEEL
Bossier City: BOH-zher CIT-ee
Breaux Bridge: BROH bridge
Calcasieu: CAL-cuh-shoo
Carencro: CARE-en-CROW
Cloutierville: CLOO-chee-vill
Erath: EEH-rath
Grand Coteau: GRAND cuh-TOE
Houma: HOAM-uh
Lafayette: LAFF-ee-ette
Lafourche: la-FOOSH
Iowa: EEH-o-way
Jeanerette: JENN-urh-ette
Mamou: MAH-moo
Monroe: MUN-roe
Natchitoches: NACK-ih-tish
Opelousas: AH-puh-loo-suss
Plaquemines: PLACK-ih-mens
Ponchatoula: PON-chuh-tool-uh
Port Barre: PORT BAR-eeh
Shreveport: SHREEV-port
Tangipahoa: TAN-jah-puh-ho
Thibodaux: TIB-uh-doe
Vacherie: VASH-er-ee

PARKS AND BODIES OF WATER

Atchafalaya (swamp/river):
  UH-cha-fuh-lye-uh
Bayou Teche (bayou): BYE-oo TESH
Bogue Chitto (river): boe-guh CHEE-tuh
Bonnet Carré (spillway):
  BONN-ett CARE-ee
Borgne (lake): BORN
Fontainebleau (park): FOWN-ten-BLOO
Manchac (bayou): MAN-shack
Maurepas (lake): MOOR-uh-paw
Ouchita (river): WAW-shuh-taw
Sabine (river): suh-BEAN
Tchefuncte (river): CHUH-funk-tuh

(504/522-8049, www.ambushmag.com). The same publication also has a website just for gay goings-on during Mardi Gras, www.gaymardigras.com.

TRAVELING WITH CHILDREN

Louisiana is an excellent, if not quite stellar, destination for families and travelers with children. The only real drawback is that the most-visited destination in the state, New Orleans, is more geared toward adults than children. This is not to say that kids won't enjoy touring some of the city's attractions, or that you won't find family-friendly hotels, inns, and restaurants. But do keep in mind that many of the city's smaller, high-end inns and fancier hotels tend to frown on children as guests, as do some of the rowdier or more sophisticated restaurants and bars.

But the New Orleans metro region has some outstanding attractions for kids, such as the Audubon Institute's facilities (which include the Audubon Zoo and Gardens, Odyssey's Shipwreck and Treasure Adventure, the Aquarium of the Americas, and the Entergy IMAX Theatre), Rivertown U.S.A., Storyland at City Park, the New Orleans Historic Voodoo Museum, Musee Conti's Wax Museum, and—of course—the Louisiana Children's Museum, right in the New Orleans CBD. Many of the excursions offered through the city and region, such as swamp tours, riverboat rides, and haunted house and voodoo tours, are a big hit with kids, especially teenagers.

Elsewhere in the state, the Konrico and Tabasco factory tours in New Iberia, and virtually all of the major attractions in Lafayette and Baton Rouge, such as Vermilionville and the U.S.S. *Kidd,* have a strong following with younger ones. In general, the plantations along the Great River Road tend to be more popular with adults, but Laura Plantation gives a lively tour that can be great fun for kids.

Many chain hotels and other accommodations throughout Louisiana allow kids to stay in their parents' rooms free or at a discount, and many restaurants in the state have kids' menus. Some of the Cajun restaurants with live music, such as Mulate's outside Lafayette and in New Orleans, are real family affairs. Fear not if you're headed to a seafood house with finicky kids who aren't wild about fish or clams—it's the very rare restaurant that doesn't offer a few chicken, burger, or grilled cheese options. Many museums and other attractions offer greatly reduced admission.

SENIOR TRAVELERS

New Orleans has a strong following among senior travelers, but much of the surrounding region is even more popular with this demographic, in part because the city has a reputation—deserved or not—for crime, nightlife, and overall rowdiness. In fact, New Orleans is as hospitable as any city toward travelers 50, 60, or older, but the wild nightlife scene around the Quarter can be off-putting to some. Many people seeking a more relaxed and slower-paced New Orleans experience prefer to stay in the Garden District, especially at one of the several hotels and inns along St. Charles Avenue. Quite a few retirees winter in the North Shore's St. Tammany and Tangipahoa parishes and also in the Lafayette and Lake Charles areas.

Louisiana is a family-friendly state, and with the growth in multigenerational travel— grandparents traveling with grandkids, or several generations of families vacationing together—the state's most family-oriented areas, such as Cajun Country and the North Shore, have become popular for these travelers.

Depending on the attraction or hotel, you may qualify for age-related discounts—the thresholds can range from 50 to 65. It can also help if you're a member of the **American Association of Retired Persons (AARP)** (800/424-3410, www.aarp.org). For a nominal annual membership fee, you'll receive all sorts of travel discounts as well as a newsletter that often touches on travel issues. **Elderhostel** (877/454-5768, www.elderhostel.org) organizes a wide variety of educationally oriented tours and vacations geared toward 55-and-over individuals or couples of whom one member is that age.

ACCESSIBILITY FOR TRAVELERS WITH DISABILITIES

Louisiana is on par with other states as far as conforming to the guidelines set by the Americans with Disabilities Act (ADA). Within new hotels, larger and recently built restaurants, and most major attractions, you can expect to find wheelchair-accessible restrooms, entrance ramps, and other fixtures. But Louisiana has many hole-in-the-wall cafes, historic house-museums with narrow staircases or uneven thresholds, tiny B&Bs, and other buildings that are not easily accessible to people using wheelchairs. If you're traveling with a guide animal, always call ahead and even consider getting written or faxed permission to bring one with you to a particular hotel or restaurant, though it's the rare instance in Louisiana that you won't be permitted to arrive with a guide dog.

A useful resource is the **Society for the Advancement of Travel for the Handicapped** (212/447-7284, www.sath.org).

Health and Safety

CRIME

As in any part of the country that is densely populated, concerns about crime and traffic are germane to planning a trip to southern Louisiana and especially to New Orleans. The city has a reputation for crime, some of it deserved, some exaggerated. Since the mid-1990s, the city's crime rate has fallen, and the New Orleans Police Department, once the subject of scandals and internal investigations, has greatly cleaned up. Furthermore, crime has declined in the city considerably since Hurricane Katrina, as many of the rougher neighborhoods were badly damaged by flooding, and many of the city's rougher residents left New Orleans for other places. Just as every aspect of

New Orleans gradually returns, so, too, will crime—there is some crime in every big city in the nation. But there's some reason to hope that crime in New Orleans may not again approach its nadir of several years ago anytime again in the near future.

One improvement in safety in recent years has been the establishment of a fleet of Hospitality Rangers, employees of the Downtown Development District whom you can spot by their yellow polo shirts and straw hats. You can ask these folks for directions, visitor maps, restaurant ideas, and other tourist advice. They work with the New Orleans Police Department to report any suspicious goings-on, broken streetlights, and other urban problems. You can also ask a ranger to escort you to your hotel or your car. The Hospitality Rangers program was suspended after Katrina because of a lack of staffing, but it was expected to resume again.

A particular concern about crime in New Orleans is that it does happen far too often in parts of the city where tourists are likely to venture. Murders of tourists are rare, but both muggings and car-jackings, while infrequent, do happen from time to time. There are a few common-sense steps you can take to minimize your likelihood of being targeted, the first being to pay attention to your surroundings and walk along well-lighted and well-traveled streets. Do not venture into dark and mostly residential areas, and never go into cemeteries after dark. Travel in groups when possible. Take cabs to parts of town with which you're unfamiliar. Don't display valuables and jewelry conspicuously, and leave all but necessary items at home. If you do visit with a laptop computer, camera, jewelry, or any type of expensive or irreplaceable item, stay at a hotel with in-room safes or store your belongings in the hotel safe.

You want to strike a balance between alert and paranoid—don't cower and fret and worry so much about crime that you end up having a bad time. Looking scared and nervous may actually increase your odds of being a victim anyway, as many criminals prey on visitors who look disoriented or uneasy about their surroundings. The most frequent targets of muggings and other crimes in New Orleans are inebriated tourists, and these, unfortunately, are easy to find in the French Quarter late at night. The simplest way to keep safe is to avoid drinking yourself into an extreme stupor.

If you're anticipating a night of revelry, try at least to venture out as part of a group. Have the name and address of your hotel written down someplace safe, but never write your hotel room number down somewhere that a thief or pickpocket could get it. If you show up at your hotel having forgotten your room number, a lobby employee can always remind you. Also be sure to carry with you the name and number of at least one or two cab companies. If you have a cell phone, carry it with you when wandering around New Orleans or just about anywhere unfamiliar to you—phones can come in extremely handy in an emergency.

Every bit of advice here should be heeded even more carefully if you're a woman, especially if traveling alone.

HOSPITALS AND HEALTH CARE

In all but a few rural parts of southern Louisiana, you're never terribly far from a hospital. In New Orleans, the best and most conveniently located is **Charity Hospital and Medical Center of Tulane** (CBD, 1532 Tulane Ave., 504/903-3000, http://gcrc.tulane.edu). Elsewhere in the southern half of the state, major facilities include **Baton Rouge General Medical Center** (8595 Picardy Ave., Suite 100, Baton Rouge, 225/387-7000, www.generalhealth.org), **Lafayette General Medical Center** (1214 Coolidge St., Lafayette, 337/289-7991, www.lafayettegeneral.com), **St. Tammany Parish Hospital** (1202 S. Tyler St., Covington, 985/898-4000, www.stph.org), and **Terrebonne General Medical Center** (8166 Main St., Houma, 985/873-4141, www.tgmc.com).

Pharmacies

You'll find pharmacies, many of them open until 9 or 10 P.M., throughout metro New

Orleans and most of the southern half of the state, the only exceptions being the more rural towns in Cajun Country. The leading chains in Louisiana are **Rite Aid** (www.riteaid.com) and **Walgreens** (www.walgreens.com), and Walgreens has many more 24-hour locations than Rite Aid, one in almost every city or large town.

WATER SAFETY

Always supervise children and exercise caution when boating, swimming, or fishing. Common sense applies—use life vests and/or other flotation devices, avoid swimming in areas that don't have lifeguards (which is the case at many of the state's swimming holes), and observe local regulations concerning boating, sailing, and fishing.

Motion sickness can be a serious, and sometimes unexpected, problem for passengers of boats. If you're at all concerned about this, or you've had bouts with seasickness in the past, consider taking Dramamine, Bonine, or another over-the-counter drug before setting sail; you may want to consult with a physician before your trip if you're interested in the Transderm Scop patch, which slowly releases medication into your system to prevent seasickness but is not without potential side effects. In general, try to avoid sailing on an empty stomach or too little sleep, keep your eyes on the horizon and avoid reading or focusing intently on anything that's small or moving with the rock of the boat, stick as close as possible to the center of the ship, and consider staying above deck (if weather permits), as breathing fresh air often helps.

If you're canoeing or even just taking a swamp tour in southern Louisiana, you should be alert about the wildlife around you. Flooding is also a danger; if you have any doubt about whether the water level is too high, consult with locals or check with one of the many canoe-rental outfitters in the region. Do not go boating on a bayou or river that has risen above its normal banks, which happens rather frequently after heavy rains. You could easily end up getting lost or caught on underbrush

in a false channel or where water has rushed onto a floodplain.

Snakes often hang in the branches of trees in the swamps and over bayous. Every now and then, you hear of a snake's falling right into a canoe or a swamp-tour boat. If you're especially nervous, take a swamp tour in a covered boat—many of them have roofs. Trees overhead also sometimes have wasps' nests in them. In general, don't linger too much beneath dense canopies of tree branches, and certainly try not to jostle branches above you. Alligators are not a serious safety threat to boaters—just give them a wide berth and consider yourself lucky if you're able to get close enough for a picture.

WILDLIFE ENCOUNTERS

Louisiana is a wonderful state for any visitor hoping to see wildlife up close, whether on swamp tours, canoe and boating expeditions, hikes, or country drives. In general, the dangers associated with such encounters are minimal.

There are plenty of animals that can hurt you—alligators and poisonous snakes being the most obvious. Louisiana has about 40 varieties of snake, of which six are poisonous and one, the water moccasin (a.k.a. the cottonmouth), is rather common in swamps, both on the ground and in tree branches overhead. Cottonmouths are one of the few snakes out there that can bite underwater. Their bite can be deadly, and they're not terribly shy, so it's up to you to back off when you come near one of these dark tan, brown, or black creatures that tend to coil and sit near stream and river borders, and on logs and stumps in the water.

Coral snakes are quite secretive. They're rarely found south of Lake Pontchartrain, near marshes and swamps, or in coastal areas—they're a greater threat in the northern part of the state, but they are sometimes found in Lake Charles and the higher parts of the Florida Parishes. Copperheads are more common but also tend toward forested areas and high ground; they're problematic chiefly because they camouflage themselves well and can easily be missed in a pile of leaves or on a log, as they tend to lie motionless. Pygmy rattlesnakes like grassy pinelands and dry coastal areas but are rarely found in the Mississippi River valley or in marshes. Eastern diamond-back rattlesnakes are somewhat common in the upland areas within the North Shore, including St. Tammany, Washington, and Tangipahoa parishes; they prefer open pinelands. The final variety of poisonous snake in the state is the timber or canebrake rattlesnake, which prefers the eastern and northern sections of the state and is especially at home in hardwood forests.

Snakes are particularly worrisome after a storm, when waterways sometimes spill over and displace wildlife; snakes can wind up in storm drains, under piles of debris, and even in homes.

The **Louisiana Department of Wildlife and Fisheries** has an excellent website, found at www.wlf.state.la.us, describing each of the state's snakes with pictures. It's worthwhile to take a look and learn what some of the common ones look like before spending a lot of time exploring.

If you're ever bitten by a water moccasin or any other snake, do not attempt to treat the bite yourself—go to the nearest hospital. And traumatized though you may be, try hard to remember what the snake looked like, as identification can be critical to correct treatment.

Alligators are great fun to watch up close, but they can cause serious bodily harm, and under no circumstances should you approach one. They can also easily be mistaken on the banks of rivers or lakes for logs, as they tend to sit up in the brush and sun themselves in warm weather. Be certain of what you're stepping on as you walk near the edge of a waterway. In general, make a bit of noise when wandering around places inhabited by snakes and alligators, as these creatures are not inherently aggressive toward humans and will generally scurry away or retreat if approached by people. In the category of things any idiot should already know: Never feed alligators, challenge or agitate them, or swim in places commonly inhabited by them, especially at dusk or at night, when they most love to hunt.

Your safest course of action is simply to go with knowledgeable locals, especially if boating, hiking, or touring swamps for the first time.

© ANDREW COLLINS

alligator in Honey Island Swamp, near Slidell on the North Shore

The animals most likely to make you miserable during a trip to Louisiana are mosquitoes, which just adore the often-still waters of the state's bayous and swamps. Bring plenty of insect repellent with you when pursing any kind of outdoor activity from March through October or even November. West Nile virus, which struck Louisiana more severely than most states since the late 1990s, can be fatal, but the odds of contracting it are quite low. Other insects that can be problematic, especially in areas popular for swamp tours and hiking, include bees, wasps, stinging caterpillars, ticks, and fire ants. In late summer and fall, so-called love-bugs (which are a species of fly often seen flying as mated pairs) can be a nuisance during picnics and outdoor gatherings, and they muck up windshields and bumpers.

Dangerous mammals are not a major issue in southern Louisiana. The state does have coyotes, black bears, red wolves, bobcats, foxes, and many other mammals that are more likely a threat to small pets than to humans. Rabies occurs rarely in Louisiana—there are typically fewer than a dozen reported cases of animals' being infected with rabies each year, and usually they're skunks and bats.

A final thing to watch for is poison ivy (and oak or sumac), common in many Louisiana state parks and preserves. Learn to identify the plants and to avoid them.

TRAVEL INSURANCE

Buying travel insurance makes sense if you've invested a great deal in a trip with prepaid accommodations, airfare, and other services, especially if you have any reason to be concerned about your ability to make the trip—perhaps impending medical concerns (check, however, the fine print regarding preexisting conditions). It's a good idea to buy insurance from a major provider, such as **Access America** (800/346-9265, www.etravelprotection.com) or **Travel Guard International** (800/826-1300, www.travelguard.com). Typically these policies can cover unexpected occurrences such as trip cancellations, interruptions, and delays, as well as medical expenses incurred during your travels.

Information and Services

MONEY
Banks, ATMs, and Credit Cards

Banks are plentiful throughout New Orleans and southern Louisiana, although fewer and farther between in the handful of rural areas, including some of the smaller villages in the Cajun Country. The French Quarter is also lacking actual banks, although businesses with ATMs (automated teller machines)—including bars, hotel lobbies, souvenir shops, and convenience stores—abound. Just keep in mind that many of these places charge a high usage fee, as much as $3–5 per transaction, whereas actual bank ATMs usually only charge $1–2. Most banks in New Orleans are adjacent to the French Quarter in the CBD, and most are open from 9 A.M. until anywhere between 3 and 5 P.M. weekdays and 9 A.M.–noon on Saturdays.

Most ATMs are available 24 hours a day and accept a wide range of bank cards (typically Cirrus and/or Plus, for example) and credit cards. Crime is a legitimate, although somewhat overblown, concern in New Orleans, but you should exercise discretion—especially if you're alone—when using ATMs late at night, particularly in the CBD, which can be desolate at times. Walk away and choose a different machine if you see anybody lurking nearby or actually loitering inside the vestibule in which the machine is situated, and never leave your car unlocked and running while you step out to use the machine.

Credit cards and bank cards are acceptable forms of payment at virtually all gas stations and hotels, many inns and B&Bs (but definitely not some of the very small ones, which will take travelers checks and sometimes personal checks), most restaurants (the exceptions tend to be inexpensive places, small cafes, diners, and the like), and most shops (again, the exception tends to be small, independent stores).

Currency

Louisiana receives relatively few international visitors directly from their countries of origin, but Louis Armstrong New Orleans International Airport does have direct flights from Canada and Honduras. The airport and the city itself do have currency exchange booths and services; at the airport, there's a branch of Whitney National Bank, in the ticket lobby next to the U.S. post office, that has a foreign-currency exchange. The ticket lobby also has a Mutual of Omaha Business Center, which has currency-exchange services. Foreign currency is not accepted anywhere in New Orleans.

Costs

Depending whether you travel mostly in New Orleans or out to the outlying towns and cities, the cost of travel in Louisiana can be as expensive as some of the most costly U.S. cities, such as Boston or New York City, or as inexpensive as many average-priced destinations. Compared with other parts of the United States, most of Louisiana is either average or even a bit less expensive. Since Hurricane Katrina struck New Orleans, however, prices for many goods and services have been altered, and even a year later, it's still hard to say what sort of long-term effect the storm will have on local costs.

For example, hotel rates have been higher than normal as properties gradually reopened (and some haven't at all), and the demand for rooms by relief and other temporary workers has been high. But by summer 2006, many of the city's relief workers had left the city or moved into more permanent housing, freeing rooms. Costs of housing, whether you're trying to buy a house or rent one, have soared because there are fewer houses than ever before. On the other hand, restaurant prices and the costs of some other goods have either remained stable or even dropped a bit, as businesses struggle to define their market and their role in post-Katrina New Orleans.

With that in mind, New Orleans, especially during the spring and fall high seasons, has some very expensive hotels, with rooms at top properties easily exceeding $300 nightly. However, the city also has a huge number of midpriced and budget motels and inns, where rates often fall well below $100 nightly, even during busy times. During Mardi Gras, Jazz Fest, and when major conventions are in town, to the extent that major conventions are gradually returning to town since Katrina, it can be tough to find a room in the city for under $150, and upscale business hotels will sometimes double their standard rates. On the positive side, because tourism numbers are still not back in full swing in New Orleans and may not be for some time, many properties offer deep discounts, especially during the slower summer months or at other periods when tourism is a bit slow. A year after Katrina, for instance, it was nearly impossible to find a hotel charging more than $200 per night, and even a number of top establishments offered deals below $100 nightly.

Elsewhere in southern Louisiana, budget chain motels typically charge $35–60 nightly, and midprice to upscale chain properties usually charge $60–100, with some high-end hotels in Lafayette and Baton Rouge charging anywhere from a bit to significantly more. Just as tourism and business visitation has dropped a great deal in New Orleans, it's increased in Baton Rouge and Lafayette. Rates at inns and B&B outside New Orleans vary greatly according to how luxurious they are, but they usually start as low as $50 for something basic to more than $200 for a fancy suite at a plantation or high-end property.

It's fairly easy to eat well in New Orleans without spending a bundle. The city is famous for its exclusive, high-end restaurants, such as Commander's Palace, Emeril's, and Brennan's. But even the ultrapopular high-end eateries charge a bit less than comparable restaurants in San Francisco and New York. And many of the fanciest restaurants offer prix-fixe set meals, which can save you money. Ordering à la carte at one of the very top New Orleans restaurants, with appetizer, entrée, dessert, wine or a couple of cocktails, and tax and tips will set you back around $100 per person, but you can get an equally good meal for about half that at many other upscale eateries around town. And for just $15–25 per person, you can enjoy a full meal at the Gumbo Shop, Praline Connection, Mulate's, Mother's, or any number of other casual restaurants serving first-rate Cajun, Creole, soul, or home-style cooking. Elsewhere in southern Louisiana, prices at lower-end restaurants are the same or slightly less than in New Orleans, and at high-end restaurants usually 10–20 percent less. The one exception can be the North Shore suburbs, such as Covington and Mandeville, which have some excellent but expensive high-end eateries that charge every bit as much as similar restaurants in New Orleans.

Shopping in Louisiana is not markedly more or less expensive than in other parts of the United States, although you'll find some very pricey upscale boutiques and galleries in New Orleans and along the North Shore. Gas stations in Louisiana charge about the same as neighboring states.

Sales Tax

The Louisiana state sales tax is 4 percent. It's the only state in the nation that offers tax-free shopping to international visitors (see the *Shopping* chapter for details). In addition, municipalities come up with many additional local taxes, most prominently car-rental and hotel taxes. In New Orleans, for example, the hotel tax is a whopping 13 percent, and the car-rental tax is 12 percent.

Tipping

In the tipping-oriented United States, it's typical to leave a 15–20 tip on a restaurant check, but in larger cities, people tip slightly higher. In New Orleans you might want to edge toward 20 percent, obviously factoring in the level of service you receive. You might round up your change or leave $1 or so when ordering a drink at a bar or a cup of espresso at a cof-

feehouse (some coffeehouses and cafes have tip jars on their counters and appreciate, but don't necessarily expect, you to drop a little change in); if you're ordering multiple drinks, tip more along the lines of 15 percent for the total bill. At nightclubs, the theater, or other places with a coat check, tip $1 per coat or bag.

Tip taxi drivers and hairstylists 15–20 percent. At hotels, tip your parking valet $1 or $2 each time he or she retrieves your car; tip bellhops $0.50–1 per bag, and leave $1 or $2 per day for hotel housecleaning staff in your room. If the concierge performs any special tasks for you, tip $5–10. Room-service gratuities are typically built into the total bill, so leaving an additional tip is unnecessary and should be done only at your discretion; tip the local pizza or other food-delivery person who brings dinner to your hotel room $2 or $3 depending on the total bill. At small inns and B&Bs, it's customary to leave somewhat more than this for cleaning and other staff. You may find an envelope left in your room especially for the purpose of tipping the staff. There seems to be no consensus about what to leave at small properties such as this, but aim for a minimum of $2 or $3 per day, and anywhere from $5 to $10 per day if you received a great deal of personal service and attention (such as help with sightseeing and restaurant reservations) or you stayed in an especially big and luxurious suite that required a great deal of cleaning. At small B&Bs that are cleaned and serviced by the owners themselves, it is not necessary or even appropriate to leave a tip.

If you use the services of an individual tour guide, consider tipping 10–15 percent of the total cost. The practice varies greatly on package tours, but drivers and guides generally expect to receive anywhere from $2 to $10 per person per day, unless gratuities have already been included in the price of the tour.

COMMUNICATION AND MEDIA
Phones and Area Codes

Southern Louisiana uses a few area codes. For New Orleans and the region immediately surrounding it, the area code is 504; much of the area surrounding New Orleans, including the North Shore and the eastern parts of the Cajun Country (such as Houma) uses 985; Baton Rouge and the rest of south-central Louisiana uses 225, and southwestern Louisiana and Lafayette use 337.

Outside your local calling region, you need to first dial 1 and the area code. For directory assistance, dial 1, the area code, and 555-1212—the charge for directory assistance calls is typically $0.50 to $0.75.

Note that in this book, where available, the local telephone number always precedes any toll-free number. Toll-free numbers have area codes of 800, 866, 877, or 888.

Pay phones generally charge $0.50 for local calls; if you're calling collect or using a calling card, there's a $0.25 surcharge. Most hotels charge anywhere from a $0.50 to $1.50 surcharge for local calls, toll-free calls, or just about any other kind of call placed from their phones; however, a number of smaller inns and also budget- to midprice chains (Motel 6, Comfort Inn, Hampton Inn, Super 8, and so on) offer free local and toll-free charges. Long-distance rates can be outrageous at many hotels, and it's generally a good idea to use a calling card or buy a prepaid one. The latter are available at many convenience stores and gas stations and at a wide range of prices. If you're a member of Costco, Sam's Club, or another wholesale discount store, consider buying one of the prepaid Sprint, MCI, or AT&T phone cards sold at these stores—often you can find cards that end up costing just $0.02 or $0.03 per minute.

Cellular Phones

Cell phones are part of life in the United States, and relatively few frequent travelers go anywhere without them. If you're a subscriber on one of the nation's major networks, such as Sprint PCS, Verizon, or Cingular, you'll find full coverage throughout most of southern Louisiana, with only a handful of rural areas being exceptions. Even in rural areas, you should have no trouble receiving "roaming" service.

It's legal to jabber away on your cell phone while driving, but it's not a good idea, especially if you're unfamiliar with where you're going and driving on local surface roads. When possible, try to pull off to the side of the road to talk on the phone; if traveling on a multilane highway, try to stay in the right or center lane and drive defensively if you must talk on your cell phone. And even if you're not speaking on your phone, be alert to drivers around you who are. Some states and cities in the United States have banned cell-phone use while driving. You can, legally, circumvent this ban by buying a hands-free attachment, which allows you to talk on your cell phone while driving without having actually to hold the phone.

It's polite to turn off your phone, or turn its ringer volume to "off" or vibrate, when in restaurants, hotel lobbies, shops, and other confined spaces; do not talk on your cell phone in libraries or fancy restaurants, and avoid doing so in general when you're in shops or even fast-food or casual venues. If you must do so, try to keep the call short and speak quietly.

Internet and Computer Access

There are an increasing number of public places in New Orleans and Baton Rouge where you can check the Internet—even some airport payphones now provide this service. And many hotels, restaurants, coffeehouses, and other public places have WiFi service, which can be free or require a fee, depending on the establishment. If you do have your WiFi-ready laptop with you, you generally won't have trouble picking up WiFi service in most cities and larger towns.

If you don't have a laptop with you, a convenient place to check email and surf the Web is the public library; there's one in virtually every Louisiana town, although only those in larger communities tend to have public computers. Libraries at Louisiana's several universities and colleges are also open to the public, but their policies vary regarding computer use; some allow computer access only to students, faculty, and staff. Libraries generally allow you to use their computers for short periods, ranging from 15 minutes to an hour.

A handful of cafes around the state have pay Internet stations, as does FedEx Kinko's, which has branches in Baton Rouge, Covington, Lafayette, Lake Charles, Metairie, and New Orleans (several locales); it's open 24 hours a day in many locations and quite late elsewhere. FedEx Kinko's is an excellent traveler's business and work resource, as it's also a place to make copies, buy some office supplies, use Federal Express and other shipping services, and rent time on computers (whether to surf the Internet, print out copies, scan photos, etc.).

Mail Services

Right in the French Quarter, Royal Mail Service (828 Royal St., 504/522-8523) can pack and ship most any gift, artwork, or other items you've picked up during your travels. It's also a pickup point for FedEx and UPS. New Orleans's main branch of the U.S. Post Office (701 Loyola Ave., just west of Poydras St. in the CBD, 504/589-1190) is a clean and efficient facility with the longest opening hours of any post office in the state. It's open 7 A.M.–7 P.M. weekdays and 8 A.M.–5 P.M. Saturday. Other branches with more limited hours are in the French Quarter at 207 North Peters Street, on Lafayette Square just off St. Charles Avenue, and Uptown at 2000 Louisiana Avenue.

Media

Louisiana has about 20 daily newspapers, and many more that run less frequently. The major daily for New Orleans, and widely read across the state, is the *Times-Picayune* (www.nola.com), which comes out daily. Other popular daily papers in southern Louisiana include Baton Rouge's *The Advocate* (www.theadvocate.com), Hammond's *Daily Star* (www.hammondstar.com), Houma's *The Courier* (www.houmatoday.com), Lafayette's *The Advertiser* (www.theadvertiser.com), *Lake Charles American Press* (www.americanpress.com), and New Iberia's *Daily Iberian* (www.iberianet.com).

Louisiana has about 30 TV stations, with major network or PBS affiliates in Baton Rouge, New Orleans, and Lafayette, plus a couple in Lake Charles.

New Orleans Magazine (www.neworleansmagazine.com) is a useful and well-produced monthly four-color glossy, with excellent dining, arts, and events coverage. *Louisiana Life* (http://louisianalife.com) comes out quarterly and has a wide variety of features on what to see and do across the state, with a focus on food, history, art, and music. An excellent resource for metro New Orleans arts, dining, shopping, clubbing, and similar such diversions is the decidedly left-of-center *Gambit Weekly* alternative newsweekly (www.bestofneworleans.com). The free Baton Rouge monthly *Country Roads* (www.countryroadsmag.com) has useful information on towns along the Mississippi River.

PRACTICALITIES
Business Hours

As of fall 2006, many businesses in areas affected by Hurricane Katrina had somewhat to extremely limited hours, especially restaurants. There was still a huge staffing shortage in New Orleans and the surrounding area, so demand was also off at many shops and restaurants. Expect hours to remain somewhat limited for at least the next couple of years, as the city rebounds and comes back into full swing.

In normal times, most restaurants in urban and suburban parts of the state serve lunch from 11 A.M. or noon until 2 or 3 P.M. and dinner from 5 or 6 P.M. until 10 P.M. In New Orleans, a handful of eateries are open 24 hours and many others serve food until midnight. In the French Quarter, many bars stay open and serve alcohol 24 hours a day; elsewhere in the city, bars are more commonly open until between 2 and 4 A.M. Elsewhere in the state, bars generally close at 2 A.M., and it's rare to find restaurants (except some fast-food chains) serving food past 10 or 11 at night. In some of the more rural parts of the state, especially the southwestern sections, expect lunch to end by 2 P.M. and dinner by 9 P.M. The post office is usually open 8 A.M.–5 P.M. on weekdays and also on Saturday mornings.

There's no reliable rule on typical shop hours, except that they seem to be getting gradually longer, to the point that major chain shops and stores in big shopping malls often stay open from 9 or 10 A.M. until 9 or 10 P.M., typically with shorter hours on Sundays. Local, independently operated boutiques and shops often don't open till late morning (especially in resort areas), and they often close by 5 or 6 P.M.; these same shops may not open at all on Sundays or even on Mondays or Tuesdays. In some densely populated areas you'll be able to find 24-hour full-service grocery stores, and 24-hour gas stations and convenience stores are found in several parts of the state, especially near highway exits of major interstate highways. Because shop hours vary so greatly, it's especially important to phone ahead if you're concerned about any one particular business's being open when you arrive.

Louisiana is pretty quiet on Sundays and Mondays outside of New Orleans; in fact, it's a good strategy to plan your visit to be in New Orleans on those days and, especially if you're not much for crowds and nightlife, in another part of the state on Fridays and Saturdays. In many towns, even places that are quite touristy, such as New Iberia or Covington, you'll find nary a shop open on Main Street on Sunday.

Many restaurants are dark on Mondays or Sundays or both, especially for dinner (as some of these serve Sunday brunch). Major attractions are often closed Monday and to a lesser extent on Sunday.

Electricity

The standard in Lousiana and the rest of the United States and Canada is AC, 110 volts/60 cycles. Plugs have two flat, parallel prongs.

Time Zone

As with Mississippi, Alabama, Arkansas, and Texas, Louisiana falls entirely within the Central Standard Time (CST) zone. Chicago is in the same zone, Los Angeles two hours behind, Denver an hour behind, and New York and Atlanta an hour ahead. The Canadian Maritimes are two hours ahead; London, England, is six hours ahead; and Israel is eight hours ahead.

Remember that hours behind and ahead are affected by the fact that Louisiana, like most but not all American states and Canadian provinces, observes Central Daylight Time (CDT): On the last Sunday in October, clocks are set back one hour through the first Sunday in April, when they are set back ahead an hour.

TOURIST INFORMATION

The state of Louisiana is broken down into numerous tourism regions. Usually each parish (like a county) has its own tourist board, and then certain cities (New Orleans, Lafayette, Baton Rouge) have their own offices of tourism. Each office has its own brochures and staff. It's wise to work directly with these offices when planning a trip to a specific area within the state—contact information for these offices is given in the appropriate chapters throughout the book. In many cases, the towns that make up a particular section of this book fall into more than one tourism region, so you may want to call two or three local offices to best plan your itinerary and cull advice on upcoming events and attractions.

The statewide information bureau is the Louisiana Office of Tourism (1051 N. 3rd St., Room 327, Baton Rouge, LA 70802, 225/346-1857 or 888/225-4003, www.louisianatravel.com), which can send you a free Louisiana travel planner.

RESOURCES
Suggested Reading

As many books have been written about New Orleans and the Cajun Country as just about any part of the country, but there are several, both fiction and nonfiction, that can especially enhance your trip to the region. Most of those listed below focus exclusively on New Orleans, but you'll also find several that cover other parts of southern Louisiana.

You may recognize the "Images of America" series, by Arcadia Publishing (888/313-2665, www.arcadiapublishing.com), from the trademark sepia covers of its hundreds of small soft-cover historic-photo essays on more than 1,000 communities across the country. These fascinating books are produced by a small firm in Charleston, South Carolina, and each title typically contains 200–250 early black-and-white photos of a particular region, along with running commentary that is usually authored by a local historian, librarian, or archivist. The books generally cost about $20, and at present there are 25 titles on Louisiana, three of them dealing specifically with New Orleans.

HURRICANE KATRINA

Brinkley, Douglas. *The Great Deluge: Hurricane Katrina, New Orleans, and the Mississippi Coast.* William Morrow, 2006. This is one of the most comprehensive and insightful accounts of Katrina, written by a noted historian and Tulane professor who experienced the storm's devastating aftermath firsthand.

Horne, Jed. *Breach of Faith: Hurricane Katrina and the Near Death of a Great American City.*

Random House, 2006. A riveting account of the storm by the metro editor of the *Times-Picayune.*

Piazza, Tom. *Why New Orleans Matters.* Regan Books, 2005. A heartfelt, first-hand celebration of the Big Easy after Katrina, making a case for why it's so important that the city rebuild and flourish.

van Heerden, Ivor, with Mike Bryan. *The Storm: What Went Wrong and Why During Hurricane Katrina—The Inside Story from One Louisiana Scientist.* Viking Adult, 2006. The name here pretty well says it all: van Heerden is deputy director of the Louisiana State University Hurricane Center, and he gives a very good sense of how Katrina was as much—if not more—a human-made catastrophe as a natural one.

DESCRIPTION AND TRAVEL

Douglas, Lake, and Jeannette Hardy. *Gardens of New Orleans: Exquisite Excess.* Chronicle Books, 2001. A companion photo book to *New Orleans: Elegance and Decadence,* this elegant tome takes readers into the many secrete and sensuous gardens of the Big Easy.

Fry, Macon, and Julie Posner. *Cajun Country Guide.* Pelican, 1998. An in-depth tour guide on the Cajun Country, with extensive anecdotes and histories on just about every town in the region, large or small.

Saxon, Lyle. *Gumbo Ya-Ya: A Collection of Louisiana Folk Tales.* Pelican, 1987 (reprint). This book, a work on Louisiana sponsored by the WPA (see other WPA listings below) in 1945, was written by one of the state's most talented and colorful writers. First editions of this title can be found used for anywhere from $25 to $75, or you can buy a relatively recent printing of this title at many bookstores.

Sexton, Richard, and Randolph Delehanty. *New Orleans: Elegance and Decadence.* Chronicle Books, 1993. A handsome photo essay that distills the essence of New Orleans's architecture, art, landscape, and culture.

Sternberg, Mary Ann. *Along the River Road.* Louisiana State University Press, 2001. An excellent and amazingly thorough history and description, mile by mile, of the towns and plantation homes strung along the Great River Road.

Sullivan, Lester. *New Orleans Then and Now.* Thunder Bay Press, 2003. This photography collection takes vintage black-and-white photos of city landmarks and streets and contrasts them with contemporary shots of the same scenes. The book offers a wonderful look at how the city has changed, and more important, how in so many places it hasn't.

Workers of the Federal Writers' Project of the Works Progress Administration for the city of New Orleans. *New Orleans City Guide.* Riverside Press Cambridge, 1938 (out of print). Arguably the best treatment of the city ever written is this dense and fascinating work compiled by the Works Progress Administration (WPA) Workers of the Federal Writers' Project. Part of the amazingly well-executed and thoroughly researched American Guide Series, the book is long since out of print (many titles within this series have been picked up in recent years and reprinted, but not yet New Orleans, alas). Your best hope of finding a copy of this wonderful tome is by scouring the racks of used bookstores or websites such as eBay. Depending on its condition and age (and whether it has its original cover and map),

this guide should sell for anywhere from $10 to $40. Or try your local library.

Workers of the Federal Writers' Project of the Works Progress Administration for the state of Louisiana. *Louisiana State Guide.* Hastings House, 1941 (out of print). The same idea as the aforementioned New Orleans city guide, this 746-page book has complete and in-depth coverage of the entire state. Used copies usually sell for between $25 and $75.

MAPS AND ORIENTATION

There are a number of decent folding maps of New Orleans, Baton Rouge, Lafayette, and Louisiana. The Louisiana Office of Tourism (1051 N. 3rd St., Room 327, Baton Rouge, LA 70802, 225/346-1857 or 888/225-4003, www.louisianatravel.com) can send you a very good general state map.

DeLorme. *Louisiana Atlas and Gazetteer.* DeLorme, 2001. DeLorme publishes a state atlas that's part of its Gazetteer series. While this series shows much greater detail than your run-of-the-mill atlas, it's not very trustworthy as a serious navigational aid. A disturbing number of errors appear on these pages—in particular, the DeLorme atlas has a tendency to show dirt roads and even trails as primary paved thoroughfares, creating the potential for all sorts of frustrating wild-goose chases.

Microsoft. *Microsoft Streets and Trips.* Microsoft, 2006. A very useful digital tool, Microsoft Streets and Trips covers the entire United States (and Canada). With this disk, you can type in virtually any street address in Louisiana (or any other state, for that matter) and instantly have it pinpointed on a full-color detailed map on your computer screen.

Rand McNally. *Rand McNally StreetFinder: New Orleans and Vicinity.* Rand McNally, 2006. Very precise maps on the city are published by Rand McNally. The easy-to-read and well-labeled *Rand McNally StreetFinder: New Orleans* is an excellent atlas with great detail, including city coverage. The 2006 edition lacks any post-Katrina updates, but it can be expected that subsequent editions will provide this. Rand McNally produces a similar atlas on Baton Rouge, and fold-out maps on New Orleans, Baton Rouge, Lafayette, Lake Charles, Houma/Thibodaux/Morgan City, and the entire state.

BIOGRAPHY AND HISTORY

Asbury, Herbert. *The French Quarter: An Informal History of the New Orleans Underworld.* Thunder's Mouth Press, 2003. In an unconventional look at the city's seamy side, Asbury's colorful account looks at the city's infamous red-light districts, illegal gaming, and other not-so-legitimate activities.

Benfey, Christopher E. G. *Degas in New Orleans: Encounters in the Creole World of Kate Chopin and George Washington Cable.* Benfey uses the brief visit by Degas to New Orleans in the early 1870s to examine the city and its Creole society during the late 19th century.

Cable, George Washington. *Old Creole Days: A Story of Creole Life.* Pelican, 1991 (reprint). Victorian novelist and essayist Cable captures life in old Creole New Orleans during the 19th century. Cable wrote many other popular books about the city.

Campanella, Richard. *Time and Place in New Orleans: Past Geographies in the Present Day.* Pelican, 2002. An eye-opening study of the unlikely establishment of New Orleans in the middle of a malaria-ridden swamp—it's filled with historic and contemporary maps and photos that trace the evolution of New Orleans.

Cowan, Walter, and John C. Chase, Charles L. Dufour, O. K. LeBlanc, and John Wilds. *New Orleans Yesterday and Today: A Guide to the City.* Louisiana State University Press, 2001. A wonderful collection of historical essays that trace the city's history by offering concise glimpses into areas such as food, music, and race. Several of the same authors penned a broader history on the state, *Louisiana Yesterday and Today: A Guide to the State,* which was published in 1996 by Louisiana State University Press.

Williams, Harry T. *Huey Long.* Random House, 1981. A superb and gripping biography of the "Kingfish," the man who shaped Louisiana politics for many years after his death.

Johnson, Walter. *Soul by Soul: Life Inside the Antebellum Slave Market.* Harvard University Press, 2001. This is a gripping and raw account of North America's largest and most notorious slave market, which was centered right in New Orleans. Narratives, court records, bills of sale, and other documents are used to trace the harrowing legacy of slavery.

Remini, Robert Vincent. *The Battle of New Orleans: Andrew Jackson and America's First Military Victory.* Penguin USA, 2001. Remini examines the great battle that secured a young America's victory against the British during the War of 1812.

SPECIAL INTEREST

Florence, Robert. *New Orleans Cemeteries: Life in the Cities of the Dead.* Batture Press, 2005. An insider's history and tour of the city's famous aboveground cemeteries.

Huber, Leonard V. *Mardi Gras: A Pictorial History of Carnival in New Orleans.* Pelican, 1989. A nice overview of the history of the city's most famous celebration.

Tallant, Robert. *Voodoo in New Orleans.* Pelican, 1983 (reprint). A classic compendium and history about one of New Orleans's most fascinating topics. Tallant is also author of the similarly informative *Voodoo Queen.*

MUSIC

Armstrong, Louis. *Satchmo: My Life in New Orleans.* DaCapo Press, 1986. The definitive autobiography by the definitive New Orleans jazz icon.

Berry, Jason. *Up from the Cradle of Jazz: New Orleans Music Since World War II.* DaCapo Press, 1992. A terrific survey tracing the history of music in the Big Easy.

Lomax, Alan. *Mister Jelly Roll: The Fortunes of Jelly Roll Morton, New Orleans Creole and Inventor of Jazz.* University of California Press, 2001. This is a fascinating examination of not only one New Orleans jazz luminary but also the development of the city's music scene.

Ondaatje, Michael. *Coming Through Slaughter.* Vintage Books, 1996. A colorful tale of Buddy Bolden, one of the earliest New Orleans jazz greats. Ondaatje is most famous for *The English Patient.*

FOOD

Fitzmorris, Tom. *Tom Fitzmorris's New Orleans Food: More than 225 of the City's Best Recipes to Cook at Home.* Stewart, Tabori, and Chang, 2006. A thorough food-lover's companion written by one of the city's top food experts.

Guste, Roy F. *The 100 Greatest New Orleans Creole Recipes.* Pelican, 1994. Guste may not be a household name like Emeril or Prudhomme, but his collection is uncompromisingly authentic and filled with colorful flavors.

Lagasse, Emeril. *Emeril's Potluck: Comfort Food with a Kicked-Up Attitude.* Morrow Cookbooks, 2004. Great recipes from the schmaltzy celebrity chef's cooking shows.

Prudhomme, Paul. *Chef Prudhomme's Louisiana Kitchen.* Morrow Cookbooks, 1984. A compendium of classic recipes by the New Orleans master of Cajun cooking.

Zagat. *Zagat 2007 New Orleans Restaurants and Nightlife.* Zagat Survey, 2006. Great reader tips and suggestions on where to eat in New Orleans and the metro area; it's an indispensable post-Katrina guide for food lovers in the Big Easy.

MEMOIR, FICTION, AND LITERATURE

Burke, James Lee. *Pegasus Descending: A Dave Robicheaux Novel.* Simon and Schuster, 2006. This is one of the more popular books in a series of gripping crime stories featuring Dave Robicheaux, a New Orleans homicide cop. In later books Robicheaux has left New Orleans and lives in the Cajun Country town of New Iberia. The tourism offices and visitors centers around New Iberia and Lafayette distribute a free brochure, "James Lee Burke's Acadiana," which lists more than a dozen real places around New Iberia that figure prominently in the Dave Robicheaux novels.

Chopin, Kate. *The Awakening and Selected Stories of Kate Chopin.* Pocket Books, 2004. One of the great literary classics of the South, Chopin's 1899 novel about a woman who flouts New Orleans Creole society by leaving her husband and family and children caused a huge scandal. The circumstances may seem tame today, but this remains an emotionally powerful work, as are her other stories.

Long, Judith. *Literary New Orleans.* Hill Street Press, 1999. A delightful anthology of works by some of the city's most notable authors, from Truman Capote to James Lee Burke to Sheila Bosworth to Zora Neale Hurston.

Percy, Walker. *The Moviegoer.* Vintage Books, 1998 (reissue). Percy, who died in 1990, was one of Louisiana's most talented writers, and this somewhat underrated existential story about a New Orleans stockbroker is one of his finest.

Rice, Anne. *Witching Hour.* Knopf, 1990. The Garden District's most famous (former) resident, Anne Rice has written a number of tales of witchcraft and vampires set throughout New Orleans. This is one of her most mesmerizing works, but also look out for the four works that make up the *Vampire Chronicles: Interview with the Vampire, The Vampire Lestat, The Queen of the Damned,* and *The Tale of the Body Thief.*

Rice, Christopher. *A Density of Souls.* Miramax, 2001. Rice's auspicious debut novel depicts the lives of four high-school students grappling with coming of age and sexual identity in New Orleans. Rice is the son of novelist Anne.

Smith, Julie. *New Orleans Mourning.* Ivy Books, 1991 (reissue). Part of a series of popular mystery books revolving around policeman Skip Langdon. Other engrossing books in the collection include *Mean Women Blues* and *Louisiana Bigshot.*

Toole, John Kennedy. *A Confederacy of Dunces.* Grove Press, 1987 (reissue). A critically acclaimed tragicomic novel published seven years after the suicide of its young author, this peculiar tale hosts an even stranger cast of Louisiana characters.

Tyree, Omar. *Leslie.* Simon and Schuster, 2003. Drugs, voodoo, and murder figure into this edgy story with compelling characters.

Walker, Rob. *Letters from New Orleans.* Garrett County Press, 2005. Released shortly before Katrina struck the city, this collection of humorous, scary, and improbable tales about the Crescent City are related by a writer who moved to the city in 2000.

Warren, Robert Penn. *All the King's Men.* Harcourt, 2005 (reissue). A thinly veiled fictional look at the controversial life of Huey Long, Warren's work goes beyond mere political rehashing to become a gripping and compelling study of one of 20th-century America's most controversial figures.

Williams, Tennessee. *A Streetcar Named Desire.* New Directions, 2004 (reissue). The seminal Williams play set in New Orleans. Less famous but more directly about life in the French Quarter is *Vieux Carré,* which Williams wrote based on notes from journals he kept while living in New Orleans.

Internet Resources

New Orleans has dozens of regional websites and several useful sites that are either statewide or focused on the southern part of Louisiana. Furthermore, a number of national sites covering everything from transportation to the outdoors have specific web pages on just Louisiana.

TOURISM AND GENERAL INFORMATION

Citysearch
www.neworleans.citysearch.com
This internationally known site contains listings and limited editorial information on new restaurants, museum exhibitions, which movies are playing where, and where to find hotels. While the coverage is chiefly about New

Orleans, you'll also find listings for the other towns and cities throughout the state. Unfortunately, outdated information appears routinely on this site.

AOL Cityguide
http://cityguide.aol.com/neworleans
The competing web company of Citysearch, Digital City has comparable coverage of New Orleans and better coverage of other parts of the state. Both sites also include ratings by site users, which can be very useful and extremely entertaining.

The New Orleans Menu
www.nomenu.com
This comprehensive site operated by local food expert Tom Fitzmorris gives details on

the city's famous food scene. There's also loads of information on which restaurants in town have opened since Katrina, and which have closed for good or are in various stages of renovation.

New Orleans Magazine
www.neworleansmagazine.com

Very useful and well-produced monthly with excellent dining, arts, and events coverage.

The Official State of Louisiana Home Page
www.state.la.us

The official state website comes in handy when you're looking for detailed information on state and local politics, regional demographics, the state library, and local laws.

The Official State of Louisiana Tourism Home Page
www.louisianatravel.com

The mother of all Louisiana travel and tourism websites, with links to the state's dozens of regional tourism sites. Some of those that promote tourism in areas covered in this book include:

New Orleans Tourism Marketing Corporation
www.neworleansonline.com

St. Tammany Parish Tourist and Convention Commission
www.neworleansnorthshore.com

Tangipahoa Parish Convention and Visitors Bureau
www.tangi-cvb.org

Baton Rouge Area Convention and Visitors Bureau
www.visitbatonrouge.com

St. James Parish Welcome Center
www.stjamesla.com

Houma Area Convention and Visitors Bureau
www.houmatourism.com

Lafayette Convention and Visitors Commission
www.lafayettetravel.com

St. Landry Parish Tourist Commission
www.cajuntravel.com

Southwest Louisiana/Lake Charles Convention and Visitors Bureau
www.visitlakecharles.org

Within each site you'll find a trove of links to regional attractions, dining, lodging, events, transportation, and other valuable information.

New Orleans *Times-Picayune*
www.nola.com

This website produced by the state's most widely read paper ranks among the most comprehensive and informative online resources in Louisiana.

TRANSPORTATION

Louis Armstrong New Orleans International Airport
www.flymsy.com

Find out about parking, airlines, check-in information, and arrivals and departures at the state's main airport.

Amtrak
www.amtrak.com

Home page for the national rail service with several stops in Louisiana.

Greyhound
www.greyhound.com

The nation's leading bus line makes a number of stops in Louisiana.

Louisiana Department of Transportation and Development
www.dotd.state.la.us

Site providing extensive information on traveler resources and road conditions, licenses and permits, upcoming roadwork and projects, and construction bid notices. You can find out about rates and scheduling for the many ferries that cross the Mississippi River and several other bodies of water around the state at www.dotd.state.la.us/operations/ferry.asp.

SPORTING AND THE OUTDOORS

Louisiana Department of Natural Resources
http://dnr.louisiana.gov

Among Louisiana's top Internet resources for outdoors enthusiasts, the DNR home page provides information and policies pertaining to boating, hiking, hunting, fishing, beachgoing, and many other activities.

Louisiana Office of State Parks
www.crt.state.la.us/crt/parks

This site provides links to every property in the state park system. It also has information on primitive camping at state parks.

Louisiana Chapter of the Nature Conservancy
http://nature.org/wherewework/ northamerica/states/louisiana

Hikers might want to visit this site, which contains information about the Conservancy's Louisiana refuges and preserves.

Orleans Audubon Society
www.jjaudubon.net

Great site for birding, with specifics on the society's New Orleans chapter.

Louisiana Golf Association
www.lgagolf.org

Here golfers can learn all about the state's many public courses.

Index

FOOD FESTIVALS

Acknowledgments

Updating this book, especially on the heels of Hurricane Katrina, has been both challenging and rewarding, and it wouldn't have been possible without assistance from numerous friends and colleagues throughout Louisiana, especially Donna O'Daniels in Mandeville, Gerald Breaux and Kelly Strenge in Lafayette, and Larry Lovell in New Orleans. I also greatly appreciate the wisdom and patience of my editor, Kathryn Ettinger, who helped ensure this book's accuracy by allowing me to include a number of late-breaking changes.

Back home in New Mexico, my furry feline and canine work assistants—Mary, Mister Grant, Foxxy, and Little Man—have provided constant cheer and warmth. And most important, I'd like to thank Michael Garcia, who has always been tremendously supportive, understanding, funny, and inspiring, through thick and thin.

www.moon.com

For helpful advice on planning a trip, visit www.moon.com for the **TRAVEL PLANNER** and get access to useful travel strategies and valuable information about great places to visit. When you travel with Moon, expect an experience that is uncommon and truly unique.

 HANDBOOKS | METRO | OUTDOORS | LIVING ABROAD

MAP SYMBOLS

▦▦▦ Expressway	**〖** Highlight	✗ Airfield	⚲ Golf Course	
▦▦▦ Primary Road	○ City/Town	✈ Airport	**P** Parking Area	
▦▦▦ Secondary Road	◉ State Capital	▲ Mountain	▲ Archaeological Site	
▫▫▫ Unpaved Road	❀ National Capital	+ Unique Natural Feature	▪ Church	
----- Trail	★ Point of Interest		🛢 Gas Station	
·········· Ferry	• Accommodation	↘ Waterfall	〰 Glacier	
▪▪▪ Railroad	▼ Restaurant/Bar	▲ Park	🗺 Mangrove	
▦▦ Pedestrian Walkway	▪ Other Location	❶ Trailhead	〰 Reef	
▥▥▥ Stairs	Λ Campground	⛷ Skiing Area	▥ Swamp	

CONVERSION TABLES

°C = (°F - 32) / 1.8
°F = (°C x 1.8) + 32
1 inch = 2.54 centimeters (cm)
1 foot = 0.304 meters (m)
1 yard = 0.914 meters
1 mile = 1.6093 kilometers (km)
1 km = 0.6214 miles
1 fathom = 1.8288 m
1 chain = 20.1168 m
1 furlong = 201.168 m
1 acre = 0.4047 hectares
1 sq km = 100 hectares
1 sq mile = 2.59 square km
1 ounce = 28.35 grams
1 pound = 0.4536 kilograms
1 short ton = 0.90718 metric ton
1 short ton = 2,000 pounds
1 long ton = 1.016 metric tons
1 long ton = 2,240 pounds
1 metric ton = 1,000 kilograms
1 quart = 0.94635 liters
1 US gallon = 3.7854 liters
1 Imperial gallon = 4.5459 liters
1 nautical mile = 1.852 km

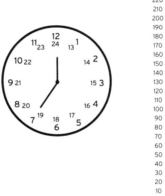

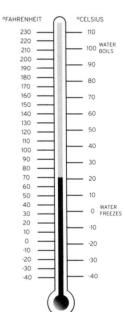

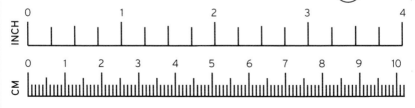

MOON NEW ORLEANS

Avalon Travel Publishing
An Imprint of
Avalon Publishing Group, Inc.

AVALON
publishing group incorporated

1400 65th Street, Suite 250
Emeryville, CA 94608, USA
www.moon.com

Editor and Series Manager: Kathryn Ettinger
Acquisitions Manager: Rebecca K. Browning
Copy Editor: Karen Gaynor Bleske
Graphics and Production Coordinator:
    Domini Dragoone
Cover Designer: Domini Dragoone
Cartography Manager: Mike Morgenfeld
Map Editor: Kevin Anglin
Cartographer: Kat Bennett
Proofreader: Marie Kent
Indexer: Judy Hunt

ISBN-10: 1-56691-931-2
ISBN-13: 978-1-56691-931-9
ISSN: 1546-4237

Printing History
1st Edition – 2004
2nd Edition – March 2007
5 4 3 2 1

KEEPING CURRENT

If you have a favorite gem you'd like to see included in the next edition, or see anything that needs updating, clarification, or correction, please drop us a line. Send your comments via email to feedback@moon.com, or use the address above.

Sacrificing Our Selves for Love

Why Women Compromise
Health and Self-Esteem…
and How to Stop

by Jane Wegscheider Hyman and

Esther R. Rome

In Cooperation with the Boston Women's Health
Book Collective

THE CROSSING PRESS
FREEDOM, CALIFORNIA

To Aunt Belle—the silence prevented her from reaching out in this life
—Esther R. Rome

To family, friends, and to J. F. H. and H. W.
—Jane Wegscheider Hyman

© Copyright 1996 by Jane Wegscheider Hyman and Esther R. Rome
Cover design by Amy Sibiga
Book design by Sheryl Karas
Cover photograph: © Ellen Shub 1995
Printed in the U.S.A.

Photo and illustration credits: p. 19, © Teresa Previte; p.25, © William Thompson/The Picture Cube; p.33, © Cathy Cade; p. 38, courtesy of The Pennsylvania Educational Network for Eating Disorders (PENED); p. 39, courtesy of Eating Disorders Awareness and Prevention (EDAP); p. 40, p. 45, © 1992, Andi Faryl Schreiber/Impact Visuals; p. 46, © 1993 Lynn Johnston Productions, Inc., distributed by Universal Press Syndicate, reprinted with permission, all rights reserved; p. 62, © 1995 Deirdre Lamb, tattoo by Chinchilla; p. 61, © Imaginative Illustration; pp. 80-81, photos of Roberta Blackgoat, Antonia Brico, and Roberta Menchú, © 1995 Ellen Shub; photos of Toni Morrison and Gro Harlem Brundtland, courtesy of Harvard University News Office; p. 83, © Marianne Gontarz; pp. 95, 100, 103, © 1991 Donna Ferrato/Domestic Abuse Awareness Project (NYC), from the book *Living with the Enemy* (Aperture); p. 96-97, adapted from the Domestic Abuse Intervention Project by Elba Crespo-Gonzalez; developed for Casa Myrna Vazquez, Inc. and sponsored by the Boston Healthy Start Initiative; p. 117, © 1992 Marian Henley, reprinted by permission of the artist; p. 136, © Esther R. Rome; p. 146, © Christine Bondante; p. 155, © Sal Lopes; p. 166, © 1995 Ellen Shub; p. 167, © Ed Howe; p. 180, courtesy of Wisconsin Pharmacal Company; p. 181, © Cathy Cade.

Library of Congress Cataloging-in-Publication Data
Hyman, Jane Wegscheider.
    Sacrificing our selves for love : why women compromise health and self-esteem-- and how to stop / by Jane Wegscheider Hyman and Esther R. Rome ; in cooperation with the Boston Women's Health Book Collective.
        p. cm.
    Includes bibliographical references (p.) and index.
    ISBN 0-89594-743-9 (paper)
    1. Women--United States--Psychology. 2. Women--Health and hygiene--United States. 3. Women--Abuse of--United States--Prevention. 4. Self-esteem in women--United States. 5. Self-help techniques--United States. I. Rome, Esther R. II. Boston Women's Health Book Collective. III. Title.
HQ1421.H96 1996
305.4--dc20   95-49713
                                                                                          CIP

ACKNOWLEDGMENTS

Our thanks to the following people who helped make this book possible by critiquing and editing the text; allowing us to learn from their experiences; and supplying us with their enthusiasm, encouragement, and advice: David Adams, Benita Adler, Kathleen Anneken, Lynn Artz, Byllye Avery, Miriam Avins, Ricardo Azziz, Elizabeth Beeson, William Bennett, Marge Berer, Annie Blais, Jessica Brantley, Melody Brazo, Jan Brin, Kate Cloud, Elizabeth Debold, Joan DiCato, Paula Doress, Kristin Engberg, J. P. Flatt, Anne Flitcrat, Judy Foreman, Candy Forster, Susan Foster, Linda Frazier, Rita Freedman, Rose E. Frisch, Betsy Frost, Dana Gallagher, Lynne Gay, Joanne Genet, Elaine Goldman Gill, John Gill, Sybil Goldrich, Anne Greenwood, Suzanne Guetter, Linda Gunnarson, Barbara Herbert, Dorrie Holmes, Peter Howley, James Hudson, Marcia Hutchinson, Charles Hyman, Jack Hyman, Peggy Schoditsch Hyman, Jenny Jones, Susan King, Suzanne Kuzmenka, Margaret Lazarus, Vicki Legion, Margorie Levenson, Paul Levenson, Beth Leventahl, Susan Levin, Jenna Luterman, Mary Maracek, Jean Baker Miller, Debi Milligan, Sonia Muchnick-Baku, Barbara Neustadt, Judy Norsigian, Jamie Penney, Jane Pincus, Kathy Price, Suzanne Repetto, Louise Rice, Tammy Richardson, Judah Rome, Micah Rome, Nathan Rome, Andee Rubin, Jama Russano, Wendy Sanford, Ellen Shub, Mildred Z. Solomon, Carole Sousa, Evan Stark, Judith Stein, Katherine Stone, Norma Swenson, Mary Waggener, Sonja Wetzsteon, Jill Wolhandler, Jane Sprague Zones, and Diana Zuckerman.

We also extend our thanks to the women of the Boston Women's Health Book Collective, their partners, and the BWHBC breast-implant support group; the women of Respond; and women from support group organizations from all over the United States.

We also thank the families of Temple B'nai Brith in Somerville, Massachusetts, the families of Cambridge Friends School, and everyone else who helped Esther Rome through her health crisis.

CONTENTS

CONTENTS

INTRODUCTION

This book is about the health hazards that can arise out of the need for love and acceptance, a theme that emerged as we researched and wrote about health issues of particular interest to women. To our surprise, in health problems as diverse as low-calorie dieting and other eating disorders; complications from cosmetic surgery; sexually transmissible diseases; and abuse and battering by partners, we found that women risk their health to appease, be liked, find approval, or feel loved.

As this theme became apparent, we realized how strongly the idea of pleasing others at any cost has been a part of our own lives. We both have memories, some of them uncomfortably recent, of giving in to a friend's suggestion, a partner's wish, or a physician's recommendation when our health and well-being would have required standing firm.

As we researched our topics, we saw that women's willingness to risk their health in order to be agreeable to others is a result of three intertwined forces: the caring attitude that characterizes many women; centuries of subordination; and cultural traditions about how we should look, behave, and be treated.

Traditionally, an important part of women's roles has been to accommodate, mediate, adapt, and soothe.[1] These are generally positive qualities, and they appear to be more common among women than men. The psychologist Carol Gilligan has shown that women define themselves in the context of relationships, and define morality in terms of their responsibilities to others.[2] Care and concern for others are part of our moral strength and form the basis on which we make many of life's decisions. For example, women tend to primarily value achievement that is not attained at someone else's expense. We are responsive to others' needs, listen to them, and include their points of view in our judgments. We recognize the importance of attachments in the cycle of life and perceive aggression as fracturing human connections. We want to prevent isolation and aggression, which oppose and jeopardize relationships.

These positive qualities can get us into trouble when combined with characteristics bred by women's subordination. As Jean Baker Miller writes:

Subordinates are...encouraged to develop personal psychological characteristics that are pleasing to the dominant group. These characteristics form a certain familiar cluster: submissiveness, passivity, docility, dependency, lack of initiative, inability to act, to decide, to think, and the like...If subordinates adopt these characteristics they are considered well adjusted...Moreover, subordinates who accept the dominants' conception of them as passive and malleable do not *openly* engage in conflict. Conflict...is forced underground.[3]

While young girls tend to speak freely, show anger, and accept differences as part of daily life, by the time we reach womanhood, we often negate our own thoughts and emotions to avoid conflict.[4] If we deny our own perceptions so that we no longer believe in our own experiences, we become easy prey to cultural traditions that tell us how we should look, behave, and be treated. When these traditions do not value women and their health—and they rarely do—our desire to please can endanger us. Also, if we do not believe in our own perceptions, we do not listen to our own voices or respond to our feelings and thoughts. The thought: "I'm *afraid* of having sex with this man" can be quickly censored to become: "If I refuse him or suggest condoms, his feelings will be hurt." "I'm *starving*!" becomes "I can't eat much, I'm already too fat." "This man *violated* me" becomes "I guess I led him on." Self-silencing leads to a sacrifice of our physical and emotional health as we deny our own inner voices and talk ourselves out of fear, hunger, and anger.

The need for money and security may make us dependent on a partner or employer, increasing our willingness to accommodate a person or adapt to a situation at the price of our health and emotional well-being. Yet, even those of us who feel independent and are financially secure often have difficulty standing up for ourselves and acting in our own interests.

This book examines a number of health problems that result from the pressures on women to conform to harmful cultural traditions. Side quotes throughout the book are excerpts from interviews by the authors or others with women who have experienced such pressures. Part I, "Trying to Look Different," discusses the health problems that arise from the belief that our bodies are ornaments (while men's bodies are instruments). For women, a major part of

being "agreeable" entails pleasing others by our appearance. We become used to being scrutinized, and instead of seeing our bodies as belonging to us, we tend to see our bodies as objects belonging to whoever is looking at us or making love to us. We think: "Is he repelled by my calves?" or "Does she admire my breasts?" We learn to look at our bodies with others' eyes and to listen to what other people and the media say about women's bodies. Many of us mold our faces and bodies at great cost to our bank accounts and health. Some eat as little as victims of famine or do not allow their bodies to digest food. Some seek surgery to reduce thighs, enlarge breasts, or make other physical changes. Though we are appalled when we read about foot binding or painful tattooing, we often do not see that with starvation diets and cosmetic surgery we also risk our health, and sometimes our lives, to look acceptable.

Part II, "Living in Abusive Relationships," discusses the great cost to women from the belief that men are supposed to "dish it out" (be strong and aggressive), and women are supposed to "take it" by enduring pain and maintaining relationships at any expense. Intimate abuse, both emotional and physical, partly arises from this splitting of roles. Since an abusive relationship is a caricature of the relationships we are encouraged to seek, women often do not recognize the beginning of abuse, mistaking coercive actions for the actions socially prescribed for men. Because we are encouraged to do the work of maintaining relationships, we may feel that a partner's mistreatment of us is evidence that we are not doing our jobs well enough.

Part III, "Dying for Love," discusses health problems that arise from the tradition that women should be receivers and men the initiators during heterosexual lovemaking. A "receiver" mentality can persist even when the partner is a woman. As subordinates in lovemaking, we are less likely to insist on protection against disease during sex, even though we are more likely than men to be infected from a single exposure to certain harmful organisms causing sexually transmissible diseases.

In all these areas—appearance, intimate relationships, and physical love—we are called upon to please by caring for others, putting their needs before our own, deferring to their wishes and opinions, and avoiding conflict, even when we are angry. Such consistent deference to others' wishes reveals that we do not take our own needs as seriously as the needs of others. Some of us experience this by feeling guilty or anxious if we do insist on something or refuse to do something solely for our own health and benefit. Some fear conflict because we are afraid of others' displeasure, disapproval, anger, and sometimes physical abuse.

However, with information and encouragement, we can counteract the social traditions that are detrimental to our health. We will be less likely to embark on a low-calorie diet when we know that starvation diets almost always leave us heavier, that body fat protects our fertility, and that the purges of bulimia can severely compromise our health. Fewer of us will choose cosmetic surgery and breast implants when we realize that an eyelid tuck might leave our eyes unable to close, that liposuction can leave puckers or kill skin, that our bodies never stop trying to reject implants, and that the silicone that leaks from implants may damage our immune system. We will be more likely to demand safer sex when we realize that we could suffer years of ill health, lose our fertility, or die from cancer, pelvic inflammatory disease, or AIDS as a result of unprotected sex. If we understand that abusive partners do not share our desire to achieve respectful intimacy, that they prefer to control us, we will not put energy into saving relationships that ruin our health and drain our spirit.

In our research, we identified a number of reasons why the information we need to save our health and lives is not always available. It suits some people to keep women ill informed about risks to their health. For example, drug companies that manufacture diet pills, dieting centers, and cosmetic surgeons profit from the risks women take, and they have actively challenged information that could help us make wise decisions. Better information for women would mean lower profits for them. Though significant progress has been made since the battered women's movement became active in the 1970s, all parts of society have been slow to recognize the extent of the problem and to take responsibility for eliminating the abuse of women. Indeed, the prevalence of women's abuse reflects the attitude that women exist for the convenience and pleasure of their partners, who are free to control them. And in the case of sexually transmissible diseases, women have traditionally been seen as reservoirs of disease, infecting men. More attention is given to how men are affected by some of these diseases, reflecting a subordination of women's needs to those of men. Better information for women would require rethinking attitudes about sexual morality and the importance of women's health. In all these areas, problems are frequently magnified for women of color and women who are poor. It is the authors' hope that this book will show readers that some women's health problems are embedded in unjust social arrangements.

Unfortunately, understanding health risks does not mean that we will safeguard our health. For this, we must learn to care for ourselves as well as for others, to take our own needs seriously, and to discourage our own self-sacrificial thoughts. Achieving a healthy self-assurance can be a difficult, lifelong process. Even women in the women's health movement are still teaching themselves not to be the objects of sacrifice—for example, the authors know a woman who teaches teenage girls how to insist that their male partners wear condoms, yet does not always insist that her own lovers wear them. We also know a woman who publicly advocates women's rights, then goes home to a partner who beats her. Nor have we achieved all the goals advocated here.

Yet, women can work toward better health, especially if we help each other. This book provides many of the tools. Each health problem is discussed along with the cultural traditions that encourage us to endanger ourselves and the larger context surrounding that choice. Other chapters tell what actions we can take to avoid or overcome these health problems. Self-esteem exercises are also included. The authors hope that this book will help empower you to protect your own physical and emotional health.

Jane Wegscheider Hyman
Esther R. Rome

Part I

Trying to Look Different

Self-Starvation

TRADITIONALLY, our culture has encouraged us to do everything possible to be attractive, even at the price of physical comfort, mobility, and health. Most of us see slenderness as the most important aspect of physical attractiveness. In search of an ideal slenderness, many women jeopardize their mental and physical health through severely restrictive low-calorie diets—that is, we starve ourselves. Self-starvation is widespread among U.S. women and can lead directly to other eating disorders, including compulsive overeating, anorexia, and bulimia. Approximately 95 percent of people who engage in self-starvation and suffer its consequences are women.[1] Severe calorie restriction is widely considered an acceptable way to try to change our bodies. Yet self-starvation—low-calorie dieting, anorexia, and bulimia—robs us of mental energy that would be better used in pursuing other goals. It also depletes physical energy and impairs our health, sometimes fatally. This chapter examines the social causes of self-starvation and explains how low-calorie dieting, anorexia, and bulimia can damage our health.

THE POWER OF SLENDERNESS

As women living in the Western world, we tend to have clearly defined images of the "ideal" female figure—and this ideal is extremely thin. For example, according to a major commercial diet center, a woman's average ideal weight is 20 pounds lower[2] than the average Metropolitan Life Insurance Company's[3] recommendation for optimal health. One survey of sophomore college women showed that three times more women strived for the thinner, cultural ideal weight than for a weight at which they would be healthiest and that women at the cultural ideal were more at risk for developing eating problems.[4] Even men tend to be more flexible than women in their views of a woman's acceptable size and weight.

Where does this "ideal" come from, and why do we strive so hard to reach it? As children and in our adult years we absorb the ideal through the images of thin women we see in movies, advertisements, and television shows. Slenderness is held up by the media as an ideal for all to

Restricting my food coincided with beginning to date and to explore sexuality with boys. I was very conscious of what my body looked like to boys, as an object to be desired, something to be wanted. At the time, the only way I felt desire in my body was to want to be wanted. I had no sense of what it was actually like to want somebody. I think that's what's given to girls: the power of the object, the power of passivity—a manipulative sort of power. But it was very powerful to be looked at. It completely blew me away to have boys looking at my body in a desirous way— wanting my body.

If I had grown up in the 1800s I would have the perfect body; you know, the curvy, voluptuous kind of body. And if today's society didn't admire thinness, I don't think that I would have developed an eating disorder. I think that there is an enormous amount of pressure—really, our society rewards the thin person, and when you're fat it's negative. And the thing that's weirdest for me is that I feel the fattest when I'm around women. Men I've met have been very accepting of my body. In a group of women, that's when I really feel like: "Oh, I wish I was as skinny as that girl over there."

achieve, and the message is strongly reinforced by the poor treatment and negative portrayal of fat women. We measure ourselves against an ideal because throughout our lives we are taught that we will be successful only if we look the "right way."

The Cultural Ideal

Magazines, movies, and television programs have played an important role in promoting an increasingly stringent ideal of thinness.[5] Every image of women that we see in magazines, on billboards, and on television suggests to us that sexual, social, and financial success come only to the very slender.

Although drawn, painted, or sculpted images of women are usually perceived as artistic creations, images of women on television and in magazines are usually considered realistic representations. Actually, though, a magazine model or television actress is often rigorously painted and sculpted. She undergoes hours of makeup and hairstyling, strict workout regimens, and perhaps self-starvation and cosmetic surgery. Her photographs are routinely touched up, further blurring the line between life and artifice. Since we are surrounded by these highly attractive media models, we see our bodies as woefully inadequate. If we try to "correct" our bodies and fail, we may feel desperate and continue rigorous dieting and exercise in an attempt to attain the lean muscularity prescribed for us. The more we try to reach this ideal, the more likely we are to develop an eating disorder.[6]

Changes in the beauty ideal for women often mirror social changes; ironically, when social rights are expanded, the ideal image tends to become unhealthfully slim. During the Victorian era, plumpness in women was considered pleasing (except for a slim waistline attainable only by wearing corsets of bone or steel). The shift in ideal from plump to slender began around 1920, at about the same time that the women's suffrage movement was gaining ground and the First International Birth

Control Congress was held. Thinness may have seemed a visible sign of the social message that women were no longer willing to be only maternal, reproductive figures. Simultaneously, the thin, straight line of the flappers became fashionable. To achieve this look, some women bound their breasts; others starved themselves. Again in the 1970s, as women began reasserting their rights in the public world and as more entered college and became professionals, the fashion line became thinner and straighter. Elizabeth Taylor's figure was considered the ideal in the 1960s, but by 1976 the 91-pound Twiggy had taken her place. Several high-fashion designers dressed women like men, with broad-shouldered, straight suits that masked curves. Curves suggest fertility, motherhood, and nurturance. The angular fashions of the 1970s suggested that only males—or male impersonators—could enter the world of professional workers and pursue the traditionally male goals of independence, personal achievement, and self-control.

In the late 1960s, the winners of the Miss America and Miss USA contests began to become taller but smaller, with decreasing bust and hips. Similarly, in 1951, Miss Sweden was 5 feet 7 inches tall and 151 pounds; in 1983, the winner was 5 feet 9 inches tall and weighed 109 pounds.[7] *Playboy* centerfold models have also changed shape. They have become taller and more linear, though their breasts remain large. In general, the ideal weight shown by the Miss America contest and *Playboy* is 13 to 19 percent below a woman's expected weight for her height and age.[8] This is a weight that we become ill trying to achieve, and one of the signs of anorexia nervosa.

Fashion models have followed this same trend. In 1894, the ideal fashion model was 5 feet 4 inches and weighed 140 pounds. By 1947 she had lost 15 pounds, and by 1975 she weighed only 118 pounds but had grown 4 inches taller.[9] Since the 1950s, fashion models have gradually become more linear, and by the early 1970s, a large bosom was less important than small buttocks. Reflecting this ideal, by 1986 women generally felt that our hips and thighs—but not our breasts—were too large.[10]

Female fashion models are an unusual size for women—tall and thin. In contrast, the male ideal is only a slightly exaggerated version of the norm for college men. Many female fashion models are genetically thin, and their actually unusual height and weight have led them to become fashion models. During times when breasts are "in fashion," the ideal woman's body is tall and thin with Marilyn Monroe-type breasts, a genetically improbable combination often requiring breast implants to achieve. Yet, because this image pervades the media, we do not perceive it as odd; instead, we endanger our health striving to achieve it.

In the 1980s, muscles became stylish. The "new woman" was not only thin but had firm, shapely muscles, like those of professional dancers or athletes. Her body suggested well-toned muscles rather than the fleshy softness traditionally associated with women's bodies, and her angularity was highlighted by broad shoulder pads. Thus, the fashion in body shape and clothes became increasingly at odds with the general biological shape of female bodies. In the 1990s, the basic message remains the same: We could all become as straight and lean as athletic boys with breasts if only we tried hard enough.

One survey shows that from 1982 to 1990, the number of articles on exercise alone and exercise combined with dieting surpassed even the number of diet articles.[11] In the future, exercise for weight loss and for a well-toned look may gradually replace dieting and purging as a method of trying to achieve the "ideal" figure. Significantly, excessive exercising is one of the compulsive habits that is a sign of anorexia nervosa or bulimia nervosa.

As the ideal has shrunk, the actual average weight of women under 30 in the general U.S. population has increased. The average U.S. woman is 5 feet 3.7 inches tall and weighs 144 pounds,[12] a far cry from the average 5 feet 8 inches, 123 pounds of fashion models.[13] In addition, we consistently overestimate our own body size, both our whole body and specific parts. This overestimation may be due to the extreme thinness of the "ideal" image we have internalized.

Learning about Looks and Food

The media's ubiquitous images of slim women might not be so harmful if we didn't learn from a very early age that our appearance is extremely important. Many women remember that some of the first comments they heard as children were about looks: "Oh, what a pretty dress!" or, "Look at those cute black curls." While such remarks are often loving, they begin to implant the idea that appearance is of primary importance in gaining attention and acceptance from others. We receive positive and negative comments about our faces and bodies throughout our lifetimes: remarks about developing breasts during puberty; casual comments about our faces, clothes, hair, body shape, and weight from family members, friends, and lovers. All reinforce the idea that for us to be loved and wanted, how we look matters more than what we think and do. Even a casual negative remark about our bodies can leave lifelong feelings of inadequacy or shame, especially if the remark is made in public.

Exposure to television, movies, and magazines teaches girls a strict ideal of the necessity of being thin and young. (In contrast, men portrayed in these media are more diverse, both in appearance and age.) By the third grade, many girls have begun feeling the pressure to be thin. Many begin dieting before adolescence, and dieting can be widespread in the fourth and fifth grades. Population samples suggest that the majority of girls have already been on a weight-loss diet before the age of 13.[14] Some girls diet out of a conviction that they are already fat; others fear gaining weight. One study of two hundred sixth-grade girls revealed that even some girls who perceive

Looking back at pictures of myself as a high school senior I realize that I was skinny then. But at the time, I thought that I had something to worry about. Partly, I think that it was the constant comparison, and the constant body watching that everybody engaged in. Not just people on the swim team, but in the school there were a lot of people constantly talking about their bodies and what they were eating and what they weren't eating, how many calories they had that day—all the time. But I think that what had more impact than anything else was that my mother would make comments about my body, saying, "You know, you're really going to have to watch it," or, "Do you really want that bowl of ice cream?" She would say things like that offhandedly. I talked to her about it years later, and she didn't even remember saying those things. But those comments were very undermining, and I don't even think she realized what she was doing.

—Woman who developed anorexia and bulimia

themselves as underweight say they restrict their food, exercise to lose weight, and are preoccupied with thoughts of food and eating.[15] Their goal is not to be thin, but to be ever thinner, and perhaps also to gain acceptance into a peer group of dieters. Dieting, and talking about diets, can become ways of making friends and of competing for other girls' attention and approval. For many young girls, counting calories and feeling guilty about eating "too much," or about eating anything, are standard aspects of food.

Girls tend to become increasingly sensitive to social expectations and to the opinions of others. At puberty, many are proud of their developing breasts and other signs of womanhood, but are dismayed at a normal increase in fat, especially the fuller hips and thighs so characteristic of women's bodies. Such changes can be particularly hard for girls who are tomboys and for those who are no longer the size or shape considered necessary for gymnastics or ballet. Some adolescent girls develop eating disorders when they lose weight through dance, gymnastics, or sports and try to maintain the lower weight; some are told to lose weight for these activities. Coaches and dance teachers can make brutal remarks and place unrealistic demands on young girls. Many girls and women mention such experiences as the precipitating events in their eating disorders. As adjuncts to diets or as independent weight-loss attempts, some adolescent girls fast, vomit, and use diet pills, laxatives, and diuretics, further jeopardizing their normal growth and distorting their eating habits, perhaps for a lifetime.

In two studies of adolescent schoolgirls in the United States, more than half who looked average in weight to others considered themselves too fat.[16] For many girls, feeling fat means feeling unattractive, unlovable, and insecure, and being afraid of being teased and being unpopular. The majority of adolescent girls and high school and college women want to lose weight regardless of what they actually weigh. One

survey showed that around 70 percent of college undergraduate and graduate women wanted to lose weight, even though 95 percent were within 10 pounds of the average weight for women of their height and frame.[17]

Studies from the 1980s suggest that about 23 percent of female students in the United States suffer from an eating disorder of some kind, not including low-calorie dieting.[18] The prevalence of all types of anorexia and bulimia appears to be rising. If low-calorie dieting were included among the eating disorders, these estimates would rise considerably.

Boarding schools and colleges often breed dysfunctional eating. A school environment can be competitive academically and socially, and living in close quarters may encourage a woman to compare her body with those of her housemates. In addition, when all three meals are abundant, often easily obtainable, and eaten in groups, students often gain weight. In fact, during their first year in college, women often gain about 15 pounds, and "You've gained weight!" may be the first thing a young woman hears from family members when she returns home for vacation. Young women then turn to the pervasive magazine articles and books on dieting—the "mass media manuals on how to develop an eating disorder."[19] Finally, in the close quarters of a college campus or boarding school, we often teach each other how to starve, binge, and purge.

Hobbies or professions that explicitly or implicitly require slimness can also accentuate our risk of an eating disorder. These include dancing, modeling, acting, and athletics. As one model said, "My job is to be thin."[20] Unless women who enter these professions are genetically extremely thin, they are at greater risk of developing dysfunctional eating than are women whose job performance is less related to appearance and weight.

In adulthood, extraordinary numbers of women engage in repeated dieting efforts.

Not surprisingly, those of us who have greater fat distribution in the hips and buttocks also report having the most problems with disordered eating. "I was bad today" has become our standard confession of enjoying more food than our diets allowed, of eating something sweet or rich, or of getting up from the table feeling full. Such a confession is usually followed by a vow to be "good" forever more. We fear the normal signal of hunger that the brain sends when our bodies require food. We think that we have no right to be hungry because we wrecked our diet the previous day and weigh "too much" anyway. We often become merciless judges of our own bodies and are determined to change the way we look in order to fit into the rigidly thin mold we are told is desirable. And when we are aware of the health hazards of food restriction, we may ignore the hazards because we feel so fat.

We have innumerable ways of restricting food learned from magazines, television advertisements, books, friends, weight-loss clinics, weight-loss camps, and physicians. Some of us skip breakfast and eat a frugal lunch so that we can have dinner without feeling guilty. Others consume diet drinks in place of meals. Some eliminate meat, cheese, and other high-fat food; or eliminate bread, potatoes, rice, pasta, and sweets; or restrict food on weekdays and gorge on weekends; or fast for a day or longer. We may try one or more of the innumerable weight-loss regimes, often using kitchen scales and tables of measurement to precisely dole out the food allotted to us by our diet. Some of us regularly take laxatives or force ourselves to vomit so that we can eat without gaining weight. Friends and family generally approve of our diets, considering a desire for thinness a natural part of being a woman.

One low-calorie diet often leads to many, each time with the belief that the regained weight was a personal failure; each time with renewed hopes and vows that the next diet will work. With such repeated damage to the body's normal signals of hunger and satiety, we may lose our ability to eat normally and develop disordered eating patterns, alternately restricting our food and eating in binges and purging. Such eating patterns are rampant among women.

The Effects of Culture, Race, and Class on Eating Habits

Exposure to the Western media and lifestyle seems to be a crucial risk factor for self-starvation. Some researchers state bluntly that the "epidemic" of eating disorders among women would not exist without our culture's thin ideal.[21] Surveys suggest that anorexia nervosa, the most severe form of self-starvation, exists mainly in North America and Western Europe, but not at all in Asia except among the Westernized upper middle class of Japan and Hong Kong. Even women from Hong Kong are still predominantly influenced by traditional Chinese culture, in which children are taught not to waste food, thinness is associated with ill health and bad luck, and "You have put on weight recently" is a compliment.

It is difficult to assess the prevalence of eating disorders among U.S. women of various income levels and cultural heritages because systematic studies are lacking. Women with higher incomes would seem more likely than poor women to emulate trends in attractiveness and fashion and therefore be at a higher risk of self-starvation. However, studies are conflicting. Some statistics show that eating disorders occur among U.S. women of all ethnic groups except those of Asian heritage; while other information suggests that many Asian women are affected. Some surveys suggest that more white women than African-American women in the U.S. consider themselves overweight, diet, binge-eat, purge, or suffer from anorexia nervosa or bulimia nervosa.

However, African-American and Latina women may get painfully mixed messages. Families and some friends may

I feel that dieting propagates itself almost. If one person's eating a certain way, like having a salad rather than meat for dinner, and the whole table's doing that, it's like a cult situation. In some groups that's common. It may influence you. You think: "Maybe I should try that too." Also, I think that cutting fats completely from your diet and exercising is very common, especially among educated young women at universities. It's like we try to be perfect in every sense: academically, the way we look, our health—and then it goes overboard.

—Woman who developed anorexia

I used to take it for granted that food and body were two of the most important things about being a girl, it's like the air you breathe. Food was the air we breathed: how much of it we had, how much of it we denied ourselves. Feeding ourselves was not just a natural part of life, it was this obsessive thing. When I look back at it now, it's surprising how unaware we all were about what was going on.

—Woman who developed anorexia and bulimia

adhere to traditions that consider different body shapes acceptable and beautiful, but some may associate thinness with "white" achievements, privileges, and social acceptance. If our schoolmates are predominantly white, we may be likely to absorb the thin body ideal; and if one or both parents have absorbed the body ideal of white U.S. culture, we are likely to feel pressure to be thin.

Economic status can also influence our families' and our own beauty ideals. One African-American woman remembers that in her family, when money was generally tight, having plenty of food, big meals, and being chubby were signs of being well off. As her family became middle class, her father began insisting that she and her mother be thin. "[I]f you were a truly well-to-do family then your family was slim and elegant."[22] Some families may continue to consider large meals and adequate food portions necessary to health, yet pressure girls to be thin. Those of us who emigrated from other countries may also remember childhoods when our families encouraged us to put on weight, but then, after emigration, they wanted thinness.

Thus, the longing for acceptance and opportunity in the United States can make the thin ideal seem supremely desirable and turn our bodies into battlefields to attain what seems like acceptance and prestige.

LOW-CALORIE DIETING

In view of the social influences surrounding us, it is not surprising that an overwhelming number of U.S. women of all ages feel too fat regardless of their actual weight. Because we equate thinness with attractiveness, many of us think that we cannot look our best and win approval or love unless we lose the fat that we perceive as "excessive." Consequently, fear of fat is pervasive among us.

At some point, a woman's attempts to control her weight involve severe restrictions on the number of calories she eats.

Our bodies interpret this as starvation. Diets of 800 calories a day or less are not unusual, especially for women who try liquid diets. Such deprivation is comparable to the most severe starvation during World War II, when people in the Warsaw ghetto and parts of western Holland subsisted on 600 to 800 calories per day.[23] (A diet of around 1000 calories per day has roughly the same effects as more severe starvation, but is rarely fatal.)

Low-calorie dieting, anorexia, and bulimia are all intense attempts to control the body's shape, and all are dangerous undertakings. Sufficient food and body fat are necessary for physical and mental health, and our bodies work hard to preserve themselves from deprivation or radical change.

The Experience of Starvation

Undernutrition can change body chemistry and affect physical and psychological functioning. Low-calorie diets can alter the functioning of the hypothalamus, which helps control sensations of hunger and fullness. As a result, the brain may lose some of its normal control of hunger and satiety: some women who have starved never feel hungry; some feel constantly hungry even if they have resumed eating meals that would have been filling in the past; some begin eating in uncontrollable binges.

Low-calorie dieters may also become fatigued, listless, hostile, aggressive, have fantasies and dreams about food and eating, have difficulty concentrating, and/or experience attacks of anxiety or depression. Both overweight and thin women are equally likely to have these symptoms of starvation while dieting.

The more restrictive a woman's diet, the more likely she is to crave food—especially "forbidden" food—and eventually give in. Binge eating is a normal reaction to starvation, not a lack of willpower. A study of men's reactions to food after a period of starvation showed that when they regained access to food, they gorged themselves and sometimes vomited. Some said

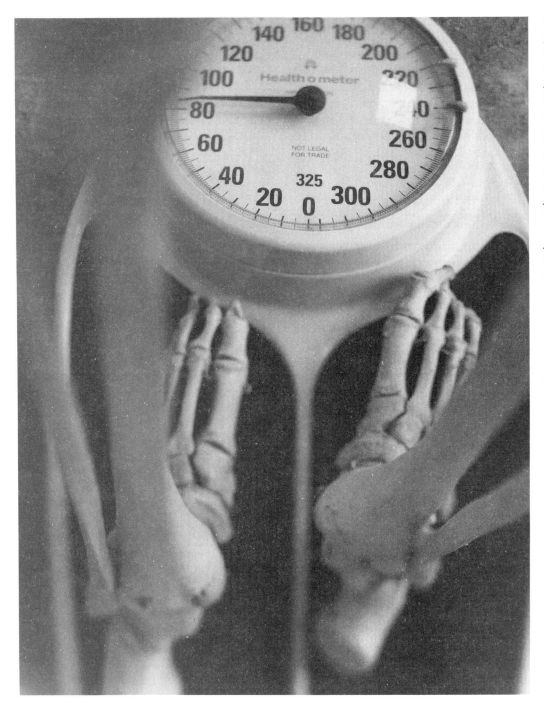

The summer after eighth grade I went to a dance camp. When I entered the camp I weighed 115 pounds. That was the first time in my life when I started to be body conscious. It was hard for me to be at this camp where there were all professional dancers and I was there because I was a very good friend of the director. He weighed us to make sure we were all the right weight for the performance at the end of the summer. He told me I had to lose 5 pounds. I was shocked that I wasn't the perfect body. I started eating less. And even though we danced all day, I would walk 3 miles down the mountain before class. And I started eating less and less and exercising more—and took it to extremes. By the end of the six-week summer I had cut my food down to 600 calories a day and weighed 90 pounds. No one even noticed that I had lost all that weight because everyone else looked so skinny.

—Woman who developed bulimia nervosa

that they were still hungry at the end of very large meals and ate as much as 7000 to 10,000 calories per day.[24] They also tended to eat snacks between meals and in the evening, and to get up at night to eat.

Similar experiences are common among women. Many of us who have dieted recently or in the past now eat feeling that we have lost the control to stop. We eat in compulsive binges accompanied by guilt and distress, a form of eating called compulsive eating or binge eating. Other women binge eat and then make themselves vomit or take diuretics to avoid adding pounds. Some women binge eat and rely on severely restrictive diets, complete fasts, or vigorous exercise in order to keep their weight down. Often women caught in such cycles gain and lose 10 or 15 pounds in a week or two.

When the cells do not receive enough fuel to burn from food, they feed on both body fat and other sources of calories, such as muscles. A starving woman loses significant amounts of fat-free body weight, especially muscle protein. Even in moderate undernutrition there is a loss of muscle tissue—including the heart muscle—and a loss of tissue in all organs except the brain.

When a woman diets, her body uses food more efficiently. To conserve sparse energy, the body lowers the rate at which it normally uses calories, called basal metabolism, by 15 to 40 percent. This has the same effect on weight as eating up to 600 more calories per day,[25] making weight loss progressively slower, until the person reaches a plateau and weight loss stops, at least for a while.

The body will continue to react to starvation even after a woman begins to feed her body adequately. Basal metabolism rises cautiously—and the less food, the slower the rise—taking up to five months or longer to return to normal. Consequently, a little bit of food goes a long way, and a woman usually regains weight rapidly until it exceeds her predieting level. With repeated self-starvation, weight loss becomes increasingly slower and weight regain increasingly faster. Some researchers refer to this inevitable result of low-calorie diets as weight-cycling or yo-yo dieting. Although many of us have experienced this yo-yo effect and have read about it, we often believe that we will be exceptions—that the next diet will work.

All women add more body fat after starvation, including those of us who were very fat to begin with. Apparently, if the body is starved once, it protects itself by storing extra energy in the form of fat in case food should become scarce again.

The repeated weight fluctuations that result from dieting efforts can increase a woman's risk of death from coronary heart disease and of premature death from all causes, no matter what she weighed before she began dieting. In addition, dieters can become dehydrated because their bodies can no longer conserve water properly; or they can develop diabetes insipidus (a disorder of the pituitary gland which causes a person to become intensely thirsty and to excrete large amounts of urine). Body temperature can begin to fail in its response to heat and cold, making a woman more vulnerable to extreme temperatures. Bones may also be affected. Some women who cut their calories by 50 percent and lose weight also lose some of their bone mass, even when they exercise regularly and take calcium and other nutritional supplements.[26] Their bones may or may not return to normal when they regain their weight. At present, no one knows how great the effects of yo-yo dieting may be on a woman's risk of osteoporosis.

Premenopausal women who lose more than 10 to 15 percent of their standard weight for height may cease menstruating or stop ovulating.[27] Rapid weight fluctuations can also stop ovulation. In a young girl, severe low-calorie dieting can delay her first menstrual cycle to as late as 20 years of age.[28] Binge eating and purging can cause women to stop menstruating and become temporarily infertile, even when their weight is considered average for their height and age. One study showed that 17 percent of women who went to an infertility clinic for treatment had anorexia nervosa, bulimia nervosa, or other eating problems related to self-starvation.[29] Among infertile women who had either ceased menstruating or had excessive menstrual bleeding, 58 percent were found to be practicing self-starvation or suffering from its aftermaths.[30] Physicians who work with women who are trying to conceive may be unaware of the prevalence of self-starvation or its possible effects on our fertility.

The Role of Body Fat

The experience of low-calorie dieting shows us that the body is remarkably protective of its fat. Body fat is not a useless mass that we can add or carve off without consequences. Fat stores energy, protects organs, and may be crucial to our ability to bear children.

Body fat, or adipose tissue, is made up of highly complex fat cells (adipocytes). We have about 30 billion fat cells, each of which contains a droplet of fat.[31] The parts of our bodies that are not fat contain mainly water; adipose tissue consists mainly of fat droplets. Fat cells specialize in storing, releasing, and regulating energy. Fats from the food we eat pass through the gut and travel in the blood to adipose tissue, where they enter the fat cells. Fat cells use fat for their own energy requirements, or, more often, transform the fat into a droplet of triglyceride that can be released if the body needs extra energy.[32] If more fat is repeatedly stored than is needed for energy, the fat cells expand. If they have already expanded to their utmost size, new fat cells may be formed to store the fat.

Our muscles store smaller amounts of readily available energy as glucose. If we eat more than we immediately require as energy, the rest is deposited as fat in adipose tissue, like money in a bank. Fat has a higher energy density than carbohydrate or protein and is therefore the most efficient way of storing energy. When we require more energy than is immediately available in our muscles, our bodies mobilize energy from our fat stores.

Research now suggests that once fat cells increase in number, dieting will not reduce them. Animal studies show that even extreme methods, such as lifelong semi-starvation or intestinal surgery, do not alter the areas of an animal's body that contain the most fat, even though the animal loses weight.

Body fat also helps produce and store the sex hormones that control our fertility. Fatty tissue in the breast, abdomen, omentum (the "apron" of fat in the abdomen), and the fatty marrow of the long bones can all produce estrogen, the female sex hormone. In addition to its effects on our reproductive organs, estrogen produced by fat tissue regulates bone metabolism, the synthesis of vital proteins in the liver, and to some extent, even behavior. For girls and for women who have reached menopause, fat is the primary source of estrogen. During our fertile years, between the first menstrual cycle and the last, the ovaries produce the most estrogen, but roughly a third comes from body fat, with important consequences for our sexual development.[33]

As they grow, girls experience a 120 percent increase in fat compared to only a 44 percent increase in lean tissue.[34] By the time growth is completed, women's bodies, if well nourished, contain about 26 to 28 percent fat. (By contrast, a man's full-grown body contains only 12 to 14 percent fat.)[35] All girls gain about 10 pounds of fat between their first menstrual cycle (menarche) and age 18.[36] This weight gain coincides with the completed growth of the ovaries, uterus, and oviducts; it also coincides with an increase in our fertile menstrual cycles in which the ovary releases an egg (ovulation).

A signal from the hypothalamus is necessary for menarche, and it seems to give its signal once it receives a message that the body has enough stored energy to meet the demands of pregnancy, birth, and lactation. In other words, our high percentage of body fat appears to be necessary for fertility. How the hypothalamus receives its signal is unclear; it may be through estrogen. Estrogen levels gradually rise along with body fat during puberty. And the estrogen in body fat accelerates the secretion of other hormones necessary for a fertile menstrual cycle. Thus, women who are fatter than others during adolescence tend to develop breasts and begin menstruating relatively young, and those who are very lean reach menarche later.

A full-term pregnancy requires about 50,000 to 80,000 calories more than a woman's normal energy needs, and breast-feeding requires from 500 to 1000 extra calories a day.[37] Women's bodies store the equivalent of approximately 144,000 calories—enough energy for pregnancy and about three months lactation even in times of food scarcity. In earlier times, and in some cultures today, when food is scarce or the supply fluctuates seasonally, stored energy is essential for the survival of both mother and child.

Women's reproductive systems are extremely sensitive to alterations in the environment, including the effects of crowding, travel, weight change, starvation, and severe stress of any kind. Body fat appears to be an important control of the "fertility switch"—a loss of the critical minimum of fat can result in infertility. Adding or losing fat is the body's efficient way of regulating itself for the differing demands of life. Accordingly, when a woman experiences a pronounced drop in weight through self-starvation, or engages in prolonged, intense physical training, she can become less fertile and even temporarily lose her ability to bear children. A high proportion of well-trained dancers and athletes have irregular cycles or cease menstruating entirely. These women may weigh as much or more than their fertile peers, but they are quite lean, their weight coming from muscle rather than fat. If a girl begins physical training before menarche, her first period can be delayed. In contrast to the usual average age of 12.6, young girls in training do not have their first menstrual periods until they are 15 years old, on average, and occasionally not until they are 19 or 20.[38] Usually, when a woman starts eating more, stops training, or reduces the intensity of her training, her cycles will return. However, she may not ovulate if she is still very lean, and she will need to gain more weight to achieve fertility.[39]

Fat and Heredity

Yet, these important roles of body fat do not explain why some of us are fatter than others. Many people think that fatness is a result of overeating—a reprehensible lack of self-control. In fact, our genetic makeup plays a far more important role than the amount of food we eat.

While studies find no consistent difference between the eating habits of fat and lean women, studies of families show a strong resemblance between parents and children in size and shape that cannot be explained by the food on the dinner table. Adopted children tend to resemble their biologic parents, especially the mother, regardless of their own eating habits. This genetic influence on our size and shape appears to increase with age, so that we are more likely to look like a parent toward the later years of our lives than during our youth. Even a woman's tendency toward fatness in certain limbs or body parts appears to be inherited.

Nonetheless, we do not inherit fatness, we inherit a susceptibility to fatness that may be brought out by our surroundings and way of life. For example, we may inherit a tendency to become fat without a lifestyle that demands high-energy activities. In the United States, we have numerous energy-saving devices, such as indoor plumbing, and many of us earn a living through activities that require sitting or standing still most of the day.

Some of us appear to be born with a particularly efficient use of the food we eat so that we use less of it as energy and store more of it as fat. This type of thrift is found among Pima Indians in the United States and among Aborigines who live in arid regions, where energy efficiency is essential to survival. When these peoples are exposed to a Western-style diet and easy access to food, they are highly susceptible to extreme fatness and to fat-related health problems.[40] In one study, people were intentionally overfed for fourteen weeks. Identical twins in the study gained at about the same rate, but unrelated people gained from 9.5 to 29 pounds on the same number of calories.[41]

Many of us apparently inherit a tendency to become fat unless we eat mainly fat-free food. When we eat food consisting mainly of complex carbohydrates or proteins, our bodies normally adjust by using these nutrients as fuel; when we eat fat foods, our bodies store the fat as body fat. Body fat is so closely associated with dietary fat that a fat cell's contents reflect the fat content of our diet. If we lower the fat in our diet, we are likely to lose weight, even if we do not restrict the total number of calories we eat. However, the amount of weight a woman loses and whether or not she keeps it off will vary depending on the extent and duration of the reduction in dietary fat, exercise habits, previous dieting attempts, age, current weight, her body's production of insulin, and her genetic tendency to be fat or lean. Population studies support the connection between high dietary fat intake and large amounts of body fat, although increased consumption of starches and sugars, decreased physical exercise, and a rise in yo-yo dieting may also have contributed to the rise in body fat.

Some women may inherit more brown fat, a somewhat mysterious, liver-colored fat that usually accounts for less than 1 percent of body weight. Brown fat is extremely important in maintaining the normal temperature of vital organs. Since this task requires energy, a trivial difference in a woman's amount of brown fat could have a profound influence on the rate at which her body uses energy. A mere 50 grams difference in brown fat could mean that one woman maintains her weight while another gains many pounds a year.[42] This might help explain why some women gain weight on the same meals that keep other women lean, and why some of us who are thin have trouble adding body fat.

A tendency to store fat rapidly after meals may run in families due to an increased activity of lipoprotein lipase, an enzyme in body fat. This enzyme is important for the storage of fatty acids derived from triglycerides. This genetic trait also helps explain why some of us add much more body fat in response to eating fats than do other women.

These inherited traits determine each woman's "setpoint weight," the weight range and body build that is uniquely her own. Our bodies strive to maintain their approximate setpoint, whether or not that setpoint corresponds to the medical world's version of "ideal weight," the culture's ideal of beauty, or our own standards of physical attractiveness.

ANOREXIA AND BULIMIA

Many of us, especially in our younger years, ignore or know nothing about the idea of setpoint weight. Enthusiastic about losing weight, we embark on low-calorie diets without realizing how little we eat, or noticing how much weight we lose.

Before we realize what we are doing to our health, food restriction has become a way of life. We may begin to dread the meals we eat with our parents for fear that they will encourage us to eat more or be angry because we only "pick" at our food. Sometimes we reduce our social life to avoid getting into situations in which we will feel obliged to violate a diet.

Articles we read on health and fitness extol the benefits of eating precisely the food we eat: fruits, salads, and low-fat yogurt, and of avoiding high-fat foods. Even our families' and peers' health-conscious eating, in itself positive and well meant, can fuel our extreme caution with food. Exercise, which countless magazines tell us is good for our health and burns calories, becomes an additional way to diet. We may adhere to an exercise regimen, not for the love of a sport or of movement, or even for improved health, but for the hope of weight loss.

During my junior year in high school, I went on a diet. I ate a lot of fruit, a lot of nonfat yogurt, a lot of salad, and just half of whatever I used to eat of chicken or meat. At first everyone said "Oh, you look so great! How did you do it?" Then after months, people started saying: "That's enough already," and people started telling me I looked sick. I wasn't looking healthy anymore, and I recognized that, and my periods had stopped. By my senior year I realized that this was a problem and that it was destructive. I went for a checkup, and my doctor said that I had to gain weight. I did gain some weight, but I didn't really feel like I needed to. I think I wanted to have an eating disorder. I didn't think that that was a terrible thing.

When I started college, I was down to 1000 calories a day. I started rowing crew. And the amount of energy you use when you do that is enormous. There's no way you can't eat—you would die. So, all of a sudden, my body, which was in this starvation mode, had to eat. And I gave into that impulse to eat. I began to eat—and I couldn't stop myself from eating. I ate, and ate, and ate. I think some smarter part of my body was saying: "Feed yourself, God damn it!" But it was very frightening. I didn't know how to control it, and I was completely freaked out about it. And I gained a lot of weight. I think that a lot of the weight I needed to gain, but it really freaked me out how big my body got. I tried to counteract it. At first, I purged by just exercising enormously even outside the regular crew work: I would go running, ride the bikes—in a totally crazed state. I didn't know how to eat moderately, I didn't know how to exercise moderately, I didn't know how to do anything moderately. That's the whole bulimic approach to life. But it got to the point that it was so bad I couldn't control it with exercise anymore, and I would purge by throwing up.

Even if we have lost enough to be pleased with our looks, we want to maintain our lower weight and fear that we will regain the pounds we lost unless we continue to starve ourselves. The experience of having lost weight and of having "control" over our weight makes us reluctant to eat more even if we notice that we look sick or emaciated. This type of eating disorder is called subclinical anorexia, or simply anorexia. It afflicts far more women than the severer types of anorexia, and some of us equate it with "successful" dieting and do not see it as a condition to be feared or avoided.

Some women don't allow their bodies to use the food they do eat. Perhaps a peer says that she occasionally sticks a spoon or finger down her throat and forces herself to vomit after a meal in order to keep her weight down. We may try this method and think, at first, that it is an easier way of reducing calories than dieting. Others use laxatives or diuretics to purge the body of partially digested food. For those of us who are, or have been, on restrictive diets, vomiting and purging may be done in desperation after finishing the enormous meals we often cannot help ourselves from eating when we are starving, or when we cannot seem to feel full no matter how much we eat. These types of calorie restrictions are called subclinical bulimia; they are also strikingly common.

Anorexia Nervosa

Women who tend toward highly obsessive thoughts and compulsive actions are particularly at risk when they diet. True obsessions are beyond voluntary control; when women who are susceptible to them feel fat and diet, their diets can be life-threatening. Society's emphasis on thinness can apparently encourage such women to focus obsessively on their appearance and to begin a lengthy and severely restrictive diet.

Usually, such a severe starvation process begins during adolescence when a girl tries to lose weight and develops a preoccupation with dieting. Compulsive dieting may replace normal eating patterns and, simultaneously, she may feel irritable, hopeless, or depressed, and even consider or attempt suicide. Depression may be part of her susceptibility to obsessive thoughts, but it could also be caused or exacerbated by the effects of self-starvation. Researchers distinguish anorexia—and bulimia—accompanied by a tendency toward highly obsessive thoughts and actions by adding the term *nervosa*. Thus, the extreme form of anorexia described here is called anorexia nervosa. The thoughts and behaviors of girls or women who develop anorexia nervosa are often quite similar to those of women with subclinical anorexia, only much more intense. Food and weight become her obsessions, and her fear of body fat is so great that she continues to starve herself after a pronounced drop in weight. She may continue to feel fat or to consider parts of her body fat even if she becomes so emaciated that she must be hospitalized. Even her fear of death does not outweigh her fear of fat. Hospitalized women in advanced stages of starvation have sometimes emptied their intravenous bottles while the nurse's back was turned. Approximately 5 percent of women with this obsessive fear of fat die of self-starvation.[43]

Not surprisingly, those of us afflicted with anorexia nervosa have our own standards for thinness: Can I put a ruler on both hip bones without having the ruler touch my abdomen? Do my legs have dimples on them? Do the inner surfaces of my thighs touch while I am standing? It doesn't matter what others say, or what the scales reveal about size and weight.

Often we find a part of our bodies grossly out of proportion: a stomach that sticks out, "excessively" wide hips. We believe these parts fat, lacking in muscle tone, and disgusting even when others find our bodies quite normal. Often we are painfully self-conscious, and think that any whispering in our presence is about our weight or that any glances are because we look

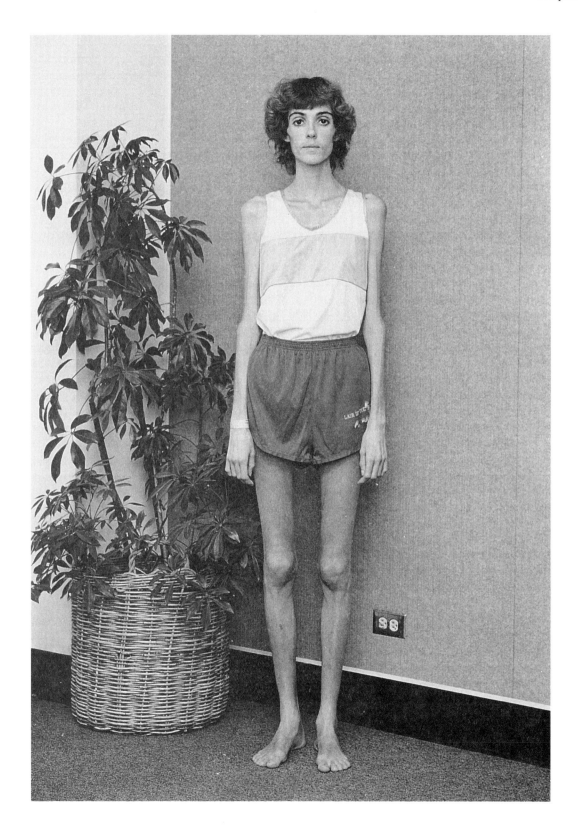

"gross." Sometimes, we avoid social outings where we think that our bodies will be scrutinized, or avoid letting a lover see or touch parts of our bodies that we find repugnant. Our self-esteem is low, we think that we are "bad," and we have an extreme dread of being rejected or abandoned.

Many women with anorexia nervosa eat much of the time to assuage chronic hunger, stretching even a few lettuce leaves over one or two hours. Others consume quantities of green vegetables, salads, and fruits, sometimes supplemented by daily vitamins, while disallowing any bread, rice, pasta, potatoes, sweets, or fatty foods. In such cases, the afflicted woman's friends may not recognize the signs of anorexia nervosa, especially since a woman who has anorexia nervosa is likely to hide her hunger and her motive for not eating normally.

Women who are starving during a food shortage become increasingly fatigued, weak, and listless; in contrast, women with anorexia nervosa are extremely active because of their fear of fat. They often have intense exercise regimens, such as running 5 or 10 miles a day or doing lengthy aerobic activities. Exercise can become an additional compulsion. Some women with anorexia nervosa become reluctant to sit down, fearing that the inactivity of sitting will cause weight gain. In extreme cases, the intensity of her fear can cause a starving woman to pace ceaselessly.

When women with anorexia nervosa do allow themselves to eat, sometimes they find that they can eat only in binges. As discussed earlier, binge eating is a natural consequence of starvation. To avoid weight gain, a woman who has anorexia nervosa and binge eats makes sure that her body cannot absorb the food. After the binge, she forces herself to vomit by sticking a finger or utensil down her throat, or she brings on diarrhea and extreme urination by taking laxatives and diuretics. She may do both. Instead of eating three meals a day, she may severely restrict food during the day, binge eat for several hours in the

middle of the night, and then purge with large amounts of laxatives. A woman who has anorexia nervosa and also binge eats and purges has bulimic anorexia nervosa. About half of the women who have anorexia nervosa are also bulimic.

Bulimia Nervosa

Some women with a tendency to obsessive behavior develop an extreme form of bulimia—eating in compulsive and uncontrollable binges, then vomiting or purging. They fear that they will be unable to stop eating and actually feel unable to stop. Often they are anxious or depressed and consider suicide. Virtually all who suffer from this type of binge eating are obsessively preoccupied with food and with body shape and weight, and all were once stringent dieters. This form of severe binge eating accompanied by profound psychological disturbances is called bulimia nervosa.

A woman with bulimia nervosa generally binge eats several times a day or week. An eating binge usually involves high carbohydrate, and often high-fat, sweet foods such as ice cream, cookies, bread, or candy, exactly the foods that she has denied herself. She may eat as many as 5000 calories during a single binge, vomit, and immediately start again. In a severe case, a woman may binge eat and vomit ceaselessly for hours, consuming 50,000 calories of food at a cost of $100 or more.

Vomiting, diarrhea, and urination cause the body to lose large amounts of water, and those of us with bulimia nervosa like the sensations associated with dehydration. These sensations include feeling washed out, drained, or empty; having loose clothes; having a flat abdomen; having protruding bones (especially cheek or hip bones): and feeling light or lightheaded. We usually dislike any sensation associated with a normal balance of body water. When we step on the scale, as we constantly do, we are frightened by the "added" weight of water, which makes us feel fat. Many of us who have bulimia nervosa abhor any sensation of food in the stomach—for us, starvation is the ideal state. We see ourselves as having failed to become or remain anorectic.

Some women do not binge in the usual sense, but vomit after eating any food, even a single cookie. For these women, eating a cookie, or eating a meal that others would consider normal, constitutes a "binge." Other women binge eat only during their sleep, a phenomenon called sleep binge eating, or somnambulistic eating. Those of us who binge while asleep are always women who are trying to diet and are very concerned about our weight, and some have had anorexia nervosa. During the night we may get up several times and walk to the kitchen to get food, yet upon awaking the next morning have no recollection of having eaten during the night. We realize that we have eaten only because we notice missing food and disarray in the kitchen. The nightly food may include items we would not eat while fully conscious, such as raw bacon and unpeeled oranges. Some women binge during their sleep over a period of fifteen years or more and, in desperation, finally have themselves locked out of their own kitchens at night.

The Hazards of Anorexia and Bulimia

Women who suffer from anorexia or bulimia face the same health risks as women on self-starvation diets, but some of the risks are intensified. They are more likely to have trouble with dehydration, diabetes insipidus, vulnerability to heat and cold, bone loss, and fertility.

Anorexia nervosa can have serious health effects related to the body's essential nutrients and lack of body fat. A woman can lose her sense of taste, especially bitter and sour tastes. Her heart rate, blood pressure, and body temperature may fall, and she may develop abnormal heart rhythms. The fatty marrow of her bones can disappear and be replaced by a gel, and the bones themselves may become more brittle,

predisposing her to fractures. Preliminary research suggests that anorexia nervosa can leave a woman with bones that are permanently compromised, increasing her risk of fractures even if she regains weight.[44] When anorexia nervosa occurs in a young girl, the lack of fatty marrow can result in permanently stunted bones.

Cycles of binge eating and purging can also cause tooth erosion and tooth loss, disruption of the body's metabolism, spasmodic seizures of the jaw muscles, inflammation of the salivary glands, kidney damage, and, in rare cases, rupture of the stomach and esophagus. Large doses of laxatives and diuretics can deplete the body of potassium and sodium. Some women have been poisoned by a plant extract called ipecac, which is used to induce vomiting. The crucial ingredient in ipecac is emetine, which in large doses can harm muscle tissue, including the heart muscle. Some women die as a result of using ipecac hundreds or thousands of times. A woman who is emaciated through anorexia and who also binge eats and purges can develop abnormalities of the heart, liver, and blood.

Two of the most pernicious drugs used for weight loss are tobacco and heroin. Cigarette companies use images of thin women to promote their products, and some have created cigarette brands aimed exclusively at women. Smoking increases the body's metabolism, so that people who quit often gain weight when their metabolism returns to its normal rate. Also, the difficulty of quitting often leads people to eat more. Cigarette companies use this knowledge in their advertising by suggesting that a woman can become or stay thin by smoking. Some women refuse to give up smoking or take up the habit with the sole aim of avoiding weight gain. Some women even take heroin to lose weight and suffer simultaneously from drug addiction, anorexia, and bulimia.

Over-the-counter diet pills may also be harmful, although their reported effects are disputed. Some studies report addiction to diet pills, anxiety, and high blood pressure if the pills are taken in large amounts. Some think that pills containing phenylpropanolamine (PPA) can be especially dangerous, in extreme cases causing cerebral hemorrhage, vasculitis, inflammation of the blood vessels, and even death, in addition to the effects already mentioned. Although the validity of reports of such extreme consequences is disputed, in 1991 PPA accounted for more reports of adverse drug reactions than any other popular over-the-counter drug, with people as young as 10 years old being affected.[45] The Food and Drug Administration requires a label on diet pills containing PPA, warning that people who have hypertension, heart disease, diabetes, or thyroid disease should not take the pills. However, many of us may have such conditions without knowing it, may not read warnings, or may read such warnings and ignore them. One survey of college women showed that 40 percent had taken pills containing PPA and many ignored label recommendations on dosage and took larger amounts than advised.[46] In spite of diet pills' possible health hazards, they are available throughout the United States with no age restrictions.

FIGHTING BACK

As more women and researchers realize that dieting is not a trivial problem and that unhealthful food restriction can cause a lifetime of problems, more of us are actively opposing thinness and body "control" as requirements for social acceptance. Our opposition will have to be long and strong. Fatness is still seen as a visible sign of a person's laziness, slovenliness, gluttony, and general lack of self-control. U.S. women who veer widely from the thin ideal are heavily penalized.[47] Even when young girls are brought up to feel positively about their looks, they may not be able to withstand social prejudice against fatness or media images of how they "should" look.

Prevention can be effective nonetheless. For example, some companies have stopped supporting weight-management programs that teach their employees to eat according to a diet plan. When Conoco, a Houston-based oil company, ceased offering traditional weight-loss seminars to its employees, binge eating dropped dramatically.[48]

Ideally, prevention should begin in elementary school, with educational programs that reveal the social influences behind our unrealistic and unhealthy weight and body image goals. (Adolescent smoking prevention programs that are based on methods for resisting social influences can serve as models.) Humorous films, skits, and comic books illustrating the absurdity and monotony of a uniform size and shape for all girls are some ways to reach young girls (and boys) in school. For young adolescents, illustrated novels with full-figured protagonists would be helpful, accompanied by classroom discussions about the pressures and rewards for being thin and the punishments for fatness. Similarly, slide shows can illustrate the manipulations of women's bodies for "beauty's" sake in other centuries and other cultures: for example, corsets, foot binding, neck or lip stretching, facial tattooing, and other practices. Such examples can be powerful—they allow us to relate other cultures' practices that we generally perceive as odd, outrageous, or unhealthy to our own culture's "beauty" practices that we often accept.

To prevent dysfunctional eating, it would be beneficial to have many skilled and well-informed teachers, counselors, and medical practitioners promoting and conducting prevention programs. Some positive action is already visible among health and medical practitioners. For example, a group called A-Help (the Association for the Health Enhancement of Large Persons) includes dieticians, nurses, physicians, therapists, and health educators who reject dieting and weight loss and promote healthy living patterns and self-acceptance. Unfortunately, many professionals still have misconceptions about what factors actually determine a woman's fatness and leanness, and many are ignorant of the danger of low-calorie diets to our mental and physical health. In fact, doctors sometimes unwittingly trigger anorexia and anorexia nervosa by putting teenage girls on diets. In general, many physicians and other medical professionals lack adequate knowledge of healthful nutrition. Some prestigious medical schools have only recently added nutrition to their basic curriculum requirements.

Therefore, it is important for those of us who are concerned and well informed to organize programs on our own or to create individual projects for the sake of our health and the health of our daughters. In addition, some women who have recovered from an eating disorder are giving talks at schools or in other public settings in order to alert other girls and women to the dangers of concern with weight. For example, according to a woman who recovered from anorexia nervosa:

I think that every school should have some kind of program that gets into more detail and explains eating disorders a little bit better, so that kids don't just ignore it. Last week I went to Marlborough High School, and next week I'm going to Lexington. I was nervous at first, and thought: "Oh, I'm not going to sit in front of all those kids and keep talking. I'm going to run out of things to say!" I didn't. I told them my whole life story, and they asked me questions. And they all wrote me thank-you notes, piles and piles of thank-you notes. I made a lot of friends. And it helps me too because the more I talk about it, the more I don't want to slip back into it.

Others are joining groups of concerned lay and professional women to discuss and carry out prevention strategies. These groups sometimes include women in recovery and family members and friends of afflicted women, as well as concerned

In school, it seemed like everybody was dieting, and even the people that weren't dieting were worrying about it. It was the constant subject of conversation—with no consciousness that it was a problem that this was so much on our minds. Looking back on it, I'm really angered that the teachers heard all of this "girl-talk" about food and bodies and didn't realize that they should help us become conscious by saying: "Don't you think that this is on your minds too much? Why is this so critical to you?"

—Woman who developed anorexia and bulimia

therapists, counselors, social workers, physicians, teachers, and nurses. (See "Resources" for a list of organizations.) Ideally, such groups could eventually work with representatives of the media, such as scriptwriters, photographers, program directors, journalists, and others to change media images to reflect the diversity of our bodies. In addition, such groups could write forceful letters of concern to manufacturers of consumer goods that promote the thin ideal in their advertisements.

Individually, in small groups, or as part of a national effort, we can help to:

➢ Educate parents and other caregivers on the possible harmful effects of restricting a daughter's calories, suggesting that she diet, making unfavorable comments about her size or weight, or making self-disparaging remarks about their own weight or eating habits.

➢ Educate coworkers, teachers, media representatives, social workers, and representatives of religious organizations about the hazards of restricted eating.

➢ Educate medical-care personnel on the possible harmful effects of advocating weight loss and on the harmful effects of low-calorie diets, weight-loss drugs, diet products, diet clinics, and "fat farms," all of which many doctors still endorse.

➢ Alert sports coaches and dance teachers to the dangers of emphasizing thinness or requiring weight loss.

➢ Boycott products whose advertisements exclusively feature thin women or imply slimness in their brand names or advertisement texts.

➢ Ban weight-loss programs, clubs, and clinics that advocate low-calorie diets. These programs promote products and services that bring in more than $30 billion dollars per year in sales by making misleading and deceptive claims and often pretending to be staffed by "experts."[49]

➢ Lobby for a law requiring written warnings on advertisements for weight-loss programs (similar to the warnings now required for cigarette advertisements).

➢ Pressure the Food and Drug Administration to remove over-the-counter weight-loss pills from the market.

➢ Censure negative remarks about fat people.

➢ Strictly penalize employers who discriminate against women because of their weight, and make all discrimination against fat people illegal, including discrimination in schools and within the medical- and life-insurance systems.

➢ Offer drug counseling for women who use amphetamines, tobacco, and other drugs for weight loss.

➢ Develop our own stories and pictures that could be used in books, comics, magazines, videos, and even television and movies. The characters would include a wide range of body types, including very fat people.

Help for Women with Eating Disorders

2

ONE OF the difficulties in getting the help we need is that so much of our harmful, weight-related behavior is widespread, encouraged, and considered normal. Also, dieting, binge eating, and other disruptive eating habits can range from barely noticeable to life threatening, depending on our genetic makeup and on the severity of our response to feeling fat. Thus, descriptions of eating disorders severe enough to require outside help may sound perfectly ordinary. For example, it might surprise you to know that a positive answer to the following questions could mean that you need help:

➤ Do you frequently think about weight and wish you were thinner? (Therapists' label: *weight obsession*)

➤ Are you afraid that you will get fat unless you constantly control what you eat? (Label: *fat phobia*)

➤ Do you feel anxious or depressed when you eat things you "shouldn't" or when you eat more than you "should"? (Label: *compulsive dieting*)

Some women recover from bulimia and anorexia by using self-help techniques. Others need outside help as they struggle to redevelop normal eating patterns. This chapter discusses both kinds of therapies.

SELF-HELP

In the 1970s, a group called Fat Liberation began rebelling against low-calorie diets and the thin ideal. These women understood that their own experiences were valid—they had found that low-calorie diets did not work, often made them fatter, and possibly damaged their health. In addition, they researched the scientific and medical literature, found that it supported their own experiences, and passed their work on to other writers.

Concerned women continue to form anti-diet groups, such as Overcoming Overeating (see National Center for Overcoming Overeating in "Resources"), which takes its name from the shared experience that low-calorie diets lead to compulsive eating. Women in self-help groups aim to normalize their eating by allowing themselves to eat whatever they like, to accept

I just felt like I couldn't go through the starving and binging and purging anymore. It was just too tiring to try to restrict my weight, and it was too tiring to binge and purge—I mean it just takes too much out of you! It's an excuse for having a life, it really is. It drains off all the vitality that you could have. It keeps you from really being alive. Now, every time it even crosses my mind, "Maybe I want to lose a little weight," this overwhelming wave of tiredness comes over me. Oh God, I don't ever want to do that again! My body remembers how awful that was.

I eat what I want. I'm not afraid of food anymore....But that is not the issue. The issue is, something clicked. When I understood how my life was almost ruined by diets, I started to understand something very basic about society. Nothing has been the same since.[1]

their bodies whatever their size, and to direct their enmity toward the culture that encouraged them to hate and mistreat their bodies. With the help of such groups, women for whom weight-loss efforts had become a way of life have stopped dieting. Some women say that such groups made them realize for the first time that they were harming themselves psychologically and physically, and were letting self-imposed starvation distract them from more important goals.

Self-help groups exist in many cities across the country and some are listed under "Resources" at the back of this book. Also, the chapter "Accepting Ourselves" may help you understand how you judge your size and shape, and it contains exercises for changing distressing thoughts and behaviors concerning eating and weight. Additionally, the bibliography includes self-help books on body image, weight, and overcoming eating problems. But simply listening to women who have recovered from dysfunctional eating may be the single most helpful thing we can do toward our own recovery. The following is one example of women's methods of self-help:

When *I* was trying to come out of it I didn't have anyone around me who had come through it. I mean, I'd read books by people who said, "You have to trust that you will not always feel like this, that it will change for you if you want it to." But I had never heard anyone talk deeply about what it was like to come through it, and how hard it is, and what you have to *do*. It was all kind of vague, and philosophical, and 12-step-y. I would think: "Yes, but what did you *do*?" So I just hit on this idea that I had to stop thinking of food as something that I deprive myself of. It had to be a process of eating; it had to be a process of taking care of myself. That was really powerful.

What I had to do was to get myself off the starvation mode and into normal eating—and before, when I'd taken myself off the starvation mode,

I'd started binging. And that's what I was afraid I was going to do. I had to *allow* my body to binge—without purging, I just had to allow it to happen, and it was *very* frightening. And I know that the people I've talked to—they're afraid that if they start eating again they won't be able to stop. That's absolutely true. That's what happens. You have to reach a certain point to let that happen.

I had to just trust that my body knew what to do and that it would correct itself, and be able to regulate itself if I just paid attention to it in a good way, not in a harsh, critical way. If I just observed it and said, "Okay, when am I hungry? What do I want to eat?" And I really had to just take myself by the hand and feed myself as if I were a little 3-year-old. I would think, "We're going into the cafeteria line, now what do you want? You want the Jell-O, okay; you want—anything—okay."

The way I finally took myself off the starvation cycle without binging was: Every time I went into the dining hall, instead of walking in, looking at all the food, and thinking, "Oh God, I can't eat that, I can't eat that—oh my God, look at all that food, it's totally overwhelming, I'm going to binge." Instead, I would walk in and think, "Okay, I now have to make sure that my body gets enough food," a reverse way of thinking about it. Instead of thinking, "Now I'm going to deprive myself," I would think, "Now I'm walking into the dining hall to take care of my body," which was a *revolutionary* way of thinking! Even if you're in the midst of binging and purging, if you can try to think that way it's helpful even if you don't totally believe it.

I gained a lot of weight. My doctor got kind of concerned because my cholesterol level went way up. I said, "That's because I've been eating hamburgers! If I want a hamburger, I'm going to *eat* a hamburger. My cholesterol level will come down eventually." And it did.

Now, I don't have to think about my body as much as I did. I feel good about my body. I don't look like the cultural ideal, I'm much bigger: I'm tall and have very broad shoulders, and I don't look like a stick. I'm healthy, and strong, and I eat fine, and I look fine.

You may also be able to help yourself by using "binge-control exercises" to help you gain control of the urge to eat compulsively. For example, you might try these adaptations of Rita Freedman's suggestions in *Bodylove*:[2]

➤ On a day-to-day basis, practice a strategy for handling stress, for instance, writing about your feelings in a journal, walking around the block, taking a bubble bath (or all three consecutively), or any other stress-coping methods that you find helpful.

➤ When you have the urge to binge, develop delay tactics to postpone a binge for a few moments, such as walking vigorously around your room, then calling the weather report. While you are walking or making the phone call, your urge to binge may subside. Then, if you can, do one or more of your antistress strategies as suggested above.

➤ Resolve always to begin a binge with an affirmation in front of the mirror. For example, stand before your reflection and repeat: "It's healthy to eat when I'm hungry and to stop when I'm full. I give myself permission to have whatever I want." This speech helps convert the binge from "bad compulsive behavior" into good permitted behavior. It may give you a sense of being in control rather than being taken over by the binge.

➤ Set a timer to interrupt a binge every five minutes. When it rings, stop eating for a moment, repeat your affirmation, and ask

You cannot overestimate how much the culture you live in is causing these struggles with eating. If you play a sport on a team where it's good to be big, or move to another country—just putting yourself into different contexts and noticing how much better you feel—you can realize how undercutting this culture is.
—Woman who recovered from bulimia

I wish I had had older women with me when I was going through this, just women noticing what I was going through and helping me put it into some sort of context, helping me realize what it was. That would have been incredibly powerful for me. And I think that in my therapy, one of the most powerful things was having an older woman really be there for me with this problem.
—Woman who recovered from bulimia

I think that the counseling helped in many ways. I think that it was good for me, just recognizing it as a problem, and dealing with it as a problem, and not trying to ignore it. The eating is just a symptom of me not feeling secure about myself as an individual. So, in a way, it's not about eating, and it's not about food, it's about me.

yourself whether you have had enough. You may want to continue binging, but make this a conscious decision. If so, reset the timer for another five minutes. If not, put away or throw out all remaining binge food.

➤ You may want to keep records of your binges. Jot down when, where, and what you eat, and any feelings or problems at that time. This will help you to accurately chart your progress and become more aware of what precipitates a binge. Stop record-keeping if it seems to become another obsession.

You may also wish to reinforce your acceptance of fat by discussing the previous chapter with other women; starting a discussion and support group on body image; reading positive sources on big women such as the magazines *Radiance* and *BBW* (stands for Big, Beautiful Woman); or actively joining other women who are rebelling against thinness as a requirement for social acceptance. Some women who have recovered from eating disorders also say that meeting people from other cultures, who often have more tolerant bodily standards, has helped them to a more relaxed and appreciative way of seeing themselves and other full, big women.

Try practicing self-acceptance exercises, such as those suggested in Chapter 6, "Accepting Ourselves." All these techniques may help you start enjoying the improved physical and mental health that can come with loving and respecting your body.

OUTSIDE HELP

You may be among the many women for whom weight concerns and dieting have led to a cycle of disordered eating that you feel unable to break without professional help. Or you may wish to combine self-help with professional help. You have several options.

Nutrition counseling may be sufficient to help you avoid the restrictive diets that lead to binge eating. Be aware, however, that some nutritionists have been trained to suggest and plan low-calorie diets. Find one who is knowledgeable about the damage done by low-calorie diets and other eating disorders and who advocates healthful eating. A self-help or support group (see "Resources") might help you find such a nutritionist. You can also ask your physician or hospital to refer you, although they may be less likely to be aware of a nutritionist's bias against fat. You might explore theories of nutrition that are more health oriented than calorie oriented, such as the Chinese or Indian (Ayurvedic) systems. If you learn from a teacher, check her or his training and attitudes about fatness.

If you are a student, a school counselor may be of help, especially one who is experienced in eating disorders. Many colleges and universities also have support groups or hotlines for eating problems.

Many therapists and hospitals run counseling and therapy groups on a regular basis for women with eating disorders. You can ask self-help or support groups, a trusted friend, or your physician for referrals, or check a feminist newspaper (if available) for ads. (Different types of talk therapy are briefly described in the following box.) Be prepared to "shop" for a counselor who is knowledgeable about the social encouragements of eating disorders and the links among self-starvation, binge eating, and purging. Also, look for one who respects you as an informed consumer of her or his expertise.

Some of the organizations listed in "Resources" may also be able to help you with information about counseling services and support groups.

Help for Anorexia Nervosa

Criteria to diagnose anorexia nervosa currently include:

➤ Refusal to maintain body weight at or above a minimally normal weight for age and height. (However, as we already pointed out, the charts that are used to judge average weight for height are controversial.)

Talk Therapies

Self-help: With this type of therapy, women who suffer from dysfunctional eating meet regularly for mutual advice, assistance, sympathy, and understanding

Behavior therapy and cognitive behavior therapy: These usually involve one-to-one conversations with a trained professional with the goal of learning specific techniques for changing a distressing behavior and, in cognitive behavior therapy, for altering the thoughts and fears underlying such behavior (for example, the fear of fat).

Psychotherapy: This involves one-to-one conversations, assessing your current problems, sometimes in relation to events in your childhood years, with the goal of increased self-awareness and self-acceptance.

Feminist therapy: This is similar to psychotherapy, but there is an emphasis on awareness of the social forces that influence women's lives.

Family therapies: These forms of therapy are similar to psychotherapy, but family members participate together with the therapist to bring about productive changes in family interactions to alleviate stress and dysfunctional eating patterns.

Group therapies: These can be based on psychotherapy, behavior therapy, feminist therapy, self-help, or a mixture of orientations. The group will consist of one or more therapists and several group members. Among the nervosas, this type of therapy is generally more helpful when bulimia nervosa is part of the problem.

➤ Intense fear of gaining weight or becoming fat even when the person is underweight according to standard charts

➤ Feeling fat or believing a body area is too fat even when the person is emaciated in others' opinions; "undue influence" of body weight or shape on self-evaluation; or denial of the seriousness of the current low body weight

➤ No menstrual blood flow for at least three consecutive menstrual cycles

Be aware that these criteria may change in response to new research. For example, some researchers now realize that feeling fat is pervasive among girls and women regardless of weight. Therefore, anorexia nervosa is increasingly recognized as the most extreme form of a self-image distortion widespread in our culture.

A woman with anorexia nervosa often does not see her behavior or her goal as unusual; therefore she is extremely resistant to help. She is likely to say that she is neither hungry nor emaciated and is proud of what she considers her achievement. She will reject all attempts of family, friends, or health care providers to reason with her. If she seeks help, it is often because she is pressured to do so by family or friends, not because she feels unwell or desires to resume normal eating. Given the fact that the brain can cease to register hunger, and given the perceived acceptability and desirability of extremely thin models, it is hard to accuse an anorectic woman of lying or of distorted perceptions. In her eyes she is doing what her society encourages: dieting; and she has become what her society rewards: a thin woman.

To make matters worse, family and friends may actually admire her control and compliment her appearance, describing her as "slender," "neat," and "fashionable." Some women who have anorexia nervosa are rewarded for their emaciation by their parents and are told that if they remain thin

they will receive further rewards. Friends who have tried and failed to lose weight may envy an anorectic woman's self-control and discipline. Even when friends and relatives perceive her as ill, they may admire her illness: she has achieved her culture's ideal of thinness and self-control; she is on a diet that works.

If a woman who has anorexia nervosa does accept help, there are no clear answers as to what form of help, if any, will be beneficial. Research on various forms of talk therapy for anorexia nervosa has been inconclusive, and studies on the use of mood- and behavior-altering drugs, such as lithium, amitriptyline, or chlorimipramine, show little benefit for anorexia nervosa so far. However, Prozac (fluoxetine) has helped some women who have anorexia nervosa: their depressed mood improves

Flyer produced by Eating Disorders Awareness and Prevention (EDAP), a national nonprofit organization that promotes awareness and prevention of eating disorders.

TRASH 'EM!!! SMASH 'EM!!! RE-HASH 'EM!!!
Breaking Free from the Oppression of Dieting

On February 9th, 1996, we are asking all our coordinators to commemorate *Eating Disorders Awareness Week*, by celebrating *Fearless Friday..A Day Without Dieting* with a national special event. This event, *Trash 'Em!!!, Smash 'Em!!! and Re-hash 'Em!!!*, will not only urge everyone across the nation to refrain from restrictive dieting and instead eat normal balanced meals, but also to *act* on this important prevention measure. On this day, ask members of your community to bring in all their diet products, which you may collectively TRASH, or their scales, which you may SMASH, or their old clothes that no longer fit, which you may RE-HASH by donating them to a worthwhile local charity. Joining together on this same day, we hope to make a strong statement denouncing unhealthy eating and dieting, the obsession in our society with weight, body dissatisfaction and discrimination, and the relentless drive for thinness. If you have any questions or need some ideas about how to organize this special event, please call the national office at (206) 382-3587.

Get active, and get going with our march against eating disorders!!!

and they eat more and gain weight as a result. If you have anorexia nervosa, you may wish to try Prozac combined with a form of talk therapy. (Fluoxetine's possible side effects are pointed out below.)

Some women who have had anorexia nervosa find that even after regaining weight their periods do not return. In such cases, some additional weight, talk therapy—or both—may help. Synthetic estrogens may also help a woman regain menstrual cycles and reduce bone loss, but their possible effects on a woman's risk of breast and endometrial cancers make them controversial.

When a woman's life is threatened by starvation, her therapy may have to take place within a hospital. Some hospitals have wards that specialize in the treatment of dysfunctional eating. Many hospitals also have what they call eating disorder centers for help on an outpatient basis. Some of the organizations listed in "Resources" offer self-help groups and may also help you find a therapist experienced in diagnosing and treating dysfunctional eating.

For some women, anorexia nervosa becomes chronic, leading to a lifetime obsession with food and weight. But despite the difficulties in treating anorexia nervosa, many women eventually improve spontaneously. Improvement can take a few months to a few years, with severe cases lasting without improvement for 10 years or more. Anorexia nervosa rarely persists after the age of 40. No one yet knows why or how spontaneous improvements occur, but the body's hormonal changes with age could play a role.

Help for Bulimic Anorexia Nervosa and Bulimia Nervosa

Women who have mild forms of bulimic anorexia nervosa or bulimia nervosa do not find their behavior very unusual or detrimental. Gorging on weekends and dieting to make up for it on weekdays is pervasive. Thus, we do not believe our eating habits are so different from those of our friends and families. Also, those of us who binge

and purge in strict secrecy may be complimented on our looks and admired for maintaining or losing weight "effortlessly." Thus, our friends and family may unwittingly encourage our continued binge eating and vomiting.

Some women use self-help methods to overcome their starve-binge-purge or binge-purge cycles. The list at the beginning of the chapter contains many useful suggestions for modifying these cycles.

Be aware that you will gain weight when you first cease to purge. This is because your body was severely dehydrated by your purges, and will gradually regain its normal water content. Even if you eat almost nothing, your weight will rise immediately. For some women, this weight gain is an obstacle to recovery—they experience their weight gain as a retribution for eating and as a result, they resume purging.

If you decide to seek professional help, studies suggest that behavior therapy, especially cognitive behavior therapy, shows the most promise in treating bulimia nervosa. If you have bulimia nervosa, you might try this form of therapy to see if it is helpful. Again, ask a trusted friend, a self-help group, or your physician or the organizations listed in "Resources" to refer a therapist. Certain drugs that alter the brain's chemistry sometimes alleviate binge eating and purging. These include imipramine (Tofranil), desipramine (Norpramin, Pertofrane), phenelzine (Nardil), isocarboxazid (Marplan), trazodone (Desyrel), and fluoxetine (Prozac). (All must be prescribed by a physician or psychiatrist.) For women with bulimia, the drugs apparently change the brain's chemistry in such a way that their preoccupations with food and body weight are alleviated and any associated depression is lifted. Interestingly, these drugs work less well against the same preoccupations in women with anorexia nervosa.

Because no one knows what makes these drugs effective, you may need to try more than one before finding a drug that is

I basically took it day to day. I would allow myself to eat breakfast and didn't allow myself to purge. You know, it was so hard for me to allow myself food. I had to teach myself to eat like a normal person. I would slip, and I would binge and purge, and want to fall back into my bad habits. And I basically had to teach myself: "I am a living organism. I need food for nourishment."

—Woman who recovered through self-help from bulimic anorexia nervosa helpful for you. You should ask about the possibility of a relapse when you stop taking the drug, or even when you continue to take it. You should also inform yourself about the possible undesirable or dangerous effects of each drug by getting a list of possible side effects from your medical practitioner and discussing the list with her or him. (You can also consult the latest *Physicians Desk Reference* at your local library.) Some possible side effects are hypertension, agitation, dizziness, nausea, insomnia, and, in a small percentage of people, a paradoxical reaction of (increased) suicidal thoughts.

General Suggestions for Women with the Nervosas

Even if you are taking an effective drug, it is crucial for you to discuss what healthful eating is and how to encourage yourself to eat healthfully. In addition, how severely and accurately we judge our appearance and what value we place on appearance seem to have a strong bearing on our risk of all types of disordered eating. For these reasons, some researchers believe that any long-term successful treatment of an eating disorder must include some form of talk therapy to change the way a woman sees her body. You will also benefit from learning stress-reduction techniques and from discussing any possible stressful events or situations that you may associate with your dysfunctional eating. According to some theories, a woman's susceptibility to obsessive thoughts or compulsive actions can be triggered by a stressful event or situation in her life, such as family difficulties, pressure at school, sexual abuse, or rape. Workshops in self-assertion may also help. An understanding and knowledgeable therapist or a group of women who have experienced eating disorders can provide comfortable settings for such learning and discussion.

Eating disorders recovery panel, one of many educational programs presented during Eating Disorders Awareness Week, observed nationally each February.

Changing Our Bodies Through Surgery

3

COSMETIC SURGEONS now claim to have answers for those of us who are discouraged by our lack of control over our body shape and size—they can sculpt our bodies with knives and chemicals. Cosmetic surgery—the permanent alteration of a person's appearance—is a medical "solution" for a purely social problem. It is based on the premise that any body part different from the current beauty ideal is pathological.

In the United States, the idea that the female body needs help goes back at least to the nineteenth century, when women were taught that their bodies were shapeless and structurally unsound and that a woman's spine and muscles could not support her breasts and stomach without help from stiff corsets.[1] Today, it is psychological relief that women are offered. According to the logic of cosmetic surgery, a physical body that causes psychological distress becomes pathological in its unaltered state. The surgeon then cures the distress by remodeling the body. Many women hope that with a change in looks, their self-esteem will increase without effort on their part.

Plastic surgery includes both reconstructive surgery (correction of an injury or disfigurement) and cosmetic or aesthetic surgery (alteration of a person's appearance to conform to an ideal standard of beauty). While some overlap exists, this chapter covers only the clearly cosmetic aspect of plastic surgery.

Many clients and doctors consider cosmetic surgery normal and natural, just as any of us might have our hair cut and styled, put on makeup, or go on vacation. As the surgery has become more widespread, pressure is increasing for it to become part of a woman's "normal" pursuit of "improving" her looks.

Procedures are made to seem easy, and the terms used by the media and cosmetic surgeons minimize any association with surgery. A face-lift is a "freshening." An abdominal rearrangement of muscles and skin—a major operation—is a "tummy tuck." Acid burn of the skin is a "face peel." One cosmetic surgeon calls his liposuction tube a "magic wand."[3] When the results of a procedure are unacceptable, corrective surgeries are "revisions" or "touch-ups."

I'm named after my mother so she lives kind of through me. In her eyes, I always had to be perfect. She told me that I needed a nose job when I was 12. We were having some sort of party at the house, and there were people over, and I remember her saying, "Well, you'll have a nose job when you're sixteen." Of course, I had one after that.[2]

Removal of stitches following cosmetic facial surgery.

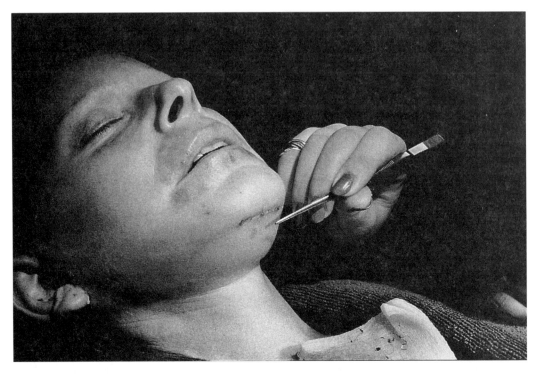

I'm responding to a letter from a 16 year old girl. I hated my nose when I was your age. I always looked directly at people so they couldn't see my profile. When I was 26 I finally saved up enough money to have cosmetic surgery. It is the most rewarding thing I've ever done! It changed my whole personality because at last I had confidence. I wish I'd done it when I was 16. My husband says I'm beautiful. If your parents can't afford it, start saving now. No matter how long it takes, it's worth it![6]

A brochure for collagen injections around the lips calls the procedure "Paris Lips." It is touted as "The New Fashion Focus for the 90s," as if it were a cosmetic. The brochure promises that: "The Paris Lip Look can be maintained with retreatments every two or three months as part of your regular beauty routine. And, it's so quick and easy, you can have it done over your lunch hour and go back to work with the new fashion look of the Paris Lip."[4] The injections, which cost $250 and up for each cubic centimeter,[5] are called "collagen replacement therapy," making them sound like a cross between a department store cosmetic and a treatment for some medical condition.

But cosmetic surgery cannot be compared to hair coloring or makeup. It is a significant intrusion into the body. A face-lift is not a gentle stretching—the skin must be separated from the underlying muscle, fat, and connective tissue, and then pulled, trimmed like a pie crust, and reattached by sewing. Various muscles may also be severed and shortened. A "nose job" often involves breaking the bridge of the nose.

Liposuction isn't a delicate sucking out of fat—the liposuction device rips up and vacuums away the underpinnings of the skin, including blood vessels and connective tissue. And, like any surgery, cosmetic surgery brings risks that can lead to long-term health problems and even death.

Why have cosmetic surgeries come to be accepted as a normal, low-risk part of women's lives? One reason is our culture's narrow standard of beauty. The cultural ideal, which affects how we see ourselves and how we are seen and treated by others, encourages us to alter our bodies for social reasons. A second reason is that little information about the risks of cosmetic surgery is readily available. Finally, the cosmetic surgery industry, with its large advertising budgets and poor research, will not provide us with the information to make thoughtful, informed decisions.

THE PRESSURE TO HAVE COSMETIC SURGERY

Slenderness is hardly the only ingredient of the cultural ideal of beauty. In our society, to be attractive, the parts of a woman's body must fall into a narrow range or "correct" proportions, as must her facial features. She must look "feminine": soft, childlike, graceful. And she must look young, a standard that every long-lived woman eventually fails.[7]

This ideal is reinforced by prejudice against the old, non-Europeans, and those who don't look like the ideal. Older women tend to be ignored more than younger women. By implication, many ethnic and racial groups are "ugly" because they deviate from the dominant ideal. And many people believe that a fat woman is too stupid and lazy to take care of herself, too unattractive to have lovers, and is ruining her health by staying fat.

Since our society judges women so heavily on their appearance, and less on their accomplishments or abilities, it is hardly surprising that we tend to internalize the ideal of beauty from the images we see. And cosmetic surgeons exploit this power of the cultural ideal. Advertisements frequently use pictures of ideally attractive models, implying that we can all look like these women. (Other ads are more explicit, with headlines such as "Classic artists create timeless beauty."[8]) These ads can heighten our sense of physical inadequacy even though nothing is functionally or aesthetically wrong with our bodies.

Unfortunately, some of us do feel that how much we are or will be loved and valued depends on how we look, and natural processes such as aging or slight variations from the ideal are deeply troubling. For example, in one study, many of the images used by women to describe facial aging were of emptied vessels: "There are bags, sacks, and pouches, which sag, hang, wrinkle, fold, and wither…The metaphors associated with facial aging are almost universally negative ones, with the possible exception of…'laugh lines'."[10] Indeed, for some of us, cosmetic surgery does improve our self-image because after it we more closely approach the heavily rewarded beauty ideal.

Some of us feel that the cultural ideal should not be so powerful, but are not willing to wait for change, which will likely take longer than our lifetimes. For others the surgery serves as a mark of increasing social status since until recently only rich people could afford it.

Some of us are pressured to undergo cosmetic surgery by parents or lovers, or we feel indirect pressure in our work lives. One researcher calls cosmetic surgery a kind of "job insurance," whether our jobs are paid labor or the unpaid work of maintaining relationships.[12] Cosmetic surgeons reinforce this view by claiming that such surgery expands women's opportunities in life. The underlying assumption is that women have more options for friendships, love, and work if they conform to the current beauty ideal. Actually, our choices will become wider if and when the range of acceptable looks becomes wider as well, and we are judged increasingly on character and/or accomplishments rather than appearance.

Although pressures to undergo cosmetic surgery are real, we may actually overestimate the extent to which others judge us on our appearance. In one experiment, some women were made up to look as though they had a facial scar, and then each woman was engaged in conversation with a stranger. However, the women did not know that the scars had been removed before the conversations and that the "strangers" were actually research assistants. Compared to women who knew they did not have a facial scar, those who believed they did reported more discomfort in themselves and more unusual gazes from the "strangers."[13] And studies of children with a cleft palate and lip or extremes of craniofacial shapes reveal that the children were not as disturbed in their adjustment as researchers had anticipated.[14]

The "Normalized" Look

Cosmetic surgeons, still overwhelmingly white upper-middle-class males, claim that they should not be the arbiters of what is

No matter how much a guy cared for me, my breasts were a distraction. . . . Other girls would look at me like I was an object. I would come home and start crying.[9]

I'd like to say that each and every person should feel comfortable with themselves and no one should ever have plastic surgery, but that's probably not going to happen. We live in a society that defines what is attractive and makes us all feel inferior if we don't measure up.
—Woman with a large nose who considered and rejected cosmetic surgery[11]

I don't really want to get a face-lift but all the women I know are doing it. I have to go to a lot of social functions for my work and it's getting so I'm the only one who looks my age. One of these days I may have to do it just to keep my business going.
—Middle-aged woman

I just didn't want to look tired anymore, and I was beginning to look older than my years.

—58-year-old woman who simultaneously had a face-lift, nose job, and under eye surgery.[17]

I said I didn't want to go out with bruises all over me. I had two black eyes, swollen. I looked like I had been beaten up, and I had. The WASP plastic surgeon was paid by my excited and very willing Jewish father to beat the Jewishness out of me—to get rid of my father's and grandmother's nose on this second-generation daughter: the daughter who looked "too Jewish."[19]

acceptable by denying surgical body changes to those who wish to conform. But by promoting cutting and reshaping the body without suggesting other options to increase self-esteem, they actually reinforce the ideal image. Surgery itself shapes standards as doctors replace a range of looks with an artificial unity. One popular teen magazine quotes a plastic surgeon as saying "the relationship between the tip of your nose and your upper lip—for a girl it should be between a 100- and 110-degree angle."[15] Perhaps the angle is right for a Greek statue, but why should this measure be applied to all women?

One surgeon suggests that cosmetic surgery be renamed "aesthetically normalizing surgery."[16] But what is the norm except a changing beauty ideal? The name suggests that every few seasons, when the ideal shape for breasts, hips, or noses changes, we should rush over to our neighborhood plastic surgeon for revamping while our clothes are at the tailor.

The idea of reshaping women to fit a certain image also meshes with the concept of woman as commodity. We start to see ourselves as if we were improvable items. Our body parts become isolated, changeable, mechanistic pieces, subject to evaluation based on appearance. Again, who we are and what we can do gets lost in the pressure to reshape ourselves into more acceptable objects.

Certain operations, in particular brow lifts and eye operations, tend to create unnatural or vacuous expressions; caricatures of normal facial expressions. Women with brow lifts have a perpetually surprised look. They look less competent, less assertive, and therefore less threatening to men.

By making age less visible, cosmetic surgery perpetuates prejudice against those of us who are older. Many of us accept society's negative view of older women and use cosmetic surgery as a way to bolster our self-esteem and avoid becoming undesirable. Some cosmetic surgeons justify their surgery by calling it "restorative," implying

that "restoration" to a cultural ideal is in the same category as surgery to reconstruct a severely injured body.

Considering the importance of being thin in our culture, it is not surprising that liposuction is one of the most common cosmetic surgery procedures.[18] With the strong social disapproval of fatness leading to condemnation and isolation of fat women, any method of slimming seems appropriate to many. And for those of us who come close to the "ideal" body weight, liposuction can give us the shape we feel we need. No longer do we need to have "sturdy ankles" or "too much" bulge around the hips. It's not just size that becomes unacceptable, now our bodies must conform to an exact shape. If prejudice against fatness and the easy availability of liposuction continues, those of us who are fat and do not choose to get surgically shrunk will be blamed for the discrimination others show toward us by denying us jobs, education, and friendships.

Many cosmetic surgeries are undertaken to minimize the extent to which we look like a member of our ethnic or racial groups. Generally, Italians and Jews seek surgery to reduce the size of their noses, especially in the bridge and length; African-Americans want narrower noses; and Asians want nose enlargements.

Northern Europeans want lip enlargements while African-Americans and Asian-Americans seek thinner lips. Eye crease operations for Asians are popular in Asia as well as in the West (the rationale is that adding an eye crease makes the eye look rounder and more expressive).

In the United States, as members of various ethnic, racial, and national groups have become more prosperous, greater numbers have turned to cosmetic surgery. But, until recently, cosmetic surgeons clearly used northern European measurement standards for all clients.[20] As one Philadelphia cosmetic surgeon said, "If they're going to be in America, they're going to look American."[21]

Discussion of ethnic differences in cosmetic surgery training programs began around 1985, perhaps because of the new pride many Americans feel in their backgrounds. Doctors now talk about improving appearance without erasing an ethnic look. But the doctors' beauty standards are still highly influenced by the northern European ideal.

THE RISKS ASSOCIATED WITH COSMETIC SURGERY

Most of us don't realize just how much we may be compromising our health by having cosmetic surgery. Sometimes there is a loss of physical functioning, such as loss of sensation from nerve damage. Sometimes the surgery is not successful and our appearance may become truly abnormal. There are rare cases of paralysis or death from anesthesia or hemorrhage. All surgery carries risks and even the most conscientious surgeons make mistakes. In addition, what works in most surgeries may not work in all—people do not always respond predictably to surgery. However, the risks are not common knowledge, and those of us who learn about them in the course of deciding to undergo cosmetic surgery often find them easy to discount.

Most information about cosmetic surgery in the lay media is provided by the cosmetic surgeons themselves, who have the most to benefit from presenting the surgery in the best possible light. In addition, some magazines and newspapers rely on cosmetic surgery advertisements as a significant source of income. As a result, magazine and television stories are almost uniformly positive about cosmetic surgery. In magazine articles, the cost of the surgery, if noted, is often more prominent than the risks.

In addition, plastic surgeons mount very active public relations campaigns through their trade organizations, the most powerful of which is the American Society of Plastic and Reconstructive Surgeons (ASPRS). One of its major roles is to provide public education to encourage people to have cosmetic surgery—"education" that glosses over the negative side effects of the surgery when side effects are mentioned at all. For example, in 1991, the U.S. Food and Drug Administration (FDA) was evaluating the safety of breast implants. The ASPRS assessed each of its members $1050 to mount a nearly $4 million campaign to influence the FDA to allow silicone-filled breast implants to remain on the market and to put the damage to some women's health "into perspective, along with the substantial benefits experienced by women with these devices."[22] The FDA ultimately decided that the research did not support manufacturers' claims of safety.[23] (See also the chapter "Inflating Our Image: Breast Implants.")

Television and radio talk show hosts, as well as writers for magazines and newspapers, rarely question any information that they receive from doctors. For instance, ASPRS has repeatedly claimed that more than 2 million women have had breast implants, but has never explained how that figure was derived. One researcher was told that the number was based on a combination of manufacturers' sales figures and a secret survey of plastic surgeons.[24] After accepting the ASPRS' figures for several years, the FDA did its own calculations, resulting in a number that was less than half of ASPRS.[25]

Those of us who are considering cosmetic surgery are told of the risks in a way that encourages us to dismiss them. Usually women don't hear much about complications until they have already decided to go ahead with the surgery. Surgeons open advertising "seminars" by saying explicitly only what cosmetic surgery can do for clients; possible complications are not mentioned. It is only relatively late in the woman's decision-making process that a surgeon discusses the possible hazards of the surgery with her. This timing gives the impression that complications are minimal, certainly less important than the rewards. In addition, the surgeon benefits from the myth that no doctor would ever

My research was based on women's magazine articles. It never occurred to me to look in medical journals or to search out stories of people who had problems. My faith was in the doctor. I still have the articles in my files on face-lifts, eye surgery, breast implants, alongside articles on makeup and hairstyles. When I heard cosmetic surgery would not be tax-deductible the following year (1991) I did it all— face-lift, eye lift, upper lip chemical peel—seven hours of surgery. The only risks I was thinking of were losing the tax-deduction and being nauseous from the anesthesia.

I can remember signing all the papers with the lists of dire results that could occur, but I would have signed my soul away. It didn't matter. I had done all the reading I wanted to do and was into fantasizing about looking ten years younger.

hurt a patient, thus giving the impression that the risks for cosmetic procedures must be remote or nonexistent. The doctor's belief in the rightness of what she or he is doing also conveys a message of safety to the client.

Even when we hear about possible side effects we usually don't believe that these complications could happen to us. One study of postoperative face-lift clients revealed that few women could list the complications that they were told about before the operation. Some denied that such complications could happen to them.[26] Women who experience complications may not talk about them because they do not want others to know about the surgery. One woman didn't want to make public her troubles with her breast implants because she had never told her husband she had had implants. However, the secretive attitude about cosmetic surgery is changing somewhat. This shift is beneficial in that more women are likely to talk about problems. On the other hand, some women, such as Abigail Van Buren and comedians Phyllis Diller and Joan Rivers actively, uncritically promote all sorts of procedures.

Because cosmetic surgeons are in the contradictory position of being required by law to explain what can go wrong with an elective surgery after touting its benefits, the tendency to downplay the risks is inherent. Although the doctor may mention complication rates, these may actually be unknown since so much cosmetic surgery takes place in isolation, out of hospitals, and without insurance coverage. Complications of these surgeries are generally not reported. While it is important for doctors to explain the risks and complications of procedures they perform, we all need an independent unbiased source of information. A few organizations do exist, but they can serve only a limited number of people, and many women do not know about them (but see "Resources"). We may also need to read medical journals to find out about possible complications.

General Risks

Some women who have conditions or habits that interfere with wound healing, such as diabetes or smoking, should not undergo cosmetic surgery. Some women form large raised scars or keloids, but the doctor may fail to ask about this predisposition or minimize the possibility of visible scars. Some unscrupulous surgeons will accept such women as clients.

Any process that involves removing the top layer of skin, such as face peeling, permanently removes some pigment from a woman's skin, so that she will always have to protect her skin from the sun and will never tan evenly. Sun exposure soon after the peel may result in permanent unsightly blotching. Even a very light-skinned woman who has had a peel on a part of her face, such as the area between the upper lip and nose, will need to wear makeup after the procedure if she wishes to disguise the difference in skin color.

All surgery disrupts the nerves and impairs feeling, at least temporarily. A woman may not be able to feel as well, or at all, things she could feel before surgery. Unless sensation returns, or until she adjusts to the lack of sensation, she may have trouble maintaining a sense of body integrity, since she may not be able to feel where all the parts of her body are. Some nerves will grow back, but the degree to which a woman recovers feeling is unpredictable and may take as long as two or three years—nerves grow slowly. After a face-lift, a woman may not be able to feel the pillow when she lies down, leading to disturbed sleep.[27] She may have permanent changes, such as differences in breathing after nose surgery, nipple numbness after breast reduction, or a sensation of skin pulling after a face-lift.

Of course, swelling, bruising and scabbing come with any cosmetic surgery. So does the risk of the possible complications of surgery—infection, hemorrhage, excess fluid accumulation, and anesthesia-related problems. With any procedure that involves separating the skin from its underpinnings,

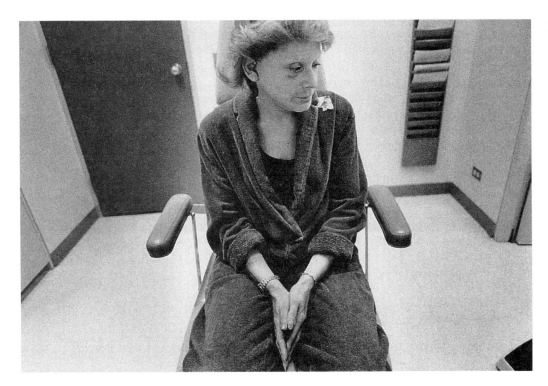

Following a neck- and face-lift, a woman's face is puffy and irritated, with dermabrasion around the mouth and black and blue areas beneath the eyes.

such as liposuction, eyelid lifts, or face-lifts, nerves are cut, leading to a loss of sensation, and skin may die if too much of the blood supply is cut. We also risk looking worse. The following are examples of problems that can accompany some procedures. These are not exhaustive lists for any of the procedures.

Liposuction

The purpose of liposuction is to remove body fat. The procedure involves sticking a plastic tube (cannula) that is attached to a suction machine through a small slit in the skin. The doctor thrusts the cannula under the skin several times in a fanlike pattern. The procedure is essentially blind—the doctor cannot actually see what the cannula is ripping through. The tube sucks out fat, blood, nerves, and connective tissue, which are all present together under the skin. After liposuction, a woman must wear a binder for a couple of weeks or more to help the skin reattach to the underlying layers. She may be black and blue and have swelling for months. Unless she is fairly young and her skin still very elastic, she will probably have bumps and ridges after the skin reattaches, which may seem so unsightly that she will always want to cover the area with clothes. If too much tissue is sucked out in one place, there may be a depression. If too much is removed altogether, she may go into shock. If the skin does not reattach properly, it can slough off, requiring skin grafts. The skin may adhere to muscle or other inappropriate underlying structures. When liposuction is performed on a women's abdomen, the doctor may accidentally puncture her intestines, which can produce a life-threatening infection. Sometimes blood clots, fat, or other tissue broken up by the cannula enters the circulatory system and can then lodge in vital organs, possibly causing life-threatening damage such as stroke. Several deaths have been documented.[28]

Removal of fat may have unexplored long-term effects. As discussed previously, fat helps regulate energy use and hormone levels, and the fat's location may affect its function.

I wanted to just have extra skin hanging from under my chin removed. However, the doctor said this had to be done with a face-lift...Most of the skin is gone but one side still hangs and he would not correct it. The right side of my head and face near the ear is numb and my neck is badly scarred. Once he got his money you were at his mercy...I looked real bad with that extra skin...One side of my face is fatter and looser than the other and my mouth is still slightly crooked.

Collagen Injections

Collagen is a fibrous protein that comprises connective tissue in humans and animals. The type used in cosmetic surgery is derived from cows or pigs and used to puff up the skin. The FDA has approved it for use in wrinkles or scars, but not for use to enlarge features or to inject it directly into the lips.

A rare but serious consequence of collagen injections involves partial loss of eyesight or death of tissue near the injection site. The required fine print on the brochure promoting collagen simply says that it is possible to accidentally inject the collagen into a blood vessel, resulting in a blockage of a flow of blood and "loss of circulation to nearby sites." It doesn't say that loss of blood results in death of tissue that may then slough off, perhaps leaving a scar.[29] Even the most common complications from collagen—severe, sometimes life-threatening allergic reactions—may not be predicted by the preliminary skin test required by the FDA. The FDA estimates that 3 percent of people are allergic to animal collagen. According to the FDA,

> Collagen allergies can take the form of rash, hives, joint and muscle pain, headache, and, in a few cases, severe reactions that include shock and difficulty breathing. Other adverse effects that have occurred after collagen injection, and which appear to have been related to the injections, include infections, abscesses, open sores, lumps, peeling of

the skin, scarring, recurrence of herpes simplex, and partial blindness.[30]

Some researchers also suspect collagen of triggering immune system diseases, primarily polymyositis and dermamyositis, in a small but unknown number of people. These diseases, which affect the muscles and skin, can be chronic, progressive, and sometimes fatal.

Eyelid Surgery (Blepharoplasty)

Eyelid surgery tightens the skin and removes fat from around the eyes, reducing droopiness of the eyelids and of the skin under the eyes. If the doctor stretches the skin around a woman's eyes too tightly, her eyelids may not close all the way, allowing the eyes to dry out and necessitating a regimen of lubricating eyedrops. (Conversely, the eyes may tear excessively.) If the eyes remain dry, the cornea may become damaged. A woman's eyes may feel like they are burning, itching, and be sore and light sensitive enough that she must always wear sunglasses. Eye damage can affect vision, leaving a woman with blurred or double vision and in the worst case, partial or total blindness.

Face-Lift (Rhytidectomy)

The most common problem after a face-lift is loss of sensation. Sometimes severing the nerves to the mouth may make one or both corners of a woman's mouth droop, and her

For Better or For Worse®   **by Lynn Johnston**

face may not be symmetrical. According to one plastic surgeon, about one in five hundred people who have face-lifts will have some kind of permanent paralysis.[31] And even with partial paralysis, a woman will not be able to show her emotions fully through her facial expressions, and her smile may change.

The skin may be pulled too tightly, creating an uncomfortable feeling, perhaps burning and itching until the skin stretches out again over time. A woman may lose hair, particularly in the temple area, or she may have poor wound healing that causes large scars behind the ears from the skin being pulled too tightly. All of the eye complications that can result from eyelid surgery can also occur with face-lifts.

MEDICAL COSMETICIANS?

Considering the complications that can result from cosmetic surgery, it would be good to know that we are buying the finest in medical care when we go under a surgeon's knife—that cosmetic surgery is conducted with the same professional standards as other branches of medicine, that it achieves its goals, that the benefits outweigh the risks, and that at least some of the claims are validated by research. In all these areas, cosmetic surgery falls short: it cannot show that it is anything more than a relatively high-risk and extremely expensive beauty treatment.

Is It Medicine?

Cosmetic surgery claims to be part of medicine. It uses the techniques and language of medicine, but its goals are different from the goals of other fields of medicine—to heal illness and injury. Instead, it seeks psychological improvement or career advancement for the client. One surgeon writes, "Self-esteem has become an important contributor to individual success in our society, and the ability of a plastic surgeon to enhance self-esteem and improve the quality of life places the specialty within the context of other health-care activities.[33] However, another

plastic surgeon calls cosmetic surgery "a medically unnecessary procedure."[34]

Cosmetic surgeons give medical terms to body parts that do not fit the narrowly defined ideal, implying defectiveness. For example, small breasts are *micromastia* or *hypomastia*, large ones *macromastia* or *gigantomastia*. A 1982 statement of the American Society for Plastic and Reconstructive Surgeons proclaims that small breasts are "deformities [that] are really a disease which in most patients result[s] in feelings of inadequacy, lack of self-confidence, distortion of body image and a total lack of well-being due to a lack of self-perceived femininity."[35] This definition has nothing to do with whether, or how well, a woman's breasts function sexually or for nursing; nor does it discuss or challenge the changing fashions in "ideal" breast size.

Cosmetic surgery seems to be the only field of medicine in which no serious discussion takes place on whether the physical risks of particular procedures are worth the benefits. Clients, often without a clear understanding of the risks, are allowed to decide what is acceptable. In most other fields, certain operations or procedures are not offered to clients because they are considered too dangerous for the benefit bestowed. In cosmetic surgery, however, no such norms about what is too dangerous seem to exist. For instance, the plastic surgery journals do not discuss an acceptable number of deaths or permanently disabled women per hundred thousand that are accepted for liposuction.

Cosmetic surgery is one of the least regulated parts of medicine, with very little oversight by peers, hospitals, or insurance companies. Almost all—95 percent—cosmetic surgery is not done in hospitals: 50 percent is done in doctors' offices and the rest in clinics.[36] No one is looking over the doctor's shoulder to see if she or he is doing a good job unless the doctor has deliberately developed some kind of peer counseling or supervision. Such a quality control mechanism is fairly common in the

After much soul-searching I adopted the policy of prepayment, which has done more to bring order to a busy practice and to diminish my fears of malpractice than any other decision I have made in office management. It virtually eliminates the threat of nuisance claims or countersuits.[32]

—Plastic surgeon

The first plastic surgeon I consulted on breast augmentation told me that his policy was payment in advance. I was stunned. I argued about how unusual that was, that I wasn't buying a car. By the time I was ready to go ahead with the prepayment and surgery, he refused to accept me as a client.

When something bothers you that bad and you're going to spend all that money to do it, you are not afraid.[45]

mental health field but rare in surgery. The office staff is unlikely to criticize even if someone there recognizes that the clients are buying inferior care.

Training and certification standards are sometimes lax. For more on this problem, see chapter 4, "Caveat Emptor: Shopping for a Cosmetic Surgeon."

Yet another difference between cosmetic surgeons and the normal practice of medicine is that cosmetic surgeons usually demand cash in advance. One plastic surgeon notes that "plastic surgery in general has already created 'special exceptions for cosmetic surgery'—and they are to the advantage of the plastic surgeon: large fees not covered by insurance....[O]ur specialty's ritual of demanding hefty fees and prepayment...have caused us more marginality with our colleagues than perhaps anything else we plastic surgeons do."[37]

Does Cosmetic Surgery Improve Psychological Health?

Determining the psychological benefits of cosmetic surgery is difficult. Popular magazine articles reflect the rhetoric of cosmetic surgeons who claim to make you "look better and feel more confident."[38] Some ads from cosmetic surgeons promise: "Life looks better when you do" and "Looking your very best can give you an added measure of self-confidence."[39] Others that: "Sometimes a small change can make a big difference and help you feel good about yourself."[40] "We give shape to your dreams."[41] One surgeon in a professional journal states, "Aesthetic surgery achieves the goal of beautifying by restoring contours and restructuring by augmenting or resecting tissues. The improvement in appearance promises increased self-confidence, leading to better jobs and friendships."[42]

Although many surgeons and women who have had cosmetic surgery report changed behaviors after surgery, little research has been done to evaluate these reports.[43] Overall, the field has not supported

claims of improvement with valid studies, but with slogans, anecdotes, and assumptions. For example, one plastic surgeon asserts that "when an individual experiences positive perceptual, cognitive, and emotional changes after surgery, then behavioral changes logically could follow."[44] A fine hypothesis, but it must be tested, and if true, the degree of change must be specified. The commonly cited evidence justifying psychological benefits consists of satisfaction surveys asking a client if she is pleased and if she would do it again. Indeed, a few weeks or months after the operation, the results are usually overwhelmingly in favor of the surgery. The surveys do not seem to recognize that the client has just paid cash in advance and has spent several weeks or months recovering from surgery. With such an investment, wouldn't most of us be inclined to think that we have improved? Believing that the surgery made little difference or was done poorly would imply that we had made a poor decision, wasted money, and possibly endangered our health for nothing.

In addition, often the doctor makes no attempt to reach a representative sample of his or her clients, including the dissatisfied, and does not repeat the questions after a few years to find out about longer-term results. Even if the samples were representative, a researcher must ask more probing questions to find out if the surgery really has fulfilled its stated purpose. Finally, client self-evaluations generally are considered more reliable when they are corroborated by another recognized method of evaluation. Usually the surgeons make no attempt to do this.

At a more detailed level, different methods of surgery are not compared through scientific research methods or even poorly executed surveys. For example, does a face-lift involving the top layer of skin and supporting tissues produce a better psychological outcome or more rapid career advancement than one that changes deeper tissue layers, including the bones?[46]

Without asking such questions the profession cannot back up its claims scientifically. If the answers to such questions don't matter, then there is no medical rationale for promoting one type of surgery over another, or promoting cosmetic surgery at all.

In fact, often cosmetic surgeons hedge on whether there are psychological benefits. In one hotel sales talk "seminar" promoting the benefits of cosmetic surgery, doctors stressed that the psychological lift might last only a few months, or perhaps even a year, but eventually the client will feel "like her old self" again. Another plastic surgeon has suggested that fear of lawsuits prompts caution about promised results.

That fear in itself indicates that cosmetic surgery cannot always deliver the psychological changes touted as its primary justification. And some women have reported that they did not feel differently, as they had hoped. The physical effects of some of the procedures, such as face-lifts, are relatively short-lived. A few years after a face-lift, perhaps five to ten years, the skin starts to show further signs of aging, and it continues to soften and wrinkle. Presumably, based on the surgeons' own statements, any psychological benefits would not outlast the physical effects. Also, doctors must compare cosmetic surgery to other therapies, including self-help techniques for building self-esteem, to discover which is the most effective method of change. Doctors sometimes recommend psychotherapy over cosmetic surgery to lessen feelings of inferiority, but no clear criteria seem to exist for providing this advice.[47]

One cause of low self-esteem for many women is physical, sexual, or emotional abuse. The resulting low self-esteem might lead to a desire for cosmetic surgery, yet cosmetic surgery might not be the most appropriate remedy. (Reconstructive surgery might be needed, though, to repair injuries.) The only recent article in *Plastic and Reconstructive Surgery* about abuse and cosmetic surgery, by a woman surgeon, suggested surgeons ask clients about childhood sexual abuse as an aid to evaluating whether cosmetic surgery will satisfy them. The author cited examples of cases in which the surgery seemed to help healing and other cases that exacerbated the previous trauma.[48]

Another area that has not been well researched is why some clients, despite "objectively" having good surgical results, still feel dissatisfied after the surgery. This phenomenon raises many questions. What are the psychological risks if the surgery goes awry? What are the psychological risks to those who are unsatisfied? For whom might the psychological effects be devastating? How many women are depressed before the surgery? What percentage develop depression after the surgery, or become recluses? How do women adjust if their bodies are asymmetrical after the surgery? How do women adjust to loss of sensation from nerve damage or to changes in strength or flexibility resulting from severed muscles?

How Clients Are "Evaluated"

Cosmetic surgeons generally do not have any significant training in psychology or psychiatry unless they make a point of getting it on their own. They do not routinely use recognized diagnostic testing for assessment. Nevertheless, they decide whether to accept each potential client based on their personal assessments of her psychological health.[49] The process seems more focused on weeding out troubled clients than identifying women whose psychological health would improve with cosmetic surgery.

A few doctors have tried to make explicit how they categorize clients who are most prone to be dissatisfied or troublesome, that is, more likely to sue—or in rare instances, even to murder them. One list includes people who are excessively concerned (in the doctor's opinion) about slight variations from the ideal, who want to become more socially adept or successful, who have unrealistic expectations of the physical changes that can occur, who come with strongly predetermined ideas of how

I had been in an abusive relationship which I finally got out of. Then I met Jim. He thought I'd look better with bigger boobs. I was unsure of myself, so I got them for him. Even after I started to have health problems he really wanted me to keep them. Finally I said to him, "If you get a penile implant in a month, I'll keep my implants. Otherwise I'm getting them out." He finally agreed it was okay for me to get the implants out.

So I figured, well, I'll go and have this done [breast implant surgery] because then my figure will be well-proportioned and—So I went and had it done—and I did it for myself—but I did it with the intent that possibly it would make the marriage better. You know, you have sometimes an underlying reason that you don't tell yourself you're doing it for—you know what I mean?[51]

they wish to look, who are unsure of what they wish to have done, who are name droppers, or who wish total secrecy about having the procedure done. Doctors generally seem to prefer women who can follow instructions well and are compliant. Another study of doctors' attitudes continues the list of preferred client characteristics: isolation of an "ugly" part of herself, pinpointing the "problem," rather than a diffuse request such as wanting to be prettier. This body partitioning, of course, allows for the "flaw" to be "corrected" or "fixed."[50]

Cosmetic surgeons do evaluate a potential client's motives for requesting the surgery. Based on the small amount of available research, the process seems to be relatively inchoate, with the plastic surgeon relying on intuition about whether a client has an underlying psychological problem. Many surgeons will say that a woman must claim that her motivation comes from her own desire for change. They concede, however, that other factors are important. They acknowledge that many women have surgery to improve their job status or have additional procedures at the surgeon's suggestion, particularly if the doctor's opinion is solicited. Many women, in fact, know by reading popular articles about cosmetic surgery that they are supposed to want the surgery for themselves. They may not tell the surgeon their real motivation if it is different from the reason stated in such articles.

Male and female potential clients are evaluated differently. One study reported that men had to show more signs of aging, such as more wrinkled skin, or have droopier eyelids in order to be accepted as clients. Surgery to promote a career was far more acceptable for men, and men tended to be far more difficult to satisfy. This indicates that the doctors use a cultural—not medical—standard. As the study notes, "If women's bodies are seen as *essentially* 'in need of repair,' then surgery on women can be seen as a moral imperative instead of an aesthetic option. But if men 'hardly ever have any problem

with that,' then surgery on men will require elaborate justification."[52]

Postsurgical assessment of the benefits of the surgery is also impressionistic. For instance, after breast surgery, the doctor looks for the "positive bathing suit sign," meaning that the woman has suntan lines showing that she was in a bathing suit. Doctors consider this a sign of improved social functioning. Presumably, the woman now feels more comfortable about allowing her body to be seen. This says nothing about how she has adjusted to her changed body or whether the quality of her relationships has improved, worsened, or remained the same. There may be a strong association among these events, but here again, research is lacking.

Research: Sloppy at Best

Plastic surgery journals are a prime source of new information for practicing cosmetic surgeons. Unfortunately, these specialty journals do not measure up to general surgery journals. Plastic surgery research tends to have more design flaws, less statistical analysis, and fewer collaborators with Ph.D.'s.[53] This should make us question the ability of the surgeon to give us an accurate assessment of the actual risks and actual benefits of any procedure.

In the most influential journal, *Plastic and Reconstructive Surgery,* the editor repeatedly bemoans the low quality of the papers submitted. He complains that surgeons write only about the best results of their surgery and that careful photography is used to enhance the differences between the "before" and "after" pictures. If the lighting, makeup, hairstyle, jewelry, and facial expression are different, the contrast can be magnified. Despite these pleas, the journal publishes articles with the very failings the editor decries. Some articles have appeared with no before and after photographs or with enhanced after photographs.[54]

The editor exhorts plastic surgeons submitting papers to include a range of results to give a truthful impression of the extent of possible results.[55] Thus, if other surgeons perform the operation and do not get the same results they will know that this is not their fault, that the operation simply has variable results. The editor also notes that many innovative procedures are reported in plastic surgery journals but later abandoned by the originating doctor because the results over time did not live up to expectations. Yet no notice or update is sent to the journals to discourage other doctors from following this fruitless path.

Proper controls are often lacking in the research. Many of the articles are based on poorly constructed experiments or deceptive reporting of results.[56] Articles reporting results for a significant number of consecutive people rather than just picking the ones with best results are so rare that one editorial lauds the fact that this particular issue contained two such studies.[57] Most articles simply report the surgeon's best results and ignore the rest. Studies using appropriate comparisons are also hard to find. One exception compared breast reduction using one technique on one breast and the other on the other breast. It is unclear, however, if the women who underwent the procedure knew that they were part of an experiment—if they were not told, the surgery was unethical. Complications are often mentioned only in passing, but they may be more prominently featured if the surgeon has found a way to correct them.

Advertising hype sometimes masquerades as science. Terms such as *cellulite*, a labeling of ordinary fat first coined by the European beauty industry, are used to transform normal body characteristics into medical problems. These labels then begin to appear as acceptable terminology in the surgical literature.

COMPETITION FOR OUR BODIES

Because it is so lucrative, the field of cosmetic surgery has grown explosively over the past decade. The average net income for plastic surgeons in 1992 was $209,840.[58]

From 1970 to 1992 the number of plastic surgeons almost tripled.[59] Projected growth in the number of plastic surgeons from 1960 to the end of the century is twenty-five times greater than the projected growth of the population.[60] This doesn't include the many other doctors now doing cosmetic procedures without specialized residency training. According to the American Medical Association, only about two-thirds of doctors whose primary activity is plastic surgery are board certified.[61] (See Chapter 4, "Caveat Emptor: Shopping for a Cosmetic Surgeon," about certification.)

Doctor Arnold Relman, the former editor of the *New England Journal of Medicine*, notes, "When doctors are as busy as they ought to be, they are much less inclined to do things of marginal medical value, or to seek patients for elective, cosmetic services."[62] Even Dr. Robert Goldwyn, *Plastic and Reconstructive Surgery* editor, admits the problem of excessive surgery. In one editorial he pleads with cosmetic surgeons to use some judgment in deciding when to do surgery. He points out that indiscriminate surgery can make women look peculiar—for example, having a tight face but wrinkled hands. He advocates avoiding surgery before it is "really necessary"—not doing it "prophylactically."[63]

Advertising campaigns are essential to cosmetic surgery not only because the surgeon must convince a client to undergo surgery without medical need but also to keep the increasing numbers of cosmetic surgeons working. Surgeons advertise directly in newspapers and magazines (especially city magazines), on TV, and hold free "seminars" (actually protracted advertisements). Carefully selected before and after photos are shown along with Greek and Roman statues. Some surgeons host "private consultations," which are usually held in fancy suites of upscale hotels. These are, of course, really sales pitches to entice women to have surgery.

If a particular doctor advertises heavily, it is especially important to be wary.

Often a large advertising budget means that the doctor must generate extra business to pay expenses. She or he may be more easily tempted to accept a person for whom an operation is medically unadvisable, such as a diabetic or heavy smoker, or implicitly promise results that are above his or her average results.

Since 1975, when the Federal Trade Commission (FTC) forced the American Medical Association to lift its ban on advertising by its members, cosmetic surgeons in particular have advertised. The FDA, which has jurisdiction over advertising, has never set clear guidelines for what is acceptable in medical advertisements, so advertisements are not well monitored. Trade organizations such as the American Medical Association, as well as state regulatory boards acting under state law, forbid deceptive advertising, but claim that the FTC discourages both state regulatory boards and organizational disciplinary committees from prosecuting all except the most blatantly deceptive advertisers.

Cosmetic surgeons also use professional qualifications and trade organizations to protect their market share. Plastic surgeons who are certified by the American Board of Plastic Surgery are very concerned, with some justification, that doctors untrained or poorly trained to perform certain procedures are doing them because the procedures are so lucrative. However, some of this concern comes not from regard for the public's welfare but from the desire to monopolize as much business as possible.

Some doctors who are not board certified for plastic surgery may be as well or better trained than plastic surgeons to do specific procedures. For instance, otolaryngologists learn to do nose-reshaping surgery and opthalmologists learn eyelid-reshaping surgery as part of their training.

One of the functions of the American Society of Plastic and Reconstructive Surgeons, the professional organization for doctors with certification by the American Board of Plastic Surgery, seems to be to protect the cosmetic surgery market for its members. It has even set up its own accrediting organization for out-of-hospital surgery facilities to keep them under the direct control of doctors certified by the American Board of Plastic Surgery. Other organizations, such as the American Board of Cosmetic Surgery, insist that performing a certain number of cosmetic operations is the only real criterion to acquire and prove skill.

Our culture's ideal of beauty has spawned a lucrative industry that has attracted an oversupply of practitioners who must fight turf wars and advertise heavily to attract new clients. Such heavy competition only increases the cosmetic surgeons' interest in reinforcing the cultural standards on which their work depends: that we all must look slender, young, and as northern European as possible. We should be aware that money often drives the doctor's claims for the surgery, and we should certainly weigh the very real risks of shaping ourselves to fit our culture's changing whims.

4

Caveat Emptor: Shopping for a Cosmetic Surgeon

IN A MORE accepting society, we would learn to feel better about our bodies without believing we need to have appearance-changing surgery that may interfere with our functioning. Even after fully understanding the risks of a particular type of surgery, some of us still may decide that the pressures, either internal or external, are so great that we will take the risks. We may feel subtle or not so subtle pressure from our workplace or partner to look younger, thinner, or different in some other way. We may find our social status changing unless we have surgery and don't wish to fight that prejudice. And we may need surgery to correct problems, such as breast implants, caused by previous cosmetic surgery.

If you are considering cosmetic surgery, try to be as clear as possible about why you want to have it and what you expect as a result of it. Please look through the exercises in Chapter 6, "Accepting Ourselves." In addition, consider answering the following questions:

➤ What are my goals for my relationships with friends, lovers, family?

➤ What do the important people in my life think about my looks? Do any make negative remarks about my looks? Have any made negative remarks about the part of my body that I want to change? If so, could these remarks have influenced my self-esteem? Do remarks from other people confirm negative remarks, or do other people say positive things about how I look?

➤ Did my family or friends make disparaging remarks about my body when I was growing up? Were these remarks related to my ethnic or racial heritage? How did that make me feel? Do I still believe those assessments?

➤ What words do I use to describe how I look? Who did I learn these words from and in what settings? Do they imply a judgment of me? If the words are negative, what positive words could substitute? For example, "droopy eyelids" could be transformed into sexy "bedroom eyes" or "wisdom curves";

"unsightly wrinkles" could become "experience lines"; and "saddlebags" could be "storehouses of energy."

➤ What do I think will change about my relationships with other people after the surgery? What can I do to work toward that goal right now?

➤ What are my work goals? Will changing the way I look actually make me more likely to advance in my career? Would learning other skills related to my job make as much difference in how far I could advance?

➤ What complications am I willing to risk? Numbness? Asymmetry? Pain? Loss of strength? What if I look worse than before the surgery? Am I willing to undergo further surgery that might or might not be able to correct the problem?

➤ Will I still be able to do all the activities I want to? (If there are specific activities that you like to do, such as gardening, playing a musical instrument, skiing, running, tennis, etc., ask your surgeon if the surgery might interfere with them.)

➤ How often will I have to repeat the surgery because its effect will lessen over time? Am I willing to do this?

➤ How much will it cost? Can I easily afford it? Do I have to give up anything in order to afford the surgery? Could I afford repeat surgery?

If you do choose surgery, be careful about choosing a doctor and a facility where it will be done to reduce your chances of having complications. Confirm with your doctor that the surgery can do what you expect of it and go over all of the possible complications. Remember that cosmetic surgery practices often lack oversight (see "Is It Medicine?" in Chapter 3).

Most cosmetic surgery is not covered by medical insurance. Surgeons usually require the client to pay in advance of the operation, although an increasing number are accepting credit card payment. "Cut now, pay later" plans to borrow money for the surgery, sponsored by plastic surgery professional organizations, are also becoming more widely promoted. But the interest on these plans often is the highest allowed by law.

Ask if there are different ways your procedure can be performed. Does your doctor plan to try a (relatively) new approach on you? One plastic surgery textbook states: "Plastic surgery is perhaps the most innovative of all specialties....many of our complex repairs [combine] some old principle with eternally evolving new approaches. I venture to say that a large part of the practice of leading, creative plastic surgeons involves the introduction of relatively or completely new techniques."[1] Ask how the doctor keeps track of the results of new techniques (follow-up procedures), what is the longest period of time that clients have been tracked, and how many have been followed for that period.

DECIPHERING THE ADS

Doctors advertise their expertise in cosmetic surgery more than practitioners of any other field of medicine.[2] In an investigation of the deceptive practices of cosmetic surgery practitioners, a congressional subcommittee identified ways ads mislead.[3] So, beware if the advertising does any of the following:

➤ Promises specific physical results

➤ Claims that the operation is innovative or claims that the surgeon invented some kind of instrument for this procedure. Generally this type of statement is hype. But, if the statement is true, find out how much practice the surgeon has with the new instrument or procedure.

➤ Invites you to look at the facilities to see how state of the art they are—Do you know what state of the art really is?

➤ Promises something free for having a consultation

➤ Makes the before and after shots not comparable—Look for changes in the angle of the photograph, different lighting or facial expressions. Check to see if the model has changed hairdo, jewelry, or makeup

➤ Provides a testimonial that implies you will get similar results

➤ Uses models deceptively—Check if the people pictured in the ad actually are clients of the surgeon. Some surgeons use hired professional models. Check to make sure that the person actually had the procedure she is helping to advertise and that it was done by the advertising surgeon

➤ Lists credentials that are not meaningful—Check to see if the board certification, if listed, is in a field related to the procedure. Find out what the requirements are for that certification. Check to see if trade organizations—which are irrelevant—such as the American Medical Association, are listed. Are there other unrelated credentials listed, such as journal publications?

➤ Lists no operating physician, just a practice name—You need a doctor's name in order to check credentials. Check any claims made about the surgeons and staff

➤ Implies or states that the surgery is painless and easy

➤ Mentions low rates or easy financing

CHOOSING A SURGEON

Always find out about the surgeon's experience in doing the procedure you are considering. Remember, the surgeon may not have received formal training during his or her residency program in the particular procedure(s) he or she intends to perform on you. Some techniques, such as liposuction, are only now being introduced into some medical schools' residency programs. Many doctors doing liposuction learned the technique on their own by apprenticing to someone who has done it or by taking a short course, sometimes over a weekend. The worst courses do not include practice. These "courses" may only include videos or the chance to observe someone else doing the procedure. That means that the first women coming to such a doctor for this procedure are experimental subjects although they probably will not know it and will probably pay several thousand dollars to have that honor. Under these circumstances the doctor should do the procedure for free or even pay women since the surgeon is the one who needs subjects on whom to practice. Of course, few of us would consent to being learning material for elective surgery, particularly if we realized that the surgeon would not be supervised during the operation. And even when the surgeon has experience with a particular technique, such as liposuction, it still is important to inquire how often the surgeon has used it in the way that you are seeking. For instance, unlike the buttocks, the lower legs have only a thin layer of fat under the skin. Your surgeon may not have the experience of knowing how that difference affects the final result if she or he has only used liposuction on the buttocks.

You can evaluate a surgeon by asking specific questions about his or her abilities. Ask how many times the surgeon has done this particular procedure and over what period of time. How many procedures does the surgeon do in a week? In a month? Can you see pictures of what the surgeon considers his or her best, worst, and average work? What complications have occurred? What complications have other surgeons seen with this procedure? (It may be easier for the doctor to talk about the problems of other surgeons.) If the surgeon denies complications, then either she or he hasn't done enough procedures or is lying. No experienced cosmetic surgeon is so good that he or she has had none. Does the cost of the initial surgery cover later corrective surgery if it becomes necessary? You may also wish to ask a doctor you trust about the surgeon's reputation although this evaluation should not substitute for your own. Whenever the surgeon suggests unrequested procedures, you would be wise to try to evaluate the doctor's motives as discussed in Chapter 3 under "Competition for Our Bodies."

It is also important to inquire at what hospital the surgeon has admitting privileges and if he or she is allowed to perform in that hospital the same procedures you plan to have. If the surgeon is allowed to perform this surgery in the hospital, it means that other doctors have confidence that this surgeon is at least minimally qualified to do the procedure. On the other hand, some cosmetic surgeons claim that restricting hospital privileges is a way to limit the number of cosmetic surgeons in an area, keeping income high. This is undoubtedly sometimes true, but treat the claim as a flag to do extra investigation. Check with the surgeon's clients who have had the surgery you are interested in, not only recently but also a number of years ago. If you can find them on your own, you are more likely to find women who have had problems, because often a doctor will only have a list of satisfied clients who are willing to talk to prospective clients. See how pleased they are with the results. It is important to talk for a while about the surgery. Many people will at first say that nothing is wrong but will later tell you about numb spots, intermittent pain in some area, or other problems.

CHECKING ON CERTIFICATION

Often people who practice crafts that affect the body, such as tattoo artists, hair-dressers, and manicurists, must be formally trained and pass a city or state exam in their specific field before they are licensed to practice. A doctor, however, "can perform any kind of specialized surgery in his office with only a general medical license."[4]

Ask if the surgeon is board certified and by what board. Not all boards have equally high standards for certification (see box "Boards for Cosmetic Surgery"). The most reliable certification for a cosmetic surgeon is from one of the boards approved by the American Board of Medical Specialties (ABMS) in plastic surgery, otolaryngology (ears, nose, and throat), dermatology (skin), and ophthalmology (eyes). These specialty boards operate under the American Medical Association. The amount of cosmetic surgery as opposed to reconstructive surgery that the doctor does while in these residency training programs varies with the hospital.

Over the years at least eight other boards besides the ones recognized by ABMS have been established to promote cosmetic surgery. All have different requirements for their own certification, some more rigorous than others. Some of these boards require that a doctor be ABMS board certified in some field of medicine, which may not necessarily be relevant to cosmetic surgery. For instance, an ABMS-board-certified internist, family practitioner, or pathologist could qualify for certification by some of these boards. Some boards require that a doctor take a written test and provide evidence of having done a certain number of pertinent surgeries. Other boards require little more than payment of a registration fee. If a doctor claims board certification, find out which board the doctor is referring to. Write down the exact name since so many are almost alike, a tactic perhaps used to confuse consumers.[5] Then ask what the doctor had to do to qualify for certification. Ask for the board's address and telephone number; most are difficult to find. Call or write the board to confirm what your doctor has told you.

Boards for Cosmetic Surgery

Approved by American Board of Medical Specialties:

For general plastic surgery:
  American Board of Plastic Surgery

Includes training in some types of plastic surgery:
  American Board of Dermatology
  American Board of Ophthalmology
  American Board of Otolaryngology

Not Approved by the American Board of Medical Specialties:

American Board of Aesthetic Plastic Surgery
American Board of Cosmetic Plastic Surgery
American Board of Cosmetic Surgery
American Board of Facial Cosmetic Surgery
American Board of Facial Plastic Surgery
American Board of Facial Plastic and Reconstructive Surgery
American Board of Maxillofacial Surgeons
American Board of Plastic Aesthetic Surgeons

Although doing all this requires a great deal of self-assertion on your part, remember that your health is at stake.

Do not confuse board certification with membership in an organization. Any group the surgeon lists that calls itself an academy, association, or a society is a trade organization. Some of these require relevant board certification and others don't, but generally the primary qualification for membership is simply payment of dues.

CHOOSING A FACILITY

Most hospitals seek accreditation from a national organization that sets standards for hospital safety. These regulations cover such areas as sterilization and emergency equipment and procedures. Surgeons working outside of a hospital, however, have no such requirements, and most cosmetic surgery is done out of a hospital in a doctor's office or clinic. Only one in ten nonhospital facilities for cosmetic surgery is certified for safety by any accrediting agency.[6]

The two national organizations that have set standards for accreditation procedures for out-of-hospital surgical facilities are the American Association for Accreditation of Ambulatory Plastic Surgery Facilities and the Accreditation Association for Ambulatory Health Care.[7] They have somewhat different rules, but both require that a plan be in place to cover cases of heart failure and, if necessary, for transferring a client to a hospital. The requirements also include regulations on patient care, such as taking a proper medical history; appropriate clinical services; use of a qualified person to administer anesthetics, such as a doctor or nurse with training in that field; the ability to monitor a patient under anesthesia and to resuscitate if necessary; and appropriate postsurgical monitoring. These are very important considerations if general anesthesia is used, and some are important with various types of local anesthesia, particularly if there is a severe allergic reaction. Some doctors are conscientious about safety precautions, which can be expensive, even if their facilities are not accredited, but many find that they can save money by skimping in this area. Chances are you won't need any of the emergency backup equipment and procedures, but make sure that they are available.

If you are considering having surgery in an office or clinic that is not accredited, ask plenty of questions before consenting to have surgery there. Find out what kind of emergency equipment is available, when it would be used, and how often employees are drilled in emergency procedures. All of this information may be hard to evaluate unless you have worked in a medical facility or know someone who does, but it is worth asking about these procedures anyway. If there is hesitation on the part of the personnel in answering such questions, then it is quite possible that the facility, personnel, or both are inadequate.

Remember that cosmetic surgery is the only surgery routinely done at the initiative of clients, mainly women. As long as cosmetic surgery remains extremely lucrative, a doctor's incentive to create a need for it and to minimize complications will be strong. So do not hesitate to get second opinions and to ask lots of questions.

Inflating Our Image: Breast Implants

PROBABLY THE dangers of breast implant surgery are more widely known than other types of cosmetic surgery because of the publicity generated during government hearings in 1991 and 1992 and the several lawsuits since 1985. The saga of breast implants is a glaring example of how beauty stereotypes have combined with suppression of information to endanger our health. We have been misled about the safety of these devices. We have been seduced into believing that we could surgically change our bodies to heighten our self-esteem and sexual appeal at no cost to our health. As many as a million women have possibly compromised their health for this elusive goal.

BEAUTY AND THE BEAST

So many of us feel inadequate about our breasts that we must believe that the size and shape of breasts are important measures of our beauty, femininity, and desirability. Few of us have escaped being influenced by the current ideal image of woman as adolescent yet voluptuous, innocent yet with latent sexuality. We are told that our breasts should be full, with taut, smooth skin and nipples pointing upward or outward from the middle. We generally do not see images of the natural progression of breast shape over a lifetime. Images that represent primarily one breast shape encourage us to deny that a large range of breast shapes is normal. "Droopy" or "sagging" breasts are disparaged. Bras, originally designed in the 1920s to flatten the breasts, now mold the breast into an imitation of eternal adolescence, so that when we are clothed we need never look as if our breasts have functioned or aged.

Yet our breasts are designed to be able to enlarge and contract as surely as the uterus. Size and shape fluctuations from pregnancy, lactation, weight changes, and age will inevitably produce relaxed breasts, which hang lower. In addition, breast shape changes can carry other meanings. Breasts that have softened after nursing may remind us that a woman may have demands on her time and energies from her children, not only from her partner. This can have serious consequences in abusive relationships in which a partner is jealous of any

My sister used to lecture me that if I didn't wear a bra I would get "Cooper's Droopers." Cooper was supposed to be some doctor who found out that bra support would keep a woman's breasts firm. But I never could figure out why I couldn't just start to wear a bra after my breasts drooped and no one would be the wiser. I guess I just didn't give sufficient weight to how my husband might respond to me in bed if I "let myself go."

When I was in the eighth grade I didn't want to go to school. It was the most horrible experience and it was the girls who started it. It wasn't boys. I do remember this one girl just started saying that I was flat-chested and started teasing me, calling me a nickname. It got so bad that even my friends joined in because they didn't realize how much it was hurting me.

And then I remember another time. I think I must have been a freshman in college when my sister met her husband, who's now a surgeon. I remember we were sitting around the kitchen table one day and he was talking about having just gone through a rotation in cosmetic surgery. He was talking about this new technique of implants and I sat there and said, "That's it. I'm going to have that done." I was absolutely, totally decided.

When I became pregnant and my breasts enlarged, my husband insisted on taking pictures of me. I hated that and it further increased my belief that to be attractive one had to have big breasts.

time a woman is directing her attention to others. In addition, if a woman no longer looks as youthful as the abusing partner wishes, she may be pressured to have implants. (For more on abusive relationships, see Part II.)

We are also often ambivalent about our breasts because they develop at a time when we are learning about and frequently are conflicted about our sexual development, and we can't easily hide breast development. We may be teased because our breasts are too large or too small.

During adolescence we desperately want to be "normal." For girls, appearance is more crucial than for boys. Girls whose breasts develop "early" or "late" have a harder time liking themselves than do boys who develop earlier or later than average.[1] Those of us who have had one breast grow noticeably larger than the other may have felt particularly embarrassed and ashamed about not looking "normal."

Advertising and soft-core pornography have turned our breasts into sexual and romantic objects for the pleasure of others without regard to our own feelings. Breasts have become fetishes. In advertising, partially uncovered breasts or very large breasts are shorthand for sexual availability. These images, of course, are designed to reinforce many men's fantasies. Women who want heterosexual relationships can hardly ignore the importance breasts have come to have in attracting men. To some extent these images affect those of us who are lesbians as well; at times, we also hope that our breasts will arouse a woman's sexual interest.

Afraid that only firm, perky breasts are attractive to others, we see ourselves through other people's eyes and forget to be concerned about our breasts' functions. We may not keep clearly in mind that our breasts are a part of *our* bodies. Even when we consider breast function, it is usually only in relationship to nursing—a way that breasts are useful for others. In fact, breast size is determined mostly by the amount of

fat in the breast and is completely unrelated to nursing ability. Only the glandular tissue, which takes up remarkably little space in our breasts when we are not lactating, determines a woman's ability to nurse. Flat-chested women can easily make enough milk to nurse a baby successfully.

We rarely discuss the sexual function of the breast for our own pleasure. For many of us, arousal is enhanced considerably by breast and nipple stimulation. Some women can have orgasms from nipple stimulation alone. Ignoring this aspect of breast function no doubt stems historically from viewing women as men's property, or at least as objects for their pleasure without regard for our own.

The current biologically unlikely beauty ideal, a body thin all over except for the breasts, has led some of us to consider surgery. In some occupations, especially in the entertainment or modeling industries, women often need large breasts to obtain work. As more women feel the necessity to surgically enlarge their breasts, the pressure to do the same for other small-breasted women will increase as they find themselves more and more discriminated against.

Plastic surgeons have reinforced our insecurities, identifying small breasts as a disease called *micromastia* and labeling relaxed breasts as *involuted*, reflecting negative prejudices about the diversity and changes in women's bodies. Breast enlargement of healthy breasts using implants is called "augmentation."

Many women think about breast surgery after having one or more children, when their breasts soften, to "restore" the youthful appearance that they had previously. We may be worried that a sexual partner will think that we don't measure up, that we will be less attractive and less desirable sexually.

We also may have formed our image of our adult bodies during adolescence and may have trouble reconciling our physical changes with these images. Because the idea of having adolescent breasts again is so enticing, we may be easily swayed to have implants. Perhaps using positive words about our breasts would help us feel more loving toward them as they matured. We might think of them as softer, more mellow, more relaxed, and draping over our chests as they become more flowing.

Those of us who have had mastectomies may feel that our bodies or our femininity have been damaged by breast amputation. Others may simply find a prosthesis uncomfortable, yet feel compelled to wear one. Most of us would be extremely embarrassed or at least uneasy about suddenly appearing in public either one-breasted or flat-chested. The social pressure to hide a mastectomy is tremendous. Audre Lorde, in *The Cancer Journals*, remembers that when she arrived at the cancer clinic without her prosthesis, one nurse told her she was bad for office morale.[2] The situation, luckily, is changing slightly with the publication of a few pictures of women showing their mastectomy scars.[3] For those of us with mastectomies, doctors have offered breast implants as the easiest solution to remove self-consciousness about a missing breast, to increase our self-esteem, and to help us forget that we have had cancer. Doctors call such breast implant surgery *reconstruction* when it is performed on a woman who has had a mastectomy.

Before 1991, approximately 20 to 35 percent of women with breast implants had them inserted after a mastectomy.[4] Since the Food and Drug Administration partially restricted the use of implants for enlargement, the proportion of women getting implants for reconstruction has risen to almost half of all implant surgeries.

THE IMPLANTS

Several types of implants have been developed to enlarge a breast or to reconstruct breast tissue removed during a mastectomy. All have a silicone rubberlike (elastomer) shell or envelope. The outside surface of the envelope may be smooth, rough, or covered with fine hairs of silicone, giving it a fuzzy appearance. Some implants have a thin layer of polyurethane foam glued to the outside and are filled with silicone gel. These implants were taken off the market in 1991, but many women still carry them inside their bodies. The filling for other types is saline (salt water), silicone gel, or both. Saline-plus-silicone implants contain two compartments, one inside the other, with one filling in each compartment. Researchers are still searching for new fillings with fewer risks than silicone gel yet with the advantages of its consistency.

It may be that some women can readjust their feelings about themselves so that they no longer feel the need for surgery, but I don't think I could have done that. I would feel better about feminist analysis that says that women should feel fine about having invisible breasts if there was any evidence that lesbian feminists did not care about such things in their prospective partners, or if there were any designers who tried to make clothing for women of that shape. I have still never seen any evidence of such acceptance, which leaves women with very small breasts still feeling that they are "freaks."

My doctor told me I needed a mastectomy and in the same breath she said I could also have reconstruction. I was so focused on the cancer that I didn't give the reconstruction part much thought. She assured me that I would feel better if I had immediate reconstruction and that problems I might have from the implant were minor. I spent months researching whether or not to have the mastectomy and now I know that I should have spent the same amount of time researching whether to have the implants. It just didn't occur to me that I would have problems from the implants, I was so worried about dying from the cancer.

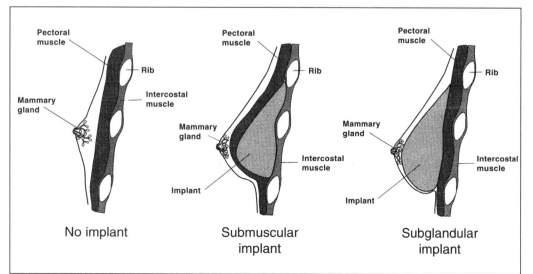

Poet/writer Andrée
O'Connor.

Implants are placed either subglandularly, behind the breast tissue and in front of the chest (pectoral) muscle, or submuscularly, behind the chest muscle and in front of the ribs. After mastectomy, the submuscular placement is almost always used. The incision for enlargement can be in the fold under the breast (submammary crease), around the bottom edge of the areola (periareola), or through the armpit (axilla). After mastectomy, a temporary implant is put in place to stretch the skin. This is replaced by a "permanent" implant through the existing scar. Each plastic surgeon has his or her preferred combination of placement and incision. Each has its benefits and problems.

Any kind of breast enlargement surgery is likely to cause a woman's breast to become numb, at least temporarily, because nerves are cut. No one can predict the regeneration of nerve cells, which grow slowly, to know how much sensation a woman may eventually regain. If the implants are inserted at the edge of the nipple, the surgeon is more likely than with other insertion methods to cut the important nerve that enters the nipple on its underside. A woman who loses feeling in her nipple loses part or all of her ability to have a sexual response from her breasts or to nurse. Some women are disturbed that their breasts feel "cooler" after the implant is inserted.

The human body tries to rid itself of foreign objects. No material can be placed in the body without eliciting this response, although some people react less than others. If we have no external reaction we may think that our bodies have accepted the implant, but our cells will never stop trying to eject it. However, because the implant cannot be removed by the immune system, the body forms a scar around it. In addition, since the implants may rupture, or leak silicone while they are intact, we may have a response to foreign bodies outside the immediate area of the implant, as discussed below.

Most women who have implants eventually need further surgery to remove them. The implants might be aging, broken, or a suspected cause of health problems. While implant removal prevents increased silicone exposure and often results in the improvement of various symptoms, it does not remove or counteract any silicone that might have escaped from the implant. Even removing the entire breast would not affect any silicone that might have migrated to other parts of the body.

Explant surgery can be done three ways: the scar capsule and the implant can be removed as a unit, the implant can be removed first and then the scar capsule, or the implant alone can be removed. The last is the simplest procedure and does not remove any breast or muscle tissue, and there is probably no need for anything more extensive if the implant is filled with saline. Removing both the implant and scar tissue as a unit reduces the possibility that the procedure will cause (more) silicone gel to spill into the body (if the implant is already ruptured or if it is broken during the removal process). However, sometimes the scar capsule is embedded in the chest muscle or around the ribs and all of it cannot be removed.

Those of us who have had implants and then decided to remove them have had a wide range of responses to our new body shapes. But almost universal is a sigh of relief that we are no longer exposed to potentially large doses of silicone on a daily basis.

KNOWN AND SUSPECTED COMPLICATIONS

The following sections discuss known and suspected complications from breast-implant surgery, many of which are associated with responses to a foreign body. Except for capsular contracture, the complications were not widely known by the general public until the well-publicized FDA hearings in November 1991 and February 1992 on silicone gel-filled implants.

I don't know if my symptoms [achiness and pain] have improved yet but I can't tell you how much better I feel psychologically to have them out.

I can't believe that the tingling and numbness in my arm has gone away. I have more sensation in my breasts, too.

I don't like the way my breasts look without the implants. I didn't expect to look attractive. There's no way that they could. But I put it all in perspective. I say, "I've got my health," and knock on wood, that's important, you know. There's a lot of other things in life that are so rewarding that something like this is a pretty minor problem.

I expected to look all flat and flabby but my breasts look younger now than before I had the implants. The doctor did such a terrific job.

I couldn't bear to have nothing so I had the silicone ones replaced with saline. I figured I already was exposed to the silicone.

My chest and arm continued to ache so I went back to my plastic surgeon. He kind of blew it off. Then I started having trouble getting appointments with him so I never went back. I thought, why should I waste my time with someone who doesn't want to help me? I think he didn't know what was going on but he didn't want to admit it. Maybe if these guys would admit their ignorance and listen a little, they might learn something.

The thing that was so horrible was moments before I went under the knife to have these things taken out— this whole thing was so terrifying—and he sits there and he goes, "Are you sure you don't want the saline?" I'm like, "Oh, my God. That's the last thing I need to hear."

Well, you just get used to it. You can adjust to anything. My chest is too tender to wear a prosthesis—so what, I'm flat-chested. That's their problem if it bothers somebody. My personality isn't in my breasts.

You know, I never thought about it until just now, but my second child didn't nurse as long as the first. And I had the implants put in after the first one because I was so saggy.

Capsular Contracture

The most common complication is a tightening of the scar tissue that always forms around a foreign object the body cannot get rid of. This tightening is called *capsular contracture*. Besides giving the breast an unnatural firmness, the more severe the contracture, the more likely a woman is to experience discomfort or pain. Her breasts will become more spherical. In the extreme they may look like and feel like baseballs. She may have difficulty lying on her stomach. Some women who have mild contracture apparently do not mind the unnatural firmness and report simply that it makes their breasts perkier. However, the more contracture, the less natural a woman's breasts look when she lies down since the contracture prevents the breasts from falling to the side in response to gravity; her breasts look the same as they do when she is standing.

No research exists on whether contracture affects a woman's ability to nurse. Any scarring that would keep the milk-producing ducts from fully expanding, however, is likely to reduce total milk production. Contracture also interferes with detection of breast cancers (see below).

Doctors use two procedures to relieve capsular contracture. In the first, open capsulotomy, the doctor removes the implant and makes many small cuts in the scar tissue before replacing the same or a different implant. In closed capsulotomy, which manufacturers do not recommend because of possible implant rupture, the doctor twists or pushes very hard on the breast to break up the scar capsule.

Silicone Gel Leakage

All intact implants with silicone gel filling constantly leak silicone through the wall of the implant. This "gel bleed" forms an oily layer on the outside of the implant. Manufacturers and plastic surgeons have claimed that the leaked silicone is harmless and that the scar tissue surrounding the implant contains it. Both assertions are unproven. In addition, manufacturers and surgeons have consistently tried to find ways to reduce the amount of scar tissue the body forms in reaction to the implant, thereby reducing any possible restriction on the movement of leaked silicone to other parts of the body.

The gel consists of two parts. The first is a polymer—that is, long chains of silicone molecules linked to each other to form a spongelike matrix. This matrix is swelled with the second component, silicone oil, which may comprise as much as 90 percent of the filling. The oil is made of short, unlinked chains of silicone. These smaller lengths of silicone, which are able to pass through the shell, are more likely to provoke a cellular response; they are more biologically active. So called "low bleed" gel-filled implants seem to reduce the total amount of leakage but may not reduce the flow of the smallest molecules at all.

Cells from the immune system can engulf small droplets of silicone and carry them to other parts of the body, or the body may try to wall off the leaked silicone with more scar tissue. Droplets of silicone that are encased in scar tissue are called granulomas. They sometimes can be felt or show up on X rays, mimicking small cancers. Women with silicone granulomas are at greater risk for having biopsies (surgical removal and examination of tissue) than women without them.

Silicone that escapes from breast implants is chemically similar to the silicone oil formerly injected into women's bodies to enlarge breasts. The FDA decided in 1965 that silicone oil was too hazardous to inject unless under strict experimental protocols. Silicone oil caused tissue hardening, inflammation, blockage of blood vessels, tissue death (necrosis), ulceration of and oozing through the skin, and sometimes necessitated amputation of the breast. Silicone from breast injections was found in women's abdomens, arms, lymph nodes, and other locations far from the breast. Sometimes the silicone was encased in scar tissue, mimicking tumors or pressing painfully on nerves. The government, manufacturers and doctors have never explained how the silicone that escapes from breast implants might be different from silicone oil injected into the body.

Rupture

Strong pressure or a sharp blow to any implant can break the shell, as will normal wear and tear over time.[5]

If a strong force breaks the implant, the gel may simultaneously be forced into the surrounding tissues, causing pain and swelling. A woman who knows her implant has broken should have it removed as soon as possible.

Sometimes the implant seems to rupture spontaneously. The strength of the shell may diminish over time as a reaction to contact with the body. A fold or seam may weaken as body movements repeatedly pull on it. Sharp crystals, called calcifications, may form on the shell to wall off the implant. These mineral deposits may cut through the implant shell as well as irritate body tissues. No one yet knows what the average life span of an implant is or whether it varies with the thickness of the shell. Small studies, however, indicate that the rate of rupture rises dramatically after about seven years.[6]

The shells of low-bleed implants may present an additional danger. They contain an added layer of fluorosilicone as part of the shell, either laminated between other layers of silicone or lining the interior surface of the shell. Although fluorosilicone is known to poison living cells on contact, manufacturers have yet to study what happens when it comes in contact with body tissues when the shell breaks or delaminates. Indeed, manufacturers do not even know whether any fluorosilicone migrates out of the shell of an unbroken implant.

Unfortunately, silicone-gel-filled implants may break without obvious external signs. This was discovered by doctors who removed implants for other reasons and found them already broken. Sometimes the shells of unbroken implants become so weak that they break during the removal process, spilling the silicone filling, which sticks to the tissues because it is oily. The shells of some implants develop pinholes through which the gel leaks as if through a sieve. Doctors try to wipe up as much loose silicone as they can. Even if a doctor claims that he or she can remove all the silicone, it is hard to see how this is possible.[7] Sometimes healthy tissue has to be removed in order to clean out the gel. (If the implant and the surrounding scar capsule are removed as a unit, the free silicone can usually be contained and removed without spilling.)

Mammography, ultrasound, and MRI (magnetic resonance imaging) sometimes can determine if an implant is ruptured, but many ruptures do not show up with any of these techniques. Some doctors and researchers are recommending a mostly outdated and hard-to-find form of breast imaging called xeromammography. Although it gives more radiation per dose (which is why it was discarded for breast cancer screening), fewer views may be required than with current mammography machines in trying to detect a rupture. The technique gives a clearer image of the edge of the implant, giving more information for this purpose than a regular mammogram. Saline-filled implant ruptures are obvious because the implant deflates when the shell breaks. Unlike silicone gel, the saline is probably harmless inside the body.

Problems with Cancer Detection

Any kind of breast implant makes mammography more difficult. The silicone shell is mostly opaque to the X rays, regardless of the filling. Gel-filled implants are nearly or completely opaque, so the implant shows up as a solid white area on the mammogram. Saline-filled implants are partly opaque to X rays as well. The technician doing the mammogram may use a special displacement technique, the Eklund technique, in which she pulls the breast tissue away from the implant as

I remember the sensation of breaking the implant. I don't know if the implant or the capsule itself broke. I gave a friend of mine a bear hug. It felt like my bra strap had snapped. He felt it, too.

much as possible. This technique has never been subjected to rigorous research to determine if it allows more cancers to be detected, or if it exerts more or less force on implants than a mammogram done in the regular way. If an implant shell is weak, a mammogram done with either technique might cause the implant to rupture. The more contracture around the implant, the less breast tissue can be seen with mammography. Even if the breast remains soft, a part of the breast still remains hidden because of the implant. Also, more views of the breast will have to be taken to see as much as possible. These extra views partially negate the safety advances in mammography that result from using less radiation.

The calcifications that develop around an implant present another problem. The radiologist will most likely assume that calcification on the edge of the implant is caused by the body's reaction to the implant. But since calcifications are a possible sign of a developing cancer, if a cancer is located on the edge of the implant it may not be recognized.

The scar tissue around the implant also impedes manual examination of the breast by the woman herself and by a medical practitioner. Again, the more contracture, the harder it is to find a developing cancer.

Changes in the Silicone

After the implant is in the body for a while, the silicone shell, gel, or both turns from clear to cloudy. One theory is that oxidizing compounds made by the body to break down foreign bodies attack the silicone. No studies seem to have been done to find out how long this process takes, whether it is significant for the integrity of the implant, or if the visible change is a sign that the implant is affecting the body.

SUSPECTED LONG-TERM RISKS

In thirty years of use, several disturbing, serious problems seem to be connected to silicone in the body. All breast implants have silicone shells, regardless of their filling, and all can cause complications. Some problems have been revealed by animal studies, others by reports from people who have had silicone implants in such places as breasts, finger joints, or in internal shunts to drain fluid from the brain. Animal experiments from as long ago as the mid-1960s indicate a link with cancer and reproductive problems. Sporadic reports in the medical literature have appeared about the development of various autoimmune problems after implanting silicone in different parts of the body. Implant manufacturers and many doctors deny the links, citing widespread and varied medical use of silicone, often with no apparent harm. At present, there is inadequate support for this claim. There are no studies that follow a woman from the time of implantation, nor do existing studies follow enough women for sufficient lengths of time to detect potential problems.

Only after recent publicity have some women realized that their sometimes mysterious health problems may be a result of having breast implants. They have developed joint achiness; stiffness; muscle weakness; extreme tiredness; burning; itching; fungal infections on their skin, in their vaginas, or under their nails; and severe, sometimes incapacitating pain in their chests, often radiating down one arm. Complaints range from common problems such as anemia to rare problems such as grain allergies or problems digesting fats. For years unsuspecting women did not report their medical problems to their plastic surgeons. Primary care providers, cancer specialists, and rheumatologists have failed to ask women if they have implants. Not until 1992 did the manufacturers and the federal government announce that each planned to study these problems seriously.

Autoimmune Conditions

The peak ages for the development of most autoimmune conditions coincides with the ages when the majority of women have gotten implants for breast enlargement. Thus, without tracking large numbers of women for a sufficient length of time, changes in autoimmune disease rates may not be apparent. Several studies in the past few years claim to show no connection between autoimmune problems and implants. These studies usually have not looked at sufficient numbers of women long enough to reach a definitive statistical conclusion. Most also look at traditional autoimmune disease categories (see box below), which do not correspond to the symptoms experienced by many women with implants. Some studies also collect data only from medical records, not patient interviews (which are much more time-consuming), relying on the records for all the relevant data. And a number of the studies were funded by plastic surgeons, the manufacturers, or both.[8]

Many women report, however, that their health problems started after getting the implants or after a known or suspected rupture of a silicone-gel-containing implant. Also, for many women, symptoms decrease after implant removal. However, this does not prove that the implant caused the symptoms; autoimmune symptoms can subside for unknown reasons. One rheumatologist researching the connection with silicone reports, however, that 70 percent of women who have had their implants removed feel better within two years.[9]

Another possible, unexplored cause of immune system problems is a compound added to all shells to keep them flexible.[10] Fumed silica is chemically identical to ordinary silica, a known immune system stimulant and the ingredient that makes asbestos so dangerous. The fumed silica is bound to the elastomer shell with

My ANA titre [an indicator of autoimmune disease] was very high when I had my implants in. Six months after removal it was negative. It's almost a year now since I had my implants removed. I feel less tired and less achy every month. But I still need to take a fungicide to control a yeast infection in my vagina.

Autoimmune Diseases

In autoimmune diseases, our immune cells do not recognize our own cells as belonging to us, but attack them as if they were foreign invaders. Most autoimmune diseases disproportionately affect women. Classic autoimmune diseases include rheumatoid arthritis, systemic lupus erythematosus, scleroderma, fibromyalgia, and Sjögren's disease. Many of these diseases are accompanied by achiness, joint swelling, changes in the skin, chronic fatigue, and changes in certain components of the blood (which can be easily measured). Symptoms can be mild to incapacitating. The course of the disease may be unpredictable, with flare-ups and remission occurring for no apparent reason. Medication doesn't always control symptoms and often has serious side effects. Some diseases, such as scleroderma, can be fatal. Each disease has some specific characteristics, such as the butterfly-shaped facial rash for lupus, or the dry eyes and other mucous membranes of Sjögren's. Many women who have implants and autoimmune symptoms do not fit into one disease category but seem to have symptoms of several diseases. Rheumatologists can help diagnose these problems.

electrostatic bonds, but no research shows how strong those bonds are. The FDA approved the use of fumed silica based on small, inadequate inhalation studies of the compound, not implantation studies that would duplicate the presence of the implant in the body. If the fumed silica separates from the shell over time, it might be quite harmful.

Reproductive Problems

Animal studies on reproductive problems after implantation with silicone are minimal and inconclusive with studies yielding contradictory results.[11] Some women who have had implants during pregnancy and nursing report unusual problems in their children, such as repeated stomachaches and other digestive problems, long-term muscle aches, and rare autoimmune conditions, and they question whether silicone in their bodies has affected their children. Some women with gel-filled implants found silicone oil leaking from their nipples. These women have now joined together to form an organization called Children Afflicted by Toxic Substances (CATS) (see "Resources"). By the end of September 1994, about 2000 families had reported that their children have difficulties ranging from gastric motility to autoimmune problems at unusually young ages. The organization collects data from its own members by questionnaire and through physicians to explore further whether there is a connection between maternal exposure to silicone and children with physical problems. It also arranges for some children to be examined by pediatric specialists as part of its research.[12]

Cancer

A connection between breast implants and cancer is particularly difficult to prove or disprove because of the long time between exposure to a cancer-causing substance and the detection of the disease. However, animal studies raise serious questions about a possible link.[13] So far, the longest study looking for cancer in women with breast implants follows them for an average of ten years after implantation. No increase in breast cancer has been identified so far, though none would be expected before 15 or 20 years have passed. Thus, the results for breast cancer mean nothing yet. This same study, however, has shown a small but statistically significant increase in lung and vulvar cancer in women with implants. The women will have to be followed further to see if this trend continues and reflects an actual increased risk.[14]

Great controversy has surrounded the relationship of polyurethane-covered implants to cancer. Polyurethane produces cancers when implanted in rats. Researchers know that it breaks down into at least two cancer-causing substances. Opinion is divided, however, on whether enough of these harmful substances accumulates to cause cancer in women. Again, surgeons and the manufacturer of polyurethane-covered breast implants have failed to track women who had the devices in the past. Although the FDA has finally required the manufacturer to monitor the women, how rigorously it will do so is still unknown.

Circulatory Problems

A few women have also reported cardiovascular problems, in particular, transient ischemic attacks (ministrokes) and mitral valve prolapse that developed after getting the implants. Again, these are problems that would occur anyway in a certain percentage of women in the same age group. No study has examined whether there is an increase in these symptoms in women with breast implants.

Theoretically, though, if small droplets of silicone find their way into the circulatory system, they might create blockages in tiny blood vessels. Circulating silicone would probably be filtered out of the blood by the lungs and perhaps accumulate there. The liver, spleen, and lymph nodes are organs that also could be a repository for circulating silicone. Again, no research exists on this.

Are Saline-filled Implants Safer?

Saline-filled implants have sometimes been promoted as safer than silicone-gel-filled ones, with some plastic surgeons encouraging women to have the saline implants because of the scare about silicone gel. Lack of research, however, means that saline-filled implants are also experimental devices. Some women experience the same serious reactions with saline-filled implants as others do with those that are gel-filled. Any implant envelope is a foreign body, and the envelope for the saline-filled implants is silicone. Although the saline used as the filler is widely used in other medical procedures without ill effects, upon removal, some saline-filled implants had fungi growing inside them.[15]

According to its legal mandate, the FDA should have required the manufacturers of saline-filled implants to submit safety and effectiveness data in 1991, at the same time as the silicone-filled implants, but it chose not to. In 1993, the FDA issued a proposal to ask the manufacturers to provide studies showing that the saline-filled implants are safe and effective. Until the FDA publishes a legally binding document called a final rule, which in this case would establish a date for submission of studies, the manufacturers can continue to sell the devices without showing evidence of safety. As of press time, the FDA and the two manufacturers still making saline-filled implants, McGhan Medical and Mentor Corporation, have agreed on a timetable for submitting data to the FDA, but it is not legally binding.

The data include the silicone envelope's strength and short- and long-term durability; possible leakage of chemicals, their toxicity, and their ability to produce mutations or affect fetal development; short-term complications such as infections, deflation, and capsular contracture; and all longer-term problems, as well as a woman's quality of life. The FDA is supposed to update its consumer information publication as new data become available.

In 1998, the FDA is planning to assess all the data to decide if the saline-filled implant should remain freely available or should be restricted partially or completely. The FDA, however, is still not requiring the manufacturers to do a ten- or fifteen-year retrospective study to examine long-term rates of capsular contracture, fungal infection, possible autoimmune reactions, or other known or suspected problems. As a result, even in 1998, presented information will be inadequate to assess long-term safety. And with the political tide again leaning toward suppression of government regulation of products, it is unclear if the manufacturers will be required to adhere to the timetable laid out for data collection.

WHY WERE WE MISLED?

Many women have been surprised and outraged to find out that the information their plastic surgeons gave them about possible complications was more opinion than fact, or that their doctors have withheld important information. In order to protect ourselves so that we are not misled again about other medical procedures, we need to understand what went wrong on the way from the manufacturers' research and development department to women's bodies.

Although they believed at the time that they were making an informed, intelligent choice, many women discovered later that they were sacrificed for profit by manufacturers and surgeons, and neglected by a weak government regulatory agency. The manufacturers of breast implants have been irresponsible in their testing and marketing. Internal memos reveal that Dow Corning Wright ignored warning signs in its own animal studies decades ago and ignored questions raised by its own employees and customers about safety, quality control, and lack of research to back up its claims before selling "improved" versions of implants.[16] In the mid-1970s, Dow cut short animal research projects and omitted clinical studies on women to rush to market an implant with

I'm angry about the fact that my surgeon never told me when they did start knowing about serious problems and he stopped using the implants. Knowing that I've been ignorant all these years, it makes me mad.

My doctor told me a Mack truck could drive over these things and they wouldn't break.

a softer gel and thinner shell to regain market share from its competitor.[17] One noted plastic surgeon has quipped that breast implants are the only device that is tested in humans before animals.[18] Long-term tracking of women was never completed; the company has yet to do sound, long-term research on the health of women with breast implants. And this lack of research was perfectly legal, though highly questionable ethically. Other companies seem to have done even less research than Dow Corning Wright.

All medical devices have a package insert for the doctor, not the patient, which lists complications and other important information. Before 1985, the insert for implants outlined few of the possible complications. In that year, after Dow Corning Wright lost a substantial lawsuit, it modified its insert to list many more complications. Although other companies also increased the amount of information on their inserts, they continued to provide less than Dow.

The U.S. public assumes that even if medical device manufacturers and pharmaceutical companies are primarily motivated by profits, the safety of medical products is assured by the FDA. This has certainly not been the case with breast implants. The FDA has only had the power to regulate medical devices since 1976. By then, breast implants had already been in use for almost fifteen years. (Silicone oil is considered a drug when injected directly into the body, so the FDA was required to regulate that. As mentioned before, the agency refused approval for general use of silicone oil injections.)

Through the 1980s, scientists at the FDA knew about serious problems experienced by women with the implants, as well as disturbing animal studies. The Reagan White House, however, discouraged and sometimes actively prevented the agency as a whole from carrying out its regulatory mandate. At the time, the head of the division to enforce medical device regulation told the *Wall Street Journal* that he thought educating business was better than forcing it to comply with regulations.[19] Some of the scientists assigned to review company data were replaced by people trained in business management. Budgetary cutbacks also reduced personnel. As a result, regulation of breast implants, along with other medical devices, languished.

It took fifteen years for the FDA to fulfill its legal mandate to make the manufacturers provide data—and this data was insufficient to prove the safety and effectiveness of silicone-gel-filled breast implants. In 1991 and 1992 reviews of the manufacturers' studies of gel-filled implants, an FDA expert advisory panel stated that the information provided showed that the implants did not meet FDA safety standards. In spite of that, the panel recommended guidelines for continued use of the implants, guidelines that the FDA adopted. The guidelines restricted the numbers of women getting gel-filled implants for breast enlargement and stated that all women having implants must be part of an approved study with long-term follow-up. (Women wishing gel-filled implants after mastectomy or for obviously asymmetrical breasts are able to get them with much less stringent testing and tracking.) Far from protecting our health, the FDA is not requiring any studies that look at the women who already have implants before allowing more women to be exposed.

All through the 1980s, before the FDA began to seek data, a handful of women's health activists and women who believed that they were damaged by the implants attempted to alert other women to the dangers of implants. In 1987, responding to their efforts, the Maryland legislature voted to require plastic surgeons in that state to distribute a booklet outlining some of the implant's problems to clients seeking implants. Surgeons were able to counter the booklet's information by giving it to clients only after they had made up their minds to have the implants, or by dismissing the complications as exceedingly rare and nothing to worry about. An informal survey about a year after distribution of the booklet started indicated that it probably made no difference in women's decisions.[20]

But public interest in implants exploded in December 1990, after Connie Chung aired a piece on network television about health problems with polyurethane-covered implants. The program resulted from the urging of activists.[21] This was the first time that women were able to learn about implant risks except from their plastic surgeons.

Before December 1990, if a woman did not know to ask for the doctor's package insert, or if her surgeon chose not to relay the information on the insert, she was unlikely to find out about many possible problems. Many surgeons also dismissed the complications listed in the insert as a legal necessity without much valid basis. In 1991. the FDA finally required the manufacturers to provide doctors with a package insert for patients, which included a partial list of complications. No doubt this action was prompted by a combination of reports to the FDA that surgeons were not adequately informing women about the risks of implants and the increased public scrutiny of the agency's lack of regulation of implants.

Few women who had problems knew that other women had problems also. Most women, encouraged by their plastic surgeons, thought that they were somehow defective because they couldn't tolerate the implants.

Some doctors who performed research in exchange for a guaranteed supply of implants probably were not willing to publicize negative results that might offend the manufacturers. Other doctors received rebates for each implant used from a particular manufacturer.[22]

The plastic surgeons' professional society, the American Society of Plastic and Reconstructive Surgeons (ASPRS) has also worked hard to stymie collection of data that might be unfavorable to implants. In 1982 it unsuccessfully opposed assigning breast implants to the most rigorously controlled of the FDA's three categories of medical devices. This category, which includes all other implants, is the only one requiring proof of safety and effectiveness of devices that were already on the market in 1976. The society promised the FDA during public hearings in 1982, 1988, and 1992 that it would start a registry to follow the health of women who had implants, but ASPRS found reasons later not to do this. The society knew that by the early 1980s the FDA was concerned that the implants might be connected with autoimmune problems and cancer.

After problems with the implants became public in 1991, ASPRS, in concert with the manufacturers, lobbied hard to keep implants on the market. It raised nearly $4 million for a publicity campaign to generate support for the implants, and 20,000 letters in favor of implants were sent to the FDA. The campaign focused on assuring women of the safety of breast implants. It insinuated that the FDA was on a witch hunt, when in fact the agency was only tardily carrying out its legal mandate. Those millions could have gone a long way toward locating women with implants and setting up the promised registry to study the long-term effects of the implants, which the ASPRS repeatedly said would be too costly to do.

The society's aggressive counterattack on the negative publicity about implants was economically driven. By the early 1990s, breast implants on average accounted for a substantial proportion of plastic surgeons' net annual income. Fortunately, the campaign backfired in some parts of the country because media interest was aroused enough to ensure that negative as well as positive stories received prominent coverage.

Although individual members of this professional society have privately expressed dismay at its actions, none have publicly criticized it. This is hardly surprising,

If my doctor had even hinted that there was any chance that I could develop autoimmune problems from these things, I would never have had them.

considering the repeated harassment by ASPRS of some of the doctors and researchers who have revealed negative information about the implants.[23] One plastic surgeon, who was among the few doctors sympathetic to women when the furor over implants was at its greatest, was grilled before the society's affiliated state association. She was forced to answer hostile questions about her advertising and fees when, in fact, she had done nothing unusual. A doctor at her hospital threatened to start proceedings to revoke her hospital privileges although no formal charges were ever brought. The chief of plastic surgery at the School of Medicine of the University of California, Los Angeles, who has conducted long-term research on explantation (or removal of an implant), was expelled from the California Society of Plastic Surgeons, ostensibly for giving medical advice over the telephone.[24]

Such intimidation, which certainly stifles scientific discourse about breast implants, highlights the need for us to be more skeptical of medical procedures that promise no significant problems. We must ask many more questions to avoid jeopardizing our health. We should also question the pressure to conform to stereotypes that lead us to seek medically unnecessary procedures that can disrupt our bodies' normal functioning.

6

Accepting Ourselves

WHEN WE have harmed our bodies by trying to change our looks, the first step toward better health is to understand what we are doing to ourselves, and why. Yet, even when we realize how and why we are harming our health, we may find it very difficult to change our attitudes and behavior. Most of us grew up saturated with pictures of an "ideal" body. As a result, self-acceptance can be a long and difficult process. It involves changing the way we see ourselves, and gradually weaning ourselves from the insidious power of images that have surrounded us all our lives.

BREAKING THE CYCLE

Over the years, each of us has developed a picture in our mind of how we look. When we think about our bodies, what our mind's eye sees is actually a complex image formed by years of experiences—with parents or other caregivers during infancy and childhood; during puberty's sexual development; from the remarks, comments, or innuendoes from others; from the way we each think that others see and judge us; and from comparisons of our faces and bodies to

those of our peers and to media images of women. Adolescence is usually a crucial time for the formation of self-images because girls between the ages of 15 and 19 are often more concerned about their appearance and more self-critical than any other age group.[1] When we look in a mirror or watch ourselves on a videotape, we see the complex picture that we have put together over the years. What we see may not match what others see. In fact, others' opinions of a woman's looks are no guideline to how she sees herself. A woman who you think is slender or beautifully featured is likely to see herself as overweight or to have a feature she cannot accept.

How we see ourselves is important to our physical and emotional health. Our most fundamental sense of ourselves is as a body; therefore, our body image is closely related to our sense of overall worthiness. Our body image affects our self-esteem, and vice versa. For example, if we have persistent negative thoughts about our looks, these thoughts can undermine confidence in our abilities. On the other hand, if our work is highly praised, or if we have

I still eat as much as I did when I was bulimic, and I weigh as much as I did then. And yet, I don't have a problem with it anymore. Now, I like my body and I think I eat well. It's all in your head—it really is.

I think that the eating and body image stuff were very much symptoms of other things that were wrong: an inability to express myself, needing to be perfect—a perfect girl. I know that when I feel good about myself and when I'm happy and feel solid, I don't worry about my body; I feel really good about it. And when I don't, then it manifests itself in how I feel about my body.

—Woman who recovered from bulimia

attracted a new lover, we may suddenly see ourselves as more appealing than before. Also, when we are happy and optimistic, our self-image may be better than when we feel lonely or pessimistic.

Our overall self-esteem is more closely related to the way we see ourselves than it is to the way others see us. For example, family, friends, lovers, and colleagues may think that we look fine, extremely attractive, or beautiful. Nonetheless, our self-esteem will not improve if we remain critical of the way we look. Conversely, if we find that we look more attractive than others think we do, our self-esteem is likely to be correspondingly high. This happy view of ourselves is a way to escape the tyranny of other people's judgments. Furthermore, believing that we are attractive fosters our social confidence and skill. In other words, accepting and liking our own appearance is a healthy state of mind because it helps us feel content with ourselves and with our lives.

Unfortunately, a healthy self-love is not common among women. Many of us have distorted views of our own bodies, finding certain features or parts unacceptable and embarrassing even when other people think we look quite normal. You probably know at least one woman whose concern over her nose, hips, or wrinkles seems exaggerated to you (just as your concerns may seem exaggerated to her). Studies suggest that the majority of women who have eating disorders or who request cosmetic surgery have self-disparaging, distorted images of certain features or parts of their bodies.[2] Those of us who are emaciated by self-starvation but still find parts or all of our bodies "too fat" are extreme examples of a tendency toward distortion now known to be widespread among women. Because of media images and other influences, many of us have irrational thoughts and unrealistic expectations of how our bodies should look. And the thoughts and expectations encourage distorted images of our own bodies. Think of

the simple act of stepping on a scale and reading the numbers. These numbers are charged with meaning and associations that you have learned from the media and possibly from physicians, friends, and family. Such associations will partly determine your reaction. Your first thought may be "I'm too heavy," meaning that you weigh more than others (a chart, a physician, a magazine article, a weight-loss clinic) say you should. This thought may lead to emotions: anxiety and self-loathing at being heavier than others say you should be. Your thoughts and emotions may trigger a reaction: you start a low-calorie diet. Eventually, the diet leads to a higher weight than before, which brings on further thoughts: "I can't even control my weight. I'm a failure." In this way, unrealistic expectations of what we should weigh and how we should look influence our thoughts, emotions, and health. They are a constant strain on our self-esteem.

We may experience a similar chain of reactions for any part or aspect of our bodies. For example, when looking in a mirror you may think, "My nose is too long," comparing your nose to those you have seen in fashion magaines or on television. This thought may trigger anxiety: "Because of my nose, no one will ever love me." This emotion may lead to a change in behavior—when you go to social events you may try to avoid letting others see your face in profile. You will probably become extremely self-conscious by being so focused on avoiding certain angles or positions vis-à-vis others, which may give the impression that you are stiff, affected, and distracted. If a prospective partner turns away from you for any reason, your thought may be: "It's just as I imagined—X is not attracted to me because of my nose." This may lead to more extreme anxiety and further destructive thoughts: "I am not worthy of love."

Other people, however, including romantically inclined partners, may find your weight or your nose quite pleasing. Unfortunately, their opinions are not likely to shake your entrenched thoughts and emotions. Instead, you may find that your life increasingly revolves around your physical self-consciousness. You may avoid social gatherings or outings where you think your body will be scrutinized, avoid bright lights, and even avoid physical intimacy, depriving yourself of the very situations that you may long for. Such self-deprivation can become a habit, a tragic result of a woman's lack of acceptance of her own body.

Changing Your Mind

Our self-destructive behaviors may begin with thoughts such as "I'm too heavy" or "My nose is too long." But such thoughts can be changed. We can exercise our imagination to begin to change the way we see ourselves. Because body images reside in the mind, our goal is to teach our minds to be our allies rather than our enemies. However, be prepared for the hard work required in a culture so hostile to our self-acceptance.

One way to begin is to write down automatic, negative thoughts about your appearance each time they arise (see accompanying box).

By using this technique, you can challenge an unlimited number of assumptions about your looks and broaden your concept

Part of my recovery from bulimia was accepting my body. I would tell myself: I'm muscular, and I'm curvaceous; I'm not 5'8" and 105 pounds and I'm never going to be.

Recognizing and Dealing with Automatic Thoughts

The psychologist Rita Freedman gives the following example of a woman who has just had her hair cut in a new way and is so appalled at the results that she feels ashamed to go to a party.[3]

Automatic Thoughts
"I look hideous. This haircut is a disaster."
"I always make such a mess of everything."
"I'm ashamed to go out. Everyone will laugh."
"I can't go. I'll die if anyone sees me."
After noting her automatic thoughts, she examines them for flaws:

Errors in Thinking
Exaggeration
Self-blame; turning one event into many
Emotional reasoning; jumping to conclusions
Jumping to conclusions; exaggeration
Then she writes down rational thoughts to use instead:

Rational Counterarguments
"It's not great, but it's not hideous. Looking scalped isn't really earthshaking."
"I wanted a new look. Just because it didn't turn out as I expected this time doesn't mean I mess up all the time."
"I'm entitled to make a mistake. Some people may laugh, others will sympathize. Most won't care."

"I can go or not go. Either way I won't die. At home I'll be safe and
lonely. If I go, I'll have more risk but more to gain."

You can use the same technique when you step on a scale or look in a
mirror:

Automatic Thoughts
"My thighs are disgusting."
"I can't lose the flab even though I've dieted. I'm a failure at
everything I try."
"I'll never find anyone to love me with thighs like this."
"I can't go to the beach today. Sam will see my thighs and be
revolted."

Errors in Thinking
Exaggeration
Irrational; self-blame
Jumping to conclusions
Jumping to conclusions

Rational Counterarguments
"My thighs are the largest part of me."
"Mother's thighs are also big. I guess big thighs run in my family."
"Some people like big thighs: they find them soft, snugly, and
sexy."
"If Sam is so easily revolted I may as well find out now. In any
case, I don't want to become a recluse. I'll go to the beach and
enjoy myself."

of beauty. For example, the thought, "I'm ashamed of these brown spots and wrinkles on my hands. They're so *ugly*!" may become, "My hands have a variety of colors and textures. I'm fascinated by the beiges and browns, and by the tiny lines on my fingers. These are hands with a *past*!"

If you begin practicing such alternative ways of thinking, try to use counterarguments based on reality, not fantasy, and that are self-affirming and persuasive. Once you have worked through a column of automatic thoughts and rational counterarguments, rehearse the counter-arguments aloud. Then practice catching automatic thoughts as soon as they occur and challenging them with ready arguments.

We can combine the above exercise with other routines to help change our body image. These routines include:

➤ Training in self-assertion, especially in regard to appearance: "My weight is my own concern, not yours." "A flat chest is normal after a mastectomy!"

➤ Beginning to overcome fears: for example, if you are afraid to appear in public in a bathing suit, you can begin by wearing just a sleeveless dress, then wearing progressively more revealing clothing until you feel comfortable in a swimsuit.

➤ Testing reality: ordering a full meal in public even if you fear ridicule; ordering dessert in front of a critical parent, friend, or lover.

➤ Scheduling pleasant events for our bodies: taking time out regularly for a massage, a long bath, a relaxing swim.

➤ Choosing dance therapy or other practices in healthful movement, such as the Alexander technique and Feldenkreis method (see "Resources").

In addition, we can practice more healthful ways of using scales and mirrors, two objects that often trigger self-disparaging thoughts about our bodies. One survey suggests that many women weigh themselves more than once a week, and that some women step on the scale once a day or more.[4] Such frequent monitoring magnifies the significance of any changes in the numbers on the scale and can repeatedly trigger negative thoughts and anxieties. Try to be aware of the number of times you step on the scale per day or week, and of your thoughts and feelings about the numbers you see. Then decide on a schedule to reduce scale use. You may decide to move your scale to a less accessible place or to remove it from your home altogether. As you learn to accept and love your body, you will find a scale unnecessary. Some women demolish their scales, which they see as a fitting end for an object that caused them so much distress.

Some of us also misuse mirrors, either refusing to look at parts of our bodies, refusing to look at ourselves unclothed, or repeatedly and compulsively looking at ourselves to check our image. Mirrors greatly influence body images. They make us more self-conscious by drawing attention to our looks, thereby encouraging critical self-scrutiny. When we see our own images we tend to compare them with media-induced ideals of beauty, inviting rejection of our own bodies, or mixed feelings at best.

We can work on constructive ways of using a mirror, such as using relaxation techniques while looking in the mirror, or rehearsing short, convincing compliments about different parts of our bodies: "My eyes are a lovely color." Some women write praise lists that are meaningful for them and that cross the boundaries set by stereotypical beauty ideals:

"These hands look strong and capable."

"My eyes are bright and humorous."

"I have a relaxed, warm expression on my face."

We can all learn to use praise lists to defend ourselves against habitual self-criticism and to help broaden our concept of beauty.

We could also decide to cover our mirrors for a month or two to allow ourselves to concentrate on how our bodies feel and whether or not our clothes are comfortable, rather than on how we look. However, if you already cover your mirrors because you intensely dislike your looks, you might uncover at least one mirror and practice the self-praise exercises above and the body image exercises later in this chapter.

Choosing Exercise

As we practice more positive approaches to our bodies, we can begin to think about healthy approaches to exercise. Movement nourishes our bodies, and exercise can be a sign of love and respect for ourselves. Even those of us who are ill, infirm, or disabled can find ways of moving certain joints or body parts to improve circulation and maintain flexibility. However, exercise can also become self-abusive. Some of us find that we have an almost compulsive urge to join yet another aerobics class, to run one more mile, or to buy yet more weights or workout machines. We may

When I looked in the mirror, it was like cutting my body up into different pieces and evaluating the pieces, as if it was some sort of thing: "That's my butt, there are my arms, and this is what my breasts look like." I was very harshly critical in a sort of splicing way. I would really focus on different parts and then rip those parts apart, being hypercritical. It was a violent way to look at my body. It's the way men look at women's bodies. It's the way people look at pornography—a violent look. In a way, I was looking at my own body the way a man looks at pornography.

continue exercising when overtired or in pain, disregarding our bodies' clear signals that we need rest. Omitting a regular exercise routine may be so frightening that we continue exercising even when injured.

If you think that you may be addicted to exercise, try to be aware of why you are exercising, how often, and how you feel when you have to miss an exercise session. If you become anxious when you miss a session, what are your fears? Over a period of months, you may want to gradually reduce your time exercising, stop timing yourself and counting, and try focusing on the fun of movement rather than on fitness or weight. Joining a folk dance group or dancing at home to music can help you feel the joy of movement and the exuberance of rhythm. Remember that loving your body means moving it to accomplish tasks and because it needs movement, not moving it to change the way it looks. You can reinforce your body love and self-esteem through positive statements as you move:

"My body is strong and comfortable."
"I enjoy my relaxed arms and legs."
"I like myself and feel easy in my body."[5]

In these ways we can help ourselves turn an oppressive addiction into an act of self-respect.

Accepting our Weight

The ultimate act of respect for the body is to nourish it sufficiently and well. However, many of us sporadically or continuously starve ourselves and therefore have lost our natural ability to know when our bodies need food and when they do not. If you feel hungry all the time, or never feel hungry, try eating breakfast, lunch, and dinner as well as a midmorning and midafternoon snack if you wish. Eat your meals and snacks at the same time each day, and eventually you will feel hungry before each meal. Be aware that chewing thoroughly helps the digestion of your food. This is healthy for all of us, and especially for those of us recovering from

bulimia, whose bodies must readjust to proper digestion.

Each of us might also practice the body image exercises given at the end of this chapter to help us accept our own setpoint weight. Techniques such as these for improved self-acceptance may help us see ourselves more positively and raise our self-esteem. If we learn such exercises as young girls, they might lower our risk of low-calorie diets and other eating disorders and make us aware early in life of the cultural pressures for weight loss and of the need to defend ourselves against them. (For this reason, it is a good idea to practice the exercises with our daughters.) Remember, however, that changing our thoughts and behavior patterns requires vigilance and continuous practice to withstand ceaseless opposing media messages; biased employers, families, partners, and medical care practitioners; and peer pressures.

We can support one another in our efforts by becoming more aware of what we say to each other about our looks. For example, notice the compliments you give and receive. How many are comments on the way you or others look? Make an agreement among trusted friends not to compliment each other's appearance, especially weight. For example, if you tell a friend: "You look like you've lost weight. Great!" you are rewarding her for being thinner; you are entrenching the idea in her mind and yours that only thinness is attractive; and you may be encouraging her to worry about maintaining her weight. Even avoid comments on haircuts and clothing. It will be harder than you think! Instead, practice greetings that have more to do with personality than appearance, such as: "You look especially lively today!" or simply warm-hearted greetings such as: "I'm so glad to see you again." Also, with a group of friends or other women interested in changing their body images, practice responding to comments about your weight. For example, your response to: "Do you think you've put on some weight?" might be: "I feel much better at this weight, thank you." In some cultures, remarks about looking heavier, such as "You look fresh and fat today," are compliments.[6]

CHALLENGING THE MEDIA

Researchers are increasingly aware of the relationship among media images, distorted body images, low self-esteem, shyness, anxiety, depression, and eating disorders. Therefore, we may find exercises that challenge the media and change our media-related habits, helpful ways to improve our self-images. By gathering data, we can learn to identify media pressures to conform to a certain body standard.

For example, ask yourself the following questions, and write down your responses and results:

➢ What television programs do I commonly watch?

➢ What items do the programs or their sponsors sell and what images associate thinness with physical attractiveness?

➢What images suggest that thinness brings glamour or goodness?

➢ How do I feel after watching such images?

➢ How do I feel about my looks after I stop watching such programs for a week? A month? Longer?

Ask the same questions of any picture magazine you habitually buy. Also, take one issue of the magazine and review it for pictures of full-figured women, women over 50, and ethnic and racial diversity. Notice if the magazine includes articles promoting more diversity in beauty ideals and warning about the dangers of diets, yet pictures only thin women for fashion and other advertising. As an antidote to such magazines, gather photographs of women whose looks are not conventional. Your photographs might include Eleanor Roosevelt, Margaret Mead, Mahalia Jackson, Grandma Moses, Toni Morrison, Helen Keller, Odetta, Golda Meir, Dorothy L. Sayers, and innumerable other women, including, perhaps, some of your own relations and friends.

Also, imagine that you live in a world without images—no television, illustrated magazines, illustrated newspapers, billboards, photographs, or mirrors. How do you think you would feel about your face and body? Would you think about your looks at all?

In addition to awareness exercises, we can form or join lay and professional organizations, such as those listed in "Resources," to help exert pressure on the media to use images that reflect the enormous diversity of our looks. Such efforts might be partly modeled on the successful use of television programs to reduce drunk driving. The media is today's most effective educator, and some people working in the media are increasingly interested in eating disorders or have friends or loved ones whose eating is disordered. Television companies could produce shows that illustrate acceptance and love of women in all our diversity. Fashion magazines could employ models who fully reflect the adult life span and humanity, rather than employing mainly white women so tall, thin, and youthful that they represent a ridiculously small fraction of women. Such changes would presumably have an impact on the way we judge ourselves. The media owes us these changes to help reverse the harm that uniformly thin, young, able-bodied images have brought about.

This culture telling us we have to be little is as much of a problem as foot-binding in China. You know, women encouraging each other to be thinner and to look a certain way; and mothers doing it to their daughters; and girls doing it to each other; and teachers doing it to girls—to break that cycle is an incredibly powerful thing. The last thing expected is that women will support each other. Usually, what happens is the competitiveness: "Oh my God, she's smaller than I am or I've got bigger breasts than her"—you know, the whole diet-competing thing which a lot of girls do together. And to have women turn that around and be supportive of each other on these issues is powerful.
—Woman who recovered from bulimia

I have begun to realize how destructive magazines are since I've been in college and become involved in feminist issues. Also, I've been dissociating myself from the media. I haven't bought a magazine like Mademoiselle since I've been in college, and I haven't watched more than an hour of television in six months.
—Woman recovering from anorexia

Page 80, top left: Roberta Blackgoat, Diné Navajo elder and activist; top right: Toni Morrison, author; bottom: Antonia Brico, conductor.

Page 81, top left: Rigoberta Menchú, 1992 Nobel Peace Prize winner; top right: Gro Harlem Brundtland, Prime Minister of Norway from 1986 to 1989.

Unrealistic media images of women encourage many of us to abuse our bodies through eating disorders and cosmetic surgery. Instead, we need images of admirable women with diverse face and body types as role models for building healthy self-esteem.

BODY IMAGE EXERCISES

Exercise I

Use the following adaptation of an exercise devised by Wendy Sanford, Jean Gillespie, and Becky Thompson, to help you understand how you see yourself and what you think about your body.[7] If you do this guided meditation with a group of women, one woman might read the text. Otherwise, record the text on tape, pausing after each question to give yourself time. Begin by getting into a comfortable position and taking a few deep breaths. Let each breath out slowly, and relax.

1. Closing your eyes if you wish, picture yourself as you look today. What clothes are you wearing? Why did you choose them? Are they comfortable, flexible? What kinds of movements do they make possible? What colors did you choose to wear? What is your hair like? Are you wearing makeup?

2. Imagine standing in front of a mirror, with your clothes on or off, as you prefer. Look at your body. What do you notice first? What next? Turn around slowly, looking at your front and your back. Lift your arms in the air. Are there any parts you feel shy to look at? To touch? What do you like about what you see? What, if anything, would you change if you could? What features or parts of your body do you find yourself judging most? Stop for a moment and ask yourself this: Whose eyes am I looking at myself with?

3. For example, as you stand there in your imagination, clothed or unclothed, ask: What would one or both of my parents see? What would they think of my body? Did someone say something to me about my body when I was younger that I can remember now? What would a woman friend or the women in my house or dormitory think of my body? How might I appear to someone with a different color skin? To someone who has just been reading *Vogue*? To a cosmetics salesperson? How does my lover (or husband or new friend) see my body? How do I see myself? How would I like to see myself? Now greet yourself in the mirror, and say something loving to your body/self.

4. If you have felt uncomfortable with your body at times in your life, when did that feeling begin? How? If you have begun to feel better about your body, when did that start? What experiences made a difference in the way you see yourself?

5. If you have ever been a weight or size you did not like, what feelings did you have about your body? What kinds of things did you do? Think about the things you did that you kept most private, how did you feel about those things then? How do you feel about them now?

6. Go inside your body for a moment. What kind of home is it for you? You might want to stretch your arms, legs, back, neck. Think of different moments when you have felt good in your body (pause)— perhaps when you were exercising, or dancing, or bathing, or masturbating, or making love, or breathing in fresh air, or eating something delicious, or perhaps in meditation. When did you last have one of these moments? How often do you have them? Now, think of the times when you have not felt good in your body. What does the difference seem to be?

7. How do you take care of your body? What do you inhale and swallow? Are you able to give yourself enough sleep? Exercise? Food that nourishes you? Think about the ways that you give your body what you need. When you don't, what hinders you? What changes would you like to make in

caring for yourself? Think of one specific change you will make this week.

8. Do you take part in any activities, such as swimming, or aerobic classes, where you worry beforehand about how you will look? If you never thought about how you look, would your activities change?

9. Now, trace the outline of your body gently and firmly with your inner eye. Let this outline feel very clear and strong. Picture yourself moving among other people with a strong sense of your physical intactness, your wholeness and beauty. (Pause.) Now, imagine someone challenging your body, perhaps with judging eyes, or a physical blow, or unwanted sexual attention. Picture yourself asserting your right to have your body respected. How do you do this?

10. Think about your sexuality for a minute. First, your sexuality when you are alone: do you have sexual fantasies, read erotic literature, or masturbate? Is this a source of enjoyment for you? If you are sexually interested in or involved with someone else, whether this means crushes, flirtation, hugging, kissing, caressing, or making love, what do you bring into the relationship by way of knowing your body's needs and wants, trusting your body, liking or disliking your body? What aspects of this relationship make you feel better about your body? Worse?

11. Now, picture your body changing in the years ahead. What kinds of changes come into your mind? (Pause.) Do you think of getting stronger or in better shape or of physical disability? Of gray hair, or dyeing your hair? Of getting fatter or thinner? Of getting wrinkles and sagging skin? Of pregnancy? Of menopause? What else? What are your feelings about these changes? As you look toward future changes, what might make a positive difference in how you will feel about and in your body over time?

12. If you are able-bodied, spend a little time with the idea that we are all only temporarily able-bodied, that an accident or illness could change our bodies and our abilities at any time. What are your feelings and thoughts about this? If you have a physical disability, either obvious or invisible, what would you want to tell others about your body image? What kinds of things in society make your condition more or less of a disability?

13. Finally, consider for a moment how you tend to look at other people. If you look sometimes with judging eyes, what are some of the reasons why? What steps can you take toward being less judgmental and more affirming of others' bodies—especially other women's bodies—and your own? If you tend to compare yourself with others, what might you and your friends do to help each other stop comparing?

As you finish this meditation, think of the images that have come to you most strongly. If the images brought painful thoughts or feelings, think of someone with whom you might discuss these. If you are doing this exercise in a group, you might share your feelings with the other group members. Remember that others may well have had thoughts and feelings similar to your own.

Personal writing: Take ten or fifteen minutes to write notes to yourself about where this journey took you, especially what you learned about the way you see yourself, how you might improve your self-image, and other points you want to remember. If you prefer, use colored paper to make a collage that expresses how you feel about your body.

Exercise II

This adaptation of an exercise by the psychologist Marcia Hutchinson uses the power of imagination for improved self-acceptance.[8] Do this exercise at least twice, once in your imagination and again with eyes open and using a mirror. You can ask a trusted friend to guide you through this exercise, or you can record it yourself on tape and play it back each time you repeat the exercise; or purchase a tape with this and other body image exercises (see "Resources").

1. Sit comfortably, close your eyes, and relax.

2. Imagine that you are standing in front of a full-length, three-sided mirror. (If you are doing this in reality, find a mirror in a warm, comfortable place.)

3. Imagine yourself closing your eyes and slowly undressing. How do you feel as you undress? Are you comfortable being naked?

4. Breathe deeply, and as you slowly exhale, feel the tension flowing from your body.

5. Keeping your eyes closed, think about a time when you looked at someone or something with feelings of love, acceptance, or awe. Perhaps it was a parent, a child, a lover, a pet, or a beautiful view. Whatever it was, bring it to your mind now.

6. Let yourself see it now, and experience the feelings that such love, acceptance, or awe inspires in you. Notice especially the feeling in your eyes. Capture the quality of your gaze—the eyes of a lover, soft and open. Let the feeling flow into your dominant hand (right if right-handed, left if left-handed). Later, when you look at yourself and squeeze your hand, you will be looking at yourself through the same eyes of love. When you look at someone or something you truly love, you do not judge or criticize them. You accept them as a beautiful whole, not as a collection of parts or flaws.

7. Now, in your imagination, open your eyes, your loving eyes, walk to the mirror, squeeze your hand, and bathe your body in your gaze. Look at yourself as if you were looking at someone you love or at a beautiful sunset or a work of art. You are looking at someone lovable and beautiful—uniquely beautiful.

8. If you feel resistance, squeeze your hand and take a few slow, deep breaths until the feeling of softness returns to your eyes.

9. Starting from the top of your head, work your way down to your toes. As you go, notice those qualities of your body that are beautiful or that you like. Acknowledge each area out loud: "I like the curve of my cheek" "I like the grace of my neck" "I like the full roundness of my belly". Find one part of your body right now and acknowledge it.

10. Find another and acknowledge it. Find five to ten more qualities of your body and acknowledge them, remembering to squeeze your hand and take a few deep, relaxing breaths if you need to.

11. What else do you like about your body?. What do you like about the way that it functions, how it serves the purposes of your life? Acknowledge these out loud.

12. Find something else lovable. Don't forget side and rear views. What else about you is beautiful? Your skin? Your carriage? Your radiance? Your character that shows through in your body? The way every part of you fits together in a whole that is unique to you? The way that you move? Smile? Really look at yourself and find as many things to acknowledge out loud as you possibly can. Squeeze your hand and take some relaxing breaths if you experience difficulty or resistance.

13. Have you neglected or overlooked any part of you? If so, acknowledge it now for its own unique quality.

14. Once again, look at yourself with tender, loving, self-accepting eyes. Really take in the fullness of your beauty. Look at yourself and say, "This is me. This is my body. This is where I live." Feel what it is like to be loved with your own eyes. See how much of this feeling you can bring back with you after you complete this exercise and open your eyes.

15. Practice applying a loving gaze to your reflection whenever you look in the mirror.

Try these and other body image exercises on your own, with a friend, or with a group of other women, using this chapter and self-help books to guide you. You can also look for a therapist to work with you specifically for improved body image, which is advisable if you feel the need of professional help or if you suspect or know that you have one of the nervosas. Look for a therapist who shows you respect and who will explore new ways of thinking and behaving with you. Your therapist should slowly encourage you to be aware of your thoughts and actions, and to try new ones.

Part II

Living in
Abusive Relationships

7

Intimate Abuse

NOBODY CHOOSES to be abused by a boyfriend, lover, or husband. Indeed, since abuse is an attempt to gain power over another person through control, abuse can deprive women of their power to choose how they wish to be treated in a relationship. The tragedy is that the beliefs we are taught by our society—beliefs about a woman's role in a relationship and what qualities are attractive in a man—blind us to clues that hint of a prospective partner's abusive tendencies. These beliefs can also keep us from recognizing abuse when it does happen. And they often cause a woman to work harder at making the relationship work or preserving her abuser's stature than at safeguarding her own safety and health. Just as we may try to change our weight and shape to suit the demands of an unhealthy ideal of beauty, we may try to change our actions and personalities to pacify our partners.

Abuse can take many forms, combining verbal, psychological, physical, sexual, or economic intimidation. An action is abusive when the person it is directed at feels intimidated, disrespected, manipulated, put down, scared, or humiliated by it. The person who is the target of the abuse has the right to decide whether an action is abusive.

This chapter uses the word *target* because the abuser directs his or her abuse at that particular person or persons, such as a girlfriend or wife or children. (Although *victim* is the term usually used to describe a woman who is abused, that word has often implied that the cause of the disaster or problem is random, unknown, or anonymous, as in a natural disaster, a disease outbreak, or random stranger violence.) In heterosexual relationships, 95 percent of the abusers are men.[2] Usually the abuser is the woman's partner, who may or may not be living with her. While romantic relationships are the focus of this chapter, a brother, sister, father, mother, son, daughter, or another person living in the same home may also be an abuser. Friends, teachers, doctors, clergy, and others in a position of trust or authority may also exercise their power in an abusive way.

Recognizing abusive and coercive behavior takes thought and practice, and many abusers are on their best behavior

When I met Pat, I was impressed with how charming and kind he really was to me. My husband had been dead for two years, and I was just starting to become interested in the possibility of having a relationship with another man. Right away I knew that Pat was a bit manipulative, but he was just so charming. I hate to say it now, but I think I was seduced rather easily.[1]

Looking back, I was actually in love with "love" itself, caught up in the glamorous myths of love as portrayed in the movies and the songs that blared from my radio. I believed that if you really loved someone, you couldn't live without him. And even when things didn't always go as smoothly as they should have, I held on to my conviction that by loving someone enough, you could change him.[3]

You know what I would do just to be loved? I've been sexually abused by almost all of my partners in my need for physical love and emotional love. I was convinced that I didn't have a brain in this head.

On TV there was this film clip of a bar scene. The man comes over to the woman's table and sits down uninvited. He stares the woman in the eye and says something like, "I've had my eye on you for a while and you're going to go out with me." He obviously doesn't care whether the woman is interested in him. All I could think of was "This looks like the early stages of stalking to me, not love. No wonder men abuse women. We're teaching them to do it."

until they have gained a woman's love. Once a woman develops ties to her abuser it becomes much harder for her to exercise choice; her abuser has too many ways to control her. These levers of control include emotional, economic, and social ties—all the needs and expectations of those outside the relationship, from a child to a community's desire to believe it doesn't have the problem of abuse. And for some women, it is safer to live in an abusive situation than to try to escape it.

Underlying the abuse of women by their partners is the second-class status of women—the core belief that allows abuse to begin and to go unchecked by society. Abusers do not think of their targets as being equal to them and deserving of the same consideration. As women, we are encouraged to put our partner's needs before our own. As a society, we minimize the importance of the problem, and often encourage women to assume all the responsibility for relationships.

This chapter identifies the cultural myths that encourage women to pick the wrong partners, as well as the beliefs that help perpetuate abuse. It shows the ways that women become increasingly trapped and outlines the health effects of abuse. And it discusses how abusers think, showing the inadequacy of what we have been taught about relationships. The last section discusses needed changes within institutions to enable them to respond better to women who are mistreated by their partners.

MYTHS THAT CONTRIBUTE TO INTIMATE ABUSE

Abuse is made more likely, and more likely to continue, by many of our culture's traditional beliefs that we learn from childhood— beliefs about the importance of relationships for women, beliefs about the privacy of the family, beliefs about the safety of the home, and beliefs that violence to women by their partners is uncommon or limited to certain groups.

Myths about Relationships

As women, we grow up with numerous, pervasive myths about relationships that underlie our beliefs about how women and men should relate to each other. Even if our families disagreed with these myths or we have consciously rejected some or all of them, we could not avoid learning from fairy tales, movies, television, music, books, magazines, and friends. Unfortunately, these myths, and the prevalence of violence in our society, have influenced nearly all of us to some degree, affecting how we view our role in a relationship, and how we view our partner's actions.

The most important myth is that having a relationship is the highest goal a woman can achieve. Such a belief exaggerates the normal tendency of most women to care greatly about relationships and our responsibilities to others, and to affirm the value of connection between people. This myth is reinforced not just in fiction, but also in the news. For example, Charles and Diana were the fairy prince and princess of the United Kingdom when their engagement was announced, and the engagement of Crown Prince Naruhito of Japan and Masako Owada even made it onto the beginning pages of the staid *New York Times* and *Wall Street Journal*. Both women gave up careers to marry their princes. Both matches were characterized as sparked by love, rather than being arranged, thus "proving" that romantic love makes up for any losses.

Some of us are taught that we will achieve the highest form of love in merging ourselves with our partner: Giving up our own needs and desires will lead us to transcendence and bliss. We learn to look forward to this obliteration almost as if it were a religious transformation. Then we will live happily ever after.

One common theme in television and movies, which are especially prone to equate love with excessive jealousy and stalking, is the man who chases after and wins "his" woman with persistence. He ignores her reluctance and disinterest; he interferes with her other activities. In the end she is swept off her feet. Her resistance to abduction or rape is to flail uselessly for a while before succumbing with pleasure and gratitude. The message is clear: Resistance is pointless, and any persistent suitor, no matter how offensive, will turn out to be a real treasure under the surface.

The final myth is that with patience and love we can tame and transform any man. We learn this from stories such as Beauty and the Beast, which encourage us to ignore our own reactions to partners who are abusive. We learn that we can and should take the responsibility to change a man's actions. With perseverance we will find the prince in the beast.

These myths condition our behavior in any relationship, and they condition our responses to abusive behavior. We try to tailor ourselves to the excessive needs of our partners. We hope that by trying to understand them just a little better, we can rescue them from whatever pain or rage set off the abuse. At the very least, we may feel that it is our responsibility as a woman to make the relationship work.

Those of us who believe that marriage should be a lifetime commitment may feel stuck. It is up to us to make the accommodations. For example, Diana's step-grandmother announced to the press that the breakup was Diana's fault because she did not put Charles's wishes first.[5] Though seemingly trivial, the fact that this comment made headlines at all indicates the persistence of the myth behind it. After hearing such messages repeatedly, we may put the onus for the abuse on ourselves. We come to believe that we deserve it, that we bring it on ourselves, that if we just try harder everything will improve—and our abusers often tell us these very things.

If only we would forgive one more time, if only we could love a little harder or remember what to do a little better, then our partners would finally stop being mad or violent and love us back. If we changed a few things about ourselves, if we always got supper on the table at the right time, then our partners wouldn't get so angry. Perhaps we are too aggressive with our demands or too mouthy in voicing them, or we fight back too often. Perhaps if we were more appealing our partners would stop using the drugs or alcohol that "make" them go out of control. This is the mindset of an abused woman.

Abuse is an exaggerated example of the norm of male entitlement taught by the same stories that teach women their role in a relationship. Many women learn that a man's interests should guide the relationship. A man is often taught that his wishes have priority over a woman's, that his needs should be met before hers, and that his opinions carry more weight. Thus, we may be blinded to clues that hint of future abuse, and we may view controlling or violent actions as a normal part of a partner's role.

We may bask in the intensity of our partner's possessive attention, not seeing in this devotion any desire to control us. And indeed, abusers are often on their best behavior, seemingly "perfect partners," until they have laid claim to us. By the time we recognize the abusive behavior, we have developed emotional bonds.

We may also confuse abuse with love. In fact, as many as one-third of women think violence is a sign of love.[6] This confusion begins in childhood. Parents often use violence to control their children—slaps, spankings, and yelling are widespread in U.S. culture. Surveys show that 84 to 97 percent of parents physically punish their children.[7] Even with goodwill, parental guidance may slide into abusive actions, so we often grow up confused about what is loving concern and what is abusive behavior.

The prevalent belief in the United States that violence is an acceptable way to get what you want also seems to set the stage for abuse. Some women grew up in homes that were so abusive that getting

I remember being in a relationship with the guy I ended up marrying. He was already abusing me. All I wanted to do was please him, like the little kindergarten student getting the star on her forehead. That kept me going a lot of times. "Well, he's going to be proud of me if—." Maybe subconsciously it was "Well, he's not going to yell, scream, and hit me if—, if I prove I'm not stupid anymore,— if I stop doing what he said is aggravating him."

The relationship was not really abusive from the beginning. At least I didn't notice it to be. I think that there was always the verbal undertone, the abuse there. The physical hitting and all that didn't start for, I don't know, maybe a year or two.

At times he hit me in anger, but I definitely felt I deserved it and never told anyone about those beatings for fear they would then know I was truly a terrible person, terrible enough that I'd make someone hit me over and over again.[4]

I didn't even know that I was in an abusive situation because my childhood was so abusive...When my husband hit me a few times, I thought I was really getting off easy. I had been so abused before that I thought I was lucky.[8]

My boyfriend slammed me against the floor, repeatedly banging my head. I had bruises on my face and arms. When his family returned fifteen minutes later, they pretended like nothing had happened. They must have felt this aura about things. They kind of walked into the living room and walked out. It was like a quick "Hi-Bye," and then we were left in that part of the house again alone.

My mother's youngest sister committed suicide about the time I was entering adolescence. It puzzled me because no one ever gave any reasons. My aunt was hardly ever mentioned again and my family lost contact with her husband and children. Years later I started to wonder if she killed herself because she was abused. Finally, I asked an older cousin who confirmed my suspicions. My cousin said one day she stopped in to visit this aunt and found her tied to the bed.

slapped or pushed around by a lover may seem like a vast improvement. They may feel grateful for the decreased level of violence, without imagining that a relationship without abuse is possible.

In addition, exposure to violence, whether in person or through the news, can make violence seem normal so that women are more likely to accept abuse and abusers' violent tendencies are reinforced—and we live in a very violent society. One study at an inner-city hospital found that one in ten children under 6 had seen a shooting or stabbing.[9] In response to the killing of a college student by several high school students, some of the murderers' classmates responded indifferently, noting that people die every day.[10] Violence against particular groups is often condoned or even applauded. Police use intimidation and force. The U.S. government tries to protect its "interests" by invading other countries. And violence bombards us through television, the movies, and music. By age 18, children have watched an estimated 200,000 acts of violence, including 26,000 to 40,000 murders, on television.[11]

While such violence does not necessarily cause anyone to be violent, these images reinforce the belief that force is acceptable, even beneficial. In fact, viewing large amounts of violence on television combined with exposure to abuse by either parent may be related to violent crime.[12] And those of us who are the targets of violence may feel that something is wrong with us. As a result, we may become genuinely confused about what is acceptable.

Myths about the Family

Once abuse is under way, several social conventions conspire to keep a woman trapped. There are strong social taboos against interfering in other people's domestic affairs. We often refuse to talk about suspected abuse. Many of us think that getting involved in other people's family affairs is meddling or rude and may possibly lead to the breakup of the family unit. Unfortu-

nately, through silence we unwittingly align ourselves with the abuser by leaving the woman isolated, entrapped, and alone, making it even harder for her to reach out for help. Yet social service agencies, mental health professionals, and judges often try to avoid breaking up a family even if individuals within it have to pay the high price of abuse. Doctors may avoid asking women if their injuries are the result of battering. We may also be afraid to interfere in another couple's violent fights, concerned that we might get hurt.

A second powerful belief is that we are safest in our homes. This may be true for the most powerful member of the family, but it is often the least safe place for the least powerful family members. At least 25 percent, and perhaps as many as 50 percent, of women are in relationships in which their partners abuse them.[13] According to one researcher:

In the United States, women are more likely to be assaulted, battered, raped, or murdered by a current or former male partner than by all other assailants combined. A 1985 study of intact couples found that approximately one of every eight husbands had performed one or more acts of physical aggression against his female intimate(s) during the survey year, with more than one third of these acts involving severe aggression, such as punching, kicking, choking, beating up, or using a knife or gun.[14]

Male partners and ex-partners murder 52 percent of the women who die violently in this country.[15]

And another researcher writes:

A man's home is his castle; rarely is it understood that the same home may be a prison for women and children. In domestic captivity, physical barriers to escape are rare...The barriers to escape are generally invisible. They are nonetheless extremely powerful. Children are rendered captive by their condition of dependency. Women are rendered captive by economic, social, psychological, and legal subordination, as well as by physical force."[16]

Who Abuses and Who Is Abused

Many of us have misconceptions about who may be the targets of abuse and who might be its perpetrators. We encourage abuse if we distance ourselves from those who are abused by thinking of them as weak or stupid. And if we don't know who might be abused, we can't design services to reach them.

Before abuse starts, women who will be battered are indistinguishable from other women.[19] A woman of any age, race, or ethnicity can find herself in a relationship in which she is abused; privileged upbringing, fame, or wealth are no protection. Olympic skier Patricia Kastle was shot by her former husband. Susan Foster, an assistant dean at Tufts University, was abducted and threatened with murder by her ex-husband. Carolyn Ramsey, now executive director of the Massachusetts Coalition of Battered Women's Service Groups, had a college degree in psychology when she fled her abuser. In her book, *Shattered Dreams* (New York: Harper & Row, 1987), Charlotte Fedders recounted her tale of abuse by her husband, a successful lawyer and former enforcement chief for the Securities and Exchange Commission. Abbe Lane, who was once married to band leader Xavier Cugat, sums up her experience: "If a woman with beauty, talent, money and ambition can get trapped, it can happen to anyone."[20]

Abuse can occur in same-sex couples. There are few studies of lesbian and gay male abusers, but the dynamics of the abusive relationships seem to be the same. Women who are abused in lesbian relationships report the same tactics, with the same effects, as women in heterosexual relationships.[21]

Abuse can start early in life. Surveys estimate that 28 percent of teenagers who date have experienced violence in their relationships.[22] Teenage girls have already learned to interpret jealousy, possessive-ness, and abuse as signs of love. They may be confused about the difference between healthy and abusive relationships. They are less experienced in negotiating relationships, but they won't necessarily get better at it if they don't recognize abuse.

Romantic media images, stories, and music with passive girls and aggressive boys are particularly directed toward teens. Geared to teenage males, MTV frequently uses very violent sexual images in which women are targets of inappropriate behavior. The violence in teen relationships can be as severe as in adult relationships, and it is not just a passing phase. Once violence occurs in a dating relationship it is likely to occur again.[24] It may be that teenagers are murdered by dates and ex-boyfriends at the same rates that adult women are murdered by their partners.[25]

Abuse sometimes occurs on a first date, though women may not talk about such incidents. Abuse on a first date may be violent, intense, predatory, and sexually exploitative. Since there isn't an emotional attachment, it may be easier for the woman not to see the abuser again, but because the incident isn't reported to the police, or perhaps even to a friend, the abuser is not hindered from repeating the violence with future dates.

Pregnant women may be at special risk for battering, which can start or increase at that time. Blows to the breasts and abdomen are particularly common. (But, for some women, battering decreases during pregnancy and escalates after the child is born.[26]) Almost one in five pregnant women are battered, and white women are more than three times more likely to be battered than African-American or Latina women.[27] Overall, 25 to 45 percent of battered women are assaulted during pregnancy.[28]

Just as we think we can single out women who are likely to be abused, many of us believe that abusers are distinguishable from others; in fact, they're not. The stereotype that abuse is confined to lower-class or immigrant families, or to certain

I am an assertive and powerful woman. I do not fit my stereotype of a battered woman...Do not think that what happened to me could not happen to you.[17]

She didn't back down from anything...You could tell that basically from her art, the way she dressed, the opinions she had.[18]
—Friend describing 21-year-old woman murdered by boyfriend

This boy came over, real mad...I opened the door, and he was yelling and screaming at me. He shook me. When boys do things like that, you don't even tell your best friend, because if the boy finds out, he might even do something worse. I think a lot of girls are walking around with a lot of secrets.[23]

Banks are very strict...in order for him to come up to the executive offices, he had to get the okay. When this abusive alcoholic is not drinking, he has a really nice appearance. He looks like you could trust him with anything or anyone.

My father never physically abused my mother, absolutely not. My parents never had a fight. My father was moody and he would be kind of a frightening figure when he yelled. She always acquiesced. He could be very nice. He wasn't consistent one way or the other. It was very confusing...She always had to check in with my father. He and my mother talked a lot on the phone. He kept her on a short leash in the sense that he always wanted to know where she was. It happened many times a day, maybe two or three.

I felt dirty, filthy, stupid, ugly, fat. I was 20 pounds underweight. He told me again and again, "You're fat." You hear it for 5 years and you believe it. I began to feel I was stupid. It took me a year to lift my eyes up.[30]

ethnic groups, couldn't be more wrong; it's just that poor and darker-skinned people are more likely to be caught by the social service and legal systems. But in Duluth, Minnesota, after a policy of mandatory arrest of all batterers took effect in 1984, the percentages of white and minority men came close to their proportions in the general population. No women were arrested for battering before 1984, but afterward 7 percent of the total arrested were women.[29]

Social status is no indicator of whether a person will be abusive, nor is political philosophy. People with nontraditional beliefs about sex roles can still be batterers, while many who espouse traditional gender roles firmly believe that hitting or otherwise intimidating another person is unacceptable.

Sometimes there is a split between the public and private behavior of abusers. How a person interacts with those outside the family is no indicator of what happens at home. Abusers may be friendly, warm, outgoing, and helpful in their communities or among friends and coworkers. They may seem to be exemplary role models in positions such as youth workers, police, or judges. Some condemn in others the actions they themselves commit.

Several studies have found some differences between husbands who physically abuse or batter and husbands who don't, but these are more a matter of degree than of each group's having distinctive personality traits. For example, batterers care less about their wives' feelings and concerns, are more blaming and critical of their wives, undermine them more, make more important decisions unilaterally, and take more time for their own pursuits. (See also the section "The Mind of an Abuser" later in this chapter.)

EXAMPLES OF ABUSE

Most of the abusive relationships that make the newspaper or come under scrutiny by researchers are physically violent. Yet an abuser may never have to use force, or perhaps just once or twice, particularly if his target is relatively compliant. Emotional outbursts of anger may be adequate to keep her in line since many of us have learned to accommodate by placating others. Nonphysical intimidation is often sufficient for control if we are quick to learn the boundaries over which we must not cross. The women in such relationships may not be aware that they are being controlled; they certainly do not think to contact a battered women's group. They may simply be confused about why they are unhappy.

Abusers can use many techniques to control their targets, and often combine several. In verbal intimidation, an abuser belittles, criticizes, threatens, shouts at a target, or calls her derogatory names. Our abusers might say we deserve what we get, or call us crazy, stupid, worthless, or ugly to undermine our self-confidence. Sexually derogatory names such as "slut," "whore," and "cunt" are especially common. Some abusers never call their targets by their given names.

Psychological intimidation is perpetrated in a variety of ways. Abusers are often emotionally unpredictable or suffocating. They may withdraw and then have outbursts, or alternate between being full of hate and being loving and remorseful. They may be intensely jealous. They may try to make us feel guilty for thinking about leaving by threatening suicide or insisting that they are helpless and dependent on us for solving their problems. Abusers may deliberately restrict their targets' friends, or not allow them to have any; restrict visits with supportive relatives; or prevent their targets from talking with anyone alone. Abusive partners may sometimes pick fights right before going out with us socially in order to upset us so we don't want to see friends. We may be confined to our homes unless we get permission to leave for specific purposes and amounts of time. We may be told what to eat, what to wear, or what entertainment we are allowed.

Abusers may also use our children to manipulate us. The abuser may be nice to the children after being abusive to us, may tell the children things to make them feel sorry for him or her and to blame us, make them take sides, tell them that they are the cause of the abuse, or wheedle information about us in order to use it against us. They may also undermine our authority with the children by degrading or humiliating us in front of them through words or actions. Some abusers threaten to harm the children if we do not do what the abusers want. They can keep us hostage if, after abusing the children themselves, they threaten to report the abuse and blame it on us, possibly leading to having our children taken away from us. We may unwittingly become the abusers' agents if we hit, yell at, or otherwise intimidate our children in an effort to preempt harsher abuse we think our partners may inflict.

Physical intimidation occurs when the abuser hits, punches, slaps, pushes, blocks his target's way, or otherwise physically attacks or threatens his (or her) partner. It can also include throwing things, breaking favorite objects, and maiming or killing a pet. Any use of physical force is abuse, regardless of whether the target is injured or not. *Battering* in this book is used to mean physical abuse. Some writers use it synonymously with *abuse*.

In sexual intimidation, the abuser forces a woman to have sex when she doesn't want to, or in ways she doesn't like. Among women who have been married, one study reports that 14 percent have been raped by a current or former husband. Another 26 percent have submitted to unwanted sex because of covert threats, psychological manipulation, or economic coercion.[31] Surveys of battered women suggest that up to 80 percent report various coerced sexual acts, which include having objects inserted into their bodies, group sex, sex with animals, bondage, and being forced to watch the abuser masturbate.[32] Some women are forced into prostitution in exchange either for money or drugs. Some shelter workers believe that nonconsensual "aberrant" sex is far more

I no longer could have my own ideas. I had to have his ideas. I had to have his ideals. I could not be my own person. And whenever I tried to be my own person that was when I was "stupid." So when I got that message very early on in the relationship, I didn't realize that I had the choice to say, "Well, I'm going to see you later. I don't want any part of this relationship." Maybe I tried to do that and I was told that I couldn't leave. They have these rules, and if they are not obeyed, then there are consequences.

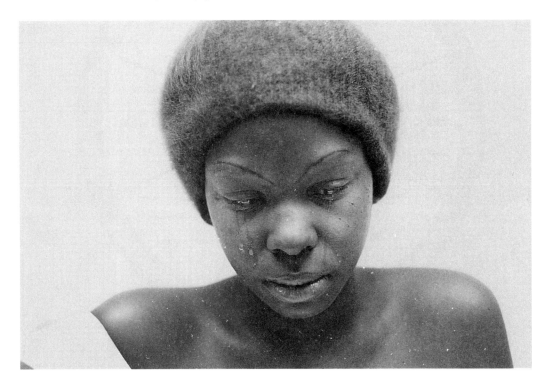

I wanted to go back to college but my lover discouraged me by telling me over and over that I was too stupid. We should use the money some other way.

widespread than current evidence suggests since women may feel too deeply degraded to report it.[33]

Economic intimidation includes being forced to give up jobs, being prevented from continuing schooling, or being forced to provide economic support. A woman may not be allowed to have a checking account, credit cards, more than a few dollars in cash, information about family finances, and the use of a car or telephone. Abusers may not allow their partners to own anything of value jointly or in their own names.

Spotting less intense abuse can be very difficult. The accompanying box, "Abusive Behaviors," indicates many of the behaviors that one person may use to try to control another person. The more of these behaviors a partner uses, the more concerned a woman should be about her safety.

The Effects on the Target
Abused women may feel that they are "walking on eggshells" all the time, or feel afraid when they are with their partners. Some can predict an outburst of violence by a change in the partner's body language or facial expression. Some are concerned that their partners would not be able to get along without them, or find themselves continually making excuses for their partners.

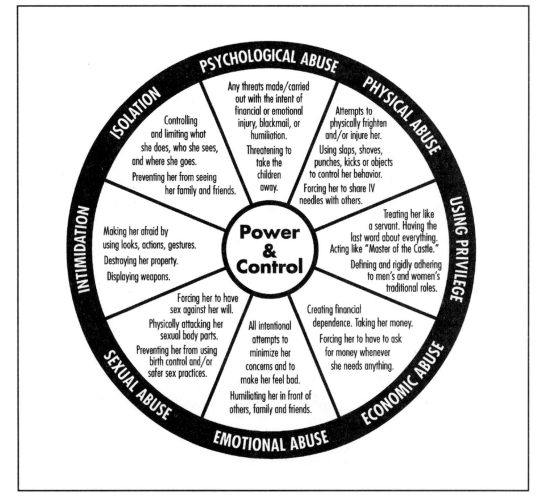

Comparison of a relationship characterized by power and control versus one based on equity.

Because abusive partners often have many appealing characteristics, we may easily recognize what we like about them—looks, charm, a way with words, strength, passion, intelligence, wit, importance, a talent for making money, good storytelling, or any number of things. Or we may feel particularly drawn to a person who has needs we think we can meet better than others. The contradiction between the abusive side and the appealing side may make us very confused. We may want to bring back the person we thought we were with, the "good" person we fell in love with. Abusers frequently alternate putting us on a pedestal while pulling the rug out from under us.

Many women learn to minimize the effects of emotional or physical abuse and tolerate some abuse as acceptable. We may have learned that physical fighting between partners is normal and natural, just a squabble of no consequence, on the order of sibling rivalry. Many people think that resolving a conflict means one side overpowers the other and that respecting the other person's opinion is a sign of weakness. As a result, women who have been abused may be reluctant to describe themselves as abused or battered out of fear that they will then be considered incompetent, victims, or losers, or that their partners will be seen as malevolent, violent criminals. It is often

(continued on p. 100)

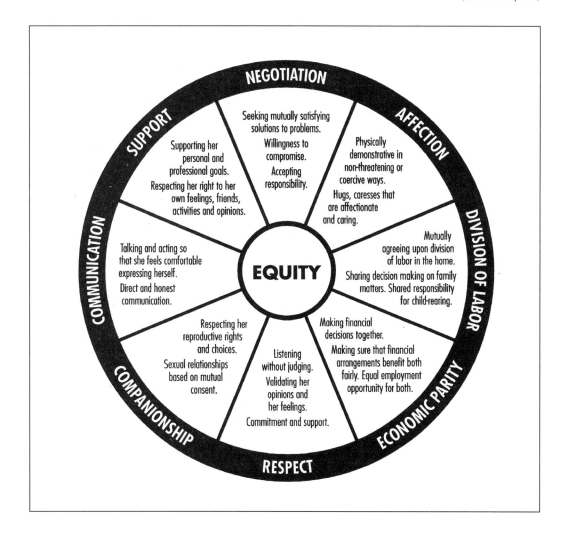

What kept me there, I know now, was a refusal to accept the reality of her rage and an insistence on seeing it through to the other side...I found it impossible to reconcile the two incongruent pictures of X. I clung to the image of "good X," as if "bad X" were the illusion...How dangerous it was for me to make that split. Whether or not she did in fact have two completely different sides, she was one person. And that one person was abusing me.[34]

—Woman in lesbian relationship

Abusive Behaviors

A man or woman regularly:

Fails to listen or respond to his or her partner, interrupts her, changes topics, outshouts her

Criticizes her, puts her down, says things that are likely to make her feel bad about herself

Doesn't give her positive attention, praise, or compliments, rarely says positive things about her to others

Talks negatively about women in general even if he or she tells the partner that she is different from or better than other women

Doesn't view her as an equal, either because he or she is older or believes him- or herself to be smarter, wealthier, or superior in other ways

Expects her to meet impossibly high standards (do other people compliment her on the very things her partner criticizes her for?)

Makes contradictory demands

Says one thing to her and does another

Tries to make her feel bad about having her own needs or her own opinions

Refuses to accept a no from her

Sulks or becomes angry when she initiates an action or idea

Doesn't allow her to make decisions, or makes decisions for her

Persists in wanting to be with her even after she says she wants to be left alone

Makes her account for all of her time

Accuses her of being sexually interested in or having affairs with others

Blames her for provoking his or her outbursts

Claims not to be able to control his or her temper

Blames stress to excuse behavior

Refuses to let her share any of the expenses of a date and gets angry when she offers to pay

Acts physically aggressive toward her or others, even if it's "just" grabbing or pushing to get his or her way

Acts physically intimidating by sitting too close, using his or her body to block her way, touching her when she says not to

Enjoys being cruel to animals, children, or people he or she can bully

Restrains his or her behavior when others are around but not when alone with her or with immediate family members

Sulks or becomes angry at emotional or sexual frustrations

Bullies her into having sex when she doesn't want to

Forces her to engage in sexual acts she doesn't feel comfortable with

Tries to get her intoxicated

Berates her for not wanting to get drunk, get high, have sex, or go with him or her to an isolated or personal place

Tells her how she should dress or what activities she should do

Controls her use of money or other resources, such as a car

Tries to isolate her by keeping her from seeing or talking to other people, especially her friends and relatives

Behaves especially nicely to her sometimes, showing the side that makes her want to stay for more.

I really have to be careful not to deny that there has been violence. There has been. I was actually battered and black and blued by an ex-husband.

I have recovered for the most part. But in the last two weeks I found myself writing in my journal (though I had not started out to) about the one incident at the end of my battering relationship when I finally acted in self-defense, leaving him with cuts and bruises, an incident about which I experienced an almost suicidal sense of shame and guilt. I hadn't realized that was something I carried like a sin.[35]

We were at a park, and I said hi to another boy. So my boyfriend smacked me. I hit him back. He hit me again. I had a big bruise on my eye.[36]

When things were bad I was too ashamed to tell anybody...I'd already had one failed marriage. I did everything I could to make this one work.[40]

When I finally called the police...it meant that I was ready to leave. I had never called them before because he is a Latino man and I knew he was going to be treated very badly by the police. And I knew it would make it bad for him because he was politically active and I had felt responsible for protecting his image.[41]

painful to admit that we cannot make a relationship work, the very thing that women are supposed to be good at. We may underestimate the severity of abuse because we don't want to believe that people we love could do us serious harm. In addition, if no one else validates what happens to us as important by ignoring our bruises or black eyes, we tend to doubt our own feelings and thoughts even more and even perhaps the severity of the violence. We may choose to deny our own experiences to keep ourselves from further social isolation.

Abusers may alternate force, threats of violence, or intimidation with attentiveness, remorse, and helplessness. Whether or not the abuser consciously sees this as a technique for control, it is very effective. Some abusers use remorse to make us think that there is hope that they will change. Others play on our guilt, perhaps threatening suicide if we leave, or pleading with us to stay to help solve their problems.

Some women do fight back. However, they are likely to be viewed as "stepping out of line."[37] The woman herself may be confused about who is the target and who is the aggressor if she has fought back in self-defense, especially if she has inflicted harm. She may loathe identifying with the abuser, yet may see herself as culpable in perpetuating the violence.

Perhaps because we sustain more injuries than men in fights, many women learn to suppress the urge to defend ourselves physically. Teenage girls may use violence in self-defense more than women who have been exposed to battering longer. Not resisting may become a survival strategy that allows us to get hurt less. Interestingly, women who hit their male dating partners are more likely to say that they were defending themselves, whereas the men who hit women are more likely to say that they were intimidating, causing fear, or coercing the partner to do something.[38]

A minuscule number of women kill their abusers; far more cases of abuse end in the death of the target, either through suicide or by being murdered by the abuser.

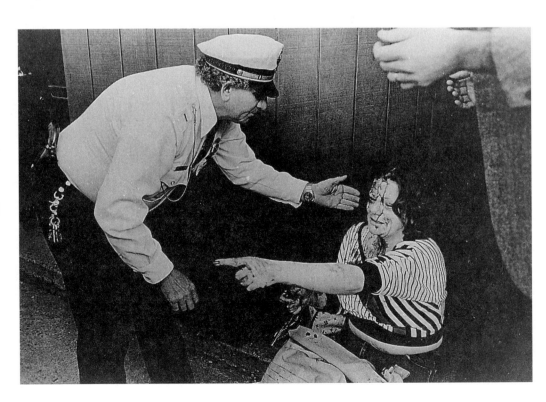

Women who kill their abusers have two factors in common—an inability to get effective help and the severity of the abuse, both of which contribute to how trapped they feel.[39]

Difficulties in Leaving Abusive Relationships

Unfortunately, leaving an abusive situation is not always a simple or safe solution. Some women, both heterosexual and lesbian, report that the idea of maintaining a relationship is so important that they would rather put up with abuse than consider themselves as failures for leaving. We may still think that we can reform our relationships to fit the cultural ideals, especially if we sometimes continue to feel a special emotional bond or sexual attraction to our partners. Our abusers will often play up this side of the relationship after a beating or when they sense that we are considering leaving. Thus, we may be inclined to give our partners one more chance. Some of us might be concerned about the effect of our leaving on our partners' reputations or jobs.

Some women find it too difficult to get help. We may be concerned that others will think something is wrong with us. Friends may feel that we are forcing them to take sides in a private dispute, or they may not believe us if our partners seem to be caring, involved community leaders. Others may want to intervene before we are ready, making our situations more dangerous. We may have fears about confidentiality.

Being a member of some cultures can make it harder to seek help. For example, we may have grown up in a culture that emphasizes that we should be strong and forbearing—the ultrastrong black woman, the Jewish *balabusta*, the stoic midwestern housewife—able to put other family members' needs first. Or we may worry about prejudice against our racial or ethnic groups. We may have been taught that our actions always represent our people and ultimately determine their reputation, so we may fear that seeking help will result in reinforcing negative stereotypes about our group.

In deciding to leave, a woman must take stock of her resources. Most abused women need emotional and practical support to figure out what to do to get away from abuse. Some are able to extricate themselves the first time they try, others must try repeatedly, and some are never able to make the break. A woman must consider many questions: How many people are willing and able to help? How much money is available? Will I become homeless or perhaps lose my children? Will social service agencies label me as criminal if I am involved with drugs or prostitution, even if my partner forced me to do this? Should I go to a shelter, or, despite the more wrenching change, should I travel to an area of the country where I will be harder to find?

A woman must also consider the chance that her bid for freedom will be unsuccessful. If she cannot find outside help, and all family resources are controlled by the abuser, there may be no realistic chance of getting away. Even if she does leave, her partner may not stop the violence and the harassment. Abusers often bring nuisance suits, violate restraining orders, attempt to get legal custody of the children, kidnap the children, and maim and kill their targets. Welfare regulations may require her to name the father of her children so he can be contacted, thereby ensuring that she loses her ability to hide from him. One of the scariest things about batterers is that some are very persistent about "owning" their targets even after the women have gone to extraordinary lengths to get away and to leave the relationship. Even after a legal separation or divorce, some targeted women may be at the same or a higher risk of being attacked as when they were living with their abusive partners. In fact, 75 percent of spousal attacks occur between people who are either separated or divorced.[44] For some women, only the jailing or death of the abuser stops the abuse.

My husband was making all these promises and all I had to do was accept the promises and I could go back home to him, to my furniture, to my house. My son would have a father, and I wouldn't have to struggle with all this welfare crap. I could just go home and be taken care of. Honey, I couldn't get to the bus fast enough.[42]

Once, when I tried to leave my ex-husband, he took my dachshund puppy and beat him against the wall. He told me to remember the dog's cries, because they could be the cries of my young niece. At that moment, I knew he was capable of every horrible threat he ever made, and my life was in grave danger.[43]

I wanted to do anything that I possibly could do for this man to love me. I'm thinking of how I sacrificed my health. I got this impression from very early on in the relationship that he loved me but I just wasn't good enough or perfect enough for him. That's when I decided I was going to have this perfect body. I decided to control the weight and control the food, and I became anorexic. He never told me that I was too fat but he told me that I was stupid. His favorite saying was "What is that on your shoulders, anyway?" referring to my brain.

I'm afraid of the dark...and I still can't walk around that much. I carry a blaster with me. And I look all the time, I'm always looking at all the cars.[48]

I started feeling real inadequate. My grades went down dramatically. I missed class a lot, because I felt sick—stomach stuff, real nervous stuff...It was probably a deep depression, but I started feeling sleepy all the time. All I wanted to do was stay in bed. It just seemed like everything just kept going down, down, down.[49]

The effects of the relationship, however, didn't go away as easily. I was scared of getting involved with a boyfriend again. During the remaining years of high school, I rarely dated and did not again have a serious relationship...Still feeling shame, I never talked with anybody about the abusive nature of this relationship until a few years ago.[51]

Several behaviors seem to indicate a high risk that an abuser will seriously hurt or kill his or her target. These warning signs are not always present before a fatal attack, but a woman should be especially alert if her partner:

➤ Shows excessive jealousy

➤ Is particularly violent or cruel during sex

➤ Says that if he or she can't have her, no one will

➤ Blames alcohol or other drugs to excuse behavior

➤ Has a fascination with weapons or threatens to use a weapon against her

➤ Threatens to commit suicide or do something that would make her too guilty to leave

THE LASTING EFFECTS OF ABUSE

Like any trauma, abuse can inflict lasting damage.[45] Psychological and physical trauma can affect mental, emotional, and physical functioning. Over the years, studies have shown that the psychological and physiological responses to single traumatic events and to repeated, prolonged trauma are predictable whether the trauma is war, sustained stress resulting from prejudice based on race or ethnicity,[46] rape or battering. The more intense or the more long-lasting a person's exposure to trauma, the more harmful it is. Some aspects of severe abuse may significantly increase harm, such as isolation, "being taken by surprise, trapped, or exposed to the point of exhaustion," and "physical violation or injury, exposure to extreme violence, or witnessing grotesque death."[47] The most important aspect of a traumatic experience is that it inspires helplessness and terror.

Abused women often say that the constant state of anxiety and terror, and the constant tearing away of their self-esteem, are the worst parts of their experiences. Many battered women report that the psychological aspects of abuse are more debilitating than the physical violence because of constant fear, nervousness, vigilance, and feeling on the defensive.

Under these circumstances, many women develop headaches, rashes, intestinal problems, high blood pressure, ulcers, chronic fatigue, chronic back or pelvic pain, disordered eating patterns, and cry frequently. Women also develop anxiety, depression, inability to sleep, nightmares, flashbacks (vivid memories that make us feel we are reliving a traumatic event), quickness to startle, constant alertness to danger, suspiciousness, or other physical and psychological problems. And there has been no thorough research on the effects of nonsexual abuse on a woman's experience of her sexuality.

We may have trouble trusting others. We may feel betrayed by those closest to us and find that our basic faith in community support is gone. Life may seem intolerable and we may feel so hopeless that we wish we were dead—42 percent of one group of battered women attempted suicide.[50]

Many women turn to legal, illegal, over-the-counter, or prescription drugs to relieve their tension or to blot out a seemingly inescapable, unbearable situation. Alcohol and tranquilizers are particularly common drugs and can be fatal when taken together. Rates of chronic drug use, including alcoholism, escalate after a woman is battered.[52] Drug use may also affect our ability to take care of ourselves. If we are the target of violence, we may find that our ability to protect ourselves is impaired when drugged by alcohol or other substances. Alcohol and other drugs used by either or both partners can increase the disparity of power between the abuser and the target. Thus, drugs can and

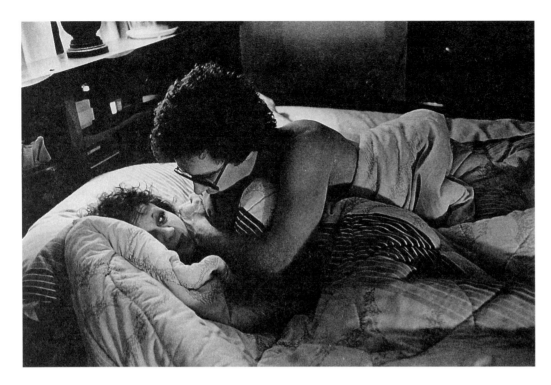

often do exacerbate an abusive situation, but they do not cause the abuse.

During a physical, verbal, or sexual attack, a woman may feel separated from her body, as if watching some other person being abused, a process called dissociation. Dissociation is a way to survive but it can lead to psychological and practical problems. For example, if we continue to react to stressful situations by dissociating, we may ignore danger signals that warn of threatening situations.

Women may become increasingly passive in an attempt to head off abusive incidents, while at the same time remaining hypervigilant for cues that will alert them to the possibility of being punished. People who feel that there is no room for mistakes are likely to avoid taking any initiative.

Physical injuries from battering can cause serious harm. In fact, targets of marital violence have higher rates of internal injuries and unconsciousness than victims of stranger violence.[53] Cuts, bruises, burns, broken bones, and wounds heal eventually,

but blows to the head and hard shaking can cause concussions and brain damage. Even seemingly minor smacks to the head, especially if they are repeated, can cause memory loss and decrease a woman's ability to function. She may also sustain permanent damage to her eyes, ears, nose, teeth or facial nerves. Broken ribs can puncture various internal organs. A broken spine can leave an abused woman paralyzed, perhaps even more at the mercy of her abuser. As abuse escalates, she is also at risk for being murdered by her abuser. The actual number fluctuates, but has been as high as one woman every eight days in Massachusetts.[54]

Repeated rape by a partner over many years can create especially severe problems. Women subjected to such chronic terror experience "emotional numbing, involuntary panics, and repetitive nightmares that often [last] for years after the relationship [has] ended and the threat of rape is gone."[55] Along with unwanted sex, an abused woman may be forced to

I would go shopping with my mother and she couldn't make a decision because my father had controlled her so much. She literally couldn't make decisions. I am not exaggerating. Maybe a year or two before she died, she was going to make some hard-boiled eggs. I can remember her saying, "George, which pot should I use?"...Also, he would tell her what to eat in restaurants as they got older. She'd ask him, "George, is it okay if I have...?" She never said, "I really want...I must have..." Never. Never. Absolutely never.

have unprotected sex. In addition to the risk of pregnancy, she is at risk for catching more than 20 sexually transmitted diseases. Although HIV/AIDS may be the scariest of these diseases because it is so clearly life-threatening, other sexually transmissible infections can lead to pelvic inflammatory disease or cervical cancer. (See Chapter 10, "The Costs of Physical Love.")

Battering is an important contributor to premature and low birthweight babies, who have a harder time surviving. One study at a private hospital noted that women battered during pregnancy were four times more likely to have low birthweight babies as women who weren't battered. The difference in a public hospital was not as great, probably because other factors that correlate with low birthweight (low income, no prenatal care, inadequate nutrition, smoking, and alcohol use) were more prevalent among the nonbattered women at the public hospital than at the private one.[56]

Nonphysical abuse is also damaging during pregnancy. An abusive partner may not allow a pregnant woman to feed herself adequately or may prevent her from seeking routine medical care during pregnancy, as well as care during illness. Psychological stress alone has been linked to complications during pregnancy and birth.

THE MIND OF AN ABUSER

Abusers have little incentive to change their behavior. They are generally well rewarded by getting the power they want—they win arguments, control resources, have their wishes immediately gratified, and demonstrate their superior power. And often, abusers experience no community censure for their activities; sometimes they receive outright support. Without a response from outsiders, abusers simply strengthen their belief that the harm they do to their targets is insignificant or unimportant. Family, friends, and the medical, mental health, academic, judicial, and religious institutions all reinforce this belief through their inadequate responses to the targets of abuse.

Knowing more about what goes on in the minds of abusers is crucial. It tells us why the strategies that women learn for improving relationships might work occasionally but won't provide a successful long-term strategy for reducing abuse. In essence, a woman's goal to improve a relationship is incompatible with the abuser's view of her as an unequal partner or as an extension of him- or herself. For example, many abusers believe that an argument is a win or lose situation, where winning is paramount. They *intend* to control rather than negotiate. Abusers believe that it is acceptable to control an intimate partner, a belief tacitly supported by society.

Most research on abuse focuses on the targets, especially those who are subject to the more violent abuse (they are easiest to identify). Not surprisingly, finding batterers who are willing to talk about their thoughts and experiences is difficult. What little research has been done on abusers concentrates on heterosexual men, usually married, who use physical violence to control their partners. Most are in counseling programs, indicating that these are the men who have been identified by the legal system as batterers. Anecdotal reports indicate that abusive men who do not batter and lesbians who abuse their partners act similarly to men who batter women. Their thinking is also likely to be similar.

An Exaggeration of the Norm

Abusers seem to display an exaggeration of how men typically perceive and act in relationships. This male paradigm, which values competition and individuality, is often considered the most powerful one in U.S. culture, so lesbian abusers may identify with it as well.

As Deborah Tannen formulates the male and female paradigms:

A man engages in the world as an individual in a hierarchical social order in which he [is] either one-up or one-down. In this world, conversations are negotiations in which people try to achieve and maintain the upper hand if they can, and protect themselves from others' attempts to put them down and push them around. Life, then, is a contest, a struggle to preserve independence and avoid failure. [A woman approaches the world] as an individual in a network of connections. In this world, conversations are negotiations for closeness in which people try to seek and give confirmation and support, and to reach consensus. They try to protect themselves from others' attempts to push them away. Life, then, is a community, a struggle to preserve intimacy and avoid isolation. Though there are hierarchies in this world too, they are hierarchies more of friendship than of power and accomplishment.[57]

In a dichotomous, hierarchical worldview, if abusers are not on top, then they are necessarily on the bottom. Abusers who feel they may have to compromise, which in their eyes is tantamount to losing, may describe themselves as victims. Batterers often describe their partners as immovable, uncompromising, and unsupportive; they see themselves as defending their own rights. Perhaps they see humiliating dependence as the only alternative to dominance; interdependence is not an option. They may view arguments as a test of their dominance, not as a way to work out differences. Staying on top may come to feel like a precariously insecure position. If they perceive love and attention as finite, limited commodities, when one person is given any, another person must lose some.

Both sexes overwhelmingly cite jealousy as the most common provocation for violence, with "uncontrollable anger" second on the list.[58] Belief by one of the partners that he or she should control the relationship rather than work toward sharing power is a strong indicator that violence may develop in a relationship, according to some studies.[59]

Batterers do not deal constructively with conflict, disagreement, or feelings of annoyance, anger, frustration, irritation, or stress. Many batterers seem to go directly from hurt to rage. They do not distinguish between anger and violence, between the emotion and the behavior. They maintain that once anger erupts, their behavior is no longer controllable. They portray themselves as at the mercy of their feelings. Because they express anger through violence, violence becomes intrinsically linked to their feelings.[60] The most insidious batterers are those who remain calm and collected during coercion. They can be so good at control and manipulation that they can obscure the true nature of their behavior.

Sometimes abuse does not escalate to battering until the abused woman tries to leave the relationship; battering may also increase to dangerous levels. At that point, abusers may panic because their former methods of ensuring compliance are no longer working. They will still insist that they were reasonable and rational, that it was the abused partners who were not accommodating.

Abusers tend to see their partners as an extension of themselves, not as separate people with their own needs and wishes. Any sign of perceived independence of the most minor kind on the targeted woman's part can be an excuse for an outburst from the abuser. This could include the most ordinary type of request, such as wanting to sleep without being woken in the middle of the night. Some abusers see this "independence" as disloyalty or deliberate humiliation by the women they're abusing.

Abusers also lack empathy for their partners. Because so many men seem unable or unwilling to give emotional support, this characteristic may not alert women to reject abusive men early on in the relationship. Abusers make little attempt to understand what their partners are saying or doing. Instead they devalue and blame their

For years my husband beat me before I finally got up the courage to file for divorce. During this time I had a restraining order out on him so we were living apart, but one evening he forced his way in and brutally raped me. I dropped the divorce proceedings because I didn't think I could go through that again.

I just didn't take her seriously, like she was a piece of furniture or something. I guess you could say I took her for granted; I belittled her looks, her intelligence, anything she did really. I used to laugh at her ways of doing things, or I'd get mad.[61]

I don't decide what's right or wrong; it's just common sense. She should know that![63]

It took me a long time to be able to recognize that I was a victim of physical and emotional abuse in this relationship. How can you be a victim when you give somebody a black eye? How can you be a victim but be stronger than the other person? I think you are the victim if you are the one who always tries to avoid arguments. I think you are the victim if you spend your life tiptoeing around the other person in order to avoid any controversy or frustration. I think you are a victim if you become silent in order to restrain or stop the violence of the other person...I think you are a victim when you give up on yourself, your dreams, your activities, your pleasures in order to please the other person.[65]

It was all booze. I didn't think. I didn't think at all. I was just like a madman. It was temporary insanity. All I wanted to do was crush her. There was nothing there but—I wanted to cause pain and mess her looks up.[66]

If [my wife] wasn't away, this never would have happened. It's all her fault. She knows I should not be left alone.[67]

—Man convicted of murdering a neighborhood woman

partners when they feel upset about something. They listen to their partners only to analyze and criticize their statements, not to offer caring and encouragement.

Batterers in particular seem to have "an exaggerated sense of individual freedoms as well as an exaggerated sense of what "services' are due" from their partners.[62] Many abusers expect their partners to know automatically, even instantaneously, what the abusers want. They believe that whatever is apparent to them should be apparent to their partners. Therefore, they need not communicate it. Abusers may interpret a partner's not knowing as a deliberate refusal to comply and an affront to their authority.

Avoiding Responsibility

Abusers' justifications of their behavior can deflect us from holding them accountable for their actions. We may become confused about where responsibility lies. For example, an abuser might declare that the targeted woman is crazy, in therapy, on medication, or that she has a history of incest, to discredit her. One researcher writes that, "After every atrocity one can expect to hear the same predictable apologies: it never happened; the victim lies; the victim exaggerates; the victim brought it upon herself; and in any case it is time to forget the past and move on. The more powerful the perpetrator, the greater is his prerogative to name and define reality, and the more completely his arguments prevail."[64]

Abusers frequently say that outside forces push them into coercive behavior. Then they may explain that they were abused or victimized previously in some way, with their controlling behavior as the inevitable result. Sometimes a batterer will deny that his or her "real" self is the one doing the battering. Batterers' claims of being out of control are belied by the facts; they are able to exercise certain kinds of control, even when in an intense rage. For example, one batterer took off an expensive watch before hitting his wife. Another

threw plates near, but just missing, her partner's head. Another only beat his girlfriend when they were alone. Commonly, batterers restrict their blows to the torso so that bruises will not show in public.

The abuser can exploit another kind of confusion if the target tries to defend herself by fighting back. The abuser may name the fighting "mutual violence" and threaten the targeted woman with calling in the police. The abused woman may feel trapped if she has hit her abuser in public. A lesbian abuser may even seek help from a battered women's service organization for "protection" from the abused partner.

Many of us still believe the excuse that alcohol and other drugs cause people to act abusively. Yet sober people intimidate, batter, and rape, while drunks or people who are high are not necessarily abusive. (When abusers do drink or take drugs, however, the combination can be very violent and destructive.) In this culture, there is a social expectation that drunk-enness, in particular, leads to a loss of control, and that being out of control often means being violent and sexual. But this hardly excuses the violence or its effects.

Researchers have found that abusive men often give contradictory reasons to explain the battering. Some agree that the action is wrong but deny responsibility by labeling it involuntary, a result of losing control, someone else's fault, or accidental. They may blame drugs or a buildup of frustration, for instance. They may even say that their actions frightened them.

Not accepting responsibility also seems to be the most common way to minimize to themselves the severity of the attack. When batterers justify their behavior, they acknowledge that they committed the action but deny or trivialize the wrongness of the act. They insist, for instance, that they couldn't have hit their partners very hard. They may report that they caused only a small bruise, when, in fact, they broke bones. Batterers also minimize the terror that they inflict.

Batterers may justify an attack by claiming that their partners are *verbally provocative* and that this merits a physical response. This reasoning, of course, assumes that limits on the partner's speech should be set by the batterer and enforced by violence. A frequent comment is that the targets provoked the action. "She drove me to it" or "she nags me" are typical excuses that batterers use, even for behavior that they would otherwise consider unacceptable. One goal of the violence is to silence their partners.

Another frequent excuse is that the partner did not fulfill her "wifely obligations." She didn't cook, clean, or have sex enough or properly, or she did not fulfill the batterer's expectations of emotional care.

CAN BATTERERS CHANGE?

True change means that a batterer must give up violence and threats of violence without simply substituting other tactics of coercion. Many must also give up drugs, including alcohol, which impair their ability to change.[73]

Unfortunately, people who work with battering men say that very few batterers care to change, and programs for batterers are only marginally successful in changing the batterers' behavior.[74] Most of the men in counseling programs are there only under court order or after a severe crisis in the relationship, such as a woman leaving or getting a restraining order to keep him away from her. If the woman returns to the batterer during the course of the counseling, he will often drop out of the program. Only 20 percent of those who entered one counseling program finished it.[75] Many batterers drop out of programs because they do not like to have their view of the relationship challenged, and one-quarter to one-third of the men who come to counseling programs do not even think that what they have done is particularly wrong.[76]

Counseling programs are generally based on the assumption that violence is learned behavior and thus is amenable to

relearning.[77] Some programs try to teach batterers how to recognize the buildup of anger, frustration, and stress and then to change their behavior when aware of these emotions. Some emphasize better communication skills, including assertiveness training, on the theory that if the batterer had nonviolent ways of expressing himself he would use them. These programs redirect the batterer away from violence but do not necessarily address the purpose of abuse or the abuser's responsibility.

Other programs—such as Emerge in Cambridge, Massachusetts, and the Duluth Abuse Intervention Project in Duluth, Minnesota—emphasize that violence is a method for maintaining power and control, that the responsibility for all coercive behavior rests with the abuser, and that the target is not to blame for the abusive behavior.

Yet very few batterers are willing to give up the power that they have to intimidate and control and the rewards they derive from it. Success rates vary, depending on how success is defined, with some as low as 2 percent.[78] In one follow-up study showing relative success, 40 percent of the abusers had contact with the criminal justice system because of their abusive behavior during the five years following treatment.[79] This statistic does not, of course, reflect battering that was not reported to the police, or abusers who stopped their physical violence but intimidated and controlled their partners in other ways. In fact, the techniques batterers learn in counseling programs (from the program itself or from other batterers) sometimes make them more skillful terrorists. They can maintain coercive control over their partners in more socially sanctioned ways, substituting non-criminal techniques for violence.[80]

However, while current programs have not effectively changed most abusers' behavior, they can serve an important function if they see maintaining the safety of the targeted women as an important goal. If the program has outreach workers who maintain regular contact with abused part-

I never beat my wife. I responded physically to her.[68]

Yeah, she is bruised. Yeah, she bruises easy anyway. If I just squeeze like that, you know, next day she'll get a mark.[69]

Women can verbally abuse you. They can rip your clothes off, without even touching you, the way women know how to talk, converse. But men don't. Well, they weren't brought up to talk as much as women do, converse as well as women do. So it was a resort to violence, if I couldn't get through to her by words.[70]

I don't think I wanted to hurt her. I just had all this rage inside, and I didn't know where to put it...I just wanted her to stop being angry at me.[71]

It was over sex, and it happened I guess because I was trying to motivate her. And she didn't seem too motivated.[72]

ners, they can alert any woman they believe is in serious danger, validate her perceptions of abuse, and help her find resources that she needs. The abused women can also corroborate (or not) the abusers' reports of changed behavior. If the abusers are lying about their behavior they can then be confronted with the discrepancy.

Sometimes workers in the justice or social service systems recommend couples' counseling on the misguided assumption that better communication between the partners will decrease violence. But, because of her partner's reprisals, couples' counseling can actually increase the danger for a targeted woman if she is truthful. If she cannot be truthful in counseling sessions, counseling is pointless. Thus, all violence must stop *before* a couple considers entering counseling together.

THE CHANGES WE NEED

In 1964, the first shelter organized specifically for battered women opened in London, England. Not until 1973 did the first U.S. shelter open in St. Paul, Minnesota.[81] Shelters started as grassroots efforts by women to help each other escape from battering relationships. Women began taking each other into their homes; when they realized doing this was too dangerous, they set up houses of refuge whose locations are kept secret.

The movement has improved the ability of many of us to protect ourselves. It is responsible for the changes in the law that have criminalized family violence, and for educating the police, prosecutors, and judges to take the law seriously.

The battered women's movement has taken an increasingly aggressive role in the education of teenagers, adults, and professionals. As a result, public consciousness has changed and made possible a somewhat broader safety net for women. School programs—which are still rare—teach male and female teens how to recognize abusive behavior in its earliest stages, strategies for stopping it, and understanding its long-lasting

effects. And programs to teach conflict resolution are increasing. The movement is pressuring government intervention services to allow each woman to shape the process to fit her own needs rather than relying on standardized problem definitions and protocols. This allows women to better recognize their ability to act on their own behalf.

In spite of some government funding, the number of U.S. battered women's shelters—about 2000—remains quite inadequate. The National Coalition Against Domestic Violence estimates that in the United States, on average, three women are turned away for every woman accommodated by a shelter. In fact, in many states funding for shelters and other battered women's programs has been cut in spite of somewhat increased public awareness—partly as a result of pressure from those who espouse a political and social agenda to keep the nuclear family together at all costs. Even progressive movements often minimize the need for women's safety in relation to "larger" causes.

The need for shelters reflects the importance of earlier intervention to stop the abusive behavior or to remove the abuser from the home—a woman should not need to leave her home and possessions and go into hiding. Much work remains to be done.

The Medical System

Medical professionals may be the first (and sometimes the only) outsiders battered women can turn to. However, doctors are not taught to recognize the social context in which injury or illness occurs. Medical schools rarely have even a few hours of training on recognizing domestic violence, suggesting that domestic violence is not a legitimate medical concern.

Unless educated about what to look for and what to do about it, doctors don't recognize abuse more than 3 to 6 percent of the time that they see its effects.[82] Doctors learn to distance themselves from clients and compartmentalize the body, so they learn to view their clients not as whole people in a context but as body parts and organ systems. They may also be fooled by the solicitousness of an accompanying partner. Batterers often appear very rational and concerned when they arrive at the hospital with their injured partners, who may seem upset or withdrawn.

Some doctors recognize that a client has been battered but consider it a personal matter between partners, not recognizing that the woman may be in serious danger. Emergency room doctors are three times more likely to label a battered woman than a nonbattered woman as having psychiatric problems; they prescribe tranquilizers for one-quarter to four-fifths of battered women compared to one-tenth of nonbattered women and are almost four times as likely to refer battered than nonbattered women to psychiatric services.[83]

Doctors are frequently so pressed for time that they are afraid of opening a Pandora's box—if they ask about abuse, they will be overwhelmed and not have time to follow up with appropriate referrals or may not even know appropriate referrals. In an emergency room, a nurse or social worker may be assigned the job of being an advocate for battered women. Nurses are more likely than doctors to have had training in recognizing partner violence. Residents, who often provide the bulk of the care, stay a year or two, while the nurses may have years of emergency room experience. But even if all the personnel are alert to battering, the hospital administration must allow time for interviewing women and following through on getting the nonhospital services the women need, such as shelter or a restraining order.

A woman who comes to the emergency room for treatment should be asked *in private* if her partner has a history of hitting her, especially if her hospital records indicate frequent emergency room visits. At least 75 percent of battered women will divulge how they were injured when asked in supportive circumstances.[84] We cannot reveal the true cause of our injury if our partners are within earshot without risking further beating in retaliation afterward. For a third of battered women, the act of seeking medical care in itself triggers further violence.[85]

Only recently have professional organizations chosen to address domestic violence. The American Medical Association and the American College of Obstetricians and Gynecologists (whose members act as primary care doctors for many women) have started to pay attention to the importance of domestic violence and their role in educating doctors about it. In 1988, the American College of Obstetricians and Gynecologists sent two pamphlets on domestic violence, one for doctors and one for clients, to all of its members. Newly certified obstetrician/gynecologists now receive these pamphlets in a batch of publications from the professional society. In 1993, the American Medical Association issued guidelines for recognizing family violence for doctors to follow while examining clients. However, no follow-up has yet been done to find out whether doctors read these materials or change their behavior in any way.

The Mental Health System

The mental health system, which is linked to the medical system, reflects many of the same biases. Historically, it has focused on the targeted woman as having a problem and on fixing her symptoms. In the 1960s and 1970s and sometimes more recently, psychiatric reports still labeled abused women as masochistic, overly aggressive, masculine, and frigid, or as helpless and with low self-esteem, essentially blaming her for her problems by implying that she asked for it or that she liked it.[86] More recently, some practitioners have shifted to looking at the woman as "codependent" or "enabling" the partner's violence by unconsciously choosing it. In either case, the professional has pathologized a situation that may be beyond the woman's ability to solve without access to outside resources. Often

When I began to seek help to escape an abusive relationship, all of the counselors I saw kept trying to fit me into this perfect battered woman thing. I couldn't be all that. I was a tough woman, I fought him all the time. The counselors kept saying you're passive, you're dependent, you're scared. I said...no, I just want out.[93]

I have seen men menacing women in the halls of the probate court...Court officers, lawyers, family services officers, and others have walked by in silence as if this were a private matter. It is not a private matter when this behavior is permitted inside the very institution that exists for her protection.[94]

the emphasis is on keeping the family intact without regard for the safety of individual members.

Although more recent writings no longer blame the targeted woman in the same way,[87] solutions still tend to revolve around the individual woman rather than working on changing the broader social context that allows abuse to continue. The mental health system still often doesn't see a woman's situation in the context of the violence of her immediate situation as well as the institutional violence of racism, homophobia, and other prejudices. Solutions often fail to provide for her safety or fail to find ways to change her underlying situation (which may require community-wide action).

Focusing on the woman is easy because her symptoms are often obvious. Battered women use psychiatric services five times as frequently as nonbattered women. Frequent triggers for seeking these services are attempted suicide, alcohol and other drug use, chronic tranquilizer use, multiple physical complaints, and anxiety.[88] In one study, 64 percent of hospitalized female psychiatric patients were battered.[89] Reflecting the uneven distribution of services and resources, twice as many suicide attempts among African-American as among white women were preceded by abuse.[90] In spite of the fact that no consistent personality profile has been found for battered women, they are more likely to have a psychiatric label (such as a personality disorder or hypochondriac) in their medical records than nonbattered women.[91] But perhaps women would not need the mental health system so much if they had access to better police protection, economic opportunities, child care, and other resources that would enable them to become more independent.

The best example of how some mental health caregivers have sought to help women is the theory of the battered woman syndrome. It was proposed by Lenore Walker, a leading theorist on battered

women and one of the few academics to take women's experiences seriously. It is frequently cited by the media and has been used as a defense for women who have killed their batterers. Walker has since gone on to modify and expand her theory, addressing many of the limitations inherent in her early work, but her original proposal lives on in the popular culture as the best-known theory used to explain women's reactions to battering.

Proponents of the battered woman syndrome characterize battered women as being passive, having low self-esteem, believing that they have no resources for help, and believing that they cause the abuser's behavior. According to this theory there is a cycle of violence that leads to the syndrome. After a buildup of tension in the relationship, which the abused woman unsuccessfully tries to defuse, the abuser batters her. The woman is grateful that she survived. The abuser becomes remorseful and may apologize; is helpful and attentive; promises never to do it again; gives the targeted woman gifts; and minimizes or denies the abuse. The woman believes that the relationship has improved. Then tension starts to build again.

This theory does describe some cases of women who are battered but it has several difficulties. First, using the term *syndrome* portrays abused women's behavior as a disorder or disease. More likely, it is the abuser who has a "syndrome." Also using the word *syndrome* implies that battering is a medical problem that needs a medical solution rather than a social problem requiring social change. Second, the theory ignores the fact that some women are not passive in the face of abuse but try to protest and fight back. Many women report that their batterers do not go through a period of remorse.[92] Also, the theory assumes that a woman's passivity is a problem rather than an effective strategy for living with an abuser. That is, if she cannot find help, passivity is a form of self-defense. Although a woman's first reaction may very well be to make accommodations and try to avert the buildup of tension, and though she may be confused by the first attack, after several attacks, most women will not be fooled into thinking that it won't happen again. That is why a feeling of "walking on eggshells" is one sign that abuse is taking place on a regular basis.

The notion of a battered woman syndrome has not served women well since it fails to examine why abusers act as they do. All theories that do not account for the abuser's role fail because, unintentionally, the blame is placed on the victim. The assumption is that a woman is exercising a real choice to stay and is not trapped. Some researchers and activists question whether the battered woman syndrome creates a class of "good victims," leaving those who don't fit with little recourse to justify their actions. We must be open to hearing individual women's stories and believing them.

The Legal and Criminal Justice System

Our legal system has traditionally supported a man's right to control his property, including his wife, who could be chastised by beating. The expression "rule of thumb" originally referred to the largest thickness of stick that was legally acceptable for wife-beating. As stated before, rape and sexual assault within marriage have only recently been made illegal, and only under certain circumstances, which vary from state to state. As recently as 1974, a man killing an adulterous wife in Texas could be charged only with justifiable homicide.

As long as the criminal justice system punishes only extreme forms of abuse, it establishes a level of abuse that is acceptable. For instance, if an abuser can hit a woman without breaking bones and suffers no legal repercussions, then that becomes a socially accepted action. Thus, how the law is defined and how police and judges enforce the law can establish whether abused women will really be safe.

The legal system can only react *after* the abused woman is perceived to be in a damaging situation. Even in cities that have a mandatory arrest law, the police cannot intervene until a woman is significantly intimidated, threatened, or injured. Without evidence of harassment, intimidation, threats, or actual physical harm, she may not be able to obtain a restraining order to keep the abuser away. Sometimes a court order is sufficient to keep the batterer away from the target; sometimes it is too little too late. In one three-week period during September 1992, 700 out of 2000 restraining orders in Massachusetts were violated.[95] The circumstances required for arrest depend on state law. In some cities or states, abusers may not be able to be arrested until they have committed a criminal offense, such as violating a restraining order or assault and battery. In others, the police can make an arrest if it appears likely that the suspect was abusive or intimidating. Until convicted, the abuser can usually be released on personal recognizance or bail.

An increasing number of municipalities now have mandatory arrest policies if police see evidence of probable domestic violence but have not witnessed the actual assault. Regulations were changed to make getting restraining and vacate orders easier, requiring an abuser to stay a certain distance from the woman or to move from the woman's home. These court orders give the woman a legal basis for keeping her batterer away from her. In Massachusetts alone, in 1991, 44,061 restraining orders were issued[96] and even more were granted in 1992.[97] Since 1990, all states have enacted antistalking laws to keep abusers from willfully, maliciously, and repeatedly following or harassing women and threatening bodily injury or death. But while all states have enacted them, the laws vary somewhat by state.[98] To prosecute under them, some only require that a targeted person fears for her physical safety; others require specific threats; and some apply only to those who previously had sexual relations.

One woman described her experience with a judge who claimed that her complaints "didn't do anyone any good." Her husband repeatedly beat her and threatened to kill her. Another woman told of a judge laughing in response to her plea for protection from her batterer.[99]

Last year...one jealous boy pinned his girlfriend against the wall at school, punched her repeatedly, and knocked her down. The principal saw it as two kids fighting and suspended both...She had bruises, he had none...The boy was told by a male counselor that the only reason he was suspended was because he was a boy.[101]

Before and after we were married I went to the priest who married us and he was absolutely no help at all. He kind of questioned me as to "Are you really afraid of him? Are you really? Now, really?" I went to him because I was afraid and I didn't think that this marriage should take place because my fiance had been beating me for eight years. I remember my mother being so afraid that she called the priest ahead of time and said, "Now she's going there to talk to you, and I think he's following her, so I want you to know that. Watch out." That's all that I basically remember, leaving that office saying, "Okay, well, we'll try again. It must be something I'm doing wrong. I'll try again. I'll try harder." I also always felt that no one was listening. There was no way out.

In practice, not all groups are equally protected under the law. Judges might not issue and police might not enforce needed restraining orders. Some women, particularly those who are poor, of color, lesbian, bisexual, recent immigrants, disabled, non-English speaking, or simply of a different ethnic group than the judge, may avoid using the criminal justice system because they have experienced it as useless or hostile. Some judges do not take battering seriously or simply are hostile to women. Some women may be made to face mediation, forcing them to work out custody, visitation, and child support face to face with their abusers, under little or no security.

Women may have trouble getting the police to respond to a domestic violence call if the neighborhood is full of violence. And if we do have our partners arrested, we may be pretty sure that they will be treated more brutally if they are not white, middle-class men. Yet, if we are better off economically and our abusers are prominent in the community (perhaps friends of police officers or judges), our stories may be discounted. Lesbians may get less protection than heterosexual women.

Women who kill in self-defense are sometimes convicted and imprisoned because of the narrow legal definition of self-defense. The legal standard of self-defense is based on what a "reasonable man" would do if attacked in a barroom brawl. Traditionally, the responsive action must be taken during the attack (immediate danger). It must be without excessively more force than the attack (equivalent response) and the responding man must escape if it is reasonably possible (duty to retreat), though he is not required to leave his home if the attack occurs there. The law assumes that the attacker and the attacked are of about equal physical strength and training and that there is no history of repeated attacks. The law is obviously based on male experience. It is unfair to women because it does not reflect women's experiences of violence. For example, a better interpretation might include new concepts of parity (equivalent response) in a fight. Because of the difference in size and strength, even though the abuser attacked with his hands, the woman would be justified in defending herself with a weapon.

Historically, abused women who kill their batterers have been given longer prison sentences than battering men convicted of killing their targets. For women, sentences have averaged fifteen to twenty years, and for men, two to six.[100] Recently a few state governors have commuted the prison sentences of some women on the grounds that all pertinent evidence was not allowed in court. Some people oppose these commutations because they are afraid that if battered women face light sentences for the murder of their batterers, "open season" would be declared for all women to kill their partners. Likewise, if targeted women were seen as justified in killing their batterers when unable to protect themselves in other ways, this would also threaten the current social order with its pandemic violence against women. Women who kill, even in self-defense, are acting outside of the cultural stereotype for women and are more likely to be seen as deviant and guilty. Currently, the battered woman syndrome defense works sporadically; some women are exonerated while others go to jail. The race and class of the defendant probably influence the judgment. Research needs to be done to verify if this is true for women as it is for men.

The Religious Community

Unfortunately, many clergy retain misogynist beliefs, preferring to think that women must be responsible for being abused because they are stepping out of their prescribed roles. Clergy of all religions may minimize the seriousness of violence in order to reduce the stigma of having domestic violence occur in their congregations. For instance, a Jewish woman who goes to her rabbi for help may be accused of failing at her religious duty of providing *shalom bayit*, a harmonious household. Some rabbis still see this solely as the woman's responsibility—if the husband beats her, she must have failed.

Traditionally, the Catholic church has supported the primary importance of the family as a unit regardless of the effects on its members. Not allowing divorce ties a woman to her batterer for life.

In October of 1992, Roman Catholic bishops made their first public statement denying that the Bible supports wife abuse. They encouraged local parishes to hold educational weekends for parishioners and to become familiar with local resources for battered women. Implementation of the education program is moving slowly.

Individual congregations of various denominations are working toward reducing battering by sponsoring shelters and promoting support groups for battered women. But change is slow and pressure is still necessary for it to continue. Until most religious leaders speak out forcefully and repeatedly against domestic violence, as well as actually implement programs to censure abusers and to help abused women, the religious establishment remains aligned with abusers.

RAISING OUR AWARENESS

The first step toward making women safer is for all of us to learn to recognize how common abuse is. For example, one worker in a teen drop-in center never came across any cases of dating violence until she read a paper about it. Then she began asking about abuse in each intake interview, and found that most teens had experienced such violence, sometimes brutal violence, with several partners.[102]

Recognizing intimate abuse requires us to become more perceptive about how much violence is a part of our culture. As one writer reflects:

> One of the most common questions I have heard is in the form, "I want to know how far you can go before an act becomes violent," or "I'm wondering where the line is drawn between normal violence and wife abuse." For these to be heard as *sensible* questions, there must be an assumption that "wife abuse" differs from "normal violence." For these to be heard as *relevant* questions, there must be an assumption that the category "normal violence" is morally tolerable and therefore not a public problem."[103]

We must also learn to see through the stereotypes telling us that abuse is inevitable among certain groups, such as Catholics, dark-skinned people, or those with lower incomes. Equally unhelpful are myths about how protective a particular group (such as Jews) is toward its women, or that lesbians have created a violence-free culture. These stereotypes make us less likely to recognize abuse, and they make it harder for abused women to look for help.

Most importantly, we must learn not to blame the target for another person's actions; instead, we must place responsibility on those who abuse and work to change the institutions that fail to respond appropriately to the abuse of women. For too long, society has searched for solutions to abuse by focusing on those of us who are the targets. This is the path of least resistance since it requires no great changes in ourselves or our society. It is also unjust. Suggestions for how to change our communities so that they will respond to women's needs are found under "Changing Our Communities" in Chapter 11.

The response of the local lesbian community to the arrest of my former lover was demoralizing. Lesbians were upset—even angry—that I had called the police. "I can see turning in a batterer and calling the cops," said one woman. "But a lover? What does that say about your ability to be intimate with anyone?"

Another woman stated flatly, "I don't feel that you were abused by your lover or that she is your batterer." Several women put a lot of pressure on me to drop the charges. They said things like, "Oh, come on. Haven't you ever hit a lover? It wasn't all that bad." "You're dragging your lover's name through the mud. It was in the newspapers." "Do you realize that the state could take away her children because of what you have done?" They suggested setting up a meeting between my former lover and me.[104]

8

About Rape

TRADITIONALLY, rape has been thought of as an attack in a dark, lonely place by a sex-crazed, unknown man leaping from behind the bushes and pointing a gun or knife at a woman's throat. This kind of story grabs the news headlines. But most rape is perpetrated by those who know their targets, and often in familiar surroundings. This very familiarity lulls us into dropping our guard and trusting the rapist.

Contrary to myth, as many as 85 percent of women who are raped know their attackers.[1] Women in their teens and early 20s seem to be particularly vulnerable to acquaintance rape, though statistics are somewhat unreliable; most rape, including marital rape, is not reported to authorities.[2] Women with disabilities may also be more vulnerable.[3]

Although people categorize acquaintance rape or date rape separately from domestic violence, it also is abuse within a relationship. The distinctions are mostly artificial, except that rape involves sex. Perhaps it is easier to see rape as a form of abuse if there is some other kind of abuse present as well because our culture harbors such confusing notions about sex. The similarities between rape and abuse, which are discussed in this chapter, demonstrate that both are aspects of coercive control, and that the same myths about the feelings and proper roles for men and women that pave the way for intimate abuse also characterize rape.

MYTHS AND REALITY

Many myths obscure the serious nature and harmful effects of rape. Rape is an act of violence with sex as the weapon. Forcing unwilling sex on someone is not an act of uncontrollable sexual impulse. Legal definitions of the crime of rape, which vary from state to state, are relatively narrow. Rape usually includes use of force or threat of force and some kind of penetration of a body cavity, whether with a penis, fingers, or an object, with someone who does not consent to it. This book will use the word *rape* in this restricted way, recognizing that many types of coercion besides physical can be used to force us to have sex against our will. Rape within a relationship, which this book focuses on, is often called *acquain-*

One night I let a male friend into my dorm room. He sat on my bed and I sat across the room on the sofa. After a while, he begged for a back rub and I agreed, thinking I could trust him, since he was a good friend. Then he insisted on giving me a back rub in return. [He proceeded to rape her at knifepoint after other threats did not work.]

Somehow people think I am at fault for letting the guy into my room. What am I supposed to do, speak to males only by telephone? After my best friend told me I was at least 50 percent responsible for what happened, I never mentioned the incident to anyone else.[4]

Most of the time, most people who get raped have short mini-skirts, and these floozy outfits, and they're shaking and doing all this and looking at men in these sexy ways. I think they're asking for it.[6]

—High school girl

tance, date, or *marital* rape. The terms *acquaintance* or *confidence rape* may also be used to include those you know more casually, implying both the trickery frequently used in setting women up for rape as well as the breach of confidence that it involves. These terms define rape by the relationship the rapist has to us, obscuring the fundamental coercion underlying all of them. Sexual harassment, which is not discussed in this chapter, is another form of sexual intimidation that may lead to confidence rape or other types of coerced sex.

With rape, as with other forms of violence, we are advised to be wary of strangers but not family and friends, and especially not romantic relationships. Believing that rape is perpetrated by strangers rather than by those we know makes date or marital rape less visible. The rape by a husband of his wife is the ultimate invisible rape. Under certain conditions, marital rape and some forms of sexual coercion within marriage are still legal in some states.

Myths about rape include the overriding belief that the person who is raped—not the perpetrator—is responsible for the rape. That is, we are to blame for our own rapes and deserve to be stigmatized if we "let it" happen. This is similar to blaming abuse on the target, not the perpetrator.

In heterosexual relationships women are supposed to be the gatekeepers for sexual activity during courtship and dating. Many of us grew up hearing that sexual intercourse is like putting a pencil into the mouth of a bottle. Since you can't stick a pencil into a spinning bottle, intercourse isn't possible if a woman is unwilling and physically resists. Many men and women still refuse to believe that a woman can be raped by someone she knows. They think a simple "Beat it, buster" message is sufficient to prevent unwanted sexual activity. But this viewpoint ignores women's experiences of pressure, intimidation, and other coercive tactics.

Equally potent is the maxim that women arouse uncontrollable sexual feel-

ings in men. Just as we are blamed for provoking our partners to abuse us, we are held responsible for "leading men on" to the point of sexual excitement at which they supposedly lose control of themselves. According to this belief, once a man claims he must continue sex to intercourse and orgasm, we have no right to tell him to stop. Thus, women become responsible for male sexual behaviors, including rape. Women who are raped are labeled "sluts," "whores," or "teases" who got what they asked for.

Our society is so preoccupied with women's responsibility for rape that *Parade* magazine ran a question-and-answer column to gather responses to the question, "Does what a girl wears provoke rape?" Though most of the women answering strongly believed that the rapist is responsible for his actions, one 30-year-old woman qualified her remarks by saying, "But a girl must take responsibility for how she presents herself and her body to the world."[5]

Unfortunately, some men and women regard certain kinds of clothing as giving blanket consent for sexual relations. Thus, we must be aware that some people will be unsympathetic to a woman's claim of unwanted sexual attention if they think that her clothes have broadcast a message that she is "asking for it." Advertising and movies, however, frequently portray "sexy" clothing as stylish and many girls and women wear it primarily for that reason.

Another myth is that women enjoy being raped. This is similar to saying that women in abusive relationships must like it or they would leave. Over and over again in books, magazines, movies, and on television, women who are raped end up falling in love and even marrying their rapists. The underlying assumption is that it is normal for men to overcome our resistance, often with repeated rapes, because we really want to have sex and won't admit it, especially if we are "good girls." Since a "good girl" is supposed to say no even if she wants sex, a man should ignore her pro-

MAXINE   by Marian Henley

tests and give her "what she wants." His satisfaction becomes her satisfaction. She will find out that she secretly enjoys it.

Particularly insidious is the conviction that if we follow certain rules we will not be raped. But, as with other forms of abuse, women do not determine when a rape will occur. We read and hear that a woman can and should protect herself from rape by her choice of partners, clothing, and body language. We are supposed to be sufficiently attractive to interest a potential partner but not so attractive that we will provoke rape, just as we are supposed to be careful not to provoke a partner to hit us. We must guess where that fine line is for each person we date, because it changes for each one. We are advised to pay attention to whether our dates show excessively possessive and controlling behavior; to stay in public places, such as restaurants; to be clear about our sexual limits; to be prepared to run away, to make a scene, to hurt our date if necessary; and above all, to trust our instincts about what we should do or not do. In other words, we must always be on our guard to avoid rape. On the other hand, men are encouraged to sow their wild oats, setting up an adversarial relationship.

We may not even recognize rape and coerced sex as such because of our immersion in culturally sanctioned sexual lore that shapes our thinking and behavior. As one researcher writes, "Conventional social attitudes not only fail to recognize most rapes as violations but also construe them as consensual sexual relations for which the victim is responsible."[7] Some people think that a woman cannot have been raped or otherwise coerced if she is not a virgin, was not threatened with a gun or knife, does not have visible injuries, didn't fight back, or was forced to have sex with a woman. If a woman "gives in" under pressure, she is seen as having consented rather than having been forced to have sex.

Many people confuse legally defined rape, which is usually based on force or the threat of force and nonconsent,[8] with other forms of coerced sex.[9] Coercion can range from mild to severe, with much controversy over what actually is mild coercion and what is consent. Many people actually deny the existence of any coerced sex. They believe that women falsely accuse men of rape as a cover for their own interest in sex or because they are vindictive.[10]

Thus, we may have trouble identifying coerced sex or rape by someone we

"I met this girl at a party, she was 12 or 13," the boy said. "She was saying she didn't want to, but she really did. So I did it. She was crying and peed the bed." [Interviewer asked the high school student why he didn't stop when she said no.] "Because it was so sweet," the boy replied.[20]

know because we somehow feel responsible—just as women often feel responsible for their abuse. This can be particularly confusing if we believe we "owe" our partner sex in return for something. We may think that if we want or allow some kinds of intimate touching we then have no right to deny our partners other forms of sex. We know we had sex unwillingly, yet do not name it as coerced sex or rape. In fact, just 27 percent of "women whose experience met legal definitions of rape labeled themselves as rape victims."[11] A *Vogue* article summarized the confusion of cultural myths and feelings:

He wants you; he would also like you to shut your feelings up. He'd like to have sex with you, baby, in spite of you. His desire sets the scene, propels the motion forward...It's all there: the overriding of deep feelings, the sense of responsibility for someone else's well-being, the overwhelming desire to be loved transferred to him—if you don't "love" him back, he'll die—the severe case of empathy.[12]

Sexual coercion clearly does not stop when a woman marries. Traditionally, marriage grants a man unlimited legal sexual access to his wife. Rape within marriage has only recently been considered a criminal act. In 1977, Nebraska was the first state to specifically delete all marital exemption for rape in the law.[13] All states now treat rape within marriage as a crime under some circumstances. More than half the states, though, still have a partial marital exemption. As an example, a husband might have to threaten his wife's life during rape before it is legally considered a crime, or the wife might have to report the rape within a few months for it to be prosecuted, a much shorter time than for stranger rape. Laws, however, continue to change. Rape and sexual abuse, like physical abuse, have a long history of being men's rightful instrument of ownership and control to coerce and terrorize women.[14]

THE SOCIAL UNDERPINNINGS OF RAPE

Just as abusers cannot be identified easily, rapists also cannot be easily distinguished. Research on dating paints contradictory pictures of rapists, indicating that they span the normal gamut of personalities.[15] For example, one study reports that "men who initiate the date, pay all expenses, and drive are more likely to be sexually aggressive."[16] In another study, "women who share dating expenses are more likely than other women to be victims of sexual aggression."[17] Actually, the situation does not make the rapist or help identify one.

Power is as much a part of rape as it is of other forms of abuse. A study corroborating this connection showed that college men who were aroused by pictures of rape were likely to batter or rape their wives and girlfriends ten years later.[18]

Boys growing up learn that conquest of women is part of the male role. Boys' first sexually aggressive behavior starts, on average, at 10 years old.[19] Boys learn that men should be dominant and that women are supposed to satisfy them.

Among teenagers, almost 40 percent of boys—and 30 percent of girls—agree that forced sex is acceptable if a girl has let a boy touch her above the waist. Over half the boys—and almost half the girls—thought that forced sex was fine if the boy was sexually aroused by the girl. Even when a boy forces a girl to have sex by threatening to spread rumors about her or threatening her with physical harm, teenagers still think that the rape is a quarter to a third the girl's fault.[21] In another study, 65 percent of the boys—and almost as many girls—believed that forced sex was okay after six months of dating. About a quarter of the boys believed spending money on a girl justified forced sex.[22] These beliefs are similar to blaming women for being attacked. Teenagers seem not to realize that it is the boy who commits the act of rape and the girl who is violated.

In one college sample, 64 percent of the men said that they get excited when a woman struggles over sex and 61 percent thought that it would be exciting to use force to subdue a woman.[23] Thus, these men do not view sex as an interaction between equals—it is for their own dominance and pleasure. Further, about a third of male college students studied were more sexually attracted by emotional distress than happiness in a woman's facial expression.[24] This group was twice as likely as the other men in the study to have committed repeated acts of sexual aggression. Other experimental studies have shown that when men who generally prefer images of consensual sex get angry at a woman, in that mood they become equally sexually aroused by images of rape. This was true even for men who had previously reacted adversely to depictions of violent actions against women. Thus, it seems that men frequently connect anger and sexual violence.[25]

In another study, close to 60 percent of college men admitted to touching a woman sexually against her will.[26] And a study on date rape disclosed that many men admitted to actions that were legally rape although they did not name their behavior as such. In fact, in one study 84 percent of the men who had actually raped denied, sometimes adamantly, that they had done so. In another, the rate was 88 percent.[27]

THE MIND OF A RAPIST

Rapists, like batterers, minimize the effects of their actions. Even convicted rapists usually deny or minimize their crimes. They believe that the women were equally or more responsible for the rape than they were. They say that the women resisted only minimally and that their own behavior was only "somewhat" forceful even if they were twisting the women's arms or holding them down. Many of the men, even after using force and injuring the women, said that they consented. Women who were raped reported that when they made their objections clearer and their resistance stronger, the violence used against them was greater than the rapists reported.

Studies of rape do not necessarily attempt to find out if a rapist's attitude or actions change according to how well he knows the targeted woman. This kind of research would let us know if there are differences between "stranger" rapists and "acquaintance" rapists. In the absence of this research the authors assume that the attitudes are similar enough so that research on "stranger" rape can be applied to all types of rapists. Also, rape research has concentrated on white male college students, probably the most advantaged group in the United States. This, of course, limits class, age, race, and ethnic representation. Lesbians aren't studied since "common sense" says women can't rape other women, although some do. (And men are not immune from being raped, though their rapists are nearly always other men.) On the one hand, because of the limitations of whom researchers study, the findings cannot be generalized. On the other hand, since the rates of rape among this privileged group are high, acquaintance rape is probably common in all groups. The men who are studied are the social arbiters of the morality of the dominant sex.

Men who rape do not consider their behavior unusual. Where studies have found a difference between men who rape and those who don't, the difference is only one of degree. For example, 50 percent of one college sample of men said if they knew they would not be caught, they would force a woman to have sex. When the action was specifically labeled rape, 30 percent were still willing to admit they would do it as long as they wouldn't get caught.[28] One rape crisis counselor points out, "There is a 'code of violence' against women and the men who abide by it are 'normal guys'."[29] It is simply "the way men treat women." Men do not take their partners' wishes into consideration. They may be unwilling to believe that what feels good to them doesn't necessarily feel good to a woman. In many

During the attack, she cried, pushed him away, and begged him to stop, "but that didn't faze him." Afterward, apparently immune to her distress, the man said, "I'll give you a call," as he headed out the door.[31]

Operating in me was a belief that I was different from other men, that I wouldn't be involved in such things as rape, certainly not; but I shared at the same time the fundamental male feeling, for example, that even if Judy said no, she didn't mean no and she could be talked out of it. I felt that way about a number of women I related to. I thought of it as persuasion, clarifying of the facts.[32]

cases, they just don't care. Some men say they feel some pride after raping a woman.[30]

Male privilege and lack of empathy leads to the common male assumption that what they want and like in sexual activity is what women want. This tendency to see a sexual partner as an extension of themselves encourages abuse, including rape and other forms of sexual coercion.

Although popular belief holds that rape is not premeditated— implying a man's lack of control over his sexual behavior— rapes are frequently planned. A rapist arranges circumstances to prevent his target from escaping or calling for help. Because of this it is particularly important for a woman to try to pick up clues that may indicate coercive control by her partner before she finds herself in a situation where she is trapped. (The box listing abusive behaviors in Chapter 7, "Intimate Abuse," will be helpful.) A perpetrator may make sure that others are out of the house or take a woman to an isolated place, perhaps telling lies about needing to do errands or dropping in to see friends. The rapist may encourage her to drink or get high in order to set up a situation in which she cannot resist or escape. Sometimes friends help the rapist and give other encouragement.

Like other kinds of abusers, rapists take advantage of the targeted woman's trust. Although they sometimes threaten or injure their dates before the rape, often they just ignore a woman's refusal to have sex. If the rapist is bigger or stronger, this difference alone may be enough to force the rape. Like batterers, rapists do not care that the woman may have wishes different from theirs.

After the rape, the rapist may act helpfully and attentively. This is similar to the apology and remorse batterers often express after administering a beating. However, if the woman presses charges, some rapists will stalk their targets afterward to intimidate them, just as some batterers stalk their targets after the woman gets a restraining order or leaves the relationship.

As with other violent behavior towards women, men who rape have little incentive to stop. Men actively encourage each other in date rape and boast of their sexual exploits. Women rarely report rape committed by someone they know. Since so few teenagers report rape to adults who have power to act on their behalf, many school-age rape survivors remain in the same classroom or school as their rapists, who serve as a constant reminder of their violation and trauma. Because of the secrecy, these rapists will not even be confronted or reprimanded, let alone punished.

THE FAILURE OF THE LEGAL SYSTEM

An especially glaring affront to women's autonomy is the failure of most of the legal system to deal with date rape as a felony. Cases of rape by someone a woman has a relationship with are harder to prosecute successfully than stranger rape. The woman is as much on trial as the rapist. Juries still tend to believe that a woman is in some way responsible for encouraging the rapist and that this constitutes consent. Rape is the only violent crime in which a person must resist to be considered a victim. That is, in all other types of crime we are traditionally expected to be passive in order to protect ourselves from more lethal harm.

Prosecutors generally decide to prosecute a rape case only if they think they can win it. Largely this is determined by whether the case fits the stereotype of unexpected rape by a stranger in which the woman fought back vigorously. In addition, if a woman does not go to an emergency room immediately after the rape, she may be accused of using the charge as revenge for being scorned. Women who state that they have been raped by another woman are often not believed. Police may also discount reports of rape from teenagers. Although prosecution of a burglary is not dependent on whether a person forgot to lock a door or window, for rape a woman is presumed to have a duty to prevent the crime by dressing conservatively and knowing in advance who might be a possible rapist and not associating with him or her. The legal system appears to ignore research showing that the rapist determines when a rape will be carried out—it is not the target's age, race, or behavior that precipitates a rape. (Some state laws are changing. New Jersey now uses the broader term *sexual assault* instead of *rape* and requires that, for each act of penetration with a body part or an object, freely given affirmative consent must be obtained.)

Some women choose to file a civil suit against the rapist, which doesn't involve the criminal justice system. The woman needs only to prove evidence of harm to her, not definitive proof of rape. The burden of proof need not be quite so strong as in a criminal court and the verdict does not require a unanimous jury. As plaintiffs, women can also require the defendants to testify. Some defendants, however, have harassed their targets by countersuing for libel.

College students may find school disciplinary boards that they turn to unsatisfactory for pursuing rape charges. Even if the board believes the woman, it may simply give the rapist a slap on the hand, perhaps suspending him or revoking his right to return to campus rather than handing evidence over to the police for criminal prosecution. But this leaves him free to rape elsewhere, and presumably does little to change his behavior. He may continue to believe that what he did was not actually rape. Colleges and universities want to hush up rape incidents because, if widely publicized, fewer students might apply. However, Congress has passed a law that requires colleges and universities to reveal campus crime statistics.

Some college students are taking matters into their own hands and warning other women by making public the names of those who have raped them. At Brown University, women repeatedly wrote rapists' names on lavatory walls even though the university kept washing them off. Finally, the university painted the walls brown in an effort to stop the underground information network. Parents and alumni can take an active role in convincing college administrations to take rape seriously.

WHAT TO DO IF YOU ARE RAPED

If you are raped, you need to get medical care and counseling as soon as possible. If you can, call a close friend and a rape crisis hotline in your area. Ask for support and information. When you feel ready, go to the emergency room—with an advocate if possible—for medical care even though the medical exam may feel like an additional trauma and violation. (If there is even the slightest possibility that you might want to take legal action later, your case will be greatly strengthened by an exam as soon after your rape as you can bear it.) Your nearest rape crisis center may be able to help you learn more about the laws that apply to your assault and help you find legal aid. (Laws covering rape and other sexual crimes vary from state to state.)

Your first instinct after rape may be to immediately wash yourself as thoroughly as possible and to try to forget about it. But in order to keep as much evidence intact as possible, do not wash even your hands. The medical practitioners can gather semen, hair, dirt, and other evidence during the exam. At the hospital you will be given a pelvic exam and possibly a rectal or oral exam, depending on how you were raped. This is to check for internal injuries as well as to gather evidence. Going to the hospital sooner rather than later may allow the medical practitioner to observe tissue injury before your body starts to heal itself. Skin inflammation in particular can subside after only a few hours. You will also be checked for external injuries.

You will probably be given a shot of antibiotics in your buttocks to prevent some sexually transmissible diseases because 30 percent of rape victims contract sexually transmissible diseases.[33] Ask what drug you are being given, what it protects against, and what tests you will need later. (Some sexually transmitted diseases, such as HIV/AIDS, often take several months to show up on tests.) If you are worried about becoming pregnant, you may be offered a high dose of hormones, which may prevent pregnancy. Ask about side effects, including their effect on fetal development if the pregnancy continues. Weigh hormone use and the likelihood that you conceived as the result of rape against your ability to get an abortion later. If abortion is an option for you, you could wait to see if you are actually pregnant.

Your emotional healing will take longer than your physical recovery. You probably will recover faster if you find one or more supportive people who believe you. People who blame you for the rape or deny that it happened may worsen your trauma. You may find that for a while even consensual sex becomes intolerable unless you continuously maintain autonomy and control. You may be able to find a support group or a counselor through a rape crisis hotline or center. If you are abused in other ways, a battered women's group may also be appropriate. And there are some positive outcomes: one researcher writes, "Among the few positive outcomes reported by rape survivors is the determination to become more self-reliant, to show greater respect for their own perceptions and feelings, and to be better prepared for handling conflict and danger."[34]

9

Saving Ourselves

BECAUSE OUR culture emphasizes the importance of developing power over others, all of us have experienced relationships as power struggles. This attitude is so pervasive that many of us accept it as the way to relate to others most of the time. If this has been your attitude and you wish to change it, the first step is to recognize coercive behaviors or situations—both when someone else is attempting to assert control over you against your wishes and when you are attempting to control other people. Remember that control is not necessarily accomplished through physical violence—threats, name calling, put-downs, teasing, jealousy, sexual harassment, and control of household or work resources are all effective.

The second step is to believe that you do not deserve to be abused, no matter what—even if you can't keep the house clean, are fat, get angry easily, use drugs, hit your partner or children, have sex with others besides your partner, or like "kinky" sex. *No one deserves to be abused.* Nor are you responsible for your abuser's actions. Always remember, no one chooses to be in an abusive relationship, especially a violent one. What we choose is a loving relationship, which sometimes turns out to be an abusive one. But the price of ignoring abuse is high.

We must remember that saying no to violence is not a sign that we are trying to destroy or emasculate our partners. We are asserting our right to safety and to a supportive, loving relationship.

HELPING OURSELVES

Following are a number of exercises that may be useful to help counter thoughts about deserving abuse or making excuses for abusers. Use the parts that work for you and don't worry about the rest. Do them with a friend or use a mirror. Some are easy to do with a tape recorder or by writing in a journal.

➤ Sit facing a friend or look in a mirror. Praise the person you are looking at for one full minute. If you are doing this

brother
i don't want to hear
about
how my real enemy
is the system.
i'm no genius,
but i do know
that system
you hit me with
is called
a fist.

— Pat Parker,
in *Movement in Black*

I guess I didn't know better. I saw my father treat my mother not physically bad, but mentally and sexually. I saw that and I guess I just figured that's the way life is. You just deal with the bad parts in relationships along with the good ones. No relationship is perfect.[1]

The pain and humiliation of living with violence went deeper than any other hurts I have ever experienced. The violation of being abused by a woman I loved has shaken the very roots of my lesbian being. I know that I will never again have the same unquestioning faith in womyn or sisterhood or lesbian utopia.[2]

I started healing one day when I was full of self-pity and guilt. Then I said, "You have comforted so many people in your life with a word or a hug. Can you do that for yourself? Can you feel compassion for Tina? Tina has a problem; she hurts, she is in pain. Can Tina give compassion to Tina? Not pity but compassion."[3]

with yourself, make sure to do it out loud and address yourself as "you," or by your name. You can record what you say and play it back. Think about including praise both for just being there or what you are like and for what you or the other person has accomplished. Use this praise list whenever you feel unlikable or as though you haven't accomplished anything. (These tend to be common feelings when self-esteem is low or when we are depressed.) If you are working with a partner, reverse the exercise, with your partner praising you. Repeat the praise you just heard in the first person, using "I am..." Write for a few minutes in a journal about what feelings you have when giving praise and when receiving praise.[4]

➤ If you usually deflect praise or compliments with comments like, "It was nothing," "X really did it," or "I don't really look so great in the morning," next time simply say, "Thank you." When you don't try to contradict your complimenter, you are helping yourself. You are also validating the other person by not questioning her or his judgment.

➤ At the end of each day, look at yourself in the mirror and tell yourself out loud two good things about what happened that day or what you liked about the day. You might make a pact with a friend to do this with each other during the day at some fixed time.

➤ Say to yourself in the mirror, or post in some prominent place in your house, any or all of these messages: "I am a worthwhile person. I like me." "I deserve more than this." "I have the right to be who I am." "God does not want me to live this way." "I have courage." "I am strong." "I will heal and be happy again." "I deserve to be loved without being hit." "I am a survivor."[5]

➤ Make a scrapbook or keep a file of images that reflect what you feel about yourself or about your interests. If possible, tell a friend why you chose those images or tell a tape recorder. You may want to ask your friend to help you hear your own story more clearly by repeating it back to you as closely as possible, but without adding any comments that indicate whether the friend thinks what you said was good or bad. You can also listen to your tape recording.[6]

➤ Write five things that you like about yourself or that you do well, one each on a slip of paper, or have five friends each write out one thing that they like about you. Collect the papers and read them aloud.[7]

➤ Finish the following sentence by writing in your journal or speaking to yourself in the mirror," If I could give myself a gift, it would be..."

➤ For each word in the following list, think back until you remember a time when the word described you. If you can't think of a time right away, just keep it in the back of your mind until you do.[8]

Determined	Friendly
Grateful	Honest
Responsible	Gentle
Generous	Helpful
Listen well	Sensitive
Funny	Loyal
Inventive	Patient
Independent	Kind

➤ Name three people you admire and what you admire about them. Name two people who have influenced you the most and how. If you know one or more people who consider you a positive role model, name them.[9]

➤ When you hear a critical voice in your head, identify where you first heard that message—from your mother, father, teacher, friend, partner, or someone else. Do you think that the meaning of the message you heard was the message that the person intended? If not, what do you think the message was supposed to be? Unless the message was intended primarily to demean you, consider how would you say the same thing without being critical. Replace the message with a more positive one.

It will be helpful to write lists for the following exercises.[10]

➤ When you ask yourself why your partner is abusive, stop and ask yourself instead what your partner gains by what he or she does.

➤ When you ask yourself what you are doing wrong, ask instead what you gain by blaming yourself.

➤ Ask yourself what you want—out of your relationship, during sex, from a counselor or support group, or just right now. If you do not know what you want sexually, explore your own body by yourself. (If you were sexually or physically abused as a child, you may have a particularly hard time figuring out what you wish, separate from your partner's wishes.)

➤ Ask yourself what is good and what is bad about your relationship, and what the costs and benefits are of maintaining it. If you are considering leaving your relationship permanently, list the costs and benefits of this also.

➤ If you decide to stay in your relationship because you think your partner will change, ask yourself what makes you think that he or she will change. Then work out a way to evaluate whether change is taking place. Think of specific ways you expect

change and how you would see it. If you are staying in your relationship out of fear of your partner's violence, then you need to think about your safety (see "If You Think You May Be in Danger" later in this chapter).

➤ Find one sentence that describes how you feel about your relationship as it was a year ago, two months ago, now, and how you imagine it six months from now.[11]

When you learn to see how you are abused, you may find that you have adopted some of the same coercive tactics to use with those who are less powerful than you, especially your children. The first step is to acknowledge that you are abusively controlling another person's behavior and that you are responsible for doing so. Consider finding a counselor, group, or class to help you examine the effects of your behavior and explore what you could use as a substitute. When choosing a counselor, find out about her or his experience working with conflict resolution techniques as well as abuse. Having an advocate will help you continue to change when you get discouraged.

If we are the ones being abusive, we are responsible for noticing how our behavior affects others. One way to start to change is to pay more attention to how the target of our actions feels. Ask and really listen. Sometimes our partners or children tell us through body language rather than directly through words. If we are the targets of an activity we don't like, we have a responsibility to let the other person know as clearly as possible before the abuse escalates. (If this person abuses you, however, speaking up may be dangerous.) If we clearly say that we do not like what has happened and the person does not stop, this is a warning to be alert to further abuse.

A particularly good book to help sort out feelings about what to do, as well as

It helped my low self-esteem to help others. I didn't articulate this to my coworkers [in the battered women's movement]. What an incredible thing I was doing in my own life bridging all these differences between women. I just basked in their energy, their sense of humor. I got so much. It changed my life completely. It was a gift. There is a thrill in seeing women's strength.[13]

A lot of counseling and a lot of friends telling me I was not a bad person [made the difference]. I had to hear it a lot of times, lots of times, QUITE A FEW TIMES, but then I heard it. And graduating from my bookkeeping course and working on my GED [were also important].[14]

I thought that I was an isolated case in society...[the group] was like a revelation.[15]

Even if I don't know what I'm looking for, I always feel better when I leave [the group].[16]

One of the things that I learned when I came to the battered women's group was the word no. I'm still learning it. I'm glad that I'm not alone.

practical suggestions for taking action, is *When Love Goes Wrong: What to Do When You Can't Do Anything Right* by Ann Jones and Susan Schecter (see "Notes). (See "Resources" for other books.) Some of the ideas in this chapter are taken from this book.

REACHING OUT

If you recognize that you are in an abusive relationship and want to change it, you need to find a way to take some action. Getting help may not be easy and may take a long time. At times you are likely to feel scared, lonely, embarrassed, enraged, uncertain, or guilty.

Explaining your positions or actions to an abuser is probably useless. The abuser is unlikely to interpret events the same way you do and will probably be unwilling to admit that your point of view is possible or valid. Thus, arguments defending yourself do not necessarily make sense to the abuser.

Remember that you can't improve a relationship by "improving" yourself. For a relationship to change, both partners must take responsibility for their own actions. Loving someone is different from being responsible for their behavior.

Getting Validation

If you find that your self-esteem is dissolving, then you need to go outside of your primary relationship for validation. You may even conclude that your self-esteem won't improve until you get a different partner.[12] The reason your abuser isolates you is to keep you from outside support.

Many women report that one of the most important steps in being able to change their situations was to find someone who believed them and believed that what they were going through was abuse. Talking with others who will listen to you and believe you is important to help you clarify your thoughts, your situation, and to check out what is real and what isn't. Help may turn up in the unlikeliest places. Develop as wide a support network as pos-

sible. Try to find friends, an advocate, a counselor, therapist, social worker, or support group to give you emotional support and practical help. Someone, such as a youth counselor or an immigration advocate, who has helped you in the past on an unrelated issue, may be willing to help you again. Make sure to tell your listener to keep what you say confidential if that is what you want. Start with people you feel safe with. If you feel betrayed by someone you talked to, if you feel you are to blame after you talk, or if he or she minimizes the abuse, don't give up reaching out. Recognize that you made a mistake in whom you told, not in the telling.

The Value of Support Groups

You may draw strength from sharing stories with those who have gone through similar experiences. Many times, simply sharing your story with a group of women who believe you is enough to solidify your resolve to escape. Although each woman's story is unique, you may find many themes of yours reflected in others'.

The women may inspire you by their actions, or offer practical advice or help. Good support groups can question your decisions while still being supportive of you as a person. For example, if you continue to stay with your batterer, others may ask you to consider the reasons you continue to do so, warn you about the dangers, and give you advice on making the transition. If you are nervous or fearful about actually following through with court procedures for restraining orders or filing criminal complaints, the other women can help you, perhaps locating an advocate to accompany you. Exchanging phone numbers gives you someone to call on a particularly hard day. Sometimes group members escort you to and from your car or give you a ride if your partner or ex-partner may be stalking you. You may find that a group gives you a perspective on your situation that you could not get in individual counseling, though you get more attention to your particular problems in one-on-one counseling.

On the other hand, cultural differences among abused women in support groups can lead to tensions and misunderstandings. For example, a woman who speaks directly may appear rude to a woman from another culture, while the more oblique approach may mystify and confuse other women. And you may find it difficult to talk about your problems with strangers, especially if they are from a different cultural group.

If you are a member of a minority group, you might want to seek out or form a network and meet with others from your culture. If your community is tightly woven, however, you may be concerned about confidentiality or be afraid to appear weak to others in your group. But this is an opportunity to open up and accept help from others who are living through the same type of experience.

If you are in a support group composed of women of different races, ethnic groups, or sexual orientation, you may feel that it is not safe to talk about conflict in your relationship. Asking for a reaction to your fears about prejudice and stereotypes is one way to judge how safe the group is for you. If you know any women who have attended mixed groups, they may be able to give you advice on their experiences and where to look for supportive groups.

Other types of support networks may also be helpful, such as Alcoholics Anonymous and related groups for people who live with alcoholics, such as Al-Anon or Alateen. Some women find yoga, self-defense, or other kinds of classes helpful. From all attempts to get help, take what is useful and discard the rest.

Individual Counseling

Individual counseling can help you focus on your own issues without having to share time with others. If you need emergency counseling, you don't need to wait for a group to meet. (However, for regular counseling, you may need to wait until the therapist you want to work with has an open slot.) Often support groups and individual counseling complement each other.

Counseling can range from a few sessions with a specifically defined goal or to longer, more wide-ranging therapy. (See the box entitled "Talk Therapies," in Chapter 2, to review the different types of therapy.) To find a counselor, call a local battered women's program; the YWCA; a local woman's center, which may be located on a college campus; or any other agency that specifically caters to women. You may also be able to find names in a local feminist newspaper.

The fees of therapists in private practice can be prohibitive for a woman with no medical insurance. Inquire at community mental health centers for sliding scale fees and at psychiatric departments of general hospitals for fee reductions. Battered women's programs are free, and some include individual counseling.

Find a counselor with whom you feel comfortable. (Many counselors will give one interview free of charge to see if you find her or him compatible. If not, you may want to try interviewing the prospective therapist by phone.) Consider if she or he takes you seriously, asks pertinent questions, listens well, is informed about your rights, and knows where to refer you for specific services you might need. Even if your counselor is already part of a battered women's service group, ask questions about her or his views on abusive relationships before entering counseling. Many counselors still accept myths about battered women, seeing the abuse as a symptom of underlying psychopathology rather than seeing your behavior and feelings as a response to the trauma. Some may even deny your reality, cause you to doubt your sanity, or focus on your childhood instead of helping you deal with being abused or in danger now. Beware of counselors who tell you what you should do rather than encourage you to decide what is best for you.

[In individual counseling] you can go into more "intimate detail" and say things you might be embarrassed by, whereas in group, there are more views, more an "I'm not alone" feeling.[17]

During a conversation with my ex-husband a few years ago he told me I was crazy and needed a lobotomy. For a moment I believed him and I thank God I was in counseling. I called my counselor immediately and she helped me get through it.

I've developed this thing which I'm trying to undevelop with my counselor, so that I don't need a man...to be a person—that my self-esteem does not come from that.

Don't live with it, don't put up with it, you don't have to, there's help out there.[18]

In some ways [when I contacted the battered women's shelter] I was in a place of "more strength" than I have ever been, because I was finally seeing something that I had lived with for seven years and I knew it had to stop.[19]

Notice if you feel shame, guilt, or despair after meeting with the counselor. These are signs that this may not be the right counselor for you.

In any setting, ask questions that might reveal prejudices against you. Many African-Americans, for instance, have shunned the mental health system because it has often used inappropriate models. Today more counselors are learning about incorporating African-American experiences and viewpoints. If you are lesbian, you may find that a heterosexual counselor sees lesbianism as the problem, with the abuse a symptom rather than the problem.

Finding the Help You Need

If you are unsure about what to do, or need help to find a relatively safe way to stop the abuse, contact a battered women's shelter or hotline or check "Resources." Someone at the hotline or battered women's group will listen to your story and may suggest possible courses of action. Many hotlines and battered women's groups have counseling services. Call even if you are unsure whether you are being abused. Many of the counselors can also explain your legal options or tell you how to get this information. For example, you may be able to obtain an emergency restraining order immediately from a court to keep your abuser away from you. Sometimes battered women's group workers are able to go to court with you and guide you through the process. They may be able to help you find temporary housing and explain how to negotiate the state aid system so that you can receive benefits if you are eligible.

If you are unsure about the advice you receive, need clarification, have further questions, or need other referrals, call back. Many hotlines and battered women's groups are staffed mostly by volunteers. Most volunteers are well trained, but you might have reached someone who is not as experienced as others. Ask to speak to a different person if you think it would help.

If you are a teenager and have a friend who believes what is happening, get that person's support. Try to enlist the help of an adult and don't give up until you find someone. This step is crucial, especially if you are under 18. If you can, get help from a parent, another adult you are close to, or someone at your school. You may fear a loss of your independence if you confide in an adult, but that may be the most effective way to get help to protect your safety.

Legally, your situation is different from an adult's if you are a minor and unmarried. For instance, in some states, a bat-

Finding Phone Numbers for Services

Phone numbers for battered women's or rape crisis hotlines and shelters are frequently in the front of the white pages of the telephone book in a section of crisis numbers. Also, look in the Yellow Pages under "Social and Human Services" or "Shelters," or call Directory Assistance for numbers. A telephone operator should also be able to connect you to a hotline or a shelter, even if none exists close to you. Ask specifically for services for battered women. Ask if there is currently a national toll-free hotline. (This hotline goes in and out of existence, depending on the availability of federal funding.)

tered women's group may be required by law to report your presence to the state department of social services, which will notify your parents. If you are under 18 but already living on your own, however, you might be able to be declared an emancipated minor with more legal rights. Call a hotline or shelter to find out where you can learn about your legal options.

IF YOU THINK YOU MAY BE IN DANGER

First of all, take seriously threats to your safety. If you are afraid of injury to yourself or your children, it is important to work out an emergency escape plan. Think about where you can go, no matter what time it is. Consider your friends or relatives. Try to find out what arrangements you need to make to reach a battered women's shelter. Think about public places you can get to where you can safely make telephone calls—a hospital emergency room, police station, perhaps a mall or restaurant.

Ask a friend or neighbor to hide a bag or suitcase. Include a change of clothes for yourself and your children, toiletries, any necessary medications, and an extra key to your home and your car, if you have one. Also include, if you can, a book or toy for each child. If you trust your friend or neighbor with money, leave cash, a checkbook or a savings passbook with her or him. Otherwise, find a hiding place at home. (However, you may not have time to retrieve the money if you need to rush out, and you also risk its discovery by your abuser.) Include emergency telephone numbers and originals or copies of identification and legal papers such as birth certificates, immigration papers, driver's license, voter registration, social security card, utility bills, and restraining orders. These papers can help you enroll your children in a new school or help you get financial assistance. If you can, include other financial records, such as rent receipts, mortgage papers, or automobile title. If your children are old enough and you think it is safe, discuss your emergency

escape plan with them so that all of you can leave together.

If you need to go to a shelter you may have to leave behind the familiar and move into an alien world of other races, ethnicities, and sexual orientation in return for safety. Shelters vary widely in size and comfort. Most are organized with a communal kitchen and living areas with bedrooms assigned to specific people. You may be assigned a bedroom for yourself and your children, if you have any, or you may have to share with others. You will be expected to do household chores and cooking as part of your duties, as well as attend regular meetings. You may feel uncomfortable about the communal lifestyle and the way domestic duties are assigned. Although shelter security rules may seem overly strict, they are designed to protect the safety of shelter residents and staff, whose lives might be at risk if batterers found out where their targets were staying. Feelings of loneliness and isolation are common, but the relief of being safe and the support of the women around you will likely help you feel more comfortable.

IF YOU NEED TO GO TO THE EMERGENCY ROOM

Many emergency rooms already have protocols for treating battered women. Those that don't will soon be required to have one in order to maintain their hospital accreditation. Having protocols, however, does not necessarily mean that medical personnel will carry them out competently and compassionately. Stereotypes do not dissolve after a few hours of training. Unfortunately, women still sometimes find their experiences at the hospital disappointing and even humiliating.

If you go to the emergency room with your batterer, you may be able to get better care if you feel able to request a private examination so that you can safely tell who injured you, how you were hurt, and whether you have been battered before. More and more emergency rooms do re-

Talk up if you are made to feel uncomfortable about the kind of food you cook, the music you listen to, or the way you comb your children's hair. A simple comment like, "I'd rather do yardwork or answer phones today instead of cooking because too much time in the kitchen makes me feel like a maid," will point out to other shelter residents that you are willing to do your fair share of chores, but not at the expense of your self-esteem.[20]

quire a private examination as part of their standard procedures, but they may be so crowded that the doctors cannot comply. Otherwise, you may need to lie about the cause of your injuries to protect yourself from further abuse later on.

If possible, ask the person taking your history to write in your medical record who hurt you, not just an anonymous description of your injury, such as "blow from fist." Make sure that the medical practitioner looks at all injuries. Most doctors are white and may not recognize the degree of severity of bruises and injuries on darker skin. Try to get someone to take instant (Polaroid) pictures of visible injuries to put in your medical records. If you decide later to take legal action, you may need these photos in court to support claims of repeated injury. Even if you don't think you will take legal action, leave yourself the option in case you change your mind.

If your partner has threatened you or your children or if you are afraid to go home, ask hospital personnel to call the police, a shelter, or other battered women's service group to help you get some immediate protection. Find someone who can help you work out a safe plan for escape. Avoid accepting tranquilizers, which generally should not be given to people with abdominal or head injuries and which can slow down your reaction time and make you less clearheaded, putting you at greater risk of injury the next time your partner attacks you.

If you have been using alcohol or other drugs and if you are aware enough, see if the staff will let you stay in the emergency room until you are more sober before receiving treatment. Then you will be able to be more cooperative. Unfortunately, the staff may otherwise label you "AOB" (alcohol on breath) or "crazy" and not take you seriously. A woman who is drunk, under the influence of other drugs, or acting bizarrely may have a particularly hard time getting a sympathetic response from the staff, who will be less likely to recognize that she has been battered. They are more likely to assume that alcoholism, drug abuse, depression, or a suicide attempt is the primary problem, and overlook the abuse.

SHOULD YOU LEAVE?

Many formerly abused women advise others to end abusive relationships as soon as possible. Many regret not leaving sooner. They remind us that we justify staying by futile hopes. Even if we don't think that we deserve the abuse, we hope that we can change ourselves to please the batterer so that we will not be beaten again. We hope that the abuser will change, especially if he or she has promised to. We hope that our own inner resources will be sufficient to change our situations. We hope that our children will not be affected by the tension and terror in the family. We hope that we can last long enough so that we can leave when the children reach a certain age or we are finally able to support ourselves. We hope that we will be able to survive one more day, even one more moment during an attack.

Each of us must decide for ourselves if leaving is the right decision and when the best time is. But be aware that the longer we wait, the harder leaving may become. Coercive control and violence often escalate as a relationship continues, while at the same time our emotional ties to our abusers may increase. We each need to trust our intuitive feelings about how dangerous the situation is. If you sense that leaving will put you in more danger than staying, take this into account when making your plans.

In some relationships, we can sever our ties to the other person and just walk away. Often, however, we cannot extricate ourselves. The nature of being a target in an abusive relationship is that the other person is trying to keep control and may not let us go. And if we have had children with our abuser, the courts may mandate contact. Or we may be in a school or work situation that is difficult to change in order to avoid contact. And when we try to protect ourselves or disentangle ourselves from our situation, we may find our abuser stalking us or harassing us in other ways.

To help you take action on what is best for you, consider the following steps. Name one thing you think is necessary to do in order to take action. It could be to fortify a personality characteristic, such as courage or assertiveness, as well as a specific skill, such as learning how to look for a job or make a budget and stick to it. After you have identified a need, name an obstacle(s) keeping you from acquiring this need. For each obstacle, identify when it occurs, with whom, and in what situation(s). Then list three steps you can take to overcome each obstacle. Rank them in the order in which they need to be done or in order of importance. Do each step in the ranked order.

Another approach is to make a list of your problems. Sort out those that you can control and those you can't. Pick an easy thing to tackle first. Also talk to someone you know to get ideas about how to solve each problem you can't control.

THE EFFECTS OF ABUSE ON CHILDREN

Many women take action only when they realize how their children are being affected.

Because many women concentrate on keeping their families intact or worry that the hardships of leaving would be bad for their children, they do not realize at first that their own abuse may be damaging for their children. As long as a woman's partner has access to her, the children cannot be assured of stability and security in their lives. Without that, adequate mothering is necessarily more difficult.

The effects of living in a home where someone is being abused are not always readily apparent. Children from abusive households usually act similarly to children from nonabusive households. Just as other children do, they cry, feel anxious when separated from a parent, hit, shove, and take things someone else is using. Upon closer examination, however, some children from abusive households are more intense doing these things, or do them more frequently. Children who witness abuse or have been abused themselves may show the same symptoms as adults who are abused: excessive nervousness, tension, stomachaches, headaches, sleeplessness, depression, eating problems, drug abuse, and so on. Some may become troublesome at school or steal. In some studies, "routine" violence, rather than extreme violence, was the best predictor of whether a child would show delinquent behavior.[21] Many children blame themselves for the abuse that they see in their households.

Children in abusive households may have more trouble being angry or responding to anger if they have learned that anger means being hit. They may be violent with their toys or with other children who are safe targets. Teenagers may abuse their parents when they become big enough to stand up to them. Children imitate abusive behavior from an early age. They often overhear arguments and fights even when the parents think that they are asleep or occupied elsewhere. Children sometimes repeat comments that abusers make about their mothers. Often the abused woman is unaware that her child has overheard disparaging remarks directed at her until she hears her child repeat them.

Children whose mothers are abused, are often not safe. Between 53 and 70 percent of batterers also physically abuse their children.[22] Your children may be relieved to get out of the abusive situation.

However, be prepared for their resentment if you decide to file for divorce. Children often side with the abuser, who is the more powerful person in the relationship, and blame their mother for causing family disruption. Children also may be indoctrinated with the abuser's view of the situation, that you cause the abuse. Children may also try to manipulate you by threatening suicide or by other coercive behaviors.

When I had Donald, just a lot of things changed, for the better. I thought more into my past. I've talked with other women too and they realize it too. I think a lot of things are triggered when you've given birth to this little infant who's so vulnerable and so dependent on you and then you look and see how something could happen.

I took a mother and her 3-year-old twins over to the shelter. One of the boys wanted me to show him around outside. I explained to him that we would do that after I spoke to his mother. He then kicked me in the shins and screamed, "Fuck you, bitch!"

The night we got to the shelter was the first time in many months that my children and I really slept. We didn't have to worry about what my husband was going to do from moment to moment.

If your children are having problems because of the trauma that they have experienced, they usually can recover with good support. Some counselors advise talking to your children about the violence they have witnessed in terms of "danger" and "safety" rather than "good" and "bad."[23] Your local battered women's service may be able to help you find services to help your children.

LIFE AFTER ABUSE: WOMEN'S VOICES

In spite of tremendous obstacles and often after years of trying, many women do manage to extricate themselves from abusive relationships. In one study, for relationships in which the abuse was physical or sexual, two-thirds of the women were not coerced in those ways two and a half years later. Almost half had achieved this by leaving the relationship; the rest were able to insist on changes in their relationships. All were offered information about a variety of resources and many used these resources to help themselves.[24] Although the number of women studied was small, the researchers believe that this group was more representative of most abused women than those of many other studies. In general, the women had not needed to go to shelters and their partners had not been sent to counseling programs.[25]

If you are able to leave, you may find that you have learned survival skills you never thought possible. Before, you may have felt depressed and constantly on edge. Along the way, your feelings are likely to change tremendously. Eventually you may find that you have a lot of confidence in yourself. Not putting up with the abuse anymore, however, may result in more difficult relationships with those you routinely acquiesced to before. You may find a book such as *The Ones Who Got Away* by Ginny NiCarthy[26] an inspiration (see also "Resources"). Other women can be role models to help you change or simply help you to understand others in abusive relationships.

Women who have successfully coped with abusive situations find themselves fundamentally stronger:

I can only say that, because of the situation and because of going to [the battered women's group], I feel that I'll never take abuse again. And that, under no circumstances would I accept my previous lover.[27]

Toward the end of the relationship I did not understand how I could want to be lovingly touched by the hands that hurt me...To help change victim attitudes I am learning to set definite limits for myself as to what I want and don't want in a relationship.[28]

I thought I was only good enough to be a housewife and to be beaten and that's literally how I thought and I was surprised to find out that I could do anything ...what I feel like I did developmentally, is grow up, from coming to [the battered women's group]...a crash course in maturation...I had help doing that, people gave me things I needed that I missed out on and I feel like I responded beautifully to it.[29]

I was separated from my husband a year ago. He was an abusive alcoholic who attempted to kill me after I left him with our two young children. Since last year, I feel like I've accomplished a lot. I started college...It's been hard...but it's been well worth the effort. My self-esteem is so much higher now, and I feel like I am headed for something, and not aimlessly drifting about...my children are so much happier and more secure and so am I...I find myself looking forward to what each day brings.[30]

I was an A student. I graduated with high honors and then I got a job. What a difference it made...All those years, Victor had told me, "No one will like you. You're fat and ugly. You'll never have a job that'll pay you anything." By going to school and getting this job, I saw that he was lying. I think that was the first step of taking control of my life...Two years ago, I thought there never would be any happiness for me.[31]

I'm just starting to taste the freedom of life, feel freer, I feel like, it's strange, it feels like being like a bird, you know, when it just comes out of its mother's nest and just starts flying away and it feels so free, that's how I do at times.[32]

CHANGING OUR COMMUNITIES

We all have the power to help change our communities' attitudes. Our tasks range from helping our best friend to advocating social policy reform.

Helping a Friend or Relative

You may notice that a friend or relative has become more fearful, depressed over time, or talks of suicide. She may stop talking to you on the telephone or stop spending time with you. You may notice that she has injuries, such as bruises or limping. If she gives you unlikely excuses for her injuries, especially more than once, be suspicious of abuse.

If you suspect an abusive situation, try to find ways to reach out to the woman who is being abused. Give her the number of the closest battered women's group. Remind her that she doesn't deserve the abuse, no matter what, and that the perpetrator is responsible for the abuse. Ask her what you could do that would be helpful to her. Be patient and show her that you believe her. Avoid analyzing her weaknesses or you may make her feel that you are judging and blaming her. In addition, beware of taking over and telling her what to do. She needs to have more control over

her life, not one authority substituting for another.

You also should try to find at least one other person you can talk to while helping someone who is abused. If confidentiality is an issue, try calling a hotline (see "Resources") to discuss your feelings; otherwise, you may find yourself overwhelmed and unable to be truly supportive. Taking care of yourself enables you to avoid abandoning the abused woman, who may be especially sensitive to abandonment because of her experience.

But without changing laws and attitudes on a wider scale, each of us will be struggling to find an individual solution to a global problem. Actually, women all over the world have been organizing and fighting back, getting their communities to pay attention.

Improving Services

We can put pressure on institutions and people who are in positions to help battered women to learn more about abusive relationships and to set up appropriate programs. We need more services like the AWAKE (Advocacy for Women and Kids in Emergencies) program at Children's Hospital in Boston. When a child who shows signs of abuse comes to that hospital, the staff knows that the mother is probably also being abused. To protect the child, the staff must get help for the mother, rather than blame the mother for not protecting the child. Their support may include telephone and in-person counseling, help in finding an emergency shelter, housing, and court advocacy; escorting women and children to hearings; referrals for legal counseling and medical care; and support groups for battered women and for children who have witnessed or experienced domestic violence.[33]

We can pressure agencies to include services for lesbians and to provide access and accommodation for handicapped women, interpreters for non-English speakers, advocates for immigrants, and cultur-

I got tired of pretending that my friend's excuses were real. Finally I said to her, "I don't believe you fell off your bicycle. I think your boyfriend gave you that black eye. You know, I'm afraid for you. I value you in my life and I want you to stay alive."

I remember that I had a friend at work who was studying to be a lawyer. She was incredible. She loved me and she began to take an interest in me. She said things like, "You don't have to take that." And I thought, "I don't have to? I don't have to take that?" It was maybe something my mother should have said when she saw me come home after that first beating.

Police officers have family problems like anyone else. Do you single police officers out and take their job away because of [a court order to stay away from someone they were battering]? Do you lose your job because of a speeding ticket?

—Comment from a deputy chief of police[34]

ally appropriate services for different ethnic, racial, and religious groups.

We can reinforce the work of battered women's shelter workers who continue to educate police, judges, and legislators. Ask if your town or city has a domestic violence unit as part of the police force and what its policies are. You can show your police force that you consider domestic violence an important issue by inquiring about its policies. Call your police chief and ask about the police policy on domestic violence and the training police officers receive. Does written policy require mandatory arrests when police see evidence of domestic violence? Can police make arrests based on probable cause even when they have not witnessed the violent action? Ask for statistics to verify how well the policies are being carried out. Ask how the police document a situation that involves domestic violence. Do they write up a detailed description or take instant pictures? What is the department's response when someone violates a restraining order?

How officers treat each other is a paradigm of how they treat others around them. Find out what the department does to reduce abusive behavior such as put-downs and harassment among officers. All too often domestic violence perpetrated by one police officer is not taken seriously by others on the police force.

Investigate how your local courts handle requests for restraining orders. Some courts have advocate programs to help targets of abuse file restraining orders, go through with criminal prosecution, and also find services for the women so that they don't have to return to their abusive situations. Programs that work in conjunction with the police department have made it possible to increase the number of criminal prosecutions, even if a woman decides not to press charges herself. Conviction rates have increased.

Ask battered women's shelter workers how the judges in your district treat battered women. If one or more of the

judges are contemptuous of abused women, you can organize women's testimony and news coverage to pressure the courts to prevent those judges from hearing cases of domestic violence.

Find out if local high schools and colleges have policies to cover battering, sexual harassment, and confidence rape. Ask if they call in the police—that is, treat the action as the crime it is. Find out if schools perform speedy investigations or if they drag out the process over months. Do they make disciplinary actions public or do they protect perpetrators by insisting on secrecy? What steps do they take to protect women from retaliation by their abusers? Tell the schools what you think would improve their policies. Ask your local newspaper or TV station to do its own investigation and publicize it. Schools do not like bad publicity, so public scrutiny can be a powerful force for change.

Changing Procedures and Laws

Services for battered women need to be coordinated instead of separated. Without coordination, both batterers and abused women fall through the cracks. And a fragmented system is potentially dangerous for an abused woman. For instance, if a woman is being encouraged to stand up for herself by taking out a restraining order, yet the police are not prepared to respond quickly when she calls to say that her abuser has violated the restraining order, she may be in greater danger of increased violence or of being killed than if she had done nothing. Also, if a woman requests a restraining order, the judge needs to know if the batterer has weapons that need to be confiscated. Police need to know what restraining orders have been issued so they can help the courts tightly supervise batterers. If a batterer is required to go to counseling and stops, the court needs to be told so that a different sentence can be instituted. Police and medical practitioners need to know about shelter and counseling services for battered women. Divorce court judges need information about abuse to issue safe and sensible child custody and visitation rights. Women need police escorts to shelters and to their homes to retrieve their belongings if they must leave. They need advocates to help them through the legal and social service bureaucracies.

In response to political pressure, more states have enacted laws requiring stronger penalties for violation of restraining orders. Bail laws should require consideration of whether the accused is likely to harm others. Better ways to coordinate court records are needed so that judges can consider previous records relating to domestic violence and gun restrictions. Serious, enforceable laws against stalking must become more widespread.

The easy availability of guns has made it simpler for abusers to kill targeted women. Severely restricting access to guns would mitigate this, though restrictions obviously cannot reduce deaths from other means, such as stabbing, beating, strangulation, or suffocation. These methods, however, require more effort than pulling a trigger.

We can pressure our congresspeople to enact state and national legislation to help women become less vulnerable to being trapped in abusive relationships. We need more economic opportunities, an end to workplace harassment and discrimination, nationwide medical insurance so a woman does not need to go on welfare to get Medicaid, an end to discrimination when applying for other kinds of insurance, quality day care, and more affordable housing. We need specific legislation to make it easier to prosecute abuse; uniform antistalking laws in all states; a repeal of laws that make certain consensual sexual acts such as sodomy or cohabitation without marriage criminal (so that abused women can report abuse without fear of being charged with these crimes); consideration of abuse in setting bail, custody, and child visitation rights; and funding for a permanent national toll-free hotline, for shelters, and for more early intervention education

against abuse and violence. For information about current legislation, call your nearest battered woman's shelter, women's center, or your legislator.

Prevention and Reformation Programs

While programs attempting to change abusive men are increasing in this country, they cannot be the sole answer. The few programs that have been in existence a relatively long time have found that the number of men who change their behavior over the long run is very small. More research on how to increase the effectiveness of the programs may improve them, but so far most women are not safer because of them.

Changing attitudes about relationships may be the most important early intervention to prevent abuse because no program that helps women after abuse has occurred can keep them completely safe. However, no program to prevent abuse can work in a vacuum. As individuals, we must stop overlooking abuse in our daily lives. Speak up when you see a situation that looks like abuse (if you think you can do so safely). Tell the abuser that certain actions are not acceptable and tell the woman being abused that she deserves better.

In Cambridge, Massachusetts, Transition House, a women's shelter and counseling center, and Emerge (a program for abusive men) have combined forces to establish the Dating Violence Intervention Project. This project has created a three-part curriculum, taught by volunteers in high school classes in the greater Boston area. The curriculum encourages the students to define abusive behavior on the basis of their own experiences. (Students never seem to lack abusive experiences on which to draw.) They study how gender stereotyping encourages disrespectful and violent behavior and develop ways to counteract the pressures to accept abusive behavior. This project organizes support groups for teenage targets of abuse and consciousness-raising groups for young

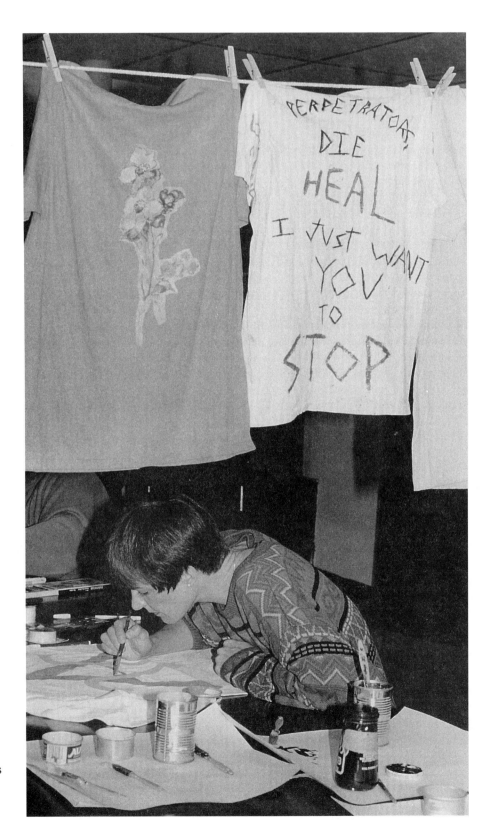

The Clothesline Project has inspired efforts nationwide to memorialize victims of domestic violence.

men. The project also founded and facilitates the "Can't Be Beat" high school theater troupe, in which teens develop educational improvisations to be performed at high school assemblies. Some of the participants go on to become peer educators on teen dating violence.

Reducing the general level of violence in our society is necessary as a first step to decrease violence against women. Curricula to teach children about abusive relationships should start well before adolescence. Some schools already have programs that concentrate on inappropriate sexual touching, but the focus needs to be broadened to include a more general understanding of how to recognize coercive control and, when possible, how to change it. Some communities mandate a violence intervention or abuse prevention curriculum as part of all levels of public school education. Already, teachers report less violence in some of these schools.[35] Duluth has developed the only curriculum covering kindergarten through high school specifically to promote awareness and prevention of abuse in relationships.

Early intervention can also come in other forms. For example, in Brooklyn, New York, the Center for Anti-Violence Education runs self-defense classes with an emphasis on self-esteem for children, women, and gay men. The program for children includes learning to recognize sexual abuse.

The news and entertainment media need to be held accountable and pressured to become advocates for preventing abuse. Write or call newspapers and TV or radio shows to compliment them if they portray individuals in ways that help people understand the actual dynamics of abusive relationships and the effects of abuse. Complain if the men and women are drawn in stereotypical ways that do not address subtle and overt methods of coercive control. Violence portrayed in TV dramas usually gives viewers no hint of the trauma that violence brings to the target's life, or to the family of the targeted person. By denying the damaging effects, the media is broadcasting the message that violence has no long-lasting consequences. No wonder some people ignore the pain they cause to someone they hit.

Movies are just as bad as TV because the official rating system puts far fewer restrictions on violence than on sex. PG-13 movies are full of violence and frequently portray women as bimbos in need of male protection.

A few years ago, the movie *Thelma and Louise* included a scene portraying a woman shooting a man who had raped her friend. There was intense furor over the violence in this film, although the total body count in the movie was three: the rapist and, at the very end, Thelma and Louise. MTV refused to air a Garth Brooks video showing a woman taking revenge on a lying, philandering husband. This passionate reaction against showing abused women responding with violence occurred while men in the movies shot and killed thousands of people and MTV regularly displayed sexual violence against women and used women as background sex objects. Clearly, violence itself was not what was objectionable. The real problem seems to have been twofold— portraying women as disturbed by the abuse rather than enjoying it and showing women taking decisive action against their abusers, removing control from the men.

Marches, fund-raising walks, billboard and transit advertising, feature dramas on TV, and more prominent news stories are becoming more common ways to raise awareness of how widespread the problem of abuse is. The Cape Cod Women's Agenda has started the Clothesline Project, inspired by the Names Project (also known as the AIDS quilt). People decorate shirts, blouses, or tee shirts memorializing a woman who has suffered physical or sexual violence. The shirts are displayed in exhibits on clotheslines. Women across the country are now mak-

One time last year when my family went to the movies together, I had an eye-opening experience. My husband and I went to an R-rated movie that portrayed a man's fight against prejudice. Our two boys went to a PG-13 adventure flick. I was confused about the rating of my film until I remembered that in two scenes "dirty words" were used. When I listened to my kids' description of their movie I was appalled at all the killing and the way that the women were clearly peripheral sex objects put into the movie for the pleasure of the men even if the women didn't actually take off their clothes.

ing their own clothesline displays. These activities proclaim that not everybody accepts abusive behavior.

As women, we have a lot of work ahead of us to root out abusive behavior and replace it with respectful behavior. Our culture, which stresses competition, individualism, and individual solutions to problems, frequently works against conflict resolution in which all parties benefit. Unless we continue to change our social attitudes about the acceptability of coercive relationships, we and our children will continue to be trapped, raped, beaten, and killed at an alarming rate in the name of affection and love.

Part III

Dying for Love

10

The Costs of Physical Love

EVERY DAY, women put themselves at risk of infertility, illness, and death by having sex without protection against disease. There are more than twenty-three sexually transmissible diseases, with effects ranging from abdominal pain to death. This chapter examines three diseases that can be fatal: cervical cancer, which is primarily caused by human papillomavirus (HPV); pelvic inflammatory disease (PID), mainly caused by gonorrhea or chlamydia; and acquired immune deficiency syndrome (AIDS), which is caused by human immunodeficiency virus (HIV). The chapter also examines the difficulties we have in approaching the subject of safer sex; the government's inadequate approach to prevention; and some of the larger social forces that have slowed efforts to halt the spread of these diseases.

The next chapter suggests how we can bring up the subject of safe sex with our partners, discusses how to practice safer sex, and explains how the diseases discussed here can be detected and treated.

SUBSERVIENCE IN THE BEDROOM

One of the most powerful ways of feeling needed and wanted is to know that someone desires to touch and kiss us and to have sex with us. Such physical affection is an affirmation that we are accepted and loved. For many of us, when a love relationship ends, the loss of physical intimacy is hard to bear. It is not surprising that we often find ourselves unwilling to jeopardize, alter, or delay an opportunity to feel loved through physical intimacy, even at the risk of our health: "[Our] sense of self becomes very much organized around being able to make and then to maintain affiliations and relationships. Eventually, for many women the threat of disruption of a relationship is perceived not as just a loss of a relationship but as something closer to a total loss of self."[1]

However, we are at a disadvantage in heterosexual love relationships because of the long tradition of male dominance. The right to dominate women is considered the essence of maleness in some societies. Also,

I can almost physically feel my identity going. I slip back into an old passive mold. I don't have anything to say about what's happening. It's just happening to me.[2]

Love is the most beautiful acknowledgement and fulfillment of who I am as a woman, and passionate lovemaking is a deep expression of love. I know that someone who truly loves me would never do anything to hurt me.

some religious traditions, laws, and social mores still support the idea that our marital duty is to be sexually available to our husbands.

Being assertive, a traditionally "male" attribute, may seem most difficult or out of place in the bedroom, one of the last places where we still adhere to the traditional female ideal. Even when we habitually stand up for ourselves and deal honestly and directly with friends, as soon as we become sexually involved, our assertiveness often weakens. We lose our sense of who we are and what we want.

For example, one woman physician informally asked about a hundred of her female colleagues whether they had equal decision-making power in the bedroom. Ninety percent said no.[3] Women physicians are among the most highly educated and well-paid women in the United States. They are accustomed to being assertive and to making crucial decisions. Their sexual subservience highlights women's deeply rooted habits and fears.

Part of this subservience in the bedroom involves our wish to please—"Giving you pleasure is my pleasure." Giving pleasure is unquestionably part of the joy of lovemaking. As women, we often ask ourselves if we are giving enough and are upset if we feel we are not. Thus, giving pleasure can be a joy that seems worth the sacrifice of our own needs and preferences. But such giving also puts us at risk of becoming servants to another person's desires, no longer recognizing and acknowledging our own needs or concerns for our health.

When we lose our sense of self, we tend to stop thinking for ourselves and leave actions and decisions to our partners. Our preferences, objections, reservations, or fears may remain unspoken, with consequences for our self-respect, sexual pleasure, and health. We may fail to protect ourselves against sexually transmissible diseases because we want to please or because we feel disempowered.

Speaking up about safe sex can also be hard because of the stigma attached to sexually transmissible diseases. Many of us distance ourselves from diseases by trying to believe that they happen only to other people, especially people different in some way: sexually, culturally, racially, or behaviorally. And sexually transmissible diseases raise questions about our most intimate behaviors: whether we have sex, how often, with whom and how, and what kind of protection we might use. For example, cervical cancer and PID have long been associated with behavior judged immoral for a woman, though this stigma has faded somewhat. The social ostracism that results from testing positive for HIV, however, is pronounced.

Because we do not want to identify with a stigmatized group, some of us refuse to realize that we may be at risk of contracting a sexually transmitted infection. Or we may understand the risk but be reluctant to bring up the subject of safe sex—it may seem to us that we are accusing our lovers of a social sin.

Protection against disease usually involves a physical barrier. For many women, this barrier symbolizes an emotional barrier or a lack of trust and makes protection with our partners difficult. However, love and trust are no protection against bacteria, viruses, and other infectious microorganisms. What happens at the microscopic level has nothing to do with trust or intentions.

Most of the microorganisms that cause sexually transmissible diseases, including gonorrhea, chlamydia, and AIDS, are fragile outside the body. If the fluid they are in dries, these organisms die; they need the warmth, moisture, and nourishment of the human body to survive. The human papillomavirus (HPV) is an exception since it appears to be able to survive in the skin around and on the genitals. Most sexually transmissible diseases spread from one person to another only if the bacteria or viruses can move directly from one body into another, or if direct skin contact is made

Could I Have a Sexually Transmissible Infection?

Nearly every woman who has ever been sexually active with a partner could have a sexually transmissible infection. Even if you have had unprotected sex only once, your partner's prior experiences may put you at risk. To demonstrate how vulnerable all women are, ask yourself the following questions.[4] (For AIDS only, the time period to consider begins with 1977.)

Have I had vaginal, anal, or oral sex with a man without a condom? This could have been by consent or by force, or to conceive. Have I received an untested semen donation in order to conceive?

Could I have had unprotected sex with a partner who has had unprotected sex with someone else (male or female)?

Have I ever used drugs or alcohol to the point of impaired judgment and memory loss, so that I cannot remember whether I had unprotected sex?

Have I had sex involving oral contact with my partner's semen or vaginal mucus or blood, including menstrual blood?

Could I have had sex in which there was any bleeding, even small amounts?

Could I have had oral contact with semen or vaginal mucus when I or my partner had a reproductive tract infection? (Many reproductive tract infections are signs of sexually transmissible diseases and may have no symptoms in the early stages, or ever. Even an infection that is not contagious can make you more susceptible to one that is.)

Have I shared unsterilized hypodermic needles or other drug works, or shared unsterilized needles for tattooing or piercing the skin?

Could I have had sex involving oral or manual contact with blood, vaginal fluids, or semen of a partner who has shared unsterilized needles with someone else?

Have I had a needlestick injury involving an HIV-positive blood sample or one that was unknown?

Did I receive a blood transfusion or blood products, such as immunoglobulin, before March 1985?

Any yes answer means that you are at risk for having a sexually transmissible infection. (Few can answer no to all these questions.) If you have answered yes to any question, please read "Detection and Treatment" in Chapter 11.

After all of the hoopla I went through with cervical problems, you would think I would know more than most people. In fact, I'm surprised to hear that cervical cancer is related to a sexually transmitted virus. The medical community that I dealt with didn't explain it that way. My doctor specifically said: "We don't know what causes this."

between vulnerable parts of the body. We can become infected through intimate physical contact, such as unprotected vaginal or anal intercourse with an infected man or unprotected oral sex with an infected woman. (For information on reducing the risk of infection, see Chapter 11.)

In unprotected heterosexual sex, women are generally at greater risk for contracting sexually transmissible diseases from men than the other way around. A woman usually retains the ejaculate from an infected man in her vagina or rectum for a number of hours, while a man is in contact with a woman's fluids only until his penis dries off, and the quantity of infected fluid that a man might get inside his urethra is much smaller. Perhaps for that reason the infection is easier for his immune system to destroy. In a single act of unprotected sex with an infected partner, a woman's risk of contracting chlamydia is 40 percent, while a man's risk is 20 percent.[5] Women are as much as 17.5 times more likely to contract HIV from a man than vice versa.[6] Gonorrhea, chlamydia, HPV, and HIV all can be transmitted at certain times to a woman's fetus either during pregnancy or birth, and in some cases, both. In addition, HIV can infect a nursing baby through breast milk from an infected mother.

CERVICAL CANCER

The spread of cervical cancer, a potentially fatal disease, was not clearly linked to heterosexually transmissible viruses until recently. Yet, since the nineteenth century, some researchers suspected that cervical cancer was related to intercourse in some way. They noticed that commercial sex workers frequently suffered from this type of cancer, but that among celibate Catholic nuns and other women believed to be virgins, the disease was almost nonexistent. The causes of cervical cancer are still subjects of controversy and continuing research, but approximately 84 percent of cervical cancers appear to be primarily caused by the human papillomavirus (HPV)

passed from an infected man to a woman during intercourse.[7] The causes of the remaining 16 percent are not known.

The Human Papillomavirus

Cervical cancer is the last stage of abnormal cervical cell changes set in motion by an infection with a few types of the large family of HPV viruses. There are more than sixty-five HPVs that cause visible warts or microscopic lesions on different parts of the body. About twenty are associated with sexual activities,[8] and only a few are linked to genital- and anal-tract infections. (Microscopic lesions are also sometimes called flat warts, microscopic warts, or simply warts.)

Many of the sexually transmitted HPV infections can cause abnormal cell changes, but few cause the changes that lead to cervical cancer. Types 6, 11, 16, 18, 31, 33, and 35 are most commonly found in abnormal cervical cells. Types 6 and 11 are usually associated with warts that never develop into cancer, while types 31, 33, 16, and 18 are associated with cancer, with the latter two implicated in approximately 70 percent of cervical cancers.[9]

The virus can infect the outer genital area, anus, vagina, cervix, or inside the cervical canal that leads to the uterus. Genital warts that are visible to the naked eye are called condyloma acuminata and occur more often on the outer genitals than inside the vagina or on the cervix. These are not likely to progress into cancer. The more dangerous types of virus do not produce changes visible to the naked eye.

Human papillomavirus is present in 85 to 95 percent of women with squamous cell cancer of the cervix.[10] In the laboratory, high-risk human papillomaviruses can transform cervical cells from a normal to a premalignant state. Certain abnormal cells can further progress to become cancer cells. Although HPV seems to be necessary for the development of abnormal cervical cells, it is not sufficient by itself. Other factors, such as smoking and having a weakened immune system, also play a role. Only a small percentage of women who are infected with a high-risk HPV ever develop cervical cancer.[11]

Data suggest that among Americans who have vaginal intercourse, a minimum of 10 percent have been infected by the virus,[12] with about half carrying the high-risk type of virus. The incidence of HPV has increased an estimated 500 percent since 1975,[13] but this figure may partly reflect the increased detection of HPV through Pap tests or through visual detection of warts, rather than an actual increase in infected people. As the reported incidence of HPV infections has increased, so have the numbers of women with seriously abnormal Pap smears.[14]

Another sexually transmitted virus, herpes simplex virus, may play a role along with HPV in the development of cervical cancer. In the late 1960s and early 1970s, the herpes virus was suspected of being the main cause of cervical cancer. Some researchers now think that the herpes simplex virus may be a cofactor in cervical cancer, acting with HPV to harm cells.[15]

Even among women infected with a high-risk HPV, more than 97 percent will never develop cervical cancer.[16] Nonetheless, infection by a high-risk HPV is now considered the first step in a progression of cell changes that can eventually lead to cervical cancer. Infected cells can develop abnormalities that result in lesions called cervical dysplasia or cervical intraepithelial neoplasia (CIN). A cell that enters this abnormal state can do one of four things: it can return to normal; it can remain abnormal for a period of time without causing any further problems; it can become more abnormal but never threaten your health; or it can become malignant (cancerous). Cervical cancer is the last stage of a gradually developing abnormality in cervical cells that begins with an HPV infection. It can take approximately 20 to 25 years to progress into cancer, or it may develop more rapidly, especially if a woman contracts HPV during adolescence.

How HPV Is Transmitted

How someone becomes infected with HPV is not entirely certain, but most likely the virus is passed through contact between the skin of our genitals and our partners' genitals. Some kind of abrasion is probably necessary for transfer of the virus; unfortunately, the rubbing involved in most kinds of sex is probably sufficient even if no irritation is obvious. Physicians have found HPV lesions in women on the outer genital area, vagina, anus, cervix, and cervical canal; and in men on the penis and the skin that immediately surrounds the penis; and in both women and men, in the urethra, anus, and mouth. However, only through vaginal penetration can your partner's virus spread to your cervix, so that unprotected heterosexual vaginal intercourse carries the greatest risk of harm. (Unprotected anal intercourse with an infected partner can lead to cancer of the anus and rectum.) A woman with microscopic lesions or visible warts in her vagina may possibly also spread HPV onto her cervix by using tampons.

Little research has been done on the possibility of spreading the virus by acts other than intercourse: for example, by the lovemaking of two women, or by a man and woman who do not have intercourse. Theoretically, if a woman rubs her genitals against the genitals of a woman who has HPV on her vulva or a man who has HPV on his penis, she could catch the virus. And a significant number of lesbians do have HPV, according to one clinic that treats many lesbians.[17] Anecdotal evidence suggests that some lesbians become infected from other women rather than from previous relationships with men.[18]

PELVIC INFLAMMATORY DISEASE

Pelvic inflammatory disease (PID) has long been linked to sexual transmission: two of the main organisms responsible are *Neisseria gonorrhea*, or simply gonorrhea, and *Chlamydia trachomatis*, also known

Around 1980 when I started working in the STD clinic, warts were a novelty. Sometime around 1984 or 1985, the numbers just skyrocketed. By the late '80s, one-third of our caseload was warts. We didn't have enough time to take care of all of the people with warts.

I started having pain with intercourse, and my husband carried me into the emergency room a couple of times, I had such severe pelvic pain. They were saying: "You don't have gonorrhea. You're fine." And I was saying: "You know, I have the feeling that something is wrong with my reproductive system and that I'm getting sterile!" I kept thinking that it was something terrible about me, that I had some kind of terrible disease that they weren't catching. It was true.

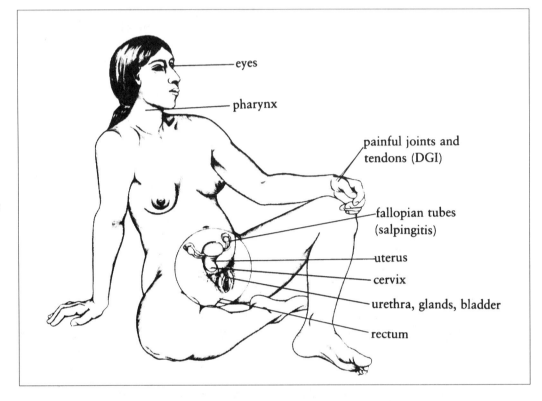

eyes

pharynx

painful joints and tendons (DGI)

fallopian tubes (salpingitis)

uterus

cervix

urethra, glands, bladder

rectum

simply as chlamydia. While PID can also be caused by many other organisms, this chapter discusses only gonorrhea and chlamydia because they are responsible for most PID in the United States. Gonorrhea is the more contagious disease, but chlamydia is the most widespread sexually transmitted bacterial infection in the United States, infecting about 4 million people each year.[19] Almost a fifth of all adolescents have chlamydia.[20] And gonorrhea infects approximately 1,100,000 people annually.[21] Some people become infected by chlamydia and gonorrhea simultaneously, and an estimated 30 to 40 percent of women who have gonorrhea also have chlamydia.[22] If a woman has intercourse even only once with a man infected with both gonorrhea and chlamydia, she is more likely to contract gonorrhea, but could contract chlamydia, or both. Data suggest that we contract chlamydia infection from our infected male partners an average of 40 percent of the time and gonorrhea 80 percent of the time.[23]

Pelvic inflammatory disease refers to the inflammation of pelvic organs caused primarily by bacteria that enter the body during vaginal intercourse. Many of us spend years of our lives with chronic pelvic pain or experience the sadness and distress of infertility because of PID. Actually, PID is a catchall term for the results of specific sexually transmitted diseases, or of a combination of such diseases, which can cause inflammations of the cervix, uterus, fallopian tubes, and perhaps the ovaries and the lining of the pelvis. The medical terms for inflammations of these organs are: cervicitis, endometritis, salpingitis, oophoritis, and peritonitis. Some researchers think that the term pelvic inflammatory disease should be replaced by these more specific terms.

Because many of us who experience pain as part of PID feel it only when the disease has spread to our fallopian tubes, many medical practitioners equate acute salpingitis with PID. Yet, some statistics suggest that the PID that causes symptoms and produces detectable salpingitis probably accounts for less than half of all women actually infected with PID.[24] The disease often spreads quietly, not revealing itself through symptoms until it has already caused considerable, sometimes irreversible, damage.

Estimates show that in industrialized countries, about 10 to 14 percent of premenopausal women suffer from acute PID at some time.[25] Each year more than 1 million women in the U.S. experience an episode of PID, with at least a quarter of those afflicted suffering a minimum of one long-term, serious health problem as a result.[26] And because large numbers of women are now believed to have PID with no symptoms, the number of women with this disease may be much higher.

What Gonorrhea and Chlamydia Do in the Body

When gonorrhea or chlamydia bacteria enter the vagina, the bacteria must reach the cervix or else they die. The cervix and the cervical canal, with their mucus secretions and tiny hairs (cilia), act as natural barriers to keep harmful organisms out of the uterus. This protective system may become less effective when the mucus is expelled during menstruation by the flow of blood, or during ovulation, when the mucus is thinner.

However, the cervix itself is relatively exposed to invasion by foreign organisms even when the organisms are prevented from traveling further upward. Both gonorrhea and chlamydia are parasites, entering normal cells on which they depend for nutrients, releasing harmful substances, and ultimately destroying those cells. If the bacteria remain in the cervix, they can cause cervical cells to become inflamed, a condition called cervicitis.

Researchers suspect that cervicitis damages the cervical canal, breaking down the cervical barrier and permitting the infection to ascend. This is perhaps the most frequent way in which a cervical infection spreads to other parts of our reproductive organs. When chlamydia or gonococci travel up through the reproductive organs, they may also encourage other bacteria in the vagina and cervix to travel upward, increasing the damage. Researchers are still debating whether these other bacteria are normally present in our bodies, or whether some of them are sexually transmitted but harmless until roused to action. All bacteria can spread more easily if the body's natural protections are disrupted.

If the bacteria spread upward, their next destination is the main body of the uterus, where they inflame the uterine lining, a condition called endometritis. The inflammation may cause abnormal menstrual bleeding. However, a woman can have endometritis and experience neither pain nor any other symptom that would lead her to seek the help of a medical care provider.

The infection, if unchecked by proper treatment or the immune system, may proceed upward through the uterus into the fallopian tubes, which open like delicate, horn-shaped canals from both sides of the uterus. Normal periodic contractions of the uterus, so subtle we do not feel them, can spread harmful bacteria. If a woman has recently had an IUD inserted, the uterus may also increase its normal contractions, presumably as a reaction against the foreign body. In addition, the uterus may contract as part of sexual orgasm. All such contractions can push harmful bacteria further up the uterus and into the fallopian tubes. In addition, in most premenopausal women, some menstrual blood evidently enters the fallopian tubes during each menstrual period. Harmful organisms might spread with this blood. This is probably why we so often experience the first pain of PID during or immediately after menstruation. The fallopian tubes and the uterus both contain cells that grow tiny cilia, partly for the purpose of entrapping and sweeping out harmful organisms. However, the

The first time I knew that something was wrong was when I was in my doctor's office and she was giving me a Pap smear. She touched my cervix with a swab—and I nearly went off the table, it hurt so much. It wasn't until she started explaining things to me and I did research myself that I realized that I had had signs for a number of years. For example, intercourse had hurt a lot. And every time I asked a doctor about it they said: "Oh, it's because you have a tipped uterus, and he's penetrating too deeply and pushing on the ligaments." That's the only explanation I ever got. And I kept getting urinary tract infections. Eight years went by from the time I first started having pain during intercourse to the actual diagnosis of PID.

What they finally found was that because of all the infections, my whole reproductive tract was basically knitted together with scar tissue. There was no free movement of any of the organs. My left ovary was plastered to my backside. My right ovary and uterus were pulled to the right side of my abdominal wall, and the adhesions extended up into part of the lower bowel and my appendix.

inflammation caused by gonorrhea or chlamydia may weaken these cells before they can carry out this function.

During the process of infection, the fallopian tubes become inflamed, swell, and may become rigid. The fringelike extensions of the tubes at the end near the ovaries, called fimbriae, may be drawn together and may finally seal off the tubes, preventing further release of bacteria into the pelvic cavity, but also causing infertility.

If the fallopian tubes do not close completely, bacteria may escape from the tubes and infect the ovaries (a condition called oophoritis) and the entire lining of the abdomen (peritonitis). Unfortunately, abdominal pain, the symptom that most frequently brings women who have PID to seek medical help, may not begin until the infection has reached the abdominal lining. Scar tissue from the inflamed cells tend to "glue" adjacent organs to one another, so that our normally mobile reproductive organs become stiff. In severe cases, abscesses develop on the fallopian tubes or ovaries, destroying some tissue. Severe, unchecked infection can also spread to a woman's blood, appendix, liver, and spleen.

This step-by-step spread of bacteria within the reproductive organs is probably the most common form of spread. However, in some women, the bacteria may spread directly from the cervix to the pelvic cavity by traveling through the lymphatic system, which carries a fluid called lymph through the body.

Whether we have PID with or without symptoms, the harm done to our bodies can be mild or severe, depending on the aggressiveness of the bacteria involved and on the stage at which the disease is detected and treated. The pain of PID can be so acute and the fever so high that we may need to go to the emergency room or even be admitted to a hospital. Yet, our bodies are constantly repairing the damage, even while the disease is in progress. When we overcome the infection, the inflammation gradually subsides as repair continues, ei-

ther restoring our health and functioning, or leaving us with chronic pain, recurring low-grade fevers, weakness, and fatigue for months or even years, interfering with daily activities.

Permanent damage to the reproductive organs leaves some of us with varying degrees of scarring or other impairments of our ability to conceive and bear children. In most women, the lining of the uterus heals without scarring. However, sometimes our fallopian tubes are left with the normally open, fringed ends sealed; with the tubes stiff from adhesions to adjacent organs; or with inner scars caused by the process of repair or the disease. When the fallopian tubes are blocked or closed by scar tissue, an egg released by the ovary cannot pass through and reach the uterus. A fertilized egg traveling through a scarred fallopian tube can become lodged in the tube. The result is a tubal or ectopic pregnancy, a painful and potentially life-threatening condition requiring emergency surgery to prevent the tube from bursting. Women who have had PID are seven to ten times more likely to experience an ectopic pregnancy than women who have never had the disease.[27] An estimated 50 percent or more of ectopic pregnancies are caused by PID.[28]

Even if a tube is not blocked or closed, its stiffness may impair its ability to guide an egg into the tube's fringed opening. In addition, an ovary that has become covered with scar tissue may be unable to successfully release its eggs. For any of these reasons, we may become infertile as a result of PID.

Many women do not choose to have children until years after an episode of PID and therefore do not discover their infertility until long after its original cause. Some women who have "silent" PID are not aware of it until they try to conceive, only to discover that their fallopian tubes are blocked or closed. Because so many cases of PID are never detected, the numbers of women who are infertile as a result of it may be higher than any estimate. Investigators have found that more than half of women whose tubes are obstructed say that they have never had PID even though tests reveal evidence of past infection by chlamydia.[29] Investigations from fourteen countries have found a significant association between tubal infertility and previous chlamydia infection, or, in some cases, chlamydia infection combined with gonococcal infection.[30] Chlamydia is apparently more likely to cause silent tubal damage than is gonorrhea or other infections, perhaps because a tubal infection with chlamydia is more likely to be chronic, causing repeated, undetected inflammations.

How Gonorrhea and Chlamydia Are Transmitted

Because the bacteria that cause PID can only reach our reproductive organs through the vagina, they can cause the disease only if spread through vaginal intercourse, though both bacteria can infect areas other than the reproductive tract, such as the anus. In industrialized countries such as the United States, around 80 percent of women afflicted with PID have contracted it as a result of unprotected intercourse with an infected male partner.[31] For women, the areas vulnerable to gonorrhea and chlamydia infections are the cervix (not the vaginal wall), anus, and the throat. The gonococci and chlamydiae are in an infected man's semen and, during vaginal intercourse, travel from his penis through the vagina to the cervix, the first step for the possible development of PID. Even if your partner withdraws his penis before ejaculation, semen or preejaculatory secretions can leak out of his penis during intercourse and reach your cervix.

Because infected secretions must enter the vagina and reach the cervix for PID to develop, other forms of sex are less likely to lead to PID. Inserting fingers, fists, or sex toys into the vagina, even if they have infected fluids on them, usually conveys fewer bacteria and thus has less of the infectious agent to spread than does semen. However, anal intercourse is not risk-free because gonococci can migrate from the anus to the vagina and up to the cervix, or can enter the blood to cause infection in distant parts of the body, such as the joints. Gonorrhea or chlamydia can also develop in the throat through mouth-to-penis lovemaking. Both gonorrhea and chlamydia can live in the throat, but neither can live in the mouth. Therefore, mouth-to-vagina lovemaking is unlikely to transmit the bacteria.

A man can become infected with gonorrhea and chlamydia when his genitals come in contact with an infected partner's vaginal or anal secretions. When a man's urethra (the opening of his penis) becomes infected with gonococci, the disease is called gonorrhea or gonococcal urethritis. When infected by chlamydia, the symptoms are usually called nonspecific urethritis, or nongonococcal urethritis. Although some men may have no symptoms of gonorrhea, most develop symptoms within two to five days of infection, though it sometimes takes longer. Your partner may first suspect that something is wrong if urinating becomes painful, or if he experiences a discharge from his urethra. The discharge may be mild at first, but in most men becomes more profuse and filled with pus within twenty-four hours after the discharge begins. The lymph nodes in his groin may also become slightly swollen and tender. Many men who have a chlamydia infection have no symptoms. When a man does have symptoms, they generally are identical to those of gonococcal urethritis, but are usually milder.

HIV AND AIDS

Many of us still perceive AIDS (Acquired Immune Deficiency Syndrome) as a disease that affects someone else, as "that gay men's disease," or as the "drug addicts' disease." Indeed, in the early 1980s most of the diseases recognized as AIDS in the United States were found among gay men.

Even then, however, some U.S. women were dying of the disease, as were many more women in other countries. By 1992, worldwide, more than 90 percent of new infections were transmitted heterosexually.[32] Internationally, since the epidemic began, more women have been infected than have gay men or men with hemophilia, even though men have been the focus of most news stories in the United States.[33]

The human immunodeficiency virus (HIV) attacks the immune system, which protects us from infection and from the development of malignancies. When a person has the virus, she or he is "HIV positive" or "HIV+." Several distinct kinds of the virus have been identified and perhaps more will be found, but so far most cases in this country have been caused by just one type. Several subtypes, however, seem to have developed, and the virus seems able to mutate easily. The virus's changeability makes it difficult for researchers to develop a preventive vaccine or an effective treatment. The virus destroys certain immune cells in the blood called T-lymphocyte cells with CD4-type receptors. These cells are variously called CD4, T-4, T-helper, or T-cells.

Acquired immune deficiency syndrome (AIDS) develops as the end stage of an infection with HIV. A syndrome is a cluster of symptoms, and AIDS signals that the immune system is failing. According to the Centers for Disease Control and Prevention's current definition of AIDS, a woman has AIDS if she has HIV and develops particular life-threatening illnesses that are uncommon in people with healthy immune systems, or if she has low blood levels of CD4 cells—less than two hundred cells per cubic milliliter of blood.

A woman can live for ten years or more with an HIV infection before developing AIDS. For much of that time she will look and feel healthy. In fact, since no early symptoms of infection are exclusive to HIV, she will not know that she is carrying the virus unless she has a blood test for HIV.

She can also live for several years after developing AIDS, but will eventually die from it. However, some people who are HIV-positive die of other causes before developing AIDS, so no one yet knows whether all people infected with HIV inevitably develop AIDS. Also, in a handful of cases, people with previously confirmed HIV infection seem to have lost all traces of having once been infected and continue to be healthy.

Since the disease was recognized in 1981, the understanding of AIDS and its definition have changed. Because in the United States it was first seen among white gay men, the symptoms that are most prominent among those men have heavily influenced how AIDS is characterized. Originally, when the cause of the disease was unknown, it was solely defined by its symptoms. At one time, it was called "gay related immune disorder," even though the disease was spreading primarily heterosexually in Africa and the Caribbean. Doctors and researchers in the United States were unwilling to connect the patterns of disease transmission in other countries with what was happening to U.S. women.

Different symptoms are more prevalent in different groups of people with HIV disease. For example, Kaposi's sarcoma, a cancer that reveals itself as splotches on the skin or inside the mouth, affects mainly gay men. It is not nearly so common among injection drug users and women. And white gay men are still the group researched most in this country, so researchers know relatively little about female reproductive tract illnesses or other HIV-related conditions that women are more likely to have. As a result, the official definition of AIDS has excluded and continues to exclude many women. In fact, one kind of pneumonia more prevalent among HIV-positive women than among white gay men was left off the official list of symptoms until recently. Some women who were HIV-positive but were not listed officially as having AIDS have died of undiagnosed "pelvic disease," and they are not usually counted among those who have AIDS. With partial success, women activists have struggled with the Centers for Disease Control and Prevention (CDCP) to include in their AIDS definition the symptoms that women report. In 1990, the CDCP admitted that 48 percent of the women whose deaths were attributed to HIV or AIDS died of conditions not then on the official list defining AIDS.[34]

The 1993 definition of AIDS now includes invasive cervical cancer but still leaves out gynecological infections that do not yield to conventional treatments, including vaginal candidiasis (yeast); pelvic inflammatory disease; HPV on the vulva, vagina, or anus; and urinary tract infections. However, the CDCP now acknowledges that HIV infection can affect the course of these diseases. And for some women, gynecological problems are their first noticeable symptoms of HIV disease.

In general, the public falsely perceives that the number of women with AIDS is minuscule. This error is fed by official undercounting of women due to incomplete definitions. Federal money allotted to the states each year to run programs for people with AIDS is determined by the number of people reported with AIDS the previous year. Thus, with the undercounting of women, less money is allocated for our care. Furthermore, whenever the CDCP changes the definitions and thus increases the number of people who qualify as having AIDS, funding for service agencies has lagged behind.

Women have been largely ignored in this epidemic while our numbers have escalated. Although in "developed" countries such as the United States, most infections are still among gay men and injection drug users—who are predominantly male—this shows signs of changing. From 1989 to 1990 alone, the number of women with HIV infection in the United States increased by 25 percent.[35] By the year 2000, twenty years after the disease was first recognized, half

or more of new infections will be in women. The Job Corps, which tests all applicants for HIV, has found that adolescent women are almost twice as likely as men to be infected.[36] Many of these women are from rural areas of the United States, traditionally considered "low-risk" areas. One out of sixty-seven new mothers in Washington, D.C.[37] and 10 percent of women of childbearing age in Brooklyn, New York, are infected with HIV.[38]

For children under 14 or 15 years old, more girls than boys have HIV infection in places as disparate as Zambia, North America, Argentina, and Haiti.[39] The rates sometimes run as high as twice as many girls as boys, which may reflect the much higher rates of sexual abuse and exploitation of young girls. Informal reports indicate that sexual abuse by family members is common everywhere, but statistics are not available on the numbers of girls and women who are infected as a result of sexual abuse.

Women have become the fastest growing group of people with AIDS in the United States. From 1987 to 1991, AIDS cases among women who were infected heterosexually jumped from 28 to 37 percent of women diagnosed with AIDS.[40] In most major U.S. cities, it is the leading cause of death for women 20 to 40 years old.[41] Overall, it is the fifth leading killer of U.S. women ages 15 to 44.[42] Generally, prevalence rates are higher in urban, middle Atlantic, and southeastern states and Puerto Rico.[43] The highest rates of AIDS in women in the United States are in Washington, D.C., Puerto Rico, New York, Florida, and New Jersey, in that order.[44]

The death rates for women from AIDS are even higher than official figures show. Between 1981 and 1986, there was an unexplained sharp rise in deaths among women aged 15 to 44 from pneumonia, influenza, tuberculosis, septicemia, rare parasitic infections, chronic obstructive pulmonary disease, and kidney disease. Since death from these causes is rare in this age group, these women may have had unrecognized HIV disease.[45]

How HIV Affects the Body

Problems caused directly by HIV include AIDS dementia; aseptic meningitis, a type of inflammation of the sheath surrounding the brain and spinal cord; and other neurological problems. Otherwise, the virus works indirectly through opportunistic diseases. It also affects and destroys other parts of the immune system, including CD4 lymphocytes, but the full scope of destruction is not yet known. Therefore, the immediate cause of death is not usually from HIV itself but from opportunistic infections that the body can no longer control. Pneumocystis carinii pneumonia, for instance, cannot cause infection in a healthy person but can kill someone who has AIDS.

The virus also seems to accelerate the progression of some sexually transmitted diseases. Organisms that cause PID, such as chlamydia and gonorrhea, may be able to proliferate more rapidly. Even organisms not usually associated with PID in the United States, such as those that cause tuberculosis, may invade the pelvic area more readily, causing PID. And HIV-positive women will have more persistent cases of PID and may need more surgery. HIV-positive women have ten times more abnormal cell changes in the cervix than do other women.[46] These cell changes also tend to be more severe and more difficult to treat and progress more rapidly to cervical cancer. Syphilis in an HIV-infected person seems to progress to the tertiary stage, in which permanent damage occurs, much more quickly than in a non-HIV-infected person.[47] Furthermore, syphilis and herpes seem to be controlled less well by the usual drug treatments in HIV-positive people. None of this is surprising in light of the inability of our immune systems to function at their best with HIV infection.

Many women are worried that pregnancy might accelerate HIV disease. Although pregnancy does affect the immune system, no obvious link has appeared between pregnancy and an increased severity of HIV infection. Women may also be concerned whether an HIV infection will be transmitted to the developing fetus. A number of years ago, researchers and doctors suspected that HIV would always be transmitted to the fetus during pregnancy; fortunately, this has turned out not to be true. The baby is more likely than not to be born uninfected. Counselors now generally advise women that the average rate of infection is around 25 or 30 percent.[48] Taking AZT during pregnancy and labor may reduce the rate even further, to 8 percent.[49]

Ironically, though many medical professionals urge HIV-positive women to have abortions, the medical system often makes abortion especially hard to get for HIV-positive women (in addition to the barriers in various states to discourage all women from having abortions). In 1989, out of thirty clinics that a woman from the New York City Commission on Human Rights called, two-thirds canceled appointments when she said she was HIV-positive.[50] More than half of the clinics said that they had inadequate infection-control precautions!

Women who inject drugs are likely to have even more problems finding a place willing to do an abortion on an outpatient basis. Clinic staff may have trouble finding veins on such drug users and may refuse to do the procedure on those grounds. Going into a hospital for an abortion may force women to tell parents or partners what they are doing.

Prejudice

Unfortunately, women with HIV disease or AIDS do not suffer from the disease alone—they are also very likely to suffer from the prejudice of others. For some, this ostracism can seem as bad as the disease itself.

Stigma can affect some of us more than others. The popular media have tended to feed preconceived beliefs and prejudices concerning "worthy" and "unworthy" people who have AIDS. The first belief suggests that gay men, intravenous drug users, commercial sex workers, and women of color do not deserve sympathy because they get AIDS through illicit, disapproved of, and/or promiscuous sex or illegal drug activity and thus deserve to be punished by having the disease. As one reporter recounts a woman's tale, "[Ms.] Clifford has learned that [how she got it] is often the first thing people ask. Even strangers. And especially medical personnel. It is their way, she contends, of passing judgment. They are separating the victims from the nonvictims, like so much clean laundry from dirty."[52]

The second belief is that children, people who became infected through blood transfusions, and middle-class white women who contract sexually transmitted diseases from their husbands or HIV from a dentist are innocent, passive victims who are worthy of help, support, and understanding. (Actually, so far, only one dentist has spread HIV as far as anyone can document.) The third belief is that lesbians do not catch sexually transmissible diseases. These attitudes guarantee that the diseases will continue to spread and that people considered "unworthy" will suffer doubly.

How HIV Is Transmitted

Human immunodeficiency virus is spread through contact with body fluids that contain the virus: blood, including that in menstrual fluid; vaginal fluids; and semen. The most common way for HIV to travel from one person to another is through sex that allows preejaculatory penile fluid (precum), semen, vaginal or cervical secretions, menstrual fluid, or blood from an infected person to come into contact with vulnerable areas of another person. For a woman, the vulnerable sexual organs are the vagina and cervix. For a man, the glans and opening of the penis are vulnerable. For both, the virus can also enter through the lining of the rectum and wherever a

break or irritation of the skin exists, such as on fingers or hands. The virus can get into the bloodstream through cuts or abrasions anywhere on the body, or through the intact vaginal and rectal walls. The riskiest unprotected sex with an infected partner is anal intercourse (penis into anus). Second in risk is vaginal intercourse, and third is mouth-to-penis oral sex.

Small cuts or irritations in the mouth may be vulnerable to infection if fluid from a man's penis or a woman's vagina comes in contact with the mouth, though this is not yet known. The mouth may be vulnerable if a person has gum disease or perhaps for up to several hours after brushing or flossing. However, saliva probably destroys HIV, though this is not certain. The throat is probably as vulnerable to infection with HIV as it is to gonorrhea and chlamydia. A few documented cases do exist of HIV transmission through oral sex. These cases are hard to document because most couples do not only have oral sex. The risk seems very low, but current statistics may be incomplete and thus misleading.

Sweat, tears, and saliva contain either too little or no HIV and thus are not transmitters of the virus. A person would have to be injected with about 32 liters of saliva at one sitting before receiving enough virus to cause infection.[53] Thus, casual contact between people, spitting, or kissing (unless blood is drawn) will not spread the virus; nor will shaking hands, hugging, or eating food prepared by an HIV-positive person. Even cleaning the vomit of an infected person is not dangerous because stomach acid kills the virus. Unless urine and feces contain visible blood, they are unlikely to contain enough HIV to cause an infection.

There is probably a higher risk of getting the disease from someone who is either recently infected or in an advanced stage of the disease. A newly infected person has high levels of the virus but is not yet producing antibodies to counteract it. When the disease becomes more advanced,

It seems odd how much shame there is surrounding this illness. But I feel that stain inside me, too...And I hate it. That a person like me—or like them—should feel shame about this shows that something is wrong. They tell us how we catch the virus, but they do not mention how shame, which is equally damaging, arises. In my entire life I have not been prone to such feelings.[51]

the immune system becomes less effective in controlling the HIV and levels of the virus rise again.[54]

The cells particularly affected by the virus, the CD4 cells, congregate where there are infections or sores. A woman with an infection, especially in her vagina or rectum, is at a higher risk of catching HIV if fluid containing the virus comes in contact with the infected area. Likewise, if a person simultaneously has HIV and another infection, the virus will spread more easily from the infected area. Thus, other sexually transmissible diseases, such as gonorrhea and chlamydia, make us more susceptible to HIV. Having any kind of sexually transmitted infection increases the risk of being infected with HIV probably about three to five times,[55] but possibly as much as a hundred times.[56] Diseases such as syphilis, herpes, and chancroid, which produce open sores, allow HIV easier entry into the body. And in turn, HIV may prolong or augment those diseases. Discharge-producing sexually transmissible diseases, such as gonorrhea, chlamydia, and trichomoniasis, may also increase the risk of acquiring HIV because of the increase in CD4 cells. These diseases may also increase risk by making the vagina more alkaline, probably a more favorable environment for HIV, and by breaking down the cervical mucus.[57]

While HIV is not as contagious as other sexually transmitted diseases such as gonorrhea or hepatitis B, it is clear that even one exposure to it can cause infection. Researchers do not yet understand why some of us seem to be more resistant to infection than others. Different studies cite rates of infection for female partners of HIV-positive men from 9 to 70 percent.[58] And a few cases of woman-to-woman sexual transfer have been documented. Actual rates are hard to establish because the Centers for Disease Control and Prevention assumed, without statistical or factual basis, that some other method of transfer, such as injection drug use or occasional

heterosexual experiences, was the cause of the infection rather than sex between women.

We can transfer blood by sharing needles without sterilizing them between uses to pierce the skin, whether for piercing body parts, tattooing, skin popping (injecting drugs under the skin rather than into a vein), or directly injecting drugs into veins. Injection drug users may feel that sharing an uncleaned needle with a partner is a sign of love or trust, just as some people feel that not using a condom represents the same bond. And though some researchers consider drug use as a more likely route of transmission than heterosexual sex, this may not actually be true for women who inject drugs. One study found that among drug users, women are more likely than men to share injection equipment but they are also more likely to clean the needles. At the same time, their drug-using male sex partners hardly ever use condoms.[59]

THE GOVERNMENT'S EDUCATIONAL EFFORTS

The only way we can be sure to avoid infections with sexually transmissible diseases is to avoid dangerous kinds of contact—we must practice safer sex. Unfortunately, government education, especially on HIV and AIDS, has focused attention on "high-risk" groups and on reducing the number of sexual partners. This focus is misguided: in addition to being insufficient to halt the spread of the diseases, it reflects and can strengthen our belief that sexually transmissible diseases only happen to other people. (For information on avoiding infection, see "Guidelines for Safer Sex" in Chapter 11.)

Who Is Actually a High Risk?

The Centers for Disease Control and Prevention encouraged erroneous beliefs about sexually transmissible diseases by promoting the notion that there are high-risk groups of people, such as gay men,

injection drug users, and, at one time, Haitians. These are groups in which HIV is relatively common, but not for any reason inherent to the groups. Simply, the virus spread among these people before anyone understood how the infection is transmitted.

The result of designating some groups of people as high risk is the mistaken association that there are low-risk groups, such as lesbians and middle-class, heterosexual whites. Many of us not in "high risk" groups have believed that HIV and other sexually transmissible diseases would not affect us. In reality, one study showed that among 20,000 women, 35 percent of those infected with HIV did not belong to any "high-risk" groups.[60] In another study in rural Florida, which has a high prevalence of HIV infection, a fifth of the pregnant women with HIV infections did not seem to have any risk factors.[61] For example, they had "low-risk" partners, and did not have other sexually transmitted diseases.

Because of the assumption that women of certain classes do not have sexually transmissible diseases, medical practitioners may miss a diagnosis or may not provide information necessary to keep us safe. Contrary to common stereotypes, in the United States, women with the highest education have the most sex partners on average.[63]

Another result of the false dichotomy between groups of people is that not much effort has been put into preventing the spread of the disease in "low-risk" groups. And where we believe the incidence of sexually transmissible diseases is low, we tend not to practice safer sex because we don't think we need to. In fact, one study suggests that merely 17 percent of heterosexual men with multiple partners use condoms.[64] Educators may falsely assume that "low-risk" women do not need information on how to avoid the disease. In reality, anyone can be infected. On one college campus, for instance, half of the women were infected with chlamydia.[65] And 17 to 46 percent of female college students have HPV infections.[66] All groups at this point include some people with HIV infection. There are no low-risk groups of

Every woman is vulnerable to this disease. No woman should say, "That's not me." That's what I did in 1984, and I'm sorry I did it. In 1984, for me, this was a gay disease. And I made choices based on that misassumption.[62]

A few weeks ago, I had a blood test that showed an abnormally low white and red blood cell count. My doctor was concerned, and I said: "Have you tested for AIDS?" She said: "No. You can't test for AIDS without the patient's permission. We're not looking for AIDS." I guess she just assumed that since I'm white, middle class, and in my fifties, I'm not infected.

I was living with my boyfriend for a year and a half and broke up six months ago. I didn't have sex with many boy-friends—only three—and Fred—he only slept with two women. He seemed like such a sweet guy when I met him. So I figured we were safe and didn't have to use condoms. After I tested positive, I found out that Fred's first girlfriend used drugs for a time.

people, only high- and low-risk activities or behaviors.

Finally, anyone in a "high risk" group is unfairly stigmatized as likely to have the disease, regardless of behavior or actual health status. Fortunately, the Centers for Disease Control and Prevention now talk less about "high-risk groups" and classify people with HIV according to the way they were probably exposed; for example, by heterosexual sex or injection drug use.

It is clear that high-risk activities are even riskier for some of us. The younger we are when we first have intercourse, the higher is our risk of developing PID, cervical cancer, and HIV disease. Age-related cell changes in the genital tract account for some of a young girl's increased risk. Our reproductive systems are not fully mature until several years after we enter puberty. Our cervical mucus may not have built up its full array of protective proteins. Also, some vulnerable cervical cells are more exposed inside the vagina in the early years after puberty, and are more vulnerable to damage from bacteria, especially chlamydia, and to viruses such as HPV. The vaginal wall is also not fully mature, but the significance of this regarding sexually transmissible infections is not known.

Some researchers speculate that in our teenage years we may have difficulty negotiating with partners about the extent of sexual activity and about safer sex; have rapid changes of partners; have more partners infected by a sexually transmitted disease; and delay seeking medical care, compared with older women.[67] Sexually experienced teenagers are three times more likely to have PID than are sexually experienced women in their mid- to late 20s.[68] Worldwide, the incidence of HIV in women peaks in the 15 to 25 year range, ten years before the peak for men, even though the normally acid environment in a premenopausal vagina may sometimes inactivate HIV.[69] Conversely, loss of vaginal acidity after menopause results in decreased defenses against HIV, and transmission of

HIV seems then to increase for each exposure.[70] The vaginal wall also becomes thinner and is less lubricated, making vaginal irritation more likely and increasing susceptibility to HIV.

How Safe Is Your "One and Only"?

The government and some medical societies have advised us that if we take a few precautions we can reduce our risk of sexually transmissible diseases. These precautions are: to reduce the number of sex partners we have and to discuss past sexual and drug-use history with our potential sexual partners. Unfortunately, these strategies give us unwarranted reassurance without real protection.

Advising people to have fewer sex partners or to save sex for a monogamous marriage is, in fact, rational from a statistical point of view—the fewer contacts between people, the slower sexually transmissible diseases spread among the population. Knowing your statistical risk, however, does not tell you if you are going to be the one to get and spread an infection. A woman or man may have only two sexual partners, yet contract a sexually transmitted disease from the first partner and pass it on to the second partner. Restricting the number of one's partners seems to make sense because it is reinforced by social taboos against multiple sexual partners, especially for women. While playing Russian roulette with one bullet in the gun is certainly less risky than with three bullets, if you get the one bullet you are still dead.

Because of the supposed safety of monogamy, if you are currently monogamous you may have a false sense of being invulnerable to a sexually transmitted infection. However, a woman is safe in a mutually monogamous relationship only if both she and her partner start the relationship uninfected—which is not always possible to tell. Both she and her partner must remain completely monogamous and continue to avoid exposure to nonsexual sources of infection such as unscreened blood or shared needles.

However, the reality of our sex lives is often not so simple. Studies of heterosexual couples in the United States show that relatively few people in this country have one lifetime partner that they make love with only after marriage. About half of marriages end in divorce, and many people remarry. Within marriage, a 1990 Kinsey survey found that 29 percent of wives and 37 percent of husbands have affairs.[71] Premarital sex is increasingly acceptable. In the United States in the late 1980s, 17 percent of married people said that they had lived with someone prior to their first marriages,[72] and this percentage is likely to have increased. A quarter of Americans over the age of 19 have never married and those who marry are marrying later,[73] yet 97 percent of adults are sexually active at some time.[74] Half of all pregnancies in the United States are unplanned, indicating that many people do not take adequate birth control precautions.[75] Many more probably do not think about preventing infection when they have sex.

Despite popular belief, monogamy on our part in a long-term relationship does not keep us safe. A woman's risk of getting a sexually transmissible disease rises with her partner's exposure to such diseases as well as with her own. Studies from countries where heterosexual transmission of HIV is already common illustrate how, worldwide, many women who are infected have had sex with only one partner. In one Rhode Island study, 70 percent of the women who were infected with HIV were monogamous. The average number of lifetime partners of these infected women was three, the same as for those not infected.[76] In the United Kingdom, 80 percent of women with AIDS were infected by long-term partners.[77] As many as 60 to 80 percent of all women in Africa infected with HIV have had only one sexual partner.[78] In the United States, around a tenth of women considered "low risk" (defined as those who are monogamous or have not had sex with a partner for at least two months), are infected with chlamydia.[79] And a quarter of adolescent girls infected with chlamydia who attended four clinics in Atlanta, Georgia, had had only one sexual partner.[80]

In reality, the more often a woman is exposed to microorganisms, even from one or two partners, the more likely she is to become infected. Rather than reduce the number of people we have sex with, we need to eliminate or at least reduce the number of times we have *unprotected* sex with a person who may be infected, whether it is with one person repeatedly or once each with one hundred people.

WHAT YOU DON'T KNOW CAN HURT YOU

Asking our partners about past sexual and drug use history is a first step in expressing our concern about safety. And when we ask such questions, we want to believe that our partners will not lie to us; however, many of us suspect that our sexual partners are sometimes less than truthful. Statistics reveal that our suspicions are well-founded and that, indeed, we cannot rely on a partner's honesty. For example, in one survey, 20 percent of the men admitted that they would lie about their HIV status, and many said they would deliberately underreport the number of previous partners. About a third of the men and a tenth of the women admitted that they had already lied in order to have sex. Almost a quarter of the women and a third of the men had been sexually involved with more than one person at a time, and more than half did not tell their primary partners.[81]

Expecting honesty presupposes an equal relationship between two partners for whom honesty is of paramount importance. If a person fears that a partner will react angrily, be extremely hurt, or abandon the relationship, truth-telling is unlikely.

Even when partners are completely honest, they might not know that they are infected because early signs of infection are

I'm very worried about AIDS and I'm glad I know what to do: abstinence is 100 percent sure; otherwise, I should use condoms. But I use the pill because I know that if my boyfriend was lying to me about what he was doing I could just see it in his eyes.

When I finally realized that this was something that affected my husband as well as me I started asking him: "Have you been with anyone else? Have you been with anyone else?" He kept denying it—but I was pretty sure he was lying. In the end, he came through very well. He was a product of his upbringing, the male model of "cheat on your wife and don't tell her." He cut through that, and he was able to say: "God, that's what I did; that's not okay. What a terrible thing has happened to us."

—Woman who developed PID

often not present. In addition, many women erroneously believe that they can tell if their partners are infected by watching for physical dirtiness, pimples, or greasy hair. This can be a fatal assumption. Even clinical tests for a sexually transmissible disease may not be accurate because a time lag may exist between infection and a "positive" test.

Gonorrhea, for example, usually causes obvious symptoms in a man but you may not be able to inspect his penis to observe an infectious discharge. Moreover, a man can be infected for two weeks or more without having any symptoms. Some men never develop noticeable symptoms and unwittingly infect one or more partners. Men are also often unaware that they are infected with chlamydia and may therefore unknowingly spread the disease. In the United States, chlamydia incidence among men appears to have risen dramatically since the 1980s, afflicting an estimated 800,000 men annually, twice as many as suffer from gonococcal infection.[82] Up to 25 percent of infected men have no signs or symptoms of infection.[83] Both gonorrhea and chlamydia can also infect women for long periods of time, even years, without causing symptoms. During this time the women can unknowingly pass these bacteria to sexual partners. As many as 70 percent of women infected with chlamydia may be without symptoms or have symptoms so mild that they do not suspect a serious problem. At times the immune system appears to be successful in suppressing chlamydia and even in curing it. Therefore, a woman may infect her partner or partners without ever knowing that she has had the disease.

Similarly, many of those who are infected with HPV infect others without realizing it. We cannot possibly tell if a male partner is infected with a high-risk HPV, and he himself is unlikely to be aware of the fact. Even many physicians do not realize that the types of HPV infections that are most likely to lead to cervical cancer are often not visible to the naked eye. A

woman can be infected for years with no symptoms before she becomes aware, usually through a Pap test, that she is infected.

Symptoms of HIV infection often do not appear for years, even though a person is infectious during that time. While blood tests can identify the presence of antibodies to the virus, most people do not get tested until after they become ill. And commonly used HIV tests actually test for antibodies to HIV rather than for the virus itself. Because it takes time for the body to make enough of these antibodies to be found in a test, for a period of several weeks to months a person can be infected and still have a negative test.

In many cases we do not have the information we need to be able to protect ourselves. Young women are particularly at risk partly because our own, our teachers', and our physicians' educations have not caught up with the rapid changes in adolescents' sexual habits. This gap leaves us with the greater likelihood of being sexually experienced before we have learned how to protect our health, and without having the medical and social services we need. Currently, 7.5 percent of girls and 19 percent of boys are sexually active by age 14.[84] And 80 percent of urban teens have had sexual intercourse by the time they are 19.[85] In a nationwide survey almost two-thirds of the male and just over half of the female students had had sexual intercourse by age 17.[86]

Sometimes we are unaware that certain activities are risky. For example, anal intercourse is fairly common among heterosexuals in the United States. As many as 61 percent of women who responded to a variety of surveys report having anal intercourse,[87] but few heterosexuals talk about it. We may not think of anal intercourse as "real sex" or may use it as a way to avoid conception, not realizing that we need to think about protection against diseases. Because most of the health information about anal sex is directed toward gay men, women may be unaware of the relative ease of disease transmission through anal intercourse.

The fact that both men and women can have gonorrhea, chlamydia, HPV, or HIV without noticing it, at least for a while, contributes to the spread of these infections. However, even symptoms do not guarantee that people will cease the sexual activities that spread the infections or that they will seek treatment. Some of us and our partners do not recognize mild symptoms as signs of disease; do not want to believe that we could have a sexually transmitted disease; or mistake our symptoms for problems unrelated to sex. In addition, some of us continue to have unprotected sex even when we know that we have an infection. One study of people who attended a clinic specializing in sexually transmitted diseases showed that 46 percent of women and 38 percent of men who came for an evaluation reported that they had had unprotected intercourse after their symptoms occurred.[88] In addition, many of us may have difficulty asserting ourselves in sexual situations even when we know how to protect ourselves and know that we should be doing so.

CAN WE RELY ON OUR DOCTORS?

Medical practitioners are no less vulnerable than the rest of society to erroneous beliefs and prejudices. Yet many of us rely on our medical practitioners to recognize and treat our various symptoms in an honest and nonjudgmental way. Unfortunately, medical practitioners often display prejudices about women that undermine our diagnosis and treatment. For example, a double standard of sexuality persists: our need for physical love is often frowned upon while a man's need is not; and some sexually transmitted diseases are considered a "just punishment" for women but merely a regrettable, but understandable, inconvenience for men. Such a double standard impedes the free and respectful exchange of useful information we so urgently need.

For years after the link between intercourse and cervical cancer became known, researchers and physicians assumed that a woman's own sexual habits were all that counted. Women who had cervical dysplasia or cervical cancer were sometimes told by their gynecologists that they should not have had sex with so many men. Such remarks were part of the overall label "promiscuous" attached to an already frightened woman seeking help. The double-standard assumption of promiscuity and blame is even more a part of the medical approach to PID and HIV disease.

Physicians still tend to ignore or minimize men's roles in women's diseases. Many physicians do not mention the prominence of a sexually transmissible virus in cervical dysplasia and cervical cancer. Some physicians do not routinely call in the partners of women who have PID for diagnosis and treatment.[89] Often men who have a sexually transmissible disease but have no symptoms are treated only if the disease could have serious consequences for them, not in order to prevent women from being infected. Do not consider yourself adequately treated for PID unless your partner(s) have been similarly treated.

Medical schools in the United States have been slow to provide adequate training. A 1985 survey showed that only one in five U.S. medical schools provided even half of its students with training in the prevention, detection, and treatment of sexually transmitted diseases.[90] This means that many physicians still lack the knowledge and skill to counsel and treat us, leading directly to inadequate care. For example, because many doctors failed to recognize early signs of AIDS in women, many women received inadequate treatment. Probably because of late diagnosis, women have in the past survived, on average, much shorter times than men after being diagnosed with AIDS—13.4 months to men's 17 months.

Someday fewer women who have PID will suffer irreversible damage if and when

My [lesbian] lover and I wanted to have a baby and one of my longtime, close male friends agreed to donate the sperm. The doctor who was helping me insisted that my friend be tested. I thought it was ridiculous. He didn't think he could be infected. He was healthy. He had no reason to lie to me. But the doctor was adamant. Both my friend and I were in a state of shock when the test results came back. He was positive. Then he remembered that one of his lovers from five or six years ago died later of AIDS. He just denied to himself all those years that he could have been infected.

There is something about the care of women's sexual systems that includes blaming women and giving men a lot of freedom to act out. And I think we need to see that. Because I feel that part of the medical community's reluctance to bring our male partners in is giving license to the male to have sexual rela-tionships with lots of people and not be fully responsible for the outcome. And part of treating a woman with PID like she's a weak person for having this problem "down there" is blaming her. And that's where society is still at with men and women. And for women to get out of that, we need enough self-esteem to say: "This doesn't happen out of the blue. There's a reason for this." And for us to get our health back, is to understand how terrible this inequality is in our health care.

The doctor never explained to me the connection between PID and sexually transmitted diseases. After my first hospitalization I went out and started doing some research on my own. I went to the library and looked at all the medical books that had to do with women's anatomy and women's health. And I found that the literature says that most cases of PID are caused by sexually transmitted diseases. Then, during my second time in the hospital my doctor was sitting in my room, and my husband and 9-year-old son were sitting with me. And I happened to ask: "I understand that PID is caused by sexually transmitted diseases. Why wasn't I told about this?" And my doctor said: "No, that's not true." That's all he would say. Later on, when my husband and son left, I asked him again. I said: "Look, this is what I found in the book. Why can't you guys be up-front with me?" He said: "Well, I didn't want to say anything because your husband and son were there."

I started saying that I wanted my husband tested. I would say: "If you can't find anything in me maybe you can find it in him." But no one would test him. We had to go to New York to find a doctor who would test men. He worked in a fertility clinic, and he was the first one—out of thirty doctors—who told us that this was because of sexually transmitted diseases that we both had.

researchers focus more attention on PID's early stages, such as cervical infection, and symptoms other than pain. A trend in this direction is emerging, with physicians acknowledging that PID can quietly smolder throughout our reproductive organs, damaging us unnoticed. Currently, however, our symptoms may not be taken seriously until the disease becomes debilitating or life-threatening. Also, many physicians in private practice prescribe inappropriate antibiotics to treat PID.[91]

Some medical personnel still have prejudices and irrational fears about HIV infection. They may isolate women and heavily drape themselves, and some women have found that medical practitioners refused to treat them out of fear of contracting the disease. In reality, any precautions that are necessary for HIV should also be taken to prevent the spread of many other diseases. Inadequate infection-control precautions against HIV indicate overall inadequate procedures for cleanliness and sterility.

Moreover, medical professionals need training in how to ask about a person's sexual life. Fewer than one in ten physicians in the United States take an adequate sexual history of their patients.[92] Thus, they often miss important clues for diagnosing sexually transmitted diseases.

Overall, we cannot count on medical practitioners to always diagnose or treat us correctly or to educate us about disease prevention. These are further reasons for learning on our own the self-esteem and skills necessary for preventing sexually transmissible diseases. We also need to consider how we can work together toward social change so that methods of prevention and bias-free treatment become available to all women.

THE NEED FOR SOCIAL CHANGE

Ideally, social institutions would encourage and facilitate our efforts toward assertiveness and empowerment. We should expect social policies to remove social, legal, or religious barriers to our attempts to prevent sexually transmissible diseases. Unfortunately, some current social policies can obstruct disease prevention. For example, obscenity laws and postal regulations can limit our access to explicit HIV-prevention materials; regulations on male or female condoms can increase their cost or make them unavailable to us; failure to halt unemployment and discrimination in housing can render testing and counseling programs ineffective because people are too occupied with daily concerns to think about health care; and laws prohibiting possession of needles and syringes or limiting their distribution can actually increase needle sharing. In addition, girls and women are sometimes partly or entirely left out of education programs and research on prevention methods and treatment of sexually transmissible diseases. This neglect encourages us to compromise our health in love relationships.

Where Education Fails

Most of us have never had basic sex education that includes explicit information about how sexually transmissible organisms live and spread and what specific actions women can take to prevent their transmission. Left on our own, many of us underestimate the risks of unprotected sex, are unskilled in using barrier methods, and are shy about insisting that a partner use condoms. We need information and encouragement in order to help ourselves and educate our children. Yet only 15 percent of all school districts in the United States offer comprehensive health education programs, with even fewer providing education on HIV disease.[93] For teens, this lack of information through schools is particularly deplorable since they are highly vulnerable to infection and seem most open to learning about safer sex.

An accurate description of how sexually transmissible diseases spread and how to prevent them requires very explicit talk about sex and drugs. To avoid controversy, much instruction on sex-related disease prevention is so vague or mechanical that it is not helpful. For instance, for many years educational material taught that people should avoid their partners' "body fluids" to prevent the spread of HIV. As a result, many people became afraid of touching others since it was not clear from the term "body fluids" that sweat, tears, and saliva are harmless.

Curricula designed to teach about sexually transmissible diseases reveal ambivalence about explicit discussions of sex. Some schools still teach their students that abstinence until marriage is the only way to avoid pregnancy and disease. Some school systems do offer explicit material such as how to use a condom properly and how to clean needles, but not necessarily at ages early enough to prevent disease. New York City, for example, was forced by some parents to avoid these topics until seventh grade. This does nothing to help those fifth and sixth grade girls who become pregnant or infected. New Haven, Connecticut, was the first school system to make condoms available to children as early as the fifth grade. The school board acted after a survey found that almost 30 percent of sixth graders and half of eighth graders claimed to be sexually active.[94]

At times, the federal government has colluded with those who wish to keep us ignorant about how to prevent the spread of HIV. In contrast, since 1986, Switzerland has conducted a public education campaign aimed at men. Over a three-year period, condom use among a representative sample increased from 8 to 48 percent in the 27 to 30 age group. In older men, condom use stayed about the same.[95] Finland mails every 16-year-old a latex condom and a glossy graphic brochure on how to have safer sex.[96]

Much existing educational material in the United States is useless. It relays a simple "use a condom" message, without any alternatives, ignoring the possibility that a woman may not have any choice about whether her partner uses a condom or not. Some educational material ignores social contexts, even though white women in their late teens at an elite college have different concerns from those of inner-city Hispanic women of the same age group. Neither group is likely to be able to take effective action if its concerns are not addressed.

Researchers generally regard drug users, teenagers, and sex workers as unable to carry out instructions for their medical care. With the right approach, however, community outreach can be effective. In Colorado Springs, a program to dispense safer sex information and condoms, along with screening and counseling for sex workers and their clients, reduced gonorrhea 16 percent over three years.[97] After educational efforts in Rhode Island, researchers found that women drug users were more likely to request HIV antibody testing even if they had no symptoms of HIV infection, thus showing that they were willing and able to take action on behalf of their health. In one urban high school, after two years of safer sex education and condom availability, condom use increased 43 percent among sexually active students. And about half of the students were sexually active, both before and after the study.[98]

Television and radio are today's most powerful messengers, especially for teenagers, who spend an average of 23 hours each week watching television or listening to the radio.[100] Yet most sexually explicit television and radio stories do not mention birth control or sex-related disease prevention. But these media do have the potential to change attitudes about healthful behavior. For example, through public service announcements and popular TV situation comedies, the Harvard Alcohol Project promotes the concept of a designated driver. The same could be done for sexually transmissible disease prevention.

Bias in Prevention Research
Over the years, very few organizations have

For a couple of years I had a lot of pain, and a lot of fevers, but I was dragging myself around because no one could find anything. My husband and I had been to marital counseling because I had painful intercourse. What was wrong with me? Then I went to a doctor in Boston who did a test that showed that I had a bacterial infection. And he said: "Both you and your husband have to be treated because these bacteria can get into a man's prostate and infect him later." And I said: "Wait a minute! You're treating me and my husband—what is this?" Suddenly I had a different handle on what was happening to me: that I had something we both needed to be treated for.

My first sign of PID was itching and a urinary tract infection. I was a college student at the time, and someone there told me that I had a sexually transmitted infection. I went to the college health service. They did not give me a pelvic exam; they did not give me antibiotics. I was given some kind of powder that I was supposed to insert into my vagina, and I was put in the infirmary with ice bags between my legs. It sounds like the dark ages! I finally went to a doctor outside of college, who said: "You are sick!" and gave me antibiotics. I think I probably had gonorrhea. I had pelvic pain, and fever, chills, fever, chills—it was a pretty classic case of PID, but I didn't know this until seven years later.

A lot of kids who come [to the high school teen health center] are incredibly embarrassed to even ask for condoms...I wish it would be easier for them. They have fears even to admit to themselves that they are sexually active, so to admit it to an adult...I'm scared they are not safe because of that fear.[99]

voiced serious concerns about preventing the spread of sexually transmissible diseases. When they do, their efforts often focus on protecting men from infection; women are left without crucial techniques to make prevention easier. The lack of interest in developing prevention methods for women to use seems to imply that sex-related diseases in women are not as important as they are in men.

For example, prevention techniques have focused primarily on the only method under men's control: the male condom. Though a male condom theoretically offers the best protection, woman-controlled methods are likely to be more effective in actual use because women can be sure they are used each time. For example, one study showed that women who used either the diaphragm or the contraceptive sponge were less likely to contract gonorrhea, chlamydia, and trichomoniasis than those who used male condoms.[101]

Another serious problem is bias on contraceptive labeling. The Food and Drug Administration allows condom packages to state that the product is useful in preventing the spread of sexually transmitted diseases, even though testing outside of laboratories is limited. Research has also indicated that spermicides can be useful in preventing the spread of disease, yet spermicide labels cannot include any claims about preventing sexually transmissible diseases. Such information could be lifesaving.

Institutions that promote birth control are usually separate from those promoting prevention of sexually transmissible diseases. These institutions have often worked without much interaction, developing separate rather than overlapping goals, and ultimately retarding disease prevention. For years, research has focused on birth control methods that do not protect against diseases. That is, since the 1950s, contraceptive researchers have focused on hormonal methods and IUDs for women instead of developing and improving physical and chemical barrier methods. At times, this neglect has

had a class, racial, or ethnic bias: Some of those who control money for research, education, and distribution of methods are more concerned about achieving demographic goals than about women's health.[102]

Another consequence of neglecting barrier methods is that only the reproductive aspects of sex (penile-vaginal intercourse) are emphasized. As a result, heterosexual couples whose sexual practices include anal or oral sex often do not realize that these activities can also spread disease. In addition, when we use high-technology contraceptive methods such as implants and injections, we do not learn about our sexual and reproductive organs, as we tend to when using barrier methods.

There is a desperate need for more and improved barrier methods since the few methods now available are not satisfactory for all. The Contraceptive Research and Development Project has begun investigating the acceptability of the female condom; studying a variety of spermicidal compounds that might also kill HIV; investigating the effects of the birth control pill on HIV transmission; and studying the negative effects on the immune system of the contraceptive vaccines under development—all socially responsible projects.

Problems with Treatment

We cannot take advantage of medical care without medical facilities that are available and accessible to us. Unfortunately, most government money allotted to treatment of sex-related diseases goes to public clinics that primarily serve men, not women and adolescents. And these few public clinics are overextended by the increasing spread of sexually transmitted diseases. The few family planning and community-based clinics that do provide comprehensive sexually transmissible disease screening generally do not treat an infected woman's partners. Simultaneously, money and resources have shrunk, so that clinics have had to reduce the numbers of people they see each day and even turn some away.

Although Congress has authorized programs to increase outreach to and screening of women, it has not appropriated any money except for a few small model programs. Funded programs show that outreach can be effective. In the northwest states, clients of public clinics had about 50 percent less chlamydia after the clinics instituted a program using a combination of systematic screening, training of family planning and sex-related disease professionals, and treatment.[103]

In addition, lack of drug treatment programs also hinders the presentation and treatment of sexually transmissible diseases, especially AIDS. Drug abuse treatment programs are all currently in need of funding and increased availability, and programs for pregnant women are almost nonexistent. American doctors have believed that stopping drugs during pregnancy could harm the fetus, but a program in Scotland has demonstrated that this is not true, and that pregnant women are often highly motivated to stop drug use, making these programs more likely to be successful.[104] Drug treatment for women, however, must take into account that women are usually the primary caregivers for children, elderly, and disabled family members. Care for their dependents must be provided, possibly at the drug treatment site or nearby.

If drug users were not punished or discriminated against, they would be less likely to go underground, where they are much harder to reach for treatment and continue to remain contagious or to engage in risky behaviors. Also, programs that allow drug users to exchange used needles for new ones are vital for reducing the spread of HIV. One-third of all HIV cases are transmitted by dirty needles, which spread the disease to the drug users, their sexual partners, and the babies born to them.

Money, Education, and Access to Medical Care

Lack of income and a poor education hinder access to medical care. Poor medical care or none at all magnifies all of the problems women have in avoiding sex-related diseases and getting tests and treatment. Whatever our skin color or ethnic background, if we lack information and money, we are more vulnerable to the effects of sexually transmissible diseases.

Through poverty, minority status, or drug abuse a woman can find herself on the fringes of society. The more "marginal" categories a woman falls into, the less likely she is to get medical care.[105] Social neglect is a frequently overlooked contributor to the different rates of sex-related diseases between communities. The limited availability and poor quality of medical services to those of us in poor communities further increase our vulnerability to sex-related diseases. The United States has a long history of providing inadequate services to prevent and treat all curable sexually transmissible diseases among poor people, most recently contributing to HIV infection. For example, policy makers have simply accepted higher rates of sexually transmitted diseases among African-Americans (who tend, in this country, to be poor) as the norm, thus denying their responsibility to help lower the disease rates, and implicitly blaming those infected for their illnesses.[106]

Those of us who have low incomes are unable to afford medical insurance unless we qualify for Medicaid or have our insurance paid by an employer.[107] Even if we can afford medical insurance for ourselves and our children, we may be denied coverage for HIV or AIDS. Probably one-quarter of all people with AIDS have no medical insurance.[108]

Furthermore, poor people are disproportionately women of color, who often have a harder time getting medical care because of transportation problems, child-care needs, and long waits at a clinic. The time it takes to get medical care takes time away from other needs, such as food, shelter, personal safety, and caretaking, so seeking medical care becomes a priority only in a health crisis.

I hate going to the doctor, especially the white male doctors. They make me feel stupid. The foreign doctors aren't so bad. The doctors talk to me very loud because they think then I'll understand. But when I get sent for tests they never tell me why. They never explain anything.

—Woman from
Puerto Rico who speaks
accented English

And those of us who are socially disadvantaged are more likely to be wary of institutions such as hospitals, and of the professionals associated with them. African-American women in particular may be suspicious of government motives behind offers of medical care because in the past the Public Health Service has been known to lie to African-Americans about the services it was delivering.[109]

Lack of access to appropriate sex education and to medical care are two possible reasons why poor women have higher rates of sexually transmissible diseases. Not surprisingly, statistics suggest that African-American women, more likely to be poor, have a higher risk of developing PID than white women.[110] This is also true for HIV/AIDS.[111]

Data show that women who have medical insurance, a higher level of education, and are employed are more likely to have Pap tests, demonstrating a clear relationship among money, social standing, and early detection of cervical disease. Medicare did not begin covering the Pap test until 1990, so that many of us were unable to afford the test until then.

How Research Has Skewed Our Understanding of Sex-Related Diseases

In research on diseases related to sex, women are often seen as reservoirs or vectors of diseases that can infect men. In other words, according to this bias, we are important as transmitters of diseases to men and to fetuses, but the diseases' effects on us are not relevant. The implication that we are to blame for infecting others leads to the study of pregnant women, for example, as infectors of their children, without equal study of the impact of the disease on the women themselves. For example, in one government-funded study, women were given AZT, a drug that seems to slow down the replication of HIV, in their second and third trimesters of pregnancy to see if the drug would affect the rate of transmission of HIV to the fetus. Once her baby was born, however, each study participant was denied further free AZT treatment.

An inordinate amount of the research on sexually transmissible diseases in women has been done on commercial sex workers, who are assumed to infect men who then might bring diseases back to their communities. The historical roots of this research stem from early twentieth century attempts to lock up sex workers with sex-related diseases in order to protect middle-class men and their families. Often investigators have trouble imagining that men who hire sex workers may be more likely to give sex-related diseases to the sex workers than the other way around. Researchers have tended to see sex workers as reservoirs of disease that they inflict upon unsuspecting customers and their families. In fact, because women are more susceptible to sexually transmissible diseases than men, commercial sex workers are more likely to catch a disease from their clients than the other way around. Sex workers are also likely to protect themselves in business transactions whenever possible, at the same time protecting their customers.[112]

When the media report on the results of research that implicitly blames women for infecting others, our own perceptions of sex-related diseases may begin to include assumptions of blame. This faulty thinking is harmful to our self-esteem and discourages us from standing up for ourselves.

Our health has repeatedly been compromised because research has not studied the questions most useful to women. For example, the effects of the menstrual cycle on sexually transmissible diseases are for the most part unknown and unstudied. No studies exist on whether tampon use increases vulnerability to a sex-related disease. No one knows exactly how PID inflammations begin, how our tissues are injured and scarred, or what treatment is best to prevent tubal damage. During the 1980s, a number of researchers who applied for federal money to study the course of HIV and AIDS in women were repeatedly turned down. At the same time, funders refused to provide money for studies that would either enroll women in clinical trials on HIV treatments or provide women with gynecological exams. Questions about women's early HIV symptoms were not asked, and no data to document differences from men's symptoms were collected.

In addition, bias can lead researchers to incorrect conclusions. For example, preconceived notions of the sexual practices of African-American girls and women determine what is considered useful for research. Research on the sex lives of African-American women in the United States has concentrated on the sexual activity and contraceptive use of teenage girls, with little research on how sexual practices change over a lifetime and how women negotiate sexual relationships under varying circumstances. Similarly, preconceived notions have led to official "exposure categories" for HIV/AIDS. Each woman with AIDS is assigned to one category, even though she could have been infected in a number of ways. The categories are ranked based on ideas about the relative likelihood of acquiring the disease in that way. Thus, if a woman uses injection drugs and has sex with either a man or a woman, she is placed in the injection-drug category. As a result, the number of women infected through sex with men or women may be underestimated through the assumption that injection drug use is always more likely to transmit the disease than heterosexual or lesbian sex. Men, however, are placed in a category that allows for more than one possible way of exposure, a more realistic and useful approach.

TAKING ACTION

We need more community, religious, and national leaders who will speak out to create an atmosphere supportive of our efforts to protect ourselves and stop the spread of sex-related diseases. We also need to recognize social inequalities in our own lives and join together with other women to explore ways to change our situations and to support each other in these changes.

We can make ourselves heard at agencies that set public health policies and research priorities on sexually transmissible diseases by writing or calling:

➢ The Centers for Disease Control and Prevention: (1) to increase the number of HIV exposure categories for women, including multiple exposure such as sex with a man and drug injection and categories that include sex with a woman; (2) to change the definition of AIDS to include more gynecological symptoms. (See "Resources" for address and telephone numbers.)

➢ Congressional representatives to increase funding for: (1) drug-abuse treatment for women, especially pregnant women (treatment sites should have provision for children or other dependents); (2) a more active program under the Public Health Service to prevent and treat sexually transmissible diseases. We can also urge them to support greater research on methods to control the spread of such diseases, especially methods under women's control. (Call the local chapter of the League of Women Voters to find out who your representatives are and how to reach them.)

➢ Director of the National Institutes of Health: to urge more funding of research on birth control methods that protect against diseases, as well as disease-prevention methods that allow conception to take place

➢ Private agencies that develop and promote methods of birth control, such as the International Planned Parenthood Federation and the Population Council: to urge them to emphasize birth control methods that also control sexually transmissible diseases

From All Walks of Life, a 1994 fundraising walk organized by the Aids Action Committee of Boston to benefit aids research and care.

➢ Local school boards: to support accurate, explicit sex education in schools. Sex education should be mandatory for each new generation of children as they become old enough to be sexually active.

We can also:

➢ Support activist groups by working with them and by donating money if possible. (Your local health department may be able to give you the names of any groups in your area. For HIV/AIDS groups the National AIDS Information Clearinghouse [see "Resources"] can also help. Existing groups focus on HIV/AIDS. Talk with friends about starting a group to increase attention on other sexually transmissible diseases.

➢ Write or call television stations and production companies that make television dramas and situation comedies, as well as advertisers who sponsor such shows, to encourage them to include explicit messages on safer sex. (People who oppose mentioning birth control and disease prevention are already pressuring sponsors to withdraw from shows containing such messages.)

➢ Join other concerned women and men to help promote, make, and distribute videotapes geared to different audiences to be shown in schools, community health centers, on television, and to be made available in video rental stores. Subjects could include how sexually transmissible diseases spread, how to use female and male condoms and other barrier methods, and self-assertive behavior for women. Also call a local cable-TV network about guidelines on filming public service announcements.

➢ Join projects that use innovative and creative ways to teach safer sex. Some examples are street theater projects; education projects that include going to clinic waiting rooms to offer information; and organizing safer-sex-information parties in homes. Where no such project exists, organize one.

ALAS (Amigas Latinas en Acción por Salud), a Latina educational theater troupe, performs skits on sex education and women's reproductive rights. The large puppets represent church, government, and media pressure.

(See "Resouces" for ideas.)

➢ Support social programs that indirectly reduce sex-related diseases by enabling low-income people to focus on longer-term health needs rather than immediate survival. Such programs include low-income housing and medical insurance for everyone.

➢ Organize politically to increase our power to command government resources and change discriminatory laws.

However, we do not have to join a group or be politically active to make an impact. We can simply talk about sexually transmissible diseases and safer sex with family, friends, coworkers, and other people in our day-to-day lives. The more we all discuss information and issues, the less embarrassing and "unmentionable" these topics become, and the more comfortable we will be with self-assertion for our own health's sake.

11

Choosing Ourselves

KNOWING THE dangers of unprotected sex does not guarantee that we will protect our health when making love. For many of us, the hardest part of safer sex is bringing up the subject with a partner and insisting despite objections. We want to feel loved, and the temptation is strong to simply enjoy our moments of physical affection.

Also, many of us find it embarrassing to talk about safer sex with a partner. Although sex is used by advertisers to sell every conceivable product, our culture does not encourage us to talk about sex honestly, openly, and without shame. In addition, standing up for ourselves assertively and taking initiative go against what many of us learned as "proper" behavior, particularly before or during lovemaking. We are used to playing a more passive role, especially with a new partner. And we may fear that assertive insistence on protected sex could cause anger, hostility, aggression, or rejection. Even some women who know that their partners are infected with HIV are reluctant to insist on protection out of solicitude for their partners' already damaged egos. Such "considerate" thoughts and

feelings can lead to an ironic sacrifice—a woman's life for her partner's self-esteem.

Our health and our lives often depend on our ability to overcome such thoughts, fears, and habits, and to take the initiative in sexual decision-making. One of our best methods of acquiring this ability is to practice ways of introducing the subject and insisting on protected sex.

DECIDING WHAT TO DO

First, decide to practice safer sex, or not to, by making lists of what you have to gain and what you might lose. For example:

Possible Gains from Protecting Myself

1. A longer life

2. A healthier life

3. Preserve my ability to bear children

4. Preserve my ability to care for the children I have

5. Greater self-esteem through defending my health and my life

I found that through all the years of fighting PID, the hardest part for me was standing up and saying: "I'm trusting me." That's when I started getting better. I think it was the psychological turning point that made me physically get better. When I said: "I am more important than these habits of seeking approval and love." That was a hard place to get to. I had to get really, really sick to get to that rock-bottom point where I had to choose myself.

My husband doesn't like using a condom. But at this point I'm just so fed up with getting PID back again. So I say: "Okay, it's abstinence for us from now on!" I told him that I'm not having any sex until he is either tested or wears a condom.

With this guy last summer, I said, "Look, this is easy, I don't have to trust you and you don't have to trust me." So that was that. And with the next person...he just automatically said, "Do you have condoms?" and I said, "In the drawer right there." No problem.[1]

6. Greater respect from my partner because I stand up for myself and make sure we protect each other

7. Learn new ways of making love

Possible Losses from Protecting Myself

1. My partner will be angry with me

2. My partner will beat me

3. My partner will leave me

4. My partner will accuse me of cheating or of thinking that he/she is cheating

5. My partner will accuse me of having a disease or of thinking that he or she is diseased

6. The excitement of spontaneity will be lost

7. I will feel embarrassed and awkward while learning new behaviors and techniques

*Possible Gains from **No** Protection*

1. My partner will be pleased with my willingness and docility

2. I won't have to worry about negotiations and can just have fun

3. I can experience the excitement of gambling

*Possible Losses from **No** Protection*

1. My self-esteem

2. My partner's respect

3. My health

4. My fertility

5. My wages

6. My ability to care for my children and watch them grow

7. My life

Many of us will not have to worry about losing our partners. They may know little about the human papillomavirus, gonorrhea, chlamydia, and other sexually transmitted diseases, yet be terrified of getting HIV and thus be willing to use protection. Nonetheless, broaching the subject of protection can be difficult, especially the first time, and some of us will experience one or more negative reactions and must be prepared for them.

If your list about possible losses from protecting yourself frightens you, ask yourself what the consequences of each loss would be. What will happen if your lover is angry? What will happen if he or she leaves you? Some of us may feel that the possible losses are too great to bear, or fear being beaten. The possibility of future disease and death can seem less frightening than the more immediate dangers of insisting on protected sex. If you come to this conclusion, you still have choices:

➤ Suggest mutual masturbation or other forms of safe intimacy without penetration. Besides masturbation, many forms of intimacy are very safe. Kissing, massage, fondling, rubbing against your partner and vice versa, erotic talk, singing or dancing, fantasizing, and using separate sex toys can all be arousing and lead to orgasm. You can also have oral sex that involves licking the vulva, vagina, or anus, but you do need to use ordinary plastic wrap for protection (see "Safer Sex," below). Many women and their partners discover exciting new possibilities in lovemaking and have more fun than before.

➤ If you are going to have vaginal intercourse, try using the female condom (see

"The Female Condom," below) rather than broaching the subject of a male condom.

➤ If you have trouble using a female condom, or if your partner's response to it is as negative as his response to the male condom, as a last resort use a less protective method, such as the diaphragm, the sponge, or the cervical cap, together with spermicide, or use spermicide alone. Have a less risky form of sex, such as oral sex without swallowing semen. (However, remember that anal intercourse is not a safer option unless your partner uses a male condom with a water-soluble lubricant.)

➤ Or use a condom or female condom as often as possible and refuse intercourse or use less effective barrier methods at other times.

Beware that negotiating male or female condom use in one sexual encounter does not guarantee that you will be able to do so in the next, even with the same person. Your feelings of self-esteem and power may vary in each sexual encounter, as will other elements of the situation. However, unless you fear violence for any delay in sex, you do have choices.

Many of us may be more concerned about the possible consequences of disease than by any loss of a partner's attention. Of course, we would prefer that a lover not be angry or turn away. When we are seriously, emotionally involved, the thought of possible anger or separation is extremely painful. However, when we ask ourselves if sex with this person is worth risking our lives, health, or fertility, the answer seems clear—either protection against sexually transmitted diseases or no sex. We may decide that if our partners care so little about our well-being, the relationship is not worth saving.

MAKING SAFER SEX PART OF YOUR LIFE

Once you have made a commitment to safer sex, teach yourself to incorporate contraceptive barriers into your lovemaking. If your partner uses a male condom, be sure that he wears it, and wears it properly. Be prepared by buying whatever protective barriers are appropriate for your sex life. Possibilities include the male condom, the female condom, plastic wrap, and finger cots (all discussed below in "Guidelines for Safer Sex"). Unless you have sex only at home with a long-term, live-in partner, carry barriers with you at all times, even if you think that you cannot possibly need them. (When at home, keep them in a cool, dry, but easily accessible place.) Being prepared may feel strange at first because it defies taboos against "premeditated" sex for women. With time, the protection you carry will become a reassuring reminder that you care about yourself. If you feel embarrassed about purchasing male or female condoms, remind yourself that they can be more vital to your health than vitamin pills, prescription drugs, or any other item that you would purchase without the least embarrassment. Remember, too, that our culture advertises and encourages the sale of tampons, menstrual pads, douches, diapers, and underpants—why not male and female condoms?

If you are not experienced in using barriers, take a good look at their textures and shapes, and practice using them. For example, you can practice putting in a female condom and practice male condom use by putting one on a banana. Some women teach themselves to put a condom on with their mouths as well as with their hands. Talk about barrier use with one or more trusted friends, relatives, teachers, counselors, or health care practitioners. You may also find a safer-sex lecture or workshop to attend. Practice until you feel entirely familiar with the devices and their use, as well as with any spermicide or lubricant you use with them. If you

I never used condoms before I found out my boyfriend had been sleeping with everyone. I said to him: "How could you have put me at such risk?"...I could have been sacrificed...So that's the one thing that I've done for myself after being so idealistic and unrealistic. I feel that any man who would bully me or sweet-talk me into it is either a liar or someone I don't respect.[2]

have decided that spermicide alone or together with diaphragm, sponge, or cervical cap are options for you, practice inserting or using them, and carry these backup choices with you, together with condoms.

At this point, you are ready for the next step: practicing self-assertion and self-esteem so that you feel empowered to choose male condoms, female condoms, plastic wrap, other protection, safe intimacy without penetration or blood transfer, or no sex at all.

Whatever choices you make for safer sex, prepare yourself to insist that your partner cooperate. Devices such as male or female condoms are partly visible, tangible barriers. You cannot rely on subterfuge as you can with devices such as the diaphragm, sponge, cervical cap, or spermicide, all of which you can wear or use without your partner's cooperation. You can put female condoms in, but using them depends on a partner's willingness.

You could begin by making a list of what you want to learn, and of any fears you may have. Many of the following suggestions pertain to vaginal intercourse but they can be modified for other forms of sex.

1. How do I broach the subject with my partner? What should I say?

What you say depends on your personality and on your relationship with your partner. A clear, direct statement is usually best: "I want to make love with you, but I don't have intercourse without using a male or female condom." Some women feel uncomfortable with such directness and prefer using humor or sexiness: "This thing [female condom] may look odd, but it's the latest fashion." Or: "You're going to love the way I put this [male condom] on you."

Possible Opening Lines[3]

This is awkward for me, but I've been thinking it would be a good idea to use _____.

I always use _____. I always have. It just makes sense with all the things you can catch.

I was in the drugstore today and saw a _____ display they just put up. It made me start thinking how things are changing.

I was talking with some friends the other day and they're all using _____ now just to be careful. I think it makes a lot of sense.

This whole AIDS thing has got me spooked. I'm not going to give up sex, but I'm going to play it safe and insist on using _____ every time I have sex.

Have I ever shown you my _____ collection?

Look what I bought today for us to try.

Listen, if we're going any further, let's use a _____.

You could remind your partner that a male condom can make an erection last longer. Many women and their partners enjoy incorporating safer sex into their lovemaking; for example, putting a male condom on your partner can be loving and erotic.

2. What if I feel too awkward to say anything and just can't do it?

You can bring up the subject without saying a word. Some women simply hand their partners a male condom, or put on their female condoms. Others prepare "condom cards," small greeting cards, sometimes with a simple text: "I trust you, and I've been true. This is just what smart people do." Or: "Thanks for showing you care, about me, about yourself, about us." Inside the card is a male condom.

3. What should I say/do if he or she gets angry? If he or she refuses?

Your partner may have any number of objections, for example:

It won't fit.

It will spoil the mood.

Sex is no fun with that thing.

Lesbians don't have to worry about STDs.

I *love* you! Would I give you an infection?

I can't get an erection when I wear a condom.

I was just tested for HIV and know that I'm not infected.

I guess you don't trust me if you think I might be infected.

You brought a *condom* with you? You were planning to seduce me!

Unless you know your partner well and feel comfortable with him or her, it is generally best to avoid discussion or argument. In response to all remarks or objections you can simply say: "I don't have sex without protection." You need not offer reasons, excuses, or apologies. Remember that requesting protected sex does not imply that you or your partner are cheating or promiscuous. One of you may have caught something from a single relationship in the past and not realize it. However, some women say that they feel more comfortable using an excuse rather than insisting on safer sex for the sake of their health. If this is true for you, use an excuse: "It's my time, and I don't want to get pregnant." Or: "My doctor told me to use this because STDs can cause infertility." Although excuses are not as convincing or empowering as assertive honesty, if they assure safer sex, use them. You can always change your tactics later on. If you want to enter into a discussion or offer your partner options, you are at an advantage if you have decided in advance what options you are willing to offer, as discussed above.

4. What should I do if he or she threatens to end our relationship?

Your partner may have a change of mind when he or she sees that you are serious, or he or she may go away and come back later, willing to use protection. You must decide for yourself to let your lover go ("My mind is made up. Let me know if you change yours.") or to use less effective alternatives such as spermicide alone or with a diaphragm, sponge, or cervical cap.

If you can, practice role-playing these situations with a man or woman you trust. Tell him or her to coerce, plead, shout, and threaten while you repeat the statements you have decided to use. For example: "I want to make love with you, but we must use a condom." Practice role-playing several times. As you practice, be aware of thoughts and actions, your own or your partner's, that can be particularly risky. For example:

1. Drinking alcohol or taking other drugs: Alcohol affects the brain and can impede your ability to make decisions, such as a decision to stop the physical advances of a partner you do not know well, or a decision to insist on the use of a male condom. Drinking alcohol decreases the tendency to choose protection before sex. Alcohol can also dull your perception of a partner's behavior and impair your physical ability to defend yourself. Taking other drugs can have the same effects. In addition, cocaine, including crack, increases the sexual urge, and addiction to any drug can lead to the exchange of sex for drugs, increasing your risk of disease. (Also, because of a drug's effects on behavior, be especially wary of a man or woman who has been drinking alcohol or who is taking other drugs.)

2. Assuming that your partner is not infected: Even if you have unprotected sex with only one partner, you put your health at risk because that person could be infected. Remember that, in most cases, sexually transmitted diseases have no visible symptoms. Even people whose present and past behavior put them at "low risk" for disease can carry a virus or bacteria. People sometimes lie to their partners about their past sexual experiences or drug use. Don't talk yourself out of protected sex. Some women sacrifice their health with misconceptions such as these:

(Fill in the blanks)

S/He's a _____ (lawyer, doctor, businessman, professor, Rhodes scholar, etc.), s/he couldn't *possibly* be infected.

But s/he's so _____ (well-groomed, charming, clean, articulate, well-mannered, educated, wealthy), I'm sure s/he's not infected.

3. Going on a date without taking a male or female condom or other appropriate protection with you: Remember, it is up to you to be prepared with protection. You cannot assume that your partner will know or initiate safer sex practices.

4. Having unprotected anal or oral sex: Keep in mind that unprotected anal intercourse can be even riskier than unprotected vaginal intercourse.

When you begin practicing your new behavior in real-life situations, write down or mentally note your successes or difficulties. Congratulate yourself on your successes, and note why you were successful. Also, analyze any situations in which you were unable to act according to your choice, whatever that choice may have been. Recreate the situation in your mind to discover what led to your inability:

➤ Fear of your partner's reactions?

➤ Desire to please your partner at all costs?

➤ Inhibition from speaking out because you felt awkward?

➤ Willingness to take the risk?

➤ No protection with you?

➤ Affected by alcohol or other drugs?

Study all past obstacles and learn from them, and from any obstacles that may lie ahead. In your mind, reconstruct negative experiences, but use new, empowering endings. Difficulties are not causes for discouragement but valuable experiences on your way toward change.

Once you discover the thoughts or behaviors that led to your difficulty, think of what you can do to change them. For example:

1. Remind yourself of what unprotected sex can mean, and reaffirm your commitment to change.

2. Imagine ways to make sex with barriers exciting.

3. Incorporate more self-assertive practice sessions into your life.

4. Tell someone of your commitment to change so that you can discuss successes or disappointments with her or him.

5. Examine your desire to please: What might the price of pleasing be? Is there something more important to you than your lover's approval?

6. Tell yourself empowering things, such as: "Its my body and my health. I have the right to protect my health and to decide whom I want to make love with and how."

Also, repeatedly remind yourself that you have the right to stop physical intimacy whenever you wish. Stopping is often difficult because you may not want to disappoint a partner and may feel guilty if he or she seems hurt or disappointed. Also, those of us who are heterosexual often want all kinds of loving intimacy short of intercourse. This fact can be difficult to convey to men, whose sexual pleasure is more likely to be focused on penetration.

In order to help yourself, you may decide to start your own practice and support group on assertive and safer sex by calling friends and putting an announcement in your local newspaper for women in your area. Keep in mind that as a woman trying to change your behavior, you may feel more comfortable with women who are in a similar life situation as your own, especially women with the same racial, ethnic, or social background. Also, if you take drugs or have a problem with alcohol, you are more likely to learn from, and with, women who have the same problem.

Through friends or through a local community center or public health department, you may be able to find a woman of similar background who has learned to practice safer sex and who now wants to help other women learn. Such women will understand the obstacles we must overcome in order to change. For example, many of us have been taught that intercourse is the only way to experience intimacy with a man. We need to talk about touching, caressing, fondling, and mutual masturbation, and to feel free to discuss intimacy without intercourse among people we trust and wish to imitate. Also, some of us tend to be exceptionally passive, strongly believing that being feminine means being unassertive. We need women who can be role models of empowering behavior, showing us that assertiveness is acceptable.

Because sex is normally a private activity, we usually do not see other women modeling more assertive behavior in sexual situations. Therefore, during one of your first group meetings, you might show and discuss a film on this subject. Some videos present women demonstrating how safer sex can be achieved. Such videos are equally useful for our male partners; they can see role models of men who understand the severity of sexually transmitted diseases and are comfortable expressing their love and concern for a woman they care about. (See "Resources" for videotapes.) Ideally, a variety of videos for heterosexual and lesbian women should be available, each with a focus on a specific racial, ethnic, or socio-economic group. The videos you choose should focus on healthful ways to talk and behave with a partner and show assertive women taking responsibility for their health. The videos can give you and your group ideas for discussion topics and illustrate how to practice self-protection.

In some cities, workshops on safer sex exist as part of community center programs, family planning programs, sexually transmitted disease clinics, drug treatment and prison programs, and through groups

In my marriage I was saying: "My husband wouldn't cheat on me!" But I finally had to learn to say: "I'm more important than my marriage. Whatever this guy has done, I have to save myself."

I was aware my husband was having casual sex when not with me, but I was too ashamed to ask him to take precautions. I kept telling myself, next time. My advice to [women] is, don't ever wait for next time. Now I have big regrets.[4]
—Woman with HIV

PID taught me to take control over my life; to control the things I could, and to let go of the other things. The most important lesson I learned was that I had to take care of myself. As a woman, in the face of great disapproval, I had to believe myself. Because I was told I didn't have pain when I did, I went around trying to believe that for a while. It sounds crazy to say that now. I think it was my upbringing that got me doing that. I was taught to be a good girl, and believe the doctor, and believe the nurse, and believe everybody else but myself.

of commercial sex workers. If you are a student, you may find that your school offers practice sessions on insisting on safer sex. You and your classmates "set the stage" for a sexually risky situation and take turns practicing the roles of the "couple." Together you decide what behaviors and what statements are most effective and practice these until you feel comfortable with them.

When You Have a Long-Term Partner

Each woman must decide for herself at what point she considers her relationship long-term and mutually monogamous, and therefore as safe as possible for unprotected sex. A guideline might be to ask yourself how long you and your partner have already been monogamous and whether you both feel committed to remaining so indefinitely. Dating someone regularly without an explicit commitment to monogamy is not a sufficient bond for unprotected sex.

Even when you reach this point, you cannot be certain that your partner has not been infected through a prior relationship. He or she may have been tested for HIV, yet carry gonorrhea, chlamydia, herpes, or the human papillomavirus without realizing it. Nowadays, many forms of physical love cannot be called "safe," only "as safe as possible." Even those of us who have been married or living with a partner for years must take this into account.

Some women make a pact with their husbands or partners that neither of them will have sex with anyone else. Some couples make a pact that requires telling each other of any outside intimacy before making love with the regular partner again. But such pacts can be very hard to make. Love and physical affection are based on trust. Bringing up the possibility of an outside relationship seems to imply that you or your partner could break a trust, or that the commitment you both now feel could someday weaken. Here again, each woman

must decide for herself whether she wishes to suggest such a pact and use her self-esteem to carry her through the negotiation with her partner. However, you must remember that your partner might lie to you even after a pact has been made. You also may find that you are not willing to tell if you break the pact.

Learning the Hard Way

The goal of all our efforts to make safer sex a habit is to avoid the suffering and possible death resulting from sexually transmitted diseases. For these reasons, we want to learn to stand up for ourselves and be insistent and assertive. We want to act according to our belief that our health is more important than a partner's pleasure or companionship. However, too many of us have had to learn through illness what the cost of wanting to please can be. Instead of learning self-assertive sexual protection as young girls, it is the years of battling with a sexually transmitted disease that have given us the strength and determination to stop risking our health in order to please and to start protecting ourselves.

We have also learned that our desire to please and our lack of self-confidence are not limited to our relationships with our lovers. Many of us who are or have been ill with a sexually transmitted disease have experienced these same traits when we had to see a medical practitioner, especially a male physician. We do not want to offend someone by questioning his or her knowledge, and we fear challenging a medical practitioner on whom we feel dependent. We may have felt afraid of the disease and its treatments, further weakening our self-esteem. Given the authority that U.S. physicians have, and given our dependence on medical practitioners when we are ill, many of us have found self-assertion in the doctor's office a formidable challenge.

GUIDELINES FOR SAFER SEX

While the following guidelines should aid your practice of safer sex, remember that even safer sex practices are not 100 percent effective. However, consistent, correct, and regular use of safer sex will provide the best possible protection.

The words "cover up" describe all of the most effective safer sex techniques. You should use a barrier against blood and penile or vaginal secretions that might contain harmful bacteria or viruses. The barrier should block the fluids and keep them from coming into contact with your most vulnerable body surfaces: the vagina, cervix, anus, throat, cuts or open sores on your body, and at times, the mouth. For vaginal, anal, or oral intercourse with a man, cover his penis with a new male condom each time or use a female condom for vaginal intercourse. Spermicides may help provide a good barrier. For sex involving licking the vagina or anus, cover those parts with plastic wrap or latex.

If fingers penetrate a part of the body, cover them with latex gloves or finger cots (single finger covers). If you use objects for penetration, cover them with a condom. Use a different cover for each person who uses the object. With latex products, including condoms, use only water-based lubrication, no Vaseline or lotion. (See accompanying box for a list of lubricants.) Store latex in a cool place, though you can keep it in a wallet next to your body or in your purse for up to a month. If you need birth control as well as protection, remember that nonbarrier methods, such as hormonal contraceptives and IUD, do not protect you from disease. Either add a barrier to your current birth-control method or switch to a method that affords protection both from pregnancy and from disease.

Cover up from start to finish. Male condoms need to go on a male partner from his first erection through withdrawal of the penis after ejaculation. Spermicides need to be inserted before genital contact that could lead to intercourse. Do not put your mouth on your partner's genitals or anus before applying plastic wrap. However, you probably can safely lick the shaft of a man's penis and his scrotum without protection as long as no blood or sores are present.

Cover up every time. No one can say whether any one sexual experience will give you a sexually transmissible disease. Some infections spread from partner to partner nearly every time an infected person has sex. Other infections are less likely to take hold, but sometimes just one sexual contact suffices for infection. Even if you have not always covered up in the past, you are better off using safer sex precautions from now on. Remember that any sexual practices that cause bleeding or irritation can increase your vulnerability. Because we often make love in the dark or do not notice irritations until afterward, we cannot always avoid them. Also, we are generally unaware of tiny tears in the walls of the vagina and anus. These are further reasons to cover up all the time.

As a general rule, for vaginal intercourse a physical barrier plus a spermicide is the most effective protection. Either a physical barrier or a spermicide alone is the next best option. Although male condoms are currently promoted as the best single method of preventing the spread of diseases, female barriers may be just as or more effective in practice. Spermicides may be better than is generally believed. But for anal intercourse and mouth-to-penis oral sex, a male condom is best.

If you think that these precautions will inhibit pleasurable, spontaneous sex, think again. With protection, you and your partner can penetrate and lick anywhere on your bodies without worrying. You have a new set of sex toys. For instance, you can suck on a latex barrier to create little bubbles, stimulating sensitive body parts for increased pleasure. As you become more adept at using protection and also associate it with arousal, you probably will find it sexy. Gay men have generated enthusiasm for protection by eroticizing safer sex, and some lesbian women have also made efforts in this direction. Heterosexual people need to learn that safer sex brings new ways to explore and enjoy sex, not deprivation.

The following advice on specific methods of protection against sexually transmissible diseases is based on current research, which is meager. As more research is done, recommendations may change.

The Male Latex Condom

The most versatile barrier is the male latex condom. It can be used during vaginal, anal, or mouth-to-penis oral sex and on sex toys of the right shape. It probably can block all of the organisms that cause sexually transmissible diseases because (at least in laboratory tests) it is impermeable even to the tiny HIV. Although good research is limited, it does show that male condoms, when used consistently and properly, reduce the risk of infections. For couples experienced in using male condoms, this method is also very effective for birth control, as effective as the birth control pill.[5] By inference then, proper and consistent condom use should tremendously reduce your risk of catching viral and bacterial infections. In Nevada brothels, where male condom use has been mandated since 1988, the regular testing of sex workers has found few cases of sexually transmitted diseases, and no cases of HIV.[6]

Lubricant Use with Latex Barriers

With latex barriers you can safely use:

Water-soluble lubricants: K-Y Jelly, Ortho Lubricant, Astro-Glide, Probe, saliva, and water

Lubricants with spermicide: creams and jellies such as Ramses, Koromex, Conceptrol disposable or creme, and Ortho-Gynol Contraceptive Jelly

Lubricants such as ForPlay, Lubraceptic, and PrePair Lubricant Foams such as Delfen and Emko

These substances harm latex barriers:

Petroleum jelly (Vaseline and other brands); baby oil; mineral oil; suntan oils; hand cream or lotions; vegetable oils, such as olive, peanut, corn, sunflower, palm or coconut; solidified or hydrogenated vegetable oils, such as Crisco or store-brand equivalents; fish oils; butter, margarine, and coconut butter; lard; insect repellents; burn ointments; hemorrhoidal ointments; and rubbing alcohol

These substances *may* harm latex barriers:

Monistat vaginal cream for yeast infections; Estrace vaginal cream; Femstat vaginal cream; Vagisil ointment; Rendell's Cone vaginal spermicide; Pharmatex Ovule vaginal spermicide; Premarin vaginal cream; Elbow Grease and Elbow Grease Hot and Shaft sexual lubricants

Male condoms do have some drawbacks. Effectiveness depends on consistent and correct use, which is often not controlled by women. Also, many people do not realize that using a male condom incorrectly can cause leaks and breaks. Although a male condom is not complicated, even commercial sex workers who might be expected to know how to use one properly do not always know how. In one study of ninety-one sex workers, fewer than 20 percent were able to correctly put a male condom onto a plastic model of a penis, and 7 percent made errors severe enough to cause the condom to break.[7] Both women and men are sometimes embarrassed about condoms and may refuse to use them, particularly if they are trying to hide their inexperience with them. Some of us, and not only men, worry that condoms change sensations or obstruct "natural," spontaneous sex. A man may avoid condoms out of fear of losing his erection.

Also, male condoms obviously cannot prevent the spread of sexually transmissible organisms from a part of the body that the latex does not cover, such as an HPV infection on the scrotum. In addition, the condom may irritate the vagina or cause painful friction sores in women who regularly have intercourse several times a day or who have prolonged sex. Some of us are allergic to latex, and unfortunately, natural skin condoms may let viruses pass through. (Polyurethane condoms, which are not permeable to viruses and bacteria, are being developed.)

Using a spermicide together with a male condom for vaginal intercourse gives additional protection. Some male condoms are coated with a spermicide, but researchers do not know if, in actual practice, these condoms are more effective than uncoated ones. Also, spermicide-coated male condoms may be too irritating to use in the anus and would not taste good during oral sex.

With a male condom, be sure not to use too much lubrication on the inside or the condom may slide off. If you use two male condoms simultaneously ("double bagging"), do not use any lubrication between the two condoms.

You may wish to use water-based lubrication, which may come with the condom or be applied separately. Lubrication is necessary during anal sex to reduce friction and make condom breakage less likely.

The Female Condom (also called Reality Condom or Vaginal Pouch)

The female condom (see illustration) can be used for vaginal sex. Although it is still too new for extensive or long-term testing, the polyurethane of which it is made has been shown in laboratory tests to block organisms that cause diseases. Theoretically, the female condom should be able to protect us even better than the male condom because the outer part of the female condom covers the labia. In fact, statistics already suggest that the female condom is highly effective against trichomoniasis, when used properly and consistently.[8] Female condoms are packaged with lubricant and complete instructions. Studies so far show that women and men can feel comfortable using the female condom and can do so correctly, especially after the third or fourth time. Some women and men prefer the material of the female condom to latex. It is especially useful for women whose male partners cannot or will not use a male condom. One researcher in New York City has found from informal conversations that many women who use the female condom feel more empowered using it than using the male condom. These women find that men are more cooperative when they do not have to stop to put a protective condom on themselves.[9] However, the female condom is more expensive than the male condom.

Spermicides (Creams, Jellies, and Foams)

If you are not irritated by them, spermicides can be used for vaginal and anal sex.

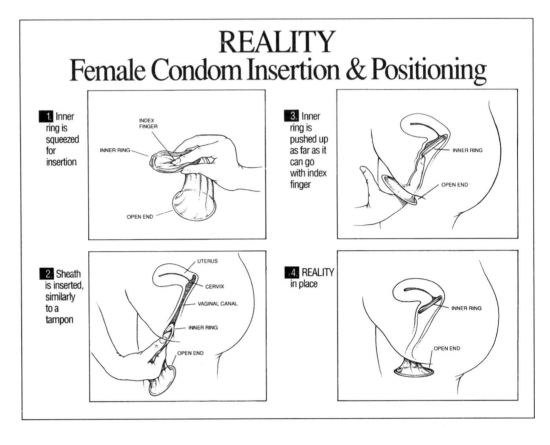

REALITY
Female Condom Insertion & Positioning

1. Inner ring is squeezed for insertion

INDEX FINGER

INNER RING

OPEN END

2. Sheath is inserted, similarly to a tampon

UTERUS

CERVIX

VAGINAL CANAL

INNER RING

OPEN END

3. Inner ring is pushed up as far as it can go with index finger

INNER RING

OPEN END

4. REALITY in place

INNER RING

OPEN END

Nonoxynol-9 and octoxynol-9 are the only two spermicides available in the United States. They are equally effective in destroying the organisms that cause sexually transmitted diseases, but nonoxynol-9 is far more common. Spermicides also provide lubrication, reducing problems caused by friction, such as small tears in the vaginal or anal walls or condom breakage. Nonoxynol-9 used alone can reduce your risk of catching chlamydia, gonorrhea, and trichomonas, and may be effective against the herpes virus. Studies on the effectiveness of nonoxynol-9 against HIV are conflicting. In the laboratory, it kills HIV. In actual practice, in one poorly done study, the spermicide did not seem to make any difference, while in two better studies it seemed to provide significant protection. A well-designed study is under way and may have results soon. Unfortunately, though, some women find spermicides irritating, especially in very high doses, and some researchers speculate that the irritation could make a woman more vulnerable to HIV infection.

To find out if you react to a spermicide, rub it on a sensitive skin area such as the inside of your arm or thigh. You might also masturbate with it. If one brand of spermicide causes irritation, itching, soreness, or redness, try another.

Nonoxynol-9's effectiveness against the human papillomavirus is currently unknown. However, retrospective studies show that women who use spermicides have lower rates of cervical cancer than those who use no protection.

The Diaphragm
Diaphragms are useful for vaginal sex. However, by itself, the diaphragm is not an effective barrier against sexually transmissible diseases and must be used with

spermicidal jelly or cream. The diaphragm holds the spermicide right around the cervix without forming a tight seal over the cervix. The placement of the spermicide is particularly effective against bacterial organisms such as gonorrhea and chlamydia that must enter the cervix to infect your reproductive tract. Spermicide and a diaphragm should also lower rates of cervical cancer. The diaphragm, however, does not protect most of the vagina, which may be important for HIV and possibly for HPV infections. If, however, the cervix is much more vulnerable to HIV infection than the walls of the vagina, as some researchers speculate, positioning the spermicide over the cervix may provide significant protection. Insert some extra nonoxynol-9 cream or jelly into your vagina after inserting the diaphragm just in case the spermicide is definitively proven effective against HPV and HIV.

The Contraceptive Sponge

The contraceptive sponge is used only in the vagina and contains the spermicide nonoxynol-9 in concentrations three to six times that of other birth control preparations. Its effectiveness against diseases is probably the same as spermicide alone since the sponge acts primarily as a holder of the spermicide rather than as a physical barrier.

The Cervical Cap

The cervical cap is effective during vaginal sex because it forms a physical barrier over the cervix to block organisms such as gonococcus and chlamydia, which can infect the cervix. As added protection, you should put spermicide in the cap before inserting it, although a properly fitted cap will form a seal around the cervix. Like the diaphragm, the cap does not prevent infection from entering through the vagina. Putting extra

nonoxynol-9 on the vaginal wall outside the cap after inserting it may increase its effectiveness.

Plastic Wrap, Gloves, and Finger Cots

Some intimacies other than vaginal or anal intercourse and mouth-to-penis oral sex can spread disease unless you use protection. These can be intimacies among women or with a male partner. Here again, the basic rule is to cover up—place a barrier between a vulnerable part of your body and your partner's body fluids. To penetrate the vagina or anus, cover fingers with latex gloves or finger cots, which you can buy in any drugstore. (You can cut single fingers from latex gloves to make your own finger cots.) If you and your partner share an object to penetrate a body part, use a fresh covering for each penetration. Never reuse a piece of plastic wrap, finger cot, glove, or condom.

Some safer sex guidelines for oral sex with a woman recommend only dental dams (small squares of latex available from dental supply houses). However, plastic wrap is much easier to get (it is available in any grocery store), is impermeable to organisms, and is not harmed by certain lubricants or foods the way latex is. (However, neither plastic wrap nor latex have been tested outside the laboratory to determine their effectiveness in actual use for oral sex.) You can use any kind of plastic wrap made for food. Other plastic films may contain toxins.

Other flat barriers can be made by cutting a condom or a latex glove. With a condom, flatten an unlubricated condom by cutting off the closed end and then slitting the cylinder lengthwise. You also can cut the fingers off a latex glove (save them for finger cots) and slit the rest of the glove on one side to get a fairly large piece of latex. To be safest, discard after one use. Remember, with latex, you must not use oil-based lubricants or oily foods.

If you stop making love and then start again, use a fresh piece of plastic or latex because you may not be able to tell which side was previously against the body. A small dab of lubrication on the side of the person being licked may increase sensation.

DETECTION AND TREATMENT OF SEXUALLY TRANSMISSIBLE DISEASES

For anyone who has ever had unprotected sex, or has used unclean needles, it is important to be aware of the symptoms of sexually transmissible diseases, as well as our options for testing and treatment. Though practicing safer sex greatly reduces infection rates, even protection cannot offer full assurance that we will not get infected.

Detecting and Treating HPV and Cervical Irregularities

Some forms of HPV can be detected easily by looking for genital warts; unfortunately, these are not the infections that are most dangerous. In addition, the effectiveness of barriers against HPV has not been well studied, but it certainly is not 100 percent. What else can we do, then, to protect ourselves from cervical cancer? Pap tests can identify early changes in cervical cells, and these abnormal cells can then be removed long before they might develop into cervical cancer. During a Pap test your medical practitioner may also be alerted to signs that you have a chlamydial, gonococcal, or other infection.

Many women are understandably confused about the purpose of a Pap test, and sometimes mistake it for a test for the AIDS virus, a pregnancy test, or think that it is a way to diagnose any abnormality in a woman's reproductive organs. Actually, the Pap test is a sample of cervical cells and indicates if the cervical cells sampled are healthy or abnormal. In other words, an abnormal Pap smear signals that there may be problems in the cervical area and that further testing is necessary to verify this finding and to ascertain what these problems might be. The Pap test gives no information on the health of the uterus, fallopian tubes, and ovaries.

Taking a Pap smear is part of a pelvic examination. Your medical care practitioner inserts a metal or plastic speculum into your vagina so that she or he can see your cervix. She or he then rubs an instrument such as a wooden or plastic scraper across the cervix to collect a sample of cells, spreads the cells onto a glass slide, and sends it to a laboratory to be examined under a microscope. The procedure should not be painful. At least two samples should be taken, including one from the cervical canal, to maximize the likelihood of getting cells from the most crucial area, the transformation zone. When you have your pelvic exam and Pap test, ask your practitioner to also look carefully for suspicious lesions or sores on your genitals, anus, or in your cervix. If any are found, she or he should take a sample to be examined at a laboratory.

Often cervical cells that are called abnormal are not cells that could ever evolve into cancer. Cell changes in the cervix are common, and most are temporary. For example, when you have a cervical or vaginal infection, or when your cervix is in the process of healing after an infection, IUD insertion, abortion, or childbirth, your Pap smear will show inflamed cells. If you use tampons, you may want to try switching to pads or reusable cloths for a few months before having another test.

Although inflammations do not progress to cancer, they can obscure other conditions, making it wise to have another Pap test once the inflammation has subsided. In addition, a cervical inflammation of any kind may make your cervical cells more susceptible to HIV. Some infections, such as trichomoniasis, that can cause inflamed cells, can increase your risk of more severe conditions later on. Other infections, such as chlamydia and gonorrhea, warrant immediate treatment to prevent their spread.

If you have abnormal cells on your Pap smear that are not obviously due to inflammation, you have a decision to make about the next step. If your abnormality is slight, some physicians suggest waiting three months, then having a second Pap smear to see if the results are still abnormal. Others suggest that it is best to have a colposcopy, an examination of your cervix through a set of magnifying binoculars. If your original Pap smear showed high-grade abnormalities, physicians agree that an immediate colposcopy should be the next step. You will not be treated to determine which type or types of HPV you might have because these tests are costly, and their usefulness as aids in making treatment choices has not been tested. If you have HIV and have any kind of abnormal Pap smear, ask about the latest medical consensus on how to proceed.

If the results of your colposcopy indicate suspicious areas in your cervix, or if your practitioner finds that problem areas may lie in the endocervical canal, which is outside the range of the colposcope, an endocervical curettage as well as a biopsy may be required. Both procedures are done in your practitioner's office. For the endocervical curettage, your practitioner takes a long-stemmed instrument called a curette and scrapes the cervix, collecting cervical tissue fragments, blood, and mucus to be sent to a pathologist for evaluation under a microscope. The procedure can cause some discomfort, but it is quickly over.

The biopsy, called a multiple punch biopsy, is done during the examination by colposcopy. Your practitioner inserts a small instrument into your cervix, and while looking through the colposcope, removes tiny tissue samples from every suspicious-looking area as well as from normal-looking areas. A pathologist then examines the samples under a microscope to make a diagnosis. The multiple punch biopsy is usually somewhat painful and may cause some bleeding. Unless your physician has discovered a suspicious lesion on your cervix visible to the naked eye, do not agree to a punch biopsy or to any further procedures unless a colposcopy has first been performed.

After a curettage and punch biopsy, if your physician is unable to make a clear diagnosis, she or he may recommend a cone biopsy, the surgical removal of a cone-shaped piece of cervical tissue. After the biopsy, a pathologist examines the tissue under a microscope to ensure that all borders of the abnormal area were removed. If a cone biopsy successfully removes all suspicious areas, it is a treatment as well as the means of diagnosis.

Unanswered questions face us if we discover that we have HPV. If warts or microscopic lesions are found, they can be removed by a number of different methods, but their removal does not eradicate the problem. No existing treatment has been proven to cure either women or men of HPV. The virus evidently remains in skin or mucous membranes that appear normal, and microscopic lesions or warts frequently reappear. Some preliminary data suggest that women who simply leave the lesions or warts alone may fare just as well as women who have them removed, and that having them removed by laser may actually worsen the condition.[10] No one knows if removal of HPV warts reduces the risk of passing HPV on to a partner. Therefore, unless a wart is irritating or uncomfortable, there is currently no reason to have it removed. We need more research to provide us with guidelines on what steps, if any, to take against the microscopic lesions or warts caused by the underlying HPV infection as well as the infection itself. Unfortunately, many of us probably undergo treatment for warts and microscopic lesions in the mistaken belief that we are eradicating the infection and eliminating our risk of developing cervical cancer.

However, if abnormal cells have already developed into cervical dysplasia or cervical intraepithelial neoplasia, treatment is important. Adequate treatment requires that your physician fully understand what is known of the process of cervical cell abnormality. If the abnormality is very mild, you and your physician may decide to wait and see if your condition heals spontaneously. Or your physician may find that the abnormal cells look too far advanced to be left alone and suggest one of two options, both of them office procedures.

The first option is for your physician to freeze cells in the cervix by applying nitrous oxide or other chemicals, a procedure called cryotherapy. The frozen cells then slough off. For severely abnormal areas, freezing the cells twice seems to bring more reliable results. Cryotherapy may cause a vaginal discharge that should subside within a maximum of six weeks.

The second option is for your physician to use a laser to destroy the abnormal tissue, a technique called laser vaporization. While looking at your cervix through a colposcope, your physician will apply the laser to the abnormal cells and vaporize them.

Both techniques are generally painless, have a high success rate, and will not interfere with your ability to conceive or bear children. However, both procedures require physicians with training and experience, especially with the use of a colposcope and laser.

If your abnormal cells extend outside of the range of vision by colposcopy, your physician may recommend a cone biopsy, as described above. If the cone biopsy fails to show a margin of normal cells, a more extensive cone biopsy may succeed. If the second attempt also fails, your physician may recommend a hysterectomy, the surgical removal of the uterus. Before you make a decision on this major surgery, try to get a second and even third opinion from other practitioners. Remember that even cells that are highly abnormal do not always progress to cancer. Besides weighing the practitioners' arguments, weigh your ability to live with uncertainty. Also, if you are premenopausal, you may also wish to consider your desire to bear children.

If your cervical cells are already cancerous, your physician will attempt to discover how far they have spread, though it is very difficult to ascertain the extent of the cancer's spread with any certainty. Cancer cells can invade some tissues without being detected by any available methods, and they can also enter the body's fluids, such as the bloodstream and lymphatic system, and then spread through the body without detection.

The appropriate treatment will depend on the (detected) extent of your cancer as well as on your age and overall health. The possibilities include some form of surgery, such as an extensive cone biopsy; removal of the cervix and uterus, called a hysterectomy; or a hysterectomy plus removal of the pelvic lymph nodes. Your therapy may also include radiation, alone or in combination with surgery or chemotherapy.

In general, if the cancer has not spread widely and can be completely surgically removed, you can consider yourself cured. Otherwise, cervical cancer may eventually spread in spite of all treatments, although the treatments may slow the disease, enabling you to live a full life for many years after diagnosis. Women who have been diagnosed as having widespread cervical cancer will want to carefully weigh the proven benefits of any treatment against the temporary or prolonged disability that the treatments themselves can cause. Try to find an experienced, knowledgeable practitioner who can tell you the results of ongoing studies, called prospective randomized trials, or who can tell you about the most recent research that pertains to your particular stage of the disease.

Detecting and Treating Pelvic Inflammatory Disease

You may first suspect that you are infected with gonorrhea, chlamydia, or both if you develop an unusual vaginal discharge, have difficult or painful urination, or need to urinate unusually frequently or urgently or, if you are premenopausal, if you experience bleeding between periods or unusually profuse menstrual bleeding. These symptoms can be mild or severe, and can occur singly or in combination. They may be signs that your cervix and probably your urethra, the opening to your bladder, are infected. When early symptoms appear, they do not usually begin until two to ten days after infection. You may not interpret mild symptoms as having any significance, and both you and your medical care practitioner may easily mistake symptoms of gonorrhea or chlamydia for a urinary tract or vaginal infection.

According to the standard definition of PID, the most common symptom is abdominal pain, the symptom of spreading gonorrhea or chlamydia that brings infected women to medical practitioners more often than any other symptom. A woman may also feel pain during intercourse, or when her cervix is moved during a pelvic exam, and experience pelvic cramping when not menstruating or more severe cramping than usual during menstruation. Other signs of PID may or may not accompany the pain. These include unusual discharge from the cervix or unusually profuse or painful menstruation, nausea, vomiting, chills, fever, and frequent stools or passing of mucus. But many women have no symptoms at all until the organisms spread to other organs, causing considerable, sometimes irreversible damage.

Most women with cervicitis, an inflamed cervix, have no revealing symptoms. As a result, many of us do not discover that we have cervicitis and therefore do nothing to prevent the infection from spreading. If you are accustomed to examining your cervix using a speculum, you may notice that it looks redder and larger than usual, or that it is secreting an unusual-looking mucus. Similarly, if you have a Pap smear that shows the presence of inflamed

I was struck by how probabilities and statistics don't really matter in the most basic way. For example, my doctor said that if I did not have a second, more extensive cone biopsy, there was a 90 percent chance things would be okay anyway. But she added: "That would leave a one out of ten chance of developing cancer." While 90 percent sounded okay, one out of ten suddenly sounded awful.

After five days in the hospital they put me on oral antibiotics and sent me home. Bang! Two weeks later I got another fever. I still had diarrhea, and they kept telling me it was because of the medication. I called my doctor, an ob/gyn, and he said: "Don't worry about it, just keep taking your medication, and take aspirin as well." When I came down with a sudden fever the third time, I called my doctor back and said: "Look, I've got another fever. Do you think the PID is back?" And he said: "No, the flu is going around. I think it's probably just the flu." When I finally went to the hospital because I was so sick I had to, they found that fluid was building in my fallopian tubes, which meant that I had salpingitis.

cervical cells, gonorrhea or chlamydia are two possible causes of the inflammation. During the examination, your physician may also discover a yellow- or green-tinged mucus in your cervix, unusual bleeding, or swelling of an area of the cervix, all signs that you should have further testing to confirm that you do have an inflammation and to find out the cause.

Gonococcus, chlamydia, and other harmful bacteria can spread past the cervix more easily if the body's natural protective system is disrupted. For example, after intercourse, after menstruation, or simply as part of routine practice, many of us regularly wash our vaginas with water and vinegar or with a store-bought solution. This procedure is called douching, and though popular, it has no proven benefit. The vagina is not meant to be sterile. It normally keeps its own healthy balance of organisms that discourage foreign bacteria from causing harm. Douching may make the vagina less effective in defending itself. In addition, the douching process usually involves squeezing the liquid into the vagina using a bulb-type bag with a nozzle. We can easily exert enough pressure in squeezing to force some liquid through the opening of the cervix, possibly flushing harmful bacteria into the uterus. Some statistics suggest that women who douche three or more times a month are over three times more likely to have PID than are women who do not douche at all.[11]

Procedures that involve inserting an instrument through the cervix into the uterus can also spread bacteria. Such procedures include the insertion of an intrauterine device (IUD) as a birth control device; the insertion of instruments for a dilation and curettage (D and C), vacuum abortion, or endometrial biopsy, or to diagnose or treat health problems involving the uterus, to perform an abortion or complete a miscarriage, or the use of an invasive procedure during childbirth, such as an internal fetal monitor or forceps. You should request a test for gonorrhea and chlamyd-

ia, as well as for other organisms that may contribute to PID before undergoing any such procedure.[12] If tests reveal an infection, treatment before undergoing the procedure is best. If this is not possible, start treatment as soon after the procedure as you can.

The best test for gonorrhea in women is a culture test. The medical practitioner takes a swab of the discharge and cells of the cervix and sends them to be cultured (growing the bacteria on a special medium in a laboratory). The results take several days. The culture test also allows the laboratory to check for drug resistance so that the most appropriate antibiotic can be selected. Another test, the gram stain, can be done in a few minutes but is only accurate for diagnosing men; it misses about half the infections in women.

Testing for chlamydia is now often done with one of several monoclonal antibody tests, using a swab from the cervix. The results are available in about fifteen minutes. Although a culture test for chlamydia is still considered the "gold standard" for accuracy, monoclonal antibody tests are nearly as accurate. The culture test is more expensive to perform and results take several days.

If gonorrhea, chlamydia, or combined gonorrhea and chlamydia infection is discovered before it spreads beyond the cervix, antibiotic treatment should cure it before it causes any damage. If you have one or more regular male partners, all of them should be treated, and women partners should probably be tested. (This may also be a good time for you to consider being tested for HIV.)

To be sure that your medical practitioner is using the most recent treatment guidelines for gonorrhea and chlamydia, contact the Centers for Disease Control and Prevention (CDCP) hotline (see "Resources") for recommendations. (They will give you general information, but for information on specific dosages, your health-care provider must call the hotline personally.) While the CDCP may lag in its educational efforts, generally it uses the latest research in treatment guidelines. Urban hospital clinics for sexually transmissible diseases, which treat large numbers of people, usually use current CDCP guidelines, while doctors in private practice are less likely to be up to date. When you contact the CDCP, ask what follow-up procedures are necessary to make sure that the treatment has completely eliminated the bacteria. Without proper follow-up, you risk having a lingering infection that could flare up later.

If scarring and abscesses have formed as a result of severe infection, you may need to be hospitalized and have intravenous antibiotics, which can be given in much higher doses than oral antibiotics. Several courses of treatment over a period of months or years may be necessary to kill all of the bacteria. If antibiotics are not sufficient, surgical removal of diseased tissue may be the only way to restore health.

Detecting and Treating HIV and AIDS

Most women (and men) probably do not know when they were exposed to HIV and are not aware of any symptoms when first infected. However, some people recall that they may have had a flu-like illness with swollen glands when they first became infected with HIV. Approximately 50 percent of newly infected people have this illness two to twelve weeks after infection.[13] The most frequent initial symptoms of HIV infection are fever, swollen glands, sore throat, rash, and muscle or joint pain. Many people who have these symptoms go to their doctors for diagnosis and treatment. However, these complaints are so common that neither patient nor medical practitioner may think of testing for HIV. A person may otherwise feel healthy for years after being infected. Other symptoms that may occur are fatigue, fever, chills, night sweats, weight loss, loss of appetite, headache, blurred vision, insomnia, confusion, concentration problems, sore mouth, trouble swallowing, cough, shortness of breath, nausea, vomiting, and/or diarrhea.

A woman may also notice recurring vaginal yeast infections. We may not seek medical care for vaginal yeast infections, which can usually be treated with over-the-counter medications. These infections are so common that it took several years for doctors to acknowledge that severe and recurrent infections could be a sign of HIV disease. Some say two to four times as many yeast infections as a woman's previous rate, others say eight or more yeast infections a year indicate immune system changes.[14] If a medical practitioner does not suspect HIV disease, she or he will not look further for other corroborating symptoms.

As the immune system declines, symptoms of opportunistic infections will increase. Opportunistic infections result from organisms that ordinarily pose no significant threat to humans and can multiply only when the immune system is not functioning well. A woman may develop white hairy-looking marks on the tongue called oral hairy leukoplakia, or shingles caused by the herpes virus. The herpes virus normally lies quiescent most of the time, occasionally causing a few very irritating and uncomfortable sores that go away on their own. If your immune system is compromised, though, you may experience a more severe outbreak of herpes sores that may erupt in your throat or lungs, or in the form of shingles with sores that can erupt on the face, scalp, torso, arms, or legs. A woman may experience skin infections caused by bacteria, fungi, or parasites. For women, many of these symptoms may be attributed to psychological causes or may not be recognized as symptoms of HIV disease because medical practitioners might not consider HIV disease as a possibility. As the immune system continues to decline, opportunistic infections and diseases will become more serious, and can include certain forms of pneumonia and cancer.

Women report a somewhat different

constellation of symptoms from men. One study showed that women most often first noticed recurrent vaginal yeast infections or oral hairy leukoplakia. Most women had these symptoms, sometimes for years, before developing more serious problems. Next, about a sixth had swollen lymph glands; slightly fewer developed bacterial pneumonia. Of all symptoms, vaginal yeast infection was by far the most prevalent, then oral, throat and esophageal yeast or thrush, herpes, bacterial pneumonia, and pneumocystis carinii pneumonia, also known as PCP. Women were less likely than men to have Kaposi's sarcoma and PCP, though other statistics suggest that PCP is the most common opportunistic infection in women. Genital warts were also common but perhaps not more so than in the general population.

You can find out whether or not you are infected by having a blood test for antibodies to HIV. The various antibody tests are easier and much cheaper to do than testing directly for the virus. Antibodies are specific proteins made by the immune system to inactivate unwanted organisms. Antibodies to HIV provide an unknown amount of protection against the virus. They usually appear a few weeks to six months after infection, though most appear within three months. Very rarely, it can take as long as eighteen months for an antibody test to become positive. When you have no antibodies, the results are called seronegative or HIV-negative. If you have antibodies or develop them after a prior negative test, the results are called seropositive or HIV-positive.

Where you go for a test for HIV, regardless of the results, can have a profound effect on many areas of your life, from job discrimination and your ability to get medical insurance, to whether you can control decisions about who is allowed to know your test results. Before getting an HIV test, be sure to find out if the testing will be done anonymously or confidentially. If you are tested anonymously, you will be given a code number to use and your name will not be recorded. Taking the test anonymously gives you the chance to decide who will know about your test and who will not. Remember, however, that if your test is HIV-positive, you owe it to yourself and your partner or partners to seek immediate professional care and advice. Do not let the initial shock keep you from taking action.

Confidential testing is different. If you are tested confidentially, you must rely on your medical practitioner not to tell anybody. If you have a primary care physician, you might prefer being tested by that person because it could affect your care. The result, whether positive or negative, will probably be put in your medical records, and laboratories that do the tests keep records, though they may use a code number rather than your name. Your state may have a law preventing the dissemination of information about your HIV status from medical records without explicit permission, yet errors can occur. If no law exists and the information is in your records, insurance companies will be able to get it. In addition, when you apply for a job, school, medical, or life insurance, you may need to show your medical records. People may then discriminate against you because of your HIV status or even for having taken the test, though you may not be able to prove blatant discrimination. You may not want your family, friends, or landlord to have any possible way to find out your HIV status unless you tell them. If you are asked to sign a form indicating that you have received pretest counseling, you are getting a confidential test, not an anonymous one. If you can only obtain confidential testing but want anonymity, consider using a false name.

Do not confuse testing to find out if you have HIV with testing for screening. Screening involves testing a group of people in order to find out which groups are most likely to have HIV and also to track the rates and spread of the virus. Another reason to screen is to discard infected products, such as blood for transfusions. Government agencies or researchers screen blood samples from people without asking their permission. This is supposed to be done anonymously, and if your blood is tested under these circumstances, you are unlikely to find out if you have the virus. If you donate blood through the Red Cross, however, and the test is positive, you will be notified. Have another test to check the result because the test for screening blood donations is different from the ones for testing individuals and sometimes gives a false positive result when no antibodies to HIV are actually present.

Treatment for HIV is still an ongoing experiment with new drugs and drug combinations continually being tested. No treatment yet can rid the body of HIV, but many drugs and procedures can slow down the progression of the disease, as well as treat opportunistic infections and cancers. As a result, many women live several years after diagnosis instead of several weeks or months. Unfortunately, research on understanding and treating HIV disease has concentrated on men and has been oblivious to the different ways that HIV affects women. Treatments are also expensive, which means that those of us who have no medical insurance, including Medicaid, often cannot afford to be treated. In addition, many treatments are experimental and thus not covered by insurance. Many people with HIV disease have also tried alternative therapies such as acupuncture, Chinese and Western herbs, and massage with some relief of symptoms. Some people say that these techniques make them feel physically better, more relaxed, and better prepared to fight the virus.

Recognizing the signs that the immune system is severely debilitated can lengthen our lives considerably. Certain medicines that inhibit the replication of HIV may be able to prolong life if medication begins around the time of the immune system's collapse. Conditions like precancerous cervical changes may need more aggressive monitoring and treatment to keep them from becoming life-threatening. Also, antibiotics used to stave off certain pneumonias that seriously threaten people with AIDS can be taken regularly as a preventive. However, to date, studies show that these drugs do not prolong life or increase health if taken while the immune system is still relatively functional. The drugs sometimes have severe side effects, and HIV becomes resistant to some of them after a while.

For more information on symptoms as the disease progresses or what kinds of tests and treatments (along with side effects) are currently available, call the AIDS information services listed in "Resources." With the rapid changes in this field, you should check to find out the latest information on testing, diagnosis, treatment, support programs, and other services.

Notes

INTRODUCTION

1. Jean Baker Miller, *Toward a New Psychology of Women* (Boston: Beacon Press, 1976), p. 125.

2. Carol Gilligan, *In a Different Voice: Psychological Theory and Women's Development* (Cambridge, MA: Harvard University Press, 1982), pp. 16–17.

3. Miller, *Toward*, pp. 7, 127.

4. Lyn Mikel Brown and Carol Gilligan, *Meeting at the Crossroads: Women's Psychology and Girls' Development* (Cambridge, MA: Harvard University Press, 1992), p. 169.

CHAPTER 1: SELF-STARVATION

1. Christopher Athas, vice president, National Association of Anorexia Nervosa and Associated Disorders, personal communication, May 16, 1991.

2. Sharlene Hesse-Biber, "Women, Weight, and Eating Disorders: A Socio-Cultural and Political-Economic Analysis," *Women's Studies International Forum* 14 (no. 3, 1991): 181.

3. The validity of the Metropolitan Life Insurance weight-for-height chart is highly controversial. Some researchers think that the chart should be considered a "historical curiosity" because the health effects of body fat can differ greatly from one person to another. See, for example, the interview with William Bennett, *Harvard Gazette*, 26 January 1990, p. 5.

4. Sharlene Hesse-Biber, "Eating Patterns and Disorders in a College Population: Are College Women's Eating Problems a New Phenomenon?" *Sex Roles* 20 (nos. 1 / 2, 1989): 83.

5. Hesse-Biber, "Women, Weight," p. 177.

6. O. Wayne Wolly and Susan Wooley, "The Beverly Hills Eating Disorder: The Mass Marketing of Anorexia Nervosa," *International Journal of Eating Disorders* 1 (no.3, 1982): 57–69.

7. April Fallon, "Culture in the Mirror: Sociocultural Determinants of Body Image," in Thomas F. Cash and Thomas Pruzinsky, *Body Images: Development, Deviance, and Change* (New York: Guilford Press, 1990), p. 89.

8. Claire V. Wiseman, et al., "Cultural Expectations of Thinness in Women: An Update," *International Journal of Eating Disorders* 11 (no.1, 1992): 89. The Society of Actuaries table was used to define "expected weight."

9. Fallon, "Culture," p. 91.

10. Ibid.

11. Wiseman, "Cultural," p. 89.

12. *New York Times*, 26 July 1992, reporting results of adult physical exams reported to the National Center for Health Statistics from 1976 to 1980.

13. J. B. Brenner and J. G. Cunningham, *Sex Differences in Eating Attitudes, Body-Concept, and Self-Esteem among Models*, poster presented at the Meeting of the American Psychological Association, San Francisco, August 1991.

14. Mark H. Thelen, Chris M. Lawrence, and Anne L. Powell, "Body Image, Weight Control, and Eating Disorders Among Children," unpublished article. (Columbia: University of Missouri, 1991), p. 9. Also, Ruth Striegel-Moore, Lisa Silberstein, and Judith Rodin, "Toward an Understanding of Risk Factors for Bulimia," *American Psychologist* 41 (1991): 41.

15. Elissa Koff and Jill Rierdan, "Perceptions of Weight and Attitudes Toward Eating in Early Adolescent Girls." *Journal of Adolescent Health* 12 (1991), 311.

16. See Regina C. Casper and Daniel Offer, "Weight and Dieting Concerns in Adolescents, Fashion or Symptom?" *Pediatrics* 86 (no.3, September 1990): 384, 388–390.

17. *Stanford (CA) News*, April 1991, p. 2.

18. Harrison G. Pope, Jr., and James I. Hudson, "Eating Disorders," in H. I. Kaplan and B. J. Sadock, eds., *Comprehensive Textbook of Psychiatry*, 5th ed. (Baltimore: Williams & Wilkens, 1989), p. 1856.

19. O. Wayne Wooley and Susan Wooley, "The Beverly Hills Eating Disorder: The Mass Marketing of Anorexia Nervosa," *International Journal of Eating Disorders* 1 (no. 3, 1982): 57–69.

20. *New York Times Magazine*, part II: "Fashions of the Times," 23 February 1992.

21. James C. Rosen, "Body-Image Disturbances in Eating Disorders," in Thomas F. Cash and Thomas Pruzinsky, *Body Images: Development, Deviance, and Change* (New York: The Guilford Press, 1990), p. 197.

22. Becky Wangsgaard Thompson, "Raisins and Smiles for Me and My Sister: A Feminist Theory of Eating Problems in Women's Lives," Ph.D diss., Brandeis University, 1990, p. 109.

23. Ancel Keys et al., *The Biology of Human Starvation*, vol. 1 (Minneapolis: University of Minnesota Press, 1950), pp. 22, 25–26.

24. Ibid., p. 119.

25. Susan C. Wooley, Orland W. Wooley, and Susan R. Dyrenforth, "Theoretical, Practical, and Social Issues in Behavioral Treatments of Obesity," *Journal of Applied Behavior Analysis* 12 (no.1, 1979): 3–25; and Keys, *Biology*, p. 338.

26. Jane Brody, "Dieting and Risk of Osteoporosis," *The New York Times*, 14 October 1992, sec. C, p. 14.

27. Rose E. Frisch, "Fatness and Fertility," *Scientific American*, March 1988, p. 88. "Standard weight" refers to the average weight (50th percentile) as indicated in chart on p. 90.

28. Ibid.

29. Donna E. Stewart et al., "Infertility and Eating Disorders," *American Journal of Obstetrics and Gynecology* 163 (no. 4, October 1990), p. 1196.

30. Ibid., p. 1196.

31. Michael Stock and Nancy Rothwell, *Obesity and Leanness: Basic Aspects* (London: John Libbey, 1982), p. 59.

32. Fat cells may communicate with the brain centers that control energy balance and feelings of hunger and satiety. See the interview with Bruce Spiegelman (of the Dana-Farber Cancer Institute, Boston) in William J. Cromie, "Gene that Controls Fat Cells Found," *Harvard Gazette*, 2 February 1995.

33. Frisch, "Fatness," p. 92.

34. Rose E. Frisch, "Body Fat, Menarche, Fitness and Fertility," in Rose E. Frisch, ed.,

Adipose Tissue and Reproduction, vol.14 of *Progress in Reproductive Biology and Medicine*, M. L'Hermite, ed., (New York: S. Karger Publishers, 1990), pp. 8-9.

35. Ibid., p. 2.

36. Frisch, "Fatness," pp. 88, 91. Note: These figures were taken from studies of European and U.S. women and may not apply to all cultures.

37. Ibid., p. 88.

38. Rose E. Frisch et al., "Delayed Menarche and Amenorrhea of College Athletes in Relation to Age of Onset of Training," *Journal of the American Medical Association* 246 (no. 14, Oct. 2, 1981): 1559; and Frisch, "Body Fat," p. 1.

39. However, extreme fatness leads to higher amounts of freely circulating testosterone, also associated with irregular menstrual cycles or with a complete loss of cycles.

40. Animal research suggests that our energy efficiency may be partly regulated by a protein secreted by fat cells. The strength of this protein might vary, causing some of us to be unusually efficient in our use of food. See Jeffrey S. Flier et al., "Severely Impaired Adipsin Expression in Genetic and Acquired Obesity." *Science*, 24 July 1987, pp. 405–408.

41. William I. Bennett, "Obesity Is Not an Eating Disorder," *Harvard Mental Health Letter* 8 (no. 4, October 1991): 4–6.

42. Stock and Rothwell, *Obesity*, p. 67.

43. Pope and Hudson, "Eating Disorders," pp. 1861–1862.

44. Nancy A. Rigotti et al., "The Clinical Course of Osteoporosis in Anorexia Nervosa," *Journal of the American Medical Association* 265 (March 6, 1991): 1138.

45. Arthur A. Levin, "Diet Pill Ingredients," *Health Facts*, January 1991, p. 3.

46. *Tufts Diet and Nutrition Letter* 9 (no.10, December 1991): 2.

47. One study shows that women who are among the top 5 percent of a weight-to-height index (for example, 5'3", 200 pounds) are more likely to lose their social and economic status, are less likely to marry, and are more likely to be poor than women whose weight is considered closer to average. This study also suggests that fat women predominantly live within the lower socioeconomic classes. Some researchers now think that this is not because poor women eat more high-fat and junk foods, but because discrimination against fat women leads to poverty. See S. L. Gortmaker et al., "Social and Economic Consequences of Overweight in Adolescence and Young Adulthood," *New England Journal of Medicine* 329 (no.14, Sept. 30, 1993): 1008–1012.

48. Molly O'Neill, "A Growing Movement Fights Diets Instead of Fat," *New York Times*, 12 April 1992, p. 43.

49. Ron Wyden, chairman of the House Subcommittee on Regulation, Business Opportunities, and Energy, "Deception and Fraud in the Diet Industry, Part IV," hearing before the House Subcommittee on Regulation, Business Opportunities, and Technology, 102 Cong. 2 sess., May 21, 1992 (Washington, DC) serial 102–78, p. 1.

CHAPTER 2:
HELP FOR WOMEN WITH EATING DISORDERS

1. Rita Freedman, *Bodylove: Learning to Like Our Looks—and Ourselves* (New York: Harper & Row, 1988), pp. 103–104.

CHAPTER 3:
CHANGING OUR BODIES THROUGH SURGERY

1. Thomas F. Cash and Thomas Pruzinsky, *Body Images: Development, Deviance, and Change* (New York: Guilford Press, 1990), p. 102.

2. Nina Berman, "Disappearing Acts," *Ms.* 3 (no. 5, March/April 1993): 41, quoting Jane, age 27, who also has bulimia.

3. Lenore Anderson, *Synthetic Beauty: American Women and Cosmetic Surgery* (Ph. D. thesis) (Ann Arbor, MI: University Microfilms, 1989), p. 342.

4. Promotional brochure of Collagen Biomedical, 1991.

5. Elizabeth Fernandez, "Scalpeled Beauty a Booming Industry," *San Francisco Examiner*, 19 January 1992, cites a figure of $250. The American Society of Plastic and Reconstructive Surgeons, on p. 9 of their booklet "1992 Statistics," claims that the national average for a cubic centimeter collagen injection is $266.

6. Quote from "Ask Beth" advice column for teenagers, *Boston Globe*, 27 September 1991.

7. For more on how the beauty ideal has affected women see the following books: Wendy Chapkis, *Beauty Secrets: Women and the Politics of Appearance* (Boston: South End Press, 1986); Rita Freedman, *Beauty Bound* (Lexington, MA: Lexington Books, 1986) and *BodyLove: Learning to Like Our Looks—and Ourselves* (New York: Harper & Row, 1989); and Naomi Wolf, *The Beauty Myth: How Images of Beauty Are Used Against Women* (New York: Anchor Books, 1991).

8. Advertisement in *D Magazine*, September 1991, p.37.

9. Marjorie Rosen and Vicki Sheff-Cahan, "'Now I Can Be Free'," *People Weekly*, 26 April 1993, p. 83, quoting a woman talking about her large breasts.

10. Anderson, p. 287.

11. Anne B., "My Nose Is Big. So What?" *Sassy*, August 1992, p. 87.

12. Anderson, pp. 277–278.

13. Thomas Pruzinsky and Thomas Cash, "Integrative Themes in Body-Image Development, Deviance, and Change," in Cash and Pruzinsky, p. 345.

14. Michael J. Pertschuk, "Reconstructive Surgery: Objective Change of Objective Deformity," in Cash and Pruzinsky, note 1, pp. 238, 240, 247.

15. Anne B., p. 116.

16. Rakesh Kumar Sandhir and Minakshi Sandhir, "Aesthetically Normalizing Surgery," *Plastic and Reconstructive Surgery*, 89 (no. 4, April 1992): 762.

17. Adam A. Dobrin, "The $10,000 Face," *Dallas Morning News*, 31 August 1992, quoting Mary Cates.

18. Actual numbers of cosmetic surgery procedures are difficult to obtain. No central office collects statistics from all the surgeons doing cosmetic surgery, many of whom are not board certified plastic surgeons and work independently of hospitals and insurance reimbursement. The American Society of Plastic and Reconstructive Surgeons and the American Academy of Facial Plastic and Reconstructive Surgery both survey their members on the numbers of each procedure that they do. Since reporting is not mandatory, numbers the organizations cite should be regarded as estimates.

19. Massachusetts Coalition of Battered Women Service Groups, *For Shelter and Beyond: Ending Violence Against Battered Women and Their Children*, 2nd ed. (Boston, MA: Author, 1990), p. 185.

20. Anne Gorman, "Surgeons Explore Ethnic Beauty," *Plastic Surgery News*, 6 (no. 4, April 1993): 1.

21. Frank Burgos, "Doctors Trade Tips on Tucks: Beauty's in the Eye of the Plastic Surgeons," *Miami Herald*, 31 October 1988, quoting Julius Newman, a Philadelphia plastic surgeon and then president of the American Academy of Cosmetic Surgery.

22. Norman Cole, M.D., then president of the ASPRS, quoted in Associated Press wire story "Plastic Surgeons Vote to Raise Money to Fight Breast Implant 'Hysteria'," 25 September 1991.

23. Diana Zuckerman, staff member, letter to Representative Ted Weiss, Chairman,

Human Resources and Intergovernmental Relations Subcommittee of the House Committee on Governmental Operations, Re: PMA Applications for Silicone Breast Implants, 21 September 1991.

24. During an FDA committee meeting to write booklets about breast implants for women, one of the authors, Esther R. Rome, asked Dr. Garry Brody to explain how the ASPRS figure was derived. This was the answer she received.

25. Roselie A. Bright, Lana L. Jeng, and Roscoe M. Moore, Jr., "National Survey of Self-Reported Breast Implants: 1988 Estimates," *Journal of Long-Term Effects of Medical Devices* 3 (no. 1, 1993): 81–89.

26. Anderson, pp. 300–303.

27. Thomas Pruzinsky and Milton T. Edgerton, "Body-Image Change in Cosmetic Plastic Surgery," in Cash and Pruzinsky, *Body Images*, p. 221.

28. Bahman Teimourian and W. Bryan Rogers, III, "A National Survey of Complications Associated with Suction Lipectomy: A Comparative Study," *Plastic and Reconstructive Surgery* 84 (no. 4, October 1989): 628–631.

29. From "Additional Information on Collagen Replacement Therapy (SM) for Discussion with Your Physician" section of several promotional brochures distributed by Collagen Biomedical, 1991.

30. Food and Drug Administration, "Collagen and Liquid Silicone Injections" (backgrounder), August 1991.

31. Anderson, p. 261. Dr. Michael Sachs, director of the Division of Facial Plastic and Reconstructive Surgery at New York Eye and Ear Infirmary and New York Medical College Affiliated Hospitals is also quoted in "Second Thoughts on Your First Face Lift," *Harper's Bazaar*, August 1985, p. 118.

32. Richard C. Webster and Richard C. Smith, "Malpractice from the Viewpoint of a Plastic Surgeon," in Robert M. Goldwyn, ed., *The Unfavorable Result in Plastic Surgery: Avoidance and Treatment*, vol. 2 (Boston: Little, Brown, 1984), p. 1112.

33. Robert Goldwyn, "AIDS, Aesthetic Surgery, and the Plastic Surgeon," *Plastic and Reconstructive Surgery*, 90 (no. 6, December 1992): 1062.

34. Ibid.

35. H. W. Porterfield, "Comments on the Proposed Classification of Inflatable Breast Prosthesis and Silicone Gel-Filled Prosthesis," comments made at a meeting of the American Society of Plastic and Reconstructive Surgeons, Chicago, 1982.

36. House Committee on Small Business, Subcommittee on Regulation, Business Opportunities, and Energy, *Hearing on Cosmetic Surgery Procedures: Standards, Quality, and Certification of Nonhospital Operating Rooms—Part III*. 28 June 1989, Serial no. 101–14. The 95 percent figure is from Ron Wyden, p. 2; the 50 percent figure is from Dr. Edward S. Truppman, p. 5.

37. Robert Goldwyn, "AIDS, Aesthetic Surgery, and the Plastic Surgeon," *Plastic and Reconstructive Surgery* 90 (no. 6, December 1992): 1062, 1063.

38. Anderson, p. 89, quoting Chawn Davis, "New Look, A New Day" *Women's Health Digest*, vol. 1, (no. 7, 26 October 1986); pp. 104-106, quoting the *Houston Post*, 12 October 1986, *Houston City Magazine*, February 1986, and *Texas Monthly*, January 1987.

39. Ibid., p. 108, quoting *Fort Bend [Texas] Advocate*, 29 October 1986.

40. Advertisement in *D Magazine*, September 1991.

41. Advertisement in *D Magazine*, December 1990, p. 75.

42. Sandhir and Sandhir, p. 762.

43. Pruzinsky and Edgerton, "Body-Image," p. 223.

44. Ibid.

45. Anderson, p. 302.

46. Pruzinsky and Edgerton, "Body-Image," p. 228.

47. Sanford Gifford, "Cosmetic Surgery and Personality Change: A Review and Some Clinical Observations," in Robert M. Goldwyn, ed., *The Unfavorable Result in Plastic Surgery* (Boston: Little, Brown, 1984), p. 27.

48. Elizabeth Morgan and Mary L. Froning, "Child Sexual Abuse Sequelae and Body-Image Surgery," *Plastic and Reconstructive Surgery* 86 (no. 3, September 1990): 475–480.

49. It is unclear whether current psychological tests would be useful for client evaluation. The point is that plastic surgeons seem not to have attempted to find this out.

50. Anderson, pp. 233–235, also Diana Dull and Candace West, "Accounting for Cosmetic Surgery: The Accomplishment of Gender," *Social Problems* 28 (no. 1, February 1991): 62–64.

51. Anderson, p. 338.

52. Dull and West, p. 66.

53. Jane Sprague Zones, "The Political and Social Context of Silicone Breast Implant Use in the United States," *Journal of Long-Term Effects of Medical Implants* 1 (no. 3, 1992): 238.

54. George Baibak, "Liposuction," letter, and Charles Ettelson, "Fat Autografting," letter, *Plastic and Reconstructive Surgery* 80 (no. 4, October 1987): 646, 647.

55. Robert F. Goldwyn, "Reality in Plastic Surgery: A Plea for Complete Disclosure of Results," *Plastic and Reconstructive Surgery* 80 (no. 5, November 1987): 713–716.

56. The quality of research in the field of cosmetic surgery continues to create controversy among surgeons. An exchange over the acceptability of how research is conducted was aired in *Plastic and Reconstructive Surgery* 93 (no. 3, March 1994): 656–660.

57. Robert F. Goldwyn, "Consecutive Patients," *Plastic and Reconstructive Surgery* 86 (no. 5, November 1990): 962.

58. Arthur Owens, "What's the Recession Done for Your Buying Power?" *Medical Economics*, 7 September 1992, p. 197.

59. Gene Roback, Lillian Randolph, and Bradley Seidman, *Physician Characteristics and Distribution in the U.S.* (Chicago: American Medical Association, 1993).

60. Zones, p. 232.

61. Roback, Randolph, and Seidman, *Physician Characteristics.*

62. Erik Eckholm, "As Doctors Become More Specialized, and Numerous, Turf Wars Erupt over Body Parts," *New York Times*, 7 July 1991.

63. Robert M. Goldwyn, "When Aesthetic Surgery Is Not Aesthetic," *Plastic and Reconstructive Surgery* 84 (no. 6, June 1990): 949–950.

CHAPTER 4:
CAVEAT EMPTOR: SHOPPING FOR A COSMETIC SURGEON

1. Richard C. Webster and Richard C. Smith, "Malpractice from the Viewpoint of a Plastic Surgeon," in Robert M. Goldwyn, ed., *The Unfavorable Result in Plastic Surgery: Avoidance and Treatment*, 2nd ed. (Boston: Little, Brown, 1984), p. 1106.

2. Leigh Page, "Clarifying the Fine Print," *American Medical News*, 5 August 1991, p. 28.

3. House Committee on Small Business, Subcommittee on Regulation, Business Opportunities, and Energy, *Hearing on Unqualified Doctors Performing Cosmetic Surgery: Policies and Enforcement Activities of the Federal Trade Commission—Part II*, 31 May 1989, Serial No. 101-111, pp. 238–239.

4. Gustave Colon, M.D., "The Office Surgical Facility: Refuge for the Unqualified Physician," in House Committee, *Hearing on Cosmetic*

Surgery Procedures: Standards, Quality, and Certification of Nonhospital Operating Rooms—Part III, 28 June 1989, Serial no. 101–14, pp. 196–197.

5. Peyton E. Weary, M.D., and Donald G. Langsley, M.D., testifying for the American Board of Medical Specialties, in House Committee, *Hearing on Cosmetic Surgery*, pp. 398–399.

6. Representative Eliot L. Engel, in House Committee, *Hearing on Cosmetic Surgery*, p. 25.

7. To get a full set of accreditation requirements for each of these groups, write to Accreditation Association for Ambulatory Health Care, 9933 Lawler Avenue, Skokie, IL 60077-3702 (telephone: 708-676-9610) or American Association for Accreditation of Ambulatory Plastic Surgery Facilities, 1202 Allanson Road, Mundelein, IL 60060 (telephone: 708-949-6058).

CHAPTER 5:
INFLATING OUR IMAGE:
BREAST IMPLANTS

1. Jill Rierdan and Elisa Koff, "Timing of Menarche and Initial Menstrual Experience," *Journal of Youth and Adolescence* 14 (no. 3, 1985): 237–243.

2. Audre Lorde, *The Cancer Journals* (Argyle, NY: Spinsters Ink, 1980), p. 52.

3. See the cover of the *New York Times Magazine*, 15 August 1993, for a picture of the artist and activist Matuschka in a dress that reveals her mastectomy.

4. Pre-1991 figures: During the FDA-sponsored task force to write informational brochures for women on breast implants, convened from 1989 to 1991, the consensus among manufacturers and surgeons was that 20 percent of the women receiving implants were getting them after a mastectomy. No statistics were presented to back up this claim. The statistics collected by the American Society of Plastic and Reconstructive Surgeons (ASPRS) indicate that the average percent of women receiving implants for reconstruction from 1981 through 1990 was about 35 percent. (But these figures were collected only from ASPRS members and thus do not include the doctors trained in other specialties who were performing cosmetic surgery.) The ASPRS figures before 1991, though, are not necessarily accurate, according to a telephone conversation by the author with an organization representative at the ASPRS executive office in February 1995. Figures for 1991 and later are from statistics supplied by ASPRS in their booklet "1992 Statistics," p. 10.

5. All human-made devices have a failure rate. For example, as much as 15 percent of shunts and 25 percent of pacemakers fail according to Nir Kossovsky, researcher on implants and pathologist at the University of California in Los Angeles. In a 1986 study, 60 percent of silicone rubber wrist implants fail after 7 years. From Sandra Blakslee, "Data Suggest that Implants May Pose Risk of Later Harm," *New York Times*, 25 July 1989.

6. Donna deCamera, James Sheridan, and Barbara Kammer. "Rupture and Aging of Silicone Gel Breast Implants," *Plastic and Reconstructive Surgery* 91 (no. 6, April 1993): 828-836. See especially pp. 829 and 831.

7. V. Leroy Young et al., "Biocompatibility of Radiolucent Breast Implants," *Plastic and Reconstructive Surgery* 88 (no. 3, September 1991): 472, states that "total removal of [silicone gel] is presently impossible" although the statement is unsubstantiated.

8. Probably the best study so far, "Silicone Breast Implants and the Risk of Connective-Tissue Diseases and Symptoms," by Jorge Sanchez-Guerrero et al., in the *New England Journal of Medicine* 332 (no. 24, 22 June 1995): 1666–70, found no connection between the implants and specific connective-tissue diseases and symptoms. However, the sample size was inadequate to detect rarely occurring problems and the study did not include the most commonly cited problems associated with the implants: fibromyalgia (musculoskeletal pain, stiffness, and fatigue) and lymphadenopathy, dismissing them as subjective. Women were fol-

lowed for an average of 10 years, an inadequate time span since reports of systemic problems generally begin to occur with increasing frequency 7 to 10 years after the initial surgery. Finally, there were major conflicts of interest related to the researchers for the study. A complete critique of the study, by Jane Zones, may be obtained from the National Women's Health Network's Information Clearinghouse, Washington, DC; (202) 628-7814.

An earlier widely publicized study was S. E. Gabriel et al., "Risk of Connective-Tissue Diseases and Other Disorders after Breast Implantation," *New England Journal of Medicine* 330 (no. 24, June 16, 1994): 1697–1702. See also "Correspondence" in the *New England Journal of Medicine* 331 (no. 18, November 3, 1994): 1231–1235, for rebuttal. The FDA expressed concern about the link to autoimmune disease in the *Federal Register*, 17 May 1990, p. 20571, with supporting references on pp. 20574–20576. For references to other studies, see the "Medical Monitor" section of *Medical•Legal Aspects of Breast Implants*, which summarizes many of the studies showing a link or no link for silicone to autoimmune disease. For those showing no link see vol. 1 (no. 6, May 1993), vol. 2 (no. 7, June 1994), vol. 2 (no. 19, September 1994), vol. 2 (no. 8, July 1994), vol. 2 (no. 10, September 1994). Mixed results are reported in vol. 2 (no. 2, January 1994). Studies linking silicone to autoimmune diseases are reported in vol. 1 (no. 5, April 1993), 2 studies, and vol. 2 (no. 1, December 1993), 16 studies.

9. Frank B. Vasey and Josh Feldstein, *The Silicone Breast Implant Controversy: What Women Need to Know* (Freedom, CA: Crossing Press, 1993), p. 34.

10. *Federal Register*, 17 May 1990, p. 20571.

11. Ibid.

12. For published references, see Jeremiah Levine and Norman T. Ilowite, "Sclerodermalike Esophageal Disease in Children Breast-Fed by Mothers with Silicone Breast Implants," *Journal of the American Medical Association* 271 (no. 3, 1994): 213–216; and the "Medical Monitor" section of *Medical•Legal Aspects of Breast Implants* 2 (no. 5, April 1994): 8, which summarizes prepublication information from Nachman Brautbar, et al., "Immunological Abnormalities in Children Born to Mothers with Silicone Breast Implants," scheduled to appear in *Archives of Environmental Health*.

13. Nirmal Mishra, "Silicone Carcinogenesis in Perspective," paper presented at the Silicone in Medical Devices Conference, February 1–2, 1991, Baltimore, Maryland. Rockville, MD: Health and Human Services Publication FDA 92-4249, December 1991.

14. Dennis M. Deapen and Garry S. Brody, "Augmentation Mammoplasty and Breast Cancer: A 5-year Update of the Los Angeles Study," *Plastic and Reconstructive Surgery* 89 (no. 4, April 1992): 660–665.

15. Pierre Blais, "Laboratory Perspective," paper presented at Command Trust Network Conference ("CTN Challenge"), Cleveland, Ohio, November 7, 1992.

16. On February 10, 1992, Dow Corning released to the public a number of internal company documents that it bound together and called "Summary of Scientific Studies and Internal Company Documents Concerning Silicone Breast Implants." The following documents are some of those of interest:

• "Two-year Studies with Miniature Silastic Mammary Implants TX-202A and TX-202B in Dogs: Dow Corning Tox. file no. 1306-3: One out of four dogs died but the company did not determine why. The dogs clearly had a response, including chronic inflammation, to the implantation. The researchers labeled the reaction as a classic foreign body response without considering if the reaction was specific to silicone.

• "Chronic Implantation Studies of Polysiloxanes in Dogs," Steven Carson, no. 86199, November 29, 1968: thirty-eight beagles were studied for three years. The report concludes that problems with capsule formation were inconsequential, but the dogs had unexplained weight gains and losses. "At the three-year period, most dogs were on a downward trend."

• "Comment on Mammary Prosthesis Quality and Request for More Information on the Scottsdale Breast Symposium," memo to Ron Kelley and Art Rathjen from Tom Talcott, January 15, 1976: Memo indicates that some members had doubts about the quality of the elastomer shell.

• "Mammary Task Force Minutes," from A. Berg to T. Abbott et al., May 23, 1975: Some task force members discouraged salesmen from showing a jar of the newly formulated gel to prospective clients "because the gel may not retain constant properties with continued manipulation such as this." No mention is made of how women were supposed to keep from moving around to avoid constantly manipulating the gel.

• Mammary Gel Migration through Envelope—Backlash from Dr. Terino's Paper at California Society of Plastic Surgeons," A. H. Rathjen to A. E. Bey et al., March 19, 1976: Author is concerned that a plastic surgeon wants to determine the amount of gel bleed through the implant and biological effects of the bleed, a test Dow has not yet done and doesn't want discovered.

• Bleed Studies for Dr. Barker," D. Petratis to R. Kelley, March 28, 1977: Author states, "I still believe that Dow Corning should convey the impression that we are indeed working in this area."

• Oily Phenomenon with New Mammary Prosthesis," Tom Salisbury to H. Backer et al., May 16, 1975: Salesmen are advised to wipe off the oily coating on the implant before showing samples to customers.

• Contracture Phenomenon," from C. Leach to B Levier, March 31, 1977: Although a research agenda for implants had been solicited by Dow Corning, "[a]s best I can tell we have not taken significant action on any of his recommendations and except for a 'half-hearted' low-priority program through Dr. Edward Kaminski at Northwestern University we have done little in the past year." In the same memo the author reports assuring several customers "with crossed fingers, that Dow Corning too had

an active 'contracture/ gel migration' study underway."

• G. Bickett Trip Report No. 504, May 4, 1976, i.e., Dr. Phares, St. Petersburg, Florida," A. H. Rathjen to A. E. Bey et al., June 8, 1976: Author states, "I have proposed again and again that we must begin an indepth [sic] study of our gel, envelope, and bleed phenomenon...Time is going to run out for us if we don't get underway."

The documents also contain a number of letters or references to letters to Dow complaining of the poor quality of the implants: Letter from Bob Schnabel to Milt Hinson, April 29, 1980; several letters from Charles A. Vinnik, January 16, 1987, September 23, 1981, and September 11, 1985, among others; from David Mobley, October 15, 1985; and "Excessive Mammary Ruptures," Frank Lewis to Milt Hinsch, March 2, 1978.

• "Review of Implantable Gel Concept," from S. Peters to J. Marlar et al., April 29, 1981: Includes mention of a rabbit study in which gel was extensively divided and walled off into many small amounts. Gel was inside of macrophages, and the possibility of it being carried to distant sites was noted.

17. Thomas D. Talcott, former employee of Dow Corning Wright, personal communication, April 20, 1995.

18. Garry S. Brody, "Discussion," reporting a comment of Dr. H. Hollis Caffee (of "Polyurethane Foam-Covered Implants and Capsular Contracture: A Laboratory Investigation"), *Plastic and Reconstructive Surgery* 86 (no. 4, October 1990): 714.

19. Bruce Ingersoll, "Amid Lax Regulation, Medical Devices Flood a Vulnerable Market," *Wall Street Journal*, 24 March 1992.

20. Sonia Muchnick-Baku, who was in charge of implementing the Maryland law on the breast-implant information booklet, personal communication, November 1988.

21. Activists also brought implants to the attention of Congress at the same time. On December 18, 1990, the House Committee on Government Operations, Human Resources

and Intergovernmental Relations Subcommittee, held a hearing *Is the FDA Protecting Patients from the Dangers of Silicone Breast Implants?* A transcript should be available in libraries that collect records of government activity.

22. See note 16, "Mammary Task Force Minutes," May 23, 1975, for rebate offered by Dow Corning. The minutes of June 6, 1975, notes that the rebate program was approved. "Health Care Business Board Meeting, April 3, 1985, Notes:" R. Steele states, "Art Rathjen made the comment that when supply is limited perhaps we should use a tactic where we ask certain surgeons to act as clinicians. They would be required to sign a commitment to supply us clinical data and also to publish the results of their clinical activity as a trade-off for being guaranteed a specified supply of product."

23. Several plastic surgeons have been told not to speak publicly about complications they have seen from implants. Except for the doctors whose examples are given in the text, they wish to remain silent in public.

24. Stated by William Shaw at Command Trust Network Conference, Los Angeles, California, May 1, 1993.

CHAPTER 6:
ACCEPTING OURSELVES

1. Thomas F. Cash, "The Psychology of Physical Appearance: Aesthetics, Attributes, and Images," in Thomas F. Cash and Thomas Pruzinsky, eds., *Body Images: Development, Deviance, and Change* (New York: Guilford Press, 1990), p. 60.

2. Thomas Pruzinsky and Thomas F. Cash, "Integrative Themes in Body-Image Development, Deviance, and Change," in Cash and Pruzinsky, *Body Images*, p. 338.

3. Rita Freedman, "Cognitive-Behavioral Perspectives on Body-Image Change," in Cash and Pruzinsky, eds., *Body Images*, p. 276.

4. Rita Freedman, *Bodylove: Learning to Like Our Looks—and Ourselves* (New York: Harper & Row, 1988), p. 101.

5. Marcia Hutchinson, *Transforming Body Image: Learning to Love the Body You Have* (Trumansburg, NY: The Crossing Press, 1985), p. 114.

6. This is a complimentary greeting of the Punjab in India, from April Fallon, "Culture in the Mirror: Sociocultural Determinants of Body Image," in Cash and Pruzinsky, *Body Images*, p. 95.

7. Wendy Sanford is a member of the Boston Women's Health Book Collective; Jean Gillespie is a former member of Boston Self-Help; and Becky Thompson is a Rockefeller Foundation fellow in Afro-American studies, Princeton University.

8. Marcia Hutchinson, *Transforming Body Image: Learning to Love the Body You Have* (Trumansburg, NY: The Crossing Press, 1985), pp. 121–122.

CHAPTER 7:
INTIMATE ABUSE

1. Lenore E. Walker, *The Battered Woman* (New York: Harper & Row, 1979), p. 132.

2. Michele Cascardi, Jennifer Langhinrichsen, and Dina Vivian, "Marital Aggression: Impact, Injury, and Health Correlates for Husbands and Wives," *Archives of Internal Medicine* 152 (June 1992): 1178–1184. Cites National Crime Survey data collected 1973–1982.)

3. Jan K. Jenson, "If Only...," in Barrie Levy, ed., *Dating Violence: Young Women in Danger* (Seattle: Seal Press, 1991), p. 46.

4. Debbie Mattson, "Belonging," in Levy, ed., *Dating Violence,* 5, p. 34.

5. William Miller, "Blame Diana for Royal Woe, Author Says," *Boston Sunday Globe,* 17 January 1993.

6. Sally A. Lloyd, James E. Koval, and Rodney M. Cate, "Conflict and Violence in Dating Relationships," in Maureen A. Pirog-Good and Jan E. Stets, eds., *Violence in Dating*

Relationships (New York: Praeger, 1989), p. 129.

7. David Carl Adams, "Empathy and Male Entitlement: A Comparison of Battering and Nonbattering Husbands," Ed.D. diss., Northeastern University, 1991, p. 16.

8. Charlene Allen et al., eds., *For Shelter and Beyond: Ending Violence Against Battered Women and Their Children* (Boston: Massachusetts Coalition of Battered Women Service Groups, 1992), p. 14.

9. Philip Bennet, "10% Of Children in Study Saw Violence," *Boston Globe*, 6 May 1992.

10. Bella English, "The Numbness That Can Kill," *Boston Globe*, 25 November 1992.

11. The 26,000 murders figure is from Myriam Miedzian, "Cultural Climate Teaches Boys Violence," *New York Times*, 21 July 1993. The 200,000 acts of violence and 40,000 murders is from Richard Harwood, "Is Television to Blame for Violence?" *Minneapolis Star Tribune*, 22 April 1993, citing statistics from the National Coalition on Television Violence.

12. Peter Jaffe, David Wolfe, with Susan Kaye Wilson, *Children of Battered Women*," vol. 21 in *Developmental Clinical Psychology and Psychiatry* series (Newbury Park, CA: Sage, 1990), p. 58.

13. Teri Randall, "Domestic Violence Begets Other Problems of which Physicians Must Be Aware to Be Effective," *Journal of the American Medical Association* 264 (no. 8, August 22/29, 1990): 940.

14. Nancy S. Jecker, "Privacy Beliefs and the Violent Family: Extending the Ethical Argument for Physician Intervention," *Journal of the American Medical Association*, 269 (no. 6, February 10, 1993): 776.

15. Judy Foreman, "Doctors Urged to Check Women for Abuse Signs," *Boston Globe*, 17 June 1992, citing statistics from the American Medical Association.

16. Judith Herman, *Trauma and Recovery: The Aftermath of Violence—From Domestic Abuse to Political Terror* (New York: Basic Books, 1992), p. 74.

17. Kerry Lobel, ed., *Naming the Violence: Speaking Out about Lesbian Battering* (Seattle: Seal Press, 1986), p. 164.

18. George Lardner, Jr., "A Father's Account of a Sparkle Snuffed Out," *Boston Globe*, 26 November 1992.

19. Evan Stark, Anne Flitcraft, and William Frazier, "Medicine and Patriarchal Violence: The Social Construction of a 'Private' Event," *International Journal of Health Sciences* 9 (no.3, 1979): 184.

20. John Robinson, "A Narrative Drawn from an Abusive Past," *Boston Globe*, 4 February 1993.

21. Lobel, p. 159.

22. David Sugarman and Gerald Hotaling, "Dating Violence: A Review of Contextual and Risk Factors," in Barrie Levy, ed., *Dating Violence: Young Women in Danger* (Seattle: Seal Press, 1991), p. 104. Because different surveys use different definitions of relationships and of violence, this figure is not firm.

23. Bella English, "Where Bruises Don't Belong," *Boston Globe*, 7 December 1992.

24. Maureen A. Pirog-Good and Jan E. Stets, eds., *Violence in Dating Relationships* (New York: Praeger, 1989): p. 11.

25. Allen, note 8, p. 71. This source claims rates are the same. Many police departments do not keep statistics by age so reliable data are difficult to find.

26. Anne Flitcraft, "Battered Women in Your Practice?" *Patient Care*, October 15, 1990, p. 110.

27. J. McFarlane, B. Parker, K. Soeken, and L. Bullock, "Assessing Abuse During Pregnancy," *Journal of the American Medical Association* 267 (no. 23, June 17, 1992): 3176–3178.

28. Anne Stuart Helton, *Protocol of Care for the Battered Woman* (White Plains, NY: March of Dimes Birth Defects Foundation, 1987), p. 3.

29. Teri Randall, "Duluth Takes Firm Stance Against Domestic Violence; Mandates Abuser Arrest, Education," *Journal of the American Medical Association* 266 (no. 9, September 4, 1991): 1180, 1183.

30. Susan Schecter, *Women and Male Violence: The Visions and Struggles of the Battered Women's Movement* (Boston: South End Press, 1982), p. 315.

31. Adams, *Empathy and Male Entitlement*, p. 26.

32. Lucy Candib, M.D., "Violence Against Women as a Gender Issue," unpublished paper, 1991.

33. Discussions with members of Respond (a Somerville, Massachusetts organization for helping abused women), 1992-1993.

34. Sarah, "Letting Out the Secret: Journal Entries, 1982–1984," in Lobel, p. 117.

35. Ibid., p. 30.

36. English, "Where Bruises Don't Belong."

37. Amy B. Kaufman, "Lesbian Battery and Its Political Implications" (senior thesis, Brandeis University, 1986–1987), p. 25.

38. Pirog-Good and Stets, p. 10.

39. Melissa Beck, "Beaten at Home, Silenced in Trial and Forgotten in Prison: Legal and Social Responses to Battered Women Who Kill" (thesis submitted to Division III, Hampshire College, April 25, 1991), pp. 40–44. Summarizes research on differences between women who kill their abusers and those who don't. Other contributing factors may be whether the men who were killed were more likely to use alcohol and other drugs, were more threatening and assaultive, or abused a child or children.

40. Tom Coakley, "Jailed Ex-Officer Accused of Hit Bid," *Boston Globe*, 21 January 1993.

41. Ginny NiCarthy, *The Ones Who Got Away* (Seattle: Seal Press, 1987), p. 217.

42. Allen et al., p. 14.

43. G. L. Bundow, "Why Women Stay," in George T. Lundberg et al., eds., *Violence: A Compendium from Journal of the American Medical Association, American Medical News, and the Specialty Journals of the American Medical Association* (Chicago: American Medical Association, 1992), p. 151.

44. Nancy Chez, "Helping the Victim of Domestic Violence," *American Journal of Nursing* 94 (no. 7, July 1994): 33–37.

45. Much of the material in this section is from Herman, *Trauma and Recovery*.

46. Jessica Henderson Daniel, "Exclusion and Emphasis Reframed as a Matter of Ethics," *Ethics and Behavior* 4 (no. 3, 1994): 229-235.

47. Herman, p. 34.

48. Constance Hays, "If That Man Is Following Her, Connecticut Is Going to Follow Him," *New York Times*, 5 June 1992.

49. Barrie Levy, *In Love and in Danger: A Teen's Guide to Breaking Free of Abusive Relationships* (Seattle: Seal Press, 1993), p. 65.

50. Herman, p. 95.

51. Barrie Levy, ed., *Dating Violence: Young Women in Danger* (Seattle: Seal Press, 1991), p. 35.

52. Sari Staver, "MDs' Responses Aggravate Battered Women's Plight, Researchers Say," *American Medical News*, August 23–30, 1985, p. 9. For battered women who seek treatment at a hospital, the risk of alcoholism is sixteen times greater than for nonbattered women, up from three times greater before the woman first came to a hospital for treatment.

53. Council on Scientific Affairs, American Medical Association, "Violence against Women: Relevance for Medical Practitioners" *Journal of the American Medical Association* 267 (no.23, June 17, 1992): 3190.

54. Figure is from the Massachusetts Office for Victim Assistance. It does not include the few men who were killed, cases where de-

tails are murky, relatives of the abused women, or suicides resulting from intolerable abuse.

55. David Finkelhor, "Marital Rape: The Misunderstood Crime," address to the New York County Lawyer's Association, May 3, 1984.

56. Anne Stewart Helton, *Protocol of Care for the Battered Woman* (White Plains, NY: March of Dimes Birth Defect Foundation, 1987): p. 5.

57. Deborah Tannen, *You Just Don't Understand: Women and Men in Conversation* (New York: Ballantine Books, 1990), pp. 24–25.

58. Pirog-Good and Stets, p. 12.

59. Ibid., p. 20.

60. Daniel Jay Sonkin and Michael Durphy, *Learning to Live without Violence: A Handbook for Men* (San Francisco: Volcano Press, 1982), p. 12.

61. Adams, "Empathy and Male Entitlement," p. 23.

62. Ibid, p. 148.

63. David Adams, "Stages of Anti-Sexist Awareness and Change for Men Who Batter," paper presented at the 92nd Annual Convention of the American Psychological Association, Toronto, August 24, 1985, p. 18.

64. Herman, p. 8.

65. Lobel, pp. 67–68.

66. James Ptacek, "Wifebeaters' Accounts of Their Violence: Loss of Control as Excuse and as Subjective Experience," Masters thesis, University of New Hampshire, May 1985, p. 50.

67. Andrew Blake, "Maimoni Faulted His Wife, Witness Says at Murder Trial," *Boston Globe*, 4 February 1993.

68. Ptacek, "Wifebeaters' Accounts," p. 53.

69. Ibid., p. 55.

70. Ibid., p. 52.

71. Ibid., p. 75.

72. Ibid., p. 56.

73. Richard H. Chacon, "New Strategy Urged on Domestic Abuse," *Boston Globe*, 30 March 1995. A report of a special commission on substance abuse appointed by the Massachusetts Supreme Court found that in 1994, 79 percent of those named as batters in restraining orders had a drug or alcohol problem.

74. David Adams, personal communication, April 1993, and Adams, "Stages of Anti-Sexist Awareness," p. 21.

75. Patricia Nealon, "Batterers: Common Characteristics," *Boston Globe*, 1 June 1992.

76. Steven Van Wagoner (counselor with men who batter, Abused Persons Program, Montgomery County, Maryland), personal communication, October 1992.

77. Experiencing violence in childhood does not mean that a person will become a batterer, though statistically it is somewhat more likely. In fact, childhood abuse motivates many men and women to make careful choices about their own behavior when they are angry so that they do not inflict abuse on others. See Adams, note 7, p. 139.

78. Eve S. Buzawa and Carl G. Buzawa, *Domestic Violence: The Criminal Justice Response* (Newbury Park, CA: Sage, 1990), p. 133.

79. Nealon, "Batterers."

80. Lobel, p. 182.

81. For more on the role of the battered women's movement, see Schecter, *Women and Male Violence*. Although this book was written more than ten years ago, most of the information is still relevant.

82. The 3 percent figure is from Lee Bowker and Lorie Maurer, "The Medical Treatment of Battered Wives," *Women and Health* 12 (no. 1, 1987): 27. The 6 percent figure is from Susan V. McLeer and Rebecca Anwar, "A Study of Battered Women Present in an Emergency Department," *American Journal of Public Health* 79 (no. 1, January 1989): 65–66.

83. Stark, Flitcraft and Frazier, p. 185.

84. Demie Kurz, "Emergency Department Responses to Battered Women: Resistance to Medicalization," *Social Problems* 34 (no. 1, February 1987): 72.

85. Bowker and Maurer, p. 37.

86. Evan Stark and Anne Flitcraft, "Violence among Intimates: An Epidemiological Review," in V. B. VanHasselt et al., eds., *A Handbook of Family Violence* (New York: Plenum Press, 1988), pp. 305–306. Labeling of this type continues to be an issue. See V. Moss, "Battered Women and the Myth of Masochism," *Journal of Psychosocial Nursing and Mental Health Services* 29 (no. 7, 1991): 18–23.

87. As an example, see Mary P. Koss et al., eds., *No Safe Haven: Male Violence Against Women at Home, at Work, and in the Community* (Washington, DC: American Psychological Association, 1994).

88. Evan Stark and Anne Flitcraft, "Medical Therapy as Repression: The Case of the Battered Woman," *Health and Medicine* 1 (no. 3, Summer/Fall 1982): 31.

89. Randall, note 13, pp. 908–913.

90. Susan McLeer and Rebecca Anwar, "The Role of the Emergency Physician in the Prevention of Domestic Violence," *Annals of Emergency Medicine* 16 (no. 10, October 1987): 1159.

91. Stark and Flitcraft, "Violence among Intimates," p. 303.

92. R. Emerson Dobash and Russell Dobash, *Violence Against Wives: A Case Against the Patriarchy* (New York: Free Press, 1979), pp. 116–117.

93. Beck, p. 26.

94. Patricia Nealon, "Troubles of Battered Women in Cambridge Court Decried," *Boston Globe*, 22 October 1992, quoting Ilene Seidman, a supervising attorney at the Harvard Legal Aid Bureau and an instructor at Harvard Law School.

95. Adrian Walker, "Third of Court Orders Flouted, Officials Say," *Boston Globe*, 30 September 1992.

96. Patricia Nealon, "Troubles of Battered Women in Cambridge Court Decried," *Boston Globe*, 22 October 1992.

97. Walker, "Third of Court Orders Flouted."

98. Peter H. Lewis, "Persistent E-Mail: Electronic Stalking or Innocent Courtship?" *New York Times*, 16 September 1994. Michigan explicitly includes electronic communication in its stalking law.

99. Sindy Siegal, "Women Testify to Cambridge Court Abuses in Domestic Violence Cases," *Somerville Women: A Publication of the Somerville Commission for Women* 2 (issue 4, Fall 1992): 1.

100. Nancy Gibbs, "'Til Death Do Us Part," *Time*, 18 January 1993, p. 42.

101. Bella English, note 22.

102. James Makepeace, "Dating, Living Together, and Courtship Violence," in Pirog-Good and Stets, eds., *Violence in Dating Relationships* (New York: Praeger, 1989), p. 105.

103. Donileen R. Loseke, *The Battered Woman and Shelters: The Social Construction of Wife Abuse* (Albany, NY: State University of New York Press, 1992), pp. 42–43.

104. Lobel, p. 159.

CHAPTER 8: ABOUT RAPE

1. Harvard Medical School, Department of Social Medicine, *Abuse and Violence in Relationships; Helping Health Care Professionals to Expand Clinical Effectiveness with Patients* (Cambridge, MA: January 13, 1993), p. 128. Also copy of flyer, "Startling Facts about Rape," citing statistics from the National Coalition Against Sexual Abuse.

2. Maureen A. Pirog-Good and Jan E. Stets, eds., *Violence in Dating Relationships* (New York: Praeger, 1989), p. 146.

3. Chris O'Sullivan, "Making the Connections: Rape, Sports, War and Profit," *New Directions for Women*, May/June 1993, p. 4.

4. Ann Landers, "Raped at Knifepoint by a 'Friend'," *Boston Globe*, 13 December 1991.

5. *Parade*, January 26, 1992.

6. Bella English, "They Just Don't Get It," *Boston Globe*, 10 August 1992.

7. Judith Herman, *Trauma and Recovery: The Aftermath of Violence—from Domestic Abuse to Political Terror* (New York: Basic Books, 1992), p. 67.

8. In some states, rape also includes sex with a person who cannot give consent because of being under the influence of drugs, including alcohol, or who is mentally incapacitated for some other reason.

9. Coerced sex often includes verbal, emotional, or financial threats, which can be as effective as physical force. A woman may agree to have sex with her partner to avoid persistent badgering or anger. Also she might be intimidated by threats such as telling her boss something she fears will get her fired.

10. Katherine Roiphe's book *The Morning After: Sex, Fear and Feminism on Campus* (Boston: Little, Brown, 1993), shows how women who want to publicize the frequency of rape and to take action to prevent it are labeled as hysterical and misguided. *Newsweek* (25 October 1993) ran a series of articles on date rape, mostly dismissing its severity. One article, however, "Balancing Act" by Susan Estrich (p. 64), notes: "Nuts and sluts is the new defense of choice in sexual-abuse cases because in many cases, it's the only choice. If you can't argue that date rape isn't really rape, or that sexual harassment comes with the job, then you have to argue that the woman is lying. If culpability isn't an issue, then credibility may be the only game in town."

11. Mary P. Koss, "Hidden Rape: Sexual Aggression and Victimization in a National Sample of Students in Higher Education," in Maureen A. Pirog-Good and Jan E. Stets, eds., *Violence in Dating Relationships* (New York: Praeger Publishers, 1989), p. 157.

12. Kathy Dobie, "Between Seduction and Rape," *Vogue*, December 1991, p. 158.

13. In 1985, a Georgia court ruled that the laws in that state had actually included marital rape as a crime since 1862, when the state passed a law making rape of a slave a crime. The court reasoned that if the rape of a slave, who was considered property at that time, was criminal, then rape of a wife must be also.

14. For a more thorough investigation of the theme of rape as an instrument of social control, see Susan Brownmiller, *Against Our Will: Men, Women and Rape* (New York: Bantam Books, 1975).

15. Allison Bass, "'Daterape' Victims Bear Scars Longer, Study Finds," *Boston Globe*, 30 September 1991.

16. Pirog-Good and Stets, p. 171.

17. Ibid. p. 172.

18. Daniel Goleman, "New Studies Map the Mind of the Rapist," *New York Times*, 10 December 1991.

19. Robin Warshaw, *I Never Called It Rape: The Ms. Report on Recognizing, Fighting, and Surviving Date and Acquaintance Rape* (New York: Harper & Row, 1988), p. 125.

20. Bella English, "Where Bruises Don't Belong," *Boston Globe*, 7 December 1992.

21. Warshaw, *I Never Called it Rape*, pp. 120–121.

22. Mary P. Koss et al., eds., *No Safe Haven: Male Violence Against Women at Home, at Work, and in the Community* (Washington, DC: American Psychological Association, 1994), p. 10, citing several studies, including a 1988 study by the Rhode Island Rape Crisis Center.

23. Warshaw, *I Never Called It Rape*, p. 93.

24. Ibid., p. 97.

25. Pirog-Good and Stets, p. 222. Also Daniel Goleman, "New Studies Map the Mind of the Rapist," *New York Times*, 10 December 1991.

26. Warshaw, *I Never Called It Rape*, pp. 96–97.

27. Pirog-Good and Stets, p. 163.

28. Warshaw, *I Never Called it Rape*, p. 97.

29. Christina Robb, "Why Do Some Men Think It's OK to Commit Rape?" *Boston Globe*, 25 July 1991.

30. Warshaw, *I Never Called It Rape*, p. 85.

31. Jane Gross, "Even the Victim Can Be Slow to Recognize Rape," *New York Times*, 28 May 1991.

32. Anne P. Glavin, *Acquaintance Rape: The Silent Epidemic* (Cambridge, MA: Campus Police Department, MIT, 1992), p. 4.

33. Lenore E. Walker, *Abused Women and Survivor Therapy: A Practical Guide for the Psychotherapist* (Washington DC: American Psychological Association, 1994), p. 29.

34. Herman, p. 69.

CHAPTER 9:
SAVING OURSELVES

1. Claire M. Renzetti, *Violent Betrayal: Partner Abuse in Lesbian Relationships* (Newbury Park, CA: Sage, 1992), p. 71.

2. Kerry Lobel, ed., *Naming the Violence: Speaking Out about Lesbian Battering* (Seattle: Seal Press, 1986), p. 169.

3. Susan Schecter, *Women and Male Violence: The Visions and Struggles of the Battered Women's Movement* (Boston: South End Press, 1982), p. 316.

4. This exercise and the next two are adapted from exercises learned from Janet Conners, personal communication, October 1993.

5. These messages are from Barb Friedmann and Cheri Brooks, *On BASE! The Step-by-Step Self-Esteem Program for Children from Birth to 18* (Kansas City, MO: BASE Systems, 1990); Ann Jones and Susan Schecter, *When Love Goes Wrong* (New York: Harper Perennial, 1992), especially p. 146; and Barrie Levy, *In Love and in Danger: A Teen's Guide to Breaking Free of Abusive Relationships* (Seattle: Seal Press, 1993).

6. Adapted from Friedmann and Brooks, *On BASE!*

7. Adapted from Janet Conners, personal communication, October 1993.

8. This exercise is adapted from Earl Hipp, *Feed Your Head: Some Excellent Stuff on Being Yourself* (Center City, MN: Hazelden Educational Materials, 1991), p. 98.

9. Adapted from "My Me Book," p. 11, photocopied exercises.

10. Unless otherwise indicated, the following exercises are adapted from Jones and Schecter, *When Love Goes Wrong*.

11. Ginny NiCarthy, Karen Merriam and Sandra Coffman, *Talking It Out: A Guide for Abused Women* (Seattle: Seal Press, 1984), pp. 91–92.

12. Jones and Schecter, *When Love Goes Wrong*, p. 123.

13. Susan Schecter, *Women and Male Violence: The Visions and Struggles of the Battered Women's Movement* (Boston: South End Press, 1982), p. 78.

14. Barrie Levy, ed., *Dating Violence: Young Women in Danger* (Seattle: Seal Press, 1991), p. 171.

15. Constance Cutter, *Voices of Recovery: How Battered Women Change* (Somerville, MA: Respond Productions, 1989), p. 28.

16. Ibid., p. 28.

17. Ibid., p. 33.

18. Ibid., p. 52.

19. Ibid., p. 26.

20. Evelyn C. White, *Chain Chain Change: For Black Women Dealing with Physical and Emotional Abuse* (Seattle: Seal Press, 1985), p. 45.

21. Peter Jaffe and David Wolfe, with Susan Kaye Wilson, *Children of Battered Women* in *Developmental Clinical Psychology and Psychiatry* series, vol. 21 (Newbury Park, CA: Sage, 1990), p. 59.

22. Joan Zorza (senior attorney, National Battered Women's Law Project), "Runaways Often Flee Domestic Violence" (Letter to the Editor), *New York Times*, 9 March 1993.

23. NiCarthy, Merriam, and Coffman, *Talking It Out*, p. 87.

24. Jacqueline Campbell, Paul Miller, Mary Cardwell, and Ruth Ann Belknap, "Relationship Status of Battered Women over Time," *Journal of Family Violence* 9 (1994): 99–111.

25. Jacqueline Campbell, personal communication, February 7, 1995.

26. Ginny NiCarthy, *The Ones Who Got Away* (Seattle: Seal Press, 1987).

27. Constance Cutter, *Voices of Recovery: How Battered Women Change* (Somerville, MA: Respond Productions, 1989), p. 40.

28. Lobel, p. 35.

29. Cutter, *Voices of Recovery*, p. 41.

30. Island Soul, "A Single Mother's New Life," *Boston Globe*, 16 March 1993.

31. Anita Diamant, "How the Quincy District Court Protects Battered Women," *Boston Globe Magazine*, 11 October 1992, pp. 54, 59.

32. Cutter, *Voices of Recovery*, p. 39.

33. "Awake: Advocacy for Women and Kids in Emergencies" (Boston: Children's Hospital). From descriptive brochure of the program, obtained January 1993.

34. Lynda Gorov, "No Unusual Trend Seen in Officers' Behavior," *Boston Globe*, 9 March 1993.

35. Sandy Pimental from the Quincy, Massachusetts, district attorney's office, personal communication, January 1995.

CHAPTER 10:
THE COSTS OF PHYSICAL LOVE

1. Jean Baker Miller, *Toward a New Psychology of Women* (Boston: Beacon Press, 1976), p. 83.

2. Ibid, p. 107.

3. Mary Guinan, M.D., personal communication, 25 September 1992.

4. Modified from exercises developed by Denise Ribble. See one version in Cynthia Chris, "Transmission Issues for Women," in ACT UP/NY Women and AIDS Book Group, *Women, AIDS, and Activism* (Boston: South End Press, 1990), p. 17.

5. Teri Randall, "New Tools Ready for Chlamydia Diagnosis, Treatment, But Teens Need Education Most," *Journal of the American Medical Association*, 269 (no. 21, June 2, 1993): 2718.

6. Nancy Padian et al., "Female-to-Male Transmission of Human Immunodeficiency Virus," *Journal of the American Medical Association* 266 (no. 1, Sept. 25, 1991): 1665.

7. P. M. Howley et al., "Oncoproteins Encoded by the Cancer-associated Human Papillomaviruses Target the Products of the Retinoblastoma and p53 Tumor Suppressor Genes," *Cold Spring Harbor Symposia on Quantitative Biology* 56 (1991): 149.

8. Karl Muenger et al., "Interactions of HPV E6 and E7 Oncoproteins with Tumour Suppressor Gene Products," *Cancer Surveys* 12 (1992): 197.

9. Howley et al., "Oncoproteins," p. 149.

10. James H. Nelson, Hervy E. Averette, and Ralph M. Richart, "Cervical Intraepithelial Neoplasia and Early Invasive Cervical Carcinoma," *CA-A Cancer Journal for Clinicians* 39 (no.3, May/June 1989): 166.

11. Muenger et al., "Interactions," p. 210.

12. Leopold G. Koss, "The Papanicolaou Test for Cervical Cancer Detection: A Triumph and a Tragedy," *Journal of the American Medical Association* 261 (no. 5, Feb. 3, 1989): 740.

13. *Health Facts* XV (no. 136, September 1990): 2.

14. William Jackson Epperson, "Preventing Cervical Cancer by Treating Genital Warts in Men: Why Male Partners Need Androscopy," *Postgraduate Medicine* 88 (no. 5, October 1990): 229.

15. "Viruses and Cancer," *Harvard Medical Area Focus*, 9 January 1992, p.4.

16. Peter Howley, M.D., personal communication, October 1992.

17. Fenway Community Health Center, Boston, personal communication, September 1993.

18. Ibid.

19. Willard Cates, Jr., and Judith N. Wasserheit, "Genital Chlamydial Infections: Epidemiology and Reproductive Sequelae," *American Journal of Obstetrics and Gynecology* 164 (no. 6, part 2, June 1991): 1771.

20. Randall, "New Tools," p. 276.

21. Centers for Disease Control and Prevention, Division of STD/HIV, *Estimated 1992 Annual Report* (Atlanta, GA, 1992).

22. Walter E. Stamm and King K. Holmes, "Chlamydia Trachomatis Infections in the Adult," in King K. Holmes et al., eds., *Sexually Transmitted Diseases* (New York: McGraw-Hill Information Services, 1990), p. 190.

23. Cates and Wasserheit, "Genital," p. 1772; and Stamm and Holmes, "Chlamydia," p. 182.

24. Cates and Wasserheit, "Genital," pp. 1775–1776.

25. Lars Westroem and Per-Anders March, "Acute Pelvic Inflammatory Disease (PID)," in King K. Holmes et al., eds., *Sexually Transmitted Diseases* (New York: McGraw-Hill Information Services, 1990), p. 593.

26. E. Eugene Washington and Patricia Katz, "Cost of and Payment Sources for Pelvic Inflammatory Disease," *Journal of the American Medical Association* 266 (no. 18, Nov. 13, 1991): 2565.

27. Westroem and March, "Acute," p. 608.

28. Pal Wolner-Hanssen et al., "Atypical Pelvic Inflammatory Disease: Subacute Chronic or Subclinical Upper Genital Tract Infection in Women," in King K. Holmes et al., eds., *Sexually Transmitted Diseases* (New York: McGraw-Hill Information Services, 1990): p. 616.

29. Cates and Wasserheit, "Genital," p. 1776.

30. Ibid.

31. Westroem and March, "Acute," p. 593.

32. Christopher J. Elias and Lori Heise, "The Development of Microbicides: A New Method of HIV Prevention for Women," in *Population Council Working Papers* (no. 6, 1993): 36.

33. Elizabeth Reid, "Gender, Knowledge and Responsibility,"in Jonathan Mann, Daniel J. M. Tarantola, and Thomas W. Netter, *AIDS in the World: A Global Report* (Cambridge, MA: Harvard University Press, 1992), pp. 663–664.

34. "Pelvic Inflammatory Disease and HIV: The Hidden Epidemic?" *WORLD*, March 1992, p. 4.

35. Nancy Kohn et al., *Searching for Women: A Literature Review on Women, HIV and AIDS in the United States* (Boston: Multicultural AIDS Coalition, 1992), p. 150.

36. George Conway et al., "Trends in HIV Prevalence among Disadvantaged Youth: Survey Results from a National Job Training Pro-

gram, 1988 through 1992," *Journal of the American Medical Association* 269 (no. 22, June 9, 1993): 2887–2889.

37. Sharon Pratt Kelly, mayor of Washington, DC, to the Health Resources and Intergovernmental Relations subcommittee of the House of Representatives Committee on Government Operations, July 2, 1992.

38. "AIDS Conference Updates State of Epidemic, Research," *Harvard University Gazette* 87 (no. 43, July 24, 1992): 12.

39. Marge Berer and Sunanda Ray, *Women and HIV/AIDS: An International Resource Book* (London: Pandora Press, 1993), p. 40. For Zambia: Alan F. Flemming, "AIDS in Africa, *Balliere's Clinical Haematology* 3 (no. 1, 1990): 177–205. For North America: Marcia Quackenbush and Sylvia Villareal, *Does AIDS Hurt?: Educating Young Children about AIDS*" (Santa Cruz, CA: Network Publications, 1988), p. 114. For Argentina and Haiti: Ann Marie Kimball et al., "AIDS among Women in Latin America and the Caribbean," *Bulletin of Pan American Health Organization*, 25 (no. 4, 1991): 367–373.

40. Delores Kong, "AIDS Data Show Spread among Women," *Boston Globe*, June 6, 1993.

41. Jonathan M. Mann et al., eds., *AIDS in the World: A Global Report* (Cambridge, MA: Harvard University Press, 1992): p. 632.

42. Elias and Heise, "Development," p. 7. Berer and Ray, *Women and HIV/AIDS*, p. 40. Mann, *AIDS*, p. 125: "In New York City, in 1988-89, AIDS was the leading cause of death among women 25 to 39 years old and the fourth leading cause of death among women 15 to 24 years old."

43. Mann et al., *AIDS*, p. 83.

44. Department of Health and Human Services, "*HIV/AIDS Surveillance Report*," vol. 5, no. 1 (Washington, DC, 1993), p. 15.

45. Berer and Ray, *Women and HIV/AIDS*, p. 38.

46. Ale Schaefer et al., "The Increased Frequency of Cervical Dysplasia-Neoplasia in Women Infected with the Human Immunodeficiency Virus Is Related to the Degree of Immunosuppression," *American Journal of Obstetrics and Gynecology* 164 (no. 2, February 1991): 598.

47. Barbara Neustadt, a nurse at the Beth Israel Hospital in Boston, and others, personal communication, July 1992.

48. Louise Rice at AIDS Action in Boston (25 percent) and Vicki Legion at Chicago Women's AIDS Project (30 percent), personal communications, Fall 1994; Mann et al., AIDS, p. 641 (30 percent).

49. Felicia R. Lee, "For Women with AIDS, Anguish of Having Babies," *New York Times*, 9 May 1995.

50. Katherine Franke, *HIV-Related Discrimination in Abortion Clinics in New York City* (New York: AIDS Discrimination Division, New York City Commission on Human Rights, 1989).

51. Fran Peavey, *A Shallow Pool of Time* (Santa Cruz, CA: New Society Publishers, 1990), p. 76.

52. Nathan Cobb, "I Am the Future of AIDS," *Boston Globe*, 16 December 1992.

53. Berer and Ray, *Women and HIV/AIDS*, p. 129.

54. Elias and Heise, note 32, p. 59.

55. Ibid., p. 8.

56. William R. Finger, "Clinic-Based Intervention Projects: STD and Family Planning Programs Get Involved," *Family Health International Network* 12 (no. 1, June 1991): 13.

57. Elias and Heise, "The Development of Microbicides," p. 63.

58. Berer and Ray, *Women and HIV/AIDS*, p. 118. Padian et al., note 6, p. 1664.

59. Berer and Ray, *Women and HIV/AIDS*, p. 40.

60. "Routine Screen Misses Many HIV-Infected Women," *AIDS Clinical Care* 3 (no. 5, 1991): 39.

61. Tedd Ellerbrock et al., "Heterosexually Transmitted Human Immunodeficiency Virus Infection among Pregnant Women in a Rural Florida Community," *New England Journal of Medicine* 327 (no. 24, Dec. 10, 1992): 1704.

62. Cobb. "I Am the Future," quoting Karen Clifford.

63. "Sex in the 90s: Some Findings of the Janus Report," *Boston Globe*, 23 February 1993.

64. "Study Finds Many Heterosexuals Are Ignoring Serious Risks of AIDS," *New York Times*, 13 November 1992.

65. Teri Randall, "New Tools Ready," *Journal of the American Medical Association* 269 (no. 21, June 2, 1993): 2716 and 2718.

66. Patricia Donovan, *Testing Positive: Sexually Transmitted Disease and the Public Health Response* (New York: Alan Guttmacher Institute, 1993), p. 9.

67. A. Eugene Washington, Willard Cates, Jr., and Judith N. Wasserheit, "Preventing Pelvic Inflammatory Disease," *Journal of the American Medical Association* 266 (no. 18, Nov. 13, 1991): 2575–2576.

68. A. Eugene Washington et al., "Assessing Risk for Pelvic Inflammatory Disease and Its Sequelae," *Journal of the American Medical Association* 266 (no. 18, Nov. 13, 1991): 2583.

69. Elias and Heise, "The Development of Microbicides," p. 63.

70. Ibid., p. 60.

71. Patty Doten, "Her Cheating Heart," *Boston Globe*, 14 July 1992.

72. *Family Planning Perspectives* 22 (no. 2, March/April 1990): 90.

73. Felicity Barringer, "Rate of Marriage Continues Decline," *New York Times*, 17 July 1992.

74. Editorial, "Trends in Sexual Behavior and the HIV Pandemic," *American Journal of Public Health* 82, (no. 11, November 1992): 1460.

75. Gina Kolata, "Panel Recommends Adding Vitamin to Food to Prevent Birth Defect," *New York Times*, 25 November 1992.

76. Charles C. J. Carpenter et al., "HIV Infection in North American Women: Experience with 200 Cases and a Review of the Literature," *Medicine* 70 (no. 5, 1991): 307–325.

77. Laura Rodrigues, "Heterosexual Transmission of HIV," *Journal of the American Medical Association* 269 (no. 7, Feb. 17, 1993): 870.

78. Gena Corea, *The Hidden Epidemic: The Story of Women and AIDS* (New York: HarperCollins, 1992), p. 86.

79. Randall, "New Tools," p. 2718.

80. Felicity Barringer, "1 in 5 in U.S. Have Sexually Caused Viral Disease," *New York Times*, 1 April 1993.

81. Susan Cochran and Vickie Mays, "Sex, Lies, and HIV," *New England Journal of Medicine* 322 (no. 11, March 15, 1990): 774.

82. Stamm and Holmes, "Chlamydia," p. 182.

83. Cates and Wasserheit, "Genital," p. 1773.

84. "Sex in the 90s."

85. Editorial, "Stop Meddling in AIDS Education," *New York Times*, 1 June 1992.

86. "Teenage Sex: Despite Aids, Many Take Risks," *Medical Abstracts Newsletter*, September 1992.

87. Jack Morin, *Anal Pleasure and Health*, 2 ed. (Burlingame, CA: Yes Press, 1986), p. 9.

88. D. M. Upchurch et al., "Behavioral Contributions to Acquisition and Transmission of *Neisseria gonorrhoeae*," *Journal of Infectious Diseases* 161 (no. 5, May 1990): 938–941.

89. J. Malcolm Pearce, "Pelvic Inflammatory Disease," *British Medical Journal* 300 (no. 28, April 1990): 1091.

90. Washington, Cates, and Wasserheit, "Preventing," p. 2577.

91. Ibid.

92. Ibid.

93. Marsha Goldsmith, "'Invisible' Epidemic Now Becoming Visible as HIV/AIDS Pandemic Reaches Adolescents," *Journal of the American Medical Association*, 20 (no. 1, July 7, 1993): 18.

94. Clifford Levy, "Fifth Graders Get Condoms in New Haven," *New York Times*, 28 July 1993.

95. Berer and Ray, *Women and HIV/AIDS*, p. 157.

96. Goldsmith, "'Invisible' Epidemic, p. 18.

97. Mann et al., eds., *AIDS in the World*, p. 187.

98. Bob Rawson, "Survey Yields Snapshot of Student Health," *Cambridge (MA) Chronicle*, 22 October 1992. Based on student surveys in 1989 and 1992.

99. Penelope Wilson, "Clinic Connects with Teens Worried about Sex, AIDS, Health," *Somerville (MA) Journal,* 25 November 1992, p. 7.

100. Washington, Cates, and Wasserheit, "Preventing," p. 2578.

101. Elias and Heise, "The Development of Microbicides," p. 45. See also M. J. Rosenberg and E. L. Gollub, "Commentary: Methods Women Can Use That May Prevent Sexually Transmitted Disease, Including HIV," *American Journal of Public Health* 82 (1992): 1473–1478. Also the critique of this article: W. Cates, Jr., F. H. Stewart, and J. Trussell, "Commentary: The Quest for Women's Prophylactic Methods—Hopes vs. Science, *American Journal of Public Health* 82 (1992): 1479–1482.

102. See Betsy Hartmann, *Reproductive Rights and Wrongs: The Global Politics of Population Control* (Boston: South End Press, 1995).

103. Peggy Clarke, president of the American Social Health Association, personal communication, 12 August 1993.

104. Berer and Ray, *Women and HIV/AIDS*, p. 64.

105. Janet L. Mitchell, John Tucker, Patricia Loftman, and Sterling Williams, "HIV and Women: Current Controversies and Clinical Relevance," *Journal of Women's Health* 1 (no. 1, Spring 1992): 38.

106. Evelynn Hammonds, "Missing Persons: African American Women, AIDS and the History of Disease," *Radical America* 24 (no. 2, 1993): 7–24. Contains an analysis of the media portrayal of African-American women and explores the roots of their higher rates of AIDS.

107. As of 1991, 32 percent of Hispanics and 20 percent of blacks did not have medical insurance. See "Blacks, Hispanics, Middle Class Lose Health Insurance," *Boston Globe*, 22 December 1992.

108. Mann et al., eds., *AIDS in the World*, p. 224.

109. One notable example, of course, is the Tuskegee experiment (1930s–1970's), in which medical personnel examined and kept records on poor, mostly illiterate African-American men who had syphilis. The men were not treated, even after effective treatment for the disease was discovered. Only after this study received public condemnation was it ended and the surviving men and their families treated.

110. Sevgi O. Aral et al., "Self-Reported Pelvic Inflammatory Disease in the United States," *Journal of the American Medical Asso-*

ciation 266 (no. 18, Nov. 13, 1991): 2572.

111. As of March 1993, black non-Hispanic women made up 53 percent of women with AIDS in the United States (white non-Hispanic women are 25 percent, and Hispanic women are 20 percent of the total). Department of Health and Human Services, "HIV/AIDS Surveillance Report," p. 8.

112. Mann et al., eds., *AIDS in the World*, p. 4.

CHAPTER 11: CHOOSING OURSELVES

1. Marcelle Clements, "Sex in the Age of Aids," *Mirabella*, July 1992, p. 118.

2. Ibid.

3. Excerpts from Kim Knutson and Paul Reed, *How to Persuade Your Lover to Use a Condom...And Why You Should* (Rocklin, CA: Prima Publishers, 1987).

4. Marge Berer and Sunanda Ray, *Women and HIV/AIDS: An International Resource Book* (London: Pandora Press, 1993), pp. 143–144, 342.

5. Willard Cates, Jr., and Katherine Stone, "Family Planning, Sexually Transmitted Diseases and Contraceptive Choice: A Literature Update—Part I," *Family Planning Perspectives* 24 (no. 2, March/April 1992): 79.

6. Carol Campbell, "Sex Work, AIDS and Preventive Health Behavior," in Berer and Ray, *Women and HIV/AIDS*, p. 225.

7. Ibid., p. 227.

8. David Soper et al., "Prevention of Vaginal Trichomoniasis by Compliant Use of the Female Condom," *Sexually Transmitted Diseases* 20 (no. 3, May-June 1993): 137.

9. Erica Gollub, D.P.H., personal communication, 4 August 1993.

10. Karyn Grimm Herndon et al., "Subclinical Human Papillomavirus Infection: The Effect of Therapeutic Modality On Outcome," abstract presented at the annual clinical meeting of the American College of Obstetrics and Gynecology, New Orleans, 8 May 1991.

11. Pal Wolner-Hanssen et al., "Association Between Vaginal Douching and Acute Pelvic Inflammatory Disease," *Journal of the American Medical Association* 263 (no. 14, April 11, 1990): 1936.

12. Other organisms to be tested for include *Streptococcus* species, *Escherichia coli*, *Haemophilus influenzae*, *Bacteroides* species, *Peptostreptococcus*, and *Peptococcus*. See Peter A. Rice and Julius Schachter, "Pathogenesis of Pelvic Inflammatory Disease," *Journal of the American Medical Association* 266 (no. 18, Nov. 13, 1991): 2587.

13. S.J. Clark et al., "High Titers of Cytopathic Virus in Plasma of Patients with Symptomatic Primary HIV-1 Infection," *New England Journal of Medicine* 324 (no. 14, April 4, 1991): 954–960.

14. Berer and Ray, *Women and HIV/AIDS*, p. 20.

Resources for Body Image and Eating Problems

PART I: TRYING TO LOOK DIFFERENT

Organizations

Eating Disorders

American Anorexia/Bulimia Association, Inc. (AABA)
418 E. 76th Street
New York, NY 10021
(212) 734-1114

Nationwide information and referral service. Publishes quarterly newsletter that includes reviews of recent books and videos, articles by specialists, research developments, and program information. Subscription price $50.00 (includes membership to AABA). Write to the above address for a complementary copy.

Anorexia Nervosa and Related Eating Disorders, Inc. (ANRED)
P.O. Box 5102
Eugene, OR 97405
(503) 344-1144

National, nonprofit organization that collects information about eating and exercise disorders and distributes that information through booklets, brochures, newsletters, and community education programs.

Eating Disorders Awareness and Prevention (EDAP)
603 Stewart Street
Seattle, WA 98101
(206) 382-3587, Fax (206) 292-9890

Nationwide network of state coordinators dedicated to the awareness and prevention of eating disorders. Sponsors National Eating Disorder Awareness Week and provides educational materials and services for the prevention of eating disorders.

National Association of Anorexia Nervosa and Associated Disorders (ANAD)
P.O. Box 7
Highland Park, IL 60035
(708) 831-3438

Educational and self-help organization. Services include self-help groups, referral list of health professionals who treat eating disorders, newsletter, education and training conferences, and national hotline.

National Center for Overcoming Overeating
Old Chelsea Station
P.O. Box 1257
New York City, NY 10113-0920
(212) 875-0442

Chicago branch:
P.O. Box 48
Deerfield, IL 60015-0048
(708) 853-1200

The national center offers workshops for women who are trying to give up dieting and end body hatred. The approach is designed to cure compulsive eating. For information on workshops, audiotapes, and newsletter, call either of the above numbers.

National Eating Disorder Organization (NEDO)

Formerly called the National Anorexic Aid Society, this organization is located in Tulsa, Oklahoma. For information on services provided, contat Craig Johnson, Ph.D., c/o Laureate Psychiatric Clinic and Hospital, at 918-481-4044.

The Pennsylvania Educational Network for Eating Disorders (PENED)
P.O. 16282
Pittsburgh, PA 15242
(412) 922-5922, Fax (412) 922-5765

Nationwide information and referral service. Publishes quarterly newsletter with information pertinent to eating disorders. Provides educational services and training, support groups, information packets, and supportive telephone line. For membership information and a complimentary newsletter, write to the above address.

Fat Acceptance

AHELP, Association for the Health Enhancement of Large Persons
St. Albans Hospital
P.O. Box 3608
Radford, VA 24143
(800) 368-3468, or in Virginia: (800) 572-3120

Founded by medical and mental health personnel who reject dieting and weight loss and who work toward helping fat women and men develop patterns of healthy living and self-acceptance.

Ample Opportunity
P.O. Box 40621
Portland, OR 97240-0621
(503) 245-1524

Promotes the mental and physical health of fat women by sponsoring workshops, physical activities, and a newsletter.

Council on Size and Weight Discrimination
P.O. Box 238
Columbia, MD 21045

Works toward ending discrimination against fat people by influencing public policy and public opinion.

Fat Lip Reader's Theatre
P.O. Box 29963
Oakland, CA 94604

A group of fat women who use humor, poetry, and dramatic skits in Reader's Theatre and video performance projects to educate people about size acceptance. Their work is available on the videotape *Nothing to Lose*, for $29.95 plus $3.00 for shipping. Send your request with a check or money order to the above address.

National Association to Advance Fat Acceptance (NAAFA)
P.O. Box 188620
Sacramento, CA 95818
(800) 442-1214, or (916) 558-6880

A network of people promoting self-acceptance of all shapes and weights and fighting discrimination based on body size. You can contact them for information on their work and also for general information on fat acceptance.

Publications

Self Starvation

Bennett, William, and Joel Gurin. *The Dieter's Dilemma*. New York: Basic Books, 1983.

One of the first publications for the general public stating that low-calorie diets are ineffective and explaining why. Discusses the setpoint weight theory and prejudices against fatness.

Bordo, Susan. *Unbearable Weight: Feminism, Western Culture, and the Body*. Berkeley: University of California Press, 1993.

Essays on the meanings attached to women's bodies, including the meanings of thinness and fatness.

Bruch, Hilde. *The Golden Cage: The Enigma of Anorexia Nervosa.* New York: Random House, 1979.

One of the first specialists in treating eating disorders discusses her insights on anorexia nervosa.

Brumberg, Joan Jacobs. *Fasting Girls: The Emergence of Anorexia Nervosa as a Modern Disease.* New York: NAL-Dutton, 1989.

Discusses the history of anorexia nervosa and of the meanings of food and eating, and the historical forces that have encouraged restricted eating among women.

Chernin, Kim. *The Hungry Self: Women, Eating, and Identity.* New York: HarperCollins, 1986.

Explores the relationship between women's roles and eating disorders.

Chernin, Kim. *Reflections on the Tyranny of Slenderness.* New York: Harper & Row, 1981.

Analysis of society's demand that women be thin.

Hall, Lindsey, and Leigh Cohn. *Bulimia: A Guide to Recovery: Understanding and Overcoming the Binge-Purge Syndrome.* Rev. ed. Carlsbad, CA: Gurze Books, 1992.

Includes a two-week program to stop binge eating, a guide for support groups, advice for loved ones, and Hall's story of self-cure.

Hirschmann, Jane R., and Carol H. Munter. *Overcoming Overeating.* New York: Fawcett Columbine, 1988.

Recognizes compulsive eating as the normal response to food restrictions and offers a self-help guide to overcoming dieting and compulsive eating. Also, four audio cassettes of strategies taped during an Overcoming Overeating workshop are available through the National Center or Chicago branch of Overcoming Overeating (see above).

Kano, Susan. *Making Peace with Food: Freeing Yourself from the Diet/Weight Obsession.* Rev. ed. New York: HarperCollins, 1989.

Thorough self-help book on overcoming eating disorders and learning self-acceptance.

Kaplan, Jane R. *A Woman's Conflict: The Special Relationship Between Women and Food.* Englewood Cliffs, NJ: Prentice-Hall, 1980.

Roth, Geneen. *Breaking Free from Compulsive Eating.* New York: NAL-Dutton, 1986.

Step-by-step approach to overcoming food restriction and binge eating. Also, four audio cassettes of Roth's strategies are available through Gurze Books, P.O. Box 2238, Carlsbad, CA 92018.

Thompson, Becky W. *A Hunger So Wide and So Deep: American Women Speak Out on Eating Problems.* Minneapolis: University of Minnesota Press, 1994.

Discussion of the experiences and healing methods of women who are lesbian or of color.

For family and friends, as well as for women who have an eating disorder:

Kinoy, Barbara P., and Estelle B. Miller, eds. *When Will We Laugh Again? Living and Dealing with Anorexia Nervosa and Bulimia.* New York: Columbia University Press, 1984.

Reindl, Sheila, and Suzanne Repetto. *What Should I Do?: Guidelines for Friends, Lovers, Roommates, and Relatives of People with Eating Disorders.*

Available by writing to the authors at 5 Linden Street, Cambridge, MA 02138. Enclose a check for $2.00 per copy, made out to either author.

Siegel, Michele, Judith Brisman, and Margot Weinshel. *Surviving an Eating Disorder: New Perspectives and Strategies for Family and Friends.* New York: HarperCollins, 1989.

Self-Acceptance

Bloom, Lynn Z., et al. *The New Assertive Woman.* New York: Dell, 1975.

Burns, David. *Feeling Good: The New Mood Therapy.* New York: Avon Books, 1992.

A guide to overcoming problems often related to eating disorders, such as lack of self-esteem and self-assertion, perfectionism, depression, and others.

Butler, Pamela E. *Self-Assertion for Women.* San Francisco: Harper & Row, 1981.

Freedman, Rita. *Bodylove: Learning to Like Our Looks—and Ourselves.* New York: HarperCollins, 1990.

Hutchinson, Marcia Germaine. *Transforming Body Image: Learning to Love the Body You Have.* Trumansburg, NY: The Crossing Press, 1985.

An accompanying single audio tape with strategies and discussion is available through Gurze Books, P.O. Box 2238, Carlsbad, CA 92018. Information on a set of seven 90-minute audio cassettes is available from Body-Mind Tapes, 88 W. Goulding Street, Sherborn, MA 01770.

Jakubowski, Patricia, and Arthur J. Lange. *The Assertive Option: Your Rights & Responsibilities.* Champaign, IL: Research Press, 1978.

McKay, Matthew, and Patrick Fanning. *Self-Esteem.* Oakland, CA: New Harbinger, 1987.

Techniques for assessing, improving, and maintaining self-esteem.

Fat Liberation

BBW-Express (Big Beautiful Woman) (fashion magazine for fat women) Larry Flynt Publications, 9171 Wilshire Blvd., Suite 300, Beverly Hills, CA 90210.

Edison, Laurie Toby, and Debbie Notkin, *Women En Large: Images of Fat Nudes.* San Francisco: Books in Focus, 1994.

Millman, Marcia. *Such a Pretty Face: Being Fat in America.* New York: Berkley Publishing Corp., 1981.

Discusses middle-class, white perspectives on cultural and personal aspects of being fat.

Radiance: The Magazine for Large Women. Alice Ansfield, Publisher, P.O. Box 30246, Oakland, CA 94604.

A magazine for fat women and their friends, promoting self-acceptance for fat women.

Schoenfielder, Lisa, and Barbara Wieser, eds. *Shadow on a Tightrope: Writings on Fat Oppression.* Iowa City, IA: Aunt Lute, 1983.

Anthology of articles about fat oppression and fat liberation.

Films and Videos

The Body Beautiful. This film reveals the profound effects of body image and the strain of racial and sexual identity through the experiences of a white mother who undergoes a mastectomy and her black daughter who embarks on a modelling career. Video/16mm. 23 minutes. Distributed by Women Make Movies, Inc., 462 Broadway, Suite 500, New York, NY 10013. (212) 925-0606.

Bulimia and the Road to Recovery. Documentary produced by a woman who recovered from bulimia. Video. 27 minutes.

Distributed by Women Make Movies, Inc., 462 Broadway, Suite 500, New York, NY 10013. (212) 925-0606. Purchase or rental.

The Famine Within. Documentary by Katherine Gilday on the cult of thinness and on eating disorders and compulsive exercise. 2 hours.

Video distributed by Direct Cinema, P.O. Box 10003, Santa Monica, CA 90410. Call (800) 525-0000 for purchase prices. (Available for rental to schools, universities, libraries, and museums, but not to the general public.)

Fear of Fat: Dieting and Eating Disorders. A film that takes a critical look at how food has become a preoccupation that can lead to eating disorders when coupled with other psychological problems. Five young women discuss their eating disorders ranging from compulsive overeating to anorexia nervosa and bulimia. The film offers encouragement to resist media manipulation and accept one's body type. Video/16mm. For grades 6–12. 26 minutes. Available from Churchill Media, 12210 Nebraska Ave., Dept. 200, Los Angeles, CA 90025-9816.

I Don't Have to Hide: A Film about Anorexia and Bulimia. Documentary presents a bulimic woman's experiences. Video. 28 minutes.

Distributed by Fanlight Productions, 47 Halifax Street, Boston, MA 02130. (617) 524-0980. Purchase or rental.

In Our Own Words: Personal Accounts of Eating Disorders. Several women, one man, and the mother of a woman who died from anorexia nervosa share their experiences of sexual abuse, pressures to be thin, lesbian support, athletics, etc. Video. 50 minutes.

Available for purchase through Gurze Books, P.O. Box 2238, Carlsbad, CA 92018. (800) 756-7533.

Learning about Eating Disorders. This series of five videos covers indications of anorexia nervosa and bulimia; the range of medical disorders associated with eating disorders; and emphasizes the possibility of recovery, outlining the components of a good treatment program. Video. 14 to 16 minutes each. Available from Churchill Media, 12210 Nebraska Ave., Dept. 200, Los Angeles, CA 90025-9816.

Mirror Mirror. On the relationship between a woman's body image and the quest for an "ideal" body. Thirteen women, of varying ages, sizes, and ethnicities, reveal their ambivalence about their own bodies. Film/video. 17 minutes.

Distributed by Women Make Movies, Inc., 462 Broadway, Suite 500, New York, NY 10013. (212) 925-0606. Purchase or rental.

Size 10. Humorous film showing how women's body images are formed and deformed by advertising and sexism. Film. 20 minutes.

Distributed by Women Make Movies, Inc., 462 Broadway, Suite 500, New York, NY 10013. (212) 925-0606. Rental.

Still Killing Us Softly: Advertising's Image of Women. Explores sex-role stereotyping in advertising and how it affects attitudes and behaviors toward women. Features Jean Kilbourne. Film/video. 30 minutes.

Distributed by Cambridge Documentary Films, P.O. Box 385, Cambridge, MA 02139. (617) 354-3677. Purchase or rental.

Other Resources

Since 1980, Gurze Books has been involved in eating disorders education and offers a wide range of books from various publishers, some of which are listed above. Includes books for parents interested in preventing eating and weight concerns in their children. For a free catalog of their offerings, call or write Gurze Books, P.O. Box 2238, Carlsbad, CA 92018, (800) 756-7533 or (619) 434-7533.

PART II: LIVING IN ABUSIVE RELATIONSHIPS

Organizations

Cape Cod Women's Agenda
P.O. Box 822
Brewster, MA 02631
For more information, call Rachel Carey-Harper (508) 385-5443.

Center for Women's Policy Studies
2000 P Street, NW
Suite 508
Washington, DC 20036

Write to this organization for a catalog of print and video resources on a variety of issues affecting women, including violence against women and health concerns.

Dating Violence Intervention Project
P.O. Box 530, Harvard Square Station
Cambridge, MA 02238
(617) 868-8328

Emerge (a Massachusetts counseling and educational program for abusive men)
Cambridge: 18 Hurley Street (617) 422-1550
Fitchburg: (617) 422-1550
Framingham: (508) 620-0010 x384
Quincy: St. John's School, Phipps Street (617)422-1550

Hetrick-Martin Institute for the Protection of Lesbian and Gay Youth
(212) 633-8920

National Clearinghouse on Marital and Date Rape
c/o Women's History Research, Inc.
2325 Oak Street
Berkeley, CA 94708
(510) 524-7770/524-1582

National Coalition Against Domestic Violence
Call (303) 839-1852 for a referral to a program in your area

National Gay and Lesbian Domestic Violence Victims Network
P.O. Box 140131
Denver, CO 80214
(800) 238-4347

Network for Battered Lesbians
P.O. Box 6011
Boston, MA 02114
(617) 424-8611

New York State Coalition Against Domestic Violence
Hotline: (800) 342-6906

For information regarding organizations in your area, consult:

NOW Legal Defense & Education Fund
99 Hudson Street
New York, NY 10013-2815
(212) 925-6635
(212) 226-1066 fax
This organization lists hotlines and organizations nationally and by state.

Sexual Assault and Child Sexual Abuse by Linda Webster (Phoenix, AZ: Oryx Press, 1989).
A national directory of victim/survivor services and prevention programs. Listings by state.

Publications

About Women on Campus. A quarterly newspaper published by the Women's Issues Project of the National Association of Women in Education, Suite 210, 1325 18th Street, NW, Washington, DC 20036-6511.

Gordon, Margaret T., and Stephanie Riger, *The Female Fear: The Social Cost of Rape.* Urbana, IL: University of Illinois Press, 1991.

Kelley, Austin. *Beyond Self-Protection.* Guidelines for women threatened by rape. Available for $12.95 from Morning Star Publishers, P.O. Box 1742, Bellaire, TX 77402-1742

Tan, Amy. *The Kitchen God's Wife.* New York: Ivy Books, 1991.

Videos and Music

But He Loves Me. Inexperienced 16-year-old Cassie McBride meets and is wooed by Charlie Taylor, one of the most popular boys in high school. Riding the crest of new love and sudden popularity as Charlie's girlfriend, Cassie overlooks his darker side: jealousy, possessiveness, and abusive behavior toward her. Cast is white and upper class. For grades 7–12. Video.

46 minutes. Available from Churchill Media, 12210 Nebraska Ave., Dept. 200, Los Angeles, CA 90025-9816.

Five Out of Five. This rap rock video features New York Women Against Rape's Acting Out Teen Theatre in a look at the problem of child and teen sexual abuse. Video. 7 minutes. Available from Women Make Movies, Inc., 462 Broadway, Suite 500C, New York, NY 10013. (212) 925-0606.

Rape by Any Name. This video on acquaintance rape features candid interviews with rape survivors, counselors, and male and female college students. Video. 60 minutes. Available from Women Make Movies, Inc., 462 Broadway, Suite 500C, New York, NY 10013 (212) 925-0606.

Rule of Thumb. This video explores domestic violence through the perspective of women who have left abusive relationships. Video. 22 minutes. Available from Women Make Movies, Inc., 462 Broadway, Suite 500C, New York, NY 10013. (212) 925-0606.

Waking Up to Rape. This film examines the personal trauma of rape, its long-term psychological effects, societal attitudes about sexual assault, and the problem of racism in the criminal justice system. Video/16mm. 35 minutes. Available from Women Make Movies, Inc., 462 Broadway, Suite 500C, New York, NY 10013. (212) 925-0606.

Tracy Chapman, "Behind the Wall" on *Tracy Chapman.* Elektra/Asylum Records, 1988. A song about domestic violence and the lack of response from the authorities.

Tori Amos, "Me and a Gun" on *Little Earthquakes*, Atlantic Recordings, 1991. A song about abusive relationships and desperation.

PART III: DYING FOR LOVE

Organizations

Centers for Disease Control and Prevention
Division of STD/HIV Prevention
1600 Clifton Road, NE
Mail Stop E 27
Atlanta, GA 30333

Hotlines

National AIDS/HIV Hotline
English Service (7 days/week, 24 hours/day)
(800) 342-2437
Spanish Service (7 days/week, 8 AM–2 PM ET)
(800) 344-7432
TTY Service for the Deaf (M–F, 10 AM–10 PM ET)
(800) 243-7889

National Aids Information Clearinghouse
English/Spanish Service (M–F, 9 AM–7 PM EST)
(800) 458-5231
TTY Service for the Deaf (M–F, 9 AM–7 PM EST)
(800) 243-7012

Centers for Disease Control

National Sexually Transmissible Diseases (STD)
Hotline (M–F, 8 AM–11 AM ET)
(800) 227-8922

National Herpes Hotline (M–F, 9 AM–7 PM ET)
(919) 361-8488

Herpes Resource Center
(to order materials about herpes)
(800) 230-6039

American Social Health Association (ASHA)
Healthline
(to order free publications about sexual health communication)
(7 days/week, 24 hours/day) (800) 972-8500

Publications

ACT UP/New York Woman and AIDS Book Group. *Women, AIDS, and Activism*. Boston: South End Press, 1990.

American Social Health Association, PO Box 13827-S, Research Triangle Park, NC 27709 (919) 361-8400. Among many publications, it has a newsletter on HPV.

Barnett, Robin, and Rebecca Fox. *A Feminist Approach to Pap Tests*. Rev. ed. Vancouver: Vancouver Women's Health Collective, 1986, with 1991 update. (Order from Vancouver Women's Health Collective, Suite 302, 1720 Grant St., Vancouver, BC V5L 2Y7 Canada.

Berer, Marge, with Sunanda Ray. *Women and HIV/AIDS: An International Resource Book*, London: Pandora Press, 1993.

Boston Women's Health Book Collective, *The New Our Bodies, Ourselves: A Book By and For Women*. New York: Touchstone, 1992.

Cherniak, Donna. *Birth Control Handbook*. Montreal: Montreal Health Press, 1991. (Order from Montreal Health Press, P.O. Box 1000, Station Place du Parc, Montreal, Quebec, Canada H2W 2N1. (514) 282-1171.) Also available in French.

Cherniak, Donna. *STD Handbook*. Montreal: Montreal Health Press, 1991. (Order from: Montreal Health Press, PO Box 1000, Station Place du Parc, Montreal, Quebec, Canada H2W 2N1. (514) 282-1171.) Also available in French.

Chicago Women's AIDS Project. *"Girls Night Out:" A Safer Sex Workshop for Women: Manual for Peer Leaders*, no date. (Order from Chicago Women's AIDS Project, 5249 Kenmore, Chicago, IL 60640. (312) 271-2242.)

Corea, Gena. *The Invisible Epidemic: The Story of Women and AIDS*. New York: Harper Collins, 1992.

Donovan, Patricia. *Testing Positive: Sexually Transmitted Disease and the Public Health Response*, New York: Alan Guttmacher Institute, 1993.

Law Center, College of Public and Community Service, University of Massachusetts-Boston, and the Multicultural AIDS Coalition. *Searching for Women: A Literature Review on Women, HIV and AIDS in the United States: A Work in Progress, 3rd ed.*, 1992. (Order from: Multicultural AIDS Coalition, 566 Columbus Ave., Boston, MA 02118.)

Mann, Jonathan, Daniel Tarantola, and Thomas Netter, eds. *AIDS in the World*, Cambridge, MA: Harvard University Press, 1992.

McKenzie, Nancy. *The AIDS Reader: Privacy, Poverty, Community*. New York: NAL/Dutton, 1990.

McKenzie, Nancy. *The AIDS Reader: Social, Political, and Ethical Issues*. New York: NAL/Dutton, 1990.

Meredith, Ann. "Until That Last Breath: Women with AIDS," in Elizabeth Fee and Daniel Fox, *AIDS: The Making of a Chronic Disease*, Berkeley: University of California Press, 1992.

Sex Information and Education Council of the U.S. (SIECUS). Numerous excellent publications regarding women and HIV. Contact Carolyn Patierno, 130 W. 42nd St., Suite 2500, New York, NY 10036.

Stoller, Nancy E. and Beth E. Schneider. *Women Resisting AIDS: Feminist Strategies of Empowerment*. Philadelphia: Temple University Press, 1994.

Films and Videos

The Afternoon Line-Up. Video. 19 minutes. Oriented toward African-American women but with multiracial cast. Combines soap-opera and talk-show formats to encourage women to insist on male condoms and to see safer sex as the new norm. For permission to copy this tape, contact Maurizio Macaluso, M.D., Department of Epidemiology, School of Public Health, Tidwell Hall Room 202, University of Alabama, Birmingham, AL 35294-0008, or call (205) 934-7835. (A videotape on female condom use may be available from the same source at a future date.)

AIDS in the Barrio. Video/film. 28 minutes. Puerto Rican women and men argue that racism, sexism, and homophobia are the main forces pushing the HIV epidemic. Distributed by Cinema Guild, 1697 Broadway, New York, NY 10019. (212) 246-5522.

AIDS Is about Secrets. Video. 37 minutes. Profiles of four African-American women whose partners use drugs. Discusses drug abuse, recurring sexually transmissible diseases, family concerns, rehabilitation, and commercial sex work. Contains some street language. Distributed by HIV Center for Clinical and Behavioral Studies, 722 W. 168th St., New York, NY 10032. (212) 740-0046.

AIDS — What Everyone Needs to Know. Video. 19 1/2 minutes. Up-to-date information and interviews with particular relevance for the 1990s. Also available in Spanish. Available from Churchill Media, 12210 Nebraska Ave., Dept. 200, Los Angeles, CA 90025-9816.

Are You with Me? Video. 17 minutes. A divorced African-American health-care worker talks to her teenage daughter about protecting herself against AIDS, but finds it difficult to practice what she preaches.
Distributed by Select Media, 74 Varick St., #305, New York, NY 10013. (212) 431-8923.

Breaking the Silence. Video. 57 minutes. A Puerto Rican cast in a drama about the complex issues involved in safer sex for women. Distributed by HIV Center for Clinical and Behavioral Studies, 722 W. 168th St., New York, NY 10032. (212) 740-0046.

Condom Talk. Video. 5 minutes. An African-American woman humorously demonstrates different approaches to condom negotiation. Encourages creativity along with prevention. Distributed by Planned Parenthood Federation of America. Marketing Dept., 810 7th Ave., New York, NY 10019. (800) 669-0156. Ask for item no. 1942 and send a check or Master Card or Visa number and expiration date with your order, or give your credit card number by phone.

Condomnation: A Dramatic Comedy About Safe Sex. Video. 14 minutes. A young woman and man, both European-Americans, go upstairs at a party to find a place to be alone, and land in bed. When she insists on protection, a desperate and comical quest for condoms ensues, and the couple learns that getting to know each other can be more fun and much less risky than having a casual fling. Distributed by Select Media, 74 Varick St., #305, New York, NY 10013. (212) 431-8923.

Dedicated to the One I Love. Video. 46 minutes. A dramatic story of teen love, life, and AIDS. For grades 7–12. Available from Churchill Media, 12210 Nebraska Ave., Dept. 200, Los Angeles, CA 90025-9816.

DiAna's Hair Ego: AIDS Info Up Front. Video. 29 minutes. Documents the growth of the South Carolina AIDS Education Network. Available from Women Make Movies, 462 Broadway, Suite 500C, New York, NY 10013. (212) 925-0606.

Fighting for Our Lives: Women Confronting AIDS. Center for Women Policy Studies. Video. 29 minutes. Available from Women Make Movies, Inc., 462 Broadway, Suite 500C, New York, NY 10013. (212) 925-0606.

(In)Visible Women. Video. 26 minutes. Documentary focusing on the heroic and empowered responses of three strong Latina women living with AIDS. (Subtitled) Available from Women Make Movies, 462 Broadway, Suite 500C, New York, NY 10013 (212) 925-0606.

Let's Do Something Different: A Condom Promotion. Video. 14 minutes. A young woman who has PID gradually realizes that she can persuade her boyfriend to use condoms. Her growing confidence is due to the advice of her brother and her girlfriend, both of whom are committed to the values of health and sexual responsibility. Multiracial cast. Distributed by Planned Parenthood Federation of America, Marketing Dept., 810 7th Ave., New York, NY 10019. (800) 669-0156. Ask for item no.1698 and send a check or MasterCard or Visa number and expiration date with your order, or give your credit card number by phone.

Mixed Messages. Horizon Films Production. Video. 12 1/2 minutes. Available from Churchill Media, 12210 Nebraska Ave., Dept. 200, Los Angeles, CA 90025-9816. For grades 9–12.

Party Safe! With DiAna and Bambi. Video. 25 minutes. DiAna and Bambi travel to New York, Chicago, Los Angeles, and Toronto where they hold safe sex informational parties. Available from Women Make Movies, 462 Broadway, Suite 500C, New York, NY 10013. (212) 925-0606.

Porque Si. Video. 17 minutes. Sensitively portrays difficult emotional issues surrounding safer sex. Developed for use in STD clinics. Distributed by Education Development Center, 55 Chapel St., Newton, MA 02160. (617) 969-7100.

Pros and Condoms. Video. 22 minutes. This humorous, explicit video presents college students and their views on condom use. Available from Churchill Media, 12210 Nebraska Ave., Dept. 200, Los Angeles, CA 90025-9816.

Vida. Video. 18 minutes. When a single Latina mother learns that her neighbor is sick with AIDS, she realizes that she too is at risk of HIV infection. She admits to a friend that she is afraid of confronting her lover about using protection. With the friend's encouragement, she asks her lover to use condoms and when he refuses, she leaves his apartment. After taking this first step to protect herself, she compassionately reaches out to her sick neighbor. Available in English or Spanish, and accompanied by a 32-page English and Spanish discussion guide including handouts, discussion questions, and fact sheets. Distributed by Select Media, 74 Varick St., #305, New York, NY 10013. (212) 431-8923.

Audio Cassette

How to Talk with a Partner about Smart Sex. $12.95. Scripted vignettes in which actors play out conversations on safer sex. Includes tips on when to raise the subject. 60 minutes. Distributed by Planned Parenthood Federation of America, Marketing Dept., 810 7th Ave., New York, NY 10019. (800) 669-0156. Ask for item no. 1984 and send a check or MasterCard or Visa number and expiration date with your order, or give your credit card number by phone.

Pamphlet

The Condom: What It Is, What It Is For, How To Use It. Illustrated pamphlet shows how to put on a condom and describes its use, care, effectiveness, and role in safer sex. Includes a playscript of supportive arguments to insist on its use with a reluctant partner. Revised May 1993. 6 pp. Reading level: 6th grade. Distributed by Planned Parenthood Federation of America, Marketing Dept., 810 7th Ave., New York, NY 10019. (800) 669-0156. Ask for item no. 1550 and send a check or MasterCard or Visa number and expiration date with your order, or give your credit card number by phone. $1 each for a single copy; $31 for 100 copies.

INDEX

Lilian Kemp Photography

Nathan Rome

Jane Wegscheider Hyman, a researcher and writer on women's health, is the author of *The Light Book: How Natural and Artificial Light Affect Our Health, Mood, and Behavior* and a co-author of *Ourselves, Growing Older* and *The New Our Bodies, Ourselves*. While living in Vienna, Austria, she organized a women's bookstore and co-founded and co-authored a feminist women's magazine. Now living in Massachusetts, she is completing her Ph.D. in psychology, specializing in women's mental health.

Esther R. Rome, a founding member of the Boston Women's Health Book Collective, co-authored *Our Bodies, Ourselves* and *The New Our Bodies, Ourselves*. A long-time women's health activist, she campaigned successfully on the national level for women's access to information on tampon safety and the dangers of silicone breast implants. Determined to complete this book before her death from breast cancer in 1995, Rome has left it as one of her many legacies to women.

The Crossing Press publishes many books of interest to women. To receive our current catalog, please call toll-free, 800-777-1048.